Introduction to Sahidic Coptic

Introduction
to
Sahidic Coptic

BY THOMAS O. LAMBDIN

Mercer University Press
Macon, Ga. 31207

ISBN 0-86554-048-9

Introduction to Sahidic Coptic

by Thomas O. Lambdin

Copyright 1983
by Mercer University Press
Macon GA 31207

All books published
by Mercer University Press
are produced on acid-free paper
that exceeds the minimum standards set by the
National Historical Publications and Records Commission.

Library of Congress Cataloging in Publication Data

Lambdin, Thomas Oden.
Introduction to Sahidic Coptic.

Bibliography: p. 364
Includes indexes.
1. Coptic language—Grammar. I. title.
PJ2035.L3   1982   493'.282421   82-14282

ISBN 0-86554-048-9

Preface

The present work is an expansion of a series of elementary lessons developed gradually during twenty years of teaching Sahidic Coptic at the college level. The Lessons are designed to provide a carefully graded introduction to the basic grammar and vocabulary of the language. The content of the Lessons and the mode of presentation were dictated by purely practical pedagogical considerations; the book is in no way intended to be a scientific reference grammar. The Reading Selections are furnished with glosses designed to facilitate the transition to unsimplified material. A thorough mastery of these and the Lessons will bring the student to the level at which any Sahidic text of average difficulty can be read with no trouble. The emphasis on basic matters has necessitated the omission of much technical linguistic data not immediately relevant to the needs of the average beginning student. Those who are interested in a detailed study of the phonology, in the relationship of Sahidic to the other Coptic dialects, or in the historical development of Coptic from ancient Egyptian may consult the standard works on these subjects as cited in the Bibliography.

A special effort has been made to provide a Glossary that will be useful to the student beyond his first year's study. In addition to covering the words used in the present text, the Glossary is intended to contain the full vocabulary of the Sahidic New Testament, including most associated phrases and idioms, as well as a generous selection of lexical items from other Biblical and literary texts. Deliberately excluded from the Glossary are words of a specialized nature, such as the names of plants, vessels, implements, drugs, and animals occurring only in technical texts that usually provide little clue to their precise meanings; nor has any effort been made to include the unusual lexical usage of Shenute. For these items the reader must consult the indispensible *A Coptic Dictionary* of W. E. Crum, which, together with M. Wilmet, *Concordance du nouveau*

iii

testament sahidique, is the main authority for the Glossary included here.

I would like to express my sincere thanks to my colleague, George W. MacRae, the Charles Chauncey Stillman Professor of Roman Catholic Theological Studies, Harvard Divinity School, for encouraging me to undertake this work and for his helpful comments on a large portion of the manuscript; to Mr. Gary A. Bisbee, for the exceptional skill and care with which he prepared the final copy for publication; to Mr. Watson E. Mills, Director of the Mercer University Press, for his part in initiating and publishing this work.

Thomas O. Lambdin

Cambridge, Mass.

June 1982

Table of Contents

Abbreviations and Conventions

adj.	adjective, adjectival	obj.	object
adv.	adverb, adverbial	oft.	often
aft.	after	p.c.	participium conjunc-
art.	article		tivum
bef.	before	part.	particle
Boh.	Bohairic	Perf. I	the First Perfect
c.pl.	common plural	pers.	person
caus.	causative	phr.	phrase
cf.	compare	pl.	plural
Circum.	the Circumstantial	pred.	predication, predicate
conj.	conjunction	prep.	preposition
Conj.	the Conjunctive	Pres. I	the First Present
coord.	coordinated, coordinating	prob.	probably
cpd.	compound, compounded	procl.	proclitic
dat.	dative	pron.	pronoun, pronominal
def.	definite	Q.	qualitative
e.g.	for example	q.v.	which see
eth.	ethical	recipr.	reciprocal
exclam.	exclamatory	reflex.	reflexive
f., fem.	feminine	Rel.	Relative Form
fig.	figuratively	s.	singular
foll.	following	s.v.	sub voce
Fut. I	the First Future	Sah.	Sahidic
Fut. II	the Second Future	sim.	similar(ly)
Fut. III	the Third Future	sing.	singular
Gk.	Greek	sthg.	something
Gr. In.	Grammatical Index (Coptic)	sub	under
Hab.	the Habitual	subj.	subject
i.e.	that is	suff.	suffix(ed)
idem	having the same meanings	tr.	transitive
	as the immediately pre-	usu.	usually
	ceding word	vb.	verb, verbal
imperf.	imperfect	Vocab.	Vocabulary
Imperf.	the Imperfect	w.	with
imptv.	imperative		
indef.	indefinite		
indep.	independent		
Inf.	Infinitive	±	with or without
Infl. Inf.	Inflected Infinitive	+	with, plus, and
intens.	intensive	=	is fully equivalent in
interrog.	interrogative		function and meaning to
intr.	intransitive		
Intro.	Introduction		
lit.	literally		
m., masc.	masculine		The names of specific conjuga-
n.	noun, nominal		tions and inflected verbal forms
neg.	negative		are capitalized throughout the
no.	number		book.

Introduction

The political unification of Egypt took place around the beginning of the third millennium B. C. with the establishment of the First Dynasty at Memphis. Soon afterward written records began to appear in the hieroglyphic script, which together with its cursive derivatives, hieratic and demotic, remained the sole medium for writing the Egyptian language until the end of the second century A. D. At that time, the missionaries of the Church, then centered in Alexandria, undertook the translation of the Bible from Greek into Egyptian in order to facilitate their task of Christianizing the country. They abandoned the three-thousand-year-old hieroglyphic writing system, probably as much because of its complexity and imperfections as for its "heathen" associations, and chose instead to employ a modified form of the Greek alphabet. Egyptian in this new guise is known as Coptic, a modern term derived from Arabic $qubt\hat{i}$, itself a corruption of the Greek word $(ai)g\acute{u}pti(os)$, Egyptian.

The conquest of Egypt by Alexander the Great in 332 B. C. and the subsequent Greek-speaking administration of the country under the Ptolemies led to the thorough Hellenization of Lower (i. e. Northern) Egypt. Egyptian-Greek bilingualism was apparently commonplace in the Delta, and it is probable that much Greek technical, legal, and commercial terminology was introduced into spoken Egyptian at this time. Rough and unsystematic attempts to transcribe Egyptian in the Greek alphabet were made as early as the third century B. C. It was only natural, then, that the Coptic translators of the Bible not only adopted the Greek alphabet but also generously supplemented the native lexicon with many more borrowings from Greek. The Greek vocabulary of any Coptic text is significantly large.

Evidence of dialectal differences is found as early as the third millennium B. C., but the general conservativism of the hieroglyphic script and the practice of standardizing a particular form of the language for long periods of time (e.g. Middle Egyptian, New Egyptian) tend to obscure the great dialectal diversity that must have existed

in the spoken language as one traveled the 750 miles down the Nile
from Aswan to the Mediterranean. The individual dialects first become
recognizable when we reach the Coptic period and see the language
spelled out in the Greek alphabet. The exact geographical location
of the dialects is still a matter of scholarly debate, but the reader
should become familiar with their names and the approximate chronolog-
ical range of their use for literary purposes.

Sahidic, the dialect treated in this book, was the dialect chosen
for the official translation of the Bible mentioned above. There is
conflicting evidence on its geographical location: the name Sahidic,
from Arabic *aṣ-ṣaˤîd*, Upper (i.e. Southern) Egypt, places it in the
south (hence its alternate name: Theban, Thebaic); linguistic considerations, however, favor a northern locale, in the neighborhood of
Memphis and the eastern Delta. One cannot rule out the possibility
that both locations are correct; the fact that Thebes and Memphis
alternated as the capital of Egypt through much of its history and
were the chief centers of religious (priestly), building, and commercial activity could have led to the development of an "urban" dialect
in these two areas, quite distinct from the dialects of the "rural"
areas that lay between. By the fourth century A. D. Sahidic was
firmly established as the standard literary dialect and retained this
status until its demise around the tenth century. Surviving texts in
Sahidic include, in addition to the New Testament and a large portion
of the Old, a considerable corpus of Church literature and some rem-
nants of secular literature, nearly all of which is translated from
Greek. Of native works we have only the writings of Pachomius (c. 300),
the founder of Egyptian monasticism; Shenute (c. 400), the administra-
tor of the White Monastery in Upper Egypt; and Besa, a disciple of
Shenute. The Coptic writings of Shenute, who attempted to mould the
language into a literary vehicle comparable to Greek, are often referred to as the "classics" of Sahidic literature. Their syntactic
complexity and unusual vocabulary usage, however, place them beyond
the scope of the present work, which is based on the language of the
more widely studied translation literature.

Bohairic replaced Sahidic as the standard literary dialect.

Bohairic texts are attested as early as the ninth century, but the dialect does not seem to have achieved wide usage until it was adopted as the official language of the Coptic Church in the eleventh century. Most Bohairic texts come from after this time, and many of them were translated from Sahidic originals. The term Bohairic comes from Arabic *al-buhairah*, Lower (i.e. Northern) Egypt; it is generally assumed that Bohairic was the dialect of the Western Delta, including Alexandria and Nitria. The designation Memphitic has also been used for this dialect.

Fayyumic, as its name implies, was the dialect of northern Middle Egypt in the vicinity of the Fayyum Basin. It is well attested in texts ranging from the fourth to the eleventh century, but it apparently never attained the status of Sahidic.

Achmimic, generally located in the area of Akhmim (Panopolis) in southern Middle Egypt, enjoyed only a brief literary period from the third to the fifth century.

Subachmimic, tentatively localized between Akhmim and Thebes, was used extensively in the fourth and fifth centuries for the translation of Manichaean and Gnostic literature. Its association with this heretical material probably had much to do with its early demise as a literary dialect. The Nag Hammadi texts are in Subachmimic or a variety of Sahidic influenced by Subachmimic in varying degrees.

For further details on the dialects the reader should consult the works of Worrell, Vergote, Kahle, and Till cited in the Bibliography.

The Arab conquest of Egypt in 641 A. D. and the subsequent suppression of the native Christian population resulted in the gradual dying out of the Egyptian language in favor of Arabic. We cannot be sure how long this process took, but it is safe to assume that by the fifteenth century Coptic had ceased to be a native spoken language, thus bringing to an end a continuous written record of over four thousand years.

The Coptic Alphabet

Sahidic Coptic is written in the Greek alphabet aug-
mented by six letters borrowed from Demotic script, the
last stage of Egyptian hieroglyphic writing. The letters
of the full alphabet, together with their conventional
transcription, are as follows:

ⲁ	a	ⲏ	ē	ⲛ	n	ⲧ	t	ⲱ	š
ⲃ	b	ⲑ	th	ⳉ	ks	ⲩ	u	ϥ	f
ⲅ	g	ⲓ	i	ⲟ	o	ⲫ	ph	ⳅ	h
ⲇ	d	ⲕ	k	ⲡ	p	ⲭ	kh	ⳃ	j, ǧ
ⲉ	e	ⲗ	l	ⲣ	r	ⲯ	ps	ⳓ	č, c
ⳅ	z	ⲙ	m	ⲥ	s	ⲱ	ō	ⲧ	ti

The following paragraphs deal with the Coptic, not the
Greek, pronunciation of this alphabet.

Spelling and Pronunciation

a. The Consonants

ⲃ was apparently pronounced like English *v* in *voice*,
but it is generally read simply as *b* in *back*.

ⲅ occurs only as a positional variant of ⲕ in a very
small set of forms. Pronounced like the *g* of *good*.

ⲇ and ⲍ do not normally occur in standard Sahidic
spelling. ⲍ may occur for ⲥ in a few words, e.g. ⲁⲛⲍⲏⲃⲉ
for ⲁⲛⲥⲏⲃⲉ school. Pronounced *d* as in *dog* and *z* as in *zoo*
respectively.

ⲫ, ⲑ, and ⲭ occur in Sahidic Coptic words only as combinations of two consonants: ⲡ + ⲍ, ⲧ + ⲍ, and ⲕ + ⲍ respectively. ⲑ is fairly frequent, e.g. ⲡⲉⲑⲟⲟⲩ evil, for ⲡⲉⲧ
ⲍⲟⲟⲩ. ⲫ and ⲭ are rare and need not be used at all. The
Copts seem to have used this same pronunciation for these
letters in Greek words, contrary to the ordinary Greek pronunciation of ⲫ as *f*, ⲑ as *th* (*thin*), and ⲭ as *ch* (German

ich, ach).

ᴋ, ⲡ, and ⲧ were like English *k*, *p*, *t*, but without aspiration. Thus, they were more like the *k*, *p*, *t* of *skin, spin, stop* than the aspirated sounds of *kin, pin, top*.

ⲗ, ⲙ, and ⲛ were probably the same as English *l*, *m*, and *n*.

ⲝ is simply a combination of ᴋ + ⲥ, rarely used. E.g. ⲝⲟⲩⲣ ring.

ⲣ is conventionally pronounced like English *r* in *road*. Its actual pronunciation is unknown.

ⲥ was like English *s* in *see*.

ⲯ is simply ⲡ + ⲥ, rarely used. E.g. ⲯⲓⲧⲉ nine (*psite*).

ⲩ was the *sh* of *shall*.

ϥ was the *f* of *foot*.

ⲍ was probably like English *h* in *hope*.

ⳮ is conventionally pronounced like the *j* of *judge*. Its actual pronunciation was probably closer to that of the [tʸ] of *tune*.[1]

ϭ, conventionally like the *ch* of *church*, was probably closer to the [kʸ] of *cue, cute*.

ϯ is merely a graphic symbol for ⲧ + ⲓ, but it was the normal way to spell this sequence of sounds. E.g. ϯⲙⲉ village (*time*).

b. The simple vowels

ⲁ like the *a* of *father*. E.g. ⲁϥ [ɑf] meat.

ⲉ like the *e* of *let*. E.g. ⲍⲉⲛ [hɛn] some.

ⲏ probably like the *a* of *hate*. E.g. ⲙⲏⲧ [met] ten.

ⲓ like the *i* of *machine*. This vowel is always spelled ⲉⲓ in initial positions: ⲉⲓⲛⲉ [íⲛⲉ] to bring, ⲉⲓⲥ [is] behold. Internally and finally the spelling alternates between ⲓ and ⲉⲓ, but ⲓ is preferred.

---

[1] Brackets are used to indicate phonetic pronunciation in standard phonetic symbols. Do not confuse these with the conventional transcriptions.

o like the o of *log, fog, dog, off, on.* E.g. топ [tɔp] edge.

ү does not appear as a simple vowel in Coptic words.

oү is the normal writing of the vowel [u], the *oo* of *food.* E.g. ноүв *noub* [nub] gold.

ω like the o of *hope.* E.g. ꝫωп [hop] to hide.

c. Semivowels and diphthongs

The consonants *y* and *w* of English *yet* and *wet* are often referred to as semivowels because they are the same sounds as the vowels [i] and [u] of *beet* and *boot* very briefly articulated. The Coptic vowels ei (ı) and oү may function as consonants in the same way. E.g. eιωτ [yot] father, oүоп [wɔp] to become pure.

The semivowels ei (ı) and oү combine with a preceding simple vowel to form various diphthongs. Many of the diph- thongs have more than one spelling; the reader should follow the spelling used in the Lessons. The diphthongs should be pronounced carefully, with the value of the single vowel as given above plus a final *y* or *w* as the case may be.

ⲁⲓ, ⲁⲉⲓ as in ⲥⲁⲉⲓⲛ [sɑyn] physician, ⲁⲓⲡⲱⲧ [ɑypót] I ran.

ⲁⲩ (rarely ⲁⲟⲩ) as in ⲛⲁⲩ [nɑw] to see, ⲁⲩⲡⲱⲧ [ɑwpót] they ran.

ⲉⲓ (less commonly ⲉⲉⲓ) as in ⲡⲉⲓⲣⲱⲙⲉ [peyróme] this man. Although a knowledge of the grammar is necessary for making the correct distinction between ⲉⲓ = [i] and ⲉⲓ = [ɛy], the problem is not a serious one: in normal Sahidic spelling ⲉⲓ has the value ⲉ + ⲓ (1) in the demonstrative adjectives ⲡⲉⲓ- ⲧⲉⲓ- ⲛⲉⲓ- (Lesson 5), (2) in the first person verbal prefixes of the forms ⲉⲓ-, ⲛⲉⲓ-, ⲙⲉⲓ- (Lesson 21 and following), and in a few isolated words like ⲉⲓⲉ [ɛyɛ] (Lesson 29).

ⲉⲩ (rarely ⲉⲟⲩ), as in ⲉⲩϣⲁⲭⲉ [ɛwšátʸɛ] while they were talking.

ⲏⲓ as in ⲡⲏⲓ [pey] the house.

ⲏⲩ (less commonly ⲏⲟⲩ) as in ⲧⲏⲩ [tew] wind.

ⲓⲉⲓ, ⲉⲓⲉⲓ is very rare and is [yi] not [iy], e.g. ₂ⲓⲉⲓⲃ [hyib] lamb.

ⲓⲟⲩ is rare, e.g. ⲥⲓⲟⲩ [siw] star.

ⲟⲉⲓ, ⲟⲓ as in ⲟⲩⲟⲉⲓⲛ [wɔyn] light.

ⲟⲟⲩ as in ⲙⲟⲟⲩ [mɔw] water, ⲙⲟⲟⲩⲧ [mɔwt] dead.

ⲱⲓ as in ⲉⲭⲱⲓ [ɛtʸóy] on me; rare except in final position.

ⲱⲟⲩ as in ⲧⲱⲟⲩⲛ [town] to stand up, ⲉⲭⲱⲟⲩ [ɛtʸów] on them.

ⲟⲩⲓ (rare) as in ⲛⲟⲩⲓ [nuy] mine; also possibly as [wi] in some words, e.g. ⲕⲟⲩⲓ [kwi] small.

ⲟⲩⲟⲩ (rare) as in ⲙⲟⲩⲟⲩⲧ [muwt] to kill, ⲛⲟⲩⲟⲩ [nuw] theirs.

Double Vowels

The double writing of any of the simple vowels is generally understood to be an indication of the presence of a glottal stop, i.e. the complete but very brief stoppage of airflow in the glottis, conventionally indicated by ꞌ in transcription. Thus ⲙⲁⲁⲃ *mâꞌăb* thirty, ⲥⲉⲉⲛⲉ *sêꞌĕpe* remainder, ϣⲟⲟⲡ *šóꞌŏp* to be. The stress is on the first vowel; the vowel after the glottal stop was probably of very brief duration.

Vowel doubling occurs in diphthongs as well, e.g. ⲙⲁⲁⲩ *mâꞌăw* mother, ⲙⲉⲉⲩⲉ *mêꞌĕwe* to think. There is no sure way of knowing whether ooy indicates [ɔw] or [ɔ́ꞌɔ̆w].

Syllabification and the Supralinear Stroke

One of the most distinctive features of Sahidic spelling is the short stroke placed over certain consonants or

groups of consonants. This supralinear stroke, as it is
called, indicates a syllable, but there is some disagreement among Coptic scholars on how this syllabification
actually sounded in the spoken language. When the stroke
is used over a voiced consonant such as ɴ, it probably
meant that the consonant is functioning as the vowel, i.e.
the most sonorous part, of the syllable in question, exactly
like the final *n* of English *button* and *sudden*, phonetically
[-tṇ] and [-dṇ]. Thus, ϣⲛ̄ⲧ (to seek me) was pronounced
[šṇt] and ⲛ̄ⲧ (to bring me) as [ṇt]. The voiced consonants
capable of having this syllabic pronunciation are ⲃ, ⲗ, ⲙ,
ⲛ, and ⲣ, known mnemonically as the *blemner* consonants.
Note that they are all voiced continuants, i.e. consonants
whose voiced duration may be prolonged at will (remember
that ⲃ is *v*, not *b*). E.g.

ⲧⲛ̄ⲥⲱⲧⲙ̄ (we hear) [tṇsótṃ]   ⲧⲃ̄ⲧ   (fish) [ty̥t]

ϣⲧⲟⲣⲧⲣ̄ (to disturb) [štɔ́rtr̥]   ⲕⲣⲙ̄ⲣⲙ̄ (to mutter) [krm̥rṃ]

The stroke over the remaining consonants may be pronounced
as a brief ⲉ or as ə (the first vowel of English *above*)
before the consonant over which the stroke is placed, e.g.
ⲥⲛ̄ⲥⲱⲡϥ̄ [səpsópəf] to entreat him. This pronunciation may
also be used with the *blemner* consonants for the sake of
convenience.

In non-standard texts, of which there are many, the
vowel ⲉ is often written instead of using the stroke (and
vice versa), but most frequently in proclitic elements and
initial clusters, e.g. ⲥⲉⲛⲥⲱⲡϥ̄ = ⲥⲛ̄ⲥⲱⲡϥ̄, ⲍⲉⲙ ⲡⲏⲓ = ⲍⲙ̄ ⲡⲏⲓ.
In standard spelling ⲉ is used regularly instead of the
stroke only when the consonant preceding the consonant that
would have had the stroke is a *blemner*; thus ⲙⲟⲕⲙⲉⲕ and
ⲛⲟⲅⲛⲉⲅ are words of the same pattern as ⲥⲟⲛⲥⲛ̄ and ⲥⲟⲗⲥⲗ̄.
This convention may have been adopted to prevent incorrect
syllabification: ⲙⲟⲕⲙⲕ could be read as [mɔ́kṃk] or [mɔ́kmək].
The chief exceptions are indeed words where a different

syllabication is required: ϣomꞪт [sɔ́mṇt] three, тѡmꞪт
[tɔ́mṇt] to befall. The Ꞥ of these words is an intrusive
(secondary) glide from the labial м to the dental т; the
earlier forms were ϣomꞦ and тѡmꞦ. The convention likewise
does not apply when the final consonant is also a *blemner:*
nѧ₂mꞪ [náhmṇ] to rescue us. Much of the variation between
є and a stroke that occurs in the writing of certain verbal prefixes (e.g. Ꞥтєрꞯ-, Ꞥтєрєч-; мѧрꞯ-, мѧрєч-) probably
results from inconsistent application of this rule.

The forms тѡoyn (to arise) and cooyꞤ (to know) have
been standardized in the Lessons. In the Reading Selections the orthography of the source has been followed.

Stress

Coptic is a highly compounding language, mostly by
prefixation. All prefixal elements are proclitic, i.e.
unstressed and bound, to the word which stands last in the
sequence, regardless of its length, e.g.

₂Ꞥ тєчmꞪтѧттѧko = ₂Ꞥ-тє-ч-mꞪт-ѧт-тѧkɔ́
in his imperishability

Any element designated as prefixal in the course of the
Lessons should be considered as proclitic. All simple
prepositions are proclitic, like ₂Ꞥ in the above example,
but for the sake of clarity they are written as separate
words in this text.

The main stress, then, is on the word standing at the
end of the compound. The successive application of the
following rules will enable the reader to apply the correct
stress in all but the rarest cases:

(1) Stress is always on one of the last two syllables
of a word.

(2) The vowels н, o, and ѡ are always stressed.

(3) Final simple -ѧ and simple -єı, -ı are always
stressed.

(4) Final -oγ is stressed except (1) when it is the suffixed pronoun of the 3rd person plural (a knowledge of the grammar will make this clear), and (2) in the words ⲡⲁ2ⲟⲩ (back), ⲥⲡⲟⲧⲟⲩ (lips), ⲥⲁ2ⲟⲩ (curse), and ⲣⲁⲥⲟⲩ (dream).

(5) Final -ⲉ is unstressed except in the adjectives introduced in Lesson 15 (thus, ⲥⲁⲃⲉ́, wise, ⲃ⳿ⲗⲗⲉ́, blind, etc.) and in a few miscellaneous words like ⲃⲉⲕⲉ́ (wages), ⲙ̄ⲛ̄ⲧⲣⲉ́ (witness), ⲕⲛ̄ⲧⲉ́ (figs), and ⲛⲁⲙⲉ́ (truly).

(6) A final syllable marked by a stroked consonant is never stressed unless it is the only syllable of the word.

Assimilation

Assimilation, for our present purposes, may be defined briefly as the alteration of a sound due to its proximity to another sound, usually resulting in greater phonetic compatibility. The final ⲛ̄ of prefixal elements (e.g. prepositions, particles, articles) is regularly assimilated to ⲙ̄ before ⲡ and ⲙ, e.g.

$$*_2\overline{ⲛ}\ ⲡ\text{ⲏ}\text{ⲓ} \rightarrow {}_2\overline{ⲙ}\ ⲡ\text{ⲏ}\text{ⲓ} \quad \text{in the house}$$
$$*\overline{ⲛ}ⲙⲁⲉⲓⲛ \rightarrow \overline{ⲙ}ⲙⲁⲉⲓⲛ \quad \text{the signs.}$$

The assimilation of consonant -ⲛ also occurs but is not standard, e.g. ⲧⲉⲙⲡⲓⲥⲧⲓⲥ for ⲧⲉⲛⲡⲓⲥⲧⲓⲥ (our faith). In some texts the particle ⲛ̄, which has several grammatical functions, assimilates completely to ⲃ, ⲗ, and ⲣ, e.g. ⲛ̄ⲃⲣ̄ⲣⲉ → ⲃ̄ⲃⲣ̄ⲣⲉ (the young), ⲛ̄ⲣⲱⲙⲉ → ⲣ̄ⲣⲱⲙⲉ (the men). This is not considered standard, but it is not uncommon; numerous examples will be met in our reading selection from the Wisdom of Solomon.

Whatever the pronunciation of the supralinear stroke was, an alternate spelling with -ⲗ- often occurs before final -2: ⲱⲛⲁ2 = ⲱⲛ2̄ to live. This represents an assimilation to the guttural quality of 2.

An alternation between -ⲱ- and -ⲟⲩ- in certain word

patterns is a result of an assimilation in the pre-Coptic stage. ⲱ was altered to ⲟⲩ after ⲙ and ⲛ; thus, words like ⲙⲟⲩ2, ⲛⲟⲩⲭⲉ, ⲙⲟⲩⲟⲩⲧ, and ⲛⲟⲩⲕ originally had the same vowel as ⲕⲱⲧ, ⲕⲱⲧⲉ, ⲧⲱⲟⲩⲛ, and ⲧⲱⲕ respectively.

The Spelling of Greek Words

Greek words in Coptic are usually spelled correctly. Certain types of errors do occasionally occur, however, resulting in part from the discrepancy between the classi-cal spelling and the contemporary pronunciation, and they must be taken into account when consulting a standard Greek dictionary. The most frequent of these are confu-sions between (1) ⲏ and ⲩ; (2) ⲉ and ⲁⲓ; (3) ⲓ and ⲏ; (4) ⲟ and ⲱ; (5) ⲅ and ⲕ; (6) ⲓ and ⲉⲓ; (7) ⲏ and ⲉ; (8) ⲧ and ⲁ; (9) initial 2 and zero. All of these are illustrated by the following words chosen from our Reading Selections.

$$\begin{aligned}
&\text{ⲃⲩⲙⲁ} = \text{ⲃⲏⲙⲁ} \quad (\beta\tilde{\eta}\mu\alpha) \\
&\text{ⲥⲡⲩⲗⲏⲟⲛ} = \text{ⲥⲡⲏⲗⲁⲓⲟⲛ} \quad (\sigma\pi\acute{\eta}\lambda\alpha\iota\text{o}\nu) \\
&\text{ⲡⲉⲣⲓⲭⲟⲣⲟⲥ} = \text{ⲡⲉⲣⲓⲭⲱⲣⲟⲥ} \quad (\pi\epsilon\rho\acute{\iota}\chi\omega\rho\text{o}\varsigma) \\
&\text{ⲟⲣⲕⲁⲛⲟⲛ} = \text{ⲟⲣⲅⲁⲛⲟⲛ} \quad (\check{o}\rho\gamma\alpha\nu\text{o}\nu) \\
&\text{ⲡⲉⲣⲉⲓⲉⲣⲕⲁⲍⲉ} = \text{ⲡⲉⲣⲓⲉⲣⲅⲁⲍⲉ} \quad (\pi\epsilon\rho\iota\epsilon\rho\gamma\acute{\alpha}\zeta\epsilon\text{-}) \\
&\text{ϯⲥⲧⲁⲍⲉ} = \text{ⲁⲓⲥⲧⲁⲍⲉ} \quad (\delta\iota\sigma\tau\acute{\alpha}\zeta\epsilon\text{-}) \\
&\text{ⲉⲑⲣⲓⲟⲛ} = \text{ⲁⲓⲑⲣⲓⲟⲛ} \quad (\alpha\check{\iota}\vartheta\rho\iota\text{o}\nu) \\
&\text{ⲕⲩⲣⲓⲥⲥⲁⲓ} = \text{ⲕⲏⲣⲩⲥⲥⲉ} \quad (\varkappa\eta\rho\acute{\upsilon}\sigma\sigma\epsilon\text{-}) \\
&\text{2ⲩⲁⲱⲛⲏ} = \text{2ⲏⲁⲟⲛⲏ} \quad (\dot{\eta}\delta\text{o}\nu\acute{\eta}) \\
&\text{ⲡⲓⲑⲉ} = \text{ⲡⲉⲓⲑⲉ} \quad (\pi\epsilon\acute{\iota}\vartheta\epsilon\text{-}) \\
&\text{ⲉⲥⲩⲭⲁⲍⲉ} = \text{2ⲏⲥⲩⲭⲁⲍⲉ} \quad (\dot{\eta}\sigma\upsilon\chi\acute{\alpha}\zeta\epsilon\text{-}) \\
&\text{2ⲉⲗⲡⲓⲍⲉ} = \text{ⲉⲗⲡⲓⲍⲉ} \quad (\dot{\epsilon}\lambda\pi\acute{\iota}\zeta\epsilon\text{-})
\end{aligned}$$

Lesson 1

1.1 Gender. There are two grammatical genders in
Coptic: masculine and feminine. Nouns denoting male
beings are usually masculine; those denoting females,
feminine. The gender of other nouns cannot, in general,
be deduced either from their form or meaning and must be
learned for each noun. Examples:

masculine		feminine	
ⲉⲓⲱⲧ	father	ⲙⲁⲁⲩ	mother
ⲕⲁϩ	earth, ground	ⲡⲉ	sky, heaven
ϩⲟⲟⲩ	day	ⲟⲩϣⲏ	night

There are some pairs of nouns where a formal relationship
exists between the masculine and the feminine form:

masculine		feminine	
ⲥⲟⲛ	brother	ⲥⲱⲛⲉ	sister
ϣⲏⲣⲉ	boy, son	ϣⲉⲉⲣⲉ	girl, daughter
ϩⲗⲗⲟ	old man	ϩⲗⲗⲱ	old woman
ⲟⲩϩⲟⲣ	dog (male)	ⲟⲩϩⲱⲣⲉ	dog (female)

These will be noted in the lesson vocabularies. The deri-
vational process involved is no longer a productive one in
Coptic: such pairs cannot be formed at will.

1.2 Number: singular and plural. Only a relatively
small number of nouns have preserved a distinct plural
form. For example:

singular		plural	
ⲉⲓⲱⲧ	father	ⲉⲓⲟⲧⲉ	fathers
ⲥⲟⲛ	brother	ⲥⲛⲏⲩ	brothers
ϫⲟⲓ	ship	ⲉϫⲏⲩ	ships

The plural is otherwise made explicit by the form of the
article (see below), the noun itself remaining unchanged.

Those plurals that are in common use will be given in the
lesson vocabularies along with the singular. They should
be learned as they occur, since there is no consistent
pattern for their formation.

     1.3 The definite article. The definite article has
the forms

       masc. sing. ⲡ, ⲡⲉ   common plural Ⲛ̄, ⲛⲉ
       fem. sing. ⲧ, ⲧⲉ

These are attached directly to the noun, as in

   ⲣⲱⲙⲉ man   ⲡⲣⲱⲙⲉ the man   Ⲛ̄ⲣⲱⲙⲉ the men
   ⲉⲓⲝ hand   ⲧⲉⲓⲝ the hand   Ⲛ̄ⲉⲓⲝ the hands

The plural article appears as ⲙ̄ before ⲡ and ⲙ (cf.
Intro., p. xvi):

   ⲡⲉ   sky   ⲧⲡⲉ   the sky   Ⲙ̄ⲡⲏⲩⲉ the heavens
   ⲙⲁⲉⲓⲛ sign   ⲡⲙⲁⲉⲓⲛ the sign Ⲙ̄ⲙⲁⲉⲓⲛ the signs

Before nouns beginning with a vowel the plural article
appears as either Ⲛ̄ or ⲛ:

   ⲉⲝⲏⲩ ships   Ⲛ̄ⲉⲝⲏⲩ or ⲛⲉⲝⲏⲩ the ships

Before initial stroked consonants there are several
possibilities:

   Ⲙ̄ⲧⲟⲛ, ⲉⲙⲧⲟⲛ repose   ⲡⲉⲙⲧⲟⲛ, ⲡⲙ̄ⲧⲟⲛ, ⲡⲉⲙ̄ⲧⲟⲛ the repose
   Ⲛ̄ⲕⲁ, ⲉⲛⲕⲁ thing   ⲛⲉⲛⲕⲁ, ⲛⲛ̄ⲕⲁ, ⲛ̄ⲛ̄ⲕⲁ   the things

The fuller forms ⲡⲉ-, ⲧⲉ-, ⲛⲉ- are used regularly before
nouns beginning with two consonants:

   ⲕⲗⲟⲙ crown   ⲡⲉⲕⲗⲟⲙ the crown ⲛⲉⲕⲗⲟⲙ the crowns
   ⲥⲍⲓⲙⲉ woman   ⲧⲉⲥⲍⲓⲙⲉ the woman ⲛⲉⲍⲓⲟⲙⲉ the women

Note that ⲟⲩ and (ⲉ)ⲓ have a consonantal value (*w* and *y*
respectively) in certain initial situations:

 ⲟⲩⲍⲟⲣ dog ⲡⲉⲩⲍⲟⲣ the dog (*pewhor*)   ⲛⲉⲩⲍⲟⲟⲣ the dogs
 ⲍⲓⲏ road ⲧⲉⲍⲓⲏ the road (*tehyē*)   ⲛⲉⲍⲓⲟⲟⲩⲉ the roads

The fuller forms are also used with certain nouns denoting
periods of time:

ⲡⲉⲟⲩⲟⲉⲓϣ	the time	ⲧⲉⲣⲟⲙⲡⲉ	the year
ⲡⲉϩⲟⲟⲩ	the day	ⲧⲉⲩϣⲏ	the night (ⲟⲩϣⲏ)
ⲧⲉⲩⲛⲟⲩ	the hour (ⲟⲩⲛⲟⲩ)		

Note that ⲟⲩⲛⲟⲩ and ⲟⲩϣⲏ fall under the two-consonant rule
above.

1.4 Prepositions. Coptic prepositions are proclitic
(i.e. unstressed and bound) to the word they govern. In
many texts some or all of the prepositions are printed as
a unit with the following word: ϩⲓⲡϫⲟⲓ on the ship, ⲉⲡⲏⲓ
to the house. In this text, however, all prepositions
will be printed as separate words: ϩⲓ ⲡϫⲟⲓ, ⲉ ⲡⲏⲓ. An
exception will be made only in the case of the preposition
ⲉ (to, for) if it is ligatured orthographically to a
following ⲟⲩ- as ⲉⲩ-.

The preposition ⲙⲛ (with) is used as the conjunction
"and" in joining two nouns: ⲡⲣⲱⲙⲉ ⲙⲛ ⲧⲉⲥϩⲓⲙⲉ the man and
the woman.

A definite noun followed by a prepositional phrase or
local adverb (e.g. ⲙⲙⲁⲩ there) constitutes a full predication (sentence) in Coptic:

ⲡⲣⲱⲙⲉ ϩⲓ ⲡϫⲟⲓ.	The man is on the ship.
ⲧⲉⲥϩⲓⲙⲉ ϩⲙ ⲡⲏⲓ.	The woman is in the house.
ⲛⲉϫⲏⲩ ⲙⲙⲁⲩ.	The ships are there.

In sentences of this type there is no overt equivalent of
English "is/are." We shall refer to sentences of this
type as sentences with adverbial predicates.

Vocabulary 1

In the lesson vocabularies all nouns will be given with
the definite article, separated from the noun by a period.
This device makes both the gender of the noun and the

correct form of the article clear at a glance. To save
space, the article is not included in the definition.
Prepositions and particles which regularly have assimilation of final ⲛ̄ to ⲙ̄ before ⲡ and ⲙ will be noted, as
e.g. ⲍⲛ̄ (ⲍⲙ̄).

ⲡ.ⲣⲱⲙⲉ man, person; mankind.

ⲧⲉ.ⲥⲍⲓⲙⲉ (pl. ⲛⲉ.ⲍⲓⲟⲙⲉ) woman,
   wife.

ⲡ.ⲍⲁ̄ⲗⲟ old man, monk.

ⲑⲁ̄ⲗⲱ old woman (= ⲧ.ⲍⲁ̄ⲗⲱ).

ⲡ.ⲭⲱⲱⲙⲉ book, book-roll,
   document.

ⲡ.ⲱⲛⲉ stone.

ⲧⲉ.ⲍⲓⲏ (pl. ⲛⲉ.ⲍⲓⲟⲟⲩⲉ) road,
   way, path.

ⲡ.ⲧⲟⲟⲩ mountain;
   monastery.

ⲡ.ⲏⲓ house.

ⲡ.ⲛⲟⲩⲃ gold.

ⲍⲛ̄ (ⲍⲙ̄) in.

ⲍⲁ under.

ⲍⲓ on, upon.

ⲍⲓ̈ⲭⲛ̄ (ⲍⲓ̈ⲭⲙ̄) on, upon.

ⲙⲛ̄ with, together with,
   in the company of;
   and.

Exercises

A.1. ⲍⲓ ⲧⲉⲍⲓⲏ

2. ⲍⲓ ⲡⲧⲟⲟⲩ

3. ⲍⲛ̄ ⲧⲉⲍⲓⲏ

4. ⲍⲙ̄ ⲡⲏⲓ

5. ⲍⲁ ⲡⲏⲓ

6. ⲍⲁ ⲡⲱⲛⲉ

7. ⲍⲓ ⲡⲭⲱⲱⲙⲉ

8. ⲙⲛ̄ ⲡⲣⲱⲙⲉ

9. ⲙⲛ̄ ⲧⲉⲥⲍⲓⲙⲉ

10. ⲍⲓ̈ⲭⲛ̄ ⲛⲉⲍⲓⲟⲟⲩⲉ

11. ⲍⲁ ⲛ̄ⲏⲓ

12. ⲍⲓ̈ⲭⲛ̄ ⲛ̄ⲧⲟⲟⲩ

13. ⲍⲛ̄ ⲛ̄ⲏⲓ

14. ⲙⲛ̄ ⲛⲉⲍⲓⲟⲙⲉ

15. ⲍⲓ ⲡⲛⲟⲩⲃ

16. ⲡⲛⲟⲩⲃ ⲙⲛ̄ ⲛ̄ⲭⲱⲱⲙⲉ

17. ⲡⲍⲁ̄ⲗⲟ ⲙⲛ̄ ⲑⲁ̄ⲗⲱ

18. ⲡⲣⲱⲙⲉ ⲙⲛ̄ ⲧⲉⲥⲍⲓⲙⲉ

19. ⲛ̄ⲣⲱⲙⲉ ⲙⲛ̄ ⲛⲉⲍⲓⲟⲙⲉ

20. ⲛ̄ⲍⲁ̄ⲗⲟ ⲙⲛ̄ ⲛ̄ⲍⲁ̄ⲗⲱ

B.1. ⲡⲱⲛⲉ ⲍⲓ̈ⲭⲛ̄ ⲧⲉⲍⲓⲏ.

2. ⲛ̄ⲍⲁ̄ⲗⲟ ⲍⲓ ⲧⲉⲍⲓⲏ.

3. ⲛ̄ⲍⲁ̄ⲗⲱ ⲍⲙ̄ ⲡⲏⲓ.

4. ⲡⲛⲟⲩⲃ ⲍⲁ ⲡⲱⲛⲉ.

5. ⲡⲭⲱⲱⲙⲉ ⲍⲓ ⲡⲱⲛⲉ.

6. ⲡⲏⲓ ⲍⲓ̈ⲭⲛ̄ ⲡⲧⲟⲟⲩ.

7. ⲛ̄ⲣⲱⲙⲉ ⲍⲓ̈ⲭⲙ̄ ⲡⲧⲟⲟⲩ.

8. ⲧⲉⲥⲍⲓⲙⲉ ⲙⲛ̄ ⲡⲣⲱⲙⲉ.

9. ⲛ̄ⲭⲱⲱⲙⲉ ⲍⲙ̄ ⲡⲏⲓ.

Lesson 2

2.1 The indefinite article. The indefinite article
for nouns of either gender is ογ in the singular, ʒ ϵν in
the plural, prefixed directly to the noun:

ογϫοι	a ship	ʒ ϵνϵϫΗγ	ships, some ships
ογρωΜϵ	a man	ʒ ϵΝρωΜϵ	men, some men
ογʒ ΙΗ	a road	ʒ ϵΝʒ ΙΟΟγϵ	roads, some roads.

The plural indefinite article may be translated as "some,
certain" or be omitted entirely in translation, as the
context requires. The plural indefinite article is frequently written as ʒ Ν̄ and is easily confused with the
preposition ʒ Ν̄. In the exercises to the lessons we shall
always distinguish between the two, but in part of the
Reading Selections the orthography of the source is maintained.

Because the use of the Coptic articles, both definite
and indefinite, corresponds closely to the use of the
articles in English, only exceptions to this general cor-
respondence will be noted in the following lessons when
appropriate. References to the omission of the article
require special attention. For the present lesson note
that indefinite nouns designating unspecific quantities of
a substance require an indefinite article in Coptic where
there is none in English:

ογΜοογ	water	ʒ ϵΝΟϵΙΚ	bread	ʒ ϵΝλϥ	meat

The choice between the singular and plural article here is
lexical, i.e. it depends on the particular noun. All such
nouns, if definite and specific, may of course appear with
the definite article: πΜοογ, ποϵΙΚ, πλϥ. Abstract nouns,
such as Μϵ truth, often appear with either article (ογΜϵ,
τΜϵ) where English employs no article.

2.2 Indefinite nouns cannot be used as subjects of

sentences with adverbial predicates unless introduced by the word oyⲛ̄- or its negative:

oyⲛ̄-oyⳉⲁⲗⲟ ⳅ ι ⲧⲉⳅ ιн.   A monk is on the road.

oyⲛ̄- is actually a predicator of existence ("there is, there are"), and the sentence given may also be translated as "There is a monk on the road."

The negative of oyⲛ̄- is мⲛ̄- (also spelled ⲙ̄мⲛ̄-). In general, an *indefinite* article is deleted (omitted) in negation in Coptic:

мⲛ̄-ⳅⲁⲗⲟ ⳅ ι ⲧⲉⳅ ιн.   There is no monk on the road.
мⲛ̄-ⲣⲱмⲉ ⳅⲙ̄ пн ι.   There is no man in the house.

oyⲛ̄- and мⲛ̄- are not used before definite nouns. The sentence пⲣⲱмⲉ ⳅⲙ̄ пн ι is negated by adding ⲁн:

пⲣⲱмⲉ ⳅⲙ̄ пн ι ⲁн.   The man is not in the house.

2.3 The genitive (or possessive) relationship between two nouns is expressed by the preposition ⲛ̄ (of):

пн ι ⲙ̄ пⲣⲱмⲉ   the house of the man, the man's house
ⲧϣⲉⲉⲣⲉ ⲛ̄ ⲧⲉⲥⳅ ιмⲉ   the woman's daughter

If the first noun is indefinite, however, the preposition ⲛ̄ⲧⲉ is used instead of ⲛ̄:

oyⳉⲱⲱмⲉ ⲛ̄ⲧⲉ пⳅⲁⲗⲟ   a book of the monk
oyⳅ̄ⳅⲁⲗ ⲛ̄ⲧⲉ пⲣ̄ⲣⲟ   a servant of the king

Vocabulary 2

п.ⳅ̄ⳅⲁⲗ, ⲧ.ⳅ̄ⳅⲁⲗ (ⲑⲙ̄ⳅⲁⲗ) slave, servant.

п.ⲣ̄ⲣⲟ (pl. ⲛ̄.ⲣ̄ⲣⲱⲟy) king; ⲧ.ⲣ̄ⲣⲱ queen.

п.ⲭⲟ ι (pl. ⲛ.ⲉⳉⲏy) ship, boat.

ⲧⲉ.мⲣⲱ (pl. ⲛ̄.ⲙ̄ⲣⲟⲟyⲉ) harbor.

п.мⲟⲟy water.

п.ⲉ ιⲉⲣⲟ river.

п.ⲧⲃ̄ⲧ fish.

п.ⲣⲁⲛ name.

п.ⲟyⲟⲉ ιⲛ light.

ⲧ.пⲉ (pl. ⲙ̄.пⲏyⲉ) sky, heaven.

ⲛ̄ (ⲙ̄) of.

ⲛ̄ⲧⲉ of.　　　　　　　　　　　　ⲉⲧⲃⲉ (prep.) about,
ⲟⲩⲛ̄- there is, there are.　　concerning; for the sake
ⲙⲛ̄-, ⲙ̄ⲙⲛ̄- there is not,　　　of, because of.
　　there are not.　　　　　　ⲁⲛ not.

Exercises

A.1. ϩ ⲓ ⲭ ⲙ̄ ⲡ ⲭ ⲟ ⲓ　　　　　　11. ⲉⲧⲃⲉ ϩⲉⲛⲣ̄ⲣⲱⲟⲩ
2. ϩⲁ ⲧⲡⲉ　　　　　　　　　12. ϩⲉⲛⲣⲱⲙⲉ ⲙⲛ̄ ϩⲉⲛϩⲓⲟⲙⲉ
3. ϩⲛ̄ ⲙ̄ⲡⲏⲩⲉ　　　　　　　13. ϩⲉⲛⲧⲟⲟⲩ ⲙⲛ̄ ϩⲉⲛϩⲓⲟⲟⲩⲉ
4. ⲉⲧⲃⲉ ⲡⲣ̄ⲣⲟ　　　　　　　14. ϩⲁ ⲟⲩⲱⲛⲉ
5. ⲙⲛ̄ ⲑⲙ̄ϩⲁⲗ　　　　　　　15. ϩ ⲓ ⲭ ⲛ̄ ⲟⲩⲧⲟⲟⲩ
6. ϩⲛ̄ ⲧⲉⲙⲣⲱ　　　　　　　16. ϩⲛ̄ ⲟⲩⲧⲃ̄ⲧ
7. ϩ ⲓ ⲡⲉ ⲓ ⲉⲣⲟ　　　　　　17. ϩ ⲓ ϩⲉⲛⲏ ⲓ
8. ⲉⲧⲃⲉ ⲡⲛⲟⲩⲃ　　　　　　18. ⲙⲛ̄ ⲟⲩϩⲁⲗⲱ
9. ϩⲛ̄ ⲛⲉⲙⲣⲟⲟⲩⲉ　　　　　19. ⲉⲧⲃⲉ ⲟⲩⲭⲱⲱⲙⲉ
10. ϩⲁ ⲡⲭⲟ ⲓ　　　　　　　20. ⲉⲧⲃⲉ ⲡⲟⲩⲟⲉ ⲓ ⲛ

B.1. ⲛ̄ⲧⲃ̄ⲧ ⲙ̄ ⲡⲉ ⲓ ⲉⲣⲟ　　　　7. ⲡⲣⲁⲛ ⲛ̄ ⲧⲣ̄ⲣⲱ
2. ⲛⲉϫⲏⲩ ⲛ̄ ⲛ̄ⲣⲱⲙⲉ　　　8. ⲛ̄ⲭⲱⲱⲙⲉ ⲙ̄ ⲡϩⲁⲗⲟ
3. ⲛ̄ⲏ ⲓ ⲙ̄ ⲡⲣ̄ⲣⲟ　　　　　9. ⲡⲙⲟⲟⲩ ⲙ̄ ⲡⲉ ⲓ ⲉⲣⲟ
4. ⲡⲣⲁⲛ ⲙ̄ ⲡϩⲁⲗⲟ　　　　10. ϩⲉⲛⲱⲛⲉ ⲛ̄ⲧⲉ ⲡⲧⲟⲟⲩ
5. ⲡⲟⲩⲟⲉ ⲓ ⲛ ⲛ̄ ⲧⲡⲉ　　　11. ⲟⲩϩⲙ̄ϩⲁⲗ ⲛ̄ⲧⲉ ⲡⲣ̄ⲣⲟ
6. ⲡⲙⲟⲟⲩ ⲛ̄ ⲧⲉⲙⲣⲱ　　　12. ⲧⲉⲥϩⲓⲙⲉ ⲙ̄ ⲡϩⲙ̄ϩⲁⲗ

C.1. ⲟⲩⲛ̄-ⲟⲩⲟⲩⲟⲉ ⲓ ⲛ ϩⲛ̄ ⲙ̄ⲡⲏⲩⲉ.　6. ⲙⲛ̄-ⲏ ⲓ ϩ ⲓ ⲭ ⲙ̄ ⲡⲧⲟⲟⲩ.
2. ⲙⲛ̄-ⲧⲃ̄ⲧ ϩⲛ̄ ⲧⲉⲙⲣⲱ.　　　　7. ⲛⲉϫⲏⲩ ϩ ⲓ ⲡⲉ ⲓ ⲉⲣⲟ ⲁⲛ.
3. ⲙⲛ̄-ⲙⲟⲟⲩ ϩⲙ̄ ⲡⲉ ⲓ ⲉⲣⲟ.　　　8. ⲙⲛ̄-ⲭⲟ ⲓ ϩ ⲓ ⲡⲉ ⲓ ⲉⲣⲟ.
4. ⲟⲩⲛ̄-ⲟⲩϩⲁⲗⲟ ϩ ⲓ ⲧⲉϩⲓⲏ.　　9. ⲛ̄ⲭⲱⲱⲙⲉ ϩ ⲓ ⲭ ⲙ̄ ⲡⲭⲟ ⲓ ⲁⲛ.
5. ⲟⲩⲛ̄-ϩⲉⲛⲱⲛⲉ ϩⲛ̄ ⲧⲉⲙⲣⲱ.　　10. ⲙⲛ̄-ⲛⲟⲩⲃ ϩⲙ̄ ⲡⲏ ⲓ ⲙ̄ ⲡϩⲙ̄ϩⲁⲗ.

Lesson 3

3.1 Relative clauses. As we shall see in subsequent lessons, relative clauses in Coptic exhibit a variety of forms, depending on the type of predication involved. In the present lesson we shall consider only those relative clauses associated with sentences with adverbial predicates. Note the transformation

ⲡⲣⲱⲙⲉ ⲍⲘ̅ ⲡⲎⲓ   →   (ⲡⲣⲱⲙⲉ) ⲉⲧ ⲍⲘ̅ ⲡⲎⲓ
The man is in the house.   (the man) who is in the house

The relative pronoun ⲉⲧ functions here as the subject of the relative clause; it is not inflected for number or gender:

ⲧⲉⲥ2ⲓⲘⲉ ⲉⲧ 2ⲓ ⲧⲉ2ⲓⲎ   the woman who is on the road
Ⲛ̅2ⲗ̅ⲗⲟ ⲉⲧ 2Ⲛ̅ ⲑⲉⲛⲉⲉⲧⲉ   the monks who are in the monastery

Negation is with ⲁⲛ: Ⲛ̅2ⲗ̅ⲗⲟ ⲉⲧ 2Ⲛ̅ ⲑⲉⲛⲉⲉⲧⲉ ⲁⲛ.

Relative clauses cannot be used to modify an indefinite noun. This is an *important general rule* of Coptic.

Any relative clause may be substantivized, i.e. converted to the status of a noun, by prefixing the appropriate form of the definite article:

ⲡⲉⲧ 2Ⲙ̅ ⲡⲎⲓ   the one who (he who, that which) is in the house
ⲧⲉⲧ ⲘⲚ̅ ⲡⲱⲏⲣⲉ   the one (f.) who is with the boy
ⲛⲉⲧ 2ⲓ ⲡⲝⲟⲓ   those who (those things which) are on the ship

Such constructions may refer to persons or things, depending on the context.

The relative clause ⲉⲧ Ⲙ̅ⲙⲁⲩ, who (which) is there, is used to express the further demonstrative "that":

ⲡⲣⲱⲙⲉ ⲉⲧ Ⲙ̅ⲙⲁⲩ   that man
ⲛⲉⲝⲏⲩ ⲉⲧ Ⲙ̅ⲙⲁⲩ   those ships

3.2 Greek nouns. The typical Coptic text contains a large number of Greek loanwords. Greek masculine and feminine nouns retain their gender; Greek neuter nouns are treated as masculine:

ὁ ἄγγελος	πⲁⲅⲅⲉⲗⲟⲥ	the angel
ἡ ἐπιστολή	ⲧⲉⲡⲓⲥⲧⲟⲗⲏ	the letter
ἡ ψυχή	ⲧⲉⲯⲩⲭⲏ	the soul
τὸ πνεῦμα	ⲡⲉⲡⲛⲉⲩⲙⲁ	the spirit
τὸ δῶρον	ⲡⲁⲱⲣⲟⲛ	the gift

Greek nouns appear in the nominative singular form of Greek and are usually not inflected in any way. Occasionally, however, a Coptic plural ending is added to a Greek noun:

ⲛ̄ⲉⲡⲓⲥⲧⲟⲗⲟⲟⲩⲉ the letters   ⲛⲉⲯⲩⲭⲟⲟⲩⲉ the souls

The Greek noun ἡ θάλασσα (the sea) was borrowed as ⲧ.ⲍⲁⲗⲁⲥⲥⲁ, i.e. θ was taken as the definite article plus ⲍ. Thus, "a sea" is ⲟⲩⲍⲁⲗⲁⲥⲥⲁ.

Initial χ, φ, θ, ψ, ξ of Greek nouns are considered two consonants in attaching the definite article (cf. Intro., p. x).

ⲧⲉ.ⲭⲱⲣⲁ   the country   ⲧⲉ.ⲯⲩⲭⲏ   the soul
ⲡⲉ.ⲫⲓⲗⲟⲥⲟⲫⲟⲥ the philosopher ⲧⲉ.ⲑⲩⲥⲓⲁ   the offering.

Vocabulary 3

ⲡ.ϯⲙⲉ (pl. ⲛⲉ.ⲧⲙⲉ) town, village.

ⲡ.ⲣⲟ (pl. ⲛ̄.ⲣⲱⲟⲩ) door, gate.

ⲡ.ϫⲟⲉⲓⲥ (pl. ⲛ̄.ϫⲓⲥⲟⲟⲩⲉ) master, owner, lord; w. art., the Lord.

ⲡ.ⲛⲟⲩⲧⲉ god; w. art., God.

ⲡⲉ.ⲕⲣⲟ (ⲛⲉ.ⲕⲣⲱⲟⲩ) shore, bank, margin-land.

ⲡ.ⲕⲁⲕⲉ darkness.

ⲡ.ϣⲏⲣⲉ son, child, boy.

ⲧ.ϣⲉⲉⲣⲉ daughter, girl.

ⲙ̅ⲙⲁⲩ (adv.) there, in that place.

ⲍ ⲓ ⲡ ⲛ̅ (ⲍ ⲓ ⲡ ⲙ̅) (prep.) at the mouth or entrance of.

ⲛⲁⲍ ⲣ ⲛ̅, ⲛ̅ⲛⲁ ⲍ ⲣ ⲛ̅ (ⲛⲁ ⲍ ⲣ ⲙ̅)   in the presence of, before.

Greek nouns:

ⲑⲁⲗⲁⲥⲥⲁ (ἡ θάλασσα) sea, ocean.

ⲧ.ⲡⲟⲗⲓⲥ (ἡ πόλις) city.

ⲧ.ⲉⲡⲓⲥⲧⲟⲗⲏ (ἡ ἐπιστολή) letter.

ⲡ.ⲁⲅⲅⲉⲗⲟⲥ (ὁ ἄγγελος)
  angel, messenger.

ⲡ.ⲧⲁⲫⲟⲥ (ὁ τάφος) tomb.

ⲡ.ⲙⲁⲑⲏⲧⲏⲥ (ὁ μαθητής)
  pupil, disciple.

ⲧ.ⲉⲕⲕⲗⲏⲥⲓⲁ (ἡ ἐκκλησία)
  church.

Proper names:

ⲡⲁⲩⲗⲟⲥ (Παῦλος) Paul.

ⲓⲏⲥⲟⲩⲥ (Ἰησοῦς) Jesus; almost always abbreviated in
  Coptic texts: ⲓ̅ⲥ̅, ⲓ̅ⲏ̅ⲥ̅.

Exercises

A.1. ⲍ ⲓ ⲡ ⲛ̅ ⲧⲉⲕⲕⲗⲏⲥ ⲓ ⲁ

2. ⲛ̅ⲛⲁ ⲍ ⲣ ⲙ̅ ⲡ̅ⲣ̅ⲣⲟ

3. ⲍ ⲙ̅ ⲡⲧⲁⲫⲟⲥ

4. ⲙⲛ̅ ⲙ̅ⲙⲁⲑⲏⲧⲏⲥ

5. ⲡⲣⲟ ⲙ̅ ⲡⲏ ⲓ

6. ⲡⲭⲟⲉ ⲓ ⲥ ⲙ̅ ⲡⲭⲟ ⲓ

7. ⲛ̅ⲭ ⲓ ⲥⲟⲟⲩⲉ ⲛ̅ ⲛⲉⲭⲏⲩ

8. ⲧⲟ̅ⲉⲉⲣⲉ ⲙ̅ ⲡⲍⲙ̅ⲍⲁⲗ

9. ⲍ ⲓ ⲡ ⲙ̅ ⲡⲣⲟ ⲙ̅ ⲡⲏ ⲓ

10. ⲟⲩⲉⲕⲕⲗⲏⲥ ⲓ ⲁ ⲛ̅ⲧⲉ ⲡ†ⲙⲉ

11. ⲟⲩⲉⲡ ⲓ ⲥⲧⲟⲗⲏ ⲛ̅ⲧⲉ ⲡⲁⲩⲗⲟⲥ

12. ⲙ̅ⲙⲁⲑⲏⲧⲏⲥ ⲛ̅ ⲓ̅ⲥ̅

13. ⲍ ⲙ̅ ⲡⲣⲁⲛ ⲙ̅ ⲡⲭⲟⲉ ⲓ ⲥ

14. ⲛⲁ ⲍ ⲣ ⲙ̅ ⲡⲛⲟⲩⲧⲉ

15. ⲡⲉⲕⲣⲟ ⲙ̅ ⲡⲉ ⲓ ⲉⲣⲟ

16. ⲍ ⲓ ⲭ ⲙ̅ ⲡⲉⲕⲣⲟ ⲛ̅ ⲑⲁⲗⲁⲥⲥⲁ

17. ⲍ ⲛ̅ ⲟⲩⲕⲁⲕⲉ

18. ⲍ ⲓ ⲣ ⲙ̅ ⲡⲣⲟ ⲙ̅ ⲡⲧⲁⲫⲟⲥ

19. ⲛ̅ⲭⲱⲱⲙⲉ ⲙ̅ ⲡⲙⲁⲑⲏⲧⲏⲥ

20. ⲛ̅ⲣⲱⲙⲉ ⲛ̅ ⲛⲉⲧⲙⲉ

B.1. ⲡⲱⲛⲉ ⲉⲧ ⲍ ⲛ̅ ⲧⲉⲙⲣⲱ

2. ⲙ̅ⲙⲁⲑⲏⲧⲏⲥ ⲉⲧ ⲙⲛ̅ ⲓ̅ⲥ̅

3. ⲡⲕⲁⲕⲉ ⲉⲧ ⲍ ⲓ ⲭ ⲛ̅ ⲧⲡⲟⲗ ⲓ ⲥ

4. ⲛ̅ⲉⲕⲕⲗⲏⲥ ⲓ ⲁ ⲉⲧ ⲍ ⲛ̅ ⲧⲡⲟⲗ ⲓ ⲥ

5. ⲡⲟⲩⲟⲉ ⲓ ⲛ ⲉⲧ ⲍ ⲛ̅ ⲙ̅ⲡⲏⲩⲉ

6. ⲛ̅ⲧⲃ̅ⲧ ⲉⲧ ⲍ ⲛ̅ ⲑⲁⲗⲁⲥⲥⲁ

7. ⲡⲍⲙ̅ⲍⲁⲗ ⲉⲧ ⲛ̅ⲛⲁ ⲍ ⲣ ⲙ̅ ⲡⲭⲟⲉ ⲓ ⲥ

8. ⲡⲙⲟⲟⲩ ⲉⲧ ⲍ ⲙ̅ ⲡⲉ ⲓ ⲉⲣⲟ

9. ⲛ̅ⲁⲅⲅⲉⲗⲟⲥ ⲉⲧ ⲍ ⲛ̅ ⲙ̅ⲡⲏⲩⲉ

10. ⲛ̅ⲍⲗⲗⲟ ⲉⲧ ⲍ ⲙ̅ ⲡⲧⲟⲟⲩ

11. ⲛ̅ⲣⲱⲙⲉ ⲛ̅ ⲧⲡⲟⲗ ⲓ ⲥ ⲉⲧ ⲙ̅ⲙⲁⲩ

12. ⲛⲉⲧⲙⲉ ⲉⲧ ⲙ̅ⲙⲁⲩ

13. ⲙ̅ⲙⲁⲑⲏⲧⲏⲥ ⲙ̅ ⲡⲣⲱⲙⲉ ⲉⲧ ⲙ̅ⲙⲁⲩ

14. ⲛ̅ⲟ̅ⲏⲣⲉ ⲙ̅ ⲡⲍⲙ̅ⲍⲁⲗ ⲉⲧ ⲙ̅ⲙⲁⲩ

15. ⲛⲉⲭⲏⲩ ⲉⲧ ⲍ ⲓ ⲭ ⲙ̅ ⲡⲉⲕⲣⲟ ⲙ̅
     ⲡⲉ ⲓ ⲉⲣⲟ

C.1. ⲡⲛⲟⲩⲧⲉ ϩⲛ̄ ⲧⲡⲉ.

2. ⲙⲛ̄-ⲉⲕⲕⲗⲏⲥⲓⲁ ϩⲙ̄ ⲡ†ⲙⲉ
ⲉⲧ ⲙ̄ⲙⲁⲩ.

3. ⲟⲩⲛ̄-ⲟⲩⲁⲅⲅⲉⲗⲟⲥ ϩⲓⲡⲙ̄
ⲡⲣⲟ ⲙ̄ ⲡⲧⲁⲫⲟⲥ.

4. ⲛ̄ⲉⲡⲓⲥⲧⲟⲗⲏ ⲙⲛ̄ ⲛ̄ϫⲱⲱⲙⲉ.

5. ⲙⲛ̄-ϫⲱⲱⲙⲉ ⲙ̄ⲙⲁⲩ.

6. ⲟⲩⲛ̄-ⲟⲩⲙⲁⲑⲏⲧⲏⲥ ⲛ̄ⲧⲉ
ⲡⲁⲩⲗⲟⲥ ϩⲓⲡⲙ̄ ⲡⲣⲟ.

7. ⲙⲛ̄-ⲟⲩⲟⲉⲓⲛ ϩⲙ̄ ⲡⲕⲁⲕⲉ.

8. ⲡϫⲟⲉⲓⲥ ⲙ̄ ⲡⲏⲓ ϩⲙ̄ ⲡⲏⲓ ⲁⲛ.

9. ⲡϫⲟⲓ ϩⲓϫⲙ̄ ⲡⲉⲓⲉⲣⲟ ⲁⲛ.

10. ⲛ̄ϣⲏⲣⲉ ⲙ̄ ⲡ†ⲙⲉ ϩⲓ ⲧⲉϩⲓⲏ.

11. ⲟⲩⲛ̄-ϩⲉⲛⲧⲁⲫⲟⲥ ϩⲛ̄ ⲛⲉⲕⲣⲱⲟⲩ
ⲉⲧ ⲙ̄ⲙⲁⲩ.

12. ⲟⲩⲛ̄-ⲟⲩⲕⲁⲕⲉ ϩⲓϫⲛ̄ ⲧⲡⲟⲗⲓⲥ.

Lesson 4

4.1 Pronominal possession is indicated by inserting a bound form of the appropriate pronoun between the definite article and the noun so modified. It is best to learn the forms, i.e. the article plus the pronoun, as a unit:

		masc. sing. noun		fem. sing. noun	
sg.	1 com.	ⲡⲁⲉⲓⲱⲧ	my father	ⲧⲁⲙⲁⲁⲩ	my mother
	2 masc.	ⲡⲉⲕⲉⲓⲱⲧ	your father	ⲧⲉⲕⲙⲁⲁⲩ	your mother
	2 fem.	ⲡⲟⲩⲉⲓⲱⲧ	your father	ⲧⲟⲩⲙⲁⲁⲩ	your mother
	3 masc.	ⲡⲉϥⲉⲓⲱⲧ	his father	ⲧⲉϥⲙⲁⲁⲩ	his mother
	3 fem.	ⲡⲉⲥⲉⲓⲱⲧ	her father	ⲧⲉⲥⲙⲁⲁⲩ	her mother
pl.	1 com.	ⲡⲉⲛⲉⲓⲱⲧ	our father	ⲧⲉⲛⲙⲁⲁⲩ	our mother
	2 com.	ⲡⲉⲧⲛ̄ⲉⲓⲱⲧ	your father	ⲧⲉⲧⲛ̄ⲙⲁⲁⲩ	your mother
	3 com.	ⲡⲉⲩⲉⲓⲱⲧ	their father	ⲧⲉⲩⲙⲁⲁⲩ	their mother

plural noun (my brothers, etc.)

sg.	1 com.	ⲛⲁⲥⲛⲏⲩ	pl.	1 com.	ⲛⲉⲛⲥⲛⲏⲩ
	2 masc.	ⲛⲉⲕⲥⲛⲏⲩ		2 com.	ⲛⲉⲧⲛ̄ⲥⲛⲏⲩ
	2 fem.	ⲛⲟⲩⲥⲛⲏⲩ			
	3 masc.	ⲛⲉϥⲥⲛⲏⲩ		3 com.	ⲛⲉⲩⲥⲛⲏⲩ
	3 fem.	ⲛⲉⲥⲥⲛⲏⲩ			

Note that there is a gender distinction in the second and
third persons of the singular but not of the plural. This
is characteristic of all pronominal paradigms in Coptic.
The term "common" (com.) refers to forms or categories
where no gender distinction is made.

4.2 The nearer demonstrative "this" is expressed by
the forms

   masc. sing. ⲡⲉⲓ-   fem. sing. ⲧⲉⲓ-   com. pl. ⲛⲉⲓ-

prefixed directly to the noun:

        ⲡⲉⲓⲣⲱⲙⲉ   this man
        ⲧⲉⲓⲥϩⲓⲙⲉ   this woman
        ⲛⲉⲓⲥⲛⲏⲩ   these brothers

After a noun with a demonstrative adjective the genitive
is usually expressed by ⲛ̄ⲧⲉ, as in

   ⲡⲉⲓϫⲱⲱⲙⲉ ⲛ̄ⲧⲉ ⲡⲁⲥⲟⲛ   this book of my brother('s)

4.3 The pronominal element -ⲕⲉ- inserted between the
article and the noun expresses "other":

   ⲡⲕⲉⲣⲱⲙⲉ the other man   ⲛ̄ⲕⲉⲣⲱⲙⲉ the other men

The indefinite article is omitted in the singular but not
in the plural:

   ⲕⲉⲣⲱⲙⲉ another man   ϩⲉⲛⲕⲉⲣⲱⲙⲉ (some) other men

-ⲕⲉ- may also be used after demonstrative or possessive
prefixes:

   ⲡⲉⲓⲕⲉⲣⲱⲙⲉ this other man   ⲡⲁⲕⲉϫⲟⲓ my other ship

-ⲕⲉ- is not inflected for number or gender in this usage.

Vocabulary 4

ⲡ.ⲥⲟⲛ (pl. ⲛⲉ.ⲥⲛⲏⲩ) brother; often of a brother monk.
ⲧ.ⲥⲱⲛⲉ sister.
ⲡ.ⲉⲓⲱⲧ (pl. ⲛ̄.ⲉⲓⲟⲧⲉ) father; (pl.) parents, ancestors.

т.мааγ mother.   ⲛ̄ⲥⲁ (prep.) behind, in back of.
п.новє sin.   ⲛ̄ (ⲙ̄) (prep.) in; mostly synon-
п.ⲏⲣⲡ̄ wine.   ymous with ⲍ̄ⲛ̄.
п.оєіⲕ bread; piece or   ⲍⲁⲍⲧⲛ̄, ⲍⲁⲧⲛ̄ (ⲍⲁⲍⲧⲙ̄) (prep.) near,
   loaf of bread.   with, beside.
п.ⲙⲁ place; ⲙ̄ пєіⲙⲁ here,
   in this place.

Greek nouns:

п.ⲕⲟⲥⲙⲟⲥ (ὁ κόσμος) world.   п.ⲙⲟⲛⲁⲭⲟⲥ (ὁ μοναχός) monk.
†ⲣⲏⲛⲏ (ἡ εἰρήνη) peace.   т.єⲛⲧⲟⲗⲏ (ἡ ἐντολή) command,
п.єпісⲕⲟпⲟⲥ (ὁ ἐπίσκοπος)   commandment.
   bishop.   т.ⲁⲅⲟⲣⲁ (ἡ ἀγορά) agora,
                                 forum, marketplace.

Exercises

A.1. ⲛ̄ⲥⲁ ⲛⲉϥⲙⲁⲑⲏⲧⲏⲥ   6. ⲛ̄ⲛⲁⲍⲣⲙ̄ пⲉⲛⲭⲟⲉⲓⲥ   11. ⲙⲛ̄ пⲉⲓⲏⲣⲡ̄
  2. ⲛⲁⲍⲣⲙ̄ пⲉⲩⲭⲟⲉⲓⲥ   7. ⲍⲓ ⲧⲉⲩⲉⲕⲕⲗⲏⲥⲓⲁ   12. ⲙⲛ̄ ⲛⲉϥⲥⲛⲏⲩ
  3. ⲍⲓⲣⲙ̄ пⲉϥⲧⲁϥⲟⲥ   8. ⲉⲧⲃⲉ пⲉⲧⲛ̄†ⲙⲉ   13. ⲉⲧⲃⲉ ⲧⲉⲛⲥⲱⲛⲉ
  4. ⲙⲛ̄ ⲧⲉϥϣⲉⲉⲣⲉ   9. ⲍⲛ̄ ⲧⲟⲩпⲟⲗⲓⲥ   14. ⲍⲙ̄ пⲕⲉⲏⲓ
  5. ⲛ̄ⲥⲁ пⲉⲥϣⲏⲣⲉ   10. ⲍⲙ̄ пⲉⲓⲕⲟⲥⲙⲟⲥ   15. ⲍⲛ̄ ⲕⲉⲙⲁ

B.1. ⲛ̄ⲉⲛⲧⲟⲗⲏ ⲛ̄ ⲛⲉⲛⲉⲓⲟⲧⲉ   11. пⲛⲟⲩⲃ ⲙ̄ пⲉⲩⲭⲟⲉⲓⲥ
  2. пⲣⲁⲛ ⲙ̄ пⲗⲉⲓⲱⲧ   12. пⲣⲁⲛ ⲛ̄ ⲧⲉⲧⲛ̄ⲙⲁⲁⲩ
  3. пⲣⲟ ⲙ̄ пⲉⲕⲏⲓ   13. ⲍⲁⲍⲧⲛ̄ ⲧⲉⲕⲉⲕⲕⲗⲏⲥⲓⲁ
  4. пⲣⲟ ⲙ̄ пⲕⲉⲏⲓ   14. ⲍⲁⲍⲧⲛ̄ ⲛⲉⲓⲧⲙⲉ
  5. ⲉⲧⲃⲉ ⲛⲉⲛⲛⲟⲃⲉ   15. ⲍⲁ ⲛⲟⲩⲛⲟⲃⲉ
  6. ⲍⲁⲍⲧⲙ̄ пⲉⲛⲏⲓ   16. ⲙⲛ̄ ⲛⲉⲧ ⲙ̄ п†ⲙⲉ
  7. ⲍⲛ̄ ⲟⲩⲉⲓⲣⲏⲛⲏ   17. ⲧⲉⲓⲉпⲓⲥⲧⲟⲗⲏ ⲛ̄ⲧⲉ пⲁⲩⲗⲟⲥ
  8. ⲛ̄ⲛⲁⲍⲣⲙ̄ пⲉⲛⲉпⲓⲥⲕⲟпⲟⲥ   18. пⲉⲓⲭⲟⲓ ⲛ̄ⲧⲉ пⲉⲛⲭⲟⲉⲓⲥ
  9. ⲧⲙⲁⲁⲩ ⲛ̄ ⲓ̄ⲥ̄   19. ⲍⲛ̄ ⲧⲁⲅⲟⲣⲁ ⲛ̄ ⲧпⲟⲗⲓⲥ
 10. пⲏⲣⲡ̄ ⲛ̄ ⲛⲉⲓⲙⲟⲛⲁⲭⲟⲥ

C.1. пⲉⲛⲭⲟⲉⲓⲥ ⲍⲓ пⲭⲟⲓ ⲁⲛ.   4. ⲙⲛ̄-ⲉⲓⲣⲏⲛⲏ ⲍⲙ̄ пⲉⲓⲕⲟⲥⲙⲟⲥ.
  2. ⲙⲛ̄-ⲏⲣⲡ̄ ⲙ̄ пⲉⲓⲙⲁ.   5. пⲗⲉⲓⲱⲧ ⲙⲛ̄ ⲧⲁⲙⲁⲁⲩ ⲍⲙ̄ пⲏⲓ.
  3. ⲟⲩⲛ̄-ⲟⲩⲍⲗ̄ⲗⲟ ⲍⲓⲣⲛ̄ ⲧⲉⲕⲕⲗⲏⲥⲓⲁ.

6. ⲟⲩⲛ̅-ⲍⲉⲛⲟⲉⲓⲕ ⲙ̅ⲙⲁⲩ.

7. ⲡⲉⲛⲥⲟⲛ ⲍⲓ ⲡⲉⲕⲣⲟ ⲛ̅ ⲑⲁⲗⲁⲥⲥⲁ.

8. ⲟⲩⲛ̅-ⲟⲩϫⲟⲓ ⲍⲁⲍⲧⲙ̅ ⲡⲉⲕⲣⲟ.

9. ⲟⲩⲛ̅-ⲟⲩⲍⲗ̅ⲗⲱ ⲍⲓⲣⲙ̅ ⲡⲣⲟ ⲙ̅ ⲡⲉϥⲏⲓ.

10. ⲛⲉⲛⲥⲛⲏⲩ ⲍⲓϫⲙ̅ ⲡⲧⲟⲟⲩ.

11. ⲡⲟⲩⲥⲟⲛ ⲍⲙ̅ ⲡⲧⲁⲫⲟⲥ ⲁⲛ.

12. ⲡⲉⲧⲛ̅ⲉⲓⲱⲧ ⲍⲓ ⲡⲁϫⲟⲓ.

13. ⲡⲉⲛϫⲟⲓ ⲍⲛ̅ ⲧⲉⲙⲣⲱ.

14. ⲡⲉϥϫⲱⲱⲙⲉ ⲍⲓ ⲡⲱⲛⲉ ⲉⲧ ⲙ̅ⲙⲁⲩ.

15. ⲙⲛ̅-ⲍⲓⲏ ⲙ̅ ⲡⲙⲁ ⲉⲧ ⲙ̅ⲙⲁⲩ.

Lesson 5

5.1 Sentences with nominal predicates. A second type
of non-verbal sentence is illustrated by

ⲡⲁⲉⲓⲱⲧ ⲡⲉ.	He is my father. It is my father.
ⲧⲁⲙⲁⲁⲩ ⲧⲉ.	She (It) is my mother.
ⲛⲁⲥⲛⲏⲩ ⲛⲉ.	They are (It is) my brothers.
ⲟⲩⲣⲱⲙⲉ ⲡⲉ.	He (It) is a man.
ⲟⲩⲥⲍⲓⲙⲉ ⲧⲉ.	She (It) is a woman.
ⲍⲉⲛⲉϫⲏⲩ ⲛⲉ.	They are (It is) ships.

The pronominal subject is expressed by ⲡⲉ (m.s.), ⲧⲉ
(f.s.), and ⲛⲉ (pl.), the choice of which depends usually
on the gender and number of the predicate noun. Simple
two-member sentences like the above are relatively rare
except in response to such questions as "Who is that?"
"What are these?" where an answer giving the predicate
alone is sufficient, the subject being understood from the
context. Modifiers of the predicate, such as a genitive
phrase, may optionally stand after the pronominal subject:

ⲡϣⲏⲣⲉ ⲡⲉ ⲙ̅ ⲡⲟⲩⲏⲏⲃ. He is the son of the priest.

A nominal subject may be added to the basic predication, producing a three-member sentence in which ⲡⲉ, ⲧⲉ,
ⲛⲉ are reduced virtually to the status of a copula. If

the predicate is indefinite, the order is almost always predicate + ⲡⲉ, the subject being placed before or after the whole unit:

ⲟⲩⲥⲁϩ ⲡⲉ ⲡⲁⲉⲓⲱⲧ.
ⲡⲁⲉⲓⲱⲧ ⲟⲩⲥⲁϩ ⲡⲉ. } My father is a teacher.

If the subject and predicate are both definite, the normal position of ⲡⲉ, ⲧⲉ, ⲛⲉ is between them:

ⲡⲉⲓⲣⲱⲙⲉ ⲡⲉ ⲡⲉⲛⲥⲁϩ.   This man is our teacher.

Identification of subject and predicate in this case can be made only on a contextual basis. The rarer order, ⲡⲉⲓⲣⲱⲙⲉ ⲡⲉⲛⲥⲁϩ ⲡⲉ, places an emphasis on the real subject: "As for this man, he is our teacher."

In the event that there is a disagreement in the number or gender of subject and predicate, the copula ⲡⲉ, ⲧⲉ, ⲛⲉ usually assumes the number and gender of the noun immediately preceding it.

All of the preceding sentences are negated by placing ⲛ̄ (ⲙ̄) before the predicate and ⲁⲛ before the ⲡⲉ, ⲧⲉ, ⲛⲉ:

ⲙ̄ ⲡⲁⲉⲓⲱⲧ ⲁⲛ ⲡⲉ.   It is not my father.
ⲡⲁⲉⲓⲱⲧ ⲛ̄ ⲟⲩⲥⲁϩ ⲁⲛ ⲡⲉ.   My father is not a teacher.
ⲙ̄ ⲡⲉⲛⲥⲁϩ ⲁⲛ ⲡⲉ ⲡⲉⲓⲣⲱⲙⲉ.   This man is not our teacher.

Note that in the case where both subject and predicate are definite, the nominal element negated is, by definition, the predicate.

Sentences with nominal predicates are converted to the status of relative clauses with ⲉⲧⲉ. For the moment we shall restrict ourselves to those clauses where ⲉⲧⲉ functions as the subject of the relative clause:

ⲡⲣⲱⲙⲉ ⲉⲧⲉ ⲟⲩⲥⲁϩ ⲡⲉ   the man who is a teacher
ⲡⲣⲱⲙⲉ ⲉⲧⲉ ⲛ̄ ⲟⲩⲥⲁϩ ⲁⲛ ⲡⲉ   the man who is not a teacher.

The phrase ⲉⲧⲉ ⲡⲁⲓ ⲡⲉ is frequently used to introduce explanatory material, much like English "namely, i.e., that is to say":

ⲡⲉⲛⲥⲱⲧⲏⲣ ⲉⲧⲉ ⲡⲁⲓ ⲡⲉ ⲓ̅ⲥ̅ ⲡⲉⲭ̅ⲥ̅ o,ur savior, i.e. Jesus Christ

    5.2 The nearer demonstrative pronouns (this, these) are ⲡⲁⲓ (m.s.), ⲧⲁⲓ (f.s.), and ⲛⲁⲓ (pl.). They are frequently employed as subjects in sentences with nominal predicates:

ⲛⲁⲓ ⲛⲉ ⲛⲉϥϣⲁⲭⲉ.	These are his words.
ⲡⲁⲓ ⲡⲉ ⲡⲁⲭⲟⲓ.	This is my ship.
ⲧⲁⲓ ⲟⲩⲍⲙ̅ⲍⲁⲗ ⲧⲉ. ⎱	This is a maidservant.
ⲟⲩⲍⲙ̅ⲍⲁⲗ ⲧⲉ ⲧⲁⲓ. ⎰	

Vocabulary 5

ⲡ.ⲥⲁⲍ teacher, master; scribe.

ⲡ.ⲟⲩⲏⲏⲃ priest (Christian or otherwise).

ⲡ.ⲍⲁⲙϣⲉ (pl. ⲛ̅.ⲍⲁⲙϣⲏⲩⲉ) carpenter.

ⲡ.ⲉⲣⲡⲉ, ⲡ.ⲣ̅ⲡⲉ (pl. ⲛ̅.ⲣ̅ⲡⲏⲩⲉ) temple.

ⲡ.ⲙⲏⲏϣⲉ crowd, throng.

ⲡ.ⲍⲁⲓ husband.

ⲧ.ϭⲟⲙ power, strength.

ⲧ.ⲙⲏⲧⲉ middle, midst; ⲛ̅/ⲍⲛ̅ ⲧⲙⲏⲧⲉ ⲛ̅ in the middle/midst of.

ⲡ.ϭⲁⲙⲟⲩⲗ (f. ⲧ.ϭⲁⲙⲁⲩⲗⲉ) camel.

ⲙⲉϣⲁⲕ (adv.) perhaps.

Greek nouns:

ⲡⲉ.ⲭⲣⲓⲥⲧⲟⲥ (ὁ χριστός) the Christ, regularly abbr. ⲭ̅ⲥ̅.

ⲡ.ⲉⲩⲁⲅⲅⲉⲗⲓⲟⲛ (τὸ εὐαγγέλιον) gospel.

ⲧ.ⲡⲁⲣⲑⲉⲛⲟⲥ (ἡ παρθένος) virgin; young woman.

ⲧ.ⲟⲣⲓⲛⲏ (ἡ ὀρεινή) mountain district, hill-country.

ⲡ.ⲁⲥⲡⲁⲥⲙⲟⲥ (ὁ ἀσπασμός) greeting.

ⲡ.ⲥⲱⲧⲏⲣ (ὁ σωτήρ) savior, redeemer; sometimes abbreviated as ⲥ̅ⲱ̅ⲣ̅.

Proper names:

ⲉⲗⲓⲥⲁⲃⲉⲧ Elizabeth.

ⲙⲁⲣⲓⲁ Mary.

ⲓⲱⲥⲏⲫ Joseph.

ⲍⲁⲭⲁⲣⲓⲁⲥ Zacharias.

ⲓⲱⲍⲁⲛⲛⲏⲥ John.

Exercises

A.1. ⲟⲩ⳿ϩⲙϩⲁⲗ ⲧⲉ ⲛ̄ⲧⲉ ⲧⲁⲙⲁⲁⲩ.
  2. ⲟⲩⲧⲃ̄ⲧ ⲡⲉ.
  3. ⲟⲩⲭⲱⲱⲙⲉ ⲡⲉ ⲛ̄ⲧⲉ ⲡⲉⲕⲥⲟⲛ.
  4. ⲟⲩⲡⲁⲣⲑⲉⲛⲟⲥ ⲧⲉ.
  5. ϩⲉⲛⲟⲩⲏⲏⲃ ⲛⲉ.
  6. ⲡϣⲏⲣⲉ ⲛ̄ ⲧⲁⲥⲱⲛⲉ ⲡⲉ.
  7. ⲧϣⲉⲉⲣⲉ ⲙ̄ ⲡϩⲁⲙϣⲉ ⲧⲉ.
  8. ⲧⲙⲁⲁⲩ ⲙ̄ ⲡⲉⲛⲥⲱⲧⲏⲣ ⲧⲉ.

  9. ⲡϩⲁⲙⲟⲩⲗ ⲡⲉ ⲙ̄ ⲡⲉϥⲉⲓⲱⲧ.
  10. ⲛ̄ ⲟⲩϩⲟⲓ ⲁⲛ ⲡⲉ.
  11. ⲟⲩⲛⲟⲃⲉ ⲡⲉ.
  12. ⲛ̄ ⲟⲩⲛⲟⲩⲧⲉ ⲁⲛ ⲡⲉ.
  13. ⲙ̄ ⲡⲉⲛⲏⲓ ⲁⲛ ⲡⲉ.
  14. ϩⲉⲛⲥⲁϩ ⲛⲉ.
  15. ⲛ̄ⲉⲛⲧⲟⲗⲏ ⲛⲉ ⲙ̄ ⲡⲉⲛϫⲟⲉⲓⲥ.

B.1. ⲧⲁⲓ ⲧⲉ ⲧϭⲟⲙ ⲙ̄ ⲡⲛⲟⲩⲧⲉ.
  2. ⲡⲁⲓ ⲙ̄ ⲡⲉⲥϩⲁⲓ ⲁⲛ ⲡⲉ.
  3. ⲟⲩϭⲁⲙⲁⲩⲗⲉ ⲧⲉ ⲧⲁⲓ.
  4. ⲛⲁⲓ ⲛⲉ ⲛ̄ϣⲁϫⲉ ⲙ̄ ⲡⲉⲩⲁⲅⲅⲉⲗⲓⲟⲛ.
  5. ⲡⲉⲩϯⲙⲉ ϩⲛ̄ ⲧⲟⲣⲓⲛⲏ.
  6. ⲡⲉϥⲏⲓ ⲛ̄ ⲧⲙⲏⲧⲉ ⲛ̄ ⲧⲡⲟⲗⲓⲥ.
  7. ⲡⲁⲉⲓⲱⲧ ⲟⲩϩⲁⲙϣⲉ ⲡⲉ.
  8. ⲡⲉϥϣⲏⲣⲉ ⲟⲩⲟⲩⲏⲏⲃ ⲡⲉ.
  9. ϩⲉⲛⲟⲩⲏⲏⲃ ⲛⲉ ⲛⲉϥⲥⲛⲏⲩ.
  10. ⲙⲉϣⲁⲕ ⲡⲉⲥϩⲁⲓ ⲡⲉ.
  11. ⲡⲟⲩϩⲁⲓ ϩⲓⲣⲙ̄ ⲡⲣⲟ.
  12. ⲡⲉⲥⲣⲁⲛ ⲡⲉ ⲉⲗⲓⲥⲁⲃⲉⲧ.
  13. ⲉⲗⲓⲥⲁⲃⲉⲧ ⲧⲙⲁⲁⲩ ⲧⲉ ⲛ̄ ⲓⲱϩⲁⲛⲛⲏⲥ.

  14. ⲓⲱϩⲁⲛⲛⲏⲥ ⲡⲉ ⲡϣⲏⲣⲉ ⲛ̄ ⲍⲁⲭⲁⲣⲓⲁⲥ.
  15. ⲡⲁⲣⲁⲛ ⲛ̄ ⲓⲱⲥⲏⲫ ⲁⲛ ⲡⲉ.
  16. ⲡⲉⲧⲛ̄ⲏⲓ ϩⲁϩⲧⲙ̄ ⲡⲉⲣⲡⲉ.
  17. ⲙⲉϣⲁⲕ ⲡⲉⲓⲣⲱⲙⲉ ⲡⲉ ⲡⲉⲭ̄ⲥ̄.
  18. ⲡⲁⲓ ⲡⲉ ⲡⲁⲥⲡⲁⲥⲙⲟⲥ ⲙ̄ ⲙⲁⲣⲓⲁ.
  19. ⲙⲁⲣⲓⲁ ⲟⲩⲡⲁⲣⲑⲉⲛⲟⲥ ⲧⲉ.
  20. ⲟⲩⲛ̄-ⲟⲩⲙⲏⲏϣⲉ ⲛ̄ ⲧⲙⲏⲧⲉ ⲛ̄ ⲧⲁⲅⲟⲣⲁ.
  21. ⲙⲛ̄-ⲉⲓⲣⲏⲛⲏ ⲙ̄ ⲡⲉⲓⲙⲁ.
  22. ⲟⲩⲛ̄-ϩⲉⲛⲧⲙⲉ ϩⲛ̄ ⲧⲟⲣⲓⲛⲏ.
  23. ⲙⲉϣⲁⲕ ⲟⲩⲛ̄-ⲟⲩⲥⲁϩ ϩⲙ̄ ⲡϯⲙⲉ.
  24. ⲛⲁⲓ ⲛⲉ ⲛⲉⲛⲛⲟⲃⲉ.
  25. ϩⲉⲛⲟⲉⲓⲕ ⲛⲉ ⲛⲁⲓ.

C.1. ⲛⲉⲧⲙⲉ ⲉⲧ ⲛ̄ⲥⲁ ⲡⲧⲟⲟⲩ
  2. ⲡⲣⲱⲙⲉ ⲉⲧⲉ ⲟⲩⲉⲡⲓⲥⲕⲟⲡⲟⲥ ⲡⲉ
  3. ⲛⲉⲓϣⲁϫⲉ ⲉⲧⲉ ⲡⲉⲥⲁⲥⲡⲁⲥⲙⲟⲥ ⲛⲉ
  4. ⲡⲙⲏⲏϣⲉ ⲉⲧ ϩⲓϫⲙ̄ ⲡⲉⲕⲣⲟ
  5. ⲧϩⲁ̄ⲗⲱ ⲉⲧⲉ ⲟⲩⲡⲁⲣⲑⲉⲛⲟⲥ ⲧⲉ
  6. ⲛⲉϩⲓⲟⲟⲩⲉ ⲉⲧ ϩⲛ̄ ⲧⲟⲣⲓⲛⲏ
  7. ⲛⲉϫⲏⲩ ⲉⲧ ϩⲛ̄ ⲧⲙⲏⲧⲉ ⲛ̄ ⲑⲁⲗⲁⲥⲥⲁ
  8. ⲡⲉⲭ̄ⲥ̄, ⲉⲧⲉ ⲡⲁⲓ ⲡⲉ ⲡⲉⲛⲥⲱⲧⲏⲣ
  9. ⲡⲉⲣⲡⲉ, ⲉⲧⲉ ⲡⲁⲓ ⲡⲉ ⲡⲏⲓ ⲙ̄ ⲡϫⲟⲉⲓⲥ
  10. ⲡⲉⲓϫⲱⲱⲙⲉ, ⲉⲧⲉ ⲡⲁⲓ ⲡⲉ ⲡⲉⲩⲁⲅⲅⲉⲗⲓⲟⲛ

Lesson 6

6.1 The independent personal pronouns.

ⲁⲛⲟⲕ	I	ⲁⲛⲟⲛ	we
ⲛ̄ⲧⲟⲕ	you (m.s.)	ⲛ̄ⲧⲱⲧⲛ̄	you (c.pl.)
ⲛ̄ⲧⲟ	you (f.s.)		
ⲛ̄ⲧⲟϥ	he, it (m.)	ⲛ̄ⲧⲟⲟⲩ	they (c.pl.)
ⲛ̄ⲧⲟⲥ	she, it (f.)		

These pronouns occur frequently in sentences with ⲡⲉ, ⲧⲉ, ⲛⲉ. When used as predicates in a two-member sentence, they are invariably followed by ⲡⲉ:

ⲁⲛⲟⲕ ⲡⲉ. It is I.   ⲁⲛⲟⲛ ⲡⲉ. It is we.
ⲛ̄ⲧⲟⲥ ⲡⲉ. It is she.

In three-member sentences they may appear in ordinary subject or predicate positions:

ⲛ̄ⲧⲟϥ ⲡⲉ ⲡⲉⲭ̄ⲥ̄.   He is the Christ.
ⲛ̄ⲧⲟϥ ⲟⲩⲛⲟⲩⲧⲉ ⲡⲉ.   He is a god.
ⲛⲉϥ₂ⲙ̄₂ⲁⲗ ⲛⲉ ⲁⲛⲟⲛ.   We are his servants.

In sentences with an indefinite nominal predicate a special construction without ⲡⲉ is used with the pronouns of the 1st and 2nd person; negation is with ⲁⲛ alone:

ⲁⲛⲟⲕ ⲟⲩ₂ⲁⲙϣⲉ (ⲁⲛ)   I am (not) a carpenter.
ⲁⲛⲟⲛ ₂ⲉⲛⲟⲩⲏⲏⲃ.   We are priests.

In this construction a reduced proclitic form of the pronoun is very often used:

ⲁⲛⲅ̄-	I	ⲁⲛ-	we
ⲛ̄ⲧⲕ̄-	you (m.s.)	ⲛ̄ⲧⲉⲧⲛ̄-	you (c.pl.)
ⲛ̄ⲧⲉ-	you (f.s.)		

as in

ⲁⲛⲅ̄-ⲟⲩⲁⲅⲅⲉⲗⲟⲥ (ⲁⲛ)   I am (not) an angel.
ⲛ̄ⲧⲕ̄-ⲟⲩ₂ⲁⲙϣⲉ.   You are a carpenter.
ⲛ̄ⲧⲉⲧⲛ̄-₂ⲉⲛⲙⲁⲑⲏⲧⲏⲥ.   You are pupils.

A 3rd person masc. form ⲚⲦϤ- also occurs, but is very rare. The reduced forms of the 1st and 2nd person pronouns may also be used with a definite predicate, but this construction is rather infrequent:

ⲀⲚⲄ̅-ⲐⲘ̅ϩⲀⲗ Ⲙ̅ ⲠⳆⲞⲉⲓⲥ.   I am the handmaiden of the Lord.

6.2 The interrogative pronouns.

ⲚⲓⲘ   who?   ⲀϢ   what?   ⲞⲨ   what?

These pronouns are used in sentences with ⲠⲈ, ⲦⲈ, ⲚⲈ:

ⲚⲓⲘ ⲠⲈ?	Who is it?
ⲀϢ ⲠⲈ?	What is it?
ⲚⲓⲘ ⲠⲈ ⲠⲈⳆⲢⲱⲘⲈ?	Who is this man?
ⲚⲓⲘ ⲠⲈ ⲠⲈⲔⲢⲀⲚ?	What is your name? (note idiom)
ⲞⲨ ⲠⲈ ⲠⲀⳆ?	What is this?
ⲞⲨ ⲚⲈ ⲚⲀⳆ?	What are these?

The interrogative pronoun normally stands first. The choice of number and gender for the copula depends on the understood or expressed subject. The pronoun ⲞⲨ is also found with the indefinite article:

ⲞⲨⲞⲨ ⲠⲈ?	What is it? (lit.: It is a what?)
ϩⲈⲚⲞⲨ ⲚⲈ?	What are they (lit.: They are whats?)

When the subject is a personal pronoun of the 1st or 2nd person, it may be placed before ⲚⲓⲘ or ⲞⲨ in normal or proclitic form:

Ⲛ̅Ⲧⲕ̅-ⲚⲓⲘ?	Who are you?
Ⲛ̅ⲦⲞⲔ ⲞⲨⲞⲨ?	What are you?

The personal pronoun may be repeated for emphasis:

ⲀⲚⲄ̅-ⲚⲓⲘ ⲀⲚⲞⲔ?   Who am I?

Note that ⲚⲓⲘ may also be used in ordinary genitive constructions:

ⲠϢⲎⲢⲈ Ⲛ̅ ⲚⲓⲘ?   whose son?

Vocabulary 6

ⲡ.ϣⲱⲥ (pl. ⲛ̄.ϣⲟⲟⲥ) shepherd.　　ⲡ.ⲙⲁⲉⲓⲛ sign, token;
ⲧ.ⲥⲱϣⲉ field, open country.　　　　marvel, miracle.
ⲛ.ⲉⲥⲟⲟⲩ sheep (pl.).　　　　　　ⲧ.ⲥⲏϥⲉ sword.
ⲡ.ⲉⲟⲟⲩ glory, honor.
Greek nouns:
ⲡ.ⲗⲁⲟⲥ (ὁ λαός) people.
ⲡ.ⲥⲩⲅⲅⲉⲛⲏⲥ (ὁ συγγενής) kinsman (usually plural).
ⲡ.ⲛⲟⲙⲟⲥ (ὁ νόμος) law.
ⲡ.ⲍ̄ⲏⲅⲉⲙⲱⲛ (ὁ ἡγεμών) governor, one in authority.
Proper names:
ⲧ.ⲥⲩⲣⲓⲁ Syria (note article).
ⲧ.ⲅⲁⲗⲓⲗⲁⲓⲁ Galilee (note article).
†ⲟⲩⲇⲁⲓⲁ Judea (ⲓⲟⲩⲇⲁⲓⲁ; note article).
ⲡ.ⲓⲥⲣⲁⲏⲗ Israel, usually abbreviated as ⲡⲓ̄ⲏ̄ⲗ̄ (use article when it denotes the people).

Exercises

A.1. ⲁⲛⲅ̄-ⲟⲩϩⲙ̄ϩⲁⲗ ⲛ̄ⲧⲉ ⲡ̄ϩⲏⲅⲉⲙⲱⲛ.
2. ⲟⲩⲛ̄-ⲟⲩϣⲱⲥ ⲙ̄ⲙⲁⲩ ϩⲓ ⲧⲥⲱϣⲉ.
3. ⲛ̄ⲧⲟⲕ ⲡⲉ ⲡⲉⲛⲥⲁϩ.
4. ⲁⲛⲟⲛ ⲛⲉ ⲛⲉϥⲉⲥⲟⲟⲩ.
5. ⲛ̄ ⲁⲛⲟⲛ ⲁⲛ ⲡⲉ.
6. ⲛ̄ⲧⲟϥ ⲡⲉ ⲡⲉⲟⲟⲩ ⲙ̄ ⲡⲉϥⲗⲁⲟⲥ.
7. ⲛ̄ⲧⲉ-ⲛⲓⲙ ⲛ̄ⲧⲟ?
8. ⲁⲛⲅ̄-ⲟⲩⲁⲅⲅⲉⲗⲟⲥ ⲛ̄ⲧⲉ ⲡⲛⲟⲩⲧⲉ.
9. ⲟⲩⲛ̄-ⲟⲩⲥⲏϥⲉ ⲙ̄ⲙⲁⲩ.
10. ⲟⲩ ⲡⲉ ⲡⲉⲓⲙⲁⲉⲓⲛ?
11. ⲛ̄ⲧⲟϥ ⲡⲉ ⲡⲟⲩϩⲁⲓ.
12. ⲡⲁⲓ ⲡⲉ ⲡⲛⲟⲙⲟⲥ ⲙ̄ ⲡⲛⲟⲩⲧⲉ.
13. ⲟⲩⲟⲩ ⲡⲉ ⲡⲉⲩⲁⲅⲅⲉⲗⲓⲟⲛ?
14. ⲡⲓ̄ⲏ̄ⲗ̄ ⲡⲉ ⲡⲉϥⲗⲁⲟⲥ.
15. ⲛ̄ⲧⲟⲟⲩ ⲡⲉ.
16. ⲛⲓⲙ ⲛⲉ? ⲛⲉⲥⲥⲩⲅⲅⲉⲛⲏⲥ ⲛⲉ.

17. ⲛ̄ⲧⲟ ⲧⲉ ⲧⲁⲥϩⲓⲙⲉ.
18. ⲛ̄ ⲟⲩⲱⲛⲉ ⲁⲛ ⲡⲉ.
19. ⲁⲛⲟⲕ ⲡⲉ ⲓⲱⲥⲏⲫ.
20. ⲡⲉⲟⲟⲩ ⲙ̄ ⲡⲭⲟⲉⲓⲥ ϩⲓⲭⲙ̄ ⲡⲉⲓⲣⲱⲙⲉ.
21. ⲁϣ ⲡⲉ ⲡⲁⲓ? ⲟⲩⲙⲁⲉⲓⲛ ⲡⲉ.
22. ⲙⲉϣⲁⲕ ⲛ̄ⲧⲟϥ ⲡⲉ ⲡⲉⲭ̄ⲥ̄.
23. ⲟⲩ†ⲙⲉ ⲛ̄ⲧⲉ ⲧⲅⲁⲗⲓⲗⲁⲓⲁ ⲡⲉ.
24. ⲡⲉⲣⲡⲉ ⲛ̄ ⲛⲓⲙ ⲡⲉ ⲡⲁⲓ?
25. ⲡⲉⲓⲭⲱⲱⲙⲉ ⲟⲩⲉⲩⲁⲅⲅⲉⲗⲓⲟⲛ ⲡⲉ.
26. ⲛ̄ⲧⲱⲧⲛ̄ ⲡⲉ.
27. ⲁϣ ⲧⲉ ⲧⲉϩⲓⲏ?
28. ⲟⲩⲛ̄-ⲟⲩϩⲏⲅⲉⲙⲱⲛ ϩⲛ̄ ⲧⲥⲩⲣⲓⲁ.
29. ⲁϣ ⲧⲉ ⲧⲉⲓϭⲟⲙ?
30. ⲛ̄ⲧⲉⲧⲛ̄-ϩⲉⲛⲟⲩⲏⲏⲃ.

31. ⲑⲗⲱ ⲛ̄ⲛⲁ2ⲣⲙ̄ ⲡ2ⲏⲅⲉⲙⲱⲛ.

32. ⲙⲛ̄-Ⳡⲙⲉ 2ⲛ̄ ⲧⲟⲣ ⲓ ⲛⲏ ⲉⲧ ⲙ̄ⲙⲁⲩ.

33. ⲡⲁ ⲓ ⲡⲉ ⲡⲛⲟⲙⲟⲥ ⲙ̄ ⲡⲣ̄ⲣⲟ.

34. ⲟⲩⲛ̄-2ⲉⲛϣⲟⲟⲥ 2 ⲓ ⲡⲧⲟⲟⲩ.

35. ⲡⲉ ⲓ ⲟⲩⲟⲉ ⲓ ⲛ ⲟⲩⲙⲁⲉ ⲓ ⲛ ⲡⲉ.

36. ⲛ̄ⲧⲟⲥ ⲟⲩⲡⲁⲣⲑⲉⲛⲟⲥ ⲧⲉ.

37. ⲛ̄ϭⲁⲙⲟⲩⲗ ⲛ̄ ⲛ ⲓ ⲙ ⲛⲉ?

38. ⲓⲱ2ⲁⲛⲛⲏⲥ ⲙ̄ ⲡⲉⲭⲥ̄ ⲁⲛ ⲡⲉ.

39. ⲡⲕⲉⲣⲱⲙⲉ ⲡⲁⲥⲩⲅⲅⲉⲛⲏⲥ ⲡⲉ.

40. ⲛ̄ⲧⲟϥ ⲡⲉ ⲡϣⲏⲣⲉ ⲙ̄ ⲡ2ⲁⲙϣⲉ.

41. ⲗϣ ⲡⲉ ⲡⲕⲁⲕⲉ ⲉⲧ 2 ⲓ ⲭⲛ̄ ⲧⲡⲟⲗ ⲓ ⲥ?

42. ⲛ̄ⲧⲟⲟⲩ ⲛⲁⲥⲛⲏⲩ ⲛⲉ.

43. ⲛⲁ ⲓ ⲛⲉ ⲛ̄ϣⲁϫⲉ ⲙ̄ ⲡⲉⲧⲛ̄ⲛⲟⲙⲟⲥ.

44. ⲛ̄ⲕⲉⲉⲥⲟⲟⲩ 2ⲛ̄ ⲧⲥⲱϣⲉ.

45. ⲛ ⲓ ⲙ ⲡⲉ ⲡⲣⲁⲛ ⲙ̄ ⲡ2ⲏⲅⲉⲙⲱⲛ?

46. ⲧⲁ ⲓ ⲧⲉ ⲧⲁⲥⲛϥⲉ.

47. ⲟⲩⲙⲁⲉ ⲓ ⲛ ⲛ̄ⲧⲉ ⲧⲉϥϭⲟⲙ ⲡⲉ.

48. ⲛ ⲓ ⲙ ⲧⲉ ⲧⲙⲁⲁⲩ ⲛ̄ ⲓⲱ2ⲁⲛⲛⲏⲥ?

Lesson 7

7.1 The First Perfect. Verbal inflection in Coptic
is commonly, but not solely, of the form: verbal prefix +
subject (noun/pronoun) + verb. The infinitive is the main
lexical form of the verb and may occur in all of the verbal conjugations. Its uses and further modifications will
be dealt with in subsequent lessons. The conjugation
known as the First Perfect is the narrative past tense par
excellence and corresponds to the English preterite
(simple past: I wrote, I wept, I sat down) or, if the context demands, the English perfect (I have written):

ⲁ ⲓ ⲃⲱⲕ	I went	ⲁⲛⲃⲱⲕ	we went
ⲁⲕⲃⲱⲕ	you (m.s.) went	ⲁⲧⲉⲧⲛ̄ⲃⲱⲕ	you (c.pl.) went
ⲁⲣⲃⲱⲕ	you (f.s.) went		
ⲁϥⲃⲱⲕ	he went	ⲁⲩⲃⲱⲕ	they went
ⲁⲥⲃⲱⲕ	she went		

The pronominal elements are for the most part familiar
from the possessive prefixes of Lesson 4. In the 1st

person singular ⲓ is normal for most of the verbal system (contrast the -ⲁ- of ⲡⲗⲉⲓⲱⲧ). The pronominal element of the 2nd person feminine exhibits much variation and should be noted carefully for each conjugation introduced: ⲁⲣⲉⲃⲱⲕ and ⲗⲃⲱⲕ are also attested in the First Perfect.

If the subject is nominal, the verbal prefix is ⲁ-:

  ⲁ-ⲡⲣⲱⲙⲉ ⲃⲱⲕ   the man went

There are two other ways in which nominal subjects may be used in a verbal phrase: (1) they may stand before the verbal unit, which in the First Perfect still requires a pronoun as well:

  ⲡⲣⲱⲙⲉ ⲁⲯⲃⲱⲕ   the man went
  ⲧⲉⲥⲍⲓⲙⲉ ⲁⲥⲃⲱⲕ   the woman went

or (2) they may stand after the verbal unit, again with a pronominal subject, introduced by the element ⲛ̄ⲉⲓ:

  ⲁⲯⲃⲱⲕ ⲛ̄ⲉⲓ ⲡⲣⲱⲙⲉ the man went
  ⲁⲥⲃⲱⲕ ⲛ̄ⲉⲓ ⲧⲉⲥⲍⲓⲙⲉ the woman went.

All three constructions are common and differ only in the emphasis accorded the subject. When the verbal prefix is followed by the indefinite article, the resulting ⲁ-ⲟⲩ... may be spelled ⲁⲩ..., as in

  ⲁ-ⲟⲩⲍⲗ̄ⲗⲟ ⲃⲱⲕ or ⲁⲩⲍⲗ̄ⲗⲟ ⲃⲱⲕ a monk went

 7.2 The prepositions ⲉ, ϣⲁ, and ⲉⲭⲛ̄ are frequent after verbs of motion.

  1) ⲉ indicates motion to or toward a place or person, less commonly motion onto or into:

  ⲁⲯⲃⲱⲕ ⲉ ⲡⲉⲕⲣⲟ. He went to the shore.
  ⲁⲩⲡⲱⲧ ⲉ ⲧⲉⲕⲕⲗⲏⲥⲓⲁ. They ran to the church.
  ⲁⲩⲁⲗⲉ ⲉ ⲡϫⲟⲓ. They got on (or into) the ship.

  Otherwise the preposition ⲉ is very frequent in a general referential sense: "to, for, in regard to," with many other nuances that will be noted in passing.

2) ϣⲁ indicates motion to, up to; it is used more frequently with persons than places:

ⲁϥⲡⲱⲧ ϣⲁ ⲡⲉϥⲉⲓⲱⲧ.   He ran to his father.

ⲁⲛⲃⲱⲕ ϣⲁ ⲡⲉⲡⲓⲥⲕⲟⲡⲟⲥ.   We went to the bishop.

3) ⲉⲭⲛ̄ indicates motion onto, on:

ⲁϥⲁⲗⲉ ⲉⲭⲙ̄ ⲡⲉⲓⲱ.   He got on the donkey.

ⲁⲥⲍⲉ ⲉⲭⲙ̄ ⲡⲕⲁⲍ.   She fell on the ground.

ⲉⲭⲛ̄ properly denotes motion onto, while ⲍⲓⲭⲛ̄ denotes static location; the two are sometimes interchanged. The same contrast exists with the less frequent pair ⲍⲓⲣⲛ̄ (at the entrance of) and ⲉⲣⲛ̄ (to the entrance of).

Several of the prepositions we have already introduced also occur freely with verbs of motion. For example ⲍⲓ, ⲍⲓⲭⲛ̄ (on or along a surface), ⲛ̄ⲥⲁ (behind, after), ⲙⲛ̄ (along with), ⲍⲛ̄ (within a circumscribed area), ⲛ̄ⲛⲁⲍⲣⲛ̄ (into the presence of), ⲍⲁⲍⲧⲛ̄ (up to, near). The preposition ⲛ̄ⲥⲁ often has the sense of English "after" in "to go after," i.e. to go to fetch, or "to run after," i.e. to try to overtake. The reader should give particular attention to the use of prepositions with verbs, since these combinations are sometimes quite idiomatic and unpredictable.

Vocabulary 7

ⲃⲱⲕ to go.

ⲙⲟⲟϣⲉ to walk, go on foot (usually).

ⲉⲓ to come; ⲉⲓ ⲛ̄ⲥⲁ to come after, come to get.

ⲁⲗⲉ to go up, climb (onto, up to: ⲉ); to mount (an animal: ⲉⲭⲛ̄).

ⲡⲱⲧ to run, to flee; ⲡⲱⲧ ⲛ̄ⲥⲁ to pursue.

ϣⲗⲏⲗ to pray (for something: ⲉ, ⲉⲧⲃⲉ, ⲉⲝⲛ̄, ⲍⲁ; for someone: ⲉ).

ⲣⲓⲙⲉ to weep (for someone: ⲉ, ⲉⲝⲛ̄).

ⲍⲙⲟⲟⲥ to sit down (at: ⲉ).

ⲡ.ⲉⲓⲱ (pl. ⲛ.ⲉⲟⲟⲩ) ass, donkey.

ⲡⲉ.ⲍⲧⲟ (f. ⲧⲉ.ⲍⲧⲱⲣⲉ; pl. ⲛⲉ.ⲍⲧⲱⲱⲣ) horse.

ⲛ̄ϭⲓ subject marker (see the lesson).

ⲉⲧⲃⲉ ⲟⲩ why?

The prepositions ⲉ, ⲉⲝⲛ̄, ϣⲁ, ⲍⲓⲣⲛ̄, ⲉⲣⲛ̄ as given in the lesson.

Greek nouns:

ⲡⲉⲑⲣⲟⲛⲟⲥ (ὁ θρόνος) throne.

ⲧⲉ.ⲧⲣⲁⲡⲉⲍⲁ (ἡ τράπεζα) table.

Exercises

1. ⲁ-ⲛⲉⲥⲛⲏⲩ ⲃⲱⲕ ⲉ ⲧⲡⲟⲗⲓⲥ.
2. ⲡϣⲏⲣⲉ ⲁϥⲉⲓ ⲉ ⲡⲉⲛⲏⲓ.
3. ⲁⲥⲃⲱⲕ ⲛ̄ϭⲓ ⲧⲉϥⲥⲱⲛⲉ ⲉⲣⲙ̄ ⲡⲣⲟ ⲛ̄ ⲧⲉⲕⲕⲗⲏⲥⲓⲁ.
4. ⲁⲩⲉⲓ ⲛ̄ⲥⲁ ⲛⲉⲩϣⲏⲣⲉ.
5. ⲁ-ⲧⲉϥⲙⲁⲁⲩ ⲙⲟⲟϣⲉ ⲉ ⲡⲧⲁⲫⲟⲥ.
6. ⲁ-ⲛⲉϥⲙⲁⲑⲏⲧⲏⲥ ⲁⲗⲉ ⲉ ⲡϫⲟⲓ.
7. ⲁϥⲃⲱⲕ ϣⲁ ⲕⲉⲥⲟⲛ.
8. ⲁⲛⲉⲓ ⲉⲣⲙ̄ ⲡⲉϥⲏⲓ.
9. ⲁϥⲙⲟⲟϣⲉ ⲛ̄ϭⲓ ⲓ̄ⲥ̄ ⲉⲝⲙ̄ ⲡⲉⲕⲣⲟ ⲛ̄ ⲑⲁⲗⲗⲁⲥⲥⲁ.
10. ⲙ̄ⲙⲟⲛⲁⲭⲟⲥ ⲁⲩⲁⲗⲉ ⲉ ⲡⲧⲟⲟⲩ.
11. ⲁ-ⲛⲉϥⲙⲁⲑⲏⲧⲏⲥ ⲡⲱⲧ ⲉ ⲕⲉⲙⲁ.
12. ⲁϥϣⲗⲏⲗ ⲉⲧⲃⲉ ⲛⲉϥϣⲏⲣⲉ.
13. ⲉⲧⲃⲉ ⲟⲩ ⲁⲧⲉⲧⲛ̄ⲡⲱⲧ ⲉⲝⲛ̄ ⲧⲉⲍⲓⲏ?
14. ⲁⲛⲙⲟⲟϣⲉ ⲙⲛ̄ ⲛⲉⲛⲍⲓⲟⲙⲉ ⲉ ⲡϯⲙⲉ.
15. ⲁⲩⲍⲗ̄ⲗⲟ ⲃⲱⲕ ϣⲁ ⲡⲉⲡⲓⲥⲕⲟⲡⲟⲥ.
16. ⲁϥϣⲗⲏⲗ ⲉⲧⲃⲉ ⲛⲉⲛⲛⲟⲃⲉ.
17. ⲁⲥⲉⲓ ⲛ̄ϭⲓ ⲑⲙ̄ⲍⲁⲗ ⲛ̄ⲛⲁⲍⲣⲙ̄ ⲡⲉⲥⲭⲟⲉⲓⲥ.
18. ⲁϥⲁⲗⲉ ⲛ̄ϭⲓ ⲡⲉⲛⲭⲟⲉⲓⲥ ⲉ ⲧⲡⲉ.

19. ⲉⲧⲃⲉ ⲟⲩ ⲁⲕⲡⲱⲧ ⲛⲥⲁ ⲡⲁⲉⲓⲱⲧ?

20. ⲉⲧⲃⲉ ⲟⲩ ⲁⲣⲣⲓⲙⲉ ⲉⲧⲃⲉ ⲛⲣⲱⲙⲉ ⲉⲧ ⲙⲙⲁⲩ?

21. ⲁϥϩⲙⲟⲟⲥ ⲉϫⲙ ⲡⲉⲕⲣⲟ ⲙ ⲡⲉⲓⲉⲣⲟ.

22. ⲁ-ⲑⲗⲗⲱ ⲣⲓⲙⲉ ⲉ ⲡⲉⲥϣⲏⲣⲉ.

23. ⲁⲩϩⲙⲟⲟⲥ ⲙⲛ ⲛⲉⲩⲥⲛⲏⲩ.

24. ⲁⲓⲙⲟⲟϣⲉ ϩⲓ ⲧⲉϩⲓⲏ ⲙⲛ ⲧⲁϣⲉⲉⲣⲉ.

25. ⲁⲩⲃⲱⲕ ϩⲓ ⲧⲉϩⲓⲏ ⲉⲧ ⲙⲙⲁⲩ ⲉ ⲧⲡⲟⲗⲓⲥ.

26. ⲁ-ⲡⲉϥϩⲧⲟ ⲡⲱⲧ ϣⲁ ⲧⲉϩⲧⲱⲣⲉ.

27. ⲁϥⲁⲗⲉ ⲉϫⲙ ⲡⲉϥϩⲧⲟ ⲛϭⲓ ⲡⲉⲡⲓⲥⲕⲟⲡⲟⲥ.

28. ⲧⲉϥⲙⲁⲁⲩ ⲁⲥⲉⲓ ϣⲁ ⲡⲣ̄ⲣⲟ ⲛ ⲧⲡⲟⲗⲓⲥ.

29. ⲁⲛϣⲗⲏⲗ ϩⲁ ⲛⲉⲛⲥⲛⲏⲩ ⲉⲧ ϩⲙ ⲡⲧⲟⲟⲩ.

30. ⲁⲓⲣⲓⲙⲉ ⲉϫⲛ ⲛⲁⲛⲟⲃⲉ.

31. ⲁ-ⲡⲣ̄ⲣⲟ ϩⲙⲟⲟⲥ ⲉϫⲙ ⲡⲉϥⲑⲣⲟⲛⲟⲥ.

32. ⲁ-ⲡⲙⲁⲑⲏⲧⲏⲥ ϩⲙⲟⲟⲥ ϩⲓⲣⲙ ⲡⲣⲟ ⲙ ⲡⲏⲓ.

33. ⲁⲩⲡⲱⲧ ⲛϭⲓ ⲛϣⲏⲣⲉ ϩⲓ ⲧⲉϩⲓⲏ ⲉ ⲧⲉⲙⲣⲱ.

34. ⲁ-ⲡⲉⲓⲱ ⲙⲟⲟϣⲉ ⲛⲥⲁ ⲡⲉϥϫⲟⲉⲓⲥ.

35. ⲁⲛⲁⲗⲉ ⲉϫⲛ ⲛⲉⲛⲉⲟⲟⲩ.

36. ⲁⲩϩⲙⲟⲟⲥ ⲉ ⲧⲉⲧⲣⲁⲡⲉⲍⲁ ⲛϭⲓ ⲧⲉϥⲥϩⲓⲙⲉ ⲙⲛ ⲛⲉϥϣⲉⲉⲣⲉ.

37. ⲁ-ϩⲉⲛⲣⲱⲙⲉ ⲉⲓ ϩⲁϩⲧⲛ ⲧⲉⲕⲕⲗⲏⲥⲓⲁ.

38. ⲉⲧⲃⲉ ⲟⲩ ⲁⲕⲙⲟⲟϣⲉ ⲛⲥⲁ ⲡⲉⲓⲱ ϩⲓϫⲛ ⲧⲉϩⲓⲏ?

39. ⲁ-ⲓ̄ⲥ̄ ϩⲙⲟⲟⲥ ϩⲁϩⲧⲛ ⲛⲉϥⲙⲁⲑⲏⲧⲏⲥ.

40. ⲁⲩⲙⲟⲟϣⲉ ⲛϭⲓ ⲛϣⲟⲟⲥ ⲛⲥⲁ ⲛⲉⲩⲉⲥⲟⲟⲩ.

41. ⲁ-ⲡϭⲁⲙⲟⲩⲗ ⲡⲱⲧ ⲉ ⲧⲥⲱϣⲉ.

42. ⲁⲛϣⲗⲏⲗ ⲉ ⲟⲩⲙⲁⲉⲓⲛ.

43. ⲁ-ⲡⲗⲁⲟⲥ ⲛ ⲧⲡⲟⲗⲓⲥ ⲉⲓ ϣⲁ ⲡϩⲏⲅⲉⲙⲱⲛ ⲛ ϯⲟⲩⲇⲁⲓⲁ.

44. ⲁ-ⲧϣⲉⲉⲣⲉ ϩⲙⲟⲟⲥ ⲙⲛ ⲛⲉⲥⲥⲩⲅⲅⲉⲛⲏⲥ.

45. ⲁϥⲃⲱⲕ ⲛϭⲓ ⲡϩⲏⲅⲉⲙⲱⲛ ⲉ ⲧⲥⲩⲣⲓⲁ.

46. ⲡⲁⲓ ⲡⲉ ⲡⲛⲟⲩⲧⲉ ⲙ ⲡⲓ̄ⲏ̄ⲗ̄.

Lesson 8

8.1 Directional adverbs. Coptic possesses a set of
directional adverbs which correspond very closely to
English adverbs of the type "up, down, in, out, over,
along, etc." As with their English counterparts, the
directional meanings found with verbs of motion are for
all practical purposes the basic meanings (e.g. to go up,
to sink down, to run in), but extended uses are equally
common (e.g. to shut up, to quiet down, to think over).
The Coptic directional adverbs consist formally of the
preposition є plus a noun, with or without the definite
article. Most of the nouns in question are seldom met
outside of these particular expressions and will be considered in more detail in a later lesson. Because these
adverbs are so frequent, we shall follow the practice of
other editors and write them as single units. The following eight are the most important:

євол	out, away	єєн	forward, ahead
єꙅoyn	in	єпаꙅoy	back, rearward
єꙅраι	up, down	єтпє	upward
єпєснт	down	єпꙍωι	upward.

The adverbs may be used alone, as in

ачвωк євол.	He went away.
ачєι єꙅoyn.	He came in.
ачпωт єпаꙅoy.	He ran back.

But they very frequently combine with a simple preposition
to form a compound prepositional phrase. Among the most
frequent of these are

євол є	out to, away to.
євол ꙅN̄	out of, out from in, away from; (rarely) out into.
євол м̄мо⸗	same as preceding.

ⲉⲃⲟⲗ ϩⲓ	away from on, out from on, away from at.
ⲉⲃⲟⲗ ϩⲓⲧⲛ̄	(1) away from (a person); (2) through, out through (a place); (3) through the agency of (a person or thing).
ⲉϩⲟⲩⲛ ⲉ	to, into, toward.
ⲉϩⲣⲁⲓ ⲉ	up to, down to.
ⲉϩⲣⲁⲓ ⲉϫⲛ̄	up onto, down upon.
ⲉⲡⲉⲥⲏⲧ ⲉ	down to, down into, down onto, down on.
ⲉⲡⲉⲥⲏⲧ ⲉϫⲛ̄	down onto, down on.
ⲉⲡⲁϩⲟⲩ ⲉ	back to.
ⲉⲑⲏ ⲉ	ahead to, forward to.

The meaning of most such compounds when used with verbs of motion is generally self-evident, but caution is in order when dealing with their use with other verbs. The dictionary should always be consulted to check on idiomatic and unpredictable meanings.

8.2 Clauses containing a First Perfect may be coordinated with the conjunction ⲁⲩⲱ (and) or follow one another with no conjunction (termed "asyndeton"):

ⲁϥϩⲙⲟⲟⲥ ⲁⲩⲱ ⲁϥⲣⲓⲙⲉ.
ⲁϥϩⲙⲟⲟⲥ, ⲁϥⲣⲓⲙⲉ.　　　　He sat down and wept.

8.3 Many infinitives are used as masculine singular nouns. This usage will be noted without further comment in the lesson vocabularies from now on ("as n.m.:"). For the infinitives in Vocabulary 7 note the nouns ⲡⲉ.ϣⲗⲏⲗ prayer, ⲡ.ⲡⲱⲧ flight, and ⲡ.ⲣⲓⲙⲉ weeping.

Vocabulary 8

ϣⲁϫⲉ to speak, talk (to, with: ⲉ, ⲙⲛ̄; about: ⲉ, ϩⲁ, ⲉⲧⲃⲉ; against: ⲛ̄ⲥⲁ, ⲟⲩⲃⲉ); as n.m.: word speech; matter, affair.

ⲧⲱⲟⲩⲛ to arise, get up (from: ⲉⲃⲟⲗ ϩⲓ, ⲉⲃⲟⲗ ϩⲛ̄); to rise up (against: ⲉ, ⲉϫⲛ̄, ⲉϩⲣⲁⲓ ⲉϫⲛ̄).

ⲧ.ⲣⲓ cell (of a monk).

ⲡ.ⳝⲱⲃ (pl. ⲛⲉ.ⳝⲃⲏⲩⲉ) work, task; thing, matter, affair.

ⲣⲁⲕⲟⲧⲉ Alexandria.

ⳝⲓⲧⲛ̄ (prep.) (1) through, by means of, by the agency of; (2) from with, from by (a person).

ⲟⲩⲃⲉ (prep.) against, opposite.

ⲁⲩⲱ (conj.) and.

Greek noun: ⲡ.ⲃⲏⲙⲁ (τὸ βῆμα) platform, dais, viewing or judgement seat.

Note: Only the less predictable combinations of verb and prepositional phrase will be given in the lesson vocabularies. Other combinations in the exercises should be self-evident from the meanings of the individual words involved.

Exercises

A.1. ⳝⲓⲧⲛ̄ ⲛⲉⲕϣⲗⲏⲗ

2. ⲟⲩⲃⲉ ⲛⲉⲛⲥⲛⲏⲩ

3. ⲉⲃⲟⲗ ⳝⲓⲧⲛ̄ ⲧⲉⳝⳝⲓⲏ

4. ⲉⲃⲟⲗ ⲉ ⲡⲉⲓⲉⲣⲟ

5. ⲉⲃⲟⲗ ⳝⲛ̄ ⲧⲡⲟⲗⲓⲥ

6. ⲉⲃⲟⲗ ⳝⲓ ⲧⲉⲧⲣⲁⲡⲉⳝⲁ

7. ⲉⲧⲃⲉ ⲡⲉϥⳝⲱⲃ

8. ⲟⲩⲃⲉ ⲛⲉⲧⲛ̄ϣⲁϫⲉ

9. ⳝⲓⲧⲛ̄ ⲛⲉϥϣⲁϫⲉ

10. ⲉⳝⲟⲩⲛ ⲉ ⲣⲁⲕⲟⲧⲉ

11. ⲉⳝⲣⲁⲓ ⲉ ⲡⲃⲏⲙⲁ

12. ⲉⳝⲣⲁⲓ ⲉⳝⲙ̄ ⲡⲧⲟⲟⲩ

13. ⲉⳝⲟⲩⲛ ⲉ ⲧⲁⲣⲓ

14. ⳝⲁ ⲛⲉⲓⳝⲃⲏⲩⲉ

15. ϣⲁ ⲛⲉϥⲙⲁⲑⲏⲧⲏⲥ

16. ⳝⲓⲣⲛ̄ ⲧⲉϥⲣⲓ

17. ⲉⲧⲃⲉ ⲡⲟⲩⲣⲓⲙⲉ

18. ⳝⲙ̄ ⲡⲉϥⲡⲱⲧ

19. ⲉⲡⲉⲥⲏⲧ ⲉ ⲑⲁⲗⲁⲥⲥⲁ

20. ⲉⲡⲉⲥⲏⲧ ⲉ ⲡⲙⲟⲟⲩ

21. ⲉⲡⲁⳝⲟⲩ ⲉ ⲡⲉⲩϯⲙⲉ

22. ⲉⲑⲏ ⲉ ⲛ̄ⲧⲟⲟⲩ

23. ⲉⲃⲟⲗ ⳝⲓ ⲡⲃⲏⲙⲁ

24. ⲉⳝⲣⲁⲓ ⲉⳝⲙ̄ ⲡⲉⳝⲧⲟ

25. ⲉⲃⲟⲗ ⳝⲓⲧⲙ̄ ⲡⲣⲟ ⲙ̄ ⲡⲏⲓ

26. ⲉⲃⲟⲗ ⳝⲙ̄ ⲡⲉⲓⲙⲁ

27. ⲟⲩⲃⲉ ⲡⲣⲁⲛ ⲙ̄ ⲡⲣ̄ⲣⲟ

28. ⲉⲃⲟⲗ ⳝⲓⲧⲙ̄ ⲡϫⲟⲉⲓⲥ

29. ⲉⲧⲃⲉ ⲡⲉⲧⲛ̄ⲡⲱⲧ

B.1. ⲁⲩⲧⲱⲟⲩⲛ, ⲁⲩⲡⲱⲧ ⲉⲃⲟⲗ.

2. ⲁⲛⲉⲓ ⲉⳝⲟⲩⲛ, ⲁⲛⳝⲙⲟⲟⲥ.

3. ⲁϥⲃⲱⲕ ⲉⲡⲁⳝⲟⲩ ⲉ ⲡⲉϥϯⲙⲉ.

4. ⲁϥⳝⲙⲟⲟⲥ ⲁⲩⲱ ⲁϥϣⲁϫⲉ ⲙⲛ̄ ⲛ̄ⲣⲱⲙⲉ.

5. ⲁⲓⲧⲱⲟⲩⲛ ⲉⲃⲟⲗ ⳝⲓ ⲧⲉⲧⲣⲁⲡⲉⳝⲁ.

6. ⲁⲛⲙⲟⲟϣⲉ ⲉⲍⲟⲩⲛ ⲉ ⲣⲁⲕⲟⲧⲉ.

7. ⲡⲕⲉⲣⲱⲙⲉ ⲁϥⲁⲗⲉ ⲉⲍⲣⲁⲓ ⲉⲭⲙ̄ ⲡⲉⲓⲱ.

8. ⲉⲧⲃⲉ ⲟⲩ ⲁⲣⲡⲱⲧ ⲉⲃⲟⲗ ⲍⲙ̄ ⲡⲟⲩⲏⲓ?

9. ⲁ-ⲡ₂ⲗ̄ⲗⲟ ⲃⲱⲕ ⲉⲍⲟⲩⲛ ⲉ ⲧⲉϥⲣⲓ.

10. ⲉⲧⲃⲉ ⲟⲩ ⲁⲧⲉⲧⲛ̄ϣⲁϫⲉ ⲛ̄ⲥⲁ ⲡⲉⲛϫⲟⲉⲓⲥ?

11. ⲁⲓⲍⲙⲟⲟⲥ ⲍⲁⲍⲧⲙ̄ ⲡⲗⲉⲓⲱⲧ.

12. ⲁⲩϣⲁϫⲉ ⲍⲁ ⲡⲉⲩⲏⲣⲡ̄.

13. ⲟⲩⲛ̄-ⲍⲉⲛⲉⲟⲟⲩ ⲙⲛ̄ ⲍⲉⲛⲍⲧⲱⲱⲣ ⲙ̄ⲙⲁⲩ.

14. ⲁϥⲉⲓ ⲉⲡⲉⲥⲏⲧ ⲉⲃⲟⲗ ⲍⲓ ⲡⲃⲏⲙⲁ.

15. ⲁⲩⲧⲱⲟⲩⲛ ⲛ̄ϭⲓ ⲛ̄ⲣⲱⲙⲉ ⲉⲍⲣⲁⲓ ⲉⲭⲙ̄ ⲡⲣ̄ⲣⲟ.

16. ⲁⲓϣⲁϫⲉ ⲉⲧⲃⲉ ⲛⲁⲛⲟⲃⲉ.

17. ⲁ-ⲛⲉⲍⲓⲟⲙⲉ ⲙⲟⲟϣⲉ ⲉⲡⲉⲥⲏⲧ ⲉ ⲡⲉⲕⲣⲟ.

18. ⲁⲛⲃⲱⲕ ⲉⲍⲣⲁⲓ ⲉ ⲛⲉⲛⲧⲙⲉ.

19. ⲁⲥⲡⲱⲧ ⲉⲃⲟⲗ ⲍⲓⲧⲛ̄ ⲛ̄ⲣⲱⲙⲉ ⲉⲧ ⲙ̄ⲙⲁⲩ.

20. ⲁⲛⲃⲱⲕ ⲉⲍⲟⲩⲛ ⲛ̄ⲛⲁⲍⲣⲙ̄ ⲡⲉⲡⲓⲥⲕⲟⲡⲟⲥ.

21. ⲉⲧⲃⲉ ⲟⲩ ⲁⲕⲃⲱⲕ ⲉⲡⲁⲍⲟⲩ ⲉ ⲧⲁⲅⲟⲣⲁ?

22. ⲁϥⲃⲱⲕ ⲉⲃⲟⲗ ⲍⲙ̄ ⲡⲉⲓⲕⲟⲥⲙⲟⲥ.

23. ⲁⲥϣⲁϫⲉ ⲙⲛ̄ ⲧⲉⲥⲙⲁⲁⲩ ⲉⲧⲃⲉ ⲛⲉⲥϣⲏⲣⲉ.

24. ⲁⲩⲁⲗⲉ ⲛ̄ϭⲓ ⲛ̄ⲣⲱⲙⲉ ⲉⲍⲣⲁⲓ ⲉⲭⲛ̄ ⲛⲉⲩⲍⲧⲱⲱⲣ.

25. ⲁⲩϣⲁϫⲉ ⲉ ⲡⲟⲉⲓⲕ ⲙⲛ̄ ⲛ̄ⲧⲃ̄ⲧ.

26. ⲁⲩϣⲁϫⲉ ⲟⲩⲃⲉ ⲛⲉϥⲉⲛⲧⲟⲗⲏ.

27. ⲁϥⲧⲱⲟⲩⲛ ⲉⲃⲟⲗ ⲍⲓ ⲡⲉⲑⲣⲟⲛⲟⲥ.

28. ⲁⲛⲙⲟⲟϣⲉ ⲉⲑⲏ ⲍⲙ̄ ⲡⲕⲁⲕⲉ.

29. ⲁϥⲁⲗⲉ ⲉⲍⲣⲁⲓ ⲉ ⲡⲃⲏⲙⲁ.

30. ⲁϥϣⲁϫⲉ ⲉⲧⲃⲉ ⲛⲉⲍⲃⲏⲩⲉ ⲙ̄ ⲡⲙⲟⲛⲁⲭⲟⲥ.

Lesson 9

9.1 Prepositions with pronominal suffixes. A pronominal object of a preposition is expressed by means of
a suffixed form of the pronoun. The preposition itself
assumes a prepronominal form which must be learned with
each preposition. For example, the preposition ∈ becomes
∈ρο⸗ before pronominal suffixes. The mark ⸗ is a convention used in Coptic grammars to indicate any form to which
a pronominal suffix is to be added. The prepronominal
forms of the prepositions introduced thus far are as
follows:

N̄	M̄MO⸗	∈	∈ρο⸗	∈ρN̄	∈ρω⸗
2N̄	N̄2HT⸗	21xN̄	21xω⸗	Nλ2ρN̄	Nλ2ρλ⸗
2λ	2λρο⸗	∈xN̄	∈xω⸗	2λ2TN̄	2λ2TH⸗
21	21ω(ω)⸗	21TN̄	21TOOT⸗	OYB∈	OYBH⸗
MN̄	NM̄Mλ⸗	N̄cλ	N̄cω⸗	∈TB∈	∈TBHHT⸗
ϣλ	ϣλρο⸗	21ρN̄	21ρω⸗		

Because the variety exhibited by the prepronominal forms is
at first puzzling, the following comments may be of some
help:

1) In ∈ρο⸗ and 2λρο⸗ the final syllable -ρο⸗ is an
original part of the preposition; it was lost in the normal prenominal form. ϣλρο⸗ is on analogy with these.

2) N̄2HT⸗ and 21ω⸗ were originally compounds: N̄ 2HT⸗
in the belly (of), 21 ω(ω)⸗ on the back (of). The prenominal form 2N̄ was originally a noun meaning "interior"
(cf. the 2OYN of ∈2OYN); 21 was a simple preposition.

3) 21xω⸗ and ∈xω⸗ are 21 and ∈ with the noun xω⸗
(head, top); the noun is reduced to -x- in 21xN̄ and ∈xN̄,
which also contain the genitival N̄.

4) 21ρω⸗ and ∈ρω⸗ are 21 and ∈ with the noun ρω⸗
mouth, door; the latter is reduced to ρ in 21ρN̄ and ∈ρN̄,
with genitival N̄.

5) ꙅⲓⲧⲟⲟⲧ* is ꙅⲓ plus the noun ⲧⲟⲟⲧ* (hand); the latter is reduced to -ⲧ- in ꙅⲓⲧⲛ̄, with genitival ⲛ̄.

6) ⲛⲁꙅⲣⲁ* contains the noun ꙅⲣⲁ* (face). The initial element is obscure. ⲛⲁꙅⲣⲛ̄ also contains the genitival ⲛ̄.

7) ꙅⲁꙅⲧⲏ* consists of ꙅⲁ plus the noun ꙅⲧⲏ* (heart, breast), reduced to -ꙅⲧ- with the genitival ⲛ̄ in ꙅⲁꙅⲧⲛ̄.

The nouns contained in these expressions will be dealt with in a later lesson.

Typical inflections of these prepositions are as follows:

ⲉⲣⲟⲓ	to me	ⲉⲣⲟⲛ	to us
ⲉⲣⲟⲕ	to you (m.s.)	ⲉⲣⲱⲧⲛ̄	to you (pl.)
ⲉⲣⲟ	to you (f.s.)		
ⲉⲣⲟϥ	to him	ⲉⲣⲟⲟⲩ	to them
ⲉⲣⲟⲥ	to her		

ⲛⲙ̄ⲙⲁⲓ	with me	ⲛⲙ̄ⲙⲁⲛ	ⲛ̄ϩⲏⲧ	in me	ⲛ̄ϩⲏⲧⲛ̄
ⲛⲙ̄ⲙⲁⲕ	etc.	ⲛⲙ̄ⲙⲏⲧⲛ̄	ⲛ̄ϩⲏⲧⲕ̄	etc.	ⲛ̄ϩⲏⲧ-ⲑⲏⲩⲧⲛ̄
ⲛⲙ̄ⲙⲉ			ⲛ̄ϩⲏⲧⲉ		
ⲛⲙ̄ⲙⲁϥ		ⲛⲙ̄ⲙⲁⲩ	ⲛ̄ϩⲏⲧϥ̄		ⲛ̄ϩⲏⲧⲟⲩ
ⲛⲙ̄ⲙⲁⲥ			ⲛ̄ϩⲏⲧⲥ̄		

ⲟⲩⲃⲏⲓ	against me	ⲟⲩⲃⲏⲛ
ⲟⲩⲃⲏⲕ	etc.	ⲟⲩⲃⲉ-ⲑⲏⲩⲧⲛ̄
[ⲟⲩⲃⲏⲧⲉ]		
ⲟⲩⲃⲏϥ		ⲟⲩⲃⲏⲩ
ⲟⲩⲃⲏⲥ		

ⲉⲧⲃⲏⲏⲧ	because of me	ⲉⲧⲃⲏⲏⲧⲛ̄
ⲉⲧⲃⲏⲏⲧⲕ̄	etc.	ⲉⲧⲃⲉ-ⲑⲏⲩⲧⲛ̄
ⲉⲧⲃⲏⲏⲧⲉ		
ⲉⲧⲃⲏⲏⲧϥ̄		ⲉⲧⲃⲏⲏⲧⲟⲩ
ⲉⲧⲃⲏⲏⲧⲥ̄		

The prepronominal form of ϩ ι appears as both ϩ ιⲱ⸗ and
ϩ ιⲱⲱ⸗; typical forms are

ϩ ιⲱⲱⲧ	on me	ϩ ιⲱⲱⲛ, ϩ ιⲱⲛ	
ϩ ιⲱⲱⲕ, ϩ ιⲱⲕ	etc.	ϩ ι-ⲧⲏ ΥⲧⲚ̄	
ϩ ιⲱⲱⲧⲉ			
ϩ ιⲱⲱϥ, ϩ ιⲱϥ		ϩ ιⲱⲟΥ	
ϩ ιⲱⲱⲥ, ϩ ιⲱⲥ			

The following details on the forms of suffixed pronouns in
general should be noted for future reference:

1) The 1st pers. sing. suffix appears as ι after a
single vowel, as zero (nothing) after -ⲧ⸗, and as ⲧ
elsewhere.

2) The suffix of the 2nd pers. fem. sing. appears as
zero after a single vowel other than -ⲗ⸗, as -ⲉ in place
of a single -ⲗ⸗, as -ⲉ after -ⲧ⸗, and as -ⲧⲉ elsewhere.

3) The suffix of the 2nd pers. pl. appears as -ⲧⲚ̄
after single -ⲟ⸗, -ⲗ⸗, -ⲱ⸗, with the change of -ⲟ⸗ to -ⲱ⸗
and -ⲗ⸗ to -ⲏ⸗. After -ⲧ⸗ one uses -ⲧⲏ ΥⲧⲚ̄. Elsewhere
-ⲧⲏ ΥⲧⲚ̄ is usually added to the prenominal form of the
preposition or other form in question, as in ϩ ⲁϩ ⲧⲚ̄-ⲧⲏ ΥⲧⲚ̄.

Vocabulary 9

ϣ ⲱ ⲡⲉ to come into being; to take place, happen; ϣ ⲱ ⲡⲉ Ⲙ̄ⲙⲟ⸗
to befall, happen to (someone). ⲁⲥϣ ⲱ ⲡⲉ it happened
that (followed directly by the principal verb, as in
ⲁⲥϣ ⲱ ⲡⲉ ⲁϥ ⲉⲓ ϣ ⲁⲣⲟⲛ it happened that he came to us).

ⲙⲟΥ to die (of, from: ⲉⲧⲃ ⲉ, ϩ ⲁ); as n.m.: death, manner of
death.

ϩ ⲉ to fall; ϩ ⲉ ⲉ to fall to, upon, into; to find, chance
upon; ϩ ⲉ ⲉⲃ ⲟ ⲗ to perish, be lost, fall away.

Ⲛ̄ⲕⲟⲧⲕ̄ to lie down, sleep; often a euphemism for dying.

ϩ ⲱ ⲛ to draw near, to approach (someone or something: ⲉ,
ⲉϩ ⲟΥⲛ ⲉ).

ϩⲓⲥⲉ to grow weary, exhausted; to be troubled, afflicted.
  As n.m. labor, toil; weariness, affliction.
ϩⲕⲟ to grow hungry; as n.m.: hunger, famine.
ⲡ.ⲕⲁϩ earth, ground.
ⲡ.ϣⲁ festival, feast day.
ⲡⲉ.ϩⲟⲟⲩ day; ⲙ̄ ⲡⲟⲟⲩ (adv.) today (note loss of ϩ);
  ϣⲁ ⲡⲟⲟⲩ up until today, until now.
ⲡⲉ.ϭⲗⲟϭ bed.
ⲙ̄ⲛ̄ⲛ̄ⲥⲁ (ⲙ̄ⲛ̄ⲛ̄ⲥⲱ⸗) (prep.) after (of time); ⲙ̄ⲛ̄ⲛ̄ⲥⲱⲥ (adv.)
  afterward.
Greek words
ⲇⲉ (δέ) postpositive conjunction: but, however.
  Frequently marks the introduction of a new subject or
  topic and has no translation value.
ⲧ.ⲥⲩⲛⲁⲅⲱⲅⲏ (ἡ συναγωγή) synagogue.

Exercises

Translate the following prepositional phrases. Replace
the nominal object with the appropriate pronominal suffix.
E.g. ⲉⲧⲃⲉ ⲡⲉⲓϩⲱⲃ → ⲉⲧⲃⲏⲏⲧϥ̄.

A.1. ⲉⲭⲙ̄ ⲡⲕⲁϩ
  2. ⲟⲩⲃⲉ ⲡⲉⲩⲭⲟⲉⲓⲥ
  3. ϩⲓ ⲡⲉϥϭⲗⲟϭ
  4. ϩⲓⲣⲙ̄ ⲡⲧⲁⲫⲟⲥ
  5. ⲙ̄ⲛ̄ⲛ̄ⲥⲁ ⲡⲉϥⲙⲟⲩ
  6. ⲛⲁϩⲣⲙ̄ ⲡⲛⲟⲩⲧⲉ
  7. ϩⲛ̄ ⲛ̄ⲉⲓⲉⲣⲟ
  8. ϩⲓⲧⲛ̄ ⲛⲉⲓϩⲓⲥⲉ
  9. ⲉ ⲛ̄ⲧⲃ̄ⲧ
  10. ⲉⲧⲃⲉ ⲡⲉⲩϩⲕⲟ
  11. ⲉ ⲡⲉⲥⲣⲁⲛ
  12. ϣⲁ ⲛⲉϥϩⲙ̄ϩⲁⲗ
  13. ϩⲓⲭⲙ̄ ⲡⲕⲁϩ
  14. ⲛ̄ⲥⲁ ⲡⲉϥϣⲏⲣⲉ
  15. ϩⲓⲧⲙ̄ ⲡⲉϩⲕⲟ

  16. ϩⲁ ⲡⲁϭⲗⲟϭ
  17. ⲙ̄ⲛ̄ⲛ̄ⲥⲁ ⲡⲉⲛⲡⲱⲧ
  18. ϩⲛ̄ ⲧⲉϥⲣⲓ
  19. ϩⲓⲭⲙ̄ ⲡⲉⲕⲭⲟⲓ
  20. ϩⲁ ⲛⲉⲧⲛ̄ϩⲓⲥⲉ
  21. ⲉⲧⲃⲉ ⲛ̄ϣⲁ
  22. ϩⲓⲣⲛ̄ ⲧⲉⲕⲕⲗⲏⲥⲓⲁ
  23. ϣⲁ ⲧ2ⲁ̄ⲗⲱ
  24. ⲟⲩⲃⲉ ⲛⲁϣⲁϫⲉ
  25. ⲛⲁϩⲣⲛ̄ ⲧⲉϥⲙⲁⲁⲩ
  26. ϩⲓⲧⲙ̄ ⲡⲟⲩⲟⲉⲓⲛ
  27. ϩⲁϩⲧⲛ̄ ⲧⲉⲙⲣⲱ
  28. ⲉⲭⲙ̄ ⲡⲃⲏⲙⲁ
  29. ⲙ̄ ⲡⲙⲟⲟⲩ
  30. ⲙ̄ⲛ̄ⲛ̄ⲥⲁ ⲡϣⲁ ⲉⲧ ⲙ̄ⲙⲁⲩ

34

B.1. ⲉⲃⲟⲗ ⲍⲓⲱⲱⲛ   6. ⲍⲁⲍⲧⲏⲛ   11. ⲚⲚⲀⲌⲢⲀⲓ

2. ⲚⲘ̄ⲘⲀⲓ   7. ⲉⲍⲢⲀⲓ ⲉⲭⲱⲛ   12. ⲉⲧⲃⲏⲏⲧⲔ̄

3. ⲉⲃⲟⲗ Ⲛ̄Ⲍⲏⲧ-ⲐⲎⲨⲦⲚ̄   8. ⲟⲨⲃⲉ-ⲐⲎⲨⲦⲚ̄   13. ⲚⲀⲌⲢⲉ

4. ⲟⲨⲃⲏⲓ   9. ⲚⲘ̄ⲘⲎⲦⲚ̄   14. ⲍⲓⲱⲕ

5. ⲉⲧⲃⲏⲏⲦⲚ̄   10. ⲉⲡⲉⲥⲏⲧ ⲉⲭⲱⲓ   15. ⲚⲘ̄ⲘⲀⲚ

C.1. ⲁ-ⲡⲘⲟⲨ ϣⲱⲡⲉ Ⲍ̄Ⲙ̄ ⲡⲕⲟⲥⲙⲟⲥ ⲉⲃⲟⲗ ⲍⲓⲧⲚ̄ ⲛⲉⲛⲛⲟⲃⲉ.

2. ⲘⲚ̄Ⲛ̄ⲤⲀ ⲚⲀⲓ Ⲇⲉ ⲀϤⲘⲟⲨ Ⲛ̄Ϭⲓ ⲡⲢ̄Ⲣⲟ ⲉⲧ Ⲙ̄ⲘⲀⲨ.

3. Ⲁ-ⲡϣⲎⲢⲉ ⲍⲉ ⲉⲡⲉⲥⲏⲧ ⲉⲭⲘ̄ ⲡⲕⲀⲍ.

4. ⲉⲧⲃⲉ ⲟⲨ Ⲁ-ⲛⲉⲓⲍⲓⲥⲉ ϣⲱⲡⲉ Ⲙ̄Ⲙⲟⲓ?

5. ⲀϤⲚ̄ⲕⲟⲧⲔ̄ ⲉⲭⲘ̄ ⲡⲉⲃⲗⲟϭ, ⲀϤⲢⲓⲙⲉ.

6. Ⲁ-Ⲛ̄Ⲣⲱⲙⲉ ⲍⲱⲛ ⲉⲍⲟⲨⲛ ⲉ ⲡⲧ†ⲙⲉ ⲉⲧ ⲍⲓⲭⲘ̄ ⲡⲧⲟⲟⲩ ⲉⲧ Ⲙ̄ⲘⲀⲨ.

7. ⲘⲚ̄Ⲛ̄Ⲥⲱⲥ Ⲇⲉ ⲀⲨⲍⲉ ⲉ ⲡⲉⲨϣⲎⲢⲉ Ⲍ̄Ⲛ̄ ⲦⲤⲨⲚⲀⲅⲱⲅⲏ.

8. ⲀⲨⲘⲟⲨ Ⲛ̄Ϭⲓ Ⲛ̄Ⲣⲱⲙⲉ Ⲛ̄ ⲧⲉⲓⲡⲟⲗⲓⲥ ⲍⲀ ⲟⲨⲍⲕⲟ.

9. Ⲁ-ⲟⲨϣⲀ ϣⲱⲡⲉ Ⲙ̄ ⲡⲉⲓⲘⲀ Ⲙ̄ ⲡⲉⲍⲟⲟⲩ ⲉⲧ Ⲙ̄ⲘⲀⲨ.

10. ⲀⲚⲌⲓⲥⲉ ⲍⲓⲧⲘ̄ ⲡⲉⲍⲕⲟ ⲀⲨⲱ ⲀⲚⲦⲱⲟⲨⲛ, ⲀⲚⲃⲱⲕ ⲉ ⲕⲉ†ⲙⲉ.

11. ⲀϤϣⲀⲭⲉ ⲚⲘ̄ⲘⲀⲚ ⲉⲧⲃⲉ Ⲛ̄ⲭⲱⲱⲙⲉ ⲉⲧ ⲍⲚ̄ Ⲧⲡⲟⲗⲓⲥ.

12. Ⲁⲓⲍⲓⲥⲉ, ⲀⲓϣⲚ̄ⲕⲟⲧⲔ̄, Ⲁⲓϣⲗⲏⲗ ⲉ ⲡⲛⲟⲩⲧⲉ ⲉⲧⲃⲉ ⲛⲉⲓϣⲀⲭⲉ.

13. ⲀϤⲍⲱⲛ ⲉⲍⲟⲨⲛ Ⲛ̄Ϭⲓ ⲡⲉⲍⲟⲟⲩ Ⲙ̄ ⲡϣⲀ.

14. Ⲁ-ⲡⲍ̄ⲗ̄ⲗⲟ ⲘⲟⲨ ⲍⲓⲢⲘ̄ ⲡⲢⲟ Ⲛ̄ ⲧⲉϤⲢⲓ.

15. ⲀⲨⲍⲕⲟ ⲀⲨⲱ ⲀⲨⲉⲓ ⲉⲡⲀⲍⲟⲨ ⲉ ⲡⲧ†ⲙⲉ.

16. ⲘⲚ̄Ⲛ̄Ⲥⲱⲥ Ⲇⲉ Ⲁ-ⲧⲉⲛⲡⲟⲗⲓⲥ ⲍⲉ ⲉⲃⲟⲗ ⲍⲓⲧⲟⲟⲦϤ̄.

17. ⲀϤⲦⲱⲟⲨⲛ Ⲛ̄Ϭⲓ ⲡϣⲎⲢⲉ ⲉⲃⲟⲗ ⲍⲓ ⲡⲕⲀⲍ, ⲀϤⲡⲱⲧ ϣⲀ ⲡⲉϤⲉⲓⲱⲧ.

18. ⲘⲚ̄Ⲛ̄ⲤⲀ ⲛⲉⲓϣⲀⲭⲉ Ⲁ-ⲡⲉⲛⲭⲟⲉⲓⲥ Ⲛ̄ⲕⲟⲧⲔ̄.

19. ⲀⲤϣⲱⲡⲉ Ⲇⲉ ⲀⲤⲍⲉ ⲉ ⲡⲛⲟⲩⲃ ⲍⲀ ⲡⲉⲃⲗⲟϭ.

20. Ⲁ-ⲛⲉⲭⲏⲩ ⲍⲱⲛ ⲉⲍⲟⲨⲛ ⲉ ⲧⲉⲘⲢⲱ.

Lesson 10

10.1 The Direct Object. The direct object of a
transitive verb is usually introduced with the preposition ⲛ̄ (ⲙ̄, ⲙ̄ⲙⲟˊ):

ⲁϥⲕⲱⲧ ⲛ̄ ⲟⲩⲏⲓ. He built a house.

ⲁϥⲕⲱⲧ ⲙ̄ⲙⲟϥ. He built it.

Many verbs, especially those denoting perception, employ ⲉ:

ⲁⲛⲥⲱⲧⲙ̄ ⲉ ⲡⲉϥϩⲣⲟⲟⲩ. We heard his voice.

ⲁⲛⲥⲱⲧⲙ̄ ⲉⲣⲟϥ. We heard it.

Occasionally other prepositions assume this function, as
for example ⲛ̄ⲥⲁ in

ⲁϥϣⲓⲛⲉ ⲛ̄ⲥⲁ ⲧⲉϥⲥϩⲓⲙⲉ. He looked for his wife.

ⲁϥϣⲓⲛⲉ ⲛ̄ⲥⲱⲥ. He looked for her.

The appropriate preposition for each transitive verb will
be given in the lesson vocabularies when a verb is introduced.

10.2 The Indirect Object (Dative). An indirect object, if present, is introduced with the preposition ⲛ̄
(ⲛⲁˊ, inflected like ⲛⲙ̄ⲙⲁˊ in §9.1):

ⲁⲓϯ ⲙ̄ ⲡⲭⲱⲱⲙⲉ ⲙ̄ ⲡⲣⲱⲙⲉ. I gave the book to the man.

ⲁⲓϯ ⲛⲁϥ ⲙ̄ ⲡⲭⲱⲱⲙⲉ. I gave him the book.

ⲁⲓϯ ⲙ̄ⲙⲟϥ ⲛⲁϥ. I gave it to him.

It is unfortunate that the prenominal forms of the most
frequent direct and indirect object markers are the same
(ⲛ̄, ⲙ̄ before ⲡ and ⲙ). In general the direct object pre-
cedes the indirect object unless the direct object is
nominal and the indirect object is pronominal. In the
latter case either order is correct, but there is a preference for placing the indirect object first. The preposition ⲉ (ⲉⲣⲟˊ) also often marks what Greek and English
regard as an indirect object (dative).

10.3 The Negative of the First Perfect. The negative forms of the First Perfect are not formally related to the positive forms:

Ⲙⲡⲓⲃⲱⲕ	I did not go	Ⲙⲡⲉⲛⲃⲱⲕ	we did not go
Ⲙⲡⲉⲕⲃⲱⲕ	you (m.s.) did not go	ⲘⲡⲉⲧⲚⲃⲱⲕ	you (pl.) did not go
Ⲙⲡⲉⲃⲱⲕ	you (f.s.) did not go		
Ⲙⲡⲉϥⲃⲱⲕ	he did not go	Ⲙⲡⲟⲩⲃⲱⲕ	they did not go
Ⲙⲡⲉⲥⲃⲱⲕ	she did not go		

With a nominal subject: Ⲙⲡⲉ-ⲡⲣⲱⲙⲉ ⲃⲱⲕ the man did not go. Variant spellings such as Ⲙⲡⲕ-, Ⲙⲡϥ-, ⲘⲡⲚ- are not uncommon.

10.4 As noted in Lesson 9, many prepositions consist of a simple preposition compounded with a noun. The nouns occurring in these expressions belong to a special group which take pronominal suffixes to indicate possession. We shall deal with the more important of these individually in later lessons, but for the moment note ⲦⲟⲟⲦ⸗, the pre-suffixal form of Ⲧⲱⲣⲉ (hand). The absolute form Ⲧⲱⲣⲉ survives only in the special meanings "handle, tool, spade" and in some compound verbal expressions (see Glossary); in the sense of "hand" it has been replaced by ϭⲓⲝ. Prepositions compounded with ⲦⲟⲟⲦ⸗, such as ⲂⲓⲦⲟⲟⲦ⸗, ⲉⲦⲟⲟⲦ⸗, ⲚⲦⲟⲟⲦ⸗, often employ a construction with an anticipatory pronominal object before the real nominal object, the latter being introduced by the particle Ⲛ (Ⲙ):

ⲂⲓⲦⲟⲟⲦϥ Ⲛ ⲡⲢⲣⲟ	by (through the agency of) the king
ⲉⲦⲟⲟⲦⲟⲩ Ⲛ ⲛⲉϥⲥⲛⲏⲩ	to (into the hands of) his brothers
ⲚⲦⲟⲟⲦⲥ Ⲛ Ⲧⲉϥⲥϩⲓⲙⲉ	from (from the hand of) his wife.

This same construction is also occasionally found with the other prepositions introduced thus far.

Vocabulary 10

ⲕⲱⲧ to build, erect (Ⲙⲙⲟ⸗).   ⲛⲁⲩ to see, look at (ⲉ).

ⲥⲱⲧⲙ̄ to hear, listen to (ⲉ); to obey (ⲛⲁˀ, ⲛ̄ⲥⲁ).

ϣⲓⲛⲉ to seek, look for, inquire after (ⲛ̄ⲥⲁ); to visit
   (ⲉ); to greet (ⲉ).

ϭⲓⲛⲉ to find (ⲙ̄ⲙⲟˀ).

ϯ to give (ⲙ̄ⲙⲟˀ); to entrust (ⲙ̄ⲙⲟˀ; to: ⲉⲧⲛ̄); ϯ ⲟⲩⲃⲉ,
   ϯ ⲙⲛ̄ to fight with; ϯ ⲙ̄ⲙⲟˀ ⲉⲃⲟⲗ to sell (to: ⲉ, ⲛⲁˀ).

ϫⲓ to take, receive (ⲙ̄ⲙⲟˀ).

ϥⲓ to lift up, take, bear, carry (ⲙ̄ⲙⲟˀ); ϥⲓ ⲙⲛ̄ to agree
   with; ϥⲓ ⲍⲁ to bear, tolerate.

ⲧⲉ.ϣⲧⲏⲛ garment, tunic.

ⲧ.ⲍⲟⲉⲓⲧⲉ, ⲡ.ⲍⲟⲉⲓⲧⲉ garment, cloak.

ⲡⲉ.ⲍⲣⲟⲟⲩ sound, voice.

ⲛ̄ⲧⲛ̄ (ⲛ̄ⲧⲟⲟⲧˀ) from; used in a wide variety of expressions,
   but very frequently with verbs of receiving, accepting,
   hearing. The separative notion lies in the verbal
   idiom; thus, with other verbs it has the sense of
   (being) near, by, with, in the hand of.

ⲉⲧⲛ̄ (ⲉⲧⲟⲟⲧˀ) to; used frequently with verbs of
   entrusting, giving, handing over, transmitting.

Exercises

A.1. ⲁϥϯ ⲛⲁⲓ ⲛ̄ ⲟⲩϣⲧⲏⲛ.

 2. ⲁⲓϯ ⲛⲁϥ ⲙ̄ ⲡⲁϫⲟⲓ ⲉⲃⲟⲗ.

 3. ⲁⲓϯ ⲙ̄ ⲡⲛⲟⲩⲃ ⲉⲧⲟⲟⲧϥ̄.

 4. ⲁⲛϯ ⲙⲛ̄ ⲛ̄ⲣⲱⲙⲉ ⲉⲧ ⲙ̄ⲙⲁⲩ.

 5. ⲁⲩϯ ⲟⲩⲃⲏⲛ.

 6. ⲁϥϯ ⲙ̄ ⲡⲛⲟⲩⲃ ⲙ̄ ⲡⲉϥϣⲏⲣⲉ.

 7. ⲁⲩϥⲓ ⲙ̄ ⲡⲱⲛⲉ ⲉⲃⲟⲗ ⲍⲓⲣⲱϥ.

 8. ⲁϥϥⲓ ⲙ̄ ⲡⲉϥϣⲏⲣⲉ ⲉⲍⲣⲁⲓ.

 9. ⲙ̄ⲡⲉⲛϥⲓ ⲛ̄ⲙ̄ⲙⲁⲩ.

10. ⲁϥϥⲓ ⲙ̄ ⲡⲉϥϭⲗⲟϭ, ⲁϥⲃⲱⲕ ⲉⲃⲟⲗ.

11. ⲁⲩⲕⲱⲧ ⲛ̄ ⲟⲩⲣ̄ⲡⲉ ⲙ̄ⲙⲁⲩ.

12. ⲙ̄ⲡⲟⲩⲥⲱⲧⲙ̄ ⲛ̄ⲥⲁ ⲡⲉⲩϫⲟⲉⲓⲥ.

13. ⲁⲓⲥⲱⲧⲙ̄ ⲉ ⲡⲉⲍⲣⲟⲟⲩ ⲙ̄ ⲡⲟⲩⲏⲏⲃ.

14. ⲙ̄ⲡⲓⲥⲱⲧⲙ̄ ⲉⲧⲃⲉ ⲡⲉⲥⲙⲟⲩ.

15. ⲁⲛⲛⲁⲩ ⲉⲩϫⲟⲓ ⲙ̄ⲙⲁⲩ.

16. ⲁⲩϣⲓⲛⲉ ⲛ̄ⲥⲱⲓ ⲍⲛ̄ ⲧⲁⲅⲟⲣⲁ.

17. ⲁⲛϭⲓⲛⲉ ⲙ̄ⲙⲟϥ ⲉϫⲙ̄ ⲡⲉⲕⲣⲟ
   ⲙⲛ̄ ⲡⲉⲛⲥⲁⲍ.

18. ⲁⲓϣⲓⲛⲉ ⲉⲣⲟϥ ⲍⲛ̄ ⲧⲉϥϥⲓ.

19. ⲁϥⲛⲁⲩ ⲉⲩⲁⲅⲅⲉⲗⲟⲥ.

20. ⲁⲓϫⲓ ⲙ̄ⲙⲟⲟⲩ ⲛ̄ⲧⲟⲟⲧϥ̄ ⲙ̄
   ⲡⲁⲉⲓⲱⲧ.

21. ⲁⲩϫⲓ ⲙ̄ⲙⲟϥ ⲛ̄ⲧⲟⲟⲧ.

22. ⲁⲛϯ ⲙ̄ⲙⲟⲥ ⲉⲧⲟⲟⲧⲉ.

23. ⲁϥϭⲓⲛⲉ ⲙ̄ⲙⲟϥ ⲍⲁ
   ⲡⲉϥϭⲗⲟϭ.

24. ⲡⲉϥⲉⲓⲱⲧ ⲇⲉ ⲙ̄ⲡⲉϥⲃⲱⲕ
   ⲉⲍⲟⲩⲛ.

25. ⲉⲧⲃⲉ ⲟⲩ ⲙ̄ⲡⲉⲧⲛ̄ⲛ̄ⲕⲟⲧⲕ̄?

26. ⲁⲛϥⲓ ⲍⲁ ⲛ̄ⲍⲓⲥⲉ ⲉⲧ ⲙ̄ⲙⲁⲩ.

27. ⲙ̄ⲡⲉⲥⲍⲱⲛ ⲉⲍⲟⲩⲛ ⲉ ⲡⲧⲁⲫⲟⲥ.

28. ⲙ̄ⲡⲓ† ⲙ̄ ⲡⲍⲟⲉⲓⲧⲉ ⲉⲃⲟⲗ.

29. ⲙ̄ⲡⲓ† ⲛⲉ ⲛ̄ ⲧⲉⲓϣⲧⲏⲛ.

30. ⲉⲧⲃⲉ ⲟⲩ ⲙ̄ⲡⲉⲉⲓ ϣⲁⲣⲟⲓ?

31. ⲙ̄ⲡⲉⲛϣⲁϫⲉ ⲛⲙ̄ⲙⲁⲩ.

32. ⲉⲧⲃⲉ ⲟⲩ ⲁⲩ† ⲛⲙ̄ⲙⲏⲧⲛ̄?

33. ⲙ̄ⲡⲉϥⲍⲉ ⲉⲣⲟⲛ ⲙ̄ⲙⲁⲩ.

34. ⲙ̄ⲡⲟⲩⲗⲉ ⲉ ⲡⲉⲩϫⲟⲓ.

35. ⲙ̄ⲡⲉⲧⲛ̄ϫⲓ ⲛ̄ ⲛⲉⲓⲉⲛⲧⲟⲗⲏ ⲛ̄ⲧⲟⲟⲧⲟⲩ ⲛ̄ ⲛⲉⲧⲛ̄ⲉⲓⲟⲧⲉ.

36. ⲙ̄ⲡⲉϥⲧⲱⲟⲩⲛ ⲉⲃⲟⲗ ⲍⲓ ⲡⲕⲁⲍ.

37. ⲁϥⲥⲱⲧⲙ̄ ⲉ ⲛⲉⲩⲍⲣⲟⲟⲩ, ⲁϥⲡⲱⲧ ⲉⲃⲟⲗ.

38. ⲁⲩϥⲓ ⲛ̄ϭⲓ ⲡⲙⲏⲏϣⲉ ⲙⲛ̄ ⲡⲉⲡⲓⲥⲕⲟⲡⲟⲥ.

39. ⲙ̄ⲡⲉⲛⲥⲱⲧⲙ̄ ⲉ ⲛⲉϥϣⲁϫⲉ.

40. ⲁϥϫⲓ ⲙ̄ ⲡⲁⲍⲟⲉⲓⲧⲉ.

41. ⲙ̄ⲡⲉ-ⲡⲉϥⲙⲁⲑⲏⲧⲏⲥ ⲥⲱⲧⲙ̄ ⲛⲁϥ.

42. ⲙ̄ⲡⲉ-ⲡⲁϣⲏⲣⲉ ⲉⲓ ⲉⲡⲁⲍⲟⲩ.

43. ⲁⲓⲥⲱⲧⲙ̄ ⲉⲧⲃⲉ ⲛⲁⲓ ⲛ̄ⲧⲟⲟⲧϥ̄ ⲙ̄ ⲡⲁⲥⲟⲛ.

44. ⲁϥ† ⲛ̄ ⲧⲉϥⲙⲁⲁⲩ ⲉⲧⲟⲟⲧⲟⲩ ⲛ̄ ⲛⲉϥⲙⲁⲑⲏⲧⲏⲥ.

45. ⲁⲩϭⲓⲛⲉ ⲙ̄ⲙⲟϥ ⲛ̄ ⲧⲙⲏⲧⲉ ⲙ̄ ⲡⲙⲏⲏϣⲉ.

46. ⲁ-ⲡⲍⲁⲙϣⲉ ⲕⲱⲧ ⲛⲁⲛ ⲛ̄ ⲟⲩⲏⲓ ⲙ̄ⲙⲁⲩ.

47. ⲙⲉϣⲁⲕ ⲁ-ⲡⲟⲩⲍⲁⲓ ⲙⲟⲩ.

48. ⲁⲓⲛⲁⲩ ⲉ ⲡⲉⲟⲟⲩ ⲙ̄ ⲡⲭⲟⲉⲓⲥ ⲙⲛ̄ ⲧⲉϥϭⲟⲙ.

49. ⲁⲩⲡⲱⲧ ⲛⲙ̄ⲙⲁⲛ ⲉ ⲧⲟⲣⲓⲛⲏ.

50. ⲁϥϣⲁϫⲉ ⲛⲙ̄ⲙⲁⲓ ⲉⲧⲃⲉ ⲡⲉⲩⲁⲅⲅⲉⲗⲓⲟⲛ.

Lesson 11

11.1 The Forms of the Infinitive. The nominal or
pronominal object of many transitive verbs may be suffixed
directly to the infinitive without the use of a prepositional object marker, as in

ⲁⲓϭⲓⲛⲉ ⲙ̄ ⲡⲁⲉⲓⲱⲧ. → ⲁⲓϭⲛ̄-ⲡⲁⲉⲓⲱⲧ.   I found my father.
ⲁⲓϭⲓⲛⲉ ⲙ̄ⲙⲟϥ.   → ⲁⲓϭⲛ̄ⲧϥ̄.   I found him.

Infinitives that allow this construction have three distinct forms: (1) the normal (absolute) dictionary form
(ϭⲓⲛⲉ), (2) the prenominal form (ϭⲛ̄-; note the conventional use of the single hyphen), and (3) the prepronominal
form (ϭⲛ̄ⲧ⸗). For infinitives of some patterns these three
forms are more or less predictable; for others there is
much irregularity. We shall deal with the most important
patterns individually in subsequent lessons. The forms of
the pronouns to be suffixed to a given infinitive are very
much the same as those suffixed to the prepronominal forms
of the prepositions as given in § 9.1. Other examples will
be given as required.

11.2 Infinitives of the pattern ⲭⲓ (i.e. consonant
+ ⲓ). Infinitives of this pattern show some irregularities, but three of these verbs (ϥⲓ, ϯ, ⲭⲓ) are especially
frequent and their forms should be learned:

ϯ	ϯ-	ⲧⲁⲁ⸗	to give
ⲭⲓ	ⲭⲓ-	ⲭⲓⲧ⸗	to take
ϥⲓ	ϥⲓ-	ϥⲓⲧ⸗	to raise, carry
ϣⲓ	ϣⲓ-	ϣⲓⲧ⸗	to measure.

The verbs ⲥⲓ (to become sated) and ⲉⲓ (to come) are intransitive and do not take direct objects. ϥⲓ, ϣⲓ, and ⲥⲓ
may also be spelled as ϥⲉⲓ, ϣⲉⲓ, and ⲥⲉⲓ; the spelling ⲧⲉⲓ
for ϯ is rare.

Object pronouns are attached to these verbs as

follows:

ϫⲓⲧ	ϫⲓⲧⲛ̄	ⲧⲁⲁⲧ	ⲧⲁⲁⲛ
ϫⲓⲧⲕ̄	ϫⲓ-ⲑⲏⲩⲧⲛ̄	ⲧⲁⲁⲕ	†-ⲑⲏⲩⲧⲛ̄
ϫⲓⲧⲉ		ⲧⲁⲁⲧⲉ	
ϫⲓⲧϥ̄	ϫⲓⲧⲟⲩ	ⲧⲁⲁϥ	ⲧⲁⲁⲩ
ϫⲓⲧⲥ̄		ⲧⲁⲁⲥ	

Note that ⲑⲏⲩⲧⲛ (2nd pers. pl.) is attached to the pre-nominal form of the infinitive; the prepronominal form is also found: ϫⲓⲧ-ⲑⲏⲩⲧⲛ̄.

Vocabulary 11

ϣⲓ ϣⲓ- ϣⲓⲧ⸗ to measure (ⲙ̄ⲙⲟ⸗); to measure out; as n.m.: measure, weight, extent; moderation.

ⲥⲓ to become sated, filled (with: ⲙ̄ⲙⲟ⸗).

ⲕⲱ (1) to put, place, set (ⲙ̄ⲙⲟ⸗); (2) to leave, abandon (ⲙ̄ⲙⲟ⸗); ⲕⲱ ⲙ̄ⲙⲟ⸗ ⲛ̄ⲥⲁ to leave, abandon, renounce; ⲕⲱ ⲙ̄ⲙⲟ⸗ ⲛⲁ⸗ ⲉⲃⲟⲗ to forgive (someone: ⲛⲁ⸗; something: ⲙ̄ⲙⲟ⸗).

ⲉⲓⲛⲉ to bring (ⲙ̄ⲙⲟ⸗; to a person: ⲛⲁ⸗, ϣⲁ); ⲉⲓⲛⲉ ⲉⲃⲟⲗ to publish.

ⲧⲛ̄ⲛⲟⲟⲩ to send (ⲙ̄ⲙⲟ⸗; to a person: ⲛⲁ⸗, ⲉ); ⲧⲛ̄ⲛⲟⲟⲩ ⲛ̄ⲥⲁ to send for.

ⲙⲉ to love, come to love (ⲙ̄ⲙⲟ⸗).

ⲙⲓⲥⲉ to bear (a child: ⲙ̄ⲙⲟ⸗); as n.m.: giving birth; offspring, progeny, one born.

ϣⲱⲛⲉ to fall ill, become sick; as n.m.: sickness, disease.

ⲣⲁϣⲉ to rejoice (at, over: ⲉ, ⲉϫⲛ̄, ⲉϩⲣⲁⲓ ⲉϫⲛ̄); as n.m.: joy, gladness.

ⲧⲉ.ⲩϣⲏ night (ⲟⲩϣⲏ).

ⲡ.ϩⲁⲧ silver, money, coins.

ⲡⲉ.ϣⲃⲏⲣ, ⲧⲉ.ϣⲃⲉⲉⲣⲉ (pl. ⲛⲉ.ϣⲃⲉⲉⲣ) friend, companion.

ⲉⲙⲁⲧⲉ (adv.) very, very much, exceedingly; also ⲙ̄ⲙⲁⲧⲉ.

Exercises

A.1. ⲀⲨⲦⲀⲀⲦ ⲈⲦⲞⲞⲦⲈ.
  2. ⲀⲚϢⲒⲦⲤ̄ ⲚⲀⲨ.
  3. ⲀⲒⲬⲒⲦϤ̄ Ⲛ̄ⲦⲞⲞⲦⲞⲨ.
  4. ⲀⲦⲈⲦⲚ̄ⲦⲀⲀϤ ⲚⲀⲚ.
  5. ⲀⲨϪⲒⲦⲞⲨ ⲈⲂⲞⲗ Ⲛ̄ϨⲎⲦⲤ̄.

  6. ⲀⲔϤⲒⲦ ⲈϨⲢⲀⲒ.
  7. ⲀⲒϢⲒⲦⲞⲨ ⲚⲎⲦⲚ̄.
  8. ⲀⲒⲦⲀⲀⲨ ⲚⲀⲤ.
  9. ⲀϤϤⲒ-ⲦⲎⲨⲦⲚ̄ ⲈⲂⲞⲗ.
  10. ⲀⲨⲦⲀⲀⲦⲈ ⲈⲦⲞⲞⲦ.

B. Translate. Replace the nominal objects with the appropriate pronominal object.

  1. ⲀⲒϮ-ⲠⲞⲈⲒⲔ ⲚⲀⲤ. (ⲀⲒⲦⲀⲀϤ ⲚⲀⲤ)
  2. Ⲙ̄ⲠⲈϤϮ-ⲠϨⲀⲦ ⲚⲀⲒ.
  3. ⲀⲚϮ-Ⲛ̄ϪⲱⲱⲘⲈ ⲈⲦⲞⲞⲦϤ̄.
  4. ⲀϤϮ-ⲠⲈϤⲎⲒ ⲚⲀⲨ ⲈⲂⲞⲗ.
  5. ⲀⲤϮ-ⲦⲈϢⲦⲎⲚ ⲚⲀⲚ.
  6. ⲀⲚϪⲒ-ⲠⲚⲞⲨⲂ Ⲛ̄ⲦⲞⲞⲦⲞⲨ.
  7. ⲀⲦⲈⲦⲚ̄ϪⲒ-ⲦⲈⲒⲈⲒⲢⲎⲚⲎ ⲈⲂⲞⲗ ϨⲒⲦⲞⲞⲦϤ̄.

  8. ⲀⲨϢⲒ-ⲦⲈϨⲒⲎ.
  9. ⲀⲒϢⲒ-ⲠⲞⲈⲒⲔ ⲚⲀⲨ.
  10. ⲀⲔϢⲒ-ⲠϨⲀⲦ ⲚⲀⲒ.
  11. ⲀϤϤⲒ-ⲠⲰⲚⲈ ⲈⲂⲞⲗ.
  12. ⲀϤϤⲒ-ⲠⲚⲞⲨⲂ, ⲀϤⲠⲰⲦ ⲈⲂⲞⲗ.
  13. ⲀⲤϢⲒ ⲚⲀⲒ Ⲙ̄ ⲠⲎⲢⲠ̄.
  14. ⲀⲢⲬⲒ-ⲠϨⲞⲈⲒⲦⲈ ⲈⲂⲞⲗ ϨⲘ̄ ⲠⲀⲎⲒ.

C.1. ⲠϢⲎⲢⲈ ⲈⲦ Ⲛ̄ⲤⲰϤ
  2. ⲠⲘⲞⲞⲨ ⲈⲦ Ⲛ̄ϨⲎⲦϤ̄
  3. ⲠⲈϢⲂⲎⲢ ⲈⲦ ⲚⲘ̄ⲘⲀϤ
  4. ⲚⲈⲦ ϨⲚ̄ ⲦⲤⲨⲚⲀⲅⲰⲄⲎ
  5. ⲦⲀⲤⲰⲚⲈ ⲘⲚ̄ ⲦⲈⲤϢⲂⲈⲈⲢⲈ
  6. ⲠⲚⲞⲨⲂ ⲘⲚ̄ ⲠϨⲀⲦ
  7. ⲠⲈϨⲞⲞⲨ ⲘⲚ̄ ⲦⲈⲨϢⲎ
  8. ϨⲀ ⲠⲈⲒϢⲰⲚⲈ
  9. Ⲉ ⲠⲈⲒϢⲒ
  10. ⲠϢⲒ Ⲙ̄ ⲠⲈⲒⲰⲚⲈ
  11. ⲠϢⲰⲤ ⲘⲚ̄ ⲚⲈϤϢⲂⲈⲈⲢ
  12. ⲘⲚ̄Ⲛ̄ⲤⲀ ⲠⲈⲤⲘⲒⲤⲈ
  13. ⲦⲈϢⲦⲎⲚ ⲈⲦ ϨⲒϪⲘ̄ ⲠⲈⲂⲖⲞϬ
  14. ⲠϢⲰⲚⲈ ⲈⲦ ϨⲚ̄ ⲚⲈⲤⲞⲞⲨ

  15. Ⲛ̄ⲦⲞⲞⲦϤ̄ Ⲙ̄ ⲠⲈϤⲈⲒⲰⲦ
  16. ⲠϢⲒ Ⲙ̄ ⲠϨⲀⲦ
  17. ⲠϨⲞⲈⲒⲦⲈ Ⲙ̄ ⲠⲀϢⲂⲎⲢ
  18. ⲞⲨⲘⲒⲤⲈ Ⲛ̄ⲦⲈ ⲠⲈϤⲎⲒ
  19. ⲈⲦⲞⲞⲦⲞⲨ Ⲛ̄ ⲚⲀϢⲂⲈⲈⲢ
  20. ⲠⲈϨⲢⲞⲞⲨ Ⲛ̄ ⲦⲀⲘⲀⲀⲨ
  21. ϨⲘ̄ ⲠⲔⲀⲔⲈ Ⲛ̄ ⲦⲈⲨϢⲎ
  22. ⲞⲨⲂⲈ ⲚⲈⲨϢⲀϪⲈ
  23. ϨⲒⲦⲞⲞⲦϤ̄ Ⲙ̄ ⲠϪⲞⲈⲒⲤ
  24. ⲘⲚ̄Ⲛ̄ⲤⲀ ⲠϢⲀ ⲈⲦ Ⲙ̄ⲘⲀⲨ
  25. ⲠⲢⲀⲚ Ⲙ̄ ⲠⲈⲒϢⲰⲚⲈ
  26. Ⲛ̄ⲢⲰⲘⲈ ⲈⲦ ϨⲀϨⲦⲎϤ
  27. ϨⲚ̄ ϨⲈⲚⲘⲀⲈⲒⲚ
  28. ϨⲚ̄ ⲞⲨⲤⲎϤⲈ

D.1. ⲀⲤϢⲰⲚⲈ Ⲛ̄ϬⲒ ⲦⲈϤⲤϨⲒⲘⲈ ⲈⲘⲀⲦⲈ.
  2. ⲀⲒⲔⲰ Ⲙ̄ ⲠⲚⲞⲨⲂ ⲘⲚ̄ ⲠϨⲀⲦ ⲈϪⲚ̄ ⲦⲈⲦⲢⲀⲠⲈⲌⲀ.

42

3. ⲁⲛⲕⲱ ⲛ̄ ⲛⲉⲛϣⲃⲉⲉⲣ ⲛ̄ⲥⲱⲛ ϩⲙ̄ ⲡ†ⲙⲉ, ⲁⲛⲃⲱⲕ ⲉⲑⲏ ⲉ ⲡⲧⲟⲟⲩ.

4. ⲙⲛ̄ⲛ̄ⲥⲱⲥ ⲇⲉ ⲁϥϣⲱⲛⲉ ⲛ̄ϭⲓ ⲡ2ⲁⲗⲟ, ⲁϥⲙⲟⲩ.

5. ⲁϥⲣⲁϣⲉ ⲉⲙⲁⲧⲉ ⲛⲙ̄ⲙⲁⲓ ⲉⲭⲙ̄ ⲡⲙⲟⲩ ⲙ̄ ⲡ̄ⲣ̄ⲣⲟ.

6. ⲁϥⲙⲉ ⲛ̄ ⲧⲉⲥ2ⲓⲙⲉ ⲉⲧ ⲙ̄ⲙⲁⲩ ⲉⲙⲁⲧⲉ.

7. ⲁ-ⲡⲛⲟⲩⲧⲉ ⲧⲛ̄ⲛⲟⲟⲩ ⲙ̄ ⲡⲉϥⲛⲟⲙⲟⲥ ⲉⲣⲟⲟⲩ.

8. ⲁϥⲧⲛ̄ⲛⲟⲟⲩ ⲛ̄ϭⲓ ⲡⲉⲡⲓⲥⲕⲟⲡⲟⲥ ⲛ̄ⲥⲁ ⲡⲙⲟⲛⲁⲭⲟⲥ.

9. ⲁⲓϣⲓ ⲛⲁⲩ ⲙ̄ ⲡⲟⲉⲓⲕ ⲙⲛ̄ ⲡⲏⲣⲡ̄.

10. ⲛ̄ⲣⲱⲙⲉ ⲁⲩϣⲓ ⲛ̄ ⲧⲥⲱϣⲉ.

11. ⲙⲛ̄-ϣⲓ 2ⲛ̄ ⲛⲉϥϣⲁϫⲉ.

12. ⲁⲩⲥⲓ, ⲁⲩⲧⲱⲟⲩⲛ ⲉⲃⲟⲗ 2ⲓ ⲧⲉⲧⲣⲁⲡⲉϫⲁ, ⲁⲩⲃⲱⲕ ⲉⲃⲟⲗ.

13. ⲁϥⲧⲛ̄ⲛⲟⲟⲩ ⲛ̄ ⲛⲉ2ⲓⲟⲙⲉ ⲙⲛ̄ ⲛⲉⲩϣⲏⲣⲉ ⲉⲃⲟⲗ 2ⲙ̄ ⲡ†ⲙⲉ.

14. ⲉⲧⲃⲉ ⲟⲩ ⲙ̄ⲡⲉ-ⲡⲛⲟⲩⲧⲉ ⲕⲱ ⲛⲏⲧⲛ̄ ⲛ̄ ⲛⲉⲧⲛ̄ⲛⲟⲃⲉ ⲉⲃⲟⲗ?

15. ⲁⲛⲥⲓ ⲛ̄ ⲛⲉϥϣⲁϫⲉ ⲁⲩⲱ ⲁⲛⲧⲛ̄ⲛⲟⲟⲩ ⲙ̄ⲙⲟϥ ⲉⲃⲟⲗ.

16. ⲁⲛⲣⲁϣⲉ ⲉ2ⲣⲁⲓ ⲉⲭⲛ̄ ⲛ̄ϣⲁϫⲉ ⲙ̄ ⲡⲉⲛϫⲟⲉⲓⲥ.

17. ⲁϥⲉⲓⲛⲉ ⲙ̄ ⲡⲉϥϣⲏⲣⲉ ⲉⲣⲛ̄ ⲧⲣⲓ ⲙ̄ ⲡⲙⲟⲛⲁⲭⲟⲥ.

18. ⲁϥⲉⲓⲛⲉ ⲙ̄ ⲡ2ⲁⲧ ϣⲁⲣⲟⲛ 2ⲛ̄ ⲧⲉⲩϣⲏ.

19. ⲁⲥⲙⲓⲥⲉ ⲙ̄ ⲡⲉⲥϣⲏⲣⲉ ⲙ̄ ⲡ†ⲙⲉ ⲉⲧ ⲙ̄ⲙⲁⲩ.

20. ⲙ̄ⲡⲉⲥⲙⲓⲥⲉ ⲙ̄ⲙⲟϥ ⲙ̄ ⲡⲉⲓⲙⲁ.

21. ⲁ-ⲡ2ⲙ̄2ⲁⲗ ⲙⲉ ⲛ̄ ⲧϣⲉⲉⲣⲉ ⲙ̄ ⲡⲉϥϫⲟⲉⲓⲥ.

22. ⲉⲧⲃⲉ ⲟⲩ ⲙ̄ⲡⲉⲉⲓⲛⲉ ⲛⲁⲓ ⲙ̄ ⲡϫⲱⲱⲙⲉ?

23. ⲁⲩⲉⲓⲛⲉ ⲛ̄ ⲛⲉϥⲉⲛⲧⲟⲗⲏ ⲉⲃⲟⲗ.

24. ⲁⲩⲉⲓⲛⲉ ⲙ̄ⲙⲟⲓ ⲛⲁ2ⲣⲁϥ.

25. ⲉⲧⲃⲉ ⲟⲩ ⲁⲕⲧⲛ̄ⲛⲟⲟⲩ ⲛ̄ⲥⲱⲓ?

Lesson 12

12.1 The relative form of the First Perfect. When
the First Perfect is used in relative clauses, it combines with the relative pronoun into a single unit:

ⲉⲛⲧⲁⲓⲥⲱⲧⲙ̄ which I heard   ⲉⲛⲧⲁⲛⲥⲱⲧⲙ̄

ⲉⲛⲧⲁⲕⲥⲱⲧⲙ̄ etc.   ⲉⲛⲧⲁⲧⲉⲧⲛ̄ⲥⲱⲧⲙ̄

ⲉⲛⲧⲁⲣⲉⲥⲱⲧⲙ̄

ⲉⲛⲧⲁ ⲝ ⲥⲱⲧⲙ̄   ⲉⲛⲧⲁⲩⲥⲱⲧⲙ̄

ⲉⲛⲧⲁⲥⲥⲱⲧⲙ̄

ⲉⲛⲧⲁ-ⲡⲣⲱⲙⲉ ⲥⲱⲧⲙ̄

These forms are very frequently spelled with ⲛ̄ for initial
ⲉⲛ-, as ⲛ̄ⲧⲁⲓ-, ⲛ̄ⲧⲁⲕ-, etc.

The relative pronoun ⲉⲛⲧ- of the preceding paradigm
and ⲉⲧ, which was introduced in § 3.1, cannot be preceded
directly by prepositions or direct object markers. The
real syntactic function of the relative pronoun within the
relative clause must be expressed by a *resumptive* pronoun.
The general construction is most clearly understood by
"Copticizing" a few English examples:

the man who went → the man who he went   ⲡⲣⲱⲙⲉ ⲉⲛⲧⲁ ⲝ ⲃⲱⲕ

the man whom I saw → the man who I saw him   ⲡⲣⲱⲙⲉ ⲉⲛⲧⲁⲓⲛⲁⲩ ⲉⲣⲟ ⲝ

the man to whom I gave the money → the man who I gave the money to him

ⲡⲣⲱⲙⲉ ⲉⲛⲧⲁⲓ†-ⲡ̄ⲍⲁⲧ ⲛⲁ ⲝ

the boat into which we climbed → the boat which we climbed into it

ⲡϫⲟⲓ ⲉⲛⲧⲁⲛⲁ ⲁ ⲉ ⲉⲣⲟ ⲝ

the sound which they heard → the sound which they heard it

ⲡⲉⲍⲣⲟⲟⲩ ⲉⲛⲧⲁⲩⲥⲱⲧⲙ̄ ⲉⲣⲟ ⲝ

This use of resumptive pronouns is required in Coptic in
all but a few instances which will be mentioned later on.
Similar constructions with ⲉⲧ will be treated in Lesson 19.

When a relative clause contains more than one verb,
the relative pronoun need not be repeated:

44

ⲡⲣⲱⲙⲉ ⲉⲛⲧⲁϥⲧⲱⲟⲩⲛ ⲁⲩⲱ ⲁϥⲃⲱⲕ ⲉⲃⲟⲗ   the man who arose and left.

12.2 The relative pronoun has the form ⲉⲧⲉ before the negative First Perfect:

ⲡⲣⲱⲙⲉ ⲉⲧⲉ ⲙ̄ⲡⲉϥⲡⲱⲧ ⲉⲃⲟⲗ   the man who did not flee
ⲛ̄ϫⲱⲱⲙⲉ ⲉⲧⲉ ⲙ̄ⲡⲉϥϭ ⲓ ⲛ ⲉ ⲙ̄ⲙ ⲟⲟⲩ the books which he did not find

12.3 As mentioned in § 3.1, all relative clauses in Coptic may be substantivized by prefixing the appropriate form of the definite article. Resumptive pronouns are required. Study the following examples carefully:

the one who (or: he who) went   ⲡⲉⲛⲧⲁϥⲃⲱⲕ
the one (m.) whom they sent   ⲡⲉⲛⲧⲁⲩⲧⲛ̄ⲛⲟⲟⲩ ⲙ̄ⲙ ⲟϥ
the one (m.) to whom I gave the money   ⲡⲉⲛⲧⲁ ⲓ ϯ ⲡ ⲍ ⲁⲧ ⲛⲁϥ
that (m.) which I took from you   ⲡⲉⲛⲧⲁ ⲓ ⲝ ⲓ ⲧ ϥ̄ ⲛ̄ⲧⲟⲟⲧⲕ̄
those who took it (m.)   ⲛⲉⲛⲧⲁⲩ ⲝ ⲓ ⲧ ϥ̄
the one (f.) whom they entrusted to us ⲧⲉⲛⲧⲁⲩⲧⲁⲁⲥ ⲉⲧⲟⲟⲧⲛ̄

12.4 Infinitives (cont.). With the exception of the verbs treated in § 9.2, monosyllabic infinitives of the pattern consonant + vowel are relatively uncommon and do not constitute any sort of unified class. Some of these verbs are very important, however, and their forms should be learned:

ⲥⲱ	ⲥ ⲉ-	ⲥⲟⲟ⸗	to drink
ⲕⲱ	ⲕⲁ-	ⲕⲁⲁ⸗	to put, place
ⲉ ⲓ ⲱ	ⲉ ⲓ ⲁ-	ⲉ ⲓ ⲁⲁ⸗	to wash
ⲝⲱ	ⲝⲉ-	ⲝⲟⲟ⸗	to say
ⲙⲉ	ⲙⲉⲣⲉ-	ⲙⲉⲣ ⲓ ⲧ⸗	to love

Some verbs of this type are intransitive and do not take direct objects: e.g. ⲙⲟⲩ (to die), ⲛⲁ (to pity), ϣⲁ (to rise: of the sun etc.), ⲍⲉ (to fall), ϭⲱ (to remain).

12.5 When introducing a direct quotation, the verb ⲝⲱ requires a "dummy" object (it: ⲙ̄ⲙⲟⲥ, -ⲥ) followed by the conjunction ⲝⲉ, as in ⲁϥϫⲟⲟⲥ ϫⲉ ⲙ̅ⲡⲓⲛⲁⲩ ⲉⲣⲟϥ. He said, "I have not seen him."

With this particular verb the alternate object form ⲭⲱ ⲙ̅ⲙⲟⲥ is not permitted in the First Perfect. ⲭⲱ may, of course, have a real direct object otherwise:

ⲙ̅ⲡⲓⲭⲉ-ⲛⲁⲓ. I did not say these things.

Vocabulary 12

ⲥⲱ ⲥⲉ- ⲥⲟⲟ⸗ to drink (ⲙ̅ⲙⲟ⸗); often with ⲉⲃⲟⲗ ϩⲛ̅ in partitive sense (drink some of); as n.m.: drinking, a drink.

ⲉⲓⲱ ⲉⲓⲁ- ⲉⲓⲁⲁ⸗ to wash (ⲙ̅ⲙⲟ⸗); + ⲉⲃⲟⲗ idem.

ⲭⲱ ⲭⲉ- ⲭⲟⲟ⸗ to say (ⲙ̅ⲙⲟ⸗).

ⲛⲁ to have pity, mercy (on: ⲛⲁ⸗, ϩⲁ); to pity; as n.m.: mercy, pity, charity.

ⲱ or ⲱⲱ to become pregnant, to conceive (ⲙ̅ⲙⲟ⸗).

ϣⲁ to rise (of sun etc.); as n.m. rising.

ϭⲱ to stop, cease, come to a stop; to delay, tarry. ϭⲱ ⲉ to wait for; ϭⲱ ⲙⲛ̅ to wait with, stay with.

ⲡ.ϩⲟ face.

ⲧ.ⲟⲩⲉⲣⲏⲧⲉ foot.

ⲡ.ⲣⲏ the sun.

ⲡ.ⲁⲡⲟⲧ (pl. ⲛ.ⲁⲡⲏⲧ) cup.

ⲡ.ϥⲱ hair.

ⲡ.ⲙⲁⲁϫⲉ ear.

ⲡ.ⲉⲣⲱⲧⲉ, ⲧ.ⲉⲣⲱⲧⲉ milk.

ⲭⲉ (conj.) introducing direct quotation.

Exercises

A.1. ⲡϣⲁ ⲉⲛⲧⲁϥϣⲱⲡⲉ ⲙ̅ⲙⲁⲩ

2. ⲡⲉⲑⲣⲟⲛⲟⲥ ⲉⲛⲧⲁϥϩⲙⲟⲟⲥ ⲉϫⲱϥ

3. ⲡⲉⲓⲱ ⲉⲛⲧⲁⲓⲁⲗⲉ ⲉϫⲱϥ

4. ⲡϩⲁⲧ ⲛ̅ⲧⲁⲓⲧⲁⲁϥ ⲛⲉ

5. ⲛⲉϩⲧⲱⲱⲣ ⲉⲛⲧⲁⲛϫⲓⲧⲟⲩ ⲛ̅ⲧⲟⲟⲧⲕ̅

6. ⲛ̅ϣⲏⲣⲉ ⲉⲛⲧⲁⲩⲙⲟⲟϣⲉ ⲛ̅ⲥⲱϥ

7. ⲧϣⲉⲉⲣⲉ ⲉⲛⲧⲁⲥϣⲱⲛⲉ

8. ⲡⲏⲣⲡ̅ ⲉⲛⲧⲁ-ⲡϩ̅ⲗⲗⲟ ⲥⲟⲟϥ

9. ⲧⲉϣⲧⲏⲛ ⲉⲛⲧⲁⲥⲉⲓⲁⲁⲥ

10. ⲛ̅ϣⲁϫⲉ ⲉⲛⲧⲁϥϫⲟⲟⲩ

11. ⲛ̅ⲣⲱⲙⲉ ⲉⲛⲧⲁⲛⲛⲁ ϩⲁⲣⲟⲟⲩ

12. ⲧⲉⲥϩⲓⲙⲉ ⲉⲛⲧⲁⲥⲱ ⲁⲩⲱ ⲁⲥⲙⲓⲥⲉ

13. ⲡⲙⲁ ⲉⲛⲧⲁ-ⲙ̅ⲙⲟⲛⲁⲭⲟⲥ ϭⲱ ⲛ̅ϩⲏⲧϥ̅

14. ΠⲈϢⲂⲎⲢ ⲈⲚⲦⲀⲨϬⲰ ⲈⲢⲞϤ

15. ⲠⲂⲀⲗⲞ ⲈⲚⲦⲀⲦⲈⲦⲚϬⲰ ⲈⲢⲞϤ

16. ⲠⲈⲌⲦⲞ ⲈⲚⲦⲀⲔⲦⲀⲁϤ ⲚⲀⲒ ⲈⲂⲞⲗ

17. ⲠⲬⲰⲰⲘⲈ ⲈⲚⲦⲀⲢⲔⲀⲁϤ ⲈⲬⲚ
    ⲦⲈⲦⲢⲀⲠⲈⲌⲀ

18. ⲠⲀⲠⲞⲦ ⲚⲦⲀⲒⲤⲰ ⲈⲂⲞⲗ ⲚⲌⲎⲦϤ

19. ⲦⲈⲢⲰⲦⲈ ⲚⲦⲀϤⲤⲰ ⲈⲂⲞⲗ ⲚⲌⲎⲦⲤ̅

20. ⲚⲈϢⲂⲈⲈⲢ ⲚⲦⲀⲚⲔⲀⲁⲨ ⲚⲤⲰⲚ

21. ⲠϢⲀⲬⲈ ⲈⲚⲦⲀϤⲢⲀϢⲈ ⲈⲬⲰϤ

22. ⲦⲈⲤⲌⲒⲘⲈ ⲈⲚⲦⲀⲤⲈⲒⲀ-ⲚⲈϤⲞⲨⲈⲢⲎⲦⲈ

23. ⲠⲤⲰ ⲈⲚⲦⲀⲒⲤⲒ ⲘⲘⲞϤ

24. ⲠⲌⲀⲦ ⲈⲚⲦⲀ-ⲠⲈⲚⲬⲞⲈⲒⲤ
    ϢⲒⲦϤ̅ ⲚⲎⲦⲚ̅

25. ⲠⲢⲰⲘⲈ ⲚⲦⲀⲔⲔⲰ ⲚⲀϤ Ⲛ̅
    ⲚⲈϤⲚⲞⲂⲈ ⲈⲂⲞⲗ

26. Ⲛ̅ⲢⲰⲘⲈ ⲈⲚⲦⲀⲨⲈⲒ ϢⲀⲢⲞⲔ ⲌⲚ̅
    ⲦⲈⲨϢⲎ

27. ⲚⲈⲤⲚⲎⲨ ⲈⲚⲦⲀϤⲘⲈⲢⲒⲦⲞⲨ

28. ⲠⲢⲰⲘⲈ ⲈⲚⲦⲀⲔⲚⲀⲨ Ⲉ ⲠⲈϤⲌⲞ

29. Ⲛ̅ⲢⲰⲘⲈ ⲈⲚⲦⲀ-ⲠⲈⲠⲒⲤⲔⲞⲠⲞⲤ
    ϢⲀⲎⲗ ⲈⲬⲰⲞⲨ

30. ⲠⲘⲀⲐⲎⲦⲎⲤ ⲈⲚⲦⲀⲨⲠⲰⲦ Ⲛ̅ⲤⲰϤ

B.1. ⲚⲈⲚⲦⲀⲨϬⲰ ⲌⲘ̅ Ⲡ†ⲘⲈ ⲈⲦ Ⲙ̅ⲘⲀⲨ

2. ⲠⲈⲚⲦⲀϤⲤⲰ ⲈⲂⲞⲗ ⲌⲘ̅ ⲠⲈⲒⲀⲠⲞⲦ

3. ⲠⲈⲚⲦⲀϤⲚⲀ ⲚⲀⲒ ⲀⲨⲰ Ⲁϥ† ⲚⲀⲒ
   Ⲛ̅ ⲞⲨⲞⲈⲒⲔ

4. ⲠⲈⲚⲦⲀϤⲬⲈ-ⲚⲈⲒϢⲀⲬⲈ

5. ⲦⲈⲚⲦⲀⲤⲰ Ⲙ̅ⲘⲞⲒ

6. ⲚⲈⲚⲦⲀⲚϬⲰ ⲈⲢⲞⲞⲨ

7. ⲠⲈⲚⲦⲀϤⲤⲈ-ⲠⲈⲢⲰⲦⲈ

8. ⲚⲈⲚⲦⲀⲨⲂⲰⲔ ⲈⲂⲞⲗ Ⲉ ⲦⲠⲞⲗⲒⲤ

9. ⲚⲈⲚⲦⲀⲨⲌⲰⲚ ⲈⲌⲞⲨⲚ ⲈⲢⲘ̅ ⲠⲈϤⲎⲒ

10. ⲠⲈⲚⲦⲀϤⲦⲚ̅ⲚⲞⲞⲨ Ⲙ̅ⲘⲞⲒ ϢⲀⲢⲰⲦⲚ̅

11. ⲦⲈⲚⲦⲀϤⲘⲈⲢⲒⲦⲤ̅

12. ⲚⲈⲚⲦⲀⲨⲈⲒⲀ-ⲚⲈⲨⲌⲞⲈⲒⲦⲈ

13. ⲚⲈⲦⲈ Ⲙ̅ⲠⲞⲨⲤⲰⲦⲘ̅ Ⲉ ⲠϢⲀⲬⲈ

14. ⲠⲈⲚⲦⲀⲒⲬⲞⲞϤ ⲚⲎⲦⲚ̅

15. ⲚⲈⲦⲈ Ⲙ̅ⲠⲈϤⲦⲚ̅ⲚⲞⲞⲨ Ⲙ̅ⲘⲞⲞⲨ

16. ⲚⲈⲦⲈ Ⲙ̅ⲠⲞⲨⲈⲒⲚⲈ Ⲙ̅ⲘⲞⲞⲨ ⲈⲂⲞⲗ

C.1. ⲀⲤⲈⲒⲰ Ⲙ̅ ⲠⲈϤⲌⲞ ⲘⲚ̅ ⲚⲈϤⲘⲀⲀⲬⲈ.

2. ⲀϤⲬⲞⲞⲤ ⲬⲈ Ⲙ̅ⲠⲒⲚⲀⲨ ⲈⲢⲞϤ.

3. ⲘⲚ̅Ⲛ̅ⲤⲀ ⲚⲀⲒ ⲀⲈ ⲀⲤⲰ Ⲛ̅ϬⲒ ⲦⲈⲤⲌⲒⲘⲈ.

4. ⲀϤⲢⲒⲘⲈ ⲈⲦⲂⲈ ⲚⲈϤϢⲂⲈⲈⲢ ⲈⲚⲦⲀⲨⲘⲞⲨ ⲌⲒ ⲦⲈⲌⲒⲎ.

5. ⲠⲌⲀⲗⲞ ⲀⲈ Ⲙ̅ⲠⲈϤⲤⲰ ⲈⲂⲞⲗ ⲌⲘ̅ ⲠⲎⲢⲠ̅.

6. ⲘⲚ̅Ⲛ̅ⲤⲀ ⲠϢⲀ Ⲙ̅ ⲠⲢⲎ ⲀⲚⲂⲰⲔ ⲈⲂⲞⲗ.

7. Ⲁ-ⲦϢⲈⲈⲢⲈ ⲈⲒⲰ Ⲙ̅ ⲠⲈⲤϢⲰ ⲌⲘ̅ ⲠⲘⲞⲞⲨ Ⲙ̅ ⲠⲈⲒⲈⲢⲞ.

8. Ⲁ-ⲠⲢⲎ ⲈⲒ ⲈⲌⲢⲀⲒ ⲈⲬⲘ̅ ⲠⲦⲞⲞⲨ.

9. ⲈⲦⲂⲈ ⲞⲨ Ⲙ̅ⲠⲈⲦⲚ̅ⲈⲒⲀ-ⲚⲈⲦⲚ̅ⲌⲞ?

10. ⲀⲨⲬⲞⲞⲤ ⲚⲀⲚ ⲬⲈ Ⲙ̅ⲠⲈⲚⲬⲒⲦϤ̅.

11. ⲀⲚϬⲰ ⲚⲘ̅ⲘⲀⲨ ⲌⲚ̅ ⲦⲈⲨϢⲎ ⲈⲦ Ⲙ̅ⲘⲀⲨ.

12. ⲀϤϢⲀⲬⲈ ⲚⲘ̅ⲘⲀⲚ ⲈⲦⲂⲈ ⲚⲈϤⲤⲚⲎⲨ ⲈⲦⲈ Ⲙ̅ⲠⲞⲨⲈⲒ ⲚⲘ̅ⲘⲀϤ.

13. Ⲁ-ⲠⲢⲎ ϢⲀ ⲀⲨⲰ ⲀⲚⲦⲰⲞⲨⲚ, ⲀⲚⲂⲰⲔ ⲈⲂⲞⲗ.

14. ⲀⲒⲤⲰⲦⲘ̅ Ⲉ ⲚⲈⲒϢⲀⲬⲈ ⲌⲚ̅ ⲚⲀⲘⲀⲀⲬⲈ.

Lesson 13

13.1 The Temporal. A special conjugation is used to express a subordinate temporal clause (English "when" with a simple past or pluperfect verb), as in

ⲚⲦⲈⲣⲓⲚⲀⲨ Ⲉⲣⲟϥ, ⲀⲓⲠⲱⲦ ϢⲀⲣⲟϥ. When I saw him, I ran to him.

ⲚⲦⲈⲣⲈϥϪⲱⲕ Ⲙ̄ ⲠⲈϥϩⲰⲂ ⲈⲂⲞⲖ, ⲀϥⲂⲰⲕ ⲈⲂⲞⲖ. When he had completed his work, he left.

The full inflection of this form, called the Temporal Conjugation, is as follows:

Ⲛ̄ⲦⲈⲣⲓⲤⲰⲦⲘ̄	when I heard	Ⲛ̄ⲦⲈⲣⲚ̄ⲤⲰⲦⲘ̄
Ⲛ̄ⲦⲈⲣⲈⲕⲤⲰⲦⲘ̄	etc.	Ⲛ̄ⲦⲈⲣⲈⲦⲚ̄ⲤⲰⲦⲘ̄
Ⲛ̄ⲦⲈⲣⲈⲤⲰⲦⲘ̄		
Ⲛ̄ⲦⲈⲣⲈϥⲤⲰⲦⲘ̄		Ⲛ̄ⲦⲈⲣⲞⲨⲤⲰⲦⲘ̄
Ⲛ̄ⲦⲈⲣⲈⲤⲤⲰⲦⲘ̄		

Ⲛ̄ⲦⲈⲣⲈ-ⲠⲣⲱⲘⲈ ⲤⲰⲦⲘ̄   when the man heard

Alternate spellings, such as Ⲛ̄ⲦⲈⲣⲈⲓ-, Ⲛ̄ⲦⲈⲣⲔ̄-, Ⲛ̄ⲦⲈⲣϤ̄-, are common.

The Temporal is negated by prefixing -ⲦⲘ̄- to the infinitive:

Ⲛ̄ⲦⲈⲣⲓⲦⲘ̄ϬⲒⲚⲈ Ⲙ̄ⲘⲞϥ   when I did not find him

With a nominal subject, -ⲦⲘ̄- usually remains with the verbal prefix:

Ⲛ̄ⲦⲈⲣⲈⲦⲘ̄-ⲠⲣⲱⲘⲈ ⲞⲨⲰϢⲂ̄   when the man did not answer

A Temporal clause usually stands before the main clause, but occurrences after the main clause are not rare:

Ⲛ̄ⲦⲈⲣⲓⲤⲰⲦⲘ̄ Ⲉ ⲚⲈϥϢⲀϪⲈ, ⲀⲓⲣⲒⲘⲈ.⎫ I wept when I heard
ⲀⲓⲣⲒⲘⲈ Ⲛ̄ⲦⲈⲣⲓⲤⲰⲦⲘ̄ Ⲉ ⲚⲈϥϢⲀϪⲈ.⎭ his words.

When a Temporal clause is continued with a second verb, the Temporal prefix is not repeated and the First Perfect is used:

ⲚⲦⲉⲣⲓⲥⲱⲧⲙ̅ ⲉ ⲡⲉϥ2ⲣⲟⲟⲩ ⲁⲩⲱ ⲁⲓⲛⲁⲩ ⲉ ⲡⲉϥ2ⲟ . . .
when I heard his voice and saw his face . . .

13.2 Relative clauses with ⲡⲉ, ⲧⲉ, ⲛⲉ. Contrast the two sentences:

ⲁ-ⲡⲁⲉⲓⲱⲧ ⲕⲁⲁⲧ ⲙ̅ⲙⲁⲩ.	My father left me there.
ⲡⲁⲉⲓⲱⲧ ⲡⲉ ⲉⲛⲧⲁϥⲕⲁⲁⲧ ⲙ̅ⲙⲁⲩ.	It was my father who left me there.

The second sentence, known in English as a type of cleft sentence ("it was . . . that/who . . ."), singles out the subject ("my father and no one else") as the actor, while the first sentence merely describes a past action with no special emphasis. The Coptic correspondent of the English cleft sentence employs ⲡⲉ, ⲧⲉ, ⲛⲉ followed by the relative form of the verb. ⲡⲉ, ⲧⲉ, ⲛⲉ usually combine with the relative form to produce ⲡⲉⲛⲧⲁⲓ-, ⲡⲉⲛⲧⲁⲕ-, etc.:

ⲡⲁⲉⲓⲱⲧ ⲡⲉⲛⲧⲁϥⲕⲁⲁⲧ ⲙ̅ⲙⲁⲩ.

This form should not be confused with the nominalized relative ⲡⲉⲛⲧⲁⲓⲥⲱⲧⲙ̅ etc., which consists of the definite article plus the relative form (see § 12.3). Contrast

ⲡⲁⲉⲓⲱⲧ ⲡⲉⲛⲧⲁϥⲕⲁⲁⲧ ⲙ̅ⲙⲁⲩ.	It was my father who left me there.
ⲡⲁⲉⲓⲱⲧ ⲡⲉ ⲡⲉⲛⲧⲁϥⲕⲁⲁⲧ ⲙ̅ⲙⲁⲩ.	My father is the one who left me there.

The second sentence is a normal ⲡⲉ sentence: ⲡⲁⲉⲓⲱⲧ is the subject, ⲡⲉⲛⲧⲁϥⲕⲁⲁⲧ ⲙ̅ⲙⲁⲩ is the predicate.

The cleft sentence with ⲡⲉ is a favorite one with the interrogative pronouns:

ⲛⲓⲙ ⲡⲉⲛⲧⲁϥⲧⲛ̅ⲛⲟⲟⲩ ⲙ̅ⲙⲟⲕ?	Who sent you? Who was it that sent you?
ⲟⲩ ⲡⲉⲛⲧⲁⲕⲧⲁⲁϥ ⲛⲁⲩ?	What did you give to them? What was it that you gave to them?

Note that in this case the English cleft sentence pattern ("who was it that") is slightly different from the one given above.

13.3 The preposition ε is used before an infinitive
to express purpose:

ⲁⲓⲉⲓ ε ϣⲁϫⲉ ⲛⲙⲙⲁⲕ.   I have come to speak with you.

The subject of the infinitive in this construction is
usually the same as that of the main verb, but some
laxness occurs, as in

ⲁϥⲧⲛ̄ⲛⲟⲟⲩ ⲙ̄ⲙⲟⲓ ε ϣⲁϫⲉ ⲛⲙⲙⲁⲕ He sent me to speak with you.

13.4 Coptic has no real passive conjugations. The
passive is expressed by using the 3rd pers. pl. of the
active form in an indefinite sense:

ⲁⲩⲧⲛ̄ⲛⲟⲟⲩ ⲙ̄ⲙⲟⲓ ϣⲁⲣⲟⲕ.   I have been sent to you.

That such expressions are to be taken in a passive sense
is most evident (1) when there is no clear reference for
the pronoun "they," or (2) when an agent is added,
usually with ⲉⲃⲟⲗ ⲍⲓⲧⲛ̄, as in

ⲁⲩⲧⲛ̄ⲛⲟⲟⲩ ⲙ̄ⲙⲟⲓ ⲉⲃⲟⲗ ⲍⲓⲧⲙ̄ ⲡⲣ̄ⲣⲟ. I have been sent by the king.

13.5 Infinitives (continued). Transitive infinitives
of the pattern ⲕⲱⲧ have the following forms:

ⲕⲱⲧ	ⲕⲉⲧ-	ⲕⲟⲧ⸗	to build
ϫⲱⲕ	ϫⲉⲕ-	ϫⲟⲕ⸗	to complete
ⲍⲱⲡ	ⲍⲉⲡ-	ⲍⲟⲡ⸗	to hide, conceal
ⲱⲡ	ⲉⲡ-	ⲟⲡ⸗	to count.

Transitive verbs of this pattern are quite common.

Vocabulary 13

ϫⲱⲕ (forms above) ± ⲉⲃⲟⲗ to finish, complete (ⲙ̄ⲙⲟ⸗); as
   n.m.: end, completion.
ⲍⲱⲡ (forms above) to hide, conceal (ⲙ̄ⲙⲟ⸗).
ⲱⲡ (forms above) to count (ⲙ̄ⲙⲟ⸗); to esteem, have regard
   for (ⲙ̄ⲙⲟ⸗); to ascribe (someone or something: ⲙ̄ⲙⲟ⸗;

50

to: є), to reckon as.

вѡл вєл- вол⸗ (1) to loosen, unfasten, undo (ⲙ̄ⲙⲟ⸗);
   (2) to interpret, explain (ⲙ̄ⲙⲟ⸗); вѡл євол = (1) and
   also: to nullify, annul (ⲙ̄ⲙⲟ⸗).

тѡм тєм- том⸗ to close, shut (ⲙ̄ⲙⲟ⸗).

оуѡм оуєм- оуом⸗ to eat (ⲙ̄ⲙⲟ⸗; partitive: євол ⲍ̄ⲛ̄);
   оуѡм ⲛ̄сл to gnaw at.

ϣѡп ϣєп- ϣоп⸗ (1) to receive, accept (ⲙ̄ⲙⲟ⸗; from: ⲛ̄ⲧⲛ̄);
   (2) to buy (ⲙ̄ⲙⲟ⸗; for a price: ⲍⲁ).

оуѡн to open (ⲙ̄ⲙⲟ⸗, є).

п.лϥ meat, flesh (human or animal); piece of meat.

пє.уⲍоⲣ (f. тє.уⲍѡⲣє; pl. нє.уⲍооⲣ) dog (оуⲍоⲣ).

п.влл eye.

п.нлу time, hour.

п.ноуⲍ rope.

Greek nouns:
тє.ⲭнⲣⲁ (ἡ χήρα) widow.
п.оⲣϥⲁнос (ὁ ὀρφανός) orphan.
т.слⲣ̇ (ἡ σάρξ) flesh.
т.пулн (ἡ πύλη) gate.

Proper names:
ллуєіⲁ David (sometimes abbreviated ⲇ̄ⲁ̄ⲇ̄).
ѳієⲣоусⲁⲗнм Jerusalem (with def. art.), regularly
   abbreviated ⲑⲓ̄ⲗ̄ⲏ̄ⲙ̄.

Exercises

A.1. пⲁпот єнтⲁіϣопϥ̄ ⲛ̄тоотϥ̄   7. тпулн єнтⲁувѡк євол
  2. пвнмⲁ єнтⲁϥтѡоун євол ⲍіѡѡϥ   ⲍітоотⲥ̄
  3. пⲍѡв єнтⲁϥхѡк ⲙ̄моϥ євол   8. пⲍѡв єнтⲁкϣⲁхє ⲍⲁроϥ
  4. пні єнтⲁукотϥ̄ ⲙ̄млу   9. тєхнⲣⲁ єнтⲁіϯ нⲁс ⲙ̄
  5. пноув єнтⲁнⲍопϥ̄ ⲍⲁ пѡнє   пⲍⲁт
  6. пѡнє єнтⲁϥⲍє єпєснт єхⲛ̄   10. пⲍ̄ⲗⲟ єнтⲁуⲍѡн єⲍоун є
     нⲁоуєⲣнтє   тєϥⲣі

B.1. ⲁівѡк є ⲣⲁкотє є нлу є плєіѡт.

2. ⲁⲩⲉⲓ ⲉ ϣⲁϫⲉ ⲛⲙ̄ⲙⲁⲓ.

3. ⲁϥⲃⲱⲕ ⲉ ⲡⲉⲓⲉⲣⲟ ⲉ ⲉⲓⲁ-ⲛⲉϥϩⲟⲉⲓⲧⲉ ⲉⲃⲟⲗ.

4. ⲁⲓϩⲙⲟⲟⲥ ⲉ ⲥⲱ ⲛ̄ ⲧⲉⲣⲱⲧⲉ ⲁⲩⲱ ⲉ ⲟⲩⲱⲙ ⲙ̄ ⲡⲁϥ.

5. ⲁⲩⲧⲛ̄ⲛⲟⲟⲩ ⲙ̄ⲙⲟⲓ ⲉ ⲉⲓⲛⲉ ⲛⲁⲕ ⲙ̄ ⲡⲉⲓϫⲱⲱⲙⲉ.

6. ⲁϥⲉⲓⲛⲉ ⲛ̄ ⲟⲩⲙⲟⲟⲩ ⲉ ⲉⲓⲁ-ⲛⲉϥⲟⲩⲉⲣⲏⲧⲉ ⲙ̄ⲙⲟϥ.

7. ⲁϥⲧⲱⲟⲩⲛ ⲉ ⲃⲱⲕ ⲉⲡⲁϩⲟⲩ ⲉ ⲑⲓ̄ⲗⲏⲙ.

8. ⲛⲓⲙ ⲡⲉⲛⲧⲁϥϫⲱⲕ ⲉⲃⲟⲗ ⲙ̄ ⲡⲉⲓϩⲱⲃ?

9. ⲛⲓⲙ ⲡⲉⲛⲧⲁⲩϩⲟⲡϥ̄ ϩⲙ̄ ⲡⲏⲓ?

10. ⲛⲉⲓⲉⲛⲧⲟⲗⲟⲟⲩⲉ ⲛⲉⲛⲧⲁⲩⲃⲟⲗⲟⲩ ⲉⲃⲟⲗ.

11. ⲧⲉⲭⲏⲣⲁ ⲧⲉ ⲛ̄ⲧⲁⲩϯ ⲛⲁⲥ ⲙ̄ ⲡⲟⲉⲓⲕ.

12. ⲛⲓⲙ ⲡⲉⲛⲧⲁϥⲃⲱⲗ ⲛⲏⲧⲛ̄ ⲙ̄ ⲡⲭⲱⲱⲙⲉ?

13. ⲛ̄ⲧⲟϥ ⲡⲉⲛⲧⲁϥⲧⲱⲙ ⲛ̄ ⲧⲡⲩⲗⲏ.

14. ⲛⲁⲓ ⲛⲉ ⲉⲛⲧⲁⲓϣⲟⲡϥ̄ ⲛ̄ⲧⲟⲟⲧⲟⲩ.

15. ⲛⲉⲩϩⲟⲟⲣ ⲛⲉ ⲉⲛⲧⲁⲩⲟⲩⲟⲙϥ̄.

16. ⲡⲉⲭⲣⲓⲥⲧⲟⲥ ⲡⲉⲛⲧⲁϥⲟⲩⲱⲛ ⲛ̄ ⲛⲁⲃⲁⲗ.

17. ⲛⲓⲙ ⲛⲉⲛⲧⲁⲩⲟⲡⲟⲩ ⲉ ⲡϯⲙⲉ ⲉⲧ ⲙ̄ⲙⲁⲩ?

18. ⲡⲥⲁϩ ⲡⲉⲛⲧⲁϥⲧⲁⲗⲩ ⲛⲁⲓ.

19. ⲡⲉⲓⲁⲥⲡⲁⲥⲙⲟⲥ ⲡⲉⲛⲧⲁ-ⲡⲁⲅⲅⲉⲗⲟⲥ ϫⲟⲟϥ ⲛⲁⲥ.

20. ⲟⲩ ⲡⲉⲛⲧⲁⲕϣⲟⲡϥ̄ ϩⲛ̄ ⲧⲁⲅⲟⲣⲁ?

21. ⲡⲉⲓⲣ̄ⲡⲉ ⲡⲉ ⲛ̄ⲧⲁⲩⲕⲟⲧϥ̄ ⲛ̄ϭⲓ ⲛⲉⲛⲉⲓⲟⲧⲉ.

22. ⲡⲉⲓⲣⲱⲙⲉ ⲡⲉⲛⲧⲁⲥϣⲁϫⲉ ⲛⲙ̄ⲙⲁϥ.

C.1. ⲛ̄ⲧⲉⲣⲉ-ⲡⲙⲟⲛⲁⲭⲟⲥ ϫⲱⲕ ⲙ̄ ⲡⲉϥϩⲱⲃ ⲉⲃⲟⲗ, ⲁϥⲧⲱⲟⲩⲛ, ⲁϥⲃⲱⲕ ⲉⲃⲟⲗ.

2. ⲁⲛϭⲱ ⲛⲙ̄ⲙⲁϥ ϣⲁ ⲡϣⲁ ⲙ̄ ⲡⲣⲏ.

3. ⲛ̄ⲧⲉⲣⲉ-ⲡⲣⲏ ϣⲁ, ⲁⲛⲁⲗⲉ ⲉϫⲛ̄ ⲛⲉⲛϩⲧⲱⲱⲣ ⲁⲩⲱ ⲁⲛⲡⲱⲧ ⲛ̄ⲥⲱϥ.

4. ⲁⲩⲟⲡϥ̄ ⲉ ⲡⲏⲓ ⲛ̄ ⲁⲗⲅⲉⲓⲁ.

5. ⲛ̄ⲧⲉⲣⲉⲥⲥⲱⲧⲙ̄ ⲉ ⲛⲁⲓ, ⲁⲥϫⲓ-ⲡⲉⲥϣⲏⲣⲉ, ⲁⲥϩⲟⲡϥ̄.

6. ⲁⲩⲧⲱⲙ ⲛ̄ϭⲓ ⲛ̄ⲣⲱⲙⲉ ⲛ̄ ⲙ̄ⲡⲩⲗⲏ ⲛ̄ ⲧⲡⲟⲗⲓⲥ.

7. ⲛ̄ⲧⲉⲣⲓⲉⲡ-ⲡϩⲁⲧ, ⲁⲓⲧⲁⲁϥ ⲛⲁⲩ.

8. ⲙ̄ⲡⲟⲩⲱⲡ ⲛ̄ ⲛ̄ϣⲁϫⲉ ⲙ̄ ⲡⲉⲛϫⲟⲉⲓⲥ.

9. ⲁⲥϣⲱⲡⲉ ⲇⲉ ⲛ̄ⲧⲉⲣⲟⲩⲟⲩⲱⲛ ⲛ̄ ⲧⲡⲩⲗⲏ ⲛ̄ ⲧⲡⲟⲗⲓⲥ, ⲁ-ⲡⲗⲁⲟⲥ ⲡⲱⲧ ⲉⲃⲟⲗ ϩⲓⲧⲟⲟⲧⲥ̄.

10. ⲛ̄ⲧⲉⲣⲓⲃⲱⲕ, ⲁⲓϫⲓ ⲙ̄ ⲡⲛⲟⲩϩ ⲛⲙ̄ⲙⲁⲓ.

11. ⲛ̄ⲧⲉⲣⲛ̄ⲥⲱⲧⲙ̄ ⲉ ⲛ̄ϣⲁϫⲉ ⲉⲛⲧⲁϥϫⲟⲟⲩ, ⲁⲛⲣⲁϣⲉ ⲉⲙⲁⲧⲉ.

12. ⲁϥⲟⲡⲛ̄ ⲉ ⲡⲗⲁⲟⲥ ⲛ̄ ⲑⲓ̄ⲗⲏⲙ.

13. ⲛ̄ⲧⲉⲣⲟⲩⲧⲙ̄ϭⲓⲛⲉ ⲛ̄ ⲛ̄ϫⲱⲱⲙⲉ ⲉⲛⲧⲁⲛϩⲟⲡⲟⲩ ϩⲙ̄ ⲡⲏⲓ, ⲁⲩⲃⲱⲕ ⲉⲃⲟⲗ.

14. ⲁ-ⲛⲉⲩ2ⲟⲟⲣ ⲟⲩⲱⲙ ⲙ̄ ⲡⲁϥ.

15. ⲛ̄ⲧⲉⲣⲉϥ2ⲉ ⲉⲣⲟⲟⲩ, ⲁϥⲃⲱⲗ ⲉⲃⲟⲗ ⲛ̄ ⲛⲉⲩⲛⲟⲩ2.

16. ⲛ̄ⲧⲉⲣ ⲓ ⲛⲁⲩ ⲉⲣⲟϥ, ⲁ ⲓ ⲛⲁ 2ⲁⲣⲟϥ.

17. ⲛ̄ⲧⲉⲣⲉϥxⲱⲕ ⲉⲃⲟⲗ ⲛ̄ ⲛⲉ ⲓ ϣⲁxⲉ, ⲁϥⲧⲱⲙ ⲛ̄ ⲛⲉϥⲃⲁⲗ, ⲁϥⲙⲟⲩ.

18. ⲛ̄ⲧⲉⲣⲉϥⲛⲁⲩ ⲉⲣⲟⲟⲩ, ⲁϥxⲟⲟⲥ ⲛⲁⲩ xⲉ ⲉⲧⲃⲉ ⲟⲩ ⲁⲧⲉⲧⲛ̄ⲉ ⲓ ⲉ ⲡⲉ ⲓ ⲙⲁ?

19. ⲁ-ⲡⲉⲩ2ⲟⲣ ⲟⲩⲱⲙ ⲛ̄ⲥⲁ ⲧⲥⲁⲣx ⲙ̄ ⲡⲉ ⲓ ⲱ.

20. ⲁⲥϣⲱⲡⲉ ⲇⲉ ⲛ̄ⲧⲉⲣⲉ-ⲡⲛⲁⲩ ⲙ̄ ⲡⲉⲥⲙ ⲓ ⲥⲉ 2ⲱⲛ ⲉ2ⲟⲩⲛ, ⲁⲥⲃⲱⲕ ⲉ ⲡⲏ ⲓ ⲛ̄ ⲧⲉⲥⲙⲁⲁⲩ.

21. ⲛ̄ⲧⲉⲣⲟⲩⲛⲁⲩ ⲉ ⲡⲟⲩⲟⲉ ⲓ ⲛ ⲙ̄ ⲡⲉϥ2ⲟ ⲁⲩⲱ ⲁⲩⲥⲱⲧⲙ̄ ⲉ ⲛⲉϥϣⲁxⲉ, ⲁⲩ2ⲉ ⲉ ⲡⲕⲁ2, ⲁⲩ2ⲉⲡ-ⲛⲉⲩ2ⲟ.

22. ⲉⲧⲃⲉ ⲟⲩ ⲁⲧⲉⲧⲛ̄ⲃⲱⲗ ⲉⲃⲟⲗ ⲛ̄ ⲛⲉⲛⲧⲟⲗⲏ ⲛ̄ ⲛⲉⲧⲛ̄ⲉ ⲓ ⲟⲧⲉ?

23. ⲛ̄ⲧⲉⲣⲉⲥⲧⲙ̄2ⲉ ⲉ ⲧⲉⲥϣⲉⲉⲣⲉ ⲙ̄ⲙⲁⲩ, ⲁⲥⲣ ⲓ ⲙⲉ.

24. ⲛ̄ⲧⲉⲣⲉϥⲧⲙ̄ⲟⲩⲱⲛ ⲙ̄ ⲡⲣⲟ ⲛ̄ ⲧⲉϥⲣ ⲓ, ⲁ ⲓ ⲃⲱⲕ ⲉⲃⲟⲗ.

Lesson 14

14.1 The Second Perfect. As we shall see in subsequent lessons, each "first" tense in Coptic has a counterpart called a second tense, the use of which places a special emphasis on some element of the sentence other than the verb, usually an adverbial phrase. Contrast the following:

First Perfect: ⲁ-ⲡⲁ ⲓ ϣⲱⲡⲉ ⲉⲧⲃⲏⲏⲧⲕ̄.
This happened because of you.

Second Perfect: ⲛ̄ⲧⲁ-ⲡⲁ ⲓ ϣⲱⲡⲉ ⲉⲧⲃⲏⲏⲧⲕ̄.
It was because of you that this happened.

As our translation indicates, the English cleft sentence is a handy way to render Coptic sentences with second tense verbal forms. Except for the special uses taken up below, the use of a second tense is not obligatory but depends on what the writer chooses to emphasize.

The Second Perfect has the same inflectional forms as the Relative of the First Perfect, but usually without the initial є: ⲚⲦⲀⲒⲤⲰⲦⲘ̄, ⲚⲦⲀⲔⲤⲰⲦⲘ̄, etc.

When phrases containing interrogative pronouns or adverbs are placed after the verb, a second tense is regularly used, but exceptions are not rare:

ⲚⲦⲀⲔⲦⲚ̄ⲚⲞⲞⲨ Ⲙ̄ⲘⲞϤ ⲈⲦⲂⲈ ⲞⲨ?   Why did you send him?

ⲚⲦⲀϤϬⲒⲚⲈ Ⲛ̄ ⲦⲈⲒⲈⲠⲒⲤⲦⲞⲖⲎ Ⲉ ⲚⲒⲘ?   To whom did he bring this
                                        letter?

But if the interrogative phrase is place first, as is usually the case with ⲈⲦⲂⲈ ⲞⲨ, the first tense is used:

ⲈⲦⲂⲈ ⲞⲨ ⲀⲔⲦⲚ̄ⲚⲞⲞⲨ Ⲙ̄ⲘⲞϤ?

14.2 Further remarks on interrogative pronouns and adverbs. The interrogative pronouns ⲚⲒⲘ (who?) and ⲞⲨ (what?) may be used as subjects or objects of verbs and as objects of prepositions. When they are used as the subject of a verb, the verb is normally in the second tense form:

Ⲛ̄ⲦⲀ-ⲞⲨ ϢⲰⲠⲈ?   What happened?

Ⲛ̄ⲦⲀ-ⲚⲒⲘ ⲂⲰⲔ ⲈⲌ̄ⲞⲨⲚ?   Who went in?

Examples of object usage, again regularly with the second tense:

Ⲛ̄ⲦⲀⲔⲚⲀⲨ Ⲉ ⲚⲒⲘ?   Whom did you see?

Ⲛ̄ⲦⲀⲔⲦⲀⲀϤ Ⲛ̄ ⲚⲒⲘ?   To whom did you give it?

Ⲛ̄ⲦⲀϤⲔⲀ-ⲞⲨ Ⲙ̄ⲘⲀⲨ?   What did he put there?

The construction introduced in § 13.2 is used much more frequently than the preceding: ⲚⲒⲘ ⲠⲈⲚⲦⲀϤⲂⲰⲔ ⲈⲌ̄ⲞⲨⲚ? ⲚⲒⲘ ⲠⲈⲚⲦⲀⲔⲚⲀⲨ ⲈⲢⲞϤ?

The interrogative adverbs ⲦⲰⲚ (where?), Ⲉ ⲦⲰⲚ (whither?), ⲈⲂⲞⲖ ⲦⲰⲚ (whence?), and ⲦⲚ̄ⲚⲀⲨ (or ⲦⲚⲀⲨ, when?) occur regularly in post-verbal position with a second tense:

ⲚⲦⲀ-ⲠⲈⲔⲈⲒⲰⲦ ⲂⲰⲔ Ⲉ ⲦⲰⲚ?	Where did your father go?
ⲚⲦⲀⲨⲘⲞⲨ ⲦⲚ̄ⲚⲀⲨ?	When did they die?

14.3 Infinitives (continued). In infinitives of the type ⲔⲰⲦ the ⲱ is modified to ⲟⲩ when the initial consonant is ⲙ or ⲛ:

ⲘⲞⲨⲢ	ⲘⲈⲢ-	ⲘⲞⲢ⸗	to bind
ⲘⲞⲨⲚ	——	——	to remain.

The o of the presuffixal form is regularly replaced by ⲁ before stem final ϩ and (usually) ϣ:

ⲞⲨⲰϨ	ⲞⲨⲈϨ-	ⲞⲨⲀϨ⸗	to put, place
ⲞⲨⲰϢ	ⲞⲨⲈϢ-	ⲞⲨⲀϢ⸗	to want, desire
ⲘⲞⲨϨ	ⲘⲈϨ-	ⲘⲀϨ⸗	to fill.

Vocabulary 14

ⲘⲞⲨⲢ ⲘⲈⲢ- ⲘⲞⲢ⸗ to bind, tie (someone: ⲘⲘⲞ⸗ or suff.; with: ⲘⲘⲞ⸗, ϨⲚ̄; to: Ⲉ, ⲈϪⲚ̄, ⲈϨⲞⲨⲚ Ⲉ).

ⲚⲞⲨϪⲈ (or ⲚⲞⲨϪ) ⲚⲈϪ- ⲚⲞϪ⸗ to cast, throw (ⲘⲘⲞ⸗; at, into: Ⲉ); ⲚⲞⲨϪⲈ ⲈⲂⲞⲖ to discard, throw away, abandon; ⲚⲞⲨϪⲈ ⲈⲠⲈⲤⲎⲦ to cast down.

ⲞⲨⲰϨ ⲞⲨⲈϨ- ⲞⲨⲀϨ⸗ (1) to put, place, set (ⲘⲘⲞ⸗); ⲞⲨⲰϨ ⲈϪⲚ̄ to add to, augment; (2) intrans.: to settle, dwell, reside (in: ϨⲚ̄; with: ⲘⲚ̄).

ⲞⲨⲰϢ ⲞⲨⲈϢ- ⲞⲨⲀϢ⸗ to want, wish, desire (ⲘⲘⲞ⸗); as n.m.: wish, desire; Ⲙ̄ ⲠⲈϤⲞⲨⲰϢ of his own volition, as he wished. ⲞⲨⲈϢ- may be compounded with another infinitive: ⲞⲨⲈϢ-ⲈⲒ to wish to come, ⲞⲨⲈϢ-ⲤⲰⲦⲘ̄ to wish to hear.

ⲘⲞⲨϨ ⲘⲈϨ- ⲘⲀϨ⸗ ± ⲈⲂⲞⲖ (1) to fill (something: ⲘⲘⲞ⸗ or suff.; with: ⲘⲘⲞ⸗, ϨⲚ̄, ⲈⲂⲞⲖ ϨⲚ̄); (2) intrans.: to become filled, full (of, with: ⲘⲘⲞ⸗). An indefinite noun after ⲘⲘⲞ⸗ (that with which something is filled) normally has no article.

ϯ ⲘⲘⲞ⸗ ϨⲒ to put (a garment: ⲘⲘⲞ⸗) on, to dress.

ⲠⲈ.ⲤⲚⲀⲨϨ bond, fetter.

ⲡⲉ.ⲱⲧⲉⲕⲟ (pl. ⲛⲉ.ⲱⲧⲉⲕⲱⲟⲩ) prison.

ⲧ.ⲣⲙ̄ⲉⲓⲏ (ⲛ̄.ⲣⲙ̄ⲉⲓⲟⲟⲩⲉ) tear(s).

ⲧ.ϭⲓϫ hand.

ⲧⲱⲛ (adv.) where? ⲉ ⲧⲱⲛ whither? ⲉⲃⲟⲗ ⲧⲱⲛ whence?

ⲧⲛ̄ⲛⲁⲩ, ⲧⲛⲁⲩ (adv.) when?

ⲡⲉ.ⲥⲭⲏⲙⲁ (Gk. τὸ σχῆμα) fashion of dress; monk's habit;
ⲙⲟⲩⲣ ⲙ̄ⲙⲟ⸗ ⲙ̄ ⲡⲉⲥⲭⲏⲙⲁ to garb someone in a monk's
habit, to accept into monkhood.

Exercises

1. ⲙ̄ⲡⲟⲩⲟⲩⲱⲱ ⲉ ϩⲱⲛ ⲉϩⲟⲩⲛ ⲉⲣⲟⲛ.
2. ⲛ̄ⲧⲁ-ⲡⲉⲕⲉⲓⲱⲧ ⲙⲟⲩ ⲧⲛ̄ⲛⲁⲩ?
3. ⲁⲥϣⲱⲡⲉ ⲇⲉ ⲛ̄ⲧⲉⲣⲓϫⲱⲕ ⲉⲃⲟⲗ ⲙ̄ ⲡⲁϩⲱⲃ, ⲁⲓⲧⲱⲟⲩⲛ, ⲁⲓⲃⲱⲕ ⲉⲃⲟⲗ.
4. ⲛⲓⲙ ⲡⲉⲛⲧⲁⲩⲛⲟϫϥ̄ ⲉ ⲡⲉⲱⲧⲉⲕⲟ? ⲡⲉⲛⲥⲁϩ ⲡⲉ.
5. ⲁ-ⲙ̄ⲡⲏⲩⲉ ⲙⲟⲩϩ ⲛ̄ ⲟⲩⲟⲉⲓⲛ.
6. ⲛ̄ⲧⲁϥⲉⲓ ⲉϩⲟⲩⲛ ⲉ ⲡⲉⲓⲕⲟⲥⲙⲟⲥ ⲙ̄ ⲡⲉϥⲟⲩⲱϣ.
7. ⲁⲓⲃⲱⲗ ⲉⲃⲟⲗ ⲛ̄ ⲛⲉⲥⲛⲁϩ ⲉⲛⲧⲁⲩⲙⲉⲣ-ⲡⲣⲱⲙⲉ ⲛ̄ϩⲏⲧⲟⲩ.
8. ⲛ̄ⲧⲁⲕϯ ⲙ̄ ⲡⲉⲥⲭⲏⲙⲁ ϩⲓⲱⲱⲕ ⲧⲛ̄ⲛⲁⲩ?
9. ⲛⲁⲓ ⲛⲉ ⲛ̄ϣⲁϫⲉ ⲉⲛⲧⲁⲩϣⲱⲡⲉ ⲙ̄ ⲡⲉϩⲟⲟⲩ ⲉⲧ ⲙ̄ⲙⲁⲩ.
10. ⲛ̄ⲧⲁⲕⲟⲩⲱϩ ϩⲛ̄ ⲧⲉⲓⲡⲟⲗⲓⲥ ⲧⲛⲁⲩ?
11. ⲁⲥϣⲱⲡⲉ ⲇⲉ ⲛ̄ⲧⲉⲣⲉⲥϩⲉ ⲉⲣⲟϥ, ⲁⲥϥⲓⲧϥ̄, ⲁⲥⲃⲱⲕ ⲉⲃⲟⲗ ⲛⲙ̄ⲙⲁϥ.
12. ⲛ̄ⲧⲁⲣϩⲟⲡⲟⲩ ⲧⲱⲛ?
13. ⲁⲩⲙⲟⲣⲧ̄ ⲛ̄ ⲛⲁⲟⲩⲉⲣⲏⲧⲉ ⲙⲛ̄ ⲛⲁϭⲓϫ ⲁⲩⲱ ⲁⲩⲕⲁⲁⲧ ⲙ̄ⲙⲁⲩ ϩⲓ ⲡⲉⲕⲣⲟ.
14. ⲛⲓⲙ ⲡⲉⲛⲧⲁⲧⲉⲧⲛ̄ϣⲉⲡ-ⲛⲁⲓ ⲛ̄ⲧⲟⲟⲧϥ̄?
15. ⲡⲁⲓ ⲡⲉ ⲡⲙⲟⲩ ⲉⲛⲧⲁϥⲟⲩⲁϣϥ̄.
16. ⲙ̄ⲡⲉϥⲟⲩⲱϩ ⲉϫⲙ̄ ⲡϩⲁⲧ ⲉⲛⲧⲁϥⲧⲁⲁϥ ⲛⲁⲩ.
17. ⲙⲛ̄ⲛⲥⲁ ⲛⲁⲓ ⲇⲉ ⲁϥⲙⲟⲩϩ ⲛ̄ ⲣⲁϣⲉ.
18. ⲁ-ⲧⲉⲕⲕⲗⲏⲥⲓⲁ ⲙⲟⲩϩ ⲛ̄ ⲛⲉϩⲣⲟⲟⲩ ⲙ̄ ⲡⲙⲏⲏϣⲉ.
19. ⲛ̄ⲧⲁ-ⲛⲓⲙ ⲕⲁⲁϥ ϩⲙ̄ ⲡⲉϣⲧⲉⲕⲟ?
20. ⲛ̄ⲧⲁⲧⲉⲧⲛ̄ⲛⲉϫ-ⲛⲉⲓϩⲟⲉⲓⲧⲉ ⲉⲃⲟⲗ ⲉⲧⲃⲉ ⲟⲩ?
21. ⲁ-ⲛ̄ⲣⲱⲙⲉ ⲙⲟⲩⲣ ⲙ̄ ⲡⲙⲟⲛⲁⲭⲟⲥ ⲉ ⲡⲉϩⲧⲟ.
22. ⲁ-ⲛⲉϥⲃⲁⲗ ⲙⲟⲩϩ ⲛ̄ ⲣⲙ̄ⲉⲓⲏ.
23. ⲛ̄ⲧⲁϥⲟⲩⲱϣ ⲉ ⲛⲁⲩ ⲉ ⲛⲓⲙ?
24. ⲛ̄ⲧⲁ-ⲛⲉⲧⲛ̄ⲉⲓⲟⲧⲉ ϩⲉ ⲉⲃⲟⲗ ⲉⲧⲃⲉ ⲛⲉⲩⲛⲟⲃⲉ.
25. ⲙⲛ̄ⲛⲥⲱⲥ ⲇⲉ ⲁⲛⲉⲓ ⲉϩⲟⲩⲛ ⲉ ⲧⲥⲩⲛⲁⲅⲱⲅⲏ.

56

26. ⲁ-ⲡⲉⲩϫⲟⲓ ⲙⲟⲩⲍ ⲙ̄ ⲙⲟⲟⲩ.

27. ⲟⲩ ⲡⲉⲛⲧⲁⲕⲟⲩⲟⲙϥ̄ ⲙ̄ ⲡⲟⲟⲩ?

28. ⲛ̄ⲧⲉⲣⲓⲧⲱⲙ ⲙ̄ ⲡⲣⲟ, ⲁⲓⲍⲙⲟⲟⲥ ⲁⲩⲱ ⲁⲓⲱⲡ ⲙ̄ ⲡⲍⲁⲧ ⲉⲛⲧⲁⲩⲧⲁⲁϥ ⲛⲁⲓ.

29. ⲁ-ⲛⲉⲩⲍⲟⲟⲣ ⲟⲩⲱⲙ ⲛ̄ⲥⲁ ⲛⲉϥⲟⲩⲉⲣⲏⲧⲉ.

30. ⲡⲁⲓ ⲡⲉ ⲡⲱⲛⲉ ⲉⲛⲧⲁⲩⲛⲟϫϥ̄ ⲉⲃⲟⲗ.

31. ⲛ̄ⲧⲁ-ⲡϣⲁ ϣⲱⲡⲉ ⲧⲛ̄ⲛⲁⲩ?

32. ⲛⲓⲙ ⲡⲉⲛⲧⲁϥⲃⲱⲗ ⲉⲃⲟⲗ ⲛ̄ ⲛⲉⲓⲥⲛⲁⲩⲍ?

33. ⲁ-ⲡⲉⲡⲓⲥⲕⲟⲡⲟⲥ ⲙⲟⲣⲛ̄ ⲛ̄ ⲛⲉⲥⲭⲏⲙⲁ.

34. ⲛ̄ⲧⲁⲛⲕⲁ-ⲡⲉⲛϯⲙⲉ ⲛ̄ⲥⲱⲛ ⲉⲧⲃⲉ ⲡⲉⲍⲕⲟ.

35. ⲛⲓⲙ ⲡⲉⲛⲧⲁϥⲟⲩⲁⲍⲕ̄ ⲍⲙ̄ ⲡⲉⲓⲙⲁ?

36. ⲁⲥⲟⲩⲉⲍ-ⲧⲉⲥϣⲉⲉⲣⲉ ⲉϫⲙ̄ ⲡⲉⲃⲗⲟϭ.

37. ⲁ-ⲛⲉϥϣⲁϫⲉ ⲙⲁⲍⲟⲩ ⲛ̄ ⲣⲁϣⲉ.

38. ⲛ̄ⲧⲁ-ⲛⲉⲓⲍⲓⲥⲉ ⲍⲉ ⲉϫⲱⲛ ⲉⲧⲃⲉ ⲟⲩ?

39. ⲛ̄ⲧⲁⲩⲟⲩⲱⲛ ⲛ̄ ⲧⲡⲩⲗⲏ ⲛ̄ ⲧⲡⲟⲗⲓⲥ ⲧⲛ̄ⲛⲁⲩ?

40. ⲟⲩ ⲡⲉⲛⲧⲁϥϣⲱⲡⲉ ⲙ̄ⲙⲟⲕ ⲍⲓⲣⲛ̄ ⲧⲡⲩⲗⲏ?

41. ⲁⲓⲛⲟⲩϫⲉ ⲙ̄ ⲡⲛⲟⲩⲍ ⲉⲡⲉⲥⲛⲧ ⲉ ⲡⲕⲁⲍ.

42. ⲙ̄ⲡⲟⲩⲟⲩⲉϣ-ⲥⲱⲧⲙ̄ ⲉ ⲛⲁϣⲁϫⲉ.

43. ⲙ̄ⲡⲓⲛⲁⲩ ⲉ ⲧⲉⲭⲏⲣⲁ ϣⲁ ⲡⲟⲟⲩ.

44. ⲁⲓⲟⲩⲱϣ ⲉ ⲛ̄ⲕⲟⲧⲕ̄.

Lesson 15

15.1 Adjectives. Although there is some debate over
the existence of adjectives as a grammatical category in
Coptic, it is nevertheless convenient to retain the designation for the words treated in this lesson. Most attributive adjectives may either precede or follow the noun
they modify, joined to the noun with a linking particle
ⲛ (ⲙ̄). The noun and adjective form a close unit; any
article, possessive adjective, or demonstrative stands
before the whole unit:

ⲟⲩⲛⲟϭ ⲙ̄ ⲡⲟⲗⲓⲥ, ⲟⲩⲡⲟⲗⲓⲥ ⲛ̄ ⲛⲟϭ	a large city
ⲡⲁⲙⲉⲣⲓⲧ ⲛ̄ ϣⲏⲣⲉ, ⲡⲁϣⲏⲣⲉ ⲙ̄ ⲙⲉⲣⲓⲧ	my beloved son
ⲡⲥⲁⲃⲉ ⲛ̄ ⲣⲱⲙⲉ, ⲡⲣⲱⲙⲉ ⲛ̄ ⲥⲁⲃⲉ	the wise man

These examples represent the normal attributive adjective
construction. There are, however, some restrictions on
certain special groups of adjectives:

1) Several adjectives show a distinct preference for
   the position before the noun in the given construction. These include ⲛⲟϭ great, ⲕⲟⲩⲓ small, ϣⲏⲙ
   small, ϣⲟⲣⲡ̄ first, ⲍⲁⲉ last, and ⲙⲉⲣⲓⲧ beloved.
2) A few adjectives may be used after a noun *without*
   the linking ⲛ̄. These include ⲁⲥ old, ⲛⲟϭ great,
   ⲕⲟⲩⲓ small, ϣⲏⲙ small, ⲟⲩⲱⲧ single, ⲟⲩⲟⲃϣ̄ white.
   With the exception of a few fixed expressions, this
   construction is rare in standard Sahidic and should
   not be imitated.

Some adjectives have distinct feminine and plural forms;
e.g.

ⲕⲁⲙⲉ	fem. ⲕⲁⲙⲏ	pl. ——		black
ⲍⲁⲉ	ⲍⲁⲏ	ⲍⲁⲉⲉⲩ(ⲉ)	last
ⲥⲁⲃⲉ	ⲥⲁⲃⲏ	ⲥⲁⲃⲉⲉⲩ(ⲉ)	wise
ϭⲁⲗⲉ	——	ϭⲁⲗⲉⲉⲩ(ⲉ)	lame
ⲙⲉⲣⲓⲧ	——	ⲙⲉⲣⲁⲧⲉ	beloved
ϣⲟⲣⲡ̄	ϣⲟⲣⲡⲉ	——	first

ⲍⲟⲩⲉⲓⲧ	ⲍⲟⲩⲉⲓⲧⲉ	ⲍⲟⲩⲁⲧⲉ	first
ϣⲙ̄ⲙⲟ	ϣⲙ̄ⲙⲱ	ϣⲙ̄ⲙⲟⲓ	alien, foreign

The plurals in -ⲉⲉⲩⲉ also occur as -ⲉⲉⲩ. The fem. forms
are used with sing. *and* plural fem. nouns. The plural
forms occur mainly in substantivized usage: ⲛ̄ⲥⲁⲃⲉⲉⲩⲉ the
wise, ⲛ̄ⲍⲟⲩⲁⲧⲉ the elders, prominent persons (e.g. of a
city).

Greek adjectives may appear (1) in the Gk. masc.
sing. form with nouns of either gender or number:

ⲡⲣⲱⲙⲉ ⲛ̄ ⲁⲅⲁⲑⲟⲥ the good man
ⲧⲉⲥⲍⲓⲙⲉ ⲛ̄ ⲁⲅⲁⲑⲟⲥ the good woman

or (2) in the Gk. fem. sing. form if the modified noun
refers to a female person:

ⲧⲉⲥⲍⲓⲙⲉ ⲛ̄ ⲁⲅⲁⲑⲏ the good woman

or (3) in the Gk. neuter form with nouns of either gender
if they denote non-humans:

ⲧⲉⲯⲩⲭⲏ ⲛ̄ ⲧⲉⲗⲉⲓⲟⲛ the perfect spirit.

Greek substantivized neuter adjectives are treated as
masculine in Coptic:

ⲡⲁⲅⲁⲑⲟⲛ good, that which is good (τὸ ἀγαθόν).

A noun may be modified by more than one adjective,
with various orders:

ⲡⲣⲱⲙⲉ ⲛ̄ ⲍⲏⲕⲉ ⲛ̄ ⲁⲓⲕⲁⲓⲟⲥ the righteous poor man
ⲡⲛⲟϭ ⲛ̄ ⲣ̄ⲣⲟ ⲛ̄ ⲁⲓⲕⲁⲓⲟⲥ the great (and) righteous king.

All Coptic adjectives may be substantivized ("one who
is . . . , that which is . . .") by prefixing the appropriate form of the article:

ⲡⲉⲃⲓⲏⲛ	the poor man	ⲛⲉⲃⲓⲏⲛ	the poor (people)
ⲡⲉⲓⲍⲏⲕⲉ	this poor man	ⲧⲉⲓⲍⲏⲕⲉ	this poor woman
ⲟⲩⲥⲁⲃⲉ	a wise man	ⲍⲉⲛⲥⲁⲃⲉⲉⲩⲉ	wise men

When the first noun in a genitive construction is followed

by an adjectival phrase, ⲚⲦⲉ may optionally be used
instead of Ⲛ̄ for the genitive:

ⲡϣⲏⲣⲉ Ⲛ̄ 6ⲁⲗⲉ Ⲛ̄ⲧⲉ ⲡⲣⲱⲙⲉ   the man's crippled child.

15.2 Adjectives as predicates are treated exactly
like noun predicates. Note the obligatory use of the
indefinite article:

ⲟⲩⲁⲅⲁⲑⲟⲥ ⲡⲉ.	He is good.
Ⲛ̄ ⳅⲉⲛⲁⲅⲁⲑⲟⲥ ⲁⲛ ⲛⲉ.	They are not good.
ⲡⲣⲱⲙⲉ ⲟⲩⲁⲅⲁⲑⲟⲥ ⲡⲉ.	The man is good.
Ⲛ̄ⲣⲱⲙⲉ ⳅⲉⲛⲁⲓⲕⲁⲓⲟⲥ ⲛⲉ.	The men are just.
ⲟⲩⲛⲟ6 ⲧⲉ ⲧⲉⲓⲡⲟⲗⲓⲥ.	This city is large.

15.3 The cardinal numbers from one to five are

one	masc.	ⲟⲩⲁ	fem.	ⲟⲩⲉⲓ
two		ⲥⲛⲁⲩ		ⲥⲚ̄ⲧⲉ
three		ϣⲟⲙⲚ̄ⲧ		ϣⲟⲙⲧⲉ
four		ϥⲧⲟⲟⲩ		ϥⲧⲟ6, ϥⲧⲟ
five		ϯⲟⲩ		ϯⲉ, ϯ

The numbers from three upward stand before the noun with
the adjectival Ⲛ̄. The noun is in the singular form, as is
the definite article when present:

ϣⲟⲙⲚ̄ⲧ Ⲛ̄ ⲭⲟⲓ	three ships
ⲡϣⲟⲙⲚ̄ⲧ Ⲛ̄ Ⲣ̄ⲣⲟ	the three kings
ⲧⲉⲓϣⲟⲙⲧⲉ Ⲛ̄ ⲣⲟⲙⲡⲉ	these three years

Note the absence of the indefinite article in the indefinite expressions.

The number one is construed in the same way, but the
linking Ⲛ̄ may be omitted:

(ⲡ)ⲟⲩⲁ ⲣⲱⲙⲉ, (ⲡ)ⲟⲩⲁ Ⲛ̄ ⲣⲱⲙⲉ   (the) one man.

The number two follows its noun, which is likewise in the
singular; no Ⲛ̄ is used:

ⲥⲟⲛ ⲥⲛⲁⲩ, ⲡⲥⲟⲛ ⲥⲛⲁⲩ	two brothers, the two brothers
ⲥⲱⲛⲉ ⲥⲚ̄ⲧⲉ, ⲧⲥⲱⲛⲉ ⲥⲚ̄ⲧⲉ	two sisters, the two sisters.

Vocabulary 15

ⲛⲟϭ large, great, important.

ⲕⲟⲩⲓ small, little; also of quantity: a little (e.g.
ⲟⲩⲕⲟⲩⲓ ⲛ̄ ⲟⲉⲓⲕ a little bread); with pl.: few (e.g.
ϩⲉⲛⲕⲟⲩⲓ ⲛ̄ ϫⲱⲱⲙⲉ a few books).

ⲙⲉⲣⲓⲧ (pl. ⲙⲉⲣⲁⲧⲉ) beloved.

ⲥⲁⲃⲉ (f. ⲥⲁⲃⲏ; pl. ⲥⲁⲃⲉⲉⲩⲉ) wise.

ϭⲁⲗⲉ (pl. ϭⲁⲗⲉⲉⲩⲉ) lame, crippled.

ϩⲏⲕⲉ poor.

ⲉⲃⲓⲏⲛ poor, wretched, miserable.

ⲧⲉ.ⲣⲟⲙⲡⲉ (pl. ⲛ̄.ⲣⲙ̄ⲡⲟⲟⲩⲉ) year; (ⲛ̄) ⲧⲣⲟⲙⲡⲉ this year.

ⲛ̄ ⲟⲩⲣⲟⲙⲡⲉ for a year. ⲛ̄ ϣⲟⲙⲧⲉ ⲛ̄ ⲣⲟⲙⲡⲉ for three years.

ⲡ.ⲉⲃⲟⲧ (pl. ⲛ.ⲉⲃⲁⲧⲉ, ⲛ.ⲉⲃⲉⲧⲉ) month.

ⲡ.ϣⲏⲣⲉ ϣⲏⲙ small child (a frequent fixed expression).

ⲡⲱϩ to reach, attain (ⲉ, ϣⲁ).

Greek adjectives:

ⲁⲅⲁⲑⲟⲥ (ἀγαθός) good.

ⲇⲓⲕⲁⲓⲟⲥ (δίκαιος) just, righteous.

ⲡⲓⲥⲧⲟⲥ (πιστός) faithful, true, believing.

ⲁⲡⲓⲥⲧⲟⲥ (ἄπιστος) unbelieving.

ⲡⲟⲛⲏⲣⲟⲥ (πονηρός) bad, wicked.

And the numbers given in the lesson.

Exercises

A.1. ⲟⲩⲭⲏⲣⲁ ⲛ̄ ϩⲏⲕⲉ

2. ⲧⲉⲓⲛⲟϭ ⲙ̄ ⲡⲩⲗⲏ

3. ⲟⲩϩⲙ̄ϩⲁⲗ ⲙ̄ ⲡⲓⲥⲧⲟⲥ

4. ⲟⲩⲣ̄ⲣⲟ ⲛ̄ ⲇⲓⲕⲁⲓⲟⲥ

5. ⲡⲉⲓⲗⲁⲟⲥ ⲛ̄ ⲁⲡⲓⲥⲧⲟⲥ

6. ⲑⲙ̄ϩⲁⲗ ⲙ̄ ⲡⲟⲛⲏⲣⲁ

7. ⲟⲩⲛⲟϭ ⲛ̄ ϩⲏⲅⲉⲙⲱⲛ

8. ⲡⲉⲛⲙⲉⲣⲓⲧ ⲛ̄ ⲉⲓⲱⲧ

9. ⲡⲕⲟⲩⲓ ⲛ̄ ⲧⲃ̄ⲧ

10. ⲟⲩϭⲁⲗⲉ ⲛ̄ ϩⲏⲕⲉ

11. ⲟⲩⲕⲟⲩⲓ ⲛ̄ ⲁϥ

12. ⲟⲩϩⲁ̄ⲗⲱ ⲛ̄ ⲥⲁⲃⲏ

13. ⲛⲉϥⲙⲁⲑⲏⲧⲏⲥ ⲙ̄ ⲡⲓⲥⲧⲟⲥ

14. ⲡⲉϩⲧⲟ ⲛ̄ ϭⲁⲗⲉ

15. ϩⲉⲛϩⲓⲟⲙⲉ ⲛ̄ ⲉⲃⲓⲏⲛ

16. ⲡⲁⲓⲕⲁⲓⲟⲥ ⲛ̄ ⲣⲱⲙⲉ

17. ⲧⲁⲙⲉⲣⲓⲧ ⲙ̄ ⲙⲁⲁⲩ

18. ⲟⲩⲕⲟⲩⲓ ⲛ̄ ϣⲧⲉⲕⲟ

19. ⲛⲉϩⲃⲏⲩⲉ ⲙ̄ ⲡⲟⲛⲏⲣⲟⲛ

20. ⲛ̄ϣⲁϫⲉ ⲛ̄ ⲛ̄ⲥⲁⲃⲉⲉⲩⲉ

21. ⲡⲉⲓⲛⲟϭ ⲛ̄ ⲛⲟⲙⲟⲥ
22. ⲡⲥⲁⲃⲉ ⲛ̄ ⲇⲓⲕⲁⲓⲟⲥ
23. ⲙ̄ⲡⲁⲣⲑⲉⲛⲟⲥ ⲛ̄ ⲥⲁⲃⲏ
24. ⲛⲉⲛⲙⲉⲣⲁⲧⲉ ⲛ̄ ϣⲏⲣⲉ
25. ⲡⲙⲏⲛϣⲉ ⲛ̄ ⲁⲡⲓⲥⲧⲟⲥ

26. ⲡⲉϥϣⲏⲣⲉ ⲛ̄ ϭⲁⲗⲉ
27. ⲛ̄ⲣ̄ⲙ̄ⲉⲓⲟⲟⲩⲉ ⲛ̄ ⲛ̄ⲍⲏⲕⲉ
28. ⲙ̄ⲡⲟⲛⲏⲣⲟⲥ ⲙⲛ̄ ⲛ̄ⲁⲅⲁⲑⲟⲥ
29. ⲟⲩⲉⲃⲓⲏⲛ ⲛ̄ ⲟⲣⲫⲁⲛⲟⲥ
30. ⲧⲉⲥϩⲓⲙⲉ ⲙ̄ ⲡⲓⲥⲧⲟⲥ

B.1. ϣⲟⲙⲛ̄ⲧ ⲛ̄ ϫⲟⲓ
 2. ϣⲟⲙⲧⲉ ⲛ̄ ϣⲧⲏⲛ
 3. ⲡⲉⲓϣⲟⲙⲛ̄ⲧ ⲛ̄ ϩⲟⲟⲩ
 4. ϥⲧⲟⲟⲩ ⲛ̄ ϩⲟⲉⲓⲧⲉ
 5. ⲡⲉϥⲧⲟⲟⲩ ⲛ̄ ⲧⲟⲟⲩ
 6. ϥⲧⲟⲉ ⲛ̄ ϫⲏⲣⲁ
 7. ⲧⲉⲓϥⲧⲟⲉ ⲛ̄ ⲉⲛⲧⲟⲗⲏ
 8. ⲟⲩⲁ ⲙ̄ ⲙⲟⲛⲁⲭⲟⲥ
 9. ⲟⲩⲉⲓ ⲙ̄ ⲡⲩⲗⲏ

10. ⲥⲛⲁⲩϩ ⲥⲛⲁⲩ
11. ⲡⲉϥⲃⲁⲗ ⲥⲛⲁⲩ
12. ⲣⲟⲙⲡⲉ ⲥⲛ̄ⲧⲉ
13. ⲉⲃⲟⲧ ⲥⲛⲁⲩ
14. ⲡⲉⲓ†ⲟⲩ ⲛ̄ ⲉⲃⲟⲧ
15. †ⲟⲩ ⲛ̄ ⲕⲟⲩⲓ ⲛ̄ ϫⲟⲓ
16. †ⲟⲩ ⲛ̄ ⲣⲱⲙⲉ ⲛ̄ ⲁⲅⲁⲑⲟⲥ
17. ⲥϩⲓⲙⲉ ⲥⲛ̄ⲧⲉ ⲛ̄ ⲁⲅⲁⲑⲟⲥ
18. ⲡⲣ̄ⲣⲟ ⲥⲛⲁⲩ

C.1. ⲛ̄ⲧⲁⲕⲡⲱϩ ⲉ ⲧⲉⲓⲡⲟⲗⲓⲥ ⲧⲏ̄ⲛⲁⲩ?
 2. ⲁⲩⲕⲱⲧ ⲛ̄ ⲟⲩⲕⲟⲩⲓ ⲙ̄ ⲡⲟⲗⲓⲥ ⲙ̄ⲙⲁⲩ.
 3. ⲁⲛⲟⲩⲱϩ ⲙ̄ⲙⲁⲩ ⲛ̄ ϥⲧⲟⲉ ⲛ̄ ⲣⲟⲙⲡⲉ.
 4. ⲛ̄ⲧⲁⲣ† ⲛⲙ̄ⲙⲁϥ ⲉⲧⲃⲉ ⲟⲩ?
 5. ⲟⲩ ⲡⲉ ⲡⲣⲁⲛ ⲙ̄ ⲡ†ⲙⲉ ⲉⲛⲧⲁⲧⲉⲧⲛ̄ⲡⲱϩ ⲉⲣⲟϥ ⲛ̄ ⲧⲉⲩϣⲏ ⲉⲧ ⲙ̄ⲙⲁⲩ?
 6. ⲛⲓⲙ ⲡⲉⲛⲧⲁϥϣⲓⲛⲉ ⲛ̄ⲥⲱⲓ?
 7. ⲡⲁⲓ ⲡⲉ ⲡⲉϩⲣⲟⲟⲩ ⲙ̄ ⲡⲉⲛⲙⲉⲣⲓⲧ ⲛ̄ ϣⲏⲣⲉ.
 8. ⲁⲓ† ⲙ̄ ⲡϩⲁⲧ ⲛ̄ ⲛⲉⲃⲓⲏⲛ.
 9. ⲙ̄ⲡⲓⲟⲩⲱϣ ⲉ ϣⲁϫⲉ ⲙⲛ̄ ⲡϭⲁⲗⲉ ⲉⲧ ⲙ̄ⲙⲁⲩ.
10. ⲟⲩ ⲡⲉ ⲡϣⲓ ⲉⲛⲧⲁϥⲡⲱϩ ⲉⲣⲟϥ ⲛ̄ϭⲓ ⲡⲉⲓϩⲗ̄ⲗⲟ ⲛ̄ ⲇⲓⲕⲁⲓⲟⲥ?
11. ⲛ̄ⲧⲁⲕⲛⲟϫⲟⲩ ⲉⲃⲟⲗ ⲧⲱⲛ?
12. ⲁⲓϭⲱ ϩⲙ̄ ⲡⲉⲩ†ⲙⲉ ⲛ̄ ⲟⲩⲣⲟⲙⲡⲉ.

Lesson 16

16.1 The interrogative pronouns ⲁϣ, ⲟⲩ, and ⲛⲓⲙ may be used adjectivally. This usage is most frequent in certain fixed expressions, the most important of which are

1) ⲁϣ ⲛ̄ ⲙⲓⲛⲉ (of) what sort? This phrase is used attributively, as in

ⲟⲩⲁϣ ⲛ̄ ⲙⲓⲛⲉ ⲛ̄ ϫⲟⲓ? what sort of ship?

or predicatively (note obligatory use of indefinite article):

ⲟⲩⲁϣ ⲛ̄ ⲙⲓⲛⲉ ⲡⲉ ⲡⲉⲓⲣⲱⲙⲉ? Of what sort is this man?

2) ⲁϣ ⲛ̄ ⳅⲉ (of) what sort? ⲛ̄ ⲁϣ ⲛ̄ ⳅⲉ in what way? how?

ⲟⲩⲁϣ ⲛ̄ ⳅⲉ ⲡⲉ ⲡⲉⲓⲙⲁⲉⲓⲛ? Of what sort is this sign?
ⲛ̄ ⲁϣ ⲛ̄ ⳅⲉ ⲁⲕϭⲓⲛⲉ ⲙ̄ⲙⲟϥ? How did you find him?

3) ⳅⲛ̄ ⲁϣ ⲛ̄ ⲟⲩⲟⲉⲓϣ? at what time?
Similar use of ⲟⲩ and ⲛⲓⲙ is rarer, e.g. ⲛⲓⲙ ⲛ̄ ⲣⲱⲙⲉ? what man? ⲟⲩ ⲛ̄ ⲙⲓⲛⲉ? what sort? In special contexts these same or similar expressions may have an indefinite value: ⲛⲓⲙ ⲛ̄ ⲣⲱⲙⲉ such and such a person, ⲁϣ ⲛ̄ ϯⲙⲉ some village or other, ⲟⲩ ⲙⲛ̄ ⲟⲩ this and that.

16.2 "Each, every" is expressed by ⲛⲓⲙ (not the same word as ⲛⲓⲙ who?) placed after a singular noun with no article: ⲣⲱⲙⲉ ⲛⲓⲙ every man, everyone; ⳅⲱⲃ ⲛⲓⲙ everything; ϯⲙⲉ ⲛⲓⲙ every village. Pronominal resumption is usually in the plural:

ϣⲁϫⲉ ⲛⲓⲙ ⲉⲛⲧⲁⲛⲥⲱⲧⲙ̄ ⲉⲣⲟⲟⲩ everything which we heard
ⳅⲱⲃ ⲛⲓⲙ ⲛ̄ ⲡⲟⲛⲏⲣⲟⲛ ⲉⲛⲧⲁϥⲉⲓⲣⲉ ⲙ̄ⲙⲟⲟⲩ every evil thing that
he did
But resumption in the singular is not rare.

16.3 The indefinite pronouns are ⲟⲩⲟⲛ anyone; ⲗⲁⲁⲩ anyone, anything. These are most frequent in negative contexts as "no one, nothing":

ⲘⲠⲒⲚⲀⲨ ⲉ ⲞⲨⲞⲚ ⲘⲘⲀⲨ.   I saw no one there.

ⲘⲠⲉϥϯ-ⲗⲀⲀⲨ ⲚⲀⲒ.   He gave me nothing.

ⲗⲀⲀⲨ also appears with the indefinite article: ⲞⲨⲗⲀⲀⲨ.

    ⲗⲀⲀⲨ is often used adjectively:

ⲘⲠⲉ-ⲗⲀⲀⲨ Ⲛ̄ ⲢⲰⲘⲉ ⲚⲀⲨ ⲉⲢⲞⲒ.   No man saw me.

ⲘⲠⲒϢⲉⲠ-ⲗⲀⲀⲨ Ⲛ̄ ⲭⲰⲰⲘⲉ Ⲛ̄ⲦⲞⲞⲦϥ̄.   I received no book from him.

When (ⲞⲨ)ⲗⲀⲀⲨ or phrases beginning with (ⲞⲨ)ⲗⲀⲀⲨ are direct objects of transitive verbs (i.e. object with ⲘⲘⲞ⸗), the use of the prenominal form of the infinitive is obligatory in the First Perfect and its negative. Thus ⲘⲠⲒϢⲰⲠ Ⲛ̄ ⲗⲀⲀⲨ ... is not permitted in the sentence above.

    As a nominal predicate ⲗⲀⲀⲨ means "nothing," even when no negative is formally involved. The indefinite article is obligatory:

ⲀⲚϥ̄-ⲞⲨⲗⲀⲀⲨ.   I am nothing.

ⲌⲉⲚⲗⲀⲀⲨ Ⲛⲉ ⲚⲉⲨⲚⲞⲨⲦⲉ.   Their gods are nothing.

Ⲛ̄ ⲗⲀⲀⲨ or ⲗⲀⲀⲨ alone may be used adverbially in the sense "(not) at all":

ⲘⲠⲒϢⲀⳆⲉ ⲚⲘ̄ⲘⲀϥ (Ⲛ̄) ⲗⲀⲀⲨ.   I didn't speak with him at all.

Note also the expression ⲞⲨⲞⲚ ⲚⲒⲘ everyone, everybody.

    16.4 "All, the whole (of)" is expressed by ⲦⲎⲢ⸗ used in apposition to a preceding noun or pronoun. A resumptive suffix is required:

Ⲛ̄ⲢⲰⲘⲉ ⲦⲎⲢⲞⲨ   all the men (lit. the men, all of them)

ⲠⲔⲞⲤⲘⲞⲤ ⲦⲎⲢϥ̄   the whole world, all the world

ⲀⲨⲉⲒ ⲉⳆⲞⲨⲚ ⲦⲎⲢⲞⲨ.   They all came in.

The pronominal suffixes are the same as those used on pre-positions and infinitives; the 2nd pers. pl. form is ⲦⲎⲢⲦⲚ̄. The 3rd pers. pl. ⲦⲎⲢⲞⲨ may also be used for 2nd pers. pl. reference.

    16.5 The numbers from six to ten:

six	masc.	cooγ	fém.	co, coє
seven		cλϣϥ		cλϣϥє
eight		ϣмoγn		ϣмoγnє
nine		ψιτ, ψιc		ψιτє, ψιcє
ten		мнт		мнтє

They are used like the numbers three to five in §15.3.

Partitive expressions with numbers employ the preposition ñ (ñмo∘):

oγλ ñ ñρωмє one of the men   ϣoмñт ñ nєхнγ three of

ϣoмñт ñмooγ three of them   the ships

The number "one," oγλ (f. oγєι) is also used as an indefinite pronoun: a certain one, a certain man (or woman), as in

λ-oγλ вωκ ϣλ πλρхιєπιcκoπoc. A certain man went to the
archbishop.

Vocabulary 16

θє (τ.2є) manner, way. ñ θє ñ prep. like, in the manner
of; with pron. suff.: ñ τλ2є like me, as I do. ñ τєι2є
in this way, thus.

τ.мιnє kind, sort, type, species. λϣ ñ мιnє of what sort?
ñ τєιмιnє of this sort, such.

πє.oγoєιϣ time, occasion. ñ oγoєιϣ nιм every time, always.
ñ oγoγoєιϣ once, on one occasion (in the past). ñ
πєoγoєιϣ at this/that time.

πє.мτo євoλ presence. ñ πємτo євoλ ñ in the presence of;
with pron. suff.: ñ πλñтo євoλ in my presence.

And the words and expressions treated in the lesson.

Greek words and names:

τє.хωρλ (ἡ χώρα) land, country.

τ.єρнмoc (ἡ ἐρῆμος) desert, wilderness.

π.κλρπoc (ὁ καρπός) fruit.   π.λρхιєρєγc (ὁ ἀρχιερεύς)

мωγcнc (Μωυσῆς) Moses.   high-priest.

π.λρхιєπιcκoπoc (ὁ ἀρχιεπίσκοπος) archbishop.

Exercises

A.1. ⲥⲟⲉⲓⲛⲉ ⲛ̄ ⲧⲉⲓⲙⲓⲛⲉ

2. ⲥⲟⲟⲩ ⲛ̄ ⲉⲥⲟⲟⲩ

3. ⲡⲍⲁⲧ ⲧⲏⲣϥ̄

4. ⲟⲩⲁ ⲛ̄ ⲛ̄ϭⲁⲗⲉⲉⲩⲉ

5. ⲟⲩⲁϣ ⲙ̄ ⲙⲓⲛⲉ ⲛ̄ ⲉⲟⲟⲩ?

6. ⲛ̄ ⲥⲁϣϥ̄ ⲛ̄ ⲍⲟⲟⲩ

7. ⲧⲉⲩϣⲏ ⲧⲏⲣⲥ̄

8. ⲍⲱⲃ ⲛⲓⲙ ⲉⲛⲧⲁⲓϣⲟⲡⲟⲩ

9. ⲟⲩⲥⲛ̄ϭⲉ ⲛ̄ ⲧⲉⲓⲙⲓⲛⲉ

10. ⲛⲉⲧⲙⲉ ⲧⲏⲣⲟⲩ ⲛ̄ⲧⲉ ⲧⲥⲩⲣⲓⲁ

11. ⲙ̄ ⲡⲉⲙⲧⲟ ⲉⲃⲟⲗ ⲙ̄
ⲡⲁⲣⲭⲓⲉⲣⲉⲩⲥ

12. ⲛ̄ ⲑⲉ ⲛ̄ ⲟⲩⲛⲟϭ ⲛ̄ ⲥⲁⲃⲉ

13. ⲡⲁⲍⲁⲧ ⲧⲏⲣϥ̄

14. ⲣⲱⲙⲉ ⲛⲓⲙ ⲉⲛⲧⲁϥⲛⲁⲩ ⲉⲣⲟⲟⲩ

15. ϣⲟⲙⲧⲉ ⲙ̄ ⲙⲓⲛⲉ

16. ⲟⲩⲟⲛ ⲛⲓⲙ ⲉⲧ ⲍⲛ̄ ⲧⲥⲩⲛⲁⲅⲱⲅⲏ

17. ⲡⲛⲟⲙⲟⲥ ⲙ̄ ⲙⲱⲩⲥⲏⲥ ⲧⲏⲣϥ̄

18. ⲥⲟⲉ ⲛ̄ ⲥⲱϣⲉ

19. ⲧⲉⲓⲙⲏⲧⲉ ⲛ̄ ⲉⲛⲧⲟⲗⲏ

20. ⲛⲉⲭⲱⲣⲁ ⲧⲏⲣⲟⲩ ⲛ̄ⲧⲉ ⲡⲉⲓⲕⲟⲥⲙⲟⲥ

21. ⲛ̄ ⲥⲁϣϥⲉ ⲛ̄ ⲣⲟⲙⲡⲉ

22. ⲛ̄ ⲑⲉ ⲛ̄ ⲟⲩⲍⲙ̄ⲍⲁⲗ ⲙ̄ ⲡⲓⲥⲧⲟⲥ

23. ⲁⲛⲟⲛ ⲧⲏⲣⲛ̄

24. ⲛ̄ⲍⲏⲕⲉ ⲛ̄ ⲧⲡⲟⲗⲓⲥ ⲧⲏⲣⲟⲩ

25. ⲍⲛ̄ ⲗⲁⲁⲩ ⲙ̄ ⲙⲁ

26. ϣⲙⲟⲩⲛ ⲛ̄ ⲛⲟϭ ⲛ̄ ϫⲟⲓ

27. ⲟⲩⲁ ⲙ̄ⲙⲟⲟⲩ

28. ϣⲁϫⲉ ⲛⲓⲙ ⲉⲛⲧⲁϥϫⲟⲟⲩ

29. ⲟⲩⲁϣ ⲙ̄ ⲙⲓⲛⲉ ⲛ̄ ϣⲱⲛⲉ?

30. ϣⲱⲥ ⲥⲛⲁⲩ

31. ⲍⲓϫⲛ̄ ⲗⲁⲁⲩ ⲛ̄ ⲍ ⲓ ⲏ

32. ⲙ̄ ⲡⲉϥⲙ̄ⲧⲟ ⲉⲃⲟⲗ

33. ⲗⲁⲁⲩ ⲛ̄ ⲕⲁⲣⲡⲟⲥ

34. ϥⲧⲟⲟⲩ ⲙ̄ ⲙⲁⲉⲓⲛ

35. ⲉ ⲁϣ ⲛ̄ ϣⲓ?

36. ⲍⲛ̄ ⲧⲉϥⲭⲱⲣⲁ ⲁⲩⲱ ⲍⲙ̄ ⲡⲉϥϯⲙⲉ

37. ⲛ̄ ϣⲙⲟⲩⲛ ⲛ̄ ⲉⲃⲟⲧ

38. ⲍⲛ̄ ⲟⲩⲛⲟϭ ⲛ̄ ⲣⲁϣⲉ

39. ⲟⲩⲁⲣⲭⲓⲉⲣⲉⲩⲥ ⲙ̄ ⲡⲟⲛⲏⲣⲟⲥ

40. ⲛⲉⲛϣⲃⲉⲉⲣ ⲧⲏⲣⲟⲩ

B.1. ⲙ̄ⲡⲓⲕⲁ-ⲗⲁⲁⲩ ⲉϫⲛ̄ ⲧⲉⲧⲣⲁⲡⲉⲍⲁ.

2. ⲟⲩⲛ̄-ⲍⲟⲉⲓⲛⲉ ⲛ̄ ⲧⲉⲓⲙⲓⲛⲉ ⲍⲙ̄
ⲡⲟⲗⲓⲥ ⲛⲓⲙ.

3. ⲛ̄ⲧⲁⲕϭⲓⲛⲉ ⲙ̄ ⲡⲉⲕⲍⲁⲡ ⲛ̄ ⲁϣ ⲛ̄ ⲍⲉ?

4. ⲟⲩⲁϣ ⲙ̄ ⲙⲓⲛⲉ ⲡⲉ ⲡⲉⲓϫⲱⲱⲙⲉ?

5. ⲍⲛ̄ ⲁϣ ⲛ̄ ⲟⲩⲟⲉⲓϣ ⲁⲥⲙⲓⲥⲉ ⲙ̄
ⲡⲉⲥϣⲏⲣⲉ?

6. ⲁⲛⲅ̄-ⲛⲓⲙ ⲁⲛⲟⲕ? ⲁⲛⲅ̄-ⲟⲩⲗⲁⲁⲩ.

7. ⲙ̄ⲡⲉϥϯ-ⲟⲩⲗⲁⲁⲩ ⲛⲁⲓ.

8. ⲁⲛⲕⲁ-ⲟⲩⲟⲛ ⲛⲓⲙ ⲛ̄ⲥⲱⲛ.

9. ⲍⲉⲛⲗⲁⲁⲩ ⲛⲉ ⲛⲉⲩϣⲁϫⲉ ⲙ̄
ⲡⲟⲛⲏⲣⲟⲛ.

10. ⲁ-ⲟⲩⲁ ⲉⲓ ϣⲁⲣⲟϥ ⲍⲛ̄
ⲧⲉⲩϣⲏ.

11. ⲁⲥϭⲱ ⲙⲛ̄ ⲟⲩⲁ ⲛ̄ ⲛⲉⲥ-
ⲥⲩⲅⲅⲉⲛⲏⲥ.

12. ⲉⲧⲃⲉ ⲟⲩ ⲛ̄ⲧⲁⲣⲉⲓⲣⲉ ⲛ̄
ⲧⲉⲓⲍⲉ?

13. ⲛ̄ ⲟⲩⲟⲩⲟⲉⲓϣ ⲁ-ⲡⲁⲣⲭⲓ-
ⲉⲡⲓⲥⲕⲟⲡⲟⲥ ⲉⲓ ⲉ ⲡⲉⲛⲧⲟⲟⲩ.

14. ⲁⲩⲉⲓⲛⲉ ⲙ̄ ⲡⲉϥⲓⲧ ⲛ̄ ⲣⲱⲙⲉ
ⲉⲍⲟⲩⲛ ⲉⲣⲟϥ.

15. ⲛ̄ⲧⲁⲩⲧⲛ̄ⲛⲟⲟⲩ ⲙ̄ⲙⲟⲓ ⲉ
ⲡⲉⲓⲗⲁⲟⲥ ⲧⲏⲣϥ̄.

16. Ⲙⲡⲓⲙⲉⲣ ⲉ-ⲗⲁⲁⲩ Ⲙ̄ ⲡⲙⲁ ⲉⲧ Ⲙ̄ⲙⲁⲩ.

17. ⲁ-ⲅⲟⲉⲓⲛⲉ ⲱⲱⲛⲉ ⲉⲙⲁⲧⲉ Ⲙ̄ ⲡⲉⲟⲩⲟⲉⲓⲱ.

18. Ⲙ̄ⲡⲉϥ†-ⲗⲁⲁⲩ Ⲛ̄ ⲟⲉⲓⲕ ⲛⲁⲛ.

19. ⲅⲚ̄ ⲁⲱ Ⲛ̄ ⲟⲩⲟⲉⲓⲱ ⲁⲧⲉⲧⲚ̄ⲡⲱⲅ ⲉ ⲡⲉⲓⲙⲁ?

20. ⲘⲚ̄-ⲗⲁⲁⲩ ⲛⲙ̄ⲙⲁϥ Ⲙ̄ⲙⲁⲩ.

Lesson 17

17.1 The Imperative of most verbs is the same as the Infinitive, with no indication of number or gender:

ⲙⲟⲟⲱⲉ Ⲛ̄ⲥⲱⲓ.	Walk behind me.
ⲙⲉⲣ-ⲡⲭⲟⲓ ⲉ ⲡⲱⲛⲉ.	Tie the boat to the rock.
ⲙⲉⲣ ⲉ-ⲡⲭⲟⲉⲓⲥ.	Love the Lord.
ⲥⲱⲧⲘ̄ ⲉ ⲛⲁⲱⲁⲭⲉ.	Listen to my words.

Negation is with the prefix Ⲙ̄ⲡⲣ̄-:

Ⲙ̄ⲡⲣ̄ⲱⲁⲭⲉ ⲛⲙ̄ⲙⲁⲩ.	Don't speak with them.
Ⲙ̄ⲡⲣ̄ⲃⲱⲕ ⲉ ⲧⲡⲟⲗⲓⲥ.	Do not go to the city.
Ⲙ̄ⲡⲣ̄Ⲛ̄ⲕⲟⲧⲕ̄ Ⲙ̄ ⲡⲉⲓⲙⲁ.	Do not lie down here.

A few verbs have special Imperative forms with prefixed ⲁ-:

ⲛⲁⲩ: ⲁⲛⲁⲩ look, see   ⲭⲱ: ⲁⲭⲓ-, ⲁⲭⲓ⸗ say, speak
ⲟⲩⲱⲛ: ⲁⲩⲱⲛ open   ⲉⲓⲛⲉ: ⲁⲛⲓ-, ⲁⲛⲓ⸗ bring
ⲉⲓⲣⲉ: ⲁⲣⲓⲣⲉ, ⲁⲣⲓ-, ⲁⲣⲓ⸗ do, make

The verb ⲙⲁ, ⲙⲁ-, ⲙⲁⲧ⸗ (or ⲙⲏⲉⲓ⸗) is used as the imperative of †, but † may also be used. The imperative of ⲉⲓ (to come) is expressed by ⲁⲙⲟⲩ, which has distinct feminine and plural forms: f. ⲁⲙⲏ, pl. ⲁⲙⲏⲉⲓⲧⲚ̄.

17.2 The vocative is expressed by using a noun with the definite article or a possessive prefix: ⲡⲣ̄ⲣⲟ O king! ⲡⲁⲱⲏⲣⲉ O my son! The Greek vocative particle ⲱ (Gk. ὦ) may also be used, but not before a designation of God.

17.3 Infinitives of the type ⲙⲓⲥⲉ, with stressed

vowel -ι- and final unstressed -ε, have the following prenominal and presuffixal forms:

ⲙⲓⲥⲉ	ⲙⲉⲥ(ⲧ̄)-	ⲙⲁⲥⲧ⸗	to bear (a child)
ⲉⲓⲱⲉ	ⲉⲱⲧ̄-	ⲁⲱⲧ⸗	to hang up, suspend.

The prenominal forms of many of these verbs occur with or
without the final -ⲧ. Several important verbs of this
type have irregularities:

ⲉⲓⲣⲉ	ⲣ̄-	ⲁⲁ⸗	to do, make
ⲉⲓⲛⲉ	ⲛ̄-	ⲛ̄ⲧ⸗	to bring
ⲱⲓⲛⲉ	ⲱⲛ̄-	ⲱⲛ̄ⲧ⸗	to seek, inquire
ⳓⲓⲛⲉ	ⳓⲛ̄-	ⳓⲛ̄ⲧ⸗	to find.

The final ⲛ̄ of ⲛ̄-, ⲱⲛ̄-, and ⳓⲛ̄- may be assimilated to ⲙ̄
before a following ⲡ or ⲙ. Note that in ⲛ̄ⲧ⸗, ⲱⲛ̄ⲧ⸗ and ⳓⲛ̄ⲧ⸗
the syllabic ⲛ̄ is the stressed vowel of the word. ⲣ̄- is
often written as ⲉⲣ-. Suffixes are added to these forms
regularly: ⳓⲛ̄ⲧ, ⳓⲛ̄ⲧⲕ̄, ⳓⲛ̄ⲧⲉ, ⳓⲛ̄ⲧϥ̄, ⳓⲛ̄ⲧⲥ̄, ⳓⲛ̄ⲧⲛ̄, ⳓⲛ̄-ⲑⲏⲩⲧⲛ̄,
ⳓⲛ̄ⲧⲟⲩ. ⲁⲁ⸗ is inflected like ⲧⲁⲁ⸗ in §11.2.

17.4 There is a certain ambiguity surrounding the
terms *transitive* and *intransitive* in classifying Coptic
verbs. The strictest definition of a transitive verb requires (1) that its direct object be marked with the "preposition" ⲛ̄ (ⲙ̄ⲙⲟ⸗) and (2) that the general equivalence
ⲕⲱⲧ ⲙ̄ⲙⲟϥ = ⲕⲟⲧϥ̄ be attested for the verb, i.e. that the
verb possess prenominal and presuffixal forms. A less
strict definition would require a transitive verb to satisfy either, but not necessarily both, of the above criteria.
This is approximately the position adopted by W. E. Crum in
his *Coptic Dictionary*, the standard lexical work in the
field. Verbs not satisfying either of these criteria are
labeled intransitive or are left unlabeled.

In the present work the designation *transitive* is
extended to include verbs having prenominal and presuffixal
forms that correspond exactly in meaning to the infinitive
with ⲉ or ⲛ̄ⲥⲁ (e.g. ⲥⲱⲧⲙ̄ ⲉ, ⲱⲓⲛⲉ ⲛ̄ⲥⲁ). Thus ⲥⲟⲧⲙⲉϥ = ⲥⲱⲧⲙ̄

ⲉⲣⲟϥ and ϣⲛ̄ⲧϥ̄ = ϣⲓⲛⲉ ⲛ̄ⲥⲱϥ are taken as fully equivalent to the criterion ⲕⲱⲧ ⲙ̄ⲙⲟϥ = ⲕⲟⲧϥ̄ above. A verb like ⲁⲙⲁ2ⲧⲉ (to seize) is considered transitive because its direct object is marked by ⲙ̄ⲙⲟ⁼, even though it does not have prenominal or presuffixal forms. It seems reasonable, therefore, to extend the designation *transitive* even further and to include verbs like ⲛⲁⲩ and ⲉⲓⲙⲉ (to understand), both of which normally have an object with ⲉ, but neither of which has prenominal or presuffixal forms. In other words, as long as there is no lexical contrast requiring the preposition ⲉ to have the semantic force of a true preposition (for, in regard to), we have generally labeled verbs with ⲉ-objects as *transitive* in the glossary of this work. Some subjectiveness remains, however, and one can sympathize with W. E. Crum in his desire to drop the terms *transitive* and *intransitive* altogether (*op. cit.*, p. vii).

Vocabulary 17

2ⲁⲣⲉ2 vb. tr. to guard, watch (ⲉ; from: ⲉ, ⲉⲃⲟⲗ 2ⲛ̄); to keep, observe, preserve (ⲉ).

ⲉⲓⲙⲉ vb. tr. to understand (ⲉ); to know, realize (that: ⲭⲉ).

ϣⲙ̄ϣⲉ vb. tr. to serve, worship (ⲛⲁ⁼); as n.m. service, worship.

ⲙⲟⲩⲧⲉ vb. tr. to call (ⲉ), summon, name. Note the constructions:

ⲁⲩⲙⲟⲩⲧⲉ ⲉⲣⲟϥ ⲭⲉ ⲓ̈ⲱ2ⲁⲛⲛⲏⲥ.　　They named him John.

ⲁⲩⲙⲟⲩⲧⲉ ⲉ ⲡⲉϥⲣⲁⲛ ⲭⲉ ⲓ̈ⲱ2ⲁⲛⲛⲏⲥ.　They called his name John.

ⲁⲩⲙⲟⲩⲧⲉ ⲉⲣⲟϥ ⲙ̄ ⲡⲣⲁⲛ ⲙ̄ ⲡⲉϥ-　They named him after his

ⲉⲓⲱⲧ.　　　　　　　　　　　　　father.

ⲁⲙⲁ2ⲧⲉ vb. tr. to grasp, seize, take possession of, take captive (ⲙ̄ⲙⲟ⁼); to learn by heart.

ⲡ.ⲭⲁⲭⲉ (pl. ⲛ̄.ⲭⲓⲭⲉⲉⲩⲉ) enemy.

ⲡ. ⲙⲁⲧⲟⲓ soldier.

ⲧⲉ.ⲥⲃⲱ (pl. ⲛⲉ.ⲥⲃⲟⲟⲩⲉ) teaching, instruction, doctrine.

пе.ⲛⲕⲁ thing (in general); property, belongings; ⲛ̄ⲕⲁ ⲛⲓⲙ
everything.

ϫⲉ (1) conj. that, introducing noun clauses after verbs of
speaking, knowing, perceiving; (2) introduces proper
name or epithet in certain contructions.

Greek words:

п.ⲇⲓⲁⲃⲟⲗⲟⲥ (ὁ διάβολος) the devil.

ⲧⲉ.ⲯⲩⲭⲏ (ἡ ψυχή) soul.

пе.ⲡⲛⲉⲩⲙⲁ (τὸ πνεῦμα) spirit, nearly always abbreviated
(пе.)ⲡⲛ̄ⲁ̄.

ⲧ.ⲡⲁⲣⲁⲃⲟⲗⲏ (ἡ παραβολή) parable.

ⲁⲕⲁⲑⲁⲣⲧⲟⲥ (ἀκάθαρτος) unclean.

<h2 style="text-align:center">Exercises</h2>

A.1. ⲡⲁⲡⲟⲧ ⲉⲛⲧⲁⲓ6ⲛ̄ⲧ9 ⲙ̄ⲙⲁⲩ

2. ⲡⲛⲟⲙⲟⲥ ⲉⲛⲧⲁ-ⲡⲭⲟⲉⲓⲥ ⲧⲁⲁ9
ⲙ̄ ⲙⲱⲩⲥⲏⲥ

3. ⲋⲱⲃ ⲛⲓⲙ ⲉⲛⲧⲁⲩⲁⲁⲩ ⲛ̄6ⲓ
ⲙ̄ⲙⲁⲑⲏⲧⲏⲥ

4. ⲡϣⲏⲣⲉ ⲉⲛⲧⲁⲥⲙⲁⲥⲧ9

5. ⲡⲉⲡⲛ̄ⲁ̄ ⲛ̄ ⲁⲕⲁⲑⲁⲣⲧⲟⲛ
ⲉⲛⲧⲁ9ⲛⲟⲭ9 ⲉⲃⲟⲗ

6. ⲡⲕⲁⲣⲡⲟⲥ ⲉⲛⲧⲁⲥⲛ̄ⲧ9 ⲙ̄ ⲡⲉⲥⲋⲁⲓ
7. ⲡⲭⲁⲭⲉ ⲉⲛⲧⲁ-ⲙ̄ⲙⲁⲧⲟⲓ ϣⲛ̄ⲧ9
8. ⲡ2ⲁⲧ ⲉⲧⲉ ⲙ̄ⲡⲉ-ⲙ̄ⲙⲁⲧⲟⲓ 6ⲛ̄ⲧ9
9. ⲡⲉⲛⲧⲁⲥⲙⲁⲥⲧ9 ⲉ ⲡⲉⲥ2ⲁⲓ
10. ⲛⲉⲛⲧⲁⲩⲛ̄ⲧⲟⲩ ϣⲁⲣⲟⲛ
11. ⲡⲉⲛⲧⲁⲧⲉⲧⲛ̄ⲁⲁ9
12. ⲛⲉⲛⲧⲁⲛ6ⲛ̄ⲧⲟⲩ ⲙ̄ⲙⲁⲩ

B.1. ⲥⲱⲧⲙ̄ ⲉ ⲧⲁⲥⲃⲱ.
2. ⲥⲉ-ⲧⲉⲣⲱⲧⲉ, ⲡⲁϣⲏⲣⲉ.
3. ⲛⲁ ⲛⲁⲓ, ⲡⲁⲭⲟⲉⲓⲥ.
4. ⲙ̄ⲡⲣ̄ⲭⲟⲟⲥ ⲛ̄ ⲁⲁⲁⲩ ⲛ̄ ⲣⲱⲙⲉ.
5. 2ⲁⲣⲉ2 ⲉ ⲛⲉⲓ ⲉⲛⲧⲟⲗⲏ ⲧⲏⲣⲟⲩ.
6. ϣⲙ̄ϣⲉ ⲙ̄ ⲡⲭⲟⲉⲓⲥ ⲡⲉⲕⲛⲟⲩⲧⲉ.
7. ⲙ̄ⲡⲣ̄6ⲱ ⲉⲣⲟⲓ.
8. ⲉⲓⲁ-ⲡⲉⲕ2ⲟ.
9. ⲙ̄ⲡⲣ̄ⲃⲱⲕ ⲉ ⲧⲉⲣⲏⲙⲟⲥ.
10. 2ⲁⲣⲉ2 ⲉ ⲧⲁⲯⲩⲭⲏ, ⲡⲁⲭⲟⲉⲓⲥ.
11. ⲙⲁ-ⲛ̄ⲕⲁ ⲛⲓⲙ ⲛ̄ ⲛⲉⲃⲓⲏⲛ.
12. 6ⲱ ⲛⲙ̄ⲙⲁⲓ 2ⲛ̄ ⲧⲉⲩϣⲏ.
13. ⲁⲛⲓ-ⲥⲟⲟⲩ ⲙ̄ ⲙⲁⲧⲟⲓ ⲛⲙ̄ⲙⲁⲕ.

14. ⲙ̄ⲡⲣ̄ϣⲙ̄ϣⲉ ⲙ̄ ⲡⲣ̄ⲣⲟ ⲙ̄ ⲡⲟⲛⲏⲣⲟⲥ
ⲉⲧ ⲙ̄ⲙⲁⲩ.
15. ⲙⲉⲣ-ⲛⲉ9ⲟⲩⲉⲣⲏⲧⲉ 2ⲛ̄ ⲛⲉⲓⲥⲛⲁⲩ2.
16. ϫⲓⲧ9 ϣⲁ ⲡⲁⲣⲭⲓⲉⲣⲉⲩⲥ.
17. ⲁⲙⲁ2ⲧⲉ ⲙ̄ⲙⲟ9.
18. ⲁⲛⲁⲩ ⲉ ⲡⲣⲏ 2ⲛ̄ ⲧⲡⲉ.
19. ⲙⲟⲩⲧⲉ ⲉ ⲡⲉⲕⲥⲟⲛ, ⲡϣⲏⲣⲉ.
20. 2ⲁⲣⲉ2 ⲉⲣⲟⲛ ⲉ ⲙ̄ⲙⲁⲧⲟⲓ.
21. ⲙ̄ⲡⲣ̄6ⲱ ⲙ̄ ⲡⲁⲙⲧⲟ ⲉⲃⲟⲗ.
22. ϯ ⲛⲁ9 ⲛ̄ ⲟⲩⲕⲟⲩⲓ ⲙ̄ ⲙⲟⲟⲩ.
23. ⲁⲣⲓ-ⲡⲁⲓ ⲛ̄ ⲧⲁ2ⲉ.
24. ⲁⲛⲓ-ⲙⲏⲧ ⲛ̄ ⲣⲱⲙⲉ ⲉ ⲡⲉⲓⲙⲁ.

25. ⲛ̄ ⲟⲩⲟⲉⲓϣ ⲛⲓⲙ ⲁⲣⲓⲣⲉ ⲛ̄ ⲧⲉϥⲍⲉ. 28. ⲁⲩⲱⲛ ⲙ̄ ⲡⲣⲟ.

26. ⲁⲙⲏⲉⲓⲧⲛ̄ ⲉⲍⲟⲩⲛ ⲉ ⲡⲉϥⲣ̄ⲡⲉ. 29. ⲙ̄ⲡⲣ̄ⲧⲉⲙ-ⲡⲣⲟ.

27. ⲁⲙⲏ ϣⲁⲣⲟⲓ, ⲧⲁϣⲉⲉⲣⲉ. 30. ϭⲱ ⲛⲙ̄ⲙⲁⲓ ⲛ̄ ϣⲙⲟⲩⲛ ⲛ̄ ⲉⲃⲟⲧ.

C.1. ⲙ̄ⲡⲟⲩⲉⲓⲙⲉ ⲉ ⲙ̄ⲡⲁⲣⲁⲃⲟⲗⲏ ⲉⲛⲧⲁϥϫⲟⲟⲩ ⲛⲁⲩ.

2. ⲁⲩⲁⲙⲁⲍⲧⲉ ⲙ̄ⲙⲟϥ ⲛ̄ϭⲓ ⲙ̄ⲙⲁⲧⲟⲓ, ⲁⲩⲙⲟⲣϥ̄, ⲁⲩⲛⲟϫϥ̄ ⲉ ⲡⲉϣⲧⲉⲕⲟ.

3. ⲙ̄ⲡⲟⲩⲉⲓⲙⲉ ⲛ̄ϭⲓ ⲡⲙⲏⲛϣⲉ ϫⲉ ⲛ̄ⲧⲟϥ ⲡⲉ ⲡⲉⲭⲣⲓⲥⲧⲟⲥ.

4. ⲛ̄ϣⲁϫⲉ ⲛⲉ ⲛⲁⲓ ⲙ̄ ⲡⲁⲓⲁⲃⲟⲗⲟⲥ. ⲙ̄ⲡⲣ̄ⲥⲟⲧⲙⲟⲩ.

5. ⲁϥⲉⲓⲙⲉ ⲙ̄ ⲡⲉⲟⲩⲟⲉⲓϣ ϫⲉ ⲁ-ⲡⲉϥⲉⲓⲱⲧ ⲙⲟⲩ.

6. ⲛⲓⲙ ⲡⲉⲛⲧⲁϥⲍⲁⲣⲉⲍ ⲉⲣⲱⲧⲛ̄ ⲉⲃⲟⲗ ⲍⲛ̄ ⲛ̄ϫⲓϫⲉⲉⲩⲉ?

7. ⲛ̄ⲧⲉⲣⲉⲥⲱ, ⲁⲩⲛ̄ⲧⲥ̄ ⲉ ⲡⲏⲓ ⲛ̄ ⲧⲉⲥⲥⲱⲛⲉ.

8. ⲁϥϫⲱⲕ ⲉⲃⲟⲗ ⲛ̄ ⲛⲉⲍⲟⲟⲩ ⲙ̄ ⲡⲉϥϣⲙ̄ϣⲉ.

9. ⲁⲩⲙⲟⲩⲧⲉ ⲉⲣⲟⲓ ⲙ̄ ⲡⲣⲁⲛ ⲛ̄ ⲧⲁⲙⲁⲁⲩ.

10. ⲁⲩⲙⲟⲩⲧⲉ ⲉ ⲡⲣⲁⲛ ⲙ̄ ⲡϣⲏⲣⲉ ϫⲉ ⲓ̄ⲥ̄.

11. ⲁⲓϣⲙ̄ϣⲉ ⲛⲁϥ ⲛ̄ ⲥⲁϣϥⲉ ⲛ̄ ⲣⲟⲙⲡⲉ.

12. ⲟⲩⲗⲁⲁⲩ ⲡⲉ ⲍⲱⲃ ⲛⲓⲙ ⲉⲛⲧⲁⲕⲁⲁⲩ. 16. ⲛ̄ⲧⲁⲕⲙⲟⲩⲧⲉ ⲉ ⲛⲓⲙ?

13. ⲁ-ⲡⲁⲓⲁⲃⲟⲗⲟⲥ ⲛ̄ⲧϥ̄ ⲉ ⲧⲉⲣⲏⲙⲟⲥ. 17. ⲛ̄ⲧⲁⲧⲉⲧⲛ̄ϭⲛ̄ⲧ ⲛ̄ ⲁϣ ⲛ̄ ⲍⲉ?

14. ⲉⲧⲃⲉ ⲟⲩ ⲙ̄ⲡⲉⲧⲛ̄ⲉⲓⲙⲉ ⲉ ⲛⲁⲥⲃⲱ? 18. ⲛ̄ⲧⲁⲕϭⲙ̄-ⲡⲉⲓⲭⲱⲱⲙⲉ ⲧⲱⲛ?

15. ⲁⲓⲁⲙⲁⲍⲧⲉ ⲙ̄ ⲡⲭⲱⲱⲙⲉ ⲧⲏⲣϥ̄. 19. ⲟⲩⲁϣ ⲙ̄ ⲙⲓⲛⲉ ⲧⲉ ⲧⲉⲓⲥⲃⲱ?

Lesson 18

18.1 The First Present (Pres. I):

ϯⲣⲓⲙⲉ	I am weeping	ⲧⲛ̄ⲣⲓⲙⲉ	we are weeping
ⲕⲣⲓⲙⲉ	you (m.s.) are weeping	ⲧⲉⲧⲛ̄ⲣⲓⲙⲉ	you (pl.) are
ⲧⲉⲣⲓⲙⲉ	you (f.s.) are weeping		weeping
ϥⲣⲓⲙⲉ	he is weeping	ⲥⲉⲣⲓⲙⲉ	they are weeping
ⲥⲣⲓⲙⲉ	she is weeping		

With nominal subject: ⲡⲣⲱⲙⲉ ⲣⲓⲙⲉ   the man is weeping

ⲟⲩⲛ̄-ⲟⲩⲣⲱⲙⲉ ⲣⲓⲙⲉ   a man is weeping.

The prefix of the 2nd pers. fem. sing. also appears as

ⲧⲉⲣ- or ⲧⲣ̄-. ⲟⲩⲛ̄ must be used to introduce an indefinite
nominal subject.

The First Present usually describes action, activity,
or process in progress at the time of speaking. It is
therefore equivalent to the English progressive present
(am weeping, am writing, etc.) except in those English
verbs that do not normally use this form (e.g. think, know,
see, hear, understand, wish, hope, believe), where its
equivalent is the simple present: ϯⲉⲓⲙⲉ I understand,
ϯⲛⲁⲩ I see, etc.

The First Present is negated with ⲛ̄ before the subject
pronoun and ⲁⲛ after the verb: ⲛ̄ϯⲣⲓⲙⲉ ⲁⲛ I am not weeping.
The second pers. ⲛ̄ⲕⲣⲓⲙⲉ ⲁⲛ usually appears as ⲛ̄ⲅⲣⲓⲙⲉ ⲁⲛ,
with ⲅ for ⲕ by assimilation to the preceding ⲛ̄ and with a
shift of the supralinear stroke: ⲛ̄ⲅⲣⲓⲙⲉ to ⲛ̄ⲅ̄ⲣⲓⲙⲉ (i.e. from
·ⲁⲛⲅ- to ⲛⲁⲅ-). A similar shift of the stroke occurs in
the 3rd pers. sing.: ⲛ̄ϥ̄ⲣⲓⲙⲉ ⲁⲛ, ⲛ̄ⲥ̄ⲣⲓⲙⲉ ⲁⲛ. ⲛ̄ is optional
before a nominal subject: (ⲛ̄) ⲡⲣⲱⲙⲉ ⲣⲓⲙⲉ ⲁⲛ. An indefinite
subject requires the negation ⲙⲛ̄; no ⲁⲛ is used: ⲙⲛ̄-(ⲟⲩ)ⲣⲱⲙⲉ
ⲣⲓⲙⲉ no man (or no one) is weeping. As in the negative of
predications of existence, the indefinite article is usually
omitted if the negation is felt as general rather than
particular.

The infinitives ⲃⲱⲕ and ⲉⲓ are not used in the First
Present.

With the sole exception of ⲟⲩⲱϣ (to wish, love), the
prenominal and presuffixal forms of the infinitive cannot
be used in the First Present. Certain compound verbs are
an exception to this rule and will be considered in a later
lesson.

The pronominal prefixes of the First Present and its
negative are also used before adverbial predicates:

    ϯ₂ⲛ̄ ⲡⲏⲓ   I am in the house.
    ⲛ̄ⲥⲉ₂ⲛ̄ ⲡⲏⲓ ⲁⲛ   They are not in the house.

18.2 The First Future (Fut. I) is formed by prefixing
ⲛⲁ- to the Infinitive. Inflection is exactly like that of
the First Present, including its negative:

ϯⲛⲁⲣⲓⲙⲉ, ⲕⲛⲁⲣⲓⲙⲉ ...	Neg. ⲛ̄ϯⲛⲁⲣⲓⲙⲉ ⲁⲛ, ⲛ̄ⲅⲛⲁⲣⲓⲙⲉ ⲁⲛ ...
ⲡⲣⲱⲙⲉ ⲛⲁⲣⲓⲙⲉ	(ⲙ̄) ⲡⲣⲱⲙⲉ ⲛⲁⲣⲓⲙⲉ ⲁⲛ
ⲟⲩⲛ-ⲟⲩⲣⲱⲙⲉ ⲛⲁⲣⲓⲙⲉ	ⲙ̄ⲛ̄-ⲣⲱⲙⲉ ⲛⲁⲣⲓⲙⲉ

The First Future corresponds to the English simple future
(I shall write, I shall go) or to the intended (planned)
future (I am going to write, going to go). The 2nd pers.
pl. commonly appears as ⲧⲉⲧⲛⲁ- for expected ⲧⲉⲧⲛ̄ⲛⲁ-.

18.3 The term *intransitive* as applied to Coptic verbs
requires a further comment (cf. § 17.4). Coptic has many
intransitive verbs, such as verbs of motion (ⲉⲓ, ⲃⲱⲕ, ⲙⲟⲟϣⲉ)
and verbs denoting activities involving no direct object
(ⲣⲓⲙⲉ, ⲛ̄ⲕⲟⲧⲕ̄, etc.), whose classification is not problema-
tic. But the intransitive use of verbs that are also transitive requires some attention. In certain situations any
transitive verb may be used intransitively: the object may
be omitted because it is understood from the context, or
the speaker may wish to predicate the action of the verb
without reference to any particular object (e.g. *we plowed
all day* as opposed to *we plowed the field*). This usage is
as commonplace in Coptic as it is in English and will not
be noted in the vocabularies or final glossary. There is
another type of intransitive usage, however, that is quite
different. Compare the following:

1) ⲛ̄ⲧⲉⲣⲉϥϫⲱⲕ ⲛ̄ ⲛⲉϥϩⲟⲟⲩ ⲉⲃⲟⲗ   when he had completed his days
2) ⲛ̄ⲧⲉⲣⲉ-ⲛⲉϥϩⲟⲟⲩ ϫⲱⲕ ⲉⲃⲟⲗ   when his days were completed.

(1) is the normal active transitive use of ϫⲱⲕ ⲉⲃⲟⲗ; (2)
involves a change in voice from active to passive (or medio-
passive, as a more general term). For speakers of English
this medio-passive usage offers no problem since many
English verbs have the same ambiguity: *he closed the door*

vs. *the door closed; he burned the paper* vs. *the paper burned*. In the vocabularies and final glossary the designation *intr.* before the meaning of a verb whose transitive meaning is given first will always refer to this medio-passive usage. Of the transitive verbs introduced up to this point, the following have important medio-passive uses:

ϫⲱⲕ ⲉⲃⲟⲗ intr. to be completed, finished, fulfilled; to die.

ϩⲱⲡ intr. to hide (oneself).

ⲃⲱⲗ ⲉⲃⲟⲗ intr. to be melted, scattered, dispersed; to come undone, be loosened; to go to pieces.

ⲧⲱⲙ intr. to shut, close (subject: door, eyes, mouth, etc.).

ⲟⲩⲱⲛ intr. to open.

ⲟⲩⲱϩ intr. to settle, dwell; to alight (on: ϩⲓϫⲛ̄, ⲉⲛⲉⲥⲏⲧ ϩⲓϫⲛ̄).

ⲙⲟⲩϩ intr. to become filled, full (of, with: ⲙ̄ⲙⲟˉ).

18.4 Infinitives of the type ⲕⲱⲧⲉ (to turn), with stressed -ⲱ- and final unstressed -ⲉ, have the same prenominal and presuffixal forms as the type ⲕⲱⲧ:

ⲕⲱⲧⲉ   ⲕⲉⲧ—   ⲕⲟⲧˉ   to turn.

ⲛⲟⲩϫⲉ (to throw), with -ⲟⲩ- for -ⲱ- because of initial ⲛ (cf. p. xvi) also belongs to this type; the infinitive ⲛⲟⲩϫ mentioned in Voc. 14 is a less frequent variant. Infinitives with -ⲱⲱ- and final -ⲉ have similar forms:

ϣⲱⲱϭⲉ   ϣⲉⲉϭⲉ—   ϣⲟⲟϭˉ   to strike, wound.

18.5 Greek verbs occur frequently in Coptic texts. These have a single fixed infinitive form resembling the Greek imperative form and are inflected like any other Coptic verb. Examples:

ⲡⲓⲥⲧⲉⲩⲉ	πιστεύω	to believe (ⲉ)
ⲉⲡⲓⲧⲓⲙⲁ	ἐπιτιμάω	to rebuke (ⲛⲁˉ)
ⲡⲉⲓⲣⲁⲍⲉ	πειράζω	to tempt (ⲙ̄ⲙⲟˉ)
ⲛⲏⲥⲧⲉⲩⲉ	νηστεύω	to fast
ⲁⲣⲭⲓ	ἄρχω	to begin (+ ⲛ̄ + Inf.: to begin to do something).

Vocabulary 18

ⲕⲱⲧⲉ ⲕⲉⲧ– ⲕⲟⲧ⸗ vb. tr. to turn (ⲙ̄ⲙⲟ⸗; away: ⲉⲃⲟⲗ; back:
ⲉⲡⲁϩⲟⲩ); intr. to rotate, circulate; to surround, go
around (ⲉ); to consort (with: ⲙⲛ̄).

ⲥϩⲁⲓ vb. tr. to write (ⲙ̄ⲙⲟ⸗; on, in: ⲉ, ⲉⲝⲛ̄, ϩⲓ, ϩⲓⲝⲛ̄, ϩⲛ̄;
to: ⲛⲁ⸗, ⲉ, ϣⲁ); to register; to draw, paint; as n.m.
writing, letter.

ϭⲱϣⲧ̄ vb. intr. to look, glance (at: ⲉ, ⲉⲝⲛ̄, ⲛ̄ⲥⲁ, ⲉϩⲟⲩⲛ ⲉ);
ϭⲱϣⲧ̄ (ⲉⲃⲟⲗ) ϩⲏⲧ⸗ to look forward to, expect, await.
Often with ⲉⲃⲟⲗ, ⲉϩⲟⲩⲛ, ⲉϩⲣⲁⲓ, ⲉⲡⲉⲥⲏⲧ.

ⲥⲟⲟⲩⲛ̄ vb. tr. to know (ⲙ̄ⲙⲟ⸗; about: ⲉⲧⲃⲉ; how to: ⲛ̄ + Inf.;
that: ϫⲉ); to recognize, be acquainted with; as n.m.
knowledge.

ⲙⲉⲉⲩⲉ vb. intr. to think, suppose (that: ϫⲉ; about: ⲉ); to
ponder, consider (often + ⲉⲃⲟⲗ); as n.m. thought, mind.

ⲕⲱⲧⲉ n.m. neighborhood, surroundings; ⲛ̄/ϩⲙ̄ ⲡⲕⲱⲧⲉ ⲛ̄ in the
neighborhood of, near, around; pron. obj. are expressed
w. poss. prefixes: ⲙ̄ ⲡⲉϥⲕⲱⲧⲉ around him.

ϩⲏⲧ⸗ prep. forward to, before; used idiomatically with certain verbs, like ϭⲱϣⲧ̄ above and ⲡⲱⲧ ⲉⲃⲟⲗ to flee (ϩⲏⲧ⸗:
from); anticipatory suffix is required.

ⲉⲃⲟⲗ ϫⲉ, ⲉⲧⲃⲉ ϫⲉ conj. because.

ⲡ.ϫⲁⲉⲓⲉ desert, wilderness.

ⲧⲉ.ϭⲣⲟⲟⲙⲡⲉ, ⲡⲉ.ϭⲣⲟⲟⲙⲡⲉ dove.

ⲃⲗ̄ⲗⲉ (pl. ⲃⲗ̄ⲗⲉⲉⲩ, ⲃⲗ̄ⲗⲉⲩⲉ) adj. blind.

And the Greek verbs in §18.5 above.

Exercises

(1) ⲁ–ⲡⲉϥϩⲱⲃ ϫⲱⲕ ⲉⲃⲟⲗ. (2) ⲥⲉⲛⲁⲙⲟⲩϩ ⲛ̄ ⲣⲁϣⲉ ⲛ̄ϭⲓ ⲛⲉⲛⲯⲩⲭⲏ.
(3) ⲛ̄ϯⲡⲓⲥⲧⲉⲩⲉ ⲉⲣⲟⲕ ⲁⲛ. (4) ϯⲛⲁϩⲱⲡ ϩⲙ̄ ⲡϫⲁⲉⲓⲉ. (5) ⲁ–
ⲡⲁⲓⲁⲃⲟⲗⲟⲥ ⲡⲉⲓⲣⲁⲍⲉ ⲙ̄ⲙⲟϥ ⲛ̄ ⲥⲁϣϥ̄ ⲛ̄ ϩⲟⲟⲩ. (6) ⲡⲉⲡⲛ̄ⲁ̄ ⲛ̄ ⲁⲕⲁⲑⲁⲣ–
ⲧⲟⲛ ⲟⲩⲱϣ ⲁⲛ ⲉ ⲉⲓ ⲉⲃⲟⲗ. (7) ⲙ̄ ⲡⲉⲟⲩⲟⲉⲓϣ ⲡⲉⲓⲕⲟⲥⲙⲟⲥ ⲧⲏⲣϥ̄ ⲛⲁ–
ⲃⲱⲗ ⲉⲃⲟⲗ. (8) ⲁ–ⲡⲃⲗ̄ⲗⲉ ϫⲟⲟⲥ ϫⲉ ⲛⲁ ⲛⲁⲓ, ⲡⲁϫⲟⲉⲓⲥ. (9) ⲁ–ⲡⲛⲁⲩ
ⲙ̄ ⲡⲉϥϣⲙ̄ϣⲉ ϫⲱⲕ ⲉⲃⲟⲗ. (10) ⲛ̄ⲧⲛ̄ⲛⲁⲟⲩⲱϩ ⲁⲛ ϩⲛ̄ ⲧⲉⲓⲭⲱⲣⲁ.

(11) ϯⲙⲉⲉⲩⲉ ϫⲉ ⲛ̄ⲧⲟⲕ ⲟⲩⲁⲓⲕⲁⲓⲟⲥ ⲡⲉ. (12) ⲛ̄ⲃⲁⲗ ⲛ̄ ⲛ̄ⲃⲗ̄ⲗⲉⲩⲉ
ⲛⲁⲟⲩⲱⲛ. (13) ⲕⲙⲉⲉⲩⲉ ϫⲉ ⲁⲛⲅ̄-ⲛⲓⲙ? (14) ⲉⲧⲃⲉ ⲟⲩ ⲧⲉⲧⲛ̄ⲕⲱⲧⲉ ⲙⲛ̄
ϩⲉⲛⲣⲱⲙⲉ ⲛ̄ ⲧⲉⲓⲙⲓⲛⲉ? (15) ⲁ-ⲛⲉϥⲥⲛⲁⲩ₂ ⲃⲱⲗ ⲉⲃⲟⲗ ⲛ̄ ⲛⲉϥⲟⲩⲉⲣⲏⲧⲉ.
(16) ⲁⲩϩⲱⲡ ⲛ̄ϭⲓ ⲛⲉⲥⲛⲏⲩ ⲉ ⲙ̄ⲙⲁⲧⲟⲓ ⲙ̄ ⲡⲣ̄ⲣⲟ. (17) ⲉⲧⲃⲉ ⲟⲩ
ⲕⲉⲡⲓⲧⲓⲙⲁ ⲛⲁⲓ? (18) ⲛ̄ⲧⲉⲧⲛ̄ⲁⲉⲓⲙⲉ ⲁⲛ ⲉ ⲛⲉϥⲡⲁⲣⲁⲃⲟⲗⲏ. (19)
ⲛ̄ⲥⲉⲛⲁⲡⲓⲥⲧⲉⲩⲉ ⲉ ⲛⲁϣⲁϫⲉ ⲁⲛ. (20) ⲛ̄ϫⲓⲭⲉⲉⲩⲉ ⲛⲁⲕⲱⲧⲉ ⲉ ⲡⲉⲛϯⲙⲉ.
(21) ⲁ-ⲧⲡⲉ ⲟⲩⲱⲛ, ⲁϥⲉⲓ ⲉⲃⲟⲗ ⲛ̄ϭⲓ ⲟⲩⲛⲟϭ ⲛ̄ ⲟⲩⲟⲉⲓⲛ. (22) ⲁ-
ⲧⲉⲥϩⲓⲙⲉ ⲁⲣⲭⲉⲓ ⲛ̄ ⲣⲓⲙⲉ. (23) ⲙⲉϣⲁⲕ ⲥⲉⲛⲁⲕⲉⲧ-ⲧⲏⲩⲧⲛ̄ ⲉⲡⲁϩⲟⲩ.
(24) ⲛ̄ϣⲟⲟⲥ ϩⲁⲣⲉϩ ⲉ ⲛⲉⲥⲟⲟⲩ ϩⲛ̄ ⲧⲥⲱϣⲉ. (25) ⲁ-ⲛⲉϥⲃⲁⲗ ⲧⲱⲙ ϩⲙ̄
ⲡⲙⲟⲩ. (26) ⲥⲉⲛⲁⲟⲩⲱϩ₂ ϩⲙ̄ ⲡⲕⲱⲧⲉ ⲛ̄ ⲑⲓ̄ⲗⲏ̄ⲙ̄. (27) ϯⲛⲁⲛⲉϫ-ⲡⲁϥ ⲉ
ⲛⲉⲩϩⲟⲟⲣ. (28) ⲧⲛ̄ⲛⲁⲙⲟⲩⲧⲉ ⲉⲣⲟϥ ⲙ̄ ⲡⲣⲁⲛ ⲙ̄ ⲡⲉϥⲉⲓⲱⲧ. (29) ⲁⲛϣⲉⲡ-
ⲧⲉⲡⲓⲥⲧⲟⲗⲏ ⲉⲛⲧⲁⲕϩⲁⲓ ⲙ̄ⲙⲟⲥ ⲛⲁⲛ. (30) ⲉⲧⲃⲉ ⲟⲩ ⲧⲉⲧⲛ̄ⲛⲏⲥⲧⲉⲩⲉ ⲛ̄
ⲟⲩⲟⲉⲓϣ ⲛⲓⲙ? (31) ⲁ-ⲛⲉⲥⲃⲁⲗ ⲙⲟⲩϩ₂ ⲛ̄ ⲣⲙ̄ⲉⲓⲟⲟⲩⲉ. (32) ⲛ̄ⲥⲉϩⲓ
ⲧⲉϩⲓⲏ ⲁⲛ. (33) ⲛ̄ⲧⲉⲣⲉϥⲥⲱⲧⲙ̄ ⲉ ⲡⲉϩⲣⲟⲟⲩ, ⲁϥϭⲱϣⲧ̄ ⲉⲃⲟⲗ. (34)
ϯⲣⲓⲙⲉ ⲉⲃⲟⲗ ϫⲉ ⲁ-ⲡⲁⲥⲟⲛ ⲙⲟⲩ. (35) ⲁ-ⲧⲉϭⲣⲟⲟⲙⲡⲉ ⲟⲩⲱϩ₂ ⲉϫⲙ̄
ⲡⲃⲏⲙⲁ. (36) ⲥⲉⲙⲉⲉⲩⲉ ϫⲉ ⲛ̄ⲧⲟϥ ⲡⲉ ⲡⲉⲭ̄ⲥ̄. (37) ⲛ̄ⲧⲉⲥⲟⲟⲩⲛ̄ ⲁⲛ ⲛ̄
ⲥϩⲁⲓ. (38) ⲉⲡⲓⲧⲓⲙⲁ ⲛⲁⲩ ⲉⲧⲃⲉ ⲛⲉⲩⲛⲟⲃⲉ. (39) ⲧⲛ̄ϭⲱϣⲧ̄ ⲉⲃⲟⲗ
ϩⲏⲧϥ̄ ⲙ̄ ⲡⲉϩⲟⲟⲩ ⲉⲧ ⲙ̄ⲙⲁⲩ. (40) ⲙ̄ⲡⲉϥⲟⲩⲱϣ ⲉ ⲛⲏⲥⲧⲉⲩⲉ. (41) ⲁ-
ⲡⲉⲡⲛ̄ⲁ̄ ⲉⲓ ⲉⲡⲉⲥⲏⲧ ⲉϫⲱϥ ⲛ̄ ⲑⲉ ⲛ̄ ⲟⲩϭⲣⲟⲟⲙⲡⲉ. (42) ⲛⲁⲓ ⲛⲉ ⲛ̄ϣⲁϫⲉ
ⲉⲛⲧⲁϥϩⲁⲓ ⲙ̄ⲙⲟⲟⲩ ϩⲙ̄ ⲡⲭⲱⲱⲙⲉ. (43) ⲛ̄ⲧⲛ̄ⲥⲟⲟⲩⲛ̄ ⲁⲛ ⲛ̄ ⲛ̄ϣⲁϫⲉ ⲛ̄ ⲁⲗⲁ.
(44) ϯⲥⲟⲟⲩⲛ̄ ϫⲉ ⲛ̄ⲧⲟⲕ ⲡⲉ ⲡϣⲏⲣⲉ ⲙ̄ ⲡⲛⲟⲩⲧⲉ. (45) ⲁⲩϩⲱⲛ ⲉϩⲟⲩⲛ ⲉ
ⲧⲡⲩⲗⲏ ⲁⲩⲱ ⲁⲩⲧⲟⲙⲥ̄. (46) ⲛ̄ⲥ̄ϩ₂ⲙ̄ ⲡⲏⲓ ⲁⲛ. (47) ⲧⲛ̄ⲥⲟⲟⲩⲛ̄ ϫⲉ ⲟⲩⲛⲟϭ
ⲧⲉ ⲧⲉϥⲥⲃⲱ. (48) ϯⲛⲁⲡⲱⲧ ⲉⲃⲟⲗ ϩⲛ̄ⲧⲟⲩ ⲉ ⲡⲭⲗⲉⲓⲉ. (49) ⲁϥ₂ⲕⲟ
ⲉⲙⲁⲧⲉ ⲉⲃⲟⲗ ϫⲉ ⲁϥⲛⲏⲥⲧⲉⲩⲉ ⲛ̄ ϣⲙⲟⲩⲛ ⲛ̄ ϩⲟⲟⲩ. (50) ⲉⲧⲃⲉ ⲟⲩ ⲧⲉⲓ-
ⲭⲏⲣⲁ ⲛ̄ ϩⲏⲕⲉ ⲙⲟⲟϣⲉ ⲛ̄ⲥⲱⲓ? (51) ⲁϥⲁⲣⲭⲓ ⲛ̄ ϣⲁϫⲉ ⲙⲛ̄ ⲡⲙⲏⲏϣⲉ.
(52) ⲁϥⲕⲱⲧⲉ ⲛ̄ ⲛ̄ϩⲏⲕⲉ ⲉⲃⲟⲗ. (53) ϯⲥⲟⲟⲩⲛ̄ ⲙ̄ⲙⲟⲕ. ⲛ̄ⲧⲟⲕ ⲡⲉ
ⲡⲁⲓⲁⲃⲟⲗⲟⲥ. (54) ⲉⲧⲃⲉ ⲟⲩ ⲕⲡⲉⲓⲣⲁⲍⲉ ⲙ̄ⲙⲟⲓ ⲛ̄ ⲧⲉⲓϩⲉ? (55) ⲛ̄ⲥⲉⲙ̄
ⲡⲉϥⲕⲱⲧⲉ ⲁⲛ. (56) ⲧⲉⲧⲛⲁⲥⲟⲟⲩⲛ̄ ϫⲉ ⲛ̄ⲧⲁⲓⲣ̄-ⲛⲁⲓ ⲉⲧⲃⲉ-ⲧⲏⲩⲧⲛ̄.
(57) ϯⲛⲁⲱⲡ ⲛ̄ ⲛⲉⲭⲛⲏⲩ ⲉⲧ ϩⲛ̄ ⲧⲉⲙⲣⲱ. (58) ⲛ̄ⲧⲉⲣⲛ̄-ⲟⲩⲱϣ ⲉ ⲃⲱⲕ
ⲉⲃⲟⲗ, ⲁⲩⲕⲟⲧⲛ̄ ⲉⲡⲁϩⲟⲩ ⲉ ⲡⲉⲛⲏⲓ.

Lesson 19

19.1 The relative forms of the First Present and
First Future employ the relative pronoun ⲉⲧ, ⲉⲧⲉ. When
the relative pronoun is the subject of the relative clause,
no further pronominal subject element is required:

ⲡⲣⲱⲙⲉ ⲉⲧ ⲣⲓⲙⲉ	the man who is weeping
ⲛⲉⲧ ⲥⲱⲧⲙ̅ ⲉ ⲛⲁϣⲁϫⲉ	those who hear my words
ⲙ̅ⲙⲁⲧⲟⲓ ⲉⲧ ⲛⲁⲁⲙⲁϩⲧⲉ ⲙ̅ⲙⲟϥ	the soldiers who will seize him
ⲛ̅ⲡⲣⲱⲙⲉ ⲉⲧ ⲛⲁⲉⲓⲛⲉ ⲙ̅ ⲡϩⲁⲧ	the men who will bring the silver.

When the relative pronoun is not the subject of the relative clause, a subject noun or pronoun and resumptive pronouns are required; the relative pronoun combines with the
various subject elements as follows:

ⲉϯ	who/which I ...	ⲉⲧⲛ̅	
ⲉⲧⲕ̅	who/which you ...	ⲉⲧⲉⲧⲛ̅	
ⲉⲧⲉ(ⲣ)	etc.		
ⲉⲧϥ̅		ⲉⲧⲟⲩ	(note this form)
ⲉⲧⲥ̅			

With nominal subject: ⲉⲧⲉⲣⲉ-ⲡⲣⲱⲙⲉ who/which the man ...
Study the following examples carefully:

ⲛ̅ϣⲁϫⲉ ⲉϯⲥϩⲁⲓ ⲙ̅ⲙⲟⲟⲩ	the words which I am writing
ⲡⲣⲱⲙⲉ ⲉⲧⲕ̅ϣⲓⲛⲉ ⲛ̅ⲥⲱϥ	the man whom you are seeking
ⲧⲡⲟⲗⲓⲥ ⲉⲧⲟⲩⲟⲩⲱϩ ⲛ̅ϩⲏⲧⲥ̅	the city in which they are settling
ⲡϣⲏⲣⲉ ⲉⲧϥ̅ⲛⲁⲕⲁⲁϥ ⲛ̅ⲥⲱϥ	the child whom he will leave behind
ⲛⲉⲛⲧⲟⲗⲏ ⲉⲧϥ̅ⲛⲁⲧⲁⲁⲩ ⲛⲁⲛ	the commandments which he will give to us
ⲡϩⲁⲧ ⲉⲧⲉⲣⲉ-ⲡⲉⲕⲉⲓⲱⲧ ⲛⲁⲧⲁⲁϥ ⲉⲧⲟⲟⲧⲕ̅	the money which your father will entrust to you

When the verb of the relative clause is negative Pres. I
or Fut. I, the relative pronoun is ⲉⲧⲉ and subject as well
as resumptive pronouns must be expressed in all constructions:

ⲚⲢⲰⲘⲈ ⲈⲦⲈ ⲚⲤⲈⲤⲰⲦⲘ̄ ⲚⲀⲒ ⲀⲚ   the men who do not heed me
ⲡⲢⲰⲘⲈ ⲈⲦⲈ ⲚϤⲚⲀⲤⲰⲦⲘ̄ ⲚⲀⲒ ⲀⲚ   the man who will not heed me
Ⲛ̄ϢⲀϪⲈ ⲈⲦⲈ Ⲛ̄ⲦⲚ̄ⲈⲒⲘⲈ ⲈⲢⲟⲞⲨ ⲀⲚ   the words which we do not understand

ⲚⲈⲦⲘⲈ ⲈⲦⲈ Ⲛ̄ⲤⲈⲚⲀⲀⲘⲀ₂ⲦⲈ   the villages which they will
     Ⲙ̄ⲘⲟⲞⲨ ⲀⲚ   not seize

    19.2 The direct object of a transitive verb may be used in a reflexive sense:

ⲀⲒⲚⲟⲬⲦ̄ ⲈⲠⲈⲤⲎⲦ Ⲉ ⲠⲔⲀ₂.   I threw myself to the ground.
ⲀϤⲈⲒⲀⲀϤ ₂Ⲙ̄ ⲠⲘⲟⲞⲨ Ⲙ̄ ⲠⲈⲒⲈⲢⲟ.   He washed himself in the water of the river.

Some verbs have special meanings in the reflexive, e.g.

   ⲞⲨⲀ₂⸗ Ⲛ̄ⲤⲀ to place oneself in the following of, go in accordance with; also simply "to follow."
   ⲔⲞⲦ⸗ (1) to return, go back (to: ⲈⲠⲀ₂ⲞⲨ Ⲉ, ⲈⲂⲟⲖ Ⲉ, ⲈⲂⲟⲖ ϢⲀ, Ⲉ₂ⲞⲨⲚ Ⲉ, Ⲉ₂ⲢⲀⲒ Ⲉ); (2) to repeat an action, usually coordinated, as in

     ⲀϤⲔⲞⲦϤ̄ ⲀϤⲢⲒⲘⲈ   he wept again

or with Ⲉ + Inf., as in

     Ⲙ̄ⲠⲈⲚⲔⲞⲦⲚ̄ Ⲉ ⲚⲀⲨ ⲈⲢⲟⲤ   we did not see her again.

The verb ⲦⲰⲞⲨⲚ occurs optionally with reflexive suffixes: ⲀϤⲦⲰⲞⲨⲚϤ̄ = ⲀϤⲦⲰⲞⲨⲚ (he arose). After stem-final -Ⲛ the 2nd pers. masc. sing. suffix -Ⲕ often appears as -Ⲅ: ⲀⲔⲦⲰⲞⲨⲚⲄ̄ you arose.

    The reflexive verb Ⲁ₂ⲈⲢⲀⲦ⸗, to stand, is actually a compound of Ⲁ₂Ⲉ (a form of the verb Ⲱ₂Ⲉ, to stand) and the preposition ⲈⲢⲀⲦ⸗ to or at the foot/feet of. ⲈⲢⲀⲦ⸗ itself consists of the prep. Ⲉ and the noun ⲢⲀⲦ⸗ foot, which belongs to that small group of nouns that may take pronominal suffixes in a possessive sense: ⲢⲀⲦ my foot, ⲢⲀⲦⲔ̄, your foot, etc.

    19.3 Infinitives of the type ⲤⲰⲦⲚ̄, to choose,

constitute the largest class of verbs in Coptic and have
the following prenominal and presuffixal forms:

ϲⲱⲧⲛ̄   ϲⲉⲧⲛ̄-   ϲⲟⲧⲡⲉ

When the final consonant of the infinitive is a *blmnr* consonant, the presuffixal form is usually written with -ⲉ-
before the suffixes -ⲧ, -ⲕ, -ϥ, -ⲥ: ϲⲟⲧⲙⲉϥ, ϲⲟⲧⲙⲉⲧ, ϲⲟⲧⲙⲉⲕ,
etc. When the final consonant is -ⲍ, spelling alternates
between -ⲍ and -ⲗⲍ in the unbound form: ⲟⲩⲱⲛⲗⲍ or ⲟⲩⲱⲛⲍ̄.

When the second consonant of the Infinitive is ⲍ
(more rarely ϣ), the presuffixal form may have -ⲗ- instead
of -ⲟ-:

ⲟⲩⲱⲍⲙ̄	ⲟⲩⲉⲍⲛ̄-	ⲟⲩⲗⲍⲙⲉ	to repeat
ⲧⲱⲍⲙ̄	ⲧⲉⲍⲛ̄-	ⲧⲗⲍⲙⲉ	to invite

When the infinitive begins with ⲙ or ⲛ, -ⲱ- is replaced
with -ⲟⲩ-:

ⲙⲟⲩⲟⲩⲧ	ⲙⲉⲩⲧ-	ⲙⲟⲟⲩⲧⲉ	to kill
ⲛⲟⲩⲍⲙ̄	ⲛⲉⲍⲛ̄-	ⲛⲗⲍⲙⲉ	to rescue.

Vocabulary 19

ϣⲓⲃⲉ ϣⲃ̄(ⲧ)- ϣⲃ̄ⲧⲉ vb. tr. to change, alter (ⲙ̄ⲙⲟⲉ); intr.
and reflex. to change, be altered (to: ⲉ; into: ⲍⲛ̄; in
form: ⲛ̄ ⲥⲙⲟⲧ).

ⲗⲍⲉⲣⲁⲧⲉ vb. reflex. to stand (before: ⲉ; against: ⲉ, ⲉⲝⲛ̄,
ⲟⲩⲃⲉ; with: ⲙⲛ̄).

ⲟⲩⲱⲛⲍ̄ ⲟⲩⲉⲛⲍ̄- ⲟⲩⲟⲛⲍⲉ (often + ⲉⲃⲟⲗ) vb. tr. to reveal, make
manifest (ⲙ̄ⲙⲟⲉ; to: ⲛⲁⲉ, ⲉ); reflex. to appear, reveal
self; intr. to appear, become manifest.

ϭⲱⲗⲡ̄ ϭⲉⲗⲡ̄- ϭⲟⲗⲡⲉ (usually + ⲉⲃⲟⲗ) vb. tr. to reveal (ⲙ̄ⲙⲟⲉ;
to: ⲉ, ⲛⲁⲉ); vb. intr. to become revealed, known, clear.

ⲣⲱⲕⲍ̄ ⲣⲉⲕⲍ̄- ⲣⲟⲕⲍⲉ vb. tr. to burn (ⲙ̄ⲙⲟⲉ); vb. intr. to burn.

ⲡⲱⲍⲧ̄ ⲡⲉⲍⲧ̄- ⲡⲗⲍⲧⲉ vb. intr. and reflex. to bow, prostrate
self.

ⲡⲉ.ⲥⲙⲟⲧ form, likeness, appearance; character, behavior.

ⲧⲉ.ⲥⲙⲏ voice, sound.

ⲡ.ⲕⲱ₂ⲧ̄ fire.

ⲃⲣ̄ⲣⲉ adj. new, young; ⲛ̄ ⲃⲣ̄ⲣⲉ recently, anew.

ⲗⲥ adj. old (not used of persons).

Greek words

ⲧⲉ.ⲅⲣⲁⲫⲏ (ἡ γραφή) writing, scripture.

ⲧ.ⲉⲝⲟⲩⲥⲓⲁ (ἡ ἐξουσία) power, authority.

ⲧ.ⲡⲓⲥⲧⲓⲥ (ἡ πίστις) faith, trust.

ⲡ.ⲙⲩⲥⲧⲏⲣⲓⲟⲛ (τὸ μυστήριον) mystery.

Exercises

A. (1) ⲡⲱⲛⲉ ⲉⲧⲟⲩⲙⲟⲩⲣ ⲙ̄ ⲡⲭⲟⲓ ⲉⲣⲟϥ   (2) ⲡⲭⲱⲱⲙⲉ ⲉϯⲟⲩⲗϣϥ̄

(3) ⲡ₂ⲟⲉⲓⲧⲉ ⲉⲧϥ̄ϯ ⲙ̄ⲙⲟϥ ₂ⲓⲱⲱϥ   (4) ⲡⲉϥⲧⲉⲕⲟ ⲉⲧⲟⲩⲛⲁⲛⲟⲭⲕ̄ ⲉⲣⲟϥ

(5) ⲡⲙⲟⲟⲩ ⲉⲧ ⲙⲟⲩ₂ ⲙ̄ ⲡⲉⲛⲭⲟⲓ   (6) ⲡ̄ⲣⲱⲙⲉ ⲉⲧ ⲛⲁⲡⲱⲧ ⲉ ⲡⲭⲗⲉⲓⲉ

(7) ⲧⲉⲭⲱⲣⲁ ⲉⲧⲛ̄ⲛ̄₂ⲏⲧⲥ̄   (8) ⲛⲉⲧ ⲛⲁⲟⲩⲁ₂ⲟⲩ ⲛ̄ⲥⲱϥ   (9) ⲧⲉⲡⲓⲥⲧⲟⲗⲏ

ⲉϯⲛⲁⲥ₂ⲁⲓ ⲙ̄ⲙⲟⲥ ϣⲁⲣⲟⲕ   (10) ⲧⲉ₂ⲓⲏ ⲉⲧⲟⲩⲙⲟⲟϣⲉ ₂ⲓⲱⲱⲥ   (11) ⲡⲥⲁ₂

ⲉⲧⲉ ⲛ̄ⲧⲉⲧⲛ̄ⲥⲟⲟⲩⲛ̄ ⲙ̄ⲙⲟϥ ⲁⲛ   (12) ⲛⲉⲧ ⲛⲁⲗ₂ⲉⲣⲁⲧⲟⲩ ⲙ̄ ⲡⲉϥⲙ̄ⲧⲟ ⲉⲃⲟⲗ

(13) ⲡⲥⲟⲛ ⲉⲧⲛ̄ⲛⲁⲙⲟⲣϥ̄ ⲙ̄ ⲡⲉⲥⲭⲏⲙⲁ   (14) ⲡⲣ̄ⲣⲟ ⲉⲧⲛ̄ⲡⲱⲧ ⲉⲃⲟⲗ ₂ⲏⲧϥ̄

(15) ⲡⲉⲧ ⲟⲩⲱⲛ ⲛ̄ ⲛ̄ⲃⲁⲗ ⲛ̄ ⲛ̄ⲃⲗ̄ⲗⲉⲉⲩ   (16) ⲡ̄ⲣⲱⲙⲉ ⲉⲧϥ̄ⲕⲱⲧⲉ ⲛ̄ⲙ̄ⲙⲁⲩ

(17) ⲛ̄ϣⲁⲭⲉ ⲉϯⲟⲩⲉϣ-ⲥⲟⲧⲙⲟⲩ   (18) ⲧⲉⲝⲟⲩⲥⲓⲁ ⲉⲧⲉⲣⲉ-ⲡⲛⲟⲩⲧⲉ ⲛⲁ-

ⲧⲁⲁⲥ ⲛⲁϥ   (19) ⲧⲡⲓⲥⲧⲓⲥ ⲉϯⲉⲓⲛⲉ ⲙ̄ⲙⲟⲥ ₂ⲛ̄ ⲧⲉⲓⲥ₂ⲓⲙⲉ   (20) ⲧⲉ-

ϭⲣⲟⲟⲙⲡⲉ ⲉⲧⲕ̄ⲛⲁⲛⲁⲩ ⲉⲣⲟⲥ   (21) ⲧⲉϥⲧⲏⲛ ⲉⲧⲉⲧⲛ̄ⲛⲟⲩϫⲉ ⲙ̄ⲙⲟⲥ ⲉⲃⲟⲗ

(22) ⲛⲉⲧϥ̄ⲛⲁⲉⲡⲓⲧⲓⲙⲁ ⲛⲁⲩ   (23) ⲡⲙⲩⲥⲧⲏⲣⲓⲟⲛ ⲉⲧϥ̄ⲛⲁϭⲟⲗⲡϥ̄ ⲛⲁⲛ ⲉ-

ⲃⲟⲗ   (24) ⲡⲏⲓ ⲉⲧⲟⲩⲛⲁⲣⲟⲕ₂ϥ̄ ⲛ̄ϭⲓ ⲙ̄ⲙⲁⲧⲟⲓ   (25) ⲡⲥⲁ₂ ⲉϯⲛⲁⲟⲩⲁ₂ⲧ̄

ⲛ̄ⲥⲱϥ   (26) ⲛ̄ϫⲓⲭⲉⲉⲩⲉ ⲉⲧ ⲕⲱⲧⲉ ⲉ ⲧⲉⲛⲡⲟⲗⲓⲥ   (27) ⲡⲃⲏⲙⲁ ⲉⲧϥ̄ⲛⲁ-

ⲁ₂ⲉⲣⲁⲧϥ̄ ₂ⲓⲭⲱϥ   (28) ⲛⲉⲧ ⲡⲉⲓⲣⲁϫⲉ ⲙ̄ⲙⲱⲧⲛ̄   (29) ⲡⲕⲱ₂ⲧ̄ ⲉⲧⲉⲣⲉ-

ⲡⲛⲟⲩⲧⲉ ⲛⲁⲛⲟⲭϥ̄ ⲉⲭⲙ̄ ⲡⲕⲁ₂   (30) ⲧⲉⲥⲙⲏ ⲉⲧⲉⲣⲥⲱⲧⲙ̄ ⲉⲣⲟⲥ   (31) ⲙ̄-

ⲙⲁⲧⲟⲓ ⲉⲧ ⲛⲁⲕⲟⲧⲕ̄ ⲉⲡⲁ₂ⲟⲩ   (32) ⲡ₂ⲟⲉⲓⲧⲉ ⲛ̄ ⲃⲣ̄ⲣⲉ ⲉⲧⲥ̄ⲛⲁϣⲟⲡϥ̄   (33)

ⲛⲉⲧ ⲡⲱ₂ⲧ̄ ⲙ̄ⲙⲟⲟⲩ ⲛ̄ⲡⲁ₂ⲣⲁⲕ   (34) ⲧⲉⲅⲣⲁⲫⲏ ⲉϯⲡⲓⲥⲧⲉⲩⲉ ⲉⲣⲟⲥ   (35)

ⲡ₂ⲁⲧ ⲉⲧⲉⲣⲉ-ⲡϣⲏⲣⲉ ⲛⲁ₂ⲉ ⲉⲣⲟϥ   (36) ⲡⲣⲱⲙⲉ ⲉⲧ ϭⲱϣⲧ̄ ⲉ₂ⲟⲩⲛ ⲉⲣⲟⲛ

(37) ⲡⲙⲁⲉⲓⲛ ⲉⲧⲟⲩⲛⲁⲟⲩⲟⲛ₂ϥ̄ ⲉⲃⲟⲗ   (38) ⲧⲉⲥ₂ⲓⲙⲉ ⲉⲧϥ̄ⲙⲉ ⲙ̄ⲙⲟⲥ

(39) ⲡⲉⲥⲙⲟⲧ ⲉⲧϥ̄ⲟⲩⲱⲛ₂̄ ⲙ̄ⲙⲟϥ ⲉⲃⲟⲗ ⲛ̄₂ⲏⲧϥ̄   (40) ⲛⲉ₂ⲟⲟⲩ ⲉⲧⲉⲧⲛⲁ-

ⲛⲏⲥⲧⲉⲩⲉ ⲛ̄₂ⲏⲧⲟⲩ

B. (1) ⲙ̄ⲡⲣ̄ϣⲃ̄-ⲗⲁⲁⲩ ⲛ̄ ⲛ̄ϣⲁϫⲉ ⲉⲧⲕ̄ⲛⲁϭ̄ⲛⲧⲟⲩ ₂ⲙ̄ ⲡⲉⲓⲭⲱⲱⲙⲉ.   (2)

ⲁⲩⲛⲟϭ ⲙ̄ ⲙⲩⲥⲧⲏⲣⲓⲟⲛ ⲟⲩⲱⲛ₂̄ ⲛⲏⲧⲛ̄   (3) ⲙ̄ ⲡⲉ₂ⲟⲟⲩ ⲉⲧ ⲙ̄ⲙⲁⲩ ⲥⲉⲛⲁ-ϭⲱⲗⲡ̄ ⲉⲃⲟⲗ ⲛ̄ϭⲓ ⲛ̄ϣⲁϫⲉ ⲙ̄ ⲡⲉⲛϫⲟⲉⲓⲥ. (4) ⲁϥϣⲃ̄ⲧϥ̄ ⲛ̄ϭⲓ ⲡⲁⲓⲁⲃⲟⲗⲟⲥ ϩⲙ̄ ⲡⲉⲥⲙⲟⲧ ⲛ̄ ⲟⲩⲁⲅⲅⲉⲗⲟⲥ ⲙ̄ ⲡⲟⲩⲟⲉⲓⲛ. (5) ⲁϥϩⲱⲛ ⲉϩⲟⲩⲛ ⲉ ⲡⲣ̄ⲣⲟ, ⲁϥⲡⲁϩⲧϥ̄, ⲁⲩⲱ ⲙ̄ⲡⲉϥϫⲉ-ⲗⲁⲁⲩ ⲛ̄ ϣⲁϫⲉ. (6) ⲁϣ ⲧⲉ ⲧⲉⲓⲥⲙⲏ ⲉⲧ̇ⲥⲱⲧⲙ̄ ⲉⲣⲟⲥ? (7) ⲁϩⲉⲣⲁⲧⲕ̄ ⲛⲙ̄ⲙⲁⲓ ⲟⲩⲃⲏϥ. (8) ⲁϥⲧ̇ ϩⲓⲱⲱϥ ⲛ̄ ⲧⲉϣⲧⲏⲛ ⲛ̄ ⲁⲥ ⲉⲛⲧⲁⲓⲛⲟϫⲥ̄ ⲉⲃⲟⲗ. (9) ⲛ̄ⲧⲁⲕϭⲓⲛⲉ ⲙ̄ ⲡⲉⲓϫⲱⲱⲙⲉ ⲛ̄ ⲁⲥ ⲧⲱⲛ? (10) ⲁⲩⲁϩⲉⲣⲁⲧⲟⲩ ⲙ̄ ⲡⲉⲙⲧⲟ ⲉⲃⲟⲗ ⲙ̄ ⲡⲛⲟϭ ⲛ̄ ⲣ̄ⲣⲟ. (11) ⲁϥϫⲟⲟⲥ ⲛ̄ϭⲓ ⲡϩⲗ̄ⲗⲟ ϫⲉ ⲧⲱⲟⲩⲛⲅ̄, ⲡⲁϣⲏⲣⲉ. ⲙ̄ⲡⲣ̄ⲡⲁϩⲧⲕ̄ ⲛ̄ ⲧⲉⲓϩⲉ. (12) ⲧⲉⲧⲛⲁⲛⲁⲩ ⲉ ⲛⲉⲧⲉ ⲙ̄ⲡⲉⲧⲛ̄ⲛⲁⲩ ⲉⲣⲟⲟⲩ ϣⲁ ⲡⲟⲟⲩ. (13) ⲥⲉⲛⲁⲣⲟⲕϩⲕ̄ ϩⲛ̄ ⲟⲩⲛⲟϭ ⲛ̄ ⲕⲱϩⲧ̄ ⲙ̄ ⲡⲉϩⲟⲟⲩ ⲉⲧ ⲙ̄ⲙⲁⲩ. (14) ⲁⲩⲧⲱⲟⲩⲛⲟⲩ, ⲁⲩⲕⲟⲧⲟⲩ ⲉϩⲣⲁⲓ ⲉ ⲡⲉⲩⲧ̇ⲙⲉ. (15) ⲙ̄ⲡⲉϥⲕⲟⲧϥ̄ ⲉ ⲁⲗⲉ ⲉ ⲡⲉⲩϫⲟⲓ. (16) ⲙ̄ⲡⲣ̄ⲕⲟⲧⲕ̄ ⲉ ϣⲁϫⲉ ⲛ̄ ⲛⲁⲓ ⲛ̄ ⲗⲁⲁⲩ ⲛ̄ ⲣⲱⲙⲉ.

Lesson 20

20.1 The Inflected (Causative) Infinitive.

ⲧⲣⲁⲥⲱⲧⲙ̄	that I hear		ⲧⲣⲉⲛⲥⲱⲧⲙ̄
ⲧⲣⲉⲕⲥⲱⲧⲙ̄	that you hear	⎰ ⲧⲣⲉⲧⲉⲧⲛ̄ⲥⲱⲧⲙ̄	
ⲧⲣⲉⲥⲱⲧⲙ̄	etc.	⎱ ⲧⲣⲉⲧⲛ̄ⲥⲱⲧⲙ̄	
ⲧⲣⲉϥⲥⲱⲧⲙ̄			ⲧⲣⲉⲩⲥⲱⲧⲙ̄
ⲧⲣⲉⲥⲥⲱⲧⲙ̄			

ⲧⲣⲉ-ⲡⲣⲱⲙⲉ ⲥⲱⲧⲙ̄ that the man hear

Negation is with ⲧⲙ̄- placed either before the whole expression or before the infinitive: ⲧⲙ̄ⲧⲣⲁⲥⲱⲧⲙ̄ or ⲧⲣⲁⲧⲙ̄ⲥⲱⲧⲙ̄ that I not hear.

The Inflected Infinitive is used in the following ways:

(1) As a complementary infinitive, with ⲉ, after appropriate verbs of wishing or commanding when the subject of the infinitive is different from that of the main verb. Contrast

ⲧ̇ⲟⲩⲱϣ ⲉ ϭⲱ ⲙ̄ ⲡⲉⲓⲙⲁ. I want to remain here.

ϯⲟⲩⲱϣ ⲉⲧⲣⲉⲕϭⲱ ⲛ̄ ⲡⲉⲓⲙⲁ.   I want you to remain here.

ⲧⲛ̄ⲟⲩⲱϣ ⲉⲧⲙ̄ⲧⲣⲉⲕⲃⲱⲕ ⲉⲃⲟⲗ.   We want you not to go away.

It is not incorrect, however to say ϯⲟⲩⲱϣ ⲉⲧⲣⲁϭⲱ ⲛ̄ ⲡⲉⲓⲙⲁ, with no change in subject.

(2) Like the ordinary infinitive with ⲉ, the Inflected Infinitive is used in a wide range of result or purpose expressions, often corresponding to English "for ... to ..."

ⲁ-ⲡⲉⲟⲩⲟⲉⲓϣ ϫⲱⲕ ⲉⲃⲟⲗ ⲉⲧⲣⲉⲛⲃⲱⲕ ⲉⲃⲟⲗ.

The time arrived (lit. was fulfilled) for us to leave.

ⲁϥϯ ⲛⲁϥ ⲛ̄ ⲧⲉϫⲟⲩⲥⲓⲁ ⲉⲧⲣⲉϥⲛⲟⲩϫⲉ ⲉⲃⲟⲗ ⲛ̄ ϩⲉⲛⲡⲛ̄ⲁ̄ ⲛ̄ ⲁⲕⲁⲑⲁⲣⲧⲟⲛ.

He gave him the power (for him) to cast out unclean spirits.

Because of the frequent use of the Inflected Infinitive with ⲉ, we shall spell this as a single unit, as in the preceding examples.

(3) With the preposition ϩⲛ̄ + the definite article ⲛ- the Inflected Inf. has the force of a temporal clause with "while, as":

ϩⲙ̄ ⲡⲧⲣⲉϥⲙⲟⲟϣⲉ   while/as he was walking

ϩⲙ̄ ⲡⲧⲣⲉ-ⲡⲟⲩⲏⲏⲃ ϣⲗⲏⲗ   as the priest was praying.

The tense of such "clauses" depends on the context. They occur frequently after introductory ⲁⲥϣⲱⲡⲉ:

ⲁⲥϣⲱⲡⲉ ⲁⲉ ϩⲙ̄ ⲡⲧⲣⲉϥϣⲙ̄ϣⲉ ϩⲙ̄ ⲡⲉⲣⲡⲉ ...

It happened, however, as he was serving in the temple, that...

(4) After the preposition ⲙⲛ̄ⲛ̄ⲥⲁ and without an article the Inflected Inf. is equivalent to a temporal clause with "after":

ⲙⲛ̄ⲛ̄ⲥⲁ ⲧⲣⲁⲛⲁⲩ ⲉⲣⲟⲟⲩ   after I saw them, ...

ⲙⲛ̄ⲛ̄ⲥⲁ ⲧⲣⲉ-ⲡⲉϥⲉⲓⲱⲧ ⲃⲱⲕ ⲉⲃⲟⲗ after his father left, ...

(5) The Inflected Inf. is used frequently with the impersonal expressions treated in the following paragraph.

Other uses will be taken up in a later lesson.

    20.2 Impersonal Expressions. The impersonal use of
ⲁⲥϣⲱⲡⲉ was introduced in Vocabulary 9. There are several
other impersonal expressions, some verbal, some anomalous,
which occur frequently:

    (1) ϩⲁⲡⲥ̄ it is necessary (neg. ⲛ̄ ϩⲁⲡⲥ̄ ⲁⲛ), followed
by the Inflected Inf. The subject of the infinitive may
be anticipated with the preposition ⲉ; an untranslatable
ⲡⲉ often co-occurs with ϩⲁⲡⲥ̄.

    ϩⲁⲡⲥ̄ (ⲡⲉ) ⲉⲧⲣⲉⲛⲡⲱⲧ ⲉⲃⲟⲗ.   It is necessary that we flee.
    ϩⲁⲡⲥ̄ (ⲡⲉ) ⲉⲣⲟⲓ ⲉⲧⲣⲁϣⲁϫⲉ   It is necessary that I speak
       ⲛⲙ̄ⲙⲁⲕ.   with you.

    (2) ⲟⲩⲛ̄-(ϣ)ϭⲟⲙ it is possible; neg.: ⲙⲛ̄-(ϣ)ϭⲟⲙ it
is not possible. The subject of a following infinitive
may be introduced with ⲙ̄ⲙⲟ⸗, with the Inflected Inf., or
both:

    ⲙⲛ̄-ϣϭⲟⲙ ⲉ ⲉⲓⲙⲉ ⲉ ⲛⲉϥϣⲁϫⲉ.   It is not possible to
                           understand his words.
    ⲙⲛ̄-ϣϭⲟⲙ ⲙ̄ⲙⲟⲛ ⲉ ⲉⲓⲙⲉ.   ⎫ It is not possible for us to
    ⲙⲛ̄-ϣϭⲟⲙ (ⲙ̄ⲙⲟⲛ) ⲉⲧⲣⲉⲛⲉⲓⲙⲉ. ⎭   understand.

    (3) ϣϣⲉ (or ⲥϣⲉ) it is appropriate, proper,
fitting; neg.: ⲛ̄ ϣϣⲉ ⲁⲛ or ⲙⲉϣϣⲉ. The subject of the infinitive may be anticipated with prep. ⲉ.

    ϣϣⲉ ⲉⲣⲟϥ ⲉ ⲃⲱⲕ ⲉϩⲟⲩⲛ.   It is proper for him to enter.
    ⲛ̄ ϣϣⲉ ⲉⲣⲱⲧⲛ̄ ⲁⲛ ⲉⲧⲣⲉⲧⲉⲧⲛ̄ϭⲱ   It is not proper for you to
       ⲙ̄ ⲡⲉⲓⲙⲁ.   remain here.

The relative forms ⲡⲉⲧⲉ ϣϣⲉ, ⲛⲉⲧⲉ ϣϣⲉ, what is proper
(neg.: ⲡⲉⲧⲉ/ⲛⲉⲧⲉ ⲙⲉϣϣⲉ) are often used as substantives.

    (4) ⲣ̄-ⲁⲛⲁ⸗ to please, used impersonally with sub-
ject ⲥ- and an object suffix, or with a personal subject
and a reflexive suffix. The suffix on ⲁⲛⲁ⸗ is required; a
nominal object is anticipated by a suffix and introduced
with ⲛ̄.

Study the following examples:

ⲁⲥⲡ̄-ⲁⲛⲁϥ ⲉⲧⲣⲉϥϭⲉⲓ ⲉ2ⲟⲩⲛ ⲉ   It pleased him to come (i.e. he
ⲡⲉⲓⲕⲟⲥⲙⲟⲥ.   came willingly) into this world.

ⲁⲥⲡ̄-ⲁⲛⲁϥ ⲛ̄ ⲡⲙⲏⲏϣⲉ ⲉⲧⲣⲉⲩⲛⲁⲩ   It pleased the crowd (for them)
ⲉ ⲡⲁⲓ.   to see this.

ⲁⲓⲡ̄-ⲁⲛⲁⲓ ⲉⲧⲣⲁⲥⲱⲧⲙ̄ ⲉ   It pleased me to hear your
ⲛⲉⲕϣⲁⲝⲉ.   words.

Note also the partially synonymous verb ⲡ̄-2ⲛⲁ⸗ to be
willing, desire, which is used only with a personal subject
and reflexive suffix:

ⲁⲓⲡ̄-2ⲛⲁⲓ ⲉⲧⲣⲁⲥ2ⲁⲓ ⲛⲁⲕ ⲛ̄   I wanted to write to you
ⲛⲉⲓϣⲁⲝⲉ.   (about) these things.

ⲡ̄-2ⲛⲁ⸗ is not used in the First Present; ⲡ̄-ⲁⲛⲁ⸗ has no such
restriction.

20.3 The verb ⲡⲉⲝⲉ-, ⲡⲉⲝⲁ⸗, followed by its subject,
is equivalent to ⲝⲱ in the First Perfect, but is used only
to report speech, with ⲝⲉ:

ⲡⲉⲝⲉ-ⲡ2ⲗ̄ⲗⲟ ⲝⲉ ...   The old man said, "...
ⲡⲉⲝⲁϥ ⲛⲁⲓ ⲝⲉ ...   He said to me, "...

20.4 Infinitives of the types ⲥⲟⲗⲥⲗ̄, to console, and
ϣⲧⲟⲣⲧⲣ̄, to disturb, have the following prenominal and presuffixal forms:

ⲥⲟⲗⲥⲗ̄   ⲥⲗ̄ⲥⲗ̄-   ⲥⲗ̄ⲥⲱⲗ⸗
ϣⲧⲟⲣⲧⲣ̄   ϣⲧⲣ̄ⲧⲣ̄-   ϣⲧⲣ̄ⲧⲱⲣ⸗

With the exceptions of the infinitives treated below in
Lesson 26, the remaining types of transitive infinitives
do not constitute regular classes of any significant size.
The following verbs of minor types have occurred in the
lessons up to this point:

ϣⲙ̄ϣⲉ   ϣⲙ̄ϣⲉ-   ϣⲙ̄ϣⲏⲧ⸗   to serve
ⲥ2ⲁⲓ   ⲥⲉ2-   ⲥ2ⲁⲓ⸗   to write
ⲥⲟⲟⲩⲛ̄   ⲥⲟⲩⲛ̄-   ⲥⲟⲩⲱⲛ⸗   to know

ⲧⲚⲚⲟⲟⲩ   ⲧⲚⲚⲉⲩ-   ⲧⲚⲚⲟⲟⲩⸯ   to send.

When the presuffixal form of the infinitive ends in a
diphthong, as in ⲥⲌⲁⲓⸯ and ⲧⲚⲚⲟⲟⲩⸯ, the object suffix of
the 3rd pers. pl. regularly appears as -ⲥⲟⲩ: ⲥⲌⲁⲓⲥⲟⲩ to
write them, ⲧⲚⲚⲟⲟⲩⲥⲟⲩ to send them. The -ⲥ- of this form
sometimes appears also before other suffixes, e.g. ⲥⲌⲁⲓⲥⲧ⳻
to write it.

Vocabulary 20

ⲥⲟⲗⲥⲗ̄ ⲥⲗ̄ⲥⲗ̄- ⲥⲗ̄ⲥⲱⲗⸯ vb. tr. to console, comfort (ⲘⲘⲟⸯ);
  intr. to be comforted; as n.m. consolation.

ϣⲧⲟⲣⲧⲣ̄ ϣⲧⲣ̄ⲧⲣ̄- ϣⲧⲣ̄ⲧⲱⲣⸯ vb. tr. to disturb, trouble (ⲘⲘⲟⸯ);
  intr. to be disturbed, troubled; as n.m. trouble,
  disturbance.

ⲥⲟⲡⲥ̄ⲡ̄ ⲥ̄ⲡⲥ̄ⲡ̄- ⲥ̄ⲡⲥⲱⲡⸯ vb. tr. to beseech, entreat (ⲘⲘⲟⸯ),
  often followed by ⲉⲧⲣⲉ-. The unbound and prenominal
  forms also occur as ⲥⲟⲡⲥ̄ and ⲥⲉⲡⲥ̄-. As n.m. prayer,
  entreaty.

ⲟⲩⲱϣⲃ̄ ⲟⲩⲉϣⲃ̄- ⲟⲩⲟϣⲃⸯ vb. tr. to respond to (ⲘⲘⲟⸯ, ⲚⲀⸯ); to
  answer.

ⲭⲚⲟⲩ ⲭⲚⲉ- ⲭⲚⲟⲩⸯ vb. tr. to ask, question (ⲘⲘⲟⸯ; for: ⲉ;
  about: ⲉⲧⲃⲉ).

ⲙⲟⲕⲙⲉⲕ ⲙⲉⲕⲙⲟⲩⲕⸯ vb. intr. or reflex. to think, ponder; as
  n.m. thought(s).

ⲙⲟⲥⲧⲉ ⲙⲉⲥⲧⲉ- ⲙⲉⲥⲧⲱⸯ vb. tr. to hate.

ⲕⲱ ⲘⲘⲟⸯ ⲉ + Inf.: to allow (someone) to do (something).
Greek words:
ⲡ.ⲥⲱⲙⲁ (τὸ σῶμα) body.
ⲡ.ⲡⲉⲓⲣⲁⲥⲙⲟⲥ (ὁ πειρασμός) temptation.
And the impersonal expressions Ⲍⲁⲡⲥ̄, ϣϣⲉ, ⲟⲩⲚ-(ϣ)ⲞⲘ,
  ⲙⲚ-(ϣ)ⲞⲘ.

Exercises

A. (1) ⲙⲚ̄Ⲛ̄ⲥⲁ ⲧⲣⲉ-ⲡϣⲏⲣⲉ Ⲛ̄ ⲃⲣ̄ⲣⲉ ⲃⲱⲕ ⲉⲃⲟⲗ (2) ⲌⲘ̄ ⲡⲧⲣⲉⲩ-
Ⲟⲱⲗⲡ̄ ⲉⲃⲟⲗ Ⲛ̄ ⲛⲉⲓⲙⲩⲥⲧⲏⲣⲓⲟⲛ (3) ⲌⲘ̄ ⲡⲧⲣⲉ-ⲡⲟⲩⲏⲏⲃ ⲗⲌⲉⲣⲁⲧ⳻ ⲌⲓⲣⲘ̄
ⲡⲉⲣⲡⲉ (4) ⲙⲚ̄Ⲛ̄ⲥⲁ ⲧⲣⲉⲥⲌⲁⲓⲥⲟⲩ ⲌⲓⲭⲘ̄ ⲡⲭⲱⲱⲙⲉ (5) ⲌⲘ̄ ⲡⲧⲣⲉⲩⲛⲟⲩⲭⲉ

ⲙ̄ ⲡⲉϥⲥⲱⲙⲁ ⲉⲭⲙ̄ ⲡⲕⲱ2ⲧ̄   (6) ⲙⲛ̄ⲛ̄ⲥⲁ ⲧⲣⲉⲛⲥⲗ̄ⲥⲱⲗⲟⲩ   (7) 2ⲙ̄ ⲡⲧⲣⲉ-
ⲡⲁⲓⲁⲃⲟⲗⲟⲥ ⲡⲉⲓⲣⲁⲍⲉ ⲙ̄ⲙⲟϥ 2ⲛ̄ ⲟⲩⲛⲟϭ ⲙ̄ ⲡⲉⲓⲣⲁⲥⲙⲟⲥ   (8) ⲙⲛ̄ⲛ̄ⲥⲁ
ⲧⲣⲉϥⲧⲛ̄ⲛⲟⲟⲩ ⲙ̄ ⲡⲉϥϣⲏⲣⲉ ⲙ̄ ⲙⲉⲣⲓⲧ ϣⲁⲣⲟⲛ   (9) ⲙⲛ̄ⲛ̄ⲥⲁ ⲧⲣⲉϥⲟⲩⲟⲛ2ϥ
ⲉⲃⲟⲗ ⲛ̄ ⲛⲉϥⲙⲁⲑⲏⲧⲏⲥ   (10) ⲙⲛ̄ⲛ̄ⲥⲁ ⲧⲣⲁⲡⲁ2ⲧ̄ ⲙ̄ ⲡⲉϥⲙ̄ⲧⲟ ⲉⲃⲟⲗ   (11)
2ⲙ̄ ⲡⲧⲣⲉϥⲥⲱ ⲉⲃⲟⲗ 2ⲙ̄ ⲡⲁⲡⲟⲧ ⲛ̄ ⲁⲥ   (12) ⲙⲛ̄ⲛ̄ⲥⲁ ⲧⲣⲉ-ⲙ̄ⲙⲁⲧⲟⲓ ⲣⲉⲕⲍ̄-
ⲛⲉⲛⲏⲓ

   ⲃ. (1) 2ⲁⲡⲥ̄ ⲡⲉ ⲉⲣⲟⲛ ⲉⲧⲣⲉⲛⲣ̄-ⲡⲉⲧⲉ ϣϣⲉ ⲛ̄ ⲟⲩⲟⲉⲓϣ ⲛⲓⲙ.   (2)
ⲛⲁⲓ ⲛⲉ ⲛ̄ϣⲁⲭⲉ ⲉⲧⲕ̄ⲛⲁⲥ2ⲁⲓⲥⲟⲩ ⲛⲁϥ.   (3) ⲡⲉⲭⲉ-ⲡ2ⲗ̄ⲗⲟ ⲭⲉ ⲟⲩⲛⲟϭ ⲧⲉ
ⲧⲉⲕⲡⲓⲥⲧⲓⲥ, ⲡⲁϣⲏⲣⲉ.   (4) ϣϣⲉ ⲉⲧⲣⲉⲛϣⲙ̄ϣⲏⲧϥ ⲛ̄ ⲟⲩⲟⲉⲓϣ ⲛⲓⲙ.   (5)
2ⲁⲡⲥ̄ ⲉⲧⲣⲉⲛϭⲱ ⲙ̄ ⲡⲉⲓⲙⲁ ⲛ̄ ⲧⲣⲟⲙⲡⲉ.   (6) ⲛ̄ⲧⲁϥⲧⲛ̄ⲛⲟⲟⲩⲧ ϣⲁⲣⲱⲧⲛ̄
ⲉⲧⲣⲁϣⲁⲭⲉ ⲛⲙ̄ⲙⲏⲧⲛ̄.   (7) ⲡⲉⲭⲉ-ⲓ̄ⲥ̄ ⲛⲁϥ ⲭⲉ †ⲟⲩⲁϣϥ.   (8) ⲁⲥϣⲱⲡⲉ
ⲁⲉ 2ⲙ̄ ⲡⲧⲣⲉϥⲛⲁⲩ ⲉ ⲛⲁⲓ, ⲁϥⲡⲁ2ⲧϥ, ⲁϥϣ̄ⲧⲟⲣⲧⲣ̄.   (9) ⲙⲛ̄-ϭⲟⲙ ⲙ̄ⲙⲟⲓ
ⲉⲧⲣⲁϣⲙ̄ϣⲏⲧⲕ̄.   (10) 2ⲁⲡⲥ̄ ⲉⲣⲟⲕ ⲡⲉ ⲉⲧⲣⲉⲕⲥⲗ̄ⲥⲗ̄-ⲧⲙⲁⲗⲁⲩ ⲙ̄ ⲡϣⲏⲣⲉ.
(11) ⲛⲓⲙ ⲡⲉⲛⲧⲁϥ† ⲛⲁϥ ⲛ̄ ⲧⲉⲝⲟⲩⲥⲓⲁ ⲉⲧⲣⲉϥⲉⲓⲣⲉ ⲛ̄ ⲛⲉⲓ2ⲃⲏⲩⲉ? (12)
ⲛ̄ⲧⲉⲣⲉϥⲥⲱⲧⲙ̄ ⲉ ⲛⲁϣⲁⲭⲉ, ⲁϥϣ̄ⲧⲟⲣⲧⲣ̄, ⲁϥⲙⲉⲕⲙⲟⲩⲕϥ.   (13) †-ⲟⲩⲱϣ
ⲉⲧⲣⲉⲕϭⲱ ⲛⲙ̄ⲙⲁⲓ ⲛ̄ ϣⲟⲙⲛ̄ⲧ ⲛ̄ ⲉⲃⲟⲧ.   (14) ϣϣⲉ ⲉⲧⲣⲉⲩⲥⲱⲧⲙ̄ ⲛ̄ⲥⲁ
ⲛ̄ϣⲁⲭⲉ ⲙ̄ ⲡⲉⲩⲭⲟⲉⲓⲥ.   (15) ⲟⲩⲛ̄-ϭⲟⲙ ⲙ̄ⲙⲟⲛ ⲉⲧⲣⲉⲛⲥⲗ̄ⲥⲱⲗϥ.   (16)
ⲛ̄ⲧⲁⲧⲉⲧⲛ̄2ⲉ ⲉ ⲧⲉⲓⲅⲣⲁⲫⲏ ⲛ̄ ⲁⲥ ⲧⲱⲛ?   (17) ⲛ̄ 2ⲁⲡⲥ̄ ⲁⲛ ⲉⲧⲣⲉⲛⲡⲱ2 ⲉ
ⲡ†ⲙⲉ ⲙ̄ ⲡⲟⲟⲩ.   (18) ⲟⲩ ⲡⲉⲧⲟⲩⲛⲁⲗⲁϥ 2ⲙ̄ ⲡⲧⲣⲉⲩⲥⲱⲧⲙ̄ ⲉ ⲧⲉϥⲥⲙⲏ?
(19) ⲁ-ⲧⲉϥⲥⲃⲱ ⲙ̄ ⲡⲟⲛⲏⲣⲟⲛ ϣⲧ̄ⲣ̄ⲧⲣ̄-ⲡⲁⲣⲭⲓⲉⲡⲓⲥⲕⲟⲡⲟⲥ ⲉⲙⲁⲧⲉ.   (20)
ⲁ-†ⲟⲩ ⲛ̄ ⲕⲟⲩⲓ ⲛ̄ ⲭⲟⲓ ⲉⲓ ⲉ2ⲟⲩⲛ ⲉ ⲧⲉⲙⲣⲱ.   (21) ⲥϣⲉ ⲉⲣⲟⲓ ⲉⲧⲣⲁϭⲱ ⲛⲙ̄ⲙⲉ.   (22) ⲧⲛ̄ⲛⲁⲥ̄ⲡ̄ⲥⲱⲡϥ ⲉⲧⲣⲉϥⲧⲛ̄ⲛⲟⲟⲩϥ ⲉⲣⲟⲛ.   (23) ⲙⲛ̄-ϣϭⲟⲙ
ⲉ ⲥⲟⲗⲥⲗ̄ ⲛ̄ ⲛ̄ⲁⲡⲓⲥⲧⲟⲥ.   (24) ⲁⲥϣⲱⲡⲉ 2ⲙ̄ ⲡⲧⲣⲉϥⲉⲓⲙⲉ ⲉ ⲛⲉⲩⲙⲟⲕⲙⲉⲕ,
ⲁϥⲁⲣⲭⲓ ⲛ̄ ⲉⲡⲓⲧⲓⲙⲁ ⲛⲁⲩ.   (25) ⲡⲉⲭⲁⲓ ⲛⲁϥ ⲭⲉ ⲛ̄ⲧⲕ̄-ⲟⲩⲁⲓⲕⲁⲓⲟⲥ.
(26) ⲥⲉⲛⲁⲭⲛⲟⲩϥ ⲉⲧⲃⲉ ⲧⲉⲝⲟⲩⲥⲓⲁ ⲉⲧϥ̄ⲛⲁⲧⲁⲁⲥ ⲛⲁⲩ.   (27) ⲙⲉϣϣⲉ
ⲉⲧⲣⲉⲩⲉⲓ ⲉ2ⲟⲩⲛ ⲉ ⲡⲉⲣⲡⲉ ⲛ̄ ⲧⲉⲓ2ⲉ.   (28) †ⲙⲟⲥⲧⲉ ⲙ̄ⲙⲟⲕ ⲙⲛ̄ ⲛⲉⲕϣⲁⲭⲉ ⲙ̄ ⲡⲟⲛⲏⲣⲟⲛ.   (29) ⲁⲩⲭⲛⲉ-ⲟⲩ2ⲗ̄ⲗⲟ ⲭⲉ ⲁϣ ⲧⲉ ⲧⲡⲓⲥⲧⲓⲥ?   (30)
ⲁⲥϣⲱⲡⲉ ⲁⲉ ⲙⲛ̄ⲛ̄ⲥⲁ ⲧⲣⲉϥⲃⲱⲕ ⲉⲃⲟⲗ, ⲁⲩⲁⲣⲭⲓ ⲛ̄ ϣⲁⲭⲉ ⲉⲧⲃⲉ ⲙ̄ⲙⲁⲉⲓⲛ
ⲉⲛⲧⲁϥⲁⲁⲩ ⲛ̄ ⲧⲉⲩⲙⲏⲧⲉ.   (31) ⲙ̄ⲡⲣⲙⲉⲥⲧⲉ-ⲗⲁⲁⲩ ⲛ̄ ⲣⲱⲙⲉ.   (32) ⲁⲓ-
ⲥ̄ⲡ̄ⲥⲱⲡϥ ⲉⲧⲣⲉϥⲟⲩⲱϣⲃ̄ ⲛⲁⲓ.   (33) ⲙ̄ⲡⲉϥⲕⲱ ⲙ̄ⲙⲟⲟⲩ ⲉ ⲭⲉ-ⲗⲁⲁⲩ ⲛ̄ ϣⲁⲭⲉ.
(34) ⲁⲩⲟⲩⲱϣⲃ̄ ⲛⲁϥ ⲛ̄ϭⲓ ⲡⲥⲟⲛ ⲥⲛⲁⲩ ⲭⲉ ⲛ̄ⲧⲁⲛⲛⲁⲩ ⲉⲣⲟϥ 2ⲓ ⲧⲉ2ⲓⲏ.
(35) ⲧⲛ̄ⲛⲁⲭⲛⲟⲩϥ ⲉⲧⲃⲉ ⲡⲉϥⲧⲟⲟⲩ ⲛ̄ ⲭⲱⲱⲙⲉ ⲛ̄ⲧⲉ ⲡⲉⲩⲁⲅⲅⲉⲗⲓⲟⲛ.

Lesson 21

21.1 The Imperfect.

ⲛⲉⲓⲕⲱⲧ	I was building	ⲛⲉⲛⲕⲱⲧ
ⲛⲉⲕⲕⲱⲧ	you were building	ⲛⲉⲧⲉⲧⲛ̄ⲕⲱⲧ
ⲛⲉⲣⲉⲕⲱⲧ	etc.	
ⲛⲉϥⲕⲱⲧ		ⲛⲉⲩⲕⲱⲧ
ⲛⲉⲥⲕⲱⲧ		

ⲛⲉⲣⲉ-ⲡⲣⲱⲙⲉ ⲕⲱⲧ   the man was building

The Imperfect is optionally, but often, followed by an untranslatable ⲡⲉ: ⲛⲉⲓⲕⲱⲧ ⲡⲉ, ⲛⲉⲕⲕⲱⲧ ⲡⲉ, etc. Negation is with ⲁⲛ: ⲛⲉⲓⲕⲱⲧ ⲁⲛ (ⲡⲉ), ⲛⲉⲕⲕⲱⲧ ⲁⲛ (ⲡⲉ), etc.

The Imperfect is used to describe an action, activity, or process as in progress in past time and is normally the equivalent of the English past progressive unless idiom requires the simple past, e.g. ⲛⲉⲩⲥⲟⲟⲩⲛ̄ they knew (not: they were knowing). It also often conveys the meaning of habitual or recurring activity in the past: they used to build, they would build.

Relative clauses containing an Imperfect are introduced with the relative pronoun ⲉⲧⲉ or, more frequently, with ⲉ- prefixed directly to the verbal form:

ⲡⲣⲱⲙⲉ ⲉⲧⲉ ⲛⲉϥⲙⲟⲟϣⲉ ϩⲓ ⲧⲉϩⲓⲏ ⎱   the man who was walking
ⲡⲣⲱⲙⲉ ⲉⲛⲉϥⲙⲟⲟϣⲉ ϩⲓ ⲧⲉϩⲓⲏ ⎰   on the road

ⲡⲏⲓ ⲉⲧⲉ ⲛⲉⲩⲕⲱⲧ ⲙ̄ⲙⲟϥ ⎱   the house which they were
ⲡⲏⲓ ⲉⲛⲉⲩⲕⲱⲧ ⲙ̄ⲙⲟϥ ⎰   building

Pronominal resumption of the subject is required. In general, the prenominal and suffixal (prepronominal) forms of the infinitive may not be used in the Imperfect.

21.2 The Qualitative. Many verbs possess a second lexical form known as the qualitative. The qualitative describes a state or quality resulting from the action, activity, or process expressed by the Infinitive; it is most conveniently taken as equivalent to English "to be" plus an adjective. The qualitative of transitive verbs is passive from the English point of view. E.g.

Inf. ⲕⲱⲧ to build ⠀⠀⠀Q. ⲕⲏⲧ to be built (i.e. in a
⠀⠀⠀⠀⠀⠀⠀⠀⠀⠀⠀⠀⠀⠀⠀⠀⠀⠀⠀⠀⠀fully constructed state)
Inf. ϩⲱⲡ to hide ⠀⠀⠀⠀Q. ϩⲏⲡ to be hidden, secret.

The form of the qualitative is more or less predictable for verbs belonging to the main classes:

⠀⠀⠀(a) type ⲕⲱⲧ: Q. ⲕⲏⲧ; ⲙⲟⲩⲣ: Q. ⲙⲏⲣ

ⲏⲡ⠀to be reckoned, ⠀⠀⠀ⲙⲏϩ, ⲙⲉϩ to be full
⠀⠀⠀ascribed to (ⲉ) ⠀⠀⠀⠀ⲟⲩⲏϩ⠀⠀to live, dwell, be
ϫⲏⲕ (ⲉⲃⲟⲗ) to be finished, ⲙⲏⲣ⠀⠀⠀to be bound
⠀⠀⠀done, perfect ⠀⠀⠀⠀⠀ⲧ�HⲙM⠀⠀⠀to be shut
ⲃⲏⲗ to be loosened, un- ⠀ⲟⲩⲏⲛ⠀⠀⠀to be open
⠀⠀⠀done, untied, dissolved
ϣⲏⲡ to be received, acceptable

⠀⠀⠀(b) type ⲕⲱⲧⲉ: Q. ⲕⲏⲧ; ⲛⲟⲩϫⲉ: Q. ⲛⲏϫ

ⲕⲏⲧ to be turned, turning, circulating
ⲛⲏϫ to be lying, reclining (esp. at table); to be

⠀⠀⠀(c) type ⲙⲓⲥⲉ: Q. ⲙⲟⲥⲉ

ⲙⲟⲥⲉ to be born ⠀⠀⠀⠀ϣⲟⲃⲉ to be different, various

⠀⠀⠀(d) type ⲥⲱⲧⲡ̅: Q. ⲥⲟⲧⲡ̅; ⲡⲱϩⲧ̅: Q. ⲡⲁϩⲧ̅

ⲟⲩⲟⲛϩ̄ to be manifest, clear, plain
ϭⲟⲗⲡ̄⠀to be known, revealed, clear
ⲣⲟⲕϩ̄⠀to be burned, destroyed by fire
ⲡⲁϩⲧ̄⠀to be prostrated, bowing

⠀⠀⠀(e) type ⲥⲟⲗⲥⲗ̅: Q. ⲥⲗ̅ⲥⲱⲗ; ϣⲧⲟⲣⲧⲣ̅: Q. ϣⲧⲣ̅ⲧⲱⲣ

ⲥⲗ̅ⲥⲱⲗ to be consoled ⠀⠀ϣⲧⲣ̅ⲧⲱⲣ to be disturbed, upset.

Otherwise, there is some irregularity:

⠀⠀⠀ⲕⲱ: Q. ⲕⲏ to be situated, lying; to be

ϭⲁⲁⲓ: Q. ϭⲏ₂ to be in writing, written

ⲥⲓ: Q. ⲥⲏⲩ to be sated, full.

Note that ⲕⲏ, ⲛⲏⲝ, and ⲟⲩⲏ₂ may all correspond to English "to be" when location or position is involved.

The qualitative is a verb and may stand in place of the Infinitive in the First Present and the Imperfect, together with their negative and relative forms. It is especially important to keep in mind that the qualitative does not express a passive action (cf. §13.4); it describes the state that the subject is (or was) in:

ⲛⲉⲣⲉ-ⲡⲣⲟ ⲧⲏⲙ ⲡⲉ.   The door was shut.

ⲛ̄ϯϣⲧⲣ̄ⲧⲱⲣ ⲁⲛ.   I am not disturbed.

ⲡⲣⲱⲙⲉ ⲛⲏⲝ ₂ⲓ ⲡⲕⲁ₂.   The man is lying on the ground.

ⲛ̄ⲣⲱⲙⲉ ⲉⲧ ⲙⲏⲣ   the men who are bound

The qualitative may not be used in any of the other conjugations introduced up to this point, including the various constructions with the Infinitive and Inflected Infinitive.

21.3 Prepositional phrases with ₂ⲛ̄ + a noun with the indefinite article occur very frequently as adverbs:

₂ⲛ̄ ⲟⲩϫⲱⲕ ⲉⲃⲟⲗ	completely	₂ⲛ̄ ⲟⲩⲣⲁϣⲉ	joyfully
₂ⲛ̄ ⲟⲩϣⲥ̄ⲛⲉ	suddenly	₂ⲛ̄ ⲟⲩ₂ⲓⲥⲉ	with difficulty,
₂ⲛ̄ ⲟⲩϭⲉⲡⲏ	hurriedly		anxiously
₂ⲛ̄ ⲟⲩⲙⲉ	truly	₂ⲛ̄ ⲟⲩϣⲧⲟⲣⲧⲣ̄	agitatedly

For ϣⲥ̄ⲛⲉ, ⲙⲉ, and ϭⲉⲡⲏ see the Vocabulary below.

Vocabulary 21

ⲙⲟⲩⲛ vb. intr. (± ⲉⲃⲟⲗ) to remain, last, endure; as n.m. perseverance, continuing. ₂ⲛ̄ ⲟⲩⲙⲟⲩⲛ ⲉⲃⲟⲗ continuously.

ⲥⲙⲟⲩ, Q ⲥⲙⲁⲙⲁⲁⲧ vb. tr. to bless (ⲉ); Q to be blessed.

ⲥⲱϭ ⲥⲉϭ- ⲥⲟϭ⸗ Q ⲥⲏϭ vb. tr. to paralyze; Q to be paralyzed.

ⲧⲉ.ⲩⲛⲟⲩ (ⲟⲩⲛⲟⲩ) hour. ⲛ̄ ⲧⲉⲩⲛⲟⲩ adv. immediately, forthwith.

ⲧⲉⲛⲟⲩ adv. now. ϣⲁ ⲧⲉⲛⲟⲩ until now. ϫⲓⲛ ⲧⲉⲛⲟⲩ from now on.

ⲉⲛⲉϩ eternity; freq. as adv. forever (with neg.: never).

ϣⲁ ⲉⲛⲉϩ, ϣⲁ ⲛⲓⲉⲛⲉϩ idem (for ⲛⲓ- see §30.8).

ϫⲓⲛ prep. from, starting from, since. ϫⲓⲛ ⲙ̄ ⲡⲟⲟⲩ ⲉⲃⲟⲗ from today onward.

ϣⲥ̄ⲛⲉ occurs only in ϩⲛ̄ ⲟⲩϣⲥ̄ⲛⲉ adv. suddenly.

ϭⲉⲡⲏ vb. intr. to hurry, hasten (to: ⲉ, ⲉⲣⲁⲧ⸗; to do: ⲉ + Inf.). ϩⲛ̄ ⲟⲩϭⲉⲡⲏ adv. quickly, hurriedly.

ⲧ.ⲙⲉ truth, justice; as adj. true. ϩⲛ̄ ⲟⲩⲙⲉ adv. truly.

ⲛⲁⲙⲉ idem.

Exercises

A. (1) ⲧⲉϫⲱⲣⲁ ⲉⲧⲛ̄ⲟⲩⲛϩ ⲛ̄ϩⲏⲧⲥ̄ (2) ⲧⲡⲁⲣⲑⲉⲛⲟⲥ ⲉⲧ ⲥⲙⲁⲙⲁⲁⲧ (3) ⲑⲁ̄ⲗⲱ ⲉⲧ ⲥⲏⲉ (4) ⲛ̄ϣⲁϫⲉ ⲉⲧ ϩⲏⲡ (5) ⲛ̄ⲣⲱⲙⲉ ⲉⲧ ⲏⲡ ⲉ ⲧⲉⲓϫⲱⲣⲁ (6) ⲡⲱⲛⲉ ⲉⲧ ⲕⲏ ϩⲓⲣⲙ̄ ⲡⲧⲁⲫⲟⲥ (7) ⲡⲛⲟⲃⲉ ⲉⲧ ⲕⲏ ⲛⲉ ⲉⲃⲟⲗ (8) ⲛⲉⲛⲧⲟⲗⲏ ⲉⲧ ⲥⲏϩ ϩⲓ ⲡⲉⲓϫⲱⲱⲙⲉ (9) ⲡⲙⲁ ⲉⲧⲟⲩⲛⲏϫ ⲛ̄ϩⲏⲧϥ̄ (10) ⲛ̄ϣⲁϫⲉ ⲉⲧ ϭⲟⲗⲡ̄ ⲉⲃⲟⲗ ⲛⲁⲛ (11) ⲛⲉⲛⲉⲓⲟⲧⲉ ⲉⲧ ⲥⲙⲁⲙⲁⲁⲧ (12) ⲡⲗⲁⲟⲥ ⲉⲧ ⲥ̄ⲥⲱⲗ (13) ϣⲁϫⲉ ⲛⲓⲙ ⲉⲧ ⲥⲏϩ ϩⲙ̄ ⲡⲛⲟⲙⲟⲥ (14) ⲡⲣⲱⲙⲉ ⲉⲧⲛ̄ⲛⲏϫ ϩⲙ̄ ⲡⲉϥⲏⲓ ⲉ ⲟⲩⲱⲙ (15) ⲡⲱⲛⲉ ⲉⲧⲉ ⲛⲉⲓϩⲙⲟⲟⲥ ϩⲓϫⲱϥ (16) ⲡϩⲓⲥⲉ ⲉⲧⲉ ⲛⲉⲛϩⲁⲣⲟϥ

B. (1) ⲛⲉϥⲥⲟⲗⲥⲗ̄ ⲛ̄ϭⲓ ⲡⲥⲁϩ ⲛ̄ ⲛⲉϥⲙⲁⲑⲏⲧⲏⲥ. (2) ⲛⲉⲣⲉ-ⲛⲉϫⲏⲩ ⲕⲏ ϩⲛ̄ ⲧⲉⲙⲣⲱ. (3) ⲛⲉⲛⲙⲟⲥⲧⲉ ⲙ̄ⲙⲟⲟⲩ ⲉⲙⲁⲧⲉ. (4) ⲛⲉⲣⲉ-ⲡⲗⲁⲟⲥ ϣⲙ̄ϣⲉ ⲛⲁϥ ϩⲛ̄ ⲟⲩⲣⲁϣⲉ. (5) ⲉⲧⲃⲉ ⲟⲩ ⲛⲉⲧⲉⲧⲛ̄ⲙⲟⲕⲙⲉⲕ ⲙ̄ⲙⲱⲧⲛ̄ ⲛ̄ ⲧⲉⲓϩⲉ? (6) ⲛⲉⲣⲉ-ⲙ̄ⲡⲛⲏⲩⲉ ⲙⲉϩ ⲛ̄ ⲟⲩⲟⲉⲓⲛ. (7) ⲧⲉⲓⲉⲕⲕⲗⲏⲥⲓⲁ ⲛⲁⲙⲟⲩⲛ ⲉⲃⲟⲗ ϣⲁ ⲉⲛⲉϩ. (8) ⲛⲉⲣⲉ-ⲡⲉⲩⲏⲓ ⲕⲏⲧ ϩⲛ̄ ⲧⲟⲣⲓⲛⲏ. (9) ϩⲁⲡⲥ̄ ⲉⲧⲣⲉⲕⲡⲱⲧ ⲉⲃⲟⲗ ϩⲛ̄ ⲟⲩϭⲉⲡⲏ. (10) ⲛⲉⲣⲉ-ⲡⲉϥϣⲏⲣⲉ ⲥⲏⲉ. (11) ⲁⲥϣⲱⲡⲉ ⲇⲉ ϩⲛ̄ ⲟⲩϣⲥ̄ⲛⲉ ⲁⲩⲥⲱⲧⲙ̄ ⲉⲩⲛⲟϭ ⲛ̄ ϩⲣⲟⲟⲩ. (12) ⲛⲉⲣⲉ-ⲡⲟⲩⲏⲏⲃ ϣⲧⲣ̄ⲧⲱⲣ ⲉⲙⲁⲧⲉ. (13) ⲛⲁⲓ ⲛⲉ ⲛⲉϥϣⲁϫⲉ ϩⲛ̄ ⲟⲩⲙⲉ. (14) ⲛⲉⲛⲥⲏⲩ ⲁⲛ. (15) ⲛ̄ⲧⲁⲩϣⲧⲟⲣⲧⲣ̄ ⲉⲧⲃⲉ ⲙ̄ⲙⲁⲉⲓⲛ ⲉⲛⲧⲁϥⲁⲁⲩ. (16) ⲛⲉⲕⲛⲟⲃⲉ ⲧⲏⲣⲟⲩ ⲕⲏ ⲛⲁⲕ ⲉⲃⲟⲗ. (17) ⲛ̄ϥⲛⲁⲙⲟⲩⲛ ⲉⲃⲟⲗ ⲁⲛ ⲛ̄ϭⲓ ⲡⲉⲓⲕⲟⲥⲙⲟⲥ. (18) ⲛⲉⲣⲉ-ⲡⲉϥϩⲱⲃ ϫⲏⲕ ⲉⲃⲟⲗ ⲛⲁⲙⲉ. (19) ⲛⲉⲣⲉ-ⲓⲱϩⲁⲛⲛⲏⲥ ⲟⲩⲏϩ ϩⲓϫⲛ̄ ⲧⲉⲣⲏⲙⲟⲥ. (20) ⲛⲉⲩⲡⲁϩⲧ̄ ⲙ̄ ⲡⲉⲙⲧⲟ ⲉⲃⲟⲗ ⲙ̄ ⲡⲣ̄ⲣⲟ. (21) ϣⲙ̄ϣⲛⲧϥ̄ ϩⲛ̄ ⲟⲩⲛⲟϭ ⲛ̄ ⲣⲁϣⲉ. (22) ⲛⲉⲣⲉ-ⲛ̄ⲣⲱⲟⲩ ⲙ̄ ⲡⲛⲟϭ ⲛ̄ ⲣ̄ⲡⲉ ⲧⲏⲙ. (23) ϣϣⲉ ⲉⲣⲱⲧⲛ̄ ⲉⲧⲣⲉⲧⲉⲧⲛ̄ⲥⲱⲧⲙ̄ ⲛ̄ⲥⲁ ⲛⲉⲓⲉⲛⲧⲟⲗⲏ. (24) ⲛ̄ⲧⲉⲣⲛ̄ⲥⲱⲧⲙ̄ ⲉ ⲡⲉϥⲁⲥⲡⲁⲥⲙⲟⲥ, ⲁⲛϭⲉⲡⲏ ⲉⲣⲁⲧϥ̄. (25) ⲛⲉⲓϩⲙⲟⲟⲥ ϩⲓϫⲙ̄ ⲡⲉⲕⲣⲟ ⲛ̄ ⲑⲁⲗⲁⲥⲥⲁ. (26) ⲙⲛ̄-ϭⲟⲙ ⲙ̄ⲙⲟⲓ ⲉⲧⲣⲁⲟⲩⲱϣⲃ̄ ⲉⲣⲟⲕ.

(27) ⲛⲉⲛⲙⲟⲟϣⲉ ⲛ̄ ⲟⲩⲟⲩⲟⲉⲓϣ ϩⲓ ⲧⲉϩⲓⲏ ⲉ ⲧⲡⲟⲗⲓⲥ. (28) ⲁⲥϣⲱⲡⲉ
ⲇⲉ ϩⲙ̄ ⲡⲧⲣⲉⲩⲭⲛⲟⲩϥ, ⲁϥⲟⲩⲱϣⲃ̄ ⲛⲁⲩ ϩⲛ̄ ⲟⲩϩⲓⲥⲉ. (29) ⲧⲛ̄ⲛⲁⲥⲙⲟⲩ ⲉ
ⲡⲉϥⲣⲁⲛ ϣⲁ ⲛⲓⲉⲛⲉϩ. (30) ⲁ-ⲡⲉⲓϣⲱⲛⲉ ⲥⲟⲃϥ̄ ⲛ̄ ⲛⲉϥⲟⲩⲉⲣⲏⲧⲉ. (31)
ⲧⲉⲛⲟⲩ ϯⲥⲟⲟⲩⲛ̄ ϫⲉ ⲛ̄ⲧⲟⲕ ⲡⲉ ⲡⲉⲭ̄ⲥ̄. (32) ⲧⲁⲓ ⲧⲉ ⲛⲁⲙⲉ ⲧⲉⲩⲛⲟⲩ ⲙ̄
ⲡⲉϥⲙⲟⲩ. (33) ⲁⲩⲡⲱⲧ ⲛ̄ ⲧⲉⲩⲛⲟⲩ ⲉⲭⲙ̄ ⲡⲉⲕⲣⲟ. (34) ϣⲁ ⲧⲉⲛⲟⲩ
ⲙ̄ⲡⲉⲛⲕⲟⲧⲛ̄ ⲉ ⲛⲁⲩ ⲉⲣⲟϥ. (35) ϯⲛⲁϭⲱ ⲛⲙ̄ⲙⲁϥ ⲛ̄ ⲥⲁϣϥ̄ ⲛ̄ ϩⲟⲟⲩ.
(36) ⲙ̄ⲡⲓϣⲁϫⲉ ⲉⲛⲉϩ ⲙⲛ̄ ϩⲟⲉⲓⲛⲉ ⲛ̄ ⲧⲉⲓⲙⲓⲛⲉ.

Lesson 22

22.1 Possession is predicated by the use of ⲟⲩⲛ̄- and
ⲙⲛ̄- compounded with the preposition ⲛ̄ⲧⲉ, ⲛ̄ⲧⲁ⸗. There are
two sets of forms:

(A)				(B)	
ⲟⲩⲛ̄ⲧⲁⲓ	I have	ⲟⲩⲛ̄ⲧⲁⲛ		ⲟⲩⲛ̄ϯ-	ⲟⲩⲛ̄ⲧⲛ̄-
ⲟⲩⲛ̄ⲧⲁⲕ	you have	ⲟⲩⲛ̄ⲧⲏⲧⲛ̄		ⲟⲩⲛ̄ⲧⲕ̄-	ⲟⲩⲛ̄ⲧⲉⲧⲛ̄-
ⲟⲩⲛ̄ⲧⲉ	etc.			ⲟⲩⲛ̄ⲧⲉ-	
ⲟⲩⲛ̄ⲧⲁϥ		ⲟⲩⲛ̄ⲧⲁⲩ		ⲟⲩⲛ̄ⲧϥ̄-	ⲟⲩⲛ̄ⲧⲟⲩ-
ⲟⲩⲛ̄ⲧⲁⲥ				ⲟⲩⲛ̄ⲧⲥ̄-	

ⲟⲩⲛ̄ⲧⲉ-ⲡⲣⲱⲙⲉ   the man has

And similarly for the negative: (A) ⲙⲛ̄ⲧⲁⲓ I do not have;
(B) ⲙⲛ̄ϯ-. Set (B) is actually a reduced proclitic form of
(A). Both sets may be accompanied by an untranslatable
ⲙ̄ⲙⲁⲩ (there).

If the possessor is pronominal (i.e. suffixal), an
immediately following object is unmarked:

(A) ⲟⲩⲛ̄ⲧⲁϥ ⲟⲩⲥϩⲓⲙⲉ.   } He has a wife.
(B) ⲟⲩⲛ̄ⲧϥ̄-ⲟⲩⲥϩⲓⲙⲉ.   }

But if some word intervenes (and this is possible only in
set A), the object is marked with ⲛ̄ (ⲙ̄ⲙⲟ⸗).

(A) ⲟⲩⲛ̄ⲧⲁϥ ⲙ̄ⲙⲁⲩ ⲛ̄ ⲟⲩⲥϩⲓⲙⲉ   He has a wife.

If the possessor is a noun, the object is usually not marked:

ⲟⲩⲛ̄ⲧⲉ-ⲡⲣⲱⲙⲉ ⲟⲩⲥϩⲓⲙⲉ.   The man has a wife.

Pronominal objects are used only with set (A) and are attached directly to the subject suffixes. These are generally limited to the third person forms:

m.s. -ϥ, -ⲥϥ̄   f.s. -ⲥ   c.pl. -ⲥⲟⲩ

as in ⲟⲩⲛ̄ⲧⲁⲓϥ, ⲟⲩⲛ̄ⲧⲁⲓⲥϥ̄ I have it (m.), ⲟⲩⲛ̄ⲧⲁⲕⲥ̄ you have it (f.), ⲟⲩⲛ̄ⲧⲁϥⲥⲟⲩ he has them.

We have seen that the genitive is expressed with ⲛ̄ⲧⲉ after indefinite nouns (ⲟⲩϩⲙ̄ϩⲁⲗ ⲛ̄ⲧⲉ ⲡⲣ̄ⲣⲟ), nouns with demonstrative prefixes (ⲡⲉⲓⲭⲱⲱⲙⲉ ⲛ̄ⲧⲉ ⲡⲁⲥⲟⲛ), and nouns with a following modifier (ⲡϣⲏⲣⲉ ⲛ̄ ϭⲁⲗⲉ ⲛ̄ⲧⲉ ⲡⲣⲱⲙⲉ). ⲛⲧⲁ* is used similarly when the possessor is pronominal:

ⲟⲩϩⲙ̄ϩⲁⲗ ⲛ̄ⲧⲁⲓ   a servant of mine
ⲡⲉⲓⲭⲱⲱⲙⲉ ⲛ̄ⲧⲁⲕ   this book of yours
ϣⲟⲙⲛ̄ⲧ ⲛ̄ ϣⲏⲣⲉ ⲛ̄ⲧⲁϥ   three sons of his

ⲛ̄ⲧⲉ, ⲛ̄ⲧⲁ* may be used predicatively:

ⲟⲩⲛ̄-ⲟⲩⲛⲟϭ ⲛ̄ ⲏⲓ ⲛ̄ⲧⲁϥ. He has a large house.
ⲡⲏⲓ ⲉⲧ ⲛ̄ⲧⲁϥ   the house that belongs to him.

ϣⲟⲟⲡ ⲛⲁ* is also sometimes used to predicate possession:

ⲙⲛ̄-ϩⲁⲧ ϣⲟⲟⲡ ⲛⲁⲓ.   I have no money.

The occasional use of ⲙ̄ⲙⲟ* to indicate possession should also be noted. We have already seen an instance of this in the idiom ⲟⲩⲛ̄-/ⲙⲛ̄-ϭⲟⲙ ⲙ̄ⲙⲟ* lit., there is/is-not power in.

22.2 Possessive pronouns, corresponding to English mine, yours, his, hers, etc., are formed by adding the appropriate pronominal suffix to m.s. ⲡⲱ*, f.s. ⲧⲱ*, c.pl. ⲛⲟⲩ*; thus, ⲡⲱⲓ, ⲡⲱⲕ, ⲡⲱ, ⲡⲱϥ, ⲡⲱⲥ, ⲡⲱⲛ, ⲡⲱⲧⲛ̄, ⲡⲱⲟⲩ, and similarly for ⲧⲱ* and ⲛⲟⲩ*. When used as predicates of ⲡⲉ-sentences, they serve to predicate possession:

92

ⲛ̄ⲭⲱⲱⲙⲉ ⲉⲧⲉ ⲛⲟⲩϥ ⲛⲉ	the books which are his
ⲡⲱⲓ ⲡⲉ.	It is mine.
ⲡⲉⲓϫⲟⲓ ⲡⲱϥ ⲡⲉ.	This ship is his.
ⲛⲟⲩⲕ ⲛⲉ.	They are yours.
ⲧⲱⲕ ⲧⲉ.	It (f.) is yours.

The proclitic pronouns ⲡⲁ-, ⲧⲁ-, and ⲛⲁ- are used to express "that of, that which pertains or belongs to." Number and gender are determined by an understood or expressed antecedent. The exact meaning must be gained from the context:

ⲛⲁ-ⲡⲁⲉⲓⲱⲧ	the affairs of my father
ⲛⲉϥϣⲏⲣⲉ ⲙⲛ̄ ⲛⲁ-ⲡⲉϥⲥⲟⲛ	his children and those of his brother
ⲛⲁ-ⲧⲡⲟⲗⲓⲥ	the inhabitants of the city
ⲛⲁ-ⲧⲉⲓⲙⲓⲛⲉ	people of this sort

22.3 The qualitative (continued). Many intransitive verbs of motion or position (e.g. ⲙⲟⲟϣⲉ, ⲁϩⲉⲣⲁⲧ⸗, ϩⲙⲟⲟⲥ) do not have a strong contrast in meaning between infinitive and qualitative, the process and state involved being about the same thing. ⲁϩⲉ and ϩⲙⲟⲟⲥ are in fact qualitative forms that have usurped the role of the infinitives ⲱϩⲉ and ϩⲙ̄ⲥⲉ for all practical purposes. But note the following:

Inf.		Q.		
ⲃⲱⲕ		ⲃⲏⲕ	to be going, be on the way there	
ⲉⲓ		ⲛⲏⲩ	to be coming, be on the way here, be about to come, be about to arrive	
ⲡⲱⲧ		ⲡⲏⲧ	to be fleeing, running, in pursuit	
ϩⲱⲛ		ϩⲏⲛ	to be near, nigh, at hand	
ϭⲱ		ϭⲉⲉⲧ	to remain, wait, stay, be	
ⲙⲟⲩⲛ		ⲙⲏⲛ	to be enduring, lasting, continual	
ⲁⲗⲉ		ⲁⲗⲏⲩ	to be riding, mounted	

The infinitives ⲉⲓ and ⲃⲱⲕ may not be used in the First Present and Imperfect; only the qualitatives ⲛⲏⲩ and ⲃⲏⲕ appear in these conjugations. For the other verbs the qualitative is preferred, but the infinitive is also found. The future nuance of ⲛⲏⲩ is especially noteworthy.

There are many intransitive verbs for which the infinitive and qualitative bear a "becoming"/"being" relationship to each other:

> Inf. ϣⲱⲡⲉ to become, come into existence; Q. ϣⲟⲟⲡ to be, to exist.

> Inf. ⲱⲱ to become pregnant; Q. ⲉⲉⲧ to be pregnant.

Included among these are many verbs with -o- or -ⲁ- in the final stem syllable:

Inf.			Q.		
ⲛ̄ϣⲟⲧ	to become hard		ⲛⲁϣⲧ̄	to be hard
ⲟⲩⲭⲁⲓ	to become well		ⲟⲩⲟⲭ	to be well
ⳍⲕⲟ	to become hungry		ⳍⲕⲁⲉⲓⲧ	to be hungry
ⲁⲓⲁⲓ	to increase		ⲟⲓ	to be great
ⲟⲩⲟⲡ	to become holy		ⲟⲩⲁⲁⲃ	to be holy

Vocabulary 22

ⲟⲩⲭⲁⲓ to become sound, whole, safe; Q ⲟⲩⲟⲭ to be sound, whole, safe; as n.m. health, safety, salvation.

ⲛ̄ϣⲟⲧ, Q ⲛⲁϣⲧ̄ to become/be hard, harsh, difficult.

ⲙ̄ⲧⲟⲛ, Q ⲙⲟⲧⲛ̄ to become/be at ease, at rest, relieved; as n.m. rest, relief. The Q is also used impersonally: ⲥⲙⲟⲧⲛ̄ it is easy (to do: ⲉ, ⲉⲧⲣⲉ).

ⲙ̄ⲕⲁⳍ, Q ⲙⲟⲕⳍ̄ to become/be painful, difficult; as n.m. (pl. ⲙ̄ⲕⲟⲟⳍ) pain, difficulty, grief. The Q is used impersonally: ⲥⲙⲟⲕⳍ̄ it is difficult (to do: ⲉ, ⲉⲧⲣⲉ).

ⲟⲩⲟⲡ, Q ⲟⲩⲁⲁⲃ to become/be pure, holy, hallowed.

ⲁⲓⲁⲓ, Q ⲟⲓ to increase (in age, size, quantity); Q to be great, honored.

ⲁϣⲁⲓ, Q ⲟϣ to become/be numerous, many.

ⲡ.ⲁⳍⲉ lifetime.

ⲕⲏⲙⲉ Egypt.

ⳍⲁⳍ adj. of quantity: many, usually before sing. noun with ⲛ̄, as in ⳍⲁⳍ ⲛ̄ ⲣⲱⲙⲉ many men.

ⲡ.ⲍⲏⲧ heart, mind, intellect.

ⲙ̄ ⲡⲉⲥⲛⲁⲩ (they) both, both (of them); used appositionally
to another pronominal element, as in ⲁⲩⲃⲱⲕ ⲙ̄ ⲡⲉⲥⲛⲁⲩ they
both went. Sim. for other numbers: ⲙ̄ ⲡϣⲟⲙⲛ̄ⲧ all three
of them.

ϣⲟⲟⲡ Q to be, to exist; a predicate adj. is introduced with
ⲛ̄ and has no article: ⲛⲉϥϣⲟⲟⲡ ⲙ̄ ⲡⲟⲛⲏⲣⲟⲥ he was wicked.

Exercises

A. (1) ⲙⲛ̄ⲧⲁⲛ ⲉⲓⲣⲏⲛⲏ ⲍⲙ̄ ⲡⲉⲓⲙⲁ. (2) ⲟⲩⲛ̄ⲧⲉ-ⲡⲁⲉⲓⲱⲧ ϥⲙⲟⲩⲛ ⲛ̄
ⲭⲟⲓ. (3) ⲟⲩⲛ̄ⲧⲁⲓ ⲙ̄ⲙⲁⲩ ⲛ̄ ⲟⲩⲕⲟⲩⲓ ⲛ̄ ⲍⲁⲧ. (4) ⲟⲩⲛ̄ⲧⲁϥ ⲍⲁⲍ ⲛ̄
ⲭⲱⲱⲙⲉ. (5) ⲟⲩⲛ̄ⲧⲁⲩ ⲙ̄ⲙⲁⲩ ⲛ̄ ⲥⲟⲟⲩ ⲛ̄ ⲉⲥⲟⲟⲩ. (6) ⲙⲛ̄ⲧⲟⲩ-ⲟⲉⲓⲕ.
(7) ⲟⲩⲛ̄ⲧϥ̄-ⲟⲩⲍⲟⲉⲓⲧⲉ ⲛ̄ ⲁⲥ. (8) ⲟⲩⲛ̄ⲧⲉ ⲙ̄ⲙⲁⲩ ⲛ̄ ⲟⲩⲍⲁⲓ? (9) ⲟⲩⲛ̄-
ⲧⲁⲥ ⲙ̄ⲙⲁⲩ ⲛ̄ ⲥⲁϣϥ̄ ⲛ̄ ϣⲏⲣⲉ. (10) ⲟⲩⲛ̄†-ⲟⲩϣⲧⲏⲛ ⲛ̄ ⲃⲣ̄ⲣⲉ.

B. (1) ⲡⲉⲓⲃⲗⲟ ⲡⲱⲓ ⲡⲉ. ⲙ̄ ⲡⲱⲕ ⲁⲛ ⲡⲉ. (2) ⲡⲁⲭⲟⲓ ⲙⲛ̄ ⲡⲁ-
ⲡⲁⲥⲟⲛ (3) ⲛⲁ-ⲡϣⲁ (4) ⲡⲉϥⲧⲁⲫⲟⲥ ⲙⲛ̄ ⲛⲁ-ⲛⲉϥⲉⲓⲟⲧⲉ (5) ⲡⲁⲟⲉⲓⲕ
ⲙⲛ̄ ⲡⲁ-ⲛⲁϣⲃⲉⲉⲣ (6) ⲧⲉⲓⲥⲛϥⲉ ⲧⲱⲕ ⲧⲉ. (7) ⲛⲉⲓⲁⲡⲏⲧ ⲛⲟⲩⲟⲩ ⲛⲉ.
(8) ⲡⲛⲟⲩⲍ ⲡⲱⲛ ⲡⲉ. (9) ⲡⲉⲛⲏⲓ ⲙⲛ̄ ⲡⲁ-ⲧⲉⲭⲏⲣⲁ (10) ⲡⲛⲟⲩⲃ ⲙ̄
ⲡⲱ ⲁⲛ ⲡⲉ.

C. (1) ⲁⲩⲱ ⲛ̄ ⲧⲉⲩⲛⲟⲩ ⲁϥⲟⲩⲭⲁⲓ ⲛ̄ϭⲓ ⲡⲉⲧ ϣⲱⲛⲉ. (2) ⲡⲟⲩⲣⲁⲛ
ⲛⲁⲟⲩⲟⲡ ⲭⲓⲛ ⲧⲉⲛⲟⲩ ϣⲁ ⲉⲛⲉⲍ. (3) ⲁϥⲁⲓⲁⲓ ⲛ̄ϭⲓ ⲡⲣⲱⲙⲉ ⲍⲛ̄ ⲛⲉϥⲍⲟⲟⲩ.
(4) ⲁⲛⲕⲟⲧⲛ̄ ⲉ ⲕⲏⲙⲉ ⲍⲛ̄ ⲟⲩϭⲉⲡⲏ. (5) ⲡⲍⲱⲃ ⲁϥⲙ̄ⲕⲁⲍ ⲉⲙⲁⲧⲉ ⲉⲭⲱⲛ.
(6) ⲛ̄ⲥ̄ⲙⲟⲧⲛ̄ ⲁⲛ ⲉⲣⲟⲛ ⲉⲧⲣⲉⲛϥⲓ ⲍⲁ ⲛⲉⲓⲙ̄ⲕⲟⲟⲍ. (7) ⲙ̄ⲡⲉϥⲥⲉ-ⲏⲣⲡ̄
ⲉⲛⲉⲍ ⲍⲙ̄ ⲡⲉϥⲁⲍⲉ ⲧⲏⲣϥ̄. (8) ⲁ-ⲡⲍⲏⲧ ⲙ̄ ⲡⲣ̄ⲣⲟ ⲛ̄ ⲕⲏⲙⲉ ⲛ̄ϣⲟⲧ ⲟⲩⲃⲏⲩ.
(9) ⲥⲉⲟⲩⲟⲭ ⲛ̄ϭⲓ ⲛⲉⲕϣⲏⲣⲉ. (10) ⲛⲉϥϣⲁⲭⲉ ⲙⲛ̄ ⲛⲉϥⲍⲃⲏⲩⲉ ⲛⲁϣⲧ̄.
(11) ⲥⲙⲟⲕⲍ̄ ⲉⲧⲣⲁⲡⲓⲥⲧⲉⲩⲉ ⲉ ⲛⲉⲕϣⲁⲭⲉ ⲙⲛ̄ ⲛⲁ-ⲛⲉⲕϣⲃⲉⲉⲣ. (12) ⲁϥ-
ⲙⲟⲩⲍ ⲙ̄ ⲡⲉⲡⲛ̄ⲁ ⲉⲧ ⲟⲩⲁⲁⲃ. (13) ⲛ̄ⲧⲉⲣⲛ̄ⲡⲱⲍ ⲉ ⲧⲡⲟⲗⲓⲥ, ⲁ-ⲡⲁⲍⲏⲧ
ⲙ̄ⲧⲟⲛ. (14) ⲥⲍⲁⲓ ⲛⲁⲛ ⲉⲧⲃⲉ ⲡⲉⲕⲟⲩⲭⲁⲓ. (15) †ⲛⲁⲥⲙⲟⲩ ⲉ ⲡⲉⲕⲣⲁⲛ ⲉⲧ ⲟⲩⲁⲁⲃ. (16) ⲛⲉⲛⲭⲓⲭⲉⲉⲩⲉ ⲟϣ. (17) ⲡⲁⲁⲍⲉ ⲭⲏⲕ ⲉⲃⲟⲗ.
(18) ⲡⲣⲟ ⲙ̄ ⲡⲉϥⲏⲓ ⲟⲩⲏⲛ. (19) ⲡⲉϥⲣⲁⲛ ⲟⲓ ⲍⲛ̄ ⲧⲉⲓⲭⲱⲣⲁ ⲧⲏⲣⲥ̄.
(20) ⲁⲩⲕⲁ-ⲡⲉϥⲑⲣⲟⲛⲟⲥ ⲉⲭⲙ̄ ⲡⲃⲏⲙⲁ.

D. (1) ⲛⲉⲛⲍⲧⲱⲱⲣ ⲍⲕⲁⲉⲓⲧ. (2) ⲛⲉⲣⲉ-ⲓⲥ̄ ⲁⲗⲏⲩ ⲉⲭⲛ̄ ⲟⲩⲉⲓⲱ.
(3) ⲧⲉϥⲥⲍⲓⲙⲉ ⲉⲉⲧ. (4) ⲛⲉⲩϭⲉⲉⲧ ⲙⲛ̄ ⲛⲉⲩⲥⲩⲅⲅⲉⲛⲏⲥ. (5) ⲛⲉⲩⲉⲥⲟⲟⲩ
ⲛⲉⲩϣⲟⲟⲡ ⲍⲛ̄ ⲧⲥⲱϣⲉ ⲡⲉ. (6) ⲧϭⲓⲭ ⲙ̄ ⲡⲭⲟⲉⲓⲥ ⲛⲉⲥϣⲟⲟⲡ ⲛⲙ̄ⲙⲁϥ ⲡⲉ.

(7) ⲛⲉⲣⲉ-ⲡⲉ2ⲟⲟⲩ ⲙ̄ ⲡⲉⲥⲙⲓⲥⲉ 2ⲏⲛ ⲉ2ⲟⲩⲛ. (8) ⲡ2ⲏⲅⲉⲙⲱⲛ ⲛⲏⲩ ⲉ
ⲣⲁⲕⲟⲧⲉ (9) ⲛⲉ4ϣⲟⲟⲡ ⲁⲉ ⲡⲉ 2ⲛ̄ ⲛ̄ⲭⲁⲓⲉ ϣⲁ ⲡⲉ2ⲟⲟⲩ ⲙ̄ ⲡⲉ4ⲟⲩⲱⲛ2̄
ⲉⲃⲟⲗ ⲙ̄ ⲡⲓ̄ⲏ̄ⲗ̄. (10) ⲛⲉⲣⲉ-2ⲁ2 ⲛ̄ ⲣⲱⲙⲉ ⲛⲏⲧ 2ⲓ ⲧⲉ2ⲓⲏ. (11) ⲛ̄†-
2ⲕⲁⲉⲓⲧ ⲁⲛ. (12) ⲛⲉⲩϣⲟⲟⲡ ⲁⲉ ⲡⲉ ⲙ̄ ⲡⲉⲥⲛⲁⲩ ⲛ̄ ⲁⲓⲕⲁⲓⲟⲥ ⲙ̄ ⲡⲉⲙⲧⲟ
ⲉⲃⲟⲗ ⲙ̄ ⲡⲛⲟⲩⲧⲉ. (13) ⲛ̄ϣⲟⲟⲥ ⲃⲏⲕ ⲉ ⲡ†ⲙⲉ. (14) ⲟⲩⲛ̄-2ⲁ2 ⲛ̄
ⲧⲃ̄ⲧ 2ⲛ̄ ⲑⲁⲗⲗⲁⲥⲥⲁ. (15) ⲡⲙⲟⲛⲁⲭⲟⲥ ⲛⲉ4ⲙⲟⲟⲥ 2ⲛ̄ ⲧⲉ4ⲣⲓ. (16)
ⲙ̄ⲙⲁⲧⲟⲓ ⲁⲗⲏⲩ 2ⲓⲭⲙ̄ ⲡⲭⲟⲓ. (17) ⲛⲉⲣⲉ-ⲡⲟⲩⲏⲏⲃ ϣⲗⲏⲗ ⲛ̄ⲧⲉⲣⲓⲉⲓ
ⲉ2ⲟⲩⲛ. (18) ⲛⲉⲣⲉ-ⲟⲩⲛⲟϭ ⲛ̄ ⲥⲛ4ⲉ 2ⲛ̄ ⲛⲉ4ϭⲓⲭ. (19) ⲡⲛⲟⲙⲟⲥ ⲙ̄
ⲡⲭⲟⲉⲓⲥ ⲙⲏⲛ ⲉⲃⲟⲗ ϣⲁ ⲛⲓⲉⲛⲉ2. (20) ⲛ̄ⲧⲉⲣⲉ4ⲛⲁⲩ ⲭⲉ ⲥⲉⲉⲧ, ⲁ4ⲛ̄ⲧⲥ̄
ⲉ ⲡⲉ4ⲏⲓ.

Lesson 23

23.1 The Circumstantial.

ⲉⲓⲥⲱⲧⲙ̄	I, hearing	ⲉⲛⲥⲱⲧⲙ̄
ⲉⲕⲥⲱⲧⲙ̄	you, hearing	ⲉⲧⲉⲧⲛ̄ⲥⲱⲧⲙ̄
ⲉⲣⲉⲥⲱⲧⲙ̄	etc.	
ⲉ4ⲥⲱⲧⲙ̄		ⲉⲩⲥⲱⲧⲙ̄
ⲉⲥⲥⲱⲧⲙ̄		

ⲉⲣⲉ-ⲡⲣⲱⲙⲉ ⲥⲱⲧⲙ̄ the man, hearing

The Circumstantial is used only in subordinate clauses
modifying either a particular element of the main clause
or the main clause as a whole. Such clauses describe an
activity or state existing simultaneously with the time
designated by the verb of the main clause and do not, in
themselves, have a tense. They correspond to various
English constructions: nominative absolutes, participial
modifiers, or temporal clauses with "as, while, when" and
a progressive verb form. Typical uses in Coptic include

(1) subject complement:

ⲉⲓⲁϩⲉⲣⲁⲧ ϩⲁϩⲧⲙ̄ ⲡⲉⲣⲡⲉ, ⲁⲓⲛⲁⲩ ⲉⲩⲛⲟϭ ⲛ̄ ⲙⲏⲏϣⲉ.
Standing near the temple, I saw a great crowd.

(2) object complement:

ⲁⲩϩⲉ ⲉ ⲡⲣⲱⲙⲉ ⲉϥϩⲙⲟⲟⲥ ϩⲛ̄ ⲧⲁⲅⲟⲣⲁ.
They found the man sitting in the marketplace.

ⲁⲛⲛⲁⲩ ⲉⲣⲟⲟⲩ ⲉⲩⲙⲟⲟϣⲉ ϩⲓ ⲧⲉϩⲓⲏ.
We saw them walking on the road.

(3) complement to the entire main clause:

ⲉⲣⲉ-ⲡⲉⲛⲥⲁϩ ϫⲱ ⲛ̄ ⲛⲉⲓϣⲁϫⲉ, ⲁⲩⲛⲟϭ ⲛ̄ ϣⲡⲏⲣⲉ ϣⲱⲡⲉ.
As our teacher was saying these things, a great
wonder occurred.

If the context requires it, circumstantial clauses may also
be translated as causal, concessive, or conditional clauses.

There are several important special uses of circumstantial clauses in Coptic:

(1) They are regularly used as relative clauses to
modify an indefinite antecedent. Contrast

ⲡⲣⲱⲙⲉ ⲉⲧ ⲉⲓⲙⲉ ⲉ ⲛⲁϣⲁϫⲉ   the man who understands my words
ⲟⲩⲣⲱⲙⲉ ⲉϥⲉⲓⲙⲉ ⲉ ⲛⲁϣⲁϫⲉ   a man who understands my words

Such indefinite antecedents include ⲗⲁⲁⲩ, ⲟⲩⲁ, ⲟⲩⲟⲛ, and
ϩⲟⲉⲓⲛⲉ. Further examples will be found in the exercises.

(2) Certain verbs are regularly followed by the Circumstantial of a complementary verb:

ⲁⲩⲙⲟⲩⲛ ⲉⲃⲟⲗ ⲉⲩϣⲁϫⲉ ⲛ̄ ⲧⲉⲩϣⲏ ⲧⲏⲣⲥ̄.
They continued talking the whole night.

ⲁⲥⲗⲟ ⲉⲥⲣⲓⲙⲉ.   She stopped crying.

(3) The Circumstantial of ϫⲱ ⲙ̄ⲙⲟⲥ ϫⲉ is regularly used
to introduce direct quotation after appropriate verbs:

ⲁϥⲟⲩⲱϣⲃ̄ ⲛⲁⲩ, ⲉϥϫⲱ ⲙ̄ⲙⲟⲥ ϫⲉ ...   He answered them, saying ...

The Circumstantial is not negated. Instead, the

circumstantial prefix ε-, also called the circumstantial converter, is added to the negative of the First Present:

ε-ⲛ̄ϯⲥⲱⲧⲙ̄ ⲁⲛ   I, not hearing

ε-ⲛ̄ⲅⲥⲱⲧⲙ̄ ⲁⲛ   you, not hearing

After ε- the syllabic pronunciation of ⲛ is given up; the stroke is not needed, but is sometimes retained.

23.2 Nouns as adjectives. In Coptic, as in English, a large number of nouns may do double duty as adjectives (cf. *pencil* sharpener, *book*store, *brick* wall, etc.). The order is reversed in Coptic, with the modifying noun second, preceded by the adjectival linking ⲛ̄ (ⲙ̄):

ⲟⲩⲁⲡⲟⲧ ⲛ̄ ⲍⲁⲧ   a silver cup

ⲟⲩⲙⲁ ⲛ̄ ϫⲁⲉⲓⲉ   a desert place

ⲡⲉϥⲥⲙⲟⲧ ⲛ̄ ⲥⲱⲙⲁ   his corporeal form (lit. body-form)

ⲟⲩⲉⲓⲉⲣⲟ ⲛ̄ ⲕⲱ₂ⲧ̄   a fiery river

Such items are very frequent, but not as freely formed as their English counterparts. In some cases two translations are possible: ⲟⲩⲁⲡⲟⲧ ⲛ̄ ⲏⲣⲡ̄ a wine cup *or* a cup of wine. Note that, as with adjectives, the construction differs from the genitive by the absence of an article on the second noun.

Several words form a large number of compounds whose meanings are more or less completely predictable. Among these are

ⲙⲁ ⲛ̄ (place of), as in ⲙⲁ ⲛ̄ ϣⲱⲡⲉ dwelling place

ⲙⲁ ⲛ̄ ⲟⲩⲱⲙ   eating place, refectory

ⲙⲁ ⲙ̄ ⲙⲟⲟϣⲉ   road, path

ⲙⲁ ⲛ̄ ⲕⲁ-ⲟⲉⲓⲕ   pantry (place for putting bread)

ⲥⲁ ⲛ̄ (seller of, vendor of, dealer in), as in

ⲥⲁ ⲛ̄ ⲧⲃ̄ⲧ fish-monger   ⲥⲁ ⲛ̄ ⲏⲣⲡ̄ wine-seller

ⲥⲁ ⲛ̄ ⲁϥ meat-seller   ⲥⲁ ⲛ̄ ⲍⲁⲧ dealer in silver.

A glance through the final Glossary will provide dozens of

further examples.

The nouns ⲣⲱⲙⲉ and ⲥϩⲓⲙⲉ often occur redundantly in this construction; the order of the nouns may be reversed:

ⲧⲉϥⲥⲱⲛⲉ ⲛ̄ ⲥϩⲓⲙⲉ	his sister (lit., woman-sister)
ⲡϩⲁⲙϣⲉ ⲛ̄ ⲣⲱⲙⲉ	the carpenter (lit., man-carpenter)
ⲡⲣⲱⲙⲉ ⲛ̄ ϫⲁϫⲉ	the enemy (lit., enemy-man)

Noun-noun modification does not always correspond exactly to English idiom, but little difficulty will be met in translating these constructions. Most of them will not be given separate listing in the vocabularies or Glossary.

Vocabulary 23

ⲙⲟⲩⲛ ⲉⲃⲟⲗ + Circum.: to continue (doing something).

ϭⲱ + Circum.: to continue, persist in (doing something).

ⲗⲟ vb. intr. (1) to cease, stop, come to an end; + Circum.: to stop (doing something); (2) to leave, depart (from: ⲙ̄ⲙⲟ⸗, ϩⲛ̄, ⲉⲃⲟⲗ ϩⲛ̄). This verb has special Imperative forms: m.s. ⲁⲗⲟⲕ; f.s. ⲁⲗⲟ; c.pl. ⲁⲗⲱⲧⲛ̄.

ⲟⲩⲱ vb. intr. to cease, stop, come to an end; + Circum.: to stop (doing something), to finish (doing something), to have already (done something).

ⲡ.ϣⲉ wood.

ⲡ.ⲃⲉⲛⲓⲡⲉ iron.

ⲑⲉⲛⲉⲉⲧⲉ monastery, convent.

ⲙⲟⲟⲩⲧ (Q of ⲙⲟⲩ) to be dead.

ⲡ.ⲓⲟⲣⲇⲁⲛⲏⲥ the Jordan River.

ⲡⲉ.ⲥⲟⲩⲟ grain, wheat.

ⲧ.ⲧⲁⲡⲣⲟ mouth (also fig.).

ⲁⲗⲗⲁ conj. but.

ⲡ.ϩⲱⲃ ⲛ̄ ϭⲓϫ handwork, handicraft.

Greek words:

ⲧ.ⲡⲉⲣⲓⲭⲱⲣⲟⲥ (ἡ περίχωρος) surrounding countryside.

ⲧ.ⲙⲉⲧⲁⲛⲟⲓⲁ (ἡ μετάνοια) repentance.

ⲧ.ⲁⲡⲟⲑⲏⲕⲏ (ἡ ἀποθήκη) storehouse, barn.

ⲡ.ⲇⲁⲓⲙⲱⲛ, ⲡ.ⲇⲉⲙⲱⲛ, ⲡ.ⲇⲉⲙⲟⲛ (ὁ δαίμων) evil spirit, demon.

ⲡⲉ.ⲥⲧⲁⲩⲣⲟⲥ (ὁ σταυρός) the Cross; usually written ⲡⲉⲥ⳨ⲟ̄ⲥ̄.

Exercises

A. (1) ⲟⲩⲟⲩϩⲟⲣ ⲉϥⲙⲟⲟⲩⲧ (2) ⲟⲩⲥⲩⲛⲁⲅⲱⲅⲏ ⲉⲥⲕⲏⲧ ϩⲁϩⲧⲛ̄

ⲧⲁⲅⲟⲣⲁ   (3) ⲟⲩⲣⲱⲙⲉ ⲉϥⲟⲩⲏⲋ ⲋ ⲡⲭⲁⲉ ⲓⲉ   (4) ⲟⲩⲋ̄ⲙ̄ϩⲁⲗ ⲉ-ⲛ̄ϥⲥⲱⲧⲙ̄
ⲁⲛ ⲛ̄ⲥⲁ ⲡⲉϥϫⲟⲉⲓⲥ   (5) ⲟⲩϣⲏⲣⲉ ϣⲏⲙ ⲉϥϯ ⲟⲩⲃⲉ ⲡⲉϥⲥⲟⲛ   (6) ⲟⲩϩⲁ̄ⲗ̄ⲱ
ⲉⲥⲥⲏⲋ   (7) ⲟⲩϩⲏⲧ ⲉϥⲛⲁϣⲧ̄   (8) ⲟⲩⲉⲓⲣⲏⲛⲏ ⲉ-ⲛ̄ⲥ̄ⲙⲏⲛ ⲉⲃⲟⲗ ⲁⲛ   (9)
ⲟⲩⲥϩⲓⲙⲉ ⲉⲥⲉⲉⲧ   (10) ϩⲉⲛϩⲏⲕⲉ ⲉⲩϩⲕⲁⲉⲓⲧ   (11) ⲟⲩϩⲓⲏ ⲉ-ⲛ̄ⲥ̄ⲙⲟⲧⲛ̄
ⲁⲛ   (12) ⲟⲩⲡⲛ̄ⲁ̄ ⲉϥⲟⲩⲁⲁⲃ   (13) ⲡⲉⲥⲟⲩⲟ ⲉⲧ ⲕⲏ ϩⲛ̄ ⲧⲁⲡⲟⲑⲏⲕⲏ
(14) ⲟⲩⲙⲏⲏϣⲉ ⲉϥⲟϣ   (15) ⲟⲩⲙⲁⲧⲟⲓ ⲉϥⲁⲗⲏⲩ ⲉⲭ̄ⲛ̄ ⲟⲩϩⲧⲟ

B. (1) ϩⲉⲛϣⲁϫⲉ ⲙ̄ ⲙⲉ   (2) ⲟⲩⲣⲟ ⲛ̄ ⲃⲉⲛⲓⲡⲉ   (3) ⲟⲩⲥⲣ̄ⲟ̄ⲥ̄ ⲛ̄ ϣⲉ
(4) ⲟⲩⲏⲓ ⲛ̄ ⲱⲛⲉ   (5) ϩⲉⲛⲥⲛⲁⲩϩ ⲛ̄ ⲃⲉⲛⲓⲡⲉ   (6) ⲛ̄ϣⲁϫⲉ ⲙ̄ ⲙⲉⲧⲁⲛⲟⲓⲁ
(7) ⲡⲁⲙⲁ ⲛ̄ ϣⲱⲡⲉ   (8) ⲟⲩⲥⲙⲟⲧ ⲛ̄ ⲁⲅⲅⲉⲗⲟⲥ   (9) ⲧⲡⲓⲥⲧⲓⲥ ⲙ̄ ⲙⲉ
(10) ⲟⲩⲥⲛϥⲉ ⲛ̄ ⲕⲱϩⲧ̄   (11) ⲟⲩⲙⲩⲥⲧⲏⲣⲓⲟⲛ ⲛ̄ ⲛⲟⲩⲧⲉ   (12) ⲡⲉⲛⲙⲁ ⲛ̄
ⲟⲩⲱⲙ   (13) ϩⲉⲛⲙⲁⲧⲟⲓ ⲛ̄ ϫⲁϫⲉ   (14) ⲟⲩⲁⲡⲟⲧ ⲛ̄ ⲉⲣⲱⲧⲉ   (15) ⲟⲩⲙⲁ
ⲛ̄ ϩⲁⲣⲉϩ

C. (1) ⲉⲛϩⲙⲟⲟⲥ ϩⲛ̄ ⲧⲁⲅⲟⲣⲁ, ⲁⲛⲛⲁⲩ ⲉ ⲡϩⲏⲅⲉⲙⲱⲛ ⲉϥϩⲱⲛ ⲉϩⲟⲩⲛ.
(2) ϯⲛⲁϭⲱ ⲙ̄ ⲡⲉⲓⲙⲁ ⲉⲓϭⲱϣⲧ̄ ⲉⲃⲟⲗ ϩⲏⲧϥ̄ ⲙ̄ ⲡⲉϩⲟⲟⲩ ⲙ̄ ⲡϫⲟⲉⲓⲥ.   (3)
ⲉⲣⲉ-ⲛⲉⲥⲛⲏⲩ ⲙⲟⲟϣⲉ ⲉ ⲑⲉⲛⲉⲉⲧⲉ, ⲁⲩϩⲉ ⲉⲩⲣⲱⲙⲉ ⲉϥⲙⲟⲟⲩⲧ ⲉϥⲕⲏ ϩⲓϫⲙ̄
ⲡⲕⲁϩ.   (4) ⲁⲩⲙⲟⲩⲛ ⲉⲃⲟⲗ ⲉⲩⲉⲓⲛⲉ ⲙ̄ ⲡⲉⲥⲟⲩⲟ ⲉ ⲧⲁⲡⲟⲑⲏⲕⲏ.   (5)
ⲁⲗⲱⲧⲛ̄! ⲛ̄ϯⲟⲩⲱϣ ⲁⲛ ⲉ ⲥⲱⲧⲙ̄ ⲉ ϩⲉⲛϣⲁϫⲉ ⲛ̄ ⲧⲉⲓⲙⲓⲛⲉ.   (6) ⲁⲛⲛⲁⲩ
ⲉⲣⲟϥ ⲉϥⲃⲏⲕ ⲉⲃⲟⲗ ϩⲛ̄ ⲑⲉⲛⲉⲉⲧⲉ.   (7) ⲙ̄ⲛ̄ⲧⲁⲛ ⲥⲟⲩⲟ ϩⲛ̄ ⲧⲉⲛⲁⲡⲟⲑⲏⲕⲏ,
ⲁⲗⲗⲁ ⲟⲩⲛ̄ⲧⲁⲛ ⲙ̄ⲙⲁⲩ ⲛ̄ ϩⲁϩ ⲛ̄ ϣⲉ.   (8) ⲥⲱⲧⲙ̄ ⲉ ⲛ̄ϣⲁϫⲉ ⲛ̄ ⲧⲁⲧⲁⲡⲣⲟ,
ⲉⲃⲟⲗ ϫⲉ ϩⲉⲛⲙⲉ ⲛⲉ.   (9) ⲁⲓⲛⲁⲩ ⲛ̄ ⲟⲩⲟⲩϩⲟⲣ ⲉϥϥⲓ ⲛ̄ ⲟⲩⲕⲟⲩⲓ ⲛ̄
ⲃⲣⲟⲟⲙⲡⲉ ϩⲛ̄ ⲧⲉϥⲧⲁⲡⲣⲟ.   (10) ⲁⲩⲉⲓ ϣⲁⲣⲟϥ ⲛ̄ϭⲓ ⲛⲉⲧ ⲟⲩⲏϩ ϩⲛ̄
ⲧⲡⲉⲣⲓⲭⲱⲣⲟⲥ ⲙ̄ ⲡⲓⲟⲣⲇⲁⲛⲏⲥ ⲧⲏⲣⲟⲩ.   (11) ⲛⲁⲓ ⲛⲉ ⲛ̄ⲣⲁⲛ ⲛ̄ ⲛⲉⲥⲛⲏⲩ
ⲉⲧ ⲏⲡ ⲉ ⲕⲏⲙⲉ.   (12) ⲛⲉⲓⲥⲟⲟⲩⲛ̄ ⲁⲛ ⲡⲉ ϫⲉ ⲛⲉⲓϫⲱⲱⲙⲉ ⲛⲟⲩⲕ ⲛⲉ.
(13) ⲉⲛϩⲏⲛ ⲉϩⲟⲩⲛ ⲉ ⲧⲡⲟⲗⲓⲥ, ⲁⲛⲛⲁⲩ ⲉⲩⲙⲏⲏϣⲉ ⲉϥⲟϣ ⲉϥⲡⲏⲧ ⲉⲃⲟⲗ
ϩⲓⲧⲛ̄ ⲧⲡⲩⲗⲏ.   (14) ⲉϥⲙⲟⲟϣⲉ ϩⲁϩⲧⲙ̄ ⲡⲉⲣⲡⲉ, ⲁϥⲛⲁⲩ ⲉⲩⲃⲁ̄ⲗⲉ ⲛ̄ ϩⲏⲕⲉ
ⲉϥϯ ⲉⲃⲟⲗ ⲙ̄ ⲡⲉϥϩⲱⲃ ⲛ̄ ϭⲓϫ.   (15) ⲙ̄ⲛ̄-ϭⲟⲙ ⲙ̄ⲙⲟⲛ ⲉ ⲛⲟⲩϫⲉ ⲉⲃⲟⲗ ⲛ̄
ϩⲉⲛⲇⲁⲓⲙⲱⲛ ⲛ̄ ⲁⲕⲁⲑⲁⲣⲧⲟⲛ.   (16) ⲁϥⲟⲩⲱ ⲉϥⲥϩⲁⲓ ⲁⲩⲱ ⲁϥϭⲱϣⲧ̄ ⲉϩⲟⲩⲛ
ⲉ ⲡⲣⲟ ⲛ̄ ⲧⲉϥⲣⲓ.   (17) ϩⲁⲡ̄ⲥ̄ ⲉⲣⲟⲛ ⲉⲧⲣⲉⲛⲗⲟ ⲉⲃⲟⲗ ϩⲙ̄ ⲡⲉⲓⲙⲁ.   (18)
ⲁⲥϭⲱ ⲉⲥⲣⲓⲙⲉ ⲉⲭⲙ̄ ⲡⲙⲟⲩ ⲙ̄ ⲡⲉⲥⲙⲉⲣⲓⲧ ⲛ̄ ϩⲁⲓ.   (19) ⲁϥⲗⲟ ⲉϥⲉⲓⲛⲉ
ⲛⲁⲛ ⲙ̄ ⲡⲉϥϩⲱⲃ ⲛ̄ ϭⲓϫ.   (20) ⲓⲥ̄ ⲇⲉ, ⲉϥϫⲏⲕ ⲉⲃⲟⲗ ⲙ̄ ⲡⲛ̄ⲁ̄ ⲉϥⲟⲩⲁⲁⲃ,
ⲁϥⲕⲟⲧϥ̄ ⲉⲃⲟⲗ ϩⲙ̄ ⲡⲓⲟⲣⲇⲁⲛⲏⲥ, ⲉϥⲙⲟⲟϣⲉ ϩⲙ̄ ⲡⲉⲡⲛ̄ⲁ̄ ϩⲓ ⲧⲉⲣⲏⲙⲟⲥ ⲛ̄ ϩⲁϩ
ⲛ̄ ϩⲟⲟⲩ, ⲉⲩⲡⲉⲓⲣⲁⲍⲉ ⲙ̄ⲙⲟϥ ϩⲓⲧⲙ̄ ⲡⲇⲓⲁⲃⲟⲗⲟⲥ, ⲁⲩⲱ ⲙ̄ⲡⲉϥⲟⲩⲉⲙ-ⲗⲁⲁⲩ ϩⲛ̄
ⲛⲉϩⲟⲟⲩ ⲉⲧ ⲙ̄ⲙⲁⲩ. ⲛ̄ⲧⲉⲣⲟⲩϫⲱⲕ ⲇⲉ ⲉⲃⲟⲗ, ⲁϥϩⲕⲟ.   (21) ⲁⲓϩⲙⲟⲟⲥ
ⲉⲓⲥϩⲁⲓ ⲛ̄ ϣⲟⲙⲧⲉ ⲛ̄ ⲟⲩⲛⲟⲩ.   (22) ⲁⲩⲙⲟⲩⲛ ⲉⲃⲟⲗ ⲉⲩⲣⲓⲙⲉ ⲛ̄ ⲧⲉⲩϣⲏ

ⲧⲏⲣⲥ̄. (23) ⲙ̄ⲡⲉⲛⲉ̄ⲱ ⲉⲛϣⲗⲏⲗ ⲛ̄ⲧⲉⲣⲛ̄ⲥⲱⲧⲙ̄ ⲉ ⲛⲁⲓ. (24) ⲛ̄ ⲧⲉⲩⲛⲟⲩ
ⲁⲥⲟⲩⲱ ⲉⲥϣⲱⲛⲉ ⲁⲩⲱ ⲁⲥⲟⲩⲭⲁⲓ. (25) ⲁⲓⲗⲟ ⲉⲓϯ ⲛ̄ ⲍⲉⲛⲟⲉⲓⲕ ⲛⲁⲩ.
(26) ⲁϥϣⲁⲝⲉ ⲛⲙ̄ⲙⲁⲩ ⲉϥⲉⲡⲓϯⲙⲁ ⲛⲁⲩ. (27) ⲙⲛ̄-ⲟⲩⲭⲁⲓ ϣⲟⲟⲡ ⲛ̄ ⲛⲉⲧⲉ
ⲛ̄ⲥⲉⲥⲱⲧⲙ̄ ⲁⲛ ⲛ̄ⲥⲁ ⲛⲉϥⲉⲛⲧⲟⲗⲏ. (28) ⲁⲩⲁⲍⲉⲣⲁⲧⲟⲩ ⲍⲁⲍⲧⲙ̄ ⲡⲉϥⲥ̄ⲣⲟ̄ⲥ̄
ⲉⲩⲣⲓⲙⲉ. (29) ⲁϥⲉⲡⲓϯⲙⲁ ⲛⲁⲩ ⲉϥⲭⲱ ⲙ̄ⲙⲟⲥ ⲭⲉ, "ⲙ̄ⲡⲣ̄ϣⲁⲝⲉ ⲛ̄ ⲗⲁⲁⲩ
ⲛ̄ ⲣⲱⲙⲉ ⲉⲧⲃⲉ ⲡⲉⲓⲍⲱⲃ."

Lesson 24

24.1 The Second Present has exactly the same inflection as the Circumstantial. This ambiguity poses a serious
difficulty for the reader of Sahidic Coptic which can be
resolved only by a careful study of the context. The uses
of the Second Present parallel those of the Second Perfect:

(1) emphasis on an adverbial element:

> ⲉⲣⲉ-ⲛⲁⲓ ϣⲟⲟⲡ ⲙ̄ⲙⲟⲓ ⲉⲧⲃⲉ ⲛⲁⲛⲟⲃⲉ.
> It is because of my sins that these things
> happen to me.

(2) preceding various interrogative expressions:

> ⲉⲕϣⲓⲛⲉ ⲛ̄ⲥⲁ ⲛⲓⲙ?　Whom do you seek?
> ⲉϥⲣⲓⲙⲉ ⲉ ⲟⲩ?　Why is he weeping?
> ⲉϥⲧⲱⲛ?　Where is he?

When ⲧⲱⲛ is used with a nominal subject, the usual idiom
is ⲉϥⲧⲱⲛ N? Where is N?, without the expected ⲛ̄ϭⲓ:

> ⲉϥⲧⲱⲛ ⲡⲉⲕⲉⲓⲱⲧ?　Where is your father?

The alternate construction (ⲉⲣⲉ-ⲡⲉⲕⲉⲓⲱⲧ ⲧⲱⲛ?) is less
frequent.

Clauses containing second tense forms are negated
with ⲁⲛ:

ⲉⲓⲟⲩⲏⲋ ⲍⲙ̄ ⲡⲉⲓⲙⲁ ⲁⲛ.   It is not here that I dwell.

ⲛ̄ⲧⲁⲓⲁⲁⲥ ⲛⲁⲕ ⲁⲛ.   It is not for you that I did it.

As may be seen from the translation, the negation applies
to the adverbial element and is not a negation of the verb
proper.

24.2 The Bipartite Conjugation (Present-Imperfect
System). The First Present, its relative forms, the
Circumstantial, the Second Present, and the Imperfect
comprise a system:

Pres. I	ⳛⲥⲱⲧⲙ̄	ⲡⲣⲱⲙⲉ ⲥⲱⲧⲙ̄
Rel. Pres. I	ⲉⲧⳛ̄ⲥⲱⲧⲙ̄	ⲉⲧⲉⲣⲉ-ⲡⲣⲱⲙⲉ ⲥⲱⲧⲙ̄
	ⲉⲧ ⲥⲱⲧⲙ̄	
Circumstantial	ⲉⳛⲥⲱⲧⲙ̄	ⲉⲣⲉ-ⲡⲣⲱⲙⲉ ⲥⲱⲧⲙ̄
Pres. II	ⲉⳛⲥⲱⲧⲙ̄	ⲉⲣⲉ-ⲡⲣⲱⲙⲉ ⲥⲱⲧⲙ̄
Imperfect	ⲛⲉⳛⲥⲱⲧⲙ̄	ⲛⲉⲣⲉ-ⲡⲣⲱⲙⲉ ⲥⲱⲧⲙ̄

Following the penetrating analysis of H. J. Polotsky (see
Bibliography), Coptic scholars now refer to this system as
the *Bipartite Conjugation*. This term arises from the fact
that the base form, the First Present, consists only of
subject + predicate, with no conjugational prefix. The
remaining forms of the system consist of this bipartite
nucleus preceded by a set of elements called *converters*:
the relative converter ⲉⲧ/ⲉⲧⲉⲣⲉ, the circumstantial converter ⲉ/ⲉⲣⲉ, the second tense converter ⲉ/ⲉⲣⲉ, and the
imperfect converter ⲛⲉ/ⲛⲉⲣⲉ. The term *tripartite* is
applied to all other Coptic verbal conjugations, which
consist of a verbal prefix + subject + predicate, e.g. the
First Perfect ⲁ̌ⳛ-ⲥⲱⲧⲙ̄, ⲁ-ⲡⲣⲱⲙⲉ ⲥⲱⲧⲙ̄. The First Future is
a special case and will be treated in the following lesson.

The conjugations belonging to the Bipartite Conjugation may have three kinds of predicates: infinitives,
qualitatives, or adverbial predicates (i.e. adverbs or
prepositional phrases). In the tripartite conjugations
only the infinitive may be used. The conjugations of the

Bipartite Conjugation, as we have already seen, character-
ize an action as durative, continuing, or (less commonly)
habitual. The following features of the Bipartite Conjugation are equally distinctive:

(1) The First Present requires the use of oyn̄- (neg.
mn̄-) before an indefinite subject (e.g. oyn̄-oyρωμε cωτm̄).
The use of oyn̄-/mn̄- is optional after the converters, e.g.
nερε-oyρωμε cωτm̄ or nε-oyn̄-oyρωμε cωτm̄.

(2) Apart from the use of mn̄- just mentioned, negation
is universally with (n̄) ... λn.

(3) An infinitive cannot, in general, be used in the
prenominal or prepronominal form, i.e. prepositional direct
object markers (m̄mo⸗, ε, etc.) must be used. This rule,
known as Jernstedt's Rule (see Bibliography), has the
following exceptions:

(a) the verb oyωϣ oyεϣ- oyλϣ⸗, which may occur in
all forms; e.g. †oyωϣ m̄moϥ or †oyλϣϥ̄.
(b) infinitives having indefinite pronominal or
numerical objects; e.g. nϥ̄†-λλλy nλn λn he is
giving us nothing.
(c) certain types of compound verbs; see 26.1.

The Imperfect may be expanded into a subsystem of its
own by the prefixation of the other converters:

Imperfect	nεϥcωτm̄	nερε-πρωμε cωτm̄
Imperfect Rel.	εnεϥcωτm̄	εnερε-πρωμε cωτm̄
	ετε nεϥcωτm̄	
Imperfect Circum.	ε-nεϥcωτm̄	ε-nερε-πρωμε cωτm̄

These forms have all the characteristics of, and belong to,
the Bipartite Conjugation. The relative forms have already
been introduced. The circumstantial forms are used syntac-
tically exactly like the Circumstantial (of Pres. I). The
past tense of the action is explicitly marked, however,
while in the Circumstantial it must be gained from the context. Second tense forms of the Imperfect may occur, but

they are too rare for consideration here. All verbal forms containing the imperfect converter may be followed by ⲛⲉ.

24.3 Numbers (continued). The 'teens are formed by prefixing ⲙⲛ̄ⲧ- to special forms of the units. ⲙⲛ̄ⲧ- is a proclitic form of ⲙⲏⲧ ten:

11 m. ⲙⲛ̄ⲧⲟⲩⲉ; f. ⲙⲛ̄ⲧⲟⲩⲉⲓ	15 m. f. ⲙⲛ̄ⲧⲏ	
12 m. ⲙⲛ̄ⲧⲥⲛⲟⲟⲩⲥ; f. ⲙⲛ̄ⲧⲥⲛⲟⲟⲩⲥ(ⲉ)	16 m. f. ⲙⲛ̄ⲧⲁⲥⲉ	
13 m. f. ⲙⲛ̄ⲧϣⲟⲙⲧⲉ	17 m. f. ⲙⲛ̄ⲧⲥⲁϣϥ(ⲉ)	
14 m. f. ⲙⲛ̄ⲧⲁϥⲧⲉ	18 m. f. ⲙⲛ̄ⲧϣⲙⲏⲛⲉ	

Construction is the same as that of the units:

ⲙⲛ̄ⲧϣⲟⲙⲧⲉ ⲛ̄ ⲣⲱⲙⲉ   thirteen men

Vocabulary 24

ⲣⲱ2ⲧ ⲣⲉ2ⲧ̄- ⲣⲁ2ⲧ⸗ Q ⲣⲁ2ⲧ̄ vb. tr. to strike, kill (ⲙ̄ⲙⲟ⸗); to strike down, cast down.

ⲥⲟⲃⲧⲉ ⲥⲃ̄ⲧⲉ- ⲥⲃ̄ⲧⲱⲧ⸗ Q ⲥⲃ̄ⲧⲱⲧ vb. tr. to prepare, make ready (ⲙ̄ⲙⲟ⸗; for: ⲉ); intr. and reflex. to get ready.

ⲝⲓⲥⲉ ⲝⲉⲥⲧ̄- ⲝⲁⲥⲧ⸗ Q ⲝⲟⲥⲉ (± ⲉ2ⲣⲁⲓ) vb. tr. to raise up, exalt (ⲙ̄ⲙⲟ⸗; over: ⲉ, ⲉ︤ⲝ︤ⲛ̄, 2ⲓⲝ︤ⲛ̄); intr. to be exalted; as n.m. heights. ⲡⲉⲧ ⲝⲟⲥⲉ the Almighty.

ⲟⲩⲉⲓⲛⲉ vb. intr. to pass (subj. usually period of time).

ⲕⲓⲙ ⲕⲉⲙⲧ̄- ⲕⲉⲙⲧ⸗ vb. tr. to touch (ⲉ; with: ⲉ); to move, shift, stir (ⲙ̄ⲙⲟ⸗, ⲉ); vb. intr. to move, stir, be moved.

ϣⲓⲛⲉ vb. intr. to be ashamed (about: ⲉⲧⲃⲉ); as n.m. shame. ϣⲓⲛⲉ 2ⲏⲧ⸗ to revere, be humbled before.

ϣⲟⲩⲉⲓⲧ Q to be empty, vain.

2ⲟⲟⲩ Q to be bad, wicked.

ⲧⲟⲛⲧⲛ̄ ⲧⲛ̄ⲧⲛ̄- ⲧⲛ̄ⲧⲱⲛ⸗ Q ⲧⲛ̄ⲧⲱⲛ vb. tr. to liken, compare (ⲙ̄ⲙⲟ⸗; to: ⲉ, ⲙⲛ̄, ⲉ︤ⲝ︤ⲛ̄).

ⲥⲱⲧⲡ̄ ⲥⲉⲧⲡ̄- ⲥⲟⲧⲡ⸗ Q ⲥⲟⲧⲡ̄ vb. tr. to choose, select (ⲙ̄ⲙⲟ⸗); Q also = to be excellent, exquisite.

ⲙⲟⲩⲟⲩⲧ ⲙⲉⲩⲧ- ⲙⲟⲟⲩⲧ⸗ vb. tr. to kill (ⲙ̄ⲙⲟ⸗).

ⲡ.ⲧⲏⲏⲃⲉ finger.

ⲉ ⲟⲩ why? for what reason?

104

ϣⲓⲏⲧ Scetis, the Lower Egyptian center of monasticism, in the Western Delta.

ⲡⲉ.ⲡⲣⲟⲫⲏⲧⲏⲥ (ὁ προφήτης) prophet.

ⲡ.ⲁⲡⲟⲥⲧⲟⲗⲟⲥ (ὁ ἀπόστολος) apostle.

Exercises

A. (1) ⲍⲉⲛⲍⲓⲟⲙⲉ ⲉ-ⲛⲉⲩⲉⲓⲱ ⲛ̄ ⲍⲉⲛⲍⲟⲉⲓⲧⲉ (2) ⲡⲉⲥⲙⲟⲧ ⲉⲛⲧⲁϥ-
ϣⲃ̄ⲧϥ̄ ⲛ̄ⲍⲏⲧϥ̄ (3) ⲟⲩⲥⲍⲓⲙⲉ ⲉ-ⲛⲉⲣⲉ-ⲡⲉⲥⲍⲁⲓ ⲙⲉ ⲙ̄ⲙⲟⲥ ⲙ̄ⲙⲁⲧⲉ (4)
ⲟⲩⲭⲏⲣⲁ ⲉ-ⲛⲉⲣⲉ-ⲡⲉⲥϣⲏⲣⲉ ϣⲱⲛⲉ (5) ⲡⲙⲏⲛϣⲉ ⲉⲛⲉⲩⲁⲍⲉⲣⲁⲧⲟⲩ ⲙ̄ ⲡⲉϥⲕⲱⲧⲉ (6) ⲡⲙⲩⲥⲧⲏⲣⲓⲟⲛ ⲉⲧⲟⲩⲛⲁⲟⲩⲟⲛⲍϥ̄ ⲉⲃⲟⲗ (7) ⲡⲉⲡⲣⲟⲫⲏⲧⲏⲥ ⲉⲛⲧⲁ-
ⲡⲙⲏⲛϣⲉ ⲙⲟⲟⲩⲧϥ̄ (8) ⲟⲩⲧⲟⲟⲩ ⲉϥϫⲟⲥⲉ (9) ⲟⲩⲛⲟϭ ⲛ̄ ⲟⲩⲟⲉⲓⲛ ⲉϥⲛⲏⲩ
ⲉⲡⲉⲥⲏⲧ ⲉⲃⲟⲗ ⲍⲙ̄ ⲡⲭⲓⲥⲉ (10) ⲟⲩⲗⲁⲟⲥ ⲉϥⲥⲃ̄ⲧⲱⲧ ⲍⲛ̄ ⲟⲩⲭⲱⲕ ⲉⲃⲟⲗ
(11) ⲟⲩⲥⲁⲍ ⲉⲛϣⲓⲡⲉ ⲍⲏⲧϥ̄ (12) ⲡⲉⲥⲟⲩⲟ ⲉⲛⲉⲣⲉ-ⲡⲉⲓⲱ ⲟⲩⲱⲙ ⲉⲃⲟⲗ
ⲙ̄ⲙⲟϥ (13) ⲙ̄ⲙⲁⲑⲏⲧⲏⲥ ⲉⲧ ⲥⲟⲧⲡ̄ ⲛ̄ⲧⲉ ⲡⲉⲛⲭⲟⲉⲓⲥ (14) ⲟⲩⲣ̄ⲣⲟ ⲉϥⲍⲟⲟⲩ
(15) ⲟⲩⲁⲡⲟⲧ ⲉϥϣⲟⲩⲉⲓⲧ (16) ⲡⲛⲟϭ ⲛ̄ ϣⲁ ⲉⲛⲉⲣⲉ-ⲙ̄ⲙⲟⲛⲁⲭⲟⲥ ⲥⲟⲃⲧⲉ
ⲉⲣⲟϥ (17) ⲡⲣⲱⲙⲉ ⲉⲛⲧⲁⲩⲣⲁⲍⲧϥ̄ ⲍⲓ ⲧⲉⲍⲓⲏ (18) ⲡϣⲉ ⲉⲛⲧⲁⲓⲛⲟⲭϥ̄
ⲉⲭⲙ̄ ⲡⲕⲱⲍⲧ̄ (19) ⲟⲩⲍⲙ̄ⲍⲁⲗ ⲉϥⲡⲁⲍⲧ̄ ⲛ̄ⲛⲁⲍⲣⲙ̄ ⲡⲉϥⲭⲟⲉⲓⲥ (20) ⲛⲉⲧⲉ
ⲛⲉⲩⲛⲏⲩ ⲉⲡⲉⲥⲏⲧ ⲉ ⲡⲓⲟⲣⲁⲁⲛⲏⲥ

B. (1) ⲡⲙⲛ̄ⲧⲥⲛⲟⲟⲩⲥ ⲛ̄ ⲁⲡⲟⲥⲧⲟⲗⲟⲥ (2) ⲡⲉⲓϣⲟⲙⲛ̄ⲧ ⲙ̄ ⲙⲁⲑⲏⲧⲏⲥ
(3) ⲙ̄ⲛ̄ⲧⲁϥⲧⲉ ⲛ̄ ⲍⲉⲛⲉⲉⲧⲉ (4) ⲥⲁϣϥ̄ ⲛ̄ ⲁⲁⲓⲙⲱⲛ (5) ϣⲙⲟⲩⲛ ⲛ̄ ⲏⲓ
ⲉⲩϣⲟⲩⲉⲓⲧ (6) ⲙⲏⲧⲉ ⲛ̄ ⲛⲟϭ ⲛ̄ ⲉⲍⲟⲩⲥⲓⲁ (7) ⲙ̄ⲛ̄ⲧⲥⲛⲟⲟⲩⲥ ⲛ̄ ⲥⲍⲓⲙⲉ
(8) ⲙ̄ⲛ̄ⲧⲏ ⲛ̄ ⲍⲟⲟⲩ (9) ⲙ̄ⲛ̄ⲧⲟⲩⲉⲓ ⲛ̄ ⲣⲟⲙⲡⲉ (10) ⲙ̄ⲛ̄ⲧⲟⲩⲉ ⲛ̄ ⲉⲃⲟⲧ

C. (1) ⲉϥⲧⲟⲛⲧⲛ̄ ⲙ̄ⲙⲟⲕ ⲉ ⲛⲓⲙ? (2) ⲉⲥⲧⲱⲛ ⲧⲁϣⲧⲏⲛ ⲛ̄ ⲃⲣ̄ⲣⲉ?
(3) ⲥⲉⲛⲁϫⲁⲥⲧⲉ ⲉⲍⲣⲁⲓ ⲉⲭⲛ̄ ⲛⲉⲍⲓⲟⲙⲉ ⲧⲏⲣⲟⲩ ⲛ̄ⲧⲉ ⲡⲉⲓⲕⲟⲥⲙⲟⲥ. (4)
ⲥⲱⲧⲡ̄ ⲛⲁⲕ ⲛ̄ ϥⲧⲟⲟⲩ ⲛ̄ ⲣⲱⲙⲉ. (5) ⲛ̄ⲧⲉⲣⲉ-ⲧⲉⲣⲟⲙⲡⲉ ⲉⲧ ⲙ̄ⲙⲁⲩ ⲟⲩⲉⲓⲛⲉ,
ⲁⲩⲕⲟⲧⲟⲩ ⲉ ⲡⲉⲩϯⲙⲉ. (6) ⲙ̄ ⲡⲉⲍⲟⲟⲩ ⲉⲧ ⲙ̄ⲙⲁⲩ ⲧⲉⲧⲛⲁϣⲓⲡⲉ ⲉⲧⲃⲉ ⲛⲉⲓ-
ⲍⲃⲏⲩⲉ ⲉⲑⲟⲟⲩ. (7) ⲁϥⲍⲉ ⲉⲭⲙ̄ ⲡⲕⲁⲍ ⲁⲩⲱ ⲙ̄ⲡⲉϥⲕⲓⲙ. (8) ⲛ̄ⲧⲁϥⲧⲛ̄-
ⲧⲱⲛⲟⲩ ⲉ ⲟⲩ? (9) ⲉⲣⲉ-ⲛⲁⲓ ϣⲏⲡ ⲉ ⲡⲉⲛⲭⲟⲉⲓⲥ ⲉⲧⲃⲉ ⲡⲉϥⲛⲁ. (10)
ⲉϥⲟⲩⲱϣ ⲉ ⲣⲁⲍⲧ̄ ⲉⲧⲃⲉ ⲡⲉⲛⲧⲁⲓⲁⲁϥ ⲟⲩⲃⲉ ⲛⲁ-ⲡⲉϥϯⲙⲉ. (11) ⲟⲩⲛ̄-
ⲟⲩⲍⲟⲟⲩ ⲛⲏⲩ ⲉϥⲍⲟⲟⲩ. (12) ⲉⲩⲧⲱⲛ ⲛⲉⲛϣⲃⲉⲉⲣ? (13) ⲁϥⲕⲓⲙ ⲉ ⲧⲉϥⲧⲁⲡⲣⲟ ⲉ ⲡⲉϥⲧⲏⲛⲃⲉ. (14) ⲧⲛ̄ⲛⲁⲥⲙⲟⲩ ⲉ ⲡⲉⲕⲣⲁⲛ ⲉⲧ ϫⲟⲥⲉ (15)
ⲉϥⲧⲛ̄ⲧⲱⲛ ⲉⲩϣⲏⲣⲉ ϣⲏⲙ. (16) ⲙⲛ̄ⲛ̄ⲥⲱⲥ ⲇⲉ ⲁ-ⲛⲉⲥⲛⲏⲩ ⲕⲟⲧⲟⲩ ⲉ ϣⲓⲏⲧ.
(17) ⲉⲧⲃⲉ ⲟⲩ ⲕⲟⲩⲱϣ ⲉ ⲙⲟⲩⲟⲩⲧ ⲛ̄ ⲛⲉⲓⲣⲱⲙⲉ? (18) ⲉⲧⲉⲧⲛ̄ⲥⲟⲃⲧⲉ
ⲙ̄ⲙⲱⲧⲛ̄ ⲉ ⲟⲩ? (19) ⲁⲩⲙⲉⲩⲧ-ⲟⲩⲟⲛ ⲛⲓⲙ ⲉⲧⲉ ⲛⲉⲩⲟⲩⲏⲍ ⲍⲙ̄ ⲡϯⲙⲉ ⲙⲛ̄
ⲧⲡⲉⲣⲓⲭⲱⲣⲟⲥ. (20) ⲁⲩⲍⲉ ⲉ ⲧⲉⲧⲣⲁⲡⲉⲭⲁ ⲉⲥⲥⲃ̄ⲧⲱⲧ.

Lesson 25

25.1 The relative, imperfect, circumstantial, and second tense converters may be used with the First Perfect, the First Future, existential and possessive predications, and copulative sentences with ⲛⲉ, ⲧⲉ, ⲛⲉ. The relative forms for all of these have already been discussed. The second tense of the First Perfect, i.e. the Second Perfect, was introduced in Lesson 14. The second tense forms of existential, possessive, and copulative sentences are too rare for inclusion here.

(a)			Neg.	
First Perfect	ⲁϥⲥⲱⲧⲙ̅			ⲙ̅ⲡⲉϥⲥⲱⲧⲙ̅
Perf. I Rel.	ⲉⲛⲧⲁϥⲥⲱⲧⲙ̅			ⲉⲧⲉ ⲙ̅ⲡⲉϥⲥⲱⲧⲙ̅
Perf. I Circum.	ⲉ-ⲁϥⲥⲱⲧⲙ̅			ⲉ-ⲙ̄ⲡⲉϥⲥⲱⲧⲙ̅
Pluperfect	ⲛⲉ-ⲁϥⲥⲱⲧⲙ̅			ⲛⲉ-ⲙ̄ⲡⲉϥⲥⲱⲧⲙ̅ (ⲛⲉ)
Second Perfect	ⲛ̄ⲧⲁϥⲥⲱⲧⲙ̅			ⲛ̄ⲧⲁϥⲥⲱⲧⲙ̅ ⲁⲛ

The imperfect of the First Perfect (ⲛⲉ-ⲁϥⲥⲱⲧⲙ̅) corresponds to the English pluperfect: he had heard, he had written. The circumstantial of the First Perfect is used to describe an action as completed prior to the tense of the verb in the main clause.

ⲉ-ⲁϥϩⲙⲟⲟⲥ, ⲁϥⲥϩⲁⲓ ... Having sat down, he wrote ...

ⲁⲛϩⲉ ⲉⲣⲟϥ ⲉ-ⲁϥⲙⲟⲩ. We found him dead (lit., having died).

(b)			
First Future	ϥⲛⲁⲥⲱⲧⲙ̅		ⲡⲣⲱⲙⲉ ⲛⲁⲥⲱⲧⲙ̅
Fut. I Rel.	ⲉⲧϥ̄ⲛⲁⲥⲱⲧⲙ̅		ⲉⲧⲉⲣⲉ-ⲡⲣⲱⲙⲉ ⲛⲁⲥⲱⲧⲙ̅
Fut. I Circum.	ⲉϥⲛⲁⲥⲱⲧⲙ̅		ⲉⲣⲉ-ⲡⲣⲱⲙⲉ ⲛⲁⲥⲱⲧⲙ̅
Fut. I Imperfect	ⲛⲉϥⲛⲁⲥⲱⲧⲙ̅		ⲛⲉⲣⲉ-ⲡⲣⲱⲙⲉ ⲛⲁⲥⲱⲧⲙ̅
Second Future	ⲉϥⲛⲁⲥⲱⲧⲙ̅		ⲉⲣⲉ-ⲡⲣⲱⲙⲉ ⲛⲁⲥⲱⲧⲙ̅

The circumstantial of the First Future describes an action as imminent, about to take place, with respect to the tense of the main clause:

ⲉⲓⲛⲁⲃⲱⲕ ⲉⲃⲟⲗ, ⲁϥⲙⲟⲩⲧⲉ ⲉⲣⲟⲓ. As I was about to leave, he summoned me.

ⲁⲛ2ⲉ ⲉⲡⲟϥ ⲉϥⲛⲁⲙⲟⲩ. We found him on the point of death.

The imperfect of the First Future describes an action as imminent in past time:

ⲛⲉⲓⲛⲁⲁⲁⲉ ⲉ ⲡ𝕏ⲟⲓ (ⲡⲉ). I was about to get on the ship.

This form is commonly called the *imperfectum futuri*. The Second Future (ⲉϥⲛⲁⲥⲱⲧⲙ̄) has all the normal uses of a second tense form. Special uses of both these conjugations will be mentioned later on.

The First Future and its related system are formally an off-shoot of the Present System, with ⲛⲁ- inserted before the infinitive. It has no other characteristics of the Bipartite Conjugation, however: (1) it is not durative (except with certain aspectually neutral verbs, e.g. ⲣⲁϣⲉ); (2) only the Infinitive may occur in predicate position; (3) the prenominal and prepronominal forms of the Infinitive occur freely.

(c) Existential and

Possessive	ⲟⲩⲛ̄-/ⲟⲩⲛ̄ⲧⲁϥ	ⲙⲛ̄-/ⲙⲛ̄ⲧⲁϥ
Relative	ⲉⲧⲉ ⲟⲩⲛ̄-/ⲟⲩⲛ̄ⲧⲁϥ	ⲉⲧⲉ ⲙⲛ̄-/ⲙⲛ̄ⲧⲁϥ
Circumstantial	ⲉ-ⲟⲩⲛ̄-/ⲟⲩⲛ̄ⲧⲁϥ	ⲉ-ⲙⲛ̄-/ⲙⲛ̄ⲧⲁϥ
Imperfect	ⲛⲉ-ⲟⲩⲛ̄-/ⲟⲩⲛ̄ⲧⲁϥ	ⲛⲉ-ⲙⲛ̄-/ⲙⲛ̄ⲧⲁϥ

The circumstantial forms describe a state simultaneous to the tense of the main clause:

ⲉ-ⲙⲛ̄-ⲟⲉⲓⲕ ⲙ̄ⲙⲁⲩ, ⲁⲛⲃⲱⲕ ⲉⲃⲟⲗ.　　There being no food there, we left.

ⲁⲛ2ⲉ ⲉⲡⲟϥ ⲉ-ⲙⲛ̄-6ⲟⲙ ⲙ̄ⲙⲟϥ ⲉ ϣⲁ𝕏ⲉ.　We found him unable to speak.

The imperfect forms simply place the state in past time:

ⲛⲉ-ⲟⲩⲛ̄- (or ⲛⲉⲩⲛ̄-) ⲟⲩⲣⲱⲙⲉ ⲙ̄ⲙⲁⲩ (ⲡⲉ).　There was a man.

ⲛⲉⲩⲛ̄ⲧⲁϥ 2ⲁ2 ⲛ̄ ⲥ2ⲓⲙⲉ (ⲡⲉ).　　　He had many wives.

(d) Copulative sentences with ⲡⲉ, ⲧⲉ, ⲛⲉ:

Relative	ⲉⲧⲉ ⲟⲩⲥⲁⳅ ⲡⲉ	ⲉⲧⲉ ⲛ̄ ⲟⲩⲥⲁⳅ ⲁⲛ ⲡⲉ
Circumstantial	ⲉ-ⲟⲩⲥⲁⳅ ⲡⲉ	ⲉ-ⲛ ⲟⲩⲥⲁⳅ ⲁⲛ ⲡⲉ
Imperfect	ⲛⲉ-ⲟⲩⲥⲁⳅ ⲡⲉ	

The circumstantial and imperfect are used as above.

The circumstantial forms of all the subsystems listed above have a frequent use as relative clauses after indefinite antecedents:

ⲟⲩⲣⲱⲙⲉ ⲉ-ⲁ̄ⲕⲉⲧ-ⲟⲩⲏⲓ	a man who had built a house
ⲟⲩⲙⲩⲥⲧⲏⲣⲓⲟⲛ ⲉⲩⲛⲁϭⲟⲗⲡ̄ϥ̄ ⲉⲃⲟⲗ	a mystery which is about to be revealed
ⲟⲩⲭⲏⲣⲁ ⲉ-ⲙⲛ̄ⲧⲁⲥ ϣⲏⲣⲉ ⲙ̄ⲙⲁⲩ	a widow who has no son
ⲟⲩϣⲏⲣⲉ ⲉ-ⲟⲩⲭⲏⲣⲁ ⲧⲉ ⲧⲉϥⲙⲁⲁⲩ	a boy whose mother is a widow

The circumstantial converter ⲉⲣⲉ- is sometimes used improperly for ⲉ- before copulative sentences.

25.2 The Conjunctive.

(ⲛ̄)ⲧⲁⲥⲱⲧⲙ̄	ⲛ̄ⲧⲛ̄ⲥⲱⲧⲙ̄	ⲛ̄ⲧⲉ-ⲡⲣⲱⲙⲉ ⲥⲱⲧⲙ̄
ⲛ̄ⲅⲥⲱⲧⲙ̄	ⲛ̄ⲧⲉⲧⲛ̄ⲥⲱⲧⲙ̄	
ⲛ̄ⲧⲉⲥⲱⲧⲙ̄		
ⲛ̄ϥⲥⲱⲧⲙ̄	ⲛ̄ⲥⲉⲥⲱⲧⲙ̄	
ⲛ̄ⲥⲥⲱⲧⲙ̄		

ⲛ̄ⲅ-, ⲛ̄ϥ-, and ⲛ̄ⲥ- also appear frequently as ⲛⲅ̄-, ⲛϥ̄-, ⲛⲥ̄-. The conjunctive is used to continue the force of a preceding verbal prefix. In a sense, it is no more than an inflected form of the conjunction "and." It is especially frequent after a First Future or an Imperative:

ϯⲛⲁⲃⲱⲕ ⲛ̄ⲧⲁϣⲁⲭⲉ ⲛⲙ̄ⲙⲁϥ.	I shall go and speak with him.
ⳅⲙⲟⲟⲥ ⲛ̄ⲅⲥⲱⲧⲙ̄ ⲉ ⲧⲁⲥⲃⲱ.	Sit down and listen to my teaching.
ⲁⲛⲓ-ⲛ̄ϫⲱⲱⲙⲉ ⲛ̄ⲧⲉⲧⲛ̄ⲧⲁⲁⲩ ⲛⲁϥ.	Bring the books and give them to him.

It may be used to continue the force of virtually any preceding verbal prefix except that of the affirmative First Perfect, but even this restriction does not hold in

the relative forms. It is also used after an Inflected
Infinitive, as in

ⲥⲁⲡⲥ̄ ⲉⲣⲟⲛ ⲉⲧⲣⲉⲛⲃⲱⲕ ⲛ̄ⲧⲛ̄ϣⲁϫⲉ ⲛⲙ̄ⲙⲁϥ.

It is necessary that we go and speak with him.

In many instances, especially where there is a change of
subject, the Conjunctive clause has the meaning of a
purpose or result clause:

ⲁⲛⲓϥ ⲉⲣⲟⲓ ⲛ̄ⲧⲁⲛⲁⲩ ⲉⲣⲟϥ. Bring him to me so that I may see him.
ⲙⲁ ⲛⲁⲩ ⲛ̄ⲥⲉⲟⲩⲱⲙ. Give them (food) so that they may eat.

This usage depends very much on the presence of an injunctive (imperative) force, implicit or explicit, in the first
clause. For the conjunctive with Greek conjunctions, see
Lesson 30.

The Conjunctive resembles the Tripartite Conjugation:
only the Infinitive may be used as its verbal component.
Negation is with -ⲧⲙ̄- before the Infinitive. If the Conjunctive continues a negative verb, however, the negation
may carry over.

Vocabulary 25

ⲟⲩⲉ, Q ⲟⲩⲏⲩ vb. intr. to become/be distant, far (from: ⲉ,
ⲙ̄ⲙⲟ⸗, ⲉⲃⲟⲗ ⲙ̄ⲙⲟ⸗); as n.m. distance. ⲉ ⲡⲟⲩⲉ away, to a
distance. ⲙ̄ ⲡⲟⲩⲉ at a distance.

ⲧⲁϩⲟ ⲧⲁϩⲉ- ⲧⲁϩⲟ⸗ Q ⲧⲁϩⲏⲩ vb. tr. (1) to cause to stand; to
create, establish (ⲙ̄ⲙⲟ⸗); (2) to reach, attain, catch
up to (ⲙ̄ⲙⲟ⸗); to seize, arrest (ⲙ̄ⲙⲟ⸗).

ϭⲱⲛⲧ̄, Q ϭⲟⲛⲧ̄ vb. intr. to become/be angry, furious (at, a-
gainst: ⲉ, ⲉϫⲛ̄); as n.m. wrath, fury.

ⲙ̄ⲡϣⲁ vb. intr. to be worthy, deserving (of: ⲙ̄ⲙⲟ⸗; to do: ⲛ̄,
ⲉ + Inf.).

ⲧⲁⲕⲟ ⲧⲁⲕⲉ- ⲧⲁⲕⲟ⸗ Q ⲧⲁⲕⲏⲩ vb. tr. to destroy, put an end to
(ⲙ̄ⲙⲟ⸗); intr. to perish; as n.m. destruction, perdition.

ⲱⲙⲥ̄ ⲉⲙⲥ̄- ⲟⲙⲥ⸗ Q ⲟⲙⲥ̄ vb. tr. to sink, dip, immerse (ⲙ̄ⲙⲟ⸗);
intr. to sink (into: ϩⲛ̄, ⲉ, ⲉϩⲟⲩⲛ ⲉ).

ⲍⲱⲗ, Q ⲍⲏⲗ vb. intr. to fly.

ⲡ.ϣⲏⲛ tree.

ⲡ.ⲧⲁⲣ branch.

ⲡ.ⲉⲗⲟⲟⲗⲉ grape.

ⲡ.ⲍⲁⲗⲏⲧ (pl. ⲍⲁⲗⲁⲧⲉ) bird.

ⲧ.ⲭⲉⲛⲉⲡⲱⲣ roof.

ⲧ.ⲃⲱ ⲛ̄ ⲉⲗⲟⲟⲗⲉ grape-vine.

ⲧ.ⲃⲱ tree, vine. ⲃⲱ is used when type of tree is mentioned; use ϣⲏⲛ otherwise.

ⲡ.ⲙⲁ ⲛ̄ ⲉⲗⲟⲟⲗⲉ vineyard.

Exercises

(1) ⲡⲙⲁ ⲛ̄ ⲉⲗⲟⲟⲗⲉ ⲟⲩⲏⲩ ⲁⲛ ⲉⲃⲟⲗ ⲍⲙ̄ ⲡϯⲙⲉ. (2) ⲉ-ⲁⲩⲧⲁⲕⲟ ⲛ̄ ⲧⲡⲟⲗⲓⲥ, ⲁⲩⲗⲟ ⲉⲃⲟⲗ. (3) ⲍⲁⲡⲥ̄ ⲉⲧⲣⲉⲕⲥⲟⲃⲧⲉ ⲛⲁϥ ⲛ̄ ⲟⲩⲙⲁ ⲛ̄ ⲛ̄ⲕⲟⲧⲕ̄. (4) ⲁⲩⲧⲁⲍⲉ-ⲛ̄ϣⲏⲣⲉ ⲉⲩⲙⲏⲣ ⲛ̄ⲛⲁⲍⲣⲙ̄ ⲡⲍⲏⲅⲉⲙⲱⲛ. (5) ⲁⲙⲏⲉⲓⲧⲛ̄ ⲛ̄ⲧⲉⲧⲛ̄-ⲥⲱⲧⲙ̄ ⲉ ⲧⲉϥⲥⲃⲱ. (6) ⲛⲉⲓⲁⲍⲉⲣⲁⲧ ⲙ̄ ⲡⲟⲩⲉ ⲉⲓⲃⲱϣⲧ̄ ⲉ ⲡⲙⲛ̄ϣⲉ. (7) ϯ-ⲛⲁⲃⲱⲕ ⲛ̄ⲧⲁⲃⲛ̄ⲧϥ̄. (8) ⲛⲉⲣⲉ-ⲛⲉⲥⲛⲏⲩ ⲉⲓⲛⲉ ⲙ̄ ⲡⲕⲁⲣⲡⲟⲥ ⲉ ⲧⲡⲟⲗⲓⲥ ⲛ̄ⲥⲉϯ ⲙ̄ⲙⲟϥ ⲉⲃⲟⲗ ⲍⲛ̄ ⲧⲁⲅⲟⲣⲁ. (9) ⲛⲉⲩⲛⲁⲣⲱⲍⲧ̄ ⲙ̄ⲙⲟϥ ⲛ̄ϭⲓ ⲙ̄ⲙⲁⲧⲟⲓ ⲛ̄ ⲭⲁⲭⲉ. (10) ⲁ-ⲡⲍⲁⲗⲏⲧ ⲍⲱⲗ ⲉ ⲧⲡⲉ ⲁⲩⲱ ⲁϥⲟⲩⲱⲍ ⲉⲭⲛ̄ ⲟⲩⲧⲁⲣ ⲛ̄ⲧⲉ ⲡϣⲏⲛ. (11) ⲛⲁⲓ ⲛⲉ ⲛ̄ϣⲁⲭⲉ ⲉⲛⲧⲁϥⲥⲍⲁⲓⲥⲟⲩ ⲍⲓ ⲡⲕⲁⲍ ⲍⲙ̄ ⲡⲉϥⲧⲏⲏⲃⲉ. (12) ⲉ-ⲁϥⲧⲱⲟⲩⲛ ⲛ̄ϭⲓ ⲡⲃⲁⲗⲉ, ⲁϥⲃⲱⲕ ⲉⲃⲟⲗ ⲉϥⲣⲁϣⲉ. (13) ⲛⲉ-ⲟⲩⲛ̄-ⲧⲁϥ ⲙ̄ⲙⲁⲩ ⲛ̄ ⲟⲩⲕⲟⲩⲓ ⲛ̄ ϣⲏⲣⲉ ⲉϥⲥⲏⲃ. (14) ⲥⲉⲛⲁⲧⲁⲍⲟϥ ⲛ̄ⲥⲉⲛⲟⲭϥ̄ ⲉ ⲡⲉϣⲧⲉⲕⲟ. (15) ⲛⲉ-ⲟⲩⲁⲡⲓⲥⲧⲟⲥ ⲡⲉ ⲡⲉⲩⲣ̄ⲣⲟ. (16) ⲕⲛⲁϣⲓⲛⲉ ⲛ̄ⲥⲱⲓ ⲙ̄ ⲡⲉⲍⲟⲟⲩ ⲉⲧ ⲙ̄ⲙⲁⲩ ⲛ̄ⲅⲧⲙ̄ϭⲓⲛⲉ ⲙ̄ⲙⲟⲓ. (17) ⲛ̄ϯⲙ̄ⲡϣⲁ ⲁⲛ ⲉⲧⲣⲉⲩ-ⲥⲟⲧⲡⲧ̄. (18) ⲁⲛⲍⲉ ⲉ ⲡⲙⲁ ⲛ̄ ⲉⲗⲟⲟⲗⲉ ⲉϥⲧⲁⲕⲏⲩ. (19) ⲉ-ⲁ-ϣⲟⲙⲛ̄ⲧ ⲛ̄ ⲉⲃⲟⲧ ⲟⲩⲉⲓⲛⲉ, ⲁⲥⲕⲟⲧⲥ̄ ⲉ ⲡⲉⲥⲛⲓ. (20) ⲛⲉ-ⲙⲛ̄-ϭⲃⲟⲙ ⲙ̄ⲙⲟϥ ⲉ ⲧⲁⲍⲉ-ⲛⲉϥϣⲃⲉⲉⲣ. (21) ⲉ-ⲁϥϭⲱⲛⲧ ⲉⲭⲙ̄ ⲡⲉϥⲥⲟⲛ, ⲁϥⲧⲱⲟⲩⲛ ⲉⲭⲱϥ, ⲁϥⲙⲟⲟⲩⲧϥ̄. (22) ⲛⲉⲣⲉ-ⲛ̄ⲍⲁⲗⲁⲧⲉ ⲛ̄ ⲧⲡⲉ ⲟⲩⲱⲙ ⲉⲃⲟⲗ ⲍⲛ̄ ⲛⲉⲗⲟⲟⲗⲉ. (23) ⲁⲛⲛⲁⲩ ⲉ ⲡⲉϫⲭⲟⲓ ⲉϥⲱⲙⲥ̄ ⲉⲡⲉⲥⲏⲧ ⲛ̄ ⲑⲁⲗⲁⲥⲥⲁ. (24) ⲛ̄ⲧⲁϥⲉⲓ ⲉ ⲧⲁⲕⲟⲛ. (25) ⲉⲓⲛⲁⲛ̄ⲕⲟⲧⲕ̄, ⲁ-ⲡⲁⲍⲙ̄ⲍⲁⲗ ⲉⲓⲛⲉ ⲛⲁⲓ ⲛ̄ ⲧⲉⲕⲉⲡⲓⲥⲧⲟⲗⲏ. (26) ⲁⲩⲁⲗⲉ ⲍⲛ̄ ⲟⲩϭⲉⲡⲏ ⲉ ⲧⲭⲉⲛⲉⲡⲱⲣ. (27) ⲛⲉⲩⲛ̄-ⲟⲩⲣ̄ⲣⲟ ⲛ̄ⲥⲁⲃⲉ ⲉ-ⲟⲩⲛ̄ⲧⲁϥ ϣⲟⲙⲛ̄ⲧ ⲛ̄ ϣⲏⲣⲉ. (28) ⲁⲓⲛⲁⲩ ⲛ̄ ⲟⲩⲛⲟϭ ⲛ̄ ⲍⲁⲗⲏⲧ ⲉϥⲟⲩⲏⲍ ⲍⲓⲭⲛ̄ ⲟⲩⲃⲱ ⲛ̄ ⲉⲗⲟⲟⲗⲉ. (29) ⲧⲛ̄ⲛⲁⲛⲁⲩ ⲛ̄ⲧⲛ̄ⲉⲓⲙⲉ ⲛ̄ⲧⲛ̄ϣⲓⲡⲉ ⲉⲙⲁⲧⲉ. (30) ⲁϥⲕⲓⲙ ⲉ ⲛⲉϥⲧⲏⲏⲃⲉ ⲉ ⲛ̄ⲃⲁⲗ ⲙ̄ ⲡⲃⲗ̄ⲗⲉ. (31) ⲛ̄ ⲧⲉⲩⲛⲟⲩ ⲁϥⲗⲟ ⲉϥϭⲟⲛⲧ̄. (32) ⲁⲩⲉⲓ ⲉ ⲃⲏⲑⲗⲉⲉⲙ ⲉⲃⲟⲗ ϫⲉ ⲛⲉ-ⲁⲩⲥⲱⲧⲙ̄ ⲉⲧⲃⲉ ⲡⲙⲓⲥⲉ ⲙ̄ ⲡⲉⲛⲥⲱⲧⲏⲣ. (33) ⲁ-ⲡⲁϫⲟⲓ ⲱⲙⲥ̄ ⲍⲙ̄ ⲡⲉⲓⲉⲣⲟ. (34) ⲛⲉ-ⲟⲩⲛ̄-ⲟⲩ-ⲛⲟϭ ⲛ̄ ϣⲧⲟⲣⲧⲣ̄ ⲍⲛ̄ ⲧⲡⲟⲗⲓⲥ. (35) ⲁ-ⲛ̄ⲍⲁⲗⲁⲧⲉ ⲟⲩⲱⲍ ⲉⲭⲛ̄ ⲧⲭⲉⲛⲉⲡⲱⲣ ⲙ̄ ⲡⲏⲓ. (36) ⲛⲉⲩⲙ̄ⲡϣⲁ ⲛ̄ ϣⲱⲡ ⲙ̄ ⲡⲉⲡⲛ̄ⲁ ⲉⲧ ⲟⲩⲁⲁⲃ ⲍⲙ̄ ⲡⲉⲩⲍⲏⲧ. (37) ⲛⲉⲩϫⲓ ⲛ̄ ⲛ̄ⲧⲁⲣ ⲛ̄ⲥⲉⲛⲟⲩϫⲉ ⲙ̄ⲙⲟⲟⲩ ⲍⲓ ⲧⲉⲍⲓⲏ.

Reading

The following selection is from the Sayings of the Fathers.
See p.146 for a brief description of this text.

ⲚⲈ-ⲞⲨⲚ̄-ⲞⲨⲀ ⲌⲚ̄ ⲔⲎⲘⲈ Ⲉ-ⲞⲨⲚ̄ⲦⲀϤ Ⲙ̄ⲘⲀⲨ Ⲛ̄ ⲞⲨϢⲎⲢⲈ ⲈϤⲤⲎⳠ. ⲀⲨⲰ ⲀϤ-
ⲈⲒⲚⲈ Ⲙ̄ⲘⲞϤ, ⲀϤⲔⲀⲀϤ ⳅⲚ̄ ⲦⲢⲒ Ⲛ̄ ⲀⲠⲀ ⲘⲀⲔⲀⲢⲒⲞⲤ, ⲀⲨⲰ ⲀϤⲔⲀⲀϤ ⲈϤⲢⲒⲘⲈ
ⳅⲀⳅⲦⲘ̄ ⲠⲢⲞ, ⲀϤⲂⲰⲔ Ⲉ ⲠⲞⲨⲈ. ⲠⳅⲀ̄ⲖⲞ ⲀⲈ ⲀϤϬⲰϢⲦ̄ ⲈⲂⲞⲖ, ⲀϤⲚⲀⲨ Ⲉ
ⲠⲔⲞⲨⲒ Ⲛ̄ ϢⲎⲢⲈ ⲈϤⲢⲒⲘⲈ, ⲀⲨⲰ ⲠⲈⲬⲀϤ ⲚⲀϤ ⳃⲈ, "ⲚⲒⲘ ⲠⲈⲚⲦⲀϤⲚ̄ⲦⲔ̄ Ⲉ
ⲠⲈⲒⲘⲀ?" Ⲛ̄ⲦⲞϤ ⲀⲈ ⲠⲈⲬⲀϤ ⳃⲈ, "ⲠⲀⲈⲒⲰⲦ ⲠⲈ. ⲀϤⲚ̄Ⲧ, ⲀϤⲚⲞⲬⲦ̄ ⲈⲂⲞⲖ,
ⲀϤⲂⲰⲔ." ⲠⲈⳃⲈ-ⲠⳅⲀ̄ⲖⲞ ⲚⲀϤ ⳃⲈ, "ⲦⲰⲞⲨⲚϤ̄ Ⲛ̄ⲄⲠⲰⲦ Ⲛ̄ⲄⲦⲀⳅⲞϤ." ⲀⲨⲰ
Ⲛ̄ ⲦⲈⲨⲚⲞⲨ ⲀϤⲞⲨⳃⲀⲒ, ⲀϤⲦⲰⲞⲨⲚ, ⲀϤⲦⲀⳅⲈ-ⲠⲈϤⲈⲒⲰⲦ, ⲀⲨⲰ Ⲛ̄ ⲦⲈⲒⳅⲈ
ⲀⲨⲂⲰⲔ Ⲉ ⲠⲈⲨⲎⲒ ⲈⲨⲢⲀϢⲈ.

Note: The term ⲀⲠⲀ is a title of respect, ultimately from
Aramaic *'abbā*, father. ⲘⲀⲔⲀⲢⲒⲞⲤ is a proper name.

Lesson 26

26.1 Compound verbs. Coptic vocabulary is particularly rich in compound verbs. Most compound verbs consist of
a simple infinitive in the prenominal form plus a nominal
element, usually without an article, e.g. ϯ-ⲈⲞⲞⲨ to praise,
ⳃⲒ-ⲂⲀⲠⲦⲒⲤⲘⲀ to be baptized. Meanings are for the most part
predictable from those of the components.

The verbs most frequently occurring in compounds are
ϯ- to give, ⳃⲒ- to take, ϤⲒ- to raise, carry, ϬⲚ̄- to find,
ⲔⲀ- to put, and Ⲣ̄- to do, make. Some examples:

ϯ-ⲔⲀⲢⲠⲞⲤ to produce fruit
ϯ-ⲘⲈⲦⲀⲚⲞⲒⲀ to repent; to humble or abase one's self
ϯ-ⲈⲞⲞⲨ ⲚⲀⸯ to praise
ϯ-ⲤⲂⲰ ⲚⲀⸯ to teach someone (something: Ⲉ)
ⳃⲒ-ⲤⲂⲰ to receive instruction, be taught (something: Ⲉ)
ϬⲚ̄-Ⲙ̄ⲦⲞⲚ to find rest

ϭⲛ̄-ϩⲱⲃ ⲙⲛ̄ to have dealings with

ϭⲙ̄-ϭⲟⲙ (ϭⲛ̄-ϭⲟⲙ) to have power, prevail (over); to be able (to do: ⲉ + Inf.)

ϥⲓ-ⲣⲟⲟⲩⲱ to take heed, be concerned (for, about: ⲉ, ⲛⲁˀ, ⲉⲧⲃⲉ, ϩⲁ).

Compounds with ⲣ̄- are the most frequent of all and fall into two groups. In the first group ⲣ̄- has its basic meaning "to do, make, perform":

ⲣ̄-ⲛⲟⲃⲉ to sin (against: ⲉ)   ⲣ̄-ⲡⲁⲓ to do this, thus

ⲣ̄-ⲟⲩ   to do what?

ⲣ̄-X ⲛ̄ ⲣⲟⲙⲡⲉ (X is a number) has two meanings: (1) to reach the age of X; (2) to pass X years.

In the second group of ⲣ̄- compounds ⲣ̄- has the meaning "to become," e.g. ⲣ̄-ⲣ̄ⲣⲟ to become king (over: ⲉϫⲛ̄). The second element may be virtually any noun or adjective in the language, so that a complete catalogue is impossible. Qualitatives are uniformly ⲟ ⲛ̄, as in ⲟ ⲛ̄ ⲣ̄ⲣⲟ to be king. Further examples:

ⲣ̄-ϩⲗ̄ⲗⲟ to grow old; ⲟ ⲛ̄ ϩⲗ̄ⲗⲟ to be old

ⲣ̄-ϩⲏⲅⲉⲙⲱⲛ to become governor; ⲟ ⲛ̄ ϩⲏⲅⲉⲙⲱⲛ to be governor.

ⲣ̄-ϫⲟⲉⲓⲥ to become lord, master (over: ⲉ, ⲉϫⲛ̄); ⲟ ⲛ̄ ϫⲟⲉⲓⲥ to be lord, master.

The distinction between these two groups is often blurred, however, with qualitatives of the ⲟ ⲛ̄ type being extended to the first group as well, e.g. ⲣ̄-ϣⲡⲏⲣⲉ to marvel, become amazed (at: ⲙ̄ⲙⲟˀ, ⲉ, ⲉⲧⲃⲉ, ⲉϫⲛ̄), to admire; Ϙ ⲟ ⲛ̄ ϣⲡⲏⲣⲉ to be amazed.

Less frequently the nominal element of a compound verb has the definite article:

ⲣ̄-ⲡⲱⲃϣ̄   to forget (ⲛ̄)

ⲣ̄-ⲡⲙⲉⲉⲩⲉ   to remember (ⲛ̄)

†-ⲑⲉ ⲛⲁˀ   to provide the means to someone (so that: ⲉ, ⲉⲧⲣⲉ).

In the case of ⲣ̄-ⲡⲱⲃϣ̄, ⲣ̄-ⲡⲙⲉⲉⲩⲉ, and many others of this type a pronominal object is expressed by a possessive prefix on the noun: ⲣ̄-ⲡⲉϥⲱⲃϣ̄ to forget him, ⲣ̄-ⲡⲉϥⲙⲉⲉⲩⲉ to remember him.

Because compound verbs employ the prenominal form of the infinitive, the question arises concerning their occurrence in the Bipartite Conjugation, where the prenominal form is usually prohibited. In general, compound verbs are an exception to Jernstedt's Rule and may be used freely as they stand in the Bipartite Conjugation. Two types of compounds, however, do tend to follow Jernstedt's Rule:

(1) the type ⲣ̄-ⲡⲙⲉⲉⲩⲉ, with the definite article on the noun. In the Bipartite Conjugation the full form of the infinitive is used. Contrast

ⲁⲓⲣ̄-ⲡⲉϥⲙⲉⲉⲩⲉ.	I remembered him.
ϯⲉⲓⲣⲉ ⲙ̄ ⲡⲉϥⲙⲉⲉⲩⲉ.	I remember him.

(2) many compounds whose nominal element is a part of the body. Contrast

ⲁⲓϯ-ⲧⲟⲟⲧⲥ̄.	I helped her.
ϯϯ ⲛ̄ ⲧⲟⲟⲧⲥ̄.	I am helping her.

26.2 The element ϣ-, ⲉϣ-, originally a full verb "to know, know how to," may be prefixed to any infinitive to express "can, be able." E.g.

ⲙ̄ⲡⲉϥϣⲃⲱⲕ	He was not able to go.
ⲛ̄ϯⲛⲁϣϯ-ⲧⲟⲟⲧⲕ̄ ⲁⲛ.	I shall not be able to help you.

It occurs redundantly and optionally in the compounds of ϭⲟⲙ: ⲟⲩⲛ̄-(ϣ)ϭⲟⲙ, ⲙⲛ̄-(ϣ)ϭⲟⲙ, ϭⲛ̄-(ϣ)ϭⲟⲙ.

26.3 Infinitives of the type ⲧⲁⲕⲟ. There is a fairly large group of verbs whose infinitives begin with ⲧ- and end in -ⲟ, e.g. ⲧⲁⲕⲟ ⲧⲁⲕⲉ- ⲧⲁⲕⲟ⸗ Q ⲧⲁⲕⲏⲩ to destroy. At an older stage of Egyptian these verbs were compound causatives with a form of ϯ (to give) plus a verbal form inflected by suffixation. Thus, the original construction

involved two verbs (e.g. I *caused* that he *pay* a fine) which
coalesced into a single verb with two objects (I caused *him*
to pay a *fine*). Traces of the older construction survive
in Sahidic, e.g. Luke 3:14 ⲙ̄ⲡⲣ̄ⲧⲧⲉ-ⲗⲁⲁⲩ ⲟⲥⲉ Do not make anyone
pay a fine (i.e. suffer a loss). ⲧⲧⲟ ⲧⲧⲉ- is the causative
of ϯ itself. The lack of an object marker on the second
object is characteristic of the construction, but the
absence of an article in this particular example stems from
its association with the compound verb ϯ-ⲟⲥⲉ to pay a fine,
suffer a loss. In general, however, there is no need to
take the older construction into account in Coptic, since
most of these verbs are simply transitive. Some examples:

ⲧⲁⲙⲟ ⲧⲁⲙⲉ- ⲧⲁⲙⲟ⸱ vb. tr. to tell, inform (ⲙ̄ⲙⲟ⸱; of,
  about: ⲉ, ⲉⲧⲃⲉ; that: ϫⲉ); causative of ⲉⲓⲙⲉ.

ⲧⲁⲗⲟ ⲧⲁⲗⲉ- ⲧⲁⲗⲟ⸱ Q ⲧⲁⲗⲏⲩ (± ⲉ₂ⲣⲁⲓ) vb. tr. to cause to
  go up, cause to board, cause to mount; to raise up,
  offer up, send up (ⲙ̄ⲙⲟ⸱); caus. of ⲁⲗⲉ.

ⲧⲁⲛ₂ⲟ ⲧⲁⲛ₂ⲉ- ⲧⲁⲛ₂ⲟ⸱ Q ⲧⲁⲛ₂ⲏⲩ vb. tr. to bring (back) to
  life, let live, keep alive (ⲙ̄ⲙⲟ⸱); caus. of ⲱⲛⲍ̄.

ⲧ + ϣ results in initial ϫ:

ϫⲡⲟ ϫⲡⲉ- ϫⲡⲟ⸱ vb. tr. to give birth to (ⲙ̄ⲙⲟ⸱); to acquire, obtain, get (ⲙ̄ⲙⲟ⸱; often with reflex. dative
  ⲛⲁ⸱ for one's self); caus. of ϣⲱⲡⲉ.

ϫⲡⲓⲟ ϫⲡⲓⲉ- ϫⲡⲓⲟ⸱ Q ϫⲡⲓⲏⲧ vb. tr. to put to shame, to
  blame, scold, reproach (ⲙ̄ⲙⲟ⸱; for: ⲉⲧⲃⲉ, ⲉϫⲛ̄, ⲍⲁ);
  caus. of ϣⲓⲡⲉ.

Sometimes the initial ⲧ- is lost, as in

ⲕⲧⲟ ⲕⲧⲉ- ⲕⲧⲟ⸱ Q ⲕⲧⲏⲩ vb. tr. to turn; this verb has
  become completely synonymous with its base ⲕⲱⲧⲉ.

A few verbs have retained a final -ⲥ or -ⲟⲩ (a frozen
subject suffix):

ϫⲟⲟⲩ ϫⲉⲩ- ϫⲟⲟⲩ⸱ vb. tr. to send (ⲙ̄ⲙⲟ⸱; to: ⲉⲣⲁⲧ⸱, ⲛⲁ⸱,
  ⲉϫⲛ̄, ϣⲁ); + ⲉⲃⲟⲗ away, out, off; + ⲍⲁⲑⲏ ahead.

т͊нооγ to send (already introduced). Originally хооγ
meant "to cause to go" (caus. of ϣε to go) and т͊ноογ
meant "to cause to bring" (caus. of εινε).

тоγνοс тоγνεс- тоγνοс⸗ vb. tr. to awaken, arouse, raise
up (ͯмο⸗); caus. of тωογν (probably).

The Imperative of these verbs may optionally have a prefixed мα-: мαтαмо, мαтαλο, etc. Cf. §17.1.

Vocabulary 26

(The compound verbs given in 26.1, the prefix ϣ- in 26.2,
and the verbs тамо, тαλο, тαν₂ο, хпο, хпιο, кто, хооγ, and
тоγνос in 26.3)

ωвϣ εвϣ- овϣ⸗ Q овϣ vb. tr. to forget, overlook, neglect
(ͯмο⸗); intr. to sleep, fall asleep; as n. forgetting,
sleep.

ωⲛ₂, Q оⲛ₂ vb. intr. to become/be alive, live; as n.m. life.
о the Q of ειре.

п.рооγϣ care, concern, anxiety. р̄-рооγϣ (Q о ͷ) to be-
come/be a care or concern (for: нα⸗).

те.ϣпнре wonder, amazement, miracle.

†-тоοт⸗, † ͷ тоот⸗ to help, assist (object suffix is
required; nominal object with ͷ).

те.θγсια (ἡ θυσία) offering, sacrifice.

п.вαптιсмα (τὸ βάπτισμα) baptism. †-вαптιсмα to baptize.

Exercises

(1) пειϣнн ⲇε нϥ†-кαрпос αⲛ. (2) нϥϭͷ-ϭом αⲛ ε тако ͷ не-
ψγхн ͷ ͷⲇικαιος. (3) пειсⲁ₂ петͷхι-свω ͷтоотϥ. (4) αϥ†-
мεтανοια εϥхω ͯмос хε αιр̄-новε, пαхоειс. (5) тͷⲛαхιсε ͯмоϥ
εн†-εооγ ͷ пеϥрαн ет оγααв. (6) ειⲛαр̄-оγ? (7) ͷтереϥр̄-
мͷтсноογс ͷ ромпе, α-неϥειоте ͷтϥ ε перпе. (8) с₂αι нαι
нϥтαмοι ετвε не₂внγε ετⲕειре ͯмооγ ͯмαγ. (9) αγω ͷ теγноγ
α-твω ͷ ελοολε †-₂α₂ ͷ кαрпос. (10) εнⲛαϭͷ-ͯтоⲛ тωⲛ ͷ
пεικосмос? (11) ϥι-рооγϣ ετвε неιϣнре ͷтετͷ₂αре₂ εрооγ
εвол ₂ͷ ппеθооγ. (12) неϥ†-свω нαγ ε нентоλн ͷ пхоειс.

(13) ⲛ̄ϯⲟⲩⲱϣ ⲁⲛ ⲉ ϭⲛ̄-ϩⲱⲃ ⲙⲛ̄ ⲛⲁ-ⲧⲉⲓⲙⲓⲛⲉ. (14) ⲙ̄ⲡⲓⲣ̄-ⲛⲟⲃⲉ
ⲉⲣⲱⲧⲛ̄ ⲉⲛⲉϩ. (15) ⲛ̄ⲧⲟϥ ⲡⲉⲧ ⲛⲁϯ-ⲙ̄ⲧⲟⲛ ⲛⲁⲛ. (16) ⲡϩⲁⲗⲏⲧ ⲇⲉ
ⲙ̄ⲡⲉϥϣϭⲙ̄-ϭⲟⲙ ⲉ ϩⲱⲗ ⲉⲃⲟⲗ. (17) ⲉ-ⲁϥⲉⲓ ⲉϩⲟⲩⲛ ⲉ ⲡⲉⲣⲡⲉ, ⲁϥⲧⲁⲗⲟ
ⲛ̄ ⲟⲩⲑⲩⲥⲓⲁ. (18) ⲥⲉⲛⲁⲥⲙⲟⲩ ⲉⲣⲟϥ ⲛ̄ⲥⲉϯ-ⲉⲟⲟⲩ ⲛⲁϥ. (19) ⲙ̄ ⲡⲉⲟⲩⲟⲉⲓϣ ⲧⲉⲧⲛⲁϣϭⲙ̄-ϭⲟⲙ ⲉ ⲧⲁⲛϩⲉ-ⲛⲉⲧ ⲙⲟⲟⲩⲧ. (20) ⲡⲁⲓ ⲡⲉ ⲡⲙⲁ
ⲉⲧⲥ̄ⲛⲁϫⲡⲟ ⲙ̄ ⲡⲉⲥϣⲏⲣⲉ ⲛ̄ϩⲏⲧϥ̄. (21) ϣϣⲉ ⲉⲣⲱⲧⲛ̄ ⲉⲧⲣⲉⲧⲉⲧⲛ̄ϥⲓ-ⲣⲟⲟⲩϣ
ϩⲁ ⲛⲉⲭⲏⲣⲁ ⲙⲛ̄ ⲛ̄ⲟⲣⲫⲁⲛⲟⲥ. (22) ⲁϥϫⲡⲟ ⲛⲁϥ ⲛ̄ ⲛ̄ⲕⲁ ⲛⲓⲙ ⲉⲛⲧⲁ-
ⲡⲉϥϩⲏⲧ ⲟⲩⲁϣⲟⲩ. (23) ⲛ̄ⲧⲁⲕⲣ̄-ⲟⲩ ϩⲛ̄ ⲧⲡⲟⲗⲓⲥ? (24) ⲉⲓⲛⲁϯ-ⲥⲃⲱ
ⲛⲏⲧⲛ̄ ⲉ ⲟⲩ? (25) ⲁ-ⲛⲉϥϣⲁϫⲉ ⲭⲡⲓⲟⲟⲩ ⲁⲩⲱ ⲁⲩⲡⲱⲧ ⲉⲃⲟⲗ. (26) ⲙ̄ⲡⲉ-
ⲡⲥⲟⲛ ϭⲛ̄-ϩⲱⲃ ⲙⲛ̄ ⲛ̄ⲣⲱⲙⲉ ⲛ̄ ⲧⲡⲉⲣⲓⲭⲱⲣⲟⲥ. (27) ⲉ-ⲁϥϫⲱⲕ ⲉⲃⲟⲗ ⲙ̄
ⲡⲉϥϩⲱⲃ, ⲁϥⲕⲧⲟϥ ⲉ ⲡⲉϥϯⲙⲉ. (28) ⲁⲛⲣ̄-ⲙⲛ̄ⲧϣⲟⲙⲧⲉ ⲛ̄ ⲣⲟⲙⲡⲉ ⲉⲛϣⲙ̄ϣⲉ
ⲛⲁϥ. (29) ⲧⲛ̄ⲛⲁϫⲟⲟⲩ ⲙ̄ⲙⲟⲕ ϩⲁⲑⲏ ⲉⲧⲣⲉⲕⲥⲟⲃⲧⲉ ⲛⲁⲛ ⲛ̄ ⲟⲩⲙⲁ. (30)
ⲛ̄ⲧⲁⲧⲉⲧⲛ̄ⲣ̄-ⲡⲁⲓ ⲉ ⲟⲩ? (31) ⲁⲓⲣ̄-ⲙⲁⲧⲟⲓ ⲉⲣⲉ-ϩⲏⲣⲱⲁⲏⲥ ⲟ ⲛ̄ ϩⲏⲅⲉⲙⲱⲛ.
(32) ⲛ̄ⲧⲉⲣⲉϥⲧⲟⲩⲛⲟⲥ ⲙ̄ⲙⲟⲥ, ⲁⲥⲟⲩϫⲁⲓ ⲛ̄ ⲧⲉⲩⲛⲟⲩ. (33) ⲉϥⲟ ⲛ̄ ϩⲗ̄ⲗⲟ,
ⲙⲛ̄-ϭⲟⲙ ⲙ̄ⲙⲟϥ ⲉ ⲃⲱⲕ ⲉⲩⲡⲟⲗⲓⲥ ⲉⲥⲟⲩⲏⲩ. (34) ⲥⲉⲛⲁⲉⲓ ⲛ̄ⲥⲉⲧⲁⲕⲟ ⲙ̄
ⲡⲉⲓⲣ̄ⲡⲉ. (35) ⲙ̄ⲡⲣ̄ⲣ̄-ⲡⲱⲃϣ̄ ⲛ̄ ⲛⲉⲛⲧⲟⲗⲏ ⲙ̄ ⲡⲛⲟⲙⲟⲥ. (36) ⲁⲩⲧⲁϩⲟϥ
ⲉϥⲙⲟⲟϣⲉ ⲙⲛ̄ ⲛⲉϥⲙⲁⲑⲏⲧⲏⲥ. (37) ⲙ̄ⲡⲣ̄ⲣ̄-ⲡⲱⲃϣ̄ ⲙ̄ ⲡⲁϯ-ⲥⲃⲱ. (38)
ϯⲟⲩⲱϣ ⲉ ⲧⲁⲙⲟⲕ ϫⲉ ⲡⲉⲕϣⲏⲣⲉ ⲟⲩⲟϫ. (39) ⲛⲓⲙ ⲡⲉⲛⲧⲁϥϯ-ⲑⲉ ⲛⲏⲧⲛ̄
ⲉⲧⲣⲉⲧⲉⲧⲛ̄ⲕⲱⲧ ⲛ̄ ⲟⲩⲏⲓ ⲛ̄ ⲧⲉⲓⲙⲓⲛⲉ? (40) ϯⲛⲁⲣ̄-ⲡⲉⲕⲙⲉⲉⲩⲉ ⲛ̄ⲧⲁⲧⲙⲟⲃϣ̄ⲕ̄.
(41) ⲕⲛⲁⲣ̄-ϫⲟⲉⲓⲥ ⲉ ⲛⲉⲓⲙⲟⲕⲙⲉⲕ ⲙ̄ ⲡⲟⲛⲏⲣⲟⲛ. (42) ⲁ-ⲛⲉϥⲙⲁⲑⲏⲧⲏⲥ
ⲧⲁⲗⲟϥ ⲉ ⲡϫⲟⲓ. (43) ⲛ̄ⲧⲉⲣⲟⲩⲥⲱⲧⲙ̄ ⲉ ⲛⲁⲓ, ⲁⲩⲣ̄-ϣⲡⲏⲣⲉ. (44) ⲟⲩ
ⲡⲉⲧ ⲛⲁϯ-ⲑⲉ ⲛⲁⲛ ⲉⲧⲣⲉⲛⲱⲛϩ̄ ϣⲁ ⲛⲓⲉⲛⲉϩ? (45) ⲡⲁϩⲧⲕ̄ ϩⲁⲣⲁⲧ ⲛ̄ⲅⲣ̄-
ϫⲟⲉⲓⲥ ⲉϫⲛ̄ ⲛⲉⲓⲉϫⲟⲩⲥⲓⲁ ⲧⲏⲣⲟⲩ. (46) ⲛ̄ⲧⲉⲣⲛ̄ⲣ̄-ⲡⲉϥⲙⲉⲉⲩⲉ, ⲁⲛⲁⲣⲭⲉⲓ
ⲛ̄ ⲣⲓⲙⲉ. (47) ⲛ̄ⲧⲉⲣⲉ-ⲡⲉϩⲟⲟⲩ ⲙ̄ ⲡⲉⲥⲙⲓⲥⲉ ϫⲱⲕ ⲉⲃⲟⲗ, ⲁⲥϫⲡⲟ ⲛ̄
ⲟⲩϣⲏⲣⲉ ⲙ̄ ⲡⲉⲥϩⲁⲓ. (48) ⲛⲉϩⲃⲏⲩⲉ ⲛ̄ ⲛ̄ⲇⲓⲕⲁⲓⲟⲥ ⲛⲁϩⲡⲓⲟ ⲛ̄ ⲛⲉⲑⲟⲟⲩ.
(49) ⲧⲉⲧⲛⲁⲥⲟⲟⲩⲛ̄ ⲛ̄ⲧⲉⲧⲛ̄ⲣ̄-ϣⲡⲏⲣⲉ. (50) ⲛ̄ⲧⲟϥ ⲇⲉ ⲛ̄ ⲟⲩⲛⲟⲩⲧⲉ ⲁⲛ
ⲡⲉ ⲛ̄ⲧⲉ ⲛⲉⲧ ⲙⲟⲟⲩⲧ, ⲁⲗⲗⲁ ⲛⲉⲧ ⲟⲛϩ̄. (51) ⲟⲩⲛⲟϭ ⲛ̄ ϣⲡⲏⲣⲉ ⲧⲉ ⲧⲁⲓ.

Lesson 27

27.1 Negative adjective compounds. The prefix ⲁⲧ- is used to form negative adjectives from verbs and nouns:

ⲁⲧⲥⲟⲟⲩⲛ̄	ignorant	ⲁⲧⲥⲱⲧⲙ̄	disobedient
ⲁⲧⲙⲟⲩ	immortal	ⲁⲧⲧⲁⲕⲟ	imperishable
ⲁⲑⲏⲧ	senseless, foolish	ⲁⲧϭⲟⲙ	powerless, impotent
		ⲁⲧⲟⲩⲱⲛⲍ̄ ⲉⲃⲟⲗ	invisible.

This prefix was originally a negative relative pronoun; a trace of this older usage is found in the resumptive pronoun required in some expressions, e.g.

ⲁⲧⲛⲁⲩ ⲉⲣⲟ⸗	unseeable, unseen
ⲁⲧϣⲁϫⲉ ⲉⲣⲟ⸗	ineffable; without ⲉⲣⲟ⸗: speechless
ⲁⲧⲕⲓⲙ ⲉⲣⲟ⸗	immovable.

The resumptive pronoun agrees with the modified noun:

ⲟⲩⲙⲩⲥⲧⲏⲣⲓⲟⲛ ⲛ̄ ⲁⲧϣⲁϫⲉ ⲉⲣⲟϥ	an ineffable mystery
ⲟⲩϭⲟⲙ ⲛ̄ ⲁⲧⲕⲓⲙ ⲉⲣⲟⲥ	an immovable power.

Nearly all ⲁⲧ- adjectives freely compound with ⲣ̄- (Ⲟ o ⲛ̄), as in ⲣ̄-ⲁⲧⲥⲟⲟⲩⲛ̄ to become/be ignorant, ⲣ̄-ⲁⲧⲟⲩⲱⲛⲍ̄ ⲉⲃⲟⲗ to become/be invisible.

27.2 Compound nouns. The distinction between a compound noun and a noun + ⲛ̄ + noun phrase is somewhat arbitrary. As a working definition we shall assume (1) that the first noun of a true compound noun must be in a reduced form different from the free (unbound) form, if indeed the latter exists; (2) that the linking ⲛ̄ be absent or at least optional. The most productive compounding prefixes are ⲙⲛ̄ⲧ-, ⲣⲙ̄(ⲛ̄)-, ⲣⲉϥ-, and ϭⲓⲛ.

(a) ⲣⲉϥ- forms agent or actor nouns; the second element is normally a simple or compound infinitive, but occasionally a qualitative:

ⲣⲉϥⲣ̄-ⲛⲟⲃⲉ	sinner	ⲣⲉϥϣⲙ̄ϣⲉ	server, worshipper

ⲣⲉϥⲙⲟⲟⲩⲧ   dead person   ⲣⲉϥϫⲓⲟⲩⲉ   thief
ⲣⲉϥⲧⲁⲕⲟ   destroyer; perishable

These may be used nominally or adjectivally, e.g.

ⲟⲩⲥ2ⲓⲙⲉ ⲛ̄ ⲣⲉϥⲡ̄-ⲛⲟⲃⲉ   a sinful woman
ⲟⲩⲡⲛⲉⲩⲙⲁ ⲛ̄ ⲣⲉϥⲧⲁⲕⲟ   a destructive spirit
ⲧⲉⲓⲥⲁⲣⲝ ⲛ̄ ⲣⲉϥⲧⲁⲕⲟ   this perishable flesh,

and may be formed freely from virtually any appropriate
verb in the language.

(b) ⲣⲙ̄-, ⲣⲙ̄ⲛ̄-, a reduced form of ⲣⲱⲙⲉ ⲛ̄, man of:

ⲣⲙ̄ⲛ̄ⲕⲏⲙⲉ an Egyptian
ⲣⲙ̄ⲛ̄2ⲏⲧ a wise, discerning person
ⲣⲙ̄ⲛ̄ⲛⲁⲍⲁⲣⲉⲑ a person from Nazareth
ⲣⲙ̄ⲧⲱⲛ a person from where? as in ⲛ̄ⲧⲉⲧⲛ̄-2ⲉⲛⲣⲙ̄ⲛ̄ⲧⲱⲛ?
Where are you from?

(c) ⲙⲛ̄ⲧ- is used to form feminine abstract nouns from
adjectives or other nouns. Compounds in ⲙⲛ̄ⲧ- are extremely
numerous; the following is a typical sampling:

ⲙⲛ̄ⲧⲟⲩⲏⲏⲃ priesthood	ⲙⲛ̄ⲧⲣⲙ̄ⲛ̄2ⲏⲧ wisdom, prudence
ⲙⲛ̄ⲧⲉⲣⲟ kingdom, kingship;	ⲙⲛ̄ⲧ2ⲗ̄ⲗⲟ old age (of a man)
the spelling ⲙⲛ̄ⲧⲣ̄ⲣⲟ is	ⲙⲛ̄ⲧ2ⲗ̄ⲗⲱ old age (of woman)
less frequent.	ⲙⲛ̄ⲧⲛⲟ6 greatness; seniority
ⲙⲛ̄ⲧⲥⲁⲃⲉ wisdom	ⲙⲛ̄ⲧⲙⲟⲛⲁⲭⲟⲥ monkhood
ⲙⲛ̄ⲧⲃⲣ̄ⲣⲉ youth; newness	ⲙⲛ̄ⲧⲁⲧⲧⲁⲕⲟ imperishability;
	incorruptibility.

ⲙⲛ̄ⲧ- is also used to designate languages:

ⲙⲛ̄ⲧⲣⲙ̄ⲛ̄ⲕⲏⲙⲉ	Egyptian	ⲙⲛ̄ⲧⲟⲩⲉⲉⲓⲉⲛⲓⲛ	Greek
ⲙⲛ̄ⲧ2ⲉⲃⲣⲁⲓⲟⲥ	Hebrew	ⲙⲛ̄ⲧ2ⲣⲱⲙⲁⲓⲟⲥ	Latin

(d) 6ⲓⲛ- is used to form a feminine noun of action or
gerund from any infinitive. The meaning ranges from con-
crete to abstract, e.g. 6ⲓⲛⲛⲁⲩ sight, vision; 6ⲓⲛⲟⲩⲱⲙ food
(pl. 6ⲓⲛⲟⲩⲟⲟⲙ). These are so predictable in meaning that
they have been systematically excluded from the Glossary

unless they have acquired meanings not immediately obvious from that of the base verb.

Less frequent compounding prefixes are ⲁⲛ-, ⲉⲓⲉⲛ-
(ⲉⲓⲟⲡⲉ), ⲉⲓⲉⲍ- (ⲉⲓⲱⲍⲉ), ⲣⲁ- ⲥ†- (ⲥⲧⲟⲓ), ϣⲟⲩ- (ϣⲁⲩ), ϣⲃⲣ̄-
(ϣⲃⲏⲣ), ϣⲛ̄- (ϣⲏⲣⲉ), ϣⲥⲛ̄- (ⲥⲁϣ), and ⲍⲁⲙ-. The reader may check these out in the Glossary.

Nominalized relative clauses are sometimes taken as compound nouns, occurring with an extra article, e.g.
(ⲡ)ⲡⲉⲧ ϣⲟⲩⲉⲓⲧ vanity, (ⲡ)ⲡⲉⲑⲟⲟⲩ evil, ⲟⲩⲡⲉⲧ ⲟⲩⲁⲁⲃ a saint.

A similar usage is found with ⲉⲃⲟⲗ ⲍⲛ̄, designating origin or affiliation (the def. art. appears as ⲡⲉ-, ⲧⲉ-, ⲛⲉ-):

ⲟⲩⲉⲃⲟⲗ ⲍⲛ̄ ⲧⲥⲩⲣⲓⲁ ⲡⲉ.　　　He is a Syrian.

ⲛⲉⲉⲃⲟⲗ ⲍⲙ̄ ⲡⲏⲓ ⲛ̄ ⲇⲁⲩⲉⲓⲇ ⲛⲉ.　They are the ones from the house of David.

27.3 There is a form of the verb known as the *participium conjunctivum* (proclitic participle) used only for forming compounds with a following nominal element:

ⲥⲱ	p. c.	ⲥⲁⲩ-ⲏⲣⲡ̄	wine-drinking, a wine-drinker
ⲟⲩⲱⲙ		ⲟⲩⲁⲙ-ⲣⲱⲙⲉ	man-eating
ϫⲓⲥⲉ		ϫⲁⲥⲓ-ⲍⲏⲧ	arrogant
ⲙⲟⲟⲛⲉ		ⲙⲁⲛ-ⲉⲥⲟⲟⲩ	shepherd, tender of sheep.

It is uniformly vocalized with -ⲁ-. For most verbs the p. c. is rare or non-existent; a few verbs like the above account for most of the examples encountered. Note especially the compounds of ⲙⲉ: ⲙⲁⲓ- (one who loves):

ⲙⲁⲓ-ⲉⲟⲟⲩ　desirous of fame or glory
ⲙⲁⲓ-ⲛⲟⲩⲃ, ⲙⲁⲓ-ⲍⲁⲧ　desirous of wealth
ⲙⲁⲓ-ⲛⲟⲩⲧⲉ pious, God-loving
ⲙⲁⲓ-ⲣⲱⲙⲉ　kind, philanthropic
ⲙⲁⲓ-ⲟⲩⲱⲙ　gluttonous.

27.4 The Third Future and its negative:

ειϲωτⲙ	ⲉⲛⲉϲⲱⲧⲙ	neg.	ⲛⲛⲁϲⲱⲧⲙ	ⲛⲛⲉⲛϲⲱⲧⲙ
ⲉⲕⲉϲⲱⲧⲙ	ⲉⲧⲉⲧⲛⲉϲⲱⲧⲙ		ⲛⲛⲉⲕϲⲱⲧⲙ	ⲛⲛⲉⲧⲛϲⲱⲧⲙ
ⲉⲣⲉϲⲱⲧⲙ			ⲛⲛⲉϲⲱⲧⲙ	
ⲉϥⲉϲⲱⲧⲙ	ⲉⲩⲉϲⲱⲧⲙ		ⲛⲛⲉϥϲⲱⲧⲙ	ⲛⲛⲉⲩϲⲱⲧⲙ
ⲉϲⲉϲⲱⲧⲙ			ⲛⲛⲉϲϲⲱⲧⲙ	
ⲉⲣⲉ-ⲡⲣⲱⲙⲉ ϲⲱⲧⲙ			ⲛⲛⲉ-ⲡⲣⲱⲙⲉ ϲⲱⲧⲙ	

The negative forms are also spelled as ⲉⲛⲛⲁ-, ⲉⲛⲛⲉⲕ- etc. The 1st pers. sing. also occurs as ⲛⲛⲉιϲⲱⲧⲙ.

The Third Future is an emphatic or vivid future with a wide variety of nuances; in an independent clause it describes a future event as necessary, inevitable, or obligatory. The English translation will depend on the context: ⲉϥⲉϲⲱⲧⲙ he shall hear, he is to hear, he is bound to hear, he must inevitably hear, he will surely hear, and similarly for the negative. The 2nd person is often used in commands and prohibitions:

> ⲛⲛⲉⲕⲡⲉιⲣⲁⲍⲉ ⲉ ⲡⲭⲟⲉιϲ ⲡⲉⲕⲛⲟⲩⲧⲉ.
> You shall not tempt the Lord your God.

> ⲉⲧⲉⲧⲛⲉ²ⲁⲣⲉ² ⲉ ⲛⲉιⲉⲛⲧⲟⲗⲏ.
> You shall keep these commandments.

One of the most frequent uses of the Third Future is to express purpose or result after the conjunctions ⲭⲉ and ⲭⲉⲕⲁ(ⲁ)ϲ:

ⲁιϲⲍⲁι ⲛⲏⲧⲛ ⲭⲉⲕⲁϲ ⲉⲧⲉⲧⲛⲉϲⲟⲩⲛ-ⲛⲉⲛⲧⲁⲩϣⲱⲡⲉ ⲙⲙⲟι ⲙ ⲡⲉιⲙⲁ.
I have written to you so that you may know what has befallen me here.

ⲧⲛⲛⲁⲧⲛⲛⲟⲟⲩϥ ⲉⲣⲱⲧⲛ ⲭⲉ ⲉϥⲉϣⲁⲭⲉ ⲛⲙⲙⲏⲧⲛ.
We shall send him to you so that he may speak with you.

The same type of clause may be used as an object clause instead of the Inflected Infinitive after verbs of commanding, exhorting, and the like:

> ⲁⲛϲⲡϲⲱⲡϥ ⲭⲉⲕⲁϲ ⲛⲛⲉϥⲭⲟⲟϲ ⲉ ⲗⲁⲁⲩ.
> We entreated him not to tell it to anyone.

It may occasionally replace the Inflected Infinitive in other situations:

ⲛ̄ϯⲙ̄ⲡϣⲁ ⲁⲛ ϫⲉⲕⲁⲥ ⲉⲓⲉⲉⲓ ⲉⲍⲟⲩⲛ. I am not worthy to enter.

The Third Future is tripartite; only the infinitive may be used in the verbal slot. The Second Future is sometimes used instead of the Third Future after ϫⲉⲕⲁⲥ and ϫⲉ.

Vocabulary 27

[The adjectival and nominal compounds given in 27.1, 2.]

ϫⲓⲟⲩⲉ vb. tr. to steal (ⲙ̄ⲙⲟ⸵; from: ⲍⲛ̄, ⲉⲃⲟⲗ ⲍⲛ̄); as n.m. theft. ⲛ̄ ϫⲓⲟⲩⲉ adv. stealthily, secretly.

ⲡ.ⲙⲛ̄ⲧⲣⲉ witness, testimony. ⲧ.ⲙⲛ̄ⲧⲙⲛ̄ⲧⲣⲉ testimony. ⲣ̄-ⲙⲛ̄ⲧⲣⲉ to testify, bear witness (to, about: ⲙ̄ⲙⲟ⸵, ⲉⲧⲃⲉ, ⲉϫⲛ̄, ⲉ, ⲍⲁ, ⲙⲛ̄).

ⲧ.ⲍⲟⲧⲉ fear. ⲁⲧⲍⲟⲧⲉ fearless. ⲣ̄-ⲍⲟⲧⲉ (Q ⲟ ⲛ̄) to become/be afraid (of: ⲉ, ⲉϫⲛ̄, ⲉⲧⲃⲉ, ⲍⲏⲧ⸵). ⲣⲉϥⲣ̄-ⲍⲟⲧⲉ fearing, respectful. ⲙⲛ̄ⲧⲣⲉϥⲣ̄-ⲍⲟⲧⲉ fear, respect.

ⲍⲱⲛ ⲉⲧⲟⲟⲧ⸵ to command, order someone (to do: ⲉ, ⲉⲧⲣⲉ, ϫⲉⲕⲁⲥ).

ⲧ.ⲣⲁⲥⲟⲩ dream.

ⲧⲁⲗϭⲟ ⲧⲁⲗϭⲉ- ⲧⲁⲗϭⲟ⸵ Q ⲧⲁⲗϭⲏⲩ vb. tr. to heal, cure (ⲙ̄ⲙⲟ⸵; of, from: ⲍⲛ̄, ⲉⲃⲟⲗ ⲍⲛ̄).

ⲡ.ⲥⲁⲉⲓⲛ physician.

ⲡ.ⲥⲱⲙⲁ (τὸ σῶμα) body; the indef. art. is often deleted with this word in prep. phrases.

ⲣ̄-ⲟⲩⲟⲉⲓⲛ to shine, make light.

ⲣ̄-ⲕⲁⲕⲉ (Q ⲟ ⲛ̄) to become/be dark.

Exercises

(1) ⲁⲓⲥⲍⲁⲓ ⲛⲁⲕ ⲛ̄ ⲛⲉⲓϣⲁϫⲉ ϫⲉⲕⲁⲁⲥ ⲛ̄ⲛⲉⲕⲣ̄-ⲡⲱⲃϣ̄ ⲛ̄ ⲍⲱⲃ ⲛⲓⲙ ⲉⲛⲧⲁⲓ-ϯ-ⲥⲃⲱ ⲛⲁⲕ ⲉⲣⲟⲟⲩ. (2) ⲛⲉⲩⲧⲁⲗⲟ ⲛ̄ ⲍⲁⲍ ⲛ̄ ⲑⲩⲥⲓⲁ ϫⲉⲕⲁⲥ ⲉⲣⲉ-ⲡⲛⲟⲩⲧⲉ ⲥⲱⲧⲙ̄ ⲉ ⲛⲉⲩϣⲗⲏⲗ. (3) ⲁⲩϭⲉⲡⲏ ⲉⲣⲁⲧϥ̄ ⲙ̄ ⲡ2ⲏⲅⲉⲙⲱⲛ ϫⲉⲕⲁⲥ ⲉⲩⲉⲧⲁⲙⲟϥ ⲉⲧⲃⲉ ⲛⲉⲛⲧⲁⲩϣⲱⲡⲉ ⲍⲙ̄ ⲡϯⲙⲉ. (4) ⲛ̄ⲛⲉⲧⲛ̄ⲥⲱⲧⲙ̄ ⲉ ⲛ̄ϣⲁϫⲉ ⲛ̄ ⲛⲁⲑⲏⲧ. (5) ⲥⲉⲙⲉⲉⲩⲉ ϫⲉ ⲛⲉⲩⲛⲟⲩⲧⲉ ⲍⲉⲛⲁⲧⲙⲟⲩ ⲛⲉ. (6) ⲁⲩⲕⲧⲟⲟⲩ

ⲙ̄ ⲡⲉⲥⲛⲁⲩ ⲉ ⲡⲏⲓ ⲭⲉⲕⲁⲥ ⲉⲩⲉϯ-ⲧⲟⲟⲧϥ̄ ⲙ̄ ⲡⲉⲩⲉⲓⲱⲧ ⲛ̄ ⲍ̅ⲝ̅ⲗⲟ. (7) ⲛⲉⲣⲉ-
ⲛ̄ϣⲏⲣⲉ ⲙ̄ ⲡⲟⲩⲏⲏⲃ ⲟ ⲛ̄ ⲁⲧⲥⲱⲧⲙ̄. (8) ⲉⲛⲛⲁⲛⲟⲩϫⲉ ⲉⲃⲟⲗ ⲙ̄ ⲡⲉⲓⲥⲱⲙⲁ ⲛ̄
ⲣⲉϥⲧⲁⲕⲟ ⲧⲛ̄ⲛⲁⲩ? (9) ⲁ-ⲡⲉⲩϫⲟⲉⲓⲥ ⲍⲱⲛ ⲉⲧⲟⲟⲧⲟⲩ ⲛ̄ ⲛⲉϥⲍⲙ̄ⲍⲁⲗ ϫⲉⲕⲁⲥ
ⲉⲩⲉⲉⲓⲛⲉ ⲙ̄ ⲙ̄ⲙⲁⲧⲟⲓ ⲉⲍⲟⲩⲛ ϣⲁⲣⲟϥ. (10) ⲛ̄ⲛⲉⲕϫⲓⲟⲩⲉ ⲛ̄ ⲛⲉⲛⲕⲁ ⲛ̄
ⲛⲉⲕⲥⲛⲏⲩ. (11) ⲁⲩⲉⲓ ⲛ̄ ϫⲓⲟⲩⲉ ⲛ̄ ⲧⲉⲩϣⲏ ⲁⲩⲱ ⲁⲩϫⲓ ⲙ̄ ⲡⲉϥⲥⲱⲙⲁ ⲉⲃⲟⲗ
ⲍⲙ̄ ⲡⲧⲁⲫⲟⲥ. (12) ϯⲟ ⲛ̄ ⲁⲧϭⲟⲙ ⲙ̄ ⲡⲉⲙⲧⲟ ⲉⲃⲟⲗ ⲛ̄ ⲟⲩⲣⲱⲙⲉ ⲛ̄ ⲧⲉⲓⲙⲓⲛⲉ. (13) ⲟⲩⲙⲁⲓ-ⲟⲩⲱⲙ ⲡⲉ ⲡⲉⲕⲥⲟⲛ. (14) ⲛⲓⲙ ⲡⲉⲧ ⲛⲁⲣ̄-ⲙⲛ̄ⲧⲣⲉ
ⲉ ⲧⲡⲓⲥⲧⲓⲥ ⲙ̄ ⲙⲉ? (15) ⲛⲉⲓⲙⲁⲧⲟⲓ ⲍⲉⲛⲁⲑⲟⲧⲉ ⲛⲉ. (16) ⲁ-ⲡⲁⲅⲅⲉⲗⲟⲥ ⲉⲓ ⲛⲁⲓ ⲍⲛ̄ ⲟⲩⲣⲁⲥⲟⲩ ⲛ̄ ⲧⲉⲩϣⲏ ⲁⲩⲱ ⲁϥⲧⲁⲙⲟⲓ ⲉⲧⲃⲉ ⲛⲉⲓϣⲁϫⲉ.
(17) ⲛ̄ ⲧⲉⲩⲛⲟⲩ ⲁ-ⲧⲡⲉ ⲣ̄-ⲕⲁⲕⲉ. (18) ⲛⲓⲙ ⲡⲉⲛⲧⲁϥⲧⲁⲗϭⲟⲕ ⲉⲃⲟⲗ ⲍⲙ̄
ⲡⲉⲕϣⲱⲛⲉ? (19) ⲡⲉⲓⲣⲱⲙⲉ ⲟⲩⲥⲁⲉⲓⲛ ⲛ̄ ⲥⲁⲃⲉ ⲡⲉ. (20) ⲙ̄ⲡⲣ̄-ⲍⲟⲧⲉ,
ⲡⲁϣⲏⲣⲉ. (21) ⲁⲩⲱ ⲛ̄ ⲧⲉⲩⲛⲟⲩ ⲁϥⲣ̄-ⲁⲧⲟⲩⲱⲛⲍ̅ ⲉⲃⲟⲗ ⲛ̄ϭⲓ ⲡⲁⲓⲁⲃⲟⲗⲟⲥ.
(22) ⲟⲩⲛⲟϭ ⲧⲉ ⲧⲉϥⲙⲛ̄ⲧⲉⲣⲟ. (23) ⲍⲛ̄ ⲧⲉϥⲙⲛ̄ⲧⲍⲗ̄ⲗⲟ ⲛⲉϥⲉⲓⲣⲉ ⲙ̄
ⲡⲙⲉⲉⲩⲉ ⲁⲛ ⲛ̄ ⲛⲉⲍⲟⲟⲩ ⲛ̄ ⲧⲉϥⲙⲛ̄ⲧϣⲏⲣⲉ ϣⲏⲙ. (24) ⲙ̄ⲡⲉⲛⲡⲓⲥⲧⲉⲩⲉ ⲉ
ⲧⲉⲩⲙⲛ̄ⲧⲙⲛ̄ⲧⲣⲉ. (25) ⲁⲩⲣ̄-ϣⲡⲏⲣⲉ ⲁⲩⲱ ⲁⲩⲛⲟϭ ⲛ̄ ⲍⲟⲧⲉ ϣⲱⲡⲉ ⲛ̄ ⲧⲉⲩⲙⲏⲧⲉ. (26) ⲁϥⲍⲱⲛ ⲉⲧⲟⲟⲧⲟⲩ ⲉⲧⲣⲉⲩⲙⲟⲩⲣ ⲙ̄ ⲡϣⲏⲣⲉ ⲛ̄ⲥⲉⲛⲟϫϥ̄ ⲉ ⲡⲉϣⲧⲉⲕⲟ. (27) ⲛ̄ⲧⲕ̄-ⲟⲩⲙⲁⲓ-ⲉⲟⲟⲩ ⲉϥϣⲟⲩⲉⲓⲧ. (28) ⲟⲩⲣⲙ̄ⲛ̄ⲧⲱⲛ ⲡⲉ
ⲛ̄ⲧⲟⲕ? ⲁⲛⲅ̄-ⲟⲩⲣⲙ̄ⲛ̄ⲕⲏⲙⲉ. (29) ⲙ̄ⲡⲉⲥϣⲃⲙ̄-ϭⲟⲙ ⲉ ⲧⲟⲩⲛⲟⲥϥ̄. (30)
ⲍⲉⲛⲍⲙ̄ⲍⲁⲗ ⲛ̄ ⲣⲉϥⲣ̄-ⲍⲟⲧⲉ ⲛⲉ. (31) ⲙⲛ̄-ϣϭⲟⲙ ⲙ̄ⲙⲟⲓ ⲉ ϣⲁϫⲉ ⲛⲙ̄ⲙⲏⲧⲛ̄
ⲙ̄ ⲙⲛ̄ⲧⲟⲩⲉⲉⲓⲉⲛⲓⲛ. (32) ⲁϫⲓⲥ ⲛⲁϥ ϫⲉⲕⲁⲥ ⲉϥⲉϫⲟⲟⲩ ⲙ̄ ⲡⲟⲉⲓⲕ ⲉ ⲛ̄-
ⲍⲏⲕⲉ ⲛ̄ ⲧⲡⲟⲗⲓⲥ. (33) ϯⲛⲁϭⲱ ⲛⲙ̄ⲙⲁⲕ ϫⲉⲕⲁⲥ ⲛ̄ⲛⲉⲩⲙⲟⲟⲩⲧ. (34)
ⲟⲩⲁⲧⲧⲁⲕⲟ ⲡⲉ ⲡⲛⲟⲙⲟⲥ ⲙ̄ ⲡϫⲟⲉⲓⲥ. (35) ⲛ̄ⲧⲁ-ⲙⲁⲣⲓⲁ ⲧⲁⲙⲁⲁⲩ ϫⲡⲟⲓ
ⲍⲛ̄ ⲟⲩⲙⲩⲥⲧⲏⲣⲓⲟⲛ ⲛ̄ ⲁⲧϣⲁϫⲉ ⲉⲣⲟϥ, ⲉ-ⲙⲛ̄-ⲗⲁⲁⲩ ⲛ̄ ⲣⲱⲙⲉ ⲍⲙ̄ ⲡⲕⲟⲥⲙⲟⲥ
ⲧⲏⲣϥ̄ ⲛⲁⲉⲓⲙⲉ ⲉⲣⲟϥ. (36) ⲁⲩⲙⲟⲩⲍ ⲇⲉ ⲧⲏⲣⲟⲩ ⲛ̄ ϭⲱⲛⲧ̄ ⲍⲛ̄ ⲧⲥⲩⲛⲁⲅⲱⲅⲏ ⲉⲩⲥⲱⲧⲙ̄ ⲉ ⲛⲁⲓ. (37) ⲁϫⲓⲥ ⲙ̄ ⲡⲉⲓⲱⲛⲉ ϫⲉ ⲉϥⲉⲣ̄-ⲟⲉⲓⲕ. (38)
ⲁⲩⲉⲓⲛⲉ ⲛ̄ ⲟⲩⲛⲟϭ ⲛ̄ ⲥⲁⲉⲓⲛ ⲉⲧⲣⲉϥⲧⲁⲗϭⲟ ⲙ̄ ⲡϣⲏⲣⲉ, ⲁⲗⲗⲁ ⲙ̄ⲡⲉϥϭⲙ̄-ϭⲟⲙ
ⲉ ⲧⲁⲗϭⲟϥ.

Lesson 28

28.1 The Habitual and its negative.

ϣⲁⲓⲥⲱⲧⲙ̄	ϣⲁⲛⲥⲱⲧⲙ̄	Neg.	ⲙⲉⲓⲥⲱⲧⲙ̄	ⲙⲉⲛⲥⲱⲧⲙ̄
ϣⲁⲕⲥⲱⲧⲙ̄	ϣⲁⲧⲉⲧⲛ̄ⲥⲱⲧⲙ̄		ⲙⲉⲕⲥⲱⲧⲙ̄	ⲙⲉⲧⲉⲧⲛ̄ⲥⲱⲧⲙ̄
ϣⲁⲣ(ⲉ)ⲥⲱⲧⲙ̄			ⲙⲉⲣⲉⲥⲱⲧⲙ̄	
ϣⲁϥⲥⲱⲧⲙ̄	ϣⲁⲩⲥⲱⲧⲙ̄		ⲙⲉϥⲥⲱⲧⲙ̄	ⲙⲉⲩⲥⲱⲧⲙ̄
ϣⲁⲥⲥⲱⲧⲙ̄			ⲙⲉⲥⲥⲱⲧⲙ̄	
ϣⲁⲣⲉ–ⲡⲣⲱⲙⲉ ⲥⲱⲧⲙ̄			ⲙⲉⲣⲉ–ⲡⲣⲱⲙⲉ ⲥⲱⲧⲙ̄	

The Habitual (or *praesens consuetudinis*) describes an action or activity as characteristic or habitual. It may usually be translated by the English general present (I write, I work, etc.):

ϣⲁⲩⲙⲟⲩⲧⲉ ⲉⲣⲟϥ ϫⲉ ⲓⲱ²ⲁⲛⲛⲏⲥ	They call him John.
ϣⲁⲣⲉ–ⲧⲥⲟⲫⲓⲁ ⲟⲩⲱ² ²ⲙ̄ ⲡ²ⲏⲧ ⲛ̄ ⲛ̄ⲁⲓⲕⲁⲓⲟⲥ.	Wisdom resides in the heart of the righteous.
ⲙⲉϥⲥⲉ–ⲏⲣⲡ̄.	He doesn't drink wine.

The Habitual forms a regular system with the converters:

relative: ⎰ ⲉϣⲁϥⲥⲱⲧⲙ̄   Neg. ⲉⲧⲉ ⲙⲉϥⲥⲱⲧⲙ̄
         ⎱ ⲉⲧⲉ ϣⲁϥⲥⲱⲧⲙ̄

circumstantial: ⲉ–ϣⲁϥⲥⲱⲧⲙ̄   ⲉ–ⲙⲉϥⲥⲱⲧⲙ̄

imperfect: ⲛⲉ–ϣⲁϥⲥⲱⲧⲙ̄   ⲛⲉ–ⲙⲉϥⲥⲱⲧⲙ̄

second tense: ⲉϣⲁϥⲥⲱⲧⲙ̄   ————————

The Habitual is basically tenseless (hence the designation *aorist* in some grammars) and gains its translation value from the context. The imperfect converter makes a past tense explicit, e.g. ⲛⲉ–ϣⲁϥⲥ²ⲁⲓ he used to write. Note that subject resumption is required in the relative form: ⲡⲣⲱⲙⲉ ⲉϣⲁϥⲣ̄–ⲡⲁⲓ the man who does thus. The Habitual belongs to the Tripartite Conjugation: only the Infinitive may be used in the verbal slot.

28.2 Emphasis. The typical non-emphatic word order

in a verbal clause is

> (verbal prefix) + subject + verb + object + adverbial elements

We have seen that the conversion of the verbal prefix to a second tense form places a strong emphasis on the adverbial element, requiring in most cases a cleft sentence in the English translation. The use of the Coptic cleft sentence pattern, with пе, те, не + a relative form is a further device for giving special prominence to a subject or object. A somewhat weaker emphasis is achieved by placing a specific element of the clause at the beginning. Such preposed elements are usually resumed pronominally within the clause unless they are simple adverbial phrases. This transformation, known also as fronting or topicalization, is very common in Coptic; examples abound on every page. The element preposed may be completely unmarked as such, but the Greek particle ᴧє is ubiquitous in this function. Fronted personal pronouns are always in the independent form. E.g.

ᴧNOK ᴧє ᴎneчбιne ᴍᴍoι.	*Me* he didn't find.
neчϣнpe ᴧє ᴧγpᴧ₂тч̄.	*His son,* however, they killed.
ᴎ̄тoк ᴧє ᴎ̄ϯ-nᴧϯ nᴧk ᴧn ᴍ̄ n₂ᴧт.	I will not give the money to *you.*

The independent pronouns may be used appositionally to emphasize any suffixed pronoun, e.g. ₂ᴍ̄ nтpᴧcωтᴍ̄ ᴧє ᴧNOK but when *I* heard; єтвннтк̄ ᴎ̄тoк for *your* sake. We have already mentioned the repetition in ᴎ̄тк̄-nιᴍ ᴎ̄тoк? Who are you? They may even stand before a relative clause, as in nᴍᴧ ᴧNOK єϯ-ᴍ̄ᴍoч the place which *I* am in.

The particles єιc and єιc ₂ннтє add a certain vividness or immediacy to a following statement. If an element is topicalized, єιc generally occurs before nouns and єιc ₂ннтє before pronouns.

> єιc ₂ннтє ᴧnг̄-eᴍ̄₂ᴧᴧ ᴍ̄ nxoєιc.
> Behold, I am the maidservant of the Lord.

ⲉⲓⲥ ⳍⲏⲏⲧⲉ ⲉⲕⲉϣⲱⲡⲉ ⲉⲕⲕⲱ ⲛ̄ ⲣⲱⲕ.
Behold, you shall remain (being) mute. (Cf. §30.11)

ⲉⲓⲥ ⳍⲏⲏⲧⲉ ⲧⲉⲛⲁⲱ ⲛ̄ⲧⲉⳝⲡⲟ ⲛ̄ ⲟⲩϣⲏⲣⲉ.
Behold you shall conceive and bear a son.

The translation "behold" is purely conventional, but it is
difficult to find a better English equivalent. The forms
ⲉⲓⲥ ⳍⲏⲏⲡⲉ, ⲉⲓⲥⲧⲉ, ⲉⲓⲥⲡⲉ, and ⲉⲓⲥ ⳍⲏⲏⲧⲉ ⲉⲓⲥ also occur. ⲉⲓⲥ
has several other functions: (1) with a following noun, as
a complete predication:

ⲉⲓⲥ ⲧⲉⲕⲥⲱⲛⲉ. *Here is* your sister.

(2) as a "preposition" before temporal expressions, as in

ⲉⲓⲥ ϣⲟⲙⲧⲉ ⲛ̄ ⲣⲟⲙⲡⲉ ⲙ̄ⲡⲉⲛⲛⲁⲩ ⲉⲣⲟϥ.
We have not seen him *for* three years.

28.3 Emphatic and intensive pronouns.

(a) ⲙⲁⲩⲁⲁ⸗, ⲙⲁⲩⲁⲧ⸗, less frequently ⲟⲩⲁⲁ(ⲧ)⸗, is
used in apposition to a preceding noun or pronoun: alone,
sole, self, only. E.g.

ⲁⲛⲟⲕ ⲙⲁⲩⲁⲁⲧ   I alone, I by myself, only I
ⲛⲁϥ ⲙⲁⲩⲁⲁϥ   to him alone, to him only
ⲡⲣ̄ⲣⲟ ⲙⲁⲩⲁⲁϥ   the king himself, the king alone.

(b) ⳍⲱⲱ⸗ (1 c.s. ⳍⲱ or ⳍⲱⲱⲧ; 2 f.s. ⳍⲱⲱⲧⲉ, 2 c.pl.
ⳍⲱⲧ-ⲑⲏⲩⲧⲛ̄), similar to the preceding, but often with the
added nuance of "also, too, moreover." E.g.

ⲛ̄ⲧⲟⲕ ⲇⲉ ⳍⲱⲱⲕ, ⲡⲁϣⲏⲣⲉ, ⲥⲉⲛⲁⲙⲟⲩⲧⲉ ⲉⲣⲟⲕ ⳝⲉ ⲡⲉⲡⲣⲟⲫⲏⲧⲏⲥ ⲙ̄
ⲡⲉⲧ ⳝⲟⲥⲉ. And you, moreover, my son, will be called
the prophet of the Most High.
ⲉⲓⲥ ⲉⲗⲓⲥⲁⲃⲉⲧ ⲧⲟⲩⲥⲩⲅⲅⲉⲛⲏⲥ ⲛ̄ⲧⲟⲥ ⳍⲱⲱⲥ ⲟⲛ ⲁⲥⲱ ⲛ̄ ⲟⲩϣⲏⲣⲉ
ⳍⲛ̄ ⲧⲉⲥⲙⲛ̄ⲧⳍⲗ̄ⲗⲱ. Behold, Elisabeth your kinsman has also
conceived a child in her old age.

The form ⳍⲱⲱϥ also serves as an adverb/conjunction "however,
on the other hand" without any pronominal force. ⲛ̄ⲧⲟϥ is
used likewise.

(c) ⲙ̄ⲙⲓⲛ ⲙ̄ⲙⲟ⸗, an intensive pronoun, used in apposition to a preceding pronoun, usually possessive or reflexive:

    ⲡⲁⲏⲓ ⲙ̄ⲙⲓⲛ ⲙ̄ⲙⲟⲓ   my own house

    ₂ⲙ̄ ⲡⲉϥ†ⲙⲉ ⲙ̄ⲙⲓⲛ ⲙ̄ⲙⲟϥ   in his own village.

28.4 The reciprocal pronoun "each other, one another" is expressed by possessive prefixes on -ⲉⲣⲏⲩ (fellow, companion), e.g.

    ⲁⲛⲙⲓϣⲉ ⲙⲛ̄ ⲛⲉⲛⲉⲣⲏⲩ.   We fought with one another.

    ⲛⲉⲩϣⲁϫⲉ ⲙⲛ̄ ⲛⲉⲩⲉⲣⲏⲩ.   They were talking with each other.

28.5 Further remarks on -ⲕⲉ-. In addition to the use of -ⲕⲉ- as an adjective "other, another" introduced in 4.3, -ⲕⲉ- may have a purely emphasizing function, e.g.

    ⲡⲕⲉⲣⲱⲙⲉ   the man *too*, the man *as well*.

Both uses are frequent, and the correct translation will depend on a careful examination of the context.

There is a related set of pronouns: m.s. ⲕⲉ or ⲕⲉⲧ, f.s. ⲕⲉⲧⲉ, c.pl. ⲕⲟⲟⲩⲉ. These occur alone mostly in negative expressions, e.g. ⲙ̄ⲡⲓⲛⲁⲩ ⲉ ⲕⲉ I saw no one else. Otherwise the articles are added, as in ⲧⲕⲉⲧⲉ the other one (f.), ⲛ̄ⲕⲟⲟⲩⲉ the others, ₂ⲉⲛⲕⲟⲟⲩⲉ some others. For the indefinite singular ⲕⲉⲟⲩⲁ and f. ⲕⲉⲟⲩⲉⲓ, another (one), are used.

28.6 Nouns with pronominal suffixes. It was noted earlier that there is a small group of nouns which take pronominal suffixes in a possessive sense. Among the more important of these are

(a) ⲭⲱ⸗ head, mostly replaced by ⲁⲡⲉ in normal usage, occurs frequently in compound expressions. The prepositions ⲉⲭⲛ̄, ⲉⲭⲱ⸗ and ₂ⲓⲭⲛ̄, ₂ⲓⲭⲱ⸗ have already been introduced. Note also ₂ⲁⲭⲛ̄, ₂ⲁⲭⲱ⸗ before, in front of; ϥⲓ-ⲭⲱ⸗ to raise one's head; ⲕⲁ-ⲭⲱ⸗ to submit (reflex.), to compel (not reflex.); †-ⲭⲱ⸗ ⲉ₂ⲟⲩⲛ ⲉ to submit to; ⲟⲩⲉ₂-ⲭⲱ⸗ to bow the head. There are other similar verbal compounds.

(b) ειλ, ειλτ⸗ eye; mainly in compounds, e.g. κτε-
ειλτ⸗ to look around; μεϩ-ειλτ⸗ ⲙ̅ⲙⲟ⸗ to stare at; τογⲛ-
ειλτ⸗ εβολ to instruct, inform; cf. also ⲛλιλτ⸗ in the
following lesson.

(c) ⲣⲱ⸗ mouth. The unbound form ⲛ.ⲣⲟ appears often
in the sense of "door, entrance," but in the sense of
"mouth" it is usually replaced by τλⲡⲣⲟ except in compounds, e.g. the prepositions ⲉⲣⲛ̅, ⲉⲣⲱ⸗ and ϩιⲣⲛ̅, ϩιⲣⲱ⸗;
κλ-ⲣⲱ⸗, κⲱ ⲛ̅ ⲣⲱ⸗ to become/remain silent (Q κλⲣⲁⲉιⲧ);
ⲧⲙ̅-ⲣⲱ⸗ idem (as imptv.); ϫι-ⲣⲱϥ ⲙ̅ⲙⲟ⸗ to obstruct, block.

(d) ⲧⲟⲟⲧ⸗ hand, already commented upon in §10.4. The
more important verbal compounds include ϯ-ⲧⲟⲟⲧ⸗ (Vocab.
26), κλ-ⲧⲟⲟⲧ⸗ εβολ to cease (doing: Circum.), and ϩι-ⲧⲟⲟⲧ⸗
to begin (see Vocab. below).

28.7 The nouns underlying the directional adverbs of
Lesson 8 are used in several other important adverbial and
prepositional expressions. With ⲛ̅, ϩι, and ⲥλ they form
adverbs of static location: e.g. ⲛ̅ βολ outside, ϩι ϩⲟγⲛ
inside, ⲥλ-ⲡⲉⲥⲏⲧ underneath, below. Each of these may be
converted into a prepositional phrase by adding ⲛ̅, ⲙ̅ⲙⲟ⸗:
ϩι βολ ⲛ̅ outside of, beyond; ⲥλ-ϩⲟγⲛ ⲛ̅ within, inside of.
Nearly all the possible combinations occur: (ⲛ̅, ϩι, ⲥλ) +
(βολ, ϩⲟγⲛ, ϩⲣλι up, ϩⲣλι down, ⲡⲉⲥⲏⲧ, ⲧⲡⲉ, ⲡλϩⲟγ, ⲡϣⲱι) ±
ⲙ̅ⲙⲟ⸗ (sometimes also + ⲉ). Their meanings are usually
obvious from the context. The noun ⲛ.ⲥλ in these expressions means "side, direction." It is the same ⲥλ we have
in ⲛ̅ⲥλ and ⲙⲛ̅ⲛ̅ⲥλ. Note also the phrase (ⲛ̅) ⲥλ ⲥλ ⲛιⲙ on
every side, everywhich way.

Vocabulary 28

(ⲉιⲥ, ⲉιⲥ ϩⲏⲏⲧⲉ, ⲙλγλλ⸗, ϩⲱⲱ⸗, ⲙ̅ⲙιⲛ ⲙ̅ⲙⲟ⸗, κλ-ⲣⲱ⸗, ⲧⲙ̅-ⲣⲱ⸗,
ϩⲉⲛκⲟⲟγⲉ, ⲛ̅κⲟⲟγⲉ, -ⲉⲣⲏγ from the lesson)

ⲥⲱⲟγϩ ⲥⲉγϩ- ⲥⲟⲟγϩ⸗ Q ⲥⲟⲟγϩ vb. tr. (± ⲉϩⲟγⲛ) to gather,
collect (ⲙ̅ⲙⲟ⸗; at: ⲉ, ⲉϫⲛ̅, ϩⲛ̅); intr. idem.

сллнϣ слⲁнϣ- слноуϣ⸍ Q слнлϣⲧ vb. tr. to nourish, rear,
tend to (ⲙ̅ⲙⲟ⸍); Q to be well-fed.

п.ⲁⲣⲓⲕⲉ fault, blame. ϭⲛ̅-ⲁⲣⲓⲕⲉ ⲉ to find fault with, blame.

ⲣⲟⲩ2ⲉ evening. ⲉ/ⲛ̅/21 ⲣⲟⲩ2ⲉ in the evening. ϣⲁ ⲣⲟⲩ2ⲉ until
evening.

2ⲧⲟⲟⲩⲉ dawn, morning. ⲉ/ⲛ̅/21 2ⲧⲟⲟⲩⲉ at dawn.

ⲣⲁⲥⲧⲉ tomorrow. ⲡⲣⲁⲥⲧⲉ, ⲛ̅ ⲣⲁⲥⲧⲉ, ⲉ ⲣⲁⲥⲧⲉ, ⲙ̅ ⲡⲉϥⲣⲁⲥⲧⲉ adv.
tomorrow.

21-ⲧⲟⲟⲧ⸍ to begin, undertake (to do: ⲉ + Inf.); for 21-
see Glossary sub 21ⲟⲩⲉ.

ⲟⲛ adv. again, further, moreover.

Exercises

(1) ⲛⲓⲙ ⲡⲉ ⲡⲉ1ⲣⲙ̅ⲛ̅ⲛⲟⲩⲧⲉ ⲉϣⲁⲩⲙⲟⲩⲧⲉ ⲉⲣⲟϥ ϫⲉ 1ⲱ2ⲁⲛⲛⲏⲥ? (2) ⲛ̅ⲧⲟϥ
ⲇⲉ 2ⲱⲱϥ ⲛⲁⲉ1 ϣⲁⲣⲟⲛ ⲙ̅ ⲡⲉϥⲣⲁⲥⲧⲉ. (3) ⲁⲛ2ⲉ ⲉⲣⲟϥ ⲉϥⲙⲟⲟϣⲉ ⲙⲁⲩⲁⲁϥ ⲉ ⲑⲉⲛⲉⲉⲧⲉ. (4) ⲁ-2ⲟⲉ1ⲛⲉ ⲡⲓⲥⲧⲉⲩⲉ ⲉⲣⲟϥ, 2ⲉⲛⲕⲟⲟⲩⲉ ⲇⲉ ⲙ̅ⲡⲟⲩ-
ⲡⲓⲥⲧⲉⲩⲉ. (5) ⲙⲉⲣⲉ-ⲛ̅ⲇⲓⲕⲁⲓⲟⲥ ⲥⲱⲧⲙ̅ ⲉ ⲛ̅ϣⲁϫⲉ ⲛ̅ ⲛ̅ⲣⲉϥⲣ̅-ⲛⲟⲃⲉ. (6)
ⲛⲉ-ϣⲁⲣⲉ-ⲙ̅ⲙⲟⲛⲁⲭⲟⲥ ⲧ-ⲛⲉⲩ2ⲱⲃ ⲛ̅ ϭⲓϫ ⲉⲃⲟⲗ 2ⲛ̅ ⲛⲉ2ⲟⲟⲩ ⲉⲧ ⲙ̅ⲙⲁⲩ.
(7) ⲛⲉⲣⲉ-ⲟⲩⲛⲟϭ ⲙ̅ ⲙⲛⲏϣⲉ ⲥⲟⲟⲩ2 21ⲣⲙ̅ ⲡⲉϥⲏ1. (8) ⲙ̅ⲡⲣ̅6ⲛ̅-ⲁⲣⲓⲕⲉ
ⲉⲣⲟ1, ⲡⲁⲉ1ⲱⲧ. ⲙ̅ⲡⲓⲣ̅-ⲗⲁⲁⲩ. (9) ⲛ̅ ⲣⲟⲩ2ⲉ ⲁ-ⲡⲥⲟⲛ ⲕⲧⲟϥ ⲟⲛ ⲉ ⲧⲉϥ-
ⲣ1. (10) ⲙⲛ̅-ⲗⲁⲁⲩ ⲙ̅ ⲡⲣⲟⲫⲏⲧⲏⲥ ϣⲏⲡ 2ⲙ̅ ⲡⲉϥ⳾ⲙⲉ ⲙ̅ⲙⲓⲛ ⲙ̅ⲙⲟϥ. (11)
ⲁⲛⲟⲕ ⲇⲉ 2ⲱ ⳾ⲛⲁ21-ⲧⲟⲟⲧ ⲉ ⲥ2ⲁ1 ⲛ̅ ⲛ̅ϣⲁϫⲉ ⲉⲛⲧⲁⲩϣⲱⲡⲉ. (12)
ϣⲁϥⲥⲗⲁⲛϣ̅ ⲛ̅ ⲛⲉϥϣⲏⲣⲉ ⲛ̅ ⲑⲉ ⲛ̅ ⲟⲩⲉ1ⲱⲧ ⲛ̅ ⲁⲅⲁⲑⲟⲥ. (13) ⲁϥϫⲟⲟⲥ
ⲛⲁ1 ϫⲉ ⲧⲙ̅-ⲣⲱⲕ ⲛ̅ⲃⲱⲕ ⲉⲃⲟⲗ. (14) ⲁⲕⲉ1ⲣⲉ ⲛ̅ ⲛⲁ1 ⲛ̅ⲧⲟⲕ ⲙⲁⲩⲁⲁⲕ?
(15) ⲛⲓⲙ ⲡⲉⲧ ⲛⲁⲥⲁⲛⲟⲩϣ̅ⲛ̅ ⲉ-ⲁ-ⲛⲉⲛⲉ1ⲟⲧⲉ ⲙⲟⲩ? (16) ⲁϥⲕⲁ-ⲣⲱϥ,
ⲙ̅ⲡⲉϥⲟⲩⲉϣ̅ⲃ̅-ⲗⲁⲁⲩ. (17) 1ⲱ2ⲁⲛⲛⲏⲥ ⲇⲉ 2ⲱⲱϥ ⲁϥⲙⲟⲩⲛ ⲉⲃⲟⲗ ⲉϥⲟⲩⲏ2
21 ⲡⲭⲁⲉ1ⲉ. (18) ⲛ̅ⲧⲉⲣⲉ-ⲣⲟⲩ2ⲉ ⲇⲉ ϣⲱⲡⲉ, ⲛⲉϥⲙⲁⲑⲏⲧⲏⲥ ⲁⲩⲥⲱⲟⲩ2
2ⲙ̅ ⲡⲙⲁ ⲉⲧ ⲙ̅ⲙⲁⲩ. (19) ⲛ̅⳾ⲟⲩⲱϣ ⲁⲛ ⲉⲧⲣⲉⲕϭⲱ ⲙ̅ ⲡⲉ1ⲙⲁ. ⲕⲟⲧⲕ̅ ⲉ
ⲡⲉⲕⲏ1 ⲙ̅ⲙ1ⲛ ⲙ̅ⲙⲟⲕ. (20) ⲁⲩ21-ⲧⲟⲟⲧⲟⲩ ⲉ ⲕⲱⲧ ⲛ̅ ⲟⲩⲛⲟϭ ⲛ̅ ⲣ̅ⲡⲉ ⲉⲣⲉ-
ⲧⲉϥϭⲁⲡⲉ ⲛⲁⲡⲱ2 ⲉ ⲧⲡⲉ ⲙⲁⲩⲁⲁⲥ. (21) ⲁ-ϣⲟⲙⲛ̅ⲧ ⲙ̅ⲙⲟⲟⲩ ϭⲱ ⲛ̅ⲙ̅ⲙⲁ1,
ⲛ̅ⲕⲟⲟⲩⲉ ⲇⲉ ⲁⲩⲕⲧⲟⲟⲩ ⲉ ⲧⲡⲟⲗⲓⲥ. (22) ⲛ̅ⲕⲟⲟⲩⲉ ⲇⲉ ⲥⲏ2 2ⲛ̅ ⲕⲉⲭⲱⲱⲙⲉ.
(23) ⲛ̅ⲣⲉϥⲣ̅-ⲛⲟⲃⲉ ⲇⲉ ⲙⲉⲩⲥⲁⲁⲛϣ̅-ⲛⲉⲩϣⲏⲣⲉ 2ⲛ̅ ⲛⲉⲛⲧⲟⲗⲏ ⲙ̅ ⲡϫⲟⲉ1ⲥ.
(24) ⲁⲩⲕⲟⲧⲟⲩ ⲟⲛ ⲉ ⲥⲡ̅ⲥⲱⲡϥ̅. (25) ⲉⲧⲃⲉ ⲟⲩ ⲧⲉⲧⲛ̅ⲙ1ϣⲉ ⲙⲛ̅ ⲛⲉⲧⲛ̅-
ⲉⲣⲏⲩ ⲛ̅ ⲧⲉ12ⲉ? (26) 21 2ⲧⲟⲟⲩⲉ ⲇⲉ ⲁ-ⲛ̅ⲣⲱⲙⲉ ⲛ̅ ⲧⲡⲟⲗⲓⲥ ⲥⲱⲟⲩ2
ⲉ ⲧⲁⲅⲟⲣⲁ. (27) ⲁⲥⲣ̅-2ⲟⲧⲉ ⲉⲃⲟⲗ ϫⲉ ⲁ-ⲡⲉⲥ2ⲁ1 ϭⲛ̅-ⲁⲣⲓⲕⲉ ⲉⲣⲟⲥ.

(28) ⲛⲓⲙ ⲡⲉϣⲁϥⲧⲁⲗⲟⲉ-ⲡⲥⲁⲉⲓⲛ ⲙⲁⲩⲁⲁϥ? (29) ⲁⲛ₂ⲉ ⲉ ⲛⲉⲛⲥⲛⲏⲩ ⲉⲩⲥⲁⲛⲁϣⲧ ⲧⲏⲣⲟⲩ ⲉ-ⲙⲛ̄-ⲟⲩⲁ ⲉϥ₂ⲕⲁⲉⲓⲧ ⲛ̄₂ⲏⲧⲟⲩ. (30) ⲧⲛ̄ⲛⲁⲟⲱ ⲉⲛ-ϣⲗⲏⲗ ϣⲁ ⲣⲟⲩ₂ⲉ.

Reading

(from the Sayings of the Fathers)

ⲁ-ⲟⲩⲁ ⲛ̄ ⲛⲉⲛⲉⲓⲟⲧⲉ ⲧⲛ̄ⲛⲟⲟⲩ ⲙ̄ ⲡⲉϥⲙⲁⲑⲏⲧⲏⲥ ⲉ ⲙⲉ₂-ⲙⲟⲟⲩ. ⲛⲉⲣⲉ-ⲧϣⲱⲧⲉ ⲇⲉ ⲡⲉ ⲟⲩⲏⲩ ⲛ̄ ⲧⲣⲓ ⲙ̄ⲙⲁⲧⲉ. ⲁϥⲣ̄-ⲡⲱⲃϣ̄ ⲇⲉ ⲉ ϫⲓ-ⲡⲛⲟⲩ₂ ⲛⲙ̄ⲙⲁϥ. ⲛ̄ⲧⲉⲣⲉϥⲉⲓ ⲇⲉ ⲉϫⲛ̄ ⲧϣⲱⲧⲉ, ⲁϥⲉⲓⲙⲉ ϫⲉ ⲙ̄ⲡⲉϥⲉⲓⲛⲉ ⲛⲙ̄ⲙⲁϥ ⲙ̄ ⲡⲛⲟⲩ₂. ⲁϥⲉⲓⲣⲉ ⲛ̄ ⲟⲩϣⲗⲏⲗ, ⲁϥⲙⲟⲩⲧⲉ ⲉϥϫⲱ ⲙ̄ⲙⲟⲥ ϫⲉ, "ⲡϣⲏⲓ, ⲡⲗⲉⲓⲟⲧ ⲡⲉⲧ ϫⲱ ⲙ̄ⲙⲟⲥ ϫⲉ, 'ⲙⲟⲩ₂ ⲙ̄ ⲡⲁⲅⲅⲓⲟⲛ ⲙ̄ ⲙⲟⲟⲩ.'" ⲁⲩⲱ ⲛ̄ ⲧⲉⲩⲛⲟⲩ ⲁ-ⲡⲙⲟⲟⲩ ⲉⲓ ⲉⲡϣⲱⲓ, ⲁ-ⲡⲥⲟⲛ ⲙⲟⲩ₂ ⲙ̄ ⲡⲉϥϣⲟϣⲟⲩ, ⲁⲩⲱ ⲁ-ⲡⲙⲟⲟⲩ ₂ⲙⲟⲟⲥ ⲟⲛ ⲉ ⲡⲉϥⲙⲁ.

New words: ⲧ.ϣⲱⲧⲉ, ⲡ.ϣⲏⲓ well, cistern.

ⲙⲉ₂-ⲙⲟⲟⲩ to fetch water.

ⲡ.ⲁⲅⲅⲓⲟⲛ (τὸ ἀγγεῖον), ⲡ.ϣⲟϣⲟⲩ names of vessels.

Lesson 29

29.1 The Conditional and conditional clauses.

ⲉⲓϣⲁⲛⲥⲱⲧⲙ̄	if I hear	ⲉⲛϣⲁⲛⲥⲱⲧⲙ̄
ⲉⲕϣⲁⲛⲥⲱⲧⲙ̄	if you hear	ⲉⲧⲉⲧⲛ̄ϣⲁⲛⲥⲱⲧⲙ̄
ⲉⲣⲉϣⲁⲛⲥⲱⲧⲙ̄	etc.	
ⲉϥϣⲁⲛⲥⲱⲧⲙ̄		ⲉⲩϣⲁⲛⲥⲱⲧⲙ̄
ⲉⲥϣⲁⲛⲥⲱⲧⲙ̄		

ⲉⲣϣⲁⲛ-ⲡⲣⲱⲙⲉ ⲥⲱⲧⲙ̄

Negation is with -ⲧⲙ̄-: ⲉϥϣⲁⲛⲧⲙ̄ⲥⲱⲧⲙ̄, ⲉⲣϣⲁⲛⲧⲙ̄-ⲡⲣⲱⲙⲉ ⲥⲱⲧⲙ̄. ϣⲁⲛ may be omitted in the negative: ⲉϥⲧⲙ̄ⲥⲱⲧⲙ̄, ⲉⲣⲉⲧⲙ̄-ⲡⲣⲱⲙⲉ ⲥⲱⲧⲙ̄. The Conditional occurs only in the protasis of conditional sentences. Only the Infinitive may occur in the verbal slot.

Conditional sentences in Coptic fall formally into two clearly defined groups: (1) real, and (2) contrary-to-fact. The protasis of real conditional sentences in present time has a variety of forms:

(a) a clause with the Conditional:

ⲉⲕϣⲁⲛⲡⲓⲥⲧⲉⲩⲉ ⲉ ⲛⲁⲓ   if you believe this

(b) ⲉϣⲱⲡⲉ (if) or ⲉϣⲭⲉ (if) followed by the First Present, the Circumstantial, the Conditional, or any type of nonverbal predication:

ⲉϣⲱⲡⲉ/ⲉϣⲭⲉ ⲕⲡⲓⲥⲧⲉⲩⲉ ⲉ ⲛⲁⲓ	
" ⲉⲕⲡⲓⲥⲧⲉⲩⲉ ⲉ ⲛⲁⲓ	if you believe this
" ⲉⲕϣⲁⲛⲡⲓⲥⲧⲉⲩⲉ ⲉ ⲛⲁⲓ	
" ⲛ̄ⲧⲟⲕ ⲡⲉ ⲡⲉϥⲉⲓⲱⲧ	if you are his father
" ⲟⲩⲛ̄ⲧⲁⲕ ⲡ2ⲁⲧ	if you have the money
" ⲛ̄ϯⲙ̄ⲡϣⲁ ⲁⲛ	if I am not worthy

(c) the Circumstantial alone often serves as protasis:

ⲉⲛⲙ̄ ⲡⲉⲓⲙⲁ,...   since we are here,...

The apodosis of such conditions may be any variety of verbal clause appropriate for the required sense (e.g. Fut. I, II, III; Habitual; Imperative). The apodosis may optionally be introduced with ⲉⲓⲉ (ⲉⲉⲓⲉ). For examples, see the exercises.

The protasis of contrary-to-fact conditions is in fact an Imperfect circumstantial clause, or, in the case of nonverbal clauses, a circumstantial of the clause with the imperfect converter:

ⲉ-ⲛⲉϥⲟ ⲛ̄ ⲣ̄ⲣⲟ	if he were king
ⲉ-ⲛⲉ-ⲛ̄ⲧⲟϥ ⲡⲉ ⲡⲣ̄ⲣⲟ	if he were the king
ⲉ-ⲛⲉ-ⲟⲩⲛ̄ⲧⲁⲛ ⲟⲩⲣ̄ⲣⲟ	if we had a king
ⲉ-ⲛⲉⲧⲉⲧⲛ̄ⲙ̄ ⲡⲉⲓⲙⲁ	if you were here

In past time ⲉ-ⲛⲉ- is followed by the affirmative Second Perfect or negative First Perfect:

ⲉ-ⲛⲉ-ⲛⲧⲁⲕϯ-ⲡ₂ⲁⲧ ⲛⲁⲓ   if you had given me the money

ⲉ-ⲛⲉ-ⲙⲡⲉⲕϫⲓ-ⲡ₂ⲁⲧ   if you had not taken the money

If the clause is nonverbal, ⲉ-ⲛⲉ- alone is used. Thus, ⲉ-ⲛⲉⲕⲙ̄ ⲡⲉⲓⲙⲁ means both "if you were here" and "if you had been here."

The conditional prefix ⲉ-ⲛⲉ- is not to be confused with the particle ⲉⲛⲉ which serves to introduce a question, e.g. ⲉⲛⲉ ⲁⲕⲛⲁⲩ ⲉⲣⲟϥ? Did you see him?

The apodosis of both tenses is in the imperfect of the Future:

ⲉ-ⲛⲉⲕⲡⲓⲥⲧⲉⲩⲉ, ⲛⲉⲣⲉ-ⲡⲁⲓ ⲛⲁϣⲱⲡⲉ ⲁⲛ.

If you believed, this would not happen.

ⲉ-ⲛⲉ-ⲛⲧⲁⲕⲡⲓⲥⲧⲉⲩⲉ, ⲛⲉⲣⲉ-ⲡⲁⲓ ⲛⲁϣⲱⲡⲉ ⲁⲛ.

If you had believed, this would not have happened.

The Greek conjunctions ⲉⲓⲙⲏⲧⲓ (εἰ μή τι) and ⲕⲁⲛ (κἄν) are also used to introduce protases of both real and contrary-to-fact conditions.

ⲛ̄ⲥⲁⲃⲏⲗ ϫⲉ (except that, unless, if not) is often used to introduce the protasis of a contrary-to-fact condition; the clause usually contains a Pres. I, Perf. I, or non-verbal predication:

ⲛ̄ⲥⲁⲃⲏⲗ ϫⲉ ⲕⲡⲓⲥⲧⲉⲩⲉ   if you did not believe

"   ⲁⲕⲡⲓⲥⲧⲉⲩⲉ   if you had not believed

"   ⲛ̄ⲧⲟⲕ ⲡⲉ ⲡⲁⲉⲓⲱⲧ   if you were not my father

29.2 Inflected predicate adjectives. There is a small set of predicate adjectives inflected by means of pronominal suffixes or by proclisis to a nominal subject, e.g.

ⲛⲉⲥⲉ-ⲧⲉϥⲥ₂ⲓⲙⲉ.   His wife is beautiful.

ⲛⲉⲥⲱⲥ.   She is beautiful.

The more important of these are ⲛⲁⲁ- ⲛⲁⲁ⸗ great, ⲛⲁⲛⲟⲩ- ⲛⲁⲛⲟⲩ⸗ good, ⲛⲉⲥⲉ- ⲛⲉⲥⲱ⸗ beautiful, ⲛⲉⲥⲃⲱⲱ⸗ wise, ⲛⲁϣⲉ- ⲛⲁϣⲱ⸗ numerous, ⲛⲉϭⲱ⸗ ugly. When used in relative clauses, they are treated like the First Present: ⲡⲣⲱⲙⲉ ⲉⲧ ⲛⲁⲛⲟⲩϥ

the good man, ⲡⲣⲱⲙⲉ ⲉⲧⲉ ⲛⲉⲥⲉ-ⲧⲉϥⲥⲁⲓⲙⲉ the man whose wife is
beautiful.   They may also be preceded by the imperfect and
circumstantial converters: ⲛⲉ-ⲛⲁⲛⲟⲩϥ (ⲡⲉ) he was good; ⲟⲩⲣⲱⲙⲉ ⲉ-ⲛⲁⲛⲟⲩϥ (ⲡⲉ) a good man.   ⲛⲁⲓⲁⲧ⸗ (blessed is/are) belongs to this group, but a following nominal subject must
be anticipated with a suffix: ⲛⲁⲓⲁⲧⲟⲩ ⲛ̄ ⲛ̄ⲣⲉϥⲣ̄-ⲉⲓⲣⲏⲛⲏ
blessed are the peacemakers.

29.3 The comparison of both attributive and predicate
adjectives is expressed by placing the preposition ⲉ before
the item on which the comparison is based: ⲛⲟϭ ⲉ ⲡⲁⲓ greater
than this, ⲥⲁⲃⲉ ⲉ ⲛⲉϥⲥⲛⲏⲩ wiser than his brothers.   In
addition to simple adjectives, both Coptic and Greek, the
predicate adjectives of the preceding paragraph as well as
appropriate qualitatives and other verbal constructions
may be used in this construction.   E.g.

ⲛⲉϥⲟ ⲛ̄ ⲛⲟϭ ⲉ ⲛⲉϥⲥⲛⲏⲩ.	He was more important than his brothers.
ϥϫⲟⲥⲉ ⲉ ⲡⲉϥϫⲟⲉⲓⲥ.	He is more exalted than his master.
ⲛⲉϥⲟ ⲛ̄ ⲟⲩⲟⲉⲓⲛ ⲉ ⲡⲣⲏ.	It was brighter than the sun.
ⲛⲉⲥⲱⲥ ⲉ ⲧⲉⲥⲥⲱⲛⲉ.	She is more beautiful than her sister.

A comparison may be strengthened by using ⳉⲟⲩⲟ (more) in
various combinations: ⲛ̄ ⳉⲟⲩⲟ ⲉ, ⲉ ⳉⲟⲩⲟ ⲉ, ⲉ ⳉⲟⲩⲉ, all
meaning "more than."   ⲛ̄ ⳉⲟⲩⲟ alone may express an absolute
comparative: ⲡⲛⲟϭ ⲛ̄ ⳉⲟⲩⲟ the greater.

The Greek preposition ⲡⲁⲣⲁ (or ⲙ̄ ⲡⲁⲣⲁ) may be used instead of ⲉ.   Suffixes may be attached: ⲡⲁⲣⲟⲓ, ⲡⲁⲣⲟⲕ, ⲡⲁⲣⲟ etc.

29.4 Nouns with possessive suffixes (continued).

(a) ⲣⲁⲧ⸗ (foot) was mentioned in §19.2 in connection
with ⲉⲣⲁⲧ⸗ and ⲁⳉⲉⲣⲁⲧ⸗.   Other compounds include ⳉⲁ ⲣⲁⲧ⸗
prep. under, at the foot of; ⲕⲁ-ⲣⲁⲧ⸗ to set foot (+ ⲉⲃⲟⲗ:
to start out); ⲙⲟⲟϣⲉ ⲛ̄ ⲣⲁⲧ⸗ to go on foot.

(b) ⳉⲣⲁ⸗ is the presuffixal form of two words: (1)
ⳉⲟ ⳉⲣⲁ⸗ face; (2) ⳉⲣⲟⲟⲩ ⳉⲣⲁ⸗ voice.   Both of these words

are common in their unbound forms. Compounds worth noting
are ⲉⲍⲣⲛ̄ ⲉⲍⲣⲁⸯ prep. toward (the face of); (ⲛ̄) ⲛⲁⲍⲣⲛ̄
(ⲛ̄)ⲛⲁⲍⲣⲁⸯ prep. in the presence of; ⲭⲓ-ⲍⲣⲁⸯ (Q ⲭⲓ-ⲍⲣⲁⲉⲓⲧ)
to amuse oneself, be diverted, distracted (suff. is reflex.);
ϥⲓ-ⲍⲣⲁⸯ to raise one's voice, utter (± ⲉⲃⲟⲗ, ⲉⲍⲣⲁⲓ).

(c) ⲍⲧⲏⸯ is the presuffixal form of (1) ⲍⲏⲧ heart,
mind, and (2) ⲍⲏⲧ tip, edge. Compounds using the form include ϯ-ⲍⲧⲏⸯ to observe, pay attention to (ⲉ, ⲉⲭⲛ̄); ϣⲛ̄-ⲍⲧⲏⸯ
to have pity (on: ⲉⲭⲛ̄, ⲉⲍⲣⲁⲓ ⲉⲭⲛ̄); and the prep. ⲍⲁⲍⲧⲛ̄ ⲍⲁⲍ-
ⲧⲏⸯ.

(d) ⲍⲏⲧⸯ is the presuffixal form of (1) ⲧ.ⲍⲏ belly,
womb, and (2) ⲧ.ⲍⲏ front. ⲍⲏⲧⸯ (belly, womb) may be used
in its plain sense, as in ⲍⲛ̄ ⲍⲏⲧⲥ̄ in her womb; otherwise
it appears only as part of the prep. ⲍⲛ̄ ⲛ̄ⲍⲏⲧⸯ. ⲍⲏⲧⸯ (front)
is used as a preposition with certain verbs, e.g. ϣⲓⲛⲉ
ⲍⲏⲧⸯ, ⲣ̄-ⲍⲟⲧⲉ ⲍⲏⲧⸯ.

(e) ⲧⲟⲩⲱⸯ (bosom) is found in the prepositions ⲉⲧⲟⲩⲛ̄-
ⲉⲧⲟⲩⲱⸯ and ⲍⲓⲧⲟⲩⲛ̄- ⲍⲓⲧⲟⲩⲱⸯ near, beside. The latter is
frequent in the relative construction ⲡⲉⲧ ⲍⲓⲧⲟⲩⲱⸯ neighbor,
e.g. ⲡⲉⲧ ⲍⲓⲧⲟⲩⲱϥ his neighbor.

Other nouns used with pronominal suffixes are ⲁⲣⲏⲭⸯ
end, ⲕⲟⲩⲛ̄(ⲧ)ⸯ bosom, ⲣⲓⲛ(ⲧ)ⸯ name, ⲥⲟⲩⲛ̄ⲧⸯ price, and ϣⲁⲁⲛⲧⸯ
nose. The Glossary may be consulted for these.

Vocabulary 29

(ⲉϣⲱⲡⲉ, ⲉϣⲭⲉ, ⲛ̄ⲥⲁⲃⲏⲗ ⲭⲉ, ⲛⲁⲛⲟⲩ-, ⲛⲉⲥⲉ-, ⲛⲁϣⲉ-, ⲛⲁⲓⲁⲧⸯ, ⲛ̄
ⲍⲟⲩⲟ ⲉ, ϥⲓ-ⲍⲣⲁⸯ, ϣⲛ̄-ⲍⲧⲏⸯ ⲉⲭⲛ̄, ⲡⲉⲧ ⲍⲓⲧⲟⲩⲱⸯ from the lesson)

ⲱⲥⲕ̄, Q ⲟⲥⲕ̄ vb. intr. to delay, tarry; to be prolonged, con-
     tinue; + Circum.: to continue (doing).
ⲥⲟⲟⲍⲉ ⲥⲁⲍⲉ- ⲥⲁⲍⲱ(ⲱ)ⸯ Q ⲥⲁⲍⲏⲩ vb. reflex. + ⲉⲃⲟⲗ to withdraw,
     leave (from: ⲙ̄ⲙⲟⸯ).
ⲧⲁⲙⲓⲟ ⲧⲁⲙⲓⲉ- ⲧⲁⲙⲓⲟⸯ Q ⲧⲁⲙⲓⲏⲩ vb. tr. to create, make; to
     prepare, make ready (ⲙ̄ⲙⲟⸯ); as n.m. creation, creature.
ⲑⲃ̄ⲃⲓⲟ ⲑⲃ̄ⲃⲓⲉ- ⲑⲃⲃⲓⲟⸯ Q ⲑⲃ̄ⲃⲓⲏⲩ vb. tr. to humble, humiliate;
     intr. and reflex. to become humble; as n.m. humility

(often + ⲛ̄ ϩⲏⲧ).

ⲡⲉ.ϩⲙⲟⲧ grace, gift, favor; gratitude. ϣⲡ̄-ϩⲙⲟⲧ ⲛ̄ⲧⲛ̄ to give
thanks to (for: ⲉⲝⲛ̄, ϩⲓ, ϩⲁ); ϭⲛ̄-ϩⲙⲟⲧ to find favor.
ϣⲟⲣⲡ̄ (f. ϣⲟⲣⲡⲉ) adj. first, before or after n. with ⲛ̄. ⲛ̄
ϣⲟⲣⲡ̄ adv. formerly, at first.
ⲣ̄-ϩⲟⲩⲟ ⲉ (Q ⲟ ⲛ̄) to exceed, be more than; to be in excess,
more than enough for.
ϩⲛ̄ ⲟⲩⲱⲣⲝ adv. firmly, surely, certainly, diligently.

Exercises

A. (1) ⲉⲧⲃⲉ ⲡⲉⲕⲟⲃ̄ⲃ̄ⲓⲟ ⲛ̄ ϩⲏⲧ ϥⲛⲁϣⲛ̄-ϩⲧⲏϥ ⲉⲭⲱⲕ. (2) ⲛⲓⲙ
ⲡⲉⲛⲧⲁϥⲧⲁⲙⲓⲟ ⲙ̄ ⲡϣⲟⲣⲡ̄ ⲛ̄ ⲣⲱⲙⲉ? (3) ⲛⲁϣⲉ-ⲛⲉⲓⲣⲱⲙⲉ ⲛ̄ ϩⲟⲩⲟ ⲉⲣⲟⲛ.
(4) ⲛⲉⲥⲉ-ⲧⲉⲓⲡⲟⲗⲓⲥ ⲛ̄ ϩⲟⲩⲟ. (5) ⲛⲁⲓⲁⲧⲟⲩ ⲛ̄ ⲛ̄ϩⲏⲕⲉ. (6) ⲁ-ⲡⲛⲟⲩⲧⲉ
ⲧⲁⲙⲓⲉ-ⲧⲡⲉ ⲙⲛ̄ ⲡⲕⲁϩ. (7) ⲛⲓⲙ ⲡⲉ ⲡⲉⲧ ϩⲓⲧⲟⲩⲱⲕ? (8) ⲧⲁⲓ ⲧⲉ
ⲧϣⲟⲣⲡⲉ ⲛ̄ ⲉⲛⲧⲟⲗⲏ. (9) ⲛⲁⲛⲟⲩ-†-ϩⲁϩ ⲙ̄ ⲙⲉⲧⲁⲛⲟⲓⲁ. (10) ⲥⲉⲛⲁⲥⲙⲟⲩ
ⲉⲣⲟⲕ ⲛ̄ ϩⲟⲩⲟ ⲉ ⲣⲱⲙⲉ ⲛⲓⲙ. (11) ⲛⲉⲩⲛ̄ⲧⲁϥ ⲟⲩⲥϩⲓⲙⲉ ⲉ-ⲛⲉⲥⲱⲥ ⲉⲙⲁⲧⲉ.
(12) ⲁⲥⲧⲁⲙⲓⲟ ⲛⲁϥ ⲛ̄ ⲟⲩⲕⲟⲩⲓ ⲛ̄ ϭⲓⲛⲟⲩⲱⲙ. (13) ⲛⲁⲓⲁⲧϥ̄ ⲙ̄ ⲡⲉⲛⲧⲁϥ-
ϭⲛ̄-ϩⲙⲟⲧ ⲛ̄ⲛⲁϩⲣⲙ̄ ⲡⲭⲟⲉⲓⲥ. (14) ⲟⲩ ⲡⲉⲧ ⲛⲁϣⲟⲃ̄ⲃ̄ⲓⲟⲕ? (15) ⲟⲩ
ⲡⲉⲧⲛ̄ⲛⲁⲁⲁϥ ϫⲉ ⲉⲛⲉⲟⲩϫⲁⲓ? (16) ⲥⲁϩⲉ-ⲧⲏⲩⲧⲛ̄ ⲉⲃⲟⲗ ⲙ̄ⲙⲟⲓ.

B. (1) ⲉϥϣⲁⲛϭⲛ̄ⲧ, ϥⲛⲁⲙⲟⲩⲟⲩⲧ ⲙ̄ⲙⲟⲓ. (2) ⲉⲕϣⲁⲛⲥⲟⲧⲡ̄, ⲉⲓⲉ
ⲛⲁⲥⲛⲏⲩ ⲛⲁϭⲱⲛⲧ̄ ⲙ̄ⲙⲁⲧⲉ. (3) ⲉⲕϣⲁⲛⲕⲁⲁⲧ ⲉ ⲃⲱⲕ, †ⲛⲁⲕⲧⲟⲓ ⲉ ϣⲓⲛⲧ.
(4) ⲉϥϣⲁⲛϩⲱⲛ ⲉⲧⲟⲟⲧⲕ̄ ⲉⲧⲣⲉⲕⲁⲁⲥ, ⲉⲕⲉⲁⲁⲥ ϩⲛ̄ ⲟⲩⲱⲣⲝ. (5) ⲉϣⲱⲡⲉ
ⲙ̄ⲙⲁⲧⲟⲓ ⲉⲓ ⲉϩⲟⲩⲛ ⲉ ⲧⲡⲟⲗⲓⲥ, ⲥⲉⲛⲁⲣⲁϩⲧⲛ̄ ⲧⲏⲣⲛ̄. (6) ⲉϣⲱⲡⲉ ϥⲥⲱⲧⲙ̄
ⲉ ⲧⲉⲕⲥⲙⲏ, ϥⲛⲁⲥⲁϩⲱϥ. (7) ⲉϣⲱⲡⲉ ⲟⲩⲛ̄ⲧⲏⲧⲛ̄ ϩⲉⲛⲟⲉⲓⲕ ⲙ̄ⲙⲁⲩ ⲉⲩⲣ̄-
ϩⲟⲩⲟ ⲉⲣⲱⲧⲛ̄, ⲧⲉⲧⲛⲉⲧⲁⲁⲩ ⲛ̄ ⲛⲉⲧ ϩⲕⲁⲉⲓⲧ. (8) ⲉⲣϣⲁⲛ-ⲛⲉⲥⲛⲏⲩ ⲕⲧⲟⲟⲩ
ⲉ ⲡ†ⲙⲉ ϩⲓ ⲣⲟⲩϩⲉ, †ⲛⲁⲃⲱⲕ ⲛⲙ̄ⲙⲁⲩ. (9) ⲉϫⲭⲉ ⲡⲉⲕⲉⲓⲱⲧ ⲉⲡⲓ†ⲙⲁ ⲛⲁⲕ,
ⲛ̄ⲛⲉⲕϭⲱⲛⲧ̄. (10) ⲉϫⲭⲉ ⲡⲉⲕⲥⲟⲛ ⲣ̄-ⲡⲉⲑⲟⲟⲩ ⲛⲁⲕ, ⲉⲕⲉⲣ̄-ⲡⲡⲉⲧ ⲛⲁⲛⲟⲩϥ
ⲛⲁϥ. (11) ⲉⲣϣⲁⲛ-ⲧⲉⲕⲥⲱⲛⲉ ⲉⲓ ϣⲁⲣⲟⲓ ⲛ̄ ⲣⲁⲥⲧⲉ, †ⲛⲁⲧⲁⲙⲟⲥ ⲉⲧⲃⲉ
ⲡⲉⲓϣⲁϫⲉ. (12) ⲉ-ⲛⲉ-ⲟⲩⲁⲓⲕⲁⲓⲟⲥ ⲡⲉ ⲛ̄ⲧⲟⲕ, ⲛⲉⲕⲛⲁⲉⲓⲣⲉ ⲛ̄ ⲧⲉⲓϩⲉ ⲁⲛ.
(13) ⲁⲣϭⲛ̄-ϩⲙⲟⲧ ⲛ̄ⲛⲁϩⲣⲙ̄ ⲡⲛⲟⲩⲧⲉ. (14) ⲉ-ⲛⲉⲕⲙ̄ ⲡⲉⲓⲙⲁ, ⲛⲉⲣⲉ-ⲡⲁⲥⲟⲛ
ⲛⲁⲙⲟⲩ ⲁⲛ ⲡⲉ. (15) ⲧⲛ̄ϣⲡ̄-ϩⲙⲟⲧ ⲛ̄ⲧⲟⲟⲧⲕ̄ ϩⲁ ⲡⲉⲕⲛⲟϭ ⲛ̄ ⲛⲁ. (16)
ⲉ-ⲛⲉ-ⲛⲧⲁⲓⲉⲓⲙⲉ ϫⲉ ⲛ̄ⲧⲟⲕ ⲡⲉ ⲡⲣ̄ⲣⲟ, ⲛⲉⲓⲛⲁⲡⲁϩ̄ⲧ ⲛⲁϩⲣⲁⲕ ⲡⲉ ⲉⲓϣⲓⲡⲉ
ϩⲏⲧⲕ̄. (17) ⲉϫⲭⲉ ⲕⲱⲥⲕ̄ ⲉⲕⲟ ⲛ̄ ⲣⲉϥⲣ̄-ⲛⲟⲃⲉ, ⲛ̄ⲥⲉⲛⲁϣⲛ̄-ϩⲧⲏⲩ ⲉⲭⲱⲕ ⲁⲛ
ⲙ̄ ⲡⲉϩⲟⲟⲩ ⲉⲧ ⲙ̄ⲙⲁⲩ. (18) ⲉϣⲱⲡⲉ ⲥⲉⲉⲓⲣⲉ ⲙ̄ ⲡⲉⲧ ⲛⲁⲛⲟⲩϥ, ⲥⲉⲛⲁϭⲛ̄-
ϩⲙⲟⲧ ⲛ̄ⲛⲁϩⲣⲙ̄ ⲡⲭⲟⲉⲓⲥ. (19) ⲉ-ⲛⲉ-ⲛⲧⲁ-ⲛⲉⲓϩⲓⲥⲉ ⲱⲥⲕ̄, ⲛⲉⲛⲛⲁⲙⲟⲩ

134

ⲡⲉ. (20) ⲉϣⲱⲡⲉ ⲉⲩⲡⲓⲥⲧⲉⲩⲉ ⲍⲛ̄ ⲟⲩⲱⲣϫ, ⲥⲉⲛⲁⲥⲕ̄ⲥⲱⲗⲟⲩ. (21) ϣϣⲉ
ⲉⲣⲟⲛ ⲉⲧⲣⲉⲛϣⲡ̄-ⲍⲙⲟⲧ ⲛ̄ⲧⲟⲟⲧϥ̄ ⲛ̄ ⲟⲩⲟⲉⲓϣ ⲛⲓⲙ. (22) ⲍⲁⲡⲥ̄ ⲉⲣⲟⲛ
ⲉⲧⲣⲉⲛϯ-ⲧⲟⲟⲧⲟⲩ ⲛ̄ ⲛⲉⲧ ⲍⲓⲧⲟⲩⲱⲛ. (23) ⲥⲙⲟⲕⲍ̄ ⲉ ⲥⲍⲁⲓ ⲙ̄ ⲙⲛ̄ⲧⲣⲙⲛ̄-
ⲕⲏⲙⲉ. (24) ⲉⲓⲥ ⲡⲉⲓⲛⲟϭ ⲙ̄ ⲙⲁⲉⲓⲛ ⲛⲁϭⲱⲗⲡ̄ ⲉⲃⲟⲗ ⲛⲏⲧⲛ̄. (25)
ⲛ̄ⲥⲁⲃⲏⲗ ϫⲉ ⲛ̄ⲧⲟⲕ ⲡⲉ ⲡⲁⲉⲓⲱⲧ, ⲛⲉⲓⲛⲁⲙⲟⲟⲩⲧⲕ̄.

Reading

(from the Sayings of the Fathers)

1. ⲁϥϫⲟⲟⲥ ⲛ̄ϭⲓ ⲟⲩⲍⲗⲗⲟ ϫⲉ "ⲍⲙ̄ ⲡⲓⲣⲁⲥⲙⲟⲥ ⲛⲓⲙ ⲙ̄ⲡⲣ̄ϭⲛ̄-ⲁⲣⲓⲕⲉ
ⲉ-ⲣⲱⲙⲉ, ⲁⲗⲗⲁ ϭⲛ̄-ⲁⲣⲓⲕⲉ ⲉⲣⲟⲕ ⲙⲁⲩⲗⲁⲕ ⲉⲕϫⲱ ⲙ̄ⲙⲟⲥ ϫⲉ 'ⲉⲣⲉ-ⲛⲁⲓ
ϣⲟⲟⲡ ⲙ̄ⲙⲟⲓ ⲉⲧⲃⲉ ⲛⲁⲛⲟⲃⲉ.'"

2. ⲁ-ⲟⲩⲁ ⲛ̄ ⲛ̄ⲍⲗⲗⲟ ⲃⲱⲕ ϣⲁ ⲕⲉⲍⲗⲗⲟ ⲁⲩⲱ ⲡⲉϫⲁϥ ⲙ̄ ⲡⲉϥⲙⲁⲑⲏⲧⲏⲥ
ϫⲉ, "ⲧⲁⲙⲓⲟ ⲛⲁⲛ ⲛ̄ ⲟⲩⲕⲟⲩⲓ ⲛ̄ ⲁⲣϣⲓⲛ." ⲁⲩⲱ ⲁϥⲧⲁⲙⲓⲟϥ. ⲡⲉϫⲁϥ ϫⲉ,
"ⲍⲉⲣⲡ̄-ⲍⲉⲛⲟⲉⲓⲕ ⲛⲁⲛ." ⲁⲩⲱ ⲁϥⲍⲟⲣⲡⲟⲩ. ⲛ̄ⲧⲟⲟⲩ ⲇⲉ ⲁⲩⲙⲟⲩⲛ ⲉⲃⲟⲗ
ⲉⲩϣⲁϫⲉ ⲉ ⲛⲉⲡⲛ̄ⲧⲓⲕⲟⲛ ⲙ̄ ⲡⲉⲍⲟⲟⲩ ⲧⲏⲣϥ̄ ⲙⲛ̄ ⲧⲉⲩϣⲏ ⲧⲏⲣⲥ̄.

3. ⲁⲩϫⲟⲟⲥ ⲛ̄ϭⲓ ⲛ̄ⲍⲗⲗⲟ ϫⲉ, "ⲕⲁⲛ ⲛⲁⲙⲉ ⲉⲣϣⲁⲛ-ⲟⲩⲁⲅⲅⲉⲗⲟⲥ
ⲟⲩⲱⲛⲁⲍ ⲛⲁⲕ ⲉⲃⲟⲗ, ⲙ̄ⲡⲣ̄ϣⲟⲡϥ̄ ⲉⲣⲟⲕ, ⲁⲗⲗⲁ ⲑⲃ̄ⲃⲓⲟⲕ ⲛ̄ⲅ̄ⲭⲟⲟⲥ ϫⲉ,
'ⲛ̄ϯⲙ̄ⲡϣⲁ ⲁⲛ ⲉ ⲛⲁⲩ ⲉ ⲡⲁⲅⲅⲉⲗⲟⲥ ⲉ-ⲁⲓⲱⲛⲍ̄ ⲍⲛ̄ ⲛ̄ⲛⲟⲃⲉ.'"

New words: ⲡ.ⲡⲓⲣⲁⲥⲙⲟⲥ (ὁ πειρασμός) temptation.

ⲡ.ⲁⲣϣⲓⲛ lentils.

ⲍⲱⲣⲡ̄ ⲍⲉⲣⲡ̄- ⲍⲟⲣⲡ⸗ vb. tr. to moisten.

ⲡⲛ̄ⲧⲓⲕⲟⲛ = ⲡⲛⲉⲩⲙⲁⲧⲓⲕⲟⲛ spiritual matter(s).

Lesson 30

30.1 The Injunctive (also called the Optative):

ⲙⲁⲣⲓⲥⲱⲧⲙ̄   let me hear   ⲙⲁⲣⲛ̄ⲥⲱⲧⲙ̄   let us hear
ⲙⲁⲣⲉϥⲥⲱⲧⲙ̄   let him hear   ⲙⲁⲣⲟⲩⲥⲱⲧⲙ̄   let them hear
ⲙⲁⲣⲉⲥⲥⲱⲧⲙ̄   let her hear

ⲙⲁⲣⲉ-ⲡⲣⲱⲙⲉ ⲥⲱⲧⲙ̄   let the man hear

The Injunctive occurs only in the 1st and 3rd persons in
standard Sahidic. The 1st person corresponds to the cohor-
tative, the 3rd person to the jussive; theoretically, the
Imperative may be said to occupy the 2nd person position.
The negative of the Injunctive is expressed by using the
negative Imperative prefix ⲙ̄ⲡⲣ̄- with the corresponding form
of the Inflected Infinitive: ⲙ̄ⲡⲣ̄ⲧⲣⲉϥⲃⲱⲕ don't let him go,
ⲙ̄ⲡⲣ̄ⲧⲣⲉⲩⲙⲟⲟⲩⲧϥ̄ don't let them kill him. The Injunctive is
tripartite and is used only with the Infinitive. The free
form of the 1st person, ⲙⲁⲣⲟⲛ, is used alone in the sense
"Let's go."

30.2 The Future Conjunctive of Result (also called
the Finalis).

————————	ⲧⲁⲣⲛ̄ⲥⲱⲧⲙ̄	ⲧⲁⲣⲉ-ⲡⲣⲱⲙⲉ ⲥⲱⲧⲙ̄
ⲧⲁⲣⲉⲕⲥⲱⲧⲙ̄	ⲧⲁⲣⲉⲧⲛ̄ⲥⲱⲧⲙ̄	
ⲧⲁⲣⲉⲥⲱⲧⲙ̄		
ⲧⲁⲣⲉϥⲥⲱⲧⲙ̄	ⲧⲁⲣⲟⲩⲥⲱⲧⲙ̄	
ⲧⲁⲣⲉⲥⲥⲱⲧⲙ̄		

ⲛ̄ may occur optionally before all of these forms. For the
1st person sing. the simple Conjunctive ⲧⲁ- may be used.
    The Future Conjunctive is basically a result clause;
it is especially frequent after an Imperative, e.g.

ⲥⲱⲧⲙ̄ ⲉⲣⲟⲓ ⲧⲁⲣⲉⲕⲣ̄-ⲥⲁⲃⲉ.   Listen to me and you will
            become wise (or: so as to become wise).

Although the Conjunctive itself may occasionally have the

value of a result/purpose clause after an Imperative, the
Future Conjunctive always has this meaning. The nuance of
the form can best be understood if it is viewed as the transformation of an underlying conditional sentence:

ⲁⲙⲟⲩ ⲧⲁⲣⲉⲕⲛⲁⲩ ⟵ ⲉⲕϣⲁⲛⲉⲓ ⲉⲉⲓⲉ ⲕⲛⲁⲛⲁⲩ.

It may also occur after a question, e.g.

ⲛⲓⲙ ⲡⲉⲛⲧⲁϥⲛⲁⲩ ⲉⲣⲟϥ ⲧⲁⲣⲉϥϣⲁϫⲉ ⲉⲣⲟϥ?

Who has seen him so as to be able to describe him?

If the question is rhetorical, as in this example, negation
is generally implied: "No one has seen him so as.... If
the question is real, the implication is "Tell me the answer
so that ...," as in

ⲉϥⲧⲱⲛ ⲡⲉⲕⲥⲟⲛ ⲧⲁⲣⲛϣⲁϫⲉ ⲛⲙⲙⲁϥ?

Where is your brother that we may speak with him?

30.3 The Clause Conjugations. A distinction is made
between sentence conjugations (Bipartite and Tripartite)
and clause conjugations. The latter are so named because
they correspond to a conjunction plus a clause in normal
translation. To this category belong the Temporal, the
Conjunctive, the Conditional, the Future Conjunctive of
Result, and most uses of the Inflected Infinitive (ⲉⲧⲣⲉϥ-
ⲥⲱⲧⲙ, ϩⲙ ⲡⲧⲣⲉϥⲥⲱⲧⲙ, ⲙⲛⲛⲥⲁ ⲧⲣⲉϥⲥⲱⲧⲙ). Characteristic of
this category is (1) negation with -ⲧⲙ-, and (2) the use
of the Infinitive only.

A further clause conjugation is ϣⲁⲛⲧϥⲥⲱⲧⲙ (until he
hears):

ϣⲁⲛϯⲥⲱⲧⲙ	until I hear	ϣⲁⲛⲧⲛⲥⲱⲧⲙ	
ϣⲁⲛⲧⲕⲥⲱⲧⲙ	until you hear	ϣⲁⲛⲧⲉⲧⲛⲥⲱⲧⲙ	
ϣⲁⲛⲧⲉⲥⲱⲧⲙ	etc.		
ϣⲁⲛⲧϥⲥⲱⲧⲙ		ϣⲁⲛⲧⲟⲩⲥⲱⲧⲙ	
ϣⲁⲛⲧⲥⲥⲱⲧⲙ			

ϣⲁⲛⲧⲉ-ⲡⲣⲱⲙⲉ ⲥⲱⲧⲙ until the man hears

Translation is regularly with "until," e.g.

ⲦⲚⲚⲀϬⲰ Ⲙ̄ ⲠⲈⲒⲘⲀ ϢⲀⲚⲦϥⲈⲒ. We shall remain here until he comes.

Similar in appearance to a clause conjugation is the form ⲬⲒⲚ(Ⲛ̄)ⲦⲀϥⲤⲰⲦⲘ̄ (from the time that he heard). This consists, however, of the conjunction ⲬⲒⲚ followed by the Second Perfect. Even more frequent are the compound expressions with ⲔⲀⲦⲀ ⲐⲈ and Ⲛ̄ ⲐⲈ (as, according as, just as), both of which are followed by relative constructions, e.g.

ⲀⲨ2Ⲉ ⲈⲢⲟϥ Ⲛ̄ ⲐⲈ Ⲛ̄ⲦⲀϥϪⲟⲟⲤ ⲚⲀⲨ.
They found it just as he had told them.

ⲔⲀⲦⲀ ⲐⲈ ⲈⲚⲦⲀⲒⲀⲀⲤ ⲚⲎⲦⲚ̄, ⲈⲦⲈⲦⲚⲈⲀⲀⲤ 2ⲰⲦ-ⲦⲎⲨⲦⲚ̄ ...
According as I have done to you, you too are to do ...

ⲔⲀⲦⲀ ⲐⲈ ⲈⲦ ⲤⲎ2 ⲈⲦⲂⲎⲎⲦϥ̄
as it is written concerning him

ⲔⲀⲦⲀ ⲐⲈ ⲈⲦⲟⲨⲚⲀϢⲤⲰⲦⲘ̄ Ⲙ̄ⲘⲟⲤ
according as they would be able to hear (i.e. understand)

The feminine resumptive -ⲥ in these constructions refers back to ⲐⲈ and should not be translated as a pronominal object. If a real pronominal object is required, the resumptive -ⲥ is omitted, e.g.

ⲔⲀⲦⲀ ⲐⲈ Ⲛ̄ⲦⲀ-ⲠⲀⲈⲒⲰⲦ ⲦⲚ̄ⲚⲟⲟⲨⲦ, ⲀⲚⲞⲔ 2Ⲱ ϯϪⲞⲞⲨ Ⲙ̄ⲘⲰⲦⲚ̄.
Just as my Father sent me, so I too am sending you.

Other constructions with ⲐⲈ are treated similarly, e.g.

ⲦⲀⲒ ⲦⲈ ⲐⲈ Ⲛ̄ⲦⲀ-ⲠϪⲞⲈⲒⲤ ⲀⲀⲤ ⲚⲀⲒ.
Thus has the Lord acted for me.

30.4 When the Inflected Infinitive is used instead of a simple Infinitive after a verbal prefix, it has the value of a causative (hence its alternate name, the Causative Infinitive):

ⲀⲒⲦⲢⲈⲨⲈⲒ Ⲉ2ⲞⲨⲚ.   I caused them to enter.

ϯⲚⲀⲦⲢⲈⲔⲢⲒⲘⲈ.   I shall cause you to weep.

30.5 The form ⲙ̅ⲡⲁⲧ̅ϥ̅ⲥⲱⲧⲙ̅ describes an action as expected but not yet done. It is conveniently translated as "he has not yet heard." The form is fully inflected:

ⲙ̅ⲡⲁϯⲥⲱⲧⲙ̅	ⲙ̅ⲡⲁⲧⲛ̅ⲥⲱⲧⲙ̅	ⲙ̅ⲡⲁⲧⲉ-ⲡⲣⲱⲙⲉ ⲥⲱⲧⲙ̅
ⲙ̅ⲡⲁⲧⲕ̅ⲥⲱⲧⲙ̅	ⲙ̅ⲡⲁⲧⲉⲧⲛ̅ⲥⲱⲧⲙ̅	
ⲙ̅ⲡⲁⲧⲉⲥⲱⲧⲙ̅		
ⲙ̅ⲡⲁⲧϥ̅ⲥⲱⲧⲙ̅	ⲙ̅ⲡⲁⲧⲟⲩⲥⲱⲧⲙ̅	
ⲙ̅ⲡⲁⲧⲥ̅ⲥⲱⲧⲙ̅		

It may occur in circumstantial clauses with the circumstantial converter ⲉ-; the resultant form appears ambiguously as ⲉ-ⲙⲡⲁⲧⲉ- or simply ⲙ̅ⲡⲁⲧⲉ-. In this usage it is best translated as an affirmative clause with "before":

ⲧⲛ̅ⲛⲁⲧⲁⲍⲟϥ ⲉ-ⲙⲡⲁⲧϥ̅ⲡⲱⲋ ⲉ ⲧⲡⲟⲗⲓⲥ.

We shall overtake him before he reaches the city.

With the imperfect converter ⲛⲉ-ⲙⲡⲁⲧϥ̅ⲥⲱⲧⲙ̅ corresponds to the pluperfect: he had not yet heard.

30.6 An untranslatable dative with ⲛⲁ⸗ or ⲉⲣⲟ⸗ occurs optionally with many verbs, especially in the Imperative. This reflexive dative is called the ethical dative, following standard terminology. E.g.

ⲃⲱⲕ ⲛⲁⲕ ⲉ ⲡⲉⲕⲏⲓ.	Go home!
ⲥⲱ ⲛⲏⲧⲛ̅.	Drink!

Verbs with which this occurs with some frequency are noted in the Glossary.

30.7 Higher numbers, ordinals, and fractions.

20	ⲭⲟⲩⲱⲧ (f. ⲭⲟⲩⲱⲧⲉ) ⲭⲟⲩⲧ-	70	ϣϥⲉ, ⲥϣ̅ϥⲉ, ϣⲃⲉ				
30	ⲙⲁⲁⲃ (f. ⲙⲁⲁⲃⲉ) ⲙⲁⲃ-	80	ⲍⲙⲉⲛⲉ, ⲍⲙ̅ⲛⲉ-				
40	ⲍⲙⲉ	90	ⲡⲥ̅ⲧⲁⲓⲟⲩ				
50	ⲧⲁⲓⲟⲩ	100	ϣⲉ	200	ϣⲏⲧ		
60	ⲥⲉ	1000	ϣⲟ	10,000	ⲧⲃⲁ		

The tens combine with the forms of the units used in the 'teens (§24.3). The -ⲧ- of -ⲧⲏ (5) is not repeated after another -τ-:

ϫογτογε	21	μαβψιτε	39
ϫογτη	25	ϣϥετη	75

An intrusive -τ- appears before -λϥτε (4) and -λϲε (6):

μαβταϥτε	34	ϲετλϲε	66

The numbers ϣε 100, ϣο 1000, and τβλ 10,000 are masculine:

ϣο ϲναγ	2000	μ̄ν̄ϲνοογϲ ν̄ τβλ	120,000
ϣομ̄ν̄τ ν̄ ϣο	3000		

Proclitic forms of the units are frequent here, e.g.

ϣm̄τ-ϣο	3000	ϲεγ-ϣο	6000

Combinations of these higher numbers with tens and units
vary in form, e.g.

ϣε μλλβ = ϣε μ̄ν̄ μλλβ	130
ϲεγ-ϣο λγω ϣμογν ν̄ ϣε	6800

Ordinal numbers are formed from the cardinals with the prefix μεʒ-. The ordinals are treated as adjectives before the
noun with linking ν̄. Gender distinctions are maintained:

πμεʒϲναγ ν̄ ʒοογ	the second day
τμεʒϲν̄τε ν̄ ρομπε	the second year

For "first" the adjectives ϣορπ̄ (f. ϣορπε) and ʒογειτ (f.
ʒογειτε) are used.

Fractional numbers worth noting are τ.πλϣε (half) and
ϭοϲ, ϭιϲ- (half). Other fractions are expressed by ρε-
prefixed to the denominator, as in ρε-μητ one-tenth, or
with ογων (ογν̄-), as in ογν̄-ν̄-ϥτοογ a fourth.

30.8 The remote (or further) demonstrative pronouns
(that) are m.s. πη, f.s. τη, and pl. νη. These occur much
less frequently than πλι, τλι, νλι because of the preference for using phrases with ετ m̄μαγ, such as πετ m̄μαγ.

The prefixal forms πι-, †-, and νι- are usually de-
scribed as the reduced forms of πη, τη, and νη, parallel

in usage to ⲡⲉⲓ-, ⲧⲉⲓ-, and ⲛⲉⲓ-. While such a formal relationship may exist, the use of ⲡⲓ-, ϯ-, and ⲛⲓ- in standard Sahidic is quite restricted. The form ⲡⲓ- occurs mainly in a few temporal and local adverbial expressions, such as ⲙ̄ ⲡⲓⲟⲩⲟⲉⲓϣ (at that time) and ⲡⲓⲥⲁ (that side, as opposed to this side). The form ⲛⲓ- occurs most frequently in expressions involving comparison with ⲛ̄ ⲑⲉ ⲛ̄ (like) or ⲣ̄-ⲑⲉ ⲛ̄ (to become like); it sometimes corresponds more closely to an English generic noun, e.g. ⲛ̄ ⲑⲉ ⲛ̄ ⲛⲓϭⲣⲟⲟⲙⲡⲉ like doves, like a dove. It is also found in the expression ϣⲁ ⲛⲓⲉⲛⲉϩ. Elsewhere ⲡⲓ-, ϯ-, and ⲛⲓ- are frequent as scribal variants of ⲡⲉⲓ-, ⲧⲉⲓ-, ⲛⲉⲓ- or have the force of an emphatic article.

30.9 When it is necessary to express a durative or continuous process or state in the future, a periphrastic construction is employed using the Circumstantial. Contrast

ⲕⲛⲁⲟⲩⲟⲡ	you will become holy
ⲕⲛⲁϣⲱⲡⲉ ⲉⲕⲟⲩⲁⲁⲃ	you will be holy
ⲉⲕⲉⲕⲁ-ⲣⲱⲕ	you shall become silent
ⲉⲕⲉϣⲱⲡⲉ ⲉⲕⲕⲱ ⲛ̄ ⲣⲱⲕ	you shall remain silent

The difference is sometimes slight, but not infrequently spelled out. The same construction occasionally appears with other tripartite conjugational forms. A full discussion of the aspectual problem involved here lies beyond the scope of this book.

30.10 Greek conjunctions, adverbs, and prepositions that occur frequently in Coptic (for reference only). The term *postpositive* means that the word in question must follow immediately after the first element of the sentence, as in ⲡⲣⲱⲙⲉ ⲇⲉ ⲁϥⲃⲱⲕ.

ⲁⲗⲗⲁ ἀλλά but, rather.
ⲁⲣⲁ ἆρα (introduces question).
ⲅⲁⲣ γάρ for, because, since (postpositive).

ⲁⲉ δέ but, however (postpositive).

ⲉⲓⲙⲏⲧⲓ εἰ μή τι (1) if not, unless, except that (+ Conj.);
(2) elliptically, e.g. ⲙ̄ⲡⲟⲩⲭⲉⲩ-ⲍⲏⲗⲓⲁⲥ ϣⲁ ⲗⲁⲁⲩ ⲙ̄ⲙⲟⲟⲩ
ⲉⲓⲙⲏⲧⲓ ⲉ ⲥⲁⲣⲉⲡⲧⲁ Elias was not sent to any of them
except Sarepta. Note the independent pronoun in this
usage: ⲙ̄ⲛ̄-ⲗⲁⲁⲩ ⲛ̄ ⲣⲱⲙⲉ ⲛⲁⲉⲓⲙⲉ ⲉⲣⲟϥ ⲉⲓⲙⲏⲧⲓ ⲁⲛⲟⲕ No one
will understand it but me.

ⲉⲓⲧⲉ ... ⲉⲓⲧⲉ εἴτε ... εἴτε either ... or.

ⲉⲡⲉⲓ ἐπεί because, since.

ⲉⲡⲉⲓⲁⲏ ἐπειδή because, since, when.

ⲉⲡⲉⲓⲁⲏⲡⲉⲣ ἐπειδήπερ inasmuch as, since.

ⲉⲧⲓ ἔτι yet, still, while yet (+ Circum.).

ⲏ ἤ or.

ⲕⲁⲓ ⲅⲁⲣ καὶ γάρ for truly.

ⲕⲁⲓⲧⲟⲓ καίτοι although, albeit.

ⲕⲁⲛ κἄν even if.

ⲕⲁⲧⲁ κατά (prep.) in accordance with, according to; also
in distributive sense, e.g. ⲕⲁⲧⲁ ⲥⲁⲃⲃⲁⲧⲟⲛ every sabbath.
Note the absence of the article here.

ⲙⲉⲛ ... ⲁⲉ μέν ... δέ balances two statements: on the one
hand ... but on the other. Both postpositive.

ⲙⲏ μή introduces a rhetorical question presuming a simple
yes or no answer.

ⲙⲏⲡⲟⲧⲉ μήποτε so that not, lest (+ Conj.).

ⲙⲏⲡⲱⲥ μήπως so that not, lest (+ Conj.).

ⲙⲏⲧⲓ μήτι like ⲙⲏ, but with strong element of surprise.

ⲙⲟⲅⲓⲥ μόγις hardly, scarcely.

ⲟⲩⲛ οὖν therefore (postpositive).

ⲟⲩⲁⲉ οὐδέ and not, nor; the negation is often repeated
in Coptic as well.

ⲟⲩⲧⲉ ... ⲟⲩⲧⲉ οὔτε ... οὔτε neither ... nor.

ⲡⲣⲟⲥ πρός (prep.) used like ⲕⲁⲧⲁ.

ⲡⲱⲥ πῶς how? why?

ⲧⲟⲧⲉ τότε then, thereupon, next.

ⲍⲟⲗⲁⲛ ὅταν when, whenever, if (+ Cond.).

₂ocoɴ, ̄ɴₐocoɴ ὅσον as long as (+ Circum.).

₂ⲱc ὡς (1) as if; (2) although; (3) when, while as (all + Circum.).

₂ⲱcⲧⲉ ὥστε so that (+ Conj. or Infl. Inf.).

xⲱpⲓc χωρίς (prep.) without; a following noun has no indefinite article.

30.11 Final remarks on Coptic conjunctions and particles.

(a) The main coordinating conjunctions are ⲁⲩⲱ and ⲙ̄ⲛ̄. ⲙ̄ⲛ̄ is used primarily to join nouns or nominalized expressions; ⲁⲩⲱ is used elsewhere. ⲁⲩⲱ is sometimes used for ⲙ̄ⲛ̄, but this poses no particular translation problem. ⲁⲩⲱ often appears redundantly before the Conjunctive or before the apodosis of a conditional sentence. When nouns have no article (for whatever reason), they may be joined with the preposition ₂ⲓ instead of ⲙ̄ⲛ̄, as in ⲙ̄ⲛ̄-ⲙⲟⲟⲩ ₂ⲓ ⲟⲉⲓⲕ ⲙ̄ⲙⲁⲩ There is neither water nor food. ₂ⲓ is also used to form compound nominal expressions of a special type, e.g. cⲁpx ₂ⲓ cⲛⲟ⳽ flesh and blood. These expressions function as a unit: any article occurs only with the first word, as in ₂ⲉⲛcⲁpx ₂ⲓ cⲛⲟ⳽ ⲛⲉ They are flesh and blood.

(b) The main uses of the conjunction xⲉ have already been introduced: (1) in naming-constructions (see Vocab. 17); (2) to introduce noun clauses (object clauses) after appropriate verbs of speaking, perception, and the like; (3) to introduce purpose/result clauses with the Second or Third Future. xⲉ is also frequent in the sense "for, since, because," which is less ambiguously expressed by ⲉⲃⲟⲗ xⲉ and ⲉⲧⲃⲉ xⲉ. In many instances xⲉ is the equivalent of English "namely, i.e." in introducing explanatory appositions, e.g. ⲟⲩⲉⲩcⲓⲁ ... xⲉ ⲟⲩcⲟⲉⲓ⳽ ̄ⲛ 6pⲙ̄ⲛⲱⲁⲛ an offering ... namely a pair of turtle-doves. xⲉ is also used in some compound conjunctions, such as ̄ⲛcⲁⲃⲏⲗ xⲉ (if not, unless) and ̄ⲛ ⲑⲉ xⲉ (as if, as though).

(c) ⲉⲱxⲉ and ⲉⲓⲉ, in addition to their role in

conditional sentences, may be placed before any statement
to mark it as a question.

(d) ⲅⲉ is a postpositive particle with very much the
same function as Greek ⲇⲉ. It is especially frequent in
the phrase ⲧⲉⲛⲟⲩ ⲅⲉ and now, so now therefore.

(e) ⲛⲧⲟⲟⲩⲛ: then, thereupon, next, forthwith.

(f) ⲛⲥⲁ may mean "except" after a negative statement:
ⲙⲡⲉ-ⲗⲁⲁⲩ ⲙⲙⲟⲟⲩ ⲧⲃⲃⲟ ⲛⲥⲁ ⲛⲁⲓⲙⲁⲛ ⲡⲥⲩⲣⲟⲥ None of them became
cleansed except Naiman the Syrian.

(g) Certain temporal expressions may occur with a
following relative clause without resumptive pronouns.
These function virtually as compound conjunctions. E.g.

    ⲡⲉⲍⲟⲟⲩ ⲉⲧⲉⲣⲉ-ⲛⲁⲓ ⲛⲁϣⲱⲡⲉ   the day *when* this will happen

    ⲍⲙ ⲡⲉⲍⲟⲟⲩ ⲛⲧⲁϥϭⲱϣⲧ   on the day *when* he looked.

(h) The Conditional is frequently used in a temporal
sense: when, whenever.

Vocabulary 30

ⲧⲉⲗⲏⲗ vb. intr. to rejoice (over: ⲉⲍⲛ); as n.m. joy.

ⲧⲁϣⲟ ⲧⲁϣⲉ- ⲧⲁϣⲟ⸗ vb. tr. to increase (ⲙⲙⲟ⸗); often prefixed
    to another Inf.: to do something more, much. ⲧⲁϣⲉ-ⲟⲉⲓϣ
    to preach, proclaim (ⲙⲙⲟ⸗).

ⲧⲃⲃⲟ ⲧⲃⲃⲉ- ⲧⲃⲃⲟ⸗ Q ⲧⲃⲃⲏⲩ vb. tr. to purify, cleanse, heal
    (ⲙⲙⲟ⸗; of, from: ⲉ, ⲉⲃⲟⲗ ⲍⲛ, ⲍⲁ); as n.m. purity, puri-
    fication.

ⲧⲁⲩⲟ ⲧⲁⲩⲉ- ⲧⲁⲩⲟ⸗ (± ⲉⲃⲟⲗ) vb. tr. to send forth, cast forth,
    proclaim, tell (ⲙⲙⲟ⸗). ⲧⲁⲩⲉ-ⲕⲁⲣⲡⲟⲥ to produce fruit.

ⲧⲁⲉⲓⲟ ⲧⲁⲉⲓⲉ- ⲧⲁⲉⲓⲟ⸗ Q ⲧⲁⲉⲓⲏⲩ vb. tr. to honor, respect.
    value, esteem (ⲙⲙⲟ⸗); Q to be honored etc., valuable.

ⲧⲁϫⲣⲟ ⲧⲁϫⲣⲉ- ⲧⲁϫⲣⲟ⸗ Q ⲧⲁϫⲣⲏⲩ vb. tr. to strengthen, confirm
    (ⲙⲙⲟ⸗); intr. to become strengthened, firm, resolute.

ⲡ.ⲥⲟⲡ time, occasion. ⲛ ⲟⲩⲥⲟⲡ once. ⲍⲓ ⲟⲩⲥⲟⲡ all at once,
    altogether. ⲛ ⲕⲉⲥⲟⲡ again. ⲥⲟⲡ ⲛⲓⲙ always, on every
    occasion. ⲛ ⲍⲁⲍ ⲛ ⲥⲟⲡ many times, often. ⲕⲁⲧⲁ ⲥⲟⲡ ⲛ

(+ Inf.) on every occasion of.

ⲡ.ⲍⲟⲟⲩⲧ male (of animals or humans); freq. as adj.: male,
wild, savage. ⲥⲍⲓⲙⲉ is used as the corresponding female.

ⲡⲉ.ⲕⲗⲟⲙ crown, wreath. ⳨-ⲕⲗⲟⲙ ⲉⲝⲛ̅ to crown. ⲝⲓ-ⲕⲗⲟⲙ to
receive a crown, become a martyr.

ⲑⲁⲉⲓⲃⲉ̅ shade, shadow. ⲣ̅-ⲍⲁⲉⲓⲃⲉ̅ to shade, protect (ⲉ, ⲉⲝⲛ̅).

ⲡ.ⲥⲉⲉⲡⲉ remainder, rest (often in plural sense). A redundant -ⲕⲉ appears frequently: ⲡⲕⲉⲥⲉⲉⲡⲉ the rest.

ⲣ̅-ⲭⲣⲓⲁ to need (ⲙ̅ⲙⲟⲋ); to have to (do: ⲉ + Inf.); ⲭⲣⲓⲁ
is Gk. ἡ χρεία

ϭⲙ̅-ⲡϣⲓⲛⲉ ⲛ̅, ϭⲙ̅-ⲡ(ⲋ)ϣⲓⲛⲉ to search out, visit.

ⲍⲣⲁⲓ is often used to reinforce a following preposition,
esp. ⲍⲛ̅, with no real difference in sense.

Exercises

(1) ⲡⲉϫⲁϥ ϫⲉ ⲙⲁⲣⲟⲛ, ⲧⲉⲩⲛⲟⲩ ⲍⲏⲛ ⲉⲍⲟⲩⲛ. (2) ⲁϥⲧⲣⲉ-ⲡⲉϥⲍⲙⲍⲁⲗ
ⲧⲁⲙⲓⲟ ⲛⲁϥ ⲛ̅ ⲟⲩⲕⲟⲩⲓ ⲛ̅ ⲟⲉⲓⲕ. (3) ⲁϥⲧⲁϣⲉ-ⲟⲉⲓϣ ⲙ̅ ⲡⲉⲩⲁⲅⲅⲉⲗⲓⲟⲛ
ⲍⲛ̅ ⲧⲉⲭⲱⲣⲁ ⲧⲏⲣⲥ̅ ϣⲁⲛⲧϥ̅ⲥⲁⲍⲱϥ ⲉⲃⲟⲗ ⲛ̅ⲍⲏⲧⲥ̅. (4) ⲙ̅ⲡⲣⲧⲣⲉ-ⲛ̅ⲍⲁⲗⲗⲁⲧⲉ
ⲟⲩⲱⲙ ⲉⲃⲟⲗ ⲍⲛ̅ ⲛⲉⲓⲉⲗⲟⲟⲗⲉ. (5) ⲁ-ⲛⲁⲓ ⲧⲏⲣⲟⲩ ϣⲱⲡⲉ ⲕⲁⲧⲁ ⲑⲉ ⲉⲧ
ⲥⲏⲍ ⲍⲙ̅ ⲡϫⲱⲱⲙⲉ. (6) ⲍⲣⲁⲓ ⲍⲛ̅ ⲧⲙⲉⲍⲙⲛ̅ⲧⲥⲛⲟⲟⲩⲥ ⲛ̅ ⲣⲟⲙⲡⲉ ⲛ̅ ⲧⲉϥ-
ⲙⲛ̅ⲧⲉⲣⲟ ⲁϥⲙⲟⲩ ⲛ̅ϭⲓ ⲡⲉⲛⲣ̅ⲣⲟ. (7) ⲁⲙⲏⲉⲓⲧⲛ̅ ϣⲁⲣⲟⲓ ⲧⲁⲣⲉⲧⲛ̅ϭⲓⲛⲉ ⲙ̅
ⲡⲉⲙⲧⲟⲛ. (8) ⲍⲁⲡⲥ̅ ⲉⲣⲟⲛ ⲉⲧⲣⲉⲛϣⲁϫⲉ ⲛⲙ̅ⲙⲁϥ ⲉ-ⲙⲡⲁⲧⲉ-ⲧⲉϥⲧⲁⲡⲣⲟ ⲧⲱⲙ
ⲍⲙ̅ ⲡⲙⲟⲩ. (9) ⲙⲁⲣⲉ-ⲡϫⲟⲉⲓⲥ ϣⲛ̅-ⲍⲧⲏϥ ⲉϫⲱⲕ ⲛ̅ϥⲧⲁⲗϭⲟⲕ. (10) ϣⲁⲣⲉ-
ⲟⲩϣⲏⲛ ⲉ-ⲛⲁⲛⲟⲩϥ ⲧⲁⲩⲉ-ⲕⲁⲣⲡⲟⲥ ⲉ-ⲛⲁⲛⲟⲩϥ. (11) ⳨ⲛⲁⲱⲥⲕ̅ ⲙ̅ ⲡⲉⲓⲙⲁ
ϣⲁⲛⲧ̅ϥⲕⲧⲟϥ. (12) ⲉⲧⲃⲉ ⲡⲁⲓ ⲧⲉⲧⲛⲁϫⲓ ⲙ̅ ⲡⲉⲕⲗⲟⲙ ⲙ̅ ⲡⲉⲟⲟⲩ ⲍⲛ̅ ⲙ̅ⲡⲏⲩⲉ.
(13) ⲛ̅ ϣϣⲉ ⲁⲛ ⲉⲧⲣⲉⲕⲧⲣⲉ-ⲡⲉⲧ ⲍⲓⲧⲟⲩⲱⲕ ϭⲱⲛⲧ̅. (14) ⲡⲕⲉⲥⲉⲉⲡⲉ ⲁⲉ
ⲁⲩⲁⲣϫⲉⲓ ⲛ̅ ⲣⲓⲙⲉ ⲍⲓ ⲟⲩⲥⲟⲡ. (15) ⲁ-ⲡⲁⲡⲛ̅ⲁ̅ ⲧⲉⲗⲏⲗ ⲉⲝⲙ̅ ⲡⲛⲟⲩⲧⲉ
ⲡⲁⲥⲱⲧⲏⲣ. (16) ⲁ-ⲡⲉⲧ ϣⲱⲛⲉ ϫⲟⲟⲥ ⲛⲁϥ ϫⲉ ⲡϫⲟⲉⲓⲥ, ⲟⲩⲛ̅-ϭⲟⲙ ⲙ̅ⲙⲟⲕ
ⲉ ⲧⲃ̅ⲃⲟⲓ. (17) ⲛ̅ⲛⲉⲧⲛ̅ⲧⲁⲩⲉ-ⲛⲉⲛⲧⲁⲧⲉⲧⲛ̅ⲛⲁⲩ ⲉⲣⲟⲟⲩ ⲉ ⲗⲁⲁⲩ. (18)
ⲛ̅ⲍⲁⲗⲗⲁⲧⲉ ⲛ̅ ⲧⲡⲉ ϣⲁⲩⲟⲩⲱⲍ ⲍⲁ ⲑⲁⲓⲃⲉ̅ ⲙ̅ ⲡϣⲏⲛ ⲉⲧ ⲙ̅ⲙⲁⲩ. (19) ⲡⲉⲧⲉ
ⲟⲩⲛ̅ⲧⲁϥ ϣⲧⲏⲛ ⲥⲛ̅ⲧⲉ ⲙⲁⲣⲉϥ⳨-ⲟⲩⲉⲓ ⲙ̅ ⲡⲉⲧⲉ ⲙⲛ̅ⲧⲁϥ. (20) ⲧⲛ̅ⲥⲟⲟⲩⲛ
ϫⲉ ⲡϫⲟⲉⲓⲥ ⲛⲁϭⲓⲛⲉ ⲙ̅ ⲡⲉⲛϣⲓⲛⲉ ⲛ̅ ⲕⲉⲥⲟⲡ ⲙ̅ ⲡⲉⲍⲟⲟⲩ ⲉⲧ ⲙ̅ⲙⲁⲩ. (21)
ⲙ̅ⲡⲉⲛⲉⲓⲣⲉ ⲕⲁⲧⲁ ⲑⲉ ⲉⲛⲧⲁϥⲍⲱⲛ ⲉⲧⲟⲟⲧⲛ̅ ⲉ ⲁⲁⲥ. (22) ⲁϥⲧⲣⲉ-
ⲡⲕⲉⲥⲉⲉⲡⲉ ⲍⲙⲟⲟⲥ ϫⲉⲕⲁⲥ ⲉⲩⲉⲥⲱⲧⲙ̅ ⲉ ⲧⲉϥⲥⲃⲱ. (23) ϥⲛⲁ⳨-ⲕⲗⲟⲙ
ⲉⲝⲛ̅ ⲛⲉⲧ ⲛⲁⲣ̅-ⲙⲛ̅ⲧⲣⲉ ⲉⲧⲃⲉ ⲡⲉϥⲣⲁⲛ ⲉⲧ ⲟⲩⲁⲁⲃ. (24) ⲧϭⲟⲙ ⲙ̅ ⲡⲉⲧ

ⲭⲟⲥⲉ ⲧⲉⲧ ⲛⲁⲣ̄-ϩⲁⲉⲓⲃⲉ̄ ⲉⲣⲟ. (25) ⲥⲱⲧⲙ̄ ⲉ ⲛⲁϣⲁϫⲉ ⲧⲁⲣⲉⲕⲧⲁⲭⲣⲟ ϩⲛ̄
ⲧⲡⲓⲥⲧⲓⲥ ϩⲛ̄ ⲟⲩⲱⲣⲝ̄. (26) ⲁ-ⲡⲭⲟⲉⲓⲥ ⲧⲁϣⲉ-ⲡⲉϥⲛⲁ ⲛⲙ̄ⲙⲁⲥ. (27)
ⲟⲩϩⲟⲟⲩⲧ ⲙⲛ̄ ⲟⲩⲥϩⲓⲙⲉ ⲁϥⲧⲁⲙⲓⲟⲟⲩ ⲛ̄ϭⲓ ⲡⲭⲟⲉⲓⲥ. (28) ⲛ̄ⲧⲁϥⲉⲓ ⲉ
ⲧⲃ̄ⲃⲟⲟⲩ ⲉⲃⲟⲗ ϩⲛ̄ ⲛⲉⲩⲛⲟⲃⲉ. (29) ⲙⲁⲣⲛ̄ⲣⲁϣⲉ ⲛ̄ⲧⲛ̄ⲧⲉⲗⲏⲗ ⲛ̄ⲧⲛ̄ϯ-ⲉⲟⲟⲩ
ⲛⲁϥ. (30) ⲛ̄ⲧⲛ̄ⲣ̄-ⲭⲣⲓⲁ ⲁⲛ ⲛ̄ ⲛⲉⲕϣⲁϫⲉ ⲉⲧ ⲧⲁⲉⲓⲏⲩ. (31) ⲛⲉ-ⲟⲩⲛ̄-
ⲧⲁϥ ϩⲉⲛ2ⲙ̄ϩⲁⲗ ⲛ̄ ϩⲟⲟⲩⲧ ⲙⲛ̄ ϩⲉⲛ2ⲙ̄ϩⲁⲗ ⲛ̄ ⲥϩⲓⲙⲉ. (32) ⲟⲩⲛ̄-ϭⲟⲙ ⲇⲉ
ⲙ̄ ⲡⲛⲟⲩⲧⲉ ⲉ ⲧⲁϣⲉ-ϩⲙⲟⲧ ⲛⲓⲙ. (33) ⲡⲁⲓ ⲡⲉ ⲡⲣⲁⲛ ⲉⲛⲧⲁ-ⲡⲁⲅⲅⲉⲗⲟⲥ
ⲧⲁⲁϥ ⲛⲁϥ ⲉ-ⲙⲡⲁⲧⲉ-ⲧⲉϥⲙⲁⲁⲩ ⲱⲱ ⲙ̄ⲙⲟϥ ϩⲛ̄ ⲑⲏ. (34) ⲡⲉⲓϩⲟⲉⲓⲧⲉ
ⲧⲁⲉⲓⲏⲩ ⲛ̄ ϩⲟⲩⲟ ⲉ ⲡⲏ. (35) ⲁⲥⲣ̄-ⲭⲏⲣⲁ ϣⲁⲛⲧⲥ̄ⲣ̄-ϩⲙⲉⲛⲉⲧⲁϥⲧⲉ ⲛ̄
ⲣⲟⲙⲡⲉ. (36) ϣⲁⲩⲭⲟⲟⲥ ϫⲉ ⲉⲛⲉⲭⲓ-ⲕⲗⲟⲙ ϩⲛ̄ ⲙ̄ⲡⲏⲩⲉ ϩⲁ ⲛⲉⲓⲛⲟϭ ⲛ̄
ϩⲓⲥⲉ.

The Lord's Prayer

ⲡⲉⲛⲉⲓⲱⲧ ⲉⲧ ϩⲛ̄ ⲙ̄ⲡⲏⲩⲉ, ⲙⲁⲣⲉ-ⲡⲉⲕⲣⲁⲛ ⲟⲩⲟⲡ. ⲧⲉⲕⲙⲛ̄ⲧⲣ̄ⲣⲟ ⲙⲁⲣⲉⲥⲉⲓ.
ⲡⲉⲕⲟⲩⲱϣ ⲙⲁⲣⲉϥϣⲱⲡⲉ ⲛ̄ ⲑⲉ ⲉⲧϥ̄ϩⲛ̄ ⲧⲡⲉ ⲛ̄ϥϣⲱⲡⲉ[1] ⲟⲛ ϩⲓϫⲙ̄ ⲡⲕⲁϩ.
ⲡⲉⲛⲟⲉⲓⲕ ⲉⲧ ⲛⲏⲩ[2] ⲛ̄ϥ̄ϯ ⲙ̄ⲙⲟϥ ⲛⲁⲛ ⲙ̄ ⲡⲟⲟⲩ, ⲛ̄ϥ̄ⲕⲱ ⲛⲁⲛ ⲉⲃⲟⲗ ⲛ̄ ⲛⲉⲧ
ⲉⲣⲟⲛ[3] ⲛ̄ ⲑⲉ ϩⲱⲱⲛ ⲟⲛ ⲉⲧⲛ̄ⲕⲱ ⲉⲃⲟⲗ ⲛ̄ ⲛⲉⲧⲉ ⲟⲩⲛ̄ⲧⲁⲛ ⲉⲣⲟⲟⲩ, ⲛ̄ϥ̄ⲧⲙ̄-
ϫⲓⲧⲛ̄ ⲉϩⲟⲩⲛ ⲉ ⲡⲉⲓⲣⲁⲥⲙⲟⲥ ⲁⲗⲗⲁ ⲛ̄ϥ̄ⲛⲁϩⲙⲛ̄[4] ⲉⲃⲟⲗ ϩⲓⲧⲟⲟⲧϥ̄ ⲙ̄ ⲡⲡⲟⲛⲏ-
ⲣⲟⲥ, ϫⲉ ⲧⲱⲕ ⲧⲉ ⲧϭⲟⲙ ⲙⲛ̄ ⲡⲉⲟⲟⲩ ϣⲁ ⲛⲓⲉⲛⲉϩ. ϩⲁⲙⲏⲛ.

1. The repetition of the verb is apparently an attempt
   to clarify what was felt as an awkward construction
   in the Greek.
2. ⲉⲧ ⲛⲏⲩ renders Gk. ἐπιούσιον "for the coming (day)."
   Note that the 2nd pers. Conjunctives continue, with
   the force of Imperatives, the 3rd pers. Injunctive
   forms at the beginning.
3. The prep. ⲉ has the special sense of "due from (as
   indebtedness)." Thus, ⲛⲉⲧ ⲉⲣⲟⲛ "those things which
   are due from us," ⲛⲉⲧⲉ ⲟⲩⲛ̄ⲧⲁⲛ ⲉⲣⲟⲟⲩ "those from
   whom we have (something) due."
4. ⲛⲟⲩϩⲙ̄ vb. tr. to rescue, save.

Reading Selections

Introductory Remarks

A. Luke I - V

The text given here is based on that of G. Horner, *The Coptic Version of the New Testament in the Southern Dialect, otherwise called Sahidic or Thebaic* (Oxford, 1911-24), Vol. II, pp. 3-95. The only orthographic changes made are in the division of the words in order to bring the text into conformity with the style of the present work. The Coptic version should be studied in conjunction with the original Greek; only in this way can the reader gain a clear understanding of the translation techniques employed and of the influence the original has had on the grammar, vocabulary, and style of the Coptic translation. The opening verses are rather difficult, but the remainder of the text is fairly simple and straightforward.

B. Apophthegmata Patrum

The Sahidic version of the *Apophthegmata Patrum*, or *Sayings of the Fathers*, survives in a single manuscript, parts of which are preserved in five different European libraries. The largest fragment, some forty-four leaves, now in the Biblioteca Nazionale of Naples, was published by G. Zoega in his *Catalogus codicum copticorum manu scriptorum qui in Museo Borgiano Velitris adservantur* (Rome, 1810). Sayings from this particular set of pages are often denoted by the siglum Z. These and the smaller fragments of Paris, Vienna, Venice, and London have all been assembled and edited by M. Chaîne, *Le manuscrit de la version copte en dialecte sahidique des "Apophthegmata Patrum"* (Cairo, 1960). The enumeration and text of this edition, which is unfortunately not without printing errors, have been followed for the selections given here. Chaîne supplies a French translation of the text and a valuable concordance of each "saying" with extant Greek and Latin versions, which the interested reader may wish to consult.

146

The contents of the Sayings are quite varied, including anecdotes about individual desert Fathers, the miracles they unwittingly performed because of their excessive virtue, their pithy statements on the perfections and imperfections of fellow-monks and the monastic way of life, and even quite serious digressions on important theological issues of the day. The collection is probably no more "historically authentic" than any similar collection of traditional material, but it does, as a whole, shed light on the early days of Christian monasticism and on the personalities of the dedicated men and women of the Egyptian desert communities.

Apart from a revision of word division, very few changes have been made in the text: (1) ₂ⲛ̄ and ₂ⲉⲛ have been adjusted throughout; (2) ϣⲱⲡⲉ for the unusual ϣⲱⲱⲡⲉ, passim; (3) ⲛⲉⲕ⁻ for ⲛ̄ⲉⲕ⁻ on the first ⲉⲥⲟ̄ⲑⲏⲣⲓⲟⲛ of No. 5; (4) ⲁⲩ₂ⲉ for ⲁⲛ₂ⲉ in No. 17; (5) ⲉⲛⲧⲟⲁⲏ for ⲛ̄ⲧⲟⲁⲏ in No. 24; (6) ⲛ̄ ⲛ̄ⲥⲩⲛⲕⲁⲏⲧⲓⲕⲟⲥ for ⲛ̄ ⲉⲛⲥ⁻ in No. 26; (7) ⲟⲩⲟⲩⲱⲛ for ⲟⲩⲱⲛ in No. 31; (8) ⲁϥ₂ⲟⲣⲡⲛ̄ϥ for ⲁϥ₂ⲟⲡⲛ̄ϥ in No. 38; (9) two lines transposed in No. 38 (a printing error in Chaîne); (10) restore [ⲙ̄ⲙⲟϥ] for Chaîne's [ⲉⲃⲟⲁ] in No. 70; (11) ⲣⲉϥⲣ̄⁻₂ⲱⲃ for ⲣⲉϥ₂ⲱⲃ in No. 175; (12) ₂ⲱⲥ ⲭⲉ for ₂ⲱⲥⲭ̄ in No. 175; (13) ⲟⲩⲥⲭⲩⲙⲁ for ⲟⲩⲟⲭⲩⲙⲁ in No. 175; (14) ₂ⲛ̄ ⲙ̄ⲡⲏⲩⲉ for ₂ⲛ̄ⲛ̄ ⲙ̄ⲡⲏⲩⲉ in No. 175. Note the frequent use of ⲛ̄₂ⲏⲧ⁴ for ₂ⲏⲧ⁴ in this text.

C. Wisdom of Solomon

The text given here is based on P. de Lagarde, *Aegyptiaca* (Göttingen, 1883), pp. 65-82. *Sapienta Solomonis*, or *The Wisdom of Solomon*, well preserved in Greek, Latin, Syriac, Coptic, and Armenian versions, is an intertestamental work in the tradition of Hebrew wisdom literature (Proverbs, Ecclesiastes, Ben Sirach), but by a writer well acquainted with the major schools of Greek philosophy. The date and provenance of the work are both disputed, and the interested reader may consult the discussion in R. H. Charles, *The Apocrypha and Pseudepigrapha of the Old Testament* (Oxford, 1913), Vol. I, pp. 518-68, where an annotated translation and an extensive bibliography may also be found. The short essay of Moses Hadas in *The Interpreter's*

Dictionary of the Bible (Abingdon Press, Nashville, 1962), *sub* Wisdom of Solomon, may also be read with profit. No changes have been made in the text other than in the division of the words. The minor restorations of Lagarde have been accepted without comment.

D. The Life of Joseph the Carpenter

As an apocryphal work dealing with the life, but mainly the death, of Joseph, the father "according to the flesh" of Jesus, *The Life of Joseph the Carpenter* is one of that large number of spurious gospels, acts, epistles, etc. that sprang from the imaginative pens of Christian writers attempting to fill in biographical details missing from the canonical New Testament. Although useless in a quest for "the historical Jesus," each of these works has its own intrinsic interest, reflecting as it does the peculiar doctrinal, nationalistic, sectarian, or other preoccupations of its writer and his circle. *The Life of Joseph* is fully preserved in a Bohairic Coptic version and a brief Arabic paraphrase, both of which were published by P. de Lagarde, *Aegyptiaca* (Göttingen, 1883), together with the Sahidic version of Chapters 14-21.1. Two further fragments (Chapters 5-8.1; 13) of the Sahidic version were published by F. Robinson, *Coptic Apocryphal Gospels* (Texts and Studies IV, 2; Cambridge, 1896), where a full translation of the Sahidic version may be found. The second fragment (Chap. 13) has been omitted from the text given here because of its poorly preserved state. S. Morenz has devoted a short monograph to the study of certain motifs in this text, especially the Egyptian background of the death scene in Chapters 21-23; that work, *Die Geschichte von Joseph dem Zimmermann* (*Texte und Untersuchungen* 56; Berlin, 1951) also contains a German translation of Chapters 14-24.1 of the Sahidic version. The text is presented as it appears in the published sources except for the division of the words. There are many unusual spellings, but the reader should be able to cope with them by this stage. The text is narrated by Jesus, who delivers a brief aside to his apostles in 22:3.

ⲉⲩⲁⲅⲅⲉⲗⲓⲟⲛ ⲕⲁⲧⲁ ⲗⲟⲩⲕⲁⲥ

Chapter I

(1) ⲉⲡⲉⲓⲇⲏⲡⲉⲣ ⲁ-ⲍⲁⲍ ⲍⲓ-ⲧⲟⲟⲧⲟⲩ ⲉ ⲥⲍⲁⲓ ⲛ̄ ⲛ̄ϣⲁⲝⲉ ⲉⲧⲃⲉ ⲛⲉⲍⲃⲏⲩⲉ
ⲉⲛⲧⲁⲩⲧⲱⲧ ⲛ̄ ⲍⲏⲧ ⲍⲣⲁⲓ ⲛ̄ⲍⲏⲧⲛ̄, (2) ⲕⲁⲧⲁ ⲑⲉ ⲉⲛⲧⲁⲩⲧⲁⲁⲥ ⲉⲧⲟⲟⲧⲛ̄
ⲛ̄ϭⲓ ⲛⲉⲛⲧⲁⲩⲛⲁⲩ ⲍⲛ̄ ⲛⲉⲩⲃⲁⲗ ⲭⲓⲛ ⲛ̄ ϣⲟⲣⲡ̄, ⲉ-ⲁⲩϣⲱⲡⲉ ⲛ̄ ⲍⲩⲡⲉⲣⲉⲧⲏⲥ
ⲙ̄ ⲡϣⲁⲝⲉ, (3) ⲁⲓⲣ̄-ⲍⲛⲁⲓ ⲍⲱ, ⲉ-ⲁⲓⲟⲩⲁⲍⲧ̄ ⲛ̄ⲥⲁ ⲍⲱⲃ ⲛⲓⲙ ⲭⲓⲛ ⲛ̄
ϣⲟⲣⲡ̄ ⲍⲛ̄ ⲟⲩⲱⲣⲝ̄, ⲉⲧⲣⲁⲥⲍⲁⲓⲥⲟⲩ ⲛⲁⲕ ⲟⲩⲁ ⲟⲩⲁ, ⲕⲣⲁⲧⲓⲥⲧⲉ ⲑⲉⲟⲫⲓⲗⲉ,
(4) ⲭⲉⲕⲁⲥ ⲉⲕⲉⲉⲓⲙⲉ ⲉ ⲡⲱⲣⲝ̄ ⲛ̄ ⲛ̄ϣⲁⲝⲉ ⲉⲛⲧⲁⲩⲕⲁⲑⲏⲅⲉⲓ ⲙ̄ⲙⲟⲕ ⲛ̄ⲍⲏⲧⲟⲩ.
(5) ⲁϥϣⲱⲡⲉ ⲍⲛ̄ ⲛⲉⲍⲟⲟⲩ ⲛ̄ ⲍⲏⲣⲱⲇⲏⲥ ⲡⲣ̄ⲣⲟ ⲛ̄ ⲧⲟⲩⲇⲁⲓⲁ ⲛ̄ϭⲓ ⲟⲩⲏⲏⲃ
ⲉ-ⲡⲉϥⲣⲁⲛ ⲡⲉ ⲍⲁⲭⲁⲣⲓⲁⲥ, ⲉϥⲏⲡ ⲉ ⲛⲉⲍⲟⲟⲩ ⲛ̄ ⲁⲃⲓⲁ, ⲉ-ⲟⲩⲛ̄ⲧϥ̄
ⲟⲩⲥⲍⲓⲙⲉ ⲉⲃⲟⲗ ⲍⲛ̄ ⲛ̄ϣⲉⲉⲣⲉ ⲛ̄ ⲁⲁⲣⲱⲛ ⲉ-ⲡⲉⲥⲣⲁⲛ ⲡⲉ ⲉⲗⲓⲥⲁⲃⲉⲧ.
(6) ⲛⲉⲩϣⲟⲟⲡ ⲇⲉ ⲡⲉ ⲙ̄ ⲡⲉⲥⲛⲁⲩ ⲛ̄ ⲇⲓⲕⲁⲓⲟⲥ ⲙ̄ ⲡⲉⲙⲧⲟ ⲉⲃⲟⲗ ⲙ̄
ⲡⲛⲟⲩⲧⲉ, ⲉⲩⲙⲟⲟϣⲉ ⲍⲛ̄ ⲛ̄ⲉⲛⲧⲟⲗⲏ ⲧⲏⲣⲟⲩ ⲙⲛ̄ ⲛ̄ⲇⲓⲕⲁⲓⲱⲙⲁ ⲙ̄ ⲡⲭⲟⲉⲓⲥ
ⲉⲩⲟⲩⲁⲁⲃ. (7) ⲁⲩⲱ ⲛⲉ-ⲙⲙⲛ̄ⲧⲟⲩ ϣⲏⲣⲉ ⲙ̄ⲙⲁⲩ ⲡⲉ, ⲉⲃⲟⲗ ⲭⲉ ⲛⲉ-ⲟⲩⲁ6ⲣⲏⲛ
ⲧⲉ ⲉⲗⲓⲥⲁⲃⲉⲧ, ⲁⲩⲱ ⲛ̄ⲧⲟⲟⲩ ⲙ̄ ⲡⲉⲥⲛⲁⲩ ⲛⲉ-ⲁⲩⲁⲓⲁⲓ ⲡⲉ ⲍⲛ̄ ⲛⲉⲩⲍⲟⲟⲩ.
(8) ⲁⲥϣⲱⲡⲉ ⲇⲉ ⲍⲙ̄ ⲡⲧⲣⲉϥϣⲙ̄ϣⲉ ⲍⲛ̄ ⲧⲧⲁⲝⲓⲥ ⲛ̄ ⲛⲉϥⲍⲟⲟⲩ ⲙ̄ ⲡⲉⲙⲧⲟ
ⲉⲃⲟⲗ ⲙ̄ ⲡⲛⲟⲩⲧⲉ, (9) ⲕⲁⲧⲁ ⲡⲥⲱⲛⲧ ⲛ̄ ⲧⲙⲛ̄ⲧⲟⲩⲏⲏⲃ ⲁⲥⲣⲁⲧⲱϥ ⲉ
ⲧⲁⲗⲉ-ϣⲟⲩ2ⲏⲛⲉ ⲉⲍⲣⲁⲓ, ⲉ-ⲁϥⲃⲱⲕ ⲉⲍⲟⲩⲛ ⲉ ⲡⲉⲣⲡⲉ ⲙ̄ ⲡⲭⲟⲉⲓⲥ.

---

1. ⲉⲡⲉⲓⲇⲏⲡⲉⲣ (ἐπειδήπερ) conj. inasmuch as. ⲧⲱⲧ ⲧⲉⲧ-
ⲧⲟⲧˢ Q ⲧⲏⲧ to become agreeable; to agree (on, upon, to: ⲉ,
ⲉⲭⲛ̄; with: ⲙⲛ̄); ⲧⲱⲧ ⲛ̄ ⲍⲏⲧ ⲍⲣⲁⲓ ⲍⲛ̄ to become agreeable,
acceptable to or among.

2. ⲡ.ⲍⲩⲡⲉⲣⲉⲧⲏⲥ (ὑπηρέτης) assistant; custodian.

3. ⲕⲣⲁⲧⲓⲥⲧⲉ: voc. of ⲕⲣⲁⲧⲓⲥⲧⲟⲥ (κράτιστος): O most
excellent Theophilos.

4. ⲕⲁⲑⲏⲅⲉⲓ ⲙ̄ⲙⲟˢ ⲍⲛ̄ (καθηγέομαι) to instruct in.

6. ⲡ.ⲇⲓⲕⲁⲓⲱⲙⲁ (τὸ δικαίωμα) act of justice; ordinance.

7. ⲁ6ⲣⲏⲛ (adj. or n.f.) barren (woman).

8. ⲧ.ⲧⲁⲝⲓⲥ (ἡ τάξις) order, arrangement; rank, post.

9. ⲡ.ⲥⲱⲛⲧ custom; ⲉⲓⲣⲉ ⲙ̄ ⲡⲥⲱⲛⲧ to follow the custom.
ⲁⲥⲣⲁⲧⲱϥ: it became his turn; an impers. expression, the
exact analysis of which is uncertain. ⲡ.ϣⲟⲩ2ⲏⲛⲉ incense.

150

(10) ⲁⲩⲱ ⲛⲉⲣⲉ-ⲡⲙⲏⲛϣⲉ ⲧⲏⲣϥ̄ ⲙ̄ ⲡⲗⲁⲟⲥ ϣⲗⲏⲗ ⲙ̄ ⲡⲥⲁ ⲛ̄ ⲃⲟⲗ ⲙ̄ ⲡⲛⲁⲩ
ⲙ̄ ⲡϣⲟⲩⲍⲏⲛⲉ. (11) ⲁ-ⲡⲁⲅⲅⲉⲗⲟⲥ ⲇⲉ ⲙ̄ ⲡϫⲟⲉⲓⲥ ⲟⲩⲱⲛⲍ̄ ⲛⲁϥ ⲉⲃⲟⲗ
ⲉϥⲁⲍⲉⲣⲁⲧϥ̄ ⲛ̄ ⲥⲁ ⲟⲩⲛⲁⲙ ⲙ̄ ⲡⲉⲑⲩⲥⲓⲁⲥⲧⲏⲣⲓⲟⲛ ⲙ̄ ⲡϣⲟⲩⲍⲏⲛⲉ.
(12) ⲁϥϣⲧⲟⲣⲧⲣ̄ ⲇⲉ ⲛ̄ϭⲓ ⲍⲁⲭⲁⲣⲓⲁⲥ ⲛ̄ⲧⲉⲣⲉϥⲛⲁⲩ, ⲁⲩⲱ ⲁⲩⲍⲟⲧⲉ ⲍⲉ
ⲉⲍⲣⲁⲓ ⲉϫⲱϥ. (13) ⲡⲉϫⲉ-ⲡⲁⲅⲅⲉⲗⲟⲥ ⲇⲉ ⲛⲁϥ ϫⲉ
ⲙ̄ⲡⲣ̄ⲣ̄-ⲍⲟⲧⲉ ⲍⲁⲭⲁⲣⲓⲁⲥ, ϫⲉ ⲁⲩⲥⲱⲧⲙ̄ ⲉ ⲡⲉⲕⲥⲟⲡⲥ̄. ⲁⲩⲱ ⲧⲉⲕⲥⲍⲓⲙⲉ
ⲉⲗⲓⲥⲁⲃⲉⲧ ⲥⲛⲁϫⲡⲟ ⲛⲁⲕ ⲛ̄ ⲟⲩϣⲏⲣⲉ, ⲛⲅ̄ⲙⲟⲩⲧⲉ ⲉ ⲡⲉϥⲣⲁⲛ ϫⲉ
ⲓⲱⲁⲛⲛⲏⲥ. (14) ⲟⲩⲛ̄-ⲟⲩⲣⲁϣⲉ ⲛⲁϣⲱⲡⲉ ⲛⲁⲕ ⲙⲛ̄ ⲟⲩⲧⲉⲗⲏⲗ, ⲁⲩⲱ
ⲟⲩⲛ̄-ⲍⲁⲍ ⲛⲁⲣⲁϣⲉ ⲉϫⲙ̄ ⲡⲉϥϫⲡⲟ. (15) ϥⲛⲁⲣ̄-ⲟⲩⲛⲟϭ ⲅⲁⲣ ⲙ̄
ⲡⲉⲙⲧⲟ ⲉⲃⲟⲗ ⲙ̄ ⲡϫⲟⲉⲓⲥ, ⲁⲩⲱ ⲛ̄ⲛⲉϥⲥⲉ-ⲏⲣⲡ̄ ⲍⲓ ⲥⲓⲕⲉⲣⲁ, ⲁⲩⲱ
ϥⲛⲁⲙⲟⲩⲍ ⲉⲃⲟⲗ ⲍⲙ̄ ⲡⲉⲡⲛ̄ⲁ ⲉⲧ ⲟⲩⲁⲁⲃ ϫⲓⲛ ⲉϥ2ⲛ̄ ⲍⲏⲧⲥ̄ ⲛ̄
ⲧⲉϥⲙⲁⲁⲩ. (16) ⲁⲩⲱ ϥⲛⲁⲕⲧⲉ-ⲟⲩⲙⲏⲛϣⲉ ⲛ̄ ⲛ̄ϣⲏⲣⲉ ⲙ̄ ⲡⲓ̄ⲏ̄ⲗ̄ ⲉ
ⲡϫⲟⲉⲓⲥ ⲡⲉⲩⲛⲟⲩⲧⲉ. (17) ⲁⲩⲱ ⲛ̄ⲧⲟϥ ϥⲛⲁⲙⲟⲟϣⲉ ⲍⲁ ⲧⲉϥⲍⲏ ⲍⲙ̄
ⲡⲉⲡⲛ̄ⲁ ⲙⲛ̄ ⲧϭⲟⲙ ⲛ̄ ⲍⲏⲗⲓⲁⲥ, ⲉ ⲕⲧⲟ ⲛ̄ ⲛ̄ⲍⲏⲧ ⲛ̄ ⲛ̄ⲉⲓⲟⲧⲉ ⲉ
ⲛⲉⲩϣⲏⲣⲉ ⲁⲩⲱ ⲛ̄ⲁⲧⲥⲱⲧⲙ̄ ⲍⲛ̄ ⲧⲙⲛ̄ⲧⲣⲙ̄ⲛ̄2ⲏⲧ ⲛ̄ ⲛ̄ⲇⲓⲕⲁⲓⲟⲥ, ⲉ ⲥⲟⲃⲧⲉ
ⲛ̄ ⲟⲩⲗⲁⲟⲥ ⲙ̄ ⲡϫⲟⲉⲓⲥ ⲉϥⲥⲃ̄ⲧⲱⲧ.
(18) ⲁⲩⲱ ⲡⲉϫⲉ-ⲍⲁⲭⲁⲣⲓⲁⲥ ⲙ̄ ⲡⲁⲅⲅⲉⲗⲟⲥ ϫⲉ
ⲍⲛ̄ ⲟⲩ †ⲛⲁⲉⲓⲙⲉ ⲉ ⲡⲁⲓ? ⲁⲛⲟⲕ ⲅⲁⲣ ⲁⲓⲣ̄-ⲍⲗ̄ⲗⲟ ⲁⲩⲱ ⲧⲁⲥⲍⲓⲙⲉ
ⲁⲥⲁⲓⲁⲓ ⲍⲛ̄ ⲛⲉⲥⲍⲟⲟⲩ.
(19) ⲁ-ⲡⲁⲅⲅⲉⲗⲟⲥ ⲇⲉ ⲟⲩⲱϣⲃ̄, ⲡⲉϫⲁϥ ⲛⲁϥ ϫⲉ
ⲁⲛⲟⲕ ⲡⲉ ⲅⲁⲃⲣⲓⲏⲗ, ⲡⲉⲧ ⲁⲍⲉⲣⲁⲧϥ̄ ⲙ̄ ⲡⲉⲙⲧⲟ ⲉⲃⲟⲗ ⲙ̄ ⲡⲛⲟⲩⲧⲉ.
ⲁⲩⲧⲛ̄ⲛⲟⲟⲩⲧ ⲉ ϣⲁϫⲉ ⲛⲙ̄ⲙⲁⲕ ⲁⲩⲱ ⲉ ⲧⲁϣⲉ-ⲟⲉⲓϣ ⲛⲁⲕ ⲛ̄ ⲛⲁⲓ.
(20) ⲉⲓⲥ ⲍⲏⲏⲧⲉ ⲉⲕⲉϣⲱⲡⲉ ⲉⲕⲕⲱ ⲛ̄ ⲣⲱⲕ, ⲙ̄ⲙⲛ̄-ϭϭⲟⲙ ⲙ̄ⲙⲟⲕ ⲉ
ϣⲁϫⲉ ϣⲁ ⲡⲉⲍⲟⲟⲩ ⲉⲧⲉⲣⲉ-ⲛⲁⲓ ⲛⲁϣⲱⲡⲉ, ⲉⲧⲃⲉ ϫⲉ ⲙ̄ⲡⲕ̄ⲡⲓⲥⲧⲉⲩⲉ ⲉ
ⲛⲁϣⲁϫⲉ, ⲛⲁⲓ ⲉⲧ ⲛⲁϫⲱⲕ ⲉⲃⲟⲗ ⲍⲙ̄ ⲡⲉⲩⲟⲩⲟⲉⲓϣ.
(21) ⲡⲗⲁⲟⲥ ⲇⲉ ⲛⲉϥϭⲱϣⲧ̄ ⲍⲏⲧϥ̄ ⲛ̄ ⲍⲁⲭⲁⲣⲓⲁⲥ ⲡⲉ, ⲁⲩⲱ ⲛⲉⲩⲣ̄-ϣⲡⲏⲣⲉ
ⲛ̄ⲧⲉⲣⲉϥⲱⲥⲕ̄ ⲍⲙ̄ ⲡⲉⲣⲡⲉ. (22) ⲛ̄ⲧⲉⲣⲉϥⲉⲓ ⲇⲉ ⲉⲃⲟⲗ, ⲙ̄ⲡⲉϥϭⲙ̄-ϭⲟⲙ ⲉ

---

11. ⲡⲉ.ⲑⲩⲥⲓⲁⲥⲧⲏⲣⲓⲟⲛ (τὸ θυσιαστήριον) altar.

13. ⲡ.ⲥⲟⲡⲥ̄ entreaty, prayer; ⲥⲟⲡⲥ̄ ⲥⲉⲡⲥ̄- or ⲥⲟⲡⲥⲡ̄ ⲥⲡ̄ⲥⲡ̄-
ⲥⲡ̄ⲥⲱⲡ⸗ Q ⲥⲡ̄ⲥⲱⲡ to entreat, implore (ⲙ̄ⲙⲟ⸗).

15. ⲡ.ⲥⲓⲕⲉⲣⲁ (τὸ σίκερα) strong drink.

22. ⲭⲱⲣⲙ̄, Q ⲭⲟⲣⲙ̄ to make a sign, beckon (to: ⲉ, ⲟⲩⲃⲉ;
with: ⲙ̄ⲙⲟ⸗, ⲍⲛ̄). ⲙ̄ⲡⲟ, ⲉⲙⲡⲟ adj. dumb, mute; ⲣ̄-ⲙ̄ⲡⲟ (Q ⲟ ⲛ̄
ⲙ̄ⲡⲟ) to become mute.

ϣⲁϫⲉ ⲛⲙ̅ⲙⲁⲩ, ⲁⲩⲱ ⲁⲩⲉⲓⲙⲉ ϫⲉ ⲛ̅ⲧⲁϥⲛⲁⲩ ⲉⲩϭⲱⲗⲡ̅ ⲉⲃⲟⲗ ϩⲙ̅ ⲡⲉⲣⲡⲉ.
ⲛ̅ⲧⲟϥ ⲇⲉ ⲛⲉϥⲭⲱⲣⲙ̅ ⲟⲩⲃⲏⲩ ⲡⲉ, ⲁⲩⲱ ⲁϥϭⲱ ⲉϥⲟ ⲛ̅ ⲉⲙⲡⲟ. (23) ⲁⲥϣⲱⲡⲉ
ⲇⲉ ⲛ̅ⲧⲉⲣⲉ-ⲛⲉϩⲟⲟⲩ ⲙ̅ ⲡⲉϥϣⲙ̅ϣⲉ ϫⲱⲕ ⲉⲃⲟⲗ, ⲁϥⲃⲱⲕ ⲉϩⲣⲁⲓ ⲉ ⲡⲉϥⲏⲓ.
(24) ⲙⲛ̅ⲛ̅ⲥⲁ ⲛⲉⲓϩⲟⲟⲩ ⲇⲉ ⲁⲥⲱ ⲛ̅ϭⲓ ⲉⲗⲓⲥⲁⲃⲉⲧ ⲧⲉϥⲥϩⲓⲙⲉ, ⲁⲩⲱ
ⲁⲥϩⲟⲡⲥ̅ ⲛ̅ ϯⲟⲩ ⲛ̅ ⲉⲃⲟⲧ, ⲉⲥϫⲱ ⲙ̅ⲙⲟⲥ (25) ϫⲉ

    ⲧⲁⲓ ⲧⲉ ⲑⲉ ⲛ̅ⲧⲁ-ⲡϫⲟⲉⲓⲥ ⲁⲁⲥ ⲛⲁⲓ ϩⲙ̅ ⲡⲉϩⲟⲟⲩ ⲛ̅ⲧⲁϥϭⲱϣⲧ̅
    ⲉ ϥⲓ ⲙ̅ ⲡⲁⲛⲟϭⲛⲉ̅ ⲉⲃⲟⲗ ϩⲛ̅ ⲛ̅ⲣⲱⲙⲉ.

(26) ϩⲙ̅ ⲡⲙⲉϩ ⲥⲟⲟⲩ ⲇⲉ ⲛ̅ ⲉⲃⲟⲧ ⲁⲩϫⲟⲟⲩ ⲛ̅ ⲅⲁⲃⲣⲓⲏⲗ ⲡⲁⲅⲅⲉⲗⲟⲥ ⲉⲃⲟⲗ
ϩⲓⲧⲙ̅ ⲡⲛⲟⲩⲧⲉ ⲉⲩⲡⲟⲗⲓⲥ ⲛ̅ⲧⲉ ⲧⲅⲁⲗⲓⲗⲁⲓⲁ ⲉ-ⲡⲉⲥⲣⲁⲛ ⲡⲉ ⲛⲁⲍⲁⲣⲉⲑ,
(27) ϣⲁ ⲟⲩⲡⲁⲣⲑⲉⲛⲟⲥ ⲉ-ⲁⲩϣⲡ̅-ⲧⲟⲟⲧⲥ̅ ⲛ̅ ⲟⲩϩⲁⲓ ⲉ-ⲡⲉϥⲣⲁⲛ ⲡⲉ ⲓⲱⲥⲏⲫ
ⲉⲃⲟⲗ ϩⲙ̅ ⲡⲏⲓ ⲛ̅ ⲇⲁⲩ̅ⲇ, ⲁⲩⲱ ⲡⲣⲁⲛ ⲛ̅ ⲧⲡⲁⲣⲑⲉⲛⲟⲥ ⲡⲉ ⲙⲁⲣⲓⲁ. (28) ⲁⲩⲱ
ⲛ̅ⲧⲉⲣⲉϥⲃⲱⲕ ⲛⲁⲥ ⲉϩⲟⲩⲛ, ⲡⲉϫⲁϥ ⲛⲁⲥ ϫⲉ

    ⲭⲁⲓⲣⲉ, ⲧⲉⲛⲧⲁⲥϭⲛ̅-ϩⲙⲟⲧ. ⲡϫⲟⲉⲓⲥ ⲛⲙ̅ⲙⲉ.

(29) ⲛ̅ⲧⲟⲥ ⲇⲉ ⲁⲥϣⲧⲟⲣⲧⲣ̅ ⲉϫⲙ̅ ⲡϣⲁϫⲉ, ⲁⲩⲱ ⲛⲉⲥⲙⲟⲕⲙⲉⲕ ⲙ̅ⲙⲟⲥ ϫⲉ
ⲟⲩⲁϣ ⲙ̅ ⲙⲓⲛⲉ ⲡⲉ ⲡⲉⲓⲁⲥⲡⲁⲥⲙⲟⲥ. (30) ⲡⲉϫⲉ-ⲡⲁⲅⲅⲉⲗⲟⲥ ⲛⲁⲥ ϫⲉ

    ⲙ̅ⲡⲣ̅ⲣ̅-ϩⲟⲧⲉ, ⲙⲁⲣⲓⲁ. ⲁⲣϭⲓⲛⲉ ⲅⲁⲣ ⲛ̅ ⲟⲩϩⲙⲟⲧ ⲛ̅ⲛⲁϩⲣⲙ̅ ⲡⲛⲟⲩⲧⲉ.
    (31) ⲁⲩⲱ ⲉⲓⲥ ϩⲏⲏⲧⲉ ⲧⲉⲛⲁⲱ, ⲛ̅ⲧⲉⲭⲡⲟ ⲛ̅ ⲟⲩϣⲏⲣⲉ, ⲛ̅ⲧⲉⲙⲟⲩⲧⲉ ⲉ
    ⲡⲉϥⲣⲁⲛ ϫⲉ ⲓⲥ̅. (32) ⲡⲁⲓ ϥⲛⲁϣⲱⲡⲉ ⲛ̅ ⲟⲩⲛⲟϭ, ⲁⲩⲱ ⲥⲉⲛⲁⲙⲟⲩⲧⲉ
    ⲉⲣⲟϥ ϫⲉ ⲡϣⲏⲣⲉ ⲙ̅ ⲡⲉⲧ ϫⲟⲥⲉ. ⲡϫⲟⲉⲓⲥ ⲡⲛⲟⲩⲧⲉ ⲛⲁϯ ⲛⲁϥ ⲙ̅
    ⲡⲉⲑⲣⲟⲛⲟⲥ ⲛ̅ ⲇⲁⲩⲉⲓⲇ ⲡⲉϥⲉⲓⲱⲧ. (33) ⲁⲩⲱ ϥⲛⲁⲣ̅-ⲣ̅ⲣⲟ ⲉϫⲙ̅ ⲡⲏⲓ
    ⲛ̅ ⲓⲁⲕⲱⲃ ϣⲁ ⲛⲓⲉⲛⲉϩ, ⲁⲩⲱ ⲙ̅ⲙⲛ̅-ϩⲁⲏ ⲛⲁϣⲱⲡⲉ ⲛ̅ ⲧⲉϥⲙⲛ̅ⲧⲉⲣⲟ.

(34) ⲡⲉϫⲉ-ⲙⲁⲣⲓⲁ ⲇⲉ ⲙ̅ ⲡⲁⲅⲅⲉⲗⲟⲥ ϫⲉ

    ⲛ̅ ⲁϣ ⲛ̅ ϩⲉ ⲡⲁⲓ ⲛⲁϣⲱⲡⲉ ⲙ̅ⲙⲟⲓ? ⲙ̅ⲡⲉⲓⲥⲟⲩⲛ̅-ϩⲟⲟⲩⲧ.

(35) ⲁ-ⲡⲁⲅⲅⲉⲗⲟⲥ ⲟⲩⲱϣⲃ̅, ⲡⲉϫⲁϥ ⲛⲁⲥ ϫⲉ

    ⲟⲩⲡⲛ̅ⲁ ⲉϥⲟⲩⲁⲁⲃ ⲡⲉⲧ ⲛⲏⲩ ⲉϩⲣⲁⲓ ⲉϫⲱ, ⲁⲩⲱ ⲧϭⲟⲙ ⲙ̅ ⲡⲉⲧ ϫⲟⲥⲉ
    ⲧⲉⲧ ⲛⲁⲣ̅-ϩⲁⲓⲃⲥ̅ ⲉⲣⲟ. ⲉⲧⲃⲉ ⲡⲁⲓ ⲡⲉⲧⲉⲛⲁϫⲡⲟϥ ϥⲟⲩⲁⲁⲃ.

---

25. ⲛⲟϭⲛⲉ̅ ⲛⲉϭⲛⲉϭ- ⲛⲉϭⲛⲟⲩϭⲋ ⲧⲟ ⲙⲟⲥⲕ, reproach (ⲙ̅ⲙⲟⲋ);
as n.m. reproach, scorn.

27. ϣⲡ̅-ⲧⲟⲟⲧⲋ ⲛⲁⲋ lit., to grasp the hand of (someone)
for, i.e. to betroth (a woman) to (a man); the Q is expressed as ⲧⲟⲟⲧⲥ̅ ϣⲏⲡ ⲛⲁϥ, she is betrothed to him (II, 5).

28. ⲭⲁⲓⲣⲉ (χαῖρε) Greetings.   33. Text has ϥⲛⲁⲣ̅ⲣⲟ.

34. ⲥⲟⲩⲛ̅-ϩⲟⲟⲩⲧ to know a man (sexually); ⲥⲟⲟⲩⲛ̅ + ϩⲟⲟⲩⲧ.

сєнамоуте єроч хє пϣнрє м̄ пноутє. (36) ауω єіс
єлісавєт тоусуггєннс н̄тос 2ωωс он асω н̄ оуϣнрє 2н̄
тєсмн̄т2ⲗ̄лω, ауω пєсмє2сооу н̄ євот пє паі, таі
єϣаумоутє єрос хє та6рнн, (37) хє н̄нє-лаау н̄ ϣахє
р̄-ат6ом н̄на2рм̄ пноутє.
(38) пєхас дє н̄6і маріа хє
єіс 2ннтє ан̄г̄-ⲑм̄2ал м̄ пхоєіс. марєсϣωпє наі ката
пєкϣахє.
ауω а-пͰаггєлос вωк євол 2ітоотс̄. (39) астωоунс̄ дє н̄6і
маріа 2н̄ нєі2ооу, асвωк є торінн 2н̄ оу6єпн є тполіс н̄
†оуалıа. (40) асвωк є2оун є пнı н̄ захаріас, асаспазє н̄
єлісавєт. (41) асϣωпє дє н̄тєрє-єлісавєт сωтм̄ є паспасмос
м̄ марıа, а-пϣнрє ϣнм кім 2раı н̄2нтс̄, ауω а-єлісавєт моу2
євол 2м̄ пєпн̄а єт оуаав. (42) асчі-2рас євол 2н̄ оуно6 н̄
смн, пєхас хє
тєсмамаат н̄то 2н̄ нє2іомє, ауω чсмамаат н̄6і пкарпос н̄
2нтє, (43) хє ан̄г̄-нім анок хє єрє-тмаау м̄ пахоєіс єі
єрат? (44) єіс 2ннтє гар н̄тєрє-тєсмн м̄ поуаспасмос
та2є-намаахє, а-пϣнрє ϣнм кім 2н̄ оутєлнл н̄2нт.
(45) ауω наıатс̄ н̄ тєнтаспістєує хє оун̄-оухωк євол
наϣωпє н̄ нєнтаухооу нас 2ıтм̄ пхоєіс.
(46) ауω пєхє-марıа хє
а-таψухн хісє м̄ пхоєіс. (47) а-папн̄а тєлнл єхм̄ пноутє
пасωтнр; (48) хє ачбωϣт̄ єхм̄ пєⲑвıо н̄ тєч2м̄2ал, єіс
2ннтє гар хін тєноу сєнатмаıоı н̄6і гєнєа нім, (49) хє
ачєірє наı н̄ 2єнмн̄тно6 н̄6і пєтєун̄-6ом м̄моч, ауω
пєчран оуаав. (50) пєчна хін оухωм ϣа оухωм єхн̄ нєт

---

40. аспазє (ἀσπάζομαι) to greet.

48. тмаіо тмаıє- тмаıо⸗ Q тмаıну to justify (м̄мо⸗), to
consider just or justified; intr. to become justified.
т.гєнєа (ἡ γενεά) generation.

50. п.хωм generation.

ⲣ̄-ϩⲟⲧⲉ ϩⲏⲧϥ̄. (51) ⲁϥⲉⲓⲣⲉ ⲛ̄ ⲟⲩ6ⲟⲙ ϩⲙ̄ ⲡⲉϥ6ⲃⲟⲓ; ⲁϥ⳽ⲱⲣⲉ
ⲉⲃⲟⲗ ⲛ̄ ⲛ̄ϫⲁⲥⲓ-ϩⲏⲧ ϩⲙ̄ ⲡⲙⲉⲉⲩⲉ ⲛ̄ ⲛⲉⲩϩⲏⲧ. (52) ⲁϥⳉⲟⲣⳉⲣ̄ ⲛ̄
ⲛⲁⲩⲛⲁⲥⲧⲏⲥ ϩⲛ̄ ⲛⲉⲩⲑⲣⲟⲛⲟⲥ; ⲁϥ⳽ⲓⲥⲉ ⲛ̄ ⲛⲉⲧ ⲑⲃ̄ⲃⲓⲏⲩ.
(53) ⲁϥⲧⲥⲓⲉ-ⲛⲉⲧ ϩⲕⲁⲉⲓⲧ ⲛ̄ ⲁⲅⲁⲑⲟⲛ; ⲁϥⲭⲉⲩ-ⲛ̄ⲣⲙ̄ⲙⲁⲟ
ⲉⲩⳉⲟⲩⲉⲓⲧ. (54) ⲁϥ-ϯ-ⲧⲟⲟⲧϥ̄ ⲙ̄ ⲡⲓⲏ̄ⲗ ⲡⲉϥϩⲙ̄ϩⲁⲗ ⲉ ⲣ̄-ⲡⲙⲉⲉⲩⲉ
ⲙ̄ ⲡⲛⲁ (55) ⲕⲁⲧⲁ ⲑⲉ ⲉⲛⲧⲁϥⳉⲁⲭⲉ ⲙⲛ̄ ⲛⲉⲛⲉⲓⲟⲧⲉ ⲁⲃⲣⲁϩⲁⲙ ⲙⲛ̄
ⲡⲉϥⲥⲡⲉⲣⲙⲁ ⳉⲁ ⲉⲛⲉϩ.
(56) ⲁ-ⲙⲁⲣⲓⲁ ⲇⲉ 6ⲱ ϩⲁϩⲧⲏⲥ ⲛ̄ ⳉⲟⲙⲛ̄ⲧ ⲛ̄ ⲉⲃⲟⲧ, ⲁⲩⲱ ⲁⲥⲕⲟⲧⲥ̄
ⲉϩⲣⲁⲓ ⲉ ⲡⲉⲥⲏⲓ. (57) ⲁ-ⲡⲉⲟⲩⲟⲉⲓ⳽ ⲇⲉ ⲭⲱⲕ ⲉⲃⲟⲗ ⲛ̄ ⲉⲗⲓⲥⲁⲃⲉⲧ
ⲉⲧⲣⲉⲥⲙⲓⲥⲉ, ⲁⲩⲱ ⲁⲥⲭⲡⲟ ⲛ̄ ⲟⲩⳉⲏⲣⲉ. (58) ⲁⲩⲥⲱⲧⲙ̄ ⲇⲉ ⲛ̄6ⲓ
ⲛⲉⲥⲣⲙ̄ⲣⲁⲩⲏ ⲙⲛ̄ ⲛⲉⲥⲥⲩⲅⲅⲉⲛⲏⲥ ⲭⲉ ⲁ-ⲡⲭⲟⲉⲓⲥ ⲧⲁⳉⲉ-ⲡⲉϥⲛⲁ ⲛⲙ̄ⲙⲁⲥ,
ⲁⲩⲣⲁⳉⲉ ⲛⲙ̄ⲙⲁⲥ. (59) ⲁⲥⳉⲱⲡⲉ ⲇⲉ ϩⲙ̄ ⲡⲙⲉϩⳉⲙⲟⲩⲛ ⲛ̄ ϩⲟⲟⲩ ⲁⲩⲉⲓ
ⲉⲩⲛⲁⲥⲃ̄ⲃⲉ ⲙ̄ ⲡⳉⲏⲣⲉ ⳉⲏⲙ. ⲁⲩⲙⲟⲩⲧⲉ ⲉⲣⲟϥ ⲙ̄ ⲡⲣⲁⲛ ⲙ̄ ⲡⲉϥⲉⲓⲱⲧ ⲭⲉ
ⲍⲁⲭⲁⲣⲓⲁⲥ. (60) ⲁ-ⲧⲉϥⲙⲁⲁⲩ ⲇⲉ ⲟⲩⲱⳉⲃ̄, ⲡⲉⲭⲁⲥ ⲭⲉ
ⲙ̄ⲙⲟⲛ. ⲁⲗⲗⲁ ⲉⲩⲛⲁⲙⲟⲩⲧⲉ ⲉⲣⲟϥ ⲭⲉ ⲓⲱϩⲁⲛⲛⲏⲥ.
(61) ⲡⲉⲭⲁⲩ ⲇⲉ ⲛⲁⲥ ⲭⲉ
ⲙⲛ̄-ⲗⲁⲁⲩ ϩⲛ̄ ⲧⲟⲩⲣⲁⲓⲧⲉ ⲉⲩⲙⲟⲩⲧⲉ ⲉⲣⲟϥ ⲙ̄ ⲡⲉⲓⲣⲁⲛ.
(62) ⲛⲉⲩⲭⲱⲣⲙ̄ ⲇⲉ ⲟⲩⲃⲉ ⲡⲉϥⲉⲓⲱⲧ ⲭⲉ
ⲕⲟⲩⲉⳉ-ⲙⲟⲩⲧⲉ ⲉⲣⲟϥ ⲭⲉ ⲛⲓⲙ?

---

51. ⲡⲉ.6ⲃⲟⲓ arm (of man), leg (of animal). ⲭⲱⲱⲣⲉ ⲭⲉⲉⲣⲉ-
ⲭⲟⲟⲣ⳽ Q ⲭⲟⲟⲣⲉ (± ⲉⲃⲟⲗ) to scatter, disperse (ⲙ̄ⲙⲟ⳽); also
more generally: to bring to naught.

52. ⳉⲟⲣⳉⲣ̄ ⳉⲣ̄ⳉⲣ̄- ⳉⲣ̄ⳉⲱⲣ⳽ Q ⳉⲣ̄ⳉⲱⲣ to overturn, upset
(ⲙ̄ⲙⲟ⳽); as n.m. overthrow, destruction. ⲡ.ⲁⲩⲛⲁⲥⲧⲏⲥ
(ὁ δυνάστης) ruler.

53. ⲁⲅⲁⲑⲟⲛ (τὸ ἀγαθόν) n. good, what is good.

55. ⲡⲉ.ⲥⲡⲉⲣⲙⲁ (τὸ σπέρμα) seed; offspring, issue.

58. ⲣ̄ⲙ̄ⲣⲁⲩⲏ cpd. of ⲣⲙ̄- (27.2) and ⲧ.ⲣⲁⲩⲏ neighborhood,
town-quarter; hence: neighbor.

59. ⲥⲃ̄ⲃⲉ ⲥⲃ̄ⲃⲉ- ⲥⲃ̄ⲃⲏⲧ⳽ Q ⲥⲃ̄ⲃⲏⲩ to circumcise (ⲙ̄ⲙⲟ⳽); as
n.m. circumcision. 60. ⲙ̄ⲙⲟⲛ No. ⲉⳉⲱⲡⲉ ⲙ̄ⲙⲟⲛ otherwise.

61. ⲧ.ⲣⲁⲓⲧⲉ kin, kindred; ⲣⲙ̄ⲣⲁⲓⲧⲉ kinsman.

(63) ⲁϥⲁⲓⲧⲉⲓ ⲇⲉ ⲛ̄ ⲟⲩⲡⲓⲛⲁⲕⲓⲥ, ⲁϥⲥϩⲁⲓ ⲉϥϫⲱ ⲙ̄ⲙⲟⲥ ϫⲉ ⲓⲱϩⲁⲛⲛⲏⲥ ⲡⲉ ⲡⲉϥⲣⲁⲛ. ⲁⲩⲱ ⲁⲩⲣ̄-ϣⲡⲏⲣⲉ ⲧⲏⲣⲟⲩ. (64) ⲁ-ⲣⲱϥ ⲇⲉ ⲟⲩⲱⲛ ⲛ̄ ⲧⲉⲩⲛⲟⲩ ⲙⲛ̄ ⲡⲉϥⲗⲁⲥ, ⲁϥϣⲁϫⲉ, ⲉϥⲥⲙⲟⲩ ⲉ ⲡⲛⲟⲩⲧⲉ. (65) ⲁⲩϩⲟⲧⲉ ⲇⲉ ϣⲱⲡⲉ ⲉϫⲛ̄ ⲟⲩⲟⲛ ⲛⲓⲙ ⲉⲧ ⲟⲩⲏϩ ϩⲙ̄ ⲡⲉⲩⲕⲱⲧⲉ, ⲁⲩⲱ ϩⲛ̄ ⲧⲟⲣⲓⲛⲏ ⲧⲏⲣⲥ̄ ⲛ̄ ϯⲟⲩⲇⲁⲓⲁ ⲛⲉⲩϣⲁϫⲉ ⲡⲉ ϩⲛ̄ ⲛⲉⲓϣⲁϫⲉ ⲧⲏⲣⲟⲩ. (66) ⲁ-ⲛⲉⲛⲧⲁⲩⲥⲱⲧⲙ̄ ⲇⲉ ⲧⲏⲣⲟⲩ ⲕⲁⲁⲩ ϩⲙ̄ ⲡⲉⲩϩⲏⲧ, ⲉⲩϫⲱ ⲙ̄ⲙⲟⲥ ϫⲉ

ⲉⲣⲉ-ⲡⲉⲓϣⲏⲣⲉ ϣⲏⲙ ⲛⲁⲣ̄-ⲟⲩ?

ⲕⲁⲓ ⲅⲁⲣ ⲧϭⲓϫ ⲙ̄ ⲡϫⲟⲉⲓⲥ ⲛⲉⲥϣⲟⲟⲡ ⲛⲙ̄ⲙⲁϥ ⲡⲉ. (67) ⲁ-ⲍⲁⲭⲁⲣⲓⲁⲥ ⲇⲉ ⲡⲉϥⲉⲓⲱⲧ ⲙⲟⲩϩ ⲉⲃⲟⲗ ϩⲙ̄ ⲡⲉⲡⲛ̄ⲁ ⲉⲧ ⲟⲩⲁⲁⲃ, ⲁϥⲡⲣⲟⲫⲏⲧⲉⲩⲉ, ⲉϥϫⲱ ⲙ̄ⲙⲟⲥ (68) ϫⲉ

ϥⲥⲙⲁⲙⲁⲁⲧ ⲛ̄ϭⲓ ⲡⲛⲟⲩⲧⲉ ⲙ̄ ⲡⲓ̅ⲏ̅ⲗ̅, ϫⲉ ⲁϥϭⲙ̄-ⲡⲉϥϣⲓⲛⲉ ⲁⲩⲱ ⲁϥⲉⲓⲣⲉ ⲛ̄ ⲟⲩⲥⲱⲧⲉ ⲙ̄ ⲡⲉϥⲗⲁⲟⲥ. (69) ⲁϥⲧⲟⲩⲛⲟⲥ ⲛ̄ ⲟⲩⲧⲁⲡ ⲛ̄ ⲟⲩϫⲁⲓ ⲛⲁⲛ ϩⲙ̄ ⲡⲏⲓ ⲛ̄ ⲇⲁⲩⲉⲓⲇ ⲡⲉϥϩⲙ̄ϩⲁⲗ. (70) ⲕⲁⲧⲁ ⲑⲉ ⲛ̄ⲧⲁϥϣⲁϫⲉ ϩⲓⲧⲛ̄ ⲧⲧⲁⲡⲣⲟ ⲛ̄ ⲛⲉϥⲡⲣⲟⲫⲏⲧⲏⲥ ⲉⲧ ⲟⲩⲁⲁⲃ ϫⲓⲛ ⲉⲛⲉϩ, (71) ⲛ̄ ⲟⲩⲟⲩϫⲁⲓ ⲉⲃⲟⲗ ϩⲓⲧⲛ̄ ⲛⲉⲛϫⲁϫⲉ ⲁⲩⲱ ⲉⲃⲟⲗ ϩⲛ̄ ⲧϭⲓϫ ⲛ̄ ⲟⲩⲟⲛ ⲛⲓⲙ ⲉⲧ ⲙⲟⲥⲧⲉ ⲙ̄ⲙⲟⲛ, (72) ⲉ ⲉⲓⲣⲉ ⲛ̄ ⲟⲩⲛⲁ ⲙⲛ̄ ⲛⲉⲛⲉⲓⲟⲧⲉ, ⲉ ⲣ̄-ⲡⲙⲉⲉⲩⲉ ⲛ̄ ⲧⲉϥⲇⲓⲁⲑⲏⲕⲏ ⲉⲧ ⲟⲩⲁⲁⲃ, (73) ⲡⲁⲛⲁϣ ⲛ̄ⲧⲁϥⲱⲣⲕ̄ ⲙ̄ⲙⲟϥ ⲛ̄ ⲁⲃⲣⲁϩⲁⲙ ⲡⲉⲛⲉⲓⲱⲧ, ⲉ ϯ-ⲑⲉ ⲛⲁⲛ (74) ⲁϫⲛ̄ ϩⲟⲧⲉ, ⲉ-ⲁⲛⲛⲟⲩϩⲙ̄ ⲉⲃⲟⲗ ϩⲓⲧⲛ̄ ⲛⲉⲛϫⲁϫⲉ, ⲉ ϣⲙ̄ϣⲉ ⲛⲁϥ (75) ϩⲛ̄ ⲟⲩⲟⲩⲟⲡ ⲙⲛ̄ ⲟⲩⲇⲓⲕⲁⲓⲟⲥⲩⲛⲏ ⲙ̄ ⲡⲉϥⲙ̄ⲧⲟ ⲉⲃⲟⲗ ⲛ̄ ⲛⲉⲛϩⲟⲟⲩ ⲧⲏⲣⲟⲩ. (76) ⲛ̄ⲧⲟⲕ ⲇⲉ ϩⲱⲱⲕ,

---

63. ⲁⲓⲧⲉⲓ (αἰτέω) to ask, ask for. ⲡ.ⲡⲓⲛⲁⲕⲓⲥ (ὁ πίναξ) writing-tablet.

65. ϣⲁϫⲉ ϩⲛ̄ to talk of, about.

66. ⲕⲁⲓ ⲅⲁⲣ (καὶ γάρ) conj. for, for truly.

67. ⲡⲣⲟⲫⲏⲧⲉⲩⲉ (προφητεύω) to prophesy.

68. ⲥⲱⲧⲉ ⲥⲉⲧ- ⲥⲟⲧ⸗ to redeem, rescue (ⲙ̄ⲙⲟ⸗); as n.m. redemption; ⲉⲓⲣⲉ ⲛ̄ ⲟⲩⲥⲱⲧⲉ ⲛⲁ⸗ to make a redemption for.

69. ⲡ.ⲧⲁⲡ horn; trumpet.

72. ⲉⲓⲣⲉ ⲛ̄ ⲟⲩⲛⲁ ⲙⲛ̄ to do a kindness to, for. ⲧ.ⲇⲓⲁⲑⲏⲕⲏ (ἡ διαθήκη) will, testament, covenant.

73. ⲡ.ⲁⲛⲁϣ (pl. ⲛ.ⲁⲛⲁⲩϣ) oath. ⲱⲣⲕ̄ ⲟⲣⲕ⸗ to swear (an oath: ⲙ̄ⲙⲟ⸗; by: ⲙ̄ⲙⲟ⸗; to: ⲉ, ⲛⲁ⸗).

75. ⲧ.ⲇⲓⲕⲁⲓⲟⲥⲩⲛⲏ (ἡ δικαιοσύνη) justice, righteousness.

пафнрє, сєнамоутє єрок хє пєпрофнтнс м̄ ппєт хосє.

кнамоофє гар 2ι θн м̄ пхоєιс є совтє н̄ нєч2ιооує;

(77) є † н̄ оусооун̄ н̄ оухаι м̄ пєчλλος 2м̄ пкω євоλ н̄

нєунові (78) єтвє тмн̄тфн̄-2тнч мн̄ пна м̄ пєнноутє 2н̄

нєтєчнα6м̄-пєнфінє н̄2нтоу н̄6ι поуоєιн євоλ 2м̄ пхιсє,

(79) є ϥ̄-оуоєιн є нєт 2моос 2м̄ пкакє мн̄ нєт 2моос 2н̄

θλιвс̄ м̄ пмоу, є сооутн̄ н̄ нєноуєрнтє є тє2ιн н̄ †рннн.

(80) пфнрє дє фнм αϥαγ2анє αγω αϥ6м̄-6ом 2м̄ пєпн̄а. нєчфооп

дє пє 2н̄ н̄хαιє фа пє2ооу м̄ пєчоуωн2̄ євоλ м̄ пιн̄λ.

Chapter II

(1) асфωпє дє 2н̄ нє2ооу єт м̄мау αγдогма єι євоλ 2ιтм̄ пр̄ро

αγгоустос єтрє-тоικоумєнн тнрс̄ с2αι н̄са нєстмє. (2) таι

тє тфорпє н̄ апографн єнтасфωпє єрє-кγрінос о н̄ 2нгємωн є

тсγріа. (3) αγω нєувнк тнроу пє поуа поуα є с2αιϥ н̄са

тєϥполιс. (4) αϥвωк є2ραι 2ωωϥ н̄6ι ιωснф євоλ 2н̄ тгαλιλαια

євоλ 2н̄ назарєθ тполιс є †оудαια є тполιс н̄ дαγєιд,

тєфαγмоутє єрос хє внθλєєм, хє оуєвоλ 2м̄ пни пє мн̄ тпатρια

н̄ дαγєιд, (5) єтрєϥтααϥ є2оун мн̄ марια, тєтєрє-тоотс̄ фнп

нαϥ, єсєєт. (6) асфωпє дє 2м̄ птрєуфωпє 2м̄ пма єт м̄мау

αγхωк євоλ н̄6ι нє2ооу єтрєсмισє. (7) асхпо м̄ пєсфнрє,

---

79. сооутн̄ соутн̄- соутωн⸵ Q соутωн to straighten,
stretch out (м̄мо⸵); intr. to become straight, upright;
сооутн̄ м̄мо⸵ є to direct toward, make fit for.

80. αγ2анє (αὐξάνω) to grow up.

1. п.догма (τὸ δόγμα) decree. т.оικоумєнн
(ἡ οἰκουμένη) the world. с2αι н̄са to register by, according
to; note the medio-passive intransitive use of с2αι.

2. т.апографн (ἡ ἀπογραφή) enrollment, registry.

4. т.патρια (ἡ πατριά) family, clan; people, nation.

5. тααϥ є2оун reflex.: to register himself (from †).

7. 6ωωλє 6єєлє- 6ооλ⸵ Q 6ооλє to swathe, clothe (м̄мо⸵).
т.тоєις rag, piece of cloth; swaddling-clothes. хто хтє-
хто⸵ Q хтну to lay down (м̄мо⸵). п.оуомϥ manger.

ΠΕϢΡΠ-Μ̄-ΜΙСΕ, ΛС６ΟΟΛΕϤ Ν̄ ２ΕΝΤΟΕΙС, ΛСΧΤΟϤ ２Ν̄ ΟΥΟΥΟΜϤ,
ΧΕ ΝΕ-Μ̄ΜΝ̄-ΜΛ ϢΟΟΠ ΝΛΥ ΠΕ ２Μ̄ ΠΜΛ Ν̄ ６ΟΙΛΕ. (8) ΝΕΥΝ̄-２ΕΝϢΟΟС
ΛΕ ΠΕ ２Μ̄ ΠΜΛ ΕΤ Μ̄ΜΛΥ, ΕΥϢΟΟΠ ２Ν̄ ΤСΩϢΕ ΕΥ２ΛΡΕ２ ２Ν̄ Ν̄ΟΥΡ̄ϢΕ Ν̄
ΤΕΥϢΗ Ε ΠΕΥΟ２Ε Ν̄ ΕСΟΟΥ. (9) Λ-ΠΛΓΓΕΛΟС Μ̄ ΠΧΟΕΙС ΟΥΩΝ＝ ΝΛΥ
ΕΒΟΛ, ΛΥΩ Λ-ΠΕΟΟΥ Μ̄ ΠΧΟΕΙС Ρ̄-ΟΥΟΕΙΝ ΕΡΟΟΥ; ΛΥΡ̄-２ΟΤΕ ２Ν̄
ΟΥΝΟ６ Ν̄ ２ΟΤΕ. (10) ΠΕΧΕ-ΠΛΓΓΕΛΟС ΛΕ ΝΛΥ ΧΕ

    Μ̄ΠΡ̄Ρ̄-２ΟΤΕ. ΕΙС ２ΗΗΤΕ ΓΛΡ †ΤΛϢΕ-ΟΕΙϢ ΝΗΤΝ̄ Ν̄ ΟΥΝΟ６ Ν̄
    ΡΛϢΕ, ΠΛΙ ΕΤ ΝΛϢΩΠΕ Μ̄ ΠΛΛΟС ΤΗΡϤ, (11) ΧΕ ΛΥΧΠΟ ΝΗΤΝ̄
    Μ̄ ΠΟΟΥ Μ̄ ΠСΩΤΗΡ, ΕΤΕ ΠΛΙ ΠΕ ΠΕΧ＝С ΠΧΟΕΙС, ２Ν̄ ΤΠΟΛΙС Ν̄
    ΛΛΥΕΙΛ. (12) ΛΥΩ ΟΥΜΛΕΙΝ ΝΗΤΝ̄ ΠΕ ΠΛΙ: ΤΕΤΝΛ２Ε ΕΥϢΗΡΕ
    ϢΗΜ ΕϤ６ΟΟΛΕ Ν̄ ２ΕΝΤΟΕΙС ΕϤΚΗ ２Ν̄ ΟΥΟΥΟΜϤ.

(13) ΛΥϢΩΠΕ ２Ν̄ ΟΥϢ＝СΝΕ Μ̄Ν ΠΛΓΓΕΛΟС Ν̄６Ι ΟΥΜΗΗϢΕ Ν̄ ΤΕСΤΡΛΤΙΛ
Ν̄ ΤΠΕ ΕΥСΜΟΥ Ε ΠΝΟΥΤΕ ΕΥΧΩ Μ̄ΜΟС (14) ΧΕ

    ΠΕΟΟΥ Μ̄ ΠΝΟΥΤΕ ２Ν̄ ΝΕΤ ΧΟСΕ, ΛΥΩ †ΡΗΝΗ ２ΙΧΜ̄ ΠΚΛ２ ２Ν̄
    Ν̄ΡΩΜΕ Μ̄ ΠΕϤΟΥΩϢ.

(15) ΛСϢΩΠΕ ΛΕ Ν̄ΤΕΡΕ-Ν̄ΛΓΓΕΛΟС ΒΩΚ Ε２ΡΛΙ ２ΙΤΟΟΤΟΥ Ε ΤΠΕ,
ΝΕΡΕ-Ν̄ϢΟΟС ϢΛΧΕ Μ̄Ν ΝΕΥΕΡΗΥ ΧΕ

    ΜΛΡΝ̄ΒΩΚ ϢΛ ΒΗΘΛΕΕΜ, Ν̄ΤΝ̄ΝΛΥ Ε ΠΕΙϢΛΧΕ ΕΝΤΛϤϢΩΠΕ
    ΕΝΤΛ-ΠΧΟΕΙС ΟΥΟΝ２Ϥ ΕΡΟΝ.

(16) ΛΥ６ΕΠΗ ΛΕ, ΛΥΕΙ, ΛΥ２Ε Ε ΜΛΡΙΛ Μ̄Ν ΙΩСΗΦ Μ̄Ν ΠϢΗΡΕ ϢΗΜ
ΕϤΚΗ ２Μ̄ ΠΟΥΟΜϤ. (17) Ν̄ΤΕΡΟΥΝΛΥ ΛΕ, ΛΥΕΙΜΕ Ε ΠϢΛΧΕ
ΕΝΤΛΥΧΟΟϤ ΝΛΥ ΕΤΒΕ ΠϢΗΡΕ ϢΗΜ. (18) ΛΥΩ ΟΥΟΝ ΝΙΜ ΕΝΤΛΥСΩΤΜ̄
ΛΥΡ̄-ϢΠΗΡΕ ΕΧΝ̄ ΝΕΝΤΛ-Ν̄ϢΟΟС ΧΟΟΥ ΝΛΥ. (19) ΜΛΡΙΛ ΛΕ ΝΕС２ΛΡΕ２
Ε ΝΕΙϢΛΧΕ ΤΗΡΟΥ ΠΕ, ΕСΚΩ Μ̄ΜΟΟΥ ２ΡΛΙ ２Μ̄ ΠΕС２ΗΤ. (20) ΛΥΚΟΤΟΥ
ΛΕ Ν̄６Ι Ν̄ϢΟΟС, ΕΥ†-ΕΟΟΥ ΛΥΩ ΕΥСΜΟΥ Ε ΠΝΟΥΤΕ ΕΧΝ̄ ΝΕΝΤΛΥСΟΤΜΟΥ
ΤΗΡΟΥ ΛΥΩ ΛΥΝΛΥ ΚΛΤΛ ΘΕ ΕΝΤΛΥΧΟΟΥ ΝΛΥ. (21) Ν̄ΤΕΡΕ-ϢΜΟΥΝ ΛΕ
Ν̄ ２ΟΟΥ ΧΩΚ ΕΒΟΛ ΕΤΡΕΥС＝ΒΒΗΤϤ, ΛΥΜΟΥΤΕ Ε ΠΕϤΡΛΝ ΧΕ Ι＝С,
ΠΕΝΤΛ-ΠΛΓΓΕΛΟС ΤΛΛϤ ΕΡΟϤ ΕΜΠΛΤ＝СΩΩ Μ̄ΜΟϤ ２Ν̄ ΘΗ. (22) ΛΥΩ
Ν̄ΤΕΡΟΥΧΩΚ ΕΒΟΛ Ν̄６Ι ΝΕ２ΟΟΥ Μ̄ ΠΕϤΤ＝ΒΒΟ ΚΛΤΛ ΠΝΟΜΟС Μ̄
ΜΩΥСΗС, ΛΥΧ̣ΙΤϤ ２ΡΛΙ Ε ΘΙΕΡΟСΟΛΥΜΛ Ε ΤΛ２ΟϤ ΕΡΛΤϤ Μ̄ ΠΧΟΕΙС,

    8. Τ.ΟΥΡ̄ϢΕ watch. Π.Ο２Ε flock, herd; pasture; fold.

    13. ΤΕ.СΤΡΛΤΙΛ (ἡ στρατιά) army, host.

    14. Μ̄ ΠΕϤΟΥΩϢ: this renders Gk. εὐδοκίας (men *of* his
favor) rather than the alternate reading εὐδοκία.

(23) ⲕⲁⲧⲁ ⲑⲉ ⲉⲧ ⲥⲏ2 2ⲙ̄ ⲡⲛⲟⲙⲟⲥ ⲙ̄ ⲡ̄ⲭⲟⲉⲓⲥ ⲭⲉ 2ⲟⲟⲩⲧ ⲛⲓⲙ ⲉⲧ
ⲛⲁⲟⲩⲱⲛ ⲛ̄ ⲧⲟⲟⲧⲉ ⲉⲩⲛⲁⲙⲟⲩⲧⲉ ⲉⲣⲟ4 ⲭⲉ ⲡⲉⲧ ⲟⲩⲁⲁⲃ ⲙ̄ ⲡⲭⲟⲉⲓⲥ,
(24) ⲁⲩⲱ ⲉ † ⲛ̄ ⲟⲩⲑⲩⲥⲓⲁ ⲕⲁⲧⲁ ⲡⲉⲛⲧⲁⲩⲭⲟⲟ4 2ⲙ̄ ⲡⲛⲟⲙⲟⲥ ⲙ̄ ⲡⲭⲟⲉⲓⲥ
ⲭⲉ ⲟⲩⲥⲟⲉⲓⲱ ⲛ̄ ⲃⲣ̄ⲙ̄ⲡⲱⲁⲛ ⲏ ⲙⲁⲥ ⲥⲛⲁⲩ ⲛ̄ ⲃⲣⲟⲟⲙⲡⲉ. (25) ⲉⲓⲥ 2ⲏⲏⲧⲉ
ⲇⲉ ⲛⲉⲩⲛ̄-ⲟⲩⲣⲱⲙⲉ ⲡⲉ 2ⲛ̄ ⲑⲓⲉⲣⲟⲩⲥⲁⲗⲏⲙ ⲉ-ⲡⲉ4ⲣⲁⲛ ⲡⲉ ⲥⲩⲙⲉⲱⲛ. ⲁⲩⲱ
ⲡⲉⲓⲣⲱⲙⲉ ⲛⲉⲩⲇⲓⲕⲁⲓⲟⲥ ⲡⲉ ⲛ̄ ⲣⲉ4ⲱⲙ̄ⲱⲉ ⲙ̄ ⲡⲛⲟⲩⲧⲉ, ⲉ4ϭⲱⲱⲧ̄ ⲉⲃⲟⲗ
2ⲏⲧ4 ⲙ̄ ⲡⲥⲟⲗⲥⲗ̄ ⲙ̄ ⲡ̄ⲓ̄ⲏ̄ⲗ̄, ⲉ-ⲟⲩⲛ̄-ⲟⲩⲡ̄ⲛ̄ⲁ̄ ⲉ4ⲟⲩⲁⲁⲃ ⲱⲟⲟⲡ ⲛⲙ̄ⲙⲁ4,
(26) ⲉ-ⲁⲩⲧⲁⲙⲟ4 ⲉⲃⲟⲗ 2ⲓⲧⲙ̄ ⲡⲉⲡ̄ⲛ̄ⲁ̄ ⲉⲧ ⲟⲩⲁⲁⲃ ⲭⲉ ⲛ4ⲛⲁⲙⲟⲩ· ⲁⲛ
ⲉ-ⲙⲡ4ⲛⲁⲩ ⲉ ⲡⲉⲭ̄ⲥ̄ ⲙ̄ ⲡⲭⲟⲉⲓⲥ. (27) ⲁⲩⲱ ⲁ4ⲉⲓ 2ⲙ̄ ⲡⲉⲡ̄ⲛ̄ⲁ̄ ⲉ ⲡⲉⲣⲡⲉ.
2ⲙ̄ ⲡⲧⲣⲉ-ⲛ̄ⲉⲓⲟⲧⲉ ⲇⲉ ⲭⲓ ⲙ̄ ⲡⲱⲏⲣⲉ ⲱⲏⲙ ⲉ2ⲟⲩⲛ, ⲓ̄ⲥ̄, ⲉⲧⲣⲉⲩⲉⲓⲣⲉ ⲙ̄
ⲡⲥⲱⲛⲧ̄ ⲙ̄ ⲡⲛⲟⲙⲟⲥ 2ⲁⲣⲟ4, (28) ⲛ̄ⲧⲟ4 ⲇⲉ ⲁ4ⲭⲓⲧ4 ⲉ ⲡⲉ42ⲁⲙⲏⲣ,
ⲁ4ⲥⲙⲟⲩ ⲉ ⲡⲛⲟⲩⲧⲉ, ⲉ4ⲭⲱ ⲙ̄ⲙⲟⲥ (29) ⲭⲉ

ⲧⲉⲛⲟⲩ ⲕⲛⲁⲕⲱ ⲉⲃⲟⲗ ⲙ̄ ⲡⲉⲕ2ⲙ̄2ⲁⲗ, ⲡⲭⲟⲉⲓⲥ, ⲕⲁⲧⲁ ⲡⲉⲕⲱⲁⲭⲉ 2ⲛ̄
ⲟⲩⲉⲓⲣⲏⲛⲏ, (30) ⲭⲉ ⲁ-ⲛⲁⲃⲁⲗ ⲛⲁⲩ ⲉ ⲡⲉⲕⲟⲩⲭⲁⲓ, (31) ⲡⲁⲓ
ⲉⲛⲧⲁⲕⲥⲃ̄ⲧⲱⲧ4 ⲙ̄ ⲡⲉⲙⲧⲟ ⲉⲃⲟⲗ ⲛ̄ ⲛ̄ⲗⲁⲟⲥ ⲧⲏⲣⲟⲩ, (32) ⲡⲟⲩⲟⲉⲓⲛ
ⲉⲩϭⲱⲗⲡ̄ ⲉⲃⲟⲗ ⲛ̄ ⲛ̄2ⲉⲑⲛⲟⲥ ⲁⲩⲱ ⲉ ⲡⲉⲟⲟⲩ ⲙ̄ ⲡⲉⲕⲗⲁⲟⲥ ⲡ̄ⲓ̄ⲏ̄ⲗ̄.
(33) ⲡⲉ4ⲉⲓⲱⲧ ⲇⲉ ⲙⲛ̄ ⲧⲉ4ⲙⲁⲁⲩ ⲛⲉⲩⲣ̄-ⲱⲡⲏⲣⲉ ⲡⲉ ⲉⲭⲛ̄ ⲛⲉⲧⲟⲩⲭⲱ
ⲙ̄ⲙⲟⲟⲩ ⲉⲧⲃⲏⲏⲧ4. (34) ⲁ-ⲥⲩⲙⲉⲱⲛ ⲇⲉ ⲥⲙⲟⲩ ⲉⲣⲟⲟⲩ, ⲡⲉⲭⲁ4 ⲙ̄ ⲙⲁⲣⲓⲁ
ⲧⲉ4ⲙⲁⲁⲩ ⲭⲉ

ⲉⲓⲥ ⲡⲁⲓ ⲕⲏ ⲉⲩ2ⲉ ⲙⲛ̄ ⲟⲩⲧⲱⲟⲩⲛ ⲛ̄ 2ⲁ2 2ⲙ̄ ⲡ̄ⲓ̄ⲏ̄ⲗ̄, ⲁⲩⲱ ⲟⲩⲙⲁⲉⲓⲛ
ⲉ ⲟⲩⲱ2ⲙ̄ 2ⲓⲱⲱ4. (35) ⲛ̄ⲧⲟ ⲇⲉ ⲟⲩⲛ̄-ⲟⲩⲥⲏ4ⲉ ⲛⲏⲩ ⲉⲃⲟⲗ 2ⲓⲧⲛ̄
ⲧⲟⲩⲯⲩⲭⲏ, ⲭⲉⲕⲁⲥ ⲉⲩⲉϭⲱⲗⲡ̄ ⲉⲃⲟⲗ ⲛ̄ϭⲓ ⲛ̄ⲙⲟⲕⲙⲉⲕ ⲛ̄ 2ⲁ2 ⲛ̄ 2ⲏⲧ.
(36) ⲛⲉ-ⲟⲩⲛ̄-ⲟⲩⲡⲣⲟⲫⲏⲧⲏⲥ ⲇⲉ ⲭⲉ ⲁⲛⲛⲁ ⲧⲱⲉⲉⲣⲉ ⲙ̄ ⲫⲁⲛⲟⲩⲏⲗ ⲧⲉ

---

23. ⲧ.ⲟⲟⲧⲉ womb.

24. ⲧⲉ.ⲑⲩⲥⲓⲁ (ἡ θυσία) sacrifice. ⲡ.ⲥⲟⲉⲓⲱ pair.
ⲧⲉ.ⲃⲣ̄ⲙ̄ⲡⲱⲁⲛ turtle-dove. ⲏ (ἤ) conj. or. ⲡ.ⲙⲁⲥ the young
of any animal.

28. ⲡ.2ⲁⲙⲏⲣ embrace, arms.

32. ⲡ.2ⲉⲑⲛⲟⲥ (τὸ ἔθνος) nation, people.

34. ⲟⲩⲱ2ⲙ̄ 2ⲓ to contradict, object to; note ⲟⲩⲱ2ⲙ̄ ⲟⲩⲃⲉ
in the same meaning.

36. The exact function of ⲧⲉ is not clear; it is not
required in the sentence as it stands. ⲧⲉ.ⲫⲩⲗⲏ (ἡ φυλή)
tribe, people, nation. ⲧ.ⲙⲛ̄ⲧⲣⲟⲟⲩⲛⲉ virginity; ⲡ.ⲣⲟⲟⲩⲛⲉ

ⲉⲃⲟⲗ ⲋⲛ̄ ⲧⲉⲫⲩⲗⲏ ⲛ̄ ⲁⲥⲏⲣ.   ⲧⲁⲓ ⲁⲉ ⲁⲥⲁⲓⲁⲓ ⲋⲛ̄ ⲋⲉⲛⲋⲟⲟⲩ ⲉ-ⲛⲁϣⲱⲟⲩ,

ⲉ-ⲁⲥⲣ̄-ⲥⲁϣϥⲉ ⲛ̄ ⲣⲟⲙⲡⲉ ⲙⲛ̄ ⲡⲉⲋⲁⲓ ϫⲓⲛ ⲧⲉⲥⲙⲛ̄ⲧⲣⲟⲟⲩⲛⲉ (37) ⲁⲩⲱ

ⲁⲥⲣ̄-ⲭⲏⲣⲁ ϣⲁⲛⲧⲥ̄ⲣ̄-ⲋⲙⲉⲛⲉⲧⲁϥⲧⲉ ⲛ̄ ⲣⲟⲙⲡⲉ.   ⲧⲁⲓ ⲁⲉ ⲙⲉⲥⲥⲛ̄-ⲡⲉⲣⲡⲉ

ⲉⲃⲟⲗ, ⲉⲥϣⲙ̄ϣⲉ ⲛ̄ ⲧⲉⲩϣⲏ ⲙⲛ̄ ⲡⲉ²ⲟⲟⲩ ²ⲛ̄ ⲋⲉⲛⲛⲏⲥⲧⲉⲓⲁ ⲙⲛ̄ ⲋⲉⲛⲥⲟⲡⲥ̄.

(38) ²ⲛ̄ ⲧⲉⲩⲛⲟⲩ ⲁⲉ ⲉⲧ ⲙ̄ⲙⲁⲩ ⲁⲥⲁ²ⲉⲣⲁⲧⲥ̄, ⲁⲥⲉ²²ⲟⲙⲟⲗⲟⲅⲉⲓ ⲙ̄

ⲡ̄ⲭⲟⲉⲓⲥ, ⲁⲩⲱ ⲛⲉⲥϣⲁϫⲉ ⲙⲛ̄ ⲟⲩⲟⲛ ⲛⲓⲙ ⲉⲧ 6ⲱϣⲧ̄ ⲉⲃⲟⲗ ²ⲏⲧϥ̄ ⲙ̄ ⲡⲥⲱⲧⲉ

ⲛ̄ ⲑⲓ̄ⲗⲏ̄ⲙ̄.   (39) ⲛ̄ⲧⲉⲣⲟⲩⲭⲱⲕ ⲁⲉ ⲉⲃⲟⲗ ⲛ̄6ⲓ ²ⲱⲃ ⲛⲓⲙ ⲕⲁⲧⲁ ⲡⲛⲟⲙⲟⲥ

ⲙ̄ ⲡ̄ⲭⲟⲉⲓⲥ, ⲁⲩⲕⲧⲟⲟⲩ ⲉ²ⲣⲁⲓ ⲉ ⲧⲅⲁⲗⲓⲗⲁⲓⲁ ⲉ ⲧⲉⲩⲡⲟⲗⲓⲥ ⲛⲁ²ⲁⲣⲉⲑ.

(40) ⲡϣⲏⲣⲉ ⲁⲉ ϣⲏⲙ ⲁϥⲁⲓⲁⲓ, ⲁⲩⲱ ⲛⲉϥ6ⲙ̄-6ⲟⲙ, ⲉϥⲙⲉ² ⲛ̄ ⲥⲟⲫⲓⲁ,

ⲉⲣⲉ-ⲧⲉⲭⲁⲣⲓⲥ ⲙ̄ ⲡⲛⲟⲩⲧⲉ ²ⲓϫⲱϥ.   (41) ⲛⲉⲣⲉ-ⲛⲉϥⲉⲓⲟⲧⲉ ⲁⲉ ⲃⲏⲕ ⲡⲉ

ⲧⲣ̄ⲣⲟⲙⲡⲉ ⲉ ⲑⲓ̄ⲗⲏ̄ⲙ̄ ⲙ̄ ⲡϣⲁ ⲙ̄ ⲡⲡⲁⲥⲭⲁ.   (42) ⲛ̄ⲧⲉⲣⲉϥⲣ̄-ⲙⲛ̄ⲧⲥⲛⲟⲟⲩⲥ ⲁⲉ

ⲛ̄ ⲣⲟⲙⲡⲉ, ⲉⲩⲛⲁⲃⲱⲕ ⲉ²ⲣⲁⲓ ⲕⲁⲧⲁ ⲡⲥⲱⲛⲧ̄ ⲙ̄ ⲡϣⲁ, (43) ⲁⲩⲱ

ⲛ̄ⲧⲉⲣⲟⲩⲭⲱⲕ ⲉⲃⲟⲗ ⲛ̄ ⲛⲉ²ⲟⲟⲩ, ⲉⲩⲛⲁⲕⲧⲟⲟⲩ, ⲁϥ6ⲱ ⲛ̄6ⲓ ⲡϣⲏⲣⲉ ϣⲏⲙ ⲓ̄ⲥ̄

²ⲛ̄ ⲑⲓ̄ⲗⲏ̄ⲙ̄.   ⲙ̄ⲡⲟⲩⲉⲓⲙⲉ ⲁⲉ ⲛ̄6ⲓ ⲛⲉϥⲉⲓⲟⲧⲉ, (44) ⲉⲩⲙⲉⲉⲩⲉ ϫⲉ ϥ²ⲛ̄

ⲧⲉ²ⲓⲏ ⲛ̄ⲙ̄ⲙⲁⲩ.   ⲛ̄ⲧⲉⲣⲟⲩⲣ̄-ⲟⲩ²ⲟⲟⲩ ⲁⲉ ⲙ̄ ⲙⲟⲟϣⲉ, ⲁⲩϣⲓⲛⲉ ⲛ̄ⲥⲱϥ ²ⲛ̄

ⲛⲉⲩⲥⲩⲅⲅⲉⲛⲏⲥ ⲙⲛ̄ ⲛⲉⲧ ⲥⲟⲟⲩⲛ̄ ⲙ̄ⲙⲟⲟⲩ.   (45) ⲁⲩⲱ ⲛ̄ⲧⲉⲣⲟⲩⲧⲙ̄²ⲉ ⲉⲣⲟϥ,

ⲁⲩⲕⲧⲟⲟⲩ ⲉ²ⲣⲁⲓ ⲉ ⲑⲓ̄ⲗⲏ̄ⲙ̄ ⲉⲩϣⲓⲛⲉ ⲛ̄ⲥⲱϥ.   (46) ⲁⲥϣⲱⲡⲉ ⲁⲉ ⲙⲛ̄ⲛⲥⲁ

ϣⲟⲙⲛ̄ⲧ ⲛ̄ ²ⲟⲟⲩ ⲁⲩ²ⲉ ⲉⲣⲟϥ ²ⲙ̄ ⲡⲉⲣⲡⲉ, ⲉϥ²ⲙⲟⲟⲥ ⲛ̄ ⲧⲙⲏⲧⲉ ⲛ̄ ⲛ̄ⲥⲁ²,

ⲉϥⲥⲱⲧⲙ̄ ⲉⲣⲟⲟⲩ, ⲉϥϫⲛⲟⲩ ⲙ̄ⲙⲟⲟⲩ.   (47) ⲁⲩⲣ̄-ϣⲡⲏⲣⲉ ⲁⲉ ⲧⲏⲣⲟⲩ ⲛ̄6ⲓ

---

virgin, virginity.

37. ⲥⲓⲛⲉ ⲥⲛ̄- ⲥⲁⲁⲧ⸗ to pass through, across; ⲥⲓⲛⲉ ⲙ̄ⲙⲟ⸗
ⲉⲃⲟⲗ to leave, pass out of.   ⲧ.ⲛⲏⲥⲧⲉⲓⲁ (ἡ νηστεία) fasting.

38. ⲉ²²ⲟⲙⲟⲗⲟⲅⲉⲓ (ἐξομολογέω) to confess, acknowledge.

40. ⲧ.ⲥⲟⲫⲓⲁ (ἡ σοφία) wisdom. ⲧⲉ.ⲭⲁⲣⲓⲥ (ἡ χάρις) grace.

41. ⲧⲣ̄ⲣⲟⲙⲡⲉ, ⲧⲛ̄ⲣⲟⲙⲡⲉ adv. yearly, annually.   ⲡ.ⲡⲁⲥⲭⲁ
(τὸ πάσχα) Passover.

42. ⲉⲩⲛⲁⲃⲱⲕ is difficult. If Circumstantial of Fut. I,
there is no main verb; if Fut. II, the tense is incorrect.
It appears to be due to a slavish rendering of the Gk.,
but fails to carry the construction into the next verse,
as the Gk. requires.

44. ⲣ̄-ⲟⲩ²ⲟⲟⲩ ⲙ̄ ⲙⲟⲟϣⲉ lit., to spend a walking-day, i.e.
to walk for a day.

ⲛⲉⲧ ⲥⲱⲧⲙ̄ ⲉⲣⲟϥ ⲉϫⲛ̄ ⲧⲉϥⲙⲛ̄ⲧⲥⲁⲃⲉ ⲙⲛ̄ ⲛⲉϥϭⲓⲛⲟⲩⲱⲱⲃ. (48) ⲁⲩⲛⲁⲩ
ⲇⲉ ⲉⲣⲟϥ, ⲁⲩⲣ̄-ϣⲡⲏⲣⲉ. ⲡⲉϫⲉ-ⲧⲉϥⲙⲁⲁⲩ ⲛⲁϥ ϫⲉ
ⲡⲁϣⲏⲣⲉ, ⲛ̄ⲧⲁⲕⲣ̄-ⲟⲩ ⲛⲁⲛ ⲍ ⲛⲁⲓ? ⲉⲓⲥ ⲍ̄ⲏⲏⲧⲉ ⲁⲛⲟⲕ ⲙⲛ̄
ⲡⲉⲕⲉⲓⲱⲧ ⲉⲛⲙⲟⲕⲍ̄ ⲛ̄ ⲍⲏⲧ ⲉⲛϣⲓⲛⲉ ⲛ̄ⲥⲱⲕ.
(49) ⲡⲉϫⲁϥ ⲇⲉ ⲛⲁⲩ ϫⲉ
ⲉⲧⲃⲉ ⲟⲩ ⲧⲉⲧⲛ̄ϣⲓⲛⲉ ⲛ̄ⲥⲱⲓ? ⲛ̄ⲧⲉⲧⲛ̄ⲥⲟⲟⲩⲛ̄ ⲁⲛ ϫⲉ ⲍⲁⲡⲥ̄ ⲉⲧⲣⲁϭⲱ
ⲍⲛ̄ ⲛⲁ-ⲡⲁⲉⲓⲱⲧ?
(50) ⲛ̄ⲧⲟⲟⲩ ⲇⲉ ⲙ̄ⲡⲟⲩⲉⲓⲙⲉ ⲉ ⲡϣⲁϫⲉ ⲛ̄ⲧⲁϥϫⲟⲟϥ ⲛⲁⲩ. (51) ⲁϥⲉⲓ ⲇⲉ
ⲉⲡⲉⲥⲏⲧ ⲛⲙ̄ⲙⲁⲩ ⲉⲍⲣⲁⲓ ⲉ ⲛⲁⲍⲁⲣⲉⲑ, ⲁⲩⲱ ⲛⲉϥⲥⲱⲧⲙ̄ ⲛ̄ⲥⲱⲟⲩ. ⲧⲉϥⲙⲁⲁⲩ
ⲇⲉ ⲛⲉⲥⲍⲁⲣⲉⲍ ⲉ ⲛⲉⲓϣⲁϫⲉ ⲧⲏⲣⲟⲩ ⲍⲙ̄ ⲡⲉⲥⲍⲏⲧ. (52) ⲓ̄ⲥ̄ ⲇⲉ
ⲛⲉϥⲡⲣⲟⲕⲟⲡⲧⲉⲓ ⲍⲛ̄ ⲧⲥⲟⲫⲓⲁ ⲙⲛ̄ ⲑⲏⲗⲓⲕⲓⲁ ⲙⲛ̄ ⲧⲉⲭⲁⲣⲓⲥ ⲛⲁⲍⲣⲙ̄ ⲡⲛⲟⲩⲧⲉ
ⲙⲛ̄ ⲛ̄ⲣⲱⲙⲉ.

Chapter III

(1) ⲍⲛ̄ ⲧⲥⲡ̄ⲙⲛ̄ⲧⲏ ⲇⲉ ⲛ̄ ⲑⲏⲅⲉⲙⲟⲛⲓⲁ ⲛ̄ ⲧⲓⲃⲓⲣⲓⲟⲥ ⲕⲁⲓⲥⲁⲣ, ⲉϥⲟ ⲛ̄
ⲍⲏⲅⲉⲙⲱⲛ ⲉϫⲛ̄ ϯⲟⲩⲇⲁⲓⲁ ⲛ̄ϭⲓ ⲡⲟⲛⲧⲓⲟⲥ ⲡⲓⲗⲁⲧⲟⲥ, ⲉⲣⲉ-ⲍⲏⲣⲱⲇⲏⲥ ⲟ ⲛ̄
ⲧⲉⲧⲣⲁⲁⲣⲭⲏⲥ ⲉϫⲛ̄ ⲧⲅⲁⲗⲓⲗⲁⲓⲁ, ⲉⲣⲉ-ⲫⲓⲗⲓⲡⲡⲟⲥ ⲡⲉϥⲥⲟⲛ ⲡⲧⲉⲧⲣⲁⲁⲣⲭⲏⲥ
ⲉϫⲛ̄ ⲓⲇⲟⲩⲣⲁⲓⲁ ⲙⲛ̄ ⲧⲧⲣⲁⲭⲱⲛⲓⲧⲓⲥ ⲛ̄ ⲭⲱⲣⲁ ⲙⲛ̄ ⲗⲩⲥⲁⲛⲓⲁⲥ ⲡⲧⲉⲧⲣⲁⲁⲣⲭⲏⲥ
ⲉϫⲛ̄ ⲧⲁⲃⲓⲗⲏⲛⲏ, (2) ⲉⲣⲉ-ⲁⲛⲛⲁⲥ ⲡⲁⲣⲭⲓⲉⲣⲉⲩⲥ ⲡⲉ ⲙⲛ̄ ⲕⲁⲓⲫⲁⲥ,
ⲁ-ⲡϣⲁϫⲉ ⲙ̄ ⲡⲛⲟⲩⲧⲉ ϣⲱⲡⲉ ϣⲁ ⲓⲱⲍⲁⲛⲛⲏⲥ ⲡϣⲏⲣⲉ ⲛ̄ ⲍⲁⲭⲁⲣⲓⲁⲥ ⲍⲁⲧⲉ
ⲧⲉⲣⲏⲙⲟⲥ. (3) ⲁϥⲉⲓ ⲉⲍⲣⲁⲓ ⲉ ⲧⲡⲉⲣⲓⲭⲟⲣⲟⲥ ⲧⲏⲣⲥ̄ ⲙ̄ ⲡⲓⲟⲣⲇⲁⲛⲏⲥ

---

48. ⲍⲓ ⲛⲁⲓ adv. in this way, thus.

52. ⲡⲣⲟⲕⲟⲡⲧⲉⲓ (προκόπτω) to progress, advance. ⲑⲏⲗⲓⲕⲓⲁ
(ἡ ἡλικία) age, time of life.

1. ⲥⲡ̄- or ⲥⲉⲡ-, proclitic form of a f. noun meaning
year in date formulas: ⲧⲥⲡ̄-ⲙⲛ̄ⲧⲏ the fifteenth year.
ⲑⲏⲅⲉⲙⲟⲛⲓⲁ (ἡ ἡγεμονία) rule, administration. ⲡ.ⲧⲉⲧⲣⲁⲁⲣⲭⲏⲥ
(ὁ τετράρχης) tetrarch, petty prince. The circumstantial
clauses ⲉⲣⲉ-ⲫⲓⲗⲓⲡⲡⲟⲥ ... and ⲉⲣⲉ-ⲁⲛⲛⲁⲥ ... are not
grammatically correct as they stand.

2. ⲍⲁⲧⲉ, ⲍⲁⲧⲛ̄ ⲍⲁⲧⲟⲟⲧ⸗ prep. near, by, with; a synonym
of ⲍⲁⲍⲧⲛ̄, with which it is virtually interchangeable.

3. ⲕⲩⲣⲓⲥⲥⲁⲓ (κηρύσσω) to announce, proclaim.

ⲉϥⲕⲩⲣⲓⲥⲥⲁⲓ ⲙ̄ ⲡⲃⲁⲡⲧⲓⲥⲙⲁ ⲙ̄ ⲙⲉⲧⲁⲛⲟⲓⲁ ⲛ̄ ⲕⲁ-ⲛⲟⲃⲉ ⲉⲃⲟⲗ, (4) ⲛ̄
ⲑⲉ ⲉⲧ ⲥⲏⲋ ⲋⲓ ⲡⲭⲱⲱⲙⲉ ⲛ̄ ⲛ̄ϣⲁϫⲉ ⲛ̄ ⲏⲥⲁⲓⲁⲥ ⲡⲉⲡⲣⲟⲫⲏⲧⲏⲥ ϫⲉ
ⲧⲉⲥⲙⲏ ⲙ̄ ⲡⲉⲧ ⲱϣ ⲉⲃⲟⲗ ϩⲛ̄ ⲧⲉⲣⲏⲙⲟⲥ ϫⲉ ⲥⲃ̄ⲧⲉ-ⲧⲉϩⲓⲏ ⲙ̄
ⲡⲭⲟⲉⲓⲥ; ⲥⲟⲟⲩⲧⲛ̄ ⲛ̄ ⲛⲉϥⲙⲁ ⲙ̄ ⲙⲟⲟϣⲉ. (5) ⲉⲓⲁ ⲛⲓⲙ ⲛⲁⲙⲟⲩϩ,
ⲛ̄ⲧⲉ-ⲧⲟⲟⲩ ⲛⲓⲙ ϩⲓ ⲥⲓⲃⲧ̄ ⲛⲓⲙ ⲑⲃ̄ⲃⲓⲟ; ⲁⲩⲱ ⲛⲉⲧ ϭⲟⲟⲙⲉ ⲛⲁϣⲱⲡⲉ
ⲉⲩⲥⲟⲩⲧⲱⲛ ⲙⲛ̄ ⲛⲉⲧ ⲛⲁϣⲧ̄ ⲉ ϩⲉⲛϩⲓⲟⲟⲩⲉ ⲉⲩⲥⲗⲉϭⲗⲱϭ. (6) ⲁⲩⲱ
ⲡⲉⲟⲟⲩ ⲙ̄ ⲡⲭⲟⲉⲓⲥ ⲛⲁⲟⲩⲱⲛϩ̄ ⲉⲃⲟⲗ, ⲛ̄ⲧⲉ-ⲥⲁⲣⲝ̄ ⲛⲓⲙ ⲛⲁⲩ ⲉ
ⲡⲟⲩϫⲁⲓ ⲙ̄ ⲡⲛⲟⲩⲧⲉ.

(7) ⲛⲉϥϫⲱ ϭⲉ ⲙ̄ⲙⲟⲥ ⲡⲉ ⲛ ⲙ̄ⲙⲏⲛϣⲉ ⲉⲧ ⲛⲏⲩ ⲉⲃⲟⲗ ⲉ ⲃⲁⲡⲧⲓⲍⲉ ⲉⲃⲟⲗ
ϩⲓⲧⲟⲟⲧϥ̄ ϫⲉ

ⲛⲉϫⲡⲟ ⲛ̄ ⲛⲉϩϥⲱ, ⲛⲓⲙ ⲡⲉⲛⲧⲁϥⲧⲁⲙⲱⲧⲛ̄ ⲉ ⲡⲱⲧ ⲉⲃⲟⲗ ϩⲏⲧⲥ̄ ⲛ̄
ⲧⲟⲣⲅⲏ ⲉⲧ ⲛⲏⲩ? (8) ⲁⲣⲓ-ϩⲉⲛⲕⲁⲣⲡⲟⲥ ⲇⲉ ⲉⲩⲙ̄ⲡϣⲁ ⲛ̄ ⲧⲙⲉⲧⲁⲛⲟⲓⲁ,
ⲛ̄ⲧⲉⲧⲛ̄ⲧⲙ̄ⲁⲣⲭⲉⲓ ⲛ̄ ϫⲟⲟⲥ ϫⲉ ⲟⲩⲛ̄ⲧⲁⲛ ⲡⲉⲛⲉⲓⲱⲧ ⲁⲃⲣⲁϩⲁⲙ. †ϫⲱ
ⲙ̄ⲙⲟⲥ ⲛⲏⲧⲛ̄ ϫⲉ ⲟⲩⲛ̄-ϭⲟⲙ ⲙ̄ ⲡⲛⲟⲩⲧⲉ ⲉ ⲧⲟⲩⲛⲉⲥ-ϩⲉⲛϣⲏⲣⲉ ⲛ̄
ⲁⲃⲣⲁϩⲁⲙ ⲉⲃⲟⲗ ϩⲛ̄ ⲛⲉⲓⲱⲛⲉ. (9) ϫⲓⲛ ⲧⲉⲛⲟⲩ ⲡⲕⲉⲗⲉⲃⲓⲛ ⲕⲏ ϩⲁ
ⲧⲛⲟⲩⲛⲉ ⲛ̄ ⲛ̄ϣⲏⲛ. ϣⲏⲛ ⲛⲓⲙ ⲉⲧⲉ ⲛ̄ϥⲛⲁ†-ⲕⲁⲣⲡⲟⲥ ⲁⲛ ⲉ-ⲛⲁⲛⲟⲩϥ
ⲥⲉⲛⲁⲕⲟⲟⲣⲉϥ ⲛ̄ⲥⲉⲛⲟϫϥ̄ ⲉ ⲡⲕⲱϩⲧ̄.

(10) ⲁ-ⲙ̄ⲙⲏⲛϣⲉ ⲇⲉ ϫⲛⲟⲩϥ, ⲉⲩϫⲱ ⲙ̄ⲙⲟⲥ ϫⲉ
ⲟⲩ ϭⲉ ⲡⲉⲧⲛ̄ⲛⲁⲁⲁϥ ϫⲉ ⲉⲛⲉⲟⲩϫⲁⲓ?

(11) ⲁϥⲟⲩⲱϣⲃ̄, ⲉϥϫⲱ ⲙ̄ⲙⲟⲥ ⲛⲁⲩ ϫⲉ
ⲡⲉⲧⲉ ⲟⲩⲛ̄ⲧϥ̄-ϣⲧⲏⲛ ⲥⲛ̄ⲧⲉ ⲙⲁⲣⲉϥ†-ⲟⲩⲉⲓ ⲙ̄ ⲡⲉⲧⲉ ⲙⲛ̄ⲧⲁϥ, ⲁⲩⲱ
ⲡⲉⲧⲉ ⲟⲩⲛ̄ⲧϥ̄-ⲟⲉⲓⲕ ⲙⲁⲣⲉϥⲉⲓⲣⲉ ⲟⲛ ϩⲓ ⲛⲁⲓ.

(12) ⲁ-ϩⲉⲛⲕⲉⲧⲉⲗⲱⲛⲏⲥ ⲇⲉ ⲉⲓ ⲉ ϫⲓ-ⲃⲁⲡⲧⲓⲥⲙⲁ ⲉⲃⲟⲗ ϩⲓⲧⲟⲟⲧϥ̄.

---

4. ⲱϣ ⲉϣ- ⲟϣ⁼ ⲉⲃⲟⲗ to cry out; to read, recite.

5. ⲡ.ⲉⲓⲁ valley, ravine. ⲧ.ⲥⲓⲃⲧ̄ hill. ϭⲟⲟⲙⲉ Q of
ϭⲱⲱⲙⲉ to twist, pervert (ⲙ̄ⲙⲟ⁼); intr. to become crooked,
twisted. ⲥⲗⲉϭⲗⲱϭ Q of ⲥⲗⲟϭⲗ̄ϭ̄ to make smooth; intr. to
become smooth.

7. ⲃⲁⲡⲧⲓⲍⲉ (βαπτίζω) to baptise; note active form with
passive meaning. ϩⲟϥ (f. ϩϥⲱ; pl. ϩⲃⲟⲩⲓ) n.m. snake,
serpent. ⲧ.ⲟⲣⲅⲏ (ἡ ὀργή) wrath.

9. ⲡ.ⲕⲉⲗⲉⲃⲓⲛ axe. ⲧ.ⲛⲟⲩⲛⲉ root. ⲕⲱⲱⲣⲉ ⲕⲉⲉⲣⲉ- ⲕⲟⲟⲣ⁼
to cut down.

12. ⲡ.ⲧⲉⲗⲱⲛⲏⲥ (ὁ τελώνης) tax-collector.

пєхⲁⲩ ⲛⲁϥ ϫє

ⲡⲥⲁ2, єⲛⲛⲁⲣ̄-ⲟⲩ?

(13) ⲛ̄ⲧⲟϥ ⲁє пєхⲁϥ ⲛⲁⲩ ϫє

ⲙ̄ⲡⲣ̄ⲣ̄-ⲗⲁⲁⲩ ⲛ̄ 2ⲟⲩⲟ ⲡⲁⲣⲁ пєⲛⲧⲁⲩⲧⲟϣϥ̄ ⲛ̄ⲏⲧⲛ̄.

(14) ⲁⲩϫⲛⲟⲩϥ ⲁє ⲛ̄ϭⲓ ⲛєⲧ ⲟ ⲙ̄ ⲙⲁⲧⲟⲓ ϫє

єⲛⲛⲁⲣ̄-ⲟⲩ 2ⲱⲱⲛ ⲟⲛ?

пєхⲁϥ ⲛⲁⲩ ϫє

ⲙ̄ⲡⲣ̄ⲧⲧє-ⲗⲁⲁⲩ ⲟⲥє, ⲁⲩⲱ ⲙ̄ⲡⲣ̄2ⲓ-ⲗⲁ є ⲗⲁⲁⲩ, ⲛ̄ⲧєⲧⲛ̄2ⲱ єⲣⲱⲧⲛ̄

є ⲛєⲧⲛ̄ⲟⲯⲱⲛⲓⲟⲛ.

(15) єⲣє-ⲡⲗⲁⲟⲥ 6ⲱϣⲧ̄ єⲃⲟⲗ, єⲩⲙєєⲩє ⲧⲏⲣⲟⲩ 2ⲛ̄ ⲛєⲩ2ⲏⲧ єⲧⲃє

ⲓⲱ2ⲁⲛⲛⲏⲥ ϫє ⲙєϣⲁⲕ ⲛ̄ⲧⲟϥ пє пєⲭ̄ⲥ̄, (16) ⲁ-ⲓⲱ2ⲁⲛⲛⲏⲥ ⲟⲩⲱϣⲃ̄,

єϥϫⲱ ⲙ̄ⲙⲟⲥ ⲛ̄ ⲟⲩⲟⲛ ⲛⲓⲙ ϫє

ⲁⲛⲟⲕ ⲙєⲛ єⲓⲃⲁⲡⲧⲓⲍє ⲙ̄ⲙⲱⲧⲛ̄ 2ⲛ̄ ⲟⲩⲙⲟⲟⲩ. ϥⲛⲏⲩ ⲁє ⲛ̄ϭⲓ пєⲧ

ϫⲟⲟⲣ єⲣⲟⲓ, ⲡⲁⲓ є-ⲛ̄ϯⲙ̄ⲡϣⲁ ⲁⲛ ⲛ̄ ⲃⲱⲗ єⲃⲟⲗ ⲙ̄ ⲡⲙⲟⲩⲥ ⲙ̄

пєϥⲧⲟⲟⲩє. ⲛ̄ⲧⲟϥ пєⲧ ⲛⲁⲃⲁⲡⲧⲓⲍє ⲙ̄ⲙⲱⲧⲛ̄ 2ⲛ̄ ⲟⲩⲡ̄ⲛ̄ⲁ̄ єϥⲟⲩⲁⲁⲃ

ⲙⲛ̄ ⲟⲩⲕⲱ2ⲧ̄, (17) ⲡⲁⲓ єⲧєⲣє-пєϥ2ⲁ 2ⲛ̄ ⲧєϥ6ⲓϫ є ⲧⲃ̄ⲃⲟ ⲙ̄

пєϥϫⲛⲟⲟⲩ, є ⲥⲱⲟⲩ2 є2ⲟⲩⲛ ⲙ̄ пєϥⲥⲟⲩⲟ є ⲧєϥⲁⲡⲟⲑⲏⲕⲏ. ⲡⲧⲱ2

ⲁє ϥⲛⲁⲣⲟⲕ2ϥ̄ 2ⲛ̄ ⲟⲩⲥⲁⲧє є-ⲙєⲥⲱϣⲙ̄.

(18) 2ⲛ̄ 2єⲛⲕєϣⲁϫє ⲁє є-ⲛⲁϣⲱⲟⲩ ⲛєϥⲡⲁⲣⲁⲕⲁⲗєⲓ ⲙ̄ⲙⲟⲟⲩ,

єϥⲧⲁϣє-ⲟєⲓϣ ⲙ̄ ⲡⲗⲁⲟⲥ. (19) 2ⲏⲣⲱⲁⲏⲥ ⲁє ⲡⲧєⲧⲣⲁⲁⲣⲭⲏⲥ, єⲩϫⲡⲓⲟ

---

13. ⲧⲱϣ ⲧєϣ- ⲧⲟϣ⸗ Q ⲧⲏϣ to bound, limit, determine, fix (ⲙ̄ⲙⲟ⸗).

14. ⲧⲧⲟ ⲧⲧє- ⲧⲧⲟ⸗ to make (someone: first object) give (second object). ⲡ.ⲟⲥє fine; loss, damage; ⲧⲧє-ⲗⲁⲁⲩ ⲟⲥє to force payment out of someone. ⲡ.ⲗⲁ slander; 2ⲓ-ⲗⲁ to slander (є). 2ⲱ є to be satisfied with; used with ethical dative єⲣⲟ⸗ (§30.6). ⲡ.ⲟⲯⲱⲛⲓⲟⲛ (τὸ ὀψώνιον) wages.

16. ϫⲟⲟⲣ Q of ϫⲱⲱⲣє to become strong, powerful. ⲡ.ⲙⲟⲩⲥ strap, band. ⲡ.ⲧⲟⲟⲩє shoe, sandal.

17. ⲡ.2ⲁ winnowing fan. ⲡє.ϫⲛⲟⲟⲩ threshing-floor. ⲡ.ⲧⲱ2 chaff. ⲧ.ⲥⲁⲧє fire. ⲱϣⲙ̄ єϣⲙ̄- ⲟϣⲙ⸗ Q ⲟϣⲙ̄ to quench (ⲙ̄ⲙⲟ⸗); intr. to become quenched.

18. ⲡⲁⲣⲁⲕⲁⲗєⲓ (παρακαλέω) to exhort (ⲙ̄ⲙⲟ⸗).

19. ⲧ.2ⲓⲙє wife.

ⲘⲘⲟϥ ⲉⲃⲟⲗ ϩⲓⲧⲟⲟⲧϥ ⲉⲧⲃⲉ ϩⲏⲣⲱⲇⲓⲁⲥ, ⲑⲓⲙⲉ Ⲙ̄ ⲡⲉϥⲥⲟⲛ ⲁⲩⲱ ⲉⲧⲃⲉ
ϩⲱⲃ ⲛⲓⲙ Ⲙ̄ ⲡⲟⲛⲏⲣⲟⲛ ⲉⲛⲧⲁ-ϩⲏⲣⲱⲇⲏⲥ ⲁⲗⲩ, (20) ⲁϥⲟⲩⲉϩ-ⲡⲉⲓⲕⲉ ⲉ-Ⲭ̄Ⲛ̄
ⲛⲉϥⲕⲟⲟⲩⲉ ⲧⲏⲣⲟⲩ: ⲁϥⲉⲧⲡ̄-ⲓⲱϩⲁⲛⲛⲏⲥ ⲉϩⲟⲩⲛ ⲉ ⲡⲱⲧⲉⲕⲟ. (21) ⲁⲥϣⲱⲡⲉ
ⲇⲉ ϩⲙ̄ ⲡⲧⲣⲉ-ⲡⲁⲗⲟⲥ ⲧⲏⲣϥ ϫⲓ-ⲃⲁⲡⲧⲓⲥⲙⲁ ⲁⲩⲱ Ⲛ̄ⲧⲉⲣⲉ-Ⲓ̄Ⲥ̄ ϫⲓ, ⲁϥϣⲗⲏⲗ,
ⲁ-ⲧⲡⲉ ⲟⲩⲱⲛ. (22) ⲁ-ⲡⲉⲡⲛ̄ⲁ̄ ⲉⲧ ⲟⲩⲁⲁⲃ ⲉⲓ ⲉⲡⲉⲥⲏⲧ ⲉ-Ⲭ̄ⲱ̄ϥ ϩⲛ̄
ⲟⲩⲥⲙⲟⲧ Ⲛ̄ ⲥⲱⲙⲁ Ⲛ̄ ⲑⲉ Ⲛ̄ ⲟⲩϭⲣⲟⲟⲙⲡⲉ, ⲁⲩⲱ ⲁⲩⲥⲙⲏ ϣⲱⲡⲉ ⲉⲃⲟⲗ ϩⲛ̄
ⲧⲡⲉ ϫⲉ

    Ⲛ̄ⲧⲟⲕ ⲡⲉ ⲡⲁϣⲏⲣⲉ, ⲡⲁⲙⲉⲣⲓⲧ. Ⲛ̄ⲧⲁⲓⲟⲩⲱϣ Ⲛ̄ϩⲏⲧ-Ⲕ̄.

The remainder of Chap. III is genealogy and has been
omitted.

Chapter IV

(1) Ⲓ̄Ⲥ̄ ⲇⲉ ⲉϥϫⲏⲕ ⲉⲃⲟⲗ Ⲙ̄ ⲡⲡⲛ̄ⲁ̄ ⲉϥⲟⲩⲁⲁⲃ, ⲁϥⲕⲟⲧϥ ⲉⲃⲟⲗ ϩⲙ̄
ⲡⲓⲟⲣⲇⲁⲛⲏⲥ, ⲉϥⲙⲟⲟϣⲉ ϩⲙ̄ ⲡⲉⲡⲛ̄ⲁ̄ ϩⲓ ⲧⲉⲣⲏⲙⲟⲥ (2) Ⲛ̄ ϩⲙⲉ Ⲛ̄ ϩⲟⲟⲩ,
ⲉⲩⲡⲉⲓⲣⲁⲍⲉ Ⲙ̄ⲙⲟϥ ϩⲓⲧⲙ̄ ⲡⲁⲓⲁⲃⲟⲗⲟⲥ, ⲁⲩⲱ Ⲙ̄ⲡϥⲟⲩⲉⲙ-ⲗⲁⲁⲩ ϩⲛ̄ ⲛⲉϩⲟⲟⲩ
ⲉⲧ Ⲙ̄ⲙⲁⲩ. Ⲛ̄ⲧⲉⲣⲟⲩϫⲱⲕ ⲇⲉ ⲉⲃⲟⲗ, ⲁϥϩⲕⲟ. (3) ⲡⲉϫⲉ-ⲡⲁⲓⲁⲃⲟⲗⲟⲥ ⲛⲁϥ ϫⲉ
    ⲉϣϫⲉ Ⲛ̄ⲧⲟⲕ ⲡⲉ ⲡϣⲏⲣⲉ Ⲙ̄ ⲡⲛⲟⲩⲧⲉ, ⲁϫⲓⲥ Ⲙ̄ ⲡⲉⲓⲱⲛⲉ ϫⲉ
    ⲉϥⲉⲣ̄-ⲟⲉⲓⲕ.

(4) ⲁϥⲟⲩⲱϣⲃ̄ ⲛⲁϥ Ⲛ̄ϭⲓ Ⲓ̄Ⲥ̄ ϫⲉ
    ϥⲥⲏϩ ϫⲉ ⲉⲣⲉ-ⲡⲣⲱⲙⲉ ⲛⲁⲱⲛϩ̄ ⲁⲛ ⲉ ⲡⲟⲉⲓⲕ Ⲙ̄ⲙⲁⲧⲉ.

(5) ⲁϥϫⲓⲧϥ ⲇⲉ ⲉϩⲣⲁⲓ, ⲁϥⲧⲟⲩⲟϥ ⲉ Ⲙ̄ⲙⲛ̄ⲧⲉⲣⲱⲟⲩ ⲧⲏⲣⲟⲩ Ⲛ̄
ⲧⲟⲓⲕⲟⲩⲙⲉⲛⲏ ϩⲛ̄ ⲟⲩⲥⲧⲓⲅⲙⲏ Ⲛ̄ ⲟⲩⲟⲉⲓϣ. (6) ⲡⲉϫⲉ-ⲡⲁⲓⲁⲃⲟⲗⲟⲥ ⲇⲉ
ⲛⲁϥ ϫⲉ
    ✝✝ ⲛⲁⲕ Ⲛ̄ ⲧⲉⲓⲉϩⲟⲩⲥⲓⲁ ⲧⲏⲣⲥ̄ ⲘⲚ̄ ⲡⲉⲩϭⲟⲟⲩ, ϫⲉ Ⲛ̄ⲧⲁⲩⲧⲁⲁⲥ ⲛⲁⲓ,
ⲁⲩⲱ ϣⲁⲓⲧⲁⲁⲥ Ⲙ̄ ⲡⲉϯⲟⲩⲁϣϥ. (7) Ⲛ̄ⲧⲟⲕ ϭⲉ ⲉⲕϣⲁⲛⲟⲩⲱϣⲧ̄ Ⲙ̄
ⲡⲁⲙ̄ⲧⲟ ⲉⲃⲟⲗ, ⲥⲛⲁϣⲱⲡⲉ ⲛⲁⲕ ⲧⲏⲣⲥ̄.

---

20. ⲱⲧⲡ̄ ⲉⲧⲡ̄- ⲟⲧⲡ⸗ Q ⲟⲧⲡ̄ (± ⲉϩⲟⲩⲛ) to imprison, enclose,
shut in (Ⲙ̄ⲙⲟ⸗).

22. Ⲛ̄ⲧⲁⲓⲟⲩⲱϣ is Perf. II since this is an independent
clause.

5. ⲧⲟⲩⲟ ⲧⲟⲩⲟ⸗ to show, teach (someone: Ⲙ̄ⲙⲟ⸗; something: ⲉ). ⲧⲉ.ⲥⲧⲓⲅⲙⲏ (ἡ στιγμή) moment.

7. ⲟⲩⲱϣⲧ̄ to worship, greet, kiss (Ⲙ̄ⲙⲟ⸗, ⲛⲁ⸗).

(8) ⲁ-ⲓ̅ⲥ̅ ⲟⲩⲱϣⲃ̅, ⲡⲉⲭⲁϥ ⲛⲁϥ ϫⲉ

ϥⲥⲏ₂ ϫⲉ ⲉⲕⲛⲁⲟⲩⲱϣⲧ̅ ⲙ̅ ⲡⲭⲟⲉⲓⲥ ⲡⲉⲕⲛⲟⲩⲧⲉ, ⲁⲩⲱ ⲉⲕⲛⲁϣⲙ̅ϣⲉ ⲛⲁϥ

ⲟⲩⲁⲁϥ.

(9) ⲁϥⲛ̅ⲧϥ̅ ⲁⲉ ⲉ ⲑⲓⲉⲣⲟⲩⲥⲁⲗⲏⲙ, ⲁϥⲧⲁϩⲟϥ ⲉⲣⲁⲧϥ̅ ϩⲓϫⲙ̅ ⲡⲧⲛ̅₂ ⲙ̅

ⲡⲉⲣⲡⲉ, ⲡⲉⲭⲁϥ ⲛⲁϥ ϫⲉ

ⲉϣϫⲉ ⲛ̅ⲧⲟⲕ ⲡⲉ ⲡϣⲏⲣⲉ ⲙ̅ ⲡⲛⲟⲩⲧⲉ, ϥⲟϭⲕ̅ ⲉⲡⲉⲥⲏⲧ ϩⲓϫⲙ̅ ⲡⲉⲓⲙⲁ,

(10) ϥⲥⲏ₂ ⲅⲁⲣ ϫⲉ ϥⲛⲁϩⲱⲛ ⲉⲧⲟⲟⲧⲟⲩ ⲛ̅ ⲛⲉϥⲁⲅⲅⲉⲗⲟⲥ ⲉⲧⲃⲏⲏⲧⲕ̅

ⲉⲧⲣⲉⲩϩⲁⲣⲉϩ ⲉⲣⲟⲕ. (11) ⲁⲩⲱ ⲥⲉⲛⲁϥⲓⲧⲕ̅ ⲉϫⲛ̅ ⲛⲉⲩϭⲓϫ, ⲙⲏⲡⲟⲧⲉ

ⲛⲅ̅ϫⲱⲣⲡ̅ ⲉⲩⲱⲛⲉ ⲛ̅ ⲧⲉⲕⲟⲩⲉⲣⲏⲧⲉ.

(12) ⲁ-ⲓ̅ⲥ̅ ⲁⲉ ⲟⲩⲱϣⲃ̅, ⲡⲉⲭⲁϥ ⲛⲁϥ ϫⲉ

ⲁⲩϫⲟⲟⲥ ϫⲉ ⲛ̅ⲛⲉⲕⲡⲉⲓⲣⲁⲍⲉ ⲙ̅ ⲡⲭⲟⲉⲓⲥ ⲡⲉⲕⲛⲟⲩⲧⲉ.

(13) ⲛ̅ⲧⲉⲣⲉϥϫⲉⲕ-ⲡⲉⲓⲣⲁⲥⲙⲟⲥ ⲁⲉ ⲛⲓⲙ ⲉⲃⲟⲗ, ⲁ-ⲡⲁⲓⲁⲃⲟⲗⲟⲥ ⲥⲁϩⲱϥ

ⲉⲃⲟⲗ ⲙ̅ⲙⲟϥ ϣⲁ ⲟⲩⲟⲩⲟⲉⲓϣ. (14) ⲁⲩⲱ ⲁϥⲕⲧⲟϥ ⲛ̅ϭⲓ ⲓ̅ⲥ̅ ϩⲛ̅ ⲧϭⲟⲙ ⲙ̅

ⲡⲉⲡⲛ̅ⲁ̅ ⲉ ⲧⲅⲁⲗⲓⲗⲁⲓⲁ. ⲁ-ⲡⲥⲟⲉⲓⲧ ⲉⲓ ⲉⲃⲟⲗ ϩⲛ̅ ⲧⲡⲉⲣⲓⲭⲱⲣⲟⲥ ⲧⲏⲣⲥ̅

ⲉⲧⲃⲏⲏⲧϥ̅. (15) ⲛ̅ⲧⲟϥ ⲁⲉ ⲛⲉϥϯ-ⲥⲃⲱ ⲡⲉ ϩⲛ̅ ⲛⲉⲩⲥⲩⲛⲁⲅⲱⲅⲏ,

ⲉⲣⲉ-ⲣⲱⲙⲉ ⲛⲓⲙ ϯ-ⲉⲟⲟⲩ ⲛⲁϥ. (16) ⲁϥⲉⲓ ⲉϩⲣⲁⲓ ⲉ ⲛⲁⲍⲁⲣⲁ, ⲡⲙⲁ

ⲉⲛⲧⲁⲩⲥⲁⲛⲟⲩϣϥ̅ ⲛ̅ϩⲏⲧϥ̅, ⲁⲩⲱ ⲁϥⲃⲱⲕ ⲉϩⲟⲩⲛ ⲕⲁⲧⲁ ⲡⲉϥⲥⲱⲛⲧ̅ ϩⲛ̅

ⲛⲉϩⲟⲟⲩ ⲙ̅ ⲡⲥⲁⲃⲃⲁⲧⲟⲛ ⲉ ⲧⲥⲩⲛⲁⲅⲱⲅⲏ. ⲁϥⲧⲱⲟⲩⲛ ⲁⲉ ⲉ ⲱϣ. (17) ⲁⲩϯ

ⲛⲁϥ ⲙ̅ ⲡϫⲱⲱⲙⲉ ⲛ̅ ⲏⲥⲁⲓⲁⲥ ⲡⲉⲡⲣⲟⲫⲏⲧⲏⲥ. ⲁϥⲟⲩⲱⲛ ⲙ̅ ⲡϫⲱⲱⲙⲉ, ⲁϥϩⲉ ⲉ

ⲡⲙⲁ ⲉⲧ ⲥⲏ₂ (18) ϫⲉ

ⲡⲉⲡⲛ̅ⲁ̅ ⲙ̅ ⲡⲭⲟⲉⲓⲥ ⲉϩⲣⲁⲓ ⲉϫⲱⲓ. ⲉⲧⲃⲉ ⲡⲁⲓ ⲁϥⲧⲁϩⲥⲧ̅,

ⲁϥⲧⲛ̅ⲛⲟⲟⲩⲧ ⲉ ⲉⲩⲁⲅⲅⲉⲗⲓⲍⲉ ⲛ̅ ⲛ̅ϩⲏⲕⲉ, ⲉ ⲧⲁϣⲉ-ⲟⲉⲓϣ ⲛ̅ ⲟⲩⲕⲱ

ⲉⲃⲟⲗ ⲛ̅ ⲛⲁⲓⲭⲙⲁⲗⲱⲧⲟⲥ ⲙⲛ̅ ⲟⲩⲛⲁⲩ ⲉⲃⲟⲗ ⲛ̅ ⲛ̅ⲃⲗ̅ⲗⲉ, ⲉ ϫⲟⲟⲩ ⲛ̅ ⲛⲉⲧ

ⲟⲩⲟϣϥ̅ ϩⲛ̅ ⲟⲩⲕⲱ ⲉⲃⲟⲗ, (19) ⲉ ⲧⲁϣⲉ-ⲟⲉⲓϣ ⲛ̅ ⲧⲉⲣⲟⲙⲡⲉ ⲙ̅

ⲡⲭⲟⲉⲓⲥ ⲉⲧ ϣⲏⲡ.

---

8. ⲡ.ⲧⲛ̅₂ wing; wing of a building. ϥⲟϭⲉ ϥⲉϭ- ϥⲟϭ⸗

Q ϥⲏϭ to leap, move quickly; reflex. idem.

11. ϫⲱⲣⲡ̅ to stumble; tr. to strike (ⲙ̅ⲙⲟ⸗) against (ⲉ).

14. ⲡ.ⲥⲟⲉⲓⲧ fame, report.

16. ⲡ.ⲥⲁⲃⲃⲁⲧⲟⲛ (τὸ σάββατον) the sabbath.

18. ⲧⲱϩⲥ̅ ⲧⲉϩⲥ- ⲧⲁϩⲥ⸗ Q ⲧⲁϩⲥ̅ to anoint (ⲙ̅ⲙⲟ⸗; with: ϩⲛ̅,

ⲙ̅ⲙⲟ⸗). ⲡ.ⲁⲓⲭⲙⲁⲗⲱⲧⲟⲥ (ὁ αἰχμάλωτος) prisoner, captive.

ⲟⲩⲱϣϥ̅ ⲟⲩⲉϣϥ- ⲟⲩⲟϣϥ⸗ Q ⲟⲩⲟϣϥ̅ to wear down, destroy; also

intr. to be worn down, destroyed.

164

(20) ⲁϥⲕ̅ⲃ̅-ⲡⲭⲱⲱⲙⲉ ⲁⲉ, ⲁϥⲧⲁⲁϥ ⲙ̅ ⲡ₂ⲩⲡⲏⲣⲉⲧⲏⲥ, ⲁϥ₂ⲙⲟⲟⲥ.
ⲛⲉⲣⲉ-ⲛ̅ⲃⲁⲗ ⲛ̅ ⲟⲩⲟⲛ ⲛⲓⲙ ⲉⲧ ₂ⲛ̅ ⲧⲥⲩⲛⲁⲅⲱⲅⲏ 6ⲱϣⲧ̅ ⲉⲣⲟϥ.

(21) ⲁϥⲁⲣⲭⲉⲓ ⲁⲉ ⲛ̅ ⲭⲟⲟⲥ ⲛⲁⲩ ⲭⲉ
ⲙ̅ ⲡⲟⲟⲩ ⲁ-ⲧⲉⲓⲅⲣⲁⲫⲏ ⲭⲱⲕ ⲉⲃⲟⲗ ₂ⲛ̅ ⲛⲉⲧⲛ̅ⲙⲁⲁⲭⲉ.

(22) ⲁⲩⲱ ⲛⲉⲣⲉ-ⲟⲩⲟⲛ ⲛⲓⲙ ⲣ̅-ⲙⲛ̅ⲧⲣⲉ ⲛⲙ̅ⲙⲁϥ, ⲉⲩⲣ̅-ϣⲡⲏⲣⲉ ⲛ̅ ⲛ̅ϣⲁⲭⲉ ⲛ̅
ⲧⲉⲭⲁⲣⲓⲥ ⲉⲧ ⲛⲏⲩ ⲉⲃⲟⲗ ₂ⲛ̅ ⲣⲱϥ, ⲉⲩⲭⲱ ⲙ̅ⲙⲟⲥ ⲭⲉ
ⲙⲏ ⲙ̅ ⲡϣⲏⲣⲉ ⲛ̅ ⲓⲱⲥⲏⲫ ⲁⲛ ⲡⲉ ⲡⲁⲓ?

(23) ⲡⲉⲭⲁϥ ⲁⲉ ⲛⲁⲩ ⲭⲉ
ⲡⲁⲛⲧⲱⲥ ⲧⲉⲧⲛⲁⲭⲱ ⲛⲁⲓ ⲛ̅ ⲧⲉⲓⲡⲁⲣⲁⲃⲟⲗⲏ, ⲭⲉ ⲡⲥⲁⲉⲓⲛ,
ⲁⲣⲓ-ⲡⲁ₂ⲣⲉ ⲉⲣⲟⲕ. ⲛⲉⲛⲧⲁⲛⲥⲱⲧⲙ̅ ⲉⲣⲟⲟⲩ ⲭⲉ ⲁⲩϣⲱⲡⲉ ₂ⲛ̅
ⲕⲁⲫⲁⲣⲛⲁⲟⲩⲙ ⲁⲣⲓⲥⲟⲩ ₂ⲱⲟⲩ ₂ⲙ̅ ⲡⲉⲓⲙⲁ ₂ⲛ̅ ⲡⲉⲕ†ⲙⲉ.

(24) ⲡⲉⲭⲁϥ ⲁⲉ ⲭⲉ
₂ⲁⲙⲏⲛ †ⲭⲱ ⲙ̅ⲙⲟⲥ ⲛⲏⲧⲛ̅ ⲭⲉ ⲙ̅ⲙⲛ̅-ⲗⲁⲁⲩ ⲙ̅ ⲡⲣⲟⲫⲏⲧⲏⲥ ϣⲏⲡ ₂ⲙ̅
ⲡⲉϥ†ⲙⲉ ⲙ̅ⲙⲓⲛ ⲙ̅ⲙⲟϥ. (25) ₂ⲛ̅ ⲟⲩⲙⲉ ⲁⲉ †ⲭⲱ ⲙ̅ⲙⲟⲥ ⲛⲏⲧⲛ̅ ⲭⲉ
ⲛⲉⲩⲛ̅-₂ⲁ₂ ⲛ̅ ⲭⲏⲣⲁ ⲡⲉ ₂ⲙ̅ ⲡⲓ̅ⲏ̅ⲗ̅ ⲛ̅ ⲛⲉ₂ⲟⲟⲩ ⲛ̅ ₂ⲏⲗⲓⲁⲥ,
ⲛ̅ⲧⲉⲣⲉ-ⲧⲡⲉ ϣⲧⲁⲙ ⲛ̅ ϣⲟⲙⲧⲉ ⲛ̅ ⲣⲟⲙⲡⲉ ⲙⲛ̅ ⲥⲟⲟⲩ ⲛ̅ ⲉⲃⲟⲧ,
ⲛ̅ⲧⲉⲣⲉ-ⲟⲩⲛⲟ6 ⲛ̅ ₂ⲉ-ⲃⲱⲱⲛ ϣⲱⲡⲉ ₂ⲓⲭⲙ̅ ⲡⲕⲁ₂ ⲧⲏⲣϥ̅. (26) ⲁⲩⲱ
ⲙ̅ⲡⲟⲩⲭⲉⲩ-₂ⲏⲗⲓⲁⲥ ϣⲁ ⲗⲁⲁⲩ ⲙ̅ⲙⲟⲟⲩ ⲉⲓⲙⲏⲧⲓ ⲉ ⲥⲁⲣⲉⲡⲧⲁ ⲛ̅ⲧⲉ
ⲧⲥⲓⲁⲱⲛⲓⲁ, ϣⲁ ⲟⲩⲥ₂ⲓⲙⲉ ⲛ̅ ⲭⲏⲣⲁ. (27) ⲁⲩⲱ ⲛⲉⲩⲛ̅-₂ⲁ₂ ⲛ̅ ⲥⲟⲃⲉ̅
₂ⲙ̅ ⲡⲓ̅ⲏ̅ⲗ̅ ₂ⲓ ⲉⲗⲓⲥⲁⲓⲟⲥ ⲡⲉⲡⲣⲟⲫⲏⲧⲏⲥ, ⲁⲩⲱ ⲙ̅ⲡⲉ-ⲗⲁⲁⲩ ⲙ̅ⲙⲟⲟⲩ
ⲧⲃ̅ⲃⲟ ⲛ̅ⲥⲁ ⲛⲁⲓⲙⲁⲛ ⲡⲥⲩⲣⲟⲥ.

(28) ⲁⲩⲙⲟⲩ₂ ⲁⲉ ⲧⲏⲣⲟⲩ ⲛ̅ 6ⲱⲛⲧ̅ ₂ⲛ̅ ⲧⲥⲩⲛⲁⲅⲱⲅⲏ ⲉⲩⲥⲱⲧⲙ̅ ⲉ ⲛⲁⲓ.

---

20. ⲕⲱⲃ ⲕⲉⲃ-, ⲕⲃ̅- ⲕⲟⲃ⸗ Q ⲕⲏⲃ to make double; to fold
(ⲙ̅ⲙⲟ⸗).

22. ⲧⲉ.ⲭⲁⲣⲓⲥ (ἡ χάρις) grace, favor.

23. ⲡⲁⲛⲧⲱⲥ (πάντως) adv. wholly, altogether. ⲣ̅-ⲡⲁ₂ⲣⲉ
to heal (ⲉ); ⲡ.ⲡⲁ₂ⲣⲉ drug, medicament. Note reflex. ⲉⲣⲟⲕ.

24. ₂ⲁⲙⲏⲛ (ἀμήν) adv. indeed, verily.

25. ϣⲧⲁⲙ vb. tr. intr. to shut, close (ⲙ̅ⲙⲟ⸗); to close,
become sealed. ⲡ.₂ⲉ-ⲃⲱⲱⲛ famine, bad harvest; cpd. of ₂ⲉ
season, ⲃⲱⲱⲛ adj. bad.

27. ⲡ.ⲥⲟⲃⲉ̅ leper; ⲥⲱⲃⲉ̅, Q ⲥⲟⲃⲉ̅ to become leprous;
ⲡ.ⲥⲱⲃⲉ̅ leprosy. Note ₂ⲓ at the time of; ⲛ̅ⲥⲁ except for.

(29) ⲁⲩⲧⲱⲟⲩⲛ, ⲁⲩⲛⲟⲭ̄ϥ ⲉⲃⲟⲗ ⲡⲃⲟⲗ ⲛ̄ ⲧⲡⲟⲗⲓⲥ, ⲁⲩⲛ̄ⲧϥ̄ ϣⲁ ⲡⲕⲟⲟϩ ⲙ̄
ⲡⲧⲟⲟⲩ ⲉⲧⲉⲣⲉ-ⲧⲉⲩⲡⲟⲗⲓⲥ ⲕⲏⲧ ϩⲓⲭⲱϥ ϩⲱⲥⲧⲉ ⲉⲧⲣⲉⲩⲛⲟⲭϥ̄ ⲉⲃⲟⲗ
ⲛ̄ⲭⲟϥⲧⲛ̄. (30) ⲛ̄ⲧⲟϥ ⲇⲉ ⲁϥⲉⲓ ⲉⲃⲟⲗ ϩⲛ̄ ⲧⲉⲩⲙⲏⲧⲉ, ⲁϥⲃⲱⲕ.

(31) ⲁϥⲉⲓ ⲉⲡⲉⲥⲏⲧ ⲉ ⲕⲁⲫⲁⲣⲛⲁⲟⲩⲙ ⲧⲡⲟⲗⲓⲥ ⲛ̄ⲧⲉ ⲧⲅⲁⲗⲓⲗⲁⲓⲁ, ⲁⲩⲱ
ⲛⲉϥϯ-ⲥⲃⲱ ⲡⲉ ϩⲛ̄ ⲛ̄ⲥⲁⲃⲃⲁⲧⲟⲛ. (32) ⲁⲩⲣ̄-ϣⲡⲏⲣⲉ ⲇⲉ ⲧⲏⲣⲟⲩ ⲉϩⲣⲁⲓ
ⲉⲭⲛ̄ ⲧⲉϥⲥⲃⲱ, ϫⲉ ⲛⲉⲣⲉ-ⲡⲉϥϣⲁϫⲉ ϣⲟⲟⲡ ⲡⲉ ϩⲛ̄ ⲟⲩⲉϩⲟⲩⲥⲓⲁ. (33) ⲁⲩⲱ
ⲛⲉⲩⲛ̄-ⲟⲩⲣⲱⲙⲉ ⲡⲉ ϩⲛ̄ ⲧⲥⲩⲛⲁⲅⲱⲅⲏ ⲉⲣⲉ-ⲟⲩⲡⲛ̄ⲁ ⲛ̄ ⲇⲁⲓⲙⲟⲛⲓⲟⲛ ⲛ̄
ⲁⲕⲁⲑⲁⲣⲧⲟⲛ ⲛ̄ϩⲏⲧϥ̄. ⲁⲩⲱ ⲁϥϫⲓ-ϣⲕⲁⲕ ⲉⲃⲟⲗ ϩⲛ̄ ⲟⲩⲛⲟϭ ⲛ̄ ⲥⲙⲏ
(34) ϫⲉ

⳿ ⲁϩⲣⲟⲕ ⲛⲙ̄ⲙⲁⲛ, ⲓⲥ̄ ⲡⲣ̄ⲙⲛⲁⲍⲁⲣⲉⲑ? ⲁⲕⲉⲓ ⲉ ⲧⲁⲕⲟⲛ. ϯⲥⲟⲟⲩⲛ̄ ϫⲉ
ⲛ̄ⲧⲕ̄-ⲛⲓⲙ ⲛ̄ⲧⲕ̄, ⲡⲉⲧ ⲟⲩⲁⲁⲃ ⲙ̄ ⲡⲛⲟⲩⲧⲉ.

(35) ⲁ-ⲓⲥ̄ ⲇⲉ ⲉⲡⲓⲧⲓⲙⲁ ⲛⲁϥ, ⲉϥϫⲱ ⲙ̄ⲙⲟⲥ ϫⲉ
ⲧⲙ̄-ⲣⲱⲕ ⲛⲅ̄ⲉⲓ ⲉⲃⲟⲗ ⲛ̄ϩⲏⲧϥ̄.

ⲁϥⲛⲟⲩϫⲉ ⲙ̄ⲙⲟϥ ⲛ̄ϭⲓ ⲡⲇⲁⲓⲙⲟⲛⲓⲟⲛ ⲉ ⲧⲙⲏⲧⲉ, ⲁϥⲉⲓ ⲉⲃⲟⲗ ⲛ̄ϩⲏⲧϥ̄
ⲉ-ⲙⲡϥ̄ⲃⲗⲁⲡⲧⲉⲓ ⲙ̄ⲙⲟϥ ⲗⲁⲁⲩ. (36) ⲁⲩϣⲧⲟⲣⲧⲣ̄ ⲇⲉ ϣⲱⲡⲉ ⲉⲭⲛ̄ ⲟⲩⲟⲛ
ⲛⲓⲙ, ⲁⲩϣⲁϫⲉ ⲙⲛ̄ ⲛⲉⲩⲉⲣⲏⲩ, ⲉⲩϫⲱ ⲙ̄ⲙⲟⲥ ϫⲉ
ⲟⲩ ⲡⲉ ⲡⲉⲓϣⲁϫⲉ? ϫⲉ ϩⲛ̄ ⲟⲩⲉϩⲟⲩⲥⲓⲁ ⲙⲛ̄ ⲟⲩϭⲟⲙ ϥⲟⲩⲉϩ-ⲥⲁϩⲛⲉ
ⲛ̄ ⲛⲉⲡⲛ̄ⲁ̄ ⲛ̄ ⲁⲕⲁⲑⲁⲣⲧⲟⲛ, ⲥⲉⲛⲏⲩ ⲉⲃⲟⲗ.

(37) ⲁ-ⲡⲥⲟⲉⲓⲧ ⲇⲉ ⲙⲟⲟϣⲉ ⲉⲧⲃⲏⲏⲧϥ̄ ϩⲙ̄ ⲙⲁ ⲛⲓⲙ ⲛ̄ ⲧⲡⲉⲣⲓⲭⲱⲣⲟⲥ.
(38) ⲁϥⲧⲱⲟⲩⲛ ⲇⲉ ⲉⲃⲟⲗ ϩⲛ̄ ⲧⲥⲩⲛⲁⲅⲱⲅⲏ, ⲁϥⲃⲱⲕ ⲉϩⲟⲩⲛ ⲉ ⲡⲏⲓ ⲛ̄
ⲥⲓⲙⲱⲛ. ⲧϣⲱⲙⲉ ⲇⲉ ⲛ̄ ⲥⲓⲙⲱⲛ ⲛⲉⲩⲛ̄-ⲟⲩⲛⲟϭ ⲛ̄ ϩⲙⲟⲙ ϩⲓⲱⲱⲥ ⲡⲉ.
ⲁⲩⲥⲉⲡⲥⲱⲡϥ̄ ⲇⲉ ⲉⲧⲃⲏⲏⲧⲥ̄. (39) ⲁϥⲁϩⲉⲣⲁⲧϥ̄ ϩⲓϫⲱⲥ, ⲁϥⲉⲡⲓⲧⲓⲙⲁ ⲙ̄
ⲡⲉϩⲙⲟⲙ, ⲁϥⲕⲁⲁⲥ. ⲛ̄ ⲧⲉⲩⲛⲟⲩ ⲁⲥⲧⲱⲟⲩⲛ, ⲁⲥⲇⲓⲁⲕⲟⲛⲉⲓ ⲛⲁⲩ.

---

29. ⲡ.ⲕⲟⲟϩ angle, corner. ⲛ̄ⲭⲟϥⲧⲛ̄ adv. headlong.

33. ϫⲓ-ϣⲕⲁⲕ ⲉⲃⲟⲗ to cry out; ⲡⲉ.ϣⲕⲁⲕ cry, shout.

34. Note use of reduced form ⲛ̄ⲧⲕ̄ for ⲛ̄ⲧⲟⲕ.

35. ⲉⲡⲓⲧⲓⲙⲁ ⲛⲁ⳽ (ἐπιτιμάω) to rebuke, reprove. ⲃⲗⲁⲡⲧⲉⲓ
ⲙ̄ⲙⲟ⳽ (βλάπτω) to harm, injure.

36. ⲟⲩⲉϩ-ⲥⲁϩⲛⲉ to order, command (ⲛⲁ⳽; that: ⲉ, ⲉⲧⲣⲉ).

38. ⲧ.ϣⲱⲙⲉ mother-in-law; ⲡ.ϣⲟⲙ father-in-law. ϩⲙⲟⲙ,
Q ϩⲏⲙ to become hot; ⲡⲉ.ϩⲙⲟⲙ heat, fever.

39. ⲇⲓⲁⲕⲟⲛⲉⲓ ⲛⲁ⳽ (διακονέω) to wait on, serve.

(40) ⲉⲣⲉ-ⲡⲣⲏ ⲇⲉ ⲛⲁϩⲱⲧⲡ̄, ⲟⲩⲟⲛ ⲛⲓⲙ ⲉⲧⲉ ⲟⲩⲛ̄ⲧⲟⲩ-ⲣⲱⲙⲉ ⲉⲩϣⲱⲛⲉ
ϩⲛ̄ ϩⲉⲛϣⲱⲛⲉ ⲉⲩϣⲟⲃⲉ ⲁⲩⲛ̄ⲧⲟⲩ ⲛⲁϥ. ⲛ̄ⲧⲟϥ ⲇⲉ ⲁϥⲧⲁⲗⲉ-ⲧⲟⲟⲧϥ̄ ⲉϫⲙ̄
ⲡⲟⲩⲁ ⲡⲟⲩⲁ ⲙ̄ⲙⲟⲟⲩ, ⲁϥⲧⲁⲗϭⲟⲟⲩ. (41) ⲛⲉⲣⲉ-ⲛ̄ⲇⲁⲓⲙⲟⲛⲓⲟⲛ ⲇⲉ ⲛⲏⲩ
ⲉⲃⲟⲗ ϩⲛ̄ ϩⲁϩ ⲡⲉ, ⲉⲩϫⲓ-ϣⲕⲁⲕ ⲉⲃⲟⲗ, ⲉⲩϫⲱ ⲙ̄ⲙⲟⲥ ϫⲉ

ⲛ̄ⲧⲟⲕ ⲡⲉ ⲡϣⲏⲣⲉ ⲙ̄ ⲡⲛⲟⲩⲧⲉ.
ⲁⲩⲱ ⲛⲉϥⲉⲡⲓⲧⲓⲙⲁ ⲛⲁⲩ ⲉ-ⲛ̄ϥⲕⲱ ⲙ̄ⲙⲟⲟⲩ ⲁⲛ ⲉ ϣⲁϫⲉ, ϫⲉ ⲛⲉⲩⲥⲟⲟⲩⲛ̄
ϫⲉ ⲛ̄ⲧⲟϥ ⲡⲉ ⲡⲉⲭⲥ̄. (42) ⲛ̄ⲧⲉⲣⲉ-ϩⲧⲟⲟⲩⲉ ⲇⲉ ϣⲱⲡⲉ, ⲁϥⲉⲓ ⲉⲃⲟⲗ,
ⲁϥⲃⲱⲕ ⲉⲩⲙⲁ ⲛ̄ ϫⲁⲓⲉ. ⲛⲉⲣⲉ-ⲙ̄ⲙⲏⲏϣⲉ ⲇⲉ ϣⲓⲛⲉ ⲛ̄ⲥⲱϥ ⲡⲉ. ⲁⲩⲉⲓ
ϣⲁⲣⲟϥ, ⲁⲩⲁⲙⲁϩⲧⲉ ⲙ̄ⲙⲟϥ ⲉ ⲧⲙ̄ⲃⲱⲕ ⲉ ⲕⲁⲁⲩ. (43) ⲛ̄ⲧⲟϥ ⲇⲉ ⲡⲉϫⲁϥ
ⲛⲁⲩ ϫⲉ

ϩⲁⲡⲥ̄ ⲉⲧⲣⲁⲉⲩⲁⲅⲅⲉⲗⲓⲍⲉ ⲛ̄ ⲛ̄ⲕⲉⲡⲟⲗⲓⲥ ⲛ̄ ⲧⲙⲛ̄ⲧⲉⲣⲟ ⲙ̄ ⲡⲛⲟⲩⲧⲉ,
ϫⲉ ⲛ̄ⲧⲁⲩⲧⲛ̄ⲛⲟⲟⲩⲧ ⲅⲁⲣ ⲉ ⲡⲉⲓϩⲱⲃ.
(44) ⲛⲉϥⲕⲏⲣⲩⲥⲥⲉ ⲇⲉ ⲡⲉ ϩⲛ̄ ⲛ̄ⲥⲩⲛⲁⲅⲱⲅⲏ ⲛ̄ †ⲟⲩⲇⲁⲓⲁ.

Chapter V

(1) ⲁⲥϣⲱⲡⲉ ⲇⲉ ϩⲙ̄ ⲡⲧⲣⲉ-ⲡⲙⲏⲏϣⲉ ϣⲟⲩⲟ ⲉϫⲱϥ ⲛ̄ⲥⲉⲥⲱⲧⲙ̄ ⲉ ⲡϣⲁϫⲉ ⲙ̄
ⲡⲛⲟⲩⲧⲉ, ⲛ̄ⲧⲟϥ ⲇⲉ ⲛⲉϥⲁϩⲉⲣⲁⲧϥ̄ ⲡⲉ ϩⲁⲧⲛ̄ ⲧⲗⲓⲙⲛⲏ ⲛ̄ ⲅⲉⲛⲛⲏⲥⲁⲣⲉⲑ.
(2) ⲁϥⲛⲁⲩ ⲉ ϫⲟⲓ ⲥⲛⲁⲩ ⲉⲩⲙⲟⲟⲛⲉ ϩⲁⲧⲛ̄ ⲧⲗⲓⲙⲛⲏ, ⲉ-ⲁ-ⲛ̄ⲟⲩⲱϩⲉ ⲡⲉ
ⲉⲓ ⲉϩⲣⲁⲓ ϩⲓⲱⲟⲩ, ⲉⲩⲉⲓⲱ ⲛ̄ ⲛⲉⲩϣⲛⲏⲩ. (3) ⲁϥⲁⲗⲉ ⲇⲉ ⲉ ⲟⲩⲁ ⲛ̄ ⲛ̄ϫⲟⲓ

---

40. ϩⲱⲧⲡ̄ ϩⲉⲧⲡ̄- ϩⲟⲧⲡ⸗ Q ϩⲟⲧⲡ̄ vb. tr. to reconcile,
adjust (ⲙ̄ⲙⲟ⸗; to: ⲉ, ⲙⲛ̄); intr. (1) to become reconciled;
(2) to set (of the sun, etc.). Note ⲣⲱⲙⲉ in indef. pron.
sense "anyone," with plural resumption in ⲉⲩϣⲱⲛⲉ.

1. ϣⲟⲩⲟ ϣⲟⲩⲉ- ϣⲟⲩⲟ⸗ vb. tr. to pour, empty out (ⲙ̄ⲙⲟ⸗;
out of: ⲉⲃⲟⲗ ϩⲛ̄); intr. to flow, pour forth. ⲧ.ⲗⲓⲙⲛⲏ
(ἡ λίμνη) lake.

2. ⲙⲟⲟⲛⲉ ⲙⲉⲛⲉ-, ⲙⲁⲛⲉ- Q ⲙⲁⲛⲟⲟⲩⲧ vb. tr. to bring
(boat) to land, into port; to moor (ⲙ̄ⲙⲟ⸗; at, to: ⲉ);
intr. to come to land, into port, be moored. ⲡ.ⲟⲩⲱϩⲉ
fisherman. ⲡⲉ.ϣⲛⲉ (pl. ⲛⲉ.ϣⲛⲏⲩ) net.

3. ϩⲓⲛⲉ to row (ⲉⲃⲟⲗ ⲛ̄: away from).

ⲉ-ⲡⲁ-ⲥⲓⲙⲱⲛ ⲡⲉ. ⲁϥϫⲟⲟⲥ ⲛⲁϥ ⲉⲧⲣⲉϥ2ⲓⲛⲉ ⲉⲃⲟⲗ ⲙ̄ ⲡⲉⲕⲣⲟ ⲛ̄
ⲟⲩⲕⲟⲩⲓ. ⲁϥ2ⲙⲟⲟⲥ ⲇⲉ 2ⲓ ⲡϫⲟⲓ, ⲁϥϯ-ⲥⲃⲱ ⲛ̄ ⲙ̄ⲙⲏⲏϣⲉ.

(4) ⲛ̄ⲧⲉⲣⲉϥⲟⲩⲱ ⲇⲉ ⲉϥϣⲁϫⲉ, ⲡⲉϫⲁϥ ⲛ̄ ⲥⲓⲙⲱⲛ ϫⲉ
ⲕⲉⲧ-ⲧⲏⲩⲧⲛ̄ ⲉ ⲛⲉⲧ ϣⲏⲕ, ⲛ̄ⲧⲉⲧⲛ̄ⲭⲁⲗⲁ ⲛ̄ ⲛⲉⲧⲛ̄ϣⲛⲏⲩ ⲉ 6ⲱⲡⲉ.

(5) ⲁ-ⲥⲓⲙⲱⲛ ⲇⲉ ⲟⲩⲱϣⲃ̄, ⲡⲉϫⲁϥ ⲛⲁϥ ϫⲉ
ⲡⲥⲁ2, ⲁⲛϣⲛ̄-2ⲓⲥⲉ ⲛ̄ ⲧⲉⲩϣⲏ ⲧⲏⲣⲥ̄, ⲙ̄ⲡⲛ̄6ⲛ̄-ⲗⲁⲁⲩ. ⲉⲧⲃⲉ
ⲡⲉⲕϣⲁϫⲉ ⲇⲉ ϯⲛⲁⲭⲁⲗⲁ ⲛ̄ ⲛⲉϣⲛⲏⲩ.

(6) ⲛ̄ⲧⲉⲣⲟⲩⲣ̄-ⲡⲁⲓ ⲇⲉ, ⲁⲩⲥⲱⲟⲩ2 ⲉ2ⲟⲩⲛ ⲛ̄ ⲟⲩⲙⲏⲏϣⲉ ⲛ̄ ⲧⲃ̄ⲧ
ⲉ-ⲛⲁϣⲱⲟⲩ. ⲛⲉⲣⲉ-ⲛⲉⲩϣⲛⲏⲩ ⲇⲉ ⲛⲁⲡⲱ2 ⲡⲉ. (7) ⲁⲩϫⲱⲣⲙ̄ ⲉ
ⲛⲉⲩϣⲃⲉⲉⲣ ⲉⲧ 2ⲓ ⲡⲕⲉϫⲟⲓ ⲉⲧⲣⲉⲩⲉⲓ ⲛ̄ⲥⲉϯ-ⲧⲟⲟⲧⲟⲩ ⲛⲙ̄ⲙⲁⲩ. ⲁⲩⲉⲓ ⲇⲉ,
ⲁⲩⲙⲉ2-ⲡϫⲟⲓ ⲥⲛⲁⲩ 2ⲱⲥⲧⲉ ⲉⲧⲣⲉⲩⲱⲙⲥ̄. (8) ⲛ̄ⲧⲉⲣⲉ-ⲥⲓⲙⲱⲛ ⲡⲉⲧⲣⲟⲥ
ⲛⲁⲩ ⲉ ⲡⲁⲓ, ⲁϥⲡⲁ2ⲧϥ̄ 2ⲁ ⲛ̄ⲟⲩⲉⲣⲏⲧⲉ ⲛ̄ ⲓ̄ⲥ̄, ⲉϥϫⲱ ⲙ̄ⲙⲟⲥ ϫⲉ
ⲥⲁ2ⲱⲕ ⲉⲃⲟⲗ ⲙ̄ⲙⲟⲓ, ϫⲉ ⲁⲛⲅ̄-ⲟⲩⲣⲱⲙⲉ ⲛ̄ ⲣⲉϥⲣ̄-ⲛⲟⲃⲉ, ⲡϫⲟⲉⲓⲥ.

(9) ⲛⲉ-ⲁⲩ2ⲟⲧⲉ ⲅⲁⲣ ⲧⲁ2ⲟϥ ⲡⲉ ⲙⲛ̄ ⲟⲩⲟⲛ ⲛⲓⲙ ⲉⲧ ⲛⲙ̄ⲙⲁϥ ⲉϫⲛ̄
ⲧⲥⲟⲟⲩ2ⲥ̄ ⲛ̄ ⲛ̄ⲧⲃ̄ⲧ ⲉⲛⲧⲁⲩ6ⲟⲡⲥ̄. (10) 2ⲟⲙⲟⲓⲱⲥ ⲇⲉ ⲡⲕⲉ ⲓⲁⲕⲱⲃⲟⲥ ⲙⲛ̄
ⲓⲱ2ⲁⲛⲛⲏⲥ, ⲛ̄ϣⲏⲣⲉ ⲛ̄ 2ⲉⲃⲉⲇⲁⲓⲟⲥ, ⲛⲉⲩⲟ ⲛ̄ ⲕⲟⲓⲛⲱⲛⲟⲥ ⲛ̄ ⲥⲓⲙⲱⲛ.
ⲡⲉϫⲉ-ⲓ̄ⲥ̄ ⲛ̄ ⲥⲓⲙⲱⲛ ϫⲉ
ⲙ̄ⲡⲣ̄ⲣ̄-2ⲟⲧⲉ. ϫⲓⲛ ⲧⲉⲛⲟⲩ ⲉⲕⲛⲁϣⲱⲡⲉ ⲉⲕ6ⲉⲡ-ⲣⲱⲙⲉ.

(11) ⲁⲩⲙⲁⲛⲉ-ⲛⲉⲭⲏⲩ ⲇⲉ ⲉ ⲡⲉⲕⲣⲟ, ⲁⲩⲕⲁ-ⲛ̄ⲕⲁ ⲛⲓⲙ ⲛ̄ⲥⲱⲟⲩ,
ⲁⲩⲟⲩⲁ2ⲟⲩ ⲛ̄ⲥⲱϥ. (12) ⲁⲥϣⲱⲡⲉ ⲇⲉ, ⲉϥ2ⲛ̄ ⲟⲩⲉⲓ ⲛ̄ ⲙ̄ⲡⲟⲗⲓⲥ, ⲉⲓⲥ
ⲟⲩⲣⲱⲙⲉ ⲉϥⲙⲉ2 ⲛ̄ ⲥⲱⲃ2̄ ⲁϥⲛⲁⲩ ⲉ ⲓ̄ⲥ̄, ⲁϥⲡⲁ2ⲧϥ̄ ⲉϫⲙ̄ ⲡⲉϥ2ⲟ,
ⲁϥⲥ̄ⲡⲥⲱⲡϥ̄, ⲉϥϫⲱ ⲙ̄ⲙⲟⲥ ϫⲉ
ⲡϫⲟⲉⲓⲥ, ⲉⲕϣⲁⲛⲟⲩⲱϣ, ⲟⲩⲛ̄-6ⲟⲙ ⲙ̄ⲙⲟⲕ ⲉ ⲧⲃ̄ⲃⲟⲓ.

---

4. ϣⲱⲕ ϣⲉⲕ- ϣⲟⲕ⸗ Q ϣⲏⲕ to dig deep; Q to be deep; ⲛⲉⲧ
ϣⲏⲕ the deep places. 6ⲱⲡⲉ 6ⲉⲡ-, 6ⲡ̄- 6ⲟⲡ⸗ Q 6ⲏⲡ to seize,
catch (ⲙ̄ⲙⲟ⸗). ⲭⲁⲗⲁ (χαλάω) to let down, lower.

5. ϣⲛ̄-2ⲓⲥⲉ to labor, work with difficulty.

6. ⲡⲱ2 ⲡⲉ2- ⲡⲁ2⸗ Q ⲡⲏ2 vb. tr. and intr. to burst, tear,
break (ⲙ̄ⲙⲟ⸗).

9. ⲧ.ⲥⲟⲟⲩ2ⲥ̄ gathering, collection; catch (of fish).

10. 2ⲟⲙⲟⲓⲱⲥ (ὁμοίως) adv. likewise. ⲡ.ⲕⲟⲓⲛⲱⲛⲟⲥ
(ὁ κοινωνός) partner.

168

(13) ⲁϥⲥⲟⲩⲧⲛ̄-ⲧⲉϥϭⲓϫ ⲁⲉ ⲉⲃⲟⲗ, ⲁϥϫⲱ2 ⲉⲣⲟϥ, ⲉϥϫⲱ ⲙ̄ⲙⲟⲥ ϫⲉ
†ⲟⲩⲱϣ. ⲧⲃ̄ⲃⲟ.
ⲁⲩⲱ ⲛ̄ ⲧⲉⲩⲛⲟⲩ ⲁ-ⲡⲥⲱⲃ2̄ ⲕⲁⲁϥ. (14) ⲛ̄ⲧⲟϥ ⲁⲉ ⲁϥⲡⲁⲣⲁⲅⲅⲉⲓⲗⲉ ⲛⲁϥ
ϫⲉ

ⲙ̄ⲡⲣ̄ϫⲟⲟⲥ ⲉ ⲗⲁⲁⲩ, ⲁⲗⲗⲁ ⲃⲱⲕ, ⲛ̄ⲅ̄ⲧⲟⲩⲟⲕ ⲉ ⲡⲟⲩⲏⲏⲃ, ⲛ̄ⲅ̄ⲧⲁⲗⲟ
ⲉ2ⲣⲁⲓ 2ⲁ ⲡⲉⲕⲧⲃ̄ⲃⲟ ⲕⲁⲧⲁ ⲑⲉ ⲉⲛⲧⲁϥⲟⲩⲉ2-ⲥⲁ2ⲛⲉ ⲙ̄ⲙⲟⲥ ⲛ̄ϭⲓ
ⲙⲱⲩⲥⲏⲥ ⲉⲩⲙ̄ⲛ̄ⲧⲙ̄ⲛ̄ⲧⲣⲉ ⲛⲁⲩ.
(15) ⲛⲉⲣⲉ-ⲡϣⲁϫⲉ ⲁⲉ ⲙⲟⲟϣⲉ ⲛ̄ 2ⲟⲩⲟ ⲉⲧⲃⲏⲏⲧϥ̄, ⲁⲩⲱ ⲛⲉⲣⲉ-ⲙ̄ⲙⲏⲏϣⲉ
ⲥⲱⲟⲩ2 ⲉ2ⲟⲩⲛ ⲉ ⲥⲱⲧⲙ̄ ⲉⲣⲟϥ ⲁⲩⲱ ⲉ ⲧⲁⲗϭⲟⲟⲩ 2ⲛ̄ ⲛⲉⲩϣⲱⲛⲉ.
(16) ⲛ̄ⲧⲟϥ ⲁⲉ ⲛⲉϥⲥⲓ2ⲉ ⲙ̄ⲙⲟϥ ⲡⲉ ⲉ 2ⲉⲛⲙⲁ ⲛ̄ ϫⲁⲓⲉ, ⲉϥϣⲗⲏⲗ.
(17) ⲁⲥϣⲱⲡⲉ ⲁⲉ, ⲉϥ†-ⲥⲃⲱ ⲛ̄ ⲟⲩ2ⲟⲟⲩ, ⲉⲣⲉ-2ⲉⲛⲫⲁⲣⲓⲥⲁⲓⲟⲥ 2ⲙⲟⲟⲥ
ⲙⲛ̄ 2ⲉⲛⲛⲟⲙⲟⲇⲓⲇⲁⲥⲕⲁⲗⲟⲥ, ⲛⲁⲓ ⲉⲛⲧⲁⲩⲉⲓ ⲉⲃⲟⲗ 2ⲛ̄ †ⲙⲉ ⲛⲓⲙ ⲛ̄ⲧⲉ
ⲧⲅⲁⲗⲓⲗⲁⲓⲁ ⲙⲛ̄ †ⲟⲩⲇⲁⲓⲁ ⲙⲛ̄ ⲑⲓⲗⲏⲙ̄, ⲛⲉⲣⲉ-ⲧϭⲟⲙ ⲁⲉ ⲙ̄ ⲡϫⲟⲉⲓⲥ ϣⲟⲟⲡ
ⲡⲉ ⲉⲧⲣⲉϥⲧⲁⲗϭⲟ. (18) ⲉⲓⲥ 2ⲉⲛⲣⲱⲙⲉ ⲁⲉ ⲁⲩⲛ̄-ⲟⲩⲣⲱⲙⲉ 2ⲓϫⲛ̄ ⲟⲩϭⲗⲟϭ
ⲉϥⲥⲏϥ, ⲁⲩⲱ ⲛⲉⲩϣⲓⲛⲉ ⲡⲉ ⲛ̄ⲥⲁ ϫⲓⲧϥ̄ ⲉ2ⲟⲩⲛ ⲉ ⲕⲁⲁϥ ⲙ̄ ⲡⲉϥⲙ̄ⲧⲟ ⲉⲃⲟⲗ.
(19) ⲉ-ⲙ̄ⲡⲟⲩ2ⲉ ⲁⲉ ⲉ ⲧⲉ2ⲓⲏ ⲉ ϫⲓⲧϥ̄ ⲉ2ⲟⲩⲛ ⲉⲧⲃⲉ ⲡⲙⲏⲏϣⲉ, ⲁⲩⲃⲱⲕ
ⲉ2ⲣⲁⲓ ⲉ ⲧϫⲉⲛⲉⲡⲱⲣ, ⲁⲩⲭⲁⲗⲁ ⲙ̄ⲙⲟϥ ⲉⲡⲉⲥⲏⲧ 2ⲓⲧⲛ̄ ⲛ̄ⲕⲉⲣⲁⲙⲟⲥ ⲙⲛ̄
ⲡⲉϭⲗⲟϭ ⲉ ⲧⲉⲩⲙⲏⲧⲉ ⲙ̄ ⲡⲉⲙⲧⲟ ⲉⲃⲟⲗ ⲛ̄ ⲓⲥ̄. (20) ⲁϥⲛⲁⲩ ⲁⲉ ⲉ
ⲧⲉⲩⲡⲓⲥⲧⲓⲥ, ⲡⲉϫⲁϥ ϫⲉ

ⲡⲣⲱⲙⲉ, ⲛⲉⲕⲛⲟⲃⲉ ⲕⲏ ⲛⲁⲕ ⲉⲃⲟⲗ.
(21) ⲁ-ⲛⲉⲅⲣⲁⲙⲙⲁⲧⲉⲩⲥ ⲁⲉ ⲙⲛ̄ ⲛⲉⲫⲁⲣⲓⲥⲁⲓⲟⲥ ⲁⲣⲭⲉⲓ ⲙ̄ ⲙⲟⲕⲙⲉⲕ,
ⲉⲩϫⲱ ⲙ̄ⲙⲟⲥ ϫⲉ

ⲛⲓⲙ ⲡⲉ ⲡⲁⲓ ⲉⲧ ϫⲓ-ⲟⲩⲁ? ⲛⲓⲙ ⲡⲉⲧⲉ ⲟⲩⲛ̄-ϭⲟⲙ ⲙ̄ⲙⲟϥ ⲛ̄

---

13. ϫⲱ2, Q ϫⲏ2 vb. tr. to touch (ⲉ).

14. ⲡⲁⲣⲁⲅⲅⲉⲓⲗⲉ ⲛⲁ⸗ (παραγγέλλω) to order, command.

16. ⲥⲓ2ⲉ ⲥⲉ2- ⲥⲁ2ⲧ⸗ vb. reflex. to withdraw, go away;
also intr. to be removed.

17. ⲛⲉ.ⲫⲁⲣⲓⲥⲁⲓⲟⲥ (οἱ φαρισαῖοι) Pharisees. ⲡ.ⲛⲟⲙⲟⲇⲓ-
ⲇⲁⲥⲕⲁⲗⲟⲥ (ὁ νομοδιδάσκαλος) teacher of the law.

19. ⲡ.ⲕⲉⲣⲁⲙⲟⲥ (ὁ κέραμος) tile.

21. ⲡⲉ.ⲅⲣⲁⲙⲙⲁⲧⲉⲩⲥ (ὁ γραμματεύς) scribe, clerk. ϫⲓ-ⲟⲩⲁ,
ϫⲉ-ⲟⲩⲁ to blaspheme (against: ⲉ); ⲡ.ⲟⲩⲁ blasphemy.

ⲔⲀ-ⲚⲞⲂⲈ ⲈⲂⲞⲖ ⲚⲤⲀ ⲠⲚⲞⲨⲦⲈ ⲘⲀⲨⲀⲀϤ?

(22) ⲚⲦⲈⲢⲈ-ⲒⲤ ⲆⲈ ⲈⲒⲘⲈ Ⲉ ⲚⲈⲨⲘⲞⲔⲘⲈⲔ, ⲠⲈⲬⲀϤ ⲚⲀⲨ ϪⲈ
ⲀϨⲢⲰⲦⲚ ⲦⲈⲦⲚⲘⲈⲈⲨⲈ ϨⲚ ⲚⲈⲦⲚϨⲎⲦ? (23) ⲀϢ ⲄⲀⲢ ⲠⲈⲦ ⲘⲞⲦⲚ Ⲉ
ϪⲞⲞⲤ ⲠⲈ, ϪⲈ ⲚⲈⲔⲚⲞⲂⲈ ⲔⲎ ⲚⲀⲔ ⲈⲂⲞⲖ, ⲬⲚ Ⲉ ϪⲞⲞⲤ ⲠⲈ, ϪⲈ
ⲦⲰⲞⲨⲚ ⲚⲦⲘⲞⲞϢⲈ? (24) ϪⲈⲔⲀⲤ ⲆⲈ ⲈⲦⲈⲦⲚⲈⲈⲒⲘⲈ ϪⲈ ⲞⲨⲚⲦⲈ-
ⲠϢⲎⲢⲈ Ⲙ ⲠⲢⲰⲘⲈ ⲈϨⲞⲨⲤⲒⲀ ϨⲒϪⲘ ⲠⲔⲀϨ Ⲉ ⲔⲀ-ⲚⲞⲂⲈ ⲈⲂⲞⲖ —
ⲠⲈⲬⲀϤ Ⲙ ⲠⲈⲦ ⲤⲎϬ ϪⲈ

ⲈⲒϪⲰ ⲘⲘⲞⲤ ⲚⲀⲔ ϪⲈ ⲦⲰⲞⲨⲚ ⲚⲦϤⲒ Ⲙ ⲠⲈⲔϬⲖⲞϬ; ⲂⲰⲔ Ⲉ ⲠⲈⲔⲎⲒ.
(25) Ⲛ ⲦⲈⲨⲚⲞⲨ ⲆⲈ ⲀϤⲦⲰⲞⲨⲚ Ⲙ ⲠⲈⲨⲘ̄ⲦⲞ ⲈⲂⲞⲖ, ⲀϤϤⲒ Ⲙ ⲠⲈϤϬⲖⲟϬ,
ⲀϤⲂⲰⲔ Ⲉ ⲠⲈϤⲎⲒ ⲈϤϯ-ⲈⲞⲞⲨ Ⲙ ⲠⲚⲞⲨⲦⲈ. (26) ⲀⲨⲢ̄-ϢⲠⲎⲢⲈ ⲆⲈ ⲦⲎⲢⲞⲨ,
ⲀⲨϯ-ⲈⲞⲞⲨ Ⲙ ⲠⲚⲞⲨⲦⲈ, ⲀⲨⲘⲞⲨϨ Ⲛ ϨⲞⲦⲈ, ⲈⲨϪⲰ ⲘⲘⲞⲤ ϪⲈ,
ⲀⲚⲚⲀⲨ Ⲉ ϨⲈⲚϢⲠⲎⲢⲈ Ⲙ ⲠⲞⲞⲨ.

(27) ⲘⲚ̄Ⲛ̄ⲤⲀ ⲚⲀⲒ ⲀϤⲈⲒ ⲈⲂⲞⲖ, ⲀϤⲚⲀⲨ ⲈⲨⲦⲈⲖⲰⲚⲎⲤ Ⲉ-ⲠⲈϤⲢⲀⲚ ⲠⲈ
ⲖⲈⲨⲈⲒ ⲈϤϨⲘⲞⲞⲤ ϨⲘ ⲠⲈϤⲦⲈⲖⲰⲚⲒⲞⲚ. ⲠⲈⲬⲀϤ ⲚⲀϤ ϪⲈ ⲞⲨⲀϨ₂Ⲕ ⲚⲤⲰⲒ.
(28) ⲀϤⲔⲀ-ⲚⲔⲀ ⲆⲈ ⲚⲒⲘ ⲚⲤⲰϤ, ⲀϤⲦⲰⲞⲨⲚ, ⲀϤⲞⲨⲀϨϤ ⲚⲤⲰϤ.
(29) ⲀⲨⲰ Ⲁ-ⲖⲈⲨⲈⲒ Ⲣ̄-ⲞⲨⲚⲞϬ Ⲛ ϢⲞⲠⲤ̄ ⲈⲢⲞϤ ϨⲘ ⲠⲈϤⲎⲒ. ⲚⲈⲨⲚ̄-
ⲞⲨⲘⲎⲎϢⲈ ⲆⲈ Ⲛ ⲦⲈⲖⲰⲚⲎⲤ ⲘⲚ ϨⲈⲚⲔⲞⲞⲨⲈ ⲚⲘⲘⲀⲨ ⲈⲨⲚⲎϪ.
(30) Ⲁ-ⲚⲈⲪⲀⲢⲒⲤⲀⲒⲞⲤ ⲘⲚ ⲚⲈⲄⲢⲀⲘⲘⲀⲦⲈⲨⲤ ⲔⲢ̄Ⲙ̄Ⲣ̄Ⲙ̄ ⲈϨⲞⲨⲚ Ⲉ
ⲚⲈϤⲘⲀⲐⲎⲦⲎⲤ, ⲈⲨϪⲰ ⲘⲘⲞⲤ ϪⲈ

ⲈⲦⲂⲈ ⲞⲨ ⲦⲈⲦⲚ̄ⲞⲨⲰⲘ ⲀⲨⲰ ⲦⲈⲦⲚ̄ⲤⲰ ⲘⲚ ⲚⲦⲈⲖⲰⲚⲎⲤ ⲀⲨⲰ
Ⲛ̄ⲢⲈϤⲢ̄-ⲚⲞⲂⲈ?
(31) Ⲁ-ⲒⲤ ⲆⲈ ⲞⲨⲰϢⲂ̄, ⲠⲈⲬⲀϤ ⲚⲀⲨ ϪⲈ
ⲚⲈⲦ ⲦⲎⲔ Ⲣ̄-ⲬⲢⲒⲀ ⲀⲚ Ⲙ ⲠⲤⲀⲈⲒⲚ, ⲀⲖⲖⲀ ⲚⲈⲦ ⲘⲞⲔⲎ̄ ⲚⲈⲦ Ⲣ̄-ⲬⲢⲒⲀ
ⲚⲀϤ. (32) Ⲛ̄ⲦⲀⲒⲈⲒ ⲀⲚ Ⲉ ⲦⲈϨⲘ̄-Ⲛ̄ⲆⲒⲔⲀⲒⲞⲤ ⲀⲖⲖⲀ Ⲛ̄ⲢⲈϤⲢ̄-ⲚⲞⲂⲈ

---

23. ⲬⲚ conj. or.

27. Ⲡ.ⲦⲈⲖⲰⲚⲒⲞⲚ (τὸ τελώνιον) tax-house.

29. ⲧ.ϢⲟⲠⲤ̄ a reception, entertainment, banquet.

30. ⲔⲢ̄Ⲙ̄Ⲣ̄Ⲙ̄ vb. intr. to murmur, complain (against: Ⲉ,
ⲈϨⲞⲨⲚ Ⲉ, ⲈϪⲚ̄, Ⲛ̄ⲤⲀ).

31. ⲦⲰⲔ ⲦⲈⲔ- ⲦⲞⲔ⸗ Q ⲦⲎⲔ vb. tr. to strengthen, confirm;
reflex. and intr. to become strong, firm, hale, hardy.

32. ⲦⲰ₂Ⲙ ⲦⲈ₂Ⲙ- ⲦⲀ₂Ⲙ⸗ Q ⲦⲀ₂Ⲙ vb. tr. to summon (ⲘⲘⲞ⸗,
Ⲉ); vb. intr. to knock at the door. ⲘⲈⲦⲀⲚⲞⲈⲒ (μετανοέω)
to repent.

ε μετλνοει.

(33) ⲛ̄ⲧⲟⲟⲩ ⲇⲉ ⲡⲉⲭⲁⲩ ⲛⲁϥ ⲭⲉ

ⲙ̄ⲙⲁⲑⲏⲧⲏⲥ ⲛ̄ ⲓⲱ₂ⲁⲛⲛⲏⲥ ⲛⲏⲥⲧⲉⲩⲉ ⲛ̄ ₂ⲁ₂ ⲛ̄ ⲥⲟⲡ ⲁⲩⲱ ⲥⲉⲥⲟⲡⲥ̄,
ⲛ̄ⲧⲟⲟⲩ ⲙⲛ̄ ⲛⲁ-ⲛⲉⲫⲁⲣⲓⲥⲁⲓⲟⲥ. ⲛⲟⲩⲕ ⲇⲉ ⲟⲩⲱⲙ, ⲥⲉⲥⲱ.

(34) ⲡⲉⲭⲉ-ⲓ̅ⲥ̅ ⲛⲁⲩ ⲭⲉ

ⲙⲏ ⲟⲩⲛ̄-6ⲟⲙ ⲙ̄ⲙⲱⲧⲛ̄ ⲉⲧⲣⲉ-ⲛ̄ϣⲏⲣⲉ ⲙ̄ ⲡⲙⲁ ⲛ̄ ϣⲉⲗⲉⲉⲧ ⲛⲏⲥⲧⲉⲩⲉ,
ⲉⲣⲉ-ⲡⲁ-ⲧϣⲉⲗⲉⲉⲧ ⲛⲙ̄ⲙⲁⲩ? (35) ⲟⲩⲛ̄-₂ⲉⲛ₂ⲟⲟⲩ ⲇⲉ ⲛⲏⲩ ⲉⲩⲛⲁϥⲓ
ⲙ̄ ⲡⲁ-ⲧϣⲉⲗⲉⲉⲧ ⲛ̄ⲧⲟⲟⲧⲟⲩ. ⲧⲟⲧⲉ ⲥⲉⲛⲁⲛⲏⲥⲧⲉⲩⲉ ₂ⲛ̄ ⲛⲉ₂ⲟⲟⲩ ⲉⲧ
ⲙ̄ⲙⲁⲩ.

(36) ⲁϥⲭⲱ ⲇⲉ ⲛⲁⲩ ⲛ̄ ⲕⲉⲡⲁⲣⲁⲃⲟⲗⲏ ⲭⲉ

ⲙⲉⲣⲉ-ⲗⲁⲁⲩ ⲥⲗ̄ⲡ-ⲟⲩⲧⲟⲉⲓⲥ ₂ⲓ ⲟⲩϣⲧⲏⲛ ⲛ̄ ϣⲁⲓ ⲛ̄ϥⲧⲟⲣⲡⲥ̄ ⲉⲩϣⲧⲏⲛ
ⲙ̄ ⲡⲗ̄6ⲉ. ⲉϣⲱⲡⲉ ⲙ̄ⲙⲟⲛ, ϥⲛⲁⲡⲉ₂-ⲧⲕⲉϣⲧⲏⲛ ⲛ̄ ϣⲁⲓ, ⲁⲩⲱ ⲛ̄ⲧⲉⲧⲙ̄-
ⲧⲧⲟⲉⲓⲥ ⲛ̄ ϣⲁⲓ ⲣ̄-ϣⲁⲩ ⲉ ⲧⲡⲗ̄6ⲉ. (37) ⲁⲩⲱ ⲙⲉⲣⲉ-ⲗⲁⲁⲩ ⲛⲟⲩⲭⲉ
ⲛ̄ ⲟⲩⲏⲣⲡ̄ ⲛ̄ ⲃⲣ̄ⲣⲉ ⲉ ₂ⲉⲛⲁⲥⲕⲟⲥ ⲛ̄ ⲁⲥ. ⲉϣⲱⲡⲉ ⲙ̄ⲙⲟⲛ, ϣⲁⲣⲉ-
ⲡⲏⲣⲡ̄ ⲛ̄ ⲃⲣ̄ⲣⲉ ⲡⲉ₂-ⲛ̄ⲁⲥⲕⲟⲥ, ⲛ̄ϥⲡⲱⲛⲉ ⲉⲃⲟⲗ, ⲛ̄ⲧⲉ-ⲛ̄ⲕⲉⲁⲥⲕⲟⲥ
ⲧⲁⲕⲟ. (38) ⲁⲗⲗⲁ ⲉϣⲁⲩⲛⲉⲭ-ⲏⲣⲡ̄ ⲛ̄ ⲃⲣ̄ⲣⲉ ⲉ ₂ⲉⲛⲁⲥⲕⲟⲥ ⲛ̄ ⲃⲣ̄ⲣⲉ.
(39) ⲙⲉⲣⲉ-ⲗⲁⲁⲩ ⲇⲉ ⲟⲩⲉϣ-ⲏⲣⲡ̄ ⲛ̄ ⲃⲣ̄ⲣⲉ, ⲉϥⲥⲉ-ⲏⲣⲡ̄ ⲁⲥ.
ϣⲁϥⲭⲟⲟⲥ ⲅⲁⲣ ⲭⲉ ⲛⲉϥⲣ̄-ⲡⲉⲣⲡ-ⲁⲥ.

---

34. ⲧ.ϣⲉⲗⲉⲉⲧ bride; ⲙⲁ ⲛ̄ ϣⲉⲗⲉⲉⲧ bridal chamber;
(ⲡ.)ⲡⲁ-ⲧϣⲉⲗⲉⲉⲧ the groom.

36. ⲥⲱⲗⲡ̄ ⲥⲗ̄ⲡ- ⲥⲟⲗⲡ⸗ Q ⲥⲟⲗⲡ̄ vb. tr. to break off, cut off
(ⲙ̄ⲙⲟ⸗); intr. to break, burst. ϣⲁⲓ adj. new. ⲧⲱⲣⲡ̄ ⲧⲟⲣⲡ⸗
Q ⲧⲟⲣⲡ̄ vb. tr. to sew (ⲙ̄ⲙⲟ⸗; to: ⲉ). ⲡ.ⲡⲗ̄6ⲉ rag; ϣⲧⲏⲛ ⲙ̄
ⲡⲗ̄6ⲉ tattered garment. ⲡ.ϣⲁⲩ use, value, profit; ⲣ̄-ϣⲁⲩ
to be useful, of value, to prosper.

37. ⲡ.ⲁⲥⲕⲟⲥ (ὁ ἀσκός) wineskin. ⲡⲱⲛ(ⲉ) ⲡⲛ̄-, ⲡⲉⲛ- ⲡⲟⲛ⸗
Q ⲡⲏⲛ (± ⲉⲃⲟⲗ) vb. tr. to pour (ⲙ̄ⲙⲟ⸗); intr. to pour, flow.

Apophthegmata Patrum

3. ⲁ-ⲟⲩⲥⲟⲛ ϫⲛⲉ-ⲟⲩⲍ̅ⲗⲟ ϫⲉ, "ⲡⲗⲉⲓⲱⲧ, ⲉⲧⲃⲉ ⲟⲩ ⲁⲛⲟⲕ ⲡⲁ2ⲏⲧ
ⲛⲁϣ̅ⲧ, ⲛ̅ϥ̅ⲣ̅-2ⲟⲧⲉ ⲁⲛ ⲛ̅2ⲏⲧϥ̅ ⲙ̅ ⲡⲛⲟⲩⲧⲉ?" ⲡⲉϫⲉ-ⲡⲍ̅ⲗⲟ ⲛⲁϥ ϫⲉ, "†-
ⲙⲉⲉⲩⲉ ϫⲉ ⲉⲣϣⲁⲛ-ⲡⲣⲱⲙⲉ ⲁⲙⲁ2ⲧⲉ ⲙ̅ ⲡⲉϫⲡⲓⲟ 2ⲙ̅ ⲡⲉϥ2ⲏⲧ, ϥⲛⲁϫⲡⲟ ⲛⲁϥ
ⲛ̅ ⲑⲟⲧⲉ ⲙ̅ ⲡⲛⲟⲩⲧⲉ." ⲡⲉϫⲉ-ⲡⲥⲟⲛ ⲛⲁϥ ϫⲉ, "ⲟⲩ ⲡⲉ ⲡⲉϫⲡⲓⲟ?" ⲡⲉϫⲉ-
ⲡⲍ̅ⲗⲟ, "ϫⲉⲕⲁⲥ ⲉⲣⲉ-ⲡⲣⲱⲙⲉ ⲛⲁϫⲡⲓⲉ-ⲧⲉϥⲯⲩⲭⲏ 2ⲛ̅ 2ⲱⲃ ⲛⲓⲙ, ⲉϥϫⲱ
ⲙ̅ⲙⲟⲥ ⲛⲁⲥ ϫⲉ, 'ⲁⲣⲓ-ⲡⲙⲉⲉⲩⲉ ϫⲉ 2ⲁⲡⲥ̅ ⲉⲣⲟⲛ ⲡⲉ ⲉⲧⲣⲉⲛⲁⲡⲁⲛⲧⲁ[1] ⲉ
ⲡⲛⲟⲩⲧⲉ,' ⲛ̅ϥ̅ϫⲟⲟⲥ ⲟⲛ ϫⲉ, 'ⲁ2ⲣⲟⲓ ⲁⲛⲟⲕ ⲙⲛ̅ ⲣⲱⲙⲉ?' ⲉⲣϣⲁⲛ-ⲟⲩⲁ ⲇⲉ
ⲙⲟⲩⲛ ⲉⲃⲟⲗ 2ⲛ̅ ⲛⲁⲓ, ⲥⲛⲏⲩ ⲛⲁϥ ⲛ̅61 ⲑⲟⲧⲉ ⲙ̅ ⲡⲛⲟⲩⲧⲉ."

4. ⲁϥϫⲟⲟⲥ ⲛ̅61 ⲁⲡⲁ ⲡⲟⲓⲙⲏⲛ ϫⲉ, "ⲁ-ⲟⲩⲥⲟⲛ ϫⲟⲟⲥ ⲛ̅ ⲁⲡⲁ ⲡⲁⲛⲥⲉ
ϫⲉ, 'ⲉⲓⲛⲁⲣ̅-ⲟⲩ ⲙ̅ ⲡⲁ2ⲏⲧ ⲉϥⲛⲁϣ̅ⲧ? ⲛ̅†ⲣ̅-2ⲟⲧⲉ ⲁⲛ ⲛ̅2ⲏⲧϥ̅ ⲙ̅ ⲡⲛⲟⲩⲧⲉ.'
ⲡⲉϫⲁϥ ⲛⲁϥ ϫⲉ, 'ⲃⲱⲕ ⲛ̅ⲅ̅ⲧⲟ6ⲕ̅[1] ⲉⲩⲥⲟⲛ ⲉϥⲣ̅-2ⲟⲧⲉ ⲛ̅2ⲏⲧϥ̅ ⲙ̅ ⲡⲛⲟⲩⲧⲉ,
ⲁⲩⲱ ⲉⲃⲟⲗ 2ⲛ̅ ⲧⲙⲛ̅ⲧⲣⲉϥⲣ̅-2ⲟⲧⲉ ⲙ̅ ⲡⲉⲧ ⲙ̅ⲙⲁⲩ ⲕⲛⲁⲣ̅-2ⲟⲧⲉ 2ⲱⲱⲕ ⲛ̅2ⲏⲧϥ̅
ⲙ̅ ⲡⲛⲟⲩⲧⲉ.'"

5. ⲁ-ⲟⲩⲁ ϫⲛⲉ-ⲟⲩ2ⲗⲟ ϫⲉ, "ⲉⲧⲃⲉ ⲟⲩ, ⲉⲓ2ⲙⲟⲟⲥ 2ⲙ̅ ⲡⲁⲙⲁ ⲛ̅
ϣⲱⲡⲉ, ⲡⲁ2ⲏⲧ ⲕⲱⲧⲉ ⲥⲁ ⲥⲁ ⲛⲓⲙ?" ⲁϥⲟⲩⲱϣ̅ⲃ̅ ⲛⲁϥ ⲛ̅61 ⲡⲍ̅ⲗⲟ ϫⲉ,
"ⲉⲃⲟⲗ ϫⲉ ⲥⲉϣⲱⲛⲉ ⲛ̅61 ⲛⲉⲕⲉⲥⲑⲏⲧⲏⲣⲓⲟⲛ[1] ⲉⲧ 2ⲓ ⲃⲟⲗ: ⲧ6ⲓⲛⲛⲁⲩ,
ⲧ6ⲓⲛⲥⲱⲧⲙ̅, ⲧ6ⲓⲛϣⲱⲗⲙ̅,[2] ⲧ6ⲓⲛϣⲁϫⲉ. ⲛⲁⲓ 6ⲉ ⲉϣⲱⲡⲉ ⲉⲕϣⲁⲛϫⲡⲟ ⲛ̅
ⲧⲉⲩⲉⲛⲉⲣⲅⲓⲁ[3] 2ⲛ̅ ⲟⲩⲙⲛ̅ⲧⲕⲁⲑⲁⲣⲟⲥ,[4] ϣⲁⲣⲉ-ⲛ̅ⲕⲉⲉⲥⲑⲏⲧⲏⲣⲓⲟⲛ ⲉⲧ 2ⲓ
2ⲟⲩⲛ ϣⲱⲡⲉ 2ⲛ̅ ⲟⲩⲥ6ⲣⲁ2ⲧ̅[5] ⲙⲛ̅ ⲟⲩⲟⲩϫⲁⲓ.

6. ⲁ-ⲟⲩⲁ ⲟⲛ ϫⲛⲉ-ⲟⲩ2ⲗⲟ ϫⲉ, "ⲉⲧⲃⲉ ⲟⲩ †2ⲙⲟⲟⲥ 2ⲙ̅ ⲡⲁⲙⲁ ⲛ̅
ϣⲱⲡⲉ, †2ⲁⲡ̅ⲗⲱⲡ?"[1] ⲁϥⲟⲩⲱϣ̅ⲃ̅ ⲛⲁϥ ϫⲉ, "ⲉⲃⲟⲗ ϫⲉ ⲙ̅ⲡⲁⲧⲉⲕⲉⲓⲱⲣ2̅[2] ⲙ̅

---

3. (1) ⲁⲡⲁⲛⲧⲁ ⲉ (ἀπαντάω) to meet, confront.

4. (1) ⲧⲱ6ⲉ ⲧⲉ6- ⲧⲟ6ⸯ Q ⲧⲏ6 vb. tr. to join, attach
(ⲙ̅ⲙⲟⸯ; to: ⲉ); used reflex. here.

5. (1) ⲡ.ⲉⲥⲑⲏⲧⲏⲣⲓⲟⲛ (τὸ αἰσθητήριον) sense-organ. (2)
ϣⲱⲗⲙ̅ vb. tr. to smell. (3) ⲧ.ⲉⲛⲉⲣⲅⲓⲁ (ἡ ἐνεργία) function,
action. (4) ⲕⲁⲑⲁⲣⲟⲥ (καθαρός) pure; ⲙⲛ̅ⲧⲕⲁⲑⲁⲣⲟⲥ purity.
(5) ⲥ6ⲣⲁ2ⲧ̅ vb. intr. to pause, rest, become still.

6. (1) 2ⲗⲟⲡⲗ̅ⲡ, Q 2ⲗⲏ̅ⲗⲱⲡ vb. intr. to become despondent. (2) ⲉⲓⲱⲣ2̅ ⲉⲓⲉⲣ2̅- ⲉⲓⲟⲣ2ⸯ vb. tr. to perceive, see
(ⲙ̅ⲙⲟⸯ).

ⲡⲘⲦⲟⲛ ⲉⲧⲚ₂ⲉⲗⲡⲓⲍⲉ³ ⲉⲣⲟ� ⲟⲩⲗⲉ ⲧⲕⲟⲗⲁⲥⲓⲥ⁴ ⲉⲧ ⲛⲁϣⲱⲡⲉ. ⲉⲛⲉⲗⲕ
ⲉⲓⲉⲣⲍ̅-ⲛⲁⲓ ₂Ⲛ ⲟⲩⲱⲣⲬ, ⲗⲩⲱ Ⲛⲧⲉⲡⲉⲕⲙⲁ Ⲛ ϣⲱⲡⲉ ⲙⲟⲩ₂ Ⲛ ⲃⲚⲧ⁵ⲉⲣⲟⲕ
ϣⲁⲛⲧⲟⲩⲡⲱ₂ ⲉ₂ⲣⲁⲓ ⲉ ⲡⲉⲕⲙⲟⲧⲉ,⁶ ⲛⲉⲕⲛⲁⲃⲱ ⲉ₂ⲣⲁⲓ Ⲛ₂ⲏⲧⲟⲩ ⲡⲉ ⲛⲧ̅ϥⲓ
₂ⲁⲣⲟⲟⲩ ⲛⲅⲧⲘ̅₂ⲗⲟⲡⲗⲡ̅."

9. ⲗϥⲭⲟⲟⲥ ⲟⲛ ⲭⲉ, "ⲧⲛⲏⲥⲧⲓⲁ ⲡⲉ ⲡⲉⲭⲁⲗⲓⲛⲟⲥ¹ Ⲙ ⲡⲙⲟⲛⲁⲭⲟⲥ ⲉϥϯ
ⲟⲩⲃⲉ ⲡⲛⲟⲃⲉ. ⲡⲉⲧ ⲛⲟⲩⲭⲉ Ⲛ ⲧⲁⲓ ⲥⲁⲃⲟⲗ Ⲙ̅ⲙⲟϥ ⲟⲩ₂ⲧⲟ Ⲛ ⲗⲁⲃ-ⲥ₂ⲓⲙⲉ
ⲡⲉ.

10. ⲗϥⲭⲟⲟⲥ ⲟⲛ ⲭⲉ, "ⲡⲥⲱⲙⲁ ⲉⲧ ϣⲟⲩⲱⲟⲩ¹ Ⲛⲧⲉ ⲡⲙⲟⲛⲁⲭⲟⲥ ⲉϥ-
ⲥⲱⲕ² Ⲛ ⲧⲉⲯⲩⲭⲏ ⲉ₂ⲣⲁⲓ ₂Ⲛ Ⲛϣⲓⲕ³ Ⲛⲧⲉ ⲡⲉⲥⲛⲧ, ⲗⲩⲱ ⲛⲧ̅ⲧⲣⲉ-Ⲛ₂ⲩⲗⲱⲛⲏ⁴
ϣⲟⲟⲩⲉ ₂ⲓⲧⲚ ⲧⲛⲏⲥⲧⲓⲁ."

11. ⲗϥⲭⲟⲟⲥ ⲟⲛ ⲭⲉ, "ⲡⲙⲟⲛⲁⲭⲟⲥ Ⲛ ₂ⲁⲕ¹ ϣⲁⲩϯ-ⲕⲗⲟⲙ ⲉⲭⲱϥ ₂Ⲙ
ⲡⲕⲁ₂, ⲗⲩⲱ ⲟⲛ ₂Ⲛ Ⲙ̅ⲡⲏⲩⲉ ϣⲁⲩϯ-ⲕⲗⲟⲙ ⲉⲭⲱϥ Ⲙ ⲡⲘ̅ⲧⲟ ⲉⲃⲟⲗ Ⲙ ⲡⲛⲟⲩⲧⲉ."

12. ⲗϥⲭⲟⲟⲥ ⲟⲛ ⲭⲉ, "ⲡⲙⲟⲛⲁⲭⲟⲥ ⲉⲧ ⲁⲙⲁ₂ⲧⲉ ⲁⲛ Ⲙ ⲡⲉϥⲗⲁⲥ ⲙⲁ-
ⲗⲓⲥⲧⲁ¹ Ⲙ ⲡⲛⲁⲩ Ⲙ ⲡⲉⲱⲛⲧ̅ ⲙⲉⲣⲉ-ⲡⲁⲓ Ⲛ ⲧⲉⲓⲙⲓⲛⲉ ⲉⲣ-ⲭⲟⲉⲓⲥ ⲉ ⲗⲁⲗⲩ Ⲙ
ⲡⲗⲑⲟⲥ² ⲉⲛⲉ₂."

13. ⲗϥⲭⲟⲟⲥ ⲟⲛ ⲭⲉ, "Ⲙ̅ⲡ̅ⲣⲧⲁⲟⲩⲉ-ⲗⲁⲗⲩ Ⲛ ϣⲁⲭⲉ ⲉϥ₂ⲟⲟⲩ ⲉⲃⲟⲗ ₂Ⲛ
ⲧⲉⲕⲧⲁⲡⲣⲟ. ⲧⲃⲱ Ⲛ ⲉⲗⲟⲟⲗⲉ ⲅⲁⲣ ⲙⲉⲥⲧⲁⲟⲩⲉ-ϣⲟⲛⲧⲉ¹ ⲉⲃⲟⲗ."

---

(3) ₂ⲉⲗⲡⲓⲍⲉ ⲉ (ἐλπίζω) to hope for. (4) ⲧ.ⲕⲟⲗⲁⲥⲓⲥ (ἡ κόλα-
ⲥⲓⲥ) punishment, correction. (5) ⲧ.ϥⲚⲧ (ⲧ.ⲃⲚⲧ) worm.
(6) ⲡ.ⲙⲟⲧⲉ neck.

9. (1) ⲡⲉ.ⲭⲁⲗⲓⲛⲟⲥ (ὁ χαλινός) bridle. (2) ⲗⲁⲃ-ⲥ₂ⲓⲙⲉ
adj. lusty, lecherous; lit. female-crazed, from ⲗⲓⲃⲉ, Q
ⲗⲟⲃⲉ to rage, be mad, p.c. ⲗⲁⲃ-.

10. (1) ϣⲟⲟⲩⲉ, Q ϣⲟⲩⲱⲟⲩ vb. intr. to become dry, dry up.
(2) ⲥⲱⲕ ⲥⲉⲕ- ⲥⲟⲕ⸗ Q ⲥⲏⲕ vb. tr. to draw, drag, impel (Ⲙ̅ⲙⲟ⸗);
also intr. to be drawn, move swiftly, flowingly. (3) ⲡ.ϣⲓⲕ
depth(s). (4) ⲑⲩⲗⲱⲛⲏ (ἡ ἡδονή) pleasure, delight.

11. (1) ₂ⲁⲕ adj. sober, mild, prudent.

12. (1) ⲙⲁⲗⲓⲥⲧⲁ (μάλιστα) adv. especially. (2) ⲡ.ⲡⲗⲑⲟⲥ
(τὸ πάθος) suffering, misfortune, calamity.

13. (1) ⲧ.ϣⲟⲛⲧⲉ the acacia nilotica, a thorn tree;
hence: thorns.

14. ⲁϥϫⲟⲟⲥ ⲟⲛ ϫⲉ, "ⲛⲁⲛⲟⲩ-ⲟⲩⲉⲙ-ⲁⲃ[1] ⲁⲩⲱ ⲉ ⲥⲉ-ⲏⲣⲡ̄ ⲛ̄ⲧⲙ̄-
ⲟⲩⲱⲙ[2] ⲁⲉ ⲛ̄ ⲛ̄ⲥⲁⲣⲝ ⲛ̄ ⲛⲉⲕⲥⲛⲏⲩ ⳨ⲧⲛ̄ ⲧⲕⲁⲧⲁⲗⲁⲗⲓⲁ."[3]

15. ⲁϥϫⲟⲟⲥ ⲟⲛ ϫⲉ, "ⲛⲧⲁ-ⲡ⳩ⲟϥ[1] ⲕⲟⲥⲕⲉⲥ[2] ⲉ ⲉⲩ⳩ⲁ[3] ϣⲁⲛⲧⲟⲩ-
ⲛⲟϫⲥ̄ ⲉⲃⲟⲗ ⳩ⲙ̄ ⲡⲡⲁⲣⲁⲇⲓⲥⲟⲥ.[4] ⲉⲣⲉ-ⲡⲉⲧ ⲕⲁⲧⲁⲗⲁⲗⲓ[5] ⲙ̄ ⲡⲉϥⲥⲟⲛ
ⲧⲛ̄ⲧⲱⲛ ⲉ ⲡⲁⲓ. ϣⲁϥⲧⲁⲕⲟ ⲅⲁⲣ ⲛ̄ ⲧⲉⲯⲩⲭⲏ ⲙ̄ ⲡⲉⲧ ⲥⲱⲧⲙ̄, ⲁⲩⲱ ⲧⲉϥ-
ⲕⲉⲟⲩⲉⲓ[6] ⲙ̄ⲙⲓⲛ ⲙ̄ⲙⲟϥ ⲙⲉϥⲧⲁⲛ⳩̄ⲟⲥ.

16. ⲁⲩϣⲁ ⲁⲉ ϣⲱⲡⲉ ⲛ̄ ⲟⲩⲟⲉⲓϣ ⳩ⲛ̄ ϣⲏⲧ, ⲁⲩⲱ ⲁⲩϯ ⲛ̄ ⲟⲩⲁⲡⲟⲧ ⲛ̄
ⲏⲣⲡ̄ ⲛ̄ ⲟⲩ⳩ⲁⲗⲟ. ⲡⲉϫⲁϥ ϫⲉ, "ϥⲓ ⲉⲃⲟⲗ ⲙ̄ⲙⲟⲓ ⲙ̄ ⲡⲓⲙⲟⲩ." ⲛ̄ⲧⲉⲣⲉ-
ⲡⲕⲉⲥⲉⲉⲡⲉ ⲁⲉ ⲛⲁⲩ ⲉⲧ ⲟⲩⲱⲙ ⲛⲙ̄ⲙⲁϥ, ⲙ̄ⲡⲟⲩϫⲓ.

17. ⲁⲩϫⲓ ⲁⲉ ⲟⲛ ⲛ̄ ⲟⲩⲥⲁⲓⲁⲓⲟⲛ[1] ⲛ̄ ⲏⲣⲡ̄ ⲛ̄ ⲁⲡⲁⲣⲭⲏ[2] ϫⲉ ⲉⲩⲉⲧⲁⲁϥ
ⲛ̄ ⲛⲉⲥⲛⲏⲩ ⲕⲁⲧⲁ ⲟⲩⲁⲡⲟⲧ ⲉ ⲡⲟⲩⲁ. ⲁ-ⲟⲩⲁ ⲁⲉ ⲛ̄ ⲛⲉⲥⲛⲏⲩ ⲃⲱⲕ ⲉ⳩ⲣⲁⲓ
ⲉϫⲛ̄ ⲧⲕⲩⲡⲏ,[3] ⲁϥⲡⲱⲧ ⲉⲃⲟⲗ ⳩ⲓϫⲱⲥ, ⲁⲩⲱ ⲛ̄ ⲧⲉⲩⲛⲟⲩ ⲁⲥ⳩ⲉ ⲛ̄ϭⲓ ⲧⲕⲩⲡⲏ.
ⲁⲩⲃⲱⲕ ⲁⲉ ⲉ ⲛⲁⲩ ⲉⲧⲃⲉ ⲡⲉ⳩ⲣⲟⲟⲩ ⲛ̄ⲧⲁϥϣⲱⲡⲉ, ⲁⲩ⳩ⲉ ⲉ ⲡⲥⲟⲛ ⲉϥⲛⲏϫ ⳩ⲓ
ⲡⲉⲥⲏⲧ. ⲁⲩ⳩ⲓ-ⲧⲟⲟⲧⲟⲩ ⲉ ⲥⲱϣ[4] ⲙ̄ⲙⲟϥ, ⲉⲩϫⲱ ⲙ̄ⲙⲟⲥ ϫⲉ, "ⲛ̄ⲧⲕ̄-ⲟⲩⲙⲁⲓ-
ⲉⲟⲟⲩ ⲉϥϣⲟⲩⲉⲓⲧ. ⲕⲁⲗⲱⲥ[5] ⲁ-ⲡⲁⲓ ϣⲱⲡⲉ ⲙ̄ⲙⲟⲕ." ⲁ-ⲡ⳩ⲁⲗⲟ ⲁⲉ ⲱⲗⲙ̄[6]
ⲉⲣⲟϥ, ⲉϥϫⲱ ⲙ̄ⲙⲟⲥ ϫⲉ, "ⲁⲗⲱⲧⲛ̄ ⳩ⲁ ⲡⲁϣⲏⲣⲉ. ⲟⲩ⳩ⲱⲃ ⲅⲁⲣ ⲉ-ⲛⲁⲛⲟⲩϥ
ⲡⲉ ⲛ̄ⲧⲁϥⲁⲁϥ. ϥⲟⲛ⳩̄[7] ⲛ̄ϭⲓ ⲡϫⲟⲉⲓⲥ ϫⲉ ⲛ̄ⲛⲉⲩⲕⲉⲧ-ⲧⲉⲓⲕⲩⲡⲏ ⳩ⲙ̄ ⲡⲁ-
ⲟⲩⲟⲉⲓϣ ⲧⲁⲣⲉ-ⲧⲟⲓⲕⲟⲩⲙⲉⲛⲏ ⲧⲏⲣⲥ̄ ⲉⲓⲙⲉ ϫⲉ ⲁⲩⲕⲏⲡⲏ ⳩ⲉ ⳩ⲛ̄ ϣⲓⲏⲧ ⲉⲧⲃⲉ

---

14. (1) ⲁⲃ = ⲁϥ. (2) The Conj. continues the infinitives: (and it is good) that you not eat the flesh of your
brothers (i.e. calumniate them). (3) ⲧ.ⲕⲁⲧⲁⲗⲁⲗⲓⲁ (ἡ καταλαλία) slander.

15. (1) ⲡ.⳩ⲟϥ (f. ⲧⲉ.⳩ϥⲱ) snake, serpent. (2) ⲕⲟⲥⲕⲉⲥ =
ⲕⲁⲥⲕⲥ̄ to whisper. (3) ⲉⲩ⳩ⲁ Eve. (4) ⲡ.ⲡⲁⲣⲁⲇⲓⲥⲟⲥ (ὁ παράδεισος) Paradise, Eden. (5) ⲕⲁⲧⲁⲗⲁⲗⲓ (καταλαλέω) to slander. (6) ⲟⲩⲉⲓ is used pronominally: his own one (soul).

17. (1) ⲡ.ⲥⲁⲓⲁⲓⲟⲛ (τὸ σαίτιον) keg. (2) ⲧ.ⲁⲡⲁⲣⲭⲏ (ἡ
ἀπαρχή) first-fruits; ⲏⲣⲡ̄ ⲛ̄ ⲁⲡⲁⲣⲭⲏ new wine. (3) ⲧ.ⲕⲩⲡⲏ,
ⲧ.ⲕⲏⲡⲏ arch, vault, vaulted place. (4) ⲥⲱϣ ⲥⲉϣ- ⲥⲟϣ⸗ Q
ⲥⲏϣ vb. tr. to scorn, treat with contempt (ⲙ̄ⲙⲟ⸗). (5) ⲕⲁⲗⲱⲥ (καλῶς) adv. well. (6) ⲱⲗⲙ̄ ⲉⲗⲙ⸗ Q ⲟⲗⲙ̄ vb. tr. to embrace (ⲉ). (7) An oath: "As the Lord lives,..."

ΟΥΔΠΟΤ Ν̄ ΗΡΠ̄.

18. ΔΥΣΟΝ ΚΙΜ 2Μ̄ ΠΕϤϬΩΝΤ̄ Ε 2ΟΥΝ Ε ΟΥΔ. ΔϤΔ 2ΕΡΔΤϤ̄ Ε
ΠΕϢΛΗΛ, ΔϤΔΙΤΕΙ Ε ΧΙ Ν̄ ΟΥΜΝ̄Τ2ΔΡϢ̄2ΗΤ[1] ΕΧΜ̄ ΠΕϤΣΟΝ ΔΥΩ Ε ΠΔΡΔ-
ΓΕ[2] Μ̄ ΠΠΙΡΔΣΜΟΣ ΔΧΜ̄ ΠΩΛΔ2.[3] ΔΥΩ Ν̄ ΤΕΥΝΟΥ ΔϤΝΔΥ ΕΥΚΔΠΝΟΣ[4]
ΕϤΝΗΥ ΕΒΟΛ 2Ν̄ ΤΕϤΤΔΠΡΟ. Ν̄ΤΕΡΕ-ΠΔΙ ΔΕ ϢΩΠΕ, ΔϤΛΟ ΕϤϬΟΝΤ̄.

19. ΔϤΒΩΚ Ν̄ ΟΥΟΕΙϢ Ν̄ϬΙ ΠΕΠΡΕΣΒΥΤΕΡΟΣ[1] Ν̄ ϢΙΗΤ ϢΔ ΠΔΡ-
ΧΗΕΠΙΣΚΟΠΟΣ Ν̄ ΡΔΚΟΤΕ ΔΥΩ Ν̄ΤΕΡΕϤΚΤΟϤ Ε ϢΙΗΤ, ΔΥΧΝΟΥϤ Ν̄ϬΙ
ΝΕΣΝΗΥ ΧΕ, "ΕΡΕ-ΤΠΟΛΙΣ Ρ̄-ΟΥ?" Ν̄ΤΟϤ ΔΕ ΠΕΧΔϤ ΝΔΥ ΧΕ,
"ΦΥΣΙ,[2] ΝΔΣΝΗΥ, ΔΝΟΚ Μ̄ΠΙΝΔΥ Ε Π2Ο Ν̄ ΛΔΔΥ Ν̄ ΡΩΜΕ Ν̄ΣΔ ΠΔΡ-
ΧΗΕΠΙΣΚΟΠΟΣ ΜΔΥΔΔϤ." Ν̄ΤΟΟΥ ΔΕ Ν̄ΤΕΡΟΥΣΩΤΜ̄, ΔΥΤΔΧΡΟ[3] ΕΤΒΕ
ΠϢΔΧΕ ΧΕ ΕΥΕ2ΔΡΕ2 ΕΡΟΟΥ 2ΔΒΟΛ 2Δ ΠΧΙ-2ΡΔϤ[4] Ν̄ Ν̄ΒΔΛ.

21. Δ-ΟΥΔ Ν̄ Π2Λ̄ΛΟ ΒΩΚ ϢΔ ΚΕ2Λ̄ΛΟ, ΔΥΩ ΠΕΧΔϤ Μ̄ ΠΕϤΜΔΘΗ-
ΤΗΣ ΧΕ, "ΤΔΜΙΟ ΝΔΝ Ν̄ ΟΥΚΟΥΙ Ν̄ ΔΡϢΙΝ,"[1] ΔΥΩ ΔϤΤΔΜΙΟϤ. ΠΕΧΔϤ
ΧΕ, "2ΕΡΠ̄-2ΕΝΟΕΙΚ[2] ΝΔΝ," ΔΥΩ ΔϤ2ΟΡΠΟΥ. Ν̄ΤΟΟΥ ΔΕ ΔΥΜΟΥΝ
ΕΒΟΛ ΕΥϢΔΧΕ Ε ΝΕΠΝ̄ΙΚΟΝ[3] Μ̄ ΠΕ2ΟΟΥ ΤΗΡϤ̄ ΜΝ̄ ΤΕΥϢΗ ΤΗΡΣ̄.

23. ΔϤΧΟΟΣ Ν̄ϬΙ ΔΠΔ ΙΣΔΚ ΧΕ, "ΝΕΝΕΙΟΤΕ ΜΕΝ ΔΠΔ ΠΔΜΒΩ[1]
ΝΕΥΦΟΡΕΙ[2] Ν̄ 2ΕΝϢΤΗΝ Μ̄ ΠΕΛϬΕ ΕΥ2Ν̄ Ν̄ΤΟΕΙΣ ΜΝ̄ 2ΕΝϢΤΗΝ Ν̄ ϢΒ̄-
ΒΝ̄ΝΕ.[3] Ν̄ΤΩΤΝ̄ ΔΕ ΤΕΝΟΥ ΤΕΤΝ̄ΦΟΡΕΙ 2ΕΝϢΤΗΝ ΕΥΤΔΕΙΗΥ. ΒΩΚ

---

18. (1) 2ΔΡϢ̄-2ΗΤ adj. patient, long-suffering; ΜΝ̄Τ2ΔΡϢ̄-
2ΗΤ patience. (2) ΠΔΡΔΓΕ (παράγω) to pass, pass by, away.
(3) ΠΩΛ2̄ ΠΟΛ2⸗ Q ΠΟΛ2̄ vb. tr. to wound, damage, offend.
(4) Π.ΚΔΠΝΟΣ (ὁ καπνός) smoke.

19. (1) ΠΡΕΣΒΥΤΕΡΟΣ (ὁ πρεσβύτερος) elder. (2) ΨΥΣΙ an
expletive of some sort, but cf. gloss 175(5) below. (3)
ΤΔΧΡΟ ΤΔΧΡΕ- ΤΔΧΡΟ⸗ Q ΤΔΧΡΗΥ vb. tr. to affirm, confirm,
strengthen (Μ̄ΜΟ⸗); intr. to be confirmed, resolute. (4)
ΧΙ-2ΡΔ⸗ to amuse or divert self; as n.m. diversion, distraction.

21. (1) Π.ΔΡϢΙΝ lentil(s). (2) 2ΩΡΠ̄ 2ΕΡΠ̄- 2ΟΡΠ⸗ Q 2ΟΡΠ̄
vb. tr. to moisten (Μ̄ΜΟ⸗); also intr. to get wet, drenched.
(3) ΝΕ.ΠΝ(ΕΥΜΔΤ)ΙΚΟΝ (τὰ πνευματικά) spiritual matters.

23. (1) Perhaps insert ΜΝ̄ before ΔΠΔ ΠΔΜΒΩ. (2) ΦΟΡΕΙ
(φορέω) to wear. (3) Π.ϢΒ̄ΒΝ̄ΝΕ palm-fiber.

ⲛ̄ⲧⲱⲧⲛ̄ ⲙ̄ ⲡⲉⲓⲙⲁ! ⲁⲧⲉⲧⲛ̄ⲧⲁⲕⲟϥ."

24. ⲉⲩⲛⲁⲃⲱⲕ ⲁⲉ ⲉ ⲡⲱ₂ⲥ̄,[1] ⲡⲉⲭⲁϥ ⲛⲁⲩ ϫⲉ, "ⲛ̄ϯⲛⲁⲃⲱⲕ ⲁⲛ ⲉ ⲕⲟⲧⲧ ⲉ ϯ-ⲉⲛⲧⲟⲗⲏ ⲛⲏⲧⲛ̄; ⲛ̄ⲧⲉⲧⲛ̄₂ⲁⲣⲉ₂ ⲅⲁⲣ ⲁⲛ."

25. ⲛ̄ⲧⲁϥ ⲟⲛ ⲁϥϫⲟⲟⲥ ϫⲉ, "ⲁ-ⲁⲡⲁ ⲡⲁⲙⲃⲱ ϫⲟⲟⲥ ϫⲉ, 'ⲧⲁⲓ ⲧⲉ ⲑⲉ ⲉⲧⲉ ϣϣⲉ ⲉ ⲡⲙⲟⲛⲁⲭⲟⲥ ⲉ ⲫⲟⲣⲉⲓ ⲛ̄ ⲛⲉϥ₂ⲟⲓⲧⲉ: ₂ⲱⲥⲧⲉ ⲉ ⲛⲉⲭ-ⲧⲉϥϣⲧⲏⲛ ⲙ̄ ⲡⲃⲟⲗ ⲛ̄ ⲧⲉϥⲣⲓ ⲛ̄ ϣⲟⲙⲛ̄ⲧ ⲛ̄ ₂ⲟⲟⲩ, ⲛ̄ⲧⲉⲧⲙ̄-ⲁⲗⲁⲩ ⲧⲁⲓⲟⲥ[1] ⲉ ϥⲓⲧⲥ̄, ⲧⲟⲧⲉ ⲉϥⲉⲫⲟⲣⲓ ⲙ̄ⲙⲟⲥ.'"

26. ⲁϥϫⲟⲟⲥ ⲛ̄ϭⲓ ⲁⲡⲁ ⲕⲁⲥⲓⲁⲛⲟⲥ ϫⲉ, "ⲟⲩⲁ ⲛ̄ ⲛ̄ⲥⲩⲛⲕⲗⲏⲧⲓⲕⲟⲥ,[1] ⲉ-ⲁϥⲁⲡⲟⲧⲁⲥⲥⲉ[2] ⲛ̄ ⲛⲉϥⲭⲣⲏⲙⲁ[3] ⲧⲏⲣⲟⲩ, ⲁϥⲧⲁⲁϥ ⲛ̄ ⲛ̄₂ⲏⲕⲉ. ⲁϥⲕⲁ-₂ⲉⲛⲕⲟⲩⲓ ⲛⲁϥ ⲉⲧⲃⲉ ⲧⲉϥⲭⲣⲓⲁ ⲙⲁⲩⲁⲁϥ. ⲙ̄ⲡⲉϥⲟⲩⲱϣ ⲉ ⲱⲛ₂ ₂ⲛ̄ ⲟⲩ-ⲙ̄ⲛ̄ⲧⲁⲡⲟⲧⲁⲕⲧⲓⲕⲟⲥ[4] ⲉⲧ ϫⲏⲕ ⲉⲃⲟⲗ ⲛ̄ⲧⲉ ⲡⲉⲑⲃ̄ⲃⲓⲟ ⲛ̄ ₂ⲏⲧ. ⲡⲁⲓ ⲁⲉ ⲁϥϫⲱ ⲛ̄ ⲟⲩϣⲁϫⲉ ⲛⲁ₂ⲣⲁϥ ⲛ̄ϭⲓ ⲃⲁⲥⲓⲙⲟⲥ, ⲡⲉⲧ ϣⲟⲟⲡ ₂ⲛ̄ ⲛⲉⲧ ⲟⲩⲁⲁⲃ, ⲉϥϫⲱ ⲙ̄ⲙⲟⲥ ϫⲉ, 'ⲧⲙ̄ⲛ̄ⲧⲥⲩⲛⲕⲗⲏⲧⲓⲕⲟⲥ ⲁⲕⲥⲟⲣⲙⲉⲥ,[5] ⲁⲩⲱ ⲧⲙ̄ⲛ̄ⲧⲙⲟⲛⲁⲭⲟⲥ ⲙ̄ⲡⲉⲕ₂ⲉ ⲉⲣⲟⲥ.'"

27. ⲁ-ⲟⲩⲁ ⲛ̄ ⲛⲉⲥⲛⲏⲩ ϫⲛⲉ-ⲁⲡⲁ ⲡⲁⲥⲧⲁⲙⲱⲛ ϫⲉ, "ⲟⲩ ⲡⲉⲧⲓⲛⲁⲁⲁϥ, ϫⲉ ⲥⲉⲑⲗⲓⲃⲉ[1] ⲙ̄ⲙⲟⲓ ⲉⲓϯ ⲙ̄ ⲡⲁ₂ⲱⲃ ⲛ̄ ϭⲓϫ ⲉⲃⲟⲗ?" ⲁϥⲟⲩⲱϣⲃ̄ ⲛ̄ϭⲓ ⲡ₂ⲗ̄ⲗⲟ, ⲡⲉⲭⲁϥ ϫⲉ, "ⲡⲕⲉ-ⲁⲡⲁ ϫⲓϫⲱⲓ ⲙ̄ⲛ̄ ⲡⲕⲉⲥⲉⲉⲡⲉ ϣⲁⲩϯ-ⲡⲉⲩ₂ⲱⲃ ⲛ̄ ϭⲓϫ ⲉⲃⲟⲗ. ⲡⲁⲓ ⲛ̄ ⲟⲩⲟⲥⲉ ⲁⲛ ⲡⲉ. ⲉⲕϣⲁⲛⲛⲟⲩ[2] ⲁⲉ ⲉ ϯ, ⲁϫⲓ-ⲧϯⲙⲏ[3]

---

24. (1) ⲱ₂ⲥ̄ ⲉ₂ⲥ̄- ⲟ₂ⲥ⸗ vb. tr. to reap, harvest; as n.m. harvesting, reaping. ₂ and ⲥ are often interchanged in this word. Note -ⲧ for zero (1st pers. obj.) on ⲕⲟⲧⲧ.

25. (1) The sense is that if no one thought it worth taking, it was suitable to be worn by a monk.

26. (1) ⲥⲩⲛⲕⲗⲏⲧⲓⲕⲟⲥ (συγκλητικός) adj. of noble rank; ⲧ.ⲙⲛ̄ⲧⲥⲩⲛⲕⲗⲏⲧⲓⲕⲟⲥ nobility. (2) ⲁⲡⲟⲧⲁⲥⲥⲉ (ἀποτάσσω) to renounce, give up. (3) ⲡⲉ.ⲭⲣⲏⲙⲁ (τὸ χρῆμα) goods, money. (4) ⲡ.ⲁⲡⲟⲧⲁⲕⲧⲓⲕⲟⲥ (ἀποτακτικός) anchorite, hermit monk; ⲧ.ⲙⲛ̄ⲧⲁⲡⲟⲧⲁⲕⲧⲓⲕⲟⲥ status of anchorite. (5) ⲥⲱⲣⲙ̄ ⲥⲉⲣⲙ̄- ⲥⲟⲣⲙ⸗ Q ⲥⲟⲣⲙ̄ vb. tr. to lose (ⲙ̄ⲙⲟ⸗); intr. to go astray, be lost.

27. (1) ⲑⲗⲓⲃⲉ (θλίβω) to afflict, distress; passive construction here. (2) ⲛⲟⲩ vb. intr. (aux.) to be about to, be going to (do: ⲉ + Inf.). (3) ⲧ.ϯⲙⲏ (ἡ τιμή) price, value.

176

ⲛ̄ ⲟⲩⲥⲟⲡ ⲛ̄ ⲟⲩⲱⲧ ⲛ̄ⲧⲉ ⲡⲓⲁⲟⲥ.⁴ ⲉⲕϣⲁⲛⲟⲩⲱϣ ⲁⲉ ⲉ ⲕⲁ-ⲟⲩⲕⲟⲩⲓ ⲉⲃⲟⲗ
ⲍⲛ̄ ⲥⲟⲩⲛ̄ⲧϥ,⁵ ⲛ̄ⲧⲟⲕ ⲉⲧ ⲧⲱϣ. ⲧⲁⲓ ⲧⲉ ⲑⲉ ⲉⲧⲉⲕⲛⲁϭⲛ̄-ⲙ̄ⲧⲟⲛ." ⲡⲉϫⲉ-
ⲡⲥⲟⲛ ⲛⲁϥ ϫⲉ, "ⲉϣⲱⲡⲉ ⲟⲩⲛ̄ⲧⲁⲓ ⲧⲁⲭⲣⲓⲁ ⲙ̄ⲙⲁⲩ, ⲕⲟⲩⲱϣ ⲉⲧⲙ̄ⲧⲣⲁϥⲉⲓ-
ⲣⲟⲟⲩϣ⁶ ⲍⲁ ⲍⲱⲃ ⲛ̄ ϭⲓϫ?" ⲁϥⲟⲩⲱϣⲃ̄ ⲛ̄ϭⲓ ⲡ₂ⲗ̄ⲗⲟ ϫⲉ, "ⲕⲁⲛ⁷ ⲟⲩⲛ̄ⲧⲁⲕ
ⲍⲱⲃ ⲛⲓⲙ, ⲙ̄ⲡⲣ̄ⲕⲁ-ⲡ₂ⲱⲃ ⲛ̄ ϭⲓϫ ⲉⲃⲟⲗ. ⲡⲉⲧⲉ ⲟⲩⲛ̄-ϭⲟⲙ ⲙ̄ⲙⲟⲕ ⲉ ⲁⲁϥ,
ⲁⲣⲓϥ, ⲙⲟⲛⲟⲛ⁸ ⲍⲛ̄ ⲟⲩϣⲧⲟⲣⲧⲣ̄ ⲁⲛ."

28. ⲁ-ⲟⲩⲥⲟⲛ ϫⲛⲉ-ⲁⲡⲁ ⲥⲁⲣⲁⲡⲓⲟⲛ ϫⲉ, "ⲁϫⲓ-ⲟⲩϣⲁϫⲉ ⲉⲣⲟⲓ."
ⲡⲉϫⲉ-ⲡ₂ⲗ̄ⲗⲟ ⲛⲁϥ ϫⲉ, "ⲉⲓⲛⲁϫⲉ-ⲟⲩ ⲛⲁⲕ? ϫⲉ ⲁⲕϥⲓ-ⲡ̄ⲉⲛⲕⲁ ⲛ̄ ⲛ̄₂ⲏⲕⲉ
ⲙ̄ⲛ̄ ⲛⲉⲭⲏⲣⲁ ⲙ̄ⲛ̄ ⲛ̄ⲟⲣⲫⲁⲛⲟⲥ, ⲁⲕⲕⲁⲁⲩ ⲍⲙ̄ ⲡϣⲟⲩϣⲧ̄."¹ ⲁϥⲛⲁⲩ ⲅⲁⲣ ⲉ
ⲡϣⲟⲩϣⲧ̄ ⲉϥⲙⲉⲍ ⲛ̄ ⲭⲱⲱⲙⲉ.

31. ⲛⲉ-ⲟⲩⲛ̄-ⲟⲩⲁ ⲁⲉ ⲛ̄ⲧⲉ ⲛⲉⲧ ⲟⲩⲁⲁⲃ ⲉϣⲁⲩⲙⲟⲩⲧⲉ ⲉⲣⲟϥ ϫⲉ ⲫⲓ-
ⲗⲁⲅⲣⲓⲟⲥ ⲉϥⲟⲩⲏⲍ ⲍⲛ̄ ⲑ̄ⲗ̄ⲏⲙ̄, ⲉϥⲣ̄-ⲍⲱⲃ ⲍⲛ̄ ⲟⲩₐⲓⲥⲉ ϣⲁⲛⲧⲉϥϫⲡⲟ ⲛⲁϥ ⲙ̄
ⲡⲉϥⲟⲉⲓⲕ ⲙ̄ⲙⲓⲛ ⲙ̄ⲙⲟϥ. ⲛ̄₂ⲱⲥⲟⲛ ⲁⲉ ⲉϥⲁⲍⲉⲣⲁⲧϥ̄ ⲍⲛ̄ ⲧⲁⲅⲱⲣⲁ ⲉ † ⲙ̄
ⲡⲉϥⲍⲱⲃ ⲛ̄ ϭⲓϫ ⲉⲃⲟⲗ, ⲉⲓⲥ ⲍⲏⲏⲧⲉ ⲍⲛ̄ ⲟⲩϣ̄ⲛⲉ ⲁϥⲉⲓⲛⲉ ⲛ̄ ⲟⲩⲃⲁⲗⲗⲁⲧⲓⲟⲛ¹
ⲉⲩⲛ̄-ⲙⲏⲧ ⲛ̄ ϣⲉ ⲛ̄ ₂ⲟⲗⲟⲕⲟⲧⲧⲓⲛⲟⲥ² ₂ⲓⲱⲱⲥ. ⲁϥⲁⲍⲉⲣⲁⲧϥ̄ ⲙ̄ ⲡⲉϥⲙⲁ, ⲉϥϫⲱ ⲙ̄ⲙⲟⲥ ϫⲉ, "ⲍⲁⲡⲥ̄ ⲡⲉ ⲉⲧⲣⲉ-ⲡⲉⲛⲧⲁϥⲥⲟⲣⲙⲉⲥ ⲉⲓ." ⲁⲩⲱ ⲉⲓⲥ ⲡⲉⲧ
ⲙ̄ⲙⲁⲩ ⲁϥⲉⲓ ⲉϥⲣⲓⲙⲉ. ⲁϥϭⲟⲡϥ̄ ⲁⲉ ⲛ̄ϭⲓ ⲡ₂ⲗ̄ⲗⲟ, ⲁϥϫⲓⲧϥ̄ ⲛ̄ ⲥⲁ ⲟⲩⲥⲁ,
ⲁϥⲧⲁⲁⲥ ⲛⲁϥ. ⲡⲉⲧ ⲙ̄ⲙⲁⲩ ⲁⲉ ⲁϥⲁⲙⲁⲍⲧⲉ ⲙ̄ⲙⲟϥ, ⲉϥⲟⲩⲱϣ ⲉ † ⲛ̄ ⲟⲩ-
ⲟⲩⲱⲛ³ ⲛⲁϥ. ⲡ₂ⲗ̄ⲗⲟ ⲁⲉ ⲙ̄ⲡⲉϥⲟⲩⲱϣ ⲉ ϫⲓ. ⲧⲟⲧⲉ ⲁϥₐⲓ-ⲧⲟⲟⲧϥ̄ ⲉ ϫⲓ-
ϣⲕⲁⲕ ⲉⲃⲟⲗ, ⲉϥϫⲱ ⲙ̄ⲙⲟⲥ ϫⲉ, "ⲁⲙⲏⲓⲧⲛ̄ ⲛ̄ⲧⲉⲧⲛ̄ⲛⲁⲩ ⲉⲩⲣⲱⲙⲉ ⲛ̄ⲧⲉ ⲡⲛⲟⲩⲧⲉ
ϫⲉ ⲛ̄ⲧⲁϥⲣ̄-ⲟⲩ." ⲡ₂ⲗ̄ⲗⲟ ⲁⲉ ⲁϥⲡⲱⲧ ⲛ̄ ϫⲓⲟⲩⲉ, ⲁϥⲉⲓ ⲉⲃⲟⲗ ⲍⲛ̄ ⲧⲡⲟⲗⲓⲥ
ϫⲉ ⲡ̄ⲛⲉⲩⲥⲟⲩⲱⲛϥ̄.

38. ⲁϥⲃⲱⲕ ⲛ̄ϭⲓ ⲁⲡⲁ ⲙⲁⲕⲁⲣⲓⲟⲥ ⲡⲛⲟϭ ϣⲁ ⲁⲡⲁ ⲁⲛⲧⲱⲛⲓⲟⲥ, ⲁⲩⲱ

---

(4) ⲡ.ⲓⲁⲟⲥ (τὸ εἶδος) kind, sort.   (5) ⲥⲟⲩⲛ̄ⲧ⸗ price, value
(w. suff. only); ⲕⲁ-ⲟⲩⲕⲟⲩⲓ ⲉⲃⲟⲗ ₂ⲛ̄ to deduct a little from.
(6) ϥⲓ-ⲣⲟⲟⲩϣ to be concerned, anxious (about: ⲉ, ⲉⲧⲃⲉ, ₂ⲁ),
to care about.   (7) ⲕⲁⲛ (κἄν) even if.   (8) ⲙⲟⲛⲟⲛ (μόνον)
only, alone; but (w. neg.).

28. (1) ⲡ.ϣⲟⲩϣⲧ̄ window; niche, alcove.

31. (1) ⲃⲁⲗⲗⲁⲧⲓⲟⲛ (τὸ βαλλάντιον) purse; note resumption as fem. in ₂ⲓⲱⲱⲥ, ⲥⲟⲣⲙⲉⲥ, ⲧⲁⲁⲥ.   (2) ⲡ.₂ⲟⲗⲟⲕⲟⲧⲧⲓⲛⲟⲥ (ὁ
ὁλοκόττινος) a gold coin.   (3) ⲡ.ⲟⲩⲱⲛ part, share.

ⲚⲦⲉⲢⲉϤⲕⲱⲗⲍ̄¹ ⲉ ⲡⲢⲟ, ⲀϤⲉⲓ ⲉⲂⲟⲗ ϢⲀⲢⲟϤ, ⲡⲉⲬⲀϤ ⲚⲀϤ Ⲭ(ⲉ), "Ⲛ̄Ⲧⲕ̄-
ⲚⲓⲘ?" Ⲛ̄ⲦⲟϤ Ⲁⲉ ⲀϤⲟⲨⲰϢⲂ̄ ⲉϤⲬⲰ Ⲙ̄Ⲙⲟⲥ Ⲭⲉ, "ⲀⲚⲟⲕ ⲡⲉ ⲘⲀⲕⲀⲢⲓⲟⲥ."
ⲀⲨⲱ ⲀϤϢⲦⲀⲘ² Ⲙ̄ ⲡⲢⲟ, ⲀϤⲂⲰⲕ ⲉⲌⲟⲨⲚ, ⲀϤⲕⲀⲀϤ. Ⲛ̄ⲦⲉⲢⲉϤⲚⲀⲨ ⲉ ⲦⲉϤ-
ⲌⲨⲡⲟⲘⲟⲚⲏ,³ ⲀϤⲟⲨⲰⲚ ⲚⲀϤ, ⲀⲨⲱ ⲀϤⲟⲨⲢⲟⲦ⁴ Ⲛ̄Ⲙ̄ⲘⲀϤ, ⲉϤⲬⲰ Ⲙ̄Ⲙⲟⲥ Ⲭⲉ,
"ⲉⲓⲥ ⲟⲨⲚⲟϬ Ⲛ̄ ⲟⲨⲟⲉⲓϢ ⲉⲓⲟⲨⲰϢ ⲉ ⲚⲀⲨ ⲉⲢⲟⲕ. ⲀⲓⲥⲰⲦⲘ̄ ⲄⲀⲢ ⲉⲦⲂⲎⲎⲦⲕ̄."
ⲀⲨⲱ ⲀϤϢⲟⲡϤ̄ ⲉⲢⲟϤ Ⲍ̄Ⲛ̄ ⲟⲨⲘⲚ̄ⲦⲘⲀⲓⲢⲰⲘⲉ, ⲀϤϯ-Ⲙ̄ⲦⲟⲚ ⲚⲀϤ, Ⲛ̄ⲦⲀϤⲉⲓ ⲄⲀⲢ
ⲉⲂⲟⲗ Ⲍ̄Ⲛ̄ ⲌⲉⲚⲚⲟϬ Ⲛ̄ Ⲍⲓⲥⲉ. Ⲛ̄ⲦⲉⲢⲉ-ⲢⲟⲨⲌⲉ Ⲁⲉ ϢⲰⲡⲉ, Ⲁ-ⲀⲡⲀ ⲀⲚⲦⲰⲚⲓ-
ⲟⲥ ⲌⲰⲢⲡ̄ ⲚⲀϤ Ⲛ̄ ⲌⲉⲚⲕⲟⲨⲓ Ⲛ̄ ⲂⲎⲦ.⁵ ⲡⲉⲬⲉ-ⲀⲡⲀ ⲘⲀⲕⲀⲢⲓⲟⲥ ⲚⲀϤ Ⲭⲉ,
"ⲕⲉⲗⲉⲨⲉ⁶ ⲚⲀⲓ ⲦⲀⲌⲰⲢⲡ̄ ⲚⲀⲓ ⲘⲀⲨⲀⲀⲦ." Ⲛ̄ⲦⲟϤ Ⲁⲉ ⲡⲉⲬⲀϤ Ⲭⲉ, "ⲌⲰⲢⲡ̄."
ⲀⲨⲱ ⲀϤⲦⲀⲘⲓⲟ Ⲛ̄ ⲟⲨⲚⲟϬ Ⲛ̄ Ϣⲟⲗ⁷ Ⲛ̄ ⲂⲎⲦ, ⲀϤⲌⲟⲢⲡϤ̄. ⲀⲨⲌⲘⲟⲟⲥ, ⲀⲨ-
ϢⲀⲬⲉ ⲉ ⲦⲘⲚ̄ⲦⲢⲉϤϯ-ⲌⲎⲨ⁸ Ⲛ̄ ⲦⲉⲯⲨⲬⲏ ⲬⲓⲚ Ⲙ̄ ⲡⲚⲀⲨ Ⲛ̄ ⲢⲟⲨⲌⲉ. ⲀⲨⲚⲟⲂ-
ⲦⲟⲨ,⁹ ⲀⲨⲱ ⲦⲚⲎⲂⲦⲉ¹⁰ ⲀⲥⲂⲰⲕ ⲉⲡⲉⲥⲎⲦ ⲉ ⲡⲉⲥⲡⲨⲗⲏⲟⲚ¹¹ ⲉⲂⲟⲗ ⲌⲓⲦⲘ̄
ⲡϢⲟⲨⲰϢⲦ. ⲀϤⲂⲰⲕ ⲉⲌⲟⲨⲚ ⲉ ⲌⲦⲟⲟⲨⲉ Ⲛ̄Ϭⲓ ⲡⲘⲀⲕⲀⲢⲓⲟⲥ¹² ⲀⲡⲀ ⲀⲚⲦⲰⲚⲓⲟⲥ,
ⲀϤⲚⲀⲨ ⲉ ⲡⲀϢⲀⲓ¹³ Ⲛ̄ ⲦⲚⲎⲂⲦⲉ Ⲛ̄ ⲀⲡⲀ ⲘⲀⲕⲀⲢⲓⲟⲥ, ⲀϤⲢ̄-ϢⲡⲎⲢⲉ, ⲀⲨⲱ
ⲀϤϯ-ⲡⲓ¹⁴ ⲉ Ⲛ̄Ϭⲓ Ⲭ Ⲛ̄ ⲀⲡⲀ ⲘⲀⲕⲀⲢⲓⲟⲥ, ⲉϤⲬⲰ Ⲙ̄Ⲙⲟⲥ Ⲭⲉ, "Ⲁ-ⲌⲀⲌ Ⲛ̄ ϬⲟⲘ
ⲉⲓ ⲉⲂⲟⲗ Ⲍ̄Ⲛ̄ ⲚⲉⲓϬⲓⲬ."

48. Ⲛⲉ-ⲟⲨⲚ̄-ⲟⲨⲥⲟⲚ ⲀⲬⲚ̄ ⲥⲂ̄ⲢⲀⲍⲦ̄ Ⲍ̄Ⲛ̄ ⲟⲨⲌⲉⲚⲉⲉⲦⲉ. ⲌⲀⲍ Ⲁⲉ Ⲛ̄
ⲥⲟⲡ ϢⲀϤⲕⲓⲘ ⲉⲨⲟⲢⲅⲏ. ⲡⲉⲬⲀϤ Ϭⲉ ⲌⲢⲀⲓ Ⲛ̄ⲌⲎⲦϤ̄ Ⲭⲉ, "ϯⲚⲀⲂⲰⲕ ⲦⲀϬⲰ
ⲘⲀⲨⲀⲀⲦ ⲉⲓⲀⲚⲀⲬⲰⲢⲉⲓ.¹ ⲀⲨⲱ Ⲍ̄Ⲙ̄ ⲡⲦⲢⲀⲦⲘ̄ϬⲚ̄-ⲌⲱⲂ ⲘⲚ̄ ⲗⲀⲀⲨ ϯⲚⲀⲥⲂ̄ⲢⲀⲌⲦ̄
ⲀⲨⲱ ⲡⲡⲁⲑⲟⲥ ⲚⲀⲗⲟ Ⲛ̄ⲌⲎⲦ." ⲀϤⲉⲓ Ⲁⲉ ⲉⲂⲟⲗ, ⲀϤⲟⲨⲱⲌ ⲘⲀⲨⲀⲀϤ Ⲍ̄Ⲛ̄

---

38. (1) ⲕⲱⲗⲍ̄ ⲕⲗ̄ⲍ- ⲕⲟⲗⲍˀ Q ⲕⲟⲗⲍ̄ vb. intr. to strike,
knock (at: ⲉ). (2) ϢⲦⲀⲘ vb. tr. to shut (Ⲙ̄Ⲙⲟˀ). (3) Ⲧ.ⲌⲨⲡⲟ-
ⲘⲟⲚⲏ (ἡ ὑπομονή) patience, endurance; he apparently made
him wait a long time. (4) ⲟⲨⲢⲟⲦ, Q ⲢⲟⲟⲨⲦ vb. intr. to be
happy, glad. (5) ⲡ.ⲂⲎⲦ palm leaves (moistened and used for
weaving). (6) ⲕⲉⲗⲉⲨⲉ (κελεύω) to order, bid, command.
(7) ⲡ.Ϣⲟⲗ bundle. (8) ϯ-ⲌⲎⲨ to benefit, profit; ⲢⲉϤϯ-ⲌⲎⲨ
beneficial; ⲘⲚ̄ⲦⲢⲉϤϯ-ⲌⲎⲨ benefit, profit, what is beneficial. (9) ⲚⲟⲨⲂⲦ̄ ⲚⲟⲂⲦˀ vb. tr. to weave (Ⲙ̄Ⲙⲟˀ). (10) Ⲧ.ⲚⲎⲂⲦⲉ
weaving, basketry. (11) ⲡⲉ.ⲥⲡⲨⲗⲏⲟⲚ (τὸ σπήλαιον) cave.
(12) ⲘⲀⲕⲀⲢⲓⲟⲥ (μακάριος) blessed; used here as epithet of
Apa Antonios; do not confuse with Apa Makarios. (13) ⲡ.ⲗϢⲀⲓ
multitude, large amount. (14) ϯ-ⲡⲓ to kiss (ⲉ).
48. (1) ⲀⲚⲀⲬⲰⲢⲉⲓ (ἀναχωρέω) to retire, withdraw; to go

ΟΥⲤΠΥλλΙΟΝ. ²Ⲛ ΟΥⲤΟⲠ λⲈ λϥⲘⲈ₂-ⲠⲈϥⲔⲈλⲱλ² Ⲙ ⲘΟΟΥ, λϥΟΥλ₂ϥ
Ⲉ ⲠⲔλ₂, λΥⲱ Ⲛ ⲦⲈΥΝΟΥ λϥⲤⲔΟⲢⲔⲢ.³ ⲚⲦⲈⲢⲈϥϬⲱⲚⲦ λⲈ, λϥϥ ΙⲦϥ,
λϥΟΥΟϬⲠϥ.⁴ λ-ⲠⲈϥ₂ⲎⲦ λⲈ ⲈΙ ⲈⲢΟϥ, λϥⲈΙⲘⲈ ⲭⲈ Πλ ⲈⲘⲱⲚ ⲠⲈⲦ ┼
ⲚⲘⲘλϥ, λΥⲱ ⲠⲈⲭλϥ ⲭⲈ, "ⲈΙⲤ ₂ⲎⲎⲦⲈ ΟⲚ ┼λⲚλⲭⲱⲢⲈΙ ⲘλΥλλⲦ λΥⲱ
┼ϬΟⲚⲦ. ⲈΙⲚλⲂⲱⲔ ⲚⲦΟΟΥⲚ Ⲉ ⲐⲈⲚⲈⲈⲦⲈ. ⲤⲢ-ⲭⲢΙλ ⲄλⲢ Ⲉ ⲘΙϢⲈ ⲈⲢΟϥ
Ⲙ Ⲙλ ⲚΙⲘ λΥⲱ Ⲛ ₂ΟΥΟ ₂ΥⲠΟⲘΙⲚⲈ⁵ Ⲉ ⲦⲂΟⲎⲐΙλ⁶ Ⲙ ⲠⲚΟΥⲦⲈ." λϥⲔⲦΟϥ
λⲈ, λϥⲂⲱⲔ Ⲉ ⲠⲈϥⲘλ.

70. λ-ΟΥⲤΟⲚ ⲭΙ Ⲙ ⲠⲈⲤⲬⲎⲘλ, λϥλΝλⲭⲱⲢⲈΙ Ⲛ ⲦⲈΥΝΟΥ, Ⲉϥⲭⲱ
ⲘⲘΟⲤ ⲭⲈ, "λⲚⲄ-ΟΥλⲚλⲭⲱⲢΙⲦⲎⲤ."¹ λΥⲤⲱⲦⲘ λⲈ ⲚϬΙ Ⲛ₂λⲗΟ, λΥⲂⲱⲔ,
λΥ┼-ⲦΟΟⲦΟΥ² ⲘⲘΟϥ, λΥⲱ λΥⲦⲢⲈϥⲔⲱⲦⲈ³ Ⲉ Ⲛ Ⲣ Ι Ⲛ ⲚⲈⲤⲚⲎΥ ⲈϥⲘⲈⲦλⲚΟΙ,
Ⲉϥⲭⲱ ⲘⲘΟⲤ ⲭⲈ, "Ⲕⲱ Ⲛλ Ι ⲈⲂΟλ. λⲚⲄ-ΟΥλⲚλⲭⲱⲢⲎⲦⲎⲤ λⲚ, λλλλ
λⲚⲄ-ΟΥⲢⲱⲘⲈ Ⲛ ⲢⲈϥⲢ-ⲚΟⲂⲈ λΥⲱ Ⲛ ⲂⲢⲢⲈ."

71. ⲠⲈⲭλΥ λⲈ ⲚϬΙ Ⲛ₂λⲗΟ ⲭⲈ, "ⲈⲔϢλⲚⲚλΥ ⲈΥϢⲎⲢⲈ ϢⲎⲘ ⲈϥⲂⲎⲔ
Ⲉ₂Ⲣλ Ι ⲈⲦⲠⲈ ₂Ⲙ ⲠⲈϥΟΥⲱϢ ⲘⲘΙⲚ ⲘⲘΟϥ, ϬⲈⲠ-ⲦⲈϥΟΥⲈⲢⲎⲦⲈ, ⲤΟⲔϥ Ⲉ-
ⲠⲈⲤⲚⲦ ⲘⲘλΥ; ⲤⲢ-ⲚΟⲂⲢⲈ Ⲅλⲣ Ⲛλϥ λⲚ."

102. ⲈⲢⲈ-λⲠλ ⲘλⲔλⲢΙΟⲤ ⲘΟΟϢⲈ Ⲛ ΟΥΟⲈΙϢ Ⲙ ⲠⲔⲱⲦⲈ Ⲙ Ⲡ₂ⲈλΟⲤ,¹
ⲈϥⲦⲱΟΥⲚ² Ⲛ ₂ⲈⲚⲂⲎⲦ, λΥⲱ ⲈΙⲤ ⲠλΙλⲂΟλΟⲤ λϥⲦⲱⲘⲚⲦ³ ⲈⲢΟϥ ₂Ⲛ
ⲦⲈϥ₂ΙⲎ, ⲈⲢⲈ-ΟΥΟ₂Ⲥ⁴ ⲚⲦΟΟⲦϥ, λΥⲱ Ⲉ-ⲚⲈϥΟΥⲱϢ ⲠⲈ Ⲉ Ⲣλ₂Ⲧϥ,
ⲘⲠⲈϥϬⲘ-ϬΟⲘ. λΥⲱ ⲠⲈⲭλϥ Ⲛλϥ ⲭⲈ, "ΟΥⲚΟϬ ⲠⲈ ⲠλⲭΙ Ⲛ ϬΟⲚⲤ⁵ ⲈⲂΟλ

---

into the desert and live as a hermit monk. (2) ⲡ.ⲕⲉⲗⲱⲗ jar,
pitcher. (3) ⲥⲕⲟⲣⲕⲅ ⲥⲕⲣ̄ⲕⲣ̄- ⲥⲕⲣ̄ⲕⲱⲣ⸴ Q ⲥⲕⲣ̄ⲕⲱⲣ to roll away
(tr. or intr.). (4) ⲟⲩⲱϭⲡ̄ ⲟⲩⲉϭⲡ̄- ⲟⲩⲟϭⲡ⸴ Q ⲟⲩⲟϭⲡ̄ vb. tr. to
break, smash (ⲙⲙⲟ⸴). (5) ₂ⲩⲡⲟⲙⲓⲛⲉ (ὑπομένω) to be patient
(with, under: ⲉ), submit to; to endure, last. (6) ⲧ.ⲃⲟⲏⲑⲓⲁ
(ἡ βοήθεια) help, aid, support.

70. (1) ⲡ.ⲁⲛⲁⲭⲱⲣⲓⲧⲏⲥ (ὁ ἀναχωρητής) anchorite; the
status of a true anchorite was viewed as a very advanced
stage of spiritual development. (2) ┼-ⲧⲟⲟⲧ⸴ ⲙⲙⲟ⸴ to lay
hold of (suff. on ⲧⲟⲟⲧ⸴ is reflex.). (3) In causative
sense: "they made him go around to the cells ..."

102. (1) ⲡ.₂ⲉⲗⲟⲥ (τὸ ἕλος) marsh. (2) ⲧⲱⲟⲩⲛ as tr. vb.
to carry (ⲙⲙⲟ⸴). (3) ⲧⲱⲙⲛ̄ⲧ, Q ⲧⲟⲙⲛ̄ⲧ to meet, befall (ⲉ).
(4) ⲡ.ⲟ₂ⲥ̄ scythe. (5) ⲭⲓ ⲙⲙⲟ⸴ Ⲛ ϭⲟⲛⲥ̄ to ill-treat, harm,

ⲘⲘⲞⲔ, ϫⲉ ⲘⲚ̄-ϬⲞⲘ ⲘⲘⲞⲒ ⲈⲢⲞⲔ.⁶ ⲈⲒⲤ ⲌⲎⲎⲦⲈ ⲄⲀⲢ ⲌⲰⲂ ⲚⲒⲘ ⲈⲦⲈⲔⲈⲒⲢⲈ
ⲘⲘⲞⲨ ⳨ⲈⲒⲢⲈ ⲘⲘⲞⲞⲨ ⲌⲰ. Ⲛ̄ⲦⲞⲔ ϢⲀⲔⲚⲎⲤⲦⲈⲨⲈ Ⲛ̄ ⲌⲈⲚⲌⲞⲞⲨ; ⲀⲚⲞⲔ ⲀⲈ
ⲘⲈⲒⲞⲨⲰⲘ Ⲉ ⲠⲦⲎⲢϤ̄.⁷ ϢⲀⲔⲢ̄-ⲞⲨϢⲎ Ⲛ̄ ⲢⲞⲈⲒⲤ⁸ Ⲛ̄ ⲌⲈⲚⲤⲞⲠ; ⲀⲚⲞⲔ ⲀⲈ
ⲘⲈⲒⲚ̄ⲔⲞⲦⲔ̄ ⲈⲚⲈⲌ. ⲞⲨⲌⲰⲂ Ⲛ̄ ⲞⲨⲰⲦ ⲠⲈⲦⲈⲔⲬⲢⲀⲈⲒⲦ ⲈⲢⲞⲒ Ⲛ̄ⲌⲎⲦϤ̄."
ⲠⲈϪⲈ-ⲀⲠⲀ ⲘⲀⲔⲀⲢⲒⲞⲤ ϪⲈ, "ⲞⲨ ⲠⲈ?" Ⲛ̄ⲦⲞϤ ⲀⲈ ⲠⲈϪⲀϤ ϪⲈ, "ⲠⲈⲔ-
ⲐⲂ̄ⲂⲒⲞ ⲠⲈ. ⲀⲚⲞⲔ ⲀⲈ ⲘⲈⲒϬⲘ̄-ϬⲞⲘ Ⲉ ⲐⲂ̄ⲂⲒⲞⲒ ⲈⲚⲈⲌ. ⲈⲦⲂⲈ ⲠⲀⲒ
Ⲙ̄ⲠⲒϬⲘ̄-ϬⲞⲘ ⲈⲢⲞⲔ."

124. ⲀϤϪⲞⲞⲤ Ⲛ̄ϬⲒ ⲀⲠⲀ ⲌⲰⲢⲤⲒⲎⲤⲒ Ϫⲉ, "ⲞⲨⲦⲰⲰⲂⲈ¹ Ⲛ̄ ⲞⲘⲈ²
ⲈⲨϢⲀⲚⲚⲞϪⲤ̄ ⲈⲨⲤⲚ̄ⲦⲈ³ ⲌⲀⲦⲘ̄ ⲠⲒⲈⲢⲞ, Ⲛ̄ϬⲚⲀⲌⲨⲠⲞⲘⲒⲚⲈ ⲀⲚ Ⲛ̄ ⲞⲨⲌⲞⲞⲨ Ⲛ̄
ⲞⲨⲰⲦ. ⲦⲦⲈⲢⲠⲞⲤⲈ⁴ ⲀⲈ ϢⲀⲤⲘⲞⲨⲚ ⲈⲂⲞⲖ Ⲛ̄ ⲐⲈ Ⲙ̄ ⲠⲰⲚⲈ. ⲦⲀⲒ ⲦⲈ ⲐⲈ Ⲙ̄
ⲠⲢⲰⲘⲈ Ⲉ-ⲞⲨⲚ̄ⲦⲀϤ Ⲙ̄ⲘⲀⲨ Ⲙ̄ ⲠⲈϤⲘⲈⲈⲨⲈ Ⲙ̄ ⲘⲚ̄ⲦⲔⲰⲤⲘⲒⲔⲞⲚ.⁵ Ⲛ̄ϤⲠⲞⲤⲈ⁶ ⲀⲚ
ⲌⲚ̄ ⲐⲞⲦⲈ Ⲙ̄ ⲠⲚⲞⲨⲦⲈ. ⲈϤϢⲀⲚⲈⲒ ⲈⲌⲢⲀⲒ ⲈⲨⲘⲚ̄ⲦⲚⲞϬ,⁷ ϢⲀϤⲂⲰⲖ ⲈⲂⲞⲖ.
ⲌⲀⲌ ⲄⲀⲢ ⲚⲈ Ⲙ̄ⲠⲒⲢⲀⲤⲘⲞⲤ Ⲛ̄ ⲚⲀ-ⲦⲈⲒⲘⲒⲚⲈ ⲘⲀⲖⲒⲤⲦⲀ ⲈⲨϢⲞⲞⲠ ⲌⲚ̄ ⲦⲘⲎⲦⲈ
Ⲛ̄ Ⲛ̄ⲢⲰⲘⲈ. ⲚⲀⲚⲞⲨⲤ ⲀⲈ ⲈⲦⲢⲈ-ⲠⲢⲰⲘⲈ ⲤⲞⲨⲈⲚ-ⲠⲈϤϢⲒ Ⲙ̄ⲘⲒⲚ Ⲙ̄ⲘⲞϤ,
ⲈⲦⲢⲈϤⲠⲰⲦ ⲀⲈ ⲈⲂⲞⲖ Ⲙ̄ ⲠⲈⲌⲢⲞϢ⁸ Ⲛ̄ ⲦⲘⲚ̄ⲦⲚⲞϬ. ⲚⲈⲦ ⲦⲀⲬⲢⲎⲨ ⲀⲈ ⲌⲒⲦⲚ̄
ⲦⲠⲒⲤⲦⲒⲤ ⲌⲈⲚⲀⲦⲔⲒⲘ ⲈⲢⲞⲞⲨ ⲚⲈ.

141. ⲀϤϢⲰⲠⲈ ⲌⲚ̄ ⲚⲈⲠⲢⲰⲀⲤⲦⲒⲞⲚ¹ Ⲛ̄ ⲔⲰⲤⲦⲀⲚⲦⲒⲚⲞⲨⲠⲞⲖⲒⲤ Ⲛ̄ϬⲒ
ⲞⲨⲘⲞⲚⲀⲬⲞⲤ Ⲛ̄ ⲢⲘ̄ⲚⲔⲎⲘⲈ ⲌⲒ ⲐⲈⲰⲀⲞⲤⲒⲞⲤ Ⲡ̄ⲢⲢⲞ. Ⲡ̄ⲢⲢⲞ ⲀⲈ ⲈϤⲂⲎⲔ ⲌⲚ̄
ⲦⲈⲌⲒⲎ ⲈⲦ Ⲙ̄ⲘⲀⲨ, ⲀϤⲔⲀ-ⲠⲘⲚⲎϢⲈ Ⲛ̄ⲤⲰϤ, ⲀϤⲈⲒ ⲘⲀⲨⲀⲀϤ, ⲀϤⲦⲰⲌⲘ̄ ⲈⲌⲞⲨⲚ
Ⲉ ⲠⲘⲞⲚⲀⲬⲞⲤ. ⲀⲨⲰ ⲀϤⲤⲞⲨⲰⲚϤ̄ ⲘⲈⲚ Ϫⲉ ⲚⲒⲘ ⲠⲈ, ⲀϤϢⲞⲠϤ̄ ⲀⲈ ⲈⲢⲞϤ Ⲛ̄

---

do violence to; to constrain; ϫⲓ Ⲛ̄ ϬⲞⲚⲤ̄ (ϪⲒⲚϬⲞⲚⲤ̄) n.m.
violence, physical constraint. The genitive (my) is objective here: "the constraint I feel from you." (6) ⲘⲚ̄-ϬⲞⲘ
Ⲙ̄ⲘⲞⲒ ⲈⲢⲞⲔ I have no power over you. (7) ⲉ ⲠⲦⲎⲢϤ̄ (not) at
all. (8) ⲢⲞⲈⲒⲤ vb. intr. to remain awake, keep watch
(over: ⲉ).

124. (1) ⲡ.ⲧⲱⲱⲃⲉ, ⲧ.ⲧⲱⲱⲃⲉ brick. (2) ⲡ.ⲟⲙⲉ, ⲧ.ⲟⲙⲉ clay,
mud. (3) ⲧ.ⲥⲛ̄ⲧⲉ foundation. (4) ⲧ.ⲧⲉⲣⲡⲟⲥⲉ(ⲛ) baked brick.
(5) ⲕⲟⲥⲙⲓⲕⲟⲥ (κοσμικός) worldly, secular; ⲙⲛ̄ⲧⲕⲟⲥⲙⲓⲕⲟⲥ
worldliness. (6) ⲡⲓⲥⲉ ⲡⲉⲥ(ⲧ̄)- ⲡⲁⲥⲧˀ Q ⲡⲟⲥⲉ vb. tr. to bake,
cook (ⲙ̄ⲙⲟˀ). (7) In sense: "if he achieves a position of
importance." (8) ⲡⲉ.ⲌⲢⲟϢ burden, responsibility.

141. (1) ⲡⲉ.ⲡⲣⲱⲁⲥⲧⲓⲟⲛ (τὸ προάστειον) suburbs, environs.

180

ⲑⲉ ⲛ̄ ⲟⲩⲁ ⲉⲃⲟⲗ ⲍ̄ⲛ̄ ⲧⲁⲗⲝⲓⲥ.[2] ⲛ̄ⲧⲉⲣⲟⲩⲃⲱⲕ ⲁⲉ ⲉⲍⲟⲩⲛ, ⲁⲩϣⲗⲏⲗ,
ⲁⲩⲍⲙⲟⲟⲥ. ⲁϥⲁⲣⲭⲉⲓ ⲛ̄ϭⲓ ⲡⲣ̄ⲣⲟ ⲛ̄ ⲍⲟⲧⲍⲧ̄[3] ⲙ̄ⲙⲟϥ, ⲉϥϫⲱ ⲙ̄ⲙⲟⲥ ϫⲉ,
"ⲛⲉⲛⲉⲓⲟⲧⲉ ⲉⲧ ⲍ̄ⲛ̄ ⲕⲏⲙⲉ ⲣ̄-ⲟⲩ?" ⲛ̄ⲧⲟϥ ⲁⲉ ⲡⲉⲭⲁϥ ϫⲉ, "ⲥⲉϣⲗⲏⲗ ⲧⲏⲣⲟⲩ ⲉⲭⲙ̄ ⲡⲉⲕⲟⲩϫⲁⲓ." ⲁⲩⲱ ⲁϥϫⲟⲟⲥ ⲛⲁϥ ⲉⲧⲣⲉϥⲟⲩⲱⲙ ⲛ̄ ⲟⲩⲕⲟⲩⲓ ⲛ̄
ⲟⲉⲓⲕ. ⲁϥϯ-ⲟⲩϣⲏⲙ ⲛ̄ ⲛⲉⲍ[4] ⲍ̄ⲓ ⲍⲙⲟⲩ[5] ⲛⲁϥ, ⲁϥⲟⲩⲱⲙ. ⲁⲩⲱ ⲁϥϯ-
ⲟⲩϣⲏⲙ ⲙ̄ ⲙⲟⲟⲩ ⲛⲁϥ, ⲁϥⲥⲱ. ⲡⲉϫⲁϥ ⲁⲉ ⲛⲁϥ ⲛ̄ϭⲓ ⲡⲣ̄ⲣⲟ ϫⲉ, "ⲕⲥⲟⲟⲩⲛ
ϫⲉ ⲁⲛⲅ̄-ⲛⲓⲙ?" ⲛ̄ⲧⲟϥ ⲁⲉ ⲡⲉϫⲁϥ ϫⲉ, "ⲡⲛⲟⲩⲧⲉ ⲥⲟⲟⲩⲛ ⲙ̄ⲙⲟⲕ." ⲧⲟⲧⲉ
ⲡⲉϫⲁϥ ϫⲉ, "ⲁⲛⲅ̄ ⲡⲉ ⲑⲉⲱⲇⲟⲥⲓⲟⲥ ⲡⲣ̄ⲣⲟ," ⲁⲩⲱ ⲛ̄ ⲧⲉⲩⲛⲟⲩ ⲁϥⲡⲁⲍⲧϥ̄
ⲛⲁϥ ⲛ̄ϭⲓ ⲡⲍⲗ̄ⲗⲟ. ⲡⲉϫⲁϥ ⲛⲁϥ ⲛ̄ϭⲓ ⲡⲣ̄ⲣⲟ ϫⲉ, "ⲛⲁⲓⲁⲧ-ⲧⲏⲩⲧⲛ̄ ϫⲉ
ⲧⲉⲧⲛ̄ⲟ ⲛ̄ ⲁⲧⲣⲟⲟⲩϣ[6] ⲍ̄ⲙ̄ ⲡⲉⲓⲕⲟⲥⲙⲟⲥ. ⲍ̄ⲛ̄ ⲟⲩⲙⲉ ⲛ̄ϫⲓⲛⲧⲁⲩϫⲡⲟⲓ ⲍ̄ⲛ̄ ⲧ-
ⲙⲛ̄ⲧⲣ̄ⲣⲟ ⲙ̄ⲡⲓⲙⲉⲍ-ⲍⲏⲧ[7] ⲛ̄ ⲟⲉⲓⲕ ⲉⲛⲉⲍ ⲟⲩⲁⲉ ⲙⲟⲟⲩ ⲛ̄ ⲑⲉ ⲙ̄ ⲡⲟⲟⲩ, ⲟⲩⲁⲉ
ⲙ̄ⲡⲓⲉⲓⲙⲉ ϫⲉ ⲥⲉⲍⲟⲗϭ[8] ⲛ̄ ⲧⲉⲓⲍⲉ ϫⲓⲛ ⲡⲉⲍⲟⲟⲩ ⲉⲧ ⲙ̄ⲙⲁⲩ." ⲁϥⲁⲣⲭⲉⲓ ⲛ̄
ϯ-ⲉⲟⲟⲩ ⲛⲁϥ ⲛ̄ϭⲓ ⲡⲣ̄ⲣⲟ. ⲡⲍⲗ̄ⲗⲟ ⲁⲉ ⲁϥⲧⲱⲟⲩⲛ, ⲁϥⲡⲱⲧ, ⲁϥⲕⲧⲟϥ ⲟⲛ
ⲉ ⲕⲏⲙⲉ.

175. ⲁϥϫⲟⲟⲥ ⲟⲛ ⲛ̄ϭⲓ ⲁⲡⲁ ⲁⲁⲛⲓⲏⲗ ϫⲉ ⲁ-ⲡⲉⲛⲉⲓⲱⲧ ⲁⲡⲁ ⲁⲣⲥⲉ-
ⲛⲓⲟⲥ ϫⲟⲟⲥ ⲉⲧⲃⲉ ⲟⲩⲁ ⲍ̄ⲛ̄ ϣⲓⲏⲧ ϫⲉ ⲟⲩⲛⲟϭ ⲙ̄ⲙⲁⲧⲉ ⲡⲉ ⲛ̄ ⲣⲉϥⲣ̄-ⲍⲱⲃ[1]
ⲉϥⲟ ⲁⲉ ⲛ̄ ⲁⲫⲉⲗⲗⲏⲥ[2] ⲍ̄ⲛ̄ ⲧⲡⲓⲥⲧⲓⲥ ⲁⲩⲱ ⲛⲉϥϣⲟⲃⲧ̄[3] ⲡⲉ ⲉⲧⲃⲉ ⲧⲙⲛ̄ⲧ-
ⲍⲓⲁⲓⲱⲧⲏⲥ. ⲁⲩⲱ ⲛⲉϥϫⲱ ⲙ̄ⲙⲟⲥ ϫⲉ ⲡⲟⲉⲓⲕ ⲉⲧⲛ̄ϫⲓ ⲙ̄ⲙⲟϥ ⲍⲓϫⲙ̄ ⲡⲙⲁ[4]
ⲛ̄ⲧⲟϥ ⲁⲛ ⲡⲉ ⲡⲥⲱⲙⲁ ⲙ̄ ⲡⲉⲭ̄ⲥ̄ ⲫⲩⲥⲓ[5] ⲁⲗⲗⲁ ⲡⲉϥⲥⲙⲟⲧ ⲡⲉ. ⲁⲩⲥⲱⲧⲙ̄ ⲁⲉ
ⲛ̄ϭⲓ ⲍⲗ̄ⲗⲟ ⲥⲛⲁⲩ ϫⲉ ⲁϥϫⲉ-ⲡⲉⲓϣⲁϫⲉ, ⲁⲩⲱ ⲉⲩⲥⲟⲟⲩⲛ ⲙ̄ⲙⲟϥ ϫⲉ ⲟⲩⲛⲟϭ
ⲡⲉ ⲍ̄ⲙ̄ ⲡⲉϥⲃⲓⲟⲥ,[6] ⲁⲩⲉⲓⲙⲉ ϫⲉ ⲉϥϫⲱ ⲙ̄ ⲡⲁⲓ ⲍ̄ⲛ̄ ⲟⲩⲙⲛ̄ⲧⲃⲁⲗ-ⲍⲏⲧ[7] ⲙⲛ̄

_____

(2) sense here: the ranks of ordinary soldiers. (3) ⲍⲟⲧⲍⲧ̄
ⲍⲉⲧⲍⲧ̄- ⲍⲉⲧⲍⲱⲧ⸗ Q ⲍⲉⲧⲍⲱⲧ vb. tr. to examine, inquire into
(ⲙ̄ⲙⲟ⸗). (4) ⲡ.ⲛⲉⲍ oil. (5) ⲡⲉ.ⲍⲙⲟⲩ salt. (6) ⲁⲧⲣⲟⲟⲩϣ adj.
carefree, free from anxieties. (7) ⲙⲉⲍ-ⲍⲏⲧ ⲙ̄ⲙⲟ⸗ to be sated,
satisfied with. (8) ⲍⲗⲟϭ, Q ⲍⲟⲗϭ̄ vb. tr. to be sweet, pleasant.
175. (1) ⲣⲉϥⲣ̄-ⲍⲱⲃ worker, doer; here in monkish sense:
ascetic, practitioner. (2) ⲁⲫⲉⲗⲗⲏⲥ (ἀφελής) simple. (3)
ϣⲱϥⲧ̄ (ϣⲱⲃⲧ̄), Q ϣⲟϥⲧ̄ (ϣⲟⲃⲧ̄) vb. intr. to stumble, err.
ⲧ.ⲙⲛ̄ⲧⲍⲓⲁⲓⲱⲧⲏⲥ being uninformed; ἰδιώτης non-professional,
layman, uninformed person. (4) ⲡ.ⲙⲁ here = the altar. (5)
ⲫⲩⲥⲓ in fact, for real (φύσει by nature, naturally); ⲧⲉ.
ⲫⲩⲥⲓⲥ (ἡ φύσις) nature. (6) ⲡ.ⲃⲓⲟⲥ (ὁ βίος) life. (7) ⲃⲁⲗ-
ⲍⲏⲧ guileless, innocent; ⲙⲛ̄ⲧⲃⲁⲗ-ⲍⲏⲧ guilelessness.

ОУМ̄ТАТNОІ.⁸ ΑΥШ ΑΥ6Ι ФΑРОϥ, ΑΥΧООС NΑϥ Χ6, "ΑПΑ, ΑNСШΤ̄М
6ΤВ6 ОУФΑΧ6 N̄ ΑПΙСΤОN, Χ6 Α-ОУΑ ΧООϥ Χ6 ПО6ΙΚ 6ΤN̄ΧΙ М̄МОϥ
ₗШС⁹ Χ6 N̄ТОϥ NΑМ6 ΑN П6 ПСШМΑ М̄ П6Χ͞С ΑΛΛΑ П6ϥСМОΤ П6."
П₂Χ̄ΛО Δ6 П6ΧΑϥ Χ6, "ΑNОΚ ΑΙΧ6-ПΑΙ." N̄ТООУ Δ6 ΑΥΚШР̄Ф⁻¹⁰
6РОϥ, 6УΧШ М̄МОС Χ6, "М̄ПШР. М̄П̄РΤΑΧРОΚ ₂М̄ ПΑΙ, ΑПΑ, ΑΛΛΑ
ΚΑΤΑ Θ6 6Τ6Р6-ΤΚΑΘОΛΙΚΗ¹¹ 6ΚΚΛΗСΙΑ ΧШ М̄МОС ПΙСΤ6У6 Χ6
ПО6ΙΚ 6ΤN̄ΧΙ М̄МОϥ N̄ТОϥ П6 ПСШМΑ М̄ П6Χ͞С ₂N̄ ОУМ6, ΑΥШ ₂N̄
ОУСМОΤ ΑN, ΑΥШ П6ΙПОΤΗРΙОN¹² П6ϥСNОϥ П6 ₂N̄ ОУМ6 ΑΥШ ₂N̄
ОУСΧΥМΑ¹³ ΑN. ΑΛΛΑ N̄ Θ6¹⁴ N̄ ΤΑРΧΗ 6-ΑϥΧΙ N̄ ОУΚΑ₂ 6ВОΛ ₂М̄
ПΚΑ₂,¹⁵ ΑϥПΛΑСС6¹⁶ М̄ ПРШМ6 ΚΑΤΑ Τ6ϥₗΙΚШN¹⁷ ΑΥШ М̄N̄-6ОМ N̄
ΛΛΑУ N̄ ΧООС Χ6 N̄ ΘΙΚШN М̄ ПNОУΤ6 ΑN Τ6 ΤΑΙ, ΚΑΙΤОΙ¹⁸ ОУΑ-
ΚΑΤΑΛΥМПΤОС П6 N̄ ΑΤΤΑ₂Оϥ, ΤΑΙ ОN Τ6 Θ6 М̄ ПО6ΙΚ N̄ΤΑϥΧООС
Χ6 ПΑΙ П6 ПΑСШМΑ. ΤN̄ПΙСΤ6У6 Χ6 ₂N̄ ОУМ6 ПΑΙ П6 ПСШМΑ М̄
П6Χ͞С." П6ΧΑϥ N̄6Ι П₂Χ̄ΛО Χ6, "6Τ6ΤN̄ΤМ̄ПΙΘ6¹⁹ М̄МОΙ 6ВОΛ ₂М̄
П₂ШВ, N̄†NΑΤШΤ ΑN N̄₂ΗΤ." N̄ТООУ Δ6 П6ΧΑУ Χ6, "МΑР6NΤШВ₂⁻²⁰
М̄ ПNОУΤ6 ₂N̄ Τ6Ι₂6ВΔШМΑС 6ΤВ6 П6ΙМУСΤΗРΙОN, ΑΥШ ΤN̄ПΙСΤ6У6
Χ6 ПNОУΤ6 NΑ6ОΛП̄ϥ NΑN 6ВОΛ." П₂Χ̄ΛО Δ6 ΑϥФП̄-ПШΧ6 6РОϥ ₂N̄
ОУРΑФ6, ΑΥШ ΑϥСОП͞С М̄ ПNОУΤ6 6ϥΧШ М̄МОС Χ6, "ПΧО6ΙС, N̄ТОΚ 6Τ

---

(8) NОΙ (νοέω) to think; ΑΤNОΙ unthinking; ₂N̄ ОУМ̄ТΑΤNОΙ
without thinking. (9) Text has ₂ШС͞Χ; prob. ₂ШС (ὡς) with
Χ6, as given above. (10) ΚШР̄Ф Κ6Р̄Ф- ΚОРФ⁼ vb. tr. to persuade, cajole (6). (11) ΚΑΘОΛΙΚΗ (καθολικός) adj. f. universal, catholic. (12) П.ПОΤΗРΙОN (τὸ ποτήριον) wine-cup.
(13) ₂N̄ ОУСΧΥМΑ in form, in appearance. (14) N̄ Θ6 N̄ is
coordinated with ΤΑΙ Τ6 Θ6 below. Τ.ΑРΧΗ (ἡ ἀρχή) beginning (of creation). (15) Note ΚΑ₂ in two senses: a clod
of earth; the ground. (16) ПΛΑСС6 (πλάσσω) to form, mould.
(17) ΘΙΚШN (ἡ εἰκών) likeness. (18) ΚΑΙΤОΙ (καίτοι) and
yet, although, albeit. ΑΚΑΤΑΛΥМПΤОС (ἀκατάληπτος) incomprehensible; used as noun here. (19) ПΙΘ6 (πείθω) to persuade. 6ВОΛ ₂М̄ П₂ШВ in sense:by a demonstration from the
matter itself. (20) ΤШВ₂ (ΤШВΑ₂) Τ6В₂- ΤОВ₂⁼ vb. tr. to
pray, make entreaty (to: М̄МО⁼; for: 6, 6ΤВ6, 6ΧN̄, ₂Λ).

сооүн хе ᷒ ειο λν ᷒ λпιстос κλτλ оүκλκιλ[21] λλλλ хе ᷒᷒νει-
плλнλ[22] 2᷒ оүм᷒᷒тλпιстос м᷒ оүм᷒᷒тλтсооүн, 6ωλᷘ νλι εвολ,
пхоεις τ̄с̄ пεх̄с̄." ᷒2λ̄λο λε он λүвωκ ε νεүρι, λүтωвλ2 ᷒
пноүтε, εүхω ᷘмос хε, "τ̄с̄ пεх̄с̄, εκε6ωλᷘ εвολ ᷒ пει2λ̄λο ᷒
пειмүстнрιон хε εчεпιстεүε λүω ν̄ч̄т̄ᷘ̄+-осε[23] ᷒ пεч2ιсε."
λ-пноүтε λε сωт̄ᷘ̄ εрооү 21 оүсоп. ᷒тεрε-ε̄в̄λωмλс λε хωκ
εвολ, λүει ε τεκκλнсιλ ᷒ τκүριλκн,[24] λү2мооς ᷒ пꙅом᷒᷒т
мλүλλү 21 <оү>оүрωм[25] ᷒ оүωт. нεрε-п2λ̄λο λε 2᷒ τεүмнтε.
λүоүωн ᷒61 νεүвλλ ετ 21 2оүн, λүω ᷒τεроүκω ε2рλι ᷒ поεικ
εх᷒ τετрλпүхλ ετ оүλλв, λчоүωνλ2 εвολ ᷒ пꙅом᷒᷒т мλүλλү ᷒ θε
᷒ оүꙅнрε κоүι, λүω ᷒τεрε-пεпрεсвүτεрос сооүт᷒ εвολ ᷒ τεч-
6ιх ε хι ᷒ поεικ ε пoꙅч̄,[26] εις оүλⲅⲅελос λчει εвολ 2᷒
ᷘпнүε, ε-оүᷘ-оү6oртε[27] ᷒тооτч̄, λүω λчꙅωωт[28] ᷒ пκоүι ᷒
ꙅнрε, λчпω2т̄[29] ᷒ пεчсноч ε ппотнрιон. ᷒тεрε-пεпрεсвүτεрос
λε εр-поεικ ᷒ ⲅλλсмλ κλλсмλ,[30] нεрε-пλⲅⲅελος 2ωωч пoꙅ ᷘ
пꙅнрε κоүι ꙅнм ꙅнм. λүω ᷒тεроү+ ᷘ пεүоⲅоι[31] ε хι εвολ 2᷒
нεт оүλλв, λчхι ᷒61 п2λ̄λο ᷒ оүκλλсмλ нλч εчпнꙅ ᷒ сноч, λүω
᷒тεрεчнλү, λч р̄-2отε, λчхι-ꙅκλκ εвολ хε, "+пιстεүε, пхоεις,
хε поεικ пε пεκсωмλ λүω ппотнрιон пε пεκсноч." λүω ᷒
τεүноү λ-пλч ετ 2᷒ τεч6ιх р̄-оεικ κλτλ пεооү ᷘ пмүстнрιон.
λчнохч̄ ε2оүн ε рωч, λүω λчхι εчεүхλριстι[32] ᷘ пхоεις.
пεхλч нλч ᷒61 п2λ̄λо хε, "пноүтε сооүн ᷒ τεφүсις ᷒ ᷒рωмε хε

т.2εв̄λωмλс, θ̄λωмλс (ἡ ἐβδομάς) week. (21) т.κλκιλ (ἡ κακία) evil, badness. (22) плλнλ (πλανάω) to deceive, lead
astray; middle: to err. (23) +-осε to suffer a loss (of:
᷒). (24) т.κүριλκн (ἡ κυριακή) Sunday. (25) оүрωм var. of
ᷘрωм) pillow, seat. (26) пoꙅ пεꙅ- пoꙅ′ Q пнꙅ vb. tr. to
divide (ᷘмо′). (27) т.6oртε knife, sword. (28) ꙅωωт ꙅεετ-
ꙅλλт′ Q ꙅλλт vb. tr. to cut, slay (ᷘмо′). (29) пω2т̄, нε2т̄-
пλ2т′ Q пλ2т̄ vb. tr. to pour (ᷘмо′). (30) пε.κλλсмλ (τὸ
κλάσμα) piece; repeated to express distributive: into pieces; cf. the following ꙅнм ꙅнм into small pieces. (31) +-
ᷘ п(′)оⲅоι to advance, proceed (suff. is reflex.). (32)
εүхλριстι (εὐχαριστέω) to give thanks.

ⲙⲛ̄-ϭⲟⲙ ⲙ̄ⲙⲟⲟⲩ ⲉ ⲟⲩⲉⲙ-ⲗⲃ ⲉϥⲟⲩⲱⲧ.[33] ⲉⲧⲃⲉ ⲡⲁⲓ ϣⲁϥⲧⲣⲉ-ⲡⲉϥⲥⲱⲙⲁ
ϣⲱⲡⲉ ⲙ̄ ⲡⲟⲉⲓⲕ ⲁⲩⲱ ⲡⲉϥⲥⲛⲟϥ ⲛ̄ ⲏⲣⲡ̄ ⲛ̄ ⲛⲉⲧ ϫⲓ ⲙ̄ⲙⲟϥ ⲍⲛ̄ ⲟⲩⲡⲓⲥⲧⲓⲥ."
ⲁⲩⲱ ⲁⲩϣⲡ̄-ⲍⲙⲟⲧ[34] ⲛ̄ⲧⲙ̄ ⲡⲛⲟⲩⲧⲉ ⲍⲓⲭⲙ̄ ⲡⲉⲛⲧⲁϥϣⲱⲡⲉ, ϫⲉ ⲙ̄ⲡⲉϥⲕⲁ-
ⲡⲍⲭ̄ⲗⲟ ⲛ̄ ⲣⲱⲙⲉ ⲉ ϯ-ⲟⲥⲉ ⲙ̄ ⲡⲉϥⲍⲓⲥⲉ, ⲁⲩⲱ ⲁⲩⲃⲱⲕ ⲙ̄ ⲡϣⲟⲙⲛ̄ⲧ ⲉ ⲛⲉⲩⲣⲓ
ⲍⲛ̄ ⲟⲩⲣⲁϣⲉ.

240. ⲁ-ⲁⲡⲁ ⲥⲁⲣⲁⲡⲓⲱⲛ ⲛⲁⲩ ⲉⲩⲡⲟⲣⲛⲏ.[1] ⲡⲉϫⲁϥ ϫⲉ, "ϯⲛⲏⲩ
ϣⲁⲣⲟ ⲙ̄ ⲡⲛⲁⲩ ⲛ̄ ⲣⲟⲩⲍⲉ. ⲥⲃ̄ⲧⲱⲧⲉ ⲉⲃⲟⲗ." ⲁⲩⲱ ⲛ̄ⲧⲉⲣⲉϥ<ⲉⲓ> ⲛⲁⲥ
ⲉⲍⲟⲩⲛ, ⲡⲉϫⲁϥ ⲛⲁⲥ ϫⲉ, "ϭⲱ ⲉⲣⲟⲓ ⲛ̄ ⲟⲩⲕⲟⲩⲓ, ϫⲉ ⲟⲩⲛ̄ⲧⲁⲓ-ⲟⲩⲛⲟⲙⲟⲥ
ⲙ̄ⲙⲁⲩ, ϣⲁⲛϯϫⲟⲕϥ ⲉⲃⲟⲗ." ⲛ̄ⲧⲟⲥ ⲇⲉ ⲡⲉϫⲁⲥ ϫⲉ, "ⲕⲁⲗⲱⲥ, ⲡⲁⲉⲓⲱⲧ."
ⲛ̄ⲧⲟϥ ⲇⲉ ⲁϥⲁⲣⲭⲉⲓ ⲙ̄ ⲯⲁⲗⲗⲉⲓ[2] ϫⲓⲛ ⲡϣⲟⲣⲡ̄ ⲙ̄ ⲯⲁⲗⲙⲟⲥ ϣⲁⲛⲧⲉϥϫⲱⲕ
ⲉⲃⲟⲗ ⲙ̄ ⲡϣⲉⲧⲁⲓⲟⲩ ⲙ̄ ⲯⲁⲗⲙⲟⲥ, ⲁⲩⲱ ⲕⲁⲧⲁ ⲥⲟⲡ ⲛ̄ ⲕⲁ-ⲣⲱϥ ⲉⲃⲟⲗ ϣⲁϥ-
ⲉⲓⲣⲉ ⲛ̄ ϣⲟⲙⲛ̄ⲧ ⲛ̄ ⲕⲗ̄ϫ̄-ⲡⲁⲧ.[3] ⲛ̄ⲧⲟⲥ ⲍⲱⲱⲥ ⲁⲥϭⲱ ⲉⲥϣⲗⲏⲗ ⲍⲓ ⲡⲁⲍⲟⲩ
ⲙ̄ⲙⲟϥ ⲍⲛ̄ ⲟⲩⲍⲟⲧⲉ ⲙⲛ̄ ⲟⲩⲥⲧⲱⲧ.[4] ⲁϥⲙⲟⲩⲛ ⲇⲉ ⲉⲃⲟⲗ ⲉϥϣⲗⲏⲗ ⲍⲁⲣⲟⲥ
ⲧⲁⲣⲉⲥⲟⲩϫⲁⲓ, ⲁⲩⲱ ⲁ-ⲡⲛⲟⲩⲧⲉ ⲥⲱⲧⲙ̄ ⲉⲣⲟϥ. ⲧⲉⲥⲍⲓⲙⲉ ⲇⲉ ⲁⲥⲡⲁⲍⲧⲥ̄ ⲍⲁ-
ⲣⲁⲧⲟⲩ ⲛ̄ ⲛⲉϥⲟⲩⲉⲣⲏⲧⲉ ⲉⲥⲣⲓⲙⲉ ⲉⲥϫⲱ ⲙ̄ⲙⲟⲥ ϫⲉ, "ⲁⲣⲓ-ⲧⲁⲅⲁⲡⲏ,[5] ⲡⲁⲉⲓⲱⲧ. ⲡⲙⲁ ⲉⲧⲉⲕⲥⲟⲟⲩⲛ ϫⲉ ϯⲛⲁⲟⲩϫⲁⲓ ⲛ̄ⲍⲏⲧϥ ϫⲓⲧ ⲉⲙⲁⲩ. ⲛ̄ⲧⲁ-
ⲡⲛⲟⲩⲧⲉ ⲅⲁⲣ ⲧⲛ̄ⲛⲟⲟⲩⲕ ϣⲁⲣⲟⲓ ⲉ ⲡⲁⲓ." ⲁⲩⲱ ⲁϥϫⲓⲧⲥ̄ ⲉⲩⲍⲉⲛⲉⲉⲧⲉ ⲙ̄
ⲡⲁⲣⲑⲉⲛⲟⲥ.[6] ⲡⲉϫⲁϥ ⲇⲉ ⲛ̄ ⲧⲙⲁⲁⲩ ⲛ̄ ⲑⲉⲛⲉⲉⲧⲉ ϫⲉ, "ϫⲓ ⲛ̄ ⲧⲉⲓⲥⲱⲛⲉ,
ⲁⲩⲱ ⲙ̄ⲡⲣ̄ⲧⲁⲗⲉ-ⲛⲁⲍⲃ̄[7] ⲉϫⲱⲥ ⲏ ⲉⲛⲧⲟⲗⲏ, ⲁⲗⲗⲁ ⲛ̄ ⲑⲉ ⲉⲧⲉⲥⲟⲩⲁϣⲥ̄
ⲙⲁⲣⲉⲥⲁⲁⲥ. ⲕⲁⲁⲥ ⲍⲙ̄ ⲡⲭⲟⲉⲓⲥ." ⲁⲩⲱ ⲙⲛ̄ⲛ̄ⲥⲁ ⲍⲉⲛⲕⲟⲩⲓ ⲛ̄ ⲍⲟⲟⲩ ⲡⲉϫⲁⲥ
ϫⲉ, "ⲁⲛⲟⲕ ⲟⲩⲣⲉϥⲣ̄-ⲛⲟⲃⲉ. ⲉⲓⲟⲩⲱϣ ⲉ ⲟⲩⲱⲙ ⲛ̄ ⲟⲩⲥⲟⲡ ⲙ̄ ⲙⲏⲛⲉ."
ⲙⲛ̄ⲛ̄ⲥⲁ ⲕⲉⲟⲩⲟⲉⲓϣ ⲟⲛ ⲡⲉϫⲁⲥ ϫⲉ, "ⲉⲓⲟⲩⲱϣ ⲉ ⲟⲩⲱⲙ ⲛ̄ ⲟⲩⲥⲟⲡ ⲕⲁⲧⲁ
ⲥⲁⲃⲃⲁⲧⲟⲛ."[8] ⲙⲛ̄ⲛ̄ⲥⲱⲥ ⲟⲛ ⲡⲉϫⲁⲥ ϫⲉ, "ⲉⲡⲓⲇⲏ[9] ⲁⲓⲣ̄-ⲍⲁⲍ ⲛ̄ ⲛⲟⲃⲉ,

---

(33) ⲟⲩⲱⲧ vb. intr. to be raw, green, fresh. ϣⲡ̄-ⲍⲙⲟⲧ ⲛ̄ⲧⲛ̄
to thank.

240. (1) ⲧ.ⲡⲟⲣⲛⲏ (ἡ πόρνη) prostitute. (2) ⲯⲁⲗⲗⲉⲓ
(ψάλλω) here: to recite psalter; ⲡⲉ.ⲯⲁⲗⲙⲟⲥ (ὁ ψαλμός)
psalm. (3) ⲕⲗ̄ϫ̄-ⲡⲁⲧ bow, genuflection; ⲕⲱⲗϫ̄ vb. tr. to bend,
bow; ⲧ.ⲡⲁⲧ knee, leg. (4) ⲡⲉ.ⲥⲧⲱⲧ trembling. (5) ⲁⲣⲓ-ⲧⲁⲅⲁⲡⲏ
be charitable, do a kindness; ⲧ.ⲁⲅⲁⲡⲏ (ἡ ἀγαπή) love. (6)
ⲟⲩⲍⲉⲛⲉⲉⲧⲉ ⲙ̄ ⲡⲁⲣⲑⲉⲛⲟⲥ a convent. (7) ⲡ.ⲛⲁⲍⲃ̄ yoke; here in
monastic sense: imposed penance. ⲏ (ἤ) or. (8) once a
week. (9) ⲉⲡⲓⲇⲏ (ἐπειδή) because, since.

184

оπ⸏‾‾⁻¹⁰ є2оүн єүрι λүω пєⲧ̇нλоүомϥ̄ тλλϥ нλι 2Ⲛ̄ оүϣоүϣⲦ̄ мⲚ̄ пλ-
2ⲱв Ⲛ̄ бιⲭ." λүω λүєιрє 2ι нλι, λүω λсⲢ̄-λнλϥ Ⲙ̄ пноүтє, λс-
Ⲛ̄котⲕ̄ λє 2Ⲙ̄ пмλ єт Ⲙ̄мλү 2Ⲙ̄ пⲭоєιс.

---

(10) оπⲦ̄ is for отп⸜т, from ωтⲎ̄.

ⲧⲥⲟⲫⲓⲁ ⲛ̄ ⲥⲟⲗⲟⲙⲱⲛ

Chapter 1

(1) ⲙⲉⲣⲉ-ⲧⲁⲓⲕⲁⲓⲟⲥⲩⲛⲏ, ⲛⲉⲧ ⲕⲣⲓⲛⲉ ⲙ̄ ⲡⲕⲁϩ.

ⲁⲣⲓ-ⲡⲙⲉⲉⲩⲉ ⲙ̄ ⲡⲭⲟⲉⲓⲥ ϩⲛ̄ ⲟⲩⲙⲛ̄ⲧⲁⲅⲁⲑⲟⲥ,

ⲛ̄ⲧⲉⲧⲛ̄ϣⲓⲛⲉ ⲛ̄ⲥⲱϥ ϩⲛ̄ ⲟⲩⲙⲛ̄ⲧϩⲁⲡⲗⲟⲩⲥ ⲛ̄ⲧⲉ ⲡⲉⲧⲛ̄ϩⲏⲧ.

(2) ϫⲉ ϣⲁⲩϩⲉ ⲉⲣⲟϥ ⲛ̄ϭⲓ ⲛⲉⲧⲉ ⲛ̄ⲥⲉⲡⲉⲓⲣⲁⲍⲉ ⲙ̄ⲙⲟϥ ⲁⲛ.

ϣⲁϥⲟⲩⲱⲛϩ̄ ⲇⲉ ⲉⲃⲟⲗ ⲛ̄ ⲛⲉⲧⲉ ⲛ̄ⲥⲉⲟ ⲛ̄ ⲁⲧⲛⲁϩⲧⲉ ⲉⲣⲟϥ ⲁⲛ.

(3) ϣⲁⲣⲉ-ⲡⲙⲉⲉⲩⲉ ⲅⲁⲣ ⲉⲑⲟⲟⲩ ⲡⲟⲣϫⲟⲩ ⲉ ⲡⲛⲟⲩⲧⲉ,

ⲁⲩⲱ ⲧⲉϥϭⲟⲙ ⲉⲧ ⲟⲩⲟⲛϩ̄ ⲉⲃⲟⲗ ϣⲁⲥϫⲡⲓⲉ-ⲛⲁⲑⲏⲧ.

(4) ϫⲉ ⲙⲉⲣⲉ-ⲧⲥⲟⲫⲓⲁ ⲅⲁⲣ ⲃⲱⲕ ⲉϩⲟⲩⲛ ⲉⲩⲯⲩⲭⲏ ⲉⲥϩⲟⲟⲩ,

ⲟⲩⲇⲉ ⲙⲉⲥⲟⲩⲱϩ ϩⲛ̄ ⲥⲱⲙⲁ ⲣ̄ ⲣⲉϥⲣ̄-ⲛⲟⲃⲉ.

(5) ⲡⲉⲡⲛ̄ⲁ̄ ⲅⲁⲣ ⲉⲧ ⲟⲩⲁⲁⲃ ⲛ̄ ⲧⲥⲟⲫⲓⲁ ϣⲁϥⲡⲱⲧ ⲉⲃⲟⲗ ⲛ̄ ⲕⲣⲟϥ,

ⲁⲩⲱ ϣⲁϥⲟⲩⲉ ⲛ̄ ⲙ̄ⲙⲟⲕⲙⲉⲕ ⲛ̄ ⲛⲁⲑⲏⲧ,

ⲁⲩⲱ ϣⲁϥϫⲡⲓⲉ-ⲡϫⲓⲛϭⲟⲛⲥ̄ ⲉϥϣⲁⲛⲉⲓ.

(6) ⲟⲩⲙⲁⲓ-ⲣⲱⲙⲉ ⲅⲁⲣ ⲡⲉ ⲡⲉⲡⲛ̄ⲁ̄ ⲛ̄ ⲧⲥⲟⲫⲓⲁ,

ⲁⲩⲱ ⲛ̄ϥⲛⲁⲧⲙⲁⲓⲉ-ⲡϫⲓ-ⲟⲩⲁ ⲁⲛ ϩⲛ̄ ⲛⲉϥⲥⲡⲟⲧⲟⲩ;

ϫⲉ ⲡⲛⲟⲩⲧⲉ ⲡⲉ ⲡⲙⲛ̄ⲧⲣⲉ ⲛ̄ ⲛⲉϥϭⲗⲟⲧⲉ,

ⲁⲩⲱ ⲡⲉⲧ ⲙⲟⲩϣⲧ̄ ⲛⲁⲙⲉ ⲙ̄ ⲡⲉϥϩⲏⲧ, ⲁⲩⲱ ⲡⲉⲧ ⲥⲱⲧⲙ̄ ⲉ ⲡⲉϥⲗⲁⲥ.

(7) ϫⲉ ⲡⲉⲡⲛ̄ⲁ̄ ⲙ̄ ⲡⲭⲟⲉⲓⲥ ⲁϥⲙⲉϩ-ⲧⲟⲓⲕⲟⲩⲙⲉⲛⲏ,

ⲁⲩⲱ ⲡⲉⲧ ϣⲱⲡ ⲙ̄ ⲡⲧⲏⲣϥ̄ ϥⲥⲟⲟⲩⲛ ⲙ̄ ⲡⲉⲩϩⲣⲟⲟⲩ.

I. (1) κρίνω to judge. ἁπλοῦς adj. simple, frank, sincere. (2) ⲛⲁϩⲧⲉ, Q ⲛ̄ϩⲟⲩⲧ vb. tr. to believe, trust (ⲉ); ⲁⲧ-ⲛⲁϩⲧⲉ adj. unbelieving. (3) ⲡⲱⲣϫ̄ ⲡⲉⲣϫ̄- ⲡⲟⲣϫ⸗ Q ⲡⲟⲣϫ̄ vb. tr. to divide, separate (ⲙ̄ⲙⲟ⸗; from: ⲉ). (5) ⲡⲉ.ⲕⲣⲟϥ deceit, guile. ⲟⲩⲉ, Q ⲟⲩⲏⲩ vb. intr. to be distant (from: ⲉ, ⲙ̄ⲙⲟ⸗), remain aloof from. (6) ⲡⲉ.ⲥⲡⲟⲧⲟⲩ lip(s), shore, edge. ϭⲗⲱⲧ (pl. ϭⲗⲟⲧⲉ, ϭⲗⲟⲟⲧⲉ) n.m.f. kidney; here in OT sense as seat of emotions. ⲙⲟⲩϣⲧ̄ ⲙⲉϣⲧ̄- ⲙⲟϣⲧ⸗ Q ⲙⲟϣⲧ̄ vb. tr. to to examine, search out (ⲙ̄ⲙⲟ⸗). (7) ⲡⲧⲏⲣϥ̄ the universe, everything.

186

(8) ⲉⲧⲃⲉ ⲡⲁⲓ ⲙⲛ̄-ⲗⲁⲁⲩ ⲛⲁϩⲱⲡ ⲉϥϣⲁϫⲉ ϩⲛ̄ ⲟⲩϫⲓⲛϭⲟⲛⲥ̄,
ⲟⲩⲇⲉ ⲛϥⲛⲁⲣ̄-ⲃⲟⲗ ⲁⲛ ⲉ ⲧⲉⲕⲣⲓⲥⲓⲥ ⲉⲧ ⲛ̄ⲛⲏⲩ.

(9) ⲥⲉⲛⲁϭⲙ̄-ⲡϣⲓⲛⲉ ⲅⲁⲣ ⲙ̄ ⲡϣⲟⲭⲛⲉ ⲙ̄ ⲡⲁⲥⲉⲃⲏⲥ,
ⲁⲩⲱ ⲡϫⲟⲉⲓⲥ ⲛⲁⲥⲱⲧⲙ̄ ⲉ ⲛⲉϥϣⲁϫⲉ ⲉ ⲡⲟⲩⲱⲛϩ̄ ⲉⲃⲟⲗ ⲛ̄ ⲛⲉϥⲁⲛⲟⲙⲓⲁ.

(10) ϫⲉ ⲡⲙⲁⲗϫⲉ ⲙ̄ ⲡⲉϥⲕⲱϩ ϣⲁϥⲥⲱⲧⲙ̄ ⲉ ϩⲱⲃ ⲛⲓⲙ,
ⲁⲩⲱ ⲡⲉϩⲣⲟⲟⲩ ⲛ̄ ⲛⲉⲕⲣⲙ̄ⲣⲙ̄ ⲛⲁϩⲱⲡ ⲁⲛ.

(11) ϩⲁⲣⲉϩ ϭⲉ ⲉⲣⲱⲧⲛ̄ ⲉ ⲡⲉⲕⲣⲙ̄ⲣⲙ̄ ⲉⲧ ϣⲟⲩⲉⲓⲧ,
ⲁⲩⲱ ϯ-ⲥⲟ ⲉ ⲡⲉⲧⲛ̄ⲗⲁⲥ ⲉⲃⲟⲗ ϩⲛ̄ ⲧⲕⲁⲧⲁⲗⲁⲗⲓⲁ;
ϫⲉ ⲙⲛ̄-ⲟⲩϣⲁϫⲉ ⲉϥϣⲟⲩⲉⲓⲧ ⲛⲁϩⲱⲡ.
ⲟⲩⲧⲁⲡⲣⲟ ⲉⲥϫⲓ-ϭⲟⲗ ϣⲁⲥⲧⲁⲕⲉ-ⲧⲉⲯⲩⲭⲏ.

(12) ⲙ̄ⲡⲣ̄ⲕⲱϩ ϭⲉ ⲉ ⲡⲙⲟⲩ ϩⲛ̄ ⲧⲉⲡⲗⲁⲛⲏ ⲙ̄ ⲡⲉⲧⲛ̄ⲱⲛϩ̄,
ⲟⲩⲇⲉ ⲙ̄ⲡⲣ̄ⲥⲱⲕ ⲛⲏⲧⲛ̄ ⲙ̄ ⲡⲧⲁⲕⲟ ϩⲛ̄ ⲛⲉϩⲃⲏⲩⲉ ⲛ̄ ⲛⲉⲧⲛ̄ϭⲓϫ.

(13) ϫⲉ ⲙ̄ⲡⲉ-ⲡⲛⲟⲩⲧⲉ ⲧⲁⲙⲓⲉ-ⲡⲙⲟⲩ,
ⲟⲩⲇⲉ ⲛϥ̄ⲣⲁϣⲉ ⲁⲛ ⲉϫⲙ̄ ⲡⲧⲁⲕⲟ ⲛ̄ ⲛⲉⲧ ⲟⲛϩ̄.

(14) ⲛ̄ⲧⲁϥⲥⲟⲛⲧⲟⲩ ⲅⲁⲣ ⲧⲏⲣⲟⲩ ⲉⲧⲣⲉⲩϭⲱ ϣⲁ ⲃⲟⲗ
ⲁⲩⲱ ⲉⲧⲣⲉⲩⲟⲩϫⲁⲓ ⲛ̄ϭⲓ ⲛ̄ⲥⲱⲛⲧ ⲙ̄ ⲡⲕⲟⲥⲙⲟⲥ.
ⲙ̄ⲙⲛ̄-ⲡⲁϩⲣⲉ ⲙ̄ ⲙⲟⲩ ϩⲣⲁⲓ ⲛ̄ϩⲏⲧⲟⲩ,
ⲟⲩⲇⲉ ⲙⲛ̄ⲧⲉⲣⲟ ⲛ̄ ⲁⲙⲛ̄ⲧⲉ ϩⲓϫⲙ̄ ⲡⲕⲁϩ.

{(15) ⲧⲁⲓⲕⲁⲓⲟⲥⲩⲛⲏ ⲅⲁⲣ ⲟⲩⲁⲧⲙⲟⲩ ⲧⲉ.}

(16) ⲛ̄ⲁⲥⲉⲃⲏⲥ ⲇⲉ ϩⲛ̄ ⲛⲉⲩϭⲓϫ ⲙⲛ̄ ⲛⲉⲩϣⲁϫⲉ ⲁⲩⲥⲟⲧⲡϥ̄ ⲛⲁⲩ;

---

(8) ⲣ̄-ⲃⲟⲗ ⲉ to avoid, escape. ⲛ̄ⲛⲏⲩ for ⲛⲏⲩ. (9) ϣⲟⲭⲛⲉ vb.
intr. to take counsel (concerning: ⲉ); as n.m. counsel.
ἀσεβής adj. ungodly, impious. ἡ ἀνομία lawlessness.
(10) ⲡ.ⲕⲱϩ envy, jealousy; vb. intr. to be envious,
jealous, zealous (for: ⲉ). (11) ϯ-ⲥⲟ ⲉ to restrain; to
refrain from. ϫⲓ-ϭⲟⲗ to tell a lie. (12) ἡ πλάνη error,
erring. (14) ⲥⲱⲛⲧ ⲥⲛ̄ⲧ- ⲥⲟⲛⲧ⸗ Q ⲥⲟⲛⲧ vb. tr. to create,
found (ⲙ̄ⲙⲟ⸗); as n.m. creation, creature. ϣⲁ ⲃⲟⲗ adv.
forever, for good. ⲡⲁϩⲣⲉ ⲙ̄ ⲙⲟⲩ poison. ⲁⲙⲛ̄ⲧⲉ Hades, Hell.
(15) Verse 15 is intrusive and incomplete. Omit.

ⲁⲩⲧⲁⲁϥ ⲛⲁⲩ ⲛ̄ ϣⲃⲏⲣ, ⲁⲩⲃⲱⲗ ⲉⲃⲟⲗ,

ⲁⲩⲥⲙⲓⲛⲉ ⲛ̄ ⲟⲩⲇⲓⲁⲑⲏⲕⲏ ⲛⲉⲙⲁϥ,

ϫⲉ ⲥⲉⲙ̄ⲡϣⲁ ⲛ̄ ⲧⲙⲉⲣⲓⲥ ⲙ̄ ⲡⲉⲧ ⲙ̄ⲙⲁⲩ.

Chapter II
The Reasoning of the Wicked

(1) ⲁⲩϫⲟⲟⲥ ⲅⲁⲣ, ⲉ-ⲁⲩⲙⲉⲉⲩⲉ ⲉⲣⲁⲓ ⲛ̄ϩⲏⲧⲟⲩ ϩⲛ̄ ⲟⲩⲥⲟⲟⲩⲧⲛ̄ ⲁⲛ,

ϫⲉ ⲟⲩⲕⲟⲩⲓ ⲡⲉ ⲡⲉⲛⲁϩⲉ, ⲉϥⲙⲉϩ ⲝ̄ ⲗⲩⲡⲏ,

ⲁⲩⲱ ⲙ̄ⲙⲛ̄-ⲙ̄ⲧⲟⲛ ϣⲟⲟⲡ ϩⲙ̄ ⲡⲙⲟⲩ ⲙ̄ ⲡⲣⲱⲙⲉ,

ⲟⲩⲇⲉ ⲙ̄ⲡⲛ̄ⲥⲟⲩⲛ̄-ⲟⲩⲁ ⲉ-ⲁϥⲉⲓ ⲉ2ⲣⲁⲓ ϩⲛ̄ ⲁⲙⲛ̄ⲧⲉ.

(2) ϫⲉ ⲛ̄ⲧⲁⲛϣⲱⲡⲉ ⲉ ⲡⲡⲉⲧ ϣⲟⲩⲉⲓⲧ.

ⲙⲛ̄ⲛ̄ⲥⲱⲥ ⲉⲛⲛⲁⲣ̄-ⲑⲉ ⲛ̄ ⲛⲉⲧⲉ ⲙ̄ⲡⲟⲩϣⲱⲡⲉ,

ϫⲉ ⲟⲩⲕⲁⲡⲛⲟⲥ ⲡⲉ ⲡⲛⲓϥⲉ ⲉⲧ ϩⲛ̄ ϣⲁⲛⲧⲛ̄,

ⲁⲩⲱ ⲟⲩϯⲕ ⲡⲉ ⲡϣⲁϫⲉ ⲉⲧ ⲕⲓⲙ ϩⲙ̄ ⲡⲉⲛϩⲏⲧ.

(3) ⲡⲁⲓ ⲉϥϣⲁⲛⲱϣⲙ̄, ⲉⲣⲉ-ⲡⲥⲱⲙⲁ ⲧⲏⲣϥ̄ ⲛⲁⲣ̄-ⲑⲉ ⲛ̄ ⲟⲩϫⲃ̄ⲃⲉⲥ,

ⲁⲩⲱ ⲡⲉⲛⲡⲛ̄ⲁ̄ ⲛⲁⲃⲱⲗ ⲉⲃⲟⲗ ⲛ̄ ⲑⲉ ⲙ̄ ⲡⲁⲏⲣ ⲉⲧ ϫⲟⲟⲣⲉ ⲉⲃⲟⲗ,

(4) ⲛ̄ⲥⲉⲣ̄-ⲡⲱⲃϣ̄ ⲙ̄ ⲡⲉⲛⲣⲁⲛ ϩⲙ̄ ⲡⲉⲛⲟⲩⲟⲉⲓϣ,

ⲛ̄ⲧⲉⲧⲙ̄-ⲗⲁⲁⲩ ⲉⲣ̄-ⲡⲙⲉⲉⲩⲉ ⲛ̄ ⲛⲉⲛϩⲃⲏⲩⲉ,

ⲁⲩⲱ ⲡⲉⲛⲁϩⲉ ⲛⲁⲟⲩⲉⲓⲛⲉ ⲛ̄ ⲑⲉ ⲛ̄ ⲟⲩⲕⲗⲟⲟⲗⲉ,

ⲁⲩⲱ ϥⲛⲁϫⲱⲱⲣⲉ ⲉⲃⲟⲗ ⲛ̄ ⲑⲉ ⲛ̄ ⲟⲩⲛⲓϥⲉ ⲉ-ⲁϥⲃⲱⲗ ⲉⲃⲟⲗ ϩⲓⲧⲛ̄

ⲡⲁⲕⲧⲓⲛ ⲙ̄ ⲡⲣⲏ,

ⲁⲩⲱ ⲉ-ⲁ-ⲧⲉϥ2ⲙ̄ⲙⲉ ϩⲣⲟϣ ⲉϫⲱϥ.

(5) ⲟⲩ2ⲁⲉⲓⲃⲉⲥ ⲉ-ⲁⲥⲟⲩⲉⲓⲛⲉ ⲡⲉ ⲡⲉⲛⲟⲩⲟⲉⲓϣ,

---

(16) ⲥⲙⲓⲛⲉ ⲥⲙⲛ̄- ⲥⲙⲛ̄ⲧ⸗ Q ⲥⲙⲟⲛⲧ̄ vb. tr. to establish, set up (ⲙ̄ⲙⲟ⸗). ἡ μερίς portion, share; party, faction.

II. (1) ϩⲛ̄ ⲟⲩⲥⲟⲟⲩⲧⲛ̄ ⲁⲛ incorrectly, not rightly. ⲝ̄ ⲗⲩⲡⲏ = ⲛ̄ ⲗⲩⲡⲏ; ἡ λύπη grief, pain. (2) ⲣ̄-ⲑⲉ ⲛ̄ to become like. ⲡ.ⲛⲓϥⲉ breath. ϣⲁⲛⲧ⸗ nose. ⲡ.ϯⲕ spark. (3) ⲧ. ϫⲃ̄ⲃⲉⲥ (glowing) coal. ὁ, ἡ ἀήρ air, atmosphere. (4) ⲧⲉ. ⲕⲗⲟⲟⲗⲉ cloud. ⲡ.ⲁⲕⲧⲓⲛ (ἡ ἀκτίς, -ῖνος) ray, beam. ⲧ.2ⲙ̄ⲙⲉ heat. 2ⲣⲟϣ, Q 2ⲟⲣϣ̄ vb. intr. to become heavy, difficult. (5) ⲧ.2ⲁⲓⲃⲉⲥ shadow, shade.

ⲁⲩⲱ ⲙ̄ⲙⲛ̄-ⲕⲧⲟ ϣⲟⲟⲡ ⲙ̄ ⲡⲉⲛⲙⲟⲩ;
ϫⲉ ⲁⲩⲧⲱⲱⲃⲉ ⲉⲣⲱⲟⲩ, ⲁⲩⲱ ⲛ̄ⲛⲉ-ⲗⲁⲁⲩ ⲕⲟⲧϥ̄.

(6) ⲁⲙⲏⲉⲓⲧⲛ̄ ⳓⲉ ⲛ̄ⲧⲛ̄ⲧⲥⲓⲟⲛ ⲛ̄ ⲛ̄ⲁⲅⲁⲑⲟⲛ ⲉⲧ ϣⲟⲟⲡ,
ⲛ̄ⲧⲛ̄ⲭⲣⲱ ⲛ̄ ⲧⲉⲕⲧⲓⲥⲓⲥ ⳁⲛ̄ ⲟⲩⳓⲉⲡⲏ ⲛ̄ ⲑⲉ ⲛ̄ ⲟⲩⲙⲛ̄ⲧⲃⲣ̄ⲣⲉ.

(7) ⲙⲁⲣⲛ̄ⲧⲥⲓⲟⲛ ⲛ̄ ⲏⲣⲡ̄ ⲉ-ⲛⲁⲛⲟⲩϥ ⳁ ⲥⲧⲓ-ⲛⲟⲩϥⲉ,
ⲁⲩⲱ ⲙ̄ⲡⲣ̄ⲧⲣⲉⲩⲥⲗⲁⲧⲛ̄ ⲛ̄ⳓⲓ ⲛ̄ⲕⲁⲣⲡⲟⲥ ⲙ̄ ⲡⲁⲏⲣ.

(8) ⲙⲁⲣⲛ̄ϯ ⲉϫⲱⲛ ⲛ̄ ⳁⲛ̄ⲕⲗⲟⲙ ⲛ̄ ⲟⲩⲣⲧ̄ ⲉⲙⲡⲁⲧⲟⲩⳁⲱⳓⲉ̄,

(9) ⲙ̄ⲡⲣ̄ⲧⲣⲉ-ⲗⲁⲁⲩ ⲙ̄ⲙⲟⲛ ϣⲱⲡⲉ ⲙ̄ ⲡⲃⲟⲗ ⲛ̄ ⲛⲉⲛⲙⲛ̄ⲧⲱⲛⲁ.
ⲙⲁⲣⲛ̄ⲕⲁ-ⲥⲩⲙⲃⲟⲩⲗⲏ ⲛ̄ ⲟⲩⲛⲟϥ ⳁⲙ̄ ⲙⲁ ⲛⲓⲙ,
ϫⲉ ⲧⲁⲓ ⲧⲉ ⲧⲉⲛⲙⲉⲣⲓⲥ ⲁⲩⲱ ⲡⲉⲛⲕⲗⲏⲣⲟⲥ.

(10) ⲟⲩⳁⲏⲕⲉ ⲛ̄ ⲁⲓⲕⲁⲓⲟⲥ ⲙⲁⲣⲛ̄ϫⲓⲧϥ̄ ⲛ̄ ⳓⲟⲛⲥ̄.
ⲙ̄ⲡⲣ̄ⲧⲣⲉⲛϯ-ⲥⲟ ⲉ ⲧⲉⲭⲏⲣⲁ,
ⲟⲩⲇⲉ ⲙ̄ⲡⲣ̄ⲧⲣⲉⲛϣⲓⲡⲉ ⳁⲏⲧⲟⲩ ⲛ̄ ⲛⲉⲥⲕⲓⲙ ⲛ̄ ⲟⲩⳁⲗⲗⲟ ⲛ̄ ⲛⲟⳓ ⲛ̄ ⲁⳁⲉ.

(11) ⲙⲁⲣⲉ-ⲧⲉⲛⳓⲟⲙ ϣⲱⲡⲉ ⲛⲁⲛ ⲛ̄ ⲛⲟⲙⲟⲥ ⲛ̄ ⲁⲓⲕⲁⲓⲟⲥⲩⲛⲏ;
ⲧⲙⲛ̄ⲧⳓⲱⲃ ⲅⲁⲣ ⲉϣⲗⲩϫⲡⲓⲟⲥ ⳁⲱⲥ ⲁⲧϣⲁⲩ.

(12) ⲙⲁⲣⲛ̄ⳓⲱⲣⳓ̄ ⲉ ⲡⲁⲓⲕⲁⲓⲟⲥ,
ϫⲉ ϥⲙⲟⲕⳁ̄ ⲉ ⲣ̄-[ⲭⲣⲏⲥⲧⲟⲥ] ⲛⲁⲛ,
ⲁⲩⲱ ϥϯ ⲟⲩⲃⲉ ⲛⲉⲛⳁⲃⲏⲩⲉ.
ϥⲛⲟⳓⲛⲉⳓ ⲙ̄ⲙⲟⲛ ⲛ̄ ⲛⲉⲛⲛⲟⲃⲉ ⳁⲓⲧⲙ̄ ⲡⲛⲟⲙⲟⲥ,
ⲁⲩⲱ ϥⲟⲩⲱⲛⳁ̄ ⲉⲃⲟⲗ ⲛ̄ ⲛⲉⲛⲛⲟⲃⲉ ⳁⲓⲧⲛ̄ ⲧⲉⲥⲃⲱ.

---

(5) ⲧⲱⲱⲃⲉ ⲧⲟⲟⲃ⸗ Q ⲧⲟⲟⲃⲉ vb. tr. to set a seal (on: ⲙ̄ⲙⲟ⸗,
ⲉⲣⲛ̄). (6) χράομαι to use. ἡ κτίσις the world, creation.
(7) ⲥⲧⲓ-ⲛⲟⲩϥⲉ perfume, incense (cf. ⲥⲧⲟⲓ). ⲡ.ⲁⲏⲣ is probably Gk. error for ἔαρ springtime. (8) ⲟⲩⲣⲧ̄ rose. ⳁⲱⳓⲉ̄
ⳁⲉⳓⲃ̄- ⳁⲟⳓⲃ⸗ Q ⳁⲟⳓⲃ̄ vb. tr. and intr. to wither. (9) ⲙⲛ̄ⲧϣⲛⲁ
profligacy. ⲥⲩⲙⲃⲟⲩⲗⲏ prob. for ⲥⲩⲙⲃⲟⲗⲟⲛ τὸ σύμβολον mark,
token. ⲟⲩⲛⲟϥ vb. intr. to rejoice; n.m. joy. ὁ κλῆρος
portion, share, inheritance. (10) ⲡⲉ.ⲥⲕⲓⲙ gray hair.
(11) ⲙⲛ̄ⲧⳓⲱⲃ weakness; ⳓⲱⲃ adj. weak. (12) ⳓⲱⲣⳓ̄, Q ⳓⲟⲣⳓ̄ vb.
to hunt, waylay, ambush (ⲉ). ⲣ̄-ⲭⲣⲏⲥⲧⲟⲥ ⲛⲁ⸗ to benefit, do
a good service to; χρηστός useful, beneficial.

(13) ϥϫⲱ ⲙ̄ⲙⲟⲥ ϫⲉ ϯⲥⲟⲟⲩⲛ ⲙ̄ ⲡⲛⲟⲩⲧⲉ,
ⲁⲩⲱ ϥⲉⲓⲣⲉ ⲙ̄ⲙⲟϥ ⲛ̄ ϣⲏⲣⲉ ⲙ̄ ⲡⲭⲟⲉⲓⲥ.

(14) ϣⲁϥϣⲱⲡⲉ ⲛⲁⲛ ⲉⲩϫⲡⲓⲟ ⲛ̄ ⲛⲉⲛⲙⲉⲉⲩⲉ,
ϥ₂ⲟⲣϣ̄ⲟ ⲛⲁⲛ ⲉ ⲛⲁⲩ ⲉⲣⲟϥ,

(15) ϫⲉ ⲙ̄ ⲡⲉϥⲃⲓⲟⲥ ⲉⲓⲛⲉ ⲁⲛ ⲙ̄ ⲡⲁ-ⲟⲩⲟⲛ ⲛⲓⲙ,
ⲁⲩⲱ ⲛⲉϥ₂ⲓⲟⲟⲩⲉ ⲥⲉϣⲟⲃⲉ.

(16) ⲉⲛⲏⲡ ⲛ̄ⲧⲟⲟⲧϥ̄ ⲉ ₂ⲉⲛϫⲟⲟⲩⲧ,
ⲁⲩⲱ ϥⲥⲁ₂ⲏⲩ ⲉⲃⲟⲗ ⲛ̄ ⲛⲉⲛ₂ⲓⲟⲟⲩⲉ ⲛ̄ ⲑⲉ ⲛ̄ ⲛⲓⲁⲕⲁⲑⲁⲣⲥⲓⲁ.
ϥⲙⲁⲕⲁⲣⲓⲍⲉ ⲛ̄ ⲑⲁⲏ ⲛ̄ ⲛ̄ⲁⲓⲕⲁⲓⲟⲥ,
ⲁⲩⲱ ϥϣⲟⲩϣⲟⲩ ⲙ̄ⲙⲟϥ ϫⲉ "ⲡⲁⲓⲱⲧ ⲡⲉ ⲡⲛⲟⲩⲧⲉ."

(17) ⲙⲁⲣ̄ⲛⲛⲁⲩ ϫⲉ ₂ⲙ̄ⲙⲉ ⲛⲉ ⲛⲉϥϣⲁϫⲉ,
ⲁⲩⲱ ⲛ̄ⲧ̄ⲛⲡⲉⲓⲣⲁⲍⲉ ⲛ̄ ⲧⲉϥ₂ⲁⲏ.

(18) ⲉϣϫⲉ ⲡⲁⲓⲕⲁⲓⲟⲥ ⲅⲁⲣ ⲡⲉ ⲡϣⲏⲣⲉ ⲙ̄ ⲡⲛⲟⲩⲧⲉ,
ϥⲛⲁϣⲟⲡϥ̄ ⲉⲣⲟϥ, ⲛϥ̄ⲛⲁ₂ⲙⲉϥ ⲛ̄ⲧⲟⲟⲧⲟⲩ ⲛ̄ ⲛⲉⲧ ϯ ⲟⲩⲃⲏϥ.

(19) ⲙⲁⲣ̄ⲛ₂ⲉⲧⲁⲍⲉ ⲙ̄ⲙⲟϥ ₂ⲛ̄ ₂ⲉⲛϣⲱϣ ⲙⲛ̄ ₂ⲉⲛⲃⲁⲥⲁⲛⲟⲥ,
ϫⲉⲕⲁⲥ ⲉⲛⲉⲉⲓⲙⲉ ⲉ ⲧⲉϥⲙⲛ̄ⲧ₂ⲁⲕ,
ⲁⲩⲱ ⲛ̄ⲧⲛ̄ⲁⲟⲕⲓⲙⲁⲍⲉ ⲛ̄ ⲧⲉϥⲙⲛ̄ⲧ₂ⲁⲣϣ̄ⲟ-₂ⲏⲧ.

(20) ⲙⲁⲣ̄ⲛⲧⲉⲗⲉⲓⲟϥ ₂ⲛ̄ ⲟⲩⲙⲟⲩ ⲉϥⲥⲛϣ;
ⲥⲉⲛⲁϭⲙ̄-ⲡⲉϥϣⲓⲛⲉ ⲅⲁⲣ ⲕⲁⲧⲁ ⲛⲉϥϣⲁϫⲉ.

(21) ⲛⲁⲓ ⲁⲩⲙⲉⲉⲩⲉ ⲉⲣⲟⲟⲩ ⲁⲩⲱ ⲁⲩⲥⲱⲣⲙ̄;
ⲁ-ⲧⲉⲩⲕⲁⲕⲓⲁ ⲅⲁⲣ ⲧⲱⲙ ⲙ̄ ⲡⲉⲩ₂ⲏⲧ.

---

(14) ϥ₂ⲟⲣϣ̄ⲟ: "he is hard for us to look at (i.e. countenance)."
(15) ⲉⲓⲛⲉ vb. tr. to resemble, be like (ⲙ̄ⲙⲟ⸗); as n.m.
likeness, aspect. (16) ϫⲟⲟⲩⲧ adj. base, rejected. ἡ ἀκαθαρσία uncleanness; ⲛⲓ- §30.8. μακαρίζω to bless, deem
blessed. ϣⲟⲩϣⲟⲩ vb. intr. to brag, boast. (18) ⲛⲟⲩ₂ⲙ̄
ⲛⲉ₂ⲙ̄- ⲛⲁ₂ⲙ⸗ Q ⲛⲁ₂ⲙ̄ vb. tr. to save, rescue (ⲙ̄ⲙⲟ⸗). (19)
₂ⲉⲧⲁⲍⲉ ἑτάζω to examine, test. ϣⲱϣ vb. tr. to twist; here
apparently as n. torture. ἡ βάσανος torture, anguish.
δοκιμάζω to prove, test. (20) ⲧⲉⲗⲉⲓⲟ ⲧⲉⲗⲉⲓⲉ- ⲧⲉⲗⲉⲓⲟ⸗ Q
ⲧⲉⲗⲉⲓⲏⲩ vb. tr. to condemn, disgrace (ⲙ̄ⲙⲟ⸗).

190

(22) ⲁⲩⲱ ⲙ̄ⲡⲟⲩⲥⲟⲩⲛ̄-ⲙ̄ⲙⲩⲥⲧⲏⲣⲓⲟⲛ ⲙ̄ ⲡⲛⲟⲩⲧⲉ,
ⲟⲩⲇⲉ ⲙ̄ⲡⲟⲩⲕⲁ-ⲍⲧⲏⲩ ⲉ ⲡⲃⲉⲕⲉ ⲛ̄ ⲧⲁⲓⲕⲁⲓⲟⲥⲩⲛⲏ;
ⲙ̄ⲡⲟⲩⲡⲓⲥⲧⲉⲩⲉ ⲉ ⲡⲧⲁⲓⲟ ⲛ̄ ⲛⲉⲯⲩⲭⲏ ⲛ̄ ⲛⲉⲧ ⲟⲩⲁⲁⲃ.

(23) ϫⲉ ⲡⲛⲟⲩⲧⲉ ⲁϥⲥⲱⲛⲧ̄ ⲙ̄ ⲡⲣⲱⲙⲉ ⲉⲩⲙⲛ̄ⲧⲁⲧⲧⲁⲕⲟ,
ⲁⲩⲱ ⲁϥⲧⲁⲙⲓⲟϥ ⲍⲛ̄ ⲑⲓⲕⲱⲛ ⲙ̄ ⲡⲉϥⲉⲓⲛⲉ.

(24) ⲍⲙ̄ ⲡⲉⲫⲑⲟⲛⲟⲥ ⲇⲉ ⲙ̄ ⲡⲁⲓⲁⲃⲟⲗⲟⲥ ⲁ-ⲡⲙⲟⲩ ⲉⲓ ⲉⲍⲟⲩⲛ ⲉ ⲡⲕⲟⲥⲙⲟⲥ.

(25) ⲥⲉⲡⲉⲓⲣⲁⲍⲉ ⲇⲉ ⲙ̄ⲙⲟϥ ⲛ̄ϭⲓ ⲧⲙⲉⲣⲓⲥ ⲙ̄ ⲡⲉⲧ ⲙ̄ⲙⲁⲩ.

Chapter V

The Remorse of the Wicked at the Judgement

(1) ⲧⲟⲧⲉ ⲡⲁⲓⲕⲁⲓⲟⲥ ⲛⲁⲁⲍⲉⲣⲁⲧϥ̄ ⲍⲛ̄ ⲟⲩⲛⲟϭ ⲙ̄ ⲡⲁⲣⲍⲏⲥⲓⲁ ⲉ ⲛⲁϣⲱⲥ ⲙ̄
ⲡⲉⲙⲧⲟ ⲉⲃⲟⲗ ⲛ̄ ⲛⲉⲛⲧⲁⲩⲑⲗⲓⲃⲉ ⲙ̄ⲙⲟϥ ⲁⲩⲱ ⲛⲉⲛⲧⲁⲩⲁⲑⲉⲧⲓ ⲛ̄
ⲛⲉϥⲍⲓⲥⲉ.

(2) ⲥⲉⲛⲁⲛⲁⲩ, ⲛ̄ⲥⲉϣⲧⲟⲣⲧⲣ̄ ⲍⲛ̄ ⲟⲩⲍⲟⲧⲉ ⲉⲥⲛⲁϣⲧ̄,
ⲛ̄ⲥⲉⲡⲱϣⲥ̄ ⲉⲭⲛ̄ ⲧⲙⲟⲉⲓⲍⲉ ⲙ̄ ⲡⲉϥⲟⲩϫⲁⲓ,

(3) ⲛ̄ⲥⲉⲭⲟⲟⲥ ⲍⲣⲁⲓ ⲛ̄ⲍⲏⲧⲟⲩ, ⲉⲩⲙⲉⲧⲁⲛⲟⲓ
ⲁⲩⲱ ⲉⲩⲁϣ-ⲁⲍⲟⲙ ⲉⲧⲃⲉ ⲡⲗⲱⲭⲍ̄ ⲙ̄ ⲡⲉⲩⲡ̄ⲛ̄ⲁ̄,
ϫⲉ "ⲡⲁⲓ ⲡⲉⲛⲉⲛⲥⲱⲃⲉ ⲛ̄ⲥⲱϥ ⲙ̄ ⲡⲓⲟⲩⲟⲉⲓϣ,
ⲉϥϣⲟⲟⲡ ⲛⲁⲛ ⲙ̄ ⲡⲁⲣⲁⲃⲟⲗⲏ ⲛ̄ ⲛⲟϭⲛⲉϭ ⲛ̄ ⲛⲓⲁⲑⲏⲧ,

(4) ⲉⲛⲱⲡ ⲙ̄ ⲡⲉϥⲁⲍⲉ ⲉⲩⲗⲓⲃⲉ, ⲁⲩⲱ ⲡⲉϥⲙⲟⲩ ⲉⲩⲥⲱϣ.

---

(22) ⲕⲁ-ⲍⲧⲏ⸗ ⲉ to set one's mind on/to. ⲡ.ⲃⲉⲕⲉ reward,
pay. (24) ὁ φθόνος ill-will, jealousy. (25) ⲧ.ⲙⲉⲣⲓⲥ is
taken as collective: "those who belong to that one."
πειράζω in the sense "to experience."

V. (1) ἡ παρρησία freedom, openness; ⲍⲛ̄ ⲟⲩⲡⲁⲣⲍⲏⲥⲓⲁ
openly, publicly. ἀθετέω to disregard. (2) ⲡⲱϣⲥ̄ ⲡⲉϣⲥ̄⸗
ⲡⲟϣⲥ⸗ Q ⲡⲟϣⲥ̄ vb. tr. to amaze (ⲙ̄ⲙⲟ⸗); intr. to be amazed
(at: ⲉⲭⲛ̄). ⲧ.ⲙⲟⲉⲓⲍⲉ wonder, marvel. (3) ⲁϣ-ⲁⲍⲟⲙ vb. intr.
to sigh; as n.m. sigh. ⲡ.ⲗⲱⲭⲍ̄ anguish, oppression. ⲥⲱⲃⲉ
vb. tr. to mock, ridicule (ⲙ̄ⲙⲟ⸗, ⲛ̄ⲥⲁ). ⲡⲁⲣⲁⲃⲟⲗⲏ in sense:
model, exemplar. (4) ⲗⲓⲃⲉ as n.m. madness.

(5) ⲛ̄ ⲁϣ ⲛ̄ ϩⲉ ⲁⲩⲟⲡϥ̄ ϩⲛ̄ ⲛ̄ϣⲏⲣⲉ ⲙ̄ ⲡⲛⲟⲩⲧⲉ,
ⲁⲩⲱ ⲡⲉϥⲕⲗⲏⲣⲟⲥ ϩⲛ̄ ⲛⲉⲧ ⲟⲩⲁⲁⲃ?

(6) ⲉⲉⲓⲉ ⲛ̄ⲧⲁⲛⲡⲗⲁⲛⲁ ⲛ̄ⲧⲟⲟⲩⲛ ⲉⲃⲟⲗ ϩⲛ̄ ⲛⲉϩⲓⲟⲟⲩⲉ ⲛ̄ ⲧⲙⲉ,
ⲁⲩⲱ ⲙ̄ⲡ̄ϥϣⲁ ⲛⲁⲛ ⲛ̄ϭⲓ ⲡⲟⲩⲟⲉⲓⲛ ⲛ̄ ⲧⲁⲓⲕⲁⲓⲟⲥⲩⲛⲏ,
ⲁⲩⲱ ⲡⲣⲏ ⲙ̄ⲡ̄ϥⲡⲉⲓⲣⲉ ⲛⲁⲛ.

(7) ⲁⲛⲙⲟⲩϩ ⲛ̄ ⲁⲛⲟⲙⲓⲁ ϩⲓ ⲧⲁⲕⲟ ⲛ̄ ⲛⲉⲛϩⲓⲟⲟⲩⲉ.
ⲁⲛⲃⲱⲕ ϩⲓⲧⲛ̄ ⲛ̄ⲭⲁⲓⲉ ⲉⲙⲉⲩⲙⲟⲟϣⲉ ⲛ̄ϩⲏⲧⲟⲩ;
ⲧⲉϩⲓⲏ ⲇⲉ ⲙ̄ ⲡⲭⲟⲉⲓⲥ ⲙ̄ⲡⲛ̄ⲥⲟⲩⲱⲛⲥ̄.

(8) ⲛ̄ⲧⲁⲥϯ-ⲟⲩ ⲙ̄ⲙⲟⲛ ⲛ̄ ⲟⲩ ⲛ̄ϭⲓ ⲧⲙ̄ⲙⲛ̄ⲧϫⲁⲥⲓ-ϩⲏⲧ?
ⲏ ⲧⲙⲛ̄ⲧⲣⲙ̄ⲙⲁⲟ ⲙⲛ̄ ⲧⲙⲛ̄ⲧⲃⲁⲃⲉ-ⲣⲱⲙⲉ ⲛ̄ⲧⲁⲥϯ-ⲟⲩ ⲛⲁⲛ?

(9) ⲁ-ⲛⲏ ⲧⲏⲣⲟⲩ ⲟⲩⲉⲓⲛⲉ ⲛ̄ ⲑⲉ ⲛ̄ ⲟⲩϩⲁⲓⲃⲉⲥ,
ⲁⲩⲱ ⲛ̄ ⲑⲉ ⲛ̄ <ⲟⲩ>ⲟⲩⲱ ⲉ-ⲁϥⲡⲁⲣⲁⲅⲉ,

(10) ⲏ ⲛ̄ ⲑⲉ ⲛ̄ ⲟⲩϫⲟⲓ ⲉϥⲥϭⲏⲣ ϩⲛ̄ ⲟⲩϩⲟⲉⲓⲙ ⲙ̄ ⲙⲟⲟⲩ
ⲉ-ⲙⲛ̄-ⲑⲉ ⲛ̄ ϭⲛ̄-ⲛⲉϥⲧⲁϭⲥⲉ
ⲏ ⲧⲉϩⲓⲏ ⲙ̄ ⲡⲉϥⲧⲟⲡ ϩⲛ̄ ⲛ̄ϩⲟⲉⲓⲙ.

(11) ⲏ ⲛ̄ ⲑⲉ ⲛ̄ ⲟⲩϩⲁⲗⲏⲧ ⲉ-ⲁϥϩⲱⲗ ⲉⲃⲟⲗ,
{ⲉ-ⲙⲉⲩϭⲛ̄-ⲙⲁⲉⲓⲛ ⲙ̄ ⲡⲉϥϩⲱⲗ ⲉⲃⲟⲗ}
ⲉϥϩⲓⲟⲩⲉ ⲛ̄ ⲛⲉϥⲧⲛ̄ϩ ⲉ ⲡⲁⲏⲣ ⲉⲧ ⲁⲥⲱⲟⲩ,
ⲉϥⲡⲱϩ ⲙ̄ⲙⲟϥ ⲛ̄ ϭⲟⲛⲥ̄ ϩⲙ̄ ⲡⲟⲩⲟⲉⲓ,
ⲉϥⲕⲓⲙ ⲛ̄ ⲛⲉϥⲧⲛ̄ϩ, ⲉϥϩⲁⲗ,
ⲙ̄ⲛ̄ⲛⲥⲱⲥ ⲉ-ⲙⲉⲩϭⲛ̄-ⲙⲁⲉⲓⲛ ⲙ̄ ⲡⲉϥϩⲱⲗ ⲉⲃⲟⲗ.

(12) ⲏ ⲛ̄ ⲑⲉ ⲛ̄ ⲟⲩⲥⲟⲧⲉ ⲉ-ⲁⲩⲛⲟϫϥ̄ ⲉ ⲡⲥⲟⲟⲩⲧⲛ̄,
ⲉ-ⲁϥⲡⲉϩ-ⲡⲁⲏⲣ, ⲛ̄ ⲧⲉⲩⲛⲟⲩ ⲟⲛ ⲁϥⲧⲱϭⲉ, ⲉ-ⲙⲉⲩⲥⲟⲩⲛ̄-ⲧⲉϥϩⲓⲏ.

---

(6) ⲡⲉⲓⲣⲉ, Q ⲡⲟⲣⲉ vb. intr. to come forth; to shine (of sun). (8) ϯ-ⲟⲩ ⲙ̄ⲙⲟⲛ ⲛ̄ ⲟⲩ is not clear; read perhaps ϯ-ⲟⲩ ⲛⲁⲛ as at end of verse. ⲃⲁⲃⲉ-ⲣⲱⲙⲉ boaster; ⲙⲛ̄ⲧⲃⲁⲃⲉ-ⲣⲱⲙⲉ boastfulness. (9) ⲡ.ⲟⲩⲱ news, report. (10) ⲥϭⲏⲣ vb. intr. to sail. ⲡ.ϩⲟⲉⲓⲙ wave. ⲧ.ⲧⲁϭⲥⲉ foot-print, track, trace. ⲡ.ⲧⲟⲡ keel. (11) ⲁⲥⲱⲟⲩ (Q of ⲁⲥⲁⲓ) vb. intr. to be light, swift. ⲡ.ⲟⲩⲟⲉⲓ rush, swift movement. ⲡⲱϩ in sense: to split, cleave. (12) ⲡ.ⲥⲟⲧⲉ arrow. ⲉ ⲡⲥⲟⲟⲩⲧⲛ̄ straight (ahead), on target. ⲧⲱϭⲉ: i.e. the air joins (or closes

(13) ⲦⲀⲓ ⲦⲈ ⲐⲈ ⳅⲱⲱⲚ ⲞⲚ Ⲉ-Ⲁ ⲨⲬ ⲠⲞⲚ Ⲁ ⲚⲱⲬⲚ̄;
ⲘⲠⲚ̄ⳅ Ⲉ Ⲉ ⲨⲘⲀ Ⲉ ⲓⲚ Ⲛ̄ ⲀⲢ Ⲉ ⲦⲎ Ⲉ ⲞⲨⲞⲚⳅⳁ Ⲉ ⲂⲞⲗ.
ⳅ ⲢⲀⲓ ⲀⲈ ⳅⲚ̄ ⲦⲈⲚ ⲔⲀ Ⲕ ⲓⲀ [...

(14) ⲬⲈ ⲐⲈ Ⲁ ⲠⲓⲤ Ⲙ̄ ⲠⲀⲤⲈ ⲂⲎⲤ [Ⲟ Ⲛ̄] ⲐⲈ Ⲛ̄ ⲞⲨ ⳧ⳅ ⲓ Ⲉ Ⲉ ⲢⲈ-ⲠⲦⲎⲨ ⳁ[ⲓ
Ⲙ̄Ⲙ ⲟ ⳁ],
ⲀⲨⲱ Ⲛ̄ ⲐⲈ Ⲛ̄ ⲞⲨⳅⲀ ⲗ ⲟ ⲨⲤ Ⲉ ⳁ ⳧ ⲞⲞ ⲘⲈ, Ⲉ-Ⲁ ⲨⲐ ⲗ ⲟ ⳁ Ⲉ ⲂⲞⲗ ⳅ ⲓ ⲦⲚ̄
ⲞⲨⳅ ⲀⲦⲎⲨ,
Ⲏ Ⲛ̄ ⲐⲈ Ⲛ̄ ⲞⲨ ⲔⲀ ⲠⲚⲞⲤ Ⲉ-Ⲁ Ⲩⳅ ⲀⲦⲎⲨ ⲂⲞⲗ ⳁ Ⲉ ⲂⲞⲗ,
Ⲛ̄ ⲐⲈ Ⲙ̄ ⲠⲢ̄-ⲠⲘⲈ Ⲉ ⲨⲈ Ⲛ̄ ⲞⲨⲢⲘⲚ̄ ⳃ ⲟ Ⲉ ⲓⲗ Ⲉ Ⲛ̄ ⲞⲨⳅ ⲟ ⲟ Ⲩ ⲞⲨⲱⲦ
Ⲉ-Ⲁ ⳁ ⲠⲀ ⲢⲀⳍ Ⲉ.

Chapter VII

The Attributes of Wisdom

(22) ⲞⲨⲚ̄-ⲞⲨ ⲠⲚ̄Ⲁ̄ ⲄⲀⲢ Ⲛ̄ⳅ ⲎⲦⳞ̄ Ⲉ ⳁ ⲞⲨⲀ ⲀⲂ, Ⲛ̄ ⲢⲈ ⳁⲚ ⲟ ⲓ, Ⲛ ⲞⲨ ⲤⲘⲞⲦ Ⲛ̄
ⲞⲨⲱⲦ, Ⲛ̄ ⲀⲦⲈ-ⲤⲘⲞⲦ, Ⲉ ⳁ Ⲁ Ⲥⲱ ⲟ Ⲩ, Ⲣ̄ ⲢⲈ ⳁⲢ̄-ⳅ ⲱⲂ, Ⲉ ⳁ ⳃⲘ̄-ⳃ ⲟ Ⲙ,
Ⲉ ⳁ ⲟ Ⲛ̄ Ⲁ ⲦⲦⲱ ⲗ Ⲙ̄, Ⲛ̄ ⲤⲀ ⲂⲈ, Ⲛ̄ ⲀⲦ ⲚⲞ ⲂⲈ, Ⲙ̄ ⲘⲀ ⲓ-ⲀⲄⲀ ⲐⲞⲚ,
Ⲉ ⳁ ⲦⲞⲢⳅ̄, Ⲉ-ⲘⲈⲨ ⳧ ⲀⲘⲀ ⳅ ⲦⲈ Ⲙ̄Ⲙ ⲟ ⳁ, Ⲣ̄ ⲢⲈ ⳁⲢ̄-ⲠⲈⲦ ⲚⲀ ⲚⲞⲨ ⳁ,

(23) Ⲙ̄ ⲘⲀ ⲓ-ⲢⲱⲘⲈ, Ⲉ ⳁ ⲦⲀⲬ ⲢⲎⲨ, Ⲉ ⳁ ⲟ ⲢⳜ̄, Ⲉ ⳁ ⲟ Ⲛ̄ ⲀⲦ ⲢⲞ ⲟ Ⲩ ⳧, Ⲉ ⳁ ⳃⲘ̄-ⳃ ⲟ Ⲙ
Ⲉ ⳅ ⲱⲂ Ⲛ ⲓⲘ, Ⲉ ⳁ ⳃ ⲱ ⳧ Ⲉ ⲬⲘ̄ ⲠⲦⲎ Ⲣ ⳁ, Ⲉ ⳁ Ⲭⲱ ⲦⲈ ⳅ ⲓ ⲦⲚ̄ ⲚⲈ ⲠⲚ̄Ⲁ̄
ⲦⲎⲢ ⲞⲨ Ⲉ Ⲧ ⲞⲨⲀ ⲀⲂ, Ⲣ̄ ⲢⲈ ⳁⲚ ⲟ ⲓ, Ⲉ Ⲧ ⳧ ⲟ ⲟ ⲘⲈ.

---

up) after the passage of the arrow. (13) ⲱⲬⲚ̄ Ⲉ ⲬⲚ̄- ⲟ ⲬⲚ⸗ vb.
tr. to destroy; intr. to perish, cease to be. ἡ ἀρετή
goodness, virtue. The end of the verse is missing: "In
wickedness [we were utterly consumed.]" (14) ἡ ἐλπίϲ hope.
ⲠⲈ.ⳅ ⳧ ⲓ ⲟ dust. Ⲡ.ⳅ Ⲁ ⲗ ⲟ ⲨⲤ spiderweb. ⳧ ⲟ ⲟ ⲘⲈ Q to be light,
fine. Ⲑ ⲗ ⲟ vb. tr. to cause to fly, chase away. Ⲧ.ⳅ ⲀⲦⲎⲨ
whirlwind. ⲠⲢⲘⲚ̄ ⳃ ⲟ Ⲉ ⲓⲗ Ⲉ lodger; ⳃ ⲟ Ⲉ ⲓⲗ Ⲉ vb. intr. to dwell,
visit, sojourn.

VII. (22) ⲀⲦⲈ-ⲤⲘⲞⲦ adj. of various sorts. Ⲧⲱ ⲗ Ⲙ̄ vb. tr.
to defile, pollute; ⲀⲦⲦⲱ ⲗ Ⲙ̄ unpolluted. ⲦⲱⲢⳅ̄, Q ⲦⲞⲢⳅ̄ vb.
intr. to become sober, alert. (23) Ⲭⲱ ⲦⲈ ⲬⲈⲦ- ⲬⲞⲦ⸗ vb. tr.
to penetrate, pierce, permeate.

(24) ⲧⲥⲟⲫⲓⲁ ⲅⲁⲣ ⲕⲓⲙ ⲉⲍⲟⲩⲉ ⲛⲉⲧ ⲕⲓⲙ ⲧⲏⲣⲟⲩ;
     ⲥⲭⲱⲧⲉ ⲁⲩⲱ ⲥⲛⲏⲩ ⲉⲃⲟⲗ ⲍⲓⲧⲙ̅ ⲡⲧⲏⲣϥ̅ ⲉⲧⲃⲉ ⲡⲉⲥⲧⲃ̅ⲃⲟ.

(25) ⲉⲥⲛⲏⲩ ⲅⲁⲣ ⲉⲃⲟⲗ ⲍⲓⲧⲛ̅ ⲧϭⲟⲙ ⲙ̅ ⲡⲛⲟⲩⲧⲉ,
     ⲁⲩⲱ ⲉⲃⲟⲗ ⲍⲙ̅ ⲡⲉⲟⲟⲩ ⲉⲧ ⲟⲩⲁⲁⲃ ⲛ̅ⲧⲉ ⲡⲡⲁⲛⲧⲟⲕⲣⲁⲧⲱⲣ.
     ⲉⲧⲃⲉ ⲡⲁⲓ ⲙⲉⲣⲉ-ⲗⲁⲁⲩ ⲉϥϫⲁⲍⲙ̅ ⲧⲱⲙⲛ̅ⲧ ⲉⲣⲟⲥ.

(26) ⲟⲩⲉⲓⲛⲉ ⲅⲁⲣ ⲧⲉ ⲛ̅ⲧⲉ ⲡⲟⲩⲟⲉⲓⲛ ⲛ̅ ϣⲁ ⲉⲛⲉⲍ,
     ⲁⲩⲱ ⲟⲩⲉⲓⲁⲗ ⲉⲥⲟⲩⲁⲁⲃ ⲛ̅ⲧⲉ ⲧⲉⲛⲉⲣⲅⲓⲁ ⲙ̅ ⲡⲛⲟⲩⲧⲉ,
     ⲁⲩⲱ ⲑⲓⲕⲱⲛ ⲛ̅ ⲧⲉϥⲙⲛ̅ⲧⲁⲅⲁⲑⲟⲥ.

(27) ⲉ-ⲟⲩⲉⲓ ⲇⲉ ⲧⲉ, ⲉⲥϭⲙ̅-ϭⲟⲙ ⲉ ⲍⲱⲃ ⲛⲓⲙ;
     ⲁⲩⲱ ⲉⲥϭⲉⲉⲧ ⲍⲁⲣⲓⲍⲁⲣⲟⲥ, ⲉⲥⲉⲓⲣⲉ ⲙ̅ ⲡⲧⲏⲣϥ̅ ⲙ̅ ⲃⲣ̅ⲣⲉ;
     ⲁⲩⲱ ⲕⲁⲧⲁ ⲅⲉⲛⲉⲁ ⲥⲃⲏⲕ ⲉⲍⲟⲩⲛ ⲉ ⲛⲉⲯⲩⲭⲏ ⲛ̅ ⲛⲉⲧ ⲟⲩⲁⲁⲃ,
     ⲥⲉⲓⲣⲉ ⲙ̅ⲙⲟⲟⲩ ⲛ̅ ϣⲃⲏⲣ ⲉ ⲡⲛⲟⲩⲧⲉ ⲁⲩⲱ ⲙ̅ⲡⲣⲟⲫⲏⲧⲏⲥ.

(28) ⲙ̅ ⲡⲛⲟⲩⲧⲉ ⲅⲁⲣ ⲙⲉ ⲗ̅ ⲗⲁⲁⲩ ⲁⲛ ⲉⲓⲙⲏⲧⲓ ⲡⲉⲧ ⲟⲩⲏⲍ ⲍⲛ̅ ⲧⲥⲟⲫⲓⲁ.

(29) ⲧⲁⲓ ⲅⲁⲣ ⲛⲉⲥⲱⲥ ⲉⲍⲟⲩⲉ ⲡⲣⲏ,
     ⲁⲩⲱ ⲉⲍⲟⲩⲉ ⲡⲉⲥⲙⲓⲛⲉ ⲛ̅ ⲛ̅ⲥⲓⲟⲩ ⲧⲏⲣⲟⲩ.
     ⲉⲩϣⲁⲛⲧⲛ̅ⲧⲱⲛⲥ̅ ⲉ ⲡⲟⲩⲟⲉⲓⲛ, ⲥⲛⲁⲣ̅-ϣⲟⲣⲡ̅ ⲉⲣⲟϥ:

(30) ⲡⲁⲓ ⲙⲉⲛ ⲅⲁⲣ ϣⲁⲣⲉ-ⲧⲉⲩϣⲏ ⲉⲓ ⲉ ⲡⲉϥⲙⲁ;
     ⲧⲥⲟⲫⲓⲁ ⲇⲉ ⲙⲉⲣⲉ-ⲧⲕⲁⲕⲓⲁ ϭⲙ̅ϭⲟⲙ ⲉⲣⲟⲥ.

Chapter IX

(Solomon's) Prayer for Wisdom

(1) ⲡⲛⲟⲩⲧⲉ ⲛ̅ ⲛⲁⲉⲓⲟⲧⲉ, ⲡϫⲟⲉⲓⲥ ⲙ̅ ⲡⲛⲁ,
    ⲡⲉⲛⲧⲁϥⲧⲁⲙⲓⲉ-ⲡⲧⲏⲣϥ̅ ⲍⲙ̅ ⲡⲉϥϣⲁϫⲉ,

---

(25) ὁ παντοκράτωρ the Almighty. ⲭⲱⲍⲙ̅ ⲭⲉⲍⲙ̅- ⲭⲁⲍⲙ⸗ Q ⲭⲁⲍⲙ̅ vb. tr. to defile, pollute (ⲙ̅ⲙⲟ⸗); intr. to become defiled. (26) ⲧ.ⲉⲓⲁⲗ mirror. (27) ⲍⲁⲣⲓⲍⲁⲣⲟ⸗ intensive pron. (she) alone, by (her)self. ⲙ̅ ⲃⲣ̅ⲣⲉ adv. anew. ⲕⲁⲧⲁ ⲅⲉⲛⲉⲁ from generation to generation. (29) ⲡⲉ.ⲥⲙⲓⲛⲉ here prob. in sense: constellations, order. (30) ⲉⲓ ⲉ ⲡ(⸗)ⲙⲁ to succeed, take place of.

194

(2) ⲀⲔⲤⲚⲦ-ⲡⲣⲱⲘⲉ ⲈⲚ ⲦⲉⲔⲤⲞⲫⲒⲀ,
ⲬⲉⲔⲀⲤ ⲈⲨⲈⲢ̄-ⲬⲞⲈⲒⲤ ⲉ ⲚⲈⲔⲤⲰⲚⲦ̄ ⲈⲚⲦⲀⲔⲦⲀⲘⲒⲞⲞⲨ,

(3) ⲚⲨⲢ̄-ⲈⲘ̄Ⲙⲉ Ⲙ̄ ⲡⲕⲟⲤⲘⲟⲤ ⲈⲚ ⲞⲨⲦⲂ̄ⲂⲞ ⲘⲚ̄ ⲞⲨⲆⲒⲔⲀⲒⲞⲤⲨⲚⲎ,
ⲚⲨⲔⲢ ⲒⲚⲉ Ⲛ̄ ⲞⲨⲈⲀⲡ ⲈⲘ̄ ⲡⲤⲞⲞⲨⲦⲚ̄ Ⲛ̄ ⲦⲉⲨⲮⲨⲬⲎ,

(4) ⲘⲀ ⲚⲀⲒ Ⲛ̄ ⲦⲤⲞⲫⲒⲀ, ⲦⲀⲒ ⲈⲦ ⲀⲈⲈⲢⲀⲦⲤ̄ ⲉ ⲚⲈⲔⲐⲢⲞⲚⲞⲤ,
Ⲛ̄ⲦⲘ̄ⲦⲤ̄ⲦⲞⲈⲒ ⲈⲂⲞⲀ ⲈⲚ̄ ⲚⲈⲔⲈⲘ̄ⲈⲀⲀ,

(5) Ⲭⲉ ⲀⲚⲨⲢ̄-ⲡⲉⲔⲈⲘ̄ⲈⲀⲀ ⲀⲨⲰ ⲡⳠⲎⲢⲉ Ⲛ̄ ⲦⲉⲔⲈⲘ̄ⲈⲀⲀ,
ⲀⲚⲨⲢ̄-ⲞⲨⲢⲰⲘⲉ Ⲛ̄ ⲀⲤⲐⲈⲚⲎⲤ, Ⲛ̄ ⲔⲞⲨⲒ Ⲛ̄ ⲀⲈⲉ,
ⲈⲒⳠⲀⲀⲦ Ⲙ̄ ⲘⲚ̄ⲦⲢⲘ̄Ⲙ̄ⲚⲈⲎⲦ ⲈⲚ ⲞⲨⲈⲀⲡ ⲘⲚ̄ ⲞⲨⲚⲞⲘⲞⲤ.

(6) ⲔⲀⲚ ⲞⲨⲦⲉⲀⲉⲒⲞⲤ ⲡⲉ ⲞⲨⲀ ⲈⲚ̄ Ⲛ̄ⳠⲎⲢⲉ Ⲛ̄ Ⲣ̄ⲢⲰⲘⲉ,
ⲉ-ⲘⲚ̄ⲦⲀⲨ Ⲙ̄ⲘⲀⲨ Ⲛ̄ ⲦⲉⲔⲤⲞⲫⲒⲀ, ⲈⲨⲚⲀⲞⲡⲨ̄ ⲈⲨⲀⲀⲀⲨ·

(7) Ⲛ̄ⲦⲞⲔ ⲀⲔⲤⲞⲦⲡ̄Ⲧ̄ ⲈⲨⲢ̄ⲢⲞ Ⲙ̄ ⲡⲉⲔⲀⲀⲞⲤ,
ⲀⲨⲰ ⲞⲨⲢⲉⲨⲦ†-ⲈⲀⲡ Ⲛ̄ ⲚⲈⲔⳠⲎⲢⲉ ⲘⲚ̄ ⲚⲈⲔⳠⲉⲈⲢⲉ.

(8) ⲀⲔⲬⲞⲞⲤ ⲉ ⲔⲰⲦ ⲚⲀⲔ Ⲛ̄ ⲞⲨⲢⲡⲉ ⲈⲘ̄ ⲡⲉⲔⲦⲞⲞⲨ ⲈⲦ ⲞⲨⲀⲀⲂ,
ⲀⲨⲰ ⲞⲨⲐⲨⲤⲒⲀⲤⲦⲎⲢⲒⲞⲚ ⲈⲚ̄ ⲦⲡⲞⲀⲒⲤ Ⲙ̄ ⲡⲉⲔⲘⲀ Ⲛ̄ ⳠⲰⲡⲉ,
ⲡⲉⲒⲚⲉ Ⲛ̄ ⲦⲉⲔⲤⲔⲎⲚⲎ ⲈⲦ ⲞⲨⲀⲀⲂ ⲈⲚⲦⲀⲔⲤⲂ̄ⲦⲰⲦⲨ̄ ⲬⲒⲚ Ⲛ̄ⳠⲞⲢⲡ̄.

(9) ⲀⲨⲰ ⲈⲢⲉ-ⲦⲤⲞⲫⲒⲀ ⲚⲈⲘⲀⲔ, ⲦⲉⲦ ⲤⲞⲞⲨⲚ Ⲛ̄ ⲚⲈⲔⲈⲂⲎⲨⲉ,
ⲀⲨⲰ ⲚⲈⲤⲀⲈⲈⲢⲀⲦⲤ̄ ⲡⲉ Ⲛ̄ⲦⲉⲢⲈⲔⲦⲀⲘⲒⲉ-ⲡⲕⲟⲤⲘⲟⲤ,
ⲈⲤⲤⲞⲞⲨⲚ Ⲭⲉ ⲞⲨ ⲡⲉⲦ Ⲣ̄-ⲀⲚⲀⲔ Ⲙ̄ ⲡⲉⲔⲘ̄ⲦⲞ ⲈⲂⲞⲀ,
ⲀⲨⲰ ⲞⲨ ⲡⲉⲦ ⲤⲞⲨⲦⲰⲚ ⲈⲚ̄ ⲚⲈⲔⲈⲚⲦⲞⲀⲎ.

(10) ⲘⲀⲦⲚ̄ⲚⲞⲞⲨⲤ ⲈⲂⲞⲀ ⲈⲚ̄ ⲚⲈⲔⲡⲎⲨⲉ ⲈⲦ ⲞⲨⲀⲀⲂ
ⲀⲨⲰ ⲈⲂⲞⲀ ⲈⲘ̄ ⲡⲉⲐⲢⲞⲚⲞⲤ Ⲙ̄ ⲡⲉⲔⲈⲞⲞⲨ,
ⲬⲉⲔⲀⲤ ⲈⲤⲉⳠⲡ̄-ⲈⲒⲤⲉ ⲚⲘ̄ⲘⲀⲒ, ⲈⲤⲈⲀⲦⲎⲒ,

IX. (3) Ⲣ̄-ⲈⲘ̄Ⲙⲉ to steer, guide (Ⲙ̄Ⲙⲟ⸗). ⲡ.ⲈⲀⲡ judgement.
(4) ⲦⲤ̄Ⲧⲟ ⲦⲤ̄Ⲧⲉ- ⲦⲤ̄Ⲧⲟ⸗ Q ⲦⲤ̄ⲦⲎⲨ vb. tr. to bring back (Ⲙ̄Ⲙⲟ⸗);
+ ⲈⲂⲟⲀ: to reject. (5) ἀσθενής weak, without strength.
ⲡ.ⲀⲈⲉ lifetime. ⳠⲀⲀⲦ Q to be lacking (in: Ⲙ̄Ⲙⲟ⸗, ⲈⲚ̄); "I
am intellectually lacking in (knowledge of) judgement and
law." (6) τέλειος perfect, complete; perhaps read ⲈⲨⲦ. for
ⲞⲨⲦ. (8) ⲬⲟⲟⲤ ⲉ + Inf. to order, command (that something
be done). ἡ σκηνή tent, "tabernacle." (10) Ⳡⲡ̄-ⲈⲒⲤⲉ ⲘⲚ̄ to

ⲚⲦⲀⲈⲒⲘⲈ ϫⲉ ⲞⲨ ⲠⲈⲦ ϢⲎⲠ ⲚⲚⲀϨⲢⲀⲔ.

(11) Ⲥ̄ⲤⲞⲞⲨⲚ ⲄⲀⲢ Ⲛ̄ⲦⲞⲤ Ⲛ̄ ϨⲰⲂ ⲚⲒⲘ, ⲀⲨⲰ ⲤⲚⲞⲒ Ⲙ̄ⲘⲞⲞⲨ,
ⲀⲨⲰ ⲤⲚⲀϪⲒ-ⲘⲞⲈⲒⲦ ϨⲎⲦ Ϩ̄Ⲛ ⲚⲀϨⲂⲎⲨⲈ Ϩ̄Ⲛ ⲞⲨⲘⲚ̄ⲦⲢⲘ̄Ⲛ̄ϨⲎⲦ,
Ⲛ̄Ⲥ̄ϨⲀⲢⲈϨ ⲈⲢⲞⲒ Ϩ̄Ⲙ̄ ⲠⲈⲤⲈⲞⲞⲨ,

(12) Ⲛ̄ⲦⲈ-ⲚⲀϨⲂⲎⲨⲈ ϢⲰⲠⲈ ⲈⲨϢⲎⲠ,
ⲀⲨⲰ ϯⲚⲀⲔⲢⲒⲚⲈ Ⲙ̄ ⲠⲈⲔⲖⲀⲞⲤ Ϩ̄Ⲛ ⲞⲨⲆⲒⲔⲀⲒⲞⲤⲨⲚⲎ,
Ⲛ̄ⲦⲀϢⲰⲠⲈ ⲈⲒⲘ̄ⲠϢⲀ Ⲛ̄ ⲚⲈⲐⲢⲞⲚⲞⲤ Ⲙ̄ ⲠⲀⲈⲒⲰⲦ.

(13) ⲚⲒⲘ ⲄⲀⲢ Ⲣ̄ ⲢⲰⲘⲈ ⲠⲈⲦ ⲚⲀⲤⲞⲨⲚ̄-ⲠϢⲞϪⲚⲈ Ⲙ̄ ⲠⲚⲞⲨⲦⲈ?
Ⲏ ⲚⲒⲘ ⲠⲈⲦ ⲚⲀⲈⲒⲘⲈ ϫⲉ ⲞⲨ ⲠⲈⲦⲈⲢⲈ-ⲠϪⲞⲈⲒⲤ ⲞⲨⲀϢϥ̄?

(14) Ⲙ̄ⲘⲞⲔⲘⲈⲔ ⲄⲀⲢ Ⲛ̄ Ⲣ̄ⲢⲰⲘⲈ ϬⲞⲞⲂ, ⲀⲨⲰ ⲤⲈⲖⲞⲞϬⲈ Ⲛ̄ϬⲒ ⲚⲈⲨⲘⲈⲈⲨⲈ.

(15) ⲠⲤⲰⲘⲀ ⲄⲀⲢ ⲠⲢⲈϤⲦⲀⲔⲞ ϢⲀϤϨⲢⲞϢ ⲈϪⲚ̄ ⲦⲈϤⲮⲨⲬⲎ,
ⲀⲨⲰ ⲠⲘⲀ Ⲛ̄ ϢⲰⲠⲈ Ⲛ̄ⲦⲈ ⲠⲔⲀϨ ϢⲀϤⲢ̄-ⲔⲀⲔⲈ Ⲉ ⲪⲎⲦ Ⲛ̄ ϤⲀⲒ-ⲢⲞⲞⲨϢ.

(16) ⲘⲞⲄⲒⲤ ⲈⲚⲦⲞⲚⲦⲚ̄ Ⲛ̄ ⲚⲈⲦ ϨⲒϪⲘ̄ ⲠⲔⲀϨ;
ⲈⲚϬⲒⲚⲈ <Ⲛ> ⲚⲈⲦ ϨⲀ ⲚⲈⲚϬⲒϪ Ϩ̄Ⲛ ⲞⲨϨⲒⲤⲈ.
ⲚⲈⲦ Ϩ̄Ⲛ Ⲙ̄ⲠⲎⲨⲈ ⲆⲈ ⲚⲒⲘ ⲠⲈⲚⲦⲀϤϨⲈⲦϨⲰⲦⲞⲨ?

(17) Ⲏ ⲚⲒⲘ ⲠⲈⲚⲦⲀϤⲈⲒⲘⲈ Ⲉ ⲠⲈⲔϢⲞϪⲚⲈ
Ⲛ̄ⲤⲀⲂⲎⲖ ϫⲉ Ⲛ̄ⲦⲞⲔ ⲀⲔϯ Ⲛ̄ ⲦⲤⲞⲪⲒⲀ,
ⲀⲔⲦⲚ̄ⲚⲞⲞⲨ Ⲙ̄ ⲦⲈⲔⲠⲚ̄Ⲁ̄ ⲈⲦ ⲞⲨⲀⲀⲂ ⲈⲂⲞⲖ Ϩ̄Ⲙ̄ ⲠϪⲒⲤⲈ?

(18) ⲦⲀⲒ ⲦⲈ ⲐⲈ Ⲛ̄ⲦⲀⲨⲤⲞⲞⲨⲦⲚ̄ Ⲛ̄ϬⲒ ⲚⲈϨⲒⲞⲞⲨⲈ Ⲛ̄ ⲚⲈⲦ ϨⲒϪⲘ̄ ⲠⲔⲀϨ,
Ⲁ-ⲚⲢⲰⲘⲈ ⲤⲂⲞ Ⲉ ⲚⲈⲦ Ⲣ̄-ⲀⲚⲀⲔ,
ⲀⲨⲰ ⲀⲨⲞⲨϪⲀⲒ Ϩ̄Ⲛ ⲦⲤⲞⲪⲒⲀ.

---

labor, toil with. ϨⲀⲦⲎ⸵ = ϨⲀϨⲦⲎ⸵. (11) ⲚⲞⲒ Ⲙ̄ⲘⲞ⸵ to understand. ϪⲒ-ⲘⲞⲈⲒⲦ ϨⲎⲦ⸵ to guide; ⲡ.ⲘⲞⲈⲒⲦ road, path. (14) ϬⲞⲞⲂ Q to be weak, feeble. ⲖⲞⲞϬⲈ Q to be in a state of collapse or decay. (15) ⲠⲢⲈϤⲦⲀⲔⲞ is in apposition to ⲡ.ⲤⲰⲘⲀ. Ⲣ̄-ⲔⲀⲔⲈ Ⲉ to darken. ϤⲀⲒ-ⲢⲞⲞⲨϢ adj. full of cares. (16) μόγις adv. with great difficulty, hardly, scarcely. ⲦⲞⲚⲦⲚ̄ ⲦⲚ̄ⲦⲚ̄- ⲦⲚ̄ⲦⲰⲚ⸵ vb. tr. to speculate about (Ⲙ̄ⲘⲞ⸵, Ⲉ). (18) ⲤⲂⲞ Ⲉ to learn.

The Life of Joseph the Carpenter

V

(1) ϩⲣⲁⲓ ⲇⲉ ϩⲛ̅ ⲧⲙⲉϩⲙⲛ̅ⲧⲁϥⲧⲉ ⲛ̅ ⲣⲟⲙⲡⲉ ⲙ̅ ⲡⲱⲛϩ̅ ⲙ̅ ⲙⲁⲣⲓⲁ ⲧⲁⲙⲁⲁⲩ ⲁⲓⲉⲓ ϩⲙ̅ ⲡⲁⲟⲩⲱϣ, ⲁⲓⲟⲩⲱϩ ⲛ̅ϩⲏⲧⲥ̅ ⲕⲁⲧⲁ ⲡⲉⲧⲉ ϩⲛⲁⲓ, ⲉ-ⲁⲛⲟⲕ ⲡⲉ ⲡⲉⲧⲛ̅ⲱⲛⲁϩ. (2) ⲁⲩⲱ ⲛ̅ⲧⲉⲣⲉⲥⲣ̅-ϣⲟⲙⲛ̅ⲧ ⲛ̅ ⲉⲃⲟⲧ ⲛ̅ ⲱ, ⲁ-ⲡⲁⲧⲕⲣⲟϥ ⲓⲱⲥⲏⲫ, ⲡⲁⲙⲉⲣⲓⲧ ⲛ̅ ⲓⲱⲧ, ⲉⲓ ⲉϩⲟⲩⲛ ϩⲱⲱϥ ϩⲛ̅ ⲛⲉⲙⲁ ⲛ̅ ⲕⲱⲧ, ⲁϥϭⲉⲛ-ⲧⲁⲙⲁⲁⲩ ⲛ̅ⲧⲁⲥⲟⲩⲱⲛϩ̅ ⲉⲃⲟⲗ ϫⲉ ⲥⲉⲉⲧ. ⲁϥⲉⲣ-ϩⲟⲧⲉ ⲁⲩⲱ ⲁϥϣⲧⲟⲣⲧⲣ̅. ⲁϥⲟⲩⲱϣ ⲉ ⲛⲁϫⲉⲥ ⲉⲃⲟⲗ ⲛ̅ ϫⲓⲟⲩⲉ. (3) ⲁⲩⲱ ⲉⲃⲟⲗ ϩⲉⲛ ⲧⲁⲩⲡⲏ, ⲁϥ-ⲛ̅ⲕⲟⲧⲕ̅, ⲙ̅ⲡⲉϥⲟⲩⲉⲙ-ⲗⲁⲁⲩ ⲉ ⲡⲧⲏⲣϥ̅ ϩⲛ̅ ⲧⲉⲣⲟⲩϩⲉ ⲉⲧ ⲙ̅ⲙⲟⲟⲩ.

VI

(1) ϩⲛ̅ ⲧⲡⲁϣⲉ ⲇⲉ ⲛ̅ ⲧⲉⲩϣⲏ ⲉⲓⲥ ⲡⲁⲣⲭⲁⲅⲅⲉⲗⲟⲥ ⲅⲁⲃⲣⲓⲏⲗ ⲁϥ-ⲃⲱⲕ ϣⲁⲣⲟϥ ϩⲛ̅ ⲟⲩⲣⲁⲥⲟⲩ ϩⲓⲧⲛ̅ ⲧⲉϫⲟⲩⲥⲓⲁ ⲙ̅ ⲡⲁⲓⲱⲧ ⲛ̅ ⲁⲅⲁⲑⲟⲥ. ⲡⲉϫⲁϥ ⲛⲁϥ ϫⲉ, "ⲓⲱⲥⲏⲫ, ⲡϣⲏⲣⲉ ⲛ̅ ⲇⲁⲩⲉⲓⲇ, ⲙ̅ⲡⲣ̅ⲣ̅-ϩⲟⲧⲉ. ϫⲓ ⲙ̅ ⲙⲁⲣⲓⲁ ⲧⲉⲕⲥϩⲓⲙⲉ; ⲡⲉⲧⲉⲥⲛⲁϫⲡⲟϥ ⲅⲁⲣ ⲟⲩⲁⲁⲃ. (2) ⲁⲩⲱ ⲉⲕⲉⲙⲟⲩⲧⲉ ⲉ ⲡⲉϥⲣⲁⲛ ϫⲉ ⲓⲥ̅. ⲛ̅ⲧⲟϥ ⲡⲉⲧ ⲛⲁⲙⲟⲟⲛⲉ ⲙ̅ ⲡⲉϥⲗⲁⲟⲥ ϩⲛ̅ ⲟⲩϭⲉⲣⲱⲃ ⲙ̅ ⲡⲉⲛⲓⲡⲉ." (3) ⲁϥⲧⲱⲟⲩⲛ ⲇⲉ ⲛ̅ϭⲓ ⲓⲱⲥⲏⲫ ⲉⲃⲟⲗ ϩⲙ̅ ⲡϩⲓⲛⲏⲃ, ⲁϥⲉⲓⲣⲉ ⲕⲁⲧⲁ ⲑⲉ ⲛ̅ⲧⲁϥϩⲱⲛ ⲉⲧⲟⲟⲧϥ̅ ⲛ̅ϭⲓ ⲡⲁⲅⲅⲉⲗⲟⲥ ⲙ̅ ⲡϫⲟⲉⲓⲥ. ⲁϥϩⲁⲣⲉϩ ⲉ ⲧⲡⲁⲣⲑⲉⲛⲟⲥ ⲉⲧ ⲟⲩⲁⲁⲃ ⲉϩⲟⲩⲛ ⲉ ⲡⲉϥⲏⲓ.

VII

(1) ⲙⲛ̅ⲛ̅ⲥⲁ ⲛⲁⲓ ⲁⲩⲇⲟⲅⲙⲁ ⲉⲓ ⲉⲃⲟⲗ ϩⲓⲧⲙ̅ ⲡⲣ̅ⲣⲟ ⲁⲩⲅⲟⲩⲥⲧⲟⲥ ⲉⲧⲣⲉ-

V. (1) ⲕⲁⲧⲁ ⲡⲉⲧⲉ ϩⲛⲁⲓ according to my desire; see Glos. sub ϩⲛⲉ-. (2) ϩⲛ̅ ⲛⲉⲙⲁ for ϩⲛ̅ ⲙ̅ⲙⲁ (ⲛ̅ ⲕⲱⲧ) from the work-shops. ⲛ̅ⲧⲁⲥⲟⲩⲱⲛϩ̅ is presumably a relative form instead of an expected circumstantial: "he found that my mother had become evident as being pregnant." ⲛⲁϫⲉⲥ = ⲛⲟϫⲥ̅.
(3) ⲙ̅ⲙⲟⲟⲩ is an error for ⲙ̅ⲙⲁⲩ.

VI. ⲧ.ⲡⲁϣⲉ half; ⲧ.ⲡⲁϣⲉ ⲛ̅ ⲧⲉⲩϣⲏ midnight. (2) ⲙⲟⲟⲛⲉ ⲙⲉⲛⲉ- ⲙⲁⲛⲟⲩ⸗ vb. tr. to pasture, shepherd (ⲙ̅ⲙⲟ⸗). ⲡ.ϭⲉⲣⲱⲃ (pl. ϭⲉⲣⲟⲟⲃ) rod, staff. ⲡⲉⲛⲓⲡⲉ = ⲃⲉⲛⲓⲡⲉ iron. (3) ϩⲓⲛⲏⲃ vb. intr. to sleep; as n.m. sleep.

ⲧⲟⲓⲕⲟⲩⲙⲉⲛⲏ ⲧⲏⲣⲥ̄ ⲥ₂ⲁⲓⲥ ⲛ̄ⲥⲁ ⲛⲉⲥⲧⲙⲉ. (2) ⲁϥⲧⲱⲟⲩⲛ ⲁⲉ ⲛ̄ϭⲓ ⲓⲱⲥⲏϥ, ⲡⲁ-ⲧⲙⲛ̄ⲧ₂ⲁ̄ⲗⲟ ⲉⲧ ⲛⲁⲛⲟⲩⲥ, ⲁϥϫⲓ ⲛ̄ ⲧⲡⲁⲣⲑⲉⲛⲟⲥ ⲛ̄ ⲥⲉⲙⲛⲏ, ⲁϥⲉⲓⲛⲉ ⲙ̄ⲙⲟⲥ ⲉ₂ⲣⲁⲓ ⲉ ⲡⲉϥⲏⲓ ⲙ̄ⲙⲓⲛ ⲙ̄ⲙⲟϥ ⲉ ⲃⲏⲑⲗⲉⲉⲙ, ⲉ-ⲁⲥ₂ⲱⲛ ⲉ₂ⲟⲩⲛ
ⲉ ⲙⲓⲥⲉ. ⲁϥⲁⲡⲟⲅⲣⲁⲫⲏ ⲛ̄ ⲡⲉϥⲣⲁⲛ ₂ⲁⲧⲛ̄ ⲛⲉⲅⲣⲁⲙⲁⲧⲉⲩⲥ ⲛ̄ ⲃⲏⲑⲗⲉⲉⲙ,
ϫⲉ ⲓⲱⲥⲏϥ ⲡϣⲏⲣⲉ ⲛ̄ ⲓⲁⲕⲱⲃ ⲙⲛ̄ ⲙⲁⲣⲓⲁ ⲧⲉϥⲥ₂ⲓⲙⲉ ⲙⲛ̄ ⲓ̄ⲥ̄ ⲡⲉⲩϣⲏⲣⲉ,
ⲉ-ⲛⲉⲉⲃⲟⲗ ⲛⲉ ₂ⲙ̄ ⲡⲏⲓ ⲛ̄ ⲁⲁⲩⲉⲓⲁ, ⲡⲁ-ⲧⲉⲫⲩⲗⲏ ⲛ̄ ⲉⲓⲟⲩⲇⲁ. (3) ⲁ-
ⲙⲁⲣⲓⲁ ⲧⲁⲙⲁⲁⲩ ⲙⲓⲥⲉ ⲙ̄ⲙⲟⲓ ⲛ̄₂ⲟⲩⲛ ⲉ ⲡⲙⲁ ⲛ̄ ϭⲟⲓⲗⲉ ⲛ̄ ⲃⲏⲑⲗⲉⲉⲙ ₂ⲓ-
ⲧⲟⲩⲱϥ ⲛ̄ ⲡⲧⲁⲫⲟⲥ ⲛ̄ ₂ⲣⲁⲭⲏⲗ ⲧⲉⲥ₂ⲓⲙⲉ ⲛ̄ ⲓⲁⲕⲱⲃ ⲡⲡⲁⲧⲣⲓⲁⲣⲭⲏⲥ,
ⲡⲉⲓⲱⲧ ⲛ̄ ⲓⲱⲥⲏϥ ⲙⲛ̄ ⲃⲉⲛⲓⲁⲙⲓⲛ.

VIII

(1) ⲁ-ⲡⲥⲁⲧⲁⲛⲁⲥ ⲥⲩⲙⲃⲟⲩⲗⲉⲩⲉ ₂ⲙ̄ ⲡ₂ⲏⲧ ⲛ̄ ₂ⲏⲣⲱⲇⲏⲥ ⲡⲛⲟϭ,
ⲡⲓⲱⲧ ⲛ̄ ⲁⲣⲭⲏ[ⲗⲗⲟⲥ ... (end of fragment I).

XIV

(1) ⲁⲥϣⲱⲡⲉ ⲁⲉ, ⲛ̄ⲧⲉⲣⲉϥϫⲉ-ⲛⲁⲓ, ⲁϥⲧⲱⲟⲩⲛ, ⲁϥⲉⲓ ⲉ ⲡⲉϥⲏⲓ
ⲛⲁⲍⲁⲣⲉⲑ, ⲧⲡⲟⲗⲓⲥ ⲉⲧⲉϥⲟⲩⲏ₂ ⲛ̄₂ⲏⲧⲥ̄, ⲁⲩⲱ ⲛ̄ ⲧⲉⲓ₂ⲉ ⲁϥϫⲧⲟ ⲉ ⲡϣⲱⲛⲉ
ⲉⲧⲉϥⲛⲁⲙⲟⲩ ⲛ̄₂ⲏⲧϥ̄ ⲡⲣⲟⲥ ⲡⲉⲧ ⲕⲏ ⲉ₂ⲣⲁⲓ ⲛ̄ ⲣⲱⲙⲉ ⲛⲓⲙ. (2) ⲁⲩⲱ ⲉⲓⲥ
₂ⲏⲏⲧⲉ ⲛⲉⲣⲉ-ⲡⲉϥϣⲱⲛⲉ ₂ⲟⲣϣ̄ ⲉⲙⲁⲧⲉ ⲛ̄ ₂ⲟⲩⲟ ⲉ ⲥⲟⲡ ⲛⲓⲙ ⲛ̄ⲧⲁϥϣⲱⲛⲉ
ϫⲓⲛⲧⲁⲩϫⲡⲟϥ ⲉ ⲡⲕⲟⲥⲙⲟⲥ. (3) ⲧⲁⲓ ⲧⲉ ⲧⲁⲛⲁⲥⲧⲣⲟⲫⲏ ⲙ̄ ⲡⲁⲙⲉⲣⲓⲧ ⲛ̄
ⲉⲓⲱⲧ ⲓⲱⲥⲏϥ. (4) ⲁϥⲣ̄-₂ⲙⲉ ⲛ̄ ⲣⲟⲙⲡⲉ ⲙ̄ⲡⲁⲧⲟⲩϫⲓ-ⲥ₂ⲓⲙⲉ ⲛⲁϥ, ⲁⲩⲱ
ⲕⲉⲯⲓⲧⲉ ⲛ̄ ⲣⲟⲙⲡⲉ ⲁϥⲁⲁⲩ ₂ⲙ̄ ⲡⲕⲟⲥⲙⲟⲥ ⲙⲛ̄ ⲧⲉϥⲥ₂ⲓⲙⲉ, ⲁⲩⲱ ⲛ̄ⲧⲉⲣⲉⲥⲙⲟⲩ,
ⲁϥⲣ̄-ⲕⲉⲣⲟⲙⲡⲉ ⲉϥϭⲉⲉⲧ ⲙⲁⲩⲁⲁϥ. (5) ⲁ-ⲧⲁⲙⲉⲣⲓⲧ ⲙ̄ ⲙⲁⲁⲩ ⲣ̄-ⲕⲉⲥⲛ̄ⲧⲉ ⲛ̄
ⲣⲟⲙⲡⲉ ₂ⲙ̄ ⲡⲉϥⲏⲓ ϫⲓⲛⲛ̄ⲧⲁⲩϣⲡ̄-ⲧⲟⲟⲧⲥ̄ ⲛⲁϥ ⲛ̄ ⲥ₂ⲓⲙⲉ, ⲉ-ⲁⲩ₂ⲱⲛ ⲉⲧⲟⲟⲧϥ̄
₂ⲓⲧⲛ̄ ⲛ̄ⲟⲩⲏⲏⲃ ϫⲉ, "₂ⲁⲣⲉ₂ ⲉⲣⲟⲥ ϣⲁ ⲡⲉⲟⲩⲟⲉⲓϣ ⲛ̄ ⲧϣⲉⲗⲉⲉⲧ."

VII. (2) σεμνή f. adj. holy, august. ἀπογράφω to register. (3) ⲡ.ⲙⲁ ⲛ̄ ϭⲟⲓⲗⲉ inn. ὁ τάφος tomb. ₂ⲣⲁⲭⲏⲗ Rachel.

VIII. (1) συμβουλεύω to advise, give counsel. ⲁⲣⲭⲏ[ⲗⲗⲟⲥ
Archilaus.

XIV. (1) ϫⲧⲟ ϫⲧⲉ- ϫⲧⲟ⸗ Q ϫⲧⲏⲩ vb. tr. to lay down (ⲙ̄ⲙⲟ⸗);
intr. to lie down, to succumb (to: ⲉ). ⲡⲣⲟⲥ ⲡⲉⲧ etc.: "according to what is ordained for every man." (3) ἡ ἀναστροφή
lit. turning; here = lifetime, biography.

(6) ⲀⲨⲰ Ⲁ-ⲘⲀⲢⲒⲀ ⲦⲀⲘⲀⲀⲨ ⲬⲠⲞⲒ ⲌⲚ ⲦⲀⲢⲬⲎ Ⲛ ⲦⲘⲈⲌⳘⲞⲘⲦⲈ Ⲛ ⲢⲞⲘⲠⲈ, ⲈⲤⲌⲘ ⲠⲎⲒ Ⲛ ⲒⲰⲤⲎⳋ. ⲌⲚ ⲦⲘⲈⲌⲘⲚⲦⲎ Ⲛ ⲢⲞⲘⲠⲈ ⲚⲦⲀ-ⲘⲀⲢⲒⲀ ⲦⲀⲘⲀⲀⲨ ⲬⲠⲞⲒ ⲌⲚ ⲞⲨⲤⲠⲈⲀⲀⲒⲞⲚ ⲈⲚ ⲀⲦⲰⲀⲬⲈ ⲈⲢⲞⳋ ⲞⲨⲀⲈ Ⲛ ⲀⲦⲌⲈⲦⲌⲰⲦⳋ ⲞⲨⲀⲈ ⲘⲚ-ⲀⲀⲀⲨ Ⲛ ⲢⲰⲘⲈ ⲌⳘ ⲠⲤⲰⲚⲦ ⲦⲎⲢⳋ ⲚⲀⲈⲒⲘⲈ ⲈⲢⲞⳋ ⲈⲒⲘⲎⲦⲈⲒ ⲀⲚⲞⲔ ⲘⲚ ⲠⲀⲈⲒⲰⲦ ⲘⲚ ⲠⲈⲠⲚⲀ ⲈⲦ ⲞⲨⲀⲀⲂ.

XV

(1) ⲚⲈⲌⲞⲞⲨ ⲀⲈ ⲦⲎⲢⲞⲨ Ⲙ ⲠⲀⲈⲒⲰⲦ ⲒⲰⲤⲎⳋ, ⲠⲀ-ⲦⲘⲚⲦⲌⲀⲀⲞ ⲈⲦ ⲤⲘⲀⲘⲀⲀⲦ, ⲤⲈⲈⲒⲢⲈ Ⲛ ⳝⲈ ⲘⲚⲦⲞⲨⲈⲒ Ⲛ ⲢⲞⲘⲠⲈ ⲔⲀⲦⲀ ⲠⲞⲨⲈⲌ-ⲤⲀⲌⲚⲈ Ⲛ ⲠⲀⲈⲒⲰⲦ. (2) Ⲁ-ⲠⲈⲌⲞⲞⲨ Ⲙ ⲠⲈⳋⲈⳘ-ⲠⳝⲒⲚⲈ ⲈⲒ ⲚⲀⳋ, ⲈⲦⲈ ⲤⲞⲨ-ⲬⲞⲨⲦⲀⲤⲈ ⲠⲈ Ⲙ ⲠⲈⲂⲞⲦ ⲈⲠⲎⳋ, (3) <ⲀⲨⲰ ⲀⳋⲀⲢⲬⲈⲒ Ⲛ ⳝⲒⲂⲈ ⲚϬⲒ ⲠⲚⲞⲨⲂ ⲈⲦ ⲤⲞⲦⲠ, ⲈⲦⲈ ⲦⲤⲀⲢⳤ ⲦⲈ Ⲙ ⲠⲀⲈⲒⲰⲦ ⲒⲰⲤⲎⳋ, ⲀⲨⲰ> Ⲁ-ⲠⲌⲀⲦ ⲠⲰⲰⲚⲈ, ⲈⲦⲈ ⲠⲚⲞⲨⲤ ⲠⲈ ⲘⲚ ⲦⲤⲞⳋⲒⲀ. (4) ⲀⳋⲠⲰⲰⲚⲈ Ⲉ ⲠⲔⲈⲀⲒⲰⲚ, ⲀⳋⲢ̄-ⲠⲰⲂⳝ Ⲙ ⲠⲞⲨⲰⲘ ⲘⲚ ⲠⲤⲰ, Ⲉ-Ⲁ-ⲦⲤⲞⳋⲒⲀ ⲘⲚ ⲦⲘⲚⲦⲦⲈⲬⲚⲒⲦⲎⲤ ⲔⲞⲦⲤ̄ ⲈⲨⲤⲞⲢⲘⲈⲤ ⲘⲚ ⲞⲨⲘⲚⲦ-ⲀⲦⲞⲠⲞⲚ. (5) ⲀⲤⳝⲰⲠⲈ ⲀⲈ, ⲚⲦⲈⲢⲈ-ⲠⲞⲨⲞⲈⲒⲚ ⲀⲢⲬⲈⲒ Ⲛ ⲤⲰⲢ ⲈⲂⲞⲀ Ⲙ ⲠⲈⲌⲞⲞⲨ ⲈⲦ ⲘⲘⲀⲨ, Ⲁ-ⲠⲀⲘⲈⲢⲒⲦ Ⲛ ⲒⲰⲦ ⲒⲰⲤⲎⳋ ⲀⲢⲬⲈⲒ Ⲛ ⳝⲦⲞⲢⲦⲢ̄ ⲈⲘⲀⲦⲈ

---

(6) ⲚⲦⲀ-ⲘⲀⲢⲒⲀ should perhaps be emended (with Lagarde) to ⲚⲦⲀⲤ Ⲁ-ⲘⲀⲢⲒⲀ, "in *her* 15th year Mary bore me." This verse makes much better sense if ⲘⲨⲤⲦⲎⲢⲒⲞⲚ is read for ⲤⲠⲈⲀⲀⲒⲞⲚ; this is supported by the Bohairic version. ⲈⲚ for Ⲛ. ⲀⲦⲌⲈⲦⲌⲰⲦⲊ inscrutable, unfathomable.

XV. (2) "the day of his visitation," i.e. of his final illness and death. ⲤⲞⲨ- day (in datings), prefixed to the number: ⲤⲞⲨ-ⲬⲞⲨⲦⲀⲤⲈ the 26th day. ⲈⲠⲎⳋ, ⲈⲠⲎⲠ Coptic month name. (3) The portion in < > is missing from the ms.; I have restored it on the basis of the Boh. version. ⲠⲰⲰⲚⲈ ⲠⲈⲈⲚⲈ- ⲠⲞⲞⲚⲈⲊ Q ⲠⲞⲞⲚⲈ vb. tr. to turn, change, transfer (ⳘⲘⲞⲊ); intr. to change, be altered. ὁ ⲫⲟῦⲥ mind. (4) ὁ αἰών period of time; age, generation; eternity, world. ὁ τεχνίτης craftsman; ⲘⲚⲦⲦⲈⲬⲚⲒⲦⲎⲤ technical skill. ⲔⲞⲦⲊ Ⲉ to turn into, become. Ⲧ.ⲤⲞⲢⲘⲈⲤ error. ἄτοπος strange, odd; ⲘⲚⲦⲀⲦⲞⲠⲞⲚ confusion, unreasonableness. (5) ⲤⲰⲢ ⲤⲈⲢ-ⲤⲞⲢⲊ Q ⲤⲎⲢ vb. tr. and intr. (± ⲈⲂⲞⲀ) to scatter, spread.

ⲉⲓⲭⲙ̄ ⲡⲉϥⲙⲁ ⲛ̄ ⲛ̄ⲕⲟⲧⲕ̄, ⲁⲩⲱ ⲛ̄ ⲧⲉⲓ2ⲉ ⲁϥⲉⲱ-ⲡⲉⲓⲛⲟ6 ⲛ̄ ⲗⲱ-ⲗ2ⲟⲙ, ⲁⲩⲱ
ⲁϥⲣⲱ2ⲧ̄ ⲛ̄ ⲛⲉϥ6ⲓⲭ ⲉⲭⲛ̄ ⲛⲉⲩⲉⲣⲏⲩ ⲛ̄ ϣⲟⲙⲛ̄ⲧ ⲛ̄ ⲥⲟⲡ, ⲁϥⲱϣ ⲉⲃⲟⲗ 2ⲛ̄ ⲟⲩ-
ⲛⲟ6 ⲛ̄ ϣⲧⲟⲣⲧⲣ̄ ⲙⲛ̄ ⲟⲩⲛⲟ6 ⲛ̄ 2ⲃⲗ ⲭⲉ

XVI

(1) "ⲟⲩⲟⲓ ⲛⲁⲓ ⲙ̄ ⲡⲟⲟⲩ. ⲟⲩⲟⲓ ⲙ̄ ⲡⲉ2ⲟⲟⲩ ⲛ̄ⲧⲁ-ⲧⲁⲙⲁⲁⲩ ⲭⲡⲟⲓ
ⲛ̄2ⲏⲧϥ̄. (2) ⲟⲩⲟⲓ ⲛ̄ ⲛⲉⲕⲓⲃⲉ ⲛ̄ⲧⲁⲓⲧⲥ̄ⲛ̄ⲕⲟ ⲛ̄2ⲏⲧⲟⲩ. (3) ⲟⲩⲟⲓ ⲛ̄ ⲛ̄-
ⲡⲁⲧ ⲛ̄ⲧⲁⲓ2ⲙⲟⲟⲥ 2ⲓⲭⲱⲟⲩ. (4) ⲟⲩⲟⲓ ⲛ̄ ⲛⲉ6ⲗⲟⲟⲧⲉ ⲛ̄ⲧⲁⲩ2ⲗⲟⲟⲗⲉ ⲙ̄ⲙⲟⲓ
ϣⲁⲛⲧⲉⲓⲉⲓ ⲉ ⲡⲧⲉ ⲛ̄ⲧⲁⲙⲉⲧⲉⲭⲉ ⲉ ⲡⲛⲟⲃⲉ. (5) ⲟⲩⲟⲓ ⲙ̄ ⲡⲁⲗⲁⲥ ⲙⲛ̄ ⲛⲁ-
ⲥⲡⲟⲧⲟⲩ, ⲭⲉ ⲁⲩ6ⲗⲟⲙⲗⲙ̄ ⲛ̄ ⲟⲩⲙⲏⲏϣⲉ ⲛ̄ ⲥⲟⲡ 2ⲙ̄ ⲡⲭⲓⲛ6ⲟⲛⲥ̄ ⲙⲛ̄ ⲧⲕⲁⲧⲁⲗⲁⲗⲓⲁ ⲙⲛ̄ ⲧⲙⲛ̄ⲧⲗⲁⲥ ⲥⲛⲁⲩ ⲙⲛ̄ ϣⲁⲭⲉ ⲛⲓⲙ ⲛ̄ ⲃⲱⲗ ⲉⲃⲟⲗ. (6) ⲟⲩⲟⲓ ⲛ̄
ⲛⲁⲃⲁⲗ, ⲭⲉ ⲁⲩ6ⲱϣⲧ̄ 2ⲛ̄ ⲟⲩⲥⲕⲁⲛⲇⲁⲗⲟⲛ ⲁⲩⲱ ⲁⲩⲙⲉⲣⲉ-ⲧⲙⲛ̄ⲧⲣⲉϥⲉⲓⲣ̄-
ⲃⲟⲟⲛⲉ. (7) ⲟⲩⲟⲓ ⲛ̄ ⲛⲁⲙⲁⲁⲭⲉ, ⲭⲉ ⲁⲩⲙⲉⲣⲉ-ⲛ̄ϣⲁⲭⲉ ⲛ̄ ⲕⲁⲥⲕⲥ̄ ⲙⲛ̄
ⲛ̄ϣⲁⲭⲉ ⲧⲏⲣⲟⲩ ⲙ̄ ⲡⲱⲙⲥ̄. (8) ⲟⲩⲟⲓ ⲛ̄ ⲛⲁ6ⲓⲭ, ⲭⲉ ⲁⲩ2ⲱⲃⲧ̄ ⲛ̄ ⲛⲉⲧⲉ
ⲛⲟⲩⲓ ⲁⲛ ⲛⲉ. (9) ⲟⲩⲟⲓ ⲛ̄ ⲙ̄ⲙⲁ2ⲧ̄ ⲙⲛ̄ ⲑⲏ, ⲛⲁⲓ ⲉⲧ ⲉⲡⲉⲓⲑⲩⲙⲉⲓ ⲉ
2ⲉⲛⲧⲣⲟⲫⲏ ⲛ̄ ⲛⲟⲩⲓ ⲁⲛ ⲛⲉ, ⲁⲩⲱ 2ⲟⲗⲁⲛ ⲉⲩϣⲁⲛ6ⲛ̄-ⲛ̄ⲕⲁ ⲛⲓⲙ, ϣⲁⲩ-

ⲡⲉ.2ⲃⲗ difficulty, straits.

XVI. (1) ⲟⲩⲟⲓ ⲛⲁ⸗ woe unto.... (2) ⲧ.ⲉⲕⲓⲃⲉ breast.
ⲧⲥ̄ⲛ̄ⲕⲟ vb. tr. to nurse, suckle (ⲙ̄ⲙⲟ⸗); here intr. to nurse.
(4) 6ⲗⲟⲟⲧⲉ in sense: internal organs in general. 2ⲗⲟⲟⲗⲉ
vb. tr. to nurse (a child: ⲙ̄ⲙⲟ⸗); to carry (a child) during
pregnancy. ⲉⲓ ⲉ ⲡⲧⲉ to grow up; ⲡ.ⲧⲉ time, season.
μετέχω to partake (of: ⲉ). (5) 6ⲗⲟⲙⲗⲙ̄ 6ⲗⲙ̄ⲗⲱⲙ⸗ Q 6ⲗⲙ̄ⲗⲱⲙ
vb. intr. to become twisted, implicated, involved. ⲙⲛ̄ⲧ-
ⲗⲁⲥ ⲥⲛⲁⲩ deceit (lit. two-tonguedness). (6) τὸ σκάνδαλον
impediment (a term applied to any behavior or situation
that can be regarded as an impediment on the road to per-
fection). ⲙⲛ̄ⲧⲣⲉϥⲉⲓⲣ̄-ⲃⲟⲟⲛⲉ greed; see Glos. sub ⲃⲟⲟⲛⲉ, ⲉⲓⲁ.
(7) ⲛ̄ϣⲁⲭⲉ ⲙ̄ ⲡⲱⲙⲥ̄ lit. the words of sinking; this curious
expression comes from Ps. 51:4 τὰ ῥήματα καταποντισμοῦ,
taken to mean "destructive words." (8) 2ⲱⲃⲧ̄ = 2ⲱϥⲧ̄ 2ⲉϥⲧ̄-
2ⲟϥⲧ⸗ vb. tr. to steal (ⲙ̄ⲙⲟ⸗). (9) ⲡ.ⲙⲁ2ⲧ̄ bowels, intestines. ἐπιθυμέω to desire, be eager (for: ⲉ). ἡ τροφή
food, nourishment.

200

ροκ2ογ Π 2ογο εγτριρ Π κω2Τ. (12) ειΝα℗-ογ τεΝογ? ΑΙωρℙ
ε2ογΝ Π cα cα ΝΙΜ. (13) ΑΛΗθωc ογοΙ ογοΙ Π ρωμε ΝΙΜ ετ
Ναℙ-ΝΟβε. (14) †χω ℗ΜΟc ΝΗΤΠ, ω Ναϣηρε ΜΠ Ναϣεερε, χε
ΠΝΟ6 Π 2βΑ ΠΤΑΙΝΑγ ερο4 2ΙΤℙ ΠΛΕΙωτ ΙΑΚωβ ε4ΝΗγ εβΟΛ 2Π
cωΜΑ ΠΤΟ4 πε ΠΑΙ ΠΤΑ4ΤωΜΠΤ εροΙ 2ω ℗ ΠΟογ, ΑΝΟΚ πειεβΙΗΝ
Π ΤΑΛΑΙπωρΟc Αγω Π 2ΗΚε. (15) ΑΛΛΑ ΠχΟειc ΠαΝΟγτε πε πΜε-
ϲΙΤΗc Π ΤΑΨγΧΗ ΜΠ ΠΑcωΜΑ ΜΠ ΠΑΠΠ̄Ν̄Ᾱ."

XVII

(1) ΝΑΙ Δε ε4χω ℗ΜΟογ Π6Ι ΠΑΜεριτ Π ειωτ Ιωϲηφ, ΑΙ-
ΤωΟγΝ, ΑΙΜΟΟϣε ερο4 ε4Π̄ΚΟΤℙ ε4ϣΤ̄ρΤωρ 2Π τε4ΨγΧΗ ΜΠ πε4-
ΠΠ̄Ν̄Ᾱ. πεχαΙ ΝΑ4 χε, "χαΙρε, ΠΑΜεριτ Π ειωτ, ΠΑ-ΤΜΠΤ2ℕΛΟ
ετ ΝΑΝΟγc." (2) Α4ΤΑϣε-ογωϣ℗ ΝΑΙ 2Π ογΝΟ6 Π ϣΤΟρΤℙ ΜΠ
ογ2βΑ ΜΠ ογ2Οτε Πτε πΜΟγ, ε4χω ℗ΜΟc χε, "χαΙρε Π ογΜΗΗϣε
Π ϲΟΠ, ΠΑΜεριτ Π ϣΗρε. Α-ΤΑΨγΧΗ ℗ΤΟΝ εροΙ Π ογΚΟγΙ Πτερε-
ΤεΚϲΜΗ ετ ΝΟΤℙ ΤΑ2ΟΙ. (3) ῙϹ̄ ΠΑχΟειc, ῙϹ̄ ΠΑℙρΟ ℗ Με, ῙϹ̄
ΠΑϲωΤΗρ, ῙϹ̄ ΠΑρε4ΤΟγχΟ, ῙϹ̄ ΠΑρε4ΝΟγ2℗, ω ῙϹ̄ πετ ϲΚεΠΑ2ε ℗
ΠΤΗΡ4̄, ω ῙϹ̄ πετ ΑΜΑ2τε ℗ ΠΤΗΡ4̄ 2℗ Πογωϣ Π τε4ΜΠΤΑΓΑθΟc, ω
ῙϹ̄ πετερε-πε4ραΝ Κ̄Ν̄Νε Αγω ε4ΚΙωογ εΜΑτε, ω ῙϹ̄ πειβαΛ ετ
Ναγ, ΠΙΜΑΛχε ετ ϲωΤℙ, ϲωΤℙ εροΙ 2ωωΤ ℗ ΠΟογ, ΑΝΟΚ πεΚ2ℙ̄2αΛ
ειϲΟΠϲ̄ ℗ΜΟΚ Αγω ειΠω2Τ̄ Π ΝΑℙΜειΟΟγε ℗ πεΚℙΤΟ εβΟΛ. (4) χε
Πτοκ πε ΠΝΟγτε 2Π ογΜε ΜΠ ογχωΚ ΚΑΤΑ θε Πτα-πεΚΑΓΓεΛΟc

_____

ρωΚ2̄ in sense: to consume. τε.τρΙρ furnace, oven. Vss.
10-11 (acc. to Boh. version) are omitted in the ms.
(12) ωρℙ ερℙ- ορβ℗ Q ορℙ vb. tr. to enclose, shut in
(℗ΜΟ℗); intr. to be shut in. (13) ἀληθῶς adv. truly.
(14) ταλαίπωρος wretched, miserable. (15) ὁ μεσίτης
mediator, intercessor.

XVII. (2) ΤΑϣε- + Inf. to do sthg. much; ΤΑϣε-ογωϣ℗ to
answer profusely. ΝΟγΤℙ, Q ΝΟΤℙ vb. intr. to be sweet,
pleasant. (3) ΤΟγχΟ ΤΟγχε- ΤΟγχΟ℗ Q ΤΟγχΗγ vb. tr. to make
sound, whole (℗ΜΟ℗); to rescue, save; as n.m. safety, salvation. σκεπάζω to cover, shelter. Κ̄Ν̄Νε vb. intr. to be
sweet, fat. ΚΙωογ Q to be fat, soft, productive, fertile.

ⲧⲟⲩⲛ-ⲓⲁⲧ ⲉⲃⲟⲗ ⲛ̄ ⲍⲁⲍ ⲛ̄ ⲥⲟⲡ, ⲛ̄ ⲍⲟⲩⲟ ⲁⲉ ⲡⲉⲍⲟⲟⲩ ⲛ̄ⲧⲁ-ⲡⲁⲍⲏⲧ ⲙ̄ⲕⲁⲍ
ⲉⲣⲟⲓ ⲉⲧⲃⲉ ⲟⲩⲙⲉⲉⲩⲉ ⲙ̄ ⲙ̄ⲛ̄ⲧⲣⲱⲙⲉ ⲉⲧⲃⲉ ⲧⲉⲧ ⲥⲙⲁⲙⲁⲁⲧ ⲙⲁⲣⲓⲁ ⲧⲡⲁⲣⲑⲉⲛⲟⲥ, ⲁⲓⲡⲉⲣⲉⲓⲉⲣⲕⲁⲍⲉ ⲭⲉ ⲗⲥⲱⲱ, ⲗⲩⲱ ⲛⲉⲓⲭⲱ ⲙ̄ⲙⲟⲥ ⲭⲉ, 'ⲉⲍⲣⲁⲓ ⲍⲛ̄
ⲧⲉⲓⲟⲩⲱⲏ, †ⲛⲁⲛⲟⲭⲥ̄ ⲉⲃⲟⲗ ⲛ̄ ⲭⲓⲟⲩⲉ.' (5) ⲛⲁⲓ ⲁⲉ ⲉⲓⲙⲉⲉⲩⲉ ⲉⲣⲟⲟⲩ,
ⲁ-ⲡⲁⲅⲅⲉⲗⲟⲥ ⲟⲩⲱⲛ̄ⲍ ⲛⲁⲓ ⲉⲃⲟⲗ ⲍⲛ̄ ⲟⲩⲣⲁⲥⲟⲩ, ⲉⲩⲭⲱ ⲙ̄ⲙⲟⲥ ⲛⲁⲓ ⲭⲉ,
'ⲓⲱⲥⲏⲫ ⲡϣⲏⲣⲉ ⲛ̄ ⲇⲁⲩⲉⲓⲇ, ⲙ̄ⲡⲣ̄ⲣ̄-ⲍⲟⲧⲉ <ⲉ> ⲭⲓ ⲙ̄ ⲙⲁⲣⲓⲁ ⲧⲉⲕⲥⲍⲓⲙⲉ,
ⲟⲩⲇⲉ ⲙ̄ⲡⲣ̄†ⲥⲧⲁⲍⲉ ⲉⲭⲛ̄ ⲧⲉⲥϭⲓⲛⲱⲱ, ⲭⲉ ⲛ̄ⲧⲁⲥⲱⲱ ⲅⲁⲣ ⲉⲃⲟⲗ ⲍⲛ̄ ⲟⲩⲡⲛ̄ⲁ
ⲉⲩⲟⲩⲁⲁⲃ. (6) ⲥⲛⲁⲭⲡⲟ ⲁⲉ ⲛ̄ ⲟⲩϣⲏⲣⲉ ⲛ̄ⲅ̄ⲙⲟⲩⲧⲉ ⲉ ⲡⲉ⳿ⲣⲁⲛ ⲭⲉ ⲓⲥ̄.'
(7) ⲧⲉⲛⲟⲩ ⲁⲉ, ⲡⲁⲭⲟⲉⲓⲥ, ⲡⲥⲱⲧⲏⲣ ⲛ̄ ⲧⲁⲯⲩⲭⲏ ⲙ̄ⲛ̄ ⲡⲁⲡⲛ̄ⲁ, ⲙ̄ⲡⲣ̄ⲅⲛ̄-
ⲁⲣⲓⲕⲉ ⲉⲣⲟⲓ, ⲁⲛⲟⲕ ⲁⲛⲅ̄-ⲡⲉⲕⲍⲙ̄ⲍⲁⲗ ⲁⲩⲱ ⲡⲍⲱⲃ ⲛ̄ ⲛⲉⲕϭⲓⲭ. ⲛ̄ⲧⲁⲓⲡⲉⲣⲉⲓ-
ⲉⲣⲕⲁⲍⲉ ⲁⲛ, ⲱ ⲡⲁⲭⲟⲉⲓⲥ, (8) ⲁⲗⲗⲁ ⲙ̄ⲡⲁ†ⲥⲟⲩⲛ̄-ⲡⲉⲟⲟⲩ ⲙ̄ ⲡⲉⲓⲛⲟϭ ⲙ̄
ⲙⲩⲥⲧⲏⲣⲓⲟⲛ, ⲉⲧⲉ ⲡⲉⲕⲭⲡⲟ ⲉⲧ ⲟⲩⲁⲁⲃ ⲡⲉ, ⲟⲩⲁⲉ ⲟⲛ ⲙ̄ⲡⲉⲓⲥⲱⲧⲙ̄ ⲉⲛⲉⲍ
ⲭⲉ ϣⲁⲣⲉ-ⲥⲍⲓⲙⲉ ⲱⲱ ⲉⲭⲛ̄ ⲍⲟⲟⲩⲧ. (9) ⲱ ⲡⲁⲭⲟⲉⲓⲥ ⲁⲩⲱ ⲡⲁⲛⲟⲩⲧⲉ,
ⲉⲛⲉ ⲡⲧⲱϣ ⲙ̄ ⲡⲉⲓⲛⲟϭ ⲙ̄ ⲙⲩⲥⲧⲏⲣⲓⲟⲛ ⲁⲛ ⲡⲉ, ⲛ̄ⲧⲉⲓⲛⲁⲡⲓⲥⲧⲉⲩⲉ ⲉⲣⲟⲕ ⲁⲛ
ⲡⲉ ⲙ̄ⲛ̄ ⲡⲉⲕⲭⲡⲟ ⲉⲧ ⲟⲩⲁⲁⲃ, ⲧⲁ†-ⲉⲟⲟⲩ ⲛ̄ ⲧⲉⲛⲧⲁⲥⲭⲡⲟⲕ, ⲙⲁⲣⲓⲁ, ⲧⲉⲓⲉⲍⲁⲓⲃⲉ ⲙ̄ ⲙⲉ. (10) †ⲉⲓⲣⲉ ⲙ̄ ⲡⲙⲉⲉⲩⲉ ⲙ̄ ⲡⲍⲟⲟⲩ ⲛ̄ⲧⲁ-ⲧⲕⲉⲣⲁⲥⲧⲏⲥ
ⲟⲩⲱⲙ ⲙ̄ ⲡϣⲏⲣⲉ ϣⲏⲙ ⲉ ⲧⲉⲩⲟⲩⲉⲣⲏⲧⲉ, ⲁⲩⲙⲟⲩ. (11) ⲁ-ⲛⲉⲩⲣⲱⲙⲉ
ⲥⲱⲟⲩⲍ ⲉⲣⲟⲕ ⲉⲩⲟⲩⲱϣ ⲉ ϭⲟⲡⲕ̄ ⲛ̄ⲥⲉⲧⲁⲁⲕ ⲛ̄ ⲍⲏⲣⲱⲧⲏⲥ ⲡⲡⲁⲣⲁⲛⲟⲙⲟⲥ.
(12) ⲁⲩⲱ ⲁⲓⲍⲉ ⲉⲣⲟⲥ, ⲁ-ⲧⲉⲕⲙ̄ⲛ̄ⲧⲛⲟⲩⲧⲉ ⲧⲁⲍⲟⲩ, ⲁⲩⲱⲛ̄ⲍ, ⲁⲩⲱ ⲍⲙ̄
ⲡⲧⲣⲉⲕⲧⲟⲩⲛⲟⲥⲩ ⲉ ⲛⲉⲩⲉⲓⲟⲧⲉ ⲁⲩⲛⲟϭ ⲛ̄ ⲣⲁϣⲉ ϣⲱⲡⲉ ⲛⲁⲩ. (13) ⲁⲓⲭⲛⲟⲩⲕ
ⲁⲉ, ⲱ ⲡⲁⲙⲉⲣⲓⲧ ⲛ̄ ϣⲏⲣⲉ, ⲭⲉ ⲉⲥⲩⲭⲁⲍⲉ ⲙ̄ⲙⲟⲕ ⲍⲛ̄ ⲍⲱⲃ ⲛⲓⲙ. ⲁⲓⲁⲙⲁⲍⲧⲉ

(4) ⲧⲟⲩⲛ-ⲓⲁⲧ⸗ ⲉⲃⲟⲗ to inform, instruct. περιεργάζομαι to
be overly concerned, meddlesome. (5) διστάζω to hesitate,
be in doubt. (7) There is an ellipsis or omission after
ⲁⲓⲡⲉⲣⲉⲓⲉⲣⲕⲁⲍⲉ ⲁⲛ: "I became overly concerned not (for any
other reason than that) I did not yet know ..." (8) ⲉⲭⲛ̄
for ⲁⲭⲛ̄. (9) The meaning of this verse is obscure. If ⲉⲛⲉ
introduces a contrary-to-fact condition, the apodosis
should be ⲛⲉⲓⲛⲁⲡⲓⲥⲧⲉⲩⲉ; cf. vs. 14 below for a similar
problem. ⲧⲉⲓⲉⲍⲁⲓⲃⲉ for ⲧⲉⲓⲍⲁⲓⲃⲉ; ⲧ.ⲍⲁⲓⲃⲉ lamb. (10) ἡ
κεραστής horned-(viper). ⲟⲩⲱⲙ here: to bite. (11) ⲛⲉⲩ-
ⲣⲱⲙⲉ = his kin etc. παράνομος lawless, unjust. (12) Perhaps read ⲧⲁⲛⲍⲟⲩ for ⲧⲁⲍⲟⲩ. (13) ἡσυχάζω to be still,
quiet; ⲙ̄ⲙⲟⲕ is reflexive.

ⲙ̄ ⲡⲉⲕⲙⲁⲁϫⲉ ⲛ̄ ⲟⲩⲛⲁⲙ, ⲁⲓⲥⲟⲕϥ̄. (14) ⲁⲕⲟⲩⲱϣⲃ̄ ⲉⲕϫⲱ ⲙ̄ⲙⲟⲥ ⲛⲁⲓ ϫⲉ,
'ⲛ̄ⲥⲁⲃⲏⲗ ϫⲉ ⲛ̄ⲧⲟⲕ ⲡⲉ ⲡⲁⲉⲓⲱⲧ ⲕⲁⲧⲁ ⲥⲁⲣⲝ, ⲉⲡⲉⲓ ϯⲛⲁⲧⲁⲙⲟⲕ ϫⲉ
ⲁⲕⲥⲉⲕⲥⲉⲕ-ⲡⲁⲙⲁⲁϫⲉ ⲛ̄ ⲟⲩⲛⲁⲙ.' (15) ⲧⲉⲛⲟⲩ ⲇⲉ, ⲱ ⲡⲁⲙⲉⲣⲓⲧ ⲛ̄
ϣⲏⲣⲉ, ⲡⲁϫⲟⲉⲓⲥ ⲁⲩⲱ ⲡⲁⲛⲟⲩⲧⲉ, ⲉϣⲱⲡⲉ ⲛ̄ⲧⲁⲕϥⲓ-ⲗⲟⲅⲟⲥ ⲛⲙ̄ⲙⲁⲓ ⲉⲧⲃⲉ
ⲡⲉⲍⲟⲟⲩ ⲉⲧ ⲙ̄ⲙⲁⲩ, ⲁⲕⲧⲣⲉ-ⲛⲉⲓⲙⲁⲉⲓⲛ ⲛ̄ ⲍⲟⲧⲉ ⲉⲓ ⲉⲍⲣⲁⲓ ⲉϫⲱⲓ, ϯⲡⲁⲣⲁ-
ⲕⲁⲗⲉⲓ ⲙ̄ⲙⲟⲕ, ⲱ ⲡⲁϫⲟⲉⲓⲥ ⲛ̄ ⲁⲅⲁⲑⲟⲥ, ⲕⲱ ⲛⲁⲓ ⲉⲃⲟⲗ ⲛⲅ̄ⲧⲙ̄ϥⲓ-ⲱⲡ
ⲛⲙ̄ⲙⲁⲓ. (16) ⲁⲛⲟⲕ ⲅⲁⲣ ⲁⲛⲅ̄-ⲡⲉⲕⲍⲙ̄ϩⲁⲗ, ⲁⲛⲟⲕ ⲡϣⲏⲣⲉ ⲛ̄ ⲧⲉⲕⲍⲙ̄ϩⲁⲗ.
(17) ⲉⲕϣⲁⲛⲥⲱⲗⲡ̄ ⲛ̄ ⲛⲁⲙⲉⲣⲣⲉ, ϯⲛⲁϣⲱⲧ ⲛⲁⲕ ⲛ̄ ⲟⲩⲑⲩⲥⲓⲁ ⲛ̄ ⲥⲙⲟⲩ,
ⲉⲧⲉ ⲧⲁⲓ ⲧⲉ ⲧⲍⲟⲙⲟⲗⲟⲅⲉⲓⲁ ⲛ̄ ⲧⲉⲕⲙⲛ̄ⲧⲛⲟⲩⲧⲉ, ϫⲉ ⲛ̄ⲧⲕ̄-ⲟⲩⲛⲟⲩⲧⲉ ⲍⲛ̄
ⲟⲩⲙⲉ, ⲁⲩⲱ ⲛ̄ⲧⲕ̄-ⲟⲩϫⲟⲉⲓⲥ ⲍⲛ̄ ⲟⲩϫⲱⲕ."

XVIII

(1) ⲛⲁⲓ ⲇⲉ ⲉϥϫⲱ ⲙ̄ⲙⲟⲟⲩ ⲛ̄ϭⲓ ⲡⲁ-ⲧⲙⲛ̄ⲧⲍⲗ̄ⲗⲟ ⲉⲥⲕⲓⲱⲟⲩ ⲡⲗⲉⲓⲱⲧ
ⲉⲓⲱⲥⲏⲫ, ⲙ̄ⲡⲉⲓⲉϣϭⲱ ⲛ̄ⲟⲩⲉϣ ⲣⲓⲙⲉ ⲉⲓⲛⲁⲩ ⲉⲣⲟϥ ⲉ-ⲁϥⲟⲩⲱ ⲉϥϫⲓ ⲍⲉⲛ
ⲛ̄ⲍⲁϭⲉ ⲙ̄ ⲡⲙⲟⲩ ⲁⲩⲱ ⲉⲓⲥⲱⲧⲙ̄ ⲛ̄ϣⲁϫⲉ ⲙ̄ ⲙⲛ̄ⲧⲉⲃⲓⲏⲛ ⲉⲧⲉϥϫⲱ ⲙ̄ⲙⲟⲟⲩ ⲛⲁⲓ.
(2) ⲙⲛ̄ⲛ̄ⲥⲁ ⲛⲁⲓ ⲁⲓⲣ̄-ⲡⲙⲉⲉⲩⲉ ⲙ̄ ⲡⲉⲍⲟⲟⲩ ⲙ̄ ⲡⲁⲙⲟⲩ, ⲙ̄ ⲡⲛⲁⲩ ⲉⲧⲉⲣⲉ-
ⲛⲉⲓⲟⲩⲇⲁⲓ ⲛⲁⲧⲁⲗⲟⲓ ⲉ ⲡⲉⲥ-ⲣ̄ⲟⲥ ⲍⲁ ⲡⲟⲩϫⲁⲓ ⲙ̄ ⲡⲕⲟⲥⲙⲟⲥ ⲧⲏⲣϥ̄. (3) ⲛ̄
ⲧⲉⲩⲛⲟⲩ ⲁⲓⲃⲱⲕ ⲉ ⲡⲉⲑⲣⲓⲟⲛ ⲉⲧ ⲍⲓ ⲃⲟⲗ, ⲁⲩⲱ ⲁⲥⲧⲱⲟⲩⲛ ⲛ̄ϭⲓ ⲙⲁⲣⲓⲁ

---

(14) For ⲉⲡⲉⲓ ϯⲛⲁⲧⲁⲙⲟⲕ read prob. ⲛⲉⲓⲛⲁⲙⲟⲟⲩⲧ ⲙ̄ⲙⲟⲕ: "If you
were not my father according to the flesh, I would kill
you ..." or ⲛⲉⲓⲛⲁⲉⲡⲉⲓϯⲙⲁ ⲛⲁⲕ: "I would rebuke you." Joseph
obviously believes that his present illness is a result of
this incident. ⲥⲟⲕⲕ̄ ⲥⲉⲕⲥⲉⲕ- ⲥⲉⲕⲥⲱⲕ⸗ vb. tr. to pull,
stretch. (15) ϥⲓ-ⲗⲟⲅⲟⲥ ⲙⲛ̄ to hold accountable (for: ⲉⲧⲃⲉ);
ϥⲓ-ⲱⲡ ⲙⲛ̄ idem. (17) ⲥⲱⲗⲡ̄ ⲥⲗ̄ⲡ- ⲥⲟⲗⲡ⸗ Q ⲥⲟⲗⲡ̄ vb. tr. to
break off, cut off. ⲧ.ⲙⲉⲣⲣⲉ bond, fetter. ϣⲱⲧ ϣⲉⲉⲧ-
ϣⲁⲁⲧ⸗ Q ϣⲁⲁⲧ vb. tr. to cut, slaughter (as sacrifice). ⲏ̀
ⲑⲩⲥⲓⲁ sacrifice, victim. ⲏ̀ ⲟⲙⲟⲗⲟⲅⲓⲁ confession, agreement.

XVIII. (1) ⲛ̄ⲟⲩⲉϣ (ⲛ̄) prep. without; ϭⲱ ⲛ̄ⲟⲩⲉϣ is best
translated "to keep from (weeping)"; cf. vs. 4 below. ϫⲓ
is for Q ϫⲏⲩ caught. ⲡ.ⲍⲁϭⲉ snare. ⲉ is required before
ⲛ̄ϣⲁϫⲉ. (2) ⲛⲉⲓⲟⲩⲇⲁⲓ the Jews. ⲧⲁⲗⲟ ⲧⲁⲗⲉ- ⲧⲁⲗⲟ⸗ Q ⲧⲁⲗⲏⲩ
vb. tr. to raise up, offer up. (3) τὸ αἴθριον atrium,
courtyard.

ⲦⲀⲘⲀⲀⲨ, ⲀⲤⲈⲒ ⲈⲂⲞⲖ Ⲉ ⲠⲘⲀ ⲈⲦⲈⲒⲚ̄ϨⲎⲦϤ̄, ⲠⲈⲬⲀⲤ ⲚⲀⲒ Ϩ︤Ⲛ︥ ⲞⲨⲚⲞϬ Ⲛ̄
ⲖⲨⲠⲎ Ⲙ︤Ⲛ︥ ⲞⲨⲰⲖ︤Ⲥ︥ Ⲛ̄ ϨⲎⲦ ⲬⲈ, "ⲞⲨⲞⲒ ⲚⲀⲒ, ⲠⲀⲘⲈⲢⲒⲦ Ⲛ̄ ϢⲎⲢⲈ, ⲀⲢⲎⲨ
ⲈϤⲚⲀⲘⲞⲨ Ⲛ̄ϬⲒ ⲠⲀ-ⲦⲘ︤Ⲛ︦Ⲧ︥Ϩ︤Ⲗ︦Ⲗ︥Ⲟ ⲈⲦ ⲚⲀⲚⲞⲨⳞ ⲒⲰⲤⲎⲪ, ⲠⲈⲔⲈⲒⲰⲦ ⲔⲀⲦⲀ ⲤⲀⲢⳜ."
(4) ⲠⲈⲬⲀⲒ ⲚⲀⲤ ⲬⲈ, "ⲱ ⲦⲀⲘⲈⲢⲒⲦ Ⲙ̄ ⲘⲀⲀⲨ, ⲚⲒⲘ ⲈⲚⲈϨ Ϩ︤Ⲙ︥ ⲠⲄⲈⲚⲞⲤ Ⲛ̄
Ⲛ̄ⲢⲰⲘⲈ Ⲛ̄ⲦⲀⲨϤⲞⲢⲈⲒ Ⲛ̄ †ⲤⲀⲢⳜ ⲠⲈⲦ ⲚⲀϬⲰ Ⲛ̄ⲞⲨⲈϢ ⲘⲞⲨ? (5) ⲠⲘⲞⲨ ⲄⲀⲢ
ⲠⲈ ⲠⲀⲢⲬⲰⲚ Ⲙ̄ ⲠⲔⲞⲤⲘⲞⲤ ⲦⲎⲢϤ̄ ⲘⲈⲬⲢⲒ Ⲛ̄ⲦⲞ, ⲱ ⲘⲀⲢⲒⲀ ⲦⲀⲘⲀⲀⲨ ⲈⲦ ⲤⲘⲀ-
ⲘⲀⲀⲦ. (6) ⲦⲀⲚⲀⲄⲄⲎ ⲦⲈ ⲈⲢⲞ Ⲛ̄ⲦⲈⲘⲞⲨ ϨⲰⲰⲦⲈ Ⲛ̄ ⲐⲈ Ⲛ̄ ⲢⲰⲘⲈ ⲚⲒⲘ.
(7) ⲀⲖⲖⲀ ⲈⲒⲦⲈ ⲠⲀⲘⲈⲢⲒⲦ Ⲛ̄ ⲈⲒⲰⲦ ⲒⲰⲤⲎⲪ ⲈⲒⲦⲈ Ⲛ̄ⲦⲞ, ⲱ ⲦⲀⲘⲈⲢⲒⲦ Ⲙ̄
ⲘⲀⲀⲨ, Ⲛ̄ ⲞⲨⲘⲞⲨ ⲀⲚ ⲠⲈ ⲠⲈⲦⲚ̄ⲘⲞⲨ, ⲀⲖⲖⲀ ⲞⲨⲰⲚ︤Ϩ︥ ϢⲀ ⲈⲚⲈϨ ⲠⲈ. (8)
ⲀⲖⲖⲀ ⲀⲚⲞⲔ ϨⲰⲰⲦ †ⲚⲀⲬⲠⲒ-ⲘⲞⲨ Ϩⲁ ⲠⲦⲎⲢϤ̄ ⲈⲦⲂⲈ ⲦⲤⲀⲢⳜ Ⲛ̄ⲦⲀⲒϤⲞⲢⲈⲒ
Ⲙ̄ⲘⲞⲤ. (9) ⲦⲈⲚⲞⲨ ϬⲈ, ⲱ ⲦⲀⲘⲈⲢⲒⲦ Ⲙ̄ ⲘⲀⲀⲨ, ⲦⲰⲞⲨⲚ̄ Ⲛ̄ⲦⲈⲂⲰⲔ ⲈϨⲞⲨⲚ
Ϩⲁ︤Ⲧ︦Ⲛ︥ ⲠϨ︤Ⲗ︦Ⲗ︥Ⲟ ⲈⲦ ⲤⲘⲀⲘⲀⲀⲦ Ⲛ̄ⲦⲈⲚⲀⲨ Ⲉ ⲠⲦⲰϢ ⲠⲈⲈⲂⲞⲖ Ϩ︤Ⲛ︥ ⲦⲠⲈ."

XIX

(1) ⲀⲨⲰ ⲀⲒⲦⲰⲞⲨⲚ̄, ⲀⲒⲂⲰⲔ ⲈϨⲞⲨⲚ Ⲉ ⲠⲈⲐⲢⲒⲞⲚ ⲈⲦϤ̄Ⲛ̄ⲔⲞⲦ︤Ⲕ︥ Ⲛ̄ϨⲎⲦϤ̄,
ⲀⲒϨⲈ ⲈⲢⲞϤ Ⲉ-Ⲁ-ⲠⲘⲀⲈⲒⲚ Ⲙ̄ ⲠⲘⲞⲨ ⲞⲨⲰⲚϨ︦ ⲈⲂⲞⲖ Ⲛ̄ϨⲎⲦϤ̄. (2) ⲀⲚⲞⲔ ⲆⲈ
ⲀⲒϨⲘⲞⲞⲤ Ϩⲁ︤Ⲧ︦Ⲛ︥ ⲦⲈϤⲀⲠⲈ, Ⲁ-ⲦⲀⲘⲈⲢⲒⲦ Ⲙ̄ ⲘⲀⲀⲨ ϨⲘⲞⲞⲤ Ϩⲁ︤Ⲧ︦Ⲛ︥ ⲚⲈϤⲞⲨⲈ-
ⲢⲎⲦⲈ. (3) ⲀϤϤⲒ Ⲛ̄ ⲚⲈϤⲂⲀⲖ ⲈϨⲢⲀⲒ Ϩⲁ ⲠⲀϨⲞ, Ⲙ̄ⲠⲈϤⲈϢϬ︦Ⲙ̄ϬⲞⲘ Ⲉ ϢⲀϪⲈ
Ⲛ̄Ⲙ̄ⲘⲀⲒ ⲈⲂⲞⲖ ⲬⲈ Ⲁ-ⲦⲘⲛ̄Ⲧ︦Ⲙ̄ⲠⲞ Ⲙ̄ ⲠⲘⲞⲨ Ⲣ̄-ϪⲞⲈⲒⲤ ⲈϨⲢⲀⲒ ⲈϪⲰϤ. (4) ⲀϤ-
ϤⲒ Ⲛ̄ ⲦⲈϤϬⲒϪ Ⲛ̄ ⲞⲨⲚⲀⲘ, ⲀϤⲈϢ-ⲠⲈⲒⲚⲞϬ Ⲛ̄ ⲀϢ-ⲀϨⲞⲘ ⲈϤⲚⲀϢⲦ̄. (5) ⲀϤ-
ϬⲰ ⲈϤⲀⲘⲀϨⲦⲈ Ⲛ̄ ⲦⲀϬⲒϪ Ⲛ̄ ⲞⲨⲚⲀⲘ ⲈϤⲈⲒⲞⲢ︤Ⲙ︥ Ⲛ̄ⲤⲰⲒ Ⲛ̄ ⲞⲨⲚⲞϬ Ⲛ̄ ⲚⲀⲨ ϨⲰⲥ
ⲈϤⲔⲰⲢϢ︦ ⲈⲢⲞⲒ ⲬⲈ, "ⲱ ⲠⲀⲬⲞⲈⲒⲤ, Ⲙ̄Ⲡ︤Ⲣ︥ⲔⲀⲀⲨ Ⲉ ϤⲒⲦ." (6) ⲀⲒⲦⲈⲒ Ⲛ̄
ⲦⲀϬⲒϪ ⲈϨⲞⲨⲚ Ϩⲁ ⲠⲈϤⲤⲦⲎⲐⲞⲤ, ⲀⲒϨⲈ Ⲉ ⲦⲈϤⲮⲨⲬⲎ Ⲉ-ⲀⲤⲦⲀϨⲈ-ⲦⲈϤ-
ϢⲞⲨⲰⲂⲈ ⲬⲈ ⲈⲨⲚⲀⲈⲚⲦ︦Ⲥ︥ ⲈϨⲢⲀⲒ, ⲀⲨⲰ ⲈⲢⲈ-ⲚⲈⲂⲀⲒ-ϢⲒⲚⲈ Ⲙ̄ ⲠⲘⲞⲨ ϬⲰϢⲦ̄

ⲡ.ⲞⲨⲰⲖ︤Ⲥ︥ Ⲛ̄ ϨⲎⲦ discouragement. ⲀⲢⲎⲨ perhaps; often simply
indicates question, as here: "Is he to die?" Note Fut. II.
(4) ⲧⲟ̀ ⲅⲉⲛⲟⲥ race. (5) ⲟ̀ ⲁ̓ⲣⲭⲱⲛ ruler, Archon. ⲙⲉⲭⲣⲓ prep.
even up to, even including. (6) ⲏ̀ ⲁ̓ⲛⲁ́ⲅⲕⲏ necessity;
ⲦⲀⲚⲀⲄⲄⲎ ⲦⲈ ⲈⲢⲞ⸗ + Conj. is an impersonal construction: "It
is necessary that (you) die also ..." (7) ⲉⲓ̓́ⲧⲉ ... ⲉⲓ̓́ⲧⲉ
either ... or, whether ... or. (8) ⲬⲠⲒ- aux. vb. must; usu.
prefixed to Inf., as here. For ⲠⲈ.ⲈⲂⲞⲖ see 27.2 (end).

XIX. (3) ⲘⲚ̄Ⲧ︦Ⲙ̄Ⲡⲟ muteness. (6) ⲧⲟ̀ ⲥⲧⲏ̃ⲑⲟⲥ chest, breast.
Ⲧ.ϢⲞⲨⲰⲂⲈ throat. ⲂⲀⲒ-ϢⲒⲚⲈ = ϤⲀⲒ-ϢⲒⲚⲈ messenger.

ⲉⲃⲟⲗ ϩⲏⲧϥ̄ ⲉⲧⲣⲉϥⲉⲓ ⲉⲃⲟⲗ ϩⲛ̄ ⲥⲱⲙⲁ, ⲁⲗⲗⲁ ⲙ̄ⲡⲉ-ⲑⲗⲏ ⲛ̄ ⲟⲩⲛⲟⲩ ϫⲱⲕ ⲉⲃⲟⲗ, ϫⲉⲕⲁⲥ ⲉϥϣⲁⲛⲉⲓ ⲛ̄ϭⲓ ⲡⲙⲟⲩ, ⲙ̄ⲙⲛ̄ⲧϥ̄-ⲁⲛⲟⲭⲏ ⲙ̄ⲙⲁⲩ, ϫⲉ ⲉⲣⲉ-ⲡⲉϣⲧⲟⲣⲧⲣ̄ ⲟⲩⲏϩ ⲛ̄ⲥⲱϥ ⲁⲩⲱ ⲡⲣⲓⲙⲉ ⲙⲛ̄ ⲡⲧⲁⲕⲟ ⲛ̄ⲛⲉⲧ ⲙⲟⲟϣⲉ ϩⲁ ⲧⲉϥϩⲏ.

XX

(1) ⲁ-ⲧⲁⲙⲁⲁⲩ ⲛ̄ ⲃⲁⲗ-ϩⲏⲧ ⲛⲁⲩ ⲉⲣⲟⲓ ⲉⲓϭⲟⲙϭⲙ̄ ⲉ ⲡⲉϥⲥⲱⲙⲁ, ⲁⲥϭⲟⲙϭⲙ̄ ϩⲱⲱⲥ ⲛ̄ϭⲟⲡ ⲛ̄ ⲛⲉϥⲟⲩⲉⲣⲏⲧⲉ, ⲁⲩⲱ ⲁⲥϩⲉ ⲉⲣⲟⲟⲩ ⲉ-ⲁ-ⲡⲛⲓⲃⲉ ⲙ̄ ⲡⲉϩⲙⲟⲙ ⲕⲁⲁⲩ. (2) ⲡⲉϫⲁⲥ ⲛⲁⲓ ϩⲛ̄ ⲟⲩⲙⲛ̄ⲧⲁⲧⲥⲟⲟⲩⲛ̄ ϫⲉ, "ⲡⲉⲕϩⲙⲟⲧ ϣⲏⲡ ⲧⲉⲛⲟⲩ, ⲱ ⲡⲁⲙⲉⲣⲓⲧ ⲛ̄ ϣⲏⲣⲉ, ϫⲉ ϫⲓⲛ ⲧⲉⲩⲛⲟⲩ ⲛ̄ⲧⲁⲕϫⲉ-ⲧⲉⲕϭⲓϫ ⲉⲃⲟⲗ ϩⲙ̄ ⲡⲉϥⲥⲱⲙⲁ, ⲁ-ⲡⲕⲱϩⲧ̄ ⲉⲣ-ϩⲟⲧⲉ, ⲁϥⲁⲛⲁⲭⲱⲣⲉⲓ ⲛⲁϥ. (3) ⲉⲓⲥ ⲛⲉϥϭⲟⲧ ⲙⲛ̄ ⲛ̄ⲥⲏⲃⲉ ⲛ̄ ⲣⲁⲧϥ̄ ⲁⲩⲱϭⲃ̄ ⲁⲩⲱ ⲁⲩⲕⲃⲟ ⲛ̄ ⲑⲉ ⲛ̄ ⲟⲩⲕⲗⲩⲥⲧⲁⲗⲗⲟⲥ ⲙⲛ̄ ⲟⲩⲭⲓⲱⲛ." (4) ⲁⲓⲕⲓⲙ ⲉ ⲧⲁⲁⲡⲉ ⲁⲩⲱ ⲁⲓⲙⲟⲩⲧⲉ ⲉ ⲛⲉϥϣⲏⲣⲉ ⲉⲓϫⲱ ⲙ̄ⲙⲟⲥ ϫⲉ, "ⲧⲱⲟⲩⲛ̄ ⲛ̄ⲧⲉⲧⲛ̄ϣⲁϫⲉ ⲙⲛ̄ ⲡⲉⲧⲛ̄ⲉⲓⲱⲧ ⲉⲧ ⲥⲙⲁⲙⲁⲁⲧ ϫⲉ ⲡⲉⲟⲩⲟⲉⲓϣ ⲛ̄ ϣⲁϫⲉ ⲡⲉ ⲡⲁⲓ ⲙ̄ⲡⲁⲧⲉ-ⲧⲧⲁⲡⲣⲟ ⲉⲧ ϣⲁϫⲉ ⲉⲃⲟⲗ ϩⲛ̄ ⲧⲥⲁⲣⲝ ⲛ̄ ⲉⲃⲓⲏⲛ ⲧⲱⲙ." (5) ⲧⲟⲧⲉ ⲁⲩⲧⲱⲟⲩⲛ̄ ⲛ̄ϭⲓ ⲛ̄ϣⲏⲣⲉ ⲙⲛ̄ ⲛ̄ϣⲉⲉⲣⲉ ⲙ̄ ⲡⲁⲙⲉⲣⲓⲧ ⲛ̄ ⲓⲱⲧ ⲉⲓⲱⲥⲏⲫ, ⲁⲩⲉⲓ ϣⲁ ⲡⲉⲩⲉⲓⲱⲧ, ⲁⲩϩⲉ ⲉⲣⲟϥ ⲉϥⲕⲓⲛⲇⲩⲛⲉⲩⲉ ⲉ ⲡⲙⲟⲩ ⲉ-ⲁϥϩⲱⲛ ⲉϩⲟⲩⲛ ⲉ ⲡⲱⲗϭ̄ ⲉⲃⲟⲗ ⲙ̄ ⲡⲓⲃⲓⲟⲥ. (6) ⲁⲥⲟⲩⲱϣⲃ̄ ⲛ̄ϭⲓ ⲗⲩⲥⲓⲁ ⲧⲉϥⲛⲟϭ ⲛ̄ ϣⲉⲉⲣⲉ, ⲉⲧⲉ ⲧⲥⲁ ⲛ̄ ϫⲏϭⲉ ⲧⲉ, ⲡⲉϫⲁⲥ ⲛ̄ ⲛⲉⲥⲥⲛⲏⲩ ϫⲉ, "ⲟⲩⲟⲓ ⲛⲁⲓ, ⲛⲁⲥⲛⲏⲩ, ⲡⲁⲓ ⲡⲉ ⲡϣⲱⲛⲉ ⲛ̄ⲧⲁϥϣⲱⲡⲉ ⲛ̄ ⲧⲁⲙⲉⲣⲓⲧ ⲙ̄ ⲙⲁⲁⲩ, ⲁⲩⲱ ϣⲁ ⲧⲉⲛⲟⲩ ⲙ̄ⲡⲉⲛⲕⲟⲧⲛ̄ ⲉ ⲛⲁⲩ ⲉⲣⲟⲥ. (7) ⲡⲁⲓ ⲟⲛ ⲧⲉⲛⲟⲩ ⲡⲉⲧ ⲛⲁϣⲉⲉⲛⲉ-ⲡⲉⲛⲉⲓⲱⲧ ⲉⲣⲟⲛ ⲉ ⲧⲙ̄ⲛⲁⲩ ⲉⲣⲟϥ ϣⲁ ⲉⲛⲉϩ." (8) ⲧⲟⲧⲉ ⲁⲩϥⲓ-ϩⲣⲁⲩ ⲉⲃⲟⲗ, ⲁⲩⲣⲓⲙⲉ ϩⲓ ⲟⲩⲥⲟⲡ ⲛ̄ϭⲓ ⲛ̄ϣⲏⲣⲉ ⲙⲛ̄ ⲛ̄ϣⲉⲉⲣⲉ ⲙ̄ ⲡⲁⲉⲓⲱⲧ ⲉⲓⲱⲥⲏⲫ, ⲁⲩⲱ ⲁⲛⲟⲕ ϩⲱⲱⲧ ⲟⲛ ⲙⲛ̄ ⲙⲁⲣⲓⲁ ⲧⲁⲙⲁⲁⲩ ⲙ̄ ⲡⲁⲣⲑⲉⲛⲟⲥ ⲛⲉⲛⲣⲓⲙⲉ ⲛ̄ⲙ̄ⲙⲁⲩ ⲡⲉ, ⲉⲛⲥⲟⲟⲩⲛ̄ ϫⲉ ⲁ-ⲧⲉⲩⲛⲟⲩ ⲙ̄ ⲡⲙⲟⲩ ⲉⲓ.

For ϫⲉⲕⲁⲥ read ϫⲉ. ἡ ἀνοχή a holding back. ⲛ̄ⲛⲉⲧ = ⲛⲉⲧ.

XX. (1) ϭⲟⲙϭⲙ̄ ϭⲙ̄ϭⲱⲙ⸗ vb. tr. to touch (ⲉ). ⲉ required before ⲛ̄ϭⲟⲡ. ⲧ.ϭⲟⲡ sole of foot. ⲡ.ⲛⲓⲃⲉ = ⲡ.ⲛⲓϥⲉ. ⲡⲉϩⲙⲟⲙ heat, fever, warmth. (2) ⲡⲉⲕϩⲙⲟⲧ ϣⲏⲡ thanks be to you; a Q equivalent of ϣⲡ̄-ϩⲙⲟⲧ. ϫⲟ ϫⲉ- ϫⲟ⸗ ⲉⲃⲟⲗ vb. tr. to extend (ⲙ̄ⲙⲟ⸗). (3) ⲥⲏⲃⲉ ⲛ̄ ⲣⲁⲧ⸗ shin-bone. ⲱϭⲃ̄ vb. tr. to become cold. ⲕⲃⲟ, Q ⲕⲏⲃ vb. tr. to make cool; intr. to become cool. ὁ κρύσταλλος ice. ἡ χιών snow. (5) κινδυνεύω to be in danger (of: ⲉ). ⲡⲱⲗϭ̄ ⲡⲗ̄ϭ- ⲡⲟⲗϭ⸗ vb. tr. to free from; intr. to be freed from (ⲉ, ⲛ̄, ϩⲛ̄). (7) ϣⲱⲱⲛⲉ ϣⲉⲉⲛⲉ- ϣⲟⲟⲛ⸗ vb. tr. to remove (ⲙ̄ⲙⲟ⸗; from: ⲉ); to deprive (ⲉ) of (ⲙ̄ⲙⲟ⸗).

XXI

(1) ⲧⲟⲧⲉ ⲁⲓⲅ̅ⲱ̅ϣⲧ̅ ⲙ̅ ⲡⲥⲁ ⲙ̅ ⲡⲣⲏⲥ ⲙ̅ ⲡⲣⲟ, ⲁⲓⲛⲁⲩ ⲉ ⲡⲙⲟⲩ, ⲁϥⲉⲓ
ⲉⲣⲉ-ⲁⲙⲛ̅ⲧⲉ ⲟⲩⲏⲍ ⲛ̅ⲥⲱϥ, ⲉⲧⲉ ⲡⲁⲓ ⲡⲉ ⲡⲉⲧ ⲟ ⲛ̅ ⲥⲩⲙⲃⲟⲩⲗⲟⲥ ⲁⲩⲱ
ⲡⲡⲁⲛⲟⲩⲣⲅⲟⲥ, ⲡⲁⲓⲁⲃⲟⲗⲟⲥ ϫⲓⲛ ⲧⲉⲍⲟⲩⲉⲓⲧⲉ, ⲉⲣⲉ-ⲟⲩⲙⲏⲛϣⲉ ⲛ̅ ϣⲁⲃ-ⲛ̅-
ⲍⲟ ⲛ̅ ⲧⲉⲕⲁⲛⲟⲥ ⲟⲩⲏⲍ ⲛ̅ⲥⲱϥ, ⲉⲩϫⲓ-ⲍⲱⲕ ⲛ̅ ⲕⲱⲍⲧ̅ ⲧⲏⲣⲟⲩ, ⲉ-ⲙⲛ̅-ⲏⲡⲉ
ⲉⲣⲟⲟⲩ, ⲉⲣⲉ-ⲟⲩⲑⲏⲛ ⲙⲛ̅ ⲟⲩⲕⲁⲡⲛⲟⲥ ⲛ̅ ⲕⲱⲍⲧ̅ ⲛⲏⲩ ⲉⲃⲟⲗ ⲍ̅ⲛ̅ ⲧⲉⲩⲧⲁⲡⲣⲟ.
(2) ⲁ-ⲡⲁⲉⲓⲱⲧ ⲉⲓⲱⲥⲏϥ ⲅ̅ⲱ̅ϣⲧ̅, ⲁϥⲛⲁⲩ ⲉ ⲛⲉⲛⲧⲁⲅⲉⲓ ⲛ̅ⲥⲱϥ ⲉⲅⲟ ⲛ̅
ⲑⲩⲙⲟⲥ ⲉⲙⲁⲧⲉ ⲕⲁⲧⲁ ⲑⲉ ⲉϣⲁⲩⲙⲟⲩⲍ ⲉⲛ ⲟⲣⲅⲏ ⲍⲓ ϭⲱⲛⲧ̅ ⲉⲍⲟⲩⲛ ⲉ ⲯⲩⲭⲏ
ⲛⲓⲙ ⲛ̅ ⲣⲱⲙⲉ ⲉⲧ ⲛⲏⲩ ⲉⲃⲟⲗ ⲍ̅ⲛ̅ ⲥⲱⲙⲁ, ⲛ̅ ⲍⲟⲩⲟ ⲇⲉ ⲛ̅ ⲣⲉϥⲣ̅-ⲛⲟⲃⲉ,
ⲉϣⲱⲡⲉ ⲉⲩϣⲁⲛϭⲓⲛⲉ ⲛ̅ ⲟⲩⲙⲁⲉⲓⲛ ⲉ-ⲡⲱⲟⲩ ⲡⲉ ⲛ̅ⲍ̅ⲏⲧϥ̅. (3) ⲛ̅ⲧⲉⲣⲉ-ⲡⲁ-
ⲧⲙⲛ̅ⲧⲍⲗ̅ⲗⲟ ⲉⲧ ⲛⲁⲛⲟⲩⲥ ⲛⲁⲩ ⲉ ⲛⲉⲛⲧⲁⲅⲉⲓ ⲛ̅ⲥⲱϥ, ⲁϥϣⲧⲟⲣⲧⲣ̅ ⲁⲩⲱ ⲁ-
ⲛⲉϥⲃⲁⲗ †-ⲣ̅ⲙⲉⲓⲏ. (4) ⲁ-ⲧⲉⲯⲩⲭⲏ ⲙ̅ ⲡⲁⲉⲓⲱⲧ ⲓⲱⲥⲏϥ ⲟⲩⲱϣ ⲉⲓ ⲉⲃⲟⲗ
ⲍ̅ⲛ̅ ⲟⲩⲛⲟϭ ⲛ̅ ⲍⲃⲁ, ⲁⲩⲱ ⲉⲥϣⲓⲛⲉ ⲛ̅ⲥⲁ ⲙⲁ ⲛ̅ ⲍⲟⲡⲥ̅ ⲛ̅ⲍ̅ⲏⲧϥ̅ ⲙ̅ⲡⲉⲥⲍⲉ ⲙⲁ.
(5) ⲛ̅ⲧⲉⲣⲉⲓⲛⲁⲩ ⲇⲉ ⲉ ⲡⲛⲟϭ ⲛ̅ ϣⲧⲟⲣⲧⲣ̅ ⲛ̅ⲧⲁϥⲧⲁⲍⲉ-ⲧⲉⲯⲩⲭⲏ ⲙ̅ ⲡⲁⲉⲓⲱⲧ
ⲉⲓⲱⲥⲏϥ, ⲁⲩⲱ ϫⲉ ⲁϥⲑⲉⲱⲣⲉⲓ ⲛ̅ ⲍⲉⲛⲙⲟⲣⲫⲏ ⲉⲩϣⲟⲃⲉ ⲉⲙⲁⲧⲉ ⲉ-ⲟⲩ-ⲍⲟⲧⲉ
ⲡⲉ ⲛⲁⲩ ⲉⲣⲟⲟⲩ, ⲁⲓⲧⲱⲟⲩⲛ̅ ⲛ̅ ⲧⲉⲩⲛⲟⲩ, ⲁⲓⲉⲡⲉⲓ†ⲙⲁ ⲙ̅ ⲡⲉⲧ ⲟ ⲛ̅
ⲟⲣⲕⲁⲛⲟⲛ ⲙ̅ ⲡⲁⲓⲁⲃⲟⲗⲟⲥ ⲙⲛ̅ ⲛ̅ⲧⲁⲍⲓⲥ ⲉⲧ ⲟⲩⲏⲍ ⲛ̅ⲥⲱϥ. (6) ⲁⲩⲡⲱⲧ ⲍ̅ⲛ̅
ⲟⲩⲛⲟϭ ⲛ̅ ϣⲓⲡⲉ. (7) ⲁⲩⲱ ⲙ̅ⲡⲉ-ⲗⲁⲁⲩ ⲛ̅ ⲣⲱⲙⲉ ⲍ̅ⲛ̅ ⲛⲉⲧ ⲥⲟⲟⲩⲍ̅ ⲉ ⲡⲁⲉⲓⲱⲧ
ⲉⲓⲱⲥⲏϥ ⲉⲓⲙⲉ, ⲟⲩⲇⲉ ⲙⲁⲣⲓⲁ ⲧⲁⲙⲁⲁⲩ. (8) ⲛ̅ⲧⲉⲣⲉϥⲛⲁⲩ ⲇⲉ ⲛ̅ϭⲓ ⲡⲙⲟⲩ
ϫⲉ ⲁⲓⲉⲡⲉⲓ†ⲙⲁ ⲛ̅ ⲛⲉⲍⲟⲩⲥⲓⲁ ⲙ̅ ⲡⲕⲁⲕⲉ ⲉⲧ ⲟⲩⲏⲍ ⲛ̅ⲥⲱϥ, ⲁⲓⲛⲟⲭⲟⲩ ⲉⲃⲟⲗ,
ⲁⲩⲱ ϫⲉ ⲙⲛ̅ⲧⲁⲩ ⲗⲁⲁⲩ ⲛ̅ ⲉⲍⲟⲩⲥⲓⲁ ⲉⲍⲟⲩⲛ ⲉ ⲡⲁⲙⲉⲣⲓⲧ ⲛ̅ ⲉⲓⲱⲧ ⲓⲱⲥⲏϥ,
ⲁϥⲣ̅-ⲍⲟⲧⲉ ⲛ̅ϭⲓ ⲡⲙⲟⲩ, ⲁϥⲡⲱⲧ, ⲁϥⲍⲟⲡϥ̅ ⲍⲓ ⲡⲁⲍⲟⲩ ⲙ̅ ⲡⲣⲟ. (9) ⲁⲓⲧⲱⲟⲩⲛ̅

XXI. (1) ⲡ.ⲣⲏⲥ the south. ὁ σύμβουλος counsellor. ὁ
πανοῦργος villain. ⲧⲉ.ⲍⲟⲩⲉⲓⲧⲉ the first, the beginning.
ϣⲁⲃ-ⲛ̅-ⲍⲟ fearsome (lit. changing of face). οἱ δεκανοί a
group of 36 divinities (or demons) who ruled over the Zodi-
ac; originally an Egyptian astronomical division for time
computation, but later debased into astrology. ϫⲓ-ⲍⲱⲕ ⲛ̅
to be girded with. ⲧ.ⲏⲡⲉ number. ⲡⲉ.ⲑⲏⲛ sulfur, brim-
stone. (2) ⲣ̅-ⲑⲩⲙⲟⲥ (Q ⲟ ⲛ̅ ⲑⲩⲙⲟⲥ) to be wrathful. ⲉⲛ for ⲛ̅.
ⲟⲩⲙⲁⲉⲓⲛ ⲉ-ⲡⲱⲟⲩ ⲡⲉ a token of their own (lit. which is
theirs). (4) Read ⲉ ⲉⲓ for ⲉⲓ. ⲙⲁ ⲛ̅ ⲍⲟⲡⲥ̅ ⲛ̅ⲍ̅ⲏⲧϥ̅ a place in
which to hide. (5) θεωρέω to look at, observe. ἡ μορφή
form, shape. τὸ ὄργανον instrument.

ⲛ̄ ⲧⲉⲩⲛⲟⲩ, ⲁⲓⲭⲱ ⲛ̄ ⲟⲩⲡⲣⲟⲥⲉⲩⲭⲏ ⲉ ⲡⲁⲉⲓⲱⲧ ⲛ̄ ⲁⲅⲁⲑⲟⲥ, ⲉⲓⲭⲱ ⲙ̄ⲙⲟⲥ ⲭⲉ,

XXII

(1) "ⲡⲁⲉⲓⲱⲧ, ⲧⲛⲟⲩⲛⲉ ⲧⲏⲣⲥ̄ ⲛ̄ ⲧⲙ̄ⲛⲧⲁⲅⲁⲑⲟⲥ, ⲡⲉⲓⲱⲧ ⲛ̄ ⲧⲙⲉ,
ⲡⲓⲃⲁⲗ ⲛ̄ ⲣⲉϥⲛⲁⲩ, ⲡⲓⲙⲁⲁϫⲉ ⲛ̄ ⲣⲉϥⲥⲱⲧⲙ̄, ⲥⲱⲧⲙ̄ ⲉ ⲡⲉⲕϣⲏⲣⲉ ⲙ̄ ⲙⲉⲣⲓⲧ
ⲉⲧⲉ ⲁⲛⲟⲕ ⲡⲉ, ⲉⲓⲥⲟⲡⲥ̄ ⲙ̄ⲙⲟⲕ ⲉⲧⲃⲉ ⲡ2ⲱⲃ ⲛ̄ ⲛⲉⲕϭⲓϫ ⲉⲧⲉ ⲡⲁⲉⲓⲱⲧ ⲓⲱⲥⲏⲫ ⲡⲉ, ⲛⲅ̄ⲧⲛ̄ⲛⲟⲟⲩ ⲛⲁⲓ ⲛ̄ ⲟⲩⲛⲟϭ ⲛ̄ ⲭⲁⲓⲣⲟⲩⲃⲓⲛ ⲙⲛ̄ ⲡⲉⲭⲟⲣⲟⲥ ⲛ̄
ⲛⲁⲅⲅⲉⲗⲟⲥ ⲙⲛ̄ ⲙⲓⲭⲁⲏⲗ, ⲡⲟⲓⲕⲟⲛⲟⲙⲟⲥ ⲛ̄ ⲛⲁⲅⲁⲑⲟⲛ, ⲙⲛ̄ ⲅⲁⲃⲣⲓⲏⲗ ⲡⲃⲁⲓ-
ϣⲙ̄-ⲛⲟⲩϥⲉ ⲛ̄ ⲛⲁⲓⲱⲛⲉ ⲡⲟⲩⲟⲉⲓⲛ, ⲛ̄ⲥⲉⲣⲟⲉⲓⲥ ⲉ ⲧⲉⲯⲩⲭⲏ ⲙ̄ ⲡⲁⲉⲓⲱⲧ ⲉⲓⲱⲥⲏⲫ, ⲛ̄ⲥⲉⲭⲓ-ⲙⲟⲉⲓⲧ 2ⲁ ⲧⲉⲥ2ⲏ ϣⲁⲛⲧⲉⲥⲟⲩⲱⲧⲃ̄ ⲙ̄ ⲡⲥⲁϣϥ̄ ⲛ̄ ⲁⲓⲱⲛ ⲛ̄
ⲕⲁⲕⲉ, ⲁⲩⲱ ⲛ̄ⲥⲉⲡⲁⲣⲁⲅⲉ ⲛ̄ ⲛⲉ2ⲓⲟⲟⲩ ⲉⲧ 2ⲧⲙ̄ⲧⲱⲙ, ⲛⲁⲓ ⲉⲩⲛⲟϭ ⲛ̄ 2ⲟⲧⲉ
ⲡⲉ ⲙⲟⲟϣⲉ ⲡ2ⲏⲧⲟⲩ ⲁⲩⲱ ⲟⲩⲛⲟϭ ⲛ̄ 2ⲃⲁ ⲡⲉ ⲛⲁⲩ ⲛ̄ⲁⲩⲙⲓⲟⲥ ⲉⲧ 2ⲓⲭⲱⲟⲩ.
ⲙⲁⲣⲉ-ⲡⲉⲓⲉⲣⲟ ⲛ̄ ⲕⲱ2ⲧ̄ ⲉⲣ-ⲑⲉ ⲛ̄ ⲟⲩⲙⲟⲟⲩ ⲁⲩⲱ ⲛ̄ⲧⲉ-ⲑⲁⲗⲁⲥⲥⲁ ⲛ̄ ⲣⲉϥϣⲁⲁⲣ ⲟⲩⲱ ⲉⲥⲉⲛⲟⲭⲗⲉⲓ. (2) ⲙⲁⲣⲉϥϣⲱⲡⲉ 2ⲛ̄ ⲟⲩⲙⲛ̄ⲧ2ⲏⲙⲉⲣⲟⲥ ⲉ2ⲟⲩⲛ
ⲉ ⲧⲉⲯⲩⲭⲏ ⲙ̄ ⲡⲁⲉⲓⲱⲧ ⲓⲱⲥⲏⲫ, ϫⲉ ⲧⲁⲓ ⲧⲉ ⲧⲉⲩⲛⲟⲩ ⲉⲧϥ̄ⲣ̄-ⲭⲣⲓⲁ ⲙ̄ ⲡⲛⲁ
ⲛ̄2ⲏⲧⲥ̄." (3) ϯⲭⲱ ⲙ̄ⲙⲟⲥ ⲛⲏⲧⲛ̄, ⲱ ⲛⲁⲙⲉⲣⲟⲥ ⲉⲧ ⲟⲩⲁⲁⲃ, ⲛⲁⲁⲡⲟⲥⲧⲟ-
ⲗⲟⲥ ⲉⲧ ⲥⲙⲁⲙⲁⲁⲧ, ϫⲉ ⲣⲱⲙⲉ ⲛⲓⲙ ⲉⲧⲟⲩⲛⲁϫⲡⲟϥ ⲉ ⲡⲕⲟⲥⲙⲟⲥ ⲁϥⲉⲓⲙⲉ ⲉ
ⲡⲡⲉⲧ ⲛⲁⲛⲟⲩϥ ⲙⲛ̄ ⲡⲡⲉⲑⲟⲟⲩ. ⲉϥϣⲁⲛⲣ̄-ⲡⲉϥⲟⲩⲟⲉⲓϣ ⲧⲏⲣϥ̄ ⲉϥϣⲉ ⲉ2ⲣⲁⲓ
ⲛ̄ⲥⲁ ⲛⲉⲗⲟⲟⲩⲉ ⲛ̄ ⲛⲉϥⲃⲁⲗ, ⲉϥϣⲁⲛⲉⲓ ⲉϥⲛⲁⲙⲟⲩ, ϥⲣ̄-ⲭⲣⲓⲁ ⲙ̄ ⲡⲛⲁ ⲙ̄
ⲡⲁⲉⲓⲱⲧ ⲉⲧ 2ⲛ̄ ⲙ̄ⲡⲏⲩⲉ ⲉ ⲧⲉⲩⲛⲟⲩ ⲙ̄ ⲡⲙⲟⲩ ⲙⲛ̄ ⲧϭⲓⲙⲡⲁⲣⲁⲅⲉ ⲛ̄ ⲛⲉ-
2ⲓⲟⲟⲩⲉ ⲁⲩⲱ ⲧϭⲓⲛⲁⲡⲟⲗⲟⲅⲓⲍⲉ 2ⲙ̄ ⲡⲃⲩⲙⲁ ⲉⲧ 2ⲁ 2ⲟⲧⲉ. (4) ⲡⲗⲏⲛ ϯ-

---

(9) ἡ προσευχή prayer.

XXII. (1) ⲧ.ⲛⲟⲩⲛⲉ root. ⲭⲁⲓⲣⲟⲩⲃⲓⲛ Cherubim. ὁ χορός
chorus, choir. ὁ οἰκονόμος steward, manager. ⲃⲁⲓ- = ϥⲁⲓ-.
ϣⲙ̄-ⲛⲟⲩϥⲉ good news. ⲣⲟⲉⲓⲥ vb. tr. to guard, keep watch (ⲉ).
ⲟⲩⲱⲧⲃ̄ ⲟⲩⲉⲧⲃ̄- ⲟⲩⲟⲧⲃ゠ Q ⲟⲩⲟⲧⲃ̄ vb. tr. to pass through (ⲙ̄ⲙⲟ゠).
2ⲧⲟⲙⲧⲙ̄, Q 2ⲧⲙ̄ⲧⲱⲙ to become dark. ὁ δήμιος executioner.
ⲣⲉϥϣⲁⲁⲣ demon; as adj. ἐνοχλέω to trouble, disturb. (2)
ἥμερος mild, tame; ⲙⲛ̄ⲧ2ⲏⲙⲉⲣⲟⲥ calm. (3) τὸ μέρος part; used
fig. here of the apostles as Christ's members. ⲉⲓϣⲉ ⲉϣⲧ-
ⲁϣⲧ゠ Q ⲁϣⲉ vb. tr. to hang, suspend (ⲙ̄ⲙⲟ゠); Q with ⲛ̄ⲥⲁ: to
be captivated by. ⲉⲗⲟⲟⲩⲉ prob. pl. of ⲉⲗⲱ, ⲁⲗⲱ snare, trap.
ⲉⲓ + Circum.: to be about to. ⲧ.ϭⲓⲙⲡⲁⲣⲁⲅⲉ passage, passing.
ⲧ.ϭⲓⲛⲁⲡⲟⲗⲟⲅⲓⲍⲉ defense. ⲡ.ⲃⲩⲙⲁ = ⲡ.ⲃⲏⲙⲁ. ⲉⲧ 2ⲁ 2ⲟⲧⲉ fearful. (4) πλήν here as conj.: but, however.

ⲛⲁⲕⲧⲟⲓ ⲉ2ⲣⲁⲓ ⲉⲭⲛ̄ ⲧ6ⲓⲛⲭⲱⲕ ⲉⲃⲟⲗ ⲙ̄ ⲡⲗⲉⲓⲱⲧ ⲓⲱⲥⲏⲫ, ⲡⲗ ⲡⲉⲓⲉⲣ-
ⲡⲙⲉⲉⲩⲉ ⲉⲧ ⲛⲁⲛⲟⲩ9.

XXIII

(1) ⲗⲥ ⲱⲡⲉ ⲇⲉ, ⲛ̄ⲧⲉⲣⲉⲓⲭⲱ ⲙ̄ ⲡ2ⲁⲙⲏⲛ, ⲉⲣⲉ-ⲙⲁⲣⲓⲁ ⲧⲁⲙⲉⲣⲓⲧ ⲙ̄
ⲙⲁⲁⲩ ⲟⲩⲱ2ⲙ̄ ⲛ̄ⲥ ⲱⲓ ⲛ̄ ⲧⲁⲥⲡⲉ ⲛ̄ ⲛⲁ-ⲙ̄ⲡⲏⲩⲉ, (2) ⲗⲩ ⲱ ⲛ̄ ⲧⲉⲩⲛⲟⲩ ⲉ ⲓⲥ
ⲙⲓⲭⲁⲏⲗ ⲙⲛ̄ ⲅⲁⲃⲣⲓⲏⲗ ⲙⲛ̄ ⲡⲉⲭⲟⲣⲟⲥ ⲛ̄ ⲛⲁⲅⲅⲉⲗⲟⲥ ⲁⲩⲉⲓ ⲉⲃⲟⲗ 2ⲛ̄ ⲧⲡⲉ,
ⲁⲩⲉⲓ, ⲁⲩ<ⲁ>2ⲉⲣⲁⲧⲟⲩ ⲉⲭⲙ̄ ⲡⲥ ⲱⲙⲁ ⲙ̄ ⲡⲗⲉⲓⲱⲧ ⲓⲱⲥⲏⲫ. (3) ⲁⲩ ⲱ ⲛ̄
ⲧⲉⲩⲛⲟⲩ ⲁ-ⲧ2ⲉⲗ2ⲓⲗⲉ ⲙⲛ̄ ⲡⲉⲭⲉⲗ2ⲏⲥ ⲧⲱⲟⲩⲛ ⲉⲭ ⲱ9 ⲉⲙⲁⲧⲉ, ⲁⲩ ⲱ ⲁⲓⲉⲓⲙⲉ
ⲭⲉ ⲁ-ⲧⲉⲩⲛⲟⲩ ⲉⲧ ⲭⲏ9 ⲉⲓ. (4) ⲁⲩ ⲱ ⲁ96 ⲱ ⲉ9†-ⲛⲁⲁⲅⲉ ⲛ̄ ⲑⲉ ⲛ̄ ⲧⲉⲧ
ⲛⲁⲙⲓⲥⲉ, ⲉⲣⲉ-ⲡ2ⲁⲭ † ⲛ̄ⲥ ⲱ9 ⲛ̄ ⲑⲉ ⲛ̄ ⲟⲩⲧⲏⲩ ⲉ9ⲛⲁ ⲱ̄ⲧ ⲙⲛ̄ ⲟⲩⲕⲱ2ⲧ̄ ⲉ9-
ⲟ ⲱ ⲉ9ⲟⲩ ⲱⲙ ⲛ̄ⲥⲁ ⲟⲩ2ⲏⲗⲏ ⲉⲥⲟ ⲱ. (5) ⲡⲙⲟⲩ ⲇⲉ 2 ⲱ ⲱ9 ⲙ̄ⲡⲉ-ⲑⲟⲧⲉ ⲕⲁⲗ9
ⲛ̄ ⲉⲓ ⲉ2ⲟⲩⲛ ⲉⲭⲙ̄ ⲡⲥ ⲱⲙⲁ ⲙ̄ ⲡⲁⲙⲉⲣⲓⲧ ⲛ̄ ⲓ ⲱⲧ ⲓ ⲱⲥⲏⲫ ⲛ̄9ⲡⲟⲣⲭ9 ⲉⲃⲟⲗ,
ⲭⲉ ⲉ96 ⲱ ⲱ̄ⲧ ⲉ2ⲟⲩⲛ ⲉ9ⲛⲁⲩ ⲉⲣⲟⲓ ⲉⲓ2ⲙⲟⲟⲥ 2ⲁ2ⲧⲛ̄ ⲧⲉ9ⲁⲡⲉ, ⲉⲓⲁⲙⲁ2ⲧⲉ
ⲉⲭⲛ̄ ⲛⲉ9ⲥⲙⲁⲩ. (6) ⲁⲩ ⲱ ⲛ̄ⲧⲉⲣⲉⲓⲉⲓⲙⲉ ⲭⲉ ⲁ9ⲣ̄-2ⲟⲧⲉ ⲛ̄6ⲓ ⲡⲙⲟⲩ ⲛ̄ ⲉⲓ
ⲉ2ⲟⲩⲛ ⲉⲧⲃⲏⲏⲧ, ⲁⲓⲧ ⲱⲟⲩⲛ̄, ⲁⲓⲃ ⲱⲕ ⲉ ⲡⲥⲁ ⲛ̄ ⲃⲟⲗ ⲙ̄ ⲡⲙⲁ ⲙ̄ ⲡⲣⲟ,
ⲁⲓ6ⲛ̄ⲧ9 ⲉ96ⲉⲉⲧ ⲙⲁⲩⲁⲁ9 2ⲛ̄ ⲟⲩⲛⲟ6 ⲛ̄ 2ⲟⲧⲉ. (7) ⲁⲩ ⲱ ⲛ̄ ⲧⲉⲩⲛⲟⲩ
ⲡⲉⲭⲁⲓ ⲛⲁ9 ⲭⲉ, 'ⲱ ⲡⲉⲛⲧⲁ9ⲉⲓ ⲉⲃⲟⲗ 2ⲛ̄ ⲛ̄ⲧⲟⲡⲟⲥ ⲙ̄ ⲡⲥⲁ ⲙ̄ ⲡⲣⲏⲥ, ⲃ ⲱⲕ
ⲛⲁⲕ ⲉ2ⲟⲩⲛ ⲧⲁⲭⲏ ⲛ̄ⲧⲭⲱⲕ ⲉⲃⲟⲗ ⲙ̄ ⲡⲉⲛⲧⲁ-ⲡⲗⲉⲓⲱⲧ ⲟⲩⲉ2-ⲥⲁ2ⲛⲉ ⲙ̄ⲙⲟ9
ⲛⲁⲕ. (8) ⲁⲗⲗⲁ ⲣⲟⲉⲓⲥ ⲉⲣⲟ9 ⲛ̄ ⲑⲉ ⲙ̄ ⲡⲟⲩⲟⲉⲓⲛ ⲛ̄ ⲛⲉⲕⲃⲁⲗ, ⲭⲉ ⲛ̄ⲧⲟ9
ⲡⲉ ⲡⲗⲉⲓⲱⲧ ⲕⲁⲧⲁ ⲥⲁⲣⲝ, ⲁⲩ ⲱ ⲁ9 ⲱ ⲡ̄-2ⲓⲥⲉ ⲛ̄ⲙⲙⲁⲓ 2ⲉⲛ ⲛⲉ2ⲟⲟⲩ ⲛ̄
ⲧⲁⲙⲛ̄ⲧ ⲱ ⲏⲣⲉ ⲱ ⲏⲙ, ⲉ9ⲡⲏⲧ ⲛ̄ⲙⲙⲁⲓ ⲉⲃⲟⲗ 2ⲛ̄ ⲟⲩⲙⲁ ⲉⲩⲙⲁ ⲉⲧⲃⲉ ⲧⲉⲡⲉⲓ-

---

ⲡⲉⲓⲉⲣ- for ⲡⲉⲓⲣ̄-.

XXIII. (1) ⲡ.2ⲁⲙⲏⲛ the amen. ⲟⲩ ⲱ2ⲙ̄ vb. intr. to repeat,
answer, respond (to: ⲉ, ⲉⲭⲛ̄, ⲛⲁ⸍, ⲛ̄ⲥⲁ). ⲧ.ⲁⲥⲡⲉ tongue,
language. (2) ⲉⲭⲛ̄ often means "by, beside, at" with verbs
of standing or stopping. (3) ⲧ.2ⲉⲗ2ⲓⲗⲉ death-rattle. ⲡⲉ-
ⲭⲉⲗ2ⲏⲥ panting, exhaustion. ⲭⲏ9 Q to be bitter, sharp.
(4) †-ⲛⲁⲁⲅⲉ to be in labor; ⲧ.ⲛⲁⲁⲕⲉ labor pains. ⲡ.2ⲁⲭ
meaning uncertain; prob. related to 2 ⲱⲭ to be in straits,
dying. † ⲛ̄ⲥⲁ to pursue. ⲡ.ⲧⲏⲩ wind. ἡ ὕλη woods, forest.
(5) ⲡⲉ.ⲥⲙⲁⲩ temple (of head). (7) τάχα adv. quickly. (8)
ⲉⲃⲟⲗ 2ⲛ̄ ⲟⲩⲙⲁ ⲉⲩⲙⲁ from one place to another. ἡ ἐπιβουλή
plot. ἡ ὠφελία advantage, profit.

ⲃⲟⲩⲗⲏ ⲛ̄ ⲍ̇ⲩⲣⲱⲧⲏⲥ, ⲁⲩⲱ ⲁⲓⲭⲓ-ⲥⲃⲱ ⲛ̄ⲧⲟⲟⲧϥ̄ ⲛ̄ ⲑⲉ ⲛ̄ ⲛ̄ϣⲏⲣⲉ ⲧⲏⲣⲟⲩ,
ⲉϣⲁⲣⲉ-ⲛⲉⲩⲉⲓⲟⲧⲉ ⲧⲓ-ⲥⲃⲱ ⲛⲁⲩ ⲉ ⲧⲉⲩⲱⲫⲉⲗⲓⲁ. (9) ⲧⲟⲧⲉ ⲁⲃⲃⲁⲧⲟⲛ
ⲁϥⲃⲱⲕ ⲉⲍⲟⲩⲛ, ⲁϥⲭⲓ ⲛ̄ ⲧⲉⲯⲩⲭⲏ ⲙ̄ ⲡⲗⲉⲓⲱⲧ ⲉⲓⲱⲥⲏⲫ, ⲁϥⲉⲓⲛⲉ ⲙ̄ⲙⲟⲥ
ⲉⲃⲟⲗ ⲍ̄ⲛ ⲥⲱⲙⲁ ⲙ̄ ⲡⲛⲁⲩ ⲙ̄ ⲡⲣⲏ ⲉϥⲛⲁϣⲁ ⲍ̄ⲛ ⲧⲉϥⲃⲁⲥⲓⲥ, ⲛ̄ ⲥⲟⲩ-ⲭⲟⲩⲧⲁⲥⲉ ⲙ̄ ⲡⲉⲃⲟⲧ ⲉⲡⲏⲡ ⲍ̄ⲛ ⲟⲩⲉⲓⲣⲏⲛⲏ. (10) ⲛⲉⲍⲟⲟⲩ ⲧⲏⲣⲟⲩ ⲙ̄ ⲡⲱⲛⲍ̄ ⲙ̄
ⲡⲁⲙⲉⲣⲓⲧ ⲛ̄ ⲉⲓⲱⲧ ⲓⲱⲥⲏⲫ ⲥⲉⲉⲓⲣⲉ ⲛ̄ ϣⲉ ⲙ̄ⲛ̄ⲧⲟⲩⲉⲓ ⲛ̄ ⲣⲟⲙⲡⲉ. (11) ⲁ-
ⲙⲓⲭⲁⲏⲗ ⲁⲙⲁⲍⲧⲉ ⲙ̄ ⲡⲧⲟⲡ ⲥⲛⲁⲩ ⲛ̄ ⲟⲩⲙⲁⲡⲡⲁ ⲛ̄ ⲍⲟⲗⲟⲥⲓⲗⲓⲕⲟⲛ ⲉⲥⲧⲁⲉⲓⲏⲩ,
ⲁ ⲅⲁⲃⲣⲓⲏⲗ ⲁⲙⲁⲍⲧⲉ ⲙ̄ ⲡⲕⲉⲧⲟⲡ ⲥⲛⲁⲩ. ⲁⲩⲁⲥⲡⲁⲍⲉ ⲛ̄ ⲧⲉⲯⲩⲭⲏ ⲙ̄ ⲡⲁⲙⲉⲣⲓⲧ ⲛ̄ ⲉⲓⲱⲧ ⲉⲓⲱⲥⲏⲫ, ⲁⲩⲧⲁⲁⲥ ⲉⲡⲉⲥⲏⲧ ⲉ ⲧⲙⲁⲡⲡⲁ. (12) ⲙ̄ⲡⲉ-
ⲗⲁⲁⲩ ⲇⲉ ⲍ̄ⲛ ⲛⲉⲧ ⲍ̄ⲙⲟⲟⲥ ⲍⲁⲍⲧⲏϥ ⲉⲓⲙⲉ ⲭⲉ ⲁϥⲙⲟⲩ, ⲟⲩⲇⲉ ⲧⲕⲉⲙⲁⲣⲓⲁ
ⲧⲁⲙⲁⲁⲩ ⲙ̄ⲡⲉⲥⲉⲓⲙⲉ. (13) ⲁⲩⲱ ⲁⲓⲧⲣⲉ-ⲙⲓⲭⲁⲏⲗ ⲙ̄ⲛ̄ ⲅⲁⲃⲣⲓⲏⲗ ⲣⲟⲉⲓⲥ
ⲉ ⲧⲉⲯⲩⲭⲏ ⲙ̄ ⲡⲁⲙⲉⲣⲓⲧ ⲛ̄ ⲉⲓⲱⲧ ⲓⲱⲥⲏⲫ ⲉⲧⲃⲉ ⲛ̄ⲣⲉϥⲧⲱⲣⲡ̄ ⲉⲧ ⲍ̇ⲓ
ⲛⲉⲍⲓⲟⲟⲩⲉ, ⲁⲩⲱ ⲁⲓⲧⲣⲉ-ⲛⲁⲅⲅⲉⲗⲟⲥ ⲛ̄ ⲁⲥⲱⲙⲁⲧⲟⲥ ⲉ̄ⲱ ⲉⲩⲍ̇ⲩⲙⲛⲉⲩⲉ ⲍⲁ
ⲧⲉϥⲍⲏ ϣⲁⲛⲧⲟⲩⲭⲓⲧϥ̄ ⲉ ⲙ̄ⲡⲏⲩⲉ ϣⲁ ⲡⲗⲉⲓⲱⲧ ⲛ̄ ⲁⲅⲁⲑⲟⲥ.

XXIV

(1) ⲁⲩⲱ ⲁⲓⲕⲧⲟⲓ ⲉⲭⲙ̄ ⲡⲥⲱⲙⲁ ⲉϥⲛⲏⲭ ⲉⲃⲟⲗ ⲛ̄ ⲑⲉ ⲛ̄ ⲟⲩⲕⲟⲩⲫⲟⲛ,
ⲁⲓⲍ̇ⲙⲟⲟⲥ, ⲁⲓⲉⲓⲛⲉ ⲛ̄ ⲛⲉϥⲃⲁⲗ ⲉⲡⲉⲥⲏⲧ, ⲁⲓ6ⲱϣⲧ̄ ⲉⲡⲉⲥⲏⲧ ⲉⲭⲱϥ ⲛ̄
ⲟⲩⲛⲟ6 ⲛ̄ ⲛⲁⲩ, ⲉⲓⲣⲓⲙⲉ ⲉⲣⲟϥ. (2) ⲡⲉⲭⲁⲓ ... (End of Fragment
III).

---

(9) ⲁⲃⲃⲁⲧⲟⲛ Death, Abbadon (Gk., ultimately from Hebrew).
ἡ βάσις here: course. (11) ⲛ.ⲧⲟⲡ edge, hem. ⲧ.ⲙⲁⲡⲡⲁ
cloth, handkerchief. ὁλοσηρικός silken. (13) ⲣⲉϥⲧⲱⲣⲡ̄
plunderer; ⲧⲱⲣⲡ̄ ⲧⲉⲣⲡ̄- ⲧⲟⲣⲡ⸗ vb. tr. to seize, rob (ⲙ̄ⲙⲟ⸗).
ἀσώματος incorporeal. ὑμνέω to sing hymns.
XXIV. (1) τὸ κοῦφον (empty) vessel.

Glossary

Words are arranged alphabetically according to the order given
on page x, with the following exceptions: (1) initial ει- and oγ-
occupy the place of ι and γ respectively; in all other positions they
are alphabetized simply as є + ι and o + γ; (2) ϕ, θ, x, ψ, ϫ are
alphabetized as π₂, τ₂, κ₂, πc, κc; (3) ϯ is alphabetized as τι.

Verbs are entered under the free (unbound) form of the Infinitive. In the rare instances when this form is not attested, a suppo-
sitious entry is used when there is no doubt about its pattern; otherwise the entry is under the first actually attested form. Other parts
of speech are entered under their unbound forms when they are attested.
The Grammatical Index should be consulted for most of the prefixed
elements. I have followed Crum (*A Coptic Dictionary*) in listing most
verbal and nominal compounds under the final element. Also following
Crum, derivatives are listed under leading verbal entries; the cross-
references must be consulted in locating these. In order to provide
space for less predictable compounds, nouns of action in ειN-, which
may be formed freely from nearly any verb, have been systematically
excluded, as have many agent nouns with peϥ-.

Where space has permitted, a selection of variant forms has been
given. Under verbal entries these are placed in parentheses; otherwise they are listed serially after the main entry. These variants
fall into two types: (1) simple spelling variants, especially between
є and a supralinear stroke; (2) dialectal or "substandard" spellings
that occur in otherwise fairly standard texts. The latter have been
included to increase the utility of the Glossary; many of them are not
rare, and their inclusion will give the reader some idea of the variety to be encountered in non-standard manuscripts.

Cross-references are grouped at the end of each letter. The
completely predictable forms of the two verb types κωτ κєτ- κoτ⸗ Q
κΗτ and cωτπ̄ cєτπ̄- coτπ⸗ Q coτπ̄ have been systematically excluded from the cross-references; all other bound forms and qualitatives have been listed. Many spelling variants involving ει/ι and
stroke/є have also been excluded.

ⲁ

ⲁ adv. of approximation, as in ⲁ ϯⲟⲩ about five, ⲁ ⲟⲩⲏⲣ
about how much? Cpd. as ⲛⲁ, as in ⲛⲁ ϣⲉ ⲛ̄ ⲙⲁ2ⲉ to the
extent of about a hundred cubits.

ⲁⲁⲥ, ⲁⲥ n. a blow, slap (usu. on face). ϯ-ⲁⲁⲥ, ϯ ⲛ̄ ⲟⲩⲁⲁⲥ
to slap, strike (ⲛⲁ⸗). ϣⲥ̄-ⲛ̄-ⲁⲥ n. = ⲁⲁⲥ.

ⲁⲃⲁ6ⲏ6ⲓⲛ, ⲁⲃⲓ6ⲏ6ⲓⲛ, ⲁⲃⲁⲕⲏⲓⲛ6, ⲁ96666ⲛ6 n.m.f. glass.

ⲁⲃⲱ (pl. ⲁⲃⲟⲟⲩ6) n.f. net (for fishing or hunting).

ⲁⲃⲱⲕ, ⲁⲃⲟⲕ (f. ⲁⲃⲟⲕ6; pl. ⲁⲃⲟⲟⲕ6) n.m. crow, raven.

ⲁ6ⲓⲕ n.m. consecration. ⲭⲓ-ⲁ6ⲓⲕ to consecrate; as n.m.
consecration.

ⲁⲓⲁⲓ, Q ⲟⲓ vb. intr. to increase (in age, size, stature);
Q to be great, honored; as n.m. increase, growth.
ⲁ6ⲓⲏⲥ, ⲁⲏⲥ, ⲁ6ⲏⲥ n.f. greatness, size, quantity.

ⲁⲕⲏⲥ, ⲁⲕ6ⲥ, ⲁⲕⲓⲥ n.m. girdle, clothing.

ⲁⲕⲱ, ⲁⲅⲱ, ⲅⲱ n.f. filth; carrion; anything ruined.

ⲁⲗ adj. deaf. ⲣ̄-ⲁⲗ (Q ⲟ ⲛ̄ ⲁⲗ) to become deaf.

ⲁⲗ n.m. pebble; hail-stone in ⲁⲗ ⲛ̄ ⲡ6.

ⲁⲗ n. only in ⲁϣ-ⲁⲗ n.m. a cry (cf. ⲱϣ).

ⲁⲗⲁⲩ, ⲁⲗ6ⲩ, ⲁⲗⲏⲩ adj. white.

ⲁⲗ6 ⲁⲗⲟ⸗ Q ⲁⲗⲏⲩ (imptv. ⲁⲗⲱⲧⲛ̄) vb. intr. to go up, ascend
(to, up to, onto: 6, 62ⲣⲁⲓ 6, 6ⲭⲛ̄, 62ⲣⲁⲓ 6ⲭⲛ̄); to
mount (an animal), to board (a ship); rarely tr. with
ⲙ̄ⲙⲟ⸗. ⲣ6ϥⲁⲗ6 rider.

ⲁⲗⲓⲗ n.m. field-mouse or sim.

ⲁⲗⲕ6, ⲁⲗⲕⲏ n.m. last day of month; ⲛ̄ ⲁⲗⲕ6 (ⲛ̄) on the last
day of (+ month name).

ⲁⲗⲟⲕ n.m. corner, angle; prob. not Sah. (cf. ⲕⲗ̄ⲝ6).

ⲁⲗⲟⲙ n.m. bosom.

ⲁⲗⲟⲩ n.m. child, servant; not properly Sah. (cf. ϣⲏⲣ6).

ⲁⲗⲟ6 n.m. thigh.

ⲁⲗⲧⲕⲁⲥ n.m. bone-marrow.

ⲁⲗⲱ, 6ⲗⲱ (pl. ⲁⲗⲟⲟⲩ6, 6ⲗⲟⲟⲩ6) n. snare, trap.

ⲁⲗⲱ, ⲁⲗⲟⲩ (pl. ⲁⲗⲟⲟⲩ6, ⲁⲗⲁⲩ6, ⲁⲣⲟⲟⲩ6) n.f. pupil of eye.

ⲁⲗⲱⲧ n.f. forced labor; term of service; a measure.

ⲁⲗⲱⲟⲩ6 n.pl. bunch (of grapes) or sim.

ⲁⲙⲁ Ama; fem. title of respect or reverence; cf. ⲁⲡⲁ.

ⲁⲙⲁϩⲧⲉ vb. intr. to prevail, take control, rule (over: ⲉⲭⲛ̄, ϩⲓⲭⲛ̄); to be valid, hold good; to persevere, continue; vb. tr. to grasp, seize, take possession of (ⲙ̄ⲙⲟ⸱); to retain, detain, take or keep captive; to learn by heart; to hold (ⲙ̄ⲙⲟ⸱) liable (for: ⲉ). As n.m. power, possession. ⲁⲧⲁⲙⲁϩⲧⲉ unrestrained, uncontrollable; ⲙⲛ̄ⲧⲁⲧⲁⲙⲁϩⲧⲉ lack of restraint, incontinence. ⲣⲉϥⲁⲙⲁϩⲧⲉ self-controlled person.

ⲁⲙⲉ (pl. ⲁⲙⲏⲩ, ⲁⲙⲏⲩⲉ) n.m. herder, herdsman.

ⲁⲙⲏ n.m. wasp.

ⲁⲙⲛ̄ⲧⲉ n.m. the underworld, Hades.

ⲁⲙⲟⲩ 2nd pers. m.s. imptv. of ⲉⲓ; f.s. ⲁⲙⲏ; pl. ⲁⲙⲏⲓⲛ, ⲁⲙⲏⲉⲓⲧⲛ̄.

ⲁⲙⲣⲉ, ⲁⲙⲣⲏ (pl. ⲁⲙⲣⲏⲩ) n.m. baker; ⲙⲛ̄ⲧⲁⲙⲣⲉ baking.

ⲁⲙⲣⲏϩⲉ, ⲁⲙⲣⲉϩⲉ n.m. bitumen, asphalt.

ⲁⲛ neg. part. not; for uses see Gr. In.

ⲁⲛ- one who is in charge of; only in cpds. with nos.: ⲁⲛⲙⲏⲧ decadarch, ⲁⲛ-ϣⲟ chiliarch, ⲙⲛ̄ⲧⲁⲛ-ϣⲟ chiliarchy.

ⲁⲛ- prefix for forming collective nouns from numbers, as in ⲁⲛ-ϣⲟ (group of) a thousand, ⲁⲛ-ⲧⲁⲓⲟⲩ (group of) 50.

ⲁⲛⲁⲓ vb. intr. to become pleasing, better. As n.m. beauty; ⲣ̄-ⲁⲛⲁⲓ to be(come) pleasing, good. ⲣ̄-ⲁⲛⲁ⸱ to please; see § 20.2 for usage. -ⲁⲛ in ⲥϯ-ⲁⲛ n.m. perfume (cf. ⲥⲧⲟⲓ).

ⲁⲛⲁϣ (pl. ⲁⲛⲁⲩϣ) n.m. oath; used with ⲉⲓⲣⲉ, ⲥⲙⲓⲛⲉ, ⲱⲣⲕ̄, ϯ, ⲧⲁⲣⲕⲟ. ⲉ ⲡⲁⲛⲁϣ under oath.

ⲁⲛⲟⲕ, ⲁⲛⲅ̄- indep. pron. 1st pers. sing.: I.

ⲁⲛⲟⲛ, ⲁⲛ-, ⲁⲛⲛ̄- indep. pron. 1st pers. pl.: we.

ⲁⲛⲟⲩⲣ̄ϣⲉ n.m. watchman, guard (ⲁⲛ + ⲟⲩⲣ̄ϣⲉ).

ⲁⲛⲭⲃⲉ, ⲁⲛⲭⲃ(ⲉⲛ), ⲁⲛⲍⲏⲃⲉ, ⲁⲛⲍⲏⲃ(ⲉⲛ) n.f. school.

ⲁⲛⲧⲁϣ n.m. sneeze.

ⲁⲛⲑⲁⲙ̄, ⲁⲛⲧⲉⲁⲙ̄ n.m. skull.

ⲁⲛϩ̄, ⲟⲛϩ̄ n.m. courtyard.

ⲁⲡⲁ Apa, masc. title of respect or reverence (saints,

martyrs, respected monks, etc.).

ⲁⲡⲁⲥ adj. old; syn. of ⲁⲥ q.v.

ⲁⲡⲉ (pl. ⲁⲡⲏⲩⲉ) n.f. head (lit. and fig.); total sum (of
money), capital; also n.m. chief, village head.
ⲙⲛ̄ⲧⲁⲡⲉ headship. ⲁⲧⲁⲡⲉ headless. ⲣ̄-ⲁⲡⲉ to become
head, leader (of: ⲉ). ϥⲓ-ⲧⲁⲡⲉ to behead.

ⲁⲡⲟⲧ (pl. ⲁⲡⲏⲧ) n.m. cup; ⲥⲁ ⲛ̄ ⲁⲡⲟⲧ cup-maker, cup-seller.

ⲁⲡⲣⲏⲧⲉ n.f. period of time; ⲛ̄ ⲟⲩⲕⲟⲩⲓ ⲛ̄ ⲁⲡⲣⲏⲧⲉ for a little
while; ⲛ̄ ⲟⲩⲛⲟϭ ⲛ̄ ⲁⲡⲣⲏⲧⲉ for a long time; ⲣ̄-ⲟⲩⲛⲟϭ ⲛ̄
ⲁⲡⲣⲏⲧⲉ to spend a long time.

ⲁⲡⲥ̄, ⲏⲡⲥ̄, ⲉⲡⲥ̄ n.f. a number (of), several.

ⲁⲣⲏⲃ, ⲉⲣⲏⲃ, ⲣⲏⲃ n.m. pledge, deposit, guarantee.

ⲁⲣⲏⲩ, ⲍⲁⲣⲏⲩ adv. perhaps.

ⲁⲣⲏⲭⲋ n. end, limit (suff. required, as in ⲁⲣⲏⲭϥ̄ ⲙ̄ ⲡⲕⲁⲍ
the end of the earth; 3rd pers. pl. sometimes -ⲛⲟⲩ);
ⲁⲧⲁⲣⲏⲭⲋ boundless.

ⲁⲣⲓⲕⲉ n.m. fault, blame; ⲁⲧⲁⲣⲓⲕⲉ blameless; ϭⲛ̄-ⲁⲣⲓⲕⲉ to
find fault (with: ⲉ), to blame (ⲉ); ⲣⲉϥϭⲛ̄-ⲁⲣⲓⲕⲉ fault-
finder; ⲙⲛ̄ⲧⲣⲉϥϭⲛ̄-ⲁⲣⲓⲕⲉ criticism.

ⲁⲣⲓⲙ n. name of an edible plant.

ⲁⲣⲟⲟⲩⲉ, ⲁⲣⲱⲟⲩ n.pl. burrs, thistles; ⲥⲣ̄-ⲁⲣⲟⲟⲩⲉ idem.

ⲁⲣⲟϣ to become cold; as n.m. cold, chill.

ⲁⲣϣⲁⲛ n. name of a skin disease.

ⲁⲣϣⲓⲛ n.m. lentils.

ⲁⲥ, ⲁⲁⲥ adj. old (usu. not of people); ⲏⲣⲡ̄ ⲁⲥ, ⲉⲣⲡ-ⲁⲥ old
wine; ⲙⲛ̄ⲧⲁⲥ oldness; ⲣ̄-ⲁⲥ to become old.

ⲁⲥⲁⲓ, Q ⲁⲥⲱⲟⲩ, ⲁⲥⲉⲓⲱⲟⲩ vb. intr. to become light, slight,
casual; to be swift; as n.m. lightness, hastiness,
alleviation. ⲍⲛ̄ ⲟⲩⲁⲥⲁⲓ easily, casually.

ⲁⲥⲏⲣ n.m. one's belongings.

ⲁⲥⲓⲕ, ⲥⲓⲕ n.m. an illness, related to fever, chills.

ⲁⲥⲟⲩ n.f. price, value; †-ⲁⲥⲟⲩ to pay; ⲣ̄-ⲁⲥⲟⲩ ⲍⲁ to set a
price on.

ⲁⲥⲡⲉ n.f. language, speech; ⲁⲥⲡⲉ ⲛ̄ ⲗⲁⲥ idem.

ⲁⲧ- prefix for the formation of negative adj.; §27.1.

ⲁⲧⲟ, ⲁⲧⲁ n. a lot, multitude; usu. with indef. art.; ⲁⲧⲟ ⲛ̄
ⲥⲙⲟⲧ, ⲁⲧⲉ-ⲥⲙⲟⲧ adj. phrase: of various or many sorts.

ⲁⲩ, ⲁⲩⲉ, ⲁⲩⲉⲓⲥ, ⲁⲩⲉⲓ imptv. vb. (1) bring here, give!   All
forms occur prenominally; with pron. suff.: ⲁⲩⲉⲓⲥ⸗.
(2) come! come, let's ...! (with Conjunctive).

ⲁⲩⲁⲛ, ⲁⲩⲁⲁⲛ, ⲁⲩⲉⲓⲛ n.m. color, appearance, complexion;
ⲥⲉⲕ-ⲁⲩⲁⲛ to tend toward (a certain color); ⲁⲩⲁⲛ ⲁⲩⲁⲛ
(of or in) a variety of colors.

ⲁⲩⲉⲓⲛ, ⲁⲩⲁⲛ n.m. (ship's) cargo.

ⲁⲩⲏⲧ n.m. company of people; monastic congregation.

ⲁⲩⲱ conj. and; for uses see Gr. In.

ⲁϣ n.m. furnace, oven.

ⲁϣ interrog. pron. what?   See §§ 14.2, 16.1 for usage.

ⲁϣⲁⲓ, Q ⲟϣ vb. intr. to be(come) many, numerous, to multi-
ply; Q is very frequent.   As n.m. multitude, amount.
ⲣⲉϥⲁϣⲁⲓ one who multiplies.   ⲁϣⲏ n.f. multitude.

ⲁϥ, ⲁⲁϥ, ⲁⲃ n.m. a fly; ⲁϥ ⲛ̄ ⲉⲃⲓⲱ bee; ⲁϥ ⲛ̄ ⲟⲩⲍⲟⲣ dog-fly.

ⲁϥ, ⲁⲁϥ, ⲁⲃ (pl. ⲁϥⲟⲩⲓ, ⲁⲃⲟⲩⲓ) n.m. flesh (human or animal),
piece of flesh, meat.   ⲥⲁ ⲛ̄ ⲁϥ meat-seller.   ϣⲁⲧ-ⲁϥ
butcher.   ⲟⲩⲉⲙ-ⲁϥ to eat meat.   ϣⲉⲡ-ⲁϥ to buy meat.

ⲁⲍⲉ n.m. lifetime, extent of lifetime; ⲣ̄-ⲁⲍⲉ to pass one's
life; ϣⲁⲣ-ⲁⲍⲉ short-lived; ⲣ̄-ϣⲁⲣ-ⲁⲍⲉ (Q ⲟ ⲛ̄ ϣⲁⲣ-ⲁⲍⲉ) to
be short-lived; ⲙⲛ̄ⲧϣⲁⲣ-ⲁⲍⲉ a short life.

ⲁⲍⲉ vb. intr. to be in need (of: ⲛⲁ⸗).

ⲁⲍⲟ (pl. ⲁⲍⲱⲱⲣ) n.m. treasure, treasure house, storehouse.

ⲁⲍⲟⲙ n. only in ⲁϣ-ⲁⲍⲟⲙ to sigh, groan (at: ⲉ, ⲉⲭⲛ̄, ⲉⲍⲣⲁⲓ
ⲉⲭⲛ̄); as n.m. groan, yawn, roar.

ⲁⲍⲣ̄, ⲁⲍⲣⲉ n.m. marsh herbage, sedge.

ⲁⲍⲣⲟ⸗ interrog. adv. requiring anticipatory suff. re-
ferring to subject of clause.   (1) with foll. verb:
why? as in ⲁⲍⲣⲱⲧⲛ̄ ⲧⲉⲧⲛ̄ⲣⲓⲙⲉ why do you weep?   (2) with
suff. alone or with foll. noun: what about ...? what's
the matter with ...?   (3) with ⲙⲛ̄: what has ... to do
with ...?

ⲁⲍⲱⲙ, ⲁⲍⲱⲙⲉ, ⲁⲍⲱⲱⲙⲉ n.m. eagle (originally: falcon).

ⲁⲝⲉ, ⲁⲗⲝⲉ (or ⲟⲩⲁⲝⲉ?) n. blow, cuff.

ⲁⲝⲛ̄, ⲉⲝⲛ̄ (ⲁⲝⲛ̄ⲧ⸗, ⲉⲝⲛ̄ⲧ⸗) prep. without; a foll. indef. n. has no article.

ⲁⲅⲃⲉⲥ, ⲁⲧⲃⲉⲥ n.f. moisture.

ⲁⲅⲟⲗⲧⲉ, ⲁⲕⲟⲗⲧⲉ n.f. wagon, cart.

ⲁⲅⲣⲏⲛ n.f. a barren woman; also adj.; ⲙⲛ̄ⲧⲁⲅⲣⲏⲛ barrenness; ⲣ̄-ⲁⲅⲣⲏⲛ to become barren.

ⲁⲗ⸗: ⲉⲓⲣⲉ	ⲁⲙⲏⲓⲛ: ⲁⲙⲟⲩ	ⲁⲥⲱⲟⲩ: ⲁⲥⲁⲓ
ⲁⲗⲥ: ⲁⲥ	ⲁⲙⲏⲩ(ⲉ): ⲁⲙⲉ	ⲁⲥ2ϥ̄: ⲱ2ⲥ̄
ⲁⲗϥ: ⲁϥ	ⲁⲙⲟⲩ: ⲉⲙⲟⲩ	ⲁⲧⲁ, ⲁⲧⲉ: ⲁⲧⲟ
ⲁⲗⲝⲉ: ⲁⲝⲉ	ⲁⲙⲣⲉ2ⲉ: ⲁⲙⲣⲏ2ⲉ	ⲁⲧⲃⲉⲥ: ⲁⲅⲃⲉⲥ
ⲁⲃ: ⲁϥ	ⲁⲛ-: ⲁⲛⲟⲛ	ⲁⲧⲉⲥⲙⲟⲧ: ⲁⲧⲟ
ⲁⲃⲉⲛ: ⲟⲃⲛ̄	-ⲁⲛ: ⲁⲛⲁⲓ	ⲁⲩⲁⲁⲛ: ⲁⲩⲁⲛ
ⲁⲃⲓⲅⲏⲉⲓⲛ: ⲁⲃⲁⲅⲏⲉⲓⲛ	ⲁⲛⲁ⸗: ⲁⲛⲁⲓ	ⲁⲩⲁⲛ: ⲁⲩⲉⲓⲛ
ⲁⲃⲟⲕ: ⲁⲃⲱⲕ	ⲁⲛⲁⲩ: ⲛⲁⲩ	ⲁⲩⲉ, ⲁⲩⲉⲓ: ⲁⲩ
ⲁⲃⲟⲕⲉ: ⲁⲃⲱⲕ	ⲁⲛⲁⲩϣ: ⲁⲛⲁϣ	ⲁⲩⲉⲓⲛ: ⲁⲩⲁⲛ
ⲁⲃⲟⲟⲕⲉ: ⲁⲃⲱⲕ	ⲁⲛϥ̄-: ⲁⲛⲟⲕ	ⲁⲩⲉⲓⲥ(⸗): ⲁⲩ
ⲁⲃⲟⲟⲩⲉ: ⲁⲃⲱ	ⲁⲛⲅⲓⲛⲉ: ⲅⲓⲛⲉ	ⲁϣ⸗: ⲉⲓϣⲉ
ⲁⲃⲟⲩⲓ: ⲁϥ	ⲁⲛⲍⲏⲃ(ⲅⲛ): ⲁⲛⲭⲏⲃⲉ	ⲁϣⲁⲗ: ⲁⲗ
ⲁⲅⲱ: ⲁⲕⲱ	ⲁⲛⲓ-, ⲁⲛⲓⲛⲉ: ⲅⲓⲛⲉ	ⲁϣⲁ2ⲟⲙ: ⲱϣ, ⲁ2ⲟⲙ
ⲁⲉⲏⲥ, ⲁⲉⲓⲏⲥ: ⲁⲓⲁⲓ	ⲁⲛⲓ⸗: ⲅⲓⲛⲉ	ⲁϣⲉ: ⲉⲓϣⲉ
ⲁⲏⲥ: ⲁⲓⲁⲓ	ⲁⲛⲛ̄-: ⲁⲛⲟⲛ	ⲁϣⲏ: ⲁϣⲁⲓ
ⲁⲕⲉⲥ: ⲁⲕⲏⲥ	ⲁⲛⲭⲓⲣ: ⲝⲓⲣ	ⲁϣⲕⲁⲕ: ϣⲕⲁⲕ
ⲁⲕⲓⲥ: ⲁⲕⲏⲥ	ⲁⲛⲭⲱⲭ: ⲭⲱⲭ	ⲁϣⲧ-/⸗: ⲉⲓϣⲉ
ⲁⲕⲟⲗⲧⲉ: ⲁⲅⲟⲗⲧⲉ	ⲁⲟⲩⲏⲣ: ⲟⲩⲏⲣ	ⲁϥⲉⲅⲉⲉⲛⲉ: ⲁⲃⲁⲅⲏⲉⲓⲛ
ⲁⲗⲁⲩⲉ: ⲁⲗⲱ	ⲁⲟⲩⲱⲛ: ⲟⲩⲱⲛ	ⲁϥⲧⲉ: ϥⲧⲟⲟⲩ
ⲁⲗⲉⲩ, ⲁⲗⲏⲩ: ⲁⲗⲁⲩ	ⲁⲡⲏⲧ: ⲁⲡⲟⲧ	ⲁϥⲟⲩⲓ: ⲁϥ
ⲁⲗⲏⲩ, ⲁⲗⲟ⸗: ⲁⲗⲉ	ⲁⲡⲏⲩⲉ: ⲁⲡⲉ	ⲁ2ⲁ: ⲉ2ⲉ
ⲁⲗⲟ: ⲗⲟ	ⲁⲣⲉ2: 2ⲁⲣⲉ2	ⲁ2ⲉ: ⲉ2ⲉ, ⲱ2ⲉ
ⲁⲗⲟⲕ: ⲗⲟ	ⲁⲣⲟⲟⲩⲉ: ⲣⲟⲟⲩⲉ	ⲁ2ⲉⲣⲁⲧ⸗: ⲱ2ⲉ
ⲁⲗⲟⲟⲩⲉ: ⲁⲗⲱ	ⲁⲣⲟⲟⲩⲉ: ⲁⲗⲱ	ⲁ2ⲱⲙⲉ: ⲁ2ⲱⲙ
ⲁⲗⲟⲩ: ⲁⲗⲱ	ⲁⲣⲱⲟⲩ: ⲁⲣⲟⲟⲩⲉ	ⲁ2ⲱⲣ: ⲁ2ⲟ
ⲁⲗⲱⲧⲛ̄: ⲗⲟ, ⲁⲗⲉ	ⲁⲥ: ⲁⲗⲥ	ⲁⲭⲓ-/⸗: ⲭⲱ
ⲁⲙ-, ⲁⲙⲉ: ⲟⲙⲉ	ⲁⲥⲉⲓⲱⲟⲩ: ⲁⲥⲁⲓ	ⲁⲭⲱ: ⲉⲭⲱ
ⲁⲙⲏ, ⲁⲙⲏⲉⲓⲧⲛ̄: ⲁⲙⲟⲩ	ⲁⲥⲕⲉ: ⲱⲥⲕ̄	

B

ⲃⲁ, ⲃⲁⲉ, ⲃⲁⲉⲓ, ⲃⲟⲓ n.m. branch of date-palm.

ⲃⲁⲁⲃⲉ, ⲃⲁⲃⲱ⸗ (ⲃⲁⲃⲱⲱ⸗) Q ⲃⲁⲃⲟⲧ (ⲃⲁⲃⲱ) vb. tr. to despise (ⲙ̄ⲙⲟ⸗), regard as foolish; intr. to be insipid, foolish.

ⲃⲁ(ⲗ)ⲃⲉ-ⲣⲱⲙⲉ n.m. boaster; ⲙⲛ̄ⲧⲃⲁⲁⲃⲉ-ⲣⲱⲙⲉ boastfulness.

ⲃⲁⲁⲙⲡⲉ, ⲃⲁⲙⲡⲉ n. goat; ⲃⲁⲁⲙⲡⲉ ⲛ̄ 2ⲟⲟⲩⲧ he-goat; ⲃⲁⲁⲙⲡⲉ ⲛ̄ ⲥ2ⲓⲙⲉ she-goat; ϣⲁⲁⲣ ⲛ̄ ⲃⲁⲁⲙⲡⲉ goatskin; ϥⲱ ⲛ̄ ⲃⲁⲁⲙⲡⲉ goat's hair; ⲙⲁⲛⲉ-ⲃⲁⲁⲙⲡⲉ goatherd.

ⲃⲁⲓ, ϥⲁⲓ n.m. night raven, screech-owl.

ⲃⲁⲗ n.m. eye. ⲁⲧⲃⲁⲗ shameless; ⲙⲛⲧⲁⲧⲃⲁⲗ shamelessness.

ⲃⲁⲗⲟⲧ n.f. skin garment; skin bag.

ⲃⲁⲣⲱⲧ, ⲃⲁⲣⲟⲧ, ⲃⲁⲗⲱⲧ, ⲃⲁⲣⲁⲧⲉ n.m. brass, bronze; ϩⲟⲙⲛ̅ⲧ (ⲛ̅) ⲃⲁⲣⲱⲧ idem or sim.

ⲃⲁⲥⲛ̅ⲅ, ⲃⲁⲥⲉⲛⲅ, ⲃⲁⲥⲛ̅ⲅ, ⲃⲁⲥⲛⲅ, ⲃⲁⲥⲓⲅ, ⲃⲁⲥⲓⲛⲅ n.m. tin.

ⲃⲁϣⲟⲣ, ⲃⲁϣⲁⲣ, ⲃⲁϣⲁⲁⲣ, ⲃⲁϣⲟⲟⲣⲉ n.f. fox.

ⲃⲁϣⲟⲩⲣ n.f. saw; ⲣⲁ ⲛ̅ ⲃⲁϣⲟⲩⲣ adj. saw-toothed.

ⲃⲁϣⲟⲩϣ n.m. rue.

ⲃⲁϩⲥⲉ n.f. heifer.

ⲃⲉⲉⲃⲉ (ⲃⲉⲃⲉ) vb. tr. to pour forth, rain down (ⲙ̅ⲙⲟ⸗); intr. to well up, be poured forth.

ⲃⲉⲕⲉ (pl. ⲃⲉⲕⲏⲩⲉ, ⲃⲉⲕⲉⲉⲩⲉ, ⲃⲉⲕⲉⲩⲉ) n.m. wages; ϯ-ⲃⲉⲕⲉ, ϯ ⲙ̅ ⲡⲃⲉⲕⲉ to pay, reward; ⲧⲁⲓ-ⲃⲉⲕⲉ employer; ⲣⲉϥϯ-ⲃⲉⲕⲉ idem. ϫⲓ-ⲃⲉⲕⲉ, ϫⲓ ⲙ̅ ⲡⲃⲉⲕⲉ to receive wages; ϫⲓ ⲉ ⲃⲉⲕⲉ to hire (ⲙ̅ⲙⲟ⸗); ϫⲁⲓ-ⲃⲉⲕⲉ hireling. ⲥⲙⲛ̅-ⲃⲉⲕⲉ to fix wages. ⲣⲙ̅ⲃⲉⲕⲉ, ⲣⲙ̅ⲙⲃⲉⲕⲉ hireling.

ⲃⲉⲛⲓⲡⲉ, ⲃⲓⲛⲓⲃⲉ, ⲡⲉⲛⲓⲡⲉ, ⲃⲁⲛⲓⲡⲉ, ⲡⲁⲛⲓⲡ n.m. iron; also fig. of fetters, sword. ϯ-ⲃⲉⲛⲓⲡⲉ to put in irons, to fetter (ⲉ). ϫⲓ-ⲃⲉⲛⲓⲡⲉ to be put in irons.

ⲃⲉⲣⲱ n.f. whirlpool.

ⲃⲉⲥⲛⲏⲧ, ⲃⲉⲥⲛⲁⲧ (pl. ⲃⲉⲥⲛⲁⲧⲉ) n.m. smith; ⲙⲛ̅ⲧⲃⲉⲥⲛⲏⲧ the work or craft of a smith.

ⲃⲏ n.f. grave.

ⲃⲏⲃ, ⲃⲏⲃⲉ n.m. cave, hole, den, nest (of animals).

ⲃⲏⲕⲉ n.m. woof (of loom).

ⲃⲏⲛⲉ, ⲃⲏⲛⲛⲉ n.f. swallow (bird); ϫⲁϫ-ⲃⲏⲛⲉ swallow-sparrow.

ⲃⲏⲥⲉ n.f. bucket, pail.

ⲃⲏⲧ n.m. palm-leaf. ⲃⲏⲧ-ⲥⲡⲓⲣ n.f. rib.

ⲃⲏⲅ, ⲃⲉⲅ, ⲃⲟ̄ n.m. falcon.

ⲃⲓⲣ (pl. ⲃⲣⲏⲟⲩⲉ) n.m. basket (of palm-leaf). ⲃⲓⲣⲉ, ⲃⲁⲓⲣⲉ n.f. idem.

ⲃⲗ̄ⲃⲓⲗⲉ n.f. a single grain (of grain, mustard, sand); a single piece (of fruit, etc.).

ⲃⲗ̄ⲗⲉ (f. ⲃⲗ̄ⲗⲏ; pl. ⲃⲗ̄ⲗⲉⲉⲩ, ⲃⲗ̄ⲗⲉⲉⲩⲉ) adj. blind; as n. a blind person; ⲙⲛ̅ⲧⲃⲗ̄ⲗⲉ blindness; ⲣ̄-ⲃⲗ̄ⲗⲉ to become blind

(Q o ⲛ̄ ⲃⲗ̄ⲗⲉ), to make blind.

ⲃⲗ2ⲙⲟⲩ (pl. ⲃⲗ2ⲙⲟⲟⲩⲉ) name of a people (Gk. Βλέμυες); usu. located on east bank of Nile in Nubia. Other spellings include ⲃⲗⲉ2ⲙⲟⲩ, ⲃⲉⲗⲉ2ⲙⲟⲟⲩⲉ, ⲃⲁⲗⲉ2ⲙⲟⲩ.

ⲃⲗ̄ⲭⲉ, ⲃⲗ̄ⲗⲭⲉ n.m.f. pottery, earthenware; ⲣ̄-ⲃⲗ̄ⲭⲉ to be made of clay.

ⲃⲛ̄ⲛⲉ n.f. date-palm, date(s); ⲃⲛ̄-ⲡⲁⲩⲛⲉ virgin palm; ⲃⲛ̄-ϣⲟⲟⲩⲉ dried dates; ⲃⲁ ⲛ̄ ⲃⲛ̄ⲛⲉ palm-branch; ⲃⲁⲗ ⲛ̄ ⲃⲛ̄ⲛⲉ date-stone; ⲉⲃⲓⲱ ⲛ̄ ⲃⲛ̄ⲛⲉ date-honey; ⲕⲁϥ ⲛ̄ ⲃⲛ̄ⲛⲉ stem, trunk of palm; ⲗⲟⲟⲩ ⲛ̄ ⲃⲛ̄ⲛⲉ cluster of dates; ⲥⲁ ⲛ̄ ⲃⲛ̄ⲛⲉ date-seller; ⲥⲣ̄-ⲃⲛ̄ⲛⲉ date-palm thorn; ⲧⲁⲋ ⲛ̄ ⲃⲛ̄ⲛⲉ date cake; ϣⲛ̄-ⲃⲛ̄ⲛⲉ, ϣⲉ-ⲃⲛ̄ⲛⲉ, ϣⲉ̄-ⲃⲛ̄ⲛⲉ, ⲥⲟⲩⲛ-ⲃⲛ̄ⲛⲉ palm-fiber.

ⲃⲟⲓⲛⲉ n. harp or sim. musical instrument.

ⲃⲟⲗⲃⲗ̄ ⲃⲗ̄ⲃⲱⲗᵉ (p.c. ⲃⲁⲗⲃⲗ̄-) vb. tr. to dig, dig up, dig out (ⲙ̄ⲙⲟᵉ); to burrow, delve; vb. intr. to be undermined. ⲃⲟⲗⲃⲗ̄ ⲉⲃⲟⲗ vb. tr. to undo, take apart; intr. to be dug up, out.

ⲃⲟⲛⲧⲉ, ⲃⲁⲛⲧⲉ (ⲃⲛ̄ⲧ-) n.f. gourd, cucumber; gourd-garden(?); ⲥⲁⲣⲃⲟⲛⲧⲉ gourd-seller. ⲃⲛ̄ⲧ-ⲛ̄-ⲉⲉⲗⲟ6 pumpkin.

ⲃⲟⲥⲧ̄ Q to be dry, parched.

ⲃⲟⲩⲃⲟⲩ vb. intr. to shine, glitter; as n.m. shine, glitter.

ⲃⲟⲩ2ⲉ, ⲃⲱ2ⲉ n.m. eyelid.

ⲃⲣ̄ⲃⲣ̄ vb. intr. to boil; ⲃⲣ̄ⲃⲣ̄ ⲉ2ⲣⲁⲓ ⲙ̄ⲙⲟᵉ to boil up with, cast up; as n.m. boiling.

ⲃⲣⲉϣⲏⲩ, ⲃⲉⲣⲉϣⲏⲩ, ⲃⲣ̄ϣⲏⲩ n.m. coriander seed.

ⲃⲣ̄ⲣⲉ, ⲃⲏⲣⲉ adj. new, young; ⲙⲛ̄ⲧⲃⲣ̄ⲣⲉ youth, newness; ⲛ̄ ⲃⲣ̄ⲣⲉ adv. anew, recently; ⲣ̄-ⲃⲣ̄ⲣⲉ to renew; to become new.

ⲃⲣ̄6ⲟⲟⲩⲧ, ⲃⲉⲣⲉ6ⲱⲟⲩⲧ n.f. chariot.

ⲃⲱ n.f. tree (when fruit is specified; otherwise use ϣⲏⲛ).

ⲃⲱⲕ, Q ⲃⲏⲕ vb. intr. to go, depart; to die; to be about to (+ ⲉ + Inf.). Used with most prep. and directional adv. in regular senses. Note ⲃⲱⲕ ⲉⲣⲁⲧᵉ to visit; ⲃⲱⲕ 2ⲓ to undergo (as well as "to go upon").

ⲃⲱⲕⲉ vb. tr. to tan (leather: ⲙ̄ⲙⲟᵉ); ⲃⲁⲕ-ϣⲁⲁⲣ tanner.

ⲃⲱⲗ ⲃⲉⲗ- ⲃⲟⲗᵉ Q ⲃⲏⲗ (± ⲉⲃⲟⲗ except when indicated) vb. tr.

to loosen, untie, unfasten (ⲙ̄ⲙⲟ⁶); (not + ⲉⲃⲟⲗ) to explain, interpret; to weaken, enfeeble; to nullify; to dissolve. Vb. intr. to be(come) loosened, undone, loose, scattered, melted, dissolved, weakened, paralysed, faint; to become dissolute; to be terminated, to die, perish. As n.m. solution, interpretation (not + ⲉⲃⲟⲗ); weakening, slackening; laxness, unrestraint; dissolution, destruction. ⲃⲱⲗ ⲙ̄ⲛ̄ to come to terms with. ⲁⲧⲃⲱⲗ ⲉⲃⲟⲗ indissoluble, unending. ⲣⲉϥⲃⲱⲗ interpreter.

ⲃⲟⲗ n.m. the outside. ⲛⲃⲟⲗ, ⲛ̄ ⲛⲃⲟⲗ prep. on or to the outside of, outside; independent of, beyond, free from; contrary to. ⲉⲃⲟⲗ adv. out, outward, away; usu. with verbs, but occasionally after prep. phrases with sense: onward, and so on, henceforth; for ⲉⲃⲟⲗ + prep. see sub prep. ⲉⲃⲟⲗ ϫⲉ conj. because. ⲛ̄ ⲃⲟⲗ adj. phr. outer, external; adv. outside, extant, in existence. ⲥⲁⲃⲟⲗ, ⲥⲁ ⲛ̄ ⲃⲟⲗ, ⲛ̄ ⲥⲁⲃⲟⲗ, ⲛ̄ ⲥⲁ ⲛ̄ ⲃⲟⲗ, ⲙ̄ ⲛⲥⲁ ⲛ̄ ⲃⲟⲗ (1) prep. (+ ⲛ̄, ⲉ) outside of, beyond, away from; (2) adv. outside, on the outside. ϣⲁⲃⲟⲗ (1) prep. (+ ⲛ̄) to the outside of; (2) adv. to the end, forever, finally, utterly. ϩⲁⲃⲟⲗ ⲛ̄ prep. from, away from. ϩⲓⲃⲟⲗ (1) adv. outside, on the outside, from the outside; (2) prep. (ⲛ̄) outside of, beyond, except for; ⲉⲧ ϩⲓⲃⲟⲗ adj. phr. external. ⲡ̄-ⲃⲟⲗ, ⲡ̄-ⲛⲃⲟⲗ vb. intr. to avoid, escape (from: ⲉ, ⲛ̄, ϩⲛ̄). ⲕⲁ-ⲃⲟⲗ vb. tr. to vomit (ⲙ̄ⲙⲟ⁶).

ⲛ̄ ⲥⲁⲃⲏⲗ ⲉ/ⲛ̄ (1) prep. except for, outside of; (2) conj. except that (+ Conj.). ⲛ̄ ⲥⲁⲃⲏⲗ ϫⲉ except that, unless, if not. ⲛ̄ⲃⲗ̄ (ⲛ̄ⲃⲗ̄ⲗⲁ⁶) prep. (± ⲛ̄) without, except for, beyond.

ⲃⲱⲱⲛ adj. bad, mainly in fixed expressions such as ⲥϯ̄-ⲃⲱⲱⲛ (ⲥⲧⲟⲓ), ⲥⲟⲩ-ⲃⲱⲱⲛ (ⲥⲓⲟⲩ), ϣⲡ̄-ⲃⲱⲱⲛ (ϣⲏⲣⲉ), ϭⲁⲩⲟⲛ ⲃⲱⲱⲛ. ⲃⲟⲟⲛⲉ n.f. evil, misfortune; ⲡ̄-ⲃⲟⲟⲛⲉ to act badly, evilly (toward: ⲛⲁ⁶); ⲙ̄ⲛ̄ⲧⲣⲉϥⲡ̄-ⲃⲟⲟⲛⲉ evil-doing. ⲉⲓⲉⲣ-ⲃⲟⲟⲛⲉ (1) the evil-eye; (2) adj. envious, greedy; ⲙ̄ⲛ̄ⲧⲉⲓⲉⲣ-ⲃⲟⲟⲛⲉ envy, greed; ⲡ̄-ⲉⲓⲉⲣ-ⲃⲟⲟⲛⲉ to become

envious of (ⲉ, ⲉⲝⲛ̅); ⲣⲉϥⲉⲓⲉⲣ-ⲃⲟⲟⲛⲉ enchanter, one who
casts evil-eye; ⲙⲛ̅ⲧⲣⲉϥⲉⲓⲉⲣ-ⲃⲟⲟⲛⲉ greed; ⲭⲓ-ⲉⲓⲉⲣ-ⲃⲟⲟⲛⲉ
to receive the evil-eye.

ⲃⲱⲱⲣⲉ ⲃⲉⲉⲣⲉ- ⲃⲟⲟⲣ⸌ Q ⲃⲟⲟⲣⲉ vb. tr. to push, drive (ⲙ̅ⲙⲟ⸌);
to repel (ⲛ̅ⲥⲁ); to prevail over, defeat (ⲙ̅ⲙⲟ⸌); intr.
(+ ⲉⲃⲟⲗ) to swell up, protrude. As n.m. protuberance.

ⲃⲱⲧⲉ (ϥⲱⲧⲉ ϥⲱ6ⲉ) ⲃⲉⲧ- (ⲃⲟⲧ- ⲃⲟⲟⲧ-) Q ⲃⲏⲧ vb. tr. to pollute
(ⲙ̅ⲙⲟ⸌), befoul; to abominate. ⲃⲟⲧⲉ n.f.(m.) abomination; ⲣ̅-ⲃⲟⲧⲉ (Q ⲟ ⲛ̅ ⲃⲟⲧⲉ) to become hateful; ⲭⲓ-ⲃⲟⲧⲉ to
loathe, abominate (ⲉ).

ⲃⲱϣ ⲃⲉϣ- ⲃⲟϣ⸌ (ⲃⲁϣ⸌) Q ⲃⲏϣ vb. tr. to strip, divest, flay
(ⲙ̅ⲙⲟ⸌); to lay bare, unsheathe; to loosen, unfasten,
undo, release; to despoil; to forsake; intr. to be undone, loosened; Q to be naked. ⲣⲉϥⲃⲱϣ robber, despoiler.

(ⲃⲱϩ) ⲃⲉϩ- (ⲛⲉϩ-) Q ⲃⲏϩ vb. tr. to bow (the head).

(ⲃⲱϩⲛ̅) ⲃⲉϩⲛ̅- Q ⲃⲁϩⲛ̅ vb. tr. to roof over (ⲙ̅ⲙⲟ⸌), cover with
awning. ⲃⲱϩⲛ̅, ⲃⲁϩⲛ̅ n.m. canopy, awning.

ⲃⲁⲃⲉ-: ⲃⲁⲁⲃⲉ	ⲃⲉⲧ-: ⲃⲱⲧⲉ	ⲃⲟⲧⲉ: ϥⲱⲧⲉ
ⲃⲁⲃⲟⲧ: ⲃⲁⲁⲃⲉ	ⲃⲉ6: ⲃⲏ6	ⲃⲟ6ⲥ̅: ϥⲱ6ⲉ
ⲃⲁⲃⲱ, ⲃⲁⲃⲱⲱ⸌: ⲃⲁⲁⲃⲉ	ⲃⲏⲛⲛⲉ: ⲃⲛ̅ⲛⲉ	ⲃⲣⲁ: ⲉⲃⲣⲁ
ⲃⲁⲉ, ⲃⲁⲉⲓ: ⲃⲁ	ⲃⲏⲣⲉ: ⲃⲣ̅ⲣⲉ	ⲃⲣ̅ⲃⲟⲣⲧ̅: 2ⲃⲟⲣⲃⲣ̅
ⲃⲁⲓⲣⲉ: ⲃⲓⲣ	ⲃⲏⲧ: ⲃⲱⲧⲉ	ⲃⲣ̅ⲃⲱⲣ: 2ⲃⲟⲣⲃⲣ̅
ⲃⲁⲕ-: ⲃⲱⲕⲉ	ⲃⲏ6: ϥⲱ6ⲉ	ⲃⲣⲉ-: ⲉⲃⲣⲁ
ⲃⲁⲗⲃⲗ̅: ⲃⲟⲗⲃⲗ̅	ⲃⲓⲛⲉ: ⲃⲏⲛⲉ	ⲃⲣⲏⲩⲉ: ⲉⲃⲣⲁ
ⲃⲁⲗⲱⲧ: ⲃⲁⲣⲱⲧ	ⲃⲓⲛⲓⲃⲉ: ⲃⲉⲛⲓⲛⲉ	ⲃⲣⲓ-: ⲉⲃⲣⲁ
ⲃⲁⲛⲓⲛⲉ: ⲃⲉⲛⲓⲛⲉ	ⲃⲓⲣⲉ: ⲃⲓⲣ	ⲃⲣⲏⲟⲩⲉ: ⲃⲓⲣ
ⲃⲁⲛⲧⲉ: ⲃⲟⲛⲧⲉ	ⲃⲁⲗⲭⲉ: ⲃⲁⲭⲉ	ⲃⲣⲏ6ⲉ: ⲉⲃⲣⲏ6ⲉ
ⲃⲁⲣⲁⲧⲉ: ⲃⲁⲣⲱⲧ	ⲃⲛ̅-: ⲃⲛ̅ⲛⲉ	ⲃⲣ̅ϣⲏⲩ: ⲃⲣⲉϣⲏⲩ
ⲃⲁⲣⲟⲧ: ⲃⲁⲣⲱⲧ	ⲃⲛ̅ⲧ-: ⲃⲟⲛⲧⲉ	ⲃⲧⲟⲟⲩ: ϥⲧⲟⲟⲩ
ⲃⲁϣ⸌: ⲃⲱϣ	ⲃⲛ̅ⲧ: ϥⲛ̅ⲧ	ⲃⲱ: ϥⲱ
ⲃⲁϣⲁⲁⲣ: ⲃⲁϣⲟⲣ	ⲃⲟⲓ: ⲃⲁ	ⲃⲱⲧⲉ: ϥⲱⲧⲉ
ⲃⲁϣⲁⲣ: ⲃⲁϣⲟⲣ	ⲃⲟⲗ: ⲃⲱⲗ	ⲃⲱ2ⲉ: ⲃⲟⲩ2ⲉ
ⲃⲁ2ⲛ̅: ⲃⲱ2ⲛ̅	ⲃⲟ: ϥⲟ	ⲃⲱ6ⲉ: ϥⲱ6ⲉ
ⲃ̅ⲃⲣⲏ6ⲉ: ⲉⲃⲣⲏ6ⲉ	ⲃⲟⲟ: ϥⲟ	ⲃⲱ6ⲥ̅: ϥⲱ6ⲥ̅
ⲃⲉⲃⲉ: ⲃⲉⲉⲃⲉ	ⲃⲟⲟⲛⲉ: ⲃⲱⲱⲛ	ⲃ6̅: ⲃⲏ6
ⲃⲉⲉⲣⲉ-: ⲃⲱⲱⲣⲉ	ⲃⲟⲟⲣ(⸌): ⲃⲱⲱⲣⲉ	
ⲃⲉⲕⲉ(ⲉ)ⲩⲉ: ⲃⲉⲕⲉ	ⲃⲟⲟⲧ-: ⲃⲱⲧⲉ	
ⲃⲉⲕⲏⲩⲉ: ⲃⲉⲕⲉ	ⲃⲟⲣⲃⲣ̅: 2ⲃⲟⲣⲃⲣ̅	ⲅⲛ̅⸌: 6ⲓⲛⲉ
ⲃⲉⲣⲉϣⲏⲩⲉ: ⲃⲣⲉϣⲏⲩ	ⲃⲟⲧ-: ⲃⲱⲧⲉ	ⲅⲣⲟⲙⲡⲉ: 6ⲣⲟⲟⲙⲡⲉ
ⲃⲉⲣⲉ6ⲱⲟⲩⲧ: ⲃⲣ̅6ⲟⲟⲩⲧ	ⲃⲟⲧⲉ: ⲃⲱⲧⲉ	ⲅⲱ: ⲁⲕⲱ

ⲉ

ⲉ (ⲉⲣⲟ⸗) prep. (1) reference: to, for, as regards, in respect to; (2) purpose: for, as; + Inf. in order to; (3) direction: to, toward, into; (4) hostility: at, against; (5) debt: against, due from; (6) ethical dative with many verbal expressions (cf. §30.6); (7) comparison: than (cf. §29.3); (8) temporal: at, in; (9) other meanings in combination with individual verbs, e.g. direct object, instrument, separation.

ⲉⲃⲏ n. darkness, only in ⲣ̄-ⲉⲃⲏ to grow dark.

ⲉⲃⲓⲏⲛ adj. poor, wretched; ⲙⲛ̄ⲧⲉⲃⲓⲏⲛ misery, wretchedness; ⲣ̄-ⲉⲃⲓⲏⲛ to become wretched.

ⲉⲃⲓⲱ (ⲉⲃⲓⲉ-) n.m. honey; ⲉⲃⲓⲱ ⲙ̄ ⲙⲉ pure honey; ⲉⲃⲓⲉ-ϩⲟⲟⲩⲧ wild honey; ⲙⲁ ⲛ̄ ⲉⲃⲓⲱ honey grove.

ⲉⲃⲟⲧ (pl. ⲉⲃⲁⲧⲉ, ⲉⲃⲉⲧⲉ) n.m. month; may be followed directly by month name without ⲛ̄. ϩⲣ̄-ⲉⲃⲟⲧ every month.

ⲉⲃⲣⲁ, ⲃⲣⲁ (ⲃⲣⲉ-, ⲃⲣⲓ-; pl. ⲉⲃⲣⲏⲩⲉ, ⲃⲣⲏⲩⲉ, ⲃⲣⲏⲏⲩⲉ) n.m. seed; ⲉⲃⲣⲁ-ⲥⲱϣⲉ n.f. seed-grain.

ⲉⲃⲣⲏϭⲉ, ⲃ̄ⲃⲣⲏϭⲉ, ⲉϥⲣⲏϭⲉ, ⲃⲣⲏϭⲉ n.f. lightning; ϯ-ⲉⲃⲣⲏϭⲉ to lightning.

ⲉⲕⲓⲃⲉ, ⲕⲓⲃⲉ, ⲕⲓⲉⲃⲉ n.f. breast; ⲛⲉⲣⲕⲓⲃⲉ n.f.m. idem; ϯ-ⲉⲕⲓⲃⲉ to suckle; ϫⲓ-ⲉⲕⲓⲃⲉ to be suckled.

ⲉⲗⲕⲱ, ⲉⲗⲕⲟ n.m. fruit of sycamore.

ⲉⲗⲟⲟⲗⲉ (ⲉⲗⲉⲗ-, ⲗⲉⲗ-, ⲗⲉⲉⲗ-, ⲗⲓⲗ-) (1) n.m. grape, grape-vine; ⲉⲗⲉⲗ-ϩⲙ̄ϫ sour grapes; ⲉⲗⲉⲗ-ϣⲟⲟⲩⲉ dried grapes, raisins; ⲃⲱ ⲛ̄ ⲉⲗⲟⲟⲗⲉ grape-vine; ⲙⲁ ⲛ̄ ⲉⲗⲟⲟⲗⲉ vineyard; ⲉⲓⲉϩ-ⲉⲗⲟⲟⲗⲉ idem; ⲉⲗⲉⲗ-ⲕⲏⲙⲉ n.m. bruise. (2) n.f. tonsil (?); pupil of eye (but cf. ⲗⲟⲟⲩⲉ).

ⲉⲗϭⲱⲃ n.m. heron.

ⲉⲙⲉ n.f. hoe, plow.

ⲉⲙⲏⲣⲉ n.f. inundation (of the Nile).

ⲉⲙⲛϣ n.m. anvil.

ⲉⲙⲓⲥⲉ n.m. dill, anise.

ⲉⲙⲛ̄ⲧ, ⲉⲓⲙⲛ̄ⲧ, ⲉⲙⲛ̄ⲧⲉ n.m. the west.

ⲉⲙⲟⲩ, ⲁⲙⲟⲩ (pl. ⲉⲙⲟⲟⲩⲉ) n.f. cat.

ⲉⲛⲉ, ⲛⲉ, ⲉⲛ interrog. part.; see §29.1.

ⲉⲛⲉ conditional part. if; see §29.1.

ⲉⲛⲉⲍ, ⲉⲛⲉⲍⲉ, ⲉⲛⲏⲍⲉ (1) n.m. eternity, age, era; (2) adj.
eternal; (3) adv. forever (with neg.: never). ϣⲁ ⲉⲛⲉⲍ
(1) adv. forever (neg.: never); (2) eternity; (3) adj.
eternal (ⲛ̄ ϣⲁ ⲉⲛⲉⲍ, ⲛ̄ⲛ̄ ϣⲁ ⲉⲛⲉⲍ). ϣⲁ ⲛⲓⲉⲛⲉⲍ adv. forever. ϣⲁ ⲉⲛⲉⲍ ⲛ̄ ⲟⲩⲟⲉⲓϣ idem. ϫⲓⲛ ⲉⲛⲉⲍ from of old.

ⲉⲛⲍ̄, ⲛ̄ⲍ n. eyebrow. ⲙ̄ⲭⲛ̄ⲍ, ⲉⲙⲭⲛ̄ⲍ n.m. idem.

ⲉⲟⲟⲩ n.m. glory, honor; ⲍⲁ ⲉⲟⲟⲩ adj. phrase: honorable,
glorious. ϯ-ⲉⲟⲟⲩ to glorify, give honor to (ⲛⲁ⸗); as
n.m. glorifying; ⲙⲛ̄ⲧⲣⲉϥϯ-ⲉⲟⲟⲩ glorification. ϫⲓ-ⲉⲟⲟⲩ
to be glorified. ⲙⲁⲓ-ⲉⲟⲟⲩ desirous of glory.

ⲉⲡⲏⲡ, ⲉⲡⲉⲓⲡ, ⲉⲡⲏⲫ name of 11th Coptic month.

ⲉⲡⲣⲁ n.pl. vanities; as adj. vain; as adv. in vain; ⲙⲛ̄ⲧ-
ⲉⲡⲣⲁ vanity.

ⲉⲡⲱ n.f. part of door fastening.

ⲉⲣⲏⲧ (ⲣⲏⲧ, ⲉⲣⲣⲏⲧ, ⲣ̄ⲣⲏⲧ) vb. tr. to vow, promise, devote
(ⲙ̄ⲙⲟ⸗; to: ⲛⲁ⸗, ⲉ); as n.m. (pl. ⲉⲣⲁⲧⲉ) vow, promise.

ⲉⲣⲏⲩ n.m.f. fellow, companion; usu. with possessive prefixes as a recipr. pron.: each other, mutually. See 28.4.

ⲉⲣⲱⲧⲉ n.m.f. milk; ⲣ̄-ⲉⲣⲱⲧⲉ to give milk; ϯ-ⲉⲣⲱⲧⲉ ⲛⲁ⸗ to
suckle; ⲟⲩⲉⲙ-ⲉⲣⲱⲧⲉ to feed on milk; ⲍⲁ ⲡⲉⲣⲱⲧⲉ still
sucking, not weaned.

ⲉⲥⲏⲧ n.m. ground, bottom, lower part; ⲉⲡⲉⲥⲏⲧ adv. down,
downward, to the ground; ⲉⲡⲉⲥⲏⲧ ⲉ prep. down to, down
into; ⲛ̄ ⲡⲉⲥⲏⲧ adv. below, down below, at the bottom of
(ⲙ̄ⲙⲟ⸗); ⲥⲁ-ⲡⲉⲥⲏⲧ adv. on the lower side, below; as prep.
(+ ⲛ̄). ⲍⲁ ⲡⲉⲥⲏⲧ adv. underneath, below ground; prep.
(+ ⲛ̄) under. ⲍⲓ ⲡⲉⲥⲏⲧ adv. on the ground, from on the
ground. ϫⲓⲛ ⲡⲉⲥⲏⲧ adv. from below. ⲣ̄-ⲡⲉⲥⲏⲧ to go
under (ⲛ̄).

ⲉⲥⲟⲟⲩ n.m. (f. ⲉⲥⲱ) sheep; ⲙⲁⲛ-ⲉⲥⲟⲟⲩ shepherd.

ⲉⲧ, ⲉⲧⲉ rel. pron.; see Gr. In.

ⲉⲧⲃⲉ (ⲉⲧⲃⲏⲏⲧ⸗) prep. because of, on account of; concerning,
about; for the sake of. ⲉⲧⲃⲉ ϫⲉ conj. because. ⲉⲧⲃⲉ
ⲡⲁⲓ adv. therefore. ⲉⲧⲃⲉ ⲟⲩ adv. why?

ετο2, ετλ2 n.m. garment or length of cloth.

εγω, εογω, ογω n.f. pledge, surety; † Ⲙ̄Ⲙⲟ⸗ Ⲛ̄ εγω to give as a pledge; ογω2 Ⲙ̄Ⲙⲟ⸗ Ⲛ̄ εγω to deposit as a pledge; κω Ⲙ̄Ⲙⲟ⸗ Ⲛ̄ εγω idem; χι Ⲙ̄Ⲙⲟ⸗ Ⲛ̄ εγω to take as a pledge.

εϣω, εϣο, ϣογ, εϣογ (pl. εϣλγ, ϣλγ) n.f. sow.

εϣχε, εϣχπε (1) conj. if (§29.1); (2) as if, as it were; (3) exclam. how! (4) adv. surely, indeed; (5) before apodosis: then.

ε2ε, 2ε, λ2ε, λ2λ part. yes; indeed, verily; also used to introduce questions. εϣχε/εϣωπε ε2ε if indeed, if so.

ε2ε (pl. ε2οογ, ε2ηγ, ε2εγ) n.f.m. ox, cow.

εχω, λχω n.f. tongs, pincers.

ε6ωϣ (f. ε6οοϣε, ε6οϣε; pl. ε6οοϣ, ε6οοϣε, ε6ωϣε, ε6λλϣ) n.m. a Nubian, Cushite, Ethiopian.

εβλτε: εβοτ	εⲛε⁻: ωⲛε	εⲥⲱ: εⲥⲟⲟγ
εβετε: εβοτ	εⲛн26: εⲛε2	εⲧ: ωω
εβιε⁻: εβιω	εⲛογⲛⲦ̄: εⲛⲦ̄	εⲧλ2: εⲧⲟ2
εβολ: βωλ	εⲛⲧλιⲣ: ⲛογⲧε	εⲧε: εⲧ
εβⲣнγε: εβⲣλ	εⲛⲧнⲣ: ⲛογⲧε	εⲧβннⲦ⸗: εⲧβε
εβⲦ⁻: ωqⲦ	εοογ: ειω	εⲧⲚ̄: ⲧωⲣε
εβω: Ⲙ̄ⲡο	εογ: ειω	εⲧοοⲦ⸗: ⲧωⲣε
εβϣε: ωβϣ̄	εογω: εγω	εⲧογⲚ̄⁻: ⲧογω⸗
εεβⲧ: ειεβⲦ	επειⲛ: επнⲡ	εⲧογⲱ⸗: ⲧογⲱ⸗
εειβⲧ: ειεβⲦ	επεⲥнⲧ: εⲥнⲧ	εⲧⲡε: ⲡε
εειε: ειε	επιⲧⲚ̄: ειⲧⲚ̄	εⲧⲡω: ωⲧⲡ̄
εειογλ: ειογλ	επογϣλⲡ: ογϣλⲡ	εⲧⲣιⲙ: ⲧⲣιⲙ
εειω: ειω	επⲥ̄: λⲡⲥ̄	εωογ: ειω
εεⲧ: ωω	εⲣ⁻: ειⲣε	εϣλⲧε: ϣωⲧ
εκλⲧε: κωⲧ	εⲣλⲧ⸗: ⲣλⲧ⸗	εϣλγ: εϣω
εκοⲧε: κωⲧ	εⲣλⲧε: εⲣнⲧ	εϣο: εϣω
εκωⲧ: κωⲧ	εⲣβε: ωⲣβ̄	εϣοⲧε: ϣωⲧ
ελελ⁻: ελοολε	εⲣβⲧ: ⲣ̄βⲦ	εϣογ: εϣω
ελοογε: λλω	εⲣε2: 2λⲣε2	εϣⲦ⸗: ειϣε
ελοο2ε: λιλοο2ε	εⲣнβ: λⲣнβ	εϣωⲡε: ϣωⲡε
ελω: λλω	εⲣн2: 2λⲣε2	εϣωⲧ: ϣωⲧ
εⲙλⲧε: ⲙλⲧε	εⲣⲚ̄: ⲣο	εϣⲧεκο: ϣⲧεκο
εⲙλγ: Ⲙ̄ⲙλγ	εⲣο⸗: ε	εϣϣε: ϣϣε
εⲙλϣο: ⲙλϣο	εⲣο: ⲣ̄ⲣο	εϣⲭⲡε: εϣⲭε
εⲙοογε: εⲙογ	εⲣⲡⲚ̄⁻: нⲣⲡ	εq⁻: ωqε
εⲙⲡⲣω: Ⲙ̄ⲣω	εⲣⲣнⲧ: εⲣнⲧ	εqⲣλ: εβⲣλ
εⲙⲥε: ωⲘⲥ̄	εⲣⲧοq: ⲣ̄ⲧοβ	εqⲣн6ε: εβⲣн6ε
εⲙⲭⲚ̄2: εⲛ2̄	εⲣω⸗: ⲣο	ε26γ: ε2ε
εⲛ: εⲛε	εⲣω, εⲣωογ: ⲣ̄ⲣο	ε2н: 2н
εⲛ⁻: ειⲛε	εⲥ: ειⲥ	ε2нγ: ε2ε

222

ε₂ιειβ: ₂ιειβ	ε₂ρπ̄: ₂ο	εχΗ: χοε
ε₂κο: ₂κο	ε₂το: ₂το	εχΗγ: χοι
ε₂Νλˢ: ₂Νλˢ	ε₂τωωρ: ₂το	ε₆λλϣ: ε₆ωϣ
ε₂Νε-: ₂Νε-	ε₂θλι: ₂τλι	ε₆λο₆: ₆λο₆
ε₂οογ: ε₂ε	εχ̄Ν̄: λχ̄Ν̄	ε₆οοϣ: ε₆ωϣ
ε₂οογτ: ₂οογτ	εχ̄Ν̄, εχωˢ: χωˢ	ε₆οοϣε: ε₆ωϣ
ε₂ρλˢ: ₂ο	εχ̄Ν̄τˢ: λχ̄Ν̄	ε₆οϣε: ε₆ωϣ

Η

Ηι n.m. house; household, family. Μεc ₂Ν̄ Ηι one born in household. ρΜ̄Ν̄Ηι, ρεΜ̄Ν̄Ηι n.m. (1) member of household, kinsman; (2) monastic superintendent; ρ̄-ρΜ̄Ν̄Ηι to be akin.

Ηι n.m. pair, couple.

ΗΝ n.m. ape.

Ηρπ̄ (ερπ̄-, ρ̄π-) n.m. wine. Ηρπ̄ λc, ερπ-λc old wine. cλγ-Ηρπ̄, cε-Ηρπ̄, wine-drinker. ρ̄-Ηρπ̄ to become wine.

Ηρχ̄ n.m.f. small bird, chick.

Ηϭε n.m. leek. cλ Ν̄ Ηϭε leek-seller.

Ηλ: ωλ	Ηπ: ωπ	Ηπϭ̄: λπϭ̄
ΗΜπω: Μ̄πο	Ηπε: ωπ	

ει (ι)

ει, Q ΝΗγ (§22.3); imptv. λΜογ (q.v.) vb. intr. to come, go; to be about to (+ Circum.); to . . . gradually (+ Ν̄ + Inf.). Used with full range of prep. and directional adv. in normal senses. Note also the following expressions: ει ερλτˢ to come to a superior; ει ετΝ̄ to come into the power of; ει εχ̄Ν̄ to be applicable to; ει Ν̄cλ to come to fetch; ει εβολ ε to sue; ει εβολ ₂ιτΝ̄ to leave, quit (a place); ει ε₂ρλι εχ̄Ν̄ to befall.

ειλ, ιλ n.m. valley, ravine.

ειλ (ειερ-, ειλτˢ, ειλλτˢ) n. eye, mostly in cpds.: κτε-ειλτˢ to look around; Με₂-ειλτˢ, Μογ₂ Ν̄ ειλτˢ to stare, look intently (at: Μ̄Μοˢ); cΜ̄Ν̄-ειλτˢ εχ̄Ν̄ to fix eye on; τcλβε-ειλτˢ, τcβ̄βε-ειλτˢ, τcλβο Ν̄ ειλτˢ εβολ to instruct, inform; τογΝ-ειλτˢ, τογΝε-ειλτˢ εβολ idem; ϥι-ειλτˢ ε₂ρλι to raise eye; ₂λ ειλτˢ before one's eyes; κω ₂λ ειλτˢ to intend to do. Νλιλτˢ exclam. pred. blessed is/are ...! Μ̄Ν̄τΝλιλτˢ blessedness.

ⲉⲓⲁⲁⲩ, ⲉⲓⲱ, ⲓⲱ n.m. linen, linen garment. ⲛⲉⲓⲁⲁⲩ, ⲛⲓⲁⲁⲩ, ⲛⲁⲁⲩ idem.

ⲉⲓⲁⲃⲉ, ⲉⲓⲁⲁⲃⲉ, ⲓⲁⲁⲃⲉ, ⲓⲁⲓⲃⲉ n.f. pus.

ⲉⲓⲁⲗ, ⲓⲁⲗ, ⲓⲏⲗ n.f. mirror.

ⲉⲓⲃ, ⲉⲓⲉⲓⲃ, ⲉⲓⲉⲃ (pl. ⲉⲓⲉⲃⲏ) n.m. hoof; claw; stinger; nail, talon.

ⲉⲓⲃⲉ, Q ⲟⲃⲉ vb. intr. to thirst, become thirsty (for: ⲙ̅ⲙⲟ⸗); as n.m. thirst.

ⲉⲓⲉ, ⲉⲉⲓⲉ, ⲉⲓ (1) conj. introducing apodosis: then (§29.1); before neg.: unless, without; (2) conj. or; ⲉⲓⲉ ... ⲏ either ... or; (3) modal or interrog. part. introducing statement; translation depends on context: well then, so.

ⲉⲓⲉⲃⲧ, ⲉⲉⲓⲃⲧ, ⲉⲓⲃⲧ, ⲉⲓⲏⲃⲧ, ⲓⲏⲧ, ⲉⲉⲃⲧ n.m. usu. with def. art.: the east. ⲥⲁ-ⲡⲉⲓⲉⲃⲧ on the east side (of: ⲛ̅).

ⲉⲓⲉⲗⲉⲗ, ⲉⲓⲉⲗⲉⲓⲉⲗ vb. intr. to shine, glitter; as n.m. brightness. ⲓⲉⲗⲗⲉ n. brightness, light.

ⲉⲓⲙⲉ, ⲉⲓⲙⲙⲉ vb. tr. to know, understand, realize (ⲉ; that: ⲭⲉ). ⲁⲧⲉⲓⲙⲉ ignorant; innocent, unaware; ⲣ̅-ⲁⲧⲉⲓⲙⲉ (Q ⲟ ⲛ̅ ⲁⲧⲉⲓⲙⲉ) to become ignorant, unaware; to be unconscious; ⲙ̅ⲛ̅ⲧⲁⲧⲉⲓⲙⲉ ignorance. ⲉⲓⲛⲉⲓⲙⲉ knowledge. ⲛⲁϣⲧ̅ⲉⲓⲙⲉ, ⲛⲁϣⲧ̅ⲙ̅ⲙⲉ, ⲛⲁϣⲧⲓⲙⲙⲉ adj. presumptuous, impudent; obdurate, stubborn; ⲙ̅ⲛ̅ⲧⲛⲁϣⲧⲙ̅ⲙⲉ stubbornness, presumptuousness.

ⲉⲓⲛⲉ ⲛ̅- (ⲙ̅-, ⲉⲛ-) ⲛ̅ⲧ⸗ (Imptv. ⲁⲛⲓⲛⲉ, ⲁⲛⲉⲓⲛⲉ, ⲁⲛⲓ- ⲁⲛⲓ⸗) vb. tr. to bring (ⲙ̅ⲙⲟ⸗), bear. Used with many prep. and directional adv. in ordinary senses. Note the following expressions: ⲉⲓⲛⲉ ⲙ̅ⲙⲟ⸗ ⲉⲝⲛ̅ or ⲉ₂ⲣⲁⲓ ⲉⲝⲛ̅ to liken something to, compare with; ⲛ̅-ⲧⲟⲟⲧ⸗ ⲉⲝⲛ̅ to seize; ⲉⲓⲛⲉ ⲙ̅ⲙⲟ⸗ ⲛ̅ⲥⲁ to bring an accusation against; ⲉⲓⲛⲉ ⲙ̅ⲙⲟ⸗ ⲉⲃⲟⲗ to complete; to extradite; to publish; to introduce; ⲉⲓⲛⲉ ⲙ̅ⲙⲟ⸗ ⲉ ⲧⲙⲏⲧⲉ to recall, bring up (in one's mind); ⲉⲓⲛⲉ ⲙ̅ⲙⲟ⸗ ⲉ₂ⲟⲩⲛ introduce; as n.m. reception.

ⲉⲓⲛⲉ vb. tr. to resemble, be like (ⲙ̅ⲙⲟ⸗); as n.m. likeness, aspect. ⲙ̅ⲛ̅ⲧⲣⲉϥⲉⲓⲛⲉ resemblance.

ⲉⲓⲛⲉ n.f. adze.

ⲉⲓⲛⲉ, ⲓⲛⲉ n.f. thumb; big toe.

ⲉⲓⲛⲉ n.m. chain.

ⲉⲓⲟⲙ, ⲓⲟⲙ n.m. (1) sea (rare in Sah.); (2) winepress.

ⲉⲓⲟⲟⲣ, ⲉⲓⲟⲟⲣⲉ n.m. canal. ⲭⲓⲟⲟⲣ vb. tr. to ferry (ⲙ̄ⲙⲟ⸗) across (to: ⲉ); to cross, ford (a river: ⲙ̄ⲙⲟ⸗); ⲅⲓⲛ-ⲭⲓⲟⲟⲣ fording, transit. ⲭⲓⲟⲟⲣ n.m. a ford, crossing; ferryboat; ferryman. ⲉⲓⲉⲣⲟ, ⲓⲉⲣⲟ (pl. ⲉⲓⲉⲣⲱⲟⲩ, ⲓⲉⲣⲱⲟⲩ) n.m. river; often spec. the Nile.

ⲉⲓⲟⲟⲩⲛ, ⲓⲟⲟⲩⲛ (f. ⲓⲟⲟⲩⲛⲉ) a title (m.f.); meaning unknown.

ⲉⲓⲟⲛⲉ n.f. a liquid measure.

ⲉⲓⲟⲛⲉ, ⲓⲟⲛⲉ (ⲉⲓⲉⲛ-) n.f. craft, occupation. Freq. cpd. with 2nd element to designate particular craft or its product, as in ⲉⲓⲉⲛ-ⲥⲁ sculpture, work in relief; ⲉⲓⲉⲛ-ⲟⲩⲟⲉⲓⲉ tillage, tilled land, produce of tillage; ⲉⲓⲉⲛ-ϣⲉ woodwork; ⲉⲓⲉⲛ-ⲛⲟⲩⲃ goldwork; ⲉⲓⲉⲛ-ⲛ̄-ϩⲁⲧ silverwork; ⲉⲓⲉⲛ-ϣⲱⲧ trade, trading, merchandise; ⲣ̄-ⲉⲓⲉⲛ-ϣⲱⲧ to engage in trade. ϩⲁⲣ-ⲉⲓⲟⲛⲉ adj. variegated. ⲣ̄-ⲉⲓⲟⲛⲉ to spin; ⲣⲉϥⲣ̄-ⲉⲓⲟⲛⲉ craftsman; ⲙⲛ̄ⲧⲣⲉϥⲣ̄-ⲉⲓⲟⲛⲉ craft.

ⲉⲓⲟⲩⲗ, ⲉⲉⲓⲟⲩⲗ, ⲉⲓⲟⲟⲩⲗ, ⲓⲟⲩⲗ n.m.f. hart, hind.

ⲉⲓⲣⲉ ⲣ̄- (ⲉⲣ-) ⲁⲁ⸗ Q ⲟ vb. tr. to do, make, perform, produce, fashion (ⲙ̄ⲙⲟ⸗); intr. to act, function, behave. For ⲉⲓⲣⲉ in cpd. vbs. see §26.1; these are listed under 2nd element. As n.m. doing, performance; ⲣⲉϥⲉⲓⲣⲉ doer, maker. ⲧⲁϣⲉ-ⲉⲓⲣⲉ to do or make even more, increase in doing.

ⲉⲓⲥ, ⲉⲥ part. behold, lo; here is/are ... (properly only before nouns). ⲉⲓⲥ ϩⲏⲏⲧⲉ, ⲉⲓⲥ ϩⲏⲧⲉ, ⲉⲓⲥ ϩⲏⲏⲡⲉ idem (before pron. or verb). ⲉⲓⲥ ϩⲏⲏⲧⲉ ⲉⲓⲥ idem (before n.). ⲉⲓⲥ ϩⲏⲏⲛⲉ idem (before n. or pron.). ⲉⲓⲥⲧⲉ = ⲉⲓⲥ ϩⲏⲏⲧⲉ. ⲉⲓⲥⲡⲉ = ⲉⲓⲥ ϩⲏⲏⲡⲉ.

ⲉⲓⲧⲛ̄, ⲓⲧⲛ̄, ⲓⲧⲛⲉ, ⲧⲛⲏ n.m. ground, earth, dust; dirt, rubbish. ⲉ ⲡⲉⲓⲧⲛ̄ = ⲉⲡⲉⲥⲏⲧ; ⲙ̄ ⲡⲉⲓⲧⲛ̄ adv. below, underneath, at the bottom.

ⲉⲓⲱ ⲉⲓⲁ- (ⲓⲁ-) ⲉⲓⲁⲁ⸗ Q ⲉⲓⲏ (± ⲉⲃⲟⲗ) vb. tr. to wash (ⲙ̄ⲙⲟ⸗); ⲉⲓⲱ ⲉⲃⲟⲗ as n.m. washing; ⲣⲉϥⲉⲓⲱ ⲉⲃⲟⲗ washer (in bath).

ειⲁ-ⲧⲟⲟⲧ⸗ ⲛ̄ⲥⲁ to renounce, despair of (suff. is reflex.).

ⲉⲓⲱ, ⲉⲉⲓⲱ, ⲉⲓⲟⲩ, ⲉⲟⲩ (pl. ⲉⲟⲟⲩ, ⲉⲱⲟⲩ, ⲉⲟⲟⲩⲉ) n.m.f. ass, donkey. ⲉⲓⲁ-ⲛ̄-ⲧⲟⲟⲩ wild ass, onager. ⲉⲓⲁ-ⲍⲟⲟⲩⲧ idem.

ⲉⲓⲱⲣⲙ̄ (ⲓⲱⲣⲙ̄) Q ⲉⲓⲟⲣⲙ̄ (± ⲉⲃⲟⲗ, ⲉⲍⲣⲁⲓ) vb. intr. to stare (at: ⲉ, ⲛ̄ⲥⲁ), stare in wonder, be astonished, dumbfounded.

ⲉⲓⲱⲣⲍ̄ (ⲉⲓⲱⲣⲁⲍ, ⲓⲱⲣⲍ̄) ⲉⲓⲉⲣⲍ̄- (ⲓⲁⲣⲍ̄-) ⲉⲓⲟⲣⲍ⸗ (ⲓⲟⲣⲍ⸗) vb. tr. to see, perceive (ⲙ̄ⲙⲟ⸗); to look (toward: ⲛ̄ⲥⲁ). As n.m. sight, vision; view, opinion; ⲣⲉϥⲉⲓⲱⲣⲍ̄ one who can see; ⲙⲛ̄ⲧⲣⲉϥⲉⲓⲱⲣⲍ̄ perception; ⲅⲓⲛⲉⲓⲱⲣⲍ̄ vision, power to see. ⲉⲓⲉⲣⲍⲉ n.f. ray (of light), sight (of eye).

ⲉⲓⲱⲧ, ⲓⲱⲧ (ⲉⲓⲧ-; pl. ⲉⲓⲟⲧⲉ) n.m. father (lit. and fig.); pl. parents, forefathers. Often used of abbots, elders and other revered persons. ⲁⲧⲉⲓⲱⲧ fatherless. ⲣ̄-ⲉⲓⲱⲧ to become father. ⲙⲛ̄ⲧⲉⲓⲱⲧ fatherhood, family. ϣⲛ̄-ⲉⲓⲱⲧ relative on father's side.

ⲉⲓⲱⲧ, ⲉⲓⲟⲩⲧ, ⲓⲱⲧ n.m. barley.

ⲉⲓⲱⲧⲉ n.f. dew.

ⲉⲓⲱⲍⲉ, ⲓⲱⲍⲉ (ⲉⲓⲉⲍ-, ⲉⲓⲱⲍ-; pl. ⲉⲓⲁⲍⲟⲩ, ⲉⲓⲁⲍⲟⲩⲉ) n.m. field. For ⲉⲓⲉⲍ-ⲉⲗⲟⲟⲗⲉ, -ϣⲏⲛ, -ⲃⲉⲣⲃⲱⲣⲉⲧ (ⲍⲃⲟⲣⲃⲣ̄) see 2nd element. ⲥⲧ̄-ⲉⲓⲱⲍⲉ, ⲥⲧⲱⲍⲉ n.f. a field measure. ϣⲓ-ⲉⲓⲱⲍⲉ to measure a field; as n.m. a field measure.

ⲉⲓϣⲉ ⲉϣⲧ̄- (ⲁϣⲧ̄-) ⲁϣⲧ⸗ (ⲁϣ⸗) Q ⲁϣⲉ vb. tr. to hang, suspend (ⲙ̄ⲙⲟ⸗; on: ⲉ; by: ⲛ̄ⲥⲁ), all ± ⲉⲍⲣⲁⲓ. Q to be suspended; to be captivated (by: ⲛ̄ⲥⲁ); to depend (on: ⲍⲛ̄); + ⲉⲃⲟⲗ: to overhang.

ⲉⲓ: ⲉⲓⲉ	ⲉⲓⲉⲟⲩⲗ: ⲉⲓⲟⲩⲗ	ⲉⲓⲟⲧⲉ: ⲉⲓⲱⲧ
ⲉⲓⲁ-: ⲉⲓⲱ	ⲉⲓⲉⲡ-: ⲉⲓⲟⲡⲉ	ⲉⲓⲟⲩ: ⲉⲓⲱ
ⲉⲓⲁⲗ⸗: ⲉⲓⲱ	ⲉⲓⲉⲣ-: ⲉⲓⲁ	ⲉⲓⲟⲩⲧ: ⲉⲓⲱⲧ
ⲉⲓⲁⲗⲃⲉ: ⲉⲓⲗⲃⲉ	ⲉⲓⲉⲣ-ⲃⲟⲟⲛⲉ: ⲃⲟⲟⲛⲉ	ⲉⲓⲥⲡⲉ: ⲉⲓⲥ
ⲉⲓⲁⲣⲍ̄-: ⲉⲓⲱⲣⲍ̄	ⲉⲓⲉⲣⲟ: ⲉⲓⲟⲟⲣ	ⲉⲓⲥⲧⲉ: ⲉⲓⲥ
ⲉⲓⲁⲁⲧ⸗: ⲉⲓⲁ	ⲉⲓⲉⲣⲱⲟⲩ: ⲉⲓⲟⲟⲣ	ⲉⲓⲧ-: ⲉⲓⲱⲧ
ⲉⲓⲁⲧ⸗: ⲉⲓⲁ	ⲉⲓⲉⲣⲍⲉ: ⲉⲓⲱⲣⲍ̄	ⲉⲓⲱ: ⲉⲓⲁⲗⲩ
ⲉⲓⲁⲍⲟⲩ: ⲉⲓⲱⲍⲉ	ⲉⲓⲉⲍ-: ⲉⲓⲱⲍⲉ	ⲉⲓϥⲧ̄: ⲱϥⲧ̄
ⲉⲓⲃⲏ: ⲉⲓⲃ	ⲉⲓⲉⲍ-ⲉⲗⲟⲟⲗⲉ: ⲉⲗⲟⲟⲗⲉ	
ⲉⲓⲃⲧ̄: ⲱϥⲧ̄	ⲉⲓⲏ: ⲉⲓⲱ	
ⲉⲓⲃⲧ̄: ⲉⲓⲉⲃⲧ̄	ⲉⲓⲏⲃⲧ̄: ⲉⲓⲉⲃⲧ̄	ⲓⲁⲓⲃⲉ: ⲉⲓⲁⲃⲉ
ⲉⲓⲉⲃ: ⲉⲓⲃ	ⲉⲓⲙⲙⲉ: ⲉⲓⲙⲉ	ⲓⲉⲗⲗⲉ: ⲉⲓⲉⲗⲉⲗ
ⲉⲓⲉⲓⲃ: ⲉⲓⲃ	ⲉⲓⲙⲛ̄ⲧ: ⲉⲙⲛ̄ⲧ	ⲓⲏⲗ: ⲉⲓⲁⲗ
ⲉⲓⲉⲗⲉⲓⲉⲗ: ⲉⲓⲉⲗⲉⲗ	ⲉⲓⲟⲣⲙ̄: ⲉⲓⲱⲣⲙ̄	ⲓⲏϥⲧ̄: ⲉⲓⲉⲃⲧ̄

K

ⲕⲁⲓⲣⲉ n.f. gullet.

ⲕⲁⲕⲉ n.m. darkness; ⲣ̄-ⲕⲁⲕⲉ to become dark.

ⲕⲁⲗⲁ₂ⲏ n.f. womb; belly.

ⲕⲁⲗⲉⲗⲉ, ⲕⲁⲗⲉⲉⲗⲉ, ⲕⲁⲗⲏⲗⲉ, ⲕⲉⲗⲉⲉⲗⲉ n.f. wooden sounding
    board struck to assemble congregation.

ⲕⲁⲗⲕⲓⲗ, ⲕⲁⲗⲕⲉⲗ, ⲕⲉⲗⲕⲓⲗ, ⳓⲉⲗⳓⲓⲗ, ⳓⲉⲓⲗⳓⲉⲓⲗ n.m. wheel.

ⲕⲁⲗⲱⲡⲟⲩ, ⲕⲁⲗⲟⲡⲟⲩ, ⳓⲁⲗⲟⲡⲟⲩ n.m.f. small dog.

ⲕⲁⲙ n.m. reed, rush.

ⲕⲁⲡ n.m. (1) thread, string, strand; (2) letter (alph.).

ⲕⲁⲣⲟⲩⲥ adj. curled (of hair); meaning not certain.

ⲕⲁⲥ, ⲕⲉⲉⲥ, ⲕⲏⲥ, ⲕⲓⲥ (pl. ⲕⲉⲉⲥ, ⲕⲁⲁⲥ) n.m. bone; fruit-
    stone. ⲙⲁⲣ-ⲕⲁⲥ, ⲙⲉⲣ-ⲕⲁⲥ n.m. bone-setter.

ⲕⲁⲥ n.m. carat (a coin).

ⲕⲁⲥⲉ, ⲕⲉⲥⲉ, ⲕⲏⲥⲉ n.m. shoemaker.

ⲕⲁⲥⲕⲥ̄ (ⲕⲟⲥⲕⲉⲥ) vb. intr. to whisper (to: ⲉ); as n.m.
    whispering. ⲣⲉϥⲕⲁⲥⲕⲥ̄ whisperer.

ⲕⲁⲧⲟ n.f. boat, skiff.

ⲕⲁϣ n.m. reed, reed pen, reed staff or pole; n.f. = ⲙⲁ ⲛ̄
    ⲕⲁϣ place where reeds grow. ϯ ⲙ̄ⲙⲟ⸗ ⲉ ⲡⲕⲁϣ to fence
    with reeds.

ⲕⲁϣⲁⲃⲉⲗ n.m. earring.

ⲕⲁϭ n.m. trunk of tree.

ⲕⲁ₂ n.m. earth, soil; the ground; land, country; ⲣ̄-ⲕⲁ₂ to
    turn to dust. ⲣⲙ̄ⲛ̄ⲕⲁ₂ a man of the earth.

ⲕⲁ₂ⲕⲥ̄ ⲕⲉ₂ⲕⲉ₂- ⲕⲉ₂ⲕⲱ₂⸗ Q ⲕⲉ₂ⲕⲱ₂ vb. tr. to hew out, clear,
    smooth out (ⲙ̄ⲙⲟ⸗); to cause (a wound) to heal; intr. to
    heal. ⲣⲉϥⲕⲉ₂ⲕⲉ₂- hewer. ⲕⲁ₂ⲕ̄ ⲕⲉ₂ⲕ̄- vb. tr. = ⲕⲁ₂ⲕⲥ̄.

ⲕⲃⲁ n.m. vengeance. ⲣ̄-ⲕⲃⲁ, ⲉⲓⲣⲉ ⲙ̄ ⲡ(⸗)ⲕⲃⲁ to do vengeance
    (for: ⲛⲁ⸗, ⲙⲛ̄, ₂ⲛ̄). ϯ-ⲕⲃⲁ to avenge. ϫⲓ-ⲕⲃⲁ to take
    vengeance (on: ⲙ̄ⲙⲟ⸗, ₂ⲛ̄); as n.m. retribution, compen-
    sation; ⲉⲓⲣⲉ ⲙ̄ ⲡϫⲓ-ⲕⲃⲁ, ϫⲓ ⲙ̄ ⲡϫⲓ-ⲕⲃⲁ to take revenge;
    ⲣⲉϥϫⲓ-ⲕⲃⲁ avenger.

ⲕⲃⲟ (ⲕⲃⲁ) ⲕⲃⲉ- Q ⲕⲏⲃ vb. tr. to make cool; intr. to

become cool; as n.m. coolness. ⲧ̄-ⲕⲃⲟ to make cool; ⲭⲓ-ⲕⲃⲟ to become refreshed, get coolness.

ⲕⲉ (1) adj. other, different; prefixed directly to noun, as in ⲕⲉⲣⲱⲙⲉ, ⲍⲉⲛⲕⲉⲣⲱⲙⲉ, ⲡⲕⲉⲣⲱⲙⲉ, ⲛ̄ⲕⲉⲣⲱⲙⲉ. In some temporal expressions: next, as in ⲧⲕⲉⲣⲟⲙⲡⲉ next year; again, in addition, as in ⲛ̄ ⲕⲉⲥⲟⲡ once again; ⲕⲉⲕⲟⲩⲓ a little more, a little longer. (2) adv. also, even, moreover; positioned as in (1), but only with def. art. This usage has led to isolation of ⲡⲕⲉ (f. ⲧⲕⲉ) as an independent element that may be prefixed to pronouns, ⲡⲕⲉ ⲁⲛⲟⲛ even we, or personal names, ⲡⲕⲉ ⲡⲁⲩⲗⲟⲥ even Paul, or used in vb. cpd. ⲣ̄-ⲡⲕⲉ- before another Inf. or Q in sense "also, even to do or be." ⲕⲉ pron. another (one), (the) other (one); pl. ⲍⲉⲛⲕⲟⲟⲩⲉ some others, (ⲛ̄)ⲕⲉⲕⲟⲟⲩⲉ the others. ⲕⲉⲧ (f. ⲕⲉⲧⲉ) pron. another; with def. art. the other. ⲕⲉⲟⲩⲁ pron. another one.

ⲕⲉⲕⲉ n.m. child; n.m.f. (var. ⲕⲁⲕⲉ, ⲕⲁⲁⲕⲉ) pupil of eye.

ⲕⲉⲗⲉⲃⲓⲛ, ⲕⲉⲗⲁⲃⲓⲛ, ⲕⲁⲗⲁⲃⲓⲛ n.m. axe.

ⲕⲉⲗⲱⲗ, ⲕⲟⲩⲗⲱⲗ, ⲕⲟⲗⲟⲗ n.m. jar, pitcher. ⲕⲉⲗⲟⲟⲗⲉ n. idem.

ⲕⲉⲍⲧⲉ n.f. hip, loin.

ⲕⲏⲡⲉ, ⲅⲏⲡⲉ, ⲅⲉⲡⲏ n.f. vaulted place, cellar, canopy; palate (of mouth). Cf. Gk. ϰύπη, γύπη.

ⲕⲓⲙ ⲕⲉⲙⲧ- ⲕⲉⲙⲧ⸗ vb. intr. to move, stir; vb. tr. to touch (ⲉ); to move, shift, stir (physically or emotionally: ⲉ, ⲙ̄ⲙⲟ⸗); as n.m. movement. ⲁⲧⲕⲓⲙ immovable. ⲅⲓⲛⲕⲓⲙ movement. ⲕⲛ̄-ⲧⲟ n.m. earthquake.

ⲕⲓⲧⲉ n.f. double drachma (half a stater), coin and weight. ⲅⲓⲥ-ⲕⲓⲧⲉ one drachma.

ⲕⲓⲱⲟⲩ Q to be fat, soft, weak; to be fertile, productive.

ⲕⲁⲗⲗ, ⲕⲗⲉⲗ, ⲕⲗⲏⲗ n.m. chain, esp. on neck.

ⲕⲁⲗⲁϥⲧ̄, ⲕⲗⲉϥⲧ̄, ⲕⲗⲃ̄ⲧ n.f. hood, cowl.

ⲕⲗⲉ, ⲕⲉⲗⲏ n.m. vessel for liquids.

ⲕⲗ̄ⲗⲉ, ⲕⲗ̄ n.m. bolt; knee, joint. ⲕⲉⲗⲉⲛⲕⲉⲍ n.m. elbow; ⲍⲁⲙ-ⲕⲉⲗⲉⲛⲕⲉⲍ bolt-smith, smith. ⲍⲁⲙ-ⲕⲗ̄ⲗⲉ idem.

ⲕⲗ̄ⲙⲉ n.f. pad, padding.

ⲕⲗⲟ n.m. poison (for arrows).

ⲕⲗⲟⲙ n.m. crown, wreath, circle. ⲧ-ⲕⲗⲟⲙ to crown (ⲉⲭⲛ̅, ⲍ ⲓⲭⲛ̅). ϫⲓ-ⲕⲗⲟⲙ to receive, bear crown; to become a martyr. ⲣⲉϥϫⲣⲟ-ⲕⲗⲟⲙ victoriously crowned; ϥⲁⲓ-ⲕⲗⲟⲙ crown-bearer.

ⲕⲗⲟⲟⲗⲉ n.f. cloud.

ⲕⲗⲟⲟⲙⲉ n.f. bruise.

ⲕⲗ̅ⲯ n. a blow; ⲣ̅-ⲕⲗ̅ⲯ ⲛⲁ⸗, ⲧ-ⲕⲗ̅ⲯ ⲉⲭⲛ̅ to strike; ϣⲥ̅-ⲛ̅-ⲕⲗ̅ⲯ a blow.

ⲕⲙ̅ⲕⲙ̅, ⲕⲟⲩⲕⲙ̅, ⲕⲟⲩⲙⲕⲙ̅ vb tr. to strike, beat (ⲉ: a musical instr.); to make a repeated sound. As n.m. drum.

ⲕⲙⲟⲙ, Q ⲕⲏⲙ vb. intr. to become black. ⲕⲁⲙⲉ, ⲕⲁⲙⲏ (f. ⲕⲁⲙⲏ; pl. ⲕⲁⲙⲁⲩⲉⲓ) adj. black; usually after n. with ⲛ̅, rarely without ⲛ̅. ⲣ̅-ⲕⲁⲙⲉ (Q ⲟ ⲛ̅ ⲕⲁⲙⲉ) to become black. ⲕⲙⲉ (?) = ⲕⲙⲏⲙⲉ n. darkness. ⲕⲏⲙⲉ n.m.(f.) Egypt; ⲣⲙ̅ⲛ̅ⲕⲏⲙⲉ an Egyptian; ⲙⲛ̅ⲧⲣⲙ̅ⲛ̅ⲕⲏⲙⲉ Egyptian (lang.).

ⲕⲛⲁⲁⲩ n.m. sheaf.

ⲕⲛ̅ⲛⲉ vb. intr. to be fat, sweet; as n.m. fatness, sweetness. ⲣ̅-ⲕⲛ̅ⲛⲉ to become fat; ⲧ-ⲕⲛ̅ⲛⲉ to make fat, to salve, anoint.

ⲕⲛⲟⲥ, ⲕⲛⲟⲟⲥ, ⲕⲛⲱⲱⲥ Q ⲕⲟⲛⲥ̅ vb. intr. to become putrid, to stink; as n.m. stench.

ⲕⲛ̅ⲧⲉ n.m. fig; ⲃⲱ ⲛ̅ ⲕⲛ̅ⲧⲉ fig-tree.

ⲕⲛ̅ⲍⲉ n.f. architectural term, precise meaning not certain: porch, shrine, side (??).

ⲕⲟⲉⲓⲥ, ⲕⲁⲉⲓⲥ n.m. vessel for liquids.

ⲕⲟⲉⲓⲍ, ⲕⲁⲓⲍ n.m. sheath, case, cover; brick-mold (?).

ⲕⲟⲓⲗⲍ̅ⲕ, ⲕⲓⲗⲍ̅ⲕ, ⲭⲟⲓⲗ(ⲍ)ⲕ, ⲭⲟⲓⲗⲭ name of 4th Copt. month.

ⲕⲟⲓⲉ, ⲕⲁⲓⲉ, ⲕⲁⲉⲓⲉ, ⲕⲟⲓ n.f. field; ⲣⲙ̅ⲛ̅ⲧⲕⲟⲓ farmer.

ⲕⲟⲙⲙⲉ, ⲕⲟⲙⲏ, ⲕⲟⲙⲓ, ⲕⲙ̅ⲙⲉ, ⲕⲏⲙ(ⲙ)ⲉ n.m. gum.

ⲕⲟⲟⲙϥ̅, ⲕⲟⲙϥ̅ n.m. blight.

ⲕⲟⲟⲩ, ⲕⲱⲟⲩ, ⲕⲁⲩ n.m. length of time; ⲟⲩⲕⲟⲩⲓ ⲛ̅ ⲕⲟⲟⲩ a little while.

ⲕⲟⲟⲍ, ⲕⲱⲍ n.m.(f.) angle, corner; point, tip, prow; piece.

ⲕⲟⲥⲕⲥ̅ ⲕⲉⲥⲕⲱⲥ⸗ ⲉⲃⲟⲗ vb. tr. to lay out, extend (ⲙ̅ⲙⲟ⸗; also

reflex.); to entwine self (reflex.).

ⲕⲟⲧ, ⲕⲁⲧ n.m. basket.

ⲕⲟⲩⲓ (ⲕⲟⲩ-) (1) adj. small, young; a little, few; used before noun (usually with ⲛ̄) or after (usually without ⲛ̄). May be cpd. as ⲕⲟⲩ-ⲛ̄. ⲕⲟⲩⲓ ⲛ̄ ϩⲏⲧ adj. impatient, easily discouraged. (2) adv., usually ⲛ̄ ⲟⲩⲕⲟⲩⲓ a little; (ⲛ̄) ⲕⲉⲕⲟⲩⲓ yet a little, a little more; ⲙⲛ̄ⲛ̄ⲥⲁ ⲟⲩⲕⲟⲩⲓ after a little while; ϩⲁⲑⲏ ⲛ̄ ⲟⲩⲕⲟⲩⲓ a little before; ϣⲁⲧⲛ̄ ⲟⲩⲕⲟⲩⲓ, ⲡⲁⲣⲁ ⲕⲉⲕⲟⲩⲓ almost, more or less; ⲡⲣⲟⲥ ⲟⲩⲕⲟⲩⲓ for a little while; ⲕⲁⲧⲁ ⲕⲉⲕⲟⲩⲓ occasionally; ⲛ̄/ⲕⲁⲧⲁ ⲕⲟⲩⲓ ⲕⲟⲩⲓ little by little; ⲣ̄-ⲕⲟⲩⲓ (Q ⲟ ⲛ̄ ⲕⲟⲩⲓ) to become small, few, young; ⲙⲛ̄ⲧⲕⲟⲩⲓ smallness, youth.

ⲕⲟⲩⲕⲗⲉ n.f. hood, cowl.

ⲕⲟⲩⲛ(ⲧ)⸗, ⲕⲟⲩⲟⲩⲛ(ⲧ)⸗, ⲕⲟⲩⲟⲛ⸗, ⲕⲟⲩⲱⲛ⸗, ⲕⲉⲛ⸗ n. bosom, breast (suff. obligatory); also sometimes: genitals.

ⲕⲟⲩⲡⲣ̄ n.m. a plant: lawsonia inermis.

ⲕⲟⲩⲣ n.m. pivot, hinge.

ⲕⲟⲩⲣ adj. deaf.

ⲕⲟⲩϫⲟⲩ, ⲕⲟⲩⲛϫⲟⲩ, ⲕⲟⲛϫⲟⲩ n.f. a type of vessel.

ⲕⲣⲓ, ⲕⲗⲓ n.m. a fragrant substance.

ⲕⲣ̄ⲙⲉⲥ n.m.f. ash, soot, dust; ⲣ̄-ⲕⲣ̄ⲙⲉⲥ to become ashes, dust. ⲣ̄-ⲁⲧⲕⲣ̄ⲙⲉⲥ to leave no ash (on burning).

ⲕⲣⲙ̄ⲣⲙ̄ vb. intr. to murmur, mutter in anger or vexation (against: ⲉϫⲛ̄, ⲛ̄ⲥⲁ, ⲉ, ⲉϩⲟⲩⲛ ⲉ); as n.m. complaint, murmuring. ⲣⲉϥⲕⲣⲙ̄ⲕⲣⲙ̄ murmurer.

ⲕⲣⲙ̄ⲧⲥ̄, ⲕⲣⲙ̄ⲛ̄ⲧⲥ̄ n.m. smoke, mist; darkness, obscurity.

ⲕⲣⲟ, ⲕⲗⲁ (pl. ⲕⲣⲱⲟⲩ) n.m. shore (of sea, river); limit or margin (of land); hill, dale.

ⲕⲣⲟⲙⲣⲙ̄ vb. intr. to become dark (in shade or color); Q ⲕⲣⲙ̄ⲣⲱⲙ to be dark. As n.m. darkness.

ⲕⲣⲟⲩⲣ n.m. frog.

ⲕⲣⲟⲩϫ, ⲕⲣⲟϫ n. a cake.

ⲕⲣⲟϥ n.m. guile, deceit; ambush; as adj. false, guileful. ⲁⲧⲕⲣⲟϥ guileless. ⲙⲛ̄ⲧⲕⲣⲟϥ guile. ⲣ̄-ⲕⲣⲟϥ (Q ⲟ ⲛ̄ ⲕⲣⲟϥ) to be guileful, lie in ambush (for: ⲉ); ⲣⲉϥⲣ̄-ⲕⲣⲟϥ

deceiver, traitor. cλ ⲛ̄ ⲕⲣⲟϥ deceiver. ϫⲓ-ⲕⲣⲟϥ to use
guile, lie in wait; ϫⲓ ⲙ̄ⲙⲟˢ ⲛ̄ ⲕⲣⲟϥ to take by guile.
ⲕⲣⲱⲙ n.m. fire (rare in Sah.). ⲕⲱⲣⲙ̄ n.m. smoke (?).
ⲕⲥⲟⲩⲣ, ϫⲟⲩⲣ, ⲅⲥⲟⲩⲣ n.m. finger-ring; key. ⲥⲁ ⲛ̄ ⲉⲕⲥⲟⲩⲣ
key-maker.
ⲕⲧⲏⲣ n.m. calf.
ⲕⲱ ⲕⲁ- ⲕⲁⲗˢ (ⲕⲉⲉˢ, ⲕⲉˢ) Q ⲕⲏ vb. tr. to put, place, set
(ⲙ̄ⲙⲟˢ; with local prep. in plain sense); to appoint,
make (ⲙ̄ⲙⲟˢ; as: ⲛ̄); to obtain, get (ⲙ̄ⲙⲟˢ; with reflex.
dat. ⲛⲁˢ); to preserve, keep; to allow, permit, grant
(ⲙ̄ⲙⲟˢ; to do: ⲉ + Inf. or Circum.; that: ϫⲉ); to be-
queathe (ⲙ̄ⲙⲟˢ; to: ⲛⲁˢ); to leave, abandon (ⲙ̄ⲙⲟˢ); to
go to (a place). Q to be situated, to lie; to be loose,
unrestrained. ⲙⲁ ⲛ̄ ⲕⲁ- a place for putting (something).

ⲕⲱ ⲙ̄ⲙⲟˢ ⲉⲃⲟⲗ (1) to release (to: ⲛ̄ⲥⲁ), loosen; (2)
to expel, dismiss; (3) to forgive (w. ⲛⲁˢ of pers.);
(4) to leave, abandon; (5) to omit, leave out; (6)
intr. to become loose, dissolved; to become desolate,
deserted. As n.m. forgiveness, remission; ⲙⲁ ⲛ̄ ⲕⲱ
ⲉⲃⲟⲗ mercy-seat; ⲣⲉϥⲕⲱ ⲉⲃⲟⲗ one who forgives.

ⲕⲱ ⲙ̄ⲙⲟˢ ⲉⲡⲉⲥⲏⲧ to lower, let down. ⲕⲱ ⲙ̄ⲙⲟˢ ⲉⲡⲁϩⲟⲩ
to leave behind. ⲕⲱ ⲙ̄ⲙⲟˢ ⲉϩⲟⲩⲛ to put or bring in; to
bring into port; ϭⲓⲛⲕⲱ ⲉϩⲟⲩⲛ entrance (to a house). ⲕⲱ
ⲉϩⲣⲁⲓ to put down, lower; to publish, expose, set forth;
Q to exist, be, be extant; ϭⲓⲛⲕⲱ ⲉϩⲣⲁⲓ nature, fashion,
what is established. ⲕⲱ ϩⲓⲃⲟⲗ to excommunicate. ⲕⲱ
ⲙ̄ⲙⲟˢ ⲛ̄ⲥⲁ to renounce, leave behind. ⲕⲱ ⲙ̄ⲙⲟˢ ⲛ̄ⲧⲟⲟⲧˢ to
keep, preserve, hold in esteem (suff. is reflex.); to
entrust to (suff. is not reflex.).
ⲕⲱⲃ ⲕⲃ̄- (ⲕⲉⲃ-) ⲕⲟⲃˢ Q ⲕⲏⲃ vb. tr. to double, fold, close
by folding (ⲙ̄ⲙⲟˢ); intr. to double, become twice the
amount; as n.m. double, double amount; repetition.
ⲕⲃ̄ⲃⲉ n. fold, crease. ⲕⲟⲟⲃⲉϥ, ⲕⲱⲃⲉϥ n.m. doubling.
ⲕⲱⲃϩ̄, ⲕⲟⲟⲃϩ̄ n. sinew, cord. ⲃⲗ̄-ⲕⲱⲃϩ̄ to cut sinews;
ⲣⲉϥϣⲉⲧ-ⲕⲱⲃϩ̄ hamstringer.

ⲕⲱⲕ ⲕⲉⲕ- ⲕⲟⲕ⸗ (ⲕⲁⲕ⸗, ⲕⲁⲁⲕ⸗) Q ⲕⲏⲕ (± ⲉⲃⲟⲗ) vb. tr. to
peel, strip of, divest (ⲙ̄ⲙⲟ⸗); intr. to peel, become
bare; as n.m. barrenness, nakedness. ⲕⲱⲕ ⲙ̄ⲙⲟ⸗ ⲁϩⲏⲩ to
strip, make naked (obj. removed: ⲛ̄); Q ⲕⲏⲕ ⲁϩⲏⲩ to be
stripped, naked; as n.m. nakedness. ⲕⲱ ⲙ̄ⲙⲟ⸗ ⲕⲁϩⲏⲩ
(ⲕⲁⲁ⸗ ⲕⲁϩⲏⲩ) to strip, make naked. ⲕⲟⲩⲕⲉ n.f. rind.
ⲕⲱⲗⲙ̄ n.m. corner of eye.
ⲕⲱⲗⲡ̄ ⲕⲉⲗⲡ- ⲕⲟⲗⲡ⸗ Q ⲕⲟⲗⲡ̄ vb. tr. to steal (ⲙ̄ⲙⲟ⸗); as n.m.
theft, stolen object; ⲁⲧⲕⲱⲗⲡ̄ inviolable. ⲕⲟⲗⲡⲉ̄ n.f.
theft.
ⲕⲱⲗϩ̄ ⲕⲗ̄ϩ- ⲕⲟⲗϩ⸗ Q ⲕⲟⲗϩ̄ vb. tr. to strike (ⲙ̄ⲙⲟ⸗), clap;
to hammer in, fix; to knock (at door: ⲉ, ⲉϩⲟⲩⲛ ⲉ); as
n.m. blow, stroke. ⲕⲗ̄ϩⲉ n.f. blow.
ⲕⲱⲗⲝ̄ ⲕⲗ̄ⲝ- (ϭⲗ̄ⲝ-) ⲕⲟⲗⲝ⸗ Q ⲕⲟⲗⲝ̄ (ϭⲟⲗⲝ̄) vb. tr. to bend,
twist (ⲙ̄ⲙⲟ⸗); reflex. to bow; intr. to bend, become
bent; as n.m. perversion, depression. ⲕⲗ̄ⲝ-ⲡⲁⲧ, ⲕⲗ̄ⲝ-
ⲁⲡⲉ to bow. ⲕⲁⲗⲁⲭⲧⲱⲣⲧ̄ n.f. part of a house. ⲕⲗ̄ⲝⲉ n.f.
corner.
ⲕⲱⲙϣ̄ ⲕⲙ̄ϣ- ⲕⲟⲙϣ⸗ vb. tr. to mock (ⲛ̄ⲥⲁ); as n.m. mockery,
contempt; ⲙⲛ̄ⲧⲣⲉϥⲕⲱⲙϣ̄ idem.
ⲕⲱⲛⲥ̄ (ⲕⲱⲱⲛⲥ̄) ⲕⲉⲛⲥ̄- ⲕⲟⲛⲥ⸗ Q ⲕⲟⲛⲥ̄ vb. tr. to pierce, slay;
as n.m. slaughter; ⲣⲉϥⲕⲱⲛⲥ̄ slayer.
ⲕⲱⲡ, Q ⲕⲏⲡ vb. tr. to hide (ⲙ̄ⲙⲟ⸗); intr. to be hidden; as
n.m. concealment. Rare in Sah.; use ϩⲱⲡ.
ⲕⲱⲣ n. measure of money.
ⲕⲱⲣϣ̄ (ϭⲱⲣϣ̄) ⲕⲉⲣϣ̄- ⲕⲟⲣϣ⸗ vb. tr. to request, persuade,
cajole (ⲉ); as n.m. entreaty, persuasion; ⲣⲉϥⲕⲱⲣϣ̄
flatterer; ⲙⲛ̄ⲧⲣⲉϥⲕⲱⲣϣ̄ flattery. ⲕⲟⲣϣϥ̄ n.m. flatterer.
ⲕⲱⲣϥ̄ (ϭⲱⲣϥ̄) Q ⲕⲟⲣϥ̄ vb. tr. to bring to naught, destroy,
cancel (ⲙ̄ⲙⲟ⸗); intr. to be idle, deficient.
ⲕⲱⲧ ⲕⲉⲧ- ⲕⲟⲧ⸗ Q ⲕⲏⲧ vb. tr. to build, form (ⲙ̄ⲙⲟ⸗); to
edify, encourage (ⲙ̄ⲙⲟ⸗); intr. to become edified; as
n.m. act of building; a building; rule, precept. ⲙⲁ ⲛ̄
ⲕⲱⲧ workshop. ⲣⲉϥⲕⲱⲧ builder. ϫⲓ-ⲕⲱⲧ to receive edi-
fication. ⲉⲕⲱⲧ (pl. ⲉⲕⲟⲧⲉ, ⲉⲕⲁⲧⲉ) n.m. builder, mason;

potter. ceκωτ, cικωτ n.f. potter's workshop.

κωτε κeτ- κοτ⸗ Q κнτ (1) vb. tr. (a) to turn, direct
(ᴍ̄мо⸗); + eвoλ to turn sthg. away; + eпλϩоγ to turn
sthg. back; + eϩoγн e to convert to, bring around to.

(2) vb. reflex. to turn (self) around, to return;
to repeat, do again (+ e + Inf. or + coord. vb.); +
eвoλ to turn away; + eпλϩoγ to turn back, return; +
eϩoγн e to return to; + eϩpλι e to return to.

(3) vb. intr. to turn, rotate, revolve; to circulate,
go or move in a cyclical way (e.g. watch, visit); to
visit (e); to go around, form circle; κωτe eхн̄ to circulate among; κωτe мн̄ to consort with, stick with; κωτe
н̄cλ to seek, go about seeking; κωτe eвoλ to go away; to
turn, return; κωτe eϩoγн to turn or incline inward;
κωτe eϩpλι to turn around. κωτe e to surround.

κωτe n.m. (1) turning, circuit; (2) surroundings,
environment; (3) seeking, inquiring; ᴍ̄/2ᴍ̄/e пκωτe adv.
round about; ᴍ̄/2ᴍ̄ пκωτe н̄, ᴍ̄/2ᴍ̄ п(⸗)κωτe prep. around,
in the neighborhood of; about, concerning. κοτ n.m.
circular motion, turn, visit; ᴘ̄-κοτ, ϯ-κοτ to make a
turn, make a visit. κοτ n.m. wheel. κοτc̄ n.f. circuit, turning; a turn, bend; knot, twist; crookedness,
guile; eιpe н̄ oγκοτc̄, ᴘ̄-κοτc̄ to make a turn, to circum-
vent; ϯ-κοτc̄ to make a circuit, circulate; хι-κοτc̄ to
be crooked; cλ н̄ κοτc̄ a guileful person; мн̄тcλ н̄ κοτc̄
guile, dishonesty.

κτο κτe- κτο⸗ Q κτнγ (κτοeιτ, κτλeιτ) vb. tr. to
cause to turn (ᴍ̄мо⸗; to: e); this verb has the same
range of meanings as κωτe above, including reflex. and
intr. uses; as n.m. turning, return; λτκτο⸗ irrevocable;
мн̄тpeчκτο good conduct.

κωτч̄ κeтч̄- κοτч⸗ Q κοτч̄ vb. tr. to gather (ᴍ̄мо⸗).

κωωвe (κωωчe) κeeвe- (κλλвe-) κοοв⸗ vb. tr. to force, compel, seize by force (ᴍ̄мо⸗). κвλ n. compulsion, forced
labor; ᴘ̄-κвλ to do forced labor.

ⲕⲱⲱⲣⲉ ⲕⲉⲉⲣⲉ- (ⲕⲉⲣⲉ-) ⲕⲟⲟⲣⲉˢ vb. tr. to cut down, chop
down (ⲙ̄ⲙⲟˢ); intr. to be cut down.

ⲕⲱⲱⲥ (ⲕⲱⲱⲥⲉ ⲕⲱⲛⲧ̄) ⲕⲟⲟⲥˢ (ⲕⲟⲟⲛⲥˢ ⲕⲟⲟⲥⲉˢ) Q ⲕⲏⲥ vb. tr. to
prepare (a corpse: ⲙ̄ⲙⲟˢ) for burial; as n.m. burial,
funeral; corpse. ⲣⲉϥⲛ̄-ⲕⲱⲱⲥ ⲉ₂ⲟⲩⲛ raiser of the dead,
necromancer. ⲣ̄-ⲕⲱⲱⲥ to become a corpse, die. ⲕⲁⲓⲥⲉ,
ⲕⲉⲓⲥⲉ, ⲕⲉⲥⲉ n.f. (1) preparation for burial; (2) grave-
clothes, shroud; (3) corpse. ⲥⲙⲟⲧ ⲛ̄ ⲕⲁⲓⲥⲉ effigy.

ⲕⲱⲱϣⲉ, Q ⲕⲟⲟϣⲉ vb. tr. to break, split (ⲙ̄ⲙⲟˢ); intr. to
become split, broken. Rare in Sah.

ⲕⲱ₂, Q ⲕⲏ₂ vb. intr. to become jealous, envious (of: ⲉ);
to become zealous, eager; to emulate, try to equal (ⲉ);
as n.m. envy, zeal. ⲣⲉϥⲕⲱ₂ zealot; rival, imitator.
†-ⲕⲱ₂ to cause (ⲛⲁˢ) to envy etc. (ⲉ). ⲕⲟⲓ₂ⲉ n.f.
rival woman.

(ⲕⲱ₂) ⲕⲉ₂- ⲕⲁ₂ˢ Q ⲕⲏ₂ vb. tr. to level, smooth out (ⲙ̄ⲙⲟˢ);
to tame, accustom (ⲙ̄ⲙⲟˢ; to: ⲉ).

ⲕⲱ₂ⲧ̄ n.m. fire. ⲣ̄-ⲕⲱ₂ⲧ̄ (Q ⲟ ⲛ̄ ⲕⲱ₂ⲧ̄) to become fire. †-
ⲕⲱ₂ⲧ̄ to set fire (to: ⲉ).

ⲕⲁ-: ⲕⲱ	ⲕⲁⲙⲟⲟⲩⲗⲉ: ⲍⲁⲙⲟⲩⲗ	ⲕⲉⲉⲃⲉ-: ⲕⲱⲱⲃⲉ
ⲕⲁⲗˢ: ⲕⲱ	ⲕⲁⲛⲕⲗⲱ: ϭⲓⲛϭⲗⲱ	ⲕⲉⲉⲣⲉ-: ⲕⲱⲱⲣⲉ
ⲕⲁⲁⲃⲉ-: ⲕⲱⲱⲃⲉ	ⲕⲁⲡ: ϭⲟⲡ	ⲕⲉⲉⲥ: ⲕⲁⲥ
ⲕⲁⲁⲕˢ: ⲕⲱⲕ	ⲕⲁⲡˢ: ϭⲱⲡⲉ	ⲕⲉⲓⲥⲉ: ⲕⲁⲓⲥⲉ
ⲕⲁⲁⲕⲉ: ⲕⲉⲕⲉ	ⲕⲁⲡⲓⲭⲉ: ϭⲁⲡⲉⲓⲭⲉ	ⲕⲉⲗ: ϭⲱⲗ
ⲕⲁⲁⲙ: ϭⲱⲙ	ⲕⲁⲣⲁⲉⲓⲧ: ⲣⲟ	ⲕⲉⲗⲉⲉⲗⲉ: ⲕⲁⲗⲉⲗⲉ
ⲕⲁⲁⲥ: ⲕⲁⲥ	ⲕⲁⲣⲱϥ: ⲣⲟ	ⲕⲉⲗⲉⲛⲕⲉ₂: ⲕ̄ⲁ̄ⲗⲉ
ⲕⲁⲉⲓⲉ: ⲕⲟⲓⲉ	ⲕⲁⲥ: ⲧⲕⲁⲥ	ⲕⲉⲗⲏ: ⲕⲁⲥ
ⲕⲁⲉⲓⲥ: ⲕⲟⲉⲓⲥ	ⲕⲁⲧ: ⲕⲟⲧ	ⲕⲉⲗⲕⲓⲗ: ⲕⲁⲗⲕⲓⲗ
ⲕⲁⲓⲉ: ⲕⲟⲓⲉ	ⲕⲁⲩ: ⲕⲟⲟⲩ	ⲕⲉⲗⲕⲱⲗˢ: ϭⲟⲗϭ̄ⲗ
ⲕⲁⲓⲥⲉ: ⲕⲱⲱⲥ	ⲕⲁⲩⲛⲁⲕⲉⲥ: ϭⲱⲛⲁϭ	ⲕⲉⲗⲗⲏⲥ: ⲭⲓⲗⲗⲉⲥ
ⲕⲁⲓ₂: ⲕⲟⲉⲓ₂	ⲕⲁⲩⲟⲛ: ϭⲗⲟⲩⲟⲛ	ⲕⲉⲗⲙ̄: ϭⲁ̄ⲙ
ⲕⲁⲕˢ: ⲕⲱⲕ	ⲕⲁϥⲕⲁϥ: ϭⲁⲃϭⲁⲃ	ⲕⲉⲗⲙⲁ: ϭⲉⲗⲙⲁⲓ
ⲕⲁⲕⲉ: ⲕⲉⲕⲉ	ⲕⲁ₂ˢ: ⲕⲱ₂	ⲕⲉⲗⲟⲟⲗⲉ: ⲕⲉⲗⲱⲗ
ⲕⲁⲗⲁⲃⲓⲛ: ⲕⲉⲗⲉⲃⲓⲛ	ⲕⲁ₂ⲏⲩ: ⲕⲱⲕ	ⲕⲉⲗⲟⲓⲧ: ϭⲟⲉⲓⲗⲉ
ⲕⲁⲗⲗⲁ₂ⲧ̄: ϭⲁⲗⲗⲁ₂ⲧ̄	ⲕⲁ₂ⲕ̄: ⲕⲁ₂ⲕ̄ⲟ̄	ⲕⲉⲙⲧ-/ˢ: ⲕⲓⲙ
ⲕⲁⲗⲏⲗⲉ: ⲕⲁⲗⲉⲗⲉ	ⲕⲁⲭⲓϥ: ϭⲁⲭⲓϥ	ⲕⲉⲛˢ: ⲕⲟⲩⲛ(ⲧ)ˢ
ⲕⲁⲗⲱⲟⲩ: ϭⲟⲉⲓⲗⲉ	ⲕⲃⲁ: ⲕⲱⲱⲃⲉ	ⲕⲉⲟⲩⲗ: ⲟⲩⲗ
ⲕⲁⲙⲁⲩⲉⲓ: ⲕⲙⲟⲙ	ⲕⲃⲁ: ⲕⲃⲟ	ⲕⲉⲡ-, ⲕⲉⲡ: ϭⲱⲡⲉ
ⲕⲁⲙⲁⲩⲗⲉ: ϭⲁⲙⲟⲩⲗ	ⲕ̄ⲃ̄ⲃⲉ: ⲕⲱⲃ	ⲕⲉⲣⲉ-: ⲕⲱⲱⲣⲉ
ⲕⲁⲙⲉ: ⲕⲙⲟⲙ	ⲕⲃⲉ-: ⲕⲃⲟ	ⲕⲉⲥⲉ: ⲕⲱⲱⲥ, ⲕⲁⲥⲉ
ⲕⲁⲙⲏ: ⲕⲙⲟⲙ	ⲕⲉˢ: ⲕⲱ	ⲕⲉⲧ-: ⲕⲱⲧ, ⲕⲱⲧⲉ
ⲕⲁⲙⲏⲗⲉ: ϭⲁⲙⲟⲩⲗ	ⲕⲉⲉˢ: ⲕⲱ	ⲕⲉⲧ: ⲕⲉ

ⲕⲉⲧⲉ: ⲕⲉ
ⲕⲉϩⲕ̄-: ⲕⲁϩⲕϩ̄
ⲕⲉϩⲕⲉϩ-: ⲕⲁϩⲕϩ̄
ⲕⲉϩⲕⲱϩ(ⲋ): ⲕⲁϩⲕϩ̄
ⲕⲏ: ⲕⲱ
ⲕⲏⲃ: ⲕⲃⲟ
ⲕⲏⲙ: ⲕⲙⲟⲙ
ⲕⲏⲙⲉ: ⲕⲟⲙⲙⲉ, ⲕⲙⲟⲙ
ⲕⲏⲡ: ϭⲱⲡⲉ
ⲕⲏⲥ: ⲕⲁⲥ
ⲕⲏⲥ: ⲕⲱⲱⲥ
ⲕⲏⲥⲉ: ⲕⲁⲥⲉ
ⲕⲏⲧ: ⲕⲱⲧ, ⲕⲱⲧⲉ
ⲕⲓⲁϩⲕ̄: ⲕⲟⲓⲁϩⲕ̄
ⲕⲓⲃⲉ: ⲉⲕⲓⲃⲉ
ⲕⲓⲉⲃⲉ: ⲉⲕⲓⲃⲉ
ⲕⲓⲛ-: ϭⲓⲛ-
ⲕⲓⲛⲃⲏⲗ: ϭⲓⲛⲟⲩⲏⲗ
ⲕⲓⲥ: ⲕⲁⲥ
ⲕⲗ̄: ⲕ̄ⲗⲉ
ⲕⲗⲁ: ϭⲗⲁ
ⲕⲗⲁ: ⲕⲣⲟ
ⲕⲗⲃ̄ⲧ: ⲕⲗⲁϥ̄ⲧ
ⲕⲗⲉⲗ: ⲕⲗⲁⲗ
ⲕⲗⲉϥⲧ̄: ⲕⲗⲁϥ̄ⲧ
ⲕⲗⲏⲗ: ⲕⲗⲁⲗ
ⲕⲗⲓ: ⲕⲣⲓ
ⲕⲗⲟϭⲉ: ϭⲗⲟⲟϭⲉ
ⲕⲗ̄ϩⲉ: ⲕⲱⲗϩ̄
ⲕⲙⲉ: ⲕⲙⲟⲙ
ⲕⲙⲏⲙⲉ: ⲕⲙⲟⲙ
ⲕ̄ⲙ̄ⲙⲉ: ⲕⲟⲙⲙⲉ
ⲕ̄ⲙ̄ⲧⲟ: ⲕⲓⲙ
ⲕ̄ⲛ̄: ⲝⲓⲛ

ⲕ̄ⲛ̄ⲙⲟⲩⲧ: ϭⲓⲛⲙⲟⲩⲧ
ⲕⲛⲟⲟⲥ: ⲕⲛⲟⲥ
ⲕⲛ̄ⲧⲋ: ϭⲓⲛⲉ
ⲕⲛⲱⲱⲥ: ⲕⲛⲟⲥ
ⲕⲟⲓϩⲉ: ⲕⲱϩ
ⲕⲟⲗⲋ: ϭⲱⲗ
ⲕⲟⲗⲟⲗ: ⲕⲉⲗⲱⲗ
ⲕⲟⲗⲡ(ⲋ): ϭⲱⲗⲡ̄
ⲕⲟⲗⲡⲥ̄: ⲕⲱⲗⲡ̄
ⲕⲟⲙ: ϭⲱⲙ
ⲕⲟⲙϥ̄: ⲕⲟⲟⲙϥ̄
ⲕⲟⲛⲭⲟⲩ: ⲕⲟⲩⲭⲟⲩ
ⲕⲟⲟⲃⲋ: ⲕⲱⲱⲃⲉ
ⲕⲟⲟⲃⲉϥ: ⲕⲱⲃ
ⲕⲟⲟⲃϩ̄: ⲕⲱⲃϩ̄
ⲕⲟⲟⲛⲥⲋ: ⲕⲱⲱⲥ
ⲕⲟⲟⲣⲉⲋ: ⲕⲱⲱⲣⲉ
ⲕⲟⲟⲥⲋ: ⲕⲱⲱⲥ
ⲕⲟⲟⲩⲉ: ⲕⲉ
ⲕⲟⲟϣⲉ: ⲕⲱⲱϣⲉ
ⲕⲟⲡⲋ: ϭⲱⲡⲉ
ⲕⲟⲣⲧⲉ: ϭⲟⲣⲧⲉ
ⲕⲟⲣϣϥ̄: ⲕⲱⲣϣ̄
ⲕⲟⲣϥⲋ: ϭⲟⲣϥⲋ
ⲕⲟⲥ: ϭⲟⲥ
ⲕⲟⲧⲋ: ⲕⲱⲧ, ⲕⲱⲧⲉ
ⲕⲟⲧ: ⲕⲱⲧⲉ
ⲕⲟⲧⲥ̄: ⲕⲱⲧⲉ
ⲕⲟⲩⲕ: ϭⲟⲩⲭ
ⲕⲟⲩⲕⲉ: ⲕⲱⲕ
ⲕⲟⲩⲕⲙ̄: ⲕ̄ⲙ̄ⲕⲙ̄
ⲕⲟⲩⲗⲱⲗ: ⲕⲉⲗⲱⲗ
ⲕⲟⲩⲙⲕⲙ̄: ⲕ̄ⲙ̄ⲕⲙ̄
ⲕⲟⲩⲛⲭⲟⲩ: ⲕⲟⲩⲭⲟⲩ

ⲕⲟⲩⲟⲛⲋ: ⲕⲟⲩⲛ(ⲧ)ⲋ
ⲕⲟⲩⲟⲩⲛ(ⲧ)ⲋ: ⲕⲟⲩⲛ(ⲧ)ⲋ
ⲕⲟⲩⲱⲛⲋ: ⲕⲟⲩⲛ(ⲧ)ⲋ
ⲕⲟⲩⲭ: ϭⲟⲩⲭ
ⲕⲟⲭⲋ: ϭⲱϭ
ⲕⲣⲙ̄ⲛ̄ⲧⲥ̄: ⲕⲣⲙ̄ⲧⲥ̄
ⲕⲣⲟϩ: ϭⲣⲱϩ
ⲕⲣⲟⲭ: ⲕⲣⲟⲩⲭ
ⲕⲣⲱⲟⲩ: ⲕⲣⲟ
ⲕⲣⲱⲱϭ: ϭⲣⲟϭ
ⲕⲣⲱϩ: ϭⲣⲱϩ
ⲕⲧⲗⲉⲓⲧ: ⲕⲱⲧⲉ
ⲕⲧⲉ-: ⲕⲱⲧⲉ
ⲕⲧⲏⲩ: ⲕⲱⲧⲉ
ⲕⲧⲟ(ⲋ): ⲕⲱⲧⲉ
ⲕⲧⲟⲉⲓⲧ: ⲕⲱⲧⲉ
ⲕⲩⲗⲙⲁⲛ: ϭⲉⲗⲙⲁⲓ
ⲕⲱⲃⲉϥ: ⲕⲱⲃ
ⲕⲱⲗ: ϭⲱⲗ
ⲕⲱⲗⲉ: ϭⲱⲱⲗⲉ
ⲕⲱⲗⲡ̄: ϭⲱⲗⲡ̄
ⲕⲱⲛⲥ̄: ⲕⲱⲱⲥ
ⲕⲱⲟⲩ: ⲕⲟⲟⲩ
ⲕⲱⲡⲋ, ⲕⲱⲡⲉ: ϭⲱⲡⲉ
ⲕⲱⲣⲙ̄: ⲕⲣⲱⲙ
ⲕⲱⲣϩ̄: ϭⲱⲣϩ̄
ⲕⲱⲧϩ̄: ϭⲱⲧϩ̄
ⲕⲱⲱⲛⲥ̄: ⲕⲱⲛⲥ̄
ⲕⲟⲟϥⲉ: ⲕⲱⲱⲃⲉ
ⲕⲱϩ: ⲕⲟⲟϩ
ⲭⲟⲓⲁⲭ: ⲕⲟⲓⲁϩⲕ̄
ⲭⲟⲓⲁ(ϩ)ⲕ: ⲕⲟⲓⲁϩⲕ̄

ⲗ

ⲗⲁ n.m. envy, slander. ⲙ̄ⲛ̄ⲧⲗⲁ slander. ϩⲓ-ⲗⲁ to slander
(ⲉ); as n.m. slander; ⲣⲉϥϩⲓ-ⲗⲁ slanderer; ⲙ̄ⲛ̄ⲧⲣⲉϥϩⲓ-ⲗⲁ
slander; ⲗⲁⲃ-ⲗⲁ eager for slander.

ⲗⲁⲁⲩ, ⲗⲁⲁⲩⲉ, ⲗⲁⲩⲉ, ⲗⲁⲟⲩⲉ (§16.3) (1) indef. pron. any, anyone; something; may take article as n., e.g. ⲟⲩⲗⲁⲁⲩ ϣⲏⲙ
a little something. ⲕⲉⲗⲁⲁⲩ any other. ⲗⲁⲁⲩ ⲛⲓⲙ everyone, everything. (2) as adj. any (usu. bef. n. w. ⲛ̄);
ⲗⲁⲁⲩ ⲙ̄ⲙⲱⲧⲛ̄ any of you. (3) Neg. context: none, no one,
nothing. (4) As pred. ⲟⲩⲗⲁⲁⲩ, ϩⲉⲛⲗⲁⲁⲩ = nothing, no
one, even when neg. is not present. (5) ⲁⲧⲗⲁⲁⲩ ⲛ̄ prep.

lacking, without; (ⲛ̄) ⲗⲁⲁⲩ adv. (not) at all.

ⲗⲁⲃⲟⲓ, ⲗⲁⲃⲁⲓ n.f. lioness; she-bear.

ⲗⲁⲓⲛ, ⲗⲁⲉⲓⲛ, ⲗⲉⲉⲓⲛ n.m. steel.

ⲗⲁⲕⲙ̄, ⲗⲁⲕⲙⲉ n.f. piece, fragment. (ⲛ̄) ⲗⲁⲕⲙ̄ ⲗⲁⲕⲙ̄ into
pieces; ⲣ̄-ⲗⲁⲕⲙ̄ ⲗⲁⲕⲙ̄ to break or tear into pieces.

ⲗⲁⲕⲛ̄ⲧ, ⲗⲁⲉⲛ̄ⲧ n.f. cauldron.

ⲗⲁⲕⲟⲟⲧⲉ, ⲗⲁⲕⲟⲧⲉ, ⲗⲁⲁⲕⲟⲧⲉ n.f. a liquid measure (wine).

ⲗⲁⲕⲍ̄ n.m. corner, edge, extremity, top.

ⲗⲁⲗⲉ (ⲗⲟⲟⲗⲉ) ⲗⲁⲗⲱ⳿ (ⲗⲁⲗⲱⲱ⳿) Q ⲗⲁⲗⲱⲟⲩ (ⲗⲁⲗⲱ, ⲗⲁⲗⲏⲩ) vb. tr.
to apply (paint, overlay: ⲙ̄ⲙⲟ⳿; to: ⲉ); to paint, smear.

ⲗⲁⲙⲭⲁⲧⲏ̄, ⲗⲁⲭⲁⲧⲏ̄, ⲗⲁⲙⲭⲁⲧ, ⲗⲁⲙⲭⲉⲧ n.m. tar, pitch.

ⲗⲁⲥ n.m. tongue; language (also ⲗⲥⲡⲉ ⲛ̄ ⲗⲁⲥ); any tongue-
shaped object. ⲗⲁⲥ ⲥⲛⲁⲩ deceitful; ⲙⲛ̄ⲧⲗⲁⲥ ⲥⲛⲁⲩ deceit.

ⲗⲁⲥ n.m. tow, flax.

ⲗⲁⲧⲃⲥ̄, ⲗⲁⲧⲃⲉⲥ n.f. a patch; ϩⲓ-ⲗⲁⲧⲃⲥ̄ ⲉ to put a patch on.

ⲗⲁⲩⲟ, ⲗⲁⲃⲱ n.m.f. sail; curtain, awning. ⲅⲓⲥ-ⲗⲁⲩⲟ n.f.
half-sail.

ⲗⲁϣⲁⲛⲉ (pl. ⲗⲁϣⲛⲏⲩ, ⲗⲁϣⲛⲓⲟⲩ) n.m. village magistrate.

ⲗⲁϩ̄ⲛ n.f. a liquid measure.

ⲗⲁϭⲉ vb. tr. to remove, cause to cease (ⲉ).

ⲗⲉⲗⲟⲩ (pl. ⲗⲉⲗⲁⲩⲉ, ⲗⲁⲩⲉ, ⲗⲁⲁⲩ) n.m.f. young man or woman.

ⲗⲉⲙⲏⲏϣⲉ n.m. warrior, champion.

ⲗⲉⲛⲧⲏⲛ, ⲗⲉⲛⲑⲏⲛ, ⲗⲁⲛⲑⲏⲛ n.m. saw.

ⲗⲉⲟⲛ n. earring, bracelet.

ⲗⲉⲯ, ⲗⲓⲯ n.m. person afflicted with eye-disease.

ⲗⲉⲡⲥⲉ, ⲗⲉⲯⲉ, ⲗⲓⲡⲥⲉ n.m. fragment.

ⲗⲉϥⲗⲓϥⲉ n.f. crumb, fragment.

ⲗⲉϩ n.m. care, anxiety.

ⲗⲉϩⲗⲱϩ Q to be high, tall. ⲗⲁϩⲗⲉϩ n.m. haughtiness.

ⲗⲓⲃⲉ ⲗⲉⲃⲧ⳿ Q ⲗⲟⲃⲉ (ⲗⲁⲃ-) vb. intr. to be mad, rage (at:
ⲉϩⲟⲩⲛ ⲉ, ⲛ̄ⲥⲁ; from: ⲛ̄ⲧⲛ̄, ϩⲁ, ϩⲛ̄, ϩⲓⲧⲛ̄); rarely tr. to
make mad. ⲗⲁⲃ-ⲗⲁ see ⲗⲁ. ⲗⲁⲃ-ⲙⲁϩⲧ̄ gluttonous. ⲗⲁⲃ-
ⲥϩⲓⲙⲉ lecherous. ⲗⲁⲃ-ϩⲏ greedy; ⲙⲛ̄ⲧⲗⲁⲃ-ϩⲏ greed; ⲣ̄-
ⲗⲁⲃ-ϩⲏ to become hungry, greedy.

ⲗⲓⲕⲧ⳿ in ⲣ̄-ⲗⲓⲕⲧ⳿ to veil, cover; ⲛ̄ ⲗⲓⲕⲧ⳿ prep. covering.

ⲁⲓⲗⲟⲟⲍⲉ, ⲗⲉⲗⲱⲍⲉ, ⲉⲗⲟⲟⲍⲉ, ⲗⲟⲍⲉ n.f. gum resin (or tree).

ⲗⲓⲙⲏⲛ n.m. portrait, image.

ⲗ̄ⲗⲏⲃ, ⲉⲗⲗⲏⲃ, ⲗ̄ⲗⲏϥ n. jesting, buffoonery.

ⲗⲟ (imptv. ⲁⲗⲟⲕ, f. ⲁⲗⲟ; pl. ⲁⲗⲱⲧⲛ̄) vb. intr. (1) to
cease, stop, come to an end, be terminated; + Circum.:
to stop doing, no longer do. (2) to leave, quit, depart
(from: ⲙ̄ⲙⲟⸯ, ⲍⲁ, ⲍⲁⲃⲟⲗ ⲛ̄, ⲍⲓ, ⲍⲛ̄, ⲉⲃⲟⲗ ⲍⲛ̄, ⲍⲓⲡⲛ̄, ⲍⲓⲭⲛ̄);
sometimes + untranslatable ⲙ̄ⲙⲁⲩ. ⲁ-ⲡⲉϥⲍⲏⲧ ⲗⲟ ⲙ̄ⲙⲟϥ he
fainted.

ⲗⲟⲓⲍⲉ n.m.(f.) mud, filth.

ⲗⲟⲓϭⲉ n.f. cause, excuse, reason; ⲁⲧⲗⲟⲓϭⲉ without cause.
ϯ-ⲗⲟⲓϭⲉ ⲛⲁⸯ to provide excuse or occasion to. ϭⲛ̄-
ⲗⲟⲓϭⲉ to find excuse. ϭⲛ̄-ⲗⲟⲓϭⲉ idem.

ⲗⲟⲕ, ⲗⲟϭ n.m. cup, bowl; also as measure. ϣⲛ̄-ⲗⲟⲕ idem.

ⲗⲟⲕⲗ̄ⲕ ⲗⲉⲕⲗⲱⲕⸯ Q ⲗⲉⲕⲗⲱⲕ vb. intr. to become soft; rarely tr.
to make soft, smooth (ⲙ̄ⲙⲟⸯ); as n.m. softness. ⲗⲁⲕⲗⲁⲕ
n. a kind of confection.

ⲗⲟⲟⲙⲉ, ⲗⲟⲩⲙⲉ, ⲙⲟⲟⲗⲉ n.f.m. bait.

ⲗⲟⲟⲩ, ⲗⲟⲟⲩⲉ, ⲗⲱⲟⲩ, ⲗⲁⲩ n.m. curl; fringe, hem; cluster.

ⲗⲟⲟϥⲉ, ⲗⲟⲟⲃⲉ, ⲗⲟⲃⲉ Q to be decayed, about to collapse.

ⲗⲟⲩⲗⲁⲓ n.m. shout. ⲱϣ/ⲉϣ-/ⲛⲉⲭ-/ⲧⲱⲕ ⲗⲟⲩⲗⲁⲓ ⲉⲃⲟⲗ to shout.

ⲗⲟϥⲗϥ̄ (ⲗⲟϥⲗⲉϥ, ⲗⲟⲃⲗⲉϥ) ⲗⲉϥⲗⲱϥⸯ Q ⲗⲉϥⲗⲱϥ, ⲗⲉϥⲗⲟϥⲧ̄ (± ⲉⲃⲟⲗ)
vb. intr. to rot, perish by decay or corruption; vb. tr.
to destroy, cause to rot (ⲙ̄ⲙⲟⸯ); as n.m. decay, rot.

ⲗⲟⲭⲗⲭ̄ vb. tr. to rub, crush, oppress (ⲙ̄ⲙⲟⸯ).

ⲗⲟⲭⲗⲭ̄ (ⲗⲟϭⲗⲉⲭ) ⲗⲉⲭⲗⲱⲭⸯ (ⲗⲉϭⲗⲱϭⸯ) Q ⲗⲉⲭⲗⲱⲭ (ⲗⲉϭⲗⲱϭ) vb.
intr. to languish, be sickly; vb. tr. to make sick
(ⲙ̄ⲙⲟⸯ); as n.m. sickness.

ⲗⲟϭ, ⲗⲁϭ n. in ⲣ̄-ⲗⲟϭ ⲉ to importune; ⲙⲛ̄ⲧⲗⲟϭ persistence.

ⲗⲟϭⲗⲉϭ n.m. girder, frame, joint.

ⲗⲱⲃϣ̄, Q ⲗⲟⲃϣ̄ vb. intr. to glow red-hot; tr. to heat red-
hot (ⲙ̄ⲙⲟⸯ); as n.m. glow.

ⲗⲱⲃϣ̄ n.m. crown, battlement; as vb. tr. to crown, adorn.

ⲗⲱⲕ, Q ⲗⲏⲕ vb. intr. to become soft, be fresh.

ⲗⲱⲕⲥ̄ (ⲗⲱϭⲥ̄, ⲗⲱⲝ, ⲗⲟⲩⲝ) ⲗⲝ- ⲗⲟⲕⲥⸯ vb. tr. to bite, stab,

pierce (ⲙ̄ⲙⲟ⸗); + ⲛ̄ⲥⲁ: to bite or snap at; as n.m. bite.
ⲣⲉϥⲗⲱⲕⲥ̄ biter, biting. ϣⲥ̄-ⲛ̄-ⲗⲱⲕⲥ̄ piercing blow.

ⲗⲱⲕϫ̄, Q ⲗⲟⲕϫ̄ vb. intr. to be weak, ineffectual; as n.m.
weakness.

ⲗⲱⲙⲥ̄ (ⲗⲁⲙⲉⲥ) Q ⲗⲟⲙⲥ̄ vb. intr. to become foul, to stink; as
n.m. foulness, putrescence.

ⲗⲱⲧⲉ (ⲗⲱⲱⲧⲉ) vb. intr. to become hard, callous (of skin).

ⲗⲱⲱⲙⲉ (ⲗⲱⲱⲙ, ⲗⲱⲙ) Q ⲗⲟⲟⲙⲉ (ⲗⲟⲙⲉ) vb. intr. to wither, fade;
to become filthy, dirty, muddy; as n.m. filth; withered
appearance. ⲁⲧⲗⲱⲱⲙⲉ unfading. Q also ⲗⲁⲁⲙ.

ⲗⲱⲱⲥ (ⲗⲱⲥ) ⲗⲉⲥ- Q ⲗⲁⲁⲥ(ⲉ) vb. tr. to crush, bruise (ⲙ̄ⲙⲟ⸗);
vb. intr. to become crushed, bruised.

ⲗⲱ₂ⲙ̄ ⲗⲉ₂ⲙ̄- ⲗⲟ₂ⲙ⸗ Q ⲗⲟ₂ⲙ̄ vb. tr. to boil (ⲙ̄ⲙⲟ⸗); vb. intr.
to be boiled. ⲗⲁ₂ⲙⲉⲥ n. boiled food (?).

ⲗⲱⲝ ⲗⲉⲝ- ⲗⲟⲝ⸗ Q ⲗⲟⲝ vb. tr. to crush, bruise (ⲙ̄ⲙⲟ⸗); to
lick (ⲙ̄ⲙⲟ⸗); vb. intr. to be sticky, adhesive; to stick
(to: ⲉ, ⲉ₂ⲟⲩⲛ ⲛ̄).

ⲗⲱⲝⲕ̄ (ⲗⲱⲝⳓ, ⲗⲱⲝⲧ̄) ⲗⲟⲝⲕ⸗ (ⲗⲟⲝ6⸗, ⲗⲟ6ⲕ⸗, ⲗⲟⲝⲧ⸗) Q ⲗⲟⲝⲧ̄ vb.
intr. to become sticky, adhesive; to stick (to: ⲉ); vb.
tr. to stick, join (ⲙ̄ⲙⲟ⸗; to: ⲉ); also to lick.

ⲗⲱⲝ₂̄ ⲗⲉⲝ₂̄- ⲗⲟⲝ₂⸗ Q ⲗⲟⲝ₂̄ (1) vb. tr. to crush (ⲙ̄ⲙⲟ⸗); intr.
to be crushed, effaced; as n.m. anguish, oppression;
(2) vb. tr. to lick (ⲙ̄ⲙⲟ⸗).

ⲗⲱ6ⲉ ⲗⲉ6- ⲗⲟ6⸗ Q ⲗⲏ6 vb. tr. to hide (ⲙ̄ⲙⲟ⸗); reflex. idem.

ⲗ̄₂ⲏⲙ (ⲗ̄₂ⲙ̄, ⲉⲗ₂ⲏⲙ, ⲣ̄₂ⲏⲙ) vb. intr. to roar; as n.m. roaring.

ⲗ̄₂ⲱⲃ, ⲗ̄₂ⲱⲱϥ n.m. steam, vapor.

ⲗⲁⲁⲕⲟⲧⲉ: ⲗⲁⲕⲟⲟⲧⲉ	ⲗⲁⲛⲑⲏⲛ: ⲗⲉⲛⲧⲏⲛ	ⲗⲉⲉⲓⲛ: ⲗⲁⲓⲛ
ⲗⲁⲁⲩ: ⲗⲉⲗⲟⲩ	ⲗⲁⲟⲩⲉ: ⲗⲁⲁⲩ	ⲗⲉⲉⲗ-: ⲉⲗⲟⲟⲗⲉ
ⲗⲁⲁⲥ(ⲉ): ⲗⲱⲱⲥ	ⲗⲁⲩ: ⲗⲟⲟⲩ	ⲗⲉⲗ-: ⲉⲗⲟⲟⲗⲉ
ⲗⲁⲃ-: ⲗⲓⲃⲉ	ⲗⲁⲩⲉ: ⲗⲉⲗⲟⲩ, ⲗⲁⲁⲩ	ⲗⲉⲗⲁⲩⲉ: ⲗⲉⲗⲟⲩ
ⲗⲁⲃⲁⲓ: ⲗⲁⲃⲟⲓ	ⲗⲁϣⲓⲏ: ϣⲓⲁⲓ	ⲗⲉⲗⲱ₂ⲉ: ⲗⲓⲗⲟⲟ₂ⲉ
ⲗⲁⲃⲱ: ⲗⲁⲩⲟ	ⲗⲁϣⲛⲏⲩ: ⲗⲁϣⲁⲛⲉ	ⲗⲉⲥ-: ⲗⲱⲱⲥ
ⲗⲁⲕⲗⲁⲕ: ⲗⲟⲕⲗⲁⲕ̄	ⲗⲁ₂ⲗⲉ₂: ⲗⲉ₂ⲗⲱ₂	ⲗⲉⲧ: ⲗⲁⲧ
ⲗⲁⲗⲏⲩ: ⲗⲁⲗⲉ	ⲗⲁ₂ⲙⲉⲥ: ⲗⲱ₂ⲙ̄	ⲗⲉϥⲗⲟϥⲧ̄: ⲗⲟϥⲗϥ̄
ⲗⲁⲗⲱ: ⲗⲁⲗⲉ	ⲗⲁⲝⲭⲁⲧⲡ̄: ⲗⲁⲙⲭⲁⲧⲡ̄	ⲗⲉ6-: ⲗⲱ6ⲉ
ⲗⲁⲗⲱⲟⲩ: ⲗⲁⲗⲉ	ⲗⲁ6: ⲗⲟ6	ⲗⲉ6ⲗⲱ6(⸗): ⲗⲟⲝⲗⲝ̄
ⲗⲁⲗⲱ(ⲱ)⸗: ⲗⲁⲗⲉ	ⲗⲁ6ⲛ̄ⲧ: ⲗⲁⲕⲛ̄ⲧ	ⲗⲏ6: ⲗⲱ6ⲉ
ⲗⲁⲙⲉⲥ: ⲗⲱⲙⲥ̄	ⲗⲉⲃⲧ⸗: ⲗⲓⲃⲉ	ⲗⲓⲗ: ⲣⲓⲣ

ⲗⲓⲗ-: ⲉⲗⲟⲟⲗⲉ   ⲗⲟⲟⲃⲉ: ⲗⲟⲟϥⲉ   ⲗⲟⲃⲗⲉⲭ: ⲗⲟⲭⲗⲉⲭ
ⲗⲓⲯ: ⲗⲉⲯ   ⲗⲟⲟⲗⲉ: ⲗⲗⲗⲉ   ⲗⲱⲙ: ⲗⲱⲱⲙⲉ
ⲗⲓⲯⲉ: ⲗⲉⲡⲥⲉ   ⲗⲟⲟⲙⲉ: ⲗⲱⲱⲙⲉ   ⲗⲱⲥ: ⲗⲱⲱⲥ
ⲗ̄ⲕ-: ⲱⲗⲕ̄   ⲗⲟⲩⲝ: ⲗⲱⲕⲥ̄   ⲗⲱⲟⲩ: ⲗⲟⲟⲩ
ⲗⲝ̄-: ⲗⲱⲕⲥ̄   ⲗⲟⲩⲙⲉ: ⲗⲟⲟⲙⲉ   ⲗⲱⲱⲧⲉ: ⲗⲱⲧⲉ
ⲗ̄ⲗⲏϥ: ⲗ̄ⲗⲏⲃ   ⲗⲟ₂ⲉ: ⲗⲓⲗⲟⲟ₂ⲉ   ⲗⲱⲭⲧ̄: ⲗⲱⲭⲕ̄
ⲗ̄ⲙ̄ⲗⲏⲙ: ⲉⲗⲟⲙⲗ̄ⲙ̄   ⲗⲟⲭⲧ(ⲋ): ⲗⲱⲭⲕ̄   ⲗⲱⲭⲟ̄: ⲗⲱⲭⲕ̄
ⲗ̄ⲙ̄ⲗⲱⲙ: ⲉⲗⲟⲙⲗ̄ⲙ̄   ⲗⲟₐⲧⲉ: ⲣⲁ₂ⲧⲉ   ⲗⲱⲃⲉ: ⲗⲱⲕⲥ̄
ⲗⲟⲃⲉ: ⲗⲓⲃⲉ   ⲗⲟⲭⲃⲋ: ⲗⲱⲭⲕ̄   ⲗ̄₂ⲙ̄: ⲗ̄₂ⲏⲙ
ⲗⲟⲃⲉ: ⲗⲟⲟϥⲉ   ⲗⲟⲃ: ⲗⲟⲕ   ⲗ̄₂ⲱⲙ: ₂ⲗⲱⲙ
ⲗⲟⲃⲗⲉϥ: ⲗⲟϥⲗ̄ϥ   ⲗⲟⲃⲋ: ⲗⲱⲃⲉ   ⲗ̄₂ⲱⲱϥ: ⲗ̄₂ⲱⲃ
ⲗⲟⲙⲉ: ⲗⲱⲱⲙⲉ   ⲗⲟⲃⲕⲋ: ⲗⲱⲭⲕ̄

ⲙ

ⲙⲁ n.m. place; often in spec. senses: dwelling-place, temple or shrine; ⲡⲉⲓⲙⲁ this world; ⲡⲕⲉⲙⲁ the other world.
ⲡ(ⲋ)ⲙⲁ ⲡⲉ it is (one's) lot or duty (to do: ⲉ). For
cpds. of ⲙⲁ ⲛ̄ see 2nd element. ⲉ ⲡⲙⲁ ⲛ̄ prep. to, toward; regarding, concerning; instead of, in the place
of. ⲉⲩⲙⲁ to one place, together. ⲕⲁⲧⲁ ⲡⲙⲁ in various,
different places. ϣⲁ ⲡⲉⲓⲙⲁ so far, up to now/here. ₂ⲁ
ⲡⲙⲁ ⲛ̄ as regards. ⲙⲁ ⲛⲓⲙ everywhere. ⲕⲁ-(ⲡ)ⲙⲁ ⲛⲁⲋ to
give an opportunity to. ⲣ̄-ⲡⲙⲁ ⲛ̄ to take the place of,
succeed. ϯ-ⲙⲁ ⲛⲁⲋ to allow, permit, give opportunity
to. ⲭⲓ-ⲙⲁ ⲛ̄ⲧⲛ̄ to usurp the place of. ⲉⲙ̄-ⲙⲁ to find
opportunity. See also § 23.2.
ⲙⲁ ⲙⲁ- ⲙⲁⲧⲋ (ⲙⲏⲉⲓⲋ) imptv. of ϯ, q.v. See also §26.3.
ⲙⲁⲁⲃ (ⲙⲁⲁⲃ-, ⲙⲁⲃ-; f. ⲙⲁⲁⲃⲉ) number: thirty. See §30.7.
ⲙⲁⲁⲩ, ⲙⲁⲩ n.f. mother; also fig. and as title. ϣⲛ̄-ⲙⲁⲁⲩ,
ϣⲏⲛ ⲙ̄ ⲙⲁⲁⲩ child having same mother as another. ⲁⲧ-
ⲙⲁⲁⲩ motherless. ⲣ̄-ⲙⲁⲁⲩ to become mother.
ⲙⲁⲁⲭⲉ n.m. ear; handle. ⲕⲁ-ⲙⲁⲁⲭⲉ ⲉ, ⲣⲓⲕⲉ ⲙ̄ ⲡⲙⲁⲁⲭⲉ ⲉ to
give ear to, incline ear to.
ⲙⲁⲁⲭⲉ, ⲙⲁⲭⲉ (ⲙⲁⲭ-) n.f. a dry measure.
ⲙⲁⲉⲓⲛ n.m. sign, mark; wonder, miracle. ⲣ̄-ⲙⲁⲉⲓⲛ to become
marked, remarkable; to indicate (ⲉ). ⲣⲉϥⲉⲓⲣⲉ ⲙ̄ ⲡⲙⲁⲉⲓⲛ
wonder-worker. ϯ-ⲙⲁⲉⲓⲛ to indicate, point at, signify
(ⲉ); to give a sign (to: ⲛⲁⲋ); ⲣⲉϥϯ-ⲙⲁⲉⲓⲛ augur.

ϫι-ⲙⲁⲉⲓⲛ to practice divination, augury; as n.m. divination; ⲣⲉϥϫⲓ-ⲙⲁⲉⲓⲛ augur, diviner; ⲙⲛ̄ⲧⲣⲉϥϫⲓ-ⲙⲁⲉⲓⲛ
augury, divination.

ⲙⲁⲕⲟⲧ, ⲙⲁⲕⲱⲧ, ⲙⲁⲕⲁ(ⲗ)ⲧ, ⲙⲁⲅⲗⲁ n.m. lance, javelin.

ⲙⲁⲕ︤ϩ︥, ⲙⲁⲭ, ⲙⲟⲕ︤ϩ︥ n.m. neck. ϯ-ⲡ(ⲥ)ⲙⲁⲕ︤ϩ︥ ϩⲁ to submit to.
ⲛⲁϣ︤ⲧ︥-ⲙⲁⲕ︤ϩ︥ adj. stiff-necked; ⲙⲛ̄ⲧⲛⲁϣ︤ⲧ︥-ⲙⲁⲕ︤ϩ︥ stiff-necked-
ness; ⲣ̄-ⲛⲁϣ︤ⲧ︥-ⲙⲁⲕ︤ϩ︥ to be stiff-necked.

ⲙⲁⲛⲅⲁⲗⲉ, ⲙⲁⲛⲅⲁⲗⲏ, ⲙⲁⲛϫⲁⲗⲉ n.m. pick, hoe; winnowing fan.

ⲙⲁⲣⲟⲩⲟϭⲉ, ⲙⲉⲣⲟⲩⲟϭⲉ, ⲙ̄ⲣⲟⲩⲟⲟϭⲉ n.f. jawbone.

ⲙⲁⲣⲭⲱϫⲉ (pl. ⲙⲁⲣⲭⲟⲟϫⲉ) n. name of woman's garment.

ⲙⲁⲧⲉ in ⲉⲙⲁⲧⲉ, ⲙ̄ⲙⲁⲧⲉ adv. very much, greatly; only.

ⲙⲁⲧⲉ (ⲙⲁⲁⲧⲉ, ⲙⲉⲧⲉ) Q ⲙⲁⲧⲱⲟⲩ vb. tr. to reach, attain, obtain, enjoy (ⲙ̄ⲙⲟⲥ); intr. to hit the mark, be success-
ful (in doing: ⲉ, ⲛ̄ + Inf.); as n.m. success. ϯ-ⲙⲁⲧⲉ
= ⲙⲁⲧⲉ tr.

ⲙⲁⲧⲟⲓ, ⲙⲁⲧⲟⲉⲓ n.m. soldier. ⲣ̄-ⲙⲁⲧⲟⲓ (Q ⲟ ⲛ̄) to become a
soldier. ⲙⲛ̄ⲧⲙⲁⲧⲟⲓ soldiering, warfare.

ⲙⲁⲧⲟⲩ n.f. poison. ⲃⲁⲕ-ⲙⲁⲧⲟⲩ poisonous, venomous.

ⲙⲁⲩⲁⲁⲥ, ⲙⲁⲩⲁⲧⲥ intens. pron. self, self alone, ownself;
used appositionally to preceding n. or pron.; see §28.3.

ⲙⲁϣⲉ n.f. balance, scales.

ⲙⲁϣⲟ in ⲉⲙⲁϣⲟ adv. very, greatly. ⲙ̄ⲙⲁϣⲟ idem.

ⲙⲁϣ︤ⲣ︥ⲧ, ⲙⲁϣⲉⲣⲧ n.m.f. cable.

ⲙⲁϩ, ⲙⲁⲁϩ n.m. nest, brood. ⲙⲁϩ-ⲟⲩⲁⲗ, -ⲃⲁⲗ, ⲙⲉϩ-ⲟⲩⲏⲗ n.m.
idem.

ⲙⲁϩⲉ n.m. cubit. ⲅⲓⲥ-ⲙⲁϩⲉ half cubit.

ⲙⲁϩⲉ n.m. flax. ⲉϥⲣⲁ-ⲙⲁϩⲉ linseed.

ⲙⲁϩ︤ⲧ︥ n.m. bowels, intestines. ⲙⲉϩⲧ-ⲟ great intestine.

ⲙⲁⲭⲉ n.m. axe, pick.

ⲙⲁⲭⲕⲉ, ⲙⲓⲭⲕⲉ, ⲙⲉⲕⲭⲉ, ⲙⲓⲭϭⲉ n. a woman's garment.

ⲙⲉ, ⲙⲉⲉ, ⲙⲏⲉ n.f. truth, justice; freq. as adj. true, real,
genuine; truthful, righteous. ⲙⲛ̄ⲧⲙⲉ truth, righteousness. ⲛⲁⲙⲉ adv. truly, in fact. ϩⲛ̄ ⲟⲩⲙⲉ idem. ⲣⲙ̄ⲙ̄ⲙⲉ
an honest person. ⲣ̄-(ⲧ)ⲙⲉ to become true, verified.
ϫⲉ-/ϫⲓ-(ⲧ)ⲙⲉ to speak the truth; ⲙⲏⲧ (archaic) adj. true.

ⲙⲉ (ⲙⲉⲓ) ⲙⲉⲣⲉ- ⲙⲉⲣⲓⲧ⸗ (p.c. ⲙⲁⲓ-) vb. tr. to love, desire, wish (ⲙ̄ⲙⲟ⸗); ⲙⲉⲣⲉ- may be used with another Inf. ϣⲟⲩⲙⲉⲣⲓⲧ⸗ worthy of love. For cpds. with ⲙⲁⲓ- see 2nd element. As n.m. love. ⲙⲉⲣⲓⲧ (pl. ⲙⲉⲣⲁⲧⲉ) adj. beloved.

ⲙⲉⲉⲣⲉ n. midday, noon. ⲙ̄ ⲙⲉⲉⲣⲉ at noon.

ⲙⲉⲉⲩⲉ (ⲙⲉⲩⲉ, ⲙⲉⲉⲩ) vb. intr. to think (about: ⲉ; that: ϫⲉ), often w. ⲉ as reflex. or ethical dative; to be about (to do: ⲛ̄ + Inf.); as n.m. (± ⲛ̄ ϩⲏⲧ) thought, mind. ⲙⲉⲉⲩⲉ ⲉϩⲟⲩⲛ ⲉ to plot against. ⲙⲉⲉⲩⲉ ⲉⲃⲟⲗ to ponder, consider. ⲙ̄ⲛ̄ⲧⲁⲧⲙⲉⲉⲩⲉ absence of thought. ⲣⲉϥⲙⲉⲉⲩⲉ one who thinks. ϯ-(ⲡ)ⲙⲉⲉⲩⲉ ⲛⲁ⸗ to remind. ⲣ̄-ⲡ(⸗)ⲙⲉⲉⲩⲉ to think of, remember (ⲛ̄); as n.m. remembrance.

ⲙⲉⲗⲱⲧ (pl. ⲙⲉⲗⲁⲧⲉ) n.f. ceiling, canopy.

ⲙⲉⲣⲉϩ, ⲙⲉϩⲣ̄ n.m. spear, javelin. ϣⲥ̄-ⲛ̄-ⲙⲉⲣⲉϩ thrust of spear. ϥⲁⲓ-ⲙⲉⲣⲉϩ spear-bearer.

ⲙⲉⲥⲧⲛ̄ϩⲏⲧ, ⲙⲉⲥⲑⲏⲧ n.f. breast, chest.

ⲙⲉⲥϩⲱⲗ n.m. a file.

ⲙⲉⲥⲟⲣⲏ, ⲙⲉⲥⲱⲣⲏ, ⲙⲉⲥⲟⲩⲣⲏ name of 12th Coptic month.

ⲙⲉϣⲉ- ⲙⲉϣⲁ⸗ vb. not to know; usu. in ⲙⲉϣⲉ-ⲛⲓⲙ so-and-so, such-and-such; ⲙⲉϣⲁⲕ, ⲙⲏϣⲁⲕ adv. perhaps.

ⲙⲉϣⲧⲓⲃⲧ̄ n.m. hinge of door.

ⲙⲉϩⲣⲟ n.m. manure; ⲣⲉϥϯ-ⲙⲉϩⲣⲟ one who manures.

ⲙⲉⲭⲡⲱⲛⲉ, ⲙⲉⲭⲡⲱⲱⲛⲉ, ⲙⲉϣⲡⲱⲛⲉ n.m.f. ulcer, eruption.

ⲙⲉϭⲧⲱⲗ n.m. tower.

ⲙⲏ, ⲙⲓ n.f. urine; ⲙⲏ ⲛ̄ ⲙⲟⲟⲩ idem. ⲙⲏ ⲟⲉⲓⲕ excrement. ⲣ̄-ⲙⲏ to urinate; to defecate. ⲙⲁ ⲛ̄ ⲣ̄-ⲙⲏ anus; latrine.

ⲙⲏⲏϣⲉ n.m. crowd, multitude; as adj. many, great, much.

ⲙⲏⲛⲉ, ⲙⲏⲏⲛⲉ in ⲙ̄ ⲙⲏⲛⲉ adv. daily, every day. ⲙ̄ ⲙⲏⲛⲉ (ⲙ̄) ⲙⲏⲛⲉ idem.

ⲙⲏⲣ n.m. shore, opposite shore (not properly Sah.).

ⲙⲏⲧ (f. ⲙⲏⲧⲉ) number: ten. ⲙ̄ⲛ̄ⲧ- prefix for 'teens; see §24.3. ⲥⲟⲩ-ⲙⲏⲧ tenth day. ⲣⲉ-ⲙⲏⲧ (pl. ⲣⲉ-ⲙⲁⲧⲉ) a tenth part, tithe.

ⲙⲏⲧⲉ, ⲙⲏⲏⲧⲉ n.f. middle. ⲉ ⲧⲙⲏⲧⲉ to, into the midst of (ⲛ̄), between; adv. forward, to a position in front.

2ⲛ̄/ⲛ̄ ⲧⲙⲏⲧⲉ in the midst (of: ⲛ̄); between; at the front.
ⲉⲃⲟⲗ ⲛ̄/2ⲛ̄ ⲧⲙⲏⲧⲉ from the midst of (ⲛ̄), from among. 2ⲓ
ⲧⲙⲏⲧⲉ in through the midst (of: ⲛ̄). ⲙⲁⲣ-ⲙⲏⲧⲉ n.f. belt.

ⲙⲏ2ⲉ, ⲙⲉ2ⲉ n.m. feather.

ⲙⲓⲕⲉ vb. intr. to rest; also reflex. (with ⲙ̄ⲙⲟ⸗); as n.m.
rest. ϯ-ⲙⲓⲕⲉ ⲛⲁ⸗ to give rest to.

ⲙⲓⲛⲉ, ⲙⲉⲓⲛⲉ n.f. kind, sort, species, quality, manner.
ⲙⲓⲛⲉ ⲛ̄ adj. sort of, kind of, manner of; ⲕⲉⲙⲓⲛⲉ ⲛ̄ other
sort of; ⲙⲓⲛⲉ ⲛⲓⲙ ⲛ̄ every sort of; ⲁϣ ⲙ̄ ⲙⲓⲛⲉ ⲛ̄ what sort,
what kind of? ⲛ̄ ⲧⲉⲓⲙⲓⲛⲉ of this sort, as follows, thus.

ⲙⲓⲟ⸗ pred. with 2nd pers. suffixes: ⲙⲓⲟⲕ, ⲙⲓⲱ, ⲙⲓⲱⲧⲛ̄ Hale!
Be well! Greetings!

ⲙⲓⲥⲉ ⲙⲉⲥ(ⲧ̄)- (ⲙⲁⲥ-) ⲙⲉⲥⲧ⸗ (ⲙⲁⲥⲧ⸗) Q ⲙⲟⲥⲉ; p.c. ⲙⲁⲥ-, ⲙⲉⲥ-
vb. tr. to bear (ⲙ̄ⲙⲟ⸗), give birth to; Q to be newly
born; as n.m. offspring; giving birth. As 2nd member
of cpd.: born, as in ⲃⲁⲗⲉ ⲛ̄ ⲙⲓⲥⲉ born lame; birth-, as
in ⲙⲁ ⲛ̄ ⲙⲓⲥⲉ birth-place, 2ⲟⲟⲩ ⲛ̄ ⲙⲓⲥⲉ birthday, ϣⲣ̄ⲡ-ⲛ̄-
ⲙⲓⲥⲉ first-born child; ⲙⲛ̄ⲧϣⲣ̄ⲡ-(ⲙ̄)ⲙⲓⲥⲉ status or right
of first born. ⲙⲓⲥⲉ ⲉ2ⲣⲁⲓ, ϯ ⲉ ⲙⲓⲥⲉ to bear, bring
forth. ⲣⲉϥⲙⲓⲥⲉ one who bears; ⲙⲛ̄ⲧⲣⲉϥⲙⲓⲥⲉ bearing,
birth. ⲁⲧⲙⲓⲥⲉ unborn. ⲙⲏⲥⲉ n.f. pregnant woman. ⲙⲁⲥ,
ⲙⲁⲥⲉ n.m. young animal; esp. bull, calf; ⲙⲛ̄ⲧⲙⲁⲥⲉ likeness of a calf. ⲙⲏⲥⲉ, ⲙⲏⲏⲥⲉ n.f. usury, interest; ϯ
ⲉ ⲙⲏⲥⲉ to lend at interest; ⲭⲓ-ⲙⲏⲥⲉ to take interest;
ⲁⲧⲙⲏⲥⲉ without interest. ⲙⲉⲥ-2ⲛ̄-ⲏⲓ n.m.f. one born in
household. ⲙⲉⲥⲓⲟ ⲙⲉⲥⲓⲟ⸗ vb. tr. to bring to birth, act
as midwife for. ⲙⲉⲥⲓⲱ, ⲙⲉⲥⲓⲟ n.f. midwife; ⲣ̄-ⲙⲉⲥⲓⲱ to
act as midwife. For cpds. with ⲙⲁⲥ- see 2nd element.

ⲙⲓϣⲉ, ⲙⲉⲓϣⲉ vb. intr. to fight, struggle, quarrel (with,
against: ⲙⲛ̄, ⲟⲩⲃⲉ, ⲉ; for, on behalf of: ⲉⲝⲛ̄, ⲉ2ⲣⲁⲓ ⲉⲝⲛ̄)
to attack (ⲉ); to strike (upon: ⲉⲝⲛ̄); as n.m. quarrel.
ⲙⲁ ⲛ̄ ⲙⲓϣⲉ arena; ⲣⲉϥⲙⲓϣⲉ fighter; ⲣ̄-ⲣⲉϥⲙⲓϣⲉ to be hos-
tile, quarrelsome; ⲥⲓⲛⲙⲓϣⲉ art of fighting.

ⲙ̄ⲕⲁ2, Q ⲙⲟⲕ2̄ vb. intr. to become painful, difficult; to be
in pain, grieved (in: ⲉ); Q to be difficult (to do: ⲉ,

ⲛ̄ + Inf.; ⲉⲧⲣⲉ); as n.m. (pl. ⲛ̄ⲕⲟⲟⲥ) pain, difficulty,
grief. ⲣ̄-ⲛ̄ⲕⲁⲥ to become pained, grieved, difficult.
ϣⲛ̄-ⲛ̄ⲕⲁⲥ to suffer pain. ⲛ̄ⲕⲁⲥ ⲛ̄ ⲁⲏⲧ vb. intr. to be pained or troubled at heart; as n.m. pain, grief. ϯ-ⲛ̄ⲕⲁⲥ
ⲛ̄ ⲁⲏⲧ to grieve, vex (ⲛⲁ⸗). ⲙⲟⲕⲁⲥ̄, ⲙⲟⲭⲥ̄ n.f. grief.

ⲙ̄ⲗⲁⲥ (pl. ⲙ̄ⲗⲟⲟⲥ) n.m. battle, -array, troops; quarrel. ⲥⲣ̄-
ⲙ̄ⲗⲁⲥ (Q ⲙ̄ⲗⲁⲥ ⲥⲏⲣ) ⲉⲃⲟⲗ to set up battle-array. ⲭⲓ-ⲙ̄ⲗⲁⲥ
to fight; ⲣⲉϥⲭⲓ-ⲙ̄ⲗⲁⲥ fighter.

ⲙ̄ⲙⲁⲩ adv. there, in that place; from there, therefrom;
thence. ⲉⲃⲟⲗ ⲙ̄ⲙⲁⲩ thence, from there. ⲉⲙⲁⲩ thither,
to there. Sometimes without translation value (§22.1).

ⲙ̄ⲙⲁⲥ prep. before (a deity; in making offerings).

ⲙ̄ⲙⲓⲛ ⲙ̄ⲙⲟ⸗ intens. pronoun, appositional to a preceding
pron., as in ⲡⲁⲏⲓ ⲙ̄ⲙⲓⲛ ⲙ̄ⲙⲟⲓ my own house. See §28.3.

ⲙ̄ⲙⲟⲛ adv. or conj. for, for surely.

ⲙⲛ̄ (archaic ⲛⲙ̄) ⲛⲙ̄ⲙⲁ⸗ (1) prep. with, together with, in
the company of; (2) conj. and, usu. joining nouns;
sometimes ⲁⲩⲱ ⲙⲛ̄.

ⲙⲛ̄-, ⲙ̄ⲙⲛ̄- pred. of nonexistence: there is/are not (§2.2);
used before indef. subj. in Present System (§18.1);
for ⲙⲛ̄-ϭⲟⲙ, ⲙⲛ̄-ϣϭⲟⲙ see ϭⲟⲙ.

ⲙ̄ⲙⲟⲛ, ⲙⲟⲛ neg. part. no (in answer to question); (ⲉϣⲱⲡⲉ)
ⲙ̄ⲙⲟⲛ adv. if not, otherwise; ⲭⲛ̄ ⲙ̄ⲙⲟⲛ, ⲭⲓⲛ ⲙ̄ⲙⲟⲛ or
rather, rather than.

ⲙ̄ⲛⲟⲩⲧ (f. ⲙ̄ⲛⲟⲧⲉ, ⲙ̄ⲛⲟⲟⲧⲉ) n.m.f. porter, doorkeeper.

ⲙⲛ̄ⲧ n.m. a grain-measure.

ⲙⲛ̄ⲧ- prefix (f.) for forming abstract nouns; see §27.2.

ⲙⲛ̄ⲧ- prefix for forming 'teens; see §24.3.

ⲙⲛ̄ⲧⲉ- ⲙⲛ̄ⲧⲁ⸗ neg. of pred. of possession; see §22.1. Also
used as nonliterary vb. prefix: lest, that not, unless.

ⲙⲛ̄ⲧⲣⲉ, ⲙⲉⲧⲣⲏ (pl. ⲙⲛ̄ⲧⲣⲉⲉⲩ) n.m. witness, testimony. ⲙⲛ̄ⲧ-
ⲙⲛ̄ⲧⲣⲉ n.f. testimony; ⲣ̄-ⲙⲛ̄ⲧⲣⲉ to testify, bear witness;
to testify (about: ⲙ̄ⲙⲟ⸗, ⲉⲧⲃⲉ, ⲉⲭⲛ̄; to a person: ⲛⲁ⸗;
against: ⲉ; for, in behalf of: ⲉ, ⲁⲗ, ⲙⲛ̄).

ⲙⲟ imptv. vb. (sing. ⲙⲟ, ⲙⲱ, ⲙ̄ⲙⲟ; pl. ⲙ̄ⲙⲏⲉⲓⲧⲛ̄) take!(ⲉ).

ⲙⲟⲉⲓⲧ n.m. road, path; rarely: place. ⲙⲟⲉⲓⲧ ⲛ̄ ⲉⲓ ⲉ2ⲟⲩⲛ
entrance; ⲙⲟⲉⲓⲧ ⲛ̄ ⲉⲓ ⲉⲃⲟⲗ exit. ⲭⲓ-ⲙⲟⲉⲓⲧ 2ⲏⲧ* to lead,
guide; ⲣⲉ4ⲭⲓ-ⲙⲟⲉⲓⲧ leader, guide; ⲭⲁⲩ-ⲙⲟⲉⲓⲧ idem; ⲙⲛ̄ⲧ-
ⲣⲉ4ⲭⲁⲩ-ⲙⲟⲉⲓⲧ leadership; ⲣ̄-ⲭⲁⲩ-ⲙⲟⲉⲓⲧ to be leader.
ⲙⲟⲉⲓⲧ ⲛ̄ ⲙⲟⲟϣⲉ track, path.

ⲙⲟⲉⲓ2, ⲙⲟⲓⲁ2 n.m. name of a measure.

ⲙⲟⲉⲓ2ⲉ, ⲙⲟⲓ2ⲉ n.m.f. wonder; ⲣ̄-ⲙⲟⲉⲓ2ⲉ to wonder, be astonished (at: ⲛ̄, ⲉⲭⲛ̄, 2ⲛ̄).

ⲙⲟⲕⲙⲉⲕ ⲙⲉⲕⲙⲟⲩⲕ* vb. intr. to think, ponder, meditate; to
intend (to do: ⲉⲧⲣⲉ); reflex. idem, to consider (that:
ⲭⲉ). ⲙⲟⲕⲙⲉⲕ ⲉⲃⲟⲗ ⲉ to reflect on, ponder. As n.m.
thought. ⲁⲧⲙⲟⲕⲙⲉⲕ unthinkable, inconceivable (ⲉⲣⲟ*).

ⲙⲟⲟⲛⲉ n.f. nurse; as adj. foster-.

ⲙⲟⲟⲛⲉ ⲙⲉⲛⲉ- (ⲙⲁⲛⲉ-, ⲙⲁⲛⲟⲩ-) Q ⲙⲁⲛⲟⲟⲩⲧ (± ⲉ2ⲟⲩⲛ) vb. tr. to
bring into port, bring to land (ⲙ̄ⲙⲟ*; to: ⲉ); vb. intr.
to come to port, moor (to: ⲉ). ⲙⲁ ⲛ̄ ⲙⲟⲟⲛⲉ harbor.

ⲙⲟⲟⲛⲉ ⲙⲉⲛⲉ- ⲙⲁⲛⲟⲩ* (ⲙⲁⲛⲟⲩⲟⲩ*), p.c. ⲙⲁⲛⲉ- vb. tr. to tend,
feed, shepherd (ⲙ̄ⲙⲟ*); to feed on, devour (ⲙ̄ⲙⲟ*); vb.
intr. to feed, graze (subj. cattle). ⲙⲁ ⲛ̄ ⲙⲟⲟⲛⲉ pasture. ⲣⲉ4ⲙⲟⲟⲛⲉ shepherd; ⲙⲛ̄ⲧⲣⲉ4ⲙⲟⲟⲛⲉ shepherding.
ⲙⲁⲛⲉ (ⲙⲁⲛ-; pl. ⲙⲁⲛⲏⲩ) n.m. herdsman, shepherd. For
ⲙⲁⲛ- in cpds. see 2nd element.

ⲙⲟⲟⲩ (pl. ⲙⲟⲩⲉⲓⲏ, ⲙⲟⲩⲏⲉⲓⲉ, ⲙⲟⲩⲉⲓⲟⲟⲩⲉ, ⲙⲟⲩⲛⲉⲓⲟⲟⲩⲉ) n.m.
water; spec. the Nile inundation. In cpds. may mean
juice, exudation, semen, urine. ⲁⲧⲙⲟⲟⲩ waterless. ⲙⲉⲥ-
ⲙⲟⲟⲩ water-containing. ⲙⲉ2-ⲙⲟⲟⲩ to draw water; ⲙⲁ ⲛ̄
ⲙⲉ2-ⲙⲟⲟⲩ place to draw water; ⲣⲉ4ⲙⲉ2-ⲙⲟⲟⲩ water-drawer.
ⲣ̄-ⲙⲟⲟⲩ to become water, liquify. ⲥⲉⲕ-ⲙⲟⲟⲩ to draw wa-
ter. ⲥⲣ̄-ⲙⲟⲟⲩ to distribute water. ϯ-ⲙⲟⲟⲩ to give wa-
ter; ⲙⲁ ⲛ̄ ϯ-ⲙⲟⲟⲩ water source. ⲧⲥⲉ-ⲙⲟⲟⲩ to slake. ⲃⲁⲓ-
ⲙⲟⲟⲩ water-bearer. ⲭⲓ-ⲙⲟⲟⲩ to receive water. 2ⲓ-ⲙⲟⲟⲩ
to rain.

ⲙⲟⲟϣⲉ (ⲙⲟϣⲉ) vb. intr. to walk, go; used with many prep.
and adv. in normal senses; as n.m. going, journey. Note
ⲙⲟⲟϣⲉ ⲙⲛ̄ to consort with; ⲙⲟⲟϣⲉ ⲛ̄ⲥⲁ to be in the

following of. ⲁⲧⲙⲟⲟϣⲉ pathless; ⲙⲁ ⲙ̄ ⲙⲟⲟϣⲉ road, path;
ⲙⲟⲉⲓⲧ ⲙ̄ ⲙⲟⲟϣⲉ road, journey; ⲍⲓⲏ ⲙ̄ ⲙⲟⲟϣⲉ road, path;
ⲣ̄-ⲍⲓⲏ ⲙ̄ ⲙⲟⲟϣⲉ to go, walk. ⲍⲟⲟⲩ ⲙ̄ ⲙⲟⲟϣⲉ day's journey.
ⲙⲟⲣⲧ̄ n.f. beard. ⲁⲧⲙⲟⲣⲧ̄ beardless. ⲣ̄-ⲙⲟⲣⲧ̄ to grow beard.
ⲙⲟⲥⲧⲉ ⲙⲉⲥⲧⲉ- ⲙⲉⲥⲧⲱ⁴ (p.c. ⲙⲁⲥⲧ̄-) vb. tr. to hate (ⲙ̄ⲙⲟ⁴);
   as n.m. hatred, object of hatred. ⲙⲁⲥⲧ̄- in cpd. hater
   of. ϣⲟⲩ-ⲙⲟⲥⲧⲉ deserving of hatred. ⲙⲉⲥⲧⲉ (f. ⲙⲉⲥⲧⲏ)
   n.m. hated person.
ⲙⲟⲩ, Q ⲙⲟⲟⲩⲧ vb. intr. to die (of: ⲉⲧⲃⲉ, ⲛ̄ⲧⲛ̄, ⲍⲁ, ⲍⲛ̄, ⲍⲓⲧⲛ̄;
   for: ⲉⲝⲛ̄); as n.m. death; plague, pestilence. ⲣⲉϥⲙⲟⲩ
   adj. mortal, dead; ⲙⲛ̄ⲧⲣⲉϥⲙⲟⲩ mortality. ⲣⲉϥⲙⲟⲟⲩⲧ dead
   person or thing. ⲡⲁϣ-ⲙⲟⲩ adj. half-dead. ⲁⲧⲙⲟⲩ immor-
   tal; ⲙⲛ̄ⲧⲁⲧⲙⲟⲩ immortality.
ⲙⲟⲩⲉ, ⲙⲟⲩⲉⲓ, ⲙⲟⲩ, ⲙⲟⲩⲓ n.f. island (usu. in Nile).
ⲙⲟⲩⲓ, ⲙⲟⲩⲉⲓ n.m.f. lion(ess); ⲙⲁⲥ ⲙ̄ ⲙⲟⲩⲓ lion cub.
ⲙⲟⲩⲕ vb. tr. to destroy; intr. to be destroyed.
ⲙⲟⲩⲕⲍ̄ ⲙⲉⲕⲍ̄- ⲙⲟⲕⲍ⁴ vb. tr. to afflict, oppress (ⲙ̄ⲙⲟ⁴); reflex. to be afflicted, oppressed; to humble oneself.
ⲙⲟⲩⲗⲍ̄ ⲙⲉⲗⲍ̄- ⲙⲟⲗⲍ⁴ Q ⲙⲟⲗⲍ̄ vb. tr. to make salty; to convert
   to salt (ⲙ̄ⲙⲟ⁴); Q to be salty. ⲙⲗ̄ⲍ, ⲙⲉⲗⲍ̄, ⲙⲏⲣⲍ̄ n. salt.
   ⲙⲉⲗⲍⲉ n.f. saltiness.
ⲙⲟⲩⲗⲍ̄, ⲙⲟⲩⲗⲗⲍ, ⲙⲟⲩⲣⲍ̄ n.m. wax; candle; honey-comb.
ⲙⲟⲩⲗⲍ̄ ⲙⲟⲗⲍ⁴ Q ⲙⲟⲗⲍ̄ vb. tr. to involve, enmesh (ⲙ̄ⲙⲟ⁴); vb.
   intr. to become hooked into, attached to (ⲉ, ⲙ̄ⲙⲟ⁴, ⲍⲛ̄).
ⲙⲟⲩⲛ, Q ⲙⲏⲛ (ⲙⲏⲛⲉ) vb. intr. ± ⲉⲃⲟⲗ to remain, last, endure; with Circum.: to continue doing. As n.m. (± ⲉⲃⲟⲗ)
   perseverance, continuing; ⲍⲛ̄ ⲟⲩⲙⲟⲩⲛ ⲉⲃⲟⲗ continuously.
ⲙⲟⲩⲛⲕ̄ (ⲙⲟⲩⲛⲅ̄) ⲙⲉⲛⲕ̄- ⲙⲟⲛⲕ⁴ (ⲙⲟⲛⲅ⁴) Q ⲙⲟⲛⲅ̄ vb. tr. to form,
   fashion, make (ⲙ̄ⲙⲟ⁴); as n.m. thing made; formation,
   fashioning; fashion, make; ⲙⲟⲩⲛⲕ̄ ⲛ̄ ⲅⲓⲝ handmade objects;
   ⲁⲧⲙⲟⲩⲛⲕ̄ ⲛ̄ ⲅⲓⲝ not handmade.
ⲙⲟⲩⲟⲩⲧ ⲙⲉⲩⲧ- ⲙⲟⲟⲩⲧ⁴ vb. tr. to kill (ⲙ̄ⲙⲟ⁴); ⲣⲉϥⲙⲟⲩⲟⲩⲧ killer.
ⲙⲟⲩⲣ ⲙⲉⲣ- (ⲙⲣ̄-) ⲙⲟⲣ⁴ Q ⲙⲏⲣ (p.c. ⲙⲁⲣ-) vb. tr. to bind,
   tie (ⲙ̄ⲙⲟ⁴; to: ⲙ̄ⲙⲟ⁴, ⲉ, ⲉⲝⲛ̄, ⲍⲛ̄; with: ⲙ̄ⲙⲟ⁴, ⲍⲛ̄); ⲙⲟⲩⲣ
   ⲙ̄ⲙⲟ⁴ ⲙ̄ ⲡⲉⲥⲭⲏⲙⲁ to gird in monastic habit; to bind by

oath, adjure; Q to be bound, girt. As n.m. band, strap,
girding. ⲙⲟⲩⲣ ⲙⲛ̅ to be at enmity with. ⲙⲁ ⲛ̅ ⲙⲟⲩⲣ prison. ⲙⲁⲣ, ⲙⲁⲁⲣ, ⲙⲉⲣ, ⲙⲏⲣ n.m. bundle. ⲙⲁⲓⲣⲉ, ⲙⲏⲣⲉ n.f.
idem. ⲙⲣ̅ⲣⲉ n.f. chain, bond, joint. ⲙⲟⲣⲥ̄ n.f. binding,
restriction; purse. For cpds. with ⲙⲁⲣ- see 2nd element.

ⲙⲟⲩⲥ n.m. strap, band; belt, girdle; thong. ⲣⲉϥⲧⲁⲙⲓⲉ-ⲙⲟⲩⲥ
strap-maker.

ⲙⲟⲩⲥⲕ̄ ⲙⲁⲥⲕⲉ Q ⲙⲟⲥⲕ̄ vb. tr. to strike (ⲙ̅ⲙⲟⲉ).

ⲙⲟⲩⲧ, ⲙⲟⲧⲉ n.m. sinew, nerve; joint; neck, shoulders.

ⲙⲟⲩⲧⲉ vb. intr. to call, name (ⲉ, rarely ⲙ̅ⲙⲟⲉ); see Vocab.
17 for usage. As n.m. call, incantation. ⲣⲉϥⲙⲟⲩⲧⲉ enchanter; ⲙⲛ̅ⲧⲣⲉϥⲙⲟⲩⲧⲉ enchantment. ⲙⲟⲩⲧⲉ ⲉⲝⲛ̅/ⲟⲩⲃⲉ to call
upon, to; ⲙⲟⲩⲧⲉ ⲉⲃⲟⲗ to call out; to summon. ⲙⲟⲩⲧⲉ ⲉ-
ⲍⲟⲩⲛ to call in (to: ⲉ); to invite in.

ⲙⲟⲩϣⲧ ⲙⲉϣⲧ̅- ⲙⲟϣⲧⲉ Q ⲙⲟϣⲧ̅ (p.c. ⲙⲁϣⲧ̅-) vb. tr. to examine,
search out (ⲙ̅ⲙⲟⲉ); to visit; reflex. (± ⲉⲃⲟⲗ) to reflect,
ponder. As n.m. consideration, opinion. ⲁⲧⲙⲟϣⲧⲉ in-
scrutible.

ⲙⲟⲩⲍ ⲙⲉⲍ- (ⲙⲁⲍ-) ⲙⲁⲍⲉ (ⲙⲟⲍⲉ) Q ⲙⲉⲍ (ⲙⲏⲍ) vb. tr. to fill
(ⲙ̅ⲙⲟⲉ; with: ⲙ̅ⲙⲟⲉ, ⲍⲛ̅, ⲉⲃⲟⲗ ⲍⲛ̅); to fulfill, complete;
to pay, repay (debt: ⲙ̅ⲙⲟⲉ ± ⲉⲃⲟⲗ; with: ⲍⲛ̅; person: obj.
suff. only); vb. intr. to become full, filled (of, with:
ⲙ̅ⲙⲟⲉ, ⲍⲛ̅, ⲍⲁ, ⲍⲓⲧⲛ̅); to get paid; + ⲉⲍⲣⲁⲓ to flood (of
the Nile); as n.m. fullness, contents; inundation. ⲙⲉⲍ-
ⲣⲱⲉ to fill the mouth (with: ⲙ̅ⲙⲟⲉ, ⲍⲛ̅, ⲉ, ⲉⲝⲛ̅). ⲙⲉⲍ-
ⲧⲟⲟⲧⲉ to fill hand, seize (ⲙ̅ⲙⲟⲉ). ⲙⲉⲍ-ⲍⲏⲧ to become
sated. For ⲙⲉⲍ- as ordinal prefix see §30.7.

ⲙⲟⲩⲍ vb. intr. to look (at: ⲉ).

ⲙⲟⲩⲍ vb. intr. to burn, glow (with fuel: ⲙ̅ⲙⲟⲉ).

ⲙⲟⲩϫϭ (ⲙⲟⲩϫⲕ̄, ⲙⲟⲩϫⲧ̅) ⲙⲉϫⲧ̅- ⲙⲟϫϭⲉ (ⲙⲟϫⲕⲉ, ⲙⲟϫⲧⲉ) Q ⲙⲟϫϭ
(ⲙⲟϫⲧ̅, ⲙⲁϫⲧ̅) vb. tr. to mix (ⲙ̅ⲙⲟⲉ; with: ⲙⲛ̅); intr. to
be mixed (with: ⲉ, ⲙⲛ̅, ⲍⲓ, ⲍⲛ̅). As n.m. mixture.
ⲣⲉϥⲙⲟⲩϫϭ mixer, confuser, disturber.

ⲙⲟϣⲧⲉ, ⲙⲟⲟϣⲧⲉ n.pl. parts, neighborhood. ⲙⲟⲟϣⲉ idem.

ⲙⲟϫⲍ̄, ⲙⲁϫⲍ̄, ⲙⲟϫⲕ̄ (and -ϥ for -ⲍ) n.m. girdle (of monk or

soldier.

ⲙ̄ⲡⲁⲓ n.m. spindle.

ⲙ̄ⲡⲉ neg. part. It was not so (in answer to question in past tense). ⲭⲛ̄ ⲙ̄ⲡⲉ or not (in double question, coord. with preceding positive statement); ⲉϣⲱⲡⲉ ⲙ̄ⲡⲉ if not.

ⲙ̄ⲡⲟ, ⲉⲙⲡⲟ, ⲉⲃⲱ (f. ⲏⲙⲡⲱ) adj. dumb, mute. ⲙⲛ̄ⲧⲙ̄ⲡⲟ muteness; ⲣ̄-ⲙ̄ⲡⲟ (Q ⲟ ⲛ̄) to become mute.

ⲙ̄ⲡⲱⲣ exclam. imptv. part. Don't! By no means! No! Also used like ⲙ̄ⲡⲣ̄- as prefix for neg. imptv. See §17.1; 30.1.

ⲙ̄ⲡϣⲁ, ⲉⲙⲡϣⲁ, ⲙ̄ϣⲁ vb. intr. to be worthy, deserving (of: ⲙ̄ⲙⲟ⁄; of doing: ⲛ̄, ⲉ + Inf.); as n.m. worth, deserts, fate. ⲁⲧⲙ̄ⲡϣⲁ worthless, undeserving; ⲙⲛ̄ⲧⲁⲧⲙ̄ⲡϣⲁ unworthiness. ⲣ̄-(ⲛ)ⲙ̄ⲡϣⲁ to become worthy, deserving.

ⲙ̄ⲣⲓⲥ n.m. new wine, must.

ⲙ̄ⲣⲟϣ (ⲙ̄ⲣⲁϣ) Q ⲙⲟⲣϣ̄ vb. intr. to become red/yellow. ⲙⲏⲣϣ̄, ⲙⲉⲣϣ̄, ⲙⲣ̄ϣ adj. red, ruddy; ⲣ̄-ⲙⲏⲣϣ̄ (Q ⲟ ⲛ̄) to be ruddy.

ⲙ̄ⲣⲱ, ⲉⲙⲣⲱ, ⲉⲙⲡⲣⲱ (pl. ⲙ̄ⲣⲟⲟⲩⲉ) n.f. harbor, landing stage.

ⲙ̄ⲣⲱⲙ, ⲟⲩⲣⲱⲙ, ⲟⲩⲗⲱⲙ n.m. pillow.

ⲙ̄ⲥⲁⲍ (pl. ⲙ̄ⲥⲟⲟⲍ) n.m. crocodile.

(ⲙ̄ⲥⲱⲃⲉ) ⲉⲙⲥⲱⲃⲉ, ⲙ̄ⲥⲱⲡⲉ n.f. large needle.

ⲙ̄ⲧⲟ ⲉⲃⲟⲗ n.m. presence, in prep. ⲙ̄ ⲡⲉⲙⲧⲟ ⲉⲃⲟⲗ ⲛ̄, ⲙ̄ ⲡ(⁄)ⲙ̄ⲧⲟ ⲉⲃⲟⲗ in the presence of, before.

ⲙ̄ⲧⲟⲛ (ⲉⲙⲧⲟⲛ) Q ⲙⲟⲧⲛ̄ vb. intr. to become at ease, at rest, content, relieved, well; Q also: to be easy (to do: ⲉ + Inf.); often impers. it is easy (ⲉ, ⲉⲧⲣⲉ). Vb. reflex. (with ⲙ̄ⲙⲟ⁄) to rest self; to go to rest, die; as n.m. rest, ease, relief; ⲙⲁⲓ-ⲙ̄ⲧⲟⲛ loving ease; ⲙⲁ ⲛ̄ ⲙ̄ⲧⲟⲛ a place to rest. ⲣ̄-ⲡ(⁄)ⲙ̄ⲧⲟⲛ to be or put at ease. ⲙ̄ⲧⲟⲛ ⲛ̄ ⳍⲏⲧ to become content; as n.m. rest, satisfaction. ϯ-ⲙ̄ⲧⲟⲛ ⲛⲁ⁄ to set at ease, give rest/respite to. ⲭⲓ-ⲙ̄ⲧⲟⲛ to get rest, be relieved. ⲙⲟⲧⲛ̄ n.m. health, ease. ⲙⲟⲧⲛⲉⲥ n.f. ease, contentment; ϯ-ⲙⲟⲧⲛⲉⲥ ⲛⲁ⁄ to give relief to; ⲣ̄-ⲙⲟⲧⲛⲉⲥ ⲛⲁ⁄ idem; ⲭⲓ-ⲙⲟⲧⲛⲉⲥ to get relief; ⳍⲛ̄ ⲟⲩⲙⲟⲧⲛⲉⲥ with ease, easily. ⲙⲟⲩⲧⲛ̄ ⲙⲉⲧⲛ̄- ⲙⲟⲧⲛ⁄ vb. tr. to set at rest (ⲙ̄ⲙⲟ⁄); also reflex.

ⲘⲦⲰ, ⲈⲘⲦⲰ, ⲘⲦⲞ n.m.f. depth (of the sea); ⲂⲰⲔ Ⲛ̄ ⲘⲦⲰ to
   founder, sink; ⲊⲓⲚⲂⲰⲔ Ⲛ̄ ⲘⲦⲞ shipwreck.

Ⲙ̄ϢⲓⲢ, ⲈⲘϢⲓⲢ, ⲘⲈϢⲓⲢ n. name of 6th Coptic month.

Ⲙ̄ϢⲦⲰⲦⲈ, ⲘⲓϢⲦⲰⲦⲈ n.f. comb.

Ⲙ̄ϨⲀⲀⲨ, Ⲙ̄ϨⲀⲖⲞⲨ n.m. tomb, cavern.

Ⲙ̄ϨⲒⲦ, ⲈⲘϨⲒⲦ n.m. north. Ⲉ ⲠⲈⲘϨⲒⲦ northward. Ⲙ̄ ⲠⲈⲘϨⲒⲦ Ⲛ̄
   on the north of. ⲤⲀ-Ⲙ̄ϨⲒⲦ (on) the north side. ⲦⲎⲨ Ⲛ̄
   Ⲙ̄ϨⲒⲦ northwind.

Ⲙ̄ⲬⲀϨⲦ̄, Ⲙ̄ⲬⲀⲦϨ̄, Ⲙ̄ⲬⲀϨⲬ̄ n.f. mortar (vessel).

Ⲙ̄ⲬⲰⲖ, ⲈⲘⲬⲰⲖ n.m. onion.

Ⲙ̄: ⲈⲓⲚⲈ	ⲘⲀⲬϤ̄: ⲘⲞⲬϨ̄	ⲘⲈϢⲠⲰⲚⲈ: ⲘⲈⲬⲠⲰⲚⲈ
ⲘⲀⲀϨ: ⲘⲀϨ	ⲘⲀⲬϨ̄: ⲘⲞⲬϨ̄	ⲘⲈϢⲦ̄-: ⲘⲞⲨϢⲦ̄
ⲘⲀⲀⲢ: ⲘⲞⲨⲢ	ⲘⲈⲈ: ⲘⲈ	ⲘⲈϢϢⲈ: ϢϢⲈ
ⲘⲀⲀⲦⲈ: ⲘⲀⲦⲈ	ⲘⲈⲒ: ⲘⲈ	ⲘⲈϨ (-): ⲘⲞⲨϨ, ⲘⲀϨ
ⲘⲀⲂ-: ⲘⲀⲀⲂ	ⲘⲈⲔⲘⲞⲨⲔˢ: ⲘⲞⲔⲘⲈⲔ	ⲘⲈϨⲈ: ⲘⲎϨⲈ
ⲘⲀⲄⲀⲖ: ⲘⲀⲔⲞⲦ	ⲘⲈⲔϨ̄-: ⲘⲞⲨⲔϨ̄	ⲘⲈϨⲦ̄-: ⲘⲀϨⲦ̄
ⲘⲀⲒ-: ⲘⲈ	ⲘⲈⲔⲬⲈ: ⲘⲀⲔⲬⲈ	ⲘⲈⲬⲦ̄-: ⲘⲞⲨⲬϬ̄
ⲘⲀⲒⲢⲈ: ⲘⲞⲨⲢ	ⲘⲈⲖⲀⲦⲈ: ⲘⲈⲖⲰⲦ	ⲘⲎⲈ: ⲘⲈ
ⲘⲀⲔⲀ(Ⲗ)Ⲧ: ⲘⲀⲔⲞⲦ	ⲘⲈⲖϨ̄ (-): ⲘⲞⲨⲖϨ̄	ⲘⲎⲈⲒˢ: ⲘⲀ
ⲘⲀⲔⲰⲦ: ⲘⲀⲔⲞⲦ	ⲘⲈⲖϨⲈ: ⲘⲞⲨⲖϨ̄	ⲘⲎⲎⲚⲈ: ⲘⲎⲚⲈ
ⲘⲀⲚ-: ⲘⲞⲞⲚⲈ	ⲘⲈⲚⲈ-: ⲘⲞⲞⲚⲈ	ⲘⲎⲎⳠⲈ: ⲘⲒⳠⲈ
ⲘⲀⳠⲈ(-): ⲘⲞⲞⲚⲈ	ⲘⲈⲚⲔ̄-: ⲘⲞⲨⲚⲔ̄	ⲘⲎⲎⲦⲈ: ⲘⲎⲦⲈ
ⲘⲀⲚⲎⲨ: ⲘⲞⲞⲚⲈ	ⲘⲈⲢ: ⲘⲞⲨⲢ	ⲘⲎⲚ(Ⲉ): ⲘⲞⲨⲚ
ⲘⲀⲚⲞⲞⲨⲦ: ⲘⲞⲞⲚⲈ	ⲘⲈⲢ-: ⲘⲞⲨⲢ	ⲘⲎⲢⲈ: ⲘⲞⲨⲢ
ⲘⲀⲚⲞⲨ-: ⲘⲞⲞⲚⲈ	ⲘⲈⲢⲈ-: ⲘⲈ	ⲘⲎⲢϢ̄: Ⲙ̄ⲢⲞϢ
ⲘⲀⲚⲞⲨⲞⲨˢ: ⲘⲞⲞⲚⲈ	ⲘⲈⲢⲒⲦ(ˢ): ⲘⲈ	ⲘⲎⲢϨ̄: ⲘⲞⲨⲖϨ̄
ⲘⲀⲚⲬⲀⲖⲈ: ⲘⲀⳠⲀⲖⲈ	ⲘⲈⲢϢ̄: Ⲙ̄ⲢⲞϢ	ⲘⲎⳠⲈ: ⲘⲒϨⲈ
ⲘⲀⲢ(-): ⲘⲞⲨⲢ	ⲘⲈⲢϨ̄: ⲘⲈⲢⲈϨ	ⲘⲎⲦ: ⲘⲈ
ⲘⲀⲢⲎⲤ: ⲢⲎⲤ	ⲘⲈⲤ-: ⲘⲒⲤⲈ	ⲘⲎⲦⲈ: ⲘⲎⲦ
ⲘⲀⲤ(-): ⲘⲒⲤⲈ	ⲘⲈⲤⲒⲞ(ˢ): ⲘⲒⲤⲈ	ⲘⲒ: ⲘⲎ
ⲘⲀⲤⲈ: ⲘⲒⲤⲈ	ⲘⲈⲤⲒⲰ: ⲘⲒⲤⲈ	ⲘⲒⲰ: ⲘⲒⲞˢ
ⲘⲀⲤⲦˢ: ⲘⲒⲤⲈ	ⲘⲈⲤⲦⲈ(-): ⲘⲞⲤⲦⲈ	ⲘⲒⲰⲦⲚ̄: ⲘⲒⲞˢ
ⲘⲀⲤⲔˢ: ⲘⲞⲨⲤⲔ̄	ⲘⲈⲤⲦ-/ˢ: ⲘⲒⲤⲈ	ⲘⲒⲬⲔⲈ: ⲘⲀⲬⲔⲈ
ⲘⲀⲤⲦ̄: ⲘⲞⲤⲦⲈ	ⲘⲈⲤⲦⲎ: ⲘⲞⲤⲦⲈ	ⲘⲒϢⲦⲰⲦⲈ: Ⲙ̄ϢⲦⲰⲦⲈ
ⲘⲀⲦˢ: ⲘⲀ	ⲘⲈⲤⲦⲰˢ: ⲘⲞⲤⲦⲈ	ⲘⲀϨ: ⲘⲞⲨⲖϨ̄
ⲘⲀⲦⲚ̄-: Ⲙ̄ⲦⲞⲚ	ⲘⲈⲤⲞⲎⲦ: ⲘⲈⲤⲦⲚ̄ϨⲎⲦ	Ⲙ̄ⲖⲞⲞϨ: Ⲙ̄ⲖⲀϨ
ⲘⲀⲦⲞⲈⲒ: ⲘⲀⲦⲞⲒ	ⲘⲈⲤⲞⲨⲢⲎ: ⲘⲈⲤⲞⲢⲎ	Ⲙ̄ⲘⲀⲦⲈ: ⲘⲀⲦⲈ
ⲘⲀⲦⲰⲞⲨ: ⲘⲀⲦⲈ	ⲘⲈⲤⲰⲢⲎ: ⲘⲈⲤⲞⲢⲎ	Ⲙ̄ⲘⲎⲈⲒⲦⲚ̄: ⲘⲞ
ⲘⲀⲨ: ⲘⲀⲀⲨ	ⲘⲈⲦⲈ: ⲘⲀⲦⲈ	Ⲙ̄ⲘⲎⳠⲈ: ⲘⲎⳠⲈ
ⲘⲀⲨⲀⲦˢ: ⲘⲀⲨⲀⲀˢ	ⲘⲈⲦⲚ̄-: Ⲙ̄ⲦⲞⲚ	Ⲙ̄ⲘⲚ̄-: ⲘⲚ̄-
ⲘⲀϢⲈⲢⲦ: ⲘⲀϢⲢ̄Ⲧ	ⲘⲈⲦⲢⲎ: ⲘⲚ̄ⲦⲢⲈ	Ⲙ̄ⲘⲞ: ⲘⲞ
ⲘⲀϢⲦ̄-: ⲘⲞⲨϢⲦ̄	ⲘⲈⲨⲈ: ⲘⲈⲈⲨⲈ	Ⲙ̄ⲘⲞˢ: Ⲛ̄
ⲘⲀϨ-/ˢ: ⲘⲞⲨϨ	ⲘⲈⲨⲦ-: ⲘⲞⲨⲞⲨⲦ	Ⲙ̄ⲘⲞⲚ: ⲘⲚ̄
ⲘⲀⲬⲦ̄: ⲘⲞⲨⲬϬ̄	ⲘⲈϢⲀˢ: ⲘⲈϢⲈ	Ⲙ̄ⲚⲞⲞⲦⲈ: Ⲙ̄ⲚⲞⲨⲦ
ⲘⲀⲬ-: ⲘⲀⲀⲬⲈ	ⲘⲈϢⲀⲔ: ⲘⲈϢⲈ	Ⲙ̄ⲚⲞⲦⲈ: Ⲙ̄ⲚⲞⲨⲦ
ⲘⲀⲬⲈ: ⲘⲀⲀⲬⲈ	ⲘⲈϢⲓⲢ: Ⲙ̄ϢⲓⲢ	ⲘⲚ̄Ⲧ-: ⲘⲎⲦ

ⲙⲛⲧⲁ⸗: ⲙⲛ	ⲙⲟⲥⲕ̄: ⲙⲟⲩⲥⲕ̄	ⲙⲟⲭⲕ⸗: ⲙⲟⲩⲭ6̄
ⲙⲛⲧⲁⲥⲉ: ⲥⲟⲟⲩ	ⲙⲟⲧⲉ: ⲙⲟⲩⲧ	ⲙⲟⲭⲕ2̄: ⲙⲟⲭ2̄
ⲙⲛⲧⲉ-: ⲙⲛ	ⲙⲟⲧⲛ̄: ⲙ̄ⲧⲟⲛ	ⲙⲟⲭⲧ(⸗): ⲙⲟⲩⲭ6̄
ⲙⲛⲧⲏ: ϯⲟⲩ	ⲙⲟⲧⲛ⸗: ⲙ̄ⲧⲟⲛ	ⲙⲟⲭϥ̄: ⲙⲟⲭ2̄
ⲙⲛⲧⲟⲩⲉ: ⲟⲩⲁ	ⲙⲟⲧⲛⲉⲥ: ⲙ̄ⲧⲟⲛ	ⲙⲟⲭ6(⸗): ⲙⲟⲩⲭ6̄
ⲙⲛⲧⲣⲉⲉⲩ: ⲙⲛⲧⲣⲉ	ⲙⲟⲩ: ⲙⲟⲩⲉ	ⲙ̄ⲡⲣ̄-: ⲙ̄ⲡⲱⲣ
ⲙⲟⲓⲁ2: ⲙⲟⲉⲓ2	ⲙⲟⲩⲉⲓ: ⲙⲟⲩⲓ, ⲙⲟⲩⲉ	ⲙⲣ̄-: ⲙⲟⲩⲣ
ⲙⲟⲕ2̄: ⲙⲁⲕ2̄	ⲙⲟⲩⲉⲓⲏ: ⲙⲟⲟⲩ	ⲙ̄ⲣⲁϣ: ⲙ̄ⲣⲟϣ
ⲙⲟⲕ2⸗: ⲙⲟⲩⲕ2̄	ⲙⲟⲩⲉⲓⲟⲟⲩⲉ: ⲙⲟⲟⲩ	ⲙ̄ⲣⲟⲟⲩⲉ: ⲙ̄ⲣⲱ
ⲙⲟⲕ2̄: ⲙ̄ⲕⲁ2	ⲙⲟⲩⲏⲉⲓⲉ: ⲙⲟⲟⲩ	ⲙ̄ⲡ̄ⲣⲉ: ⲙⲟⲩⲣ
ⲙⲟⲕ2ⲥ̄: ⲙ̄ⲕⲁ2	ⲙⲟⲩⲓ: ⲙⲟⲩⲉ	ⲙ̄ⲣⲱ2ⲉ: ⲙ̄ⲣⲱϣⲉ
ⲙⲟⲗ2(⸗): ⲙⲟⲩⲗ2̄	ⲙⲟⲩⲛⲧ̄: ⲙⲟⲩⲛⲕ̄	ⲙ̄ⲣ̄ϣ: ⲙ̄ⲣⲟϣ
ⲙⲟⲛⲧ̄⸗: ⲙⲟⲩⲛⲕ̄	ⲙⲟⲩⲛⲉⲓⲟⲟⲩⲉ: ⲙⲟⲟⲩ	ⲙ̄ⲥⲉ: ⲱⲙⲥ̄
ⲙⲟⲟⲗⲉ: ⲗⲟⲟⲙⲉ	ⲙⲟⲩⲣ2̄: ⲙⲟⲩⲗ2̄	ⲙ̄ⲥⲟⲟ2: ⲙ̄ⲥⲁ2
ⲙⲟⲟⲩⲧ: ⲙⲟⲩ	ⲙⲟⲩⲣⲭⲛⲁ2: ⲭⲛⲁ2	ⲙ̄ⲥⲱⲛⲉ: ⲙ̄ⲥⲱⲃⲉ
ⲙⲟⲟⲩⲧ⸗: ⲙⲟⲩⲟⲩⲧ	ⲙⲟⲩⲧⲛ̄: ⲙ̄ⲧⲟⲛ	ⲙ̄ⲧⲟ: ⲙ̄ⲧⲱ
ⲙⲟⲟϣ(ⲧ)ⲉ: ⲙⲟϣⲧⲉ	ⲙⲟⲩⲭⲕ̄: ⲙⲟⲩⲭ6̄	ⲙⲱ: ⲙⲟ
ⲙⲟⲣ⸗: ⲙⲟⲩⲣ	ⲙⲟⲩⲭⲧ̄: ⲙⲟⲩⲭ6̄	ⲙ̄ϣⲁ: ⲙ̄ⲡϣⲁ
ⲙⲟⲣⲥ̄: ⲙⲟⲩⲣ	ⲙⲟϣⲉ: ⲙⲟⲟϣⲉ	ⲙϣ̄ϣⲉ: ϣϣⲉ
ⲙⲟⲣϣ̄: ⲙ̄ⲣⲟϣ	ⲙⲟϣⲧ(⸗): ⲙⲟⲩϣⲧ̄	ⲙ̄ⲭⲁⲧ2̄: ⲙ̄ⲭⲁ2ⲧ̄
ⲙⲟⲥⲉ: ⲙⲓⲥⲉ	ⲙⲟ2⸗: ⲙⲟⲩ2	ⲙ̄ⲭⲛ̄2: ⲉⲛ2̄

N

N̄ prep. marking the genitive; see 2.3.

N̄ (ⲛⲁ⸗) prep. to, for (dative; see 10.2); also in ⲙⲁ ⲛⲁⲓ⸗
Give me (+ pron. suffix).

N̄ linking noun and adjective (15.1), noun and noun (23.2).

N̄ linking noun to proleptic suffix (10.4).

N̄ ... ⲁⲛ negation; see Grammatical Index.

N̄ (ⲙ̄ⲙⲟ⸗) prep. (1) place: in, into, from in; (2) time: in,
on, during; (3) agent, instrument: with, by; (4) used
to form adverbs (s.v.); (5) ⲉⲃⲟⲗ N̄ out of, from within;
(6) as marker of direct object (10.1); (7) partitive: of.

ⲛⲁ (ⲛⲁⲁ, ⲛⲁⲉ, ⲛⲁⲓ) vb. intr. to have pity (on: ⲛⲁ⸗, 2ⲁ); as
n.m. pity, mercy, charity. ⲉⲓⲣⲉ N̄ ⲟⲩⲛⲁ, ⲣ̄-ⲡⲛⲁ to treat
charitably, kindly (ⲙⲛ̄, ⲉ2ⲣⲁⲓ ⲉⲭⲛ̄). ⲁⲧⲛⲁ pitiless;
ⲣ̄-ⲁⲧⲛⲁ (Q ⲟ N̄) to become pitiless. ⲙⲛ̄ⲧⲛⲁ pity, charity; ⲣ̄-ⲙⲛ̄ⲧⲛⲁ to do charity; ⲥⲣ̄-ⲙⲛ̄ⲧⲛⲁ to distribute charity; ϯ-ⲙⲛ̄ⲧⲛⲁ to give charity; ⲭⲓ-ⲙⲛ̄ⲧⲛⲁ to receive
charity; ϣⲁ(ⲗ)ⲧ-ⲙⲛ̄ⲧⲛⲁ to ask for charity. ⲛⲁ-ϩⲧ adj.
compassionate; ⲣ̄-ⲛⲁ-ϩⲧ to be compassionate; ⲙⲁⲓ-ⲛⲁ-ϩⲧ

charity-loving; ⲙⲛ̄ⲧⲛⲁ-ⲏⲧ pity, charity.

ⲛⲁ vb. intr. to go (to: ⲉ, ⲉⲣⲁⲧ⸗); ⲛⲁ ⲉ ⲧⲱⲛ to go whither?
ⲛⲁ ⲉϩⲟⲩⲛ to enter (ⲉ, ϣⲁ); ⲛⲁ ⲉϩⲣⲁⲓ to go up. ⲛⲁ ...
ⲛⲏⲩ to come and go.

ⲛⲁⲁ- (ⲛⲁⲉ-) ⲛⲁⲁ⸗ pred. adj. to be great (29.2).

ⲛⲁⲉⲓⲱ, ⲛⲁⲓⲱ, ⲛⲉⲓⲱ n.f. peg, stake.

ⲛⲁⲁⲕⲉ n.f. labor pains; pains in general. ϯ-ⲛⲁⲁⲕⲉ to be
in labor (with: ⲙ̄ⲙⲟ⸗).

ⲛⲁⲛⲟⲩ- (ⲛⲁⲛⲉ-) ⲛⲁⲛⲟⲩ⸗ pred. adj. to be good, fair, just.
ⲛⲁⲛⲟⲩⲥ impers. it is good, right (ⲉ, ⲉⲧⲣⲉ). ⲡⲉⲧ ⲛⲁⲛⲟⲩϥ
that which is good; ⲙⲁⲓ-ⲡⲉⲧ ⲛⲁⲛⲟⲩϥ loving what is good;
ⲣ̄-ⲡⲉⲧ ⲛⲁⲛⲟⲩϥ to do good (to: ⲛⲁ⸗; ⲙⲛ̄); ⲣⲉϥⲣ̄-ⲡⲉⲧ ⲛⲁⲛⲟⲩϥ
benefactor; ⲙⲛ̄ⲧⲣⲉϥⲣ̄-ⲡⲉⲧⲛⲁⲛⲟⲩϥ benefaction.

ⲛⲁⲡⲣⲉ, ⲛⲉⲡⲣⲉ n.f. grain, seed.

ⲛⲁⲧ, ⲛⲉⲧ, ⲛⲏⲧ n.m. loom, web.

ⲛⲁⲩ (imptv. ⲁⲛⲁⲩ) vb. tr. to look at, see, behold (ⲉ;
that: ⲝⲉ); to seek out, get. ⲛⲁⲩ ⲉⲃⲟⲗ to be able to
see (i.e. not be blind). As n.m. sight, vision, view.
ⲁⲧⲛⲁⲩ ⲉⲣⲟ⸗ unseen, unseeable. ⲣⲉϥⲛⲁⲩ seer.

ⲛⲁⲩ n.m. time, hour. ⲡⲛⲁⲩ ⲛ̄ ϣⲱⲣⲡ̄ early morning. ⲡⲛⲁⲩ ⲙ̄
ⲙⲉⲉⲣⲉ noon. ⲡⲛⲁⲩ ⲛ̄ ⲣⲟⲩϩⲉ evening. ⲛⲟⲩ- may be used
for ⲛⲁⲩ in the preceding expressions. ⲟⲩⲛⲟϭ ⲛ̄ ⲛⲁⲩ a
long time. ⲛ̄ ⲛⲁⲩ ⲛⲓⲙ always. ⲛ̄ ⲁϣ ⲛ̄ ⲛⲁⲩ when? ⲙ̄ ⲡⲉⲓ-
ⲛⲁⲩ at that time, just then. ϣⲁ ⲡⲛⲁⲩ until (+ Rel.).
ⲝⲓⲛ ⲡⲛⲁⲩ since, from the time that (+ Rel.). ⲣ̄-ⲛⲁⲩ to
become time. ⲧⲛⲁⲩ, ⲧⲛ̄ⲛⲁⲩ when? ϣⲁ ⲧⲛ̄ⲛⲁⲩ until when?

ⲛⲁϣⲉ- ⲛⲁϣⲱ⸗ pred. adj. to be many, much (29.2).

ⲛⲁϩⲧⲉ ⲛ̄ϩⲉⲧ- Q ⲛ̄ϩⲟⲩⲧ (ⲛ̄ϩⲟⲧ) vb. intr./tr. to believe, trust
(in: ⲉ, ϩⲛ̄, ⲉⲝⲛ̄); Q to be trustworthy, faithful; as n.
m. trust, faith. ⲁⲧⲛⲁϩⲧⲉ unbelieving; ⲣ̄-ⲁⲧⲛⲁϩⲧⲉ to be
mistrustful, unbelieving. ⲣⲉϥⲛⲁϩⲧⲉ believer. ⲛ̄ϩⲟⲧ n.
trust, faith; ⲟ ⲛ̄ϩⲟⲧ (Q) to be trustworthy.

ⲛⲁⲝϩⲉ, ⲛⲁⲁⲝϩⲉ, ⲛⲁ(ⲗ)ⲝⲉ, ⲛⲉⲝⲉ n.f. tooth.

ⲛⲉⲉϥ, ⲛⲉϥ, ⲛⲉⲉⲃ, ⲛⲏ(ⲏ)ϥ, ⲛⲏ(ⲏ)ⲃ n.m. sailor.

ⲛⲉⲥⲃⲱⲱ⸗ pred. adj. to be wise. Cf. 29.2.

ⲛⲉⲥⲉ- ⲛⲉⲥⲱⸯ (ⲛⲉⲥⲟⸯ) pred. adj. to be beautiful. ⲡⲉⲧ ⲛⲉⲥⲱϥ,
ⲛⲉⲧ ⲛⲉⲥⲱⲟⲩ that which is beautiful. Cf. 29.2.

ⲛⲉϩ, ⲛⲉⲍ̄, ⲛⲏϩ n.m. oil. ⲁⲧⲛⲉϩ without oil. (ⲡ)ⲉⲣ-ⲛⲉϩ oil-
press. ϯ-ⲛⲉϩ to pour oil. ⲥⲁ ⲛ̄ ⲛⲉϩ oil-dealer.

ⲛⲉϩⲡⲉ vb. intr. to mourn (for: ⲉ, ⲉⲭⲛ̄); as n.m. mourning.

ⲛⲉϩⲥⲉ vb. tr. to awake, rouse (ⲙ̄ⲙⲟⸯ); also reflex.; vb.
    intr. (± ⲉϩⲣⲁⲓ) to awake, arise (from: ϩⲁ, ϩⲛ̄, ⲉⲃⲟⲗ ϩⲛ̄).

ⲛⲉϭⲱⸯ pred. adj. to be ugly, unseemly, disgraceful. Cf. 29.2.

ⲛⲏ̄ⲏⲃⲉ (ⲛⲏⲃⲉ, ⲛⲓⲃⲉ, ⲛⲓϥⲉ) vb. intr. to swim, float.

ⲛⲏⲥⲉ n.f. bench.

ⲛⲏⲩ (ⲛ̄ⲛⲏⲩ) Q to be coming, about to come, to be on the way.
    Used as Q of ⲉⲓ, q.v. for prep. and adv. complements.

ⲛⲓⲙ (1) interrog. pron. who? what? ⲛⲓⲙ ⲛ̄ adj. what? (2)
    indef. pron. so and so; ⲛⲓⲙ ⲙⲛ̄ ⲛⲓⲙ idem. See Gr. In.

ⲛⲓⲙ adj. every, each, used with articleless noun, often
    with pl. resumption. See 16.2.

ⲛⲓϥⲉ (ⲛⲓⲃⲉ) ⲛⲁϥⲧⸯ (ⲛⲉϥⲧⸯ, ⲛⲓϥⲧⸯ) vb. tr. to blow (ⲙ̄ⲙⲟⸯ; a-
    way; ⲉⲃⲟⲗ); vb. intr. (subj. wind, breath) to blow,
    with prep. in normal senses. As n.m. breath. ϯ-ⲛⲓϥⲉ
    to give breath; ϩⲙ̄-ⲛⲓϥⲉ difficult breathing.

ⲛⲕⲁ n.m. thing(s) in general; food; vessel; property, be-
    longings. ⲛ̄ⲕⲁ ⲛⲓⲙ everything.

ⲛ̄ⲕⲟⲧⲕ̄ (ⲉⲛⲕⲟⲧⲕ̄, ⲛ̄ⲕⲟⲧⲉ) vb. intr. to lie down (on: ⲉ, ⲉⲭⲛ̄,
    ϩⲓⲝⲛ̄); to die; as n.m. sleep, death. ⲁⲧⲛ̄ⲕⲟⲧⲕ̄ sleepless;
    ⲙⲁ ⲛ̄ ⲛ̄ⲕⲟⲧⲕ̄ couch. ⲣⲉϥⲛ̄ⲕⲟⲧⲕ̄ one who lies.

ⲛ̄ⲛⲟ exclam. no, it shall not be so!

ⲛⲟⲃⲉ n.m. sin. ⲁⲧⲛⲟⲃⲉ sinless. ⲙⲁⲓ-ⲛⲟⲃⲉ sin-loving. ⲣ̄-
    ⲛⲟⲃⲉ to sin (against: ⲉ); ⲣⲉϥⲣ̄-ⲛⲟⲃⲉ sinner; ⲙⲛ̄ⲧⲣⲉϥⲣ̄-
    ⲛⲟⲃⲉ sinfulness.

ⲛⲟⲉⲓⲛ vb. tr. to shake (ⲙ̄ⲙⲟⸯ); intr. to shake, tremble.
    ⲁⲧⲛⲟⲉⲓⲛ unshaken. As n.m. shaking.

ⲛⲟⲉⲓⲕ n.m. adulterer. ⲣ̄-ⲛⲟⲉⲓⲕ to commit adultery (with:
    ⲉ, ⲙⲛ̄); ⲙⲛ̄ⲧⲛⲟⲉⲓⲕ adultery.

ⲛⲟⲕⲛⲉⲕ vb. intr. to have affection (for: ⲉϩⲟⲩⲛ ⲉ); as n.m.
    affection.

ɴoм, ɴᴀм n.m. pine, tamarisk.

ɴoмтє n.f. strength, power.

ɴoʏ vb. to be about to, be going to (+ є + Inf.).

ɴoʏʙ, ɴoʏ٩ n.m. gold; money, coin. мᴀɪ-ɴoʏʙ gold-loving.
ᴈᴀм-ɴoʏʙ, ᴈᴀʏ-ɴoʏʙ, ᴈoʏ-ɴoʏʙ n.m. goldsmith.

(ɴoʏʙᴛ̄) ɴoʙᴛ⁵ vb. tr. to weave. ɴнʙᴛє n.f. plait; basket-
work.

ɴoʏɴ n.m. the abyss of hell, the depths of the sea or earth.

ɴoʏɴє n.f. root. ɴєx-ɴoʏɴє to put forth roots. xɪ-ɴoʏɴє
(± єʙoʌ) to take root.

ɴoʏpє n.f.m. vulture.

ɴoʏᴛ n. receptacle, pool.

ɴoʏᴛ ɴᴀᴛ⁵ vb. tr. to grind, pound (м̄мo⁵). мᴀ ɴ̄ ɴoʏᴛ mill.
pє٩ɴoʏᴛ grinder. ɴoєɪᴛ n.m. meal, ground grain.

ɴoʏᴛє (pl. ɴ̄ᴛнp, єɴᴛᴀɪp) god. пɴoʏᴛє God. ᴀᴛɴoʏᴛє godless; м̄ɴᴛᴀᴛɴoʏᴛє godlessness; p̄-ᴀᴛɴoʏᴛє to be godless.
м̄ɴᴛɴoʏᴛє divinity. мᴀɪ-ɴoʏᴛє God-loving; м̄ɴᴛмᴀɪ-ɴoʏᴛє
piety, godliness. мᴀc-ɴoʏᴛє, xпє-ɴoʏᴛє God-bearing.
мᴀcᴛє-ɴoʏᴛє God-hating. pм̄ɴɴoʏᴛє godly person; м̄ɴᴛpм̄ɴ-
ɴoʏᴛє godliness. ᴈᴀᴛʙ̄-ɴoʏᴛє God-slaying. pє٩ϣємϣє-
ɴoʏᴛє God-serving; м̄ɴᴛpє٩ϣємϣє-ɴoʏᴛє piety.

ɴoʏᴛм̄, Q ɴoᴛм̄ vb. intr. to be sweet, pleasant; as n.m.
sweetness. xɪᴛ-ɴoʏᴛм̄ sweet olive.

ɴoʏᴛ٩ (ɴoʏ٩ᴛ) ɴєᴛ٩- (ɴєᴛʙ̄-) Q ɴoᴛ٩ (ɴoᴛʙ̄) vb. tr. to loos-
en, relax (м̄мo⁵); ɴєᴛ٩-pω⁵, ɴєᴛ٩-п(⁵)ᴈo to smile; vb.
intr. to become relaxed, loosened; (subj. face, mouth)
to smile. As n.m. relaxation.

ɴoʏϣп̄ ɴєϣп̄- ɴoϣп̄⁵ (ɴᴀϣп̄⁵) Q ɴoϣп̄ vb. tr. to frighten
(м̄мo⁵), overawe; intr. to be frightened. ɴoʏϣп̄ єʙoʌ,
ɴ̄ cᴀʙoʌ to frighten away (from: м̄мo⁵).

ɴoʏϣc̄ ɴoϣc⁵ vb. tr. to benumb; to strike, rebuke; as n.m.
numbness. ɴoϣc٩ n.m. one who strikes.

ɴoʏϣᴛ̄ vb. intr. to become heavy, hard, difficult. Cf. ɴ̄ϣoᴛ.

ɴoʏ٩p̄ Q ɴo٩p̄ vb. intr. to be good. ɴє٩p̄- pred. adj. to be
good. ɴo٩pє, ɴoʙpє n.f. good, profit, advantage; p̄-

ночре to be profitable (to, for: нλ⸗; to do: є, єтрє).

ноучє adj. good; rare except in cpds. (стоı, 2є, ϣıнє).

ноучт̄ (ноувт̄) vb. intr. to swell, be distended.

ноу2, нω2 n.m. rope, cord. ср̄-ноу2 євоλ to stretch meas-
uring cord. ск̄-ноу2 as n.m. portion measured by cord.
ϣєϣ-ноу2 to make (lit. twist) rope.

ноу2б̄ нλ2б̄- нλ2в⸗ Q нλ2б̄ vb. tr. to yoke up (a wagon:
м̄мо⸗), to yoke (an animal: м̄мо⸗; to: є2оун є). нλ2б̄,
нλ2єв n.m. yoke. нλ2вєч n.m. idem. чλı-нλ2б̄ beast of
burden. нλ2б̄, нλ2ч̄, нλ2вє n.f. shoulders, back, neck;
ϣı н̄ нλ2б̄ shoulder's height. 2б̄с-нλ2б̄ shoulder-covering.

ноу2б̄ vb. intr. to copulate.

ноу2є (нω2є, ноу2, ноу) нє2- нλ2⸗ Q нн2 (нє2) vb. tr. (1)
to shake, cast off (м̄мо⸗; ± євоλ); (2) to separate, set
apart (м̄мо⸗ ± євоλ); vb. reflex. to separate self; to
turn, return; vb. intr. (± євоλ) to come apart, loose.

ноу2є n.f. sycamore.

ноу2м̄ нє2м̄ нλ2м⸗ Q нλ2м̄ vb. tr. to save, rescue, preserve
(м̄мо⸗; from: є, єтн̄, н̄тн̄, 2н̄, євоλ 2н̄, євоλ 2ıтн̄); vb.
intr. to be saved, rescued (preps. as above); Q to be
safe and sound. As n.m. safety. рєчноу2м̄ savior.

ноуx adj. lying, false (usu. aft. n. w. н̄); as n.m. liar.
м̄нтноуx falsehood. сλ н̄ м̄нтноуx lie-monger.

ноуxє (ноуx) нєx- ноx⸗ Q ннx vb. tr. to throw, cast (м̄мо⸗),
used with full range of prep. and adv. in normal senses;
Q to be situated, lying, reclining (at table). ноуxє
м̄мо⸗ є to cast into (prison), to launch a (ship) in
(water). ннx є to rely on. ноуxє м̄мо⸗ єxн̄ to impose
(sthg.) upon (someone); to put (clothes) on (someone).
ноуxє м̄мо⸗ є2оун to put in, introduce. As n.m. throw.

ноуxк̄ ноxк⸗ (ноx6⸗, ноx⸗) vb. tr. to sprinkle, asperge
(м̄мо⸗; upon: єxн̄); dir. obj. may be substance scattered
or object receiving it. As n.m. sprinkling, scattering.

ноу6т̄ нє6т̄- Q но6т̄ vb. intr. to become angry, furious (at,
against: є, єxн̄); as n.m. wrath. р̄-ноу6т̄ to make angry.

ᴩⲉϥⲛⲟⲩϬⲧ wrathful person. †-ⲛⲟⲩϬⲧ ⲛⲁˢ to make angry.
ⲛⲁϬϭⲉ n. wrath.

ⲛⲟϬⲛⲉϭ ⲛⲉϬⲛⲉϭ- ⲛⲉϬⲛⲟⲩϬˢ vb. tr. to reproach, mock (ⲙ̄ⲙⲟˢ);
as n.m. reproach; ⲣ̄-ⲛⲟϬⲛⲉϭ to become a reproach.

ⲛⲟϬ adj. big, great, large; elder (son, brother, sister);
bef. or aft. n. with ⲛ̄; aft. n. without ⲛ̄; as n.m.
great person or thing, old person. ⲙⲛ̄ⲧⲛⲟϬ greatness;
seniority; ⲣ̄-ⲙⲛ̄ⲧⲛⲟϬ to do great things. ⲣ̄-ⲛⲟϬ (Q o ⲛ̄)
to become great; to grow up, become of age; ⲙⲁⲓ-ⲣ̄-ⲛⲟϬ
ambitious. ⲛⲟϬ ⲉ greater, older than; ⲣ̄-ⲛⲟϬ ⲉ to become older than, superior to. ⲣ̄-ⲟⲩⲛⲟϬ, ϣⲱⲡⲉ ⲛ̄ ⲟⲩⲛⲟϬ to
become great. ⲛⲟϬ ⲛ̄ ⲣⲱⲙⲉ full-grown; old; as n.m. elder, notable; ⲙⲛ̄ⲧⲛⲟϬ ⲛ̄ ⲣⲱⲙⲉ old age. ⲛⲟϬ ⲛ̄ ⲥⲁ̀ⲓⲙⲉ sim.

ⲛ̄ⲧⲉ ⲛ̄ⲧⲁˢ prep. expressing genitive and possession; Gr. In.

ⲛ̄ⲧⲏϭ, ⲉⲛⲧⲏϭ n.m. plant, herb, weed; ⲣ̄-ⲛ̄ⲧⲏϭ to become
weedy. ϫⲓ-ⲛ̄ⲧⲏϭ to sow plants.

ⲛ̄ⲧⲟ indep. pers. pron. you (f.s.).

ⲛ̄ⲧⲟⲕ indep. pers. pron. you (m.s.).

ⲛ̄ⲧⲟⲟⲩ indep. pers. pron. they; cf. ⲛ̄ⲧⲟϥ.

ⲛ̄ⲧⲟⲟⲩⲛ̄, ⲛ̄ⲧⲱⲟⲩⲛ adv. then, next, thereupon; therefore, so.

ⲛ̄ⲧⲟⲥ indep. pers. pron. she, it (f.); cf. ⲛ̄ⲧⲟϥ.

ⲛ̄ⲧⲟϥ (1) indep. pers. pron. he, it (m.); (2) adv. but, rather, on the other hand; again, further; ⲛ̄ⲧⲟⲥ and ⲛ̄ⲧⲟⲟⲩ
may be used sim. with f. or pl. subject reference.
ⲛ̄ⲧⲟϥ ⲛ̄ⲧⲟϥ ⲡⲉ he (it) is one and the same.

ⲛ̄ⲧⲱⲧⲛ̄ indep. pers. pron. you (pl.).

ⲛ̄ϣⲟⲧ (ⲉⲛϣⲟⲧ) Q ⲛⲁϣⲧ̄ vb. intr. to become hard, strong, difficult; Q to be hard, harsh, difficult. ⲛⲁϣⲧ̄-ϩⲣⲁˢ impudent. ⲛⲁϣⲧ̄-(ⲛ̄)-ϩⲏⲧ hard-hearted; ⲙⲛ̄ⲧⲛⲁϣⲧ̄-ϩⲏⲧ hard-
heartedness; ⲣ̄-ⲛⲁϣⲧ̄-ϩⲏⲧ (Q o ⲛ̄) to become hard-hearted.
As n.m. harshness, boldness; ϩⲛ̄ ⲟⲩⲛ̄ϣⲟⲧ harshly, rough-
ly; †-ⲛ̄ϣⲟⲧ ⲛ̄/ⲉ ⲡ(ˢ)ϩⲏⲧ to encourage. ⲛⲁϣⲧⲉ n.f.
strength, protection; ⲣ̄-ⲛⲁϣⲧⲉ (Q o ⲛ̄) to become protector.

ⲛ̄Ϭⲓ particle introducing subject in post-verbal position.

N-: Π-	NЄTϥ: NOYTϥ	NOY: NOY2Є
Ñ-: ЄINЄ	NЄϢΠ-: NOYϢΠ	NOYBT̄: NOYϥT̄
NAˣ: Ñ	NЄϥ: NЄЄϥ	ÑOYЄϢÑ: OYωϢ
NA-: ΠA-, λ	NЄϥP̄-: NOYϥP̄	ÑOYOЄI: OYOЄI
NAλ: NA	NЄϥTˣ: NIϥЄ	NOYϥ: NOYB
NAAY: ЄIAAY	NЄ2(-): NOY2Є	NOYϥЄ: NOYϥP̄
NAAX(2)Є: NAX2Є	NЄ2M̄-: NOY2M̄	NOYϥT̄: NOYTϥ
NAЄ-: NAλ-	NЄX-: NOYXЄ	NOY2: NOY2Є
NAЄ: NA	NЄXЄ: NAX2Є	NOYX: NOYXЄ
NAI: ΠAI; NA	NЄϬC̄-: NOYϬC̄	NOϢΠ(ˣ): NOYϢΠ
NAIATˣ: ЄIA	NH: ΠH	NOϢCˣ: NOYϢC̄
NAM: NOM	NHBЄ: NHHBЄ	NOϥP̄: NOYϥP̄
NATˣ: NOYT	NHBTЄ: NOYBT̄	NOϥPЄ: NOYϥP̄
NAϢΠˣ: NOYϢΠ	NHHB: NЄЄϥ	NOXˣ: NOYXЄ
NAϢT(-): ÑϢOT	NHHϥ: NЄЄϥ	NOXˣ: NOYXK̄
NAϢTЄ: ÑϢOT	NHT: NAT	NOXKˣ: NOYXK̄
NAϢTIMMЄ: ЄIMЄ	NH2: NЄ2	NOXGˣ: NOYXK̄
NAϢTM̄MЄ: ЄIMЄ	NH2: NOY2Є	NOϬC̄: NOYϬC̄
NAϥTˣ: NIϥЄ	NHY: ЄI	ÑCABHλ: BωλN
NA2ˣ: NOY2Є	NHX: NOYXЄ	ÑCABOλ: BωλN
NA2Bˣ: NOY2B̄	NIλλY: ЄIλλY	ÑCλ Ñ BOλ: BωλN
NA2(Є)B: NOY2B̄	NIBЄ: NHHBЄ	ÑTˣ: ЄINЄ
NA2M(ˣ): NOY2M̄	NIBЄ: NIϥЄ	ÑTAˣ: ÑTЄ-
NA2PAˣ: 2O	NIϥЄ: NHHBЄ	ÑTЄ: TωPЄ
NA2PÑ: 2O	NIϥTˣ: NIϥЄ	ÑTÑ: TωPЄ
NA2ϥ: NOY2B̄	ÑλIKTˣ: λIKTˣ	ÑTOOTˣ: TωPЄ
NAϬCЄ: NOYϬC̄	NM̄: MÑ	ÑTωOYN: ÑTOOYÑ
ÑBX̄-, ÑBX̄λλˣ: BωλN	NM̄MAˣ: MÑ	Nω2: NOY2
NЄ: ΠЄ	NOBPЄ: NOYϥP̄	Nω2Є: NOY2Є
NЄ: ЄNЄ	NOBTˣ: NOYBT̄	N2̄: NЄ2, 9N2̄
NЄIλλY: ЄIλλY	NOЄIT: NOYT	Ñ2ЄT-: NA2TЄ
NЄIω: NλЄIω	NOTB̄: NOYTϥ	Ñ2HTˣ: 2Ñ
NЄΠPЄ: NλΠPЄ	NOTM̄: NOYTM̄	Ñ2OT: NA2TЄ
NЄT: NλT	NOTϥ: NOYTϥ	Ñ2OYT: NA2TЄ
NЄTB̄-: NOYTϥ	NOYˣ: Πωˣ	ÑXЄ: XЄ

ɔ

o, ω adj. great; archaic except as final element in cpds.:
see ЄIЄPO, P̄PO, 2X̄λO, 2X̄λω, P̄Tω, 2POYO.

OBÑ, OBЄN, λBЄN n.m. alum.

OB2Є, OB2̄ n.m. tooth, tusk; (?) hoe.

OЄIK n.m. (1) bread; loaf or piece of bread; (2) dung (cf.
MH). MA Ñ KA-/†-/OYЄ2-OЄIK storeroom, pantry. P̄-OЄIK
to become bread. PЄϥTAMIЄ-OЄIK baker.

OЄIK n.m. reed.

OЄIMЄ, OIMЄ, OЄIM n.f. hook.

oeine, oine n.f. ephah (a grain measure).

oeiϣ n. cry, only in cpds.: ⲗϣ-oeiϣ loquacious; ⲧⲁϣⲉ-oeiϣ
to preach, proclaim (ⲙⲙⲟⸯ); as n.m. preaching, procla-
mation; ⲣⲉϥⲧⲁϣⲉ-oeiϣ preacher, herald; ⲣ̄-ⲣⲉϥⲧⲁϣⲉ-oeiϣ
to become preacher, herald; ⲙⲛ̄ⲧⲣⲉϥⲧⲁϣⲉ-oeiϣ proclaiming.

oⲕⲉ n.m. sesame.

oⲗⲉⲓⲉ, oⲓⲗⲉⲓⲉ n.m. ram.

oⲙⲉ, ooⲙⲉ, ⲗⲙⲉ n.m.f. clay, mud. ⲣ̄-oⲙⲉ to become mud.
ⲗⲙ-ⲡⲏⲣϣ̄ red clay; ⲗⲙ-ⲍⲁⲧ white clay. oⲩⲗⲙ-oⲙⲉ n.f.
name of a rodent; gangrene, ulcer; ⲣ̄-oⲩⲗⲙ-oⲙⲉ to
spread like gangrene.

oⲛ adv. again, also, still, further, yet.

ooⲧ vb. (Q?) to groan or sim.

ooⲧⲉ, oⲧⲉ n.f. womb.

ooⲩϣ n.m. gruel (of bread or lentils).

ooⲍ, oⲍ, ⲱⲍ n.m. moon.

oⲣⲃⲉ n. wafer, thin cake.

oⲥⲉ n.m. loss, damage; a fine. ϯ-oⲥⲉ to suffer loss (of:
ⲙⲙⲟⸯ); to be fined.

oⲑⲉ n.f. outlet (for water); way, course.

oⲍⲉ, ooⲍⲉ, ⲱⲍⲉ n.m. courtyard; cattle pen, fold; pasture;
herd, flock.

o: ⲉⲓⲣⲉ	oⲗⲥ̄: ⲱⲗ	oⲥⲍϥ̄: ⲱⲍⲥ̄
oⲃⸯ: ⲱϥⲉ	oⲙⲕⸯ: ⲱⲛⲕ̄	oⲧⲉ: ooⲧⲉ
oⲃⲉ: ⲉⲓⲃⲉ	oⲛⲅⸯ: ⲱⲛⲕ̄	oⲧⲉⸯ: ⲱϭⲧ̄
oⲃⲉⲛ: oⲃⲛ̄	oⲛϣⸯ: ⲱϣ	oϥⸯ: ⲱϥⲉ
oⲃⲧ(ⸯ): ⲱϥⲧ̄	oⲛϣⲥ̄: ⲱⲛϣ̄	oϣ: ⲗϣⲗⲓ
oⲃϣⲥ̄: ⲱⲃϣ̄	oⲛⲍ̄: ⲗⲛⲍ̄	oⲍ: ooⲍ
oⲓ: ⲗⲓⲗⲓ	ooⲙⲉ: oⲙⲉ	oⲝⲧⸯ: ⲱϭⲧ̄
oⲓⲗⲉⲓⲉ: oⲗⲉⲓⲉ	ooⲛϣ̄: ⲱⲛϣ̄	oϭⲃⲥ̄: ⲱϭⲃ̄
oⲗⲉⲕⲥ: ⲱⲗⲕ̄	ooⲍⲉ: oⲍⲉ	oϭϥ̄: ⲱϭⲃ̄
oⲗⲕⲥ̄: ⲱⲗⲕ̄	oⲣϥⸯ: ⲱⲣⲃ̄	

ⲡ

ⲡ-, ⲧ-, ⲛ- the def. article; see 1.3.

ⲡⲗ-, ⲧⲗ-, ⲛⲗ- absolute relative pronoun, that of, that
which belongs or pertains to; see 22.2.

ⲡⲁⲓ, ⲧⲁⲓ, ⲛⲁⲓ dem. pron. this, these; see 5.2.

ⲡⲁⲓϣⲉ, ⲡⲁϣⲉ, ⲡⲉϣⲉ, ⲡⲓϣⲉ n.f. name of a disease.

ⲡⲁⲕⲉ (ⲡⲁⲁⲕⲉ) Q ⲡⲟⲕ(ⲉ) vb. intr. to become light, thin; w. ϩⲏⲧ: to become poor, mean (at heart). ⲡⲟⲕϥ̄ n.m. thin sheet, plate.

ⲡⲁⲡⲟⲓ, ⲡⲁⲡⲁⲓ n.m. bird, chicken.

ⲡⲁⲟⲡⲉ, ⲡⲟⲟⲡⲉ, ⲡⲁⲁⲡⲉ name of 2nd Coptic month.

ⲡⲁⲣⲙⲟⲩⲧⲉ, ⲡⲁⲣⲙⲟⲩϯ name of 8th Coptic month.

ⲡⲁⲣⲙ̄ϩⲟⲧⲡ̄, ⲡⲁⲣⲉⲙϩⲟⲧⲡ̄, -ϩⲟⲧ, -ϩⲁⲧ(ⲡ̄) name of 7th Coptic mo.

ⲡⲁⲧ n.f. leg, shin, knee, foot. ⲕⲗ̄ϫ-ⲡⲁⲧ to bend the knee.

ⲡⲁⲧⲁⲗⲗⲁⲥ n. unknown ethnic (?) term, abusive; prob. = pagan.

ⲡⲁⲱⲛⲉ, ⲡⲁⲱⲛⲓ, ⲡⲁⲟⲩⲛⲓ name of 10th Coptic month.

ⲡⲁϣ n.m. trap, snare. ⲡⲁϣϥ̄ n. idem.

ⲡⲁϣⲟⲛⲥ̄, ⲡⲁϣⲱⲛⲥ̄, ⲡⲁⲭⲟⲛⲥ̄ name of 9th Coptic month.

ⲡⲁϩⲣⲉ, ⲡⲁϩⲣ̄ n.m.(f.) drug, medicament; paint, color. ⲣ̄-ⲡⲁϩⲣⲉ to heal, cure (ⲉ); ⲣⲉϥⲣ̄-ⲡⲁϩⲣⲉ magician; ⲙⲛ̄ⲧⲣⲉϥⲣ̄-ⲡⲁϩⲣⲉ magic. ϯ-ⲡⲁϩⲣⲉ to heal, cure. ϫⲓ-ⲡⲁϩⲣⲉ to take medication, be healed; to take color, be dyed. ⲙⲁ ⲛ̄ ϫⲓ-ⲡⲁϩⲣⲉ place of healing.

ⲡⲁϩⲟⲩ n.m. back, hind part, buttocks; as adj. past. ⲉⲡⲁϩⲟⲩ adv. back, backward. ⲉⲡⲁϩⲟⲩ ⲉ prep. back to. ⲥⲁ-ⲡⲁϩⲟⲩ = ⲉⲡⲁϩⲟⲩ. ⲛ̄ ⲥⲁ-ⲡⲁϩⲟⲩ adv. behind, back, from behind. ϩⲁ ⲡⲁϩⲟⲩ adv. in the past. ϩⲓ ⲡⲁϩⲟⲩ behind; prep. + ⲙ̄ⲙⲟ⸗.

ⲡⲁϭⲥⲉ, ⲡⲁⲧⲥⲉ n.f. spittle; ⲛⲉϫ-ⲡⲁϭⲥⲉ to spit.

ⲡⲉ, ⲧⲉ, ⲛⲉ pron./copula. See Gr. In.

ⲡⲉ (pl. ⲡⲏⲩⲉ) n.f. sky, heaven. Note adj. use in ⲁⲩⲁⲛ ⲙ̄ ⲡⲉ sky-blue, ⲁⲗ ⲙ̄ ⲡⲉ hailstone(s), ⲣⲙ̄ⲙ̄ⲡⲉ man of heaven. ϩⲣⲟⲩ-ⲙ̄-ⲡⲉ thunder, ϩⲱⲟⲩ ⲙ̄ ⲡⲉ rain. ⲧⲡⲉ that which is above; ⲉⲧⲡⲉ adv. upward; ⲛ̄ ⲧⲡⲉ (1) adj. upper; (2) adv. above; (3) prep. above (+ ⲛ̄). ϩⲛ̄ ⲧⲡⲉ idem (2,3). (ⲛ̄) ⲥⲁ-ⲧⲡⲉ idem (2,3). ϩⲓ ⲧⲡⲉ idem (2,3). ⲣ̄-ⲧⲡⲉ to surmount, rise above (ⲙ̄ⲙⲟ⸗). ⲙ̄ ⲡⲉⲧⲡⲉ ⲛ̄, ϩⲙ̄ ⲡⲉⲧⲡⲉ ⲛ̄ prep. above, over. ⲣ̄-ⲡⲉⲧⲡⲉ = ⲣ̄-ⲧⲡⲉ.

ⲡⲉⲓ, ⲡⲓ n.f. kiss. ϯ-ⲡⲉⲓ to kiss (ⲉ, ⲉⲣⲛ̄, ⲉϫⲛ̄).

ⲡⲉⲓⲣⲉ (ⲡⲓⲣⲉ) Q ⲡⲟⲣⲉ (ⲡⲣⲉⲓⲱⲟⲩ, ⲡⲉⲣⲉⲓⲱⲟⲩ) ± ⲉⲃⲟⲗ vb. intr.

to come forth (subj. light, blossom, hair); to bloom,
blossom; to shine, be radiant. As n.m. coming forth,
shining; tale; epithet. ма ⲙ̄ ⲛⲉⲓⲣⲉ place of sunrise.

ⲡⲉⲛⲛⲉ, ⲡⲉⲛⲛⲏ n. bug.

ⲡⲉⲣⲓⲛⲉⲣⲟⲓ n.m. royal palace.

ⲡⲉⲝⲉ- ⲡⲉⲝⲁˢ vb. said (suff. is subj.), usu. + ⲭⲉ; used
only to introduce direct speech.

ⲡⲏ, ⲧⲏ, ⲛⲏ dem. pron. that, those; see 30.8.

ⲡⲏⲓ n. flea.

ⲡⲏⲣⲉ, ⲡⲏⲣⲁ n.m. quail. ⳅⲏ ⲙ̄ ⲡⲏⲣⲉ brood of quails.

ⲡⲏⲣⲟ̅ n.m. red substance; rust, blight. ⲁⲙ-ⲡⲏⲣⲟ̅ red clay.

ⲡⲓⲛ n.m. mouse.

ⲡⲓⲥⲉ (ⲡⲓⲥ) ⲡⲉⲥ(ⲧ̄)- ⲡⲁⲥⲧˢ (ⲡⲓⲥⲧˢ) Q ⲡⲟⲥⲉ (ⲡⲏⲥ) vb. tr. to
cook, boil, bake (ⲙ̄ⲙⲟˢ); to melt (e.g. wax, metal,
glass); vb. intr. to be cooked, to melt; as n.m. anything cooked. ⲡⲁⲥⲉ n. cooked food.

ⲡⲓⲧⲉ n.f. bow (for arrows); ⲣⲁ ⲙ̄ ⲡⲓⲧⲉ loop-hole.

ⲡⲓϭⲁ, ⲡⲓϭⲏ, ⲡⲓϭⲓ n. vanity; ⲙⲛ̄ⲧⲡⲓϭⲁ idem.

ⲡⲗ̄ϭⲉ, ⲡⲉⲗϭⲉ, ⲡⲉⲗⲭⲉ, ⲡⲣ̄ϭⲉ n.m. rag, torn cloth; as adj. old,
worn. ⲡⲗ̄ϭⲉ ⲛ̄ ⲧⲟⲉⲓⲥ idem; patch. ⲣ̄-ⲡⲗ̄ϭⲉ (Q o ⲛ̄) to become torn, ragged.

ⲡⲛ̄ⲛⲏ, ⲡⲛⲏ n.f. doorpost, threshhold.

ⲡⲟⲉⲓϣ n.m. rung, step.

ⲡⲟⲓ n.m. bench.

ⲡⲟⲣⲕ̄ n.m. outer mantle of clerics, pallium.

ⲡⲟⲣⲕ̄, ⲡⲟⲣⲉⲕ n.m. foal, calf. ⲙⲉⲥ-ⲡⲟⲣⲕ̄, ⲙⲁⲥ-ⲡⲟⲣⲕ̄ mule.

ⲡⲟⲧⲛ̄ⲧ̄ vb. tr. to fell, cut down (ⲙ̄ⲙⲟˢ); intr. to fall, fall
away.

ⲡⲣⲱ n.f. winter. ⲣ̄-ⲧⲉⲡⲣⲱ to pass the winter.

ⲯⲓⲥ, ⲯⲓⲧ (f. ⲯⲓⲧⲉ, ⲯⲓⲥⲉ) number: nine. ⲙⲉⳅⲯⲓⲥ ninth.
ⲡⲥ̄ⲧⲁⲓⲟⲩ ninety; ⲯⲁⲓⲧ- idem in cpd. nos.

ⲡⲱˢ, ⲧⲱˢ, ⲛⲟⲩˢ poss. pron.; see 22.2.

ⲡⲱⲗⳅ ⲡⲟⲗⳅˢ Q ⲡⲟⲗⳅ vb. tr. to wound (ⲙ̄ⲙⲟˢ); intr. to be
wounded, offended (by: ⲉ); as n.m. wound.

ⲡⲱⲗϭ ⲡⲗ̄ϭ- (ⲡⲉⲗⲕ-) ⲡⲟⲗϭˢ (-ⲕˢ, -ⲭˢ, ⲡⲁⲗϭˢ) ± ⲉⲃⲟⲗ vb. tr.

to decide, settle (a matter: ⲙⲙⲟ⸗); to relieve, free
(from: ⲉⲃⲟⲗ ⲛ̄, ⲉⲃⲟⲗ ϩⲛ̄, ϩⲁ); vb. intr. to strive for or
reach satisfaction or agreement (with: ⲙⲛ̄); to reach
conclusion; to be relieved of or freed from (ⲉⲃⲟⲗ ⲉ,
ⲉⲃⲟⲗ ⲛ̄, ⲉⲃⲟⲗ ϩⲛ̄). ⲡⲗⲟ6 n.m. part, portion. ⲡⲟⲗ6ⲥ̄ n.f.
clod, lump.

ⲡⲱⲛ (ⲡⲟⲱⲛ, ⲡⲱⲱⲛⲉ) ⲡⲉⲛ- (ⲡⲉⲉⲛ-, ⲡⲉⲛⲉ-) Q ⲡⲏⲛ vb. intr.
to pour, be poured, flow (± ⲉⲃⲟⲗ: out, forth); as n.m.
pouring, outflow.

ⲡⲱⲛⲕ̄ (ⲡⲱⲛⲅ̄, ⲡⲱⲛ6̄) ⲡⲛ̄ⲅ- (ⲡⲉⲛⲕ̄-) ⲡⲟⲛⲕ⸗ vb. tr. (± ⲉⲃⲟⲗ) to
draw, bail (water, breath: ⲙⲙⲟ⸗); to move, transfer,
carry (ⲙⲙⲟ⸗; onto, upon: ⲉxⲛ̄; from: ϩⲛ̄; into: ⲉϩⲟⲩⲛ ⲉ).

ⲡⲱⲣⲕ̄ ⲡⲣ̄ⲕ- (ⲡⲉⲣⲕ̄-) ⲡⲟⲣⲕ⸗ (± ⲉⲃⲟⲗ) vb. tr. to pluck out, up-
root (ⲙⲙⲟ⸗; from: ϩⲛ̄); vb. intr. to be uprooted, destroyed. As n.m. plucking out.

(ⲡⲱⲣⲥ̄) Q ⲡⲟⲣⲥ̄ vb. intr. to stretch, strain (uncertain).
ⲡⲟⲣⲥ̄ n.f. curtain (?), mat (?). ⲡⲣⲉⲥⲣⲁⲥⲧ̄ Q to be stiff
(of hair).

ⲡⲱⲣⲱ̄ ⲡⲣ̄ⲱ̄- (ⲡⲉⲣⲱ̄-) ⲡⲟⲣⲱ⸗ Q ⲡⲟⲣⲱ̄ vb. tr. to spread, stretch,
extend (ⲙⲙⲟ⸗; ± ⲉⲃⲟⲗ out, forth); with ⲉ, ⲉxⲛ̄, ϩⲓ,
ϩⲓxⲛ̄, ⲛⲁϩⲣⲛ̄, ⲟⲩⲃⲉ in normal senses; vb. intr. to spread, extend, be spread (prep. as preceding). As n.m. thing
spread, mat, coverlet; + ⲉⲃⲟⲗ: spreading, extending.
ⲙⲁ ⲙ̄ ⲡⲱⲣⲱ̄ couch, bed. ⲡⲟⲣⲱ̄ⲥ̄ n.f. spread table. ⲡⲣⲏⲱ
n.m. thing spread, mat, cloak, cover.

ⲡⲱⲣⲝ̄ ⲡⲣ̄x- (ⲡⲉⲣⲝ̄-) ⲡⲟⲣx⸗ Q ⲡⲟⲣⲝ̄ ± ⲉⲃⲟⲗ vb. tr. to divide,
separate (ⲙⲙⲟ⸗; from: ⲉ, ⲙⲙⲟ⸗; into: ⲉ; in half: ⲉ
ⲧ(⸗)ⲙⲏⲧⲉ; vb. intr. to divide, become divided; to part,
depart. As n.m. (± ⲉⲃⲟⲗ) parting, separation; ⲉⲓⲣⲉ ⲛ̄
ⲟⲩⲡⲱⲣⲝ̄ to make a division; ⲧ̄-ⲡⲱⲣⲝ̄, ⲧ̄ ⲛ̄ ⲟⲩⲡⲱⲣⲝ̄ idem.
ⲁⲧⲡⲱⲣⲝ̄ undivided, indivisible; ⲣ̄-ⲁⲧⲡⲱⲣⲝ̄ to become in-
separable (with: ⲉ); ⲙⲛ̄ⲧⲁⲧⲡⲱⲣⲝ̄ indivisibility. ⲙⲁ ⲙ̄
ⲡⲱⲣⲝ̄ frontier. ⲣⲉϥⲡⲱⲣⲝ̄ divider.

ⲡⲱⲧ, Q ⲡⲏⲧ vb. intr. to run, flee; to run a course; used
with full range of prep. and adv. in normal senses.

ⲡⲱⲧ ⲛ̄ⲥⲁ to pursue. ⲡⲱⲧ ⲛ̄ⲧⲛ̄ to flee from; ⲡⲱⲧ ϩⲏⲧ⸗ idem. As n.m. course, flight. ⲙⲁ ⲙ̄ ⲡⲱⲧ place of refuge; race-course; + ⲉⲃⲟⲗ: exit. ⲣⲉϥⲡⲱⲧ runner.

ⲡⲱⲧⲥ̄, Q ⲡⲟⲧⲥ̄ vb. tr. to split, divide, crack (ⲙ̄ⲙⲟ⸗, ⲉ). ⲡⲁⲧⲥⲉ n.f. plank, shelf.

ⲡⲱⲧϩ̄ ⲡⲟⲧϩ⸗ Q ⲡⲟⲧϩ̄ vb. tr. to carve, engrave, depict (ⲙ̄ⲙⲟ⸗).

ⲡⲱⲱⲛⲉ (ⲡⲱⲛⲉ) ⲡⲉⲉⲛⲉ- (ⲡⲉⲛⲉ-) ⲡⲟⲟⲛⲉ⸗ (ⲡⲁⲁⲛⲉ⸗) Q ⲡⲟⲟⲛⲉ (1) vb. tr. to turn (ⲙ̄ⲙⲟ⸗); to transfer, change, translate, copy (ⲙ̄ⲙⲟ⸗; to, into, over to: ⲉ, ⲉϩⲟⲩⲛ ⲉ, ⲉϩⲣⲁⲓ ⲉ); + ⲉⲃⲟⲗ: to remove, carry out, take out (ⲙ̄ⲙⲟ⸗; from: ⲛ̄, ϩⲛ̄, ϩⲓϫⲛ̄). (2) vb. intr. to turn, change, become altered (from: ϩⲛ̄; to: ⲉ); + ⲉⲃⲟⲗ: to move away, depart. ⲡⲱⲱⲛⲉ ⲉⲃⲟⲗ n.m. removal, change, death. ⲁⲧⲡⲱⲱⲛⲉ immovable, unchangeable; ⲙⲛ̄ⲧⲁⲧⲡⲱⲱⲛⲉ immutability. ⲣⲉϥⲡⲱⲱⲛⲉ, ⲣⲉϥⲡⲟⲟⲛⲉϥ changeable person; ⲙⲛ̄ⲧⲣⲉϥⲡⲱⲱⲛⲉ changeableness. ⲡⲱⲱⲛⲉⲥ, ⲡⲟⲟⲛⲉⲥ n.f. movement.

ⲡⲱⲱⲡⲉ ⲡⲁⲡⲉ- ⲡⲁⲡⲱ⸗ vb. tr. to make bricks (ⲧⲱⲃⲉ). ⲙⲛ̄ⲧⲡⲁⲡⲉⲧⲱⲃⲉ brick-making. ⲙⲁ ⲙ̄ ⲡⲁⲡⲉ-ⲧⲱⲃⲉ brickyard. ⲡⲁⲡⲉⲓⲧ n. brick-maker.

ⲡⲱⲱⲣⲉ ⲡⲉⲣⲉ- ⲡⲟⲟⲣ⸗ vb. tr. to dream (+ ⲣⲁⲥⲟⲩ). ⲣⲉϥⲡⲱⲱⲣⲉ dreamer.

ⲡⲱϣ (ⲡⲱϣⲉ) ⲡⲉϣ- ⲡⲟϣ⸗ Q ⲡⲏϣ vb. tr. to divide (ⲙ̄ⲙⲟ⸗; at, into: ⲉ; among: ϩⲛ̄, ⲙⲛ̄); to share (with: ⲉϩⲣⲛ̄, ⲉϫⲛ̄, ⲛⲁ⸗); vb. intr. to be divided, shared, apportioned (prep. as in preceding); as n.m. division. ⲁⲧⲡⲱϣ undivided, indivisible; ⲣⲉϥⲡⲱϣ divider. ⲡⲁϣⲉ, ⲡⲏϣⲉ, ⲡⲓϣⲉ (ⲡⲁϣ-, ⲡϣ̄-) n.f. half, division; ⲡⲁϣⲉ ⲛ̄ ⲧⲉⲩϣⲏ midnight. ⲣ̄-ⲡⲁϣⲉ (Q ⲟ ⲛ̄) to be half, midway (+ ⲛ̄ + Inf. or w. Circum.); also cpd. as ⲣ̄-ⲡⲁϣ-, as in ⲣ̄-ⲡⲁϣ-ⲙⲟⲩ be half dead.

ⲡⲱϣⲛ̄ ⲡⲉϣⲛ̄- ⲡⲟϣⲛ⸗ Q ⲡⲟϣⲛ̄ vb. tr. to ordain (ⲙ̄ⲙⲟ⸗; as: ⲛ̄); vb. intr. to serve as priest; as n.m. service, ordination. ⲣⲉϥⲡⲱϣⲛ̄ servant. ⲡⲁϣⲛⲉ n.f. service.

ⲡⲱϣⲥ̄ (ⲡⲱⲥϣ̄) ⲡⲉϣⲥ̄- ⲡⲟϣⲥ⸗ (ⲡⲁϣⲥ⸗) Q ⲡⲟϣⲥ̄ (ⲡⲟⲥϣ̄) vb. tr. to amaze (ⲙ̄ⲙⲟ⸗); to turn aside (ⲙ̄ⲙⲟ⸗); vb. intr. (± ⲉⲃⲟⲗ) to become amazed, beside oneself (at: ⲉϫⲛ̄, ⲛ̄ⲥⲁ); to

turn aside, be turned (to: ϭ). As n.m. amazement.
ⲡⲱϣⲥ̄ ⲛ̄ ⲍⲏⲧ to be amazed, disturbed (at: ⲉⲝⲛ̄, ⲛ̄ⲥⲁ);
as n.m. amazement.

ⲡⲱⲍ ⲡⲉⲍ- (ⲡⲁⲍ-) ⲡⲟⲍ⸱ (ⲡⲁⲍ⸱) Q ⲡⲏⲍ (ⲡⲉⲍ) vb. tr. to burst,
split, break, tear (ⲙ̄ⲙⲟ⸱); vb. intr. idem; as n.m.
division, piece. ⲟ ⲙ̄ ⲡⲱⲍ ⲡⲱⲍ Q to be in pieces. ⲣⲉϥ-
ⲡⲉⲍ- splitter, divider. ⲡⲁⲍⲉ n.f. fragment; ⲛ̄ ⲡⲁⲍⲉ
ⲡⲁⲍⲉ in pieces. ⲡⲁⲍⲥ̄ n.f. prey; ⲣ̄-ⲡⲁⲍⲥ̄, ⲉⲓⲣⲉ ⲙ̄ ⲡⲁⲍⲥ̄
to make as prey. ⲡⲁⲍϥ n.m. cleft.

ⲡⲱⲍ ⲡⲉⲍ- (ⲡⲍ̄-) Q ⲡⲏⲍ (1) vb. tr./intr. to reach, attain
(ⲉ, ⲉⲍⲟⲩⲛ ⲉ, ϣⲁⲣⲁⲓ ⲉ); to come upon (ⲉⲝⲛ̄); to reach
to (ϣⲁ), refer to (ϣⲁ); to mature, ripen. (2) aux. vb.
+ Inf.: to do for once, succeed in doing, just manage
to do.

ⲡⲱⲍⲥ̄ ⲡⲉⲍⲥ̄- Q ⲡⲟⲍⲥ̄ vb. tr. to bite (ⲙ̄ⲙⲟ⸱); as n.m. bite.

ⲡⲱⲍⲧ̄ ⲡⲉⲍⲧ̄- (ⲡⲁⲍⲧ̄-) ⲡⲁⲍⲧ⸱ Q ⲡⲁⲍⲧ̄ (1) vb. tr. to bend, bow
(ⲙ̄ⲙⲟ⸱); intr. and reflex. to bow, prostrate self. Used
with ⲉ, ⲉⲝⲛ̄, ⲉⲍⲣⲁⲓ ⲉⲝⲛ̄, ⲛⲁ⸱, ⲍⲁⲣⲁⲧ⸱ in usual senses.
(2) vb. tr. (± ⲉⲃⲟⲗ) to pour, shed (ⲙ̄ⲙⲟ⸱; with ⲉ, ⲉⲝⲛ̄,
ⲉⲍⲣⲁⲓ ⲉⲝⲛ̄ in usual senses); vb. intr. to pour, flow
(like preceding); ⲡⲱⲍⲧ̄ ⲉⲃⲟⲗ ⲙⲛ̄ to abandon oneself with.
As n.m. pouring, shedding. ⲁⲧⲡⲉⲍⲧ̄-ⲥⲛⲟϥ not shedding
blood. ⲣⲉϥⲡⲉⲍⲧ̄-ⲥⲛⲟϥ shedder of blood.

ⲡⲱⲭⲋ (ⲡⲱⲭⲕ̄, ⲡⲱⲭⲧ̄) Q ⲡⲟⲭⲧ̄ vb. tr. to beat flat; as n.m.
breadth, flat part.

ⲡⲱϭⲉ ⲡⲟϭ⸱ (ⲡⲟⲕ⸱, ⲡⲟⲅ⸱) Q ⲡⲟⲅⲉ vb. tr. to break, burst (ⲙ̄-
ⲙⲟ⸱); intr. idem. ⲡⲟϭⲉ, ⲡⲱϭⲉ, ⲡⲟⲕⲉ, ⲡⲁϭⲉ n.f. fragment.

пес(т)-: пісе   покˢ: пѡбє   побє: пѡбє
петвє: тѡѡвє   пок(є): пакє   пп̄г-: (пѡн̄к̄)
петпє: пє   покє: пѡбє   пнн: пꙟн̄нн
пеѳооу: ѕооу   покꙦ: пакє   пннє-: пѡѡнє
пешє: паіше   полкˢ: пѡлб̄   преіѡоу: пеірє
пеѕ-: (вѡѕ)   полхˢ: пѡлб̄   пресрасꙦ: пѡрс̄
пехаˢ, пехе-: хѡ   полб̄с̄: пѡлб̄   прнш: пѡрш̄
пнс: пісе   поонеˢ: пѡѡнє   пꙦбе: пꙠбе
пнує: пє   поонес: пѡѡнє   ѱаіт-: ѱіс
пншє: пѡш   поопе: паопє   пстаіоу: ѱіс
пі: пеі   поорˢ: пѡѡрє   пѡнꙦ: пѡн̄к̄
пініпє: вєніпє   пооу: ѕооу   пѡнє: пѡѡнє
пістˢ: пісе   порє: пеірє   пѡнб̄: пѡн̄к̄
пішє: паіше   поршꙦ: пѡрш̄   пѡсшꙷ: пѡшс̄
пкє: кє   посе: пісе   пѡѡн(є): пѡѡнє
плоб̄: пѡлб̄   посшˢ: пѡшꙦ   пѡхꙠ: пѡхб̄
погˢ: пѡбє   похꙦ: пѡхб̄   пѡхꙦ: пѡхб̄
погє: пѡбє   побˢ: пѡбє

Р

ра n.m. state, condition; cpd. with n. or vb. to give abstract or local sense, e.g. ра-(н̄)-ша the east, ра-ѡѕс̄
   the harvest. ша пра to the extent (of: н̄), until (+
   Rel.), even.

раітє n.f. kin, kindred. рм̄раітє kinsman. хі-раітє to be
   akin.

ран, пін (рен-, рн̄-; пінˢ, рн̄тˢ, рентˢ, рантˢ) n.m. name,
   fame, reputation. ꙷ-рн̄тˢ (є) хе, ꙷ-рн̄-пран хе to
   call, name. атꙷ-ран наˢ unnamed. For моутє see Vocab.
   17. таує-рінˢ to pronounce name, call by name. рм̄пран
   dignitary, notable. ѕооу н̄ ран holiday, name-day.

рампеі, рампі, раппі n. ring.

рамѡнє, рамоунє n.m. part of a door.

растє n.m. morrow. растє, прастє, н̄ растє, є растє, м̄ неꙴ-
   растє on the morrow, tomorrow. н̄са/мн̄н̄са (неꙴ)растє
   after tomorrow. ша (неꙴ)растє until tomorrow.

расоу n.f. dream. р̄-расоу to dream. реꙴоуеѕ-расоу interpreter of dreams.

ратˢ n.m. foot; lowest part, bottom. рм̄(н̄)ратˢ footman.
   ка-ратˢ to set foot; + евол to set out. моошє н̄ ратˢ

to go on foot. ⲛ̅-ⲡⲁⲧ⸗ to track; ⲁⲧⲛ̅-ⲡⲁⲧ⸗ untraceable.
ⲥⲁⲣ-ⲡⲁⲧ⸗ to defecate. ⳨ ⲉⲡⲁⲧ⸗ to put (shoe) on. ⲟⲩⲉϩ-
ⲡⲁⲧ⸗ to set foot. ϫⲓ-ⲡⲁⲧ⸗ to impede. ϭⲛ̅-ⲡⲁⲧ⸗ to trace,
search out; ⲁⲧϭⲛ̅-ⲡⲁⲧ⸗ unattainable. ⲉⲡⲁⲧ⸗ prep. to, to
the foot/feet of. ϩⲁⲣⲁⲧ⸗ prep. under. ϩⲓⲡⲁⲧ⸗ toward.

ⲣⲁⲩⲏ, ⲣⲁⲩⲉ, ⲣⲏⲩⲉ n.f. town-quarter, neighborhood. ⲣⲙ̅ⲣⲁⲩⲏ
neighbor.

ⲣⲁϣ only in ⲣⲙ̅ⲣⲁϣ mild, gentle person. ⲙⲛ̅ⲧⲣⲙ̅ⲣⲁϣ gentle-
ness; ⲣ̅-ⲣⲙ̅ⲣⲁϣ (Q ⲟ ⲛ̅) to become gentle.

ⲣⲁϣⲉ vb. intr. to rejoice (over, at: ⲉϫⲛ̅, ⲉϩⲣⲁⲓ ⲉϫⲛ̅; with:
ⲙⲛ̅); vb. tr. to mock, deride (ⲙ̅ⲙⲟ⸗); as n.m. joy.

ⲣⲁϩⲧⲉ, ⲣⲟϩⲧⲉ, ⲗⲟϩⲧⲉ n.f. cauldron.

ⲣⲁϩⲧⲟⲩ n. some sort of monk's garment.

ⲣⲃⲧ, ⲉⲣⲃⲧ̅, ⲣ̅ϥⲧ̅ adj. used with ϣⲧⲏⲛ garment.

ⲣⲏ n.m. sun; (alchemy) gold.

ⲣⲏⲥ n.m. the south. ⲉ ⲣⲏⲥ southward. ⲙ̅ ⲡⲣⲏⲥ ⲙ̅ⲙⲟ⸗ on the
south of. ϩⲁ/ϩⲓ ⲡⲣⲏⲥ ⲙ̅ⲙⲟ⸗ idem. ⲡⲁⲥ-(ⲛ̅)-ⲣⲏⲥ the south
side. ⲥⲁ-ⲣⲏⲥ on the south (of: ⲛ̅). ⲣⲙ̅ⲣⲏⲥ southerner.
ⲙⲁⲣⲏⲥ n.m. Upper Egypt.

ⲣⲏⲧⲉ n.m. manner, fashion. Rare in Sah.; use ϩⲉ.

ⲣⲓ, ⲣⲉⲓ n.f. cell (of monk, of prison); room (of house).

ⲣⲓⲕⲉ ⲣⲉⲕ(ⲧ̅)- ⲣⲁⲕ(ⲧ)⸗ (ⲣⲉⲕⲧ⸗) Q ⲣⲟⲕⲉ vb. tr. to bend, turn,
incline (ⲙ̅ⲙⲟ⸗; toward: ⲉ, ⲉϫⲛ̅, ⲛⲁ⸗, ⲛ̅ⲥⲁ, ϣⲁ; away: ⲉⲃⲟⲗ;
away from: ⲉⲃⲟⲗ ⲛ̅/ϩⲛ̅, ϩⲓ); vb. intr. and reflex. idem;
as n.m. turning, inclination. ⲣⲁⲕⲧⲉ̄ n.f. bent, direction.

ⲣⲓⲙⲉ vb. intr. to weep (about, for: ⲉ, ⲉϫⲛ̅, ⲛⲁ⸗); as n.m.
weeping. ϫⲓ-ⲣⲓⲙⲉ to weep. ⲣⲙ̅ⲉⲓⲏ, ⲣⲙ̅ⲉⲓⲉ (pl. ⲣⲙ̅ⲉⲓⲟⲟⲩⲉ)
n.f. tear(s); ⳨-ⲣⲙ̅ⲉⲓⲏ to weep.

ⲣⲓⲣ, ⲣⲏⲗ, ⲗⲓⲗ (ⲣⲡ̅-) n.m. swine, pig. ⲣⲓⲣ ⲛ̅ ⲧⲟⲟⲩ wild
swine. ⲙⲁⲛⲉ-ⲣⲓⲣ swineherd. ⲥⲁ ⲛ̅ ⲣⲓⲣ pig-dealer.

ⲣⲕ̅ⲣⲓⲕⲉ, ϩⲣⲕ̅ⲣⲓⲕⲉ n.f. nodding (in sleep); ⳨-ⲣⲕ̅ⲣⲓⲕⲉ ⲛⲁ⸗ to
give sleep to; ϫⲓ-ⲣⲕ̅ⲣⲓⲕⲉ to doze off.

ⲣⲙ̅ⲙⲁⲟ n.m. rich man, important personage; ⲙⲛ̅ⲧⲣⲙ̅ⲙⲁⲟ wealth;
ⲣ̅-ⲣⲙ̅ⲙⲁⲟ to become rich.

ⲣ̅ⲙⲟⲛⲧ, ⲣ̅ⲙⲟⲟⲧ n.f. chills, ague.

pⲘ2ⲉ (f. pⲘ2ⲏ; pl. pⲘ2ⲉⲉⲩⲉ) n.m.f. free person. ⲘⲚⲧpⲘ2ⲉ
freedom. ⲕⲱ (ⲉⲃⲟⲗ) Ⲛ pⲘ2ⲉ to set free. Ⲫ-pⲘ2ⲉ (Q o Ⲛ)
to become free; to make free (from: 2Ⲛ, ⲉⲃⲟⲗ 2Ⲛ).

pⲟ n.m. goose.

pⲟ n.m. strand, ply (of cord).

pⲟ (pⲱ⸗; pl. pⲱⲟⲩ) n.m. mouth; door, gate; edge (of sword);
ⲁⲧpⲱ⸗ not speaking the language. ⲕⲱ Ⲛ pⲱ⸗, ⲕⲁ-pⲱ⸗ (Q
ⲕⲁpⲁⲉⲓⲧ) to remain silent; ⲕⲁ-pⲱϥ n. silence; ⲁⲧⲕⲁ-pⲱϥ
never silent; ⲭⲓ-pⲱϥ to block off, obstruct (Ⲙ̄ⲙⲟ⸗); to
interrupt. ⲡⲁ-ⲡpⲟ doorkeeper. 2ⲁⲚpⲟ n.m. doorway.
pⲁ-, pⲉ- forms fractions w. foll. no.: pⲁ-ϣⲟⲙⲚ̄ⲧ a third.
ⲉpⲚ̄ (ⲉpⲱ⸗) prep. to the entrance of. 2ⲓpⲚ̄ (2ⲓpⲱ⸗) prep.
at the entrance of, on, at. 2ⲁpⲚ̄ (2ⲁpⲱ⸗) prep. before,
usu. of setting food before. ⲉⲃⲟⲗ 2ⲓpⲚ̄ from before.

pⲟⲉⲓⲥ, Q pⲏⲥ vb. intr. to remain awake, vigilant; to watch,
keep watch (over: ⲉ); to guard (ⲉ; from: ⲉ, ⲉⲃⲟⲗ 2Ⲛ);
as n.m. guard, watch. pⲉϥpⲟⲉⲓⲥ watchman. ⲙⲁ Ⲛ pⲟⲉⲓⲥ
watch, watch-tower. ⲟⲩϣⲏ Ⲛ pⲟⲉⲓⲥ vigil; Ⲫ-ⲟⲩϣⲏ Ⲛ pⲟⲉⲓⲥ
to keep vigil.

pⲟⲙⲡⲉ, pⲁⲙⲡⲉ (pⲘ̄ⲡⲉ-; pl. pⲘ̄ⲡⲟⲟⲩⲉ) n.f. year. ⲉⲓⲥ 2ⲉⲚpⲟⲙⲡⲉ
many years ago. Ⲛ ⲟⲩpⲟⲙⲡⲉ for a year. ⲕⲁⲧⲁ pⲟⲙⲡⲉ per
year. (Ⲛ) ⲧpⲟⲙⲡⲉ this year. ⲧⲠ̄pⲟⲙⲡⲉ, ⲧⲚ̄pⲟⲙⲡⲉ, ⲧⲉ-
pⲟⲙⲡⲉ yearly, annually. Ⲫ-ⲭ Ⲛ pⲟⲙⲡⲉ to reach age of x;
to pass x years.

pⲟⲟⲩⲉ, ⲁpⲟⲟⲩⲉ n.m. stubble. ⲥⲃ̄-pⲟⲟⲩⲉ n.f. stalk.

pⲟⲟⲩⲛⲉ n.m. virginity, virgin. ⲙⲚ̄ⲧpⲟⲟⲩⲛⲉ idem; puberty.

pⲟⲟⲩϣ n.m. care, concern, anxiety. ⲕⲁ-pⲟⲟⲩϣ ⲛⲁ⸗ to exercise care (suff. is reflex.). ⲛⲉⲭ-pⲟⲟⲩϣ ⲉ to transfer
cares to. Ⲫ-pⲟⲟⲩϣ (Q o Ⲛ) to become a care/concern
(for: ⲛⲁ⸗); to become anxious (ⲛⲁ⸗ reflex.); to give
heed (to: ⲛⲁ⸗). ϥⲓ-pⲟⲟⲩϣ to take heed, take care (to,
for: ⲉ, ⲉⲧⲃⲉ, ⲛⲁ⸗, 2ⲁ, or poss. prefix); as n.m. care,
anxiety; ϥⲁⲓ-pⲟⲟⲩϣ guardian, one who cares (for: 2ⲁ);
ⲙⲚ̄ⲧϥⲁⲓ-pⲟⲟⲩϣ providence. ⲁⲧpⲟⲟⲩϣ carefree; ⲙⲚ̄ⲧⲁⲧpⲟⲟⲩϣ
freedom from care.

ρογ2є n.m. evening.   ρογ2є, є/ⲛ/2ι ρογ2є in the evening.
  ϣⲁ ρογ2є until evening.   ⲡⲛⲁγ ⲛ ρογ2є the evening.   xι-
  ρογ2є to spend evening.   2ⲁρογ2є, 2ιρογ2є = ρογ2є.

ⲣ̄ⲡє, єⲣⲡє (pl. ⲣ̄ⲡнγє) n.m. temple.   ϣⲱⲗ ⲛ ογⲣ̄ⲡє, ϣⲗ̄-ⲣ̄ⲡє to
  rob a temple.   ρєϥϣⲗ̄-ⲣ̄ⲡє, ϣⲗⲗ-ⲣ̄ⲡє temple-robber.

ⲣ̄ρο, єρο (f. ⲣ̄ρⲱ, єρⲱ; pl. ⲣ̄ρⲱογ, єρⲱογ) n.m.f. king,
  queen; as adj. royal.   ⲙⲛ̄τєρο, ⲙⲛ̄τⲣ̄ρο (pl. -ⲣ̄ρⲱογ,
  -єρⲱογ) kingdom.   ⲣ̄-ⲣ̄ρο (Q o ⲛ) to become king; to rule
  (over: єⲭⲛ̄).   єιρє ⲙ̄ⲙο⸗ ⲛ ⲣ̄ρο to make king.

ⲣ̄сⲱ, єρсⲱ n.f. fold (for sheep or cattle).

ⲣ̄τοв, єρτοв, (є)ρτοϥ n.m. grain measure.

ⲣ̄τⲱ, єρτⲱ n.f. span (as measure).

ρⲱ, ρⲱⲱ enclitic part. of emphasis, usually of contrast:
  but, but then, on the other hand, on the contrary; in
  neg. context: not even, not at all.   May follow other
  particles: ⲁρнγ, ⲙєϣⲁк, єϣⲱⲡє, єϣxє, єⲛє.

ρⲱⲕ2̄ ρєⲕ2̄- ροⲕ2⸗ (ρⲁⲕ2⸗) Q ροⲕ2̄ vb. tr. to burn (ⲙ̄ⲙο⸗); vb.
  intr. to burn (aft., in pursuit of: ⲛсⲁ, є); as n.m.
  burning, fervor.   ροⲕ2є n.f. fuel.

ρⲱⲙє (ρⲱⲙ-, ρⲙ̄-, ρєⲙ-) n.m. man, person, human being; indef. usage: anyone, no one; as adj. human; male (often
  redundant).   ⲁτρⲱⲙє friendless; without a person; ⲙⲛ̄τ-
  ⲁτρⲱⲙє friendlessness.   ⲙⲁι-ρⲱⲙє kind. ⲙⲁстє-ρⲱⲙє mis-
  anthropic.   ⲙⲛ̄τρⲱⲙє humanity; humanitas.   ⲣ̄-ρⲱⲙє to become man.   For cpds. in ρⲙ̄-, ρєϥ- see 2nd elem.; cf. 27.2.

ρⲱτ ρєτ- Q ρнτ vb. intr. to sprout, grow (subj. plants
  etc.); to become covered with vegetation, become over-
  grown (with: ⲙ̄ⲙο⸗); as n.m. (pl. ρⲁτє) vegetation; wool.

ρⲱϣє ρєϣτ̄- ρⲁϣτ̄⸗ vb. tr. to satisfy, make content (ⲙ̄ⲙο⸗);
  vb. intr. to suffice, be enough (for: є, ⲛⲁ⸗); to assume responsibility (for: є), deal with.   As n.m. suf-
  ficiency, enough; є ⲡρⲱϣє adv. enough, sufficiently.
  ⲣ̄-ⲡρⲱϣє to become enough, do enough, suffice.

ρⲱ2є, Q ρⲁ2є vb. tr. to wash, clean (ⲙ̄ⲙο⸗); ρⲁ2τ̄ n.m.f.
  fuller, launderer.

ρωϩⲧ ρⲉϩⲧ- ρⲁϩⲧ⸗ (ροϩⲧ⸗) Q ρⲁϩⲧ vb. tr. to strike, strike
down, kill, cast down (ⲙⲙⲟ⸗; upon, on: ⲉ, ⲉϩⲟⲩⲛ ⲉ, ⲉϫⲛ,
ⲉϩⲣⲁⲓ ⲉϫⲛ; also + ⲉⲡⲉⲥⲏⲧ); vb. intr. to be struck, fall;
Q to lie. As n.m. stroke, blow. ρⲁϩⲧⲉ̄ n.f. slaughter.
ρ̄ϣⲱⲛ, ⲉρϣⲱⲛ n.m. cloak, covering.

ρ̄-: ⲉⲓρⲉ	ρⲉ-ⲙⲏⲧ: ⲙⲏⲧ	ρⲙ̄ρⲁϣ: ρⲁϣ
ρ̄-ⲁⲛⲁ⸗: ⲁⲛⲁⲓ	ρⲉⲕ(ⲧ̄)-: ⲡⲓⲕⲉ	ρⲙⲟⲩⲁ: ⲟⲩⲟⲉⲓⲉ
ρⲁ-: ρⲟ	ρⲉⲕⲧ⸗: ⲡⲓⲕⲉ	ρⲙⲟⲩⲉ: ⲟⲩⲟⲉⲓⲉ
ρⲁⲕ(ⲧ̄)-/⸗: ⲡⲓⲕⲉ	ρⲉⲙ-: ρⲱⲙⲉ	ρⲛ̄-: ρⲁⲛ
ρⲁⲕⲧⲉ̄: ⲡⲓⲕⲉ	ρⲉⲛ-: ρⲁⲛ	ρⲛ̄-, ρⲛ̄ⲧ⸗: ρⲁⲛ
ρⲁⲕϩ⸗: ρⲱⲕϩ̄	ρⲉⲛⲧ⸗: ρⲁⲛ	ρⲟⲕⲉ: ⲡⲓⲕⲉ
ρⲁⲙⲡⲉ: ρⲟⲙⲡⲉ	ρⲉϣⲧ̄-: ρⲱϣⲉ	ρⲟⲕϩⲉ: ρⲱⲕϩ̄
ρⲁⲛⲡⲓ: ρⲁⲙⲡⲉⲓ	ρⲏⲃ: ⲁρⲏⲃ	ρⲟⲟⲩⲧ: ⲟⲩρⲟⲧ
ρⲁⲛⲧ⸗: ρⲁⲛ	ρⲏⲁ: ρⲓρ	ρⲟϩⲧⲉ: ρⲁϩⲧⲉ
ρⲁⲧⲉ: ρⲱⲧ	ρⲏⲥ: ρⲟⲉⲓⲥ	ρⲡ̄-: ⲏρⲡ̄
ρⲁϣⲧ⸗: (ρⲱϣⲉ)	ρⲏⲧ: ⲉρⲏⲧ	ρⲡⲁⲥ: ⲁⲥ
ρⲁϩⲉ: ρⲱϩⲉ	ρⲏⲩⲉ: ρⲁⲩⲏ	ρρ̄-: ⲣⲓρ
ρⲁϩⲧ̄: ρⲱϩⲉ	ρⲓⲛ(⸗): ρⲁⲛ	ρ̄ρⲏⲧ: ⲉρⲏⲧ
ρⲁϩⲧ⸗: ρⲱϩⲧ̄	ρⲙ̄-: ρⲱⲙⲉ	ρⲱ⸗, ρⲱⲟⲩ: ρⲟ
ρⲁϩⲧⲉ̄: ρⲱϩⲧ̄	ρⲙⲉⲓⲏ: ⲣⲓⲙⲉ	ρⲱⲙ: ⲙ̄ρⲱⲙ
ρ̄ⲃⲉ: ⲱρⲃ̄	ρⲙ̄ⲉⲓⲟⲟⲩⲉ: ⲣⲓⲙⲉ	ρϭⲧ: ρⲃ̄ⲧ
ρ̄ⲃⲏⲉ: ⲉⲃρⲏⲉⲉ	ρⲙ̄ⲡⲉ-: ρⲟⲙⲡⲉ	ρ̄ϩⲙ: ⲗ̄ϩⲙ
ρⲉ-: ρⲟ	ρⲙ̄ⲡⲟⲟⲩⲉ: ρⲟⲙⲡⲉ	ρⲝ-: ⲱρϫ̄

c

ⲥⲁ n.m. side, direction, part. (ⲛ̄) ⲥⲁ ⲥⲁ ⲛⲓⲙ on every
side, everywhich way. ⲡⲓⲥⲁ (ⲙⲛ̄) ⲡⲁⲓ, ⲡⲉⲓⲥⲁ ... (ⲙⲛ̄)
ⲡⲁⲓ, ⲡⲥⲁ ⲡⲥⲁ, ⲡⲓⲥⲁ ... ⲡⲓⲕⲉⲥⲁ this way and that, this
side and that. For the cpds. of ⲥⲁ (ⲛ̄) indicating direction or location, see 2nd element and § 28.7. ⲕⲉⲥⲁ
elsewhere, apart. (ⲛ̄) ⲥⲁ ⲟⲩⲥⲁ aside, apart, alone. (ⲛ̄)
ⲥⲁ ⲗⲁⲁⲩ ⲛ̄ ⲥⲁ on any (no) side. ⲛ̄ⲥⲁ (ⲛ̄ⲥⲱ⸗) prep. (1) behind; after (place or time); (2) after (= in search of,
in pursuit of); (3) with some vbs.: against, at; (4)
except, except for, other than. ⲙⲛ̄ⲛ̄ⲥⲁ (ⲙⲛ̄ⲛ̄ⲥⲱ⸗) prep.
after (of time); ⲙⲛ̄ⲛ̄ⲥⲱⲥ adv. afterward.
ⲥⲁ, Q ⲥⲁⲉⲓⲟⲟⲩ vb. intr. to become beautiful; as n.m. beauty. ⲥⲁⲉⲓⲉ, ⲥⲁⲓⲉ, ⲥⲁⲉⲓⲏ adj. beautiful (bef. or aft. n.,
usu. w. ⲛ̄); ⲛ̄/ⲉ ⲥⲁⲉⲓⲉ adv. thoroughly. ρ̄-ⲥⲁⲉⲓⲉ (Q ⲟ ⲛ̄)
to become beautiful. ⲙⲛ̄ⲧⲥⲁⲉⲓⲉ beauty. ⳨-ⲥⲁ to beauti-
fy (ⲉ, ⲛⲁ⸗).

ⲥⲁ n.m. in cpds. maker of, dealer in, possessor of. See
2nd element and §23.2.

ⲥⲁⲁⲛ͞ϣ (ⲥⲁⲛ͞ϣ) ⲥⲁ(ⲗ)ⲛ͞ϣ- ⲥⲁⲛⲟⲩϣⲉ vb. tr. to nourish, rear,
tend, maintain (ⲙ͞ⲙⲟⲉ); vb. intr. to be alive; Q to be
nourished, well fed. As n.m. nourishment. ⲙⲁ ⲛ̄ ⲥⲁⲁⲛ͞ϣ
feeding place. ⲣⲉϥⲥⲁⲁⲛ͞ϣ nourisher, nurse; ⲙⲛ̄ⲧⲣⲉϥⲥⲁⲁⲛ͞ϣ
rearing. Q ⲥⲁⲛⲁϣ͞ⲧ.

ⲥⲁⲁⲥⲉ, ⲥⲁⲥⲉ n. tow, flax.

ⲥⲁⲃⲉ (f. ⲥⲁⲃⲏ; pl. ⲥⲁⲃⲉⲉⲩ, ⲥⲁⲃⲉⲉⲩⲉ) adj. wise; as n. wise
person; bef. or aft. n. w. ⲛ̄. ⲙⲛ̄ⲧⲥⲁⲃⲉ wisdom. ⲣ̄-ⲥⲁⲃⲉ
(Q ⲟ ⲛ̄) to become wise. ⲥⲃⲟⲩⲓ n.m. disciple, appren-
tice. ⲥⲃⲱ (pl. ⲥⲃⲟⲟⲩⲉ, ⲥⲃⲱⲟⲩⲉ) n.f. instruction, doctrine; ϯ-ⲥⲃⲱ to teach, instruct (person: ⲛⲁⲉ; subject:
ⲉ); ⲙⲁ ⲛ̄ ϯ-ⲥⲃⲱ school; ⲣⲉϥϯ-ⲥⲃⲱ teacher. ⲭⲓ-ⲥⲃⲱ to be
taught (a subj.: ⲉ) ⲣⲉϥⲭⲓ-ⲥⲃⲱ pupil; ⲙⲁ ⲛ̄ ⲭⲓ-ⲥⲃⲱ
school. ⲁⲧⲥⲃⲱ ignorant. ⲙⲁⲓ-ⲥⲃⲱ loving learning. ⲣⲙ̄-
ⲛ̄ⲥⲃⲱ knowledgeable person.

ⲥⲁⲉⲓⲛ, ⲥⲁⲓⲛⲉ n.m. physician; ⲙⲛ̄ⲧⲥⲁⲉⲓⲛ craft of physician.

ⲥⲁⲕ n.m. shape, appearance; ϯ-ⲥⲁⲕ to make a show.

ⲥⲁⲗⲟ, ⲥⲁⲗⲱ, ⲥⲁⲣⲟ n.f. basket.

ⲥⲁⲙⲓⲧ n.m. fine flour.

ⲥⲁⲙⲛ̄ⲧ n.f. pool.

ⲥⲁⲣⲁⲕⲱⲧⲉ, ⲥⲁⲣⲁⲕⲟⲧⲉ n. wanderer, vagrant.

ⲥⲁⲣⲁⲃⲱⲟⲩϣ, ⲥⲁⲣⲁⲛⲃⲱϣ, ⲥⲁⲗⲁⲃⲱⲟϣ n.m. hare, rabbit.

ⲥⲁⲧ, ⲥⲏⲧ n.m. tail. ⲥⲏⲧ, ⲥⲉⲉⲧ n.m. penis.

ⲥⲁⲧⲃⲉ vb. intr. to chew, ruminate.

ⲥⲁⲧⲉ, ⲥⲁⲁⲧⲉ, ⲥⲟⲧⲉ n.f. fire. ϣⲁⲡ ⲛ̄ ⲥⲁⲧⲉ flame of fire. ⲣ̄-
ⲥⲁⲧⲉ (Q ⲟ ⲛ̄) to be fiery.

ⲥⲁⲧⲉⲉⲣⲉ n.f. stater (coin or weight).

ⲥⲁⲧⲱ, ⲥⲁⲧⲟ n.f. fan. ⲥⲁⲧⲉ vb. to fan.

ⲥⲁϣϥ̄ (f. ⲥⲁϣϥⲉ) number: seven. ⲙⲛ̄ⲧⲥⲁϣϥ̄ (f. -ⲥⲁϣϥⲉ) seven-
teen. ⲙⲉ₂ⲥⲁϣϥ̄ seventh. ϣϥⲉ, ϣⲃⲉ, ⲥ͞ϣϥⲉ seventy.

ⲥⲁϥ n.m. yesterday. ⲥⲁϥ ⲛ̄ ₂ⲟⲟⲩ idem. ⲛ̄ ⲥⲁϥ idem.

ⲥⲁ₂, ⲥⲁ₂ϥ̄ n.m. awl, borer.

ⲥⲁ₂ⲛ̄- vb. tr. to bring near.

ⲥⲁϨⲛⲉ n.m. supply, provisions. ⲟⲩⲉϨ-ⲥⲁϨⲛⲉ to command
(something: ⲙ̄ⲙⲟˢ; someone: ⲛⲁˢ, ⲉⲧⲛ̄; to do: ⲉ, ⲉⲧⲣⲉ);
as n.m. command.

ⲥⲁϨⲧⲉ vb. tr. to kindle, to burn; as n.m. fire. ⲁⲧⲥⲁϨⲧⲉ
unheated. ⲙⲁ ⲛ̄ ⲥⲁϨⲧⲉ kitchen.

ⲥⲁϨⲟⲩ (ⲥⲁϨⲟⲩⲉ) ⲥ̄Ϩⲟⲩⲣ̄- (ⲥ̄Ϩⲟⲩⲉⲣ-) ⲥ̄Ϩⲟⲩⲱⲣˢ Q ⲥ̄Ϩⲟⲩⲟⲣⲧ̄ vb. tr.
to curse (ⲙ̄ⲙⲟˢ); as n.m. curse; ⲉ/Ϩⲁ ⲛⲥⲁϨⲟⲩ under a
curse. ϫⲓ-ⲥⲁϨⲟⲩ to be cursed. ⲣⲉϥⲥⲁϨⲟⲩ curser.

ⲥⲃ̄ⲃⲉ ⲥⲃ̄ⲃⲉ- ⲥⲃ̄ⲃⲏⲧˢ Q ⲥⲃ̄ⲃⲏⲩ(ⲧ) vb. tr. to circumcise; as n.
m. circumcision. ⲁⲧⲥⲃ̄ⲃⲉ uncircumcised; ⲟ ⲛ̄ ⲁⲧⲥⲃ̄ⲃⲉ Q to
be uncircumcised. ⲙⲛ̄ⲧⲁⲧⲥⲃ̄ⲃⲉ being uncircumcised.

ⲥⲃⲉ n.m. door.

ⲥⲃ̄ⲧⲉ, ⲥ̄ⲃⲧⲉ, ⲥ̄ϥⲧⲉ vb. intr. to roll about.

ⲥⲃⲟⲕ, Q ⲥⲟⲃⲕ̄ vb. intr. to become few, small; as n.m. fewness, smallness. ⲥⲃ̄ⲕⲉ n.m. fewness.

ⲥⲃ̄ϣⲉ, ⲥⲱ̄ⲃⲉ, ϣⲃ̄ϣⲉ n.f. shield.

ⲥⲉ affirmative particle: yes, yes but; indeed, verily.

ⲥⲉⲉⲛⲉ, ⲥⲉⲛⲉ, ⲥⲓⲛⲉ vb. intr. to remain over, be left over
(of, from: ⲉ, Ϩⲛ̄). As n.m.f. (also ⲥⲏⲏⲡⲉ, ⲥⲏⲡⲉ) remainder, rest; often with redundant -ⲕⲉ-.

ⲥⲉⲓ, ⲥⲓⲉ n.f. name of a tree (oak?).

ⲥⲉⲗⲉⲡⲓⲛ n.m. (1) spleen; (2) little finger or toe.

ⲥⲉⲣⲥⲱⲣ Q to be displayed.

ⲥⲉⲧⲏ, ⲥⲓⲧⲉ, ⲥⲛ̄ⲧⲉ n. state in development of fig.

ⲥⲉϨⲥⲱϨˢ Q ⲥⲉϨⲥⲱϨ vb. tr. to plane, rub down.

ⲥⲏⲃⲉ, ⲥⲏϥⲉ n.f. reed. ⲥⲏⲃⲉ ⲛ̄ ⲣⲁⲧˢ shin-bone; greave. ⲥⲏⲃⲉ
ⲛ̄ ϫⲱ reed flute.

ⲥⲏⲛⲉ, ⲥⲉⲛⲏ, ⲥⲉⲛⲉ n.f. granary, bin.

ⲥⲏⲧ, ⲥⲟⲧⲉ Q to be spun. ⲥⲏⲧⲉ n.f. spun fabric.

ⲥⲏⲩ (ⲥⲟⲩ-) n.m. time, season, age. ⲙ̄ ⲡⲓⲥⲏⲩ at this time.
ⲛ̄ ⲟⲩⲥⲏⲩ once, at one time. ⲛ̄ ⲥⲏⲩ ⲛⲓⲙ always. ⲙ̄/Ϩⲙ̄ ⲡ-
ⲥⲏⲩ at the time when. ⲕⲁⲧⲁ ⲥⲏⲩ from time to time. ⲁⲧ-
ⲥⲏⲩ timeless. ⲥⲟⲩ- is cpd. with no. to indicate day of
month or other specified period. ⲥⲟⲩⲁ = ⲥⲟⲩ-ⲟⲩⲁ.

ⲥⲏϥⲉ, ⲥⲏⲃⲉ n.f. sword, knife.

ϭHϭ n.m.f. foal.

ϭι (ϭϭι), Q ϭHγ vb. intr. to become sated, satisfied (with:
ⲙ̄ⲙⲟⸯ, ⸱ⲁ, ⸱ⲛ̄); to enjoy; as n.m. fullness, surfeit. ⲁⲧϭι
insatiate, greedy; ⲙ̄ⲛ̄ⲧⲁⲧϭι greed. ⲣ̄-ⲁⲧϭι to be greedy.

ϭιв n.m. tick (insect).

ϭιв̄ⲧ n.f. hill.

ϭιⲕϭ ϭⲁⲕⲧⸯ Q ϭⲟⲕϭ (ϭⲟⲟⲕϭ) vb. tr. to grind, pound (ⲙ̄ⲙⲟⸯ);
as n.m. grinding. ⲕⲟⲧ ⲛ̄ ϭιⲕϭ mill-wheel. ⲱⲛϭ ⲛ̄ ϭιⲕϭ
millstone.

ϭιⲙ (ϭⲙ̄-) n.m. grass, fodder, herbs; radish.

ϭιⲙϭιⲙ, ϭⲙ̄ϭιⲙ, ϭⲙ̄ϭⲙ̄ n.m. sesame.

ϭιⲛϭ ϭⲛ̄- (ϭϭⲛ-, ϭⲁⲁⲧ-) ϭⲁⲁⲧⸯ (ϭⲁⲧⸯ, ϭⲟⲧⸯ, ϭⲛ̄ⲧⸯ) vb. tr. to
pass through/across; + ϭвⲟⲗ to pass out of, leave; vb.
intr. idem (⸱ⲛ̄: through; ϭвⲟⲗ: out; ϭвⲟⲗ ⸱ⲛ̄ out through);
ⲁⲧϭιⲛϭ not passing.

ϭιⲛϭ n.f. plowshare.

ϭιⲟⲟγⲛ, ϭιⲁⲟγⲛ n.f. bath.

ϭιⲟγ (ϭⲟγ-) n.m. star. ϭⲟγ-ⲛ̄-ⲍⲧⲟⲟγϭ morning star; ϭⲟγ-ⲛ̄-
ⲣⲟγⲍϭ evening star; ϭⲟγ-ⲛ̄-ⲍⲱⲣ Orion; ϭιⲟγ ϭιⲟγ speckled.

ϭιⲟγⲣ n.m. eunuch.

ϭιⲣ n.m. hair; line, stripe.

ϭιⲣ, ϭϭⲣ(ϭ) n.m. leaven.

ϭιⲣ, ϭⲁϭιⲣ(ϭ), ϭHⲣϭ n.m. colostrum; butter.

ϭιⲧ, ϭιⲧϭ n.m. basilisk, serpent, dragon.

ϭιⲧϭ ϭϭⲧ- (ϭⲁⲧ-) ϭⲁⲧⸯ (ϭϭⲧⸯ, ϭιⲧⸯ) Q ϭHⲧ vb. tr. to throw,
cast (ⲙ̄ⲙⲟⸯ; upon, on, in: ϭⲝⲛ̄, ⸱ιⲝⲛ̄, ⸱ι; at, after: ϭ,
ⲛ̄ϭⲁ), esp. to sow (grain); used with adv. in usu. senses.
ϭⲟⲧϭ, ϭⲟⲟⲧϭ (pl. ϭⲟⲟⲧϭ) n.m.f. arrow, dart; ⲛϭⲝ-ϭⲟⲧϭ to
shoot arrow; ⲙⲁ ⲛ̄ ⲛϭⲝ-ϭⲟⲧϭ archery range. ⲣϭϥⲧⲕ̄-ϭⲟⲧϭ
archer. ⲝι-ϭⲟⲧϭ to be struck by arrow. ⲍⲛⲁⲁγ ⲛ̄ ⲕⲁ-
ϭⲟⲧϭ quiver.

ϭιϣϭ, Q ϭⲁϣϭ vb. intr. to become bitter, like gall. As n.m.
bitterness; ⸱ⲛ̄ ⲟγϭιϣϭ bitterly. ┼-ϭιϣϭ to make bitter.

ϭιϣ̄ϥ, ϭιϣв̄, ϣιϥ n.m. flake, chip.

ϭιϥϭ, ϭHϥϭ, ϭιвϭ, ϭHвϭ n.m. tar; ϣϭ ⲛ̄ ϭιϥϭ cedar wood.

cιϩε cεϩ- cλϩτ⸗ (cεϩτ⸗) vb. tr. reflex. to remove self,
withdraw; vb. intr. to be removed, displaced.

cιϭε = cωϭ intr.

cκλι cεκ- cοκ⸗ vb. tr. to plow (ⲙⲙⲟ⸗; with: ⲙⲙⲟ⸗, ϩⲛ̅); as
n.m. plowing. ϩⲃ̅ⲃε ⲛ̅ cκλι plow. ⲣⲉϥcκλι plowman.

cκιⲙ, cϭιⲙ n.m. grey hair; ⲣⲙ̅cκιⲙ grey-haired man.

cκⲟⲣⲕⲣ̅ cⲕⲣ̅ⲕⲣ̅- cⲕⲣ̅ⲕⲱⲣ⸗ Q cⲕⲉⲣⲕⲱⲣ vb. tr. to roll (ⲙⲙⲟ⸗);
vb. intr. to roll, be rolled; as n.m. rolling. Used
with various prep. and adv. in usu. senses. cⲕλⲣλⲕιⲣ,
cⲕⲟⲣλⲕιⲣ, cⲕⲉλλⲕιⲣ n. steep slope.

cⲭλⲧ, cⲭλλⲧ, ϣⲟⲧ, cϩλⲧ n.m. marriage gift (from groom).

cλλⲧε vb. intr. to stumble, slip; as n.m. stumbling. ϯ-
cλλⲧε to cause to stumble (ⲛλ⸗).

cλⲟⲡλⲉⲡ cλⲉⲡλⲱⲡ⸗ (± ⲉⲃⲟλ) vb. tr. to tear asunder.

cλⲟϭλϭ̅, Q cλⲉϭλⲱϭ (cλⲉⲕλⲱⲕ) vb. tr. to make smooth (ⲙⲙⲟ⸗);
vb. intr. to become smooth; as n.m. smoothness.

cⲙλⲩ n.m. temples (of head); eyelids.

cⲙλϩ n.m. bunch (of fruit, flowers, etc.).

cⲙⲏ n.f. voice, sound. ϯ-cⲙⲏ to give voice, utter sound.
ϫⲓ-cⲙⲏ to listen (to: ε). λⲧcⲙⲏ voiceless, soundless.
ϫⲁⲥⲧ̅-cⲙⲏ loquacious.

cⲙιⲛⲉ cⲙ̅ⲛ- (cⲙⲉⲛ-) cⲙ̅ⲛⲧ⸗ Q cⲙⲟⲛⲧ̅ vb. tr. to establish, con-
struct, found (ⲙⲙⲟ⸗); to set up, set right; to compose,
write; to draw up (a document); vb. intr. to be established, put right, put in order; Q to exist, be standing, extant; to be correct, in good order. As n.m. es-
tablishing, confirmation, agreement. cⲙ̅ⲛ-ⲧⲟⲟⲧ⸗ ⲙ̅ⲛ̅ to
consort with. cⲙιⲛⲉ ⲙⲙⲟ⸗ ⲙ̅ⲛ̅ to settle (sthg.) with, to
come to an agreement with .. on... cⲙιⲛⲉ ⲙⲙⲟ⸗ ε to fabricate against. cⲙ̅ⲛⲧⲥ̅ ε to resolve on (n. or Inf.).

cⲙ̅ⲙε vb. intr. to make an appeal (to: ⲛλ⸗, ϩλϩⲧ̅ⲛ̅; for,
concerning: ϩλ, ⲉϩⲣλι ϩλ, ⲉⲧⲃⲉ); to make an accusation
(against: ε, ⲟⲩⲃε); as n.m. appeal, accusation. λⲛcⲙ̅ⲙε
n. ordinance.

cⲙⲟⲧ n.m. form, likeness; appearance; pattern; character;

customary behavior. cмoт ⲛ a kind of, sort of. ⲁⲧ-
cмoт formless. ⲣ̄-(oⲩ)cмoт to become as though (ⲭⲉ); ⲣ̄-
cмoт ⲛⲓм to assume every aspect; ⲣ̄-ⲛⲉⲓcмoт to behave
thus; ⲣ̄-ⲡⲉcмoт ⲛ to behave like. ϯ-cмoт ⲉ to give form
to. ⲭⲓ-cмoт ⲛ to become like.

cмoⲩ, Q cмⲁмⲁⲁⲧ (cмⲁⲁⲧ, cмⲁмⲁⲁⲛⲧ) vb. tr. to bless (ⲉ); as
n.m. blessing, praise; ϯ-cмoⲩ to give blessing, give
sacrament; ⲭⲓ-cмoⲩ to receive sacrament; to greet, sa-
lute (someone: ⲛ̄ⲧⲛ̄).

cⲛⲁⲉⲓⲛ vb. intr. to skip, stroll, wander (also reflex.
with м̄мo⸗).

cⲛⲁⲧ vb. intr. to be afraid (of: ⲅ̄ⲏⲧ⸗).

cⲛⲁⲩ (f. cⲛ̄ⲧⲉ) number: two (§15.3). мⲛ̄ⲧcⲛooⲩc (f. -cⲛooⲩcⲉ)
twelve, and sim. with higher nos. м̄ ⲡⲉcⲛⲁⲩ, ⲛ̄ ⲧcⲛ̄ⲧⲉ
adv. both together. мⲉⲅ̄cⲛⲁⲩ (f. -cⲛ̄ⲧⲉˋ second. ⲅo
cⲛⲁⲩ adj. two-edged. ⲅ̄ⲏⲧ cⲛⲁⲩ doubt; ⲣ̄-ⲅ̄ⲏⲧ cⲛⲁⲩ to become doubtful; мⲛ̄ⲧⲅ̄ⲏⲧ cⲛⲁⲩ state of doubt. ⲣ̄-cⲛⲁⲩ to
become two; мⲛ̄ⲧⲣⲉϥⲣ̄-cⲛⲁⲩ duality.

cⲛoⲩϥ, cⲛoⲩⲃ n. last year.

cⲛoϥ, cⲛoⲃ (pl. cⲛⲱⲱϥ) n.m. blood. ⲁⲧcⲛoϥ bloodless. ⲣ̄-
cⲛoϥ to become blood.

cⲛ̄cⲛ̄ (cⲉⲛcⲉⲛ) vb. intr. to resound, echo; as n.m. echo.

co n. in ϯ-co to spare, restrain (ⲉ); to avoid, refrain
from (ⲉ + n. or Inf.). As n.m. forbearance, restraint;
ⲁⲭⲛ̄ ϯ-co unsparingly. мⲛ̄ⲧⲁⲧϯ-co lack of restraint.

coⲃⲛ̄ vb. intr. to fan, make cool breeze.

coⲃⲧ̄ n.m. wall, fence. ⲕⲧⲉ-coⲃⲧ̄ ⲉ to wall.

coⲃⲧⲉ (coϥⲧⲉ) cⲃ̄ⲧⲉ- (cⲉⲃⲧⲉ-) cⲃ̄ⲧⲱⲧ⸗ Q cⲃ̄ⲧⲱⲧ vb. tr. to prepare, make ready (м̄мo⸗; for: ⲉ); vb. intr. to become
ready, prepared; vb. reflex. to get ready. As n.m.
preparation, what is prepared; furniture; ⲣ̄-coⲃⲧⲉ to
make preparations. ⲁⲧcⲃ̄ⲧⲱⲧ⸗ unfurnished.

coⲉⲓⲧ n.m. fame, report. ⲣ̄-coⲉⲓⲧ (Q o ⲛ̄) to become famous.
ϯ-coⲉⲓⲧ to celebrate, give fame (to: ⲛⲁ⸗, ⲉ; for, in:
ⲅ̄ⲛ̄). ⲣⲙ̄ⲛcoⲉⲓⲧ famous person.

ⲥⲟⲉⲓϣ, ⲥⲟⲉⲓⵂ n.m. pair, couple.

ⲥⲟⲓ n.m. back (of man or animal).

ⲥⲟⲓ n.m.f. beam; ⲟⲩⲉⵂ-ⲥⲟⲓ n.f. roof(-beam).

ⲥⲟⲕ, ⲥⲟⲟⲕ, ⲥⲁⲕ, ⲥⲱ(ⲱ)ⲕ n.m. sack, bag; sackcloth.

ⲥⲟⲕⲥⲉⲕ ⲥⲉⲕⲥⲉⲕ- ⲥⲉⲕⲥⲟⲕˢ vb. tr. to pull, stretch.

ⲥⲟⲗ n.m. wick. ⲙⲁ ⲛ̄ ⲧ̄-ⲥⲟⲗ wick-opening.

(ⲥⲟⲗⲥⲗ̄) ⲥⲗ̄ⲥⲗ̄- ⲥⲉⲗⲥⲱⲗˢ vb. tr. to adorn (ⲙ̄ⲙⲟˢ; with: ⵂⲛ̄).

ⲥⲟⲗⲥⲗ̄ ⲥⲗ̄ⲥⲗ̄- ⲥⲗ̄ⲥⲱⲗˢ Q ⲥⲗ̄ⲥⲱⲗ vb. tr. to comfort, console
   (ⲙ̄ⲙⲟˢ; for, concerning: ⲉ, ⲉⲧⲃⲉ, ⲉⲭⲛ̄, ⵂⲁ); vb. intr. to
   become comforted, consoled, encouraged; as n.m. consolation; amusement, diversion. ϣⲱⲡⲉ (Q ϣⲟⲟⲡ) ⲛ̄ ⲥⲟⲗⲥⲗ̄
   become a consolation. ϫⲓ-ⲥⲟⲗⲥⲗ̄ to take comfort.

ⲥⲟⲗϥ̄, ⲥⲟⲣϥ̄, ⲥⲟⲗⲓⲃ, ⲥⲱⲗϥ̄ n.m. sieve.

ⲥⲟⲙⲉ̄ vb. intr. to look, see, behold (rare in Sah.).

ⲥⲟⲛ (ⲥⲛ̄-, ⲥⲉⲛ-; pl. ⲥⲛⲏⲩ) n.m. brother (lit., fig.); ⲛⲟϭ ⲛ̄
   ⲥⲟⲛ elder brother; ⲕⲟⲩⲓ ⲛ̄ ⲥⲟⲛ younger brother; ⲥⲟⲛ ⲛ̄
   ⲉⲓⲱⲧ uncle; ϣⲛ̄-ⲥⲟⲛ nephew; ⲥⲟⲛ ⲙ̄ ⲙⲟⲟⲛⲉ foster-brother.
   Freq. as monk's title. ⲙⲛ̄ⲧⲥⲟⲛ brotherhood, brotherli-
   ness. ⲙⲛ̄ⲧⲙⲁⲓ-ⲥⲟⲛ brotherly love.

ⲥⲟⲛⲧⲉ n.m. resin.

ⲥⲟⲟⲛⲉ n.m. robber. ⲙⲁ ⲛ̄ ⲥⲟⲟⲛⲉ den of thieves.

ⲥⲟⲟⲩ (ⲥⲉⲩ-; f. ⲥⲟ, ⲥⲟⲉ, ⲥⲟⲟⲩⲉ) number: six. ⲙⲛ̄ⲧⲁⲥⲉ six-
   teen. ⲥⲉ sixty. ⲙⲉⵂⲥⲟⲟⲩ sixth. ⲙⲉⵂⲥⲉ sixtieth.
   See 16.5; 24.3.

ⲥⲟⲟⲩⲛ̄ ⲥⲟⲩⲛ̄- (ⲥⲟⲩⲱⲛ-, ⲥⲟⲩⲉⲛ-) ⲥⲟⲩⲱⲛˢ vb. tr. to know (ⲙ̄ⲙⲟˢ,
   ⲉ; about: ⲉⲧⲃⲉ; that: ϫⲉ; how to: ⲛ̄ + Inf.); to recognize, be acquainted with; to know sexually; as n.m.
   knowledge. ϣⲣ̄ⲡ-ⲥⲟⲟⲩⲛ̄ foreknowledge. ⲁⲧⲥⲟⲟⲩⲛ̄ ignorant;
   ⲙⲛ̄ⲧⲁⲧⲥⲟⲟⲩⲛ̄ ignorance; ⲣ̄-ⲁⲧⲥⲟⲟⲩⲛ̄ (Q ⲟ ⲛ̄) to be ignorant
   (of: ⲉ, ⲙ̄ⲙⲟˢ). ⲣⲙ̄ⲛ̄ⲥⲟⲟⲩⲛ̄ an acquaintance. ϫⲓ-ⲥⲟⲟⲩⲛ̄ to
   get knowledge.

ⲥⲟⲟⲩⲧⲛ̄ ⲥⲟⲩⲧⲛ̄- (ⲥⲟⲩⲧⲱⲛ-) ⲥⲟⲩⲧⲱⲛˢ Q ⲥⲟⲩⲧⲱⲛ vb. tr. to make
   straight, straighten (ⲙ̄ⲙⲟˢ); ± ⲉⲃⲟⲗ: to stretch (ⲙ̄ⲙⲟˢ;
   to: ⲉ, ϣⲁ, ⲉⵂⲟⲩⲛ ⲉ); vb. intr. to become straight,
   erect; to stretch; to be right (for: ⲉ; with: ⲙⲛ̄). As

n.m. uprightness. ϩⲛ ⲟⲩⲥⲟⲟⲩⲧⲛ uprightly; forthwith.
ⲛ ⲥⲟⲟⲩⲧⲛ just now. ⲉ ⲡⲥⲟⲟⲩⲧⲛ straight, on target.

ⲥⲟⲟⲩϩⲉ n.f. egg; crown of head. ⲙⲟⲟⲩ ⲛ ⲥⲟⲟⲩϩⲉ egg-white.

ⲥⲟⲟϩⲉ (ⲥⲟϩⲉ) ⲥⲁϩⲉ- ⲥⲁϩⲱ⸗ (1) vb. tr. to set upright, set
up (ⲙⲙⲟ⸗); vb. intr. to be set up, set upright. (2) vb.
tr. to correct, reprove (ⲙⲙⲟ⸗); vb. intr. to be correc-
ted, reproved.

ⲥⲟⲟϩⲉ ⲥⲁϩⲉ- ⲥⲁϩⲱ(ⲱ)⸗ Q ⲥⲁϩⲏⲩ vb. tr. to remove; usu. reflex. w. ⲉⲃⲟⲗ: to depart, withdraw; also w. ⲉⲡⲁϩⲟⲩ, ⲉ-
ϩⲟⲩⲛ, ⲉϩⲣⲁⲓ. As n.m. departure.

ⲥⲟⲡ (ⲥⲡ-, ⲥⲉⲡ-; pl. ⲥⲱⲱⲡ, ⲥⲟⲟⲛ) n.m. time, occasion; turn,
round (e.g. of reading or prayer). ⲥⲟⲡ ... ⲥⲟⲡ now ...
again (oft. with ⲙⲉⲛ ... ⲇⲉ). ⲉ ⲡⲥⲟⲡ occasionally; all
at once. ⲙ ⲡⲥⲟⲡ at the time when (+ Rel.). ⲙ ⲡⲉⲓⲥⲟⲡ on
this occasion. ⲛ ⲟⲩⲥⲟⲡ on one occasion, once. ⲛ ⲟⲩⲥⲟⲡ
ⲉⲩⲥⲟⲡ from time to time. ϩⲓ ⲟⲩⲥⲟⲡ altogether, all at one
time. ⲕⲁⲧⲁ ⲥⲟⲡ from time to time. (ⲛ) ⲕⲉⲥⲟⲡ again.
ⲙ ⲡⲉⲓⲕⲉⲥⲟⲡ yet once more. ⲟⲩⲙⲏⲏϣⲉ/ϩⲁϩ ⲛ ⲥⲟⲡ many times.
ⲧⲙⲛⲥⲟⲡ idem. ⲥⲟⲡ ⲛⲓⲙ always.

ⲥⲟⲡⲥ ⲥⲡⲥ- (ⲥⲉⲡⲥ-) vb. tr. and n.m. = ⲥⲟⲡⲥⲡ q.v. ⲣ-ⲥⲟⲡⲥ to
make prayer. ⲭⲓ-ⲥⲟⲡⲥ to receive comfort.

ⲥⲟⲡⲥⲡ ⲥⲡⲥⲡ- ⲥⲡⲥⲱⲡ⸗ Q ⲥⲉⲡⲥⲱⲡ vb. tr. to entreat, implore
(ⲙⲙⲟ⸗, ⲉ); to pray (for: ⲉⲧⲃⲉ, ⲉⲭⲛ, ϩⲁ, ϩⲓⲭⲛ); to comfort; as n.m. prayer, entreaty, consolation.

ⲥⲟⲣⲙ, ⲥⲁⲣⲙ n.m. dregs.

ⲥⲟⲣⲧ, ⲥⲁⲣⲧ n.m.f. wool.

ⲥⲟⲧ, ⲥⲟⲟⲧ, ⲥⲁⲧ, ⲥⲁⲁⲧⲉ n.m. dung, excrement.

ⲥⲟⲧⲃⲉϥ, ⲥⲁⲧⲃⲉϥ, ⲥⲟⲧ(ϩ)ϥ n.m. tool, weapon; + ⲙ ⲙⲓϣⲉ weapon.

ⲥⲟⲩⲛⲧ⸗ n.m. price, value; ⲛⲁϣⲉ-ⲥⲟⲩⲛⲧ⸗ of great value (vb.).

ⲥⲟⲩⲟ n.m. grain, wheat.

(ⲥⲟⲩⲟⲗⲟⲩⲗ) ⲥⲟⲩⲉⲗⲟⲩⲱⲗ⸗ (ⲥⲟⲩⲗⲱⲗ⸗, ⲥⲟⲩⲗⲟⲗ⸗) Q ⲥⲟⲩⲗⲱⲗ vb. tr.
to wrap (ⲙⲙⲟ⸗; in: ⲙⲙⲟ⸗, ϩⲛ; around: ⲉ).

ⲥⲟⲩⲣⲉ (ⲥⲟⲩⲣ-, ⲥⲉⲣ- ⲥⲁⲣ- ⲥⲣ-) n.f. thorn, spike, dart, awl,
needle. For cpds. see 2nd element.

ⲥⲟⲩⲥⲟⲩ n.m. point, moment.

ⲥⲟⳕ, ⲥⲏ6ⲉ, ⲥⲉ6ⲉ n.m. fool; adj. foolish. ϣⲝ-ⲥⲟⳕ foolish talk. ⲙⲛⲧⲥⲟⳕ folly. ⲣ̄-ⲥⲟⳕ to become a fool; to make a fool.

ⲥⲟ6ⲛ̄ (ⲥⲕⲉⲛ-) n.m. ointment. ⲙⲛⲧⲥⲟ6ⲛ̄ anointing. ⲛⲉⲥ-ⲥⲟ6ⲛ̄ to make ointments; ⲛⲁⲥ-/ⲣⲉ⳽ⲛⲉⲥ-ⲥⲟ6ⲛ̄ perfumer. ⲥⲕⲉⲛ-ⲉⲛⲓⲥⲉ cooking grease.

ⲥⲛ̄-, ⲥⲉⲛ- n.f. year, in date formulas, prefixed to number, e.g. ⲍ̄ⲛ̄ (ⲧ)ⲥⲛ̄-⳽ⲧⲟⳕ in the 4th year.

ⲥⲛⲓⲣ (pl. ⲥⲛⲓⲣⲟⲟⳛⲉ) n.m. rib. ⲃⲏⲧ-ⲥⲛⲓⲣ rib. ⲛ̄/ⲍ⳽ ⲥⲁ-ⲥⲛⲓⲣ ⲙ̄ⲙⲟ⳽ prep. beside. ⲍ⳽ ⲟⳛⲥⲛⲓⲣ aside.

ⲥⲛⲟⲧⲟⳛ n.m. lips; shore, edge (used as sg. or pl.).

ⲥⲣⲁ⳽, ⲥⲉⲣⲉⳕ n.m. wound, sore.

ⲥⲣⲓⲧ ⲥⲣⲁⲧ⳽ (ⲥⲣⲓⲧ⳽) vb. tr. to glean (ⲙ̄ⲙⲟ⳽); to ravage.

ⲥⲣⲟⲙⲣ̄ⲙ ⲥⲣ̄ⲙ̄ⲣⲱⲙ⳽ Q ⲥⲣ̄ⲙ̄ⲣⲱⲙ vb. tr. to daze, stupefy (ⲙ̄ⲙⲟ⳽); vb. intr. to become dazed, move dazedly; as n.m. stupefaction.

ⲥⲣⲟ⳽ⲣⲉ⳽ (ⲥⲣⲟ̄ⲃⲣⲉⳕ) ⲥⲣⲉ⳽ⲣⲱ⳽ (ⲥⲣⲉ̄ⲃⲣⲱⲃ⳽) vb. tr. to dissipate (ⲙ̄ⲙⲟ⳽); vb. intr. to wither, fall useless; as n.m. falling, withering. ⲥⲣⲉ⳽ⲣⲓ⳽ⲉ, ⲥⲣ̄ⲣⲓⲃⲉ, ⲥⲣⲉ⳽ⲣⲉ⳽ n. droppings, crumbs.

ⲥⲣ̄⳽ⲉ (ⲥⲣ̄ⲃⲉ) Q ⲥⲣⲟⳛⲧ̄ (ⲥⲣⲟ̄ⲃⲧ̄) vb. intr. to be at leisure, unoccupied; to have time for, be occupied with (ⲉ); as n. m. leisure, perseverance. ⲙⲛ̄ⲧⲁⲧⲥⲣ̄⳽ⲉ lack of leisure.

ⲥⲧⲉⲃⲗⲉ⳵⳽ n. tool, utensil.

ⲥⲧⲏⲙ n.m. stibium, antimony, kohl.

ⲥⲧⲟ⳵ (ⲥ†-, ⲥⲧⲁ⳵-, ⲥⲧⲉ-) n.m. smell, fragrance, incense; ⲥ†-ⲛⲟⳛⳛⲉ perfume, incense; ⲥ†-ⲁⲛ idem; ⲥ†-ⲃⲱⲱⲛ stench; ⲣ̄-ⲥⲧⲟ⳵ to stink.

ⲥⲧⲣ̄ⲧⲣ̄ n.m. trembling.

ⲥⲧⲱ n.f. river bank.

ⲥⲧⲱⲧ vb. intr. to tremble (at: ⲍⲏⲧ⳽, ⲍⲁ); as n.m. trembling.

ⲥⲱ n. (mat of) soaked reeds.

ⲥⲱ (ⲥⲟⳛ) ⲥⲉ- (ⲥⲉⳛ-, ⲥⲟⳛ-) ⲥⲟⲟ⳽ vb. tr. to drink (ⲙ̄ⲙⲟ⳽); as n.m. drinking. ⲙⲁ ⲛ̄ ⲥⲱ place for drinking. ⲣⲉⳛⲥⲉ-/ⲥⲁⳛ- a drinker of.

ϭⲱⲃⲉ vb. tr. to mock, deride, ridicule (ⲙ̄ⲙⲟ⸗); vb. intr.
to laugh (at: ⲉⲝⲛ̄, ⲛ̄ⲥⲁ), to sport (with: ⲙⲛ̄); as n.m.
laughter, derision, sport. ⲣⲉϥϭⲱⲃⲉ mocker, jester.
ϣⲝ̄-ϭⲱⲃⲉ jesting speech.

ϭⲱⲃⲉ, ϭⲱⲡⲉ n.f. edge, fringe.

ϭⲱⲃⲍ̄ ϭⲟⲃⲍ̄- ϭⲟⲃ2⸗ Q ϭⲟⲃⲍ̄ vb. tr. to make leprous; vb. intr.
to become leprous; as n.m. leprosy. ϭⲟⲃⲍ̄ n.m. leper.

ϭⲱⲕ ϭⲉⲕ- (ϭⲕ̄-, ϭⲁⲕ-) ϭⲟⲕ⸗ Q ϭⲏⲕ (1) vb. tr. to pull, draw
(ⲙ̄ⲙⲟ⸗); to beguile, attract; to protract, draw out; to
bring, take, lead; (2) vb. intr. to move with smooth,
gliding motion, hence: to flow, be blown; to be drawn;
to go, proceed; vb. reflex. = intr. Used with full
range of prep. and adv. in usu. senses. ϭⲱⲕ 2ⲁ to submit to, move along with. ϭⲱⲕ as n.m. drawing; (± ⲉⲃⲟⲗ)
death.

ϭⲱⲗⲡ̄ ϭⲗ̄ⲡ- (ϭⲉⲗⲡ-) ϭⲟⲗⲡ⸗ Q ϭⲟⲗⲡ̄ (± ⲉⲃⲟⲗ) vb. tr. to break
off, cut off (ⲙ̄ⲙⲟ⸗); to decide; vb. intr. to be broken
off, cut off; to burst, break; as n.m. separation.
ϭⲗ̄ⲡⲉ n. strip.

ϭⲱⲗϭ̄ ϭⲟⲗϭ⸗ Q ϭⲟⲗ(ⲉ)ϭ vb. tr. to smear (ⲙ̄ⲙⲟ⸗; on: ⲉ) to
wipe out, obliterate; as n.m. obliteration.

ϭⲱⲙ ϭⲟⲙ⸗ (ϭⲁⲙ⸗) Q ϭⲏⲙ to pound, press, subdue.

ϭⲱⲙⲧ̄ (ϭⲱⲙⲛ̄ⲧ) ϭⲟⲙⲧ⸗ (ϭⲟⲙⲛ̄ⲧ⸗) Q ϭⲟⲙ(ⲛ̄)ⲧ vb. tr. to stretch,
extend (ⲙ̄ⲙⲟ⸗; ± ⲉⲃⲟⲗ); to bind (to: ⲉ); vb. intr. to be
stretched; to delay, tarry.

ϭⲱⲛⲉ n.f. sister. ⲛⲟϭ/ⲕⲟⲩⲓ ⲛ̄ ϭⲱⲛⲉ elder/younger sister.
ϭⲱⲛⲉ ⲙ̄ ⲙⲁ2ⲧ̄ real sister; ϭⲱⲛⲉ 2ⲁ ⲉⲓⲱⲧ step-sister.

ϭⲱⲛⲕ̄ (ϭⲱⲛϥ̄, ϭⲱⲙⲕ̄, ϭⲱⲙϥ̄) vb. tr. to suck (ⲙ̄ⲙⲟ⸗).

ϭⲱⲛⲧ̄ (ϭⲱⲱⲛⲧ̄) ϭⲛ̄ⲧ- (ϭⲉⲛⲧ̄-) ϭⲟⲛⲧ⸗ (ϭⲟⲟⲛⲧ⸗) Q ϭⲟⲛⲧ̄ vb. tr. to
found, create (ⲙ̄ⲙⲟ⸗); vb. intr. to be created; as n.m.
creature, creation. ⲁⲧϭⲟⲛⲧ⸗ uncreated. ⲣⲉϥϭⲱⲛⲧ̄ crea-
tor. ϣⲁ-ϭⲱⲛⲧ̄ first in creation. ϭⲛ̄ⲧⲉ n.f. foundation;
ⲕⲁ-ϭⲛ̄ⲧⲉ to lay a foundation; ϭⲙ̄ⲛ-/ϯ-ϭⲛ̄ⲧⲉ idem.

ϭⲱⲛⲧ̄ n.m. custom. ⲡϭⲱⲛⲧ̄ ⲛ̄ ⲛⲉ2ⲓⲟⲙⲉ menstruation. ⲉⲓⲣⲉ ⲙ̄
ⲡϭⲱⲛⲧ̄ to follow a custom.

cⲱⲛⲍ̄ cⲟⲛ2ⲋ Q cⲟⲛⲍ̄ vb. tr. to fetter, bind (ⲙ̄ⲙⲟⲋ; to: ⲉ, ⲛ̄ⲧⲛ̄; as to, e.g. feet: ⲍⲛ̄, ⲙ̄ⲙⲟⲋ); vb. intr. to be bound; as n.m. bond, fetter. cⲛⲁⲩⲍ n.m. bond, fetter.

cⲱⲟⲩⲍ cⲉⲩⲍ- cⲟⲟⲩⲍ ⲋ Q cⲟⲟⲩⲍ vb. tr. (± ⲉⲍⲟⲩⲛ) to gather, collect (ⲙ̄ⲙⲟⲋ; to, at: ⲉ, ⲉⲭⲛ̄, ⲍⲛ̄; with: ⲙⲛ̄; against: ⲉ); vb. intr. idem, to be gathered. As n.m. gathering; assembly; ⲣ̄-ⲡcⲱⲟⲩⲍ to attend service; ⲙⲁ ⲛ̄ cⲱⲟⲩⲍ meeting place. cⲟⲟⲩⲍⲧ̄ n.f. congregation, collection; ⲣ̄-cⲟⲟⲩⲍⲧ̄ to be collected.

cⲱⲡ cⲡ̄- (cⲉⲡ-) cⲟⲡⲋ vb. tr. to dip, soak (ⲙ̄ⲙⲟⲋ; in: ⲍⲛ̄).

cⲱⲣ cⲡ̄- (cⲉⲣ-) cⲟⲣⲋ Q cⲏⲣ (p.c. cⲁⲣ-) ± ⲉⲃⲟⲗ vb. tr. to scatter, spread, extend, distribute (ⲙ̄ⲙⲟⲋ); cⲱⲣ ⲛ̄cⲁ to spread (report) against; vb. intr. to scatter, spread, esp. of sunlight; as n.m. (± ⲉⲃⲟⲗ) spreading, laying out.

cⲱⲣⲙ̄ cⲉⲣⲙ̄- cⲟⲣⲙⲋ Q cⲟⲣⲙ̄ vb. tr. to lead astray, mislead. lose (ⲙ̄ⲙⲟⲋ; ± ⲉⲃⲟⲗ); cⲱⲣⲙ̄ ⲙ̄ⲙⲟⲋ ⲛ̄ⲧⲟⲟⲧⲋ (reflex.) to lose; vb. intr. to go astray, get lost, err (from: ⲍⲛ̄, ⲛ̄ cⲁ- ⲃⲟⲗ ⲛ̄); as n.m. error. ⲣⲉϥcⲱⲣⲙ̄ one who leads astray. ⲙⲟⲩ-ⲛ̄-cⲱⲣⲙ̄ torrent. cⲣ̄ⲙⲉ n. wanderer, vagrant. cⲟⲣⲙⲉc n.f. error.

cⲱc cⲟcⲋ Q cⲏc vb. tr. to upset, overthrow (ⲙ̄ⲙⲟⲋ); vb. intr. to be overthrown.

cⲱⲧ cⲟⲧⲋ (cⲟⲟⲧⲋ, cⲁⲁⲧⲋ) (1) vb. intr. or reflex. to repeat, do again (+ ⲉ + Inf. or + Circum.); (2) vb. intr. to reach (to: ⲉ; ± ⲉⲃⲟⲗ).

cⲱⲧⲉ cⲉⲧ- cⲟⲧⲋ (cⲟⲟⲧⲋ, cⲁⲧⲋ) vb. tr. to rescue, redeem (ⲙ̄- ⲙⲟⲋ; from: ⲛ̄ⲧⲛ̄, ⲉ, ⲍⲛ̄, ⲉⲃⲟⲗ ⲍⲛ̄); as n.m. ransom, price. ϯ-cⲱⲧⲉ to redeem. ϫⲓ-cⲱⲧⲉ to receive ransom. ⲣⲉϥcⲱⲧⲉ redeemer.

cⲱⲧⲙ̄ cⲉⲧⲙ̄- cⲟⲧⲙⲋ vb. tr. to hear, listen to (ⲉ); to obey, heed (ⲛⲁⲋ, ⲛ̄cⲁ); to hear from, at hand of (ⲉⲧⲛ̄, ⲛ̄ⲧⲛ̄, ⲍⲓⲧⲛ̄); as n.m. hearing, obedience. ⲁⲧcⲱⲧⲙ̄ unhearing, disobedient; ⲙⲛ̄ⲧⲁⲧcⲱⲧⲙ̄ disobedience; ⲣ̄-ⲁⲧcⲱⲧⲙ̄ (Q ⲟ ⲛ̄) to be disobedient. ⲙⲛ̄ⲧⲣⲉϥcⲱⲧⲙ̄ obedience. cⲧ̄ⲙⲏⲧ, cⲉⲧ- ⲙⲏⲧ, cⲙⲏⲧ adj. obedient; ⲁⲧcⲧ̄ⲙⲏⲧ disobedient; ⲙⲛ̄ⲧcⲧ̄ⲙⲏⲧ obedience; ⲡ̄-ⲥⲧ̄ⲙⲏⲧ (Q o ⲛ̄) to be obedient.

ⲥⲱⲧⲡ̄ ⲥⲉⲧⲡ̄- ⲥⲟⲧⲡ⸗ Q ⲥⲟⲧⲡ̄ vb. to choose, select (ⲙ̄ⲙⲟ⸗); Q to
be chosen, elect; excellent, exquisite; often in comparative w. ⲉ, ⲛ̄ ⳁⲟⲩⲟ: to be better, choicer, more advan-
tageous. As n.m. chosen or elect person; oft. adj.
ⲙⲛ̄ⲧⲥⲱⲧⲡ̄ election, choice; superiority.

ⲥⲱⲧⲡ̄, Q ⲥⲟⲧⲡ̄ vb. intr. to turn, twist.

ⲥⲱⲧϥ̄ ⲥⲉⲧϥ̄- ⲥⲟⲧϥ⸗ Q ⲥⲟⲧϥ̄ vb. tr. to purify, filter, strain,
pour (ⲙ̄ⲙⲟ⸗; ± ⲉⲃⲟⲗ); vb. intr. to be purified, pure,
clear; to pour. As n.m. purity. ⲣⲉϥⲥⲱⲧϥ̄ purifier.

ⲥⲱⲱⲙⲉ ⲥⲟⲙⲉ⸗ vb. tr. to rub, polish.

ⲥⲱⲱϥ ⲥⲉⲉϥ- (ⲥⲉⲃⲉ-, ⲥⲉϥ-) ⲥⲟⲟϥ⸗ (ⲥⲟⲟⲃ⸗, ⲥⲟϥ⸗) Q ⲥⲟⲟϥ vb.
tr. to defile, pollute (ⲙ̄ⲙⲟ⸗); vb. intr. to become defiled, polluted; as n.m. pollution, abomination.

ⲥⲱϣ ⲥⲉϣ- (ϣⲉⲥ-) ⲥⲟϣ⸗ vb. tr. to strike. ⲥⲗ̄ϣ (ⲥⲅ̄-, ϣⲉ̄-, ⲥⲉ̄-,
ϣⲥⲉ-, ϣⲉ-, ϣⲧⲉ-; pl. ⲥⲛ̄ϣⲉ) n.m.f. blow, stroke; sore,
wound; ⲡ̄-ⲥⲗ̄ϣ (Q o ⲛ̄) to cover, be covered, with sores,
wounds. ϯ-ⲥⲗ̄ϣ to give a blow (to: ⲛⲁ⸗). ϫⲓ-ⲥⲗ̄ϣ to be
wounded. For cpds. w. reduced form + ⲛ̄ see 2nd element.

ⲥⲱϣ ⲥⲉϣ- (ϣⲉⲥ-) ⲥⲟϣ⸗ (ϣⲟⲥ⸗) Q ⲥⲏϣ (ϣⲏⲥ) vb. tr. to despise,
scorn (ⲙ̄ⲙⲟ⸗); vb. intr. to be despised, scorned, humbled; as n.m. shame, contempt, scorn. ⲣⲉϥⲥⲱϣ one who
scorns; ⲙⲛ̄ⲧⲣⲉϥⲥⲱϣ scorn. ϯ-ⲥⲱϣ ⲛⲁ⸗ to scorn, despise.
ϫⲓ-ⲥⲱϣ to be scorned.

ⲥⲱϣⲉ vb. tr. to drag (ⲙ̄ⲙⲟ⸗); vb. intr. to drag, creep.

ⲥⲱϣⲉ n.f. field, open country. ⲣⲙ̄ⲛ̄ⲥⲱϣⲉ country man.

ⲥⲱϣⲙ̄ (ϣⲱⲥⲙ̄) Q ⲥⲟϣⲙ̄ (ϣⲟⲥⲙ̄) vb. intr. (± ⲛ̄ ⳁⲏⲧ) to be faint,
(for: ⲛ̄ⲥⲁ; from: ⳁⲁ), discouraged; to be annoyed (at,
with: ⲉ, ⲙⲛ̄); as n.m. faintness.

ⲥⲱϣⲧ̄ ⲥⲉϣⲧ̄- ⲥⲟϣⲧ⸗ (ⲥⲗϣⲧ⸗) Q ⲥⲟϣⲧ̄ (ⲥⲗϣⲧ̄) vb. tr. to stop,
hinder (ⲙ̄ⲙⲟ⸗; from: ⲉ + [neg.] Inf.); vb. intr. to
stop, be hindered, impeded (from: ⲉ + Inf.).

ⲥⲱϣϥ̄ ⲥⲉϣϥ̄- ⲥⲟϣϥ⸗ Q ⲥⲟϣϥ̄ vb. tr. intr. = ⲥⲱϣ despise, q.v.

ⲥⲱⳁ n.m. deaf person. ⲡ̄-ⲥⲱⳁ to become deaf.

ⲥⲱⳁⲉ ⲥⲗⳁⲧ̄- ⲥⲗⳁⲧ⸗ Q ⲥⲗⳁⲧ̄ (ⲥⲗϣⲧ̄) vb. tr. to weave (ⲙ̄ⲙⲟ⸗, ⲉ;

onto: ⲉ2ⲟⲩⲛ ⲉ); as n.m. weaving. ⲥⲁ2ⲧ̄- in cpds.: weaver of. ⲥⲁ2ⲧ̄ n.m. weaver.

ⲥⲱ2ⲙ̄ ⲥⲁ2ⲙ⸗ Q ⲥⲁ2ⲙ̄ vb. tr. to press down, crush, overwhelm
(ⲙ̄ⲙⲟ⸗); vb. intr. to sink, be pressed down, crushed; to
recede (from: 2ⲁ). ⲥⲁ2ⲙⲉⲥ n. pestle.

ⲥⲱ2ⲡ̄ ⲥⲉ2ⲡ̄- ⲥⲁ2ⲡ⸗ vb. tr. to drink, suck in (ⲙ̄ⲙⲟ⸗); vb. intr. to sink in, be swallowed. ⲥⲓ2ⲛⲉ n. drop.

ⲥⲱ2ⲣ̄ ⲥⲉ2ⲣ̄- ⲥⲁ2ⲣ⸗ (ⲥⲟ2ⲣ⸗) Q ⲥⲁ2ⲣ̄ vb. tr. to sweep (ⲙ̄ⲙⲟ⸗);
as n.m. sweeping.

ⲥⲱ6 ⲥⲉ6- ⲥⲟ6⸗ Q ⲥⲏ6 vb. tr. to stiffen, harden, paralyze
(ⲙ̄ⲙⲟ⸗); vb. intr. to become rigid, paralyzed.

ⲥ2ⲁⲓ (ⲥⲁ2ⲉⲓ, ⲥ2ⲏⲧ) ⲥⲉ2- ⲥ2ⲁⲓ⸗ (ⲥ2ⲁⲓⲥ⸗, ⲥ2ⲁⲓⲧ⸗, ⲥⲁ2⸗, ⲥⲁ2ⲧ⸗,
ⲥⲉ2ⲧ⸗) Q ⲥⲏ2 vb. tr. to write (ⲙ̄ⲙⲟ⸗; on, upon, in: ⲉ,
ⲉⲝⲛ̄, 2ⲓ, 2ⲓⲭⲛ̄, 2ⲛ̄; to: ⲉ, ⲛⲁ⸗, ⲉⲣⲁⲧ⸗, ϣⲁ; for, on behalf of: ⲉ, ⲉⲧⲛ̄, 2ⲁ); to register; to draw, paint. ⲥ2ⲁⲓ
ⲙ̄ⲙⲟ⸗ ⲛ̄ⲥⲁ to ascribe to; ⲥ2ⲁⲓ ⲛ̄ⲥⲁ to take down in writing.
ⲥ2ⲁⲓ as n.m. writing, letter, epistle; letter of alph.
ⲭⲓ-ⲥ2ⲁⲓ to receive a letter. ⲁⲧⲥ2ⲁⲓ illiterate. ⲣⲉϥ-
ⲥ2ⲁⲓ scribe. ⲥⲁ2 n.m. scribe, writer; teacher, master,
master craftsman; ⲙⲛ̄ⲧⲥⲁ2 skill, craft; ⲣ̄-ⲥⲁ2 (Q ⲟ ⲛ̄) to
become master, skilled. ⲥⲁⲭⲟ, ⲥⲁⲭⲱ n.m.f. village
scribe; also = ⲥⲁ2.

ⲥ2̄ⲃⲏⲏⲧⲉ, ⲥⲃⲏⲏⲧⲉ, ⲥⲃⲉⲉⲧⲉ, 2ⲃⲏⲏⲧⲉ n.m. foam. ⲧⲁⲩⲉ-ⲥ2̄ⲃⲏⲏⲧⲉ
ⲉⲃⲟⲗ to foam.

ⲥ2ⲓⲙⲉ (pl. 2ⲓⲟⲙⲉ) n.f. woman, wife; female. 2ⲓⲙⲉ n.f. wife.
ⲙⲛ̄ⲧⲥ2ⲓⲙⲉ womanhood. ⲣ̄-ⲥ2ⲓⲙⲉ to become wife (to: ⲛⲁ⸗).
ⲭⲓ-ⲥ2ⲓⲙⲉ to take wife; as n.m. marriage.

ⲥ6ⲏⲣ (ⲥⲕⲏⲣ, ϣ6ⲏⲣ, ϣ̄6ⲏⲣ, ϣⲕⲉⲣ) vb. intr. to sail (with
prep. in usu. senses); as n.m. sailing, voyage.

ⲥ6̄ⲣⲁ2ⲧ̄ (ⲥ6̄ⲣⲉ2ⲧ̄, ϣ6̄ⲣⲁ2ⲧ̄, ⲥϣ̄6ⲣⲁ2ⲧ̄) vb. intr. to pause, become
still, quiet, tranquil; also reflex. with ⲙ̄ⲙⲟ⸗; as n.m.
quiet, rest; 2ⲛ̄ ⲟⲩⲥ6̄ⲣⲁ2ⲧ̄ at rest, quietly.

ⲥⲁⲁⲧ⸗: ⲥⲱⲧ	ⲥⲁⲃⲏⲗ: ⲃⲱⲗ	ⲥⲁⲉⲓⲉ: ⲥⲁ
ⲥⲁⲁⲧ⸗/-: ⲥⲓⲛⲉ	ⲥⲁⲃⲟ(⸗): ⲧⲥⲁⲃⲟ	ⲥⲁⲉⲓⲟⲟⲩ: ⲥⲁ
ⲥⲁⲁⲧⲉ: ⲥⲁⲧⲉ	ⲥⲁⲃⲟⲗ: ⲃⲱⲗ	ⲥⲁⲉⲓⲣ(ⲉ): ⲥⲓⲣ

ⲤⲀⲔ: ⲤⲞⲔ
ⲤⲀⲔ-: ⲤⲰⲔ
ⲤⲀⲔⲦ⸗: ⲤⲒⲔⲈ
ⲤⲀⲬⲞ: ⲤϨⲀⲒ
ⲤⲀⲖⲖϬⲰⲰϢ: ⲤⲀⲢⲀϬⲰⲞⲨϢ
ⲤⲀⲘ⸗: ⲤⲰⲘ
ⲤⲀ-Ⲛ-ⲂⲞⲖ: ⲂⲰⲖ
ⲤⲀⲚⲞⲨϢ⸗: ⲤⲀⲀⲚϢ̄
ⲤⲀⲚϢ̄: ⲤⲀⲀⲚϢ̄
ⲤⲀⲢ-: ⲤⲰⲢ
ⲤⲀⲢ-: ⲤⲞⲨⲢ
ⲤⲀⲢⲘ̄: ⲤⲞⲢⲘ̄
ⲤⲀⲢⲞ: ⲤⲀⲖⲞ
ⲤⲀⲢⲦ̄: ⲤⲞⲢⲦ̄
ⲤⲀⲤⲈ: ⲤⲀⲀⲤⲈ
ⲤⲀⲦ: ⲤⲞⲦ
ⲤⲀⲦ-/⸗: ⲤⲒⲦⲈ
ⲤⲀⲦ⸗: ⲤⲒⲚⲈ
ⲤⲀⲦ⸗: ⲤⲰⲦⲈ
ⲤⲀⲦⲂⲈϤ: ⲤⲞⲦⲂⲈϤ
ⲤⲀⲦⲈ: ⲤⲀⲦⲰ
ⲤⲀⲨ-: ⲤⲰ
ⲤⲀⲨ-ⲎⲢⲠ̄: ⲎⲢⲠ̄
ⲤⲀϢ: ⲤⲰϢ
ⲤⲀϢⲈ: ⲤⲒϢⲈ
ⲤⲀϢⲦ̄: ⲤⲰϨⲈ
ⲤⲀϢ(Ⲧ)⸗: ⲤⲰϢⲦ̄
ⲤⲀϨ(⸗): ⲤϨⲀⲒ
ⲤⲀϨⲈ-: ⲤⲞⲞϨⲈ
ⲤⲀϨⲈⲒ: ⲤϨⲀⲒ
ⲤⲀϨⲎⲨ: ⲤⲞⲞϨⲈ
ⲤⲀϨⲘ(⸗): ⲤⲰϨⲘ̄
ⲤⲀϨⲘⲈⲤ: ⲤⲰϨⲘ̄
ⲤⲀϨⲠ⸗: ⲤⲰϨⲠ̄
ⲤⲀϨⲢ(⸗): ⲤⲰϨⲢ̄
ⲤⲀϨⲦ⸗: ⲤⲒϨⲈ
ⲤⲀϨⲦ(-/⸗): ⲤⲰϨⲈ
ⲤⲀϨⲦ⸗: ⲤϨⲀⲒ
ⲤⲀϨⲰ(Ⲱ)⸗: ⲤⲞⲞϨⲈ
ⲤⲀϨϤ̄: ⲤⲀϨ
ⲤⲂⲈⲈⲦⲈ: ⲤⲂ̄ⲂⲎⲎⲦⲈ
ⲤⲂⲎⲎⲦⲈ: ⲤⲂ̄ⲂⲎⲎⲦⲈ
ⲤⲂ̄ⲔⲈ: ⲤⲂⲞⲔ
ⲤⲂⲞ: ⲦⲤⲀⲂⲞ
ⲤⲂⲞⲞⲨⲈ: ⲤⲂⲰ
ⲤⲂⲞⲨⲒ: ⲤⲀⲂⲈ
ⲤⲂ̄ⲢⲞⲞⲨⲈ: ⲢⲞⲞⲨⲈ
ⲤⲂ̄ⲦⲈ-: ⲤⲞⲂⲦⲈ
ⲤⲂ̄ⲦⲰⲦ(⸗): ⲤⲞⲂⲦⲈ
ⲤⲂⲰ: ⲤⲀⲂⲈ
ⲤⲈ: ⲤⲞⲞⲨ
ⲤⲈ-: ⲤⲰ

ⲤⲈⲈⲦ: ⲤⲀⲦ
ⲤⲈⲈϤ-: ⲤⲰⲰϤ
ⲤⲈⲔ-: ⲤⲔⲀⲒ
ⲤⲈⲔⲰⲦ: ⲔⲰⲦ
ⲤⲈⲖϬⲀⲘ: Ϣ̄ϬⲞⲘ
ⲤⲈⲚ-: ⲤⲞⲚ
ⲤⲈⲚ-: ⲤⲒⲚⲈ
ⲤⲈⲚⲄ, ⲤⲈⲚⲎ: ⲤⲎⲚⲈ
ⲤⲈⲚⲤⲈⲚ: ⲤⲚ̄ⲤⲚ̄
ⲤⲈⲠ-: ⲤⲞⲠ
ⲤⲈⲠ-: ⲤⲠ̄
ⲤⲈⲠⲈ: ⲤⲈⲈⲠⲈ
ⲤⲈⲠⲤ̄-: ⲤⲞⲠⲤ̄
ⲤⲈⲢ-: ⲤⲞⲨⲢ
ⲤⲈⲢ(Ⲉ): ⲤⲒⲢ
ⲤⲈⲢⲈⲂ: ϬⲢⲀϤ
ⲤⲈⲦ-: ⲤⲰⲦⲈ
ⲤⲈⲦ-/⸗: ⲤⲒⲦⲈ
ⲤⲈⲦⲘⲎⲦ: ⲤⲰⲦⲘ̄
ⲤⲈⲨ-: ⲤⲰ
ⲤⲈⲨ-: ⲤⲰ
ⲤⲈⲨ-: ⲤⲞⲞⲨ
ⲤⲈϤ-: ⲤⲰⲰϤ
ⲤⲈϨ-: ⲤϨⲀⲒ
ⲤⲈϨ-: ⲤⲒϨⲈ
ⲤⲈϨⲦ⸗: ⲤϨⲀⲒ
ⲤⲈϨⲦ⸗: ⲤⲒϨⲈ
ⲤⲈϬⲈ: ⲤⲞϬ
ⲤⲎⲂⲈ: ⲤⲎϤⲈ
ⲤⲎⲂⲈ: ⲤⲒϤⲈ
ⲤⲎⲎⲠⲈ: ⲤⲈⲈⲠⲈ
ⲤⲎⲠⲈ: ⲤⲈⲈⲠⲈ
ⲤⲎⲢⲈ: ⲤⲒⲢ
ⲤⲎⲦ: ⲤⲀⲦ
ⲤⲎⲦ: ⲤⲒⲦⲈ
ⲤⲎⲨ: ⲤⲒ
ⲤⲎϢⲈ: ⲤⲰϢ
ⲤⲎϤⲈ: ⲤⲎⲂⲈ
ⲤⲎϤⲈ: ⲤⲒϤⲈ
ⲤⲎϨ: ⲤϨⲀⲒ
ⲤⲎϬⲈ: ⲤⲞϬ
ⲤⲒⲀⲞⲨⲚ̄: ⲤⲒⲞⲞⲨⲚ̄
ⲤⲒⲂⲈ: ⲤⲒⲂⲈ
ⲤⲒⲎⲨ: ⲦⲤⲒⲞ
ⲤⲒⲔ: ⲀⲤⲒⲔ
ⲤⲒⲚⲈ: ⲤⲈⲈⲠⲈ
ⲤⲒⲦ⸗: ⲤⲒⲦⲈ
ⲤⲒⲦⲈ: ⲤⲈⲦⲎ
ⲤⲒϨⲠⲈ: ⲤⲰϨⲠ̄
ⲤⲔⲀⲢⲀⲔⲒⲢ: ⲤⲔⲞⲢⲔⲢ̄
ⲤⲔⲈⲖⲖⲔⲒⲢ: ⲤⲔⲞⲢⲔⲢ̄
ⲤⲔⲈⲚ-: ⲤⲞϬⲚ̄

ⲤⲔⲎⲢ: ⲤϬⲎⲢ
ⲤⲔⲞⲢⲀⲔⲒⲢ: ⲤⲔⲞⲢⲔⲢ̄
ⲤⲖ̄ⲂⲦⲈ: ⲤⲂⲀⲦⲈ
ⲤⲖⲈⲔⲖⲰⲔ: ⲤⲖⲞϬⲂ̄
ⲤⲖ̄ⲠⲈ: ⲤⲰⲖⲠ̄
ⲤⲖ̄ϤⲦⲈ: ⲤⲂⲀⲦⲈ
ⲤⲘ̄-: ⲤⲒⲘ
ⲤⲘⲀⲀⲦ: ⲤⲘⲞⲨ
ⲤⲘⲀⲘⲀⲀⲦ: ⲤⲘⲞⲨ
ⲤⲘⲈⲚ-: ⲤⲘⲒⲚⲈ
ⲤⲘⲎⲦ: ⲤⲰⲦⲘ̄
ⲤⲘⲚ̄-: ⲤⲘⲒⲚⲈ
ⲤⲘⲚ̄Ⲧ⸗: ⲤⲘⲒⲚⲈ
ⲤⲘⲞⲚⲦ̄: ⲤⲘⲒⲚⲈ
ⲤⲘ̄ⲤⲒⲘ: ⲤⲒⲘⲤⲒⲘ
ⲤⲚ̄-: ⲤⲞⲚ
ⲤⲚⲀⲨϨ: ⲤⲰⲚ̄Ϩ̄
ⲤⲚⲎⲨ: ⲤⲞⲚ
ⲤⲚ̄ⲔⲞ: ⲦⲤⲈⲚⲔⲞ
ⲤⲚⲞⲂ: ⲤⲚⲞϤ
ⲤⲚⲞⲞⲨⲤ(Ⲉ): ⲤⲚⲀⲨ
ⲤⲚ̄-: ⲤⲒⲚⲈ
ⲤⲚ̄Ⲧ-/⸗: ⲤⲒⲚⲈ
ⲤⲚ̄ⲦⲈ: ⲤⲰⲚⲦ̄
ⲤⲚ̄ⲦⲈ: ⲤⲚⲀⲨ
ⲤⲚ̄ⲦⲈ: ⲤⲈⲦⲎ
ⲤⲚⲰⲰϤ: ⲤⲚⲞϤ
ⲤⲞ: ⲤⲞⲞⲨ
ⲤⲞⲂⲔ̄: ⲤⲂⲞⲔ
ⲤⲞⲈ: ⲤⲞⲞⲨ
ⲤⲞⲈⲒϨ: ⲤⲞⲈⲒϢ
ⲤⲞⲔ⸗: ⲤⲔⲀⲒ
ⲤⲞⲔⲈ: ⲤⲒⲔⲈ
ⲤⲞⲖⲒⲂ: ⲤⲞⲖϤ̄
ⲤⲞⲘⲈ⸗: ⲤⲰⲰⲘⲈ
ⲤⲞⲘⲚ̄Ⲧ(⸗): ⲤⲰⲘⲦ̄
ⲤⲞⲞ⸗: ⲤⲰ
ⲤⲞⲞⲔ: ⲤⲞⲔ
ⲤⲞⲞⲔⲈ: ⲤⲒⲔⲈ
ⲤⲞⲞⲦ⸗: ⲤⲰⲦ
ⲤⲞⲞⲦ⸗: ⲤⲰⲦⲈ
ⲤⲞⲞⲦ: ⲤⲞⲦ
ⲤⲞⲞⲦ⸗: ⲤⲒⲚⲈ
ⲤⲞⲞⲦⲈ: ⲤⲒⲦⲈ
ⲤⲞⲞⲨϨⲤ̄⸗: ⲤⲰⲞⲨϨ
ⲤⲞⲞϤ(⸗): ⲤⲰⲰϤ
ⲤⲞⲢⲘⲈⲤ: ⲤⲰⲢⲘ̄
ⲤⲞⲢϤ̄: ⲤⲞⲖϤ̄
ⲤⲞⲦ⸗: ⲤⲰⲦⲈ
ⲤⲞⲦ⸗: ⲤⲒⲚⲈ
ⲤⲞⲦⲈ: ⲤⲀⲦⲈ
ⲤⲞⲦⲈ: ⲤⲎⲦ

cⲟⲧⲉ: ⲥⲓⲧⲉ   cⲣⲁⲣⲟⲟⲩⲉ: ⲗⲣⲟⲟⲩⲉ   cⲱⲗϥ: ⲥⲟⲗϥ
cⲟⲧϥ̄: ⲥⲟⲧⲃⲉϥ   cⲣⲁⲧ⸗: ⲥⲣⲓⲧ   cⲱⲙⲅ̄: ⲥⲱⲛⲕ̄
cⲟⲧ₂ϥ̄: ⲥⲟⲧⲃⲉϥ   cⲣⲃⲉ: ⲥⲣ̄ϥⲉ   cⲱⲙⲕ̄: ⲥⲱⲛⲕ̄
cⲟⲩ(-): ⲥⲱ   cⲣⲃⲛ̄ⲛⲉ: ⲃⲛ̄ⲛⲉ   cⲱⲙⲛ̄ⲧ: ⲥⲱⲙⲧ̄
cⲟⲩ-: ϣⲟⲩ   cⲣⲉϥⲣⲓϥⲉ: ⲥⲣⲟϥϥ̄   cⲱⲛⲅ̄: ⲥⲱⲛⲕ̄
cⲟⲩ-: ⲥⲓⲟⲩ, ⲥⲏⲩ   cⲣ̄ⲙⲉ: ⲥⲱⲣⲙ̄   cⲱⲡⲉ: ⲥⲱⲃⲉ
cⲟⲩⲗ: ⲥⲏⲩ   cⲣⲟⲃⲣⲉⲃ: ⲥⲣⲟϥϥ̄   cⲱⲱⲛⲧ̄: ⲥⲱⲛⲧ
cⲟⲩⲃⲛ̄ⲛⲉ: ⲃⲛ̄ⲛⲉ   cⲣⲟⲃⲧ̄: ⲥⲣ̄ϥⲉ   cⲱ̄ϣ-: ⲥⲱϣ
cⲟⲩⲉⲗⲟⲩⲱⲗ⸗: ⲥⲟⲩⲟⲗⲟⲩⲗ̄   cⲣⲟϥⲧ̄: ⲥⲣ̄ϥⲉ   cⲱ̄ϣⲉ: ⲥⲃ̄ϣⲉ
cⲟⲩⲉⲛ-: ⲥⲟⲟⲩⲛ̄   cⲣϥⲣⲓⲃⲉ: ⲥⲣⲟϥϥ̄   cⲱϣⲉ: ϣϣⲉ
cⲟⲩⲗⲱⲗ(⸗): ⲥⲟⲩⲟⲗⲟⲩⲗ̄   cⲥ̄-: ⲥⲱϣ   cⲱ̄ϣⲛⲉ: ϣⲥ̄ⲛⲉ
cⲟⲩⲛ̄-: ⲥⲟⲟⲩⲛ̄   cⲧⲁⲁⲧⲉ: ⲧⲁⲁⲧⲉ   cⲱⲟⲧ: ⲥⲭⲁⲧ
cⲟⲩ-ⲟⲩⲏⲣ: ⲟⲩⲏⲣ   cⲧⲁⲓ-: ⲥⲧⲟⲓ   cⲱ̄ϣϥⲉ: ⲥⲁϣϥ̄
cⲟⲩⲥⲟⲟⲩϣⲉ: ϣⲟⲩⲥⲟⲟⲩϣⲉ   cⲧⲉ-: ⲧⲥ̄ⲧⲟ   cϣ̄ϭⲣⲁ₂ⲧ̄: ⲥϭ̄ⲣⲁ₂ⲧ̄
cⲟⲩⲧⲛ̄-: ⲥⲟⲟⲩⲧⲛ̄   cⲧⲉ-: ⲥⲧⲟⲓ   c₂ⲁⲓⲥ⸗: ⲥ₂ⲁⲓ
cⲟⲩⲧⲱⲛ(-/⸗): ⲥⲟⲟⲩⲧⲛ̄   cⲧ̄ⲉⲓⲱ₂ⲉ: ⲉⲓⲱ₂ⲉ   c₂ⲁⲓⲧ⸗: ⲥ₂ⲁⲓ
cⲟⲩⲱⲛ-/⸗: ⲥⲟⲟⲩⲛ̄   cⲧⲏⲩ: ⲧⲥ̄ⲧⲟ   c₂ⲁⲧ: ⲥⲭⲁⲧ
cⲟϥ⸗: ⲥⲱⲱϥ   c†-: ⲥⲧⲟⲓ   c₂ⲏⲧ: ⲥ₂ⲁⲓ
cⲟⲧⲉ: ⲥⲟⲃⲧⲉ   cⲧ̄ⲙⲏⲧ: ⲥⲱⲧⲙ̄   c₂ⲟⲩⲟⲣⲧ: ⲥⲁ₂ⲟⲩ
cⲟ₂ⲉ: ⲥⲟⲟ₂ⲉ   cⲧⲟ(⸗): ⲧⲥ̄ⲧⲟ(⸗)   c₂ⲟⲩⲣ̄-: ⲥⲁ₂ⲟⲩ
cⲡ̄-: ⲥⲟⲡ   cⲧⲱ₂ⲉ: ⲉⲓⲱ₂ⲉ   c₂ⲟⲩⲱⲣ⸗: ⲥⲁ₂ⲟⲩ
cⲡ̄c̄-: ⲥⲟⲡⲥ̄   cⲉⲟ: ⲧⲥ̄ⲧⲟ   cⲉⲓⲙ: ⲥⲕⲓⲙ
cⲣ̄-: ⲥⲟⲩⲣ   cⲱⲕ: ⲥⲟⲕ   cⲉⲟⲗ: ϣϭⲟⲣ

ⲧ

ⲧ-, ⲧⲉ- def. art. fem. sing.; see 1.3.

ⲧⲁ- absolute rel. fem. sing.; see 22.2.

ⲧⲁⲁⲧⲉ (ⲧⲟⲟⲧⲉ) vb. intr. to shine (with: ⲙ̄ⲙⲟ⸗; ± ⲉⲃⲟⲗ).

ⲧⲁⲁⲧⲉ, ⲥⲧⲁⲁⲧⲉ vb. tr. to clap (hands); to spread (ⲙ̄ⲙⲟ⸗).

ⲧⲁⲃⲓⲣ n.m. sanctuary (of the temple).

ⲧⲁⲉⲓⲟ (ⲧⲁⲓⲟ) ⲧⲁⲉⲓⲉ- (ⲧⲁⲓⲉ-) ⲧⲁⲉⲓⲟ⸗ (ⲧⲁⲓⲟ⸗) Q ⲧⲁⲉⲓⲏⲩ, ⲧⲁⲏⲩ
    vb. tr. to honor, pay respect to (ⲙ̄ⲙⲟ⸗); to esteem,
    have high regard for, regard as precious; Q to be
    honored, esteemed, excellent, valuable, precious; as
    n.m. honor, honored state; complimentary gift. ⲣⲉϥ-
    ⲧⲁⲉⲓⲟ honored person. †-ⲧⲁⲉⲓⲟ (ⲛⲁ⸗) to honor, give com-
    plimentary gift to. ϫⲓ-ⲧⲁⲉⲓⲟ to receive honor or gift.

ⲧⲁⲓ adv. here, in this place.

ⲧⲁⲓⲃⲉ, ⲧⲏⲏⲃⲉ, ⲧⲏⲃⲉ n.f. chest, coffin; pouch, pocket.

ⲧⲁⲕⲟ ⲧⲁⲕⲉ- ⲧⲁⲕⲟ⸗ Q ⲧⲁⲕⲏⲩ (ⲧⲁⲕⲏⲩⲧ) vb. tr. to destroy, put
    an end to (ⲙ̄ⲙⲟ⸗); vb. intr. to perish, be lost, des-
    troyed; as n.m. perdition, destruction. ⲁⲧⲧⲁⲕⲟ

indestructible, imperishable; ⲙⲛ̄ⲧⲁⲧⲧⲁⲕⲟ incorruptibility. ⲣⲉϥⲧⲁⲕⲟ (1) destroyer; (2) perishable.

ⲧⲁⲗ, ⲧⲟⲗ n.m. heap, hillock.

ⲧⲁⲗⲟ (ⲧⲁⲗⲉ, ⲧⲁⲣⲟ) ⲧⲁⲗⲉ- ⲧⲁⲗⲟ⸗ Q ⲧⲁⲗⲏⲩ vb. tr. (± ⲉϩⲣⲁⲓ) to lift, raise up, offer up, send up (ⲙ̄ⲙⲟ⸗; upon: ⲉϫⲛ̄, ϩⲓϫⲛ̄); to cause to mount (an animal); to take aboard; to weave (ⲙ̄ⲙⲟ⸗); vb. intr. to go up, ascend, mount, board; as n.m. raising up, offering.

ⲧⲁⲗϭⲟ ⲧⲁⲗϭⲉ- ⲧⲁⲗϭⲟ⸗ Q ⲧⲁⲗϭⲏⲩ vb. tr. to heal, cure (ⲙ̄ⲙⲟ⸗; of, from: ϩⲛ̄, ⲉⲃⲟⲗ ϩⲛ̄); vb. intr. to become healed; as n.m. curing, healing. ⲁⲧⲧⲁⲗϭⲟ incurable. ⲣⲉϥⲧⲁⲗϭⲟ healer. ⲣⲉϥϯ-ⲧⲁⲗϭⲟ idem. ⲙⲛ̄ⲧⲣⲉϥⲧⲁⲗϭⲟ healing power.

ⲧⲁⲙⲓⲟ ⲧⲁⲙⲓⲉ- ⲧⲁⲙⲓⲟ⸗ Q ⲧⲁⲙⲓⲏⲩ vb. tr. to create, make (ⲙ̄ⲙⲟ⸗); to prepare, make ready; as n.m. thing made, creation.

ⲧⲁⲙⲟ ⲧⲁⲙⲉ- ⲧⲁⲙⲟ⸗ vb. tr. to tell, inform (someone: ⲙ̄ⲙⲟ⸗; thing told: ⲉ, ⲉⲧⲃⲉ; that: ϫⲉ).

ⲧⲁⲛⲟ ⲧⲉⲛⲁ- (ⲧⲛⲁ-) ⲧⲁⲛⲟ⸗ vb. tr. to make, create (ⲙ̄ⲙⲟ⸗); to draw up (a deed).

ⲧⲁⲛϩⲟ ⲧⲁⲛϩⲉ- ⲧⲁⲛϩⲟ⸗ Q ⲧⲁⲛϩⲏⲩ vb. tr. to bring to life, keep alive, let live (ⲙ̄ⲙⲟ⸗); vb. intr. to become alive; as n.m. keeping alive, saving. ⲣⲉϥⲧⲁⲛϩⲟ savior, life-giver; ⲙⲛ̄ⲧⲣⲉϥⲧⲁⲛϩⲟ life-saving.

ⲧⲁⲛϩⲟⲩⲧ ⲧⲁⲛϩⲉⲧ- ⲧⲁⲛϩⲟⲩⲧ⸗ Q ⲧⲁⲛϩⲏⲩⲧ vb. tr. to believe, trust (ⲙ̄ⲙⲟ⸗; that: ϫⲉ); to entrust (ⲙ̄ⲙⲟ⸗; to: ⲉ, ⲉϫⲛ̄; also reflex.); to confide (in: ⲙⲛ̄).

ⲧⲁⲡ n.m. horn, trumpet. ⲡⲁ-ⲡⲧⲁⲡ ⲛ̄ ⲟⲩⲱⲧ unicorn. ϩⲟϥ ⲛ̄ ⲧⲁⲡ horned snake. ⲁϣ-ⲧⲁⲡ to sound trumpet; as n.m. trumpet blast.

ⲧⲁⲡⲛ̄, ⲧⲉⲡⲛ̄, ⲧⲉⲡⲛⲉ n. cumin.

ⲧⲁⲡⲣⲟ n.f. mouth; also fig. of well, sword, tomb. (ⲛ̄) ⲧⲁⲡⲣⲟ ϩⲓ ⲧⲁⲡⲣⲟ mouth to mouth, face to face.

ⲧⲁⲣ n.m. sprig, branch.

ⲧⲁⲣⲕⲟ (ⲧⲉⲣⲕⲟ) ⲧⲁⲣⲕⲉ- ⲧⲁⲣⲕⲟ⸗ (ⲧⲉⲣⲕⲟ⸗, ⲧⲣ̄ⲕⲟ⸗) vb. tr. to adjure, cause to swear (ⲙ̄ⲙⲟ⸗; by: ⲙ̄ⲙⲟ⸗, ⲕⲁⲧⲁ, ⲉ).

ⲧⲁⲩⲟ (ⲧⲁⲟⲩⲟ) ⲧⲁⲩⲉ- (ⲧⲁⲟⲩⲉ-) ⲧⲁⲩⲟ⸗ vb. tr. (1) ± ⲉⲃⲟⲗ: to

send, send forth (ⲙⲙⲟ⸗; to: ⲉ, ⲛⲁ⸗, ϣⲁ; after, for: ⲛ̄ⲥⲁ);
to put forth, produce; (2) to cast (ⲙⲙⲟ⸗; forth: ⲉⲃⲟⲗ;
down: ⲉⲡⲉⲥⲏⲧ, ⲉ₂ⲣⲁⲓ); (3) to tell, proclaim, repeat,
recite (ⲙⲙⲟ⸗; to: ⲉ, ⲉⲧⲛ̄, ⲛⲁ⸗). As n.m. mission; +
ⲉⲃⲟⲗ: product. ⲁⲧⲧⲁⲩⲟ indescribable, inexplicable.

ⲧⲁϣⲟ ⲧⲁϣⲉ- ⲧⲁϣⲟ⸗ vb. tr. to increase (ⲙⲙⲟ⸗); ⲧⲁϣⲉ- + Inf.
to do something much, more; increase in doing.

ⲧⲁϥ n.m. spittle. ⲛⲉⲝ-/ⲥⲉⲧ-ⲧⲁϥ to spit.

ⲧⲁ2ⲟ ⲧⲁ2ⲉ- ⲧⲁ2ⲟ⸗ Q ⲧⲁ2ⲏⲩ vb. tr. to cause to stand, set up,
create (ⲙⲙⲟ⸗); to reach, attain, meet, catch up to
(ⲙⲙⲟ⸗); to arrest; to befall (someone: obj. suff.; that:
ⲉ, ⲉⲧⲣⲉ); to assign (ⲙⲙⲟ⸗; to: ⲉ); vb. intr. to be able,
to manage (to do: ⲉ + Inf.). ⲁⲧⲧⲁ2ⲟ⸗ unattainable, incomprehensible; ⲙⲛ̄ⲧⲁⲧⲧⲁ2ⲟ⸗ incomprehensibility. ⲣⲉϥ-
ⲧⲁ2ⲉ- catcher. ⲧⲁ2ⲉ (ⲉ)ⲣⲁⲧ⸗ to set up, establish
(ⲙⲙⲟ⸗); as n.m. establishment, right order.

ⲧⲁ2ⲧ̄, ⲧⲁ2ⲧ2̄, ⲧⲁⲑ n.m. lead.

ⲧⲁ2ⲧ2̄ (ⲧⲁ2ⲧ̄) ⲧⲉ2ⲧⲱ2⸗ Q ⲧⲉ2ⲧⲱ2 vb. tr. to mix, confuse
(ⲙⲙⲟ⸗); as n.m. mixture, confusion.

ⲧⲁⲝⲟ vb. tr. to judge, condemn; as n.m. judgement.

ⲧⲁⲭⲣⲟ ⲧⲁⲭⲣⲉ- ⲧⲁⲭⲣⲟ⸗ Q ⲧⲁⲭⲣⲏⲩ (ⲧⲁⲭⲣⲁⲉⲓⲧ) vb. tr. to strengthen, affirm, confirm, make fast (ⲙⲙⲟ⸗; in, with: 2ⲛ̄;
on, to: ⲉ, ⲉⲭⲛ̄); to direct firmly (ⲙⲙⲟ⸗; toward: ⲉ); vb.
intr. to become strengthened, resolute; to rely (on:
ⲉⲭⲛ̄); as n.m. firmness, strength, resoluteness; 2ⲛ̄ ⲟⲩ-
ⲧⲁⲭⲣⲟ firmly, certainly. ϯ-ⲧⲁⲭⲣⲟ to give strength.
ⲭⲓ-ⲧⲁⲭⲣⲟ to receive confirmation.

ⲧⲁ6, ⲧⲁⲕ n.m. lump, cake.

ⲧⲁ6ⲥⲉ, ⲧⲁⲧⲥⲉ n.f. sole of foot; foot-print. ϣⲥ̄-ⲛ̄-ⲧⲁ6ⲥⲉ
n.f. foot-print. ⲭⲓ-ⲧⲁ6ⲥⲉ ⲛ̄ⲥⲁ to follow. ⲁⲧⲭⲓ-ⲧⲁ6ⲥⲉ
not to be tracked.

ⲧⲃⲁ n.m. ten thousand; see 30.7. 6ⲓⲥⲧⲃⲁ five thousand.

ⲧⲃ̄ⲃⲟ ⲧⲃ̄ⲃⲉ- ⲧⲃ̄ⲃⲟ⸗ Q ⲧⲃ̄ⲃⲏⲩ vb. tr. to make pure, purify
(ⲙⲙⲟ⸗: of, from: ⲉ, ⲉⲃⲟⲗ 2ⲛ̄, 2ⲁ); vb. intr. to become
pure, clean, clear; as n.m. purity, purification; 2ⲛ̄

oyⲧⲃ̄ⲃo in a ritually pure way; ⲙⲁ ⲛ̄ ⲧⲃ̄ⲃo place of
purification.

ⲧⲃⲏⲣ n.m. a kick. ⲛⲉⲭ-ⲧⲃⲏⲣ ⲉⲃoⲗ to give a kick. ϯ-ⲧⲃⲏⲣ
to kick (at: ⲉ₂oyⲛ ⲉ/₂ⲛ̄); ⲣⲉϥϯ-ⲧⲃⲏⲣ kicker.

ⲧⲃ̄ⲕⲉ- ⲧⲃ̄ⲕo⸗ to send.

ⲧⲃ̄ⲛⲏ (pl. ⲧⲃ̄ⲛooyⲉ, ⲧⲉⲃⲛⲏoy, ⲧⲩⲛⲏy, ⲧⲃ̄ⲛⲉy) n.m. beast, do-
mestic animal. ⲡⲁ-ⲛ̄ⲧⲃ̄ⲛⲏ cattleman. ⲙⲛ̄ⲧⲧⲃ̄ⲛⲏ bestial
nature. ⲣⲉϥⲥⲁⲛⲟ̄ⲟ̄-ⲧⲃ̄ⲛⲏ cattle-breeder.

ⲧⲃ̄ⲧ, ⲧⲏⲃ̄ⲧ, ⲧⲏϥⲧ̄ n.m. fish. ϭⲛ̄-ⲧⲃ̄ⲧ to catch fish; ⲣⲉϥϭⲛ̄-
ⲧⲃ̄ⲧ fisherman. ⲥⲁ ⲛ̄ ⲧⲃ̄ⲧ fish-monger.

ⲧⲉ fem. sing. pron. and copula; see 5.1.

ⲧⲉ, ⲧⲏ n.m. time, season, age. ⲛ̄/₂ⲙ̄ ⲡⲉϥⲧⲉ at the proper
time. ⲉⲓ ⲉ ⲡⲧⲉ to come of age. ⲣ̄-ⲧⲉ idem.

ⲧⲉⲗⲏⲗ vb. intr. to rejoice (over: ⲉⲭⲛ̄); also used reflex.
with ⲙ̄ⲙo⸗; as n.m. joy.

ⲧⲉⲣⲡoⲥⲉⲛ, ⲧⲉⲣⲡoⲥⲉ n.f. baked brick.

ⲧⲉ₂ⲛⲉ n.f. forehead.

ⲧⲉϭⲧⲱϭ Q to be pressed down.

ⲧⲏⲏⲃⲉ, ⲧⲏⲃⲉ, ⲧⲉⲃⲉ n.m. finger, toe; as measure: finger's
breadth, any small quantity.

ⲧⲏⲛⲉ n.m. dam, dike.

ⲧⲏⲣ⸗ adj. all, all of, the whole, every; normally follows
noun in apposition; see 16.4. ⲡⲧⲏⲣϥ̄ the whole of creation, everything; the All (Gnostic); ⲉ ⲡⲧⲏⲣϥ̄ wholly,
completely, (not) at all.

ⲧⲏy, ⲧⲏoy, ⲧⲉy (ⲧoy-) n.m. wind, breath. ⲧoy-ⲣⲏⲥ south-
wind. ⲕⲱ ⲙ̄ ⲡⲧⲏy, ⲕⲁ-ⲡⲧⲏy to die; ⲛⲉⲭ-ⲧⲏy ⲉⲃoⲗ idem.
ⲁⲛⲟ̄ⲟ̄-/ⲁⲛ₂̄-ⲧⲏy, ⲥⲉⲕ-ⲧⲏy to breathe, draw breath. ₂ⲛ-ⲧⲏy
n.m. breeze. ₂ⲁ-ⲧⲏy n.f. whirlwind. ⲭⲓⲛⲧⲏy n. wind-
blight; ⲣ̄-ⲭⲓⲛⲧⲏy to become blighted by the wind.

ϯ (ⲧⲉⲓ, ϯⲓ, ϯⲉⲓ) ϯ- ⲧⲁⲁ⸗ (ϯ⸗) Q ⲧo (ⲧⲱ) (imptv. ⲙⲁ ⲙⲁ-
ⲙⲁⲧ⸗, ⲙⲏⲉⲓ⸗) vb. tr. to give (ⲙ̄ⲙo⸗; to: ⲛⲁ⸗, ⲉ); to
pay out; to sell (for: ₂ⲁ); to put, place; vb. reflex.
to go, betake self (to: ⲉ, ⲉⲣⲛ̄, ⲉ₂oyⲛ ⲉⲣⲛ̄, ⲉ₂oyⲛ ⲉ), to
begin (to do: ⲉ, ⲉⲧⲣⲉ); vb. intr. to move, go; Q impers.

cто it suits, befits (someone: ɴⲁ⸗; to do: ⲉ + Inf.).
As n.m. gift, bounty; ⲣⲉϥϯ giver, fighter; ⲙⲛ̄ⲧⲣⲉϥϯ gen-
erosity; ⲣ̄-ⲣⲉϥϯ to become a giver. ⲧⲁⲓ- (p.c.) one who
gives. ϫⲓ-ϯ to buy and sell; to hesitate; as n.m. exchange. *Transitive idioms* (obj. ⲙ̄ⲙⲟ⸗): ⲉⲧⲛ̄, ⲛ̄ⲧⲛ̄: to entrust to, to enjoin, command. ⲉϫⲛ̄: to add to, apply to.
ⲍ ⲓ: to dress in, put on, don (Q ⲧⲟ ⲍ ⲓ being worn by).
ⲉⲃⲟⲗ: to sell, give away. ⲉⲡⲉⲥⲏⲧ: to put down (into: ⲉ).
ⲉⲍⲟⲩⲛ: to hand in, give in; to invest. ⲉⲍⲣⲁⲓ: to send,
give up (to: ⲉ). *Intransitive idioms*: ⲉϫⲛ: to fight
for. ⲙⲛ̄: to fight against, struggle with. ⲛ̄ⲥⲁ: to pursue. ⲟⲩⲃⲉ: to fight against. ⲉⲟ̄ⲏ: to move forward.
ⲉⲍⲟⲩⲛ ⲉ to strike upon, against; to oppose. For cpds.
with ϯ- see 2nd element.
ϯⲃⲉ̄, ⲧⲉⲃⲉ̄, ⲧⲃ̄ⲥ n.f. heel; ϫⲓ-ϯⲃⲉ̄ to trip (ⲙ̄ⲙⲟ⸗); ⲙⲛ̄ⲧϫⲓ-ϯⲃⲉ̄
tripping.
ϯⲙⲉ, ⲧⲓⲙⲉ (pl. ⲧⲙⲉ) n.m. village, town. ⲣⲙ̄ϯⲙⲉ villager.
ϯⲟⲩ (f. ϯⲉ, ϯ) number: five. ⲙⲛ̄ⲧⲏ fifteen. ⲧⲁⲉⲓⲟⲩ,
ⲧⲁⲓⲟⲩ fifty. ⲙⲉⲍϯⲟⲩ fifth. ⲙⲉⲍⲧⲁⲓⲟⲩ fiftieth.
ϯⲡⲉ n.f. loins.
ϯⲍⲉ, Q ⲧⲁⲍⲉ vb. intr. to become intoxicated (with: ⲍⲁ, ⲙ̄ⲙⲟ⸗,
ⲍⲛ̄); as n.m. drunkenness. ⲣⲉϥϯⲍⲉ drunkard.
ϯⲍⲙⲉⲍ n.m. box; bee-hive.
ϯⲥⲉ n.f. gourd, vegetables. ⲙⲁ ⲛ̄ ⲍⲁⲣⲉⲍ ⲛ̄ ϯ-ⲥⲉ gourd-bed.
ⲧⲕⲁⲥ, ⲕⲁⲥ n.m. pain. ϯ-ⲧⲕⲁⲥ to give pain (to: ⲉ); as
n.m. pain.
ⲧⲗⲏ n. drop; ⲏⲣⲡ̄ ⲛ̄ ⲧⲗⲏ filtered wine.
ⲧⲗⲟⲙ, ⲧⲗⲟⲟⲙ, ⲧⲛⲟⲙ n.m. furrow.
ⲧⲗ̄ⲧⲗ̄ vb. tr. to let drip (ⲙ̄ⲙⲟ⸗); intr. to drip. ⲧⲗ̄ⲧⲓⲗⲉ
n.f. drop.
ⲧⲙ̄- negative prefix for Temporal, Conjunctive, Conditional,
and Infinitives. See Gr. In.
ⲧⲙⲁⲉⲓⲟ (ⲧⲙⲁⲓⲟ) ⲧⲙⲁⲉⲓⲉ- (ⲧⲙⲁⲓⲉ-) ⲧⲙⲁⲉⲓⲟ⸗ (ⲧⲙⲁⲓⲟ⸗) Q ⲧⲙⲁⲉⲓⲏⲩ
(ⲧⲙⲁⲓⲏⲩ) vb. tr. to justify (ⲙ̄ⲙⲟ⸗), to regard or hold
as justified; intr. to become justified; as n.m.

justification.

ⲧⲙⲏ n.f. reed mat. ⲥⲁ₂ⲧ̄-(ⲧ)ⲙⲏ mat-weaver.

ⲧⲙ̄ⲙⲟ (ⲧⲙⲟ) ⲧⲙ̄ⲙⲉ- (ⲧⲙⲉ-) ⲧⲙ̄ⲙⲟ⸗ (ⲧⲙ̄ⲙⲉ⸗, ⲧⲙⲟ⸗) Q ⲧⲙ̄ⲙⲏⲩ vb. tr. to feed, nourish (ⲙ̄ⲙⲟ⸗; with: ⲙ̄ⲙⲟ⸗, ₂ⲛ̄). ⲧⲙ̄ⲙⲉ⸗ ⲟⲉⲓⲕ to feed (someone) bread.

ⲧⲙ̄ⲧⲙ̄ ⲧⲙ̄ⲧⲙ̄- Q ⲧⲙ̄ⲧⲱⲙ vb. intr. to become heavy; + ⲉⲃⲟⲗ: to resound, reverberate.

ⲧⲙ̄₂ⲟ ⲧⲙ̄₂ⲉ- ⲧⲙ̄₂ⲟ⸗ vb. tr. to kindle, set afire (ⲙ̄ⲙⲟ⸗); intr. to burn, blaze; as n.m. burning, heat.

ⲧⲛ̄ⲛⲟ (ⲧⲛⲟ, ⲧⲛⲁ) ⲧⲛ̄ⲛⲟ⸗ (ⲧⲛⲟ⸗, ⲧⲁⲛⲁ⸗) Q ⲧⲛ̄ⲛⲏⲩ vb. tr. to pound, tread down (ⲙ̄ⲙⲟ⸗); intr. to be beaten, trodden; Q to be contrite; as n.m. breaking, contrition.

ⲧⲛ̄ⲛⲟⲟⲩ ⲧⲛ̄ⲛⲉⲩ- (ⲧⲛⲉⲩ-) ⲧⲛ̄ⲛⲟⲟⲩ⸗ (ⲧⲛ̄ⲛⲟⲟⲩⲧ⸗, ⲧⲛⲟⲟⲩ⸗) vb. tr. to send (ⲙ̄ⲙⲟ⸗; to: ⲉ, ⲉⲣⲁⲧ⸗, ⲛⲁ⸗, ϣⲁ; for, after: ⲛ̄ⲥⲁ); also w. ⲉⲃⲟⲗ, ⲉ₂ⲟⲩⲛ, ⲉ₂ⲣⲁⲓ.

ⲧⲛ̄₂, ⲧⲛⲁ₂, ⲧⲉⲛⲁ₂ n.m. wing, fin; also fig. of building, ship, etc. ⲣ̄-ⲧⲛ̄₂ to become winged. ⲣⲉⲧ-ⲧⲛ̄₂ (Q ⲣⲏⲧ ⲛ̄ ⲧⲛ̄₂) idem. ⲭⲓ-ⲧⲛ̄₂ to take wing.

ⲧⲟⲃⲧⲉ̄ ⲧⲉ̄ⲧⲉ̄- ⲧⲉ̄ⲧⲱⲃ⸗ vb. tr. to form, fashion, fabricate.

ⲧⲟⲉ, ⲧⲟ, ⲧⲟⲓⲉ, ⲧⲁ, ⲧⲁⲉ n.f. part, portion, share. ⲭⲓ-ⲧⲟⲉ to partake of (₂ⲛ̄). ⲙⲁⲓ-ⲧⲟⲉ ⲛ̄ ₂ⲟⲩⲟ covetous. ⲙⲛ̄ⲧⲙⲁⲓ-ⲧⲟⲉ ⲛ̄ ₂ⲟⲩⲟ covetousness.

ⲧⲟⲉ, ⲧⲟ n.f. spot. ⲣ̄-ⲧⲟ (Q ⲟ ⲛ̄ ⲧⲟ) to become spotted.

ⲧⲟⲉⲓⲥ, ⲧⲟⲓⲥ, ⲧⲟⲉⲓⲥⲉ n.f. piece of cloth, patch, rag; purse.

ⲧⲟⲉⲓⲧ vb. intr. to mourn (for: ⲉ, ⲉⲭⲛ̄); as n.m. lament.

ⲧⲟⲓⲗⲉ vb. intr. to rise up.

ⲧⲟⲕ, ⲧⲟⲉ n.m. knife, razor.

ⲧⲟⲙ n.m. reed mat.

ⲧⲟⲛⲧⲛ̄ ⲧⲛ̄ⲧⲛ̄- ⲧⲛ̄ⲧⲱⲛ⸗ Q ⲧⲛ̄ⲧⲱⲛ (ⲧⲛ̄ⲧⲟⲛⲧ̄) (1) vb. tr. to liken, compare (ⲙ̄ⲙⲟ⸗; to: ⲉ, ⲙⲛ̄, ⲉⲭⲛ̄); intr. to be like, comparable to. (2) vb. tr. to estimate (ⲙ̄ⲙⲟ⸗, ⲉ), speculate about. As n.m. likeness, similitude; oracle. †-ⲧⲟⲛⲧⲛ̄ to guess, surmise. ⲁⲧⲧⲟⲛⲧⲛ̄ without comparison. ⲣⲉϥⲧⲟⲛⲧⲛ̄ diviner.

ⲧⲟⲛ₂⸗ Q ⲧⲟⲛ₂̄ vb. reflex. to become entangled (in: ⲉ); to

converse (with: мⲛ̄).

ⲧⲟⲟⲃⲉϥ n.m. foliage.

ⲧⲟⲟⲧⲉ (ⲧⲁⲁⲧⲉ) vb. tr. to turn; intr. idem (ⲉⲡⲁ₂ⲟⲩ: back).

ⲧⲟⲟⲩ n.m. mountain; monastery; desert cemetery; as adj.
hill-, wild, desert-. ⲣⲙ̄ⲛ̄ⲧⲟⲟⲩ mountain man. ₂ⲁⲛⲧⲟⲟⲩ
n.m. mountainous country. ⲧⲟⲩⲉⲓⲏ pl. of ⲧⲟⲟⲩ.

ⲧⲟⲟⲩ ⲧⲉⲩ- ⲧⲟⲟⲩ⁼ vb. tr. to buy.

ⲧⲟⲟⲩⲉ n.m. shoe, sandal; pair of shoes. ⲙⲟⲩⲥ ⲛ̄ ⲧⲟⲟⲩⲉ shoe-
lace. ⲋⲟⲡ ⲛ̄ ⲧⲟⲟⲩ shoe-sole.

ⲧⲟⲟⲩⲧⲉ ⲧⲟⲩⲏⲧ⁼ Q ⲧⲟⲩⲏⲧ vb. tr. to collect, gather.

ⲧⲟⲡ, ⲧⲱⲡ n.m. edge, border, hem; keel; bosom, embrace.

ⲧⲟⲣⲧⲣ̄ ⲧⲣ̄ⲧⲣ̄- ⲧⲣ̄ⲧⲱⲣ⁼ Q ⲧⲣ̄ⲧⲱⲣ vb. tr. to drive in (nail, sword:
ⲙ̄ⲙⲟ⁼; into: ⲉ, ₂ⲛ̄); to pierce (ⲙ̄ⲙⲟ⁼, ⲉ).

ⲧⲟⲩⲁ n.m.f. doorpost, lintel.

ⲧⲟⲩⲉⲓⲟ (ⲧⲟⲩⲓⲟ) ⲧⲟⲩⲓⲟ⁼ vb. tr. to repay, give back (ⲙ̄ⲙⲟ⁼);
as n.m. repayment. ⲭⲱⲱⲙⲉ ⲛ̄ ⲧⲟⲩⲉⲓⲟ bill of divorce.

(ⲧⲟⲩⲛⲟ) ⲧⲟⲩⲛ- (ⲧⲟⲩⲛⲉ-) ⲧⲟⲩⲛⲟ⁼ (ⲧⲟⲩⲛⲟⲩ⁼) vb. tr. to open.

ⲧⲟⲩⲛⲟⲥ (ⲧⲟⲩⲛⲟⲩⲥ) ⲧⲟⲩⲛⲉⲥ- ⲧⲟⲩⲛⲟⲥ⁼ vb. tr. to awaken, raise
up, set up (ⲙ̄ⲙⲟ⁼; from: ⲉⲃⲟⲗ ₂ⲛ̄); to incite (ⲙ̄ⲙⲟ⁼; against:
ⲉⲝⲛ̄); as n.m. raising; ⲣⲉϥⲧⲟⲩⲛⲉⲥ- one who raises.

ⲧⲟⲩⲟ ⲧⲟⲩⲟ⁼ vb. tr. to show, teach (to someone: ⲙ̄ⲙⲟ⁼; something: ⲉ; or vice versa); intr. to learn. Also = ⲧⲁⲩⲟ.

ⲧⲟⲩⲱ⁼ n. bosom. ⲉⲧⲟⲩⲛ̄-, ⲉⲧⲟⲩⲉⲛ-; ⲉⲧⲟⲩⲱ⁼ prep. at, near,
beside. ₂ⲓⲧⲟⲩⲛ̄-, ₂ⲓⲧⲟⲩⲉⲛ-; ₂ⲓⲧⲟⲩⲱ⁼ idem.

ⲧⲟⲩⲱⲧ, ⲧⲟⲩⲟⲟⲧⲉ n.m. pillar; idol.

ⲧⲟⲩⲭⲟ ⲧⲟⲩⲭⲉ- ⲧⲟⲩⲭⲟ⁼ Q ⲧⲟⲩⲭⲏⲩ vb. tr. to make whole (ⲙ̄ⲙⲟ⁼);
to save, rescue (from: ⲉ, ⲉⲧⲛ̄, ⲙ̄ⲙⲟ⁼, ₂ⲛ̄, ⲉⲃⲟⲗ ₂ⲛ̄, ₂ⲓⲧⲛ̄);
intr. to be saved, safe; as n.m. safety, salvation.

ⲧⲣⲁ, ⲋⲣⲁ n.f. extremity (of limbs); joint.

ⲧⲣ̄ⲃⲏⲓⲛ, ⲧⲏⲣⲃⲏⲓⲛ, ⲧⲉⲣⲃⲉⲉⲓⲛ, ⲧⲉⲣϥⲉⲉⲓⲛ n.m. papyrus plant.

ⲧⲣⲉ, ⲧⲣⲏ n.m.f. kite (bird).

ⲧⲣⲓⲙ, ⲉⲧⲣⲓⲙ n.m. clover.

ⲧⲣⲓⲣ n.f. oven.

ⲧⲣⲟ ⲧⲣⲉ- vb. tr. to cause to do; rare except as prefix of
inflected (causative) infinitive. See 20.1.

тр̅рє, Q тр̅єıωоү vb. intr. to be afraid (of: ϩнт⸗ н̅).

трωм n.m. hurricane.

тсаво тсаве- (тсеве-) тсаво⸗ (тс̅во⸗) Q тсавнү(т) vb. tr. to make wise, teach, show (м̅мо⸗ of person; є of thing taught or vice versa); as n.m. teaching, instruction. мн̅трєqтсаво teaching. саво (сво) саво⸗ to learn (є).

тсаєıо (тсаıо) тсаıє- тсаєıо⸗ Q тсаıнү vb. tr. to make beautiful.

тсано (тс̅но) тсанє- тсано⸗ Q тсаннү(т) vb. tr. to set in order (м̅мо⸗); to adorn; to furnish, provide; as n.m. propriety, order. маı-тсано⸗ fond of adorning self.

тсв̅ко тсв̅кє- тсв̅ко⸗ Q тсв̅кнү vb. tr. to diminish (м̅мо⸗).

тсєнко (тсн̅ко, сн̅ко) тсєнко⸗ vb. tr. to nurse, suckle (м̅мо⸗); аттсєнко not giving milk (of breasts).

тс̅ıо (тс̅єıо) тс̅ıє- тс̅ıо⸗ Q тс̅ıнү (сıнү) vb. tr. to sate, make satisfied (м̅мо⸗; with: м̅мо⸗, ϩн̅).

тсо тсє- тсо⸗ Q тснү vb. tr. to give a drink to, slake thirst of, water (м̅мо⸗; with: м̅мо⸗); as n.m. watering. ма н̅ тсо drinking-place; рєqтсо drink-giver.

тс̅то (сто, сѳо) тс̅тє- (стє-) тс̅то⸗ (сто⸗) Q тс̅тнү (стнү) vb. tr. to bring back, return (м̅мо⸗); reflex. to go back. тс̅то євол vb. tr. to reject, throw out (м̅мо⸗); as n.m. rejection. тс̅тє євол, стє євол, стєвол n. what is rejected. тс̅то єпаϩоү to turn (м̅мо⸗) back; also reflex. сѳо in ма н̅ сѳо n.m. lodging, retreat.

ттє- тто⸗ vb. tr. to cause to give, require of (м̅мо⸗).

тωвс̅ тєвс̅- (тв̅с-) товс⸗ vb. tr. to goad, incite (м̅мо⸗, є); as n.m. pricking of conscience, compunction.

тωвϩ̅ (тωваϩ) тєвϩ̅- (тв̅ϩ-) товϩ⸗ vb. tr. to pray, make entreaty (to: м̅мо⸗; for: є, єтвє, єϫн̅, єϩраı єϫн̅, ϩа); as n.m. prayer, entreaty. рєqтωвϩ̅ one who prays, suppliant.

тωк тєк- ток⸗ Q тнк vb. tr. to strengthen, confirm (м̅мо⸗); to stiffen, thicken; vb. intr. to become strong, firm, thick; vb. reflex. to strengthen oneself. тωк єϩоүн to persist, be confident (in doing: Circum.); to endure (є).

ϯ-ⲧⲱⲕ to strengthen, fortify (ⲛⲁ⸗). ϫⲓ-ⲧⲱⲕ to take courage. ⲧⲱⲕ ⲛ̄ ϩⲏⲧ intr. to become strong of heart, take courage, rely (upon: ⲉϫⲛ̄, ϩⲛ̄); as n.m. confidence. ϯ-ⲧⲱⲕ ⲛ̄ ϩⲏⲧ to give confidence (to: ⲛⲁ⸗); ϫⲓ-ⲧⲱⲕ ⲛ̄ ϩⲏⲧ to take courage.

ⲧⲱⲕ (ⲧⲱϭⲉ) ⲧⲉⲕ- (ⲧⲕ̄-) ⲧⲉⲕ⸗ Q ⲧⲏⲕ vb. tr. to throw (ⲙ̄ⲙⲟ⸗); ⲧⲱⲕ ⲉⲃⲟⲗ to cast forth, exude (ⲙ̄ⲙⲟ⸗). ⲣⲉϥⲧⲕ̄-ⲥⲟⲧⲉ archer.

ⲧⲱⲕ (ⲧⲱϭ, -ⲉ) ⲧⲟⲕ⸗ (ⲧⲁⲕ⸗, ⲧⲟϭ⸗) vb. tr. (1) to kindle (fire), stoke (oven), obj. w. ⲙ̄ⲙⲟ⸗ or ⲉ. ⲙⲁ ⲛ̄ ⲧⲱⲕ stoke-hole (of bath-house); ⲣⲉϥⲧⲱⲕ stoker. (2) to bake (bread: ⲙ̄ⲙⲟ⸗); as n.m. baking. ⲙⲁ ⲛ̄ ⲧⲱⲕ bakery. ⲧⲓⲕ n.m. spark.

ⲧⲱⲕⲙ̄ ⲧⲉⲕⲙ̄- ⲧⲟⲕⲙ⸗ Q ⲧⲟⲕⲙ̄ (ⲧⲁⲕⲙ̄) vb. tr. to pluck (ⲙ̄ⲙⲟ⸗); to draw (sword). ⲧⲱⲕⲙ̄ ⲛ̄ ϩⲏⲧ to become troubled.

ⲧⲱⲕⲥ̄ (ⲧⲱϭⲥ̄, ⲧⲱⲧⲥ̄) ⲧⲉⲕⲥ̄- ⲧⲟⲕⲥ⸗ (ⲧⲟϭⲥ⸗) Q ⲧⲟⲕⲥ̄ (ⲧⲟϭⲥ̄, ⲧⲟⲧⲥ̄) vb. tr. to pierce, goad, bite (ⲙ̄ⲙⲟ⸗); to drive (nail: ⲙ̄ⲙⲟ⸗; into: ⲉ); to point (finger: ⲙ̄ⲙⲟ⸗; at: ⲉ); Q to be nailed, fastened (to: ⲉ), to be inlaid (with: ⲙ̄ⲙⲟ⸗); to be pierced (with: ϩⲛ̄). ⲧⲱⲕⲥ̄, ⲧⲱϭⲥ̄ n.m. piercing. ⲧⲱϭⲥ̄, ⲧⲟⲟⲧⲥ̄ n.m. a fixed seat. ⲧⲁϩ n.m. molar tooth.

ⲧⲱⲗⲕ̄ ⲧⲟⲗⲕ⸗ vb. tr. to pluck out (ⲙ̄ⲙⲟ⸗).

ⲧⲱⲗⲙ̄ ⲧⲟⲗⲙ⸗ Q ⲧⲟⲗⲙ̄ vb. tr. to defile, besmirch, pollute (ⲙ̄ⲙⲟ⸗); vb. intr. to become defiled etc. (with, by: ϩⲛ̄, ⲙ̄ⲙⲟ⸗); as n.m. stain, pollution. ϯ-ⲧⲱⲗⲙ̄ ⲉ to stain. ⲁⲧⲧⲱⲗⲙ̄ stainless, unpolluted.

ⲧⲱⲗⲥ̄, Q ⲧⲟⲗⲥ̄ vb. intr. to become stuck, sink (in: ⲉ, ϩⲛ̄).

ⲧⲱⲙ ⲧⲉⲙ- (ⲧⲙ̄-) ⲧⲟⲙ⸗ Q ⲧⲏⲙ vb. tr. to close, shut (ⲙ̄ⲙⲟ⸗); vb. intr. idem.

ⲧⲱⲙ, Q ⲧⲏⲙ vb. tr. to sharpen; vb. intr. to become sharp.

ⲧⲱⲙⲛ̄ⲧ (ⲧⲱⲙⲧ̄), Q ⲧⲟⲙⲛ̄ⲧ vb. intr. to meet, befall (someone: ⲉ, ⲉϩⲟⲩⲛ ⲉ); as n.m. meeting, event.

ⲧⲱⲙⲛ̄ⲧ vb. intr. to become amazed, stupefied.

ⲧⲱⲙⲥ̄ ⲧⲉⲙⲥ̄- (ⲧⲙ̄ⲥ-) ⲧⲟⲙⲥ⸗ (ⲧⲟⲙⲉⲥ⸗) Q ⲧⲟⲙⲥ̄ vb. tr. to bury (ⲙ̄ⲙⲟ⸗; in: ⲉ, ϩⲛ̄); ⲙⲁ ⲛ̄ ⲧⲱⲙⲥ̄ burial place.

ⲧⲱⲛ adv. where? how? ⲉ ⲧⲱⲛ whither, where to? ⲛ̄ ⲧⲱⲛ = ⲧⲱⲛ. ⲉⲃⲟⲗ ⲧⲱⲛ whence? ϩⲛ̄ ⲧⲱⲛ where? ϣⲁ ⲧⲱⲛ whither?

ϫⲓⲛ ⲧⲱⲛ from where? ⲣⲙ̄ⲛ̄ⲧⲱⲛ a person from where?

ⲧⲱⲛ in ϯ-ⲧⲱⲛ vb. intr. to quarrel, dispute (with: ⲙⲛ̄, ⲟⲩⲃⲉ, ⲉⲍⲟⲩⲛ ⲉⲍⲣⲛ̄, ⲛ̄ⲛⲁⲍⲣⲛ̄; about: ⲉⲧⲃⲉ, ⲉϫⲛ̄); ϯ-ⲧⲱⲛ as n.m. dispute, strife. ⲁⲧϯ-ⲧⲱⲛ without strife. ⲣⲉϥϯ-ⲧⲱⲛ quarreler; ⲙⲛ̄ⲧⲣⲉϥϯ-ⲧⲱⲛ faction; discrepancy.

ⲧⲱⲛⲟⲩ, ⲧⲱⲛⲉ, ⲧⲱⲛⲁ, ⲧⲟⲛⲟⲩ, ⲧⲟⲛⲱ, ⲧⲟⲛⲛⲉ, ⲧⲟⲛⲛⲟⲩ adv. very, greatly; certainly; ⲥⲉ ⲧⲱⲛⲟⲩ yes indeed.

ⲧⲱⲟⲩⲛ ⲧⲟⲩⲛ- ⲧⲱⲟⲩⲛˢ vb. intr. and reflex. to arise, rise, rise up (± ⲉⲃⲟⲗ, ± ⲉⲍⲣⲁⲓ; against: ⲉ, ⲉϫⲛ̄; from: ⲍⲓ, ⲍⲓϫⲛ̄, ⲍⲛ̄); ⲧⲱⲟⲩⲛ ⲍⲁ to lift up, bear; vb. tr. to raise, carry (ⲙ̄ⲙⲟˢ); as n.m. rising, resurrection (± ⲉⲃⲟⲗ).

ⲧⲱⲡ ⲧⲟⲡˢ vb. tr. to stop up, plug, caulk (ⲙ̄ⲙⲟˢ). ⲙⲉⲍ-ⲧⲱⲡ needle, peg. ⲍⲁⲙ ⲛ̄ ⲧⲱⲡ idem.

ⲧⲱⲡⲉ ⲧⲉⲡ- ⲧⲟⲡˢ (ⲧⲱⲡˢ) vb. tr. to taste (ⲙ̄ⲙⲟˢ). ϯⲡⲉ n.f. taste; ϫⲓ-ϯⲡⲉ to taste (ⲙ̄ⲙⲟˢ); as n.m. tasting.

ⲧⲱⲣⲉ n. willow. ⲃⲱ ⲛ̄ ⲧⲱⲣⲉ willow tree.

ⲧⲱⲣⲉ, ⲧⲟⲣⲉ n.f. (hand); handle; spade, pick, oar. ⲣ̄-ⲧⲱⲣⲉ to clap, stamp. ϭⲛ̄-ⲧⲱⲣⲉ (to grasp hand), to be surety, stand as surety (for: ⲙ̄ⲙⲟˢ; to: ⲛⲁˢ); as n.m. surety; ϫⲓ-ϭⲛ̄-ⲧⲱⲣⲉ to take as surety; ϯ-ϭⲛ̄-ⲧⲱⲣⲉ to give surety; ⲣⲉϥϭⲛ̄-ⲧⲱⲣⲉ guarantor. ϭⲣⲱⲡⲉ, ϭⲧⲟⲣⲉ = ϭⲛ̄-ⲧⲱⲣⲉ; ⲣⲙ̄ϭⲧⲱⲣⲉ guarantor. ⲧⲟⲟⲧˢ hand, in literal sense with many verbs (cf. ⲕⲱ, ⲙⲟⲩⲍ, ⲥⲱⲕ, ⲁⲙⲁⲍⲧⲉ, ⲉⲓⲱ, ⲉⲓⲛⲉ, ⲥⲙⲓⲛⲉ, ⲟⲩⲱⲍ). ⲉⲓⲣⲉ ⲛ̄ ⲁ(ⲡⲁ)ⲧⲟⲟⲧˢ, ⲣ̄-ⲁ(ⲡⲁ)ⲧⲟⲟⲧˢ to endeavor, make an effor (to do: ⲉ, ⲉⲧⲣⲉ). ⲕⲱ ⲛ̄ ⲧⲟⲟⲧˢ ⲉⲃⲟⲗ, ⲕⲁ-ⲧⲟⲟⲧˢ ⲉⲃⲟⲗ to cease (doing: Circum.); to despair; to stay one's hand; ⲁⲧⲕⲁ-ⲧⲟⲟⲧˢ ⲉⲃⲟⲗ unceasing. ϯ ⲛ̄ ⲧⲟⲟⲧˢ, ϯ-ⲧⲟⲟⲧˢ to give a hand, to help; the suff. pron. on ⲧⲟⲟⲧˢ usu. refers to the object, as in ⲁⲓϯ-ⲧⲟⲟⲧϥ̄ I helped him. ϯ-ⲛ̄ ⲧⲟⲟⲧˢ ⲙ̄ⲙⲟˢ/ⲉ to lay hold of, seize (suff. on ⲧⲟⲟⲧˢ is reflex.). ϯ- ⲛ̄ ⲧⲟⲟⲧˢ ⲙⲛ̄ to assist, give aid to. ϯ-ⲧⲟⲟⲧˢ as n.m. help; ⲣⲉϥϯ-ⲧⲟⲟⲧˢ helper, assistant. ϭⲛ̄-ⲧⲟⲟⲧˢ to grasp hand (in greeting, promising etc.); to betroth (obj. suff. of woman; ⲛⲁˢ to man); Q ⲧⲟⲟⲧˢ ϭⲏⲡ ⲛⲁˢ she is betrothed to (see gloss on Lk. 1:27). ⲛ̄ⲥⲁ ⲧⲟⲟⲧˢ adv.

immediately, forthwith (suff. refers to subject of clause). ⲉⲧⲛ̄ (ⲉⲧⲟⲟⲧ⁼) prep. to, into the hand of; freq. with verbs of giving, entrusting, etc. ⲛ̄ⲧⲛ̄ (ⲛ̄ⲧⲟⲟⲧ⁼) prep. (1) from, from the hand of, from by; (2) with, by, beside; in the hand of; (3) because of, through. ⲉⲃⲟⲗ ⲛ̄ⲧⲛ̄ from. ⲛ̄ⲧⲉ = ⲛ̄ⲧⲛ̄. ⲍⲁⲧⲛ̄ (ⲍⲁⲧⲟⲟⲧ⁼) prep. beside, with, near; subject to, under the hand of; virtually inter-changeable with ⲍⲁⲍⲧⲛ̄ q.v. ⲍⲓⲧⲛ̄ (ⲍⲓⲧⲟⲟⲧ⁼) prep. by the hand of, through the agency of, by, from; (of time:) during, after; (of place) out through, from; ± ⲉⲃⲟⲗ: expresses agent after passive verb.

ⲧⲱⲣⲡ̄ ⲧⲉⲣⲡ̄- (ⲧⲣ̄ⲡ-) ⲧⲟⲣⲡ⁼ vb. tr. to seize, rob (ⲙ̄ⲙⲟ⁼; from: ⲛ̄ⲧⲛ̄, ⲍ̄ⲛ̄, ⲍⲓ); to master, acquire; to carry off (to: ⲉ); as n.m. plunder; ⲙⲁⲓ-ⲧⲱⲣⲡ̄ plunder-loving.

ⲧⲱⲣⲡ̄ ⲧⲟⲣⲡ⁼ Q ⲧⲟⲣⲡ̄ vb. tr. to sew, stitch (ⲙ̄ⲙⲟ⁼; to: ⲉ). ⲁⲧⲧⲱⲣⲡ unsewn. ⲛ̄ⲕⲁ ⲛ̄ ⲧⲱⲣⲡ̄ needle. ⲣⲉϥⲧⲱⲣⲡ̄ tailor.

ⲧⲱⲣⲧ̄ n.m. staircase. ⲧⲱⲣⲧⲣ̄, ⲧⲱⲧⲣ̄ n.m. ladder, step, degree.

ⲧⲱⲣϣ̄ vb. intr. to become red; as adj. red. ⲧⲣⲟϣ, Q ⲧⲟⲣϣ̄ to become red. ⲧⲣⲟϣⲣϣ̄ (ⲧⲣⲟϣⲣⲉϣ) Q ⲧⲣ̄ϣⲣⲟϣ (ⲧⲣⲉϣⲣⲟϣ) to become red; as n.m. redness.

ⲧⲱⲣⲍ̄, Q ⲧⲟⲣⲍ̄ (ⲧⲁⲣⲍ̄, ⲧⲁⲍⲣ̄) vb. intr. to become sober, alert.

ⲧⲱⲥ ⲧⲉⲥ- ⲧⲟⲥ⁼ Q ⲧⲏⲥ (ⲧⲉⲥ) ± ⲉⲃⲟⲗ vb. tr. (rare) to stiffen, fix; intr. to become stiff, hard, firm, fixed. ⲁⲧⲧⲱⲥ adj. limp. ⲧⲁⲥ-ⲃⲁⲗ impudent; ⲙ̄ⲛ̄ⲧⲁⲥ-ⲃⲁⲗ impudence.

ⲧⲱⲧ ⲧⲉⲧ- ⲧⲟⲧ⁼ Q ⲧⲏⲧ vb. tr. to join together, mingle (ⲙ̄ⲙⲟ⁼); to level; vb. intr. to be agreeable, to agree (with: ⲙ̄ⲛ̄; to: ⲉ; on, upon: ⲉϫⲛ̄); to be persuaded, satisfied; to be joined; to become even, level. As n.m. agreement, mingling. ⲧⲱⲧ ⲙ̄ ⲡ(⁼)ⲍⲏⲧ, ⲧⲉⲧ-ⲡ(⁼)ⲍⲏⲧ to persuade, satisfy. ⲧⲱⲧ ⲛ̄ ⲍⲏⲧ to consent, agree; as n.m. consent, agreement; ⲁⲧⲧⲱⲧ ⲛ̄ ⲍⲏⲧ unconvinced.

ⲧⲱⲧⲉ, ⲧⲱⲱⲧⲉ, ⲧⲟⲧⲉ n.f. fringe, border (of garment).

ⲧⲱⲱⲃⲉ, ⲧⲱⲃⲉ n.f.m. brick; ⲛⲁⲡⲉ-ⲧⲱⲱⲃⲉ to make bricks.

ⲧⲱⲱⲃⲉ, ⲧⲉⲃⲉ- ⲧⲟⲟⲃ⁼ vb. tr. to repay, requite (ⲙ̄ⲙⲟ⁼; to: ⲛⲁ⁼; for, in place of: ⲉ); as n.m. requittal, repayment. ⲣⲉϥⲧⲱⲱⲃⲉ one who repays.

ⲧⲱⲱⲃⲉ, ⲧⲟⲟⲃ⁼ Q ⲧⲟⲟⲃⲉ (ⲧⲟⲃⲉ) vb. tr. to seal, set or stamp
with a seal (ⲙ̄ⲙⲟ⁼, ⲉ, ⲉⲣⲛ̄; with: ⲙ̄ⲙⲟ⁼, ⲍⲛ̄); as n.m.
seal, stamp. ⲧⲟⲟⲃⲉⲥ n.f.; ⲧⲟⲟⲃⲉϥ, ⲧⲟⲟⲃⲧ̄ n.m. impress
of a seal. ⲧⲃ̄ⲃⲉ n.f. seal.

ⲧⲱⲱⲙⲉ, Q ⲧⲟⲟⲙⲉ vb. tr. to join; mostly in Q: to be joined
(to: ⲉ); to be fitting, suitable (for, to: ⲉ, ⲛⲁ⁼).

ⲧⲱⲱⲙⲉ, ⲧⲟⲟⲙⲉ n.f. purse, wallet.

ⲧⲱⲱⲡ (ⲧⲱⲡ) ⲧⲉⲡ- ⲧⲟⲡ⁼ Q ⲧⲏⲡ (ⲧⲏⲏⲡ) vb. tr. to accustom
(ⲙ̄ⲙⲟ⁼; to: ⲉ); intr. to become accustomed (ⲉ: to),
familiar with; as n.m. custom, usage. ⲧⲟⲡⲥ̄, ⲧⲁⲡⲥ̄,
ⲧⲁⲁⲡⲥ̄ n.f. custom, habit.

ⲧⲱⲱϭⲉ (ⲧⲱϭⲉ) ⲧⲉϭ- (ⲧⲉⲕ-) ⲧⲟⲟϭ⁼ (ⲧⲟϭ⁼, ⲧⲟⲕ⁼, ⲧⲟⲟⲕ⁼) Q ⲧⲏϭ
(ⲧⲏⲕ) (1) vb. tr. to join, attach (ⲙ̄ⲙⲟ⁼; to: ⲉ, ⲉⲝⲛ̄);
to ascribe, impute (ⲙ̄ⲙⲟ⁼; to: ⲉ); vb. intr. to join
self (to: ⲉ, ⲉⲍⲟⲩⲛ ⲉ), to cling; ⲧⲱⲱϭⲉ ⲙ̄ⲙⲟ⁼ ⲉⲃⲟⲗ to publish. (2) vb. tr. to plant (ⲙ̄ⲙⲟ⁼); as n.m. planting.

ⲧⲱϣ ⲧⲉϣ- ⲧⲟϣ⁼ Q ⲧⲏϣ vb. tr. to limit, bound, determine
(ⲙ̄ⲙⲟ⁼); to appoint, assign, destine (ⲙ̄ⲙⲟ⁼; to, for,
over: ⲉ, ⲉⲍⲟⲩⲛ ⲉ, ⲉⲝⲛ̄, ⲛⲁ⁼); vb. intr. to become fixed,
limited, determined; to be moderate. As n.m. ordinance,
destiny; manner, fashion; affair, matter. ⲁⲧⲧⲱϣ unlimited; immoderate. ⲣ̄-(ⲡ)ⲧⲱϣ to prepare, put in order.
ϯ-(ⲡ)ⲧⲱϣ to give orders (to: ⲛⲁ⁼, ⲉ), provide (for: ⲉ,
ⲛⲁ⁼). ⲣⲉϥⲧⲱϣ commander. ⲧⲟϣ, ⲧⲱϣ (pl. ⲧⲱϣ, ⲧⲟⲟϣ ?)
border, boundary, limit; nome; province, district; bish-
opric; ⲣⲙ̄ⲛ̄ⲧⲟϣ man of nome; ⲣ̄-ⲧⲟϣ ⲛⲁ⁼ to be adjacent to;
ϯ-ⲧⲟϣ ⲉ to set limits to; ⲝⲓ-ⲧⲟϣ to adjoin (ⲉ, ⲙⲛ̄).
ⲧⲉϣⲉ (pl. ⲧⲉϣⲉⲩ) n.f. neighbor; that which adjoins.

ⲧⲱⲍ ⲧⲉⲍ- (ⲧⲁⲍ-) ⲧⲁⲍ⁼ Q ⲧⲏⲍ vb. tr. to mix, stir (ⲙ̄ⲙⲟ⁼; into, with: ⲉ, ⲙⲛ̄, ⲙ̄ⲙⲟ⁼, ⲍⲓ, ⲍⲛ̄); vb. intr. to become
mixed, disturbed, clouded; as n.m. mixture, disturbance.
ⲁⲧⲧⲱⲍ unmixed, distinct. ⲙⲁⲓ-ⲧⲱⲍ meddlesome. ⲣⲉϥⲧⲱⲍ
meddler, mixer; ⲙⲛ̄ⲧⲣⲉϥⲧⲱⲍ confusion.

ⲧⲱⲍ n.m. chaff.

ⲧⲱϩⲃ̄ ⲧⲁϩⲃ˵ Q ⲧⲁϩⲃ̄ vb. tr. to moisten, soak. ⲑⲁⲃ n.m.
   leaven; ⲣ̄-ⲑⲁⲃ, ⲭⲓ-ⲑⲁⲃ to become leavened. ⲁⲧⲑⲁⲃ un-
   leavened.
ⲧⲱϩⲙ̄ ⲧⲁϩⲙ˵ vb. tr. to chase, pursue (ⲙ̄ⲙⲟ˵, ⲛ̄ⲥⲁ).
ⲧⲱϩⲙ̄ ⲧⲉϩⲙ̄- ⲧⲁϩⲙ˵ Q ⲧⲁϩⲙ̄ (± ⲉϩⲟⲩⲛ) to summon (ⲙ̄ⲙⲟ˵; to: ⲉ,
   ⲉⲭⲛ̄); to knock (on, at: ⲉ); as n.m. calling, convocation.
ⲧⲱϩⲥ̄ ⲧⲉϩⲥ̄- ⲧⲁϩⲥ˵ (ⲧⲟϩⲥ˵) Q ⲧⲁϩⲥ̄ vb. tr. to anoint (ⲙ̄ⲙⲟ˵;
   with: ⲙ̄ⲙⲟ˵, ϩⲓ, ϩⲛ̄); to pour (ⲙ̄ⲙⲟ˵; on: ⲉ); as n.m.
   anointing. ⲭⲓ-ⲧⲱϩⲥ̄ to be anointed.
ⲧⲱϭⲛ̄ ⲧⲉϭⲛ̄- (ⲧⲁϭⲛ̄-) ⲧⲟϭⲛ˵ (ⲧⲁϭⲛ˵) vb. tr. to push (ⲙ̄ⲙⲟ˵).
ⲧⲱϭⲡ̄ (ⲧⲱⲕⲡ̄, ⲧⲱⲣϭ) Q ⲧⲟϭⲡ̄ (ⲧⲟⲣⲕ̄, ⲧⲁⲕⲡ̄) vb. intr. to be joined, fixed (to: ⲉ; in: ϩⲛ̄).
ⲧⲱϭⲥ̄ ⲧⲟϭⲥ˵ (ⲧⲁϭⲥ˵) Q ⲧⲟϭⲥ̄ vb. tr. to bleach, dye (ⲙ̄ⲙⲟ˵).
ⲑⲃ̄ⲃⲓⲟ ⲑⲃ̄ⲃⲓⲉ- ⲑⲃ̄ⲃⲓⲟ˵ Q ⲑⲃ̄ⲃⲓⲏⲩ(ⲧ) vb. tr. to make humble,
   humiliate (ⲙ̄ⲙⲟ˵); intr. to become humble, be humiliated;
   as n.m. humility.
ⲑⲏⲛ n.m. sulfur.
ⲧϩⲓⲟ (ⲑⲓⲟ) ⲑⲓⲉ- ⲑⲓⲟ˵ Q ⲑⲓⲏⲩ vb. tr. to cause to fall,
   bring down (ⲙ̄ⲙⲟ˵).
ⲑⲗⲟ ⲑⲗⲟ˵ vb. tr. to cause to fly, to chase away.
ⲑⲙ̄ⲕⲟ ⲑⲙ̄ⲕⲉ- ⲑⲙ̄ⲕⲟ˵ Q ⲑⲙ̄ⲕⲏⲩ vb. tr. to afflict, treat badly
   (ⲙ̄ⲙⲟ˵); as n.m. affliction, ill-treatment.
ⲑⲙⲟ vb. tr. to warm (ⲙ̄ⲙⲟ˵).
ⲑⲙ̄ⲥⲟ ⲑⲙ̄ⲥⲉ- ⲑⲙ̄ⲥⲟ˵ Q ⲑⲙ̄ⲥⲟⲉⲓⲧ vb. tr. to seat (ⲙ̄ⲙⲟ˵).
ⲑⲛⲟ (ⲑⲛⲟ) ⲧ︤ⲥ︥ⲛⲉ- ⲑⲛⲟ˵ Q ⲑⲛⲏⲩ (± ⲉϩⲟⲩⲛ) vb. tr. to cause
   to approach (ⲙ̄ⲙⲟ˵); to hire.
ⲑⲛⲟ ⲑⲛⲟ˵ (ⲑⲛⲱ˵, ⲑⲉⲛⲟ˵, ⲑⲁⲛⲟ˵) Q ⲑⲛⲏⲩ (ⲑⲉⲛⲏⲩ) vb. tr. to
   pound, crush (ⲙ̄ⲙⲟ˵).
ⲧϩⲟ (ⲑⲟ) vb. intr. to become bad; as n.m. badness.
ⲑⲟⲟⲩⲧ, ⲑⲱⲟⲩⲧ, ⲑⲱⲑ n. name of 1st Coptic month.
ⲧ︤ⲥ︥ⲛⲟ (ⲑⲛⲟ) ⲧ︤ⲥ︥ⲛⲟ˵ vb. tr. to lead, accompany (ⲙ̄ⲙⲟ˵; ⲉⲃⲟⲗ:
   forth).
ⲧϩⲣ̄ϣⲟ (ⲑⲣ̄ϣⲟ) ⲑⲣ̄ϣⲉ- ⲑⲣ̄ϣⲟ˵ vb. tr. to terrify, oppress.
ⲧϭⲁⲉⲓⲟ (ϭⲁⲉⲓⲟ) (ⲧ)ϭⲁⲉⲓⲉ- (ⲧ)ϭⲁⲉⲓⲟ˵ Q (ⲧ)ϭⲁⲉⲓⲏⲩ vb. tr. to
   disgrace, condemn (ⲙ̄ⲙⲟ˵); vb. intr. to be disgraced,

condemned (to: ε); as n.m. disgrace, condemnation.
ϭⲁⲉⲓⲉ, ϭⲁⲉⲓⲏ adj. ugly; as n. ugly person; ⲙⲛⲧϭⲁⲉⲓⲉ
disgrace, ugliness. ⲟ ⲛ̄ ϭⲁⲉⲓⲉ to be disgraceful.
ϭⲁ n.m. ugliness.

ⲧ–: ⲡ–
ⲧⲁ: ⲧⲟⲉ
ⲧⲁ–: ⲡⲁ–
ⲧⲁⲁⲡⲥ̄: ⲧⲱⲱⲡ
ⲧⲁⲁⲧⲉ: ⲧⲟⲟⲧⲉ
ⲧⲁⲉ: ⲧⲟⲉ
ⲧⲁⲉⲓⲟⲩ: †ⲟⲩ
ⲧⲁⲓ: ⲡⲁⲓ
ⲧⲁⲕ: ⲧⲁϭ
ⲧⲁⲕ⸗: ⲧⲱⲕ
ⲧⲁⲕⲙ̄: ⲧⲱⲕⲙ̄
ⲧⲁⲕⲣ̄: ⲧⲱϭⲣ̄
ⲧⲁⳉ: ⲧⲱⲕⲥ̄
ⲧⲁⲛⲁ⸗: ⲧⲛ̄ⲛⲟ
ⲧⲁⲛ2ⲉⲧ–: ⲧⲁⲛ2ⲟⲩⲧ
ⲧⲁⲛ2ⲏⲧ: 2ⲏⲧ
ⲧⲁⲛ2ⲏⲩⲧ: ⲧⲁⲛ2ⲟⲩⲧ
ⲧⲁⲡⲉⲛ: ⲧⲁⲡⲛ̄
ⲧⲁⲡⲥ̄: ⲧⲱⲱⲡ
ⲧⲁⲣⲟ: ⲧⲁⲗⲟ
ⲧⲁⲣⲝ̄: ⲧⲱⲣⲝ̄
ⲧⲁⲥⲃⲁⲗ: ⲧⲱⲥ
ⲧⲁⲧⲥⲉ: ⲧⲁϭⲥⲉ
ⲧⲁⲑ: ⲧⲁ2ⲧ̄
ⲧⲁϣⲉ–ⲱⲣⲕ̄: ⲱⲣⲕ̄
ⲧⲁ2–/⸗: ⲧⲱ2
ⲧⲁ2ⲃ(⸗): ⲧⲱ2ⲃ̄
ⲧⲁ2ⲉ: ⲧⲓ2ⲉ
ⲧⲁ2ⲏⲩ: ⲧⲁ2ⲟ
ⲧⲁ2ⲙ(⸗): ⲧⲱ2ⲙ̄
ⲧⲁ2ⲣ̄: ⲧⲱⲣⲝ̄
ⲧⲁ2ⲥ⸗: ⲧⲱ2ⲥ̄
ⲧⲁϭⲛ(⸗): ⲧⲱϭⲛ̄
ⲧⲁϭⲥ⸗: ⲧⲱϭⲥ̄
ⲧⲃ̄ⲃⲉ: ⲧⲱⲱⲃⲉ
ⲧⲃ̄ⲛⲉⲩ: ⲧⲃ̄ⲛⲏ
ⲧⲃ̄ⲛⲟⲟⲩⲉ: ⲧⲃ̄ⲛⲏ
ⲧⲃ̄ⲥ̄: †ⲃⲥ̄
ⲧⲉ: ⲡⲉ
ⲧⲉⲃⲉ: ⲧⲏⲏⲃⲉ
ⲧⲉⲃⲉ–: ⲧⲱⲱⲃⲉ
ⲧⲉⲃⲥ̄: †ⲃⲥ̄
ⲧⲉⲕ–: ⲧⲱⲱϭⲉ
ⲧⲉⲛⲁ–: ⲧⲁⲛⲟ
ⲧⲉⲛⲁ2: ⲧⲛ̄2

ⲧⲉⲛⲟⲩ: ⲟⲩⲛⲟⲩ
ⲧⲉⲡ–: ⲧⲱⲡⲉ, ⲧⲱⲱⲡ
ⲧⲉⲡⲛ̄, ⲧⲉⲡⲛⲉ: ⲧⲁⲡⲛ̄
ⲧⲉⲣⲃⲁⲉⲓⲛ: ⲧⲣ̄ⲃⲏⲓⲛ
ⲧⲉⲣⲃⲉⲉⲓⲛ: ⲧⲣ̄ⲃⲏⲓⲛ
ⲧⲉⲣⲕⲟ(⸗): ⲧⲁⲣⲕⲟ
ⲧⲉⲣϥⲉⲉⲓⲛ: ⲧⲣ̄ⲃⲏⲓⲛ
ⲧⲉⲩ–: ⲧⲟⲟⲩ
ⲧⲉⲩ: ⲧⲏⲩ
ⲧⲉⲩⲛⲟⲩ: ⲟⲩⲛⲟⲩ
ⲧⲉϣⲉ: ⲧⲱϣ
ⲧⲉϣⲉⲩ: ⲧⲉϣⲉ
ⲧⲉ2ⲧⲱ2(⸗): ⲧⲁ2ⲧ2̄
ⲧⲉϭ–: ⲧⲱⲱϭⲉ
ⲧⲏ: ⲧⲉ, ⲡⲏ
–ⲧⲏ: †ⲟⲩ
ⲧⲏⲃⲉ: ⲧⲁⲓⲃⲉ, ⲧⲏⲏⲃⲉ
ⲧⲏⲃⲧ̄: ⲧⲃ̄ⲧ
ⲧⲏⲏⲃⲉ: ⲧⲁⲓⲃⲉ
ⲧⲏⲏⲡ: ⲧⲱⲱⲡ
ⲧⲏⲕ: ⲧⲱⲱϭⲉ
ⲧⲏⲡ: ⲧⲱⲱⲡ
ⲧⲏⲣⲃⲏⲓⲛ: ⲧⲣ̄ⲃⲏⲓⲛ
ⲧⲏϥⲧ̄: ⲧⲃ̄ⲧ
ⲧⲏ2: ⲧⲱ2
ⲧⲏϭ: ⲧⲱⲱϭⲉ
†: †ⲟⲩ
†ⲉ: †ⲟⲩ
†ⲕ: ⲧⲱⲕ
†ⲛⲉ: ⲧⲱⲡⲉ
ⲧⲗⲟⲟϭⲉ: ϭⲗⲟⲟϭⲉ
ⲧⲗⲟϭ: ϭⲗⲟϭ
ⲧⲁ̄ⲧⲓⲗⲉ: ⲧⲁ̄ⲧⲁ̄
ⲧⲗⲱϭⲉ: ϭⲗⲟⲟϭⲉ
ⲧⲙⲉ–/⸗: ⲧⲙ̄ⲙⲟ
ⲧⲙⲉ: †ⲙⲉ
ⲧⲙⲟ(⸗): ⲧⲙ̄ⲙⲟ
ⲧⲙ̄ⲡⲥⲟⲡ: ⲥⲟⲡ
ⲧⲛⲁ–: ⲧⲁⲛⲟ
ⲧⲛⲁ: ⲧⲛ̄ⲛⲟ
ⲧⲛⲉⲩ–: ⲧⲛ̄ⲛⲟⲟⲩ
ⲧⲛⲏ: ⲉⲓⲧⲛ̄
ⲧⲛ̄ⲛⲉⲩ–: ⲧⲛ̄ⲛⲟⲟⲩ
ⲧⲛⲟ(⸗): ⲧⲛ̄ⲛⲟ
ⲧⲛⲟⲙ: ⲧⲗⲟⲙ

ⲧⲛⲟⲟⲩ⸗: ⲧⲛ̄ⲛⲟⲟⲩ
ⲧⲛⲟⲩ⸗: ⲧⲛ̄ⲛⲟⲟⲩ
ⲧⲛ̄ⲣⲟⲙⲡⲉ: ⲣⲟⲙⲡⲉ
ⲧⲟ: ⲧⲟⲉ
ⲧⲟⲃⲉ: ⲧⲱⲱⲃⲉ
ⲧⲟⲓⲉ: ⲧⲟⲉ
ⲧⲟⲕ⸗: ⲧⲱⲱϭⲉ
ⲧⲟⲗ: ⲧⲁⲗ
ⲧⲟⲙⲛ̄ⲧ: ⲧⲱⲙⲛ̄ⲧ
ⲧⲟⲛⲛⲉ, ⲧⲟⲛⲛⲟⲩ: ⲧⲱⲛⲟⲩ
ⲧⲟⲛⲟⲩ: ⲧⲱⲛⲟⲩ
ⲧⲟⲛⲱ: ⲧⲱⲛⲟⲩ
ⲧⲟⲟⲃ⸗: ⲧⲱⲱⲃⲉ
ⲧⲟⲟⲃⲉ(ⲥ/ϥ): ⲧⲱⲱⲃⲉ
ⲧⲟⲟⲕ⸗: ⲧⲱⲱϭⲉ
ⲧⲟⲟⲙⲉ: ⲧⲱⲱⲙⲉ
ⲧⲟⲟⲧ⸗: ⲧⲱⲣⲉ
ⲧⲟⲟⲧⲉ: ⲧⲁⲁⲧⲉ
ⲧⲟⲟⲩⲉ: 2ⲧⲟⲟⲩⲉ
ⲧⲟⲡ⸗: ⲧⲱⲡⲉ, ⲧⲱⲱⲡ, ⲧⲱⲡ
ⲧⲟⲡⲥ̄: ⲧⲱⲱⲡ
ⲧⲟⲣⲉ: ⲧⲱⲣⲉ
ⲧⲟⲣⲕ̄: ⲧⲱϭⲣ̄
ⲧⲟⲧⲉ: ⲧⲱⲧⲉ
ⲧⲟⲧⲥ̄: ⲧⲱⲕⲥ̄
ⲧⲟⲩⲏⲧ(⸗): ⲧⲟⲟⲩⲧⲉ
ⲧⲟⲩⲛ–: ⲧⲟⲩⲱ⸗
ⲧⲟⲩⲛ–: ⲧⲱⲟⲩⲛ
ⲧⲟⲩⲛⲉⲥ–: ⲧⲟⲩⲛⲟⲥ
ⲧⲟⲩⲟⲟⲧⲉ: ⲧⲟⲩⲱⲧ
ⲧⲟⲩⲣⲏⲥ: ⲧⲏⲩ
ⲧⲟϣ: ⲧⲱϣ
ⲧⲟϭ(⸗): ⲧⲟⲕ, ⲧⲱⲕ
ⲧⲟϭ⸗: ⲧⲱⲱϭⲉ
ⲧⲟϭⲥ⸗, ⲧⲟϭⲥ̄: ⲧⲱⲕⲥ̄
ⲧⲣⲉ–: ⲧⲣⲟ
ⲧⲣⲉⲓⲟⲟⲩ: ⲧⲣ̄ⲣⲉ
ⲧⲣⲏ: ⲧⲣⲉ
ⲧⲣ̄ⲕⲟ⸗: ⲧⲁⲣⲕⲟ
ⲧⲣⲟϣ: ⲧⲱⲣϣ̄
ⲧⲣⲟϣⲣ̄ϣ: ⲧⲱⲣϣ̄
ⲧⲣ̄ⲣⲟⲙⲡⲉ: ⲣⲟⲙⲡⲉ
ⲧⲣϣⲣⲱϣ: ⲧⲱⲣϣ̄
ⲧⲥ̄ⲃⲟ⸗: ⲧⲥⲁⲃⲟ
ⲧⲥⲉⲃⲉ–: ⲧⲥⲁⲃⲟ

ⲧⲥ̄ⲛⲟ: ⲧⲥⲁⲛⲟ	ⲧⲱⲡ: ⲧⲱⲡⲉ, ⲧⲱⲱⲡ	ⲧⲱϭⲥ̄: ⲧⲱⲕⲥ̄
ⲧⲧⲟ⸗: ⲧⲧⲉ-	ⲧⲱⲣⲥ̄: ⲧⲱϭⲣ̄	ⲑⲁⲃ: ⲧⲱ₂ⲃ̄
ⲧⲱ⸗: ⲡⲱ⸗	ⲧⲱⲧⲡ̄: ⲧⲱⲣⲧ̄	ⲑⲁⲛⲟ⸗: ⲑⲛⲟ
ⲧⲱⲃⲁ₂: ⲧⲱⲃ₂̄	ⲧⲱⲧⲥ̄: ⲧⲱⲕⲥ̄	ⲑⲉⲛⲟ⸗: ⲑⲛⲟ
ⲧⲱⲃⲉ: ⲧⲱⲱⲃⲉ	ⲧⲱⲱⲧⲉ: ⲧⲱⲧⲉ	ⲑⲉⲛⲏⲩ: ⲑⲛⲟ
ⲧⲱⲕⲡ̄: ⲧⲱϭⲡ̄	ⲧⲱϭ: ⲧⲱⲕ	ⲑⲓⲏⲩ: ⲑⲓⲟ
ⲧⲱⲙⲧ̄: ⲧⲱⲙⲛ̄ⲧ	ⲧⲱϭⲉ: ⲧⲱⲱϭⲉ	ⲑⲱⲟⲩⲧ, ⲑⲱⲉ: ⲑⲟⲟⲩⲧ
ⲧⲱⲛⲁ, ⲧⲱⲛⲉ: ⲧⲱⲛⲟⲩ	ⲧⲱϭϭ: ⲧⲱⲕ	ⲧⲝⲁⲉⲓⲟ: ⲝⲁⲉⲓⲟ
ⲧⲱⲡ: ⲧⲟⲡ		

ⲟⲩ

ⲟⲩ interrog. pron. what? less commonly: who? ⲟⲩ ⲉⲣⲟ⸗ what
does it profit (me, you, etc.)? ⲟⲩ ⲛ̄ what of (partitive)? ⲟⲩⲟⲩ what? (with indef. art.). ⲣ̄-ⲟⲩ to do
what? to be like what? ⲉⲧⲃⲉ ⲟⲩ why? ⲉⲧⲃⲉ ⲟⲩ ⲛ̄ ₂ⲱⲃ
idem. ⲟⲩ ⲙⲛ̄ ⲟⲩ this and that, such and such.

ⲟⲩ indef. art. sing. See 2.1.

ⲟⲩⲁ (f. ⲟⲩⲉⲓ) (1) indef. pron. one, someone; (2) one (the
number); see 15.3. For -ⲟⲩⲉ in ⲙⲛ̄ⲧⲟⲩⲉ eleven, etc.; see
24.3. ⲟⲩⲁ ⲟⲩⲁ one by one. ⲟⲩⲁ ... ⲟⲩⲁ ... one ... the
other. ₂ⲉⲛⲟⲩⲁ ⲟⲩⲁ some (pl.), a few. ⲉ ⲡⲟⲩⲁ distributive: one each. ⲡⲟⲩⲁ ⲡⲟⲩⲁ each one. ⲕⲉⲟⲩⲁ another one.
ⲣ̄-ⲕⲉⲟⲩⲁ to become another, be altered. ⲙⲛ̄ⲧⲟⲩⲁ unity,
unison. ⲣ̄-ⲟⲩⲁ to become one; to unite with (ⲙⲛ̄).

ⲟⲩⲁ n.m. blasphemy; as adj. blasphemous. ⲭⲓ-/ⲭⲉ-ⲟⲩⲁ to
blaspheme (against: ⲉ, ⲉ₂ⲟⲩⲛ ⲉ). ⲣⲉϥⲭⲓ-ⲟⲩⲁ blasphemer.
ⲙⲛ̄ⲧⲣⲉϥⲭⲓ-ⲟⲩⲁ blasphemy. ⲭⲁⲧ-ⲟⲩⲁ blasphemer.

ⲟⲩⲁⲁ⸗ intens. pron. -self, alone, only; used appositionally, as in ⲛ̄ⲧⲟⲕ ⲟⲩⲁⲁⲕ you yourself, you alone; ⲧⲉⲥ₂ⲓⲙⲉ ⲟⲩⲁⲁⲥ the woman herself. ⲛ̄ ⲟⲩⲁⲁ⸗ idem. ⲣ̄-ⲟⲩⲁⲁ⸗
to become alone.

ⲟⲩⲁ₂ n.m. pole, stave.

ⲟⲩⲁ₂ⲃⲉϥ, ⲟⲩⲁ₂ⲙⲉϥ, ⲟⲩⲟ₂ⲃⲉϥ vb. intr. to bark, growl (of dog).

ⲟⲩⲁ₂ⲉ n. oasis.

ⲟⲩⲁ₂ⲓ₂ⲏⲧ, ⲟⲩⲁ₂ⲉⲓⲏⲧ adj. cruel. ⲙⲛ̄ⲧⲟⲩⲁ₂ⲓ₂ⲏⲧ cruelty. ⲣ̄-
ⲟⲩⲁ₂ⲓ₂ⲏⲧ to become cruel.

ⲟⲩⲁ₂ⲙⲉ n.f. storey (of a house or structure).

oⲩⲃⲁϣ, Q oⲩoⲃϣ̄ vb. intr. to become white; as n.m. white-
ness. oⲩⲱⲃϣ̄ adj. white (aft. n., with or without ⲛ̄);
ⲣ̄-oⲩⲱⲃϣ̄ to become white.

oⲩⲃⲉ (oⲩⲃⲏ⸗) prep. against; toward, opposite.

oⲩⲉ, Q oⲩⲏⲩ vb. intr. to become distant, far, far-reaching
(± ⲉⲃoⲗ); oⲩⲉ ⲉ to be distant from; idem with prep. ⲙ̄ⲙo⸗,
ⲉⲃoⲗ ⲙ̄ⲙo⸗, ⲥⲁⲃoⲗ ⲙ̄ⲙo⸗, ⲉⲃoⲗ ⳍⲛ̄. As n.m. distance; oⲩⲉ
ⲉⲡⲉⲥⲏⲧ distance downward. ⲉ ⲡoⲩⲉ to a distance (from:
ⲙ̄ⲙo⸗). ⲛ̄ ⲡoⲩⲉ at a distance. ⳍ ⲓ/ⳍ ⲙ̄ ⲡoⲩⲉ idem.

oⲩⲉ number one in higher numbers (11, 21, etc.).

oⲩⲉⲉⲓⲉⲛⲓⲛ n.m. Greek. ⲙ̄ⲛ̄ⲧoⲩⲉⲉⲓⲉⲛⲓⲛ n.f. Greek (language).

oⲩⲉⲓⲛⲉ vb. intr. to pass by (subj. usu. period of time).
ⲁⲧoⲩⲉⲓⲛⲉ not passing, permanent.

oⲩⲉⲓⲥⲉ oⲩⲁⲥⲧ⸗ vb. tr. to saw (ⲙ̄ⲙo⸗). ⲣⲉϥoⲩⲉⲓⲥⲉ sawyer.

oⲩⲉⲓⲧⲉ (oⲩⲉⲉⲧⲉ) vb. intr. to waste away, dry up; vb. tr.
to dry up, make waste away (ⲙ̄ⲙo⸗), ± ⲉⲃoⲗ.

oⲩⲉⲗoⲩⲉⲗⲉ vb. intr. to howl.

oⲩⲉⲣⲏⲧⲉ, oⲩⲣⲏⲏⲧⲉ n.f. foot, leg (of person, animal, object).

oⲩⲉⲣⲧ̄, oⲩⲣ̄ⲧ, oⲩⲁⲣ̄ⲧ n.f.m. rose.

oⲩⲉⳍ-ⲣⲁⲥoⲩ interpreter of dreams.

oⲩⲉⲥⲃⲣo n.f. doorpost.

oⲩⲏⲣ (f. oⲩⲏⲣⲉ) interrog. adj. how much? how many? how
great? oⲩⲏⲣ ⲡⲉ N? How great is N? (also exclam.). ⲣ̄-
oⲩⲏⲣ to become how much/many? to amount to how much?
ⲛ̄ oⲩⲏⲣ by how much? to what extent? ⲁ oⲩⲏⲣ how long?
how much more so (in syllogistic statement). ⲥoⲩ-oⲩⲏⲣ
such and such a day. ⲙⲉⳍoⲩⲏⲣ the how-many-eth?

oⲩⲏⲧⲉ n.f. calamity.

oⲩⲭⲗⲉ, oⲩⲉⲭⲗⲉ n.f. melody, music.

oⲩⲭⲡⲉ n. depression in skin (left by disease or sim.).

oⲩⲙoⲧ, Q oⲩoⲙⲧ̄ (oⲩoⲙⲛ̄ⲧ) vb. intr. to become thick, swollen;
as n.m. thickness, swelling.

oⲩⲛ̄- existential predicate: there is/are. See Gr. In.

oⲩⲛⲁⲙ n.f. right hand, the right side; ϭⲓⲝ ⲛ̄ oⲩⲛⲁⲙ the
right hand; ⲉ oⲩⲛⲁⲙ to the right. ⲛ̄ⲥⲁ/ⳍ ⲓ oⲩⲛⲁⲙ ⲙ̄ⲙo⸗

on the right of. ⲧⲏⲩ ⲛ̄ ⲟⲩⲛⲁⲙ favorable wind.

ⲟⲩⲛⲟⲩ (pl. ⲟⲩⲛⲟⲟⲩⲉ) n.f. hour. ⲛ̄ ⲧⲉⲩⲛⲟⲩ adv. immediately, thereupon, forthwith. ⲍⲛ̄ ⲧⲉⲩⲛⲟⲩ idem. ⲡⲣⲟⲥ ⲧⲉⲩⲛⲟⲩ for a while, for a moment, at present. ⲣⲉϥⲕⲁ-ⲟⲩⲛⲟⲩ astrologer. ⲧⲉⲛⲟⲩ adv. now; ⲧⲉⲛⲟⲩ ϭⲉ so now, now therefore; ⲉ/ⲛ̄ ⲧⲉⲛⲟⲩ now; ϣⲁ ⲧⲉⲛⲟⲩ until now; ⲝⲓⲛ ⲧⲉⲛⲟⲩ from now.

ⲟⲩⲛⲟϥ vb. intr. to rejoice (at: ⲉⲝⲛ̄, ⲍⲓⲝⲛ̄); also used reflex. with ⲙ̄ⲙⲟ⸗. As n.m. joy, gladness.

ⲟⲩⲛ̄ⲧ, ⲟⲩⲟⲛⲧ n.m. hollow place, esp. hold of a ship.

ⲟⲩⲛ̄ⲧⲉ- ⲟⲩⲛ̄ⲧⲁ⸗ pred. of possession: to have. See 22.1.

ⲟⲩⲟⲉⲓ, ⲟⲩⲟⲓ n.m. rush, swift movement. ϯ-ⲟⲩⲟⲉⲓ to go about seeking, search (for: ⲉ, ⲉⲍⲟⲩⲛ ⲉ, ⲛ̄ⲥⲁ). ϯ-ⲡⲟⲩⲟⲉⲓ, ϯ ⲙ̄ ⲡⲟⲩⲟⲉⲓ, ϯ-ⲡ(⸗)ⲟⲩⲟⲉⲓ, ϯ-ⲡ(⸗)ⲛ̄ⲟⲩⲟⲉⲓ to advance, proceed (to: ⲉ; into: ⲉⲍⲟⲩⲛ ⲉ; on to: ⲉⲍⲣⲁⲓ ⲉ, ⲉⲝⲛ̄). ⲉⲓⲛϯ-ⲡⲟⲩⲟⲉⲓ act of going, proceeding. ⲛ̄ⲟⲩⲟⲉⲓ = ⲟⲩⲟⲉⲓ.

ⲟⲩⲟⲉⲓ, ⲟⲩⲟⲓ interj. woe! (unto: ⲛⲁ⸗). Rare as n.m. woe.

ⲟⲩⲟⲉⲓⲉ (pl. ⲟⲩⲉⲉⲓⲏ, ⲟⲩⲉⲓⲏ) n.m. farmer, cultivator (of fields and vines). There are many variant spellings. ⲙⲛ̄ⲧⲟⲩⲟⲉⲓⲉ husbandry. ⲙⲁ ⲛ̄ ⲟⲩⲟⲉⲓⲉ farm. ⲣⲙ̄ⲟⲩⲟⲉⲓⲉ farmer, peasant (var. ⲣⲙ̄ⲟⲩⲉ, ⲣⲙ̄ⲟⲩⲁ). ⲣ̄-ⲟⲩⲟⲉⲓⲉ to farm.

ⲟⲩⲟⲉⲓⲛ n.m. light; dawn; eyesight. ⲁⲧⲟⲩⲟⲉⲓⲛ without light. ⲣ̄-ⲟⲩⲟⲉⲓⲛ to shine, make light (for: ⲉ, ⲛⲁ⸗; on: ⲉⲝⲛ̄, ⲍⲓⲝⲛ̄). ⲣⲉϥⲣ̄-ⲟⲩⲟⲉⲓⲛ one who gives light, illuminator. ⲝⲓ-ⲟⲩⲟⲉⲓⲛ to get, receive light.

ⲟⲩⲟⲉⲓⲧ n.m. pillar.

ⲟⲩⲟⲉⲓϣ n.m. time, occasion. ⲡⲉⲟⲩⲟⲉⲓϣ ⲉⲧ ⲙ̄ⲙⲁⲩ at that time. ⲙ̄ ⲡⲉⲓⲛⲟϭ ⲛ̄ ⲟⲩⲟⲉⲓϣ all this while. ⲛ̄ ⲟⲩⲙⲏⲏϣⲉ ⲛ̄ ⲟⲩⲟⲉⲓϣ for a long time; ⲛ̄ ⲟⲩⲟⲉⲓϣ ⲛⲓⲙ always. ⲙ̄ ⲡⲓⲟⲩⲟⲉⲓϣ, ⲙ̄ ⲡⲉⲟⲩⲟⲉⲓϣ at this/that time. ⲛ̄ (ⲟⲩ)ⲟⲩⲟⲉⲓϣ at one time (in the past). ϣⲁ ⲟⲩⲟⲉⲓϣ later on, at a later time. ⲍⲙ̄ ⲡⲉⲟⲩⲟⲉⲓϣ at the time in question. ⲡⲣⲟⲥ (ⲟⲩ)ⲟⲩⲟⲉⲓϣ for a time, transitory. ⲁⲧⲟⲩⲟⲉⲓϣ ill-timed, at a bad time. ⲍⲛ̄ ⲟⲩⲙⲛ̄ⲧⲁⲧⲟⲩⲟⲉⲓϣ adv. idem. ⲣ̄-ⲟⲩⲟⲉⲓϣ to spend, pass time. ϭⲙ̄-ⲡⲟⲩⲟⲉⲓϣ to find time, have leisure.

ⲟⲩⲟⲓ particle of assent: yes. Cf. also ⲟⲩⲟⲉⲓ.

ογομτε, ογοομτε, ογομπτε n.f. tower.

ογομϥ n.m. manger.

ογον indef. pron. someone, something, some; in neg. context: no one, nothing. Also used as pl.: ⲛ̄ογον, ϩⲉⲛ-
ογον some, some such. ογον ⲛⲓⲙ everyone (s. or pl.).

ογοοϩⲉ, ογοϩⲉ n.f. scorpion.

ογοοϭⲉ, ογοϭⲉ n.f. cheek, jaw.

ογοπ, Q ογⲁⲁⲃ vb. intr. to become pure, innocent, holy (of,
from: ⲉ, ⲉⲃⲟⲗ ϩⲛ̄); as n.m. purity; ϩⲛ̄ ογογοπ purely;
ϫⲓ-ογοπ to acquire purity, be hallowed. ⲡⲉⲧ ογⲁⲁⲃ who/
what is holy, esp. a saint; used with art. or poss. prefixes. ογⲏⲏⲃ n.m. priest (Christian or pagan); ⲣ̄-ογⲏⲏⲃ
to become a priest. ⲙⲛ̄ⲧογⲏⲏⲃ priesthood.

ογοⲥⲣ̄ n.m. oar. ⲣⲉϥⲥⲉⲕ-ογοⲥⲣ̄, ⲣⲉϥⲥⲱⲕ ⲛ̄ ⲛ̄ογοⲥⲣ̄ oarsman.

ογοⲥⲧⲛ̄, Q ογⲉⲥⲧⲱⲛ to become broad, wide, extensive; rarely
tr.: to broaden. As n.m. breadth.

ογοτογⲉⲧ, Q ογⲉⲧογⲱⲧ vb. intr. to become green, pallid; as
n.m. greenness, herbs; pallor.

ογοϣογⲉϣ ογⲉϣογⲱϣ⸗ Q ογⲉϣογⲱϣ vb. tr. to beat, strike.

ογοϥ n.m. lung.

ογοϭογⲉϭ ογⲉϭογⲱϭ⸗ vb. tr. to chew, crush (ⲙ̄ⲙⲟ⸗).

ογⲣⲁⲥ n. crutch.

ογⲣⲟⲧ, Q ⲣⲟογⲧ vb. intr. to become eager, ready, glad; Q
to be fresh, flourishing; as n.m. zeal, enthusiasm,
eagerness, gladness; ϩⲛ̄ ογογⲣⲟⲧ gladly, eagerly. ϯ-
ογⲣⲟⲧ to gladden; to incite, arouse (someone: ⲛⲁ⸗).

ογⲣⲱ n.m. bean.

ογⲣ̄ϣⲉ, ογⲉⲣϣⲉ n.f. watch, watch-tower. ⲁⲛογⲣ̄ϣⲉ n.m. guard.

ογⲥ n.m. bald person; ⲙⲛ̄ⲧογⲥ baldness.

ογⲧⲁϩ n.m. fruit, produce (rare in Sah.).

ογⲧⲉ (ογⲧⲱ⸗) prep. between, among; often in proleptic construction; ογⲧⲉ x ⲙⲛ̄ y, ογⲧⲉ x ⲙⲛ̄ ογⲧⲉ y, ογⲧⲱ⸗x ογⲧⲱ⸗y
between x and y. ⲉⲃⲟⲗ ογⲧⲉ from among, from between.
ογⲧⲉ is often followed by ⲧⲙⲏⲧⲉ in same constructions.

ογⲱ n.m. news, report. ⲛ̄-ⲡογⲱ ⲛⲁ⸗ to bring news to.

ⲣ̄-ⲟⲩⲱ to respond, reply, say (to: ⲛⲁ⸗, ⲍⲁⲣⲛ̄). ϯ-ⲟⲩⲱ to
give news. ϥⲓ-ⲟⲩⲱ, ϥⲁⲓ-ⲟⲩⲱ bearer of news, messenger.
ⲍⲉ-ⲡⲟⲩⲱ, ⲍⲉ-ⲡ(⸗)ⲟⲩⲱ to inquire (about). ϫⲓ-ⲟⲩⲱ, ϫⲓ-
ⲡⲟⲩⲱ to announce (to: ⲉ, ⲛⲁ⸗, ϣⲁ); ⲣⲉϥϫⲓ-ⲟⲩⲱ informer.
ϭⲓⲛϫⲓ-ⲟⲩⲱ Annunciation. ϭⲙ̄-ⲡⲟⲩⲱ, ϭⲙ̄-ⲡ(⸗)ⲟⲩⲱ to inquire
(about). ⲍⲁ̄-ⲟⲩⲱ n. dispute, argument.
ⲟⲩⲱ vb. intr. to cease, stop, come to an end; to cease
(from: ⲛ̄ⲧⲛ̄, ⲍⲛ̄, ⲉⲃⲟⲗ ⲛ̄); + Circum.: to stop doing, finish doing; to have already done. + ⲉ/ⲛ̄ + Inf. idem,
but rarer. Vb. tr. to stop, bring to an end (ⲙ̄ⲙⲟ⸗).
ⲁⲧⲟⲩⲱ unceasing, unending. ϯ-ⲟⲩⲱ to cease; to make
cease (ⲙ̄ⲙⲟ⸗); to release (from: ⲍⲛ̄); ⲁⲧϯ-ⲟⲩⲱ unending.
ⲟⲩⲱ n. in ϯ-ⲟⲩⲱ (± ⲉⲃⲟⲗ) to bloom, sprout; to bring forth,
produce (ⲙ̄ⲙⲟ⸗); as n.m. sprout, blossom. ϫⲓ-ⲟⲩⲱ to
conceive (a child: ⲙ̄ⲙⲟ⸗); as n.m. conception.
ⲟⲩⲱⲗⲥ̄ ⲟⲩⲉⲗⲥ̄- ⲟⲩⲟⲗⲥ⸗ Q ⲟⲩⲟⲗⲥ̄ vb. tr. to put to shame, humiliate, defeat (ⲙ̄ⲙⲟ⸗); vb. intr. to bend down (in shame,
weakness, defeat); to lean (on: ⲉϫⲛ̄, ⲍⲓϫⲛ̄, ⲉⲍⲟⲩⲛ ⲉ); as
n.m. humiliation. ⲟⲩⲱⲗⲥ̄ ⲛ̄ ⲍⲏⲧ to be discouraged.
ⲟⲩⲱⲙ ⲟⲩⲉⲙ- (ⲟⲩⲙ̄-) ⲟⲩⲟⲙ⸗ vb. tr. to eat, consume (ⲙ̄ⲙⲟ⸗);
also fig.: to submit to (e.g. punishment); (subj. the
heart) to make repentant. ⲟⲩⲱⲙ ⲛ̄ⲥⲁ to eat away at, gnaw
at. ⲟⲩⲱⲙ (ⲉⲃⲟⲗ) ⲍⲛ̄ to eat away at, consume; to eat some
of. ⲟⲩⲱⲙ as n.m. food, eating. ⲟⲩⲁⲙ- in cpds.: eater
of (e.g. ⲟⲩⲁⲙ-ⲣⲱⲙⲉ man-eating). ⲁⲧⲟⲩⲱⲙ not eating,
without food; ⲙ̄ⲛ̄ⲧⲁⲧⲟⲩⲱⲙ being without food. ⲙⲁⲓ-ⲟⲩⲱⲙ
fond of eating; ⲙ̄ⲛ̄ⲧⲙⲁⲓ-ⲟⲩⲱⲙ fondness for eating; ⲙⲁ ⲛ̄
ⲟⲩⲱⲙ eating place, refectory. ⲣⲉϥⲟⲩⲱⲙ glutton; ⲙ̄ⲛ̄ⲧⲣⲉϥ-
ⲟⲩⲱⲙ gluttony. ϭⲓⲛⲟⲩⲱⲙ (pl. ϭⲓⲛⲟⲩⲟⲟⲙ) n.m.f. food.
ⲟⲩⲱⲛ, Q ⲟⲩⲏⲛ (imptv. ⲁⲟⲩⲱⲛ, ⲟⲩⲛ̄-) vb. tr. to open (ⲙ̄ⲙⲟ⸗,
ⲉ); vb. intr. to open (out on, towards: ⲉ, ⲉϫⲛ̄, ⲉⲍⲣⲁⲓ
ⲉϫⲛ̄, ⲛ̄ⲥⲁ, ⲟⲩⲃⲉ); as n.m. opening.
ⲟⲩⲱⲛ n.m. part, portion, piece. ⲟⲩⲛ̄- in fractions 30.6.
ⲟⲩⲱⲛⲅ̄ n.m. wolf.
ⲟⲩⲱⲛⲍ̄ ⲟⲩⲉⲛⲍ̄- ⲟⲩⲟⲛⲍ⸗ Q ⲟⲩⲟⲛⲍ̄ (± ⲉⲃⲟⲗ) vb. intr. and reflex.:

to be revealed, become manifest, appear; vb. tr. to
reveal, make manifest, make clear, declare (ⲙ̄ⲙⲟ⸗; to:
ⲉ, ⲉ2ⲟⲩⲛ ⲉ, ⲛⲁ⸗). As n.m. (+ ⲉⲃⲟⲗ) manifesting,
showing, declaration; 2ⲛ̄ ⲟⲩⲟⲩⲱⲛ2̄ ⲉⲃⲟⲗ openly, publicly.
ⲁⲧⲟⲩⲱⲛ2̄ ⲉⲃⲟⲗ invisible, not manifest. ⲣ̄-ⲁⲧⲟⲩⲱⲛ2̄ ⲉⲃⲟⲗ
to become invisible.

ⲟⲩⲱⲣⲡ̄ ⲟⲩⲟⲣⲡ⸗ vb. tr. to send (Boh., rare in Sah.).

ⲟⲩⲱⲣ2̄ ⲟⲩⲉⲣ2̄- ⲟⲩⲟⲣ2⸗ Q ⲟⲩⲟⲣ2̄ vb. tr. to set free, renounce
a claim on; vb. intr. to be free, not responsible.
ⲟⲩⲉⲣ2̄ n.m. free space.

ⲟⲩⲱⲥϥ̄ ⲟⲩⲉⲥϥ̄- ⲟⲩⲟⲥϥ⸗ Q ⲟⲩⲟⲥϥ̄ vb. tr. to leave barren, idle;
to keep idle; to neglect; vb. intr. to be idle, come to
a halt (for: ⲉ); to be brought to naught. As n.m. idleness, ceasing, cessation. ⲟⲩⲁⲥϭⲉ n.f. idleness.

ⲟⲩⲱⲧ ⲟⲩⲉⲧ- ⲟⲩⲉⲧ⸗ vb. tr. to make soft, weak; vb. intr. to
become green, fresh, raw, soft, weak. ⲟⲩⲟⲧⲉ, ⲟⲩⲟⲟⲧⲉ
n.m. greens, herbs; ⲙⲁ ⲛ̄ ⲟⲩⲟⲧⲉ garden.

ⲟⲩⲱⲧ (f. ⲟⲩⲱⲧⲉ, rare) adj. single, sole, one and the same;
usu. aft. n. with ⲛ̄. ⲟⲩⲁ ⲛ̄ ⲟⲩⲱⲧ each one, a single one.
ⲙⲛ̄ⲧⲟⲩⲁ ⲛ̄ ⲟⲩⲱⲧ singleness, unity. ⲣ̄-ⲟⲩⲁ ⲛ̄ ⲟⲩⲱⲧ to make
one, amount to one and the same thing (with: ⲙⲛ̄).

ⲟⲩⲱⲧⲃ̄ ⲟⲩⲉⲧⲃ̄- ⲟⲩⲟⲧⲃ⸗ Q ⲟⲩⲟⲧⲃ̄ vb. tr. to pass through (ⲙ̄ⲙⲟ⸗);
to transform, translate, exchange; to remove, make/let
pass; vb. intr. to change, be altered (usu. of place or
situation); ⲟⲩⲱⲧⲃ̄ ⲉ to change into, to surpass; Q to
surpass. ⲟⲩⲱⲧⲃ̄ ⲉⲃⲟⲗ to cross over, spread over. ⲟⲩⲱⲧⲃ̄
ⲉ2ⲟⲩⲛ to pass in (into: ⲉ). ⲟⲩⲱⲧⲃ̄ ⲉ2ⲣⲁⲓ to pass beyond.

ⲟⲩⲱⲧⲃ̄ (forms as above) vb. to pour (into: ⲉ; upon: ⲉⲝⲛ̄;
down on: ⲉⲡⲉⲥⲏⲧ 2ⲓ).

ⲟⲩⲱⲧⲃ̄ (forms as above) vb. to pierce. ⲟⲩⲁⲧⲃⲉ n.f. hole.

ⲟⲩⲱⲧⲛ̄ ⲟⲩⲟⲧⲛ⸗ vb. tr. to pour; as n.m. libation. ⲟⲩⲱⲧⲛ̄ ⲉⲃⲟⲗ
to pour forth (tr. and intr.); as n.m. libation.

ⲟⲩⲱⲧ2̄ ⲟⲩⲉⲧ2̄- ⲟⲩⲟⲧ2⸗ vb. tr. to cast (metal), to pour (water), to draw (water); as n.m. anything cast or molten.
ⲙⲁ ⲛ̄ ⲟⲩⲱⲧ2̄ crucible, melting-pot. ⲣⲉϥⲟⲩⲱⲧ2̄ cup-bearer,

drawer of water. ⲟⲩⲟⲧⲍ̄ n.m. cup. ⲟⲩⲟⲧⲍⲉ, ⲟⲩⲁⲧⲍⲉ idem.

ⲟⲩⲱⲱⲗⲉ, ⲟⲩⲱⲗⲉ, Q ⲟⲩⲟⲟⲗⲉ (ⲟⲩⲟⲗⲉ) vb. intr. to become well off, to prosper, flourish (in: ⲙ̄ⲙⲟˀ, ⲍⲁ); as n.m. prosperity, plenty. ⲍ̄ⲛ ⲟⲩⲟⲩⲟⲟⲗⲉⲥ in abundance.

ⲟⲩⲱⲙⲉ (ⲟⲩⲱⲙⲉ) ⲟⲩⲟⲟⲙˀ (ⲟⲩⲟⲙˀ) vb. intr. to break down (emotionally); reflex.: to accommodate (someone: ⲙ̄ⲛ̄).

ⲟⲩⲱⲧⲉ (ⲟⲩⲱⲧⲉ) ⲟⲩⲁⲁⲧⲉ- ⲟⲩⲟⲟⲧˀ (ⲟⲩⲁⲁⲧˀ) Q ⲟⲩⲟⲟⲧⲉ vb. tr. (1) to send (ⲙ̄ⲙⲟˀ; forth: ⲉⲃⲟⲗ); (2) to separate, distinguish, choose (esp. in Q), ± ⲉⲃⲟⲗ. ⲟⲩⲱⲧ or ⲟⲩⲉⲧ- impers. vb. followed by subj.: is different, distinct. ⲟⲩⲉⲧ- ... ⲟⲩⲉⲧ- ... the one is ..., the other is....

ⲟⲩⲱⲱ ⲟⲩⲉⲱ- ⲟⲩⲗⲱˀ (ⲟⲩⲟⲱˀ) vb. tr. to want, wish, desire (ⲙ̄ⲙⲟˀ); to love; to be ready, on the point of (doing: ⲉ + Inf., ⲉⲧⲣⲉ, ϫⲉ). ⲟⲩⲉⲱ- may be prefixed directly to an Inf., as in ϯⲟⲩⲉⲱ-ⲉⲓⲙⲉ. ⲟⲩⲱⲱ as n.m. desire, love, wish; ⲟⲩⲱⲱ ⲛ̄ ⲍⲏⲧ heart's desire; ⲙ̄ ⲡ(ˀ)ⲟⲩⲱⲱ on one's own; voluntarily, willingly.

ⲟⲩⲱⲱ n.m. cleft, gap; interval, pause, holiday; ⲡⲟⲩⲱⲱ ⲛ̄ ⲧⲙⲏⲧⲉ Thursday (?). ⲕⲁ-ⲟⲩⲱⲱ to set an interval; ϯ- ⲟⲩⲱⲱ idem. ϥ̄-ⲟⲩⲱⲱ ⲉ to wait for. (ⲛ̄) ⲟⲩⲉⲱⲛ̄ prep. without.

ⲟⲩⲱⲱⲃ̄ ⲟⲩⲉⲱⲃ̄- ⲟⲩⲟⲱⲃˀ vb. tr. to answer (someone: ⲉ, ⲛⲁˀ, rarely suff.). ⲟⲩⲱⲱⲃ̄ ⲙ̄ⲛ̄ to converse with. ⲟⲩⲱⲱⲃ̄ ⲛ̄ⲥⲁ to repeat after (in response). ⲟⲩⲱⲱⲃ̄ ⲟⲩⲃⲉ to testify against. ⲟⲩⲱⲱⲃ̄ as n.m. answer.

ⲟⲩⲱⲱⲉ (ⲟⲩⲱⲱⲱⲉ) to consume, be consumed (fire, heat).

ⲟⲩⲱⲱⲙ̄ ⲟⲩⲉⲱⲙ̄- ⲟⲩⲟⲱⲙˀ Q ⲟⲩⲟⲱⲙ̄ vb. tr. to knead, mix, compound (ⲙ̄ⲙⲟˀ; with: ⲙ̄ⲛ̄, ⲍ̄ⲓ, ⲍ̄ⲛ̄). as n.m. dough. ⲙⲁ ⲛ̄ ⲟⲩⲱⲱⲙ̄ kneading place.

ⲟⲩⲱⲱⲥ̄ ⲟⲩⲉⲱⲥ̄- ⲟⲩⲟⲱⲥˀ Q ⲟⲩⲟⲱⲥ̄ to become broad, level, flat; to be at ease; also tr. to make broad etc. ⲟⲩⲱⲱⲥ̄ ⲉⲃⲟⲗ tr. and intr. to spread out/forth, extend; as n.m. extent, breadth; ease. ⲟⲩⲗⲱⲥⲉ, ⲟⲩⲟⲱⲥⲉ, ⲟⲩⲉⲱⲥⲉ n.f. breadth.

ⲟⲩⲱⲱⲧ̄ vb. tr. to greet, kiss; to worship (ⲙ̄ⲙⲟˀ, ⲉ, ⲛⲁˀ); ⲟⲩⲱⲱⲧ̄ ⲉⲭⲛ̄/ⲍⲁ to worship, do obeisance at. ⲱⲟⲩ-ⲟⲩⲱⲱⲧ̄ adj. to be revered. ογλϣτε n.f. worship.

ογωϣϥ ογεϣϥ- ογοϣϥˣ (ογλϣϥˣ) Q ογοϣϥ vb. tr. to break down,
crush, destroy (ⲙⲙⲟˣ); vb. intr. to be worn down, broken, crushed, destroyed. As n.m. breakage, destruction.

ογωϩ ογεϩ- ογλϩˣ Q ογнϩ (1) vb. tr. to put, place set
(ⲙⲙⲟˣ); Q to be placed, situated, set; ογωϩ ⲙⲙⲟˣ ε to
add to, set on, apply to, bring on; ογωϩ ετοοτˣ to add,
repeat, do again (vb. complement in Circum. or ε + Inf.);
ογωϩ εχⲛ to add (sthg.: ⲙⲙⲟˣ) to; ογωϩ ⲛτοοτˣ to leave
(a deposit or pledge) with; ογωϩ ϩλ to invest/deposit
for/with; ογωϩ εβολ to set (sthg.: ⲙⲙⲟˣ) down, leave;
ογωϩ επεϲнτ to set down. (2) vb. reflex. to put or
place oneself; ογλϩˣ ⲛϲλ to follow. (3) intr. to live,
dwell, reside, be situated, be; ογωϩ ε live etc. with,
by; ογωϩ εχⲛ, εϩρλι εχⲛ to live etc. on, upon; ογωϩ ⲙⲛ
to live etc. with; sim. with ϩλ, ϩⲛ, ϩι, and ϩιχⲛ. As
n.m. place where one stops, stands, dwells. ⲙλ ⲛ ογωϩ
idem. ϭιⲛογωϩ manner of life.

ογωϩε n.m. fisherman; ⲙⲛτογωϩε fisherman's profession.

ογωϩⲙ ογεϩⲙ- ογλϩⲙˣ Q ογοϩⲙ vb. tr. to repeat, interpret
(ⲙⲙⲟˣ); intr. to repeat, answer, respond (to: ε, εχⲛ,
ⲛλˣ, ⲛϲλ); to contradict, object to (ογβε, ϩλ, ϩι); reflex. to respond, repeat. ογεϩⲙ- may be prefixed to an
Inf.: to re-(do), (do) again. As n.m. answer, objec-
tion, interpretation. ⲛ ογωϩⲙ adv. again. ρεϥογωϩⲙ one
who contradicts; ⲙⲛτρεϥογωϩⲙ opposition, disobedience.
ϭιⲛογωϩⲙ opposition. ογλϩⲙεϥ n.m. interpreter.

ογωχε (ογωωχε) ογεεχε- (ογεχ-) ογοοχˣ (ογοχˣ) vb. tr. to
cut out, cut off (ⲙⲙⲟˣ).

ογωϭ n. (pl.) architectural term: entrance, portico.

ογωϭⲛ ογεϭⲛ- ογοϭⲛˣ Q ογοϭⲛ vb. tr. to break, break down,
destroy; vb. intr. to break, be broken. As n.m.
destruction, breakage. λτογωϭⲛ unbroken.

ογωϭϲ vb. to collect (a contribution); as n.m. collection.

ογϣλⲡ n.m. a loan; ε πογϣλⲡ on loan. † ε πογϣλⲡ to give

on loan (to: ɴᴀˀ); ϫı ε ⲡⲟⲩϣⲁⲡ to receive on loan.
ⲟⲩϣⲏ (pl. ⲟⲩϣⲟⲟⲩⲉ) n.f. night. ⲧⲡⲁϣⲉ ⲛ̄ ⲧⲉⲩϣⲏ midnight.
ⲛ̄ ⲟⲩⲟⲩϣⲏ during a night. ⲛ̄ ⲧⲉⲩϣⲏ by night. ⲣ̄-ⲟⲩϣⲏ to
pass the night.
ⲟⲩⲍⲟⲣ (f. ⲟⲩⲍⲟⲣⲉ, ⲟⲩⲍⲟⲟⲣⲉ, ⲟⲩⲍⲱⲣⲉ; pl. ⲟⲩⲍⲟⲟⲣ) n.m. dog.
ⲟⲩϫⲁı, Q ⲟⲩⲟϫ vb. intr. to become whole, sound, safe, saved
(in religious sense); ⲟⲩϫⲁı ε to be saved from. As n.m.
health, safety. ⲁⲧⲟⲩϫⲁı unsound, incurable. ⲙⲛ̄ⲧⲁⲧⲟⲩϫⲁı
unsoundness, unhealthiness.

ⲟⲩⲁ ⲛ̄ ⲟⲩⲱⲧ: ⲟⲩⲱⲧ	ⲟⲩⲉⲥⲧⲱⲛ: ⲟⲩⲟⲥⲧⲛ̄	ⲟⲩⲟⲟⲧⲉ: ⲟⲩⲱⲧ
ⲟⲩⲁⲁⲃ: ⲟⲩⲟⲡ	ⲟⲩⲉⲧˀ: ⲟⲩⲱⲧ	ⲟⲩⲟⲥϭˀ: ⲱⲥϭ̄
ⲟⲩⲁⲙⲟⲙⲉ: ⲟⲙⲉ	ⲟⲩⲉⲧ-: ⲟⲩⲱⲱⲧⲉ	ⲟⲩⲟⲧⲉ: ⲟⲩⲱⲧ
ⲟⲩⲁⲣⲧ̄: ⲟⲩⲉⲣⲧ̄	ⲟⲩⲉⲧⲟⲩⲱⲧ: ⲟⲩⲟⲧⲟⲩⲉⲧ	ⲟⲩⲟⲧⲍⲉ: ⲟⲩⲱⲧⲍ̄
ⲟⲩⲁⲥⲧˀ: ⲟⲩⲉıⲥⲉ	ⲟⲩⲉⲧϥ̄-: ⲟⲩⲱⲧⲃ̄	ⲟⲩⲟⲧϥ(ˀ): ⲟⲩⲱⲧⲃ̄
ⲟⲩⲁⲥϥⲉ: ⲟⲩⲱⲥϥ̄	ⲟⲩⲉϥⲛ̄: ⲟⲩⲱϣ	ⲟⲩⲟϣⲥⲉ: ⲟⲩⲱϣϭ̄
ⲟⲩⲁⲧⲃⲉ: ⲟⲩⲱⲧⲃ̄	ⲟⲩⲉϣⲟⲩⲱϣ: ⲟⲩⲟϣⲟⲩⲉϣ	ⲟⲩⲟⲥⲃⲉϥ: ⲟⲩⲁⲍⲃⲉϥ
ⲟⲩⲁⲧϥⲉ: ⲟⲩⲱⲧⲃ̄	ⲟⲩⲉϣⲥⲉ: ⲟⲩⲱϣϭ̄	ⲟⲩⲟⲍⲉ: ⲟⲩⲟⲟⲍⲉ
ⲟⲩⲁⲧⲍⲉ: ⲱⲧⲍ̄	ⲟⲩⲉϭϭ̄-: ⲱϭϭ̄	ⲟⲩⲟϫ: ⲟⲩϫⲁı
ⲟⲩⲁϣⲥⲉ: ⲟⲩⲱϣϭ̄	ⲟⲩⲏⲏⲃ: ⲟⲩⲟⲡ	ⲟⲩⲣⲱⲙ: ⲙ̄ⲣⲱⲙ
ⲟⲩⲁϣⲧⲉ: ⲟⲩⲱϣⲧ̄	ⲟⲩⲏⲛ: ⲟⲩⲱⲛ	ⲟⲩⲧⲱˀ: ⲟⲩⲧⲉ
ⲟⲩⲁ²ⲙⲉ: ⲟⲩⲱ²ⲙ̄	ⲟⲩⲏⲩ: ⲟⲩⲉ	ⲟⲩⲱ: ⲉⲩⲱ
ⲟⲩⲁ²ⲙⲉϥ: ⲟⲩⲱ²ⲙ̄	ⲟⲩⲗⲱⲙ: ⲙ̄ⲣⲱⲙ	ⲟⲩⲱⲙⲉ: ⲟⲩⲱⲱⲙⲉ
ⲟⲩⲁⲭⲉ: ⲁⲭⲉ	ⲟⲩⲛ̄-: ⲟⲩⲱⲛ	ⲟⲩⲱⲧ: ⲟⲩⲱⲱⲧⲉ, ⲱⲧ
ⲟⲩⲉⲉıⲏ: ⲟⲩⲟⲉıⲉ	ⲟⲩⲟⲙˀ: ⲟⲩⲱⲱⲙⲉ	ⲟⲩⲱⲧϥ̄: ⲟⲩⲱⲧⲃ̄
ⲟⲩⲉⲉⲧⲉ: ⲟⲩⲉıⲧⲉ	ⲟⲩⲟⲙⲡⲧⲉ: ⲟⲩⲟⲙⲧⲉ	ⲟⲩⲱⲧⲍ̄: ⲱⲧⲍ̄
ⲟⲩⲉı: ⲟⲩⲁ	ⲟⲩⲟⲙⲛ̄ⲧ: ⲟⲩⲙⲟⲧ	ⲟⲩⲱⲱⲭⲉ: ⲟⲩⲱⲭⲉ
ⲟⲩⲉıⲏ: ⲟⲩⲟⲉıⲉ	ⲟⲩⲟⲟⲗⲉⲥ: ⲟⲩⲱⲱⲗⲉ	ⲟⲩⲱϣⲙ̄: ⲱϣⲙ̄
ⲟⲩⲉⲛⲧ̄: ϥⲛ̄ⲧ	ⲟⲩⲟⲟⲙˀ: ⲟⲩⲱⲱⲙⲉ	ⲟⲩϥ: ⲱϥ
ⲟⲩⲉⲣⲍ̄: ⲟⲩⲱⲣⲍ̄	ⲟⲩⲟⲟⲙⲧⲉ: ⲟⲩⲟⲙⲧⲉ	ⲟⲩⲍⲱⲣⲉ: ⲟⲩⲍⲟⲣ

ⲱ

ⲱ interj. O, Oh.
ⲱⲃⲧ̄, ⲱϥⲧ̄ n.m. goose.
ⲱⲃϣ ⲉⲃϣ- ⲟⲃϣˀ Q ⲟⲃϣ (1) trans.: to forget, overlook,
neglect (ε); Q to be forgotten, neglected; also used
reflexively. (2) intr. to sleep, fall asleep; Q to be
asleep. As n.m. forgetfulness; sleep. ⲣ̄-ⲡⲱⲃϣ to become forgetful, to forget; n. obj. with ⲛ̄; pron. obj.
with suff. in ⲣ̄-ⲡ(ˀ)ⲱⲃϣ; as n.m. forgetfulness. ⲣⲉϥⲣ̄-
ⲡⲱⲃϣ one who forgets. ⲉⲃϣⲉ, ⲃϣⲉ n.f. forgetfulness,

carelessness, sleep; ⲣ̄-ⲉⲃϣⲉ to be forgetful; ϯ-ⲉⲃϣⲉ,
ϯ ⲛ̄ ⲟⲩⲉⲃϣⲉ ⲉ ⲡ2ⲏⲧ ⲛ̄ to make forgetful; ⲭⲓ ⲛ̄ ⲟⲩⲉⲃϣⲉ to
be forgetful. ⲟⲃϣⲧ̄ n.f. forgetfulness.

ⲱⲕ ⲛ̄ 2ⲏⲧ to be content.

ⲱⲕⲙ̄ ⲉⲕⲙ̄- Q ⲟⲕⲙ̄ vb. intr. to become dark, gloomy, changed
for the worse (toward: ⲉ, ⲉ2ⲟⲩⲛ ⲉ); rarely tr. to
darken, alter; as n.m. sadness, gloom.

ⲱⲗ ⲟⲗ⸗ Q ⲏⲗ (mainly Boh.) to lay hold of, take, gather in
(ⲙ̄ⲙⲟ⸗); reflex. to withdraw (± ⲉⲣⲟ⸗ ethical dat.); ⲱⲗ ⲉ
to bring/take to; ⲱⲗ ⲉⲃⲟⲗ to take away; ⲱⲗ ⲉ2ⲟⲩⲛ to
bring in; ⲱⲗ ⲉ2ⲣⲁⲓ to lift up; to withdraw. As n.m.
harvest, in-gathering. ⲟⲗⲧ̄ n.f. what is collected.

ⲱⲗⲕ̄, Q ⲟⲗⲕ̄ vb. intr. to become bent, turned aside, dis-
torted (toward: ⲉ); also with adv. ⲉⲃⲟⲗ, ⲉⲡⲉⲥⲏⲧ, ⲉ2ⲣⲁⲓ,
ⲛ̄ⲥⲁ ⲡⲁ2ⲟⲩ. ⲱⲗⲕ̄ ϣⲁ, ⲉⲗⲕ̄-/ⲗ̄ⲕ-ϣⲁ to turn up nose, sneer
(at: ⲛ̄ⲥⲁ). ⲟⲗⲕⲧ̄, ⲟⲗⲉⲕⲧ̄ n.f. bend, corner.

ⲱⲗⲙ̄ ⲟⲗⲙ⸗ Q ⲟⲗⲙ̄ vb. tr. to clasp, embrace (ⲉ, ⲉ2ⲟⲩⲛ ⲉ).

ⲱⲙⲕ̄ ⲉⲙⲕ̄- ⲟⲙⲕ⸗ vb. tr. to swallow (ⲙ̄ⲙⲟ⸗); intr. to be
swallowed.

ⲱⲙⲧ̄ ⲉⲙⲧ̄- ⲟⲙⲥ⸗ Q ⲟⲙⲧ̄ vb. tr. to sink, submerge, dip (ⲙ̄ⲙⲟ⸗);
vb. intr. to sink, be submerged, dive (into: ⲉ, ⲉ2ⲟⲩⲛ
ⲉ, ⲙ̄ⲙⲟ⸗, 2ⲁ, 2ⲛ̄), ± ⲉⲃⲟⲗ, ⲉⲡⲉⲥⲏⲧ. As n.m. sinking, di-
ving, baptism. ⲣⲉϥⲱⲙⲧ̄ diver. ⲉⲙⲥⲉ, ⲙ̄ⲥⲉ n. submersion.

ⲱⲙⲝ̄ ⲉⲙⲝ̄- ⲟⲙⲝ⸗ vb. tr. to wean (ⲙ̄ⲙⲟ⸗; from: ⲉⲃⲟⲗ 2ⲛ̄).

ⲱⲛⲉ n.m.(f.) stone. ⲙⲁ ⲛ̄ ⲱⲛⲉ stony place. ⲣ̄-ⲱⲛⲉ to become (like) stone. 2ⲓ-ⲱⲛⲉ to throw stones (at: ⲉ).
ⲛⲉⲭ-ⲱⲛⲉ idem. ⲃⲁⲕ-ⲱⲛⲉ stone-thrower. ϣⲁⲧ-ⲱⲛⲉ quarry.
ⲉⲛⲉ-ⲙ̄-ⲙⲉ precious stone, gem.

ⲱⲛⲕ̄ ⲟⲛⲕ⸗ (ⲟⲙⲕ⸗, ⲟⲛⲅ⸗) vb. tr. and reflex. to leap (ⲉ: at,
upon; 2ⲓⲭⲛ̄ from on; ⲉ2ⲣⲁⲓ up; ⲉ2ⲣⲁⲓ ⲉⲭⲛ̄ up onto; ⲉ2ⲣⲁⲓ
2ⲛ̄/2ⲁ/2ⲓ up from; ⲉⲃⲟⲗ out).

ⲱⲛⲧ̄ (ⲱⲛⲧ̄) vb. intr. to be pinched, contracted.

ⲱⲛϣ, Q ⲟⲛϣ (ⲟⲟⲛϣ) vb. intr. to become dazed, astonished,
dumb with astonishment; to gape (at: ⲛ̄ⲥⲁ). ⲱⲛϣ ⲉⲃⲟⲗ to
muse, be in a trance. ⲟⲛϣⲧ̄ n. astonishment.

ⲱⲛⲍ̄, Q ⲟⲛⲍ̄ vb. intr. to live, be alive; as n.m. life. ⲣⲉϥ-
ϯ-ⲱⲛⲍ̄ life-giver. ⲅⲓⲛⲱⲛⲍ̄ way of life, means of living.
ⲱⲡ ⲉⲡ- ⲟⲡ⁼ Q ⲏⲡ vb. tr. to count; to reckon, regard, consider (ⲙ̄ⲙⲟ⁼; as: ⲙ̄ⲙⲟ⁼; as belonging to: ⲉ); to ascribe
(ⲙ̄ⲙⲟ⁼; to: ⲉ); to esteem or be esteemed. Q is esp. freq.
in senses: to be ascribed, related, belonging to. ⲱⲡ
ⲙⲛ̄ to number or be numbered among/with; to become part
of. ⲱⲡ ⲛ̄ⲥⲁ to count, enumerate. As n.m. count, reck-
oning; ⲁⲧⲱⲡ unesteemed; ϯ-ⲱⲡ, ϯ ⲙ̄ ⲡⲱⲡ to render an account, give an accounting (of); ϥⲓ-ⲱⲡ to take a count
(of: ⲛ̄, ⲉ, ⲙⲛ̄). ⲏⲡⲉ n.f. number; ⲁⲧⲏⲡⲉ numberless; ⲭⲓ-
ⲏⲡⲉ to take count (of: ⲙ̄ⲙⲟ⁼); ⲁⲧⲭⲓ-ⲏⲡ countless.
ⲱⲣⲃ̄ (ⲱⲣϥ̄) ⲉⲣⲃ̄- ⲟⲣⲃ⁼ (ⲟⲣϥ⁼) Q ⲟⲣⲃ̄ (ⲟⲣϥ̄) + ⲉⲍⲟⲩⲛ vb. tr. to
enclose, shut in, restrict (ⲙ̄ⲙⲟ⁼); vb. intr. to be shut
in, enclosed; as n.m. frame, siege, enclosing, seclusion; ⲁⲧⲟⲣⲃ⁼ unlimited. ⲉⲣⲃⲉ, ⲣ̄ⲃⲉ n.f. pen, enclosure.
ⲱⲣⲕ̄ ⲟⲣⲕ⁼ vb. tr. to swear (obj. oath: ⲙ̄ⲙⲟ⁼); to adjure,
swear to (person: ⲉ, ⲛⲁ⁼; concerning: ⲉⲧⲃⲉ, ⲉⲭⲛ̄, ⲍⲁ; by,
upon: ⲉⲭⲛ̄, ⲍ ⲓ); as n.m. swearing, oath. ⲱⲣⲕ̄ ⲛ̄ ⲛⲟⲩⲭ to
swear falsely; as n. false oath; ⲣⲉϥⲱⲣⲕ̄ ⲛ̄ ⲛⲟⲩⲭ one who
swears falsely; ⲙⲛ̄ⲧⲣⲉϥⲱⲣⲕ̄ ⲛ̄ ⲛⲟⲩⲭ swearing falsely. ⲧⲁϣⲉ-
ⲱⲣⲕ̄, ⲣⲉϥⲧⲁϣⲉ-ⲱⲣⲕ̄ one who swears a lot.
ⲱⲣϣ̄, Q ⲟⲣϣ̄ (ⲍⲟⲣϣ̄) vb. intr. to become cold; tr. to scorch.
ⲱⲣⲭ̄ ⲉⲣⲭ̄- (ⲣ̄ⲭ-) ⲟⲣⲭ⁼ Q ⲟⲣⲭ̄ vb. tr. to fasten, bind, imprison; to close (ⲙ̄ⲙⲟ⁼; against: ⲉ); intr. to be firm, se-
cure. As n.m. firmness, assurance; deed of security.
ⲍ̄ⲛ ⲟⲩⲱⲣⲭ̄ with assurance, with certainty; diligently,
carefully. ⲉ ⲡⲱⲣⲭ̄ for sure. ⲙⲁ ⲛ̄ ⲱⲣⲭ̄ prison; stronghold.
ⲱⲥⲕ̄, Q ⲟⲥⲕ̄ vb. intr. to continue, be prolonged; to delay,
remain; to be long past, out of date; oft. w. Circum.:
to remain doing, continue doing; or + ⲉ + Inf. idem.
As n.m. duration, continuance, delay. ⲁⲥⲕⲉ n.f. delay.
ⲱⲥϭ̄ (ⲱϭⲥ̄) ⲉⲥϭ̄- (ⲟⲩⲉϭⲥ̄-) ⲟⲥϭ⁼ (ⲟⲩⲟⲥϭ⁼) Q ⲟⲥϭ̄ vb. tr. to a-
noint, smear (ⲙ̄ⲙⲟ⁼).
ⲱⲧ, ⲟⲩⲱⲧ n.m. fat.

ⲱⲧⲡ̄ ⲉⲧⲡ̄- ⲟⲧⲡ⳿ Q ⲟⲛⲧ̄ vb. tr. to imprison, shut in (ⲙ̄ⲙⲟ⳿; in:
ⲉ); ⲱⲧⲡ̄ ⲉⲍⲟⲩⲛ idem (ⲉ, ⲍⲛ̄). ⲙⲁ ⲛ̄ ⲱⲧⲡ̄ ⲉⲍⲟⲩⲛ place of
confinement. ⳪ⲓⲛⲱⲧⲡ̄ ⲉⲍⲟⲩⲛ seclusion.

ⲱⲧⲡ̄ ⲟⲧⲡ⳿ Q ⲟⲧⲡ̄ vb. tr. to load (ⲙ̄ⲙⲟ⳿; with: ⲙ̄ⲙⲟ⳿). ⲉⲧⲡⲱ
n.f. load, burden; Ⳙⲁⲓ-ⲉⲧⲡⲱ porter, bearer of burden.

ⲱⲧⲍ̄ (ⲟⲩⲱⲧⲍ̄) ⲟⲧⲍ⳿ Q ⲟⲧⲍ̄ vb. tr. to weave; to sew, tie (ⲙ̄ⲙⲟ⳿;
to, onto: ⲉ, ⲍⲛ̄). ⲟⲩⲁⲧⲍⲉ n.m. warp (on loom).

ⲱⲱ (ⲱ), Q ⲉⲉⲧ (ⲉⲧ) vb. intr. to become pregnant (with:
ⲙ̄ⲙⲟ⳿); to conceive (by: ⲙⲛ̄, ⲍⲛ̄, ⲉⲃⲟⲗ ⲍⲛ̄); as n.m. conception. ϯ-ⲱⲱ to be pregnant.

ⲱⳡ ⲉⳡ- ⲟⳡ⳿ (± ⲉⲃⲟⲗ) (1) vb. tr. to utter, sound (ⲙ̄ⲙⲟ⳿); to
cry out (to, for: ⲉ, ⲉⲍⲣⲁⲓ ⲉ, ⲉⲭⲛ̄, ⲉⲍⲟⲩⲛ ⲉⲍⲣⲛ̄, ⲟⲩⲃⲉ);
(2) vb. tr. to read (ⲙ̄ⲙⲟ⳿; to: ⲉ, ⲛⲁ⳿; on, about: ⲉ,
ⲉⲭⲛ̄; in: ⲍⲓ, ⲍⲛ̄); as n.m. reading. ⲙⲁⲓ-ⲱⳡ fond of reading; ⲣⲉⳡⲱⳡ reader, lector. ⳪ⲓⲛⲱⳡ art of reading.

(ⲱⳡ) ⲟⳡ⳿ (ⲍⲟⳡ⳿, ⲟⲛⳡ⳿) reflex. only, + ⲉⲍⲟⲩⲛ ⲉ: to slip into
intrude into.

ⲱⳡⲙ̄ (ⲟⲩⲱⳡⲙ̄) ⲉⳡⲙ̄- ⲟⳡⲙ⳿ Q ⲟⳡⲙ̄ vb. tr. to dry up (ⲙ̄ⲙⲟ⳿), to
quench; vb. intr. to be quenched. ⲁⲧⲱⳡⲙ̄ unquenchable.

ⲱ⳪, ⲱⲃ, ⲟⲩ⳪ n.m. lettuce.

ⲱ⳽ⲉ (ⲱⲃⲉ) ⲉ⳽- ⲟ⳽⳿ (ⲟⲃ⳿) vb. tr. to press (ⲙ̄ⲙⲟ⳿; on, onto:
ⲉⲡⲉⳬⲏⲧ ⲉ, ⲉⲍⲟⲩⲛ ⲉ, ⲉⲭⲛ̄). ⳝⲉ ⲛ̄ ⲱ⳽ⲉ fuller's club.

ⲱ⳽ⲧ̄ (ⲱⲃⲧ̄) ⲉ⳽ⲧ̄- (ⲉⲃⲧ̄-) ⲟ⳽ⲧ⳿ (ⲟⲃⲧ⳿) Q ⲟ⳽ⲧ̄ (ⲟⲃⲧ̄) vb. tr. to
nail, fix (ⲙ̄ⲙⲟ⳿; to: ⲉ, ⲉⲍⲟⲩⲛ ⲉ, ⲉⲭⲛ̄); Q ⲟ⳽ⲧ̄ ⲛ̄ studded
with. ⲉⲓ⳽ⲧ̄, ⲉⲓⲃⲧ̄ n.m. nail, spike; ⳝⳅ̄-ⲛ̄-ⲉⲓ⳽ⲧ̄ blow or
wound of nail.

ⲱⲍ interj. woe! ⲱⲍ ⲉ woe to ...!

ⲱⲍⲉ, ⲁⲍⲉ, Q ⲁⲍⲉ vb. intr. to stand, stay, remain (with:
behind: ⲉⲡⲁⲍⲟⲩ); to wait (for: ⲉ, ⲛⲁ⳿); ⲱⲍⲉ ⲟⲩⲃⲉ to
stand against, resist, oppose; idem with ⲉⲃⲟⲗ ⲉ, ⲛ̄ⲃⲟⲗ ⲉ.
ⲁⲍⲉⲣⲁⲧ⳿ (reflex. suff.) to stand (ⲉ: before), to attend,
to resist; ⲁⲍⲉⲣⲁⲧ⳿ ⲉⲭⲛ̄, ⲍⲓⲭⲛ̄ to stand upon, at, beside;
to stand against, resist. ⲁⲍⲉⲣⲁⲧ⳿ ⲙⲛ̄ to stand with.
Also w. ⲟⲩⲃⲉ against, ⲍⲓⲣⲛ̄ at, ⲍⲁⲍⲧⲛ̄, ⲍⲁⲧⲛ̄ before, in
the presence of. ⲙⲁ ⲛ̄ ⲁⲍⲉⲣⲁⲧ⳿ place for standing.

ⲱⲥⳝ ⲉⳝⳝ- ⲟⳝⲥ⸗ (ⲟⲥⳝ⸗) vb. tr. to reap, mow (ⲙ̄ⲙⲟ⸗); as n.m.
reaping, harvesting; ⲣⲁ-ⲱⲥⳝ act of reaping. ⲟⳝⳝ, ⲟⲥⳝ
n.m. sickle, scythe; ⲭⲓ-ⲟⳝⳝ to wield a sickle; ⲭⲁⲓ-ⲟⳝⳝ
sickle-bearer, reaper. ⲟⲥⳝϥ, ⲁⲥⳝϥ n.m. knife, sickle.

ⲱⲝ n. thief.

ⲱⲝⲛ̄ ⲉⲝⲛ̄- ⲟⲝⲛ⸗ vb. intr. to cease, perish (from: ⲉⲃⲟⲗ ⲛ̄,
ⲉⲃⲟⲗ ⳝⲛ̄); vb. tr. to destroy, make cease, put an end to
(ⲙ̄ⲙⲟ⸗); as n.m. ceasing, destruction. ⲁⲝⲛ̄ ⲱⲝⲛ̄ without
ceasing. ⲁⲧⲱⲝⲛ̄ unceasing.

ⲱϭ͞ⲃ (ⳝⲱϭ͞ⲃ) ⲉϭ͞ⲃ- Q ⳝⲟϭ͞ⲃ (ⲟϭϥ) vb. intr. to become cold,
freeze; as n.m. cold, frost. ⲟϭⲃ͞ⲥ n. cold.

ⲱϭ͞ⲣ ⲟϭⲣ⸗ Q ⲟϭ͞ⲣ vb. intr. to become hard, stiff, frozen;
also tr. to freeze, stiffen.

ⲱϭ͞ⲧ ⲉϭ͞ⲧ- ⲟϭⲧ⸗ (ⲟⲝⲧ⸗, ⲟⲧϭ⸗) vb. tr. to choke, throttle (ⲙ̄ⲙⲟ⸗).

ⲱ: ⲱⲱ, ⲟ	ⲱⲛ͞ϭ: ⲱⲛ͞ⲧ	ⲱⳝ: ⲟⲟⳝ
ⲱⲃ: ⲱϥ	ⲱⲣϥ: ⲱⲣ͞ⲃ	ⲱⳝⲉ: ⲟⳝⲉ
ⲱⲃⲉ: ⲱϥⲉ	ⲱϥ: ⳝⲱⲃ	ⲱϭ͞ⲥ: ⲱⲥ͞ϭ
ⲱⲃ͞ⲧ: ⲱϥ͞ⲧ	ⲱϥ͞ⲧ: ⲱⲃ͞ⲧ	

ⳡ

ⳡ- prefixed vb. (+ Inf.) to be able to, know how to, be
allowed to. See 26.2.

ⳡⲁ vb. intr. to rise (of the sun), ± ⲉⳝⲣⲁⲓ, ⲉⲃⲟⲗ. As n.m.
rising (of sun). ⲙⲁ ⲛ̄ ⳡⲁ the east. ⲣⲁ-ⳡⲁ eastern side.

ⳡⲁ- vb. to begin; only in cpds. ⳡⲁ-ⲙⲓⲥⲉ, ⳡⲁ-ⲥⲱⲛ͞ⲧ. See
second element.

ⳡⲁ n.m. festival; divine service. ⳝⲓⲃⲟⲗ ⲙ̄ ⲡⳡⲁ excommuni-
cated. ⳡⲁ ⲱ great festival. ⳝⲟⲟⲩ ⲛ̄ ⳡⲁ festival day.
ⳡⲁ is also used as vb. to keep festival (for: ⲉ, ⲙ̄ⲙⲟ⸗).
ⲣ̄-(ⲡ)ⳡⲁ to keep festival (for: ⲉ); ⲙⲁ ⲛ̄ ⲣ̄-ⳡⲁ church;
ⲙⲛ̄ⲧⲣⲉϥⲣ̄-ⳡⲁ occasion of festival; ϯ-ⳡⲁ to give communion.

ⳡⲁ, ⳡⲉ (ⳡⲁⲛⲧ⸗, ⳡⲁⲁⲧ⸗, ⳡⲁⲁⲛⲧ⸗, ⳡⲁⲧⲧ⸗, ⳡⲉⲛⲧ⸗) n.m. nose.
ⲥⲱⲃⲉ ⲛ̄ ⳡⲁ, ⲥ͞ⲃ-ⳡⲁ, ⲭⲉϥ-ⳡⲁ, ⲥ͞ⲃ-ⳡⲉ n.m.f. nostrils.

ⳡⲁ (ⳡⲁⲣⲟ⸗) prep. (1) to, toward (a person); (2) to, at (a
place); (3) till, at, by, for (a time); (4) up to, to

length of (in reckonings); (5) except (i.e. up to but
not including). See cpds. under second element.

ϣⲁⲁⲃ, ϣⲁⲁϥ, ϣⲟⲟⲃ n.m. skin.

ϣⲁⲁⲣ, ϣⲁⲣ (pl. ϣⲁⲁⲣⲉ) n.m. skin, hide, leather. ⲃⲁⲕ-ϣⲁⲁⲣ
tanner. ⲟⲩⲁⲙ-ϣⲁⲁⲣ ulcer, sore. ⲣⲙ̄ⲛ̄ϣⲁⲁⲣ man of skin
(i.e. the purely physical person).

ϣⲁⲁⲣ, ϣⲁⲣ, ϣⲁⲁⲣⲉ, ϣⲁⲣⲉ n.m. price; ⲣ̄-ϣⲁⲁⲣ to fix a price,
bargain (for: ⲉ); ϯ-ϣⲁⲁⲣ idem.

ϣⲁⲁⲣⲉ (ϣⲁⲓⲣⲉ, ϣⲁⲁⲣ) ϣⲁⲣ⸗ Q ϣⲁⲣ vb. tr. to smite (ⲉⲣⲟ⸗); as
n.m. blow, stroke; ⲣⲉϥϣⲁⲁⲣⲉ demon, smiter; ⲙⲛ̄ⲧⲣⲉϥϣⲁⲁⲣⲉ
devilry. ⲙⲛ̄ⲧϣⲟⲟⲣ idem.

ϣⲁⲓ n.m. fortune. ⲡϣⲁⲓ also as name of a god.

ϣⲁⲓ adj. new (after noun, with ⲛ̄).

ϣⲁⲓⲣⲉ n.f. couch, cohabitation; ⲣ̄-ϣⲁⲓⲣⲉ to lie down.

ϣⲁⲓⲣⲉ n.f. sheepfold.

ϣⲁⲗ n.m. myrrh.

ϣⲁⲗⲓⲟⲩ, ϣⲁⲗⲏⲩ, ϣⲁⲣⲓⲟⲩ n.m. administrative official (title).

ϣⲁⲗⲟⲟⲩ n.f. water-wheel or the like.

ϣⲁⲣⲃⲁ, ϣⲁⲃⲣⲁ, ϣⲁϥⲣⲁ n.m. scorching heat; ⲧⲏⲩ ⲛ̄ ϣⲁⲣⲃⲁ
scorching wind; ⲟ ⲛ̄ ϣⲁⲣⲃⲁ to be scorched, parched; ϯ-
ϣⲁⲣⲃⲁ to scorch (ⲉϩⲟⲩⲛ ⲉ).

ϣⲁⲣⲕⲉ n.m. lack of water, drought; ⲣ̄-ϣⲁⲣⲕⲉ to be dried up.

ϣⲁⲩ, ϣⲁⲟⲩ, ϣⲟⲩ- n.m. use, value; as adj. useful, suitable,
fitting, virtuous; ⲁⲧϣⲁⲩ useless, worthless, obscene;
ⲣ̄-ϣⲁⲩ (Q ⲟ ⲛ̄) to be useful, suitable (for: ⲉ, ⲛⲁ⸗, ⲉⲭⲛ̄);
to become prosperous; ⲙⲛ̄ⲧϣⲁⲩ usefulness; propriety, modesty; ⲣ̄-ⲁⲧϣⲁⲩ to become useless, worthless, vain; ⲙⲛ̄ⲧ-
ⲁⲧϣⲁⲩ worthlessness. ϣⲟⲩ- worthy of, fit for (in cpds.).

ϣⲁⲩ n.m. measure, extent; ⲉ/ⲛ̄/ϣⲁ ⲛϣⲁⲩ ⲛ̄ to the extent of;
ⲛⲁ ⲛϣⲁⲩ ⲛ̄ for about (the extent of).

ϣⲁⲩ (pl. ϣⲏⲩ) n.m. trunk, stump; piece, lump; (ⲛ̄) ϣⲁⲩ ϣⲁⲩ
into many pieces; ⲉⲓⲣⲉ ⲙ̄ⲙⲟ⸗ ⲛ̄ ϣⲁⲩ ϣⲁⲩ to divide into
many pieces.

ϣⲁϥⲉ, ϣⲁⲁϥⲉ, ϣⲁⲃⲉ, ϣⲉϥⲉ, ϣⲉⲃⲉ, ϣⲏϥⲉ, ϣⲏⲃⲉ, ϣⲓϥⲉ, ϣⲓⲃⲉ;
Q ϣⲟⲃⲉ vb. intr. to swell up.

ϢΑϨ n.m. flame, fire; †-ϢΑϨ to burn, be alight (± ЄΒΟΛ).

ϢΑϪЄ vb. tr. to speak, talk, say (ⲘⲘⲞⸯ). ϢΑϪЄ Є to speak
  to; to speak about, tell of; to speak against. ϢΑϪЄ
  ЄϨΟΥΝ Є, ЄϨΡΑΙ Є to speak to. ϢΑϪЄ ЄΧⲚ to speak for,
  on behalf of; ЄΠЄϹΗΤ ЄΧⲚ to speak down (from above).
  ϢΑϪЄ ⲘⲚ to speak with. ϢΑϪЄ ⲚϹΑ to speak against, ma-
  lign. Also with ΝΑϨΡⲚ before, ΟΥΒЄ against, ϨΑ concerning, ϨⲚ/Ⲛ with, in. As n.m. word, saying; thing, matter, affair; story, account, tale. ΝΟϬ Ⲛ ϢΑϪЄ boastful
  words; ΧЄ-ΝΟϬ Ⲛ ϢΑϪЄ to boast; ΡЄϤΧЄ-ΝΟϬ Ⲛ ϢΑϪЄ braggart.
  ϨΑϨ Ⲛ ϢΑϪЄ verbosity, garrulousness; ⲘⲚΤϨΑϨ Ⲛ ϢΑϪЄ idem.
  Ⲣ-ϨΑϨ Ⲛ ϢΑϪЄ to be garrulous. Ⲣ-ΟΥϢΑϪЄ Ⲛ ΟΥⲰΤ ⲘⲚ to
  make an agreement with. ΤΑϢЄ-ϢΑϪЄ to talk a lot, multi-
  ply words. ΧΙ-ϢΑϪЄ to accept the word (of: ⲚΤⲚ). ϬⲚ-
  ϢΑϪЄ to complain (against: ЄϨΟΥΝ Є). ϢⲬ- in various
  cpds. (see 2nd element). ΑΤϢΑϪЄ speechless; unspeakable,
  ineffable (± ⲘⲘΟⸯ, ЄΡΟⸯ). ΡЄϤϢΑϪЄ eloquent person. ϹΑ
  Ⲛ ϢΑϪЄ babbler. ϬΙⲚϢΑϪЄ speech, saying, tale.

ϢΒЄ, ϢϤЄ, ϢЄΒЄ n. off-scouring, filth.

ϢΒΗΡ (f. ϢΒЄЄΡЄ; pl. ϢΒЄЄΡ, ϢΒЄЄΡЄ) n.m.f. friend, comrade,
  companion. ϢΒⲢ- freq. in cpds.: companion in (often =
  Gk. prefix συν-). ⲘⲚΤϢΒΗΡ n.f. friendship, community.
  Ⲣ-ϢΒΗΡ (Q o Ⲛ) to be friend, partner (to, with: ⲘⲚ, Є).

ϢΒⲰ, ϢϤⲰ n.f. tale, fable; as adj. fabled, fabulous. ϢЄΧ-
  ϢΒⲰ, ϢⲬ-ϢΒⲰ telling of tales; ΡЄϤΧЄ-ϢΒⲰ teller of tales.

ϢΒⲰΤ, ϢΒΟΤ (pl. ϢΒΑΤЄ) n.m. rod, staff; ϤΑΙ-ϢΒⲰΤ staff-
  bearer.

ϢЄ (ϢΗ, ϢЄΙ) vb. intr. to go (± ethical dat.). This verb
  is mainly Boh.; its use with adv. and prep. is completely parallel to that of ΒⲰΚ.

ϢЄ, ϢΗ, ϢΙ n.m.(f.) wood, beam of wood; many special meanings: cross, gallows, stocks, pillory, shaft, stave.
  For various woods (ϢЄ Ⲛ) see 2nd element.

ϢЄ number: hundred. ϢΗΤ two hundred. ⲘЄϨϢЄ hundredth.
  ϢЄ ϢЄ, Є ΠЄϢЄ ϢЄ by hundreds. See 30.7.

ϣⲉ, ϣⲁ prep. by (in swearing an oath).

ϣⲉⲃⲓⲏⲩ, ϣⲉⲃⲃⲓⲏⲩ, ϣⲃⲉⲓⲁⲉⲓⲧ, ϣⲃⲃⲓⲁⲉⲓⲧ (all Q) to be changed,
different (from: ⲉ; in regard to: ⲍⲛ̄). ϣⲃⲉⲓⲱ, ϣⲃⲓⲟ,
ϣⲃⲃⲓⲱ, ϣⲃⲃⲓⲟ, ϣⲉⲃⲓⲱ, ϣⲉⲃⲃⲓⲱ, ϣⲉϥⲓⲱ n.f. change, exchange, requital; ⲡ̄-ϣⲃⲉⲓⲱ to replace, be instead (of:
ⲙ̄ⲙⲟˢ); ϫⲓ-(ⲧ)ϣⲃⲉⲓⲱ to take requital, be repaid.

ϣⲉⲉⲓ (= ϣⲉ + ⲉⲓ) to go and come, be carried to and fro,
wander. As n. derangement, madness.

ϣⲉⲗⲉⲉⲧ n.f. bride, daughter-in-law; marriage. ⲡ̄-ϣⲉⲗⲉⲉⲧ
(Q o ⲛ̄) to become a bride; to make a marriage (for: ⲉ;
with: ⲙⲛ̄; to: ⲛⲁˢ). ⲙⲁ ⲛ̄ ϣⲉⲗⲉⲉⲧ bridal-chamber, marriage. ⲡⲁ-ⲧϣⲉⲗⲉⲉⲧ bridegroom (may take def. art.).

ϣⲉⲛϥⲉ, ϣⲛ̄ϥⲉ, ϣⲛ̄ⲃⲉ, ϣⲏ(ⲛ)ϥⲉ, ϣⲏⲃⲉ, ϣⲓϥⲉ n.f. fish-scale.

ϣⲏⲃⲉ, ϣⲓⲃⲉ n.m. rust, verdigris. ⲡ̄-ϣⲏⲃⲉ to become rusted.

ϣⲏⲓ, ϣⲏⲉⲓ, ϣⲁⲓ n.m. pit, cistern.

ϣⲏⲙ n. sign, omen; only in cpds.: ϫⲓ-ϣⲏⲙ to divine, read
omens; ⲣⲉϥϫⲓ-ϣⲏⲙ diviner, augur; ⲙⲛ̄ⲧⲣⲉϥϫⲓ-ϣⲏⲙ divination.
ⲡ̄-ϣⲏⲙ to divine.

ϣⲏⲙ adj. small, few, young, humble (bef. n. with ⲛ̄; aft. n.
without ⲛ̄). ⲛ̄ ⲟⲩϣⲏⲙ adv. a little. ⲛ̄ ⲧⲉⲓⲍⲉ ϣⲏⲙ ⲁⲛ not
only, not merely. ⲕⲟⲩⲓ ϣⲏⲙ little child. ϣⲏⲙ ϣⲏⲙ little by little, (by, into) small amounts. ⲡ̄-ϣⲏⲙ ϣⲏⲙ (Q
o ⲛ̄) to make small. As n. small person, thing, quantity.

ϣⲏⲛ n.m. tree. ⲉⲓⲁⲍ-ϣⲏⲛ grove. ⲙⲁ ⲛ̄ ϣⲏⲛ idem.

ϣⲏⲣⲉ (ϣⲡ̄-; f. ϣⲉⲉⲣⲉ, ϣⲏⲏⲣⲉ; pl. ϣⲣⲏⲩ, ϣⲣⲉⲩ) n.m.f. son,
daughter, child; young of animals. ϣⲏⲣⲉ ϣⲏⲙ small child.
baby; a youth. ϣⲉⲉⲣⲉ ϣⲏⲙ f. idem. ⲙⲛ̄ⲧϣⲏⲣⲉ ϣⲏⲙ child-
hood, infancy. ⲁⲧϣⲏⲣⲉ childless; ⲙⲛ̄ⲧⲁⲧϣⲏⲣⲉ childless-
ness. ⲙⲛ̄ⲧϣⲏⲣⲉ status of son. ⲡ̄-ϣⲏⲣⲉ (Q o ⲛ̄) to become
a child. ϣⲡ̄-, ϣⲛ̄-, ϣⲉⲛ- son of, daughter of, in various
cpds.; see 2nd element: -ⲉⲓⲱⲧ, -ⲙⲁⲁⲩ, -ⲥⲟⲛ, -ⲥⲱⲛⲉ, -ⲟⲩⲱⲧ,
-ⲍⲟⲟⲩⲧ. ϣⲛⲟⲩⲁ(ⲓ), ϣⲉⲛⲟⲩⲁ, ϣⲟⲩⲟⲩⲁ n.m.f. nephew, niece.

ϣⲏⲧⲥ̄, ϣⲉⲛⲧⲥ̄, ϣⲛ̄ⲥ n.m. name of a plant.

ϣⲏⲩⲉ (pl. ? ϣⲟⲟⲩⲉ) n.f. altar.

ϣⲓ (ϣⲉⲓ) ϣⲓ- ϣⲓⲧˢ Q ϣⲏⲩ vb. tr. to measure, weigh (ⲙ̄ⲙⲟˢ);

with 2nd obj.: to measure out to the amount of; ϣι ⲉ2ⲣⲁι
to weigh (ⲉ, ⲙⲛ̄: to a given amount); as n.m. measure,
weight, extent, length; moderation. ⲁⲧϣι immeasurable;
ⲙⲛ̄ⲧⲁⲧϣι immeasurability. ⲕⲁ-ϣι to set a measure or
limit (to: ⲛⲁ⸗). ⲣ̄-ϣι (Q o ⲛ̄) to make or equal a given
weight. ϯ-ϣι to set a measure to, restrict (ⲉ); ⲁⲧϯ-ϣι
unmeasured, unrestricted; ⲙⲛ̄ⲧⲁⲧϯ-ϣι limitlessness. ⲭι-
ϣι to take measure, estimate.

ϣιⲁι, ϣⲁι, ϣⲁιⲉ, ϣιⲁⲉιⲁⲉι; Q ϣⲏⲩ vb. intr. to be long; as
n.m. length. ϣιⲏ, ϣιⲏⲉ, ϣιⲉ n.f.(m.) length; rarely vb.
to become, grow long. ⲗⲁ-ϣιⲏ adj. tall.

ϣιⲃⲉ ϣⲃ̄- (ϣⲉⲃⲧ-, ϣⲃ̄ⲧ-, ϣⲉϥⲧ-) ϣⲃ̄ⲧ⸗ (ϣⲉⲃⲧ⸗, ϣⲉϥⲧ⸗) Q ϣⲟⲃⲉ
(ϣⲟⲟⲃⲉ, ϣⲟϥⲉ) vb. tr. to change, alter (ⲙ̄ⲙⲟ⸗); vb. intr.
and reflex. to change, be altered (to: ⲉ; into: ⲛ̄, 2ⲛ̄;
in form: ⲛ̄ ⲥⲙⲟⲧ); as n.m. change, difference. ⲙⲛ̄ⲧⲙⲁι-
ϣιⲃⲉ loving change. ⲁⲧϣιⲃⲉ unchanging, unaltered; ⲙⲛ̄ⲧ-
ⲁⲧϣιⲃⲉ changelessness. ϣⲁⲃⲛ̄2ⲟ fearful, strange (lit.,
changing of aspect). ϣⲃ̄ⲧⲥ̄ n. change. Cf. Q ϣⲉⲃιⲏⲩ.

ϣιⲃⲧⲉ (ϣιϥⲧⲉ) rare synonym of ϣιⲃⲉ to change.

ϣιⲕⲉ ϣⲉⲕⲧ̄- ϣⲁⲕⲧ⸗ (ϣιⲕⲧ⸗) Q ϣⲟⲕⲉ vb. intr. to dig (in, into:
ⲉ, 2ⲛ̄; for, after: ⲛ̄ⲥⲁ; down into: ⲉⲡⲉⲥⲏⲧ ⲉ); as n.m.
depth. ϣιⲕ, ϣⲉιⲕ, ϣⲏⲕ n.m. depth, what is dug.

ϣιⲛⲉ ϣⲉⲛ(ⲧ̄)- (ϣⲛ̄-) ϣⲛ̄ⲧ⸗ vb. tr. to seek, ask, ask for, inquire after, about (ⲙ̄ⲙⲟ⸗, ⲛ̄ⲥⲁ); ϣιⲛⲉ ⲉ to visit, inquire
after, greet, bid farewell; ϣιⲛⲉ ⲙ̄ⲙⲟ⸗ ⲉ to ask someone
for something; ϣιⲛⲉ ⲙ̄ⲙⲟ⸗ ⲛ̄ⲥⲁ/ⲉⲧⲃⲉ to ask someone about.
Also with ⲛ̄ⲧⲛ̄ from; 2ⲁ for; 2ⲛ̄ in, among, into; 2ιⲧⲛ̄
through. As n.m. inquiry, request; news, report. ϣⲙ̄-
ⲛⲟⲩϥⲉ good news. ⲙⲁ ⲛ̄ ϣιⲛⲉ place of inquiry, oracle.
ⲣⲉϥϣιⲛⲉ inquirer, wizard; ⲙⲛ̄ⲧⲣⲉϥϣιⲛⲉ wizardry. ϭιⲛⲉ ⲙ̄
ⲡ(⸗)ϣιⲛⲉ, ϭⲙ̄-ⲡ(⸗)ϣιⲛⲉ to search out, visit; as n.m.
visitation. ϥⲁι-ϣιⲛⲉ news-bearer, messenger.

ϣιⲛⲉ vb. intr. to be ashamed (about: ⲉⲧⲃⲉ, ⲉⲭⲛ̄, ⲛ̄, 2ⲁ, 2ι);
rarely tr. to put to shame. ϣιⲛⲉ 2ⲏⲧ⸗ ⲛ̄ to stand in
shame before, to revere. As n.m. shame. ⲁⲧϣιⲛⲉ

unashamed; ⳣ-ⲁⲧϣⲓⲡⲉ to be unashamed; ⲙⲛ̄ⲧⲣⲉϥϣⲓⲡⲉ shyness, modesty. ⲧ̄-ϣⲓⲡⲉ to put to shame (ⲛⲁ⸗); ⲣⲉϥⲧ̄-ϣⲓⲡⲉ one who puts to shame. ϫⲓ-ϣⲓⲡⲉ to be ashamed (of: ⲉⲧⲃⲉ, ⳝⲛ̄; ⲉϫⲛ̄; before: ⲛ̄ⲛⲁ2ⲣⲛ̄). ϣⲛ̄ⲓⲏⲧ (f. ϣⲛ̄ⲓⲉⲉⲧⲉ) modest person.

ϣⲓⲣⲉ, ϣⲏⲣⲉ (f. ϣⲉⲉⲣⲉ) adj. small. 2(ⲉ)ⲣϣⲓⲣⲉ young servant, youth (opp. of 2ⲗ̄ⲗⲟ); ⲙⲛ̄ⲧ2ⲣ̄ϣⲓⲣⲉ state of youth.

ϣⲓⲧⲉ (ϣⲱⲧ) ϣⲉⲧ- (ϣⲁⲁⲧ-) ϣⲁⲧ⸗ (ϣⲁⲁⲧ⸗, ϣⲓⲧ⸗) vb. tr. to demand, extort (ⲙ̄ⲙⲟ⸗, ⲉ; from: ⲙ̄ⲙⲟ⸗; for, on account of: 2ⲁ). ϣⲓⲧⲉ ⲙ̄ⲙⲟ⸗ ⲛ̄ ⲟⲩⲟⲥⲉ to exact a fine from. ϣⲉⲧ-ⲙⲛ̄ⲧⲛⲁ to beg for charity.

ϣⲕⲁⲕ n.m. cry, shout; ϫⲓ-ϣⲕⲁⲕ ⲉⲃⲟⲗ to cry out (to: ⲉ, ⲉϫⲛ̄, ⲉ2ⲣⲁⲓ ⲉ). ⲁϣⲕⲁⲕ to cry out (= ⲁϣ-ϣⲕⲁⲕ, cf. ⲱϣ), ± ⲉⲃⲟⲗ (ⲉ, ⲉ2ⲣⲁⲓ ⲉ). ϫⲓ-ϣⲕⲁⲕ, ⲁϣⲕⲁⲕ n.m. cry.

ϣⲕⲓⲗ, ϣⲕⲏⲗ n. curl of hair.

ϣⲕⲗ̄ⲕⲉⲗ, ϣⲕⲏⲗⲕⲉⲗ n.m. gnashing, grinding of teeth.

ϣⲕⲗ̄ⲓⲗ, ϣⲕⲉⲗⲓⲗ, ϣⲕ̄ⲗⲉⲗ, ϣⲕⲓⲗⲉⲓⲗ, ϣⲟ̄ⲗⲉⲓⲗ, ϣⲉⲓⲗⲉⲓⲗ n.m. bell.

ϣⲕⲟⲗ n.m. hole. ⲟ ⲛ̄ ϣⲕⲟⲗ ϣⲕⲟⲗ to be full of holes.

ϣⲗⲁ2, ϣⲟⲗ2̄ vb. intr. to be afraid. ϣⲗ̄2ϥ, ϣⲗ̄ϥ n. fear, in cpd. ⲛⲉ2-ϣⲗ̄2ϥ, ⲛⲁ2-ϣⲗ̄2ϥ to emit fear, be terrified; also as n.m. terror; ⲙⲛ̄ⲧⲛⲉ2-ϣⲗ̄2ϥ terror.

ϣⲗⲏ to creep (into: 2ⲛ̄).

ϣⲗⲏ- in ϣⲗⲏ-ⲟⲩⲥⲧ̄-ⲛⲟⲩϥⲉ to enjoy the odor of incense.

ϣⲗⲏⲗ (ϣⲗⲏ̄ⲗ) vb. intr. to pray (to: ⲉ, ⲛⲁ⸗, ϣⲁ; for: ⲉ, ⲉⲧⲃⲉ, ⲉϫⲛ̄, 2ⲁ, 2ⲓϫⲛ̄); as n.m. prayer.

ϣⲗⲓ6, ϣⲗⲉ6, ϣⲗ̄ⲁⲓ6 n.m. spike, sharp instrument; ray, flame.

ϣⲗⲟⲡ n.m. ply, strand (of cord).

ϣⲗⲟϥ n.m. shame, disgrace; as adj. shameful, disgraceful.

ϣⲗ̄2, ϣⲉⲗ2̄, ϣⲗⲉ2 n.m. twig, shoot; stave, wand.

ϣⲗ̄6ⲟⲙ, ⲥⲉⲗ6ⲁⲙ, ϣⲗ̄ⲧⲁⲙ, ϣⲉⲗⲧⲁⲙ, ϣⲉⲗⲧⲉⲙ, ϣⲁⲗⲧⲉⲙ n.f.m. mustard.

ϣⲙⲁ, Ⳁ ϣⲟⲟⲙⲉ (ϣⲟⲙⲉ) vb. intr. to be light, fine, subtle; as n.m. fineness, subtlety. ϣⲱⲟⲙⲉ adj. light, fine.

ϣⲙ̄ⲙⲟ, ϣⲙⲟ, ϣⲙⲱ (f. ϣⲙ̄ⲙⲱ; pl. ϣⲙ̄ⲙⲟⲓ) n.m. stranger; as adj. strange. ⲉ ⲡϣⲙ̄ⲙⲟ abroad (motion); 2ⲓ ⲡϣⲙ̄ⲙⲟ abroad (static); 2ⲙ̄ ⲡϣⲙ̄ⲙⲟ idem. ⲙⲛ̄ⲧϣⲙ̄ⲙⲟ strangeness, foreignness. ⲙⲁⲓ-ϣⲙ̄ⲙⲟ hospitable; ⲙⲛ̄ⲧⲙⲁⲓ-ϣⲙ̄ⲙⲟ hospitality; ⳣ-ⲙⲛ̄ⲧⲙⲁⲓ-

ϢⲘⲘⲟ to be hospitable. ⲘⲚ̄ⲧⲘⲁⲥⲧ̄-ϢⲘⲘⲟ hatred of strangers.
Ⲣ̄-ϢⲘⲘⲟ (Q o ⲛ̄) to become a stranger, be estranged (from:
ⲉ, ⲛⲁˢ).

ϢⲘⲟⲩ, ϢⲘⲟⲩⲉ, ϢⲘⲟⲩⲓ n.f. peg, stake.

ϢⲘⲟⲩⲛ (f. ϢⲘⲟⲩⲛⲉ) number: eight. ⲘⲚ̄ⲧϢⲘⲏⲛ(ⲉ) eighteen. ⲘⲉⳆ-
ϢⲘⲟⲩⲛ eighth. See 15.3; 30.7.

ϢⲘ̄Ϣⲉ ϢⲘ̄Ϣⲉ- ϢⲘ̄Ϣⲏⲧˢ vb. tr. to serve (Ⲙ̄Ⲙⲟˢ or ⲛⲁˢ); as n.m.
service, worship, liturgy; Ⲙⲁ ⲛ̄ ϢⲘ̄Ϣⲉ place of worship.
Ⲣ̄-ϢⲘ̄Ϣⲉ to do service (to, for: ⲛⲁˢ). ⲣⲉϥϢⲘ̄Ϣⲉ server,
worshipper; ⲘⲚ̄ⲧⲣⲉϥϢⲘ̄Ϣⲉ service. ϢⲘ̄Ϣⲓⲧ n.m. servant.

ϢⲘ̄Ϣⲏⲥⲉ vb. intr. to whisper; as n. whispering. ⲉϢ-ϢⲘ̄Ϣⲏⲥⲉ,
ϥⲓ-ϢⲘ̄Ϣⲏⲥⲉ to whisper.

Ϣⲛⲁ n.m. waste-land. Ⲣ̄-Ϣⲛⲁ to become waste, dry.

Ϣⲛⲁ n.m. profligate, prodigal (person); ⲘⲚ̄ⲧϢⲛⲁ profligacy.

Ϣⲛⲉ, Ϣⲛⲏ (pl. Ϣⲛⲏⲩ, -ⲉ) n.m. net. Ϣⲛⲉ ⲛ̄ Ⳟⲓⲟⲩⲉ casting-net.

Ϣⲛⲏ n.f. garden; ⲡⲁ-ⲧⲉϢⲛⲏ gardener.

ϢⲛⲟϢ, Q ϢⲟⲛϢ̄ vb. intr. to stink; as n.m. stench.

ϢⲚ̄ⲥ n.m. linen.

ϢⲚ̄ⲧⲱ n.f. sheet, robe (of linen).

ϢⲚ̄Ϣⲱⲧⲉ, ϢⲓⲛϢⲱⲧⲉ n.f. cushion or sim.

Ϣⲟ number: thousand. See 30.7.

Ϣⲟ particle: yea!

ϢⲟⲉⲓⲘ n.m. row, course; ⲛ̄ ϢⲟⲉⲓⲘ ϢⲟⲉⲓⲘ in rows. ϢⲓⲘⲉ,
ϢⲟⲉⲓⲘⲉ n.f. courses (of stones).

Ϣⲟⲉⲓⲧ in Ⲣ̄-Ϣⲟⲉⲓⲧ (Q o ⲛ̄ Ϣⲟⲉⲓⲧ) to become inspired,
possessed, frenzied.

ϢⲟⲉⲓϢ n.m. dust; Ⲣ̄-ϢⲟⲉⲓϢ to become dusty; ⲭⲓ-ϢⲟⲉⲓϢ idem.

(ϢⲟⲕϢⲕ̄) ϢⲉⲕϢⲱⲕˢ vb. tr. to dig, hollow out, gouge out.

Ϣⲟⲗ, Ϣⲁⲗ n.m. bundle.

Ϣⲟⲗ, Ϣⲱⲗ n.m. molar tooth, tusk.

ϢⲟⲗⲘⲉⲥ n.f. gnat.

ϢⲟⲗϢⲗ̄ Ϣ(ⲉ)ⲗϢⲱⲗˢ Q ϢⲉⲗϢⲱⲗ (Ϣⲣ̄Ϣⲱⲣ) vb. tr. to sift, shake in
sieve (Ⲙ̄Ⲙⲟˢ); as n.m. shaking.

ϢⲟⲘ, ϢⲱⲟⲘ (f. ϢⲱⲘⲉ; pl. ϢⲘⲟⲩⲓ) n.m. father-in-law (mother-
in-law); son (daughter)-in-law. Ⲣ̄-ϢⲟⲘ to become

father-in-law (to: ε).

ϣομⲛ̄ⲧ, ϣⲙ̄ⲛ̄ⲧ, ϣⲉⲙⲛ̄ⲧ, ϣⲟⲙⲧ̄, ϣⲙ̄ⲛ̄(ⲧ)- number: three (f. ϣⲟⲙⲧⲉ, ϣⲟⲙⲛ̄ⲧⲉ). ϣⲙ̄(ⲛ̄)ⲧ-(ⲉ)ⲛⲟⲟⲩ three days ago, heretofore. ⲙⲉϩϣⲟⲙⲛ̄ⲧ third. ⲙⲛ̄ⲧϣⲟⲙⲧⲉ thirteen; ⲙⲉϩⲙⲛ̄ⲧϣⲟⲙⲧⲉ thirteenth. ⲙ̄ ⲛϣⲟⲙⲛ̄ⲧ all three (of them). See 15.3; 30.7.

ϣⲟⲛⲧⲉ n.f. thorn-tree (acacia nilotica); thorns; thicket of acacias; ϣⲉ ⲛ̄ ϣⲟⲛⲧⲉ acacia wood.

ϣⲟⲟⲩ, ϣⲟⲟⲩⲉ, ϣⲟⲩ- n.m. incense, perfume.

ϣⲟⲟⲩⲉ, Q ϣⲟⲩⲱⲟⲩ(ⲉ) vb. intr. to become dry, dry up, become dessicated, stale. ⲛⲛⲉⲧ ϣⲟⲩⲱⲟⲩ the dry land.

ϣⲟⲛ, ϣⲟⲟⲛ, ϣⲱⲛ n.m. palm, four-fingerbreadth; a set of four.

(ϣⲟⲛϣⲛ̄) ϣ(ⲉ)ⲛϣⲛ̄- ϣⲛ̄ϣⲱⲛ⸗ vb. tr. to take in arms, nurse.

ϣⲟⲣⲧ̄, ϣⲟⲟⲣⲧ̄ n.m. awning, veil.

ϣⲟⲣϣ̄ⲣ ϣⲣ̄ϣⲣ̄- ϣⲣ̄ϣⲱⲣ⸗ Q ϣⲣ̄ϣⲱⲣ (ϣⲣ̄ϣⲟⲣⲧ̄) vb. tr. to upset, overturn (ⲙ̄ⲙⲟ⸗, ⲉ; on, onto: ⲉⲭⲛ̄); to destroy; + ⲉⲛⲉⲥⲏⲧ idem. As n.m. overthrow, destruction; ⲣⲉϥϣⲟⲣϣ̄ⲣ destroyer.

ϣⲟⲧ, ϣⲱⲧ (pl. ϣϣⲱⲧⲉ; cf. ϣⲛ̄ϣⲱⲧⲉ) n.m. pillow, cushion.

ϣⲟⲧϣ̄ⲧ (ϣⲟⲭ̄ⲧ) ϣⲉⲧϣⲱⲧ⸗ Q ϣⲉⲧϣⲱⲧ vb. tr. to cut, carve, hollow out (ⲙ̄ⲙⲟ⸗); to make a hole in (ⲉ, ϩⲛ̄). As n.m. (also ϣⲟϣⲧ) anything carved or hollowed out.

ϣⲟⲩ, ⲥⲟⲩ in ⲛ̄ϣⲟⲩ prep. without (not standard Sah.).

ϣⲟⲩⲏⲏⲃ, ϣⲟⲩⲏⲃ, ϣⲃⲓⲃ, ϣⲟⲩⲉⲃⲉ, ϣⲟⲩⲉϥⲉ n.m. persea tree.

ϣⲟⲩⲟ ϣⲟⲩⲉ- (ϣⲟⲩ-) ϣⲟⲩⲱ⸗ (ϣⲟⲩⲟ⸗) (± ⲉⲃⲟⲗ) vb. tr. to discharge, pour out, empty (ⲙ̄ⲙⲟ⸗; from: ⲙ̄ⲙⲟ⸗, ⲉⲃⲟⲗ ⲙ̄ⲙⲟ⸗, ⲉⲃⲟⲗ ϩⲛ̄; into: ϩⲛ̄); vb. intr. to flow, pour out. ϣⲟⲩⲟ ⲉⲭⲛ̄ to pour out upon; to crowd against, throng. Also with ⲉⲛⲉⲥⲏⲧ (ⲉ), ⲉϩⲣⲁⲓ (ⲉ, ⲉⲭⲛ̄, ϩⲛ̄). ϣⲟⲩⲉⲓⲧ Q to be empty; ⲛⲉⲧ ϣⲟⲩⲉⲓⲧ emptiness, vanity (may take art.); ⲙⲛ̄ⲧⲛⲉⲧ ϣⲟⲩⲉⲓⲧ emptiness; ϩⲛ̄ ⲟⲩⲙⲛ̄ⲧⲛⲉⲧ ϣⲟⲩⲉⲓⲧ without cause, vainly; ⲣ̄-ⲛⲉⲧ ϣⲟⲩⲉⲓⲧ to act in vain.

ϣⲟⲩⲣⲏ n.f. censer, brazier, altar.

ϣⲟⲩⲥⲟⲟⲩϣⲉ, ϣⲟⲩⲥⲱⲟⲩϣⲉ, ϣⲟⲩⲥⲟⲟⲩϩⲉ n.m. sacrifice, offering.

ϣⲟⲩⲱⲃⲉ, ϣⲟⲩⲟⲃⲉ n.f. throat.

ϣⲟⲩϣⲟⲩ vb. intr. to boast, brag; reflex. (w. ⲙ̄ⲙⲟ⸗) to take pride (in, on, about: ⲉ, ⲉⲧⲃⲉ, ⲉⲭⲛ̄, ⲉϩⲣⲁⲓ ⲉⲭⲛ̄, ϩⲓ, ϩⲛ̄).

As n.m. boasting, pride; as adj. proud. ⲙ̄ⲛ̄ⲧϣⲟⲩϣⲟⲩ,
ⲙ̄ⲛ̄ⲧϣⲟⲩϣⲟ pride, impudence. ϯ-ϣⲟⲩϣⲟⲩ to glorify.
ϣⲟⲩϣⲧ̄, ϣⲱϣⲧ̄ n.m. window; niche, alcove.
ϣⲟϣ, ϣⲟⲟϣ n.m. kind of antelope (bubalis buselaphus).
ϣⲟϣⲟⲩ, ϣⲁϣⲟⲩ, ϣⲟϣⲟ n.m. pot, jar.
ϣⲟϣⲧ̄ n.m. hindrance, impediment; key. ϯ-ϣⲟϣⲧ̄ to lock
    (a door). ⲣ̄-ϣⲟϣⲧ̄ to shut, lock.
ϣⲟϥϣ̄, Q ϣϥϣⲱϥ meaning uncertain: to burrow (?).
ϣⲟⲭⲛⲉ, ϣⲁⲭⲛⲉ vb. tr. to consider (ⲙ̄ⲙⲟˢ); to take counsel
    concerning (ⲉ, ⲉⲭⲛ̄; with: ⲙⲛ̄). As n.m. counsel, design,
    plan, advice. ⲁⲧϣⲟⲭⲛⲉ ill-considered; ⲙ̄ⲛ̄ⲧⲁⲧϣⲟⲭⲛⲉ being
    without counsel, at a loss, reckless. ⲉⲓⲣⲉ ⲛ̄ ⲟⲩϣⲟⲭⲛⲉ
    ⲣ̄-ϣⲟⲭⲛⲉ to take counsel, make a decision. ⲭⲓ-ϣⲟⲭⲛⲉ idem
    (with: ⲙⲛ̄; concerning: ⲉ, ⲉ₂ⲟⲩⲛ ⲉ); ⲭⲓ-ϣⲟⲭⲛⲉ ⲛⲁˢ to
    counsel, advise; ⲣⲉϥⲭⲓ-ϣⲟⲭⲛⲉ counsellor, advisor.
ϣⲡⲏⲣⲉ n.f. wonder, amazement; miracle; as adj. wonderful,
    marvelous; ϩⲁ ϣⲡⲏⲣⲉ wonderful; ϩⲛ̄ ⲟⲩϣⲡⲏⲣⲉ wondrously.
    ⲣ̄-ϣⲡⲏⲣⲉ (Q ⲟ ⲛ̄) to become amazed, to marvel (at: ⲙ̄ⲙⲟˢ,
    ⲉ, ⲉⲧⲃⲉ, ⲉⲭⲛ̄, ⲉ₂ⲣⲁⲓ ⲉⲭⲛ̄, ⲛ̄ⲥⲁ, ϩⲛ̄).
ϣⲣⲱ n.f. menstruation; ⲣ̄-ϣⲣⲱ (Q ⲟ ⲛ̄) to be menstruous.
ϣⲥⲛⲉ, ⲥⲕ̅ⲛⲉ in ϩⲛ̄ ⲟⲩϣⲥⲛⲉ suddenly, all of a sudden.
ϣⲧⲉ, ϣⲧⲏ (pl. ϣⲧⲏⲩ) n.m. mast of a ship.
ϣⲧⲉ n. nest.
ϣⲧⲉⲕⲟ, ⲉϣⲧⲉⲕⲟ (pl. ϣⲧⲉⲕⲱⲟⲩ) n.m. prison.
ϣⲧⲏⲛ, ϣⲧⲛ̄ n.f. garment, tunic.
ϣϯ n.m. weaver; warp (on loom).
ϣⲧⲟⲣⲧⲣ̄ ϣⲧⲣ̄ⲧⲣ̄- ϣⲧⲣ̄ⲧⲱⲣˢ Q ϣⲧⲣ̄ⲧⲱⲣ vb. tr. to disturb, agitate,
    bother, upset, trouble, urge, hasten (ⲙ̄ⲙⲟˢ); vb. intr.
    to become disturbed etc.; as n.m. disturbance, trouble,
    anxiety, haste; ϩⲛ̄ ⲟⲩϣⲧⲟⲣⲧⲣ̄ hastily, quickly, anxiously.
    ⲁⲧϣⲧⲟⲣⲧⲣ̄ undisturbed, untroubled; ⲙ̄ⲛ̄ⲧⲁⲧϣⲧⲟⲣⲧⲣ̄ tranquil-
    lity; ⲣ̄-/ϯ-ϣⲧⲟⲣⲧⲣ̄ to create disturbance.
ϣⲧⲟⲩⲏⲧ in ϯ-ϣⲧⲟⲩⲏⲧ to accuse, bring accusation against (ⲉ,
    ⲛ̄, ϩⲁ); ⲣⲉϥϯ-ϣⲧⲟⲩⲏⲧ accuser.
ϣⲱ n.m. sand, gravel; ⲕⲏ ⲉ ⲡϣⲱ being in sandy condition.

ϣⲱⲃ (ϣⲟϥ) ϣⲃ̄- (ϣⲉϥ-) ϣⲟⲃˀ (ϣⲟϥˀ) Q ϣⲏⲃ (ϣⲏϥ) vb. tr. to
shave, clip, tonsure (ⲙ̄ⲙⲟˀ); ϣⲃ̄-ⲭⲱ to shave the head;
as n.m. shaving, clipping, tonsure.

ϣⲱⲃⲍ̄ ϣⲟⲃⲍˀ Q ϣⲟⲃⲍ̄ vb. tr. to scorch, wither (ⲙ̄ⲙⲟˀ); vb.
intr. to become scorched, withered.

ϣⲱⲓ n.m. what is above, high; always w. art. and usu. in
prep. phrases: ⲉ ⲡϣⲱⲓ upward; ⲙ̄ ⲡϣⲱⲓ ⲉ above; ⲉⲃⲟⲗ ⲙ̄
ⲡϣⲱⲓ from above; ⲥⲁ-ⲡϣⲱⲓ upper part or direction; ⲥⲁ
ⲡϣⲱⲓ ⲛ̄ (prep.) above; ⲉⲃⲟⲗ ⲥⲁ-ⲡϣⲱⲓ from above.

ϣⲱⲕ ϣⲉⲕ- Q ϣⲏⲕ vb. tr. to dig, dig deep; Q = to be deep;
as n.m. depth(s). Cf. ϣⲓⲕⲉ.

ϣⲱⲕⲍ̄ ϣⲉⲕⲍ̄- ϣⲟⲕⲍˀ Q ϣⲟⲕⲍ̄ vb. tr. to dig, dig deep (± ⲉⲡⲉⲥⲏⲧ). ϣⲓⲕⲍ̄ n.m. depth. Cf. preceding.

ϣⲱⲗ ϣⲉⲗ- (ϣⲗ̄-) ϣⲟⲗˀ vb. tr. to despoil (ⲙ̄ⲙⲟˀ); + ⲉⲃⲟⲗ: to
spoil, destroy; intr. to be destroyed; as n.m. spoil,
booty. ⲁⲧϣⲱⲗ ⲉⲃⲟⲗ indestructible. ϣⲟⲗⲥ̄ n.f. spoils.

ϣⲱⲗ ϣⲟⲗˀ Q ϣⲏⲗ vb. tr. to loosen, dissolve, paralyze; vb.
intr. to flow (into: ⲉ, ⲍⲛ̄, ⲉⲃⲟⲗ ⲉⲝⲛ̄); ϣⲏⲗ ⲉⲃⲟⲗ to be
paralyzed, crippled, worthless.

ϣⲱⲗⲕ̄ ϣⲗ̄ⲕ- ϣⲟⲗⲕˀ vb. tr. to stitch, weave (ⲙ̄ⲙⲟˀ).

ϣⲱⲗⲙ̄ vb. tr. to smell (ⲙ̄ⲙⲟˀ); sniff at (ⲉ); as n.m. sense
of smell; ⲙⲁ ⲛ̄ ϣⲱⲗⲙ̄ organ of smell; ϭⲓⲛϣⲱⲗⲙ̄ sense of s.

ϣⲱⲗⲍ̄ ϣⲟⲗⲍˀ Q ϣⲟⲗⲍ̄ vb. tr. to mark, trace line of, make as
a mark (ⲙ̄ⲙⲟˀ); as n.m. mark, marker, stake; ϯ-ϣⲱⲗⲍ̄ to
set a mark or boundary.

ϣⲱⲗⲥ̄ ϣⲗ̄ⲥ- ϣⲗⲗⲕˀ Q ϣⲟⲗⲥ̄ vb. tr. to cut (ⲙ̄ⲙⲟˀ); Q to be sharp,
sharpened, cutting. Cf. ϣⲗⲓϭ.

ϣⲱⲙ n.m. tax, tribute; ϯ-ϣⲱⲙ to pay tribute; ⲭⲓ-ϣⲱⲙ to
receive tribute.

ϣⲱⲙ n.m. summer. ⲍⲉ ⲛ̄ ϣⲱⲙ, ⲍⲛ̄ϣⲱⲙ n.m. spring.

ϣⲱⲙ ϣⲟⲙˀ (ϣⲟⲟⲙˀ) vb. tr. to wash (clothes: ⲙ̄ⲙⲟˀ).

ϣⲱⲙⲝ̄ ϣⲙ̄ⲝ- Q ϣⲟⲙⲝ̄ vb. tr. to pierce.

ϣⲱⲛⲉ vb. intr. to become sick, weak, ill (in, with: ⲉ, ⲛ̄,
ⲍⲛ̄); as n.m. sickness, disease. ⲙⲁ ⲛ̄ ⲛⲉⲧϣⲱⲛⲉ infirmary.
ⲣ̄-ϣⲱⲛⲉ to become sick; ⲣⲉϥϣⲱⲛⲉ sick person. For cpds.

in ϣⲛ̄-, ϣⲉⲛ-, ϣⲁⲛ- see 2nd element.

ϣⲱⲛⲧ̄ (ϣⲟⲛⲧ̄) Q ϣⲟⲛⲧ̄ vb. intr. to quarrel (with: ⲙⲛ̄, ⲟⲩⲃⲉ); as n.m. quarreling.

ϣⲱⲛⲧ̄ ϣⲛ̄ⲧ- (ϣⲉⲛⲧ̄-) ϣⲟⲛⲧ˟ Q ϣⲟⲛⲧ̄ vb. tr. to plait (ⲙ̄ⲙⲟ˟). ϣⲟⲛⲧⲉ n.f. plaited work.

ϣⲱⲛϥ (ϣⲱⲛⲃ̄) ϣⲉⲛϥ- (ϣⲉⲛⲃ̄-) ϣⲟⲛϥ˟ (ϣⲟⲛⲃ˟) Q ϣⲟⲛϥ (ϣⲟⲛⲃ̄) vb. intr. to come together, join; vb. tr. to join, connect (ⲙ̄ⲙⲟ˟; to, with: ⲉ, ⲙⲛ̄, ⲛⲁ˟); to convey (to: ϣⲁ); as n.m. union, unity. ⲍⲛ̄ ⲟⲩϣⲱⲛϥ jointly, in unison.

ϣⲱⲡ only in ϣⲉⲛⲛ̄ϣⲱⲡ, ϣⲡⲛ̄ϣⲱⲡ, ϣⲡⲉⲛϣⲱⲡ moment, instant; ⲍⲛ̄ ⲟⲩϣⲉⲛⲛ̄ϣⲱⲡ suddenly.

ϣⲱⲡ ϣⲉⲡ- (ϣⲡ̄-, ϣⲁⲡ-) ϣⲟⲡ˟ (ϣⲁⲡ˟) Q ϣⲏⲡ vb. tr. to receive, accept, take, bear, suffer (ⲙ̄ⲙⲟ˟; for, on behalf of: ⲉⲭⲛ̄, ⲛⲁ˟; from: ⲛ̄ⲧⲛ̄, ⲍⲓⲧⲛ̄); to buy (for a price: ⲍⲁ; with: ⲍⲛ̄). Freq. w. ethical dative. Q also = to be acceptable. As n.m. acceptance, purchase. ⲁⲧϣⲱⲡ, ⲁⲧϣⲟⲡ˟ which cannot be limited or contained. ϣⲟⲡⲉ̄ n.f. reception, entertainment.

ϣⲱⲡⲉ (ϣⲱⲱⲡⲉ), Q ϣⲟⲟⲡ vb. intr. to become, come into existence; to happen, take place, occur; to last, endure; Q to be, exist. ⲁⲥϣⲱⲡⲉ impers. it happened that (foll. by coord. vb.). For ϣⲱⲡⲉ as aux. vb., see §30.9. ϣⲱⲡⲉ ⲉ, ⲉⲍⲟⲩⲛ ⲉ to be for, intended for, destined for; ϣⲱⲡⲉ ⲙ̄ⲙⲟ˟ (1) to be in; (2) to happen to (a person); (3) to be + pred. noun. ϣⲱⲡⲉ ⲛⲁ˟ ⲉ to act as (ⲉ) for (ⲛⲁ˟). ϣⲱⲡⲉ ϣⲁ to last until; ϣⲱⲡⲉ ⲍⲁ to receive, get, have; ϣⲱⲡⲉ ⲍⲓ to be/live in the time of. ϣⲱⲡⲉ ⲍⲁⲧⲛ̄ to be in the care, the charge of. ϣⲱⲡⲉ ⲍⲓⲧⲛ̄, ⲉⲃⲟⲗ ⲍⲓⲧⲛ̄ to come into existence through, by means of. As n.m. existence, being. ⲙⲁ ⲛ̄ ϣⲱⲡⲉ dwelling place, residence. ⲉϣⲱⲡⲉ if, when, since, because.

ϣⲱⲡⲉ, ϣⲱⲃⲉ, ϣⲱⲱⲡⲉ, ϣⲱⲱⲃⲉ, ⲉϣⲱⲡⲉ n.m. cucumber.

ϣⲱⲡⲧ̄ n.m. arm, foreleg; shoulder; name of constellation.

ϣⲱⲣ ϣⲟⲣ˟ (ϣⲟⲟⲣ˟) Q ϣⲏⲣ vb. tr. to stop up, to pile up.

ϣⲱⲣⲡ̄ ϣⲣ̄ⲡ- (ϣⲉⲣⲡ̄-) ϣⲟⲣⲡ˟ Q ϣⲟⲣⲡ̄ vb. intr. to be early,

first (in, at, to: ⲉ); reflex. idem. ϣⲣ̄ⲡ- + Inf. to
do something first, to have done something previously,
already. ϣⲱⲣⲡ̄ n. morning; ϣⲱⲣⲡ̄ ⲙ̄ ⲡⲉϥⲣⲁⲥⲧⲉ tomorrow morning, the morning of the next day; ⲡⲛⲁⲩ ⲛ̄ ϣⲱⲣⲡ̄ the morning. ϣⲟⲣⲡ̄ (f. ϣⲟⲣⲡⲉ) adj. first, earliest; used before
of after n., with ⲛ̄; ϣⲣ̄ⲡ-ⲛ̄- idem. ⲛ̄ ϣⲱⲣⲡ̄, ⲛ̄ ϣⲟⲣⲡ̄ adv.
early. ⲛ̄ ϣⲟⲣⲡ̄ adv. formerly, at first; ⲛ̄ ϣⲟⲣⲡ̄ ⲛ̄ prep.
before. ϫⲓⲛ (ⲛ̄) ϣⲟⲣⲡ̄, ϫⲓⲛ ⲉ ϣⲟⲣⲡ̄ from the beginning.
ⲣ̄-ϣⲟⲣⲡ̄ (Q ⲟ ⲛ̄) to be first, before; + ⲉ + Inf. to do
first, beforehand; to be the first to do.
ϣⲱⲣⲧ̄ vb. intr. to be demented; tr. to derange (ⲙ̄ⲙⲟ⸗).
ϣⲱⲥ, ϣⲱⲱⲥ, ϣⲟⲟⲥ (pl. ϣⲟⲟⲥ, ϣⲱⲱⲥ) n.m. shepherd, herdsman;
ⲙⲛ̄ⲧϣⲱⲥ shepherding.
ϣⲱⲧ, ⲉϣⲱⲧ (pl. ⲉϣⲟⲧⲉ, ⲉϣⲁⲧⲉ) n.m. trader, merchant; ⲙⲁ ⲛ̄
ⲉϣⲱⲧ emporium; ⲙⲛ̄ⲧⲉϣⲱⲧ trade, commerce; ⲣ̄-ⲉϣⲱⲧ to trade,
deal, traffic (in: ⲍ̄ⲛ̄); ϭⲓⲛⲉⲣ-ⲉϣⲱⲧ trade, profit.
ϣⲱⲧⲃ̄ ϣⲉⲧⲃ̄- (ϣⲧⲃ̄-) vb. tr. to muzzle. ϣⲧⲟⲃ, ϣⲧⲟϥ n.m. a
muzzle, halter.
ϣⲱⲧⲉ, ϣⲱⲱⲧⲉ n.f. well, cistern.
ϣⲱⲧⲉ n.m. flour, dough.
ϣⲱⲧⲙ̄ ϣⲉⲧⲙ̄- (ϣⲧⲙ̄-) Q ϣⲟⲧⲙ̄ vb. tr. to close, seal (ⲙ̄ⲙⲟ⸗; a-
gainst: ⲉⲣⲛ̄); vb. intr. to be shut, sealed. ϣⲧⲁⲙ (ϣⲧⲟⲙ)
Q ϣⲧⲁⲙ vb. tr. idem. ϣⲧⲟⲙ n.m. gate, what is shut.
ϣⲧⲙ̄-ⲟⲩⲱⲛ n.pl. joints.
ϣⲱⲱⲙⲉ, ϣⲱⲙⲉ n.f. cliff, precipice.
ϣⲱⲱⲛⲉ ϣⲉ(ⲉ)ⲛⲉ- ϣⲟ(ⲟ)ⲛ⸗ Q ϣⲟⲟⲛⲉ vb. tr. to exclude, deprive
(of: ⲉ, ⲉⲃⲟⲗ ⲍ̄ⲛ̄); to remove (ⲙ̄ⲙⲟ⸗; from: ⲉ).
ϣⲱⲱⲧ (ϣⲱⲧ) ϣⲉⲧ- (ϣⲉⲉⲧ-) ϣⲁⲁⲧ⸗ (ϣⲁⲧ⸗) Q ϣⲁⲁⲧ (ϣⲁⲧ, ϣⲏⲧ)(1)
vb. tr. to cut (ⲙ̄ⲙⲟ⸗); to slaughter, slay (with: ⲍ̄ⲛ̄).
ϣⲱⲱⲧ ⲉⲃⲟⲗ to cut off, cut short; to excommunicate; to
decide; as n.m. excommunication, cutting off. ϣⲱⲱⲧ ⲉⲃⲟⲗ
ⲉϫⲛ̄ to condemn. ⲍ̄ⲛ̄ ⲟⲩϣⲱⲱⲧ ⲉⲃⲟⲗ sharply, briefly. ϣⲁⲧ-
in cpds.: who, which cuts (see 2nd elem.). ϣⲱⲱⲧ as n.m.
what is cut; sacrifice; decision, verdict. ⲁⲧϣⲱⲱⲧ
uncut. ⲣⲉϥϣⲱⲱⲧ (ⲉⲃⲟⲗ) cutter, sacrificer.

(2) vb. intr. to lack (for: ε, ⲙ̄ⲙⲟ⸗, ²ⲛ̄); to want, be
lacking; as n.m. lack, need, shortage; ⲁⲧϣⲱⲱⲧ without
needs. ϣⲁⲁⲧ ⲛ̄, ϣⲁⲧ ⲛ̄, ϣⲁⲧⲉ prep. short of, lacking; ex-
cepting, apart from. ϣⲁⲁⲧⲉ, ϣⲁⲁⲧⲉ̄ n.f. part cut off,
portion. ϣⲁⲁⲧⲉ̄, ϣⲁⲧⲉ̄ n.f. cut, ditch. ϣⲧⲁ vb. intr. to
become faulty, deficient; to have defects; as n.m. de-
fect, fault, deficiency.

ϣⲱⲱϭⲉ ϣⲉϭϭⲉ- (ϣϭϭⲉ-) ϣⲟⲟϭ⸗ (ϣⲟϭ⸗) Q ϣⲟⲟϭⲉ (ϣⲟϭⲉ) vb. tr.
to strike, smite, wound (ⲙ̄ⲙⲟ⸗); vb. intr. to be wounded
(in: ε); as n.m. blow, wound. ϣϭⲁ n.m. blow, wound; ⲣ̄-
ϣϭⲁ to wound; ϣϭⲁ-ϭⲓϫ to clap the hands.

ϣⲱϣ ϣⲉϣ- ϣⲟϣ⸗ Q ϣⲏϣ (± ⲉⲃⲟⲗ) vb. tr. to scatter, spread
(ⲙ̄ⲙⲟ⸗; esp. of odor, by wind); vb. intr. idem.

ϣⲱϣ ϣⲉϣ- Q ϣⲏϣ vb. tr. to twist (rope etc.); as n.m. twis-
ting; torture (?).

ϣⲱϣ ϣⲉϣ- ϣⲟϣ⸗ (ϣⲁϣ⸗) Q ϣⲏϣ (± ⲉⲃⲟⲗ, ⲉ²ⲣⲁⲓ) vb. tr. to make
equal (ⲙ̄ⲙⲟ⸗; to: ε, ⲙ̄ⲛ̄); to make level, straight; to lay
out straight; Q to be equal (to: ε, ⲙ̄ⲛ̄, ⲟⲩⲃⲉ). As n.m.
equality, sameness, equal status.

ϣⲱϥ ϣⲉϥ- ϣⲟϥ⸗ Q ϣⲏϥ vb. tr. to devastate, lay waste, destroy (ⲙ̄ⲙⲟ⸗); vb. intr. to become desert, laid waste,
destroyed; as n.m. devastation, destruction. ϣⲱⲱϥⲉ,
ϣⲱⲱⲃⲉ n.m. barrenness, poverty.

ϣⲱϥⲧ̄, ϣⲟϥⲧ̄ n.m. hollow of hand; handful.

ϣⲱϥⲧ̄ ϣⲉϥⲧ̄- Q ϣⲟϥⲧ̄ vb. intr. to err, make a mistake (in:
ⲙ̄ⲙⲟ⸗, ε, ²ⲛ̄); as n.m. error, fault. ⲁⲧϣⲟϥⲧ̄ unerring.
ϣⲁϥⲧⲉ adj. wicked, iniquitous; ⲙ̄ⲛ̄ⲧϣⲁϥⲧⲉ iniquity; ⲣ̄-ⲙ̄ⲛ̄ⲧ-
ϣⲁϥⲧⲉ to sin (against: ε). ϣⲟϥⲧⲉ̄, ϣⲟⲃⲧⲉ̄, ϣⲁϥⲧⲉ̄ n. error.

ϣⲱ²ⲃ̄ ϣⲉ²ⲃ̄- ϣⲟ²ⲃ⸗ vb. tr. intr. to wither, scorch.

ϣⲱϫⲉ vb. intr. to contend, wrestle, struggle (with: ⲙ̄ⲛ̄,
ⲟⲩⲃⲉ); as n.m. contest. ⲙⲁ ⲛ̄ ϣⲱϫⲉ arena; ⲣⲉϥϣⲱϫⲉ contender. ϣⲟⲉⲓϫ n.m.f. athlete, gladiator, contender;
ⲙ̄ⲛ̄ⲧϣⲟⲉⲓϫ athleticism; ⲣ̄-ϣⲟⲉⲓϫ to become an athlete,
contender. ϣⲟⲉⲓϫϥ̄ n.m. athlete, contender.

ϣⲱϫⲛ̄ ϣⲉϫⲛ̄- ϣⲟϫⲛ⸗ Q ϣⲟϫⲛ̄ vb. tr. to leave as a remainder,

to leave behind (ⲙ̄ⲙⲟ⸗); vb. intr. to be left over, remain; ± ⲉⲡⲁ₂ⲟⲩ idem. As n.m. remainder.

ϣϣⲉ, ⲉϣϣⲉ, ϣⲉ, ⲥϣⲉ (neg. ⲙⲉϣϣⲉ, ⲙ̄ϣϣⲉ) impers. vb. it is fitting, suitable, proper (to, that: ⲉ, ⲉⲧⲣⲉ; see 20.2);
ⲡⲉⲧ (ⲉ)ϣϣⲉ, ⲛⲉⲧ (ⲉ)ϣϣⲉ that which is proper.

ϣϥⲱ, ϣⲃⲱ n.f. a measure of length, schoenus, parasang.

ϣ₂ⲓⲋ, ϣ₂ⲓⲝ n.m. dust; ⲣ̄-ϣ₂ⲓⲋ (Q o ⲛ̄) to become dust.

ϣϫⲉ (pl. ϣϫⲏⲩ) n.m. locust.

ϣϫⲏⲛ n.m. garlic.

ϣϫⲓⲧ, ⲥϫⲓⲋ n.m. name of an occupation: dyer (?).

ϣϫⲱⲧ n.f. cord (?).

ϣϭⲁⲡ in ⲁϣ-ϣϭⲁⲡ to cry out.

ϣϭⲟⲣ, ϣϭⲟⲗ, ⲥϭⲟⲗ n.m. rent, hire; ⲁⲧϣϭⲟⲣ rent-free; ⲣⲙ̄ⲛ̄-
ϣϭⲟⲣ tenant.

ϣⲁ: ϣⲉ	ϣⲁⲥⲱⲛⲧ̄: ⲥⲱⲛⲧ̄	ϣⲃ̄ϣⲉ: ⲥⲃ̄ϣⲉ
ϣⲁⲁⲛⲧ⸗: ϣⲁ	ϣⲁⲧ(-/⸗): ϣⲓⲧⲉ,	ϣⲉ: ϣϣⲉ, ϣⲁ
ϣⲁⲁⲣⲉ: ϣⲁⲁⲣ	ϣⲱⲱⲧ	ϣⲉ-: ⲥⲱϣ
ϣⲁⲁⲧ(-/⸗): ϣⲁ, ϣⲓⲧⲉ,	ϣⲁⲧⲁϥ: ⲁϥ	ϣⲉⲃⲃⲓⲱ: ϣⲉⲃⲓⲏⲩ
ϣⲱⲱⲧ	ϣⲁⲧⲉ: ϣⲱⲱⲧ	ϣⲉⲃⲉ: ϣⲃⲉ
ϣⲁⲁⲧⲉ: ϣⲱⲱⲧ	ϣⲁⲧⲛ̄: ϣⲱⲱⲧ	ϣⲉⲃⲉ: ϣⲁϥⲉ
ϣⲁⲁⲧⲥ̄: ϣⲱⲱⲧ	ϣⲁⲧⲥ̄: ϣⲱⲱⲧ	ϣⲉⲃⲓ: ϣⲁϥⲉ
ϣⲁⲁϥ: ϣⲁⲁⲃ	ϣⲁⲧⲧ⸗: ϣⲁ	ϣⲉⲃⲓⲱ: ϣⲉⲃⲓⲏⲩ
ϣⲁⲁϥⲉ: ϣⲁϥⲉ	ϣⲁⲩ: ⲉϣⲱ	ϣⲉⲃⲛ̄ⲛⲉ: ⲃⲛ̄ⲛⲉ
ϣⲁⲃⲉ: ϣⲁϥⲉ	ϣⲁϣ⸗: ϣⲟϣ	ϣⲉⲃⲧ⸗: ϣⲟϥⲧ̄
ϣⲁⲃⲟⲗ: ⲃⲟⲗ	ϣⲁϣⲟⲩ: ϣⲟϣⲟⲩ	ϣⲉⲃⲧ-/⸗: ϣⲓⲃⲉ
ϣⲁⲃⲣⲁ: ϣⲁⲣⲃⲁ	ϣⲁϥ: ϣⲟϥ	ϣⲉⲉⲛⲉ: ϣⲱⲱⲛⲉ
ϣⲁⲓ: ϣⲓⲁⲓ, ϣⲏⲓ	ϣⲁϥⲣⲁ: ϣⲁⲣⲃⲁ	ϣⲉⲉⲣⲉ: ϣⲓⲣⲉ, ϣⲏⲣⲉ
ϣⲁⲓⲉ: ϣⲓⲁⲓ	ϣⲁϥⲉ(-): ϣⲓⲃⲉ, ϣⲟϥ	ϣⲉⲉⲧ-: ϣⲟⲱⲧ
ϣⲁⲓⲣⲉ: ϣⲁⲁⲣⲉ	ϣⲁⲭⲛⲉ: ϣⲟⲭⲛⲉ	ϣⲉⲉϭⲉ-: ϣⲱⲱϭⲉ
ϣⲁⲕⲧ⸗: ϣⲓⲕⲉ	ϣⲃ̄-: ϣⲓⲃⲉ, ϣⲟⲃ	ϣⲉⲓ: ϣⲓ, ϣⲉ
ϣⲁⲗ(-): ϣⲱⲗ	ϣⲃⲁⲧⲉ: ϣⲃⲱⲧ	ϣⲉⲓⲕ: ϣⲓⲕⲉ
ϣⲁⲗⲏⲩ: ϣⲁⲗⲓⲟⲩ	ϣⲃ̄ⲣⲓⲁⲉⲓⲧ, ϣⲃ̄ⲃⲓⲟ:	ϣⲉⲕⲧ̄-: ϣⲓⲕⲉ
ϣⲁⲗⲕ⸗: ϣⲱⲗϭ̄	ϣⲉⲃⲓⲏⲩ	ϣⲉⲗⲧⲁⲙ, ϣⲉⲗⲧⲉⲙ:
ϣⲁⲗⲧⲉⲙ, ϣⲁⲗⲧⲏⲙ: ϣⲗ̄ϭⲟⲙ	ϣⲃⲉ: ⲥⲁϣϥ	ϣⲗ̄ϭⲟⲙ
ϣⲁⲙⲁ-: ϣⲙⲁ	ϣⲃⲉⲉⲣ(ⲉ): ϣⲃⲏⲣ	ϣⲉⲛ-: ϣⲏⲣⲉ, ϣⲓⲛⲉ
ϣⲁⲙⲓⲥⲉ: ⲙⲓⲥⲉ	ϣⲃ̄ⲉⲓⲁⲉⲓⲧ: ϣⲉⲃⲓⲏⲩ	ϣⲉⲛ: ⲭⲓⲛ
ϣⲁⲛⲧ⸗: ϣⲁ	ϣⲃ̄ⲉⲓⲱ: ϣⲉⲃⲓⲏⲩ	ϣⲉⲛⲃ̄-: ϣⲱⲛϥ̄
ϣⲁⲟⲩ: ϣⲁⲩ	ϣⲃⲓⲃ: ϣⲟⲩⲏⲏⲃ	ϣⲉⲛⲉ-: ϣⲱⲱⲛⲉ
ϣⲁⲡ(-/⸗): ϣⲱⲡ, ϭⲱⲡⲉ	ϣⲃ̄ⲓⲱ: ϣⲉⲃⲓⲏⲩ	ϣⲉⲛⲟⲩⲗ: ϣⲏⲣⲉ
ϣⲁⲣ(⸗): ϣⲁⲁⲣⲉ, ϣⲁⲁⲣ	ϣⲃ̄ⲃⲛ̄ⲛⲉ: ⲃⲛ̄ⲛⲉ	ϣⲉⲛⲧ̄-: ϣⲓⲛⲉ, ϣⲱⲛⲧ̄
ϣⲁⲣⲁ₂ⲉ: ⲁ₂ⲉ	ϣⲃ̄ⲣ̄-: ϣⲃⲏⲣ	ϣⲉⲛⲧ⸗: ϣⲁ
ϣⲁⲣⲉ: ϣⲁⲁⲣ	ϣⲃⲟⲧ: ϣⲃⲱⲧ	ϣⲉⲛⲧⲥ̄: ϣⲏⲧⲥ̄
ϣⲁⲣⲓⲟⲩ: ϣⲁⲗⲓⲟⲩ	ϣⲃ̄ⲧ⸗, ϣⲃ̄ⲧⲥ̄: ϣⲓⲃⲉ	ϣⲉⲡⲛ̄ϣⲱⲡ: ϣⲱⲡ
ϣⲁⲣⲟ⸗: ϣⲁ	ϣⲃⲱ: ϣϥⲱ	ϣⲉⲧ-: ϣⲱⲱⲧ, ϣⲓⲧⲉ

ϣⲉϥ-: ϣⲱϥ, ϣⲱⲃ
ϣⲉϥⲉ: ϣⲁϥⲉ
ϣⲉϥⲓⲱ: ϣⲉⲃⲓⲏⲩ
ϣⲉϥⲧ̄-: ϣⲱϥⲧ̄, ϣⲓⲃⲉ
ϣⲉϥⲧˀ: ϣⲓⲃⲉ
ϣⲉϭⲉ-: ϣⲱⲱϭⲉ
ϣⲏ: ϣⲉ
ϣⲏⲃ: ϣⲱⲃ, ϣⲟⲩⲏⲏⲃ
ϣⲏⲃⲉ: ϣⲉⲛϥⲉ, ϣⲁϥⲉ
ϣⲏⲉⲓ: ϣⲏⲓ
ϣⲏⲏⲣⲉ: ϣⲏⲣⲉ
ϣⲏⲕ: ϣⲓⲕⲉ, ϣⲱⲕ
ϣⲏⲛϥⲉ: ϣⲉⲛϥⲉ
ϣⲏⲣⲉ: ϣⲓⲣⲉ
ϣⲏⲧ: ϣⲱⲱⲧ, ϣⲉ
ϣⲏⲩ: ϣⲓ, ϣⲓⲗⲓ, ϣⲁⲩ
ϣⲏⲩⲉ: ϣⲟⲩⲏⲏⲃ
ϣⲏϥ: ϣⲱϥ, ϣⲱⲃ
ϣⲏϥⲉ: ϣⲁϥⲉ: ϣⲉⲛϥⲉ
ϣⲓ: ϣⲉ
ϣⲓⲃⲉ: ϣⲏⲃⲉ, ϣⲁϥⲉ
ϣⲓⲉ: ϣⲓⲏ
ϣⲓⲏ, ϣⲓⲏⲉ: ϣⲓⲗⲓ
ϣⲓⲕ, ϣⲓⲕⲧˀ: ϣⲓⲕⲉ
ϣⲓⲕⲍ̄: ϣⲱⲕⲍ̄
ϣⲓⲙⲉ: ϣⲟⲉⲓⲙ
ϣⲓⲛϣⲱⲧⲉ: ϣⲛ̄ϣⲱⲧⲉ
ϣⲓⲧˀ: ϣⲓ, ϣⲓⲧⲉ
ϣⲓϥ: ⲥⲓϣϥ̄
ϣⲓϥⲉ: ϣⲉⲛϥⲉ, ϣⲁϥⲉ
ϣⲓϥⲧⲉ: ϣⲓⲃⲧⲉ
ϣⲕⲉⲣ: ⲥϭⲏⲣ
ϣⲕⲏⲗ: ϣⲕⲓⲗ
ϣⲕⲏⲗⲕⲉⲗ: ϣⲕⲗ̄ⲕⲗ̄
ϣⲕⲓⲗⲅⲓⲗ: ϣⲕⲗ̄ⲓⲗ
ϣⲗⲉⲓⲛ: ϣⲗⲁⲉⲓⲛ
ϣⲗⲉⲍ: ϣⲗ̄ⲍ
ϣⲗⲉϭ: ϣⲱⲗϭ̄
ϣⲗⲓϭ: ϣⲱⲗϭ̄
ϣⲗⲁⲗ̄: ϣⲗⲏⲗ
ϣⲗ̄ⲧⲁⲙ, ϣⲗ̄ⲧⲉⲙ: ϣⲗ̄ϭⲟⲙ
ϣⲗ̄ϥ: ϣⲗⲗⲍ
ϣⲙ-ⲛⲟⲩϥⲉ: ϣⲓⲛⲉ
ϣⲙⲏⲛ(ⲉ): ϣⲙⲟⲩⲛ
ϣⲙ̄ⲙⲟⲓ, ϣⲙ̄ⲙⲱ: ϣⲙ̄ⲙⲟ
ϣⲙ̄ⲛ̄ⲧ(-): ϣⲟⲙⲛ̄ⲧ
ϣⲙⲟ: ϣⲙ̄ⲙⲟ
ϣⲙⲟⲙ: ⲍⲙⲟⲙ
ϣⲙⲟⲩⲉ, ϣⲙⲟⲩⲓ: ϣⲙⲟⲩ
ϣⲙⲟⲩⲓ: ϣⲟⲙ
ϣⲙⲱ: ϣⲙ̄ⲙⲟ
ϣⲙ̄ϣⲏⲧˀ, ϣⲙ̄ϣⲓⲧ: ϣⲙ̄ϣⲉ

ϣⲛ̄-: ϣⲏⲣⲉ, ϣⲓⲛⲉ
ϣⲛ̄ⲃⲉ: ϣⲉⲛϥⲉ
ϣⲛ̄ⲃⲛ̄ⲛⲉ: ⲃⲛ̄ⲛⲉ
ϣⲛⲏ, ϣⲛⲏⲩ(ⲉ): ϣⲛⲉ
ϣⲛⲟⲩⲗ(ⲓ): ϣⲏⲣⲉ
ϣⲛ̄ⲥ: ϣⲏⲧⲥ̄
ϣⲛ̄ⲧ-/ˀ: ϣⲓⲛⲉ, ϣⲱⲛⲧ̄
ϣⲛ̄ⲧˀ: ϣⲁ
ϣⲛ̄ϥⲉ: ϣⲉⲛϥⲉ
ϣⲛ̄ϫⲱϫ: ϫⲱϫ
ϣⲟⲃⲉ: ϣⲁϥⲉ, ϣⲓⲃⲉ
ϣⲟⲃⲧ(ˀ): ϣⲱϥⲧ̄
ϣⲟⲉⲓⲙⲉ: ϣⲟⲉⲓⲙ
ϣⲟⲉⲓϫϥ̄: ϣⲱϫⲉ
ϣⲟⲕⲉ: ϣⲓⲕⲉ
ϣⲟⲗⲍ̄: ϣⲱⲗⲍ̄, ϣⲗⲗⲍ
ϣⲟⲙⲧ̄, ϣⲟⲙⲧⲉ: ϣⲟⲙⲛ̄ⲧ
ϣⲟⲛˀ: ϣⲱⲱⲛⲉ
ϣⲟⲛⲃ(ˀ): ϣⲱⲛϥ̄
ϣⲟⲛⲧⲉ: ϣⲱⲛⲧ̄
ϣⲟⲛⲱϣ: ϣⲛⲟϣ
ϣⲟⲟⲃ: ϣⲁⲁⲃ
ϣⲟⲟⲃⲉ: ϣⲓⲃⲉ, ϣⲱⲡⲉ
ϣⲟⲟⲙ: ϣⲟⲙ
ϣⲟⲟⲙˀ: ϣⲱⲙ
ϣⲟⲟⲙⲉ: ϣⲙⲁ
ϣⲟⲟⲛˀ, ϣⲟⲟⲛⲉ: ϣⲱⲱⲛⲉ
ϣⲟⲟⲡ: ϣⲟⲡ, ϣⲱⲡⲉ
ϣⲟⲟⲣˀ: ϣⲱⲣ
ϣⲟⲟⲣⲧ̄: ϣⲟⲣⲧ̄
ϣⲟⲟⲥ: ϣⲱⲥ
ϣⲟⲟⲩⲉ: ϣⲟⲟⲩ
ϣⲟⲟⲩⲉ: ϣⲏⲩⲉ
ϣⲟⲟϣ: ϣⲟϣ
ϣⲟⲟϭˀ, ϣⲟⲟϭⲉ: ϣⲱⲱϭⲉ
ϣⲟⲡⲥ̄: ϣⲟⲡ
ϣⲟⲣⲡⲉ: ϣⲱⲣⲡ̄
ϣⲟⲥⲙ̄: ⲥⲱϣⲙ̄
ϣⲟⲩ: ⲉϣⲱ
ϣⲟⲩ-: ϣⲟⲟⲩ, ϣⲁⲩ,
   ϣⲟⲩⲟ
ϣⲟⲩⲗ: ϣⲏⲣⲉ
ϣⲟⲩⲉ: ϣⲟⲩⲏⲏⲃ
ϣⲟⲩⲉ-: ϣⲟⲩⲟ
ϣⲟⲩⲉⲃⲉ: ϣⲟⲩⲏⲏⲃ
ϣⲟⲩⲉⲓⲧ: ϣⲟⲩⲟ
ϣⲟⲩⲉϥⲉ: ϣⲟⲩⲏⲏⲃ
ϣⲟⲩⲏⲟⲩ: ϣⲟⲩⲏⲏⲃ
ϣⲟⲩⲟⲃⲉ: ϣⲟⲩⲱⲃⲉ
ϣⲟⲩⲟⲩⲗ: ϣⲏⲣⲉ
ϣⲟⲩⲟⲩⲱϣⲧ̄: ⲟⲩⲱϣⲧ̄
ϣⲟⲩⲥⲟⲟⲩⲍⲉ: ϣⲟⲩⲥⲟⲟⲩϣⲉ

ϣⲟⲩⲱˀ: ϣⲟⲩⲟ
ϣⲟⲩⲱⲟⲩ(ⲉ): ϣⲟⲟⲩⲉ
ϣⲟⲩⲍⲏⲛⲉ: ⲍⲏⲛⲉ
ϣⲟϣⲧ: ϣⲟⲧϣⲧ̄
ϣⲟϥˀ: ϣⲱⲃ, ϣⲱϥ
ϣⲟϥⲉ: ϣⲓⲃⲉ
ϣⲟϫⲧ̄: ϣⲟⲧϣⲧ̄
ϣⲟϭˀ, ϣⲟϭⲉ: ϣⲱⲱϭⲉ
ϣⲡⲉⲛϣⲱⲡ: ϣⲱⲡ
ϣⲡⲓⲉⲉⲧⲉ, ϣⲡⲓⲏⲧ:
   ϣⲓⲡⲉ
ϣⲡ̄ⲛ̄ϣⲱⲡ: ϣⲱⲡ
ϣⲡ̄-: ϣⲏⲣⲉ
ϣⲣⲁ: ⲍⲣⲁ
ϣⲣⲉⲩ, ϣⲣⲏⲩ: ϣⲏⲣⲉ
ϣⲣ̄ϣⲟⲣⲧ̄: ϣⲟⲣϣ̄
ϣⲣ̄ϣⲱⲣ: ϣⲟⲣϣ̄,
   ϣⲟⲗϭⲗ̄
ϣⲥ(ⲉ)-: ⲥⲱϣ
ϣⲥ̄ⲛ̄ⲗⲥ: ⲗⲥ
ϣⲥ̄ⲛⲉⲓϥⲧ: ⲉⲓϥⲧ
ϣⲥ̄ⲛ2ⲏⲧ: 2ⲏⲧ
ϣⲥ̄ϭⲏⲣ: ⲥϭⲏⲣ
ϣⲧⲁ: ϣⲱⲱⲧ, ⲭⲧⲟ
ϣⲧⲁⲙ: ϣⲱⲧⲙ̄
ϣⲧⲏ: ϣⲧⲉ
ϣⲧⲏⲩ: ⲥⲧⲉ, ⲭⲧⲟ
ϣⲧⲛ̄: ϣⲧⲏⲛ
ϣⲧⲟ(ˀ): ⲭⲧⲟ
ϣⲧⲟⲃ: ϣⲱⲧⲃ̄
ϣⲧⲟϥ: ϣⲱⲧⲃ̄
ϣⲧⲟⲙ: ϣⲱⲧⲙ̄
ϣⲧⲟⲣⲉ: ⲧⲱⲣⲉ
ϣⲧⲣ̄ⲧⲣ̄ⲓⲡ: ϣⲧⲟⲣⲧⲣ̄
ϣⲧⲱⲣⲉ: ⲧⲱⲣⲉ
ϣⲱⲃⲧ̄: ϣⲟϥⲧ̄
ϣⲱⲛⲧ̄: ϫⲱⲛϥ̄
ϣⲱⲡⲉ: ϭⲱⲡⲉ
ϣⲱⲥⲙ̄: ⲥⲱϣⲙ̄
ϣⲱⲱⲙⲉ: ϣⲙⲁ
ϣϣⲱⲧⲉ: ϣⲟⲧ
ϣϥⲉ: ϣⲃⲉ, ⲥⲁϣϥ̄
ϣϥⲱ: ϣⲃⲱ
ϣ2ⲓϫ: ϣ2ⲓϭ
ϣⲍ̄ⲗ2ⲓϭ: ϣⲱⲗϭ̄
ϣⲭ̄-: ϣⲁϫⲉ
ϣϫⲏⲩ: ϣϫⲉ
ϣϫⲟⲥ: ⲍ2ⲟⲥ
ϣⲭ̄2ⲟⲥ: ⲍ2ⲟⲥ
ϣϭⲗ: ϣⲱⲱϭⲉ
ϣϭⲏⲣ: ⲥϭⲏⲣ
ϣϭⲗ̄ϭⲓⲗ, ϣϭⲉⲗϭⲓⲗ,

ϣ6ιλ6ιλ: ϣⲕλιλ   ϣ6ολ: ϣ6ορ   ϣⲃ̄ρλ2Т̄: Сⲃ̄ρλ2Т̄

ϥ

ϥι (ϥ6ι) ϥι- (ϥ6ι-) ϥιТ⸗ Q ϥⲏⲩ vb. tr. to take, carry,
bear, sustain (ⲙ̄ⲙⲟ⸗, 2λ); oft. w. eth. dat. (6, ⲛλ⸗).
Used w. many prep. and adv. in normal senses. ϥι ⲙ̄ⲛ̄ to
agree with. ϥι 2λ to tolerate, bear, endure. ϥι ⲙ̄ⲙⲟ⸗
6ⲃоλ to take away, remove (from: ⲙ̄ⲙⲟ⸗, 2ⲛ̄). ϥι ⲙ̄ⲙλⲩ to
carry etc. from there (± 2ⲛ̄, 2ιⲭ̄ⲛ̄: from, from on). For
ϥι- and ϥλι- in vb. and nom. cpds. see 2nd element.
ρ6ϥϥι one who bears (may have object); ⲙ̄ⲛ̄Тρ6ϥϥι state
or condition of bearing.
ϥⲛ̄Т, ⲃⲛ̄Т, ϥ6ⲛ̄Т, ⲟⲩ6ⲛ̄Т n.m.f. worm. ⲣ̄-ϥⲛ̄Т to become wormy.
ϥо, ⲃо, ⲃоо, ϥωι n.f. canal, water conduit.
ϥтⲟоⲩ, ⲃтⲟоⲩ (ϥт6ⲩ-, ϥтⲟⲩ-; f. ϥтⲟ6, ϥтⲟ, ⲃтⲟ) number: four.
ⲙ̄ⲛ̄Тλϥт6 fourteen. ⲙ6⳺ϥтⲟоⲩ (f. -ϥтⲟ6, -ϥтⲟ) fourth.
See §§15.3; 24.3; 30.7.
ϥω, ⲃω, ⲟⲩω, ϥω6 n.m. hair. ρλт-ϥω, ρⲏт ⲙ̄ ϥω hairy. ⲟⲩ6⳺-
ϥω to let hair grow.
ϥωт6, ⲃωт6 n.f.m. sweat. †-ϥωт6 to sweat.
ϥωт6 (ⲃωт6, ⲃот6) ϥ6т- ϥот⸗ vb. tr. to wipe away, off; to
obliterate, destroy (ⲙ̄ⲙⲟ⸗). ϥωт6 6ⲃоλ (1) idem; (2) intr. to be wiped out, destroyed. λтϥωт6 6ⲃоλ uneface-
able, ineradicable.
ϥω66 (ⲃω66) ϥ66- ϥо6⸗ Q ϥⲏ6 (ⲃⲏ6) vb. intr. and reflex. to
leap, spring (6ⲃоλ, 6ⲡ6Сⲏт, 66ⲏ, 62ⲟⲩⲛ, 62ρλι); as n.m.
impetuosity; ρ6ϥϥω66 impetuous person. ϥо6С̄, ⲃо6С̄ n.
leaping, dancing; esp. in ⲭι-ϥо6С̄ to dance; ⲙ̄ⲛ̄Тρ6ϥ-
ⲃо6С̄ haste.
ϥω66 (ⲃω66) ϥ66- ϥо6⸗ Q ϥⲏ6 vb. tr. to seize, snatch, rob
(6, ⲙ̄ⲙⲟ⸗); ρ6ϥϥω66 violent person. ϥо6ϥ̄ n. robber.
ϥω6С̄ (ⲃω6С̄) rare variant of ϥω66 to leap q.v.

ϥλι-: ϥι   ϥ6ⲛ̄Т: ϥⲛ̄Т   ϥⲏⲩ: ϥι
ϥλι: ⲃλι   ϥ6т-: ϥωт6   ϥⲏ6: ϥω66
ϥ6ι, ϥ6ι-: ϥι   ϥ66-: ϥω66   ϥιТ⸗: ϥι

ϧⲟⲧ⸗: ϧⲱⲧⲉ   ϧⲧⲉⲩ⁻: ϧⲧⲟⲟⲩ   ϧⲱⲓ: ϧⲟ
ϧⲟϭ⸗: ϧⲱϭⲉ   ϧⲧⲟ, ϧⲧⲟⲉ: ϧⲧⲟⲟⲩ   ϧⲱⲧⲉ: ⲃⲱⲧⲉ
ϧⲟϭⲥ̄: ϧⲱϭⲉ   ϧⲧⲟⲩ⁻: ϧⲧⲟⲟⲩ   ϧⲱϭⲉ: ⲃⲱⲧⲉ
ϧⲟϭϥ̄: ϧⲱϭⲉ

ⲍ

ⲍⲁ, ⲍⲟ n.m. winnowing fan.

ⲍⲁ, ⲍⲟ n.m. pole, mast; weaver's beam.

ⲍⲁ (ⲍⲁⲣⲟ⸗) prep. (1) under, beneath; often with meaning of bearing, carrying; (2) from under, from the presence of, from the time of; (3) from, by reason of, because of; (4) for, in respect to, on behalf of; (5) in exchange for, for; to, toward (usu. of persons).

ⲍⲁⲉ, ⲍⲁⲉⲓⲏ, ⲍⲁⲓⲏ (f. ⲍⲁⲏ, ⲍⲁⲉ; pl. ⲍⲁⲉⲩ, ⲍⲁⲉⲉⲩ, ⲍⲁⲉⲟⲩ, ⲍⲁⲉⲩⲉ) adj. last, final; as n.: end, termination, last part. ⲉ ⲡ²ⲁⲉ, ⲙ̄ ⲡ²ⲁⲉ, ⲛ̄ ⲑⲁⲉ, ⲛ̄ ⲍⲁⲉ, ⲉⲭⲛ̄ ⲍⲁⲉ, ⲍⲛ̄ ⲑⲁⲉ at last, finally. ϣⲁ ⲍⲁⲉ, ϣⲁ ⲑⲁⲉ until the last, at the last. ⲣ̄-ⲍⲁⲉ (1) to become last; to be (too) late (for: ⲉ); (2) to be in want (of: ⲉ). ⲭⲓ-ⲍⲁⲉ to lag.

ⲍⲁⲉⲓⲃⲉⲥ, ⲍⲁⲓⲃⲉⲥ, ⲍⲟⲓⲃⲉⲥ n.f. shade, shelter, shadow; ⲣ̄-ⲍⲁⲉⲓⲃⲉⲥ to make shade (for, over: ⲉ, ⲉⲭⲛ̄, ⲍⲓⲭⲛ̄). ⲭⲓ-ⲍⲁⲉⲓⲃⲉⲥ to take shade, be shaded, sheltered.

ⲍⲁⲉⲓⲧ, ⲍⲁⲓⲉⲓⲧ, ⲍⲁⲉⲓⲏⲧ n.f. gateway, forecourt, porch.

ⲍⲁⲓ n.m. husband. ⲭⲓ-ⲍⲁⲓ to take a husband.

ⲍⲁⲕ, ⲍⲁⲁⲕ n.m. tailor.

ⲍⲁⲕ adj. sober, prudent, mild (bef. or aft. n., w. ⲛ̄); ⲙⲛ̄ⲧⲍⲁⲕ sobriety, mildness. ⲣ̄-ⲍⲁⲕ (Q ⲟ ⲛ̄ ⲍⲁⲕ) to become sober, prudent.

ⲍⲁⲕⲗ̄ϥ, ⲍⲁⲕⲏⲗϥ̄, ⲍⲁⲕⲉⲗϥ̄, ⲍⲁⲛⲕⲗ̄ϥ n.m. a species of lizard.

ⲍⲁⲗ n.m.f. servant, slave; rare except in ⲍⲙ̄ⲍⲁⲗ, ⲍⲙ̄ⲉⲗ n.m.f. idem; ⲙⲛ̄ⲧⲍⲙ̄ⲍⲁⲗ status of slave or servant; ⲣ̄-ⲍⲙ̄ⲍⲁⲗ to serve, become servant (to: ⲛⲁ⸗).

ⲍⲁⲗ only in ⲣ̄-ⲍⲁⲗ to deceive (ⲙ̄ⲙⲟ⸗); as n. deceit; ⲙⲛ̄ⲧⲣ̄-ⲍⲁⲗ deceit, deception; ⲣⲉϥⲣ̄-ⲍⲁⲗ deceiver; ⲙⲛ̄ⲧⲣⲉϥⲣ̄-ⲍⲁⲗ deceit.

ⲍⲁⲗⲁⲕ, ⲍⲁⲗⲏⲕ n.f. ring.

ⲍⲁⲗⲏⲧ (pl. ⲍⲁⲗⲁⲧⲉ, ⲍⲁⲗⲁⲁⲧⲉ) n.m. bird, any flying creature.

ⲊⲀⲖⲘⲎⲀⲈ, ⲊⲀⲖⲘⲎⲀ, ⲊⲀⲖⲘⲈⲀ, ⲊⲈⲖⲘⲈⲀⲈ n.f. boat.

ⲊⲀⲖⲞⲨⲤ, ⲊⲀⲖⲖⲞⲨⲤ n.m. spiderweb.

ⲊⲀⲖⲰⲘ n.m. cheese.

ⲊⲀⲘ (pl. ⲊⲘⲎⲨ, ⲊⲘⲈⲨ) n.m. craftsman; cf. ⲊⲀⲘϣⲈ.

ⲊⲀⲘⲎⲢ n.m. embrace; ⲣ̄-ⲊⲀⲘⲎⲢ Ⲙ̄ⲘⲞ⸗; ϯ-ⲊⲀⲘⲎⲢ Ⲉ to embrace.

ⲊⲀⲘⲞⲓ interj. would that ...!

ⲊⲀⲘϣⲈ, ⲊⲀⲘϣⲓ (pl. ⲊⲀⲘϣⲎⲞⲨⲈ, ⲊⲀⲘϣⲎⲨⲈ, ⲊⲀⲘϣⲞⲞⲨⲈ) n.m. carpenter; ⲘⲚ̄ⲦⲊⲀⲘϣⲈ carpentry.

ⲊⲀⲡ, ⲊⲞⲡ n.m. judgement, inquest; ⲀⲦⲊⲀⲡ without going to court. ⲈⲓⲣⲈ ⲙ̄ ⲡ(⸗)ⲊⲀⲡ, ⲣ̄-ⲊⲀⲡ to give a judgement (for: ⲚⲀ⸗; between: ⲞⲨⲦⲈ); to go to court; to avenge, i.e. to settle one's case (against: ⲘⲚ̄). ϯ-ⲊⲀⲡ to give a judgement, pass judgement (on: Ⲉ, ⲈⲭⲚ̄); ⲘⲀ Ⲛ̄ ϯ-ⲊⲀⲡ court, place of judgement; ⲣⲈϥϯ-ⲊⲀⲡ judge; ⲣ̄-ⲣⲈϥϯ-ⲊⲀⲡ to act as judge. ⲭⲓ-ⲊⲀⲡ, ⲭⲓ Ⲛ̄ ⲞⲨⲊⲀⲡ to go to court (against, with: ⲘⲚ̄, ⲞⲨⲂⲈ, ⲊⲀ, Ⲋⲓ); as n.m. judgement.

ⲊⲀⲡⲈ n.m. the god Apis.

ⲊⲀⲡⲞⲣⲕ̄, ⲊⲀⲡⲞⲣⲦ̄ n.f. saddle, saddle-cloth.

ⲊⲀⲡⲤ̄, ⲊⲞⲡⲤ̄ impers. vb. (± ⲡⲈ) it is necessary (for someone: Ⲉ; to do: Ⲉ, ⲈⲦⲣⲈ). See §20.2.

ⲊⲀⲣⲈⲀ (ⲀⲣⲈⲀ, ⲊⲀⲣⲎⲀⲈ, ⲈⲣⲈⲀ, ⲈⲣⲎⲀ) vb. tr. to keep, observe, preserve, be careful about (Ⲉ); to guard, watch, keep (Ⲉ; from: Ⲉ, ⲈⲂⲞⲖ Ⲙ̄ⲘⲞ⸗, ⲈⲂⲞⲖ ⲊⲚ̄); as n.m. watch, guard, caution; ⲘⲚ̄ⲦⲀⲦⲊⲀⲣⲈⲀ heedlessness; ⲘⲀ Ⲛ̄ ⲊⲀⲣⲈⲀ place of watch, guardhouse; ⲣⲈϥⲊⲀⲣⲈⲀ guard, watcher, watchman.

ⲊⲀⲣⲓⲊⲀⲣⲞ⸗ intensive pron., used appositionally: (he) alone, apart; (he him)self, by (him)self; other pers. sim.

ⲊⲀⲤ n.m. dung (of animals).

ⲊⲀⲤⲓⲈ, ⲊⲀⲤⲈⲓⲈ, ⲊⲀⲤⲓⲎ n.m. a drowned person; in cpds.: ⲂⲰⲕ Ⲛ̄ ⲊⲀⲤⲓⲈ, ϣⲈ Ⲛ̄ ⲊⲀⲤⲓⲈ, ⲣ̄-ⲂⲞⲖ Ⲛ̄ ⲊⲀⲤⲓⲈ to drown, be drowned.

ⲊⲀⲦ, ⲊⲀⲦⲈ, ⲊⲀⲀⲦ n.m. silver; silver coin(s), money; as adj. silver, white. ⲘⲀⲓ-ⲊⲀⲦ money-loving. ⲘⲈⲚⲦ̄-ⲊⲀⲦ silversmith; ⲣⲈϥⲘⲈⲚⲦ̄-ⲊⲀⲦ idem. ⲤⲀ Ⲛ̄ ⲊⲀⲦ dealer in silver. ⲣ̄-ⲊⲀⲦ to work silver; (Q ⲟ Ⲛ̄ ⲊⲀⲦ) to become silver; ⲣⲈϥⲣ̄-ⲊⲀⲦ silversmith. ϯ-ⲊⲀⲦ to pay.

ⲋⲁⲧⲁⲓⲁⲅ, ⲋⲁⲧⲁⲗⲏ n. name of an eye-disease.

ⲋⲁⲧⲉ, ⲋⲁⲁⲧⲉ vb. intr. to flow; tr. to pour (ⲙ̄ⲙⲟ⸗) ± ⲉⲃⲟⲗ.
As n.m. flow. ⲙⲁ ⲛ̄ ⲋⲁⲧⲉ channel, water-course.

ⲋⲁⲧⲏⲣ, ⲋⲁⲧⲏⲣⲉ n.m.f. hammer.

ⲋⲁⲑⲱⲣ, ⲋⲉⲱⲣ name of 3rd Coptic month.

ⲋⲁⲩϭⲁⲗ n.m. anchor.

ⲋⲁϣⲏⲧ, ⲋⲁϣⲓⲧ, ⲋⲁⲣϣⲏⲧ n.m. falcon.

ⲋⲁϥⲗⲉⲉⲗⲉ, ⲋⲁϥⲗⲉⲅⲉ, ⲋⲁⲃⲗⲉⲉⲗⲉ n.f. lizard.

ⲋⲁⲗ2 pron. many; as adj. (bef. or aft. noun, with ⲛ̄) many.
ⲣ̄-ⲋⲁⲗ2 to become or do much/many (+ ⲛ̄ + noun); ⲙⲛ̄ⲧⲋⲁⲗ2
multitude.

ⲋⲁϭⲉ, ⲋⲁⲗⲁϭⲉ n.m. snare.

ⲋⲁϭⲓⲛ n.m. mint.

ⲋⲃⲁ n.m. straits, difficulty, distress; ⲣ̄-ⲋⲃⲁ (ⲱ ⲟ ⲛ̄ ⲋⲃⲁ)
to become distressed; †-ⲋⲃⲁ to distress, disturb (ⲛⲁ⸗).

ⲋⲃ̄ⲃⲉ, ⲋⲅⲃⲃⲉ, ⲋⲏⲩⲃⲅ, ⲋⲏⲃ(ⲃ)ⲉ n.m. plow; yoke of animals.

ⲋⲃⲟⲣⲃ̄ⲣ̄ (ⲃⲟⲣⲃⲣ̄) ⲋⲃⲣ̄ⲃ̄ⲣ- (ⲃⲣ̄ⲃ̄ⲣ̄-) ⲋⲃ̄ⲣ̄ⲃⲱⲣ⸗ (ⲋⲟⲩⲉⲣⲟⲩⲱⲣ⸗) ⲱ
ⲃⲣ̄ⲃⲱⲣ (ⲃⲣ̄ⲃⲟⲣⲧ̄) vb. tr. to throw down, push, cast (ⲙ̄ⲙⲟ⸗);
ⲋⲃⲟⲣⲃ̄ⲣ̄ ⲙ̄ⲙⲟ⸗ ⲉⲃⲟⲗ to cast forth (on, onto: ⲉ, ⲉⲡⲉⲥⲏⲧ ⲉ,
ⲉ2ⲣⲁⲓ ⲉ); intr. to fall to pieces. ⲕⲁⲋ-ⲃⲣ̄ⲃⲱⲣ unoccupied land; ⲉⲓⲱⲋ-ⲃⲉⲣⲃⲱⲣ idem or sim.

ⲋⲃⲟⲩⲣ n.f. left hand; as adj. left. (ⲛ̄) ⲥⲁ ⲋⲃⲟⲩⲣ, ⲋⲓ
ⲋⲃⲟⲩⲣ on, to the left.

ⲋⲃⲱ n.f. covering; tent.

ⲋⲉ (ⲋⲉⲉ, ⲋⲏⲉ) ⲱ ⲋⲏⲩ to fall (± ⲉⲡⲉⲥⲏⲧ, ⲉ2ⲣⲁⲓ down); used
with ⲉ, ⲉⲝⲛ̄, ⲋⲛ̄, ⲋⲁⲧⲛ̄, ⲋⲓⲭⲛ̄ in ordinary senses. ⲋⲉ ⲛ̄ⲥⲁ,
ⲋⲉ ⲛ̄ⲧⲛ̄ to become lost to (someone). ⲋⲉ ⲉⲃⲟⲗ to perish,
cease (from: ⲋⲛ̄; from on, from with: ⲋⲓ, ⲋⲓⲭⲛ̄); to fall
away. ⲋⲉ ⲉ to find, chance upon, light upon, discover;
ⲋⲉ ⲉⲣⲟ⸗ ⲛ̄ⲥⲁ to find something in the possession of.

ⲋⲉ, ⲋⲓⲏ n.f. way, manner. ⲧⲁⲓ ⲧⲉ ⲑⲉ this is the way (that),
thus. ⲟⲩⲛ̄-ⲑⲉ there is a way, it is possible (to: ⲉ, ⲛ̄,
ⲉⲧⲣⲉ); ⲙⲛ̄-ⲑⲉ there is no way (to: ⲉ, ⲛ̄, ⲉⲧⲣⲉ). ⲛ̄ ⲑⲉ ⲛ̄
prep. like, in the manner of. ⲛ̄ ⲑⲉ + Rel. as, even as,
in the same way that. ⲛ̄ ⲧⲉⲓⲋⲉ (1) in this way, thus;

(2) of this sort. ⲚⲦⲈⲓⲌⲈ ⲦⲎⲣⳡ so much, to such an extent. ⲚⲦ(ⲉ)ⲌⲈ like (e.g. me), as (I) do, in (my) way or manner. ⲚⲦ(ⲉ)ⲌⲈ Ⲧ(ⲉ)ⲌⲈ as (I) was before. Ⲁⳬ Ⲛ ⲌⲈ of what sort? ⲔⲀⲦⲀ ⲐⲈ like (Ⲛ); as (+ Rel.). ⲔⲀⲦⲀ ⲦⲈⲓⲌⲈ in this way, likewise. Ⲣ̄-ⲐⲈ (Q o Ⲛ ⲐⲈ) (1) to become like; (2) to make like; Ⲣ̄-Ⲧ(ⲉ)ⲌⲈ to resume one's former appearance. ϯ-ⲐⲈ to provide means (to: ⲚⲀⲉ; so that: ⲉ, ⲈⲦⲣⲈ). ⳡⲚ̄-ⲐⲈ to find means (to: Ⲛ).

ⲌⲈ, Ⲍ- n.m. season, in cpds.: ⲌⲈ-ⲂⲰⲰⲚ, Ⲍ-ⲂⲰⲰⲚ bad season, famine; Ⲣ̄-ⲌⲈ-ⲂⲰⲰⲚ to have a bad season. ⲌⲈ-ⲚⲞⲨϥⲈ good season, plenty; Ⲣ̄-ⲌⲈ-ⲚⲞⲨϥⲈ to be in plenty.

ⲌⲈⲀⲚⲈ, ⲌⲬ̄ⲚⲈ n.f. navel.

ⲌⲈⲀⲌⲓⲀⲉ n.f. death-rattle.

ⲌⲈⲚⲈⲈⲦⲈ n.f. monastery, convent. Many variant spellings: ⲉ, Ⲏ for ⲉⲉ; -Ⲏ for -ⲉ; Ⲍ Ⲏ for Ⲍⲉ-.

Ⲍ Ⲏ, ⲉⲌⲎ, ⲌⲓⲎ (ⲌⲎⲦⲉ) n.f. front, forepart, beginning; ⲌⲎⲦⲉ, ⲉ ⲌⲎⲦⲉ prep. forward (to), before, into the presence of; used idiomatically with certain verbs. ⲈⲐⲎ adv. forward, ahead, in advance; ϯ ⲈⲐⲎ to advance, progress. Ⲛ̄ⲤⲀ-ⲐⲎ adv. formerly, henceforth. ⲌⲀ ⲐⲎ, ⲌⲀ Ⲧ(ⲉ)ⲌⲎ prep. in front of, before (time or place); also used as conj. (+ ⲈⲦⲣⲉ or Ⲙ̄ⲠⲀⲦⲈ-). Ⲍⲓ ⲐⲎ, Ⲍⲓ ⲌⲎ at the front, forward, in front; Ⲍⲓ ⲐⲎ Ⲙ̄ⲘⲞⲉ in front of, before, on the front of; Ⲣ̄-ⲌⲓⲐⲎ Ⲙ̄ⲘⲞⲉ to precede.

Ⲍ Ⲏ (ⲌⲎⲦⲉ) n.f. belly, womb. Ⲙ̄Ⲛ̄ⲦⲘⲀⲓ-ⲌⲎⲦⳡ gluttony. ϢⲀⲬⲈ ⲈⲂⲞⲀ Ⲛ ⲌⲎⲦ to ventriloquize. Ⲛ̄ⲌⲎⲦⲉ see Ⲍ̄Ⲛ.

Ⲍ Ⲏ, ⲌⲈ n.f. storey (of a house).

ⲌⲎⲂⲈ, ⲌⲎⲎⲂⲈ, ⲌⲎⲓⲂⲈ n.m.f. grief, mourning; Ⲣ̄-ⲌⲎⲂⲈ to grieve, mourn (for: ⲉ, ⲈⲦⲂⲈ, ⲈⲬⲚ̄, ⲚⲀⲉ, ⲌⲓⳜⲚ̄); ⲣⲈϥⲢ̄-ⲌⲎⲂⲈ mourner.

ⲌⲎⲂ̄Ⲥ, Ⲍ̄ⲂⲤ, ⲌⲈⲂⲤ̄ n.m. lamp.

ⲌⲎⲔⲈ n.f. corn-measure.

ⲌⲎⲘⲈ, ⲌⲈⲘⲈ, ⲌⲘ̄ⲘⲈ, ⲌⲓⲘⲈ n.f. freight, fare (on ship or camel); ϯ-ⲌⲎⲘⲈ to pay fare; ⲀⲦⲌⲎⲘⲈ free of charge.

ⲌⲎⲚⲈ n.m., usu. pl., spices, incense. Ⲥϯ-ⲌⲎⲚⲈ idem;

ⲧ-ⲥ-ⲧ-ⲍⲏⲛⲉ to offer (burn) incense. ϣⲟⲩ-ⲍⲏⲛⲉ incense;
ⲧⲁⲗⲉ-ϣⲟⲩ-ⲍⲏⲛⲉ ⲉⲍⲣⲁⲓ, ⲧ-ϣⲟⲩ-ⲍⲏⲛⲉ ⲉⲍⲣⲁⲓ to offer incense.
ⲍⲏⲧ (ⲍⲧⲏ*; pl. ⲍⲧⲉⲉⲩ) tip, edge, end; ⲍⲧⲏ* ⲛ̄ is the preferred construction before nouns.
ⲍⲏⲧ n.m. north. ⲉ ⲍⲏⲧ, ⲉⲛⲍⲏⲧ, ⲁⲛⲍⲏⲧ adv. northward.
ⲧⲁⲛⲍⲏⲧ, ⲍⲁⲛⲍⲏⲧ adv. (on) the north side. ⲥⲁ ⲛ̄ ⲍⲏⲧ idem.
ⲍⲏⲧ (ⲍⲧⲏ*) n.m. heart, mind. ⲁ-ⲡⲉϥⲍⲏⲧ ⲉⲓ ⲉⲣⲟϥ he came to
his senses. ⲙⲛ̄ⲧⲍⲏⲧ ⲛ̄ ⲟⲩⲱⲧ unanimity, being of a single
mind; ⲣ̄-ⲍⲏⲧ ⲛ̄ ⲟⲩⲱⲧ to become unanimous. ⲍⲏⲧ ⲥⲛⲁⲩ doubt;
ⲙⲛ̄ⲧⲍⲏⲧ ⲥⲛⲁⲩ doubt, hesitation; ⲣ̄-ⲍⲏⲧ ⲥⲛⲁⲩ to become
doubtful, hesitant. ⲍⲏⲧ ϣⲏⲙ impatience; ⲙⲛ̄ⲧⲍⲏⲧ ϣⲏⲙ
idem; ⲣ̄-ⲍⲏⲧ ϣⲏⲙ to become impatient. ⲁⲧⲍⲏⲧ senseless;
ⲙⲛ̄ⲧⲁⲧⲍⲏⲧ senselessness; ⲣ̄-ⲁⲧⲍⲏⲧ to become senseless.
ⲃⲁⲗ-ⲍⲏⲧ guileless, simple; ⲙⲛ̄ⲧⲃⲁⲗ-ⲍⲏⲧ guilelessness.
ⲡⲙⲛ̄ⲍⲏⲧ wise, a wise person; ⲙⲛ̄ⲧⲡⲙⲛ̄ⲍⲏⲧ wisdom, understanding; ⲣ̄-ⲡⲙⲛ̄ⲍⲏⲧ to become wise. ϣⲥ̄-ⲛ̄-ⲍⲏⲧ anguish.
ⲕⲱ ⲛ̄ ⲍⲧⲏ*, ⲕⲁ-ⲍⲧⲏ* to set one's heart or mind (on, to:
ⲉ, ⲉⲭⲛ̄, ⲍⲓ), to be confident (in); ⲕⲁ-ⲍⲧⲏ* ⲉⲃⲟⲗ to relax, become careless. ⲣ̄-ⲍⲧⲏ* to regret, repent (concerning: ⲉ, ⲉⲭⲛ̄, ⲛ̄ⲥⲁ); ⲁⲧⲣ̄-ⲍⲧⲏ* unrepentant; ⲙⲛ̄ⲧⲣⲉϥⲣ̄-
ⲍⲧⲏ*, ⲙⲛ̄ⲧⲣ̄-ⲍⲧⲏ* repentance. ⲥⲉⲕ-ⲡⲍⲏⲧ ⲛ̄ to persuade.
ⲧ-ⲍⲧⲏ* to observe, notice, pay attention to, heed (ⲉ,
ⲉⲭⲛ̄, ⲍⲓ, ⲍⲛ̄); ⲙⲛ̄ⲧⲁⲧⲧ-ⲍⲧⲏ* heedlessness; ⲣⲉϥⲧ-ⲍⲧⲏ* atten-
tive; ⲙⲛ̄ⲧⲣⲉϥⲧ-ⲍⲧⲏ* attentiveness. ϣⲛ̄-ⲍⲧⲏ* to pity, have
pity (on, for: ⲉⲭⲛ̄, ⲉⲍⲣⲁⲓ ⲉⲭⲛ̄, ⲍⲁ); ⲙⲛ̄ⲧϣⲛ̄-ⲍⲧⲏ* pity,
mercy; ⲣ̄-ϣⲛ̄-ⲍⲧⲏ* to be merciful. For nouns and vbs.
cpd. with ⲛ̄ ⲍⲏⲧ see 1st element. ⲍⲁⲍⲧⲛ̄, ⲍⲁⲧⲛ̄ (ⲍⲁⲍⲧⲏ*,
ⲍⲁⲧⲏ*) prep. with, near, beside.
ⲍⲏⲩ, ⲍⲏⲟⲩ n.m. profit, benefit, usefulness, advantage.
ⲙⲁⲓ-ⲍⲏⲩ profit-loving. ⲣ̄-ⲍⲏⲩ to be profitable, useful
(to: ⲛⲁ*). ⲧ-ⲍⲏⲩ to give profit or benefit (to: ⲛⲁ*);
to gain profit or benefit (in, by, from: ⲙ̄ⲙⲟ*, ⲉ, ⲙⲛ̄,
ⲍⲛ̄). ⲋⲛ̄-ⲍⲏⲩ to find profit or benefit (in: ⲉ, ⲍⲛ̄).
ⲍⲏⲋⲉ to be disturbed, concerned.
ⲍⲓ ⲍⲓⲧ* (ⲍⲁⲧ*) vb. tr. to beat, thresh, rub (ⲙ̄ⲙⲟ*; on,

against: ϬⲝⲚ̄, ₂ⲓ). As n.m. threshing. ⲡϬϥ₂ⲓ thresher.

₂ⲓ (₂ⲓⲱˢ, ₂ⲓⲱⲱˢ) prep. (1) on, in, at; (2) (to enquire) concerning; (3) and, or, with (connecting two nouns); (4) from on, from in, from at; (5) in the time of, in the presence of. ₂ⲓ ⲚⲀⲓ adv. thus. ⲈⲂⲟⲗ ₂ⲓ from on, from. ⲈⲡⲈⲤⲎⲦ ₂ⲓ down from on, down onto; Ⲉ₂ⲟⲨⲚ ₂ⲓ in toward; Ⲉ₂ⲢⲀⲓ ₂ⲓ down from, up from, down on.

(₂ⲓⲂⲈ), Q ₂ⲟⲂⲈ (₂ⲀⲂⲈ) vb. intr. to be low, short. ₂ⲃ̄ⲂⲈ n.m. lower part or place. ₂ⲂⲀⲓ n. shortness.

₂ⲓⲂⲱⲓ, ₂ⲈⲂⲱⲓ, ₂ⲓⲂⲟⲨⲓ, ₂ⲂⲟⲨⲓ, ₂ⲀⲂⲓⲟⲨⲓ n.m. ibis.

₂ⲓⲈ, ₂ⲓⲎ (pl. ₂ⲓⲎⲨ, ₂ⲓⲎⲟⲨ, ₂ⲓⲈⲨ) n.m.f. rudder.

₂ⲓⲈⲓⲂ, Ⲉ₂ⲓⲈⲓⲂ, ₂ⲈⲓⲈⲂ, ₂ⲓⲂ (f. ₂ⲈⲓⲀⲈⲓⲂⲈ, ₂ⲓⲀⲂⲈ, ₂ⲓⲈⲓⲀⲂⲈ, ₂ⲓⲈⲈⲂⲈ, ₂ⲓⲈⲓⲂⲈ, ₂ⲓⲂⲈ, ₂ⲓⲎⲂⲈ, ₂ⲀⲓⲂⲈ) n.m.f. lamb.

₂ⲓⲈⲓⲦ, ₂ⲈⲓⲈⲓⲦ, ₂ⲓⲦ n.m. pit.

₂ⲓⲎ (pl. ₂ⲓⲟⲟⲨⲈ, ₂ⲓⲎⲨ) n.f. road, way. ₂ⲓⲎ Ⲛ̄ Ⲉⲓ ⲈⲂⲟⲗ exodus, way out. ₂ⲓⲎ Ⲛ̄ Ⲉⲓ Ⲉ₂ⲟⲨⲚ way in. ₂ⲓⲎ Ⲛ̄ Ⲃⲱⲕ way of going (in: Ⲉ₂ⲟⲨⲚ). ₂ⲓⲎ Ⲙ̄ ⲘⲟⲟⲱⲈ way, road. ₂ⲓⲎ Ⲛ̄ ⲬⲓⲟⲟⲢ a way for crossing, ford. ₂ⲓⲎ Ⲙ̄ ⲚⲢ̄Ⲣⲟ the king's road, highway. ⲢⲘ̄(Ⲛ̄)₂ⲓⲎ traveling companion. ⳨—ⲦⲈ₂ⲓⲎ ⲚⲀˢ to provide way or means to (someone).

₂ⲓⲕ n.m. magic; as adj. magical. Ⲣ̄-₂ⲓⲕ to bewitch, enchant (Ⲉ, ₂ⲓ). ⲢⲈϥⲢ̄-₂ⲓⲕ wizard, magician; ⲘⲚ̄ⲦⲢⲈϥⲢ̄-₂ⲓⲕ magic, wizardry. ₂Ⲁⲕⲟ n.m. magician; ⲘⲚ̄Ⲧ₂Ⲁⲕⲟ magic.

₂ⲓⲚ, ₂ⲈⲓⲚ n.m. cup, vessel; a liquid measure; ⲢⲈϥⲘ̄-Ⲛ₂ⲓⲚ Ⲉ₂ⲟⲨⲚ diviner (by aid of cup).

₂ⲓⲚⲈ vb. intr. to row; tr. idem (Ⲙ̄Ⲙⲟˢ). ₂ⲓⲚⲓⲈ, ₂ⲈⲚⲈⲓⲈ n.m. steering-oar, rudder.

₂ⲓⲚⲈ ₂Ⲛ̄Ⲧˢ reflex. to move forward (not properly Sah.).

₂ⲓⲚⲎⲂ, ₂ⲓⲚⲎϥ to sleep, doze; as n.m. sleep.

₂ⲓⲟⲨⲈ ₂ⲓ- ₂ⲓⲦˢ vb. tr. (1) to beat, strike (Ⲙ̄Ⲙⲟˢ, Ⲉ, ⲈⲝⲚ̄, ₂Ⲛ̄, Ⲉ₂ⲟⲨⲚ Ⲉ; with: Ⲙ̄Ⲙⲟˢ, ₂Ⲛ̄). (2) to cast, throw (Ⲙ̄Ⲙⲟˢ; ± ⲈⲂⲟⲗ, Ⲉ₂ⲢⲀⲓ); mostly Boh. in this sense. ₂ⲓ-ⲦⲟⲟⲦˢ to begin, undertake (to do: Ⲉ + inf.); also lit., to place one's hand (on: Ⲉ).

₂ⲓⲢ, ₂ⲈⲓⲢ n.m. street, town quarter, road. Ⲉ Ⲛ₂ⲓⲢ adv.

outside, to the outside. ₂ιρₐιρє, ₂єρₐιρє, ₂ₕρₐιρє n.f.
idem.

₂ιcє ₂ᴀcⲧ̄‐ ₂ᴀcⲧˢ Q ₂οcє (1) vb. intr. to become weary,
troubled (with, by, of: єⲧвє, ₂ᴧ, ₂ⲛ̄); to experience
difficulty or distress (in doing: Circum.); to be dif‐
ficult or troublesome (to, for: є, ⲛᴀˢ). (2) vb. tr.
to weary, distress, trouble. As n.m. weariness, dis‐
tress, trouble; labor, product of labor. ᴀⲧ₂ιcє un‐
wearied; without difficulty; ⲙⲛ̄ⲧⲙᴀι‐₂ιcє love of toil.
ⲣ̄‐₂ιcє to take trouble; to make trouble. ⳨‐₂ιcє to
give trouble, make trouble (to, for: ⲛᴀˢ). ογє₂‐₂ιcє
idem. ϣⲛ̄‐₂ιcє to labor, take trouble, be deeply con‐
cerned (for: є, єxⲛ̄; in, concerning: єⲧвє, ₂ⲛ̄); as n.m.
labor, product of labor; ᴀⲧϣⲛ̄‐₂ιcє unsympathetic; ρєϥ‐
ϣⲛ̄‐₂ιcє one who labors etc.; ⲙⲛ̄ⲧϣⲛ̄‐₂ιcє labor, suffer‐
ing. ϥι ₂ᴧ ₂ιcє to bear up under difficulty.

₂ιcє ₂ᴀcⲧˢ Q ₂οcє to spin (flax etc.).

₂ιⲧє ₂єⲧ‐ ₂ᴀⲧˢ (1) vb. tr. to rub, move back and forth
(ⲙ̄ⲙοˢ); to wear out (ⲙ̄ⲙοˢ); to convulse, torment (ⲙ̄ⲙοˢ);
to flay. (2) vb. intr. to become old, worn out; to
loiter, loaf around; to be convulsed, tormented. As
n.m. spasm, pain; ᴀⲧ₂ιⲧє unworn; untormented; ⲙⲛ̄ⲧρєϥ₂ιⲧє
convulsion.

₂ιⲱⲙє, ₂ιοⲙє, ₂ⲱⲙє n.f. palm, hollow of hand (ⲛ̄ ϭιx).

₂ⲕο (є₂ⲕο) Q ₂ⲕᴀєιⲧ (₂ⲕοєιⲧ, ₂οⲕⲣ̄) to become hungry (for:
ⲙ̄ⲙοˢ); as n.m. hunger, famine. ₂ⲏⲕє adj. poor (bef. or
aft. noun, with ⲛ̄); ⲙⲛ̄ⲧ₂ⲏⲕє poverty; ⲙᴀι‐₂ⲏⲕє loving
the poor; ⲙⲛ̄ⲧⲙᴀcⲧ̄‐₂ⲏⲕє hatred of the poor. ⲣ̄‐₂ⲏⲕє to
become poor.

₂ⲗ̄ⲕογ, ₂єⲗⲕογ, ₂ᴧⲗⲕογ n.f.m. sickle.

₂ⲗ̄ⲗο (f. ₂ⲗ̄ⲗⲱ, ₂ⲗ̄ⲗογ; pl. ₂ⲗ̄ⲗοι) n.m.f. an old person, el‐
der; esp. an older monk; as adj. old (bef. or aft. noun
with ⲛ̄). ⲙⲛ̄ⲧ₂ⲗ̄ⲗο (of women: ⲙⲛ̄ⲧ₂ⲗ̄ⲗⲱ) old age. ⲣ̄‐₂ⲗ̄ⲗο
(Q ο ⲛ̄ ₂ⲗ̄ⲗο) to become old.

₂ⲗοєιᴧє, ₂ⲗοєιᴧ, ₂ᴧєєιᴧє, ₂єᴧєιᴧє vb. tr. to bear, carry

(ⲙ̄ⲙⲟⳋ), usu. on surface of water; intr. to be borne, carried; to float.

ⲑⲗⲟⲙⲗ̄ⲙ̄ n.m. entanglement, snare.

ⲑⲗⲟⲟⲗⲉ vb. tr. to nurse (a child: ⲙ̄ⲙⲟⳋ); to carry a child during pregnancy or infancy. ⲣⲉ̇ϥⲑⲗⲟⲟⲗⲉ n. nurse.

ⲑⲗⲟⲡ n.m. a vessel (for pouring).

ⲑⲗⲟⲡⲗ̄ⲛ̄ (ⲑⲗⲟⲡⲗⲉⲛ) ⲑⲗ̄ⲡⲗⲱⲡⳋ Q ⲑⲗⲉⲡⲗⲱⲡ vb. tr. to weary, plague (ⲉ, ⲉⲭⲛ̄); intr. to become weary, despondent; as n.m. weariness, distress.

ⲑⲗⲟⲥⲧⲛ̄, ⲑⲗⲟⲥⲧⲉⲛ n.m. mist; ⲣ̄-ⲑⲗⲟⲥⲧⲛ̄ to become misty, dark; ϯ-ⲑⲗⲟⲥⲧⲛ̄ to darken.

ⲑⲗⲟⲩⲗⲱⲟⲩ Q to be high, exalted.

ⲑⲗⲟϭ, Q ⲑⲟⲗⲟ̄ⳓ to become sweet, delightful; ⲑⲗⲗⲟ̄ⳓ- in cpds.: sweet in, sweet of (e.g. -ϣⲗⲭⲉ speech, -ⲑⲏⲧ heart). As n.m. sweetness, delight. ⲙⲛ̄ⲧⲑⲗⲟϭ idem. ϯ-ⲑⲗⲟϭ to make sweet, pleasant. ⲑⲉⲗϭⲉ, ⲑⲗⲟ̄ϭⲉ n.f. sweetness. ⲑⲗⲏϭⲉ n.f. idem.

ⲑⲗⲱⲙ, ⲗ̄ⲑⲱⲙ, ⲑⲗⲟⲙ n.m. louse, flea.

ⲑⲗⲱϭϥ̄ vb. intr. to be easy, pleasant.

ⲑⲙⲉ number: forty (see §30.7). ⲡⲉⲑⲙⲉ ⲛ̄ ⲑⲟⲟⲩ Lent. ⲙⲉⲑⲑⲙⲉ fortieth.

ⲑⲙⲉⲛⲉ number: eighty (see §30.7).

ⲑⲙ̄ⲙⲉ in ⲣ̄-ⲑⲙ̄ⲙⲉ to steer, guide (ⲙ̄ⲙⲟⳋ). ⲣ̄-ⲑⲙ̄ⲙⲉ n.m. guidance. ⲗⲧⲣ̄-ⲑⲙ̄ⲙⲉ unguided. ⲣⲉϥⲣ̄-ⲑⲙ̄ⲙⲉ pilot, guide.

ⲑⲙ̄ⲛ̄ⲧⲱⲣⲉ, ⲑⲉⲙⲉⲧⲟⲣⲉ, ⲑⲉⲃⲉⲧⲱⲣⲉ etc. n.m. sign, token; password.

ⲑⲙⲟⲙ (ϣⲙⲟⲙ) Q ⲑⲏⲙ to become hot; as n.m. fever, heat. ⲑⲙ̄ⲙⲉ n.f.m. heat, fever; ϯ-ⲑⲙ̄ⲙⲉ to give off heat.

ⲑⲙⲟⲟⲥ vb. intr. to sit, sit down, be seated (± ⲉⲑⲣⲗⲓ); to dwell, remain. Used with most prep. in normal senses. ⲙⲗ ⲛ̄ ⲑⲙⲟⲟⲥ (1) seat; (2) privy, latrine; (3) anus. ϭⲓⲛⲑⲙⲟⲟⲥ manner of sitting, dwelling. ⲑⲙⲗⲓⲥ n.m. buttocks.

ⲑⲙⲟⲧ n.m. grace, gift, favor; gratitude, thanks, credit. ⲗⲧⲑⲙⲟⲧ graceless, thankless. ⲣ̄-ⲑⲙⲟⲧ, ⲉⲓⲣⲉ ⲛ̄ ⲟⲩⲑⲙⲟⲧ to grant a favor, give grace, give as a gift. ϯ-ⲑⲙⲟⲧ to

give grace, to benefit, be kind to (ⲛⲁ⸗); ϯ ⲙⲙⲟ⸗ ⲛ
ⲍⲙⲟⲧ to give as a gift or favor. ϣⲡ̄-ⲍⲙⲟⲧ ⲛ̄ⲧⲛ̄ to thank,
give thanks to (for: ⲉⲭⲛ̄, ⲍ ⲓ, ⲍⲁ); as n.m. thanksgiv-
ing; ⲁⲧϣⲡ̄-ⲍⲙⲟⲧ ungrateful; ⲣⲉϥϣⲡ̄-ⲍⲙⲟⲧ a grateful person; ⲙⲛ̄ⲧⲣⲉϥϣⲡ̄-ⲍⲙⲟⲧ gratitude. ⲭ ⲓ-ⲍⲙⲟⲧ to obtain grace
or favor (from: ⲉⲃⲟⲗ ⲍⲛ̄, ⲛ̄ⲧⲛ̄; for someone: ⲉⲭⲛ̄, ⲍ ⲓⲭⲛ̄).
ⲋⲛ̄-ⲍⲙⲟⲧ to find favor or grace.

ⲍⲙⲟⲩ n.m. salt. ⲣ̄-ⲍⲙⲟⲩ to become salt. ϯ-ⲍⲙⲟⲩ to add
salt. ⲭ ⲓ-ⲍⲙⲟⲩ to be salted. ⲁⲧⲍⲙⲟⲩ unsalted. ⲥⲁ ⲛ̄
ⲍⲙⲟⲩ salt-dealer, salt-seller.

ⲍⲙⲟⲭ, Q ⲍⲟⲙⲝ̄ to become sour. ⲍⲙ̄ⲭ, ⲍⲉⲙⲝ̄, ⲍ ⲏ ⲙⲝ̄ n.m. vinegar.
ⲣ̄-ⲍⲙ̄ⲭ to become sour. ϯ ⲉ ⲛⲍⲙ̄ⲭ to start to turn sour.

ⲍⲙ̄ⲥ, ⲍⲉⲙⲥ̄, ⲍ ⲏ ⲙⲥ̄ n.m. ear of grain.

ⲍⲙ̄ⲍⲙ̄ vb. intr. to roar, neigh; as n.m. neighing, roaring.
ⲣ̄-ⲍⲙ̄ⲍⲙ̄ idem.

ⲍⲛ̄ (ⲛ̄ⲍⲏⲧ⸗) prep. (1) of place: in, within, on, at, among;
from in, from; (2) of time: at, in, during; (3) of a-
gent, means, instrument: with, by, through; (4) for adv.
phrases ⲍⲛ̄ ⲟⲩ... see 21.3; (5) for ⲍⲙ̄ ⲡⲧⲣⲉϥ- see 20.1.
ⲉⲃⲟⲗ ⲍⲛ̄ from in, from within, out of; ⲉⲍⲟⲩⲛ ⲍⲛ̄ into,
toward, at, within; ⲛ̄ⲍⲟⲩⲛ ⲍⲛ̄ in, within; ⲍⲣⲁ ⲓ ⲍⲛ̄ in.

ⲍⲛⲁⲩ, ⲍⲛⲁⲁⲩ, ⲍⲛⲁⲟⲩ n.m. vessel, pot, container; thing (any
material object), property. ⲙⲛ̄ⲧⲁⲧⲍⲛⲁⲩ state of being
without property.

ⲍⲛⲉ- (ⲉⲍⲛⲉ-) ⲍⲛⲁ⸗ (ⲉⲍⲛⲁ⸗) impers. vb. it pleases (suff. is
objective); ⲡⲉⲧ ⲉⲍⲛⲉ- that which pleases (someone), that
which (someone) desires; often followed by ⲉ + inf.
ⲣ̄-ⲍⲛⲁ⸗ to be willing, desire (to do: ⲉ, ⲉⲧⲣⲉ). See 20.2.

ⲍⲛ̄ⲕⲉ n.m. beer.

ⲍⲟ, ⲍⲁ (ⲍⲣⲁ⸗) n.m. face (of man or animal); surface, side.
ⲍⲟ ⲙⲛ̄ ⲍⲟ face to face. ⲍⲟ ⲟⲩⲃⲉ ⲍⲟ, ⲍⲟ ⲍ ⲓ ⲍⲟ idem. ⲛ̄
ⲍⲟ, ⲙ̄ ⲡⲍⲟ, ⲍⲙ̄ ⲡⲍⲟ by sight. ⲍⲁ ⲡ(⸗)ⲍⲟ from before.
ϯ ⲙ̄ ⲡ(⸗)ⲍⲟ to direct one's attention (to: ⲉ, ⲉⲭⲛ̄).
ϣⲡ̄-ⲍⲣⲁ⸗ (ⲛ̄) to beseech, ask; to receive, accept. ϥ ⲓ-
ⲍⲣⲁ⸗ (ⲉⲃⲟⲗ, ⲉ ⲛ ϣ ⲱ ⲓ) to look up. ⲭ ⲓ-ⲍⲟ, ⲭ ⲓ-ⲡⲍⲟ, ⲭ ⲓ ⲙ̄ ⲡⲍⲟ

(ⲛ) to heed, pay attention to, respect, favor; ⲭⲓ-ⲍⲟ as
n.m. favoritism; ⲁⲧⲭⲓ-ⲍⲟ impartial; ⲙⲛ̄ⲧⲁⲧⲭⲓ-ⲍⲟ imparti-
ality; ⲡⲉϥⲭⲓ-ⲍⲟ one who is partial. ⲭⲓ-ⲍⲣⲁ⸗, ⲭⲓ ⲛ̄ ⲍⲟ
(Q ⲭⲓ-ⲍⲣⲁⲉⲓⲧ), suff. is reflex.: to amuse oneself, occupy oneself; to be distracted; to attend (to: ⲉ); to converse (with: ⲙⲛ̄); to reflect (on: ⲍⲓ, ⲍⲛ̄); to sport,
play (with: ⲙⲛ̄, ⲍⲛ̄); ⲙⲛ̄ⲧⲭⲓ-ⲍⲣⲁ⸗ distraction; ⲡⲉϥⲭⲓ-ⲍⲣⲁ⸗
trifler. ϯ-ⲍⲟ ⲉ to beseech (Boh., rare in Sah.).
ⲉⲍⲡⲛ̄ (ⲉⲍⲣⲁ⸗) prep. toward (the face of), among; ⲉⲃⲟⲗ
ⲉⲍⲡⲛ̄ out to; ⲉⲍⲟⲩⲛ ⲉⲍⲡⲛ̄ in to, before, at, against.
ⲛⲁⲍⲣⲛ̄, ⲛ̄ⲛⲁⲍⲣⲛ̄, (ⲛ̄)ⲛⲁⲍⲣⲁ⸗ in the presence of, before.
ⲍⲓ ⲍⲣⲁ⸗ on the surface of, on the face of.
ⲍⲟ, ⲍⲱ n.m. a grain measure.
ⲍⲟⲉⲓⲙ (pl. ⲍⲏⲙⲉ, ⲍⲓⲙⲏ) n.m. wave. ⲣ̄-ⲍⲟⲉⲓⲙ (Q ⲟ ⲛ̄ ⲍⲟⲉⲓⲙ)
to become agitated. ϯ-ⲍⲟⲉⲓⲙ, ϥⲓ-ⲍⲟⲉⲓⲙ to cast up waves.
ⲍⲟⲉⲓⲛⲉ, ⲍⲟⲓⲛⲉ indef. pron. pl. some, certain (ones, people,
things); as pred.: such, of this sort.
ⲍⲟⲉⲓⲣⲉ, ⲍⲟⲉⲓⲗⲉ, ⲍⲟⲓⲣⲉ n.f. dung (human or animal).
ⲍⲟⲉⲓⲧⲉ, ⲍⲟⲓⲧⲉ n.f. hyena.
ⲍⲟⲉⲓⲧⲉ, ⲍⲟⲓⲧⲉ n.m.f. garment; ϯ-ⲍⲟⲉⲓⲧⲉ ⲉⲍⲛ̄ to clothe.
ⲍⲟⲓ n. in ⲣ̄-ⲍⲟⲓ meaning uncertain, prob.: to make an effort, strive (to do: ⲉ, ⲛ̄ + Inf.); ϯ-ⲍⲟⲓ ⲛⲁ⸗ to vex.
ⲍⲟⲓ (pl. ⲍⲓⲉⲉⲩ, ⲍⲓⲉⲉⲩⲉ) n.m. (1) field; (2) water-wheel.
ⲍⲟⲙⲉ n.f. cup.
ⲍⲟⲙⲛ̄ⲧ, ⲍⲟⲙⲉⲧ, ⲍⲟⲙⲧ̄ n.m. copper, bronze; coin, money. ϯ-
ⲍⲟⲙⲛ̄ⲧ to pay (someone: ⲛⲁ⸗; for: ⲍⲁ). ϣⲱⲡ ⲍⲁ ⲍⲟⲙⲛ̄ⲧ to
buy with money. ⲭⲓ-ⲍⲟⲙⲛ̄ⲧ to accept a bribe. ⲙⲁⲓ-
ⲍⲟⲙⲛ̄ⲧ money-loving; ⲙⲛ̄ⲧⲙⲁⲓ-ⲍⲟⲙⲛ̄ⲧ love of money; ⲙⲛ̄ⲧ-
ⲙⲁⲥⲧ̄-ⲍⲟⲙⲛ̄ⲧ hatred of money. ⲣ̄-ⲍⲟⲙⲛ̄ⲧ to become copper;
ⲡⲉϥⲣ̄-ⲍⲟⲙⲛ̄ⲧ coppersmith; ⲥⲁ ⲛ̄ ⲍⲟⲙⲛ̄ⲧ copper-dealer.
ⲍⲟⲛⲃⲉ n.f. spring, well.
ⲍⲟⲛⲧ̄, ⲍⲱⲛⲧ̄ n.m. pagan priest.
ⲍⲟⲟⲗⲉ n.f.(m.) moth. ⲣ̄-ⲍⲟⲟⲗⲉ to become moth-eaten, to
perish. ⲁⲧⲣ̄-ⲍⲟⲟⲗⲉ incorruptible, indestructible.
ⲍⲟⲟⲩ n.m. day. ⲙ̄ ⲡⲉⲍⲟⲟⲩ in, during the day. ⲛ̄ ⲟⲩⲍⲟⲟⲩ

for a day. 2ⲛ̄ ⲟⲩ2ⲟⲟⲩ ⲉⲃⲟⲗ 2ⲛ̄ ⲟⲩ2ⲟⲟⲩ from day to day.
ⲭⲓⲛ 2ⲟⲟⲩ ⲉ 2ⲟⲟⲩ idem. 2ⲟⲟⲩ 2ⲟⲟⲩ, ⲡⲉ2ⲟⲟⲩ ⲡⲉ2ⲟⲟⲩ idem.
ⲣ̄-2ⲟⲟⲩ to spend a day. ⲡⲟⲟⲩ adv. today; ⲙ̄ ⲡⲟⲟⲩ idem;
ⲙⲛ̄ⲛ̄ⲥⲁ ⲡⲟⲟⲩ from today onward; ϣⲁ ⲡⲟⲟⲩ until today; ⲭⲓⲛ
ⲡⲟⲟⲩ (± ⲉⲃⲟⲗ, ⲉ2ⲣⲁⲓ) from today onward. ⲡⲟⲟⲩ ⲛ̄ 2ⲟⲟⲩ
adv. today (used as ⲡⲟⲟⲩ above).

2ⲟⲟⲩ Q to be bad, wicked, putrid. ⲡⲉ⊖ⲟⲟⲩ, ⲡⲉⲧ 2ⲟⲟⲩ used
as nominal: what is bad; evil, wickedness (may take
def. or indef. art.). ⲣ̄-ⲡⲉ⊖ⲟⲟⲩ, ⲉⲓⲡⲉ ⲙ̄ ⲡⲉ⊖ⲟⲟⲩ to do
evil; ⲣⲉϥⲣ̄-ⲡⲉ⊖ⲟⲟⲩ evil-doer; ⲙⲛ̄ⲧⲣⲉϥⲣ̄-ⲡⲉ⊖ⲟⲟⲩ wickedness;
ⲥⲁ ⲙ̄ ⲡⲉ⊖ⲟⲟⲩ evil-doer; ⲙⲛ̄ⲧⲥⲁ ⲙ̄ ⲡⲉ⊖ⲟⲟⲩ evil.

2ⲟⲟⲩⲧ, ⲉ2ⲟⲟⲩⲧ, 2ⲉ0ⲩⲧ, 2ⲉⲩⲧ (2ⲟⲩⲧ-) n.m. male (of men or
animals); freq. as adj., aft. n., with or without ⲛ̄:
male, wild, savage. 2ⲟⲩⲧ-ⲥ2ⲓⲙⲉ male-female, bisexual.
ⲙⲛ̄ⲧ2ⲟⲟⲩⲧ maleness.

2ⲟⲟⲩⲧⲛ̄ n.m. road, highway; a furlong.

2ⲟⲟⲩϣ to abuse, curse (ⲉ, ⲉⲭⲛ̄).

2ⲟⲡ, 2ⲟⲟⲡ (2ⲁⲡ-) n.m. marriage feast; bridle-chamber.

2ⲟⲥⲃ̄, 2ⲟⲥⲃⲉ n.f. market; ⲣⲙ̄ⲛ̄2ⲟⲥⲃ̄ market-man.

2ⲟⲥⲙ̄, 2ⲟⲥⲏⲙ, 2ⲟⲥⲙⲉ, 2ⲁⲥⲙ̄, 2ⲱⲥⲉⲙ n.m. natron.

2ⲟⲧⲉ, 2ⲟⲧ, 2ⲱⲧⲉ, 2ⲱⲧ in ⲙ̄ ⲡ(ⲉ)2ⲟⲧⲉ, ⲙ̄ ⲡ2ⲟⲧⲉ ⲛ̄ in the
vicinity of, in the presence of.

2ⲟⲧⲉ n.f. fear; as adj. fearful. ⲁⲧ2ⲟⲧⲉ fearless; ⲙⲛ̄ⲧⲁⲧ-
2ⲟⲧⲉ fearlessness; ⲣ̄-ⲁⲧ2ⲟⲧⲉ to become fearless. 2ⲁ
2ⲟⲧⲉ in fear; fearful, fearsome (as pred.). ⲣ̄-2ⲟⲧⲉ (Q
ⲟ ⲛ̄ 2ⲟⲧⲉ) to become afraid (of: ⲉ, ⲉⲭⲛ̄, ⲉⲧⲃⲉ, 2ⲁⲑⲏ ⲛ̄,
ⲉⲃⲟⲗ 2ⲛ̄, 2ⲏⲧ︦ ⲛ̄); ⲣⲉϥⲣ̄-2ⲟⲧⲉ fearing, respectful; ⲙⲛ̄ⲧ-
ⲣⲉϥⲣ̄-2ⲟⲧⲉ fear, respect. †-2ⲟⲧⲉ to terrify, frighten
(ⲉ, ⲛⲁ︦, ⲉⲭⲛ̄); ⲣⲉϥ†-2ⲟⲧⲉ dreadful. ⲭⲓ-2ⲟⲧⲉ to frighten
(ⲙ̄ⲙⲟ︦).

2ⲟⲧⲉ n.f. hour, moment; ⲣ̄-2ⲟⲧⲉ to spend time.

2ⲟⲧⲥ̄, 2ⲁⲧⲥ̄ n.f. a vessel or measure.

2ⲟⲧ2ⲧ̄ 2ⲉⲧ2ⲧ̄- 2ⲉⲧ2ⲱⲧ︦ Q 2ⲉⲧ2ⲱⲧ vb. tr. to examine, investi-
gate, inquire into (ⲙ̄ⲙⲟ︦, ⲉ, ⲛ̄ⲥⲁ, 2ⲛ̄); as n.m. inquiry,
question; ⲁⲧ2ⲉⲧ2ⲱⲧ︦ unfathomable; ⲣⲉϥ2ⲟⲧ2ⲧ̄ inquirer;

ⲙⲛ̄ⲧⲣⲉϥϩⲟⲧϩⲧ̄ inquiry.

ϩⲟⲩⲉⲓⲧ (f. ϩⲟⲩⲉⲓⲧⲉ, ϩⲟⲩⲓⲧⲉ; pl. ϩⲟⲩⲁⲧⲉ) adj. bef. or aft. n. with ⲛ̄: first, foremost, leading. ϩⲟⲩⲉⲓⲧⲉ n.f. beginning; ϩⲛ̄ ⲧⲉϩⲟⲩⲉⲓⲧⲉ in the beginning; ϫⲓⲛ ⲧⲉϩⲟⲩⲉⲓⲧⲉ from the beginning.

ϩⲟⲩⲏⲧ (pl. ϩⲟⲩⲁⲧⲉ) n. passenger, crewman (?).

ϩⲟⲩⲛ n.m. inner part, interior. ⲙ̄ ⲡϩⲟⲩⲛ ⲙ̄ⲙⲟ⸗ prep. inside, within (spatial or temporal). ⲣ̄-ⲡ(⸗)ϩⲟⲩⲛ ⲉ to enter. ⲉϩⲟⲩⲛ adv. to the inside, into, toward: ⲉϩⲟⲩⲛ ⲉ prep. to, toward, into; ⲉϩⲟⲩⲛ is also used to reinforce ⲉϩⲣ̄ⲛ̄, ⲉϫⲛ̄, ⲛⲁ⸗, ⲛⲁϩⲣ̄ⲛ̄, ϣⲁ, ϩⲁ. ⲛ̄ϩⲟⲩⲛ adv. within, inside (static location); ⲛ̄ϩⲟⲩⲛ ϩⲁ under; ⲛ̄ϩⲟⲩⲛ ϩⲛ̄ in: ⲛ̄ϩⲟⲩⲛ ⲙ̄ⲙⲟ⸗ in. ⲥⲁ-ϩⲟⲩⲛ adv. inside, within; + ⲉ/ⲙ̄ⲙⲟ⸗ idem as prep. ⲥⲁ ⲛ̄ ϩⲟⲩⲛ n.m. inner part, interior. ϣⲁ ϩⲟⲩⲛ ⲉ prep. until. ϩⲓ ϩⲟⲩⲛ adv. within; ⲉⲧ ϩⲓ ϩⲟⲩⲛ adj. phrase: inner, interior. ⲣⲙ̄ⲛ̄ϩⲟⲩⲛ title of official.

ϩⲟⲩⲟ n.m. greater part; profit, advantage; majority, greatness; as adj. bef. n. without ⲛ̄ or aft. n. with ⲛ̄: great, much; before adj.: more, greater. ϩⲟⲩⲉ- as proclitic form of adj., used like preceding entry. ϩⲟⲩⲟ ⲉ, ϩⲟⲩⲉ more than, beyond. ⲉ ϩⲟⲩⲟ ⲉ, ⲉ ϩⲟⲩⲉ (ⲉ) more than, rather than. ⲉ ⲡⲉϩⲟⲩⲟ adv. greatly, very. ⲛ̄ ϩⲟⲩⲟ adv. much, greatly, very, much more so; ⲛ̄ ϩⲟⲩⲟ ⲉ more than. ⲛ̄ ϩⲟⲩⲟ ⲛ̄ ϩⲟⲩⲟ idem (emphatic). ⲣ̄-ϩⲟⲩⲟ to exceed, be more than (ⲉ); to have or do more (than: ⲉ); with immediately following noun or verb: to be or do all the more. ⲣ̄-ϩⲟⲩⲉ- proclitic form of preceding.

ϩⲟⲩⲣⲉ- (ϩⲟⲩⲣ-, ϩⲟⲩⲣⲱ-) ϩⲟⲩⲣⲟ⸗ (ϩⲟⲩⲣⲱ⸗) vb. tr. to deprive (someone: suff. obj.) of (ⲙ̄ⲙⲟ⸗, ⲉ).

ϩⲟⲩⲣⲓⲧ, ϩⲱⲣⲓⲧ (pl. ϩⲟⲩⲣⲁⲧⲉ) n.m. watchman, guardian. ⲁⲡⲉ ⲛ̄ ϩⲟⲩⲣⲓⲧ head-watchman.

ϩⲟⲩϥ n.m. vetch, pulse.

ϩⲟⲩϩⲉ n.m. untimely birth.

ϩⲟϥ, ϩⲟⲃ, ϩⲟⲡ, ϩⲱⲃ (f. ϩϥⲱ, ϩⲃⲱ; pl. ϩⲃⲟⲩⲓ) n.m.f. snake.

ϩⲟϫϩⲝ̄ (ϩⲟϫϩⲉϫ, ϩⲟϫϩ̄ⲝ̄) ϩⲉϫϩⲝ̄- (ϩⲉϫϩ̄ⲝ̄-) ϩⲉϫϩⲱϫ⸗ Q ϩⲉϫϩⲱϫ vb.

tr. to distress, restrict, straiten (ⲙ̄ⲙⲟ⸗); to compel,
force; vb. intr. to become distressed, restricted, narrow; as n.m. distress, need.

ⲍⲡⲟⲧ, ⲍⲡⲱⲧ n. a fathom.

ⲍⲣⲁ (ϣⲣⲁ) vb. tr. to drive, compel (ⲙ̄ⲙⲟ⸗, ⲛ̄ⲥⲁ), ± ⲉⲃⲟⲗ.

ⲍⲣⲁⲓ, ⲍⲣⲉ n.m. upper part (very rare as n.); ⲍⲣⲁⲓ reinfor-
ces other prep., no diff. in meaning. ⲉⲍⲣⲁⲓ adv. upward (see §8.1). ⲉⲍⲣⲁⲓ forms cpds. with many prep. (including ⲉ, ⲉⲭⲛ̄, ⲉⲍⲣⲛ̄, ⲟⲩⲃⲉ, ⲥⲁ, ⲍⲁ, ⲍⲓ, ⲍⲛ̄), usually,
but not necessarily, with the added nuance of "up," e.g.
up to, up onto, etc. ⲛ̄ⲍⲣⲁⲓ adv. above (static; §28.7).
also freq. cpds., as in ⲛ̄ⲍⲣⲁⲓ ⲉⲭⲛ̄ up on, etc. ⲥⲁ-ⲍⲣⲁⲓ
adv. above, on the upper side. ϣⲁ ⲍⲣⲁⲓ adv. upward; ϣⲁ
ⲍⲣⲁⲓ ⲉ up to, even to. ⲍⲓ ⲍⲣⲁⲓ, ⲍⲓ ⲍⲣⲉ adv. upward.
ⲥⲁ-ⲍⲣⲉ n.m. in ⲉ ⲡ(⸗)ⲥⲁ-ⲍⲣⲉ prep. above.

ⲍⲣⲁⲓ n.m. lower part, rare except in cpds.: ⲉⲍⲣⲁⲓ adv.
downward, down; ⲉⲍⲣⲁⲓ ⲉ down to, into, onto; ⲉⲍⲣⲁⲓ ⲉⲭⲛ̄
down onto. ⲛ̄ⲍⲣⲁⲓ adv. below. ⲥⲁ-ⲍⲣⲁⲓ adv. downward,
down. ϣⲁ ⲍⲣⲁⲓ ⲉ prep. down to.

ⲍⲣ̄ⲃ n.m. form, likeness; ⲭⲓ-ⲍⲣ̄ⲃ to assume a form, likeness.

ⲍⲣ̄ⲃⲱⲧ, ⲍⲉⲣⲃⲱⲧ, ⲍⲉⲣⲃⲟⲟⲑⲉ n.f. staff, stout stick.

ⲍⲣⲉ, ⲍⲉⲣⲉ (pl. ⲍⲣⲏⲩⲉ, ⲍⲣⲉⲟⲩⲉ) n.m.f. food (of man or animals); ⲣ̄-ⲍⲣⲉ (Q ⲟ ⲛ̄ ⲍⲣⲉ) to become food; †-ⲍⲣⲉ, † ⲛ̄
ⲟⲩⲍⲣⲉ to give food (to: ⲛⲁ⸗). ⲭⲓ-ⲍⲣⲉ to get food.

ⲍⲣⲉⲃ n.m. chisel.

ⲍⲣⲏⲣⲉ n.m.(f.) flower. ⲣ̄-ⲍⲣⲏⲣⲉ to bloom, blossom. ⲧⲉⲕ-
ⲍⲣⲏⲣⲉ ⲉⲃⲟⲗ idem. ⲟⲩⲁⲙ-ⲍⲣⲏⲣⲉ beetle (lit., flower-eater).

ⲍⲣⲏⲅ, ⲍⲣⲏⲭ vb. intr. to become still, calm, quiet.

ⲍⲣⲓⲙ n.m. pelican.

ⲍⲣ̄ⲙⲁⲛ, ⲍⲉⲣⲙⲁⲛ n.m. pomegranate (tree or fruit); ⲃⲱ ⲛ̄
ⲍⲣ̄ⲙⲁⲛ pomegranate tree.

ⲍⲣⲟⲕ (ⲍⲣⲁⲕ) Q ⲍⲟⲣⲕ̄ vb. intr. or reflex. to become still,
calm, quiet; to cease; rarely tr. to still. As n.m.
stillness, quiet; †-ⲍⲣⲟⲕ to calm, quiet (ⲛⲁ⸗). ⲍⲟⲣⲕ̄ⲅ̄
adj. silent, quiet.

ϩⲣⲟⲟⲩ (ϩⲣⲟⲩ-, ϩⲣ̄-; ϩⲣⲁ⸗) n.m. voice; sound, noise, cry.
ⲁⲧϩⲣⲟⲟⲩ voiceless; ⲥⲙⲁⲓ ⲁⲧϩⲣⲟⲟⲩ a consonant. ⲛⲉⲝ-
ϩⲣⲟⲟⲩ, ⲛⲟⲩϫⲉ ⲛ̄ ⲟⲩϩⲣⲟⲟⲩ (± ⲉⲃⲟⲗ) to let out a cry. ⲥⲉⲕ-
ϩⲣⲟⲟⲩ to snort. ϯ-ϩⲣⲟⲟⲩ (± ⲉⲃⲟⲗ) to speak, give voice,
promise; ⲥⲙⲁⲓ ⲉϥϯ-ϩⲣⲟⲟⲩ a vowel. ⲉϣ-ϩⲣⲟⲟⲩ ⲉⲃⲟⲗ to make
a sound, utter a cry. ϥⲓ-ϩⲣⲟⲟⲩ, ϥⲓ-ϩⲣⲁ⸗ (± ⲉⲃⲟⲗ, ⲉϩⲣⲁⲓ)
to raise one's voice, to utter, speak. ϫⲓ ⲛ̄ ϩⲣⲁ⸗ to
cry out; ϫⲓ ⲙ̄ ⲡⲉϩⲣⲟⲟⲩ to hear the sound (of). ⲙⲛ̄ⲧ-
ⲛⲁϣⲧ̄-ϩⲣⲟⲟⲩ being hard-voiced. ϩⲣⲟⲩ-ⲙ̄-ⲡⲉ n.m. thunder.
ϩⲣⲟⲩ-ⲃⲁⲓ n.f. thunder; ϯ-ϩⲣⲟⲩ-ⲃⲁⲓ to thunder. ϩⲣⲟⲩⲟ,
ϩⲣⲟⲩⲱ boastful talk; ⲙⲛ̄ⲧϩⲣⲟⲩⲟ boastfulness; ⲣ̄-ⲙⲛ̄ⲧϩⲣⲟⲩⲟ
to boast.
ϩⲣⲟⲡⲣⲉⲡ vb. tr. to flap or spread (wings); to blink (eyes).
ϩⲣⲟⲩϫⲉ̄ n. pebbles.
ϩⲣⲟϣ ϩⲣ̄ϣ- (ϩⲉⲣϣ̄-) Q ϩⲟⲣϣ̄ vb. intr. to become heavy, difficult (for someone: ⲉ, ⲉϫⲛ̄, ⲉϩⲣⲁⲓ ⲉϫⲛ̄; in, with something: ⲙ̄ⲙⲟ⸗, ϩⲛ̄); to be slow (to do: ⲉ + Inf.); rarely
tr.: to make difficult. As n.m. weight, burden. ⲁⲧ-
ϩⲣⲟϣ weightless; ϯ-ϩⲣⲟϣ ⲛⲁ⸗ to add weight to. ϩⲣⲟϣ
ⲛ̄ ϩⲏⲧ to become long-suffering, patient; ϩⲁⲣϣ̄-ϩⲏⲧ adj.
patient, long-suffering; ⲙⲛ̄ⲧϩⲁⲣϣ̄-ϩⲏⲧ patience; ⲣ̄-ϩⲁⲣϣ̄-
ϩⲏⲧ to be patient. ϩⲣⲏϣⲉ, ϩⲉⲣϣⲉ n.f. weight.
ϩⲣⲟϫⲣⲝ̄ vb. tr. to grind or gnash (the teeth; at, against:
ⲉϩⲟⲩⲛ ⲉ, ⲉϩⲟⲩⲛ ϩⲛ̄, ⲉϩⲣⲁⲓ ⲉϫⲛ̄). As n.m. gnashing of
teeth.
ϩⲣⲱ n.f. oven, furnace.
ϩⲣⲱⲧ n.f. wine-press, vat.
ϩⲣ̄ϩⲣ̄ vb. intr. to snore.
ϩⲧⲁⲓ (ϩⲧⲁⲉⲓ, ⲉϩⲑⲁⲓ) to become fat. As n.m. fat.
ϩⲧⲏ n.f. shaft of spear; mast.
ϩⲧⲓⲧ n.m. onion.
ϩⲧⲟ, ϩⲧⲱ, ⲉϩⲧⲟ (f. ϩⲧⲱⲣⲉ, ϩⲧⲟⲟⲣⲉ; pl. ϩⲧⲱⲱⲣ, ⲉϩⲧⲱⲱⲣ, ϩⲧⲱⲣ)
n.m.f. horse. ⲙⲁⲥ ⲛ̄ ⲉϩⲧⲟ foal. ⲙⲁⲛⲉ-ϩⲧⲟ horse-groom.
ⲡⲙ̄ⲛϩⲧⲟ horseman.
ϩⲧⲟⲙⲧⲙ̄ ϩⲧⲙ̄ⲧⲙ̄- Q ϩⲧⲙ̄ⲧⲟⲙⲧ̄ to become dark, be darkened; as

n.m. darkness, mist.

₂ⲧⲟⲟⲩⲉ, ⲧⲟⲟⲩⲉ n.m. dawn, morning. ⲡⲛⲁⲩ ⲛ̄ ₂ⲧⲟⲟⲩⲉ dawn, early morning. ⲉ ₂ⲧⲟⲟⲩⲉ, ⲛ̄ ₂ⲧⲟⲟⲩⲉ, ₂ⲓ ₂ⲧⲟⲟⲩⲉ at dawn. ϣⲁ ₂ⲧⲟⲟⲩⲉ until morning. ⲝⲓⲛ ₂ⲧⲟⲟⲩⲉ from morning (on).

ₐⲧⲟⲡ n.m. (1) fall, destruction; (2) name of a measure.

ₐⲧⲟⲣ n.m. necessity, constraint; ₂ⲛ̄ ⲟⲩₐⲧⲟⲣ out of necessity. ₂ⲁ/₂ⲙ̄ ⲡ(ˀ)₂ⲧⲟⲣ of one's own accord, on one's own authority. ⲣ̄-₂ⲧⲟⲣ to constrain (ⲉ); ⲣ̄-ⲡ(ˀ)₂ⲧⲟⲣ to exercise authority. ⳨-₂ⲧⲟⲣ to constrain (ⲉ); to give authority (to: ⲉ).

ₐⲱ impers. vb. it suffices, is enough (for someone: ⲉ; to, that: ⲉ + Inf., ⲉⲧⲣⲉ, Circum.). Also used with pers. subject: to have enough, be satisfied; to cease, stop (ⲉ + Inf., ⲉⲧⲣⲉ, Circum.); often + ⲉ as ethical dative.

ₐⲱⲃ ₂ⲁⲃˀ vb. tr. to send (ⲙ̄ⲙⲟˀ; for, after: ⲛ̄ⲥⲁ).

ₐⲱⲃ, ₂ⲱϥ, ⲱϥ, ₂ⲟϥ (pl. ₂ⲃⲏⲩⲉ) n.m. (1) work, product of work; (2) thing, object; (3) matter, affair, business. ⲟⲩ ⲡⲉ ⲡ(ˀ)₂ⲱⲃ what is the matter (with ...)? ⲟⲩ ⲡⲉ ⲡ₂ⲱⲃ ⲛ̄ what is the use of? ⲟⲩ ⲛ̄ ₂ⲱⲃ what? ⲟⲩⲛ̄-₂ⲱⲃ ⲙⲛ̄ (neg. ⲙⲛ̄-₂ⲱⲃ ⲙⲛ̄ there is (not) a matter; this and the same constructions with the corresponding possessives (ⲟⲩⲛ̄-ⲧⲁ₁ etc.) express the general idea of having a (legal) problem with or involving another person. ₂ⲱⲃ ⲛ̄ ⳓⲓⲝ handiwork, handicraft. ⲣ̄-₂ⲱⲃ to work (at, on: ⲉ; for: ₂ⲁ, ₂ⲓ; in, with: ₂ⲛ̄); as n.m. work, working; ⲣⲉϥⲣ̄-₂ⲱⲃ worker; ⲙⲛ̄ⲧⲣⲉϥⲣ̄-₂ⲱⲃ work, labor; ϣⲃⲣ̄-ⲣ̄-₂ⲱⲃ fellow-worker.

ₐⲱⲃⲕ̄ vb. tr. to prick, incite. ₂ⲃⲟⲕ, ₂ⲃⲟⳓ n. prick, stab.

ₐⲱⲃⲥ̄ ₂ⲉⲃⲥ̄- (₂ⲃ̄ⲥ-) ₂ⲟⲃⲥˀ Q ₂ⲟⲃⲥ̄ vb. tr. to cover, shelter. protect, clothe (ⲙ̄ⲙⲟˀ, ⲉ, ⲉⲭⲛ̄, ₂ⲓⲭⲛ̄; with: ⲙ̄ⲙⲟˀ, ₂ⲛ̄); ₂ⲱⲃⲥ̄ ⲉⲃⲟⲗ ⲉⲭⲛ̄ idem; vb. intr. to become covered etc. ⲣⲉϥ₂ⲱⲃⲥ̄ coverer, protector. ₂ⲱⲃⲥ̄, ₂ⲟⲃⲥ̄, ₂ⲃ̄ⲥ, ₂ⲃ̄ⲃⲥ̄, ₂ⲏⲃⲥ̄, ₂ⲁⲡⲥ̄ n.m. covering, lid. ₂ⲃⲟⲟⲥ, ₂ⲃⲟⲥ (pl. ₂ⲃⲱⲱⲥ, ₂ⲃⲱⲥ) n.m.f. covering, garment; linen. ₂ⲃ̄ⲥⲱ, ₂ⲉⲃⲥⲱ (pl. ₂ⲃ̄ⲥⲟⲟⲩⲉ) n.f. garment, clothes, cloth.

ₐⲱⲕ ₂ⲉⲕ- ₂ⲟⲕˀ Q ₂ⲏⲕ vb. tr. to smite, crush (ⲙ̄ⲙⲟˀ, ⲉⲭⲛ̄).

ϨⲰⲖ, Q ϨⲎⲖ vb. intr. to fly. ϨⲰⲖ ⲈⲂⲞⲖ to fly forth; Q to
be distraught. Other adv. and prep. in normal senses.
ⲘⲀ Ⲛ̄ ϨⲰⲖ exit. ⲢⲈϤϨⲰⲖ flier.

ϨⲰⲖ (ϨⲰⲖⲈ, ϨⲰⲰⲖⲈ) vb. intr. to become hoarse.

ϨⲰⲖ ϨⲈⲖ- (ϨⲖ̄-) ϨⲞⲖ⳿ vb. tr. to throw, cast.

ϨⲰⲖⲔ̄ (ϨⲰⲖϬ) ϨⲞⲖⲔ⳿ Q ϨⲞⲖⲔ̄ vb. tr. to twist, braid, roll
(Ⲙ̄ⲘⲞ⳿); as n.m. plait, twist.

ϨⲰⲖϬ, Q ϨⲞⲖϬ vb. tr. to embrace (Ⲉ, ⲈϨⲞⲨⲚ Ⲉ); as n.m.
embrace.

ϨⲰⲘ ϨⲘ̄- (ϨⲈⲘ-) ϨⲞⲘ⳿ Q ϨⲎⲘ vb. tr. to tread, trample, beat
(Ⲙ̄ⲘⲞ⳿; on: Ⲉ, ⲈϨⲢⲀⲒ Ⲉ, ⲈⲬⲚ̄, ⲈϨⲢⲀⲒ ⲈⲬⲚ̄, ϨⲒ); as n.m.
treading, trampling.

ϨⲰⲚ ϨⲚ̄- ϨⲞⲚ⳿ Q ϨⲎⲚ (± ⲈϨⲞⲨⲚ) vb. intr. to approach, draw
near (to: Ⲉ); to be about (to do: Ⲉ + Inf.); Q to be
nigh, near; to be related (to), in compliance (with);
rarely vb. tr. or reflex. to bring near. ⲀⲦϨⲰⲚ ⲈⲢⲞ⳿
unapproachable.

ϨⲰⲚ ϨⲞⲚ⳿ vb. tr. to command, order (someone: ⲈⲦⲚ̄, Ⲛ̄ⲦⲚ̄; to
do: Ⲉ, ⲈⲦⲢⲈ); to give (an order, command: Ⲙ̄ⲘⲞ⳿; to: ⲈⲦⲚ̄,
Ⲛ̄ⲦⲚ̄). As n.m. command.

ϨⲰⲚ vb. intr. to go aground. ⲘⲀ Ⲛ̄ ϨⲰⲚ shallows. Ⲟ Ⲛ̄
ϨⲰⲚ (Q) to be shallow.

ϨⲰⲚ n. in ⲬⲒ-ϨⲰⲚ to betroth (Ⲙ̄ⲘⲞ⳿; to: ⲚⲀ⳿).

ϨⲰⲚⲈ n.f. canal.

ϨⲰⲚⲔ̄ (ϨⲰⲚϮ) ϨⲈⲚⲅ⳿ vb. tr. to consecrate, appoint.

ϨⲰⲚϮ ϨⲈⲚⲦ̄- (ϨⲚ̄Ⲧ-) ϨⲞⲚⲦ⳿ Q ϨⲎⲚⲦ̄ vb. intr. to approach; rare
in Sah.; uses parallel those of ϨⲰⲚ (approach) q.v.

ϨⲰⲚⲬ̄ vb. tr. to entreat, exhort (Ⲉ). Very rare in Sah.

ϨⲰⲞⲨ ϨⲞⲨ- vb. intr. to rain (down on: ⲈⲬⲚ̄, ⲈϨⲢⲀⲒ ⲈⲬⲚ̄; from:
ⲈⲂⲞⲖ ϨⲚ̄); also tr. As n.m. rain, moisture; ⲘⲞⲨ-Ⲛ̄-ϨⲰⲞⲨ
idem. ϨⲞⲨ-Ⲙ̄-ⲠⲈ n.m. rain.

ϨⲰⲠ ϨⲈⲠ ϨⲞⲠ⳿ Q ϨⲎⲠ vb. tr. to hide, conceal (Ⲙ̄ⲘⲞ⳿; from:
Ⲉ); intr. to hide, become hidden (from: Ⲉ). As n.m.
hiding; ϨⲚ̄ ⲞⲨϨⲰⲠ in hiding, secretly; ϨⲘ̄ ⲠϨⲰⲠ idem; Ⲛ̄
ϨⲰⲠ idem. ⲀⲦϨⲰⲠ unhidden. ⲘⲀ Ⲛ̄ ϨⲰⲠ hiding-place.

ϩⲱⲛⳉ n.m. palm-branch with hanging dates.

ϩⲱⲣ ϩⲣ̄- ϩⲟⲣ⸗ Q ϩⲏⲣ vb. reflex. to guard against, take heed
for (ⲉ).

ϩⲱⲣ ϩⲣ̄- (ϩⲉⲣ-) ϩⲟⲣ⸗ vb. tr. to milk; ϩⲣ̄-ⲉⲣⲱⲧⲉ idem.

ϩⲱⲣ the god Horus.

ϩⲱⲣⲃ̄ (ϩⲱⲣϥ) ϩⲟⲣⲃ⸗ Q ϩⲟⲣ(ⲉ)ϥ vb. tr. to break (ⲙ̄ⲙⲟ⸗); intr.
to be broken.

ϩⲱⲣⲕ̄, Q ϩⲟⲣⲕ̄ vb. intr. to sit quietly (as in ambush).

ϩⲱⲣⲛ̄, Q ϩⲟⲣⲛ̄ vb. intr. to sleep, doze.

ϩⲱⲣⲛ̄ ϩⲣ̄ⲛ- (ϩⲉⲣⲛ̄-) ϩⲟⲣⲛ⸗ Q ϩⲟⲣⲛ̄ vb. tr. to soak, drench,
wet (ⲙ̄ⲙⲟ⸗; with: ϩⲛ̄, ⲙ̄ⲙⲟ⸗); also intr.: to become wet.

ϩⲱⲣϭ̄ (ϩⲱⲗϭ̄, ϩⲱⲣⳉ) ϩⲉⲣϭ̄- ϩⲟⲣⳉ⸗ Q ϩⲟⲣϭ̄ (ϩⲟⲣⳉ) vb. tr. to
heap up, pile up (ⲙ̄ⲙⲟ⸗); to put into order, arrange;
vb. intr. to be heaped up, put into order; as n.m.
order, harmony. ϩⲣⲟⲭ vb. idem (rare).

ϩⲱⲥ, ϩⲱⲱⲥ, ϩⲟⲩⲥ n.m. thread, cord.

ϩⲱⲥ ϩⲉⲥ- ϩⲟⲥ⸗ vb. tr. to block up, cover up, stop up (ⲙ̄ⲙⲟ⸗;
ⲉⲭⲛ̄, ϩⲓⲭⲛ̄); vb. intr. to be blocked up etc.

ϩⲱⲥ vb. intr. to sing, make music; as n.m. song; ⲣⲉϥϩⲱⲥ
singer.

ϩⲱⲧ n.m. sack, bag.

ϩⲱⲧ in ⲣ̄-ϩⲱⲧ to sail, float (to: ⲉ, ϣⲁ; in, on: ϩⲛ̄); ⲙⲁ ⲛ̄
ⲣ̄-ϩⲱⲧ sailing course.

ϩⲱⲧⲃ̄ (ϩⲱⲧⲉⲃ) ϩⲉⲧⲃ̄- ϩⲟⲧⲃ⸗ Q ϩⲟⲧⲃ̄ vb. tr. to kill (ⲙ̄ⲙⲟ⸗);
ϩⲱⲧⲃ̄ ⲛ̄ⲥⲁ to massacre. ϩⲁⲧⲃ̄ in cpd.: slaying, as in
ϩⲁⲧⲃ̄-ϣⲏⲣⲉ child-slaying. As n.m. slaughter, murder;
corpse; ⲣⲉϥϩⲱⲧⲃ̄ slayer, murderer; ⲙⲛ̄ⲧⲣⲉϥϩⲱⲧⲃ̄ murder,
slaughter; ⲣ̄-ⲣⲉϥϩⲱⲧⲃ̄ to slay (ⲉ). ϩⲁⲧⲃⲉⲥ n.f. slaying;
thing slain.

ϩⲱⲧⲉ vb. to bruise, pierce.

ϩⲱⲧⲉ, ϩⲱⲧ n.f. rod, pole; ϣⲉ ⲛ̄ ϩⲱⲧ wooden pole.

ϩⲱⲧⲛ̄ (ϩⲱⲡⲧ̄) ϩⲉⲧⲛ̄- ϩⲟⲧⲛ⸗ (ϩⲟⲡⲧ⸗) Q ϩⲟⲧⲛ̄ vb. intr. to set,
sink (of celestial bodies); to become reconciled (to,
with: ⲉ, ⲙⲛ̄); vb. tr. to reconcile (ⲙ̄ⲙⲟ⸗; to, with: ⲉ,
ⲙⲛ̄); as n.m. reconciliation; sunset. ⲙⲁ ⲛ̄ ϩⲱⲧⲛ̄ the

338

west. ϥ-2ωτⲛ̄ to reconcile.

2ωτⲣ̄ (2ωτⲉⲣ) 2ⲉτⲣ̄- 2ⲟτⲣ⸳ Q 2ⲟτⲣ̄ vb. tr. to join (ⲙ̄ⲙⲟ⸳; to:
ⲉ; with: ⲙⲛ̄); to hire; vb. intr. to be joined (to: ⲉ);
to be hired (for: ⲉ); to be in harmony (with: ⲙⲛ̄). As
n.m. joining, yoke, harmony. ⲣⲉϥ2ωτⲣ̄ hireling. 2ⲁτⲣ̄
(pl. 2ⲁτⲣⲉⲉⲩ, 2ⲁτⲣⲉⲩⲉ) n.m. twin, double; as adj. doub-
led. 2ⲁτⲣⲉⲥ n.f. yoke (pair) of animals.

2ⲱⲱ⸳, 2ⲱ⸳ emphatic or intensive pronoun, used appositionally with other pronominal elements: (I) myself, (I)
too, for my part, on the contrary, on the other hand.
2ⲱⲱϥ adv. (no pron. agreement) on the other hand, however (expressing contrast or opposition).

2ⲱⲱⲕ (2ⲱⲕ) 2ⲉⲕ- 2ⲟⲕ⸳ (2ⲟⲟⲕ⸳) Q 2ⲏⲕ vb. tr. to gird, arm
(ⲙ̄ⲙⲟ⸳; with: 2ⲛ̄, ⲙ̄ⲙⲟ⸳; for, against: ⲉ, ⲟⲩⲃⲉ), ± ⲉⲃⲟⲗ,
ⲉ2ⲟⲩⲛ. 2ⲱⲕ ⲙ̄ⲙⲟ⸳ ⲛ̄ ⲙⲁτⲟⲓ to gird someone as a soldier.
As n.m. girding, breastplate, protective armor.

2ⲱⲱⲕⲉ (2ⲱⲕⲉ, 2ⲱⲱⲕ, 2ⲱⲕ) 2ⲉⲕⲉ- (2ⲉⲕⲉ-, 2ⲉⲕ-) 2ⲟⲕ⸳ (2ⲟⲟⲕ⸳)
Q 2ⲟⲟⲕⲉ vb. tr. (1) to scrape, scratch, esp. as means
of torture (ⲙ̄ⲙⲟ⸳); (2) to shave (ⲙ̄ⲙⲟ⸳); as n.m. baldness, shaven condition. 2ⲱⲱⲕⲉ n.m. fleece.

2ⲱⲱⲗⲉ (2ⲱⲗⲉ) 2ⲁⲗ- 2ⲟⲗ⸳ (2ⲟⲟⲗ⸳) vb. tr. to pluck.

2ⲱⲱⲙⲉ (2ⲱⲙⲉ, 2ⲱⲙ) Q 2ⲁⲙ (2ⲁⲁⲙ) vb. intr. to become lean,
thin; + ⲉⲃⲟⲗ: to pine away, be blighted.

2ⲱϣ 2ⲉϣ- 2ⲟϣ⸳ Q 2ⲏϣ vb. tr. to distress, afflict (ⲙ̄ⲙⲟ⸳, ⲉ);
intr. to be distressed (by, with: ⲉτⲃⲉ, 2ⲁ, ⲙⲛ̄, ⲛ̄τⲛ̄);
as n.m. distress, straits. 2ⲁϣⲧ̄ n.f. constraint.

2ⲱϥⲧ̄ (2ⲱⲃⲧ̄, 2ⲟϥⲧ̄) 2ⲉϥⲧ̄- 2ⲟϥⲧ⸳ (2ⲟⲃⲧ⸳) vb. tr. to steal
(ⲙ̄ⲙⲟ⸳; from: ⲛ̄τⲛ̄, 2ⲓ, 2ⲛ̄, ⲉⲃⲟⲗ 2ⲛ̄); as n.m. theft.
ⲣⲉϥ-2ⲱϥⲧ̄ thief.

(2ⲟϥⲧ̄) 2ⲉϥⲧ̄- 2ⲟϥⲧ⸳ ± ⲉⲃⲟⲗ vb. tr. to eject, send forth.

2ⲱ2 2ⲟ2⸳ vb. tr. to scrape, scratch (ⲙ̄ⲙⲟ⸳); vb. intr. to
be scraped; to itch; as n.m. itching, scratching.

2ⲱ2ϥ, 2ⲱ2ⲕ̄ n.f. hand (as a measure).

2ⲱϫ (2ⲟϫ) Q 2ⲏϫ vb. intr. to be in straits, be dying; vb.
tr. to distress, put in straits (ⲙ̄ⲙⲟ⸳, ⲉ); as n.m.

straits. ²ⲁⲝ n.m. illness; name of a disease.

²ⲱⲭⲡ̅ ²ⲉⲭⲡ̅- ²ⲟⲭⲡⸯ vb. tr. to shut (ⲙ̅ⲙⲟⸯ), shut in, enclose; as n.m. shutting, sealing.

²ⲱ6ⲃ̅ (²ⲱ6ⲅ̄, ²ⲱⲕⲙ̄) ²66ⲃ̅- (²66ⲙ̄-) ²о6ⲃⸯ Q ²о6ⲃ̅ (²о6ⲅ̄) vb. tr. to wither, destroy (ⲙ̅ⲙⲟⸯ); vb. intr. to wither away, fade, expire. ²ⲁ6ⲃ̅- in cpds.: weak in, feeble of. As n.m. feebleness. ⲁⲧ²ⲱ6ⲃ̅ unfading.

²ⲭⲟⲡⲭⲡ̅ (ⲭⲟⲡⲭⲡ̅, ²ⲡⲟ6ⲡ6ⲧ) vb. intr. to feel, grope (for: 6, 62ⲟⲩⲛ 6).

²ⲁ: ²ⲟ	²ⲁⲣⲟⸯ: ²ⲁ	²6: ²ⲏ, 62є
²ⲁⲁⲕ: ²ⲁⲕ	²ⲁⲣⲟⲩ²6: ⲣⲟⲩ²6	²6ⲃⲃ6: ²ⲃ̅ⲃ6
²ⲁⲁⲙ: ²ⲱⲱⲙ6	²ⲁⲣⲱⸯ: ⲣⲟ	²6ⲃ6ⲧⲱⲣ6: ²ⲙ̄ⲛ̄ⲧⲱⲣ6
²ⲁⲁⲧ: ²ⲁⲧ	²ⲁⲣⲡ̣̄-: ²ⲣⲟⲱ	²6ⲃⲥ̅: ²ⲏⲃⲥ̅
²ⲁⲁⲧ6: ²ⲁⲧ6	²ⲁⲣⲱⲏⲧ: ²ⲁⲱⲏⲧ	²6ⲃⲥⲱ: ²ⲱⲃⲥ̅
²ⲁⲁ66: ²ⲁ66	²ⲁⲥ616: ²ⲁⲥ16	²6ⲃⲱ1: ²1ⲃⲱ1
²ⲁⲃⸯ: ²ⲱⲃ	²ⲁⲥⲙ̄: ²ⲟⲥⲙ̄	²6ⲃⲱⲱⲛ: ²6-
²ⲁⲃ6: ²ⲟⲃ6	²ⲁⲥⲧ̄-/ⸯ: ²1ⲥ6	²66: ²6
²ⲁⲃ1ⲟⲩ1: ²1ⲃⲱ1	²ⲁⲧⸯ: ²1ⲧ6, ²1	²661ⲧ: ²ⲁ61ⲧ
²ⲁⲃⲗ66ⲗ6: ²ⲁⲅⲗ66ⲗ6	²ⲁⲧⲃ̅-: ²ⲱⲧⲃ̅	²61ⲁ61ⲃ6: ²161ⲃ
²ⲁⲃⲟⲗ: ⲃⲱⲗ	²ⲁⲧⲃ6ⲥ: ²ⲱⲧⲃ̅	²616ⲃ: ²161ⲃ
²ⲁ6ⲃ̅-: ²ⲱ6ⲃ̅	²ⲁⲧ6: ²ⲁⲧ	²6161ⲧ: ²1617
²ⲁ61ⲏ: ²ⲁ6	²ⲁⲧⲏⲩⸯ: ⲧⲏⲩ	²6ⲕ-: ²ⲱⲕ, ²ⲱⲱⲕ,
²ⲁ66ⲩ: ²ⲁ6	²ⲁⲧⲛ̄: ⲧⲱⲣ6	²ⲱⲱⲕ6
²ⲁ6ⲟⲩ: ²ⲁ6	²ⲁⲧⲟⲟⲧⸯ: ⲧⲱⲣ6	²6ⲕ6-: ²ⲱⲱⲕ6
²ⲁ6ⲩ(6): ²ⲁ6	²ⲁⲧⲣ̄: ²ⲱⲧⲣ̄	²6ⲗ61ⲗ6: ²ⲗⲟ61ⲗ6
²ⲁⲏ: ²ⲁ6	²ⲁⲧⲣ66ⲩ(6): ²ⲱⲧⲣ̄	²6ⲗⲕⲟⲩ: ²ⲗ̄ⲕⲟⲩ
²ⲁ1ⲃ6: ²161ⲃ	²ⲁⲧⲣ6ⲥ: ²ⲱⲧⲣ̄	²6ⲗⲙ626: ²ⲁⲗⲙⲏ²6
²ⲁ1ⲏ: ²ⲁ6	²ⲁⲧⲥ̅: ²ⲟⲧⲥ̅	²6ⲗ66: ²ⲗⲟ6
²ⲁⲕⲏⲗ̄ⲅ̄: ²ⲁⲕ̅ⲗ̄ⲅ̄	²ⲁⲱ1ⲧ: ²ⲁⲱⲏⲧ	²6ⲙ6: ²ⲏⲙ6
²ⲁⲕⲟ: ²1ⲕ	²ⲁⲱⲥ̅: ²ⲱⲱ	²6ⲙ6ⲧⲟⲣ6: ²ⲙ̄ⲛ̄ⲧⲱⲣ6
²ⲁⲗ-: ²ⲱⲱⲗ6	²ⲁⲭ: ²ⲱⲭ	²6ⲙⲝ̅: ²ⲙⲟⲭ
²ⲁⲗⲁⲧ6: ²ⲁⲗⲏⲧ	²ⲁⲭⲛ̄, ²ⲁⲭⲱⸯ: ⲭⲱⸯ	²6ⲛⲏ(ⲏ)ⲧ6: ²6ⲛ66ⲧ6
²ⲁⲗⲏⲛⲕ: ²ⲁⲗⲁⲕ	²ⲃⲁ1: ²1ⲃ6	²6ⲛⲅⸯ: ²ⲱⲛⲕ̄
²ⲁⲗⲕⲟⲩ: ²ⲗ̄ⲕⲟⲩ	²ⲃ̅ⲃ6: ²1ⲃ6	²6ⲛ616: ²1ⲛ6
²ⲁⲗⲗⲟⲩⲥ: ²ⲁⲗⲟⲩⲥ	²ⲃ̅ⲃⲥ̅: ²ⲱⲃⲥ̅	²6ⲛⲟⲩⲅ6: ²6-
²ⲁⲗⲃ̅-: ²ⲗⲟ6	²ⲃⲏⲏⲧ6: ⲥ̅²ⲃⲏⲏⲧ6	²6ⲟⲩⲧ: ²ⲟⲟⲩⲧ
²ⲁⲙ: ²ⲱⲱⲙ6	²ⲃⲏⲩ6: ²ⲱⲃ	²6ⲣⲃⲟⲟ66: ²ⲣ̄ⲃⲱⲧ
²ⲁⲙⲛ̄ⲧⲱⲣ: ²ⲙ̄ⲛ̄ⲧⲱⲣ6	²ⲃⲟⲕ: ²ⲱⲃⲕ̄	²6ⲣ6: ²ⲣ6
²ⲁⲛⲕⲗ̄ⲅ̄: ²ⲁⲕ̅ⲗ̄ⲅ̄	²ⲃⲟⲟⲥ, ²ⲃⲟⲥ: ²ⲱⲃⲥ̅	²6ⲣⲡ̣̄-: ²ⲣⲟⲱ
²ⲁⲛ²ⲏⲧ: ²ⲏⲧ	²ⲃⲟⲩ1: ²ⲟⲅ, ²1ⲃⲱ1	²6ⲣⲱ6: ²ⲣⲟⲱ
²ⲁⲛⲣⲟ: ⲣⲟ	²ⲃⲟ6: ²ⲱⲃⲕ̄	²6ⲣ²1ⲣ6: ²1ⲣ
²ⲁⲡ: ²ⲟⲡ	²ⲃ̅ⲥ: ²ⲏⲃⲥ̅, ²ⲱⲃⲥ̅	²6ⲧ-: ²1ⲧ6
²ⲁⲡⲥ̅: ²ⲱⲃⲥ̅	²ⲃ̅ⲥⲟⲟⲩ6: ²ⲱⲃⲥ̅	²6ⲩⲧ: ²ⲟⲟⲩⲧ
²ⲁⲣ61ⲟⲡ6: 61ⲟⲡ6	²ⲃ̅ⲥⲱ: ²ⲱⲃⲥ̅	²6ⲭⲝ̅-: ²ⲟⲭ²ⲭ̄
²ⲁⲣⲏⲩ: ⲁⲣⲏⲩ	²ⲃⲱ: ²ⲟⲅ	²66ⲙ̄-: ²ⲱ6ⲃ̅
²ⲁⲣⲏ²6: ²ⲁⲣ6²	²ⲃⲱⲥ, ²ⲃⲱⲱⲥ: ²ⲱⲃⲥ̅	²ⲏⲃ(ⲃ)6: ²ⲃ̅ⲃ6
²ⲁⲣⲛ̄: ⲣⲟ	²ⲃⲱⲱⲛ: ²6-	²ⲏⲃⲥ̅: ²ⲱⲃⲥ̅

ϩΗ€: ϩ€	ϩⲓⲱⲱˢ: ϩⲓ	ϩΟⲨΜ̄ⲡ€: ϩⲱΟⲨ
ϩΗ€ΙΤ: ϩλ€ΙΤ	ϩⲓϩⲣλˢ: ϩΟ	ϩΟⲨⲣ-: ϩΟⲨⲣ€-
ϩΗΒϬ€: ϩΗΒϬ€	ϩⲓⲭⲛ̄, ϩⲓⲭⲱˢ: ⲭⲱˢ	ϩΟⲨⲣλΤ€: ϩΟⲨⲣΙΤ
ϩΗΗⲡ€, ϩΗΗΤ€: ϬΙϬ	ϩΚλ€ΙΤ, ϩΚΟ€ΙΤ: ϩΚΟ	ϩΟⲨⲣⲱ(ⲱ)ˢ: ϩΟⲨⲣ€-
ϩΗΒϬ€: ϩΗΒϬ€	ϩλ€€Ιλ€: ϩλΟ€Ιλ€	ϩΟⲨϹ: ϩⲱϹ
ϩΗΚ: ϩⲱⲱΚ	ϩλΗϬ€: ϩλΟϬ	ϩΟⲨⲧ-: ϩΟΟⲨⲧ
ϩΗΚ€: ϩΚΟ	ϩλΟΜ: ϩλⲱΜ	ϩΟϣˢ: ⲱϣ
ϩΗΜ€: ϩΟ€ΙΜ	ϩλΟⲩⲱ: Οⲩⲱ	ϩΟϥ: ϩⲱΒ
ϩΗΜϬ̄: ϩΜ̄Ϭ	ϩλϬ€: ϩλΟϬ	ϩΟⲭ: ϩⲱⲭ
ϩΗΜⲭ̄: ϩΜΟⲭ	ϩΜ̄-: ϩλΜ, ϩⲱΜ	ϩΟⲭⲭ̄: ϩΟⲭϩⲭ̄
ϩΗΜ: ϩΜΟΜ	ϩΜλΙϹ: ϩΜΟΟϹ	ϩΟϬϬ̄: ⲱϬϬ̄
ϩΗΝ€Τ€: ϩ€Ν€€Τ€	ϩΜ€ⲩ, ϩΜΗⲨ: ϩλΜ	ϩΟϬϥ̄: ϩⲱϬϬ̄
ϩΗΝⲧ̄: ϩⲱΝⲧ̄	ϩΜ̄Μ€: ϩΗΜ€, ϩΜΟΜ	ϩⲡΟϬⲡϬ̄, ϩⲡΟⲭⲡⲭ̄:
ϩΗΟⲨ: ϩΗⲨ	ϩΜ̄Τⲱⲣ: ϩΜ̄Ν̄Τⲱⲣ€	ϩⲭΟⲡⲭⲡ̄
ϩΗⲣϩΙⲣ€: ϩΙⲣ	ϩΜ̄ϩλλ, ϩΜ̄ϩ€λ: ϩλλ	ϩⲡⲱΤ: ϩⲡΟΤ
ϩΗⲧˢ: ϩΗ	ϩΜⲭ̄: ϩΜΟⲭ	ϩⲣλˢ: ϩΟ, ϩⲣΟΟⲨ
ϩΗΤ€: ϬΙϬ	ϩΝλλⲨ: ϩΝλⲨ	ϩⲣλΚ: ϩⲣΟΚ
ϩΗⲨ: ϩ€	ϩΝ̄Τˢ: ϩΙΝ€	ϩⲣ€: ϩⲣλΙ
ϩΗⲨΒϬ€: ϩϬ̄Βϩ	ϩΟ: ϩλ	ϩⲣ€ΟⲨ€: ϩⲣ€
ϩΗⲭ: ϩλⲭ	ϩΟΒ: ϩΟϥ	ϩⲣΗⲨ€: ϩⲣ€
ϩⲓ-: ϩΙΟⲨ€	ϩΟΒ€: ϩΙΒ€	ϩⲣΗϣ€: ϩⲣΟϣ
ϩⲓλΒ€, ϩⲓλ€ΙΒ€:	ϩΟΒⲧ̄: ϩΟϥⲧ̄	ϩⲣΚ̄ⲣΙΚ€: ϩⲣΚ̄ⲣΙΚ€
ϩΙϬΙΒ	ϩΟϬΙλ€: ϩΟϬΙⲣ€	ϩⲣΟⲨΒ(Β)λΙ: ϩⲣΟΟⲨ
ϩΙΒ, ϩΙΒ€: ϩΙϬΙΒ	ϩΟΙΒ€Ϲ: ϩλ€ΙΒ€Ϲ	ϩⲣΟⲨΜ̄ⲡ€: ϩⲣΟΟⲨ
ϩΙΒΟλ: ϥⲱλ	ϩΟΚˢ: ϩⲱⲱΚ, ϩⲱⲱΚ€	ϩⲣΟⲨΟ, ϩⲣΟⲨⲱ:
ϩΙΒΟⲨΙ: ϩΙΒⲱΙ	ϩΟΚⲣ̄: ϩΚΟ	ϩⲣΟΟⲨ
ϩΙϬϬΒϬ€: ϩΙϬΙΒ	ϩΟλˢ: ϩⲱⲱλ€	ϩⲣΟⲨⲱⲣˢ: ϩΒΟⲣΒⲣ̄
ϩΙϬ€Ⲩ(€): ϩΟΙ	ϩΟλϬ̄: ϩλΟϬ	ϩⲣϣ̄-: ϩⲣΟϣ
ϩΙϬⲨ: ϩΙϬ	ϩΟΜ€Τ: ϩΟΜΝ̄Τ	ϩΤΗˢ: ϩΗΤ
ϩΙϬΙλΒ€, ϩΙϬΙΒ€:	ϩΟΜⲧ̄: ϩΟΜΝ̄Τ	ϩΤΟΟⲣ€: ϩΤΟ
ϩΙϬΙΒ	ϩΟΜⲱΤⲱⲣ: ϩΜ̄Ν̄Τⲱⲣ€	ϩΤⲱ: ϩΤΟ
ϩΙΗ: ϩΙϬ, ϩϬ, ϩΗ	ϩΟΜⲭ̄: ϩΜΟⲭ	ϩΤⲱⲣ€: ϩΤΟ
ϩΙΗΒϬ€: ϩΙϬΙΒ	ϩΟΟΚˢ: ϩⲱⲱΚ€, ϩⲱⲱΚ	ϩΤⲱⲱⲣ: ϩΤΟ
ϩΙΗΟⲨ: ϩΙϬ	ϩΟΟΚ€: ϩⲱⲱΚ€	ϩΘⲱⲣ: ϩλΘⲱⲣ
ϩΙΗⲨ: ϩΙϬ, ϩΙΗ	ϩΟΟλˢ: ϩⲱⲱλ€	ϩⲱ: ϩΟ
ϩΙλλ: λλ	ϩΟΟⲡ: ϩΟⲡ	ϩⲱˢ: ϩⲱⲱˢ
ϩΙΜ€: ϩΗΜ€, ϹϩΙΜ€	ϩΟⲡ: ϩΟϥ, ϩλⲡ	ϩⲱΒ: ϩΟϥ
ϩΙΜΗ: ϩΟϬΙΜ	ϩΟⲡϬ̄: ϩλⲡϬ̄	ϩⲱΒⲧ̄: ϩⲱϥⲧ̄
ϩΙΝΙϬ: ϩΙΝϬ	ϩΟⲡⲧˢ: ϩⲱⲧⲡ̄	ϩⲱΚ: ϩⲱⲱΚ
ϩΙΟΜ€: ϹϩΙΜ€,	ϩΟⲣϬϥ: ϩⲱⲣⲃ̄	ϩⲱΚ(€): ϩⲱⲱΚ€
ϩΙⲱΜ€	ϩΟⲣⲕ̄: ϩⲣΟΚ, ϩⲱⲣⲕ̄	ϩⲱΚⲙ̄: ϩⲱϬϬ̄
ϩΙΟΟⲨ€: ϩΙΗ	ϩΟⲣϣ̄: ϩⲣΟϣ, ⲱⲣϣ̄	ϩⲱλ€: ϩⲱⲱλ€, ϩⲱλ
ϩΙⲣϩΙⲣ€: ϩΙⲣ	ϩΟⲣϥ̄: ϩⲱⲣⲃ̄	ϩⲱλϬ̄: ϩⲱⲣϬ̄
ϩΙⲣⲛ̄: ⲣΟ	ϩΟⲣⲭ(ˢ): ϩⲱⲣϬ̄	ϩⲱλϬ̄: ϩⲱλⲕ̄
ϩΙⲣΟⲨϩϬ€: ⲣΟⲨϩϬ€	ϩΟϹϬ€: ϩΙϹϬ	ϩⲱΜ: ϩⲱⲱⲙ€
ϩΙⲣⲱˢ: ⲣΟ	ϩΟϹΗΜ: ϩΟϹΜ̄	ϩⲱⲙ€: ϩⲱⲱⲙ€,
ϩΙΤ: ϩΙϬΙΤ	ϩΟⲨλΤ€: ϩΟⲨ€ΙΤ,	ϩΙⲱΜ€
ϩΙΤˢ: ϩΙ, ϩΙΟⲨ€	ϩΟⲨΗΤ	ϩⲱΝⲧ̄: ϩⲱΝⲕ̄
ϩΙΤⲛ̄: Τⲱⲣ€	ϩΟⲨ€-: ϩΟⲨΟ	ϩⲱΝⲧ̄: ϩΟΝⲧ̄
ϩΙΤΟΟΤˢ: Τⲱⲣ€	ϩΟⲨ€ΙΤ€: ϩΟⲨ€ΙΤ	ϩⲱⲡⲧ̄: ϩⲱⲧⲡ̄
ϩΙΤΟⲨⲛ̄-: ΤΟⲨⲱˢ	ϩΟⲨ€ⲣΟⲨⲱⲣˢ: ϩΒΟⲣΒⲣ̄	ϩⲱⲣΙΤ: ϩΟⲨⲣΙΤ
ϩΙΤϹⲨⲱˢ: ΤΟⲨⲱˢ	ϩΟⲨΙΤ€: ϩΟⲨ€ΙΤ	ϩⲱⲣϥ̄: ϩⲱⲣⲃ̄

ⲋⲱⲧ: ⲋⲱⲧⲉ, ⲋⲟⲧ, ⲋⲟⲧⲉ   ⲋⲱⲱϥ: ⲋⲱⲱˣ   ⲋⲱⲋⲃ̄: ⲱϭⲃ̄
ⲋⲱⲧⲉ: ⲋⲟⲧ, ⲋⲟⲧⲉ   ⲋⲱⲋⲃ̄: ⲋⲱⲋϥ̄   ⲋⲱϭϥ̄: ⲋⲱϭⲃ̄
ⲋⲱⲱⲗⲉ: ⲋⲱⲗ   ⲋⲱϥ: ⲋⲱⲃ   ⲋϥⲱ: ⲋⲟϥ
ⲋⲱⲱⲥ: ⲋⲱⲥ

ϫ

ϫⲁⲁϫⲉ vb. tr. to clap (hands: ⲙ̄ⲙⲟˣ, ⲋⲛ̄).

ϫⲁⲉⲓⲉ, ϫⲁⲓⲉ, ϫⲁⲉ n.m. desert. ⲋ1/ⲋⲙ̄ ⲛϫⲁⲉⲓⲉ in the desert.
  ⲙⲁⲓ-ϫⲁⲉⲓⲉ loving solitude. ⲙⲛ̄ⲧϫⲁⲉⲓⲉ desolation. ⲕⲱ/†/
  ⲉⲓⲣⲉ ⲙ̄ⲙⲟˣ ⲛ̄ ϫⲁⲉⲓⲉ to make desert. ⲣ̄-ϫⲁⲉⲓⲉ to become
  desert, waste.

ϫⲁⲉⲓⲟ (ⲧϫⲁⲉⲓⲟ) ϫⲁⲉⲓⲟˣ vb. tr. to display (ⲙ̄ⲙⲟˣ).

ϫⲁⲕ vb. tr. to clap (hands: ⲙ̄ⲙⲟˣ); to flap (wings); as
  n.m. clapping, flapping; ⲣⲉϥϫⲁⲕ one who claps.

ϫⲁⲙⲏ n.f. calm.

ϫⲁⲛⲉ, ϫⲁⲁⲛⲉ, ϫⲟⲟⲛⲉ, ϫⲁⲛⲏ n. ark, box.

ϫⲁⲥϥⲉ n. in ϫⲓ-ϫⲁⲥϥⲉ to repair, put in order.

ϫⲁⲧⲉ (ϫⲁⲁⲧⲉ), Q ϫⲟⲧⲉ vb. intr. to become ripe, mature; to
  advance in age. ϫⲧⲁⲓ, Q ϫⲏⲧ idem.

ϫⲁⲧⲙⲉ n. heap (of grain).

ϫⲁⲧϥⲉ, ϫⲁⲧⲃⲉ n.m. snake, reptile.

ϫⲁϥ, ϫⲁⲃ n.m. frost.

ϫⲁⲋϫⲋ̄ (ϫⲁⲋⲭ̄, ϫⲁϫⲋ̄, ϭⲁⲋϫⲋ̄, ϭⲁⲋϭⲋ̄, ϭⲁⲋϭ̄, ϭⲟⲋϭ̄) ϫⲉⲋϫⲱⲋˣ vb.
  tr. to beat, strike, gnash (ⲙ̄ⲙⲟˣ; against: ⲉϫⲛ̄); as n.m.
  beating, gnashing; as adj. beaten, (of metal) refined.

ϫⲁϫ n.m. sparrow. ϫⲁϫ ⲛ̄ ⲗⲓⲗ name of a bird.

ϫⲁϫⲉ (ϫⲁⲁϫⲉ), Q ϫⲁϫⲱ(ⲟⲩ) vb. intr. to become rough, hard,
  harsh. ⲁⲧϫⲁϫⲉ not harsh (of voice).

ϫⲁϫⲉ (pl. ϫⲓϫⲉⲉⲩ, ϫⲓϫⲉⲉⲩⲉ, ϫⲓϫⲉⲟⲩ, ϫⲓⲛϫⲉⲉⲩ, ϫⲓⲛϫⲉⲉⲩⲉ, ϫⲓⲛ-
  ϫⲉⲩⲉ) n.m.f. enemy. ⲙⲁⲓ-ϫⲁϫⲉ loving enmity, quarrelsome;
  ⲙⲛ̄ⲧϫⲁϫⲉ enmity (toward: ⲉⲋⲟⲩⲛ ⲉ). ⲣ̄-ϫⲁϫⲉ (Q ⲟ ⲛ̄) to be
  at enmity (with: ⲉ, ⲙⲛ̄).

ϫⲃ̄ⲃ̄ⲥ̄, ϫⲃ̄ⲃ̄ⲉⲥ, ϫⲉⲃⲃⲉⲥ, ϫⲉⲃⲃⲥ̄, ϫⲃ̄ⲥ, ϫⲏⲏⲃⲥ̄, ϫⲏⲃⲥ̄, ϫⲏⲓⲃⲉⲥ, ϫⲁⲉⲓ-
  ⲃⲉⲥ n.f. coal, charcoal.

ϫⲃⲓⲛ n.m. blemish. ⲁⲧϫⲃⲓⲛ without blemish.

ⲭⲉ, ⲛ̄ⲭⲉ conj. see 30.11 for full discussion of uses.

ⲭⲉⲃⲏⲗ, ⲭⲃⲏⲗ, ⲭⲓⲃⲏⲗ, ⲭⲉⲃⲉⲗ n.m. spear; a shoot.

ⲭⲉⲕ n.m. shell, sherd.

ⲭⲉⲕⲁⲥ, ⲭⲉⲕⲁⲗⲥ conj. so that, in order that; usu. followed
by Future III or II. See 27.4.

ⲭⲉⲕⲭⲓⲕ n. an insect (ant?).

ⲭⲉⲗ²ⲏⲥ, ⲭⲗ̄²ⲏⲥ, ⲭⲗ̄²ⲥ̄, ⲭⲉⲗⲗⲏⲥ vb. intr. to become exhausted,
to pant; as n.m. exhaustion, panting.

ⲭⲉⲙⲡⲉ², ⲭⲙ̄ⲡⲉ², ⲭⲙ̄ⲡⲏ², ⲭⲉⲡⲏ², ⲭⲏⲡⲉ², ⲭⲓⲡⲉ² n.m. apple.

ⲭⲉⲛⲉⲡⲱⲣ n.f. roof.

ⲭⲉⲣⲟ (ⲭⲉⲣⲱ) ⲭⲉⲣⲉ– (ⲭⲉⲉⲣⲉ–) ⲭⲉⲣⲟ⸗ (ⲭⲉⲣⲱ⸗) vb. tr. to kindle,
set afire; intr. to be ablaze, burn.

ⲭⲏ n.m. speck, mote (of straw, chaff, sawdust).

ⲭⲏ n.f. dish, bowl.

ⲭⲏⲏⲥ n.f. bowl, censer.

ⲭⲏⲣ vb. intr. to be merry, enjoy oneself; to be wanton; as
n.m. merriment, fun; wanton behavior. ⲣⲉϥⲭⲏⲣ wanton.
ⲭⲉⲣⲭ̄ⲣ̄ n.m. wanton behavior.

ⲭⲏⲣⲉ, ⲭⲉⲉⲣⲉ n.f. threshing-floor; threshing season.

ⲭⲓ n.m. a metal vessel.

ⲭⲓ (ⲭⲉⲓ) ⲭⲓ– (ⲭⲉ–) ⲭⲓⲧ⸗ Q ⲭⲏⲩ̈ vb. tr. (1) to seize, take
(ⲙ̄ⲙⲟ⸗); to receive, accept; (2) to buy, acquire; (3) to
strike, reach (of arrows, teeth, etc.); (4) to learn by
heart. In basic meaning (1) all prep. and adv. occur
with normal meanings. ⲭⲓ ⲉ to affect, relate to, im-
pinge on; (± ⲉ²ⲟⲩⲛ) to lead to, be conducive to, introduce to. ⲭⲓ ⲙ̄ⲙⲟ⸗ ⲉⲭⲛ̄ to borrow (suff. on ⲉⲭⲛ̄ is reflex.).
ⲭⲓ ⲙⲛ̄ to touch, be in contact with. For ⲭⲓ– and ⲭⲁⲓ–
in vb. and nom. cpds. see 2nd element.

ⲭⲓⲉⲓⲡⲉ n.m. pod.

ⲭⲓⲗⲗⲉⲥ, ⲭⲓⲗⲗⲏⲥ, ⲭⲉⲗⲗⲏⲥ, ⲕⲉⲗⲗⲏⲥ n.m. box.

ⲭⲓⲛ, ⲭⲛ̄, ⲭⲉⲛ, ⲕⲛ̄, ϭⲛ̄, ϣⲉⲛ prep. from, since, starting from;
conj. since (see § 30.3); while yet (+ Circum.). ⲭⲓⲛ
ⲉ, ⲭⲓⲛ ⲛ̄, ⲭⲓⲛ ²ⲛ̄ = ⲭⲓⲛ. ⲭⲓⲛ X ⲉ/ϣⲁ/ϣⲁ²ⲣⲁⲓ ⲉ Y from X
to Y. ⲭⲓⲛ X ⲉⲃⲟⲗ/ⲉ²ⲣⲁⲓ from X onward. ⲭⲓⲛ is

occasionally preceded by ε, ⲛ̄, ²ⲁ, ²ⲓ.

ⲭⲓⲛⲭⲏ n.m. emptiness, nothingness; ε ⲡⲭⲓⲛⲭⲏ in vain, for no purpose, for no reason. ⲛ̄ ⲭⲓⲛⲭⲏ idem.

ⲭⲓⲟⲩⲉ vb. tr. to steal (ⲙ̄ⲙⲟ⁼; from: ²ⲛ̄, ⲉⲃⲟⲗ ²ⲛ̄); to rob (ε, ⲛ̄ⲥⲁ); as n.m. theft, fraud. ⲛ̄ ⲭⲓⲟⲩⲉ adv. stealthily secretly; unbeknownst (to: ε). ϥⲓ ⲙ̄ⲙⲟ⁼ ⲛ̄ ⲭⲓⲟⲩⲉ to steal. ⲙⲁ ⲛ̄ ⲭⲓⲟⲩⲉ secret place. ⲣⲉϥⲭⲓⲟⲩⲉ, ⲥⲁ ⲛ̄ ⲭⲓⲟⲩⲉ thief.

ⲭⲓⲣ n.m. brine; salted fish. ⲁⲛⲭⲓⲣ brine-lotion (as soap).

ⲭⲓⲥⲉ ⲭⲉⲥⲧ̄- ⲭⲁⲥⲧ⁼ (ⲭⲓⲥⲧ⁼) Q ⲭⲟⲥⲉ (± ⲉ²ⲣⲁⲓ) vb. tr. to raise up, exalt (ⲙ̄ⲙⲟ⁼; over, above: ε, ⲉⲭⲛ̄, ²ⲓⲭⲛ̄); vb. intr. to become exalted, raised up; as n.m. height(s), top. ⲡⲉⲧ ⲭⲟⲥⲉ the Most High (of God). ⲭⲓⲥⲉ ⲛ̄ ²ⲏⲧ to become arrogant, proud, vain; ⲭⲁⲥⲓ-²ⲏⲧ proud, arrogant; ⲣ̄-ⲭⲁⲥⲓ-²ⲏⲧ to become vain, proud; ⲙ̄ⲛ̄ⲧⲭⲁⲥⲓ-²ⲏⲧ pride, arrogance. ⲭⲟⲥⲉ n.m. exalted person or place.

ⲭⲓⲥⲉ n.f. back, spine.

ⲭⲓⲥⲉ, ⲭⲉⲥⲉ, ⲭⲏⲥⲉ n.f. a land measure.

ⲭⲓϥ adj. sparing, niggard.

ⲭⲓ² n.m. spittle.

ⲭⲓⲭⲱⲓ, ϭⲓⲭⲱⲓ n. single lock or braid of hair.

ⲭⲗⲱⲙ, ⲭⲗⲱⲃ, ⲭⲗⲱϥ n.m. brazier.

ⲭⲙⲁⲁⲩ n.pl. testicles.

ⲭⲛ̄, ⲭⲉⲛ, ⲭⲓⲛ, ⲭⲉ conj. or. ⲭⲛ̄ ⲙ̄ⲙⲟⲛ/ⲙ̄ⲡⲉ or not. ⲭⲛ̄ ⲙ̄ⲡⲱⲣ or rather.

ⲭⲛⲁ (ⲭⲉⲛⲁ, ⲭⲛⲉ) ⲭⲛⲉ- ⲭⲉⲛⲁ⁼ vb. tr. to quench, put out (ⲙ̄ⲙⲟ⁼); intr. to be quenched. ⲁⲧⲭⲛⲁ unquenchable.

ⲭⲛⲁ⁼ vb. tr. to send, send away.

ⲭⲛⲁ⁼ (ⲭⲛⲟ⁼, ⲭⲛⲁⲁ⁼) vb. tr. to strike (with: ⲛ̄ or zero).

ⲭⲛⲁⲩ (ⲭⲛⲁⲁⲩ) vb. intr. to delay (in doing: ε); as n.m. sloth. ⲁⲧⲭⲛⲁⲩ without delay; ⲙ̄ⲛ̄ⲧⲁⲧⲭⲛⲁⲩ promptness; ⲣⲉϥⲭⲛⲁⲩ sluggard; ⲙ̄ⲛ̄ⲧⲣⲉϥⲭⲛⲁⲩ sloth, delay.

ⲭⲛⲁ² (pl. ⲭⲛⲁⲩ²) n.m. forearm, wing; force, violence. ⲛ̄ ⲭⲛⲁ² with effort. †-ⲭⲛⲁ² ⲛⲁ⁼ to treat violently. ⲭⲓ ⲙ̄ⲙⲟ⁼ ⲛ̄ ⲭⲛⲁ² to force, compel. ⲭⲓ ⲛ̄ ⲟⲩⲭⲛⲁ² to use force; ⲙ̄ⲛ̄ⲧⲭⲓ ⲛ̄ ⲭⲛⲁ² force, violence; ⲣⲉϥⲭⲓ-ⲭⲛⲁ² violent; ⲙ̄ⲛ̄ⲧⲣⲉϥϫⲓ-ⲭⲛⲁϩ violence. ⲙⲟⲩⲣ ⲛ̄ ϫⲛⲁϩ n.f. scapular (of monk).

ϫⲛⲉ, ϫⲛⲏ, ϫⲏⲛⲏ n.m. beets, greens.

ϫⲛⲟⲟⲩ, ϫⲛⲁⲁⲩ (pl. ϫⲛⲟⲟⲩⲉ) n.m. threshing-floor, grain on threshing-floor. ⲣ̄ϫⲛⲟⲟⲩ, ⲣⲉϫⲛⲟⲟⲩ, ⲗⲉϫⲛⲟⲟⲩ, ⲣⲓϫⲛⲟⲟⲩ n.f. idem.

ϫⲛⲟⲩ ϫⲛⲉ- (ϫⲛ̄-) ϫⲛⲟⲩ⸗ (ϫⲓⲛⲟⲩ⸗, ϫⲉⲛⲟⲩⲟⲩ⸗) vb. tr. to ask, question (dir. obj. of person asked; the thing asked is indicated by ⲉ or ⲉⲧⲃⲉ); (rarely) to tell. As n.m. inquiry, questioning.

ϫⲛⲟϥ, ϫⲉⲛⲟϥ, ϫⲉⲛⲟⲃ n.m. basket, container.

ϫⲛ̄ϫⲱⲛ⸗ vb. tr. to ask about.

ϫⲟ ϫⲉ- ϫⲟ⸗ Q ϫⲏⲩ vb. tr. to sow, plant (seed: ⲙ̄ⲙⲟ⸗; in: ϩⲛ̄, ϩⲓϫⲛ̄); to plant (a field; ⲙ̄ⲙⲟ⸗, ⲉ; with: ⲙ̄ⲙⲟ⸗); as n.m. sowing, planting. ⲣⲉϥϫⲟ sower.

ϫⲟ ϫⲉ- (ϫⲓ-) ϫⲟ⸗ (usually + ⲉⲃⲟⲗ) vb. tr. (1) to spend, expend, dispose of, use up (ⲙ̄ⲙⲟ⸗); (2) to put forth, send forth (ⲙ̄ⲙⲟ⸗; to, onto: ⲉ, ⲉϫⲛ̄, ⲉϩⲟⲩⲛ ⲉ). ϫⲉ-ⲛⲟⲩⲛⲉ ⲉⲃⲟⲗ to take root.

ϫⲟ (pl. ϫⲱⲟⲩ) n.m. arm-pit; ⲟ ⲛ̄ ϫⲟ to be hunch-backed.

ϫⲟⲉ, ϫⲟⲓⲉ, ϫⲟⲉⲓ, ϫⲟⲓ, ϫⲟ (pl. ⲉϫⲏ) n.f. wall. ϫⲉ-ⲛ̄-ⲧⲙⲏⲧⲉ, ϫⲉⲛⲉⲧⲙⲏⲧⲉ n.f. middle wall.

ϫⲟⲉⲓⲥ, ϫⲟⲓⲥ (abbrev. ϫ︦ⲥ︦; pl. ϫⲓⲥⲟⲟⲩⲉ, ϫⲓⲥⲟⲟⲩ) n.m.f. lord, lady; with def. art. the Lord; master, owner. ⲣ̄-ϫⲟⲉⲓⲥ to become lord, rule (over: ⲉ, ⲉϫⲛ̄, ⲉϩⲣⲁⲓ ⲉϫⲛ̄); ⲣⲉϥⲣ̄-ϫⲟⲉⲓⲥ ruler. ⲙⲛ̄ⲧϫⲟⲉⲓⲥ lordship.

ϫⲟⲉⲓⲧ, ϫⲁⲉⲓⲧ (ϫⲓⲧ-) n.m. olive-tree, olives; n.m.f. testi-cle. ⲃⲱ ⲛ̄ ϫⲟⲉⲓⲧ olive-tree. ⲙⲁ ⲛ̄ ϫⲟⲉⲓⲧ olive grove. ϣⲉ ⲛ̄ ϫⲟⲉⲓⲧ olive wood. ϭ̄ⲃ-ⲛ̄-ϫⲟⲉⲓⲧ olive-leaf. ⲡⲧⲟⲟⲩ ⲛ̄ ϫⲟⲉⲓⲧ the Mt. of Olives.

ϫⲟⲓ, ϫⲟⲉⲓ (pl. ⲉϫⲏⲩ) n.m. ship, boat.

ϫⲟⲕ, ϫⲁⲕ n.m. hair.

ϫⲟⲕϫⲕ̄, ϫⲉⲕϫⲱⲕ⸗ Q ϫⲉⲕϫⲱⲕ (ϫⲉⲕϫⲟⲕⲧ̄) vb. tr. to stamp, brand, mark (ⲙ̄ⲙⲟ⸗); as n.m. stamp, brand.

ϫⲟⲗϩ̄ Q to be least, smallest.

ϫⲟⲗϫⲗ̄ (ϫⲟⲗϫⲉⲗ) ϫⲗ̄ϫⲗ̄- ϫⲗ̄ϫⲱⲗ⸗ vb. tr./intr. to drip, let drip.

ϫⲟⲗϫⲗ̄ ϫⲉⲗϫⲗ̄- (ϫⲗ̄ϫⲗ̄-) ϫⲗ̄ϫⲱⲗⸯ Q ϫⲗ̄ϫⲱⲗ vb. tr. to hedge in
(ⲙ̄ⲙⲟⸯ); as n.m. hedge.

ϫⲟⲟⲗⲉⲥ n.f. moth. ⲣ̄-ϫⲟⲟⲗⲉⲥ to become moth-eaten, decayed.

ϫⲟⲟⲩ (ϫⲟⲩ, ϫⲁⲩ) ϫⲉⲩ- (ϫⲟⲟⲩ-, ϫⲁⲩ-) ϫⲟⲟⲩⸯ (ϫⲟⲩⸯ) vb. tr. to
send (ⲙ̄ⲙⲟⸯ; to: ⲉ, ⲉⲣⲁⲧⸯ, ⲉϫⲛ̄, ⲛⲁⸯ, ϣⲁ) ± ⲉⲃⲟⲗ out, off,
away; ⲉϩⲟⲩⲛ in; ⲉϩⲣⲁⲓ up; ϩⲁⲑⲏ ahead. ϫⲟⲟⲩ ⲛ̄ⲥⲁ to send
after.

ϫⲟⲟⲩⲧ adj. base, lowly, rejected. ⲙⲛ̄ⲧϫⲟⲟⲩⲧ, ⲙⲛ̄ⲧⲣⲉϥϫⲟⲟⲩⲧ
baseness. ⲣ̄-ϫⲟⲟⲩⲧ to become base, lowly.

ϫⲟⲟⲩϥ n.m. papyrus.

ϫⲟⲡ n.m. bowl, dish.

ϫⲟⲣϫ̄ⲣ̄ ϭⲉⲣϭⲱⲣ Q ϫⲉⲣϫⲱⲣ vb. tr. to overcome; Q to be hard.

ϫⲟⲩⲱⲧ (ϫⲟⲩⲧ-, ϫⲁⲩⲧ-, ϫⲱⲧ-, ϫⲟⲧ-; f. ϫⲟⲩⲱⲧⲉ, ϫⲟⲩⲟⲩⲱⲧⲉ)
number: twenty. See 30.7.

ϫⲟⲩϥ (ϫⲟⲩⲃ, ϫⲛⲟⲩϥ, ϫⲱϥ) ϫⲉϥ- Q ϫⲏϥ (ϫⲏⲃ) vb. tr. to burn,
scorch (ⲙ̄ⲙⲟⸯ); intr. to be sharp, bitter; as n.m. burning, ardor. ϫⲟⲩϥ ⲛ̄ ϩⲏⲧ n.m. warmth of heart, esp. in
ϩⲛ̄ ⲟⲩϫⲟⲩϥ ⲛ̄ ϩⲏⲧ warmly, sincerely, ardently.

ϫⲟⲩϥ (ϫⲱϥ) ϫⲟⲃⸯ Q ϫⲏϥ vb. intr. to be costly, rare; tr. to
value.

ϫⲟⲩϩⲉ vb. intr. to limp.

ϫⲟⲩϫⲟⲩ, ϭⲟⲩϭⲟⲩ vb. intr. to fly (or sim., of birds).

ϫⲟϥⲧⲛ̄ in ⲛ̄ ϫⲟϥⲧⲛ̄ headlong, over the edge.

ϫⲟϥϫⲩ̄ (ϫⲟⲃϫⲃ̄, ϫⲟϥϫⲉϥ) ϫⲉϥϫⲱϥⸯ Q ϫⲉϥϫⲱϥ vb. tr. to burn,
cook; intr. idem.

ϫⲡ̄-, ϫⲉⲡ- n.m.f. hour; usually prefixed to number, as in
ϫⲡ̄-ⲙⲛ̄ⲧⲟⲩⲉ the 11th hour. ⲙ̄ ⲡⲛⲁⲩ ⲛ̄ ϫⲡ̄-X at about the
Xth hour.

ϫⲡⲓ-, ϫⲡⲉ- vb. must; usually prefixed to Inf., as in ϥⲛⲁϫⲡⲓ-
ⲃⲱⲕ; rarely impers.: it is necessary (that: ⲉⲧⲣⲉ).

ϫⲡⲓⲟ ϫⲡⲓⲉ- ϫⲡⲓⲟⸯ Q ϫⲡⲓⲏⲧ vb. tr. to blame, scold, reproach
(ⲙ̄ⲙⲟⸯ; for: ⲉⲧⲃⲉ, ⲉϫⲛ̄, ϩⲁ, ϩⲛ̄); as n.m. blame, reproach.
ⲙⲛ̄ⲧϫⲡⲓⲏⲧ modesty.

ϫⲡⲟ ϫⲡⲉ- ϫⲡⲟⸯ vb. tr. (1) to beget, give birth to (ⲙ̄ⲙⲟⸯ);
(2) to acquire, get, obtain (ⲙ̄ⲙⲟⸯ), oft. + eth. dat. w.

 naˢ. As n.m. birth, begetting; acquisition, gain, possession. ⲁⲧⲭⲡⲟϥ unbegotten. ⲣⲉϥⲭⲡⲟ maker, begetter; ⲙⲛⲧⲣⲉϥⲭⲡⲟ begetting.

ⲭⲣⲟ (ϭⲣⲟ) Q ⲭⲣⲁⲉⲓⲧ (ⲭⲣⲟⲉⲓⲧ, ϭⲣⲟⲉⲓⲧ) vb. intr. to become strong, firm, victorious (over: ⲉ, ⲉⲭⲛ); vb. tr. to make strong; as n.m. strength, victory. ϯ-ⲭⲣⲟ naˢ to encourage, confirm. ⲥⲙⲛ-ⲭⲣⲟ to establish victory. ⲁⲧ-ⲭⲣⲟ unconquerable. ⲙⲁⲓ-ⲭⲣⲟ victory-loving. ⲣⲉϥⲭⲣⲟ victor, victorious. ⲭⲟⲟⲣ Q to be strong, bold, hard. ⲭⲁⲣ-ⲃⲁⲗ bold of sight, staring; ⲙⲛⲧⲭⲁⲣ-ⲃⲁⲗ staring. ⲭⲁⲣ-ϩⲏⲧ firm of heart, bold; ⲙⲛⲧⲭⲁⲣ-ϩⲏⲧ courage, boldness; ϯ-ⲙⲛⲧⲭⲁⲣ-ϩⲏⲧ to give courage (to: naˢ); ⲭⲓ-ⲙⲛⲧⲭⲁⲣ-ϩⲏⲧ to take courage. ⲭⲱⲱⲣⲉ, ⲭⲱⲱⲣ, ⲭⲱⲣ adj. strong, bold (bef. or aft. n. with ⲛ). ⲣ̄-ⲭⲱⲱⲣⲉ to become strong. ⲙⲛⲧⲭⲱⲱⲣⲉ strength, prowess.

ⲭⲧⲟ (ϣⲧⲟ) ⲭⲧⲉ- ⲭⲧⲟˢ (ϣⲧⲟˢ, ϣⲧⲁˢ) Q ⲭⲧⲏⲩ (ϣⲧⲏⲩ) vb. tr. to lay down (ⲙ̄ⲙⲟˢ; on: ⲉ, ⲉⲭⲛ, ϩⲛ, ϩⲓⲭⲛ); intr. to lie down. ⲭⲧⲟ ⲉ ⲡϣⲱⲛⲉ to succumb to sickness.

ⲭⲱ n.m. cup.

ⲭⲱˢ n.m. head (§28.6). Rare except in prep. phrases or as the obj. in certain verbal expressions. ⲉⲭⲛ ⲉⲭⲱˢ prep. (1) on, upon, over, above; (2) for, on account of; (3) at, against; (4) to, unto; (5) in addition to. ⲉⲃⲟⲗ ⲉⲭⲛ out upon; ⲉϩⲟⲩⲛ ⲉⲭⲛ unto; ⲉϩⲣⲁⲓ ⲉⲭⲛ up/down onto, upon. ϩⲁⲭⲛ ϩⲁⲭⲱˢ prep. before, in front of. ϩⲓⲭⲛ ϩⲓⲭⲱˢ prep. (1) on, upon, over; (2) in, at, beside; (3) ± ⲉⲃⲟⲗ from on, from at; ⲡⲉⲧ ϩⲓⲭⲛ the one in command of; ϩⲣⲁⲓ ϩⲓⲭⲛ on, upon.

ⲭⲱ ⲭⲉ- ⲭⲟˢ vb. tr. to sing; as n.m. song. ⲣⲉϥⲭⲱ (pl. ⲣⲉϥ-ⲭⲟⲟⲩⲉ) singer, minstrel.

ⲭⲱ ⲭⲉ- (ⲭⲓ-) ⲭⲟⲟˢ (imptv. ⲁⲭⲓ-, ⲁⲭⲓˢ) vb. tr. to say, speak (ⲙ̄ⲙⲟˢ; to: ⲉ, naˢ; about, concerning: ⲉ, ⲉⲧⲃⲉ, ⲉⲭⲛ, ⲉϩⲣⲁⲓ ⲉⲭⲛ; against: ⲛⲥⲁ, ⲟⲩⲃⲉ). ⲁⲧⲭⲱ, ⲁⲧⲭⲟⲟˢ ineffable. ⲣⲉϥ-ⲭⲉ- one who says; ⲙⲛⲧⲣⲉϥⲭⲉ- saying, telling. ⲭⲉⲣⲟ- (for ⲭⲱ ⲉⲣⲟˢ) to mean, signify; to say to. ⲡⲉⲭⲉ-, ⲡⲉⲭⲁˢ said (before direct quotation; see 20.3).

ⲭⲱⲕ ⲭⲉⲕ- ⲭⲟⲕ⸗ Q ⲭⲏⲕ (± ⲉⲃⲟⲗ) vb. tr. to finish, complete, fulfill, accomplish (ⲙ̄ⲙⲟ⸗); vb. intr. to become finished, completed, fulfilled, ended; as n.m. completion, end; total; fulfillment. ⲁⲧⲭⲱⲕ without end.

ⲭⲱⲕⲙ̄ ⲭⲉⲕⲙ̄- ⲭⲟⲕⲙ⸗ (ⲭⲁⲕⲙ⸗) Q ⲭⲟⲕⲙ̄ vb. tr. to wet, wash (ⲙ̄ⲙⲟ⸗; in, with: ⲍ̄ⲛ̄, ⲉⲃⲟⲗ ⲍ̄ⲛ̄); as n.m. washing, cleansing. +- ⲭⲱⲕⲙ̄ ⲛⲁ⸗ to bathe, baptize. ⲭⲓ-ⲭⲱⲕⲙ̄ to be bathed, baptized. ⲁⲧⲭⲱⲕⲙ̄ unwashed; ⲙ̄ⲛ̄ⲧⲁⲧⲭⲱⲕⲙ̄ being unwashed.

ⲭⲱⲕⲡ̄ ⲭⲉⲕⲡ̄- ⲭⲟⲕⲡ⸗ Q ⲭⲟⲕⲡ̄ vb. tr. to salt, season.

ⲭⲱⲗⲕ̄ vb. tr./intr. to sink, submerge.

ⲭⲱⲗⲕ̄ ⲭⲉⲗⲕ̄- ⲭⲟⲗⲕ⸗ Q ⲭⲟⲗⲕ̄ (± ⲉⲃⲟⲗ) vb. tr. to extend, stretch ⲙ̄ⲙⲟ⸗; to: ⲉ, ⲉⲍⲟⲩⲛ ⲉ); to sew together. ⲭⲱⲗⲕ̄ ⲉⲃⲟⲗ as n.m. stretching, strain; extent; endurance, continuation. ⲭⲁⲗⲕ n.m. strain; punishment. ⲭⲟⲗⲕⲥ̄ n.f. strain, tension.

ⲭⲱⲗⲙ̄ (ⲭⲱⲣⲙ̄) Q ⲭⲟⲗⲙ̄ (ⲭⲟⲣⲙ̄) vb. intr. (1) to make merry; (2) to become implicated, involved (in, with: ⲙⲛ̄, ⲍ̄ⲛ̄); as n.m. (1) festivity, dissipation; (2) care, distraction. ⲭⲟⲗⲙ(ⲉ)ⲥ, ⲭⲟⲣⲙ(ⲉ)ⲥ n. care, distraction.

ⲭⲱⲗⲍ̄ ⲭⲗ̄ⲍ- ⲭⲟⲗⲍ⸗ vb. tr. to cut, prune.

ⲭⲱⲗⲍ̄ (ⲭⲱⲗⲁⲍ, ⲭⲱⲣⲁⲍ) ⲭⲉⲗⲉⲍ- ⲭⲟⲗⲍ⸗ (± ⲉⲃⲟⲗ) vb. tr. to draw, scoop (ⲙ̄ⲙⲟ⸗). ⲭⲟⲗⲍⲉⲥ, ⲭⲟⲗⲍⲥ̄, ⲭⲟⲗ(ⲉ)ⲥ n.f. vessel for pouring.

ⲭⲱⲙ n.m. generation. ⲭⲓⲛ ⲭⲱⲙ ϣⲁ ⲭⲱⲙ, ⲉⲩⲭⲱⲙ ⲛ̄ ⲛ̄ⲭⲱⲙ, ⲛ̄ ⲍⲉⲛ- ⲭⲱⲙ ⲛ̄ ⲭⲱⲙ from generation to generation. ϣⲁⲭⲉ ⲛ̄ ⲭⲱⲙ genealogy.

ⲭⲱⲛⲧ̄ ⲭⲛ̄ⲧ- (ⲭⲉⲛⲧ̄-) ⲭⲟⲛⲧ⸗ Q ⲭⲟⲛⲧ̄ vb. tr. (1) to try, test (ⲙ̄ⲙⲟ⸗, ⲉ; with: ⲍ̄ⲛ̄); (2) to begin, start; as n.m. trial; ⲙⲁ ⲛ̄ ⲭⲱⲛⲧ̄ place of testing. ⲭⲟⲛⲧⲥ̄ n.f. trial, test. ⲭⲛⲓⲧ in ⲭⲓ-ⲭⲛⲓⲧ to test, try (ⲙ̄ⲙⲟ⸗, ⲛ̄ⲥⲁ); as n.m. test, trial; ⲣⲉϥⲭⲓ-ⲭⲛⲓⲧ tester.

ⲭⲱⲛϥ̄ (ϣⲱⲛϥ̄) Q ⲭⲟⲟⲛⲉϥ vb. impersonal: to happen, befall by chance; personal: to happen to be; vb. tr. to meet with (ⲉ) by chance; as n.m. chance.

ⲭⲱⲣ Q ⲭⲏⲣ vb. tr. to blacken.

ϫⲱⲣ ϫⲟⲟⲣ⸗ vb. tr. to study, examine. As n.m. spy, scout.

ϫⲱⲣ ϫⲉⲣ- ϫⲟⲣ⸗ Q ϫⲏⲣ vb. tr. to sharpen; as n.m. sharpness.

ϫⲱⲣⲙ̄ Q ϫⲟⲣⲙ̄ vb. intr. to make a sign (to: ⲉ, ⲟⲩⲃⲉ; with: ⲙ̄ⲙⲟ⸗, ϩⲛ̄), to beckon; vb. tr. to indicate (ⲙ̄ⲙⲟ⸗); as n.m. sign, indication.

ϫⲱⲣⲙ̄ Q ϫⲟⲣⲙ̄ vb. tr. to urge on, hasten (ⲙ̄ⲙⲟ⸗); intr. to ride fast, hasten (after: ⲛ̄ⲥⲁ). ⲙⲁ ⲛ̄ ϫⲱⲣⲙ̄ training stable. ⲣⲉϥϫⲱⲣⲙ̄ rider.

ϫⲱⲣⲛ̄ vb. intr. to stumble, trip. ϫⲣⲟⲡ n.m. obstacle, impediment; ⲁⲧϫⲣⲟⲡ unimpeded; ⲣ̄-ϫⲣⲟⲡ to become an obstacle, difficulty; ϯ-ϫⲣⲟⲡ to trip up (ⲛⲁ⸗), cause difficulty for; ϫⲓ-ϫⲣⲟⲡ to stumble, trip, be impeded.

ϫⲱⲥ Q ϫⲏⲥ vb. tr. to load, pack (ⲙ̄ⲙⲟ⸗; with: ⲙ̄ⲙⲟ⸗); intr. to become hard, solid.

ϫⲱⲧⲉ (ϫⲱⲧ) ϫⲉⲧ- ϫⲟⲧ⸗ (± ⲉϩⲟⲩⲛ) vb. tr. to pierce, penetrate (ⲙ̄ⲙⲟ⸗; to, as far as: ⲉ, ϣⲁ, ϩⲛ̄); as n.m. penetration, separation.

ϫⲱⲧϩ̄ Q ϫⲟⲧϩ̄ vb. intr. to fail, cease.

ϫⲱⲱⲃⲉ (ϫⲱⲱϥⲉ, ϫⲱϥⲉ) ϫⲉⲉⲃⲉ- ϫⲟⲟⲃ⸗ vb. tr. to reach, pass, surpass (ⲙ̄ⲙⲟ⸗); ⲁⲧϫⲟⲟⲃ⸗ impassable.

ϫⲱⲱⲕⲉ (ϫⲱⲕⲉ, ϫⲟⲩⲟⲩⲕⲉ) ϫⲉⲉⲕⲉ- (ϫⲉⲕ-) ϫⲟⲟⲕ⸗ vb. tr. to sting, prick, goad (ⲙ̄ⲙⲟ⸗). ϫⲟⲟⲕⲉϥ n.m. goad.

ϫⲱⲱⲗⲉ Q ϫⲟⲟⲗⲉ vb. intr. to be hindered.

ϫⲱⲱⲗⲉ (ϫⲱⲗⲉ) ϫⲉⲉⲗⲉ- (ϫⲉⲗⲉ-) ϫⲟⲟⲗ⸗ (ϫⲟⲗ⸗) vb. tr. to gather, harvest (ⲙ̄ⲙⲟ⸗); as n.m. harvest. ⲣⲉϥϫⲱⲱⲗⲉ harvester. ϫⲁ̄ⲗⲉ n. gleanings, left-over crops.

ϫⲱⲱⲙⲉ, ϫⲱⲙⲉ n.m. book, document, book-roll, sheet of parchment; as adj. book- (with parts or types of books); ϫⲱⲱⲙⲉ ⲛ̄ ⲱϣ reading book.

ϫⲱⲱⲣⲉ (ϫⲱⲣⲉ) ϫⲉⲉⲣⲉ- (ϫⲉⲣⲉ-, ϭⲉⲣ-) ϫⲟⲟⲣ⸗ (ϫⲟⲣ⸗) Q ϫⲟⲟⲣⲉ vb. tr. to scatter, disperse (ⲙ̄ⲙⲟ⸗); + ⲉⲃⲟⲗ idem; to hinder, bring to naught (ⲙ̄ⲙⲟ⸗); as n.m. scattering, dissolution.

ϫⲱⲱϭⲉ (ϫⲱϭⲉ) ϫⲉϭ- ϫⲟϭ⸗ (ϫⲟϫ⸗, ϫⲁⲕ⸗) Q ϫⲏϭ vb. tr. to dye, stain (ⲙ̄ⲙⲟ⸗; with: ϩⲛ̄, ⲉⲃⲟⲗ ϩⲛ̄); intr. to become dyed, stained; as n.m. dyeing; ⲣⲉϥϫⲉϭ- dyer of. ϫⲏϭⲉ, ϫⲏⲕⲉ, ϫⲉⲕⲉ n.m. purple dye; as adj. purple; ⲉⲓⲉⲡ-ⲭⲏϭⲉ purple embroidery; ⲥⲁ ⲛ̄ ⲭⲏϭⲉ seller of purple.

ϫⲱϩ (ϫⲟϩ) ϫⲉϩ- Q ϫⲏϩ vb. tr. to touch (ⲉ, ⲉϩⲟⲩⲛ ⲉ); as n.m. touching, contagion. ⲁⲧϫⲱϩ ⲉⲣⲟ⸗ untouchable.

ϫⲱϩ ϫⲉϩ- ϫⲁϩ⸗ Q ϫⲏϩ vb. tr. to smear, anoint (ⲙ̄ⲙⲟ⸗, ⲉ; with: ⲙ̄ⲙⲟ⸗, ϩⲛ̄).

ϫⲱϩⲙ̄ ϫⲉϩⲙ̄ ϫⲁϩⲙ⸗ Q ϫⲁϩⲙ̄ vb. tr. to defile, pollute (ⲙ̄ⲙⲟ⸗); to become defiled, polluted (with, by: ϩⲛ̄, ⲉⲃⲟⲗ ϩⲛ̄); as n.m. pollution, uncleanness. ⲁⲧϫⲱϩⲙ̄ undefiled. ⲣⲉϥ-ϫⲱϩⲙ̄ defiled person.

ϫⲱϫ, ⲁⲛϫⲱϫ n.m. head, chief. ϣⲛ̄-ϫⲱϫ headache. ⲣ̄-ϫⲱϫ to become head, chief.

ϫⲁⲁⲛⲉ: ϫⲁⲛⲉ	ϫⲉⲉⲗⲉ-: ϫⲱⲱⲗⲉ	ϫⲏⲏⲃⲥ̄: ϫⲃ̄ⲃⲥ̄
ϫⲁⲁⲧⲉ: ϫⲁⲧⲉ	ϫⲉⲉⲣⲉ: ϫⲏⲣⲉ	ϫⲏⲓⲃⲉⲥ: ϫⲃ̄ⲃⲥ̄
ϫⲁⲁϫⲉ: ϫⲁϫⲉ	ϫⲉⲉⲣⲉ-: ϫⲉⲣⲟ, ϫⲱⲱⲣⲉ	ϫⲏⲕⲉ: ϫⲱⲱϭⲉ
ϫⲁⲃ: ϫⲁϥ	ϫⲉⲕ-: ϫⲱⲱⲕⲉ	ϫⲏⲛⲏ: ϫⲛⲉ
ϫⲁⲉ: ϫⲁⲉⲓⲉ	ϫⲉⲕⲉ: ϫⲏϭⲉ	ϫⲏⲡⲉ2: ϫⲉⲙⲡⲉ2
ϫⲁⲉⲓⲃⲉⲥ: ϫⲃ̄ⲃⲥ̄	ϫⲉⲗⲉ-: ϫⲱⲱⲗⲉ	ϫⲏⲥⲉ: ϫⲓⲥⲉ
ϫⲁⲉⲓⲧ: ϫⲟⲉⲓⲧ	ϫⲉⲗⲉϫ-: ϭⲱⲗϫ̄	ϫⲏⲧ: ϫⲁⲧⲉ
ϫⲁⲓ-: ϫⲓ	ϫⲉⲗⲗⲏⲥ: ϫⲉⲗ2ⲏⲥ	ϫⲏⲩ: ϫⲓ, ϫⲟ
ϫⲁⲓⲉ: ϫⲁⲉⲓⲉ	ϫⲉⲗⲗⲏⲥ: ϫⲓⲗⲗⲉⲥ	ϫⲏϥ: ϫⲟⲩϥ
ϫⲁⲕ⸗: ϫⲱⲱϭⲉ	ϫⲉⲛ: ϫⲓⲛ	ϫⲏϭ: ϫⲱⲱϭⲉ
ϫⲁⲕ: ϫⲟⲕ	ϫⲉⲛⲁ(⸗): ϫⲛⲁ	ϫⲏϭⲉ: ϫⲱⲱϭⲉ
ϫⲁⲕⲙ⸗: ϫⲱⲕⲙ̄	ϫⲉⲛⲉⲧⲙⲏⲧⲉ: ϫⲟⲉ	ϫⲓ-: ϫⲓ, ϫⲟ, ϫⲱ
ϫⲁⲙⲏ: ϭⲁϫⲙⲏ	ϫⲉⲛⲟⲃ, ϫⲉⲛⲟϥ: ϫⲛⲟϥ	ϫⲓⲃⲏⲗ: ϫⲉⲃⲏⲗ
ϫⲁⲛⲏ: ϫⲁⲛⲉ	ϫⲉⲛⲟⲩⲟⲩ⸗: ϫⲛⲟⲩ	ϫⲓⲛ: ϫⲛ̄
ϫⲁⲣ-: ϫⲣⲟ	ϫⲉⲛⲧⲙⲏⲧⲉ: ϫⲟⲉ	ϫⲓⲛⲟⲩ⸗: ϫⲛⲟⲩ
ϫⲁⲥⲓ-: ϫⲓⲥⲉ	ϫⲉⲡⲏ2: ϫⲉⲙⲡⲉ2	ϫⲓⲛⲟⲩ⸗: ϫⲛⲟⲩ
ϫⲁⲥⲧ⸗: ϫⲓⲥⲉ	ϫⲉⲣⲉ-: ϫⲱⲱⲣⲉ	ϫⲓⲛⲧⲏⲩ: ⲧⲏⲩ
ϫⲁⲧⲃⲉ: ϫⲁⲧϥⲉ	ϫⲉⲣⲉ-: ϫⲉⲣⲟ	ϫⲓⲛϫⲉⲉⲩ(ⲉ): ϫⲁϫⲉ
ϫⲁⲩ(-): ϫⲟⲟⲩ	ϫⲉⲣⲟ-: ϫⲱ	ϫⲓⲛϫⲉⲩⲉ: ϫⲁϫⲉ
ϫⲁⲩⲧ-: ϫⲟⲩⲱⲧ	ϫⲉⲣⲱ(⸗): ϫⲉⲣⲟ	ϫⲓⲛϫⲓⲛ: ϭⲛ̄ϭⲛ̄
ϫⲁ2⸗: ϫⲱ2	ϫⲉⲣⲭⲣ̄: ϫⲏⲣ	ϫⲓⲟⲟⲣ: ⲉⲓⲟⲟⲣ
ϫⲁ2ⲙ(⸗): ϫⲱ2ⲙ̄	ϫⲉⲥⲉ: ϫⲓⲥⲉ	ϫⲓⲡⲉ2: ϫⲉⲙⲡⲉ2
ϫⲁ2ϫ̄: ϫⲁ2ϫ̄2	ϫⲉⲥⲧ̄-: ϫⲓⲥⲉ	ϫⲓⲣⲱϥ: ⲣⲟ
ϫⲁϫⲱ(ⲟⲩ): ϫⲁϫⲉ	ϫⲉⲧ-: ϫⲱⲧⲉ	ϫⲓⲧ⸗: ϫⲓ, ϫⲟⲉⲓⲧ
ϫⲁϫ̄2: ϫⲁ2ϫ̄2	ϫⲉⲩ-: ϫⲟⲟⲩ	ϫⲓⲥⲟⲟⲩ(ⲉ): ϫⲟⲉⲓⲥ
ϫⲃⲏⲗ: ϫⲉⲃⲏⲗ	ϫⲉϥ-: ϫⲟⲩϥ	ϫⲓⲥⲧ⸗: ϫⲓⲥⲉ
ϫⲃ̄ⲥ: ϫⲃ̄ⲃⲥ̄	ϫⲉϥϣⲗ: ϣⲗ	ϫⲓϫⲉⲉⲩ(ⲉ),
ϫⲉ: ϫⲛ̄, ϭⲉ	ϫⲉ2ϫⲱ2⸗: ϫⲁ2ϫ̄2	ϫⲓϫⲉⲟⲩ: ϫⲁϫⲉ
ϫⲉ-: ϫⲟ, ϫⲱ, ϫⲓ	ϫⲉϫ-: ϭⲱⲱϫⲉ	ϫⲁ̄ⲗⲉ: ϫⲱⲱⲗⲉ
ϫⲉⲃⲃⲉⲥ, ϫⲉⲃⲃⲥ̄: ϫⲃ̄ⲃⲥ̄	ϫⲉϭ-: ϫⲱⲱϭⲉ	ϫⲁ̄2ⲏⲥ: ϫⲉⲗ2ⲏⲥ
ϫⲉⲃⲉⲗ: ϫⲉⲃⲏⲗ	ϫⲏ: ϫⲓⲛϫⲏ	ϫⲁ̄2ⲥ̄: ϫⲉⲗ2ⲏⲥ
ϫⲉⲉⲃⲉ-: ϫⲱⲱⲃⲉ	ϫⲏⲃ: ϫⲟⲩϥ	ϫⲙ̄ϫⲙ̄: ϭⲛ̄ϭⲛ̄
ϫⲉⲉⲕⲉ-: ϫⲱⲱⲕⲉ	ϫⲏⲃⲥ̄: ϫⲃ̄ⲃⲥ̄	ϫⲛ̄: ϫⲓⲛ, ϫⲛⲟⲩ

ϫⲛⲁⲁⲩ: ϫⲛⲁⲩ, ϫⲛⲟⲟⲩ	ϫⲟⲟⲗⲉ: ϫⲱⲱⲗⲉ	ϫⲣⲟⲡ: ϫⲱⲣⲛ̄
ϫⲛⲁⲩϩ: ϫⲛⲁϩ	ϫⲟⲟⲛⲉ: ϫⲁⲛⲉ	ϫⲣⲁⲉⲓⲧ: ϫⲣⲟ
ϫⲛⲉ(-): ϫⲛⲁ, ϫⲛⲟⲩ	ϫⲟⲟⲛⲉϥ: ϫⲱⲛϥ̄	ϫⲣⲟⲉⲓⲧ: ϫⲣⲟ
ϫⲛⲏ: ϫⲛⲉ	ϫⲟⲟⲣ': ϫⲱⲱⲣⲉ	ϫⲥ̅: ϫⲟⲉⲓⲥ
ϫⲛⲓⲧ: ϫⲱⲛⲧ̄	ϫⲟⲟⲣ': ϫⲱⲣ	ϫⲧⲁⲓ: ϫⲁⲧⲉ
ϫⲛⲟ': ϫⲛⲁ'	ϫⲟⲟⲣ: ϫⲣⲟ	ϫⲧⲉ-: ϫⲧⲟ
ϫⲛⲟⲩϥ: ϫⲟⲩϥ	ϫⲟⲟⲩⲉ: ϫⲱ	ϫⲧⲏⲩ: ϫⲧⲟ
ϫⲛ̄ϫⲛ̄: ϭⲛ̄ϭⲛ̄	ϫⲟⲡϫⲛ̄: ϩϫⲟⲡϫⲛ̄	ϫⲱⲕⲉ: ϫⲱⲱⲕⲉ
ϫⲟ': ϫⲟ, ϫⲱ	ϫⲟⲣ': ϫⲱⲱⲣⲉ	ϫⲱⲗⲉ: ϫⲱⲱⲗⲉ
ϫⲟ: ϫⲟⲉ	ϫⲟⲣⲛ̄: ϫⲱⲗⲙ̄	ϫⲱⲗϫ̄: ϭⲱⲗϫ̄
ϫⲟⲃ': ϫⲟⲩϥ	ϫⲟⲣⲙⲉⲥ: ϫⲱⲗⲙ̄	ϫⲱⲙⲉ: ϫⲱⲱⲙⲉ
ϫⲟⲃϫⲃ̄: ϫⲟϥϫϥ̄	ϫⲟⲥⲉ: ϫⲓⲥⲉ	ϫⲱⲟⲩ-: ϫⲟ
ϫⲟⲉⲓ: ϫⲟⲓ, ϫⲟⲉ	ϫⲟⲧ': ϫⲱⲧⲉ	ϫⲱⲣ(ⲉ): ϫⲱⲱⲣⲉ, ϫⲣⲟ
ϫⲟⲓ, ϫⲟⲓⲉ: ϫⲟⲉ	ϫⲟⲧ-: ϫⲟⲩⲱⲧ	ϫⲱⲣⲁϩ: ϫⲱⲗϩ̄
ϫⲟⲗ': ϫⲱⲗϩ̄	ϫⲟⲧⲉ: ϫⲁⲧⲉ	ϫⲱⲣⲛ̄: ϫⲱⲗⲙ̄
ϫⲟⲗⲉⲥ: ϫⲱⲗϩ̄	ϫⲟⲩ, ϫⲟⲩ': ϫⲟⲟⲩ	ϫⲱⲧ-: ϫⲟⲩⲱⲧ
ϫⲟⲗⲙⲉⲥ: ϫⲱⲗⲙ̄	ϫⲟⲩⲃ: ϫⲟⲩϥ	ϫⲱⲧ-: ϫⲱⲧⲉ
ϫⲟⲗⲥ̄: ϫⲱⲗϩ̄	ϫⲟⲩⲟⲩⲕⲉ: ϫⲱⲱⲕⲉ	ϫⲱⲧϩ̄: ϭⲱⲧϩ̄
ϫⲟⲗϩⲉⲥ, ϫⲟⲗϩⲥ̄: ϫⲱⲗϩ̄	ϫⲟⲩⲟⲩⲱⲧⲉ: ϫⲟⲩⲱⲧ	ϫⲱⲟⲣ: ϫⲣⲟ
ϫⲟⲗϫ', ϫⲟⲗϫ̄: ϭⲱⲗϫ̄	ϫⲟⲩⲧ-: ϫⲟⲩⲱⲧ	ϫⲱⲟⲣⲉ: ϫⲣⲟ
ϫⲟⲛⲧⲥ̄: ϫⲱⲛⲧ̄	ϫⲟϫ': ϫⲱⲱϭⲉ	ϫⲱⲱϫⲉ: ϫⲱⲱⲃⲉ
ϫⲟⲟⲃ': ϫⲱⲱⲃⲉ	ϫⲟϭ': ϫⲱⲱϭⲉ	ϫⲱϥ: ϫⲟⲩϥ
ϫⲟⲟⲕ': ϫⲱⲱⲕⲉ	ϫⲡⲉ-: ϫⲡⲟ, ϫⲡⲓ-	ϫⲱϥⲉ: ϫⲱⲱⲃⲉ
ϫⲟⲟⲕⲉϥ: ϫⲱⲱⲕⲉ	ϫⲡⲓⲉ-: ϫⲡⲓⲟ	ϫⲱϭⲉ: ϫⲱⲱϭⲉ
ϫⲟⲟⲗ': ϫⲱⲱⲗⲉ	ϫⲡⲓⲏⲧ: ϫⲡⲓⲟ	ϫϩⲟⲥ: ϭϩⲟⲥ

6

ϭⲁⲃϭⲁⲃ, ϭⲁϥϭⲁϥ, ⲕⲁϥⲕⲁϥ, ϭⲁⲃϭⲏⲃ n. chick-pea.

ϭⲁⲗⲗⲁϩⲧ̄, ⲕⲁⲗⲗⲁϩⲧ̄ n.f. pot.

ϭⲁⲗⲉ, ϭⲁⲗⲏ (pl. ϭⲁⲗⲉⲉⲩ, ϭⲁⲗⲉⲉⲩⲉ, ϭⲁⲗⲉⲩⲉ) adj. lame, crippled; ⲙⲛ̄ⲧϭⲁⲗⲉ lameness; ⲣ̄-ϭⲁⲗⲉ (Q o ⲛ̄) to become lame.

ϭⲁⲗⲓⲧⲉ n.f. name of vessel or measure.

ϭⲁⲗⲟⲩⲃⲓϩ n.m. bald-headed person.

ϭⲁⲙ n. bull. (Doubtful.)

ϭⲁⲙⲟⲩⲗ, ⲕⲁⲙⲟⲩⲗ (f. ϭⲁⲙⲁⲩⲗⲉ, ⲕⲁⲙⲟⲟⲩⲗⲉ, ⲕⲁⲙⲏⲗⲉ; pl. ϭⲁⲙⲁⲩⲗⲉ, ϭⲁⲙⲟⲩⲗⲉ, ⲕⲁⲙⲟⲟⲩⲗⲉ) n.m.f. camel, camel-load. ⲙⲁⲛ-ϭⲁ-ⲙⲟⲩⲗ camelherd. ⲙⲁⲥ ⲛ̄ ϭⲁⲙⲁⲩⲗⲉ baby camel.

ϭⲁⲛⲁϩ n. or adj. maimed; ⲣ̄-ϭⲁⲛⲁϩ (Q o ⲛ̄) to become maimed.

ϭⲁⲟⲩⲟⲛ, ϭⲁⲩⲟⲛ, ϭⲁⲩⲟⲩⲟⲛ, ⲕⲁⲩⲟⲛ n.m.f. slave, servant. ⲙⲛ̄ⲧ-ϭⲁⲟⲩⲟⲛ service, servitude. ⲣ̄-ϭⲁⲟⲩⲟⲛ (Q o ⲛ̄) to become a slave.

ϭⲁⲟⲩⲟⲛ, ϭⲁⲩⲟⲛ n.m. a beverage.

ϭⲁⲡⲉⲓϫⲉ, ϭⲁⲡⲓϫⲉ, ϭⲁⲡⲓϫⲏ, ⲕⲁⲡⲓϫⲉ, ϭⲁⲡⲓϫⲟⲩ n.m.f. a dry

measure.

ϭⲁⲛϭⲉⲡ (ϭⲉⲛϭⲛ̅) vb. intr. to be hurried, anxious.

ϭⲁⲣⲁⲧⲉ n. carob pod.

ϭⲁⲝⲉ n.m. earring.

ϭⲁⲝⲓϥ, ϭⲁⲝⲓⲃ, ⲕⲁⲝⲓϥ n.m. ant. ⲣ̅-ϭⲁⲝⲓϥ to suffer from itch
    or warts.

ϭⲁⲝⲙⲏ̅, ϭⲁⲝⲙⲉ, ⲭⲁⲙⲏ n.f. fist, handful. ϭⲁⲝⲙⲉⲥ n.f. idem.

ϭⲁϭⲓⲧⲱⲛ(ⲉ) n.m.f. coarse linen, tow; coarse linen garment.

ϭⲃ̅ⲃⲉ, Q ϭⲟⲟⲃ (ϭⲟⲟϥ) vb. intr. to become feeble, timid; as
    n.m. weakness. ϭⲁⲃ-ϩⲏⲧ weak, feeble; ⲙⲛ̅ⲧϭⲁⲃ-ϩⲏⲧ weak-
    ness, timidity; ⲣ̅-ϭⲁⲃ-ϩⲏⲧ (Q ⲟ ⲛ̅) to become feeble.
    ϭⲱⲃ adj. weak, feeble; ⲙⲛ̅ⲧϭⲱⲃ weakness, folly; ⲣ̅-ϭⲱⲃ (Q
    ⲟ ⲛ̅) to become weak; ⲉⲓⲣⲉ ⲙ̅ⲙⲟ⸗ ⲛ̅ ϭⲱⲃ to make weak.

ϭⲃⲟⲓ, ϭⲃⲟⲉ n.m. arm (of person); leg (of animal).

ϭⲉ, ⲭⲉ postpositive particle (1) then, therefore, for;
    (2) with neg.: no more, not again. ⲧⲉⲛⲟⲩ ϭⲉ now then,
    and now, now moreover.

ϭⲉⲗⲙⲁⲓ, ϭⲗ̅ⲙⲁⲓ, ϭⲉⲗⲙⲁ, ⲕⲉⲗⲙⲁ, ϭⲁⲗⲙⲁ, ϭⲉⲗⲙⲏⲛ n.m. jar, vase.

ϭⲉⲗϩ̅, ϭⲗ̅ϩ, ϭⲗⲁϩ n.m. shoulder.

ϭⲉⲛⲛⲏⲩⲧ Q to be hard, stiff.

ϭⲉⲡⲏ, ϭⲓⲡⲏ vb. intr. to hurry, hasten, come quickly; may
    be used reflex. w. ⲙ̅ⲙⲟ⸗. As adv. quickly, in haste;
    usu. in phrase ϩⲛ̅ ⲟⲩϭⲉⲡⲏ. ⲣⲉϥϭⲉⲡⲏ one who is hasty,
    quick; ⲙⲛ̅ⲧⲣⲉϥϭⲉⲡⲏ hastiness.

ϭⲉⲣⲱⲃ, ϭⲉⲣⲱϥ (pl. ϭⲉⲣⲟⲟⲃ, ϭⲉⲣⲱⲱⲃ) n.m. staff, rod. ϯ-
    ϭⲉⲣⲱⲃ to beat (ⲛⲁ⸗, ⲉ). ϣⲥ̅-ⲛ̅-ϭⲉⲣⲱⲃ a blow.

ϭⲏⲡⲉ n.f. cloud.

ϭⲓⲉ, ϭⲓⲉⲓⲉ, ϭⲓⲏ n.m. he-goat.

ϭⲓⲛ-, ⲕⲓⲛ-, ϭⲛ̅- prefix added to any inf. to form an ab-
    stract noun (f.) of action or manner of action.

ϭⲓⲛⲉ ϭⲛ̅- (ϭⲉⲛ-, ϭⲓⲛ-) ϭⲛ̅ⲧ⸗ (ϭⲉⲛⲧ⸗, ⲕⲛ̅ⲧ⸗, ϭⲏⲛⲧ⸗, ⲅⲛ̅⸗) vb.
    tr. to find (ⲙ̅ⲙⲟ⸗). ϭⲛ̅ⲧⲥ̅ to find that (+ Circum. or
    ⲭⲉ); also: perhaps, suppose that. ϭⲓⲛⲉ ⲙ̅ⲙⲟ⸗ ⲛ̅ⲥⲁ to find
    someone (ⲛ̅ⲥⲁ) guilty of (ⲙ̅ⲙⲟ⸗). ϭⲛ̅-ϩⲏⲧ to learn wisdom.
    ϭⲓⲛⲉ as n.m. finding, thing found. ⲣⲉϥϭⲓⲛⲉ finder.

352

ϭⲓⲛⲙⲟⲩⲧ, ϭⲓⲙⲙⲟⲩⲧ, ϭⲓⲛⲙⲟⲧ, ⲕⲛ̄ⲙⲟⲩⲧ, ϭⲙ̄ⲙⲟⲩⲧ n.f. the Pleiades.

ϭⲓⲛⲟⲩⲏⲗ, ϭⲉⲛⲟⲩⲏⲛ, ϭⲓⲛⲟⲩⲃⲁⲗ, ⲕⲓⲛⲃⲏⲗ n.m. kind of ship.

ϭⲓⲛ₂ⲟⲩⲧ, ϭⲓⲙ₂ⲟⲩⲧ, ϭⲛ̄₂ⲟⲩⲧ, ϭⲉⲙ₂ⲟⲩⲧ presumably = ϭⲓⲛⲙⲟⲩⲧ q.v.

ϭⲓⲛϭⲗⲱ, ϭⲓⲛϭⲗⲟ, ϭⲓⲛⲧⲗⲱ, ϭⲛ̄ϭⲉⲗⲱ, ϭⲉⲛϭⲗⲱ, ⲕⲁⲛⲕⲗⲱ n.f. bat.

ϭⲓⲛϭⲱⲣ n.m. talent (weight).

ϭⲓⲧⲣⲉ n. kind of fruit, lemon.

ϭⲓⲝ n.f. hand; script-hand; hand as measure. ϭⲓⲝ ⲛ̄ ⲟⲩⲛⲁⲙ right hand. ₂ⲁ ⲧ(ⲉ)ϭⲓⲝ under one's control. ⲣ̄-ⲛⲟϭ ⲛ̄ ϭⲓⲝ to become generous. ϯ-ϭⲓⲝ to promise (someone: ⲛⲁⲉ).

ϭⲁ̄, ϭⲁⲗ n.m. a weapon (exact meaning not clear).

ϭⲗⲁ, ϭⲗⲟ, ⲕⲗⲁ in ϯ-ϭⲗⲁ to sway, stagger.

ϭⲗⲓⲗ n.m. burnt-offering.

ϭⲁ̄ⲙ, ϭⲉⲗⲙ̄, ϭⲁ̄ⲗⲙ̄, ⲕⲉⲗⲙ̄ n. dry sticks, twigs.

ϭⲗⲟ n.m. vanity, futility.

ϭⲗⲟⲙⲗⲙ̄ ϭⲗⲙ̄ⲗⲱⲙ- (ϭⲗⲉⲙⲗⲱⲙ-) ϭⲗⲙ̄ⲗⲱⲙⲉ (ϭⲗⲉⲙⲗⲱⲙⲉ) Q ϭⲗⲙ̄ⲗⲱⲙ (ϭⲗⲙ̄ⲗⲟⲙⲧ̄, ⲗⲙ̄ⲗⲱⲙ, ⲗⲙ̄ⲗⲏⲙ) vb. intr. to become twisted (up with, up in: ⲉ, ₂ⲛ̄); to become implicated, involved, complicated; also tr. to embrace. As n.m. complication.

ϭⲗⲟⲟϭⲉ, ϭⲗⲟϭⲉ, ⲕⲗⲟⲅⲉ, ⲧⲗⲟⲟϭⲉ, ⲧⲗⲱϭⲉ n.f. ladder.

ϭⲗⲟϭ, ⲧⲗⲟϭ n.m. bed, bier.

ϭⲗⲟϭ, ⲉϭⲗⲟϭ n.m. gourd.

ϭⲗⲱ, ϭⲗⲟⲩ n.f. twigs, firewood.

ϭⲗⲱⲧ (pl. or dual: ϭⲗⲟⲟⲧⲉ, ϭⲗⲟⲧⲉ, ϭⲗⲟⲟϭⲉ) n.m.f. kidney; pl. also = internal organs in general, viscera.

ϭⲛⲟⲛ, Q ϭⲏⲛ (ϭⲟⲛ) vb. intr. to become soft, smooth, weak; as n.m. softness. ϯ-ϭⲛⲟⲛ to weaken. ϭⲟⲛ, ϭⲟⲟⲛⲉ, ϭⲱⲛ adj. soft; also of a condition of wine.

ϭⲛ̄ϭⲛ̄ (ϭⲉⲛϭⲉⲛ, ϭⲙ̄ϭⲙ̄, ⲝⲛ̄ⲝⲛ̄, ⲝⲓⲛⲝⲓⲛ, ⲝⲙ̄ⲝⲙ̄) vb. intr. to make music (vocal or instrumental); as n.m. music.

ϭⲟϭⲓⲗⲉ (ϭⲟⲓⲗⲉ) ϭⲗⲗⲉ- Q ϭⲗⲗⲱⲟⲩ (ⲕⲁⲗⲱⲟⲩ, ϭⲗⲗⲏⲩ, ϭⲗⲗⲏⲩⲧ, ϭⲗ-ⲗⲟⲟⲩⲧ) vb. intr. to dwell, sojourn, reside (at, in: ⲉ); ⲙⲁ ⲛ̄ ϭⲟϭⲓⲗⲉ dwelling-place, inn. ⲣⲙ̄ⲛ̄ϭⲟϭⲓⲗⲉ sojourner, lodger; ⲣ̄-ⲣⲙ̄ⲛ̄ϭⲟϭⲓⲗⲉ (Q ⲟ ⲛ̄) to become a sojourner. (2) (additional forms: ϭⲗⲗⲱⲉ, ϭⲗⲗⲱⲱⲉ; Q ⲕⲉⲗⲟⲓⲧ) to deposit (ⲙ̄ⲙⲟⲉ; with: ⲉ), entrust to. ϭⲟϭⲓⲗⲉ n.m. sojourn, residence; furnishings; deposit.

Ϭⲟⲗ n.m. (1) a lie; (2) a liar. ⲣ̄-Ϭⲟⲗ to lie, be false; ⲉⲓⲣⲉ ⲙ̄ⲙⲟⳟ ⲛ̄ Ϭⲟⲗ to make false, present or take as false. ⲝⲓ-Ϭⲟⲗ to tell a lie; ⲁⲧⲝⲓ-Ϭⲟⲗ sincere; ⲙ̄ⲛ̄ⲧⲁⲧⲝⲓ-Ϭⲟⲗ sincerity; ⲡⲉϥⲝⲓ-Ϭⲟⲗ liar; ⲙ̄ⲛ̄ⲧⲣⲉϥⲝⲓ-Ϭⲟⲗ lying.

Ϭⲟⲗⲃⲉ n.f. woolen garment.

Ϭⲟⲗⲝⳟ ⲉ vb. reflex. to abstain from. Ϭⲱⲗⲝ̄ n.m. abstinence.

ϬⲟⲗϬ̄ (ϬⲟⲗϬⲉⲗ) Ϭ̄Ϭⲱⲗⳟ (ϬⲉⲗϬⲱⲗⳟ, ⲕⲉⲗϬⲱⲗⳟ) Q Ϭ̄Ϭⲱⲗ vb. tr. to spread to dry (ⲙ̄ⲙⲟⳟ); as n.m. spreading to dry.

Ϭⲟⲙ n.f. power, strength, might, authority. ⲁⲧϬⲟⲙ powerless; ⲙ̄ⲛ̄ⲧⲁⲧϬⲟⲙ powerlessness, inability; ⲣ̄-ⲁⲧϬⲟⲙ (Q ⲟ ⲛ̄) to become powerless; ⲡⲙ̄ⲛ̄Ϭⲟⲙ mighty man. ⲕⲁ-Ϭⲟⲙ ⲉⲃⲟⲗ to lose strength, be exhausted. ⲣ̄-Ϭⲟⲙ, ⲉⲓⲣⲉ ⲛ̄ ⲟⲩϬⲟⲙ to do wondrous deeds. ⲉⲓⲣⲉ ⲛ̄ ⲧ(ⳟ)Ϭⲟⲙ to do one's utmost. ϯ-Ϭⲟⲙ to give power (to: ⲛⲁⳟ). ⲟⲩⲛ̄-Ϭⲟⲙ ⲙ̄ⲙⲟⳟ (one) has the strength, power, ability (to do: ⲉ, ⲉⲧⲣⲉ); ⲟⲩⲛ-ⳡϬⲟⲙ ⲙ̄ⲙⲟⳟ idem; (one) is able (to do: ⲉ, ⲉⲧⲣⲉ); (ⲙ̄)ⲙⲛ̄-(ⳡ)Ϭⲟⲙ ⲙ̄ⲙⲟⳟ neg. of preceding. Ϭⲙ̄-Ϭⲟⲙ, Ϭⲛ̄-Ϭⲟⲙ to find strength, to be able (to do: ⲉ); to prevail (over: ⲉ, ⲉⲝⲛ̄, ⲉ2ⲣⲁⲓ ⲉⲝⲛ̄, 2ⲛ̄, 2ⲓⲝⲛ̄). ⳡϬⲙ̄-Ϭⲟⲙ idem.

ϬⲟⲙϬ̄ⲙ̄ (ϬⲟⲙϬⲉⲙ) Ϭⲙ̄Ϭⲱⲙⳟ vb. tr. to touch, grope for (ⲉ); as n.m. sense of touch. ⲁⲧϬⲙ̄Ϭⲱⲙⳟ untouchable.

Ϭⲟⲛ n.m. low place, hollow. Ϭⲟⲟⲛⲉ n.f. idem.

Ϭⲟⲛⲥ̄ n. violence, might, force, usu. only in cpd. ⲝⲓ ⲛ̄ Ϭⲟⲛⲥ̄ to use violence, act violently; to harm, hurt, illtreat, constrain (ⲙ̄ⲙⲟⳟ); as n.m. violence, iniquity; ⲙ̄ⲛ̄ⲧⲝⲓ ⲛ̄ Ϭⲟⲛⲥ̄ idem; ⲣ̄-ⲝⲓ ⲛ̄ Ϭⲟⲛⲥ̄ to act violently; ⲡⲉϥⲝⲓ ⲛ̄ Ϭⲟⲛⲥ̄ violent, harmful; ⲙ̄ⲛ̄ⲧⲣⲉϥⲝⲓ ⲛ̄ Ϭⲟⲛⲥ̄ violence.

Ϭⲟⲟⲗⲉⲥ n.f. thigh.

Ϭⲟⲟⲩⲛⲉ, Ϭⲁⲩⲛⲉ n.f. hair-cloth, sack cloth; as measure: a sack. ⲥⲁ ⲛ̄ Ϭⲟⲟⲩⲛⲉ sack-seller. ⲥⲁ2(ⲧ̄)-Ϭⲟⲟⲩⲛⲉ weaver of sacks.

Ϭⲟⲟⲩⲡⲉ, Ϭⲁⲩⲡⲉ a term of contempt; slave (?).

Ϭⲟⲡ, ⲕⲁⲡ n.f. sole of foot, foot.

Ϭⲟⲡ n.f. a cutting instrument.

Ϭⲟⲡⲉ, Ϭⲟⲡ, Ϭⲁⲡⲉ, Ϭⲁⲡⲏ, Ϭⲁⲡⲉⲓ n. small vessel, small amount;
Ϭⲟⲡⲉ Ϭⲟⲡⲉ little by little.

Ϭⲟⲣⲧⲉ, ⲕⲟⲣⲧⲉ, Ϭⲁⲣⲧⲉ n.f. knife, sword. ⲁⲧϬⲟⲣⲧⲉ without a
knife; uncut.

Ϭⲟⲣϥ⸗ (ⲕⲟⲣϥ⸗) vb. tr. to nip off.

Ϭⲟⲣⲭ̄, Ϭⲟⲣⲭⲉ n.m. filth. ⲣ̄-Ϭⲟⲣⲭ̄ (Q o ⲛ̄) to become filthy.

Ϭⲟⲥ, ⲕⲟⲥ n.m. half. ⲟⲩϬⲟⲥ (added to a quantity) and a half.
Ϭⲓⲥ-, Ϭⲉⲥ- cpd. form, as in Ϭⲓⲥⲧⲏⲏⲃⲉ half a fingerbreadth.

Ϭⲟⲥⲙ̄ n.m. darkness, stormy darkness.

ϬⲟⲥϬⲉ̄ (ϬⲟⲥϬⲉⲥ) vb. intr. to dance; as n.m. dancing.

Ϭⲟⲧ n.f. size; age; form, sort. ⲛ̄ ⲧⲉⲓϬⲟⲧ of this sort,
such. ⲁϣ ⲛ̄ Ϭⲟⲧ of what sort? ⲣ̄-ⲧϬⲟⲧ (Q o ⲛ̄) to become
like (ⲛ̄ or poss. prefix).

Ϭⲟⲩⲏⲁ n.m. kind of locust.

Ϭⲟⲩⲭ, ⲕⲟⲩⲭ, Ϭⲱⲭ, ϬⲟⲩϬ, ⲕⲟⲩⲕ n.m. safflower, cardamum.

ϬⲟϣϬⲱ̄ (ϬⲟϣϬⲉϣ) ϬⲉϣϬⲉϣ- ϬⲉϣϬⲱϣ⸗ Q ϬⲉϣϬⲱϣ vb. tr. to sprinkle.

ϬⲟⲭϬⲭ̄ (ϬⲟⲭϬⲉⲭ) ϬⲉⲭϬⲱⲭ⸗ (ϬⲉⲧϬⲱⲭ⸗, ϬⲉⲧϬⲱϬ⸗) Q ϬⲉⲭϬⲟⲭⲧ̄ vb. tr.
to cut, smite, slaughter (ⲙ̄ⲙⲟ⸗); as n.m. cutting etc.

Ϭⲣⲏ vb. tr. to dig (ⲙ̄ⲙⲟ⸗).

Ϭⲣⲏⲡⲉ n.f. diadem, sceptre.

ϬⲣⲏϬⲉ n.f. dowry.

Ϭⲣⲟⲟⲙⲡⲉ, Ϭⲉⲣⲟⲙⲡⲉ n.m.f. dove, pigeon. ⲙⲁⲥ ⲛ̄ Ϭⲣⲟⲟⲙⲡⲉ baby
dove. Ϭⲣⲙ̄ⲡϣⲁⲛ n.f. turtledove.

Ϭⲣⲟⲟⲙⲡⲉ, ⲅⲣⲟⲙⲡⲉ n.m. name of a vessel and measure.

ϬⲣⲟϬ, ϬⲣⲟⲟϬ (pl. ϬⲣⲱϬ, ϬⲣⲱⲱϬ, ⲕⲣⲱⲱϬ, ϬⲣⲟⲟϬ) n.m. seed;
sperm; progeny. ⲁⲧϬⲣⲟϬ without seed, without progeny.
ⲭⲓ-ϬⲣⲟϬ to be impregnated.

Ϭⲣⲱⲍ, ⲕⲣⲱⲍ, Ϭⲣⲱⲱⲍ, ⲕⲣⲟⲍ n.m. need, want, lack. ⲣ̄-Ϭⲣⲱⲍ to
be in want (of: ⲛ̄); as n.m. need.

Ϭⲱ Q Ϭⲉⲉⲧ (Ϭⲏⲛⲧ) vb. intr. (1) to remain, wait (for: ⲉ, ⲛⲁ⸗;
with: ⲙⲛ̄; in, within: ⲍⲛ̄); (2) to continue, persist (in
doing: Circum.); (3) to cease, stop, cease functioning.

Ϭⲱⲗ Ϭⲭ̄- (Ϭⲉⲗ-) Ϭⲟⲗ⸗ (Ϭⲟⲟⲗ⸗, ⲕⲟⲗ⸗) Q ⲕⲉⲗ vb. tr. to collect,
gather. ⲣⲉϥϬⲭ̄-ϣⲉ wood-gatherer.

Ϭⲱⲗ (ⲕⲱⲗ) Ϭⲭ̄- Ϭⲟⲗ⸗ (Ϭⲟⲟⲗ⸗) Q Ϭⲏⲗ vb. tr. to roll up (like

a scroll: ⲙ̄ⲙⲟ⸗); intr. to roll up, back; to curl up.
ϭⲱⲗ ⲉⲃⲟⲗ to turn back, return (tr. or intr.).
ϭⲱⲗⲡ̄ (ⲕⲱⲗⲡ̄) ϭⲉⲗⲡ̄- (ϭⲗ̄ⲡ-) ϭⲟⲗⲡ⸗ (ⲕⲟⲗⲡ⸗) Q ϭⲟⲗⲡ̄ (ⲕⲟⲗⲡ̄) ± ⲉⲃⲟⲗ
vb. tr. to uncover, reveal (ⲙ̄ⲙⲟ⸗; to: ⲉ, ⲛ̄ⲥⲁ); vb. intr.
to become revealed, uncovered, manifest; as n.m. revela-
tion, uncovering; ⲁⲧϭⲱⲗⲡ̄ covered. ϭⲁⲗⲡ̄- in cpd. one
who uncovers.
ϭⲱⲗⲝ̄ (ⲭⲱⲗⲝ̄) ϭⲗ̄ϭ- (ϭⲉⲗⲝ̄-, ⲭⲉⲗⲉⲝ-) ϭⲟⲗⲝ⸗ (ϭⲟⲗϭ⸗, ⲭⲟⲗⲝ⸗) Q
ϭⲟⲗⲝ̄ (ⲭⲟⲗⲝ̄) vb. tr. to entangle, ensnare (ⲙ̄ⲙⲟ⸗; in, with:
ⲉ, ⲙ̄ⲙⲟ⸗); reflex. and intr. to become entangled, entwined;
to adhere, be swathed (in: ⲙ̄ⲙⲟ⸗, ϩⲛ̄); as n.m. entanglement.
ϭⲱⲙ, ϭⲟⲙ, ⲕⲟⲙ (pl. ϭⲟⲟⲙ, ⲕⲁⲁⲙ) n.m. garden, vineyard, property. ϭⲙⲉ, ϭⲙⲏ (pl. ϭⲙⲏⲩ, ϭⲙⲏⲟⲩ, ϭⲙⲉⲉⲩ) n.m. gardener,
vinedresser. ⲁⲧϭⲙⲉ untilled; ⲙⲛ̄ⲧϭⲙⲉ vinedressing.
ϭⲱⲛⲁϭ, ϭⲟⲩⲛⲁϭ, ϭⲱⲛⲅ̄, ϭⲟⲩⲛⲁϭⲉⲥ, ⲕⲁⲩⲛⲁⲕⲉⲥ n.m. cloak.
ϭⲱⲛⲧ̄, Q ϭⲟⲛⲧ̄ vb. intr. to become angry, furious, raging
(at, against: ⲉ, ⲉⲭⲛ̄); as n.m. wrath, anger, fury. ⲁⲧ-
ϭⲱⲛⲧ̄ incapable of anger; ⲙⲛ̄ⲧⲁⲧϭⲱⲛⲧ̄ ability to control
one's anger. ⲣⲉϥϭⲱⲛⲧ̄ wrathful, quick-tempered person;
ⲙⲛ̄ⲧⲣⲉϥϭⲱⲛⲧ̄ quick-temperedness. ϯ-ϭⲱⲛⲧ̄ to provoke to
anger (ⲛⲁ⸗); ⲣⲉϥϯ-ϭⲱⲛⲧ̄ one who provokes to anger; ⲙⲛ̄ⲧ-
ⲣⲉϥϯ-ϭⲱⲛⲧ̄ provoking to anger. ϭⲛⲁⲧ vb. intr. to become
angry; as n.m. anger; ⲣⲉϥϭⲛⲁⲧ given to anger; ϯ-ϭⲛⲁⲧ to
provoke to anger; ⲣⲉϥϯ-ϭⲛⲁⲧ provoking to anger.
ϭⲱⲛⲅ̄ (ϭⲱϭ) ϭⲛ̄ϭ- (ϭⲉⲛⲅ̄-) vb. tr. to wring, nip off. ϭⲟⲛϭⲛ̄
(ϭⲱⲛϭⲛ̄) ϭⲛ̄ϭⲛ̄- idem.
ϭⲱⲟⲩ ϭⲟⲟⲩ⸗ Q ϭⲏⲩ (ϭⲏⲟⲩ) vb. tr. to make narrow; intr. to
become narrow, crowded; as n.m. narrowness.
ϭⲱⲟⲩ ϭⲉⲩ- vb. tr. to push; + ⲉⲃⲟⲗ: to put (a ship: ⲙ̄ⲙⲟ⸗)
to sea, to set sail, push off.
ϭⲱⲟⲩϭ, Q ϭⲟⲟⲩϭ vb. tr. to twist, make crooked (ⲙ̄ⲙⲟ⸗); intr.
to become crooked, twisted. ϩⲛ̄ ⲟⲩϭⲱⲟⲩϭ crookedly.
ϭⲱⲡⲉ (ⲕⲱⲡⲉ, ϣⲱⲡⲉ, ϭⲱⲡ, ⲕⲱⲡ) ϭⲉⲡ- (ϭⲡ̄-, ϣⲁⲡ-, ϭⲱⲡ-, ϭⲟⲡ-,
ϭⲁⲡ-, ⲕⲉⲡ-) ϭⲟⲡ⸗ (ϭⲁⲡ⸗, ⲕⲁⲡ⸗, ⲕⲟⲡ⸗, ⲕⲱⲡ⸗, ϭⲱⲡ⸗) Q ϭⲏⲡ
(ⲕⲏⲡ, ϭⲉⲡ, ⲕⲉⲡ) vb. tr. (1) to seize, take (ⲙ̄ⲙⲟ⸗); to

take up, begin (from: ϫⲓⲛ, ϩⲛ̄); (2) to have a claim
against (ⲉ); Q to be guilty (of: ⲉ), liable for, responsible for; (3) to entrap (in, by: ϩⲛ̄), inculpate. ϭⲟⲛⲥ̄
n. capture.

ϭⲱⲣϩ̄, ⲕⲱⲣϩ̄, ϭⲱⲣⲁϩ n.m. night.

ϭⲱⲣϭ̄, Q ϭⲟⲣϭ̄ vb. tr. to hunt (ⲉ), lie in ambush for; as n.
m. snare. ⲙⲁ ⲛ̄ ϭⲱⲣϭ̄ hunting place; ⲣⲉϥϭⲱⲣϭ̄ hunter.
ϭⲟⲣϭⲥ̄ n.f. snare, ambush; prey. ϭⲉⲣⲏϭ (pl. ϭⲉⲣⲁϭⲉ) n.m.
hunter.

ϭⲱⲣϭ̄ ϭⲟⲣϭˀ Q ϭⲟⲣϭ̄ (ϭⲟⲗϭ̄) vb. tr. to prepare, provide (ⲙ̄ⲙⲟˀ).
as n.m. preparation. ⲣⲉϥϭⲱⲣϭ̄ preparer.

ϭⲱⲣϭ̄ ϭⲟⲣϭ̄- Q ϭⲟⲣϭ̄ vb. tr. to populate, people, inhabit
(ⲙ̄ⲙⲟˀ); intr. to be inhabited, peopled.

ϭⲱⲧ n.f. drinking trough.

ϭⲱⲧⲡ̄ ϭⲉⲧⲡ̄- ϭⲟⲧⲡˀ Q ϭⲟⲧⲡ̄ vb. tr. to overcome, defeat (ⲙ̄ⲙⲟˀ);
intr. to become defeated, overcome, wearied, discouraged.
as n.m. intimidation, discouragement. ϭⲱⲧⲡ̄ ⲉⲃⲟⲗ to
frighten away. ϭⲱⲧⲡ̄ ⲛ̄ ϩⲏⲧ to be afraid; as n.m. fear.
ⲁⲧϭⲱⲧⲡ̄ unconquered, undefeated; ⲙⲛ̄ⲧⲁⲧϭⲱⲧⲡ̄ invincibility.
ⲣⲉϥϭⲱⲧⲡ̄, ⲣⲉϥϭⲉⲧⲡ̄-ⲣⲱⲙⲉ ⲉⲃⲟⲗ kidnapper. ϭⲟⲧⲡⲥ̄ n.f. defeat.

ϭⲱⲧϩ̄ (ϫⲱⲧϩ̄, ⲕⲱⲧϩ̄, ϭⲱϩⲧ̄) ϭⲟⲧϩˀ Q ϭⲟⲧϩ̄ vb. tr. to pierce,
wound (ⲙ̄ⲙⲟˀ); as n.m. hole. ⲣ̄-ϭⲱⲧϩ̄ ϭⲱⲧϩ̄ (Q ⲟ ⲛ̄) to become all holes. ϭⲁⲧϩⲉ n. hole.

ϭⲱⲱⲃⲉ, ϭⲱⲃⲉ (ϭⲃ̄-) n.f. leaf. ϭⲃ̄- in cpds. e.g. ϭⲃ̄-ϫⲟⲉⲓⲧ
olive-leaf. ⲁⲧϭⲱⲱⲃⲉ leafless. ϫⲓ-ϭⲱⲱⲃⲉ to glean grapes.

ϭⲱⲱⲗⲉ, ⲕⲱⲗⲉ n.m. flat cake, loaf.

ϭⲱⲱⲗⲉ (ϭⲱⲗⲉ) ϭⲉⲉⲗⲉ- (ϭⲉⲗⲉ-, ϭⲗ̄-) ϭⲟⲟⲗˀ (ϭⲁⲗˀ) Q ϭⲟⲟⲗⲉ vb.
tr. to swathe, clothe, cover (ⲉ; with: ⲙ̄ⲙⲟˀ, ϩⲛ̄); as n.m.
cloak, covering. ϭⲟⲟⲗⲉⲥ, ϭⲟⲗⲉⲥ n.f. covering, garment.

ϭⲱⲱⲙⲉ ϭⲉⲉⲙⲉ- (ϭⲉⲙⲉ-) Q ϭⲟⲟⲙⲉ (ϭⲁⲁⲙⲉ) vb. tr. to twist, pervert (ⲙ̄ⲙⲟˀ); intr. to be twisted, crooked; as n.m. perversion; ⲙⲛ̄ⲧϭⲟⲟⲙⲉ crookedness; ⲙⲛ̄ⲧⲣⲉϥϭⲟⲟⲙⲉ perversion.

ϭⲱⲱϫⲉ (ϭⲱϫⲉ) ϫⲉϫ- ϭⲟϫϩˀ Q ϭⲟⲟϫⲉ (± ⲉⲃⲟⲗ) vb. tr. to cut,
cut off, hew (ⲙ̄ⲙⲟˀ). ⲙⲁ ⲛ̄ ϫⲉϫ-ⲱⲛⲉ quarry.

ϭⲱϣⲧ̄, Q ϭⲟϣⲧ̄ vb. intr. to look, glance, gaze (at: ⲉ, ⲉϩⲟⲩⲛ

ε, εϫⲚ, ⲚⲤⲀ, �ⲏⲧ[⸗]); to pay heed (to: ε); to look forward
(to: ε); as n.m. look, glance. ⳕⲱϣⲦ ⲉⲃⲟⲗ idem; as n.m.
idem. ⲘⲀ Ⲛ ⳕⲱϣⲦ a look-out.

ⳕⲱϫⲂ̄ (ⳕⲱϫⲠ̄) ⳕⲉϫⲂ̄- ⳕⲟϫⲃ⸗ Q ⳕⲟϫⲂ̄ (ⳕⲟϫⲡ̄, ⳕⲁϫⲂ̄) vb. intr. to
become small, less; to diminish, wane, be reduced; vb.
tr. to lessen (Ⲙ̄Ⲙⲟ⸗); as n.m. diminution, inferiority.

ⳕⲱϫⲉ (ⳕⲱⲱϫⲉ) ⳕⲉϫ- Q ⳕⲏϫ vb. tr. to dig (Ⲙ̄Ⲙⲟ⸗).

ⳕⲱϭ vb. intr. to swell. ⳕⲟⲩϭ n. swelling, boil.

ⳕⲱϭ ⳕⲉϭ- (ⳕⲉϫ-) ⳕⲟϭ⸗ (ⳕⲁϭ⸗, ⳕⲉϭ⸗, ⲕⲟϫ⸗) Q ⳕⲏϭ (ⳕⲏϫ) vb. tr.
bake, roast (Ⲙ̄Ⲙⲟ⸗). ⳕⲁⲁϭⲉ, ⳕⲁϭⲉ, ⳕⲟⲟϭⲉ n.m.f. baked loaf.

ⳕ₂ⲟⲥ, ⳕⲟ₂Ⲥ̄, ϫ₂ⲟⲥ, ϣⳕⲟⲥ, ⳕ�X̄₂ⲟⲥ, ϣ�X̄₂ⲟⲥ, ϣϫⲟⲥ, ⳕⲟ₂ϭⲉ, ⳕⲁ₂ⲥⲉ
n.f. gazelle.

ⳕⲁ: Ⲧⳕⲁⲉⲓⲟ	ⳕⲁ₂ⲥⲉ: ⳕ₂ⲟⲥ	ⳕⲉⲩ-: ⳕⲱⲟⲩ
ⳕⲁⲃ-: ⳕⲂ̄ⲃⲉ	ⳕⲁ₂ⲭ̄₂: ϫⲁ₂ⲭ̄₂	ⳕⲉϫ-: ⳕⲱⲱϫⲉ
ⳕⲁⲁⲙⲉ: ⳕⲱⲱⲙⲉ	ⳕⲁ₂Ⲥ̄, ⳕⲁ₂ⳕ̄₂: ϫⲁ₂ⲭ̄₂	ⳕⲉϫ-: ⳕⲱϭ
ⳕⲁⲁϭⲉ: ⳕⲱϭ	ⳕⲁϫⲂ̄: ⳕⲱϫⲂ̄	ⳕⲏⲏⲦ: ⳕⲱ
ⳕⲁⲉⲓⲉ, ⳕⲁⲉⲓⲏ: Ⲧⳕⲁⲉⲓⲟ	ⳕⲁϭ⸗: ⳕⲱϭ	ⳕⲏⲛ: ⳕⲛⲟⲛ
ⳕⲁⲉⲓⲟ: Ⲧⳕⲁⲉⲓⲟ	ⳕⲁϭⲉ: ⳕⲱϭ	ⳕⲏⲛⲧ⸗: ⳕⲓⲛⲉ
ⳕⲁⲗ⸗: ⳕⲱⲱⲗⲉ	ⳕⲂ̄-: ⳕⲱⲱⲃⲉ	ⳕⲏⲟⲩ: ⳕⲱⲟⲩ
ⳕⲁⲗ: ⳕⲗ̄	ⳕⲃⲟⳕ: ⳕⲃⲟⲓ	ⳕⲏⲡ: ⳕⲱⲡⲉ
ⳕⲁⲗⲉ-: ⳕⲟⲉⲓⲗⲉ	ⳕⲂ̄ϣⲗ, ⳕⲂ̄ϣⲉ: ϣⲗ	ⳕⲏⲡⲉ: ⲕⲏⲡⲉ
ⳕⲁⲗⲉⲉⲩ(ⲉ): ⳕⲁⲗⲉ	ⳕⲉ: ⲕⲉ	ⳕⲏⲩ: ⳕⲱⲟⲩ
ⳕⲁⲗⲉⲩⲉ: ⳕⲁⲗⲉ	ⳕⲉⲉⲗⲉ-: ⳕⲱⲱⲗⲉ	ⳕⲏϫ: ⳕⲱϭ, ⳕⲱⲱϫⲉ
ⳕⲁⲗⲏ: ⳕⲁⲗⲉ	ⳕⲉⲉⲙⲉ-: ⳕⲱⲱⲙⲉ	ⳕⲓⲉⲓⲉ: ⳕⲓⲉ
ⳕⲁⲗⲏⲩ(Ⲧ): ⳕⲟⲉⲓⲗⲉ	ⳕⲉⲉⲧ: ⳕⲱ	ⳕⲓⲏ: ⳕⲓⲉ
ⳕⲁⲗⲓⲗ: ⲕⲁⲁⲕⲓⲗ	ⳕⲉⲓⲁⳕⲉⲓⲗ: ⲕⲁⲁⲕⲓⲗ	ⳕⲓⲙⲙⲟⲩⲧ: ⳕⲓⲛⲙⲟⲩⲧ
ⳕⲁⲗⲙⲁ: ⳕⲉⲗⲙⲁⲓ	ⳕⲉⲗⲉ-: ⳕⲱⲱⲗⲉ	ⳕⲓⲙ₂ⲟⲩⲧ: ⳕⲓⲛ₂ⲟⲩⲧ
ⳕⲁⲗⲟⲟⲩⲧ: ⳕⲟⲉⲓⲗⲉ	ⳕⲉⳕⲓⲗ: ⲕⲁⲁⲕⲓⲗ	ⳕⲓⲛ-: ⳕⲓⲛⲉ
ⳕⲁⲗⲟⲡⲟⲩ: ⲕⲁⲗⲱⲡⲟⲩ	ⳕⲉⲙⲉ-: ⳕⲱⲱⲙⲉ	ⳕⲓⲛⲧⲁⲱ: ⳕⲓⲛⳕⲗⲱ
ⳕⲁⲗⲡ̄-: ⳕⲱⲗⲡ̄	ⳕⲉⲙ₂ⲟⲩⲧ: ⳕⲓⲛ₂ⲟⲩⲧ	ⳕⲓⲡⲏ: ⳕⲉⲡⲏ
ⳕⲁⲗⲱ⸗, ⳕⲁⲗⲱⲱ⸗: ⳕⲟⲉⲓⲗⲉ	ⳕⲉⲛ-: ⳕⲓⲛⲉ	ⳕⲓⲥ-: ⳕⲟⲥ
ⳕⲁⲗⲱⲟⲩ: ⳕⲟⲉⲓⲗⲉ	ⳕⲉⲛⲟⲩⲏⲗ: ⳕⲓⲛⲟⲩⲏⲗ	ⳕⲓϫⲱⲓ: ϫⲓϫⲱⲓ
ⳕⲁⲙⲁⲩⲗⲉ: ⳕⲁⲙⲟⲩⲗ	ⳕⲉⲛⲧ⸗: ⳕⲓⲛⲉ	ⳕⲓⳕⲗⲱ: ⳕⲓⲛⳕⲗⲱ
ⳕⲁⲡ-, ⳕⲁⲡ⸗: ⳕⲱⲡⲉ	ⳕⲉⲛⳕⲗⲱ: ⳕⲓⲛⳕⲗⲱ	ⳕⲭ̄-: ⳕⲱⲱⲗⲉ
ⳕⲁⲡⲉ, ⳕⲁⲡⲏ, ⳕⲁⲡⲉⲓ: ⳕⲟⲡⲉ	ⳕⲉⲡ-, ⳕⲉⲡ: ⳕⲱⲡⲉ	ⳕⲁⲗ₂: ⳕⲭ̄₂
ⳕⲁⲡⲓϫⲉ, ⳕⲁⲡⲓϫⲟⲩ: ⳕⲁⲡⲉⲓϫⲉ	ⳕⲉⲡⲏ: ⲕⲏⲡⲉ	ⳕⲭ̄ⲙ̄: ⳕⲭ̄ⲙ
ⳕⲁⲣⲧⲉ: ⳕⲟⲣⲧⲉ	ⳕⲉⲣ-: ϫⲱⲱⲣⲉ	ⳕⲗⲟ: ⳕⲗⲗ
ⳕⲁⲧ₂ⲉ: ⳕⲱⲧ₂	ⳕⲉⳕⲂ̄: ⳕⲁⲡ̄ⳕⲉⲡ	ⳕⲗⲟⲟⲧⲉ: ⳕⲗⲱⲧ
ⳕⲁⲩⲛⲉ: ⳕⲟⲟⲩⲛⲉ	ⳕⲉⲣⲁⳕⲉ: ⳕⲱⲣⲂ̄	ⳕⲗⲟⲟϭⲉ: ⳕⲗⲱⲧ
ⳕⲁⲩⲟⲛ: ⳕⲁⲟⲩⲟⲛ	ⳕⲉⲣⲏϭ: ⳕⲱⲣⲂ̄	ⳕⲗⲟⲧⲉ: ⳕⲗⲱⲧ
ⳕⲁⲩⲟⲩⲟⲛ: ⳕⲁⲟⲩⲟⲛ	ⳕⲉⲣⲟⲙⲡⲉ: ⳕⲣⲟⲟⲙⲡⲉ	ⳕⲗⲟⲩ: ⳕⲗⲱ
ⳕⲁⲩⲣⲉ: ⳕⲟⲟⲩⲣⲉ	ⳕⲉⲣⲟⲟⲃ: ⳕⲉⲣⲱⲃ	ⳕⲗⲟⳕⲉ: ⳕⲗⲟⲟϭⲉ
ⳕⲁϥⳕⲁϥ: ⳕⲁⲃⳕⲁⲃ	ⳕⲉⲣⲱⲱⲃ: ⳕⲉⲣⲱⲃ	ⳕⲗⲭ̄-: ⲕⲱⲗⲭ̄
	ⳕⲉⲣⳕⲱⲣ⸗: ϫⲟⲣϫⲣ̄	ⳕⲙⲉ: ⳕⲱⲙ
	ⳕⲉⲥ-: ⳕⲟⲥ	ⳕⲙⲉⲉⲩ: ⳕⲱⲙ
	ⳕⲉⲧⳕⲱϫ⸗, ⳕⲉⲧⳕⲱϭ⸗: ⳕⲟϫⳕⲭ̄	

ϭⲙⲏ: ϭⲱⲙ
ϭⲙⲏⲩ: ϭⲱⲙ
ϭⲙⲙⲟⲩⲧ: ϭⲓⲛⲙⲟⲩⲧ
ϭⲙ̅2ⲟⲩⲧ: ϭⲓⲛ2ⲟⲩⲧ
ϭⲙ̅ϭⲙ̅: ϭⲛ̅ϭⲛ̅
ϭⲛ̅-: ϭⲓⲛ-, ϭⲓⲛⲉ
ϭⲛ̅: ϫⲓⲛ
ϭⲛⲁⲧ: ϭⲱⲛⲧ̅
ϭⲛ̅ⲧ⸗: ϭⲓⲛⲉ
ϭⲛ̅ϭⲉⲗⲟ, ϭⲛ̅ϭⲉⲗⲱ: ϭⲓⲛϭⲗⲱ
ϭⲛ̅ϭⲛ̅-: ϭⲱⲛϭ
ϭⲟⲗⲉⲥ: ϭⲱⲱⲗⲉ
ϭⲟⲗⲝ̅: ⲕⲱⲗⲝ̅
ϭⲟⲗϭ⸗: ϭⲱⲗⲝ̅
ϭⲟⲗϭ̅: ϭⲱⲣϭ̅
ϭⲟⲙ: ϭⲱⲙ
ϭⲟⲟⲃ: ϭⲃ̅ⲃⲉ
ϭⲟⲟⲗ⸗: ϭⲱⲱⲗⲉ
ϭⲟⲟⲗ⸗: ϭⲱⲗ
ϭⲟⲟⲗⲉ: ϭⲱⲱⲗⲉ
ϭⲟⲟⲗⲉⲥ: ϭⲱⲱⲗⲉ
ϭⲟⲟⲙ: ϭⲱⲙ

ϭⲟⲟⲙⲉ: ϭⲱⲱⲙⲉ
ϭⲟⲟⲛⲉ: ϭⲛⲟⲛ, ϭⲟⲛ
ϭⲟⲟⲩ⸗: ϭⲱⲟⲩ
ϭⲟⲟⲩϭ: ϭⲱⲟⲩϭ
ϭⲟⲟϥ: ϭⲃ̅ⲃⲉ
ϭⲟⲟϫⲉ: ϭⲱⲱϫⲉ
ϭⲟⲟϭⲉ: ϭⲱϭ
ϭⲟⲡ: ϭⲟⲡⲉ
ϭⲟⲡ-/⸗: ϭⲱⲡⲉ
ϭⲟⲡⲥ̅: ϭⲱⲡⲉ
ϭⲟⲣϫⲉ: ϭⲟⲣⲝ̅
ϭⲟⲣϭⲥ̅: ϭⲱⲣϭ̅
ϭⲟⲧⲡⲥ̅: ϭⲱⲧⲡ̅
ϭⲟⲩⲛⲁϭ(ⲉⲥ): ϭⲱⲛⲁϭ
ϭⲟⲩϭ: ϭⲟⲩϫ, ϭⲱϭ
ϭⲟⲩϭⲟⲩ: ϫⲟⲩϫⲟⲩ
ϭⲟ2ⲥ̅: ϭ2ⲟⲥ
ϭⲟ2ϭ̅: ϫⲁ2ϫ2̅
ϭⲟϫϥ̅: ϭⲱϫⲃ̅
ϭⲟϫ2⸗: ϭⲱⲱϫⲉ
ϭⲡ̅-: ϭⲱⲡⲉ
ϭⲣⲁ: ⲧⲣⲁ
ϭⲣⲟ: ϫⲣⲟ

ϭⲣⲟⲉⲓⲧ: ϫⲣⲟ
ϭⲣⲙ̅ⲡϣⲁⲛ: ϭⲣⲟⲟⲙⲡⲉ
ϭⲣⲟⲟϭ: ϭⲣⲟϭ
ϭⲣⲱⲱ2: ϭⲣⲱ2
ϭⲣⲱⲱϭ: ϭⲣⲟϭ
ϭⲣⲱϭ: ϭⲣⲟϭ
ϭⲥⲟⲩⲣ: ⲕⲥⲟⲩⲣ
ϭⲱⲃ: ϭⲃ̅ⲃⲉ
ϭⲱⲃⲉ: ϭⲱⲱⲃⲉ
ϭⲱⲗⲉ: ϭⲱⲱⲗⲉ
ϭⲱⲗϭⲉⲗⲱ: ϭⲓⲛϭⲉⲗⲱ
ϭⲱⲛ: ϭⲛⲟⲛ
ϭⲱⲛϭ̅: ϭⲱⲛⲁϭ
ϭⲱⲛϭⲛ̅: ϭⲱⲛϭ̅
ϭⲱⲡ-/⸗, ϭⲱⲡ: ϭⲱⲡⲉ
ϭⲱⲣϭ̅: ⲕⲱⲣϭ̅
ϭⲱⲣϥ̅: ⲕⲱⲣϥ̅
ϭⲱ2ⲧ̅: ϭⲱⲧ2̅
ϭⲱϫ: ϭⲟⲩϫ
ϭⲱϫⲉ: ϭⲱⲱϫⲉ
ϭⲱϫϥ̅: ϭⲱϫⲃ̅
ϭⲱϭ: ϭⲱⲛϭ̅

Addenda

ϭⲓ ⲉⲃⲟⲗ 2ⲛ̅ to survive (an ordeal), come through successfully.

(ⲛⲟ2ⲛ2̅) ⲛⲉ2ⲛⲟⲩ2⸗ Q ⲛⲉ2ⲛⲟⲩ2 vb. tr. to shake, shake down.

ⲡⲱϣⲛ̅ ⲉ to assist.

ⲥⲗ̅2ⲟ in ⲙⲟⲩ-ⲛ̅-ⲥⲗ̅2ⲟ lukewarm water.

2ⲁⲉⲓⲟ, ⲗⲉⲓⲟ part. yea, verily; also of entreaty.

ⲃⲉⲣⲉ-: ⲃⲱⲱⲣⲉ

ⲗⲁⲁⲙ: ⲗⲱⲱⲙⲉ

ⲣⲁⲕⲧⲉ: ⲣⲓⲕⲉ

ⲥⲁⲛⲁϣⲧ̅: ⲥⲁⲗⲁϣ̅

ⲧⲟⲩⲉⲓⲏ: ⲧⲟⲟⲩ

ϣⲟⲟⲣ: ϣⲗⲁⲣⲉ

2ⲁⲃⲁϭⲏⲉⲓⲛ: ⲁⲃⲁϭⲏⲉⲓⲛ

2ⲣ̅ⲉⲃⲟⲧ: ⲉⲃⲟⲧ

Glossary of Greek Words

(Greek verbs are cited in their normal dictionary
form: 1st pers. sing. indicative active or middle.)

ἀγαθόν n. what is good.

ἀγαθός good.

ἀγαπή f. love.

ἀγγεῖον n. name of a vessel.

ἄγγελος m. angel.

ἀγορά f. agora, forum.

ἀήρ m. air, atmosphere.

ἀθετέω to disregard.

αἴθριον n. atrium, courtyard.

αἰσθητήριον n. sense-organ.

αἰτέω to ask, ask for.

αἰχμάλωτος m. prisoner.

αἰών m. period of time, age;
eternity; world.

ἀκαθαρσία f. uncleanness.

ἀκάθαρτος unclean.

ἀκατάληπτος incomprehensible.

ἀκτίς, -ῖνος f. ray, beam.

ἀλλά but, but rather.

ἀληθῶς truly.

ἀμήν amen; truly, verily.

ἀνάγκη f. necessity.

ἀναστροφή f. turning; life(-time).

ἀναχωρέω to retire, withdraw, go
and live in desert as a hermit.

ἀναχωρητής m. anchorite.

ἀνομία f. lawlessness.

ἀνοχή f. a holding back.

ἀπαντάω to meet, confront.

ἀπαρχή f. first-fruits.

ἄπιστος unbelieving.

ἁπλοῦς simple, sincere.

ἀπογραφή f. registration.

ἀπογράφω to register.

ἀποθήκη f. storehouse, barn.

ἀπόστολος m. apostle.

ἀποτακτικός m. anchorite, hermit-
monk.

ἀποτάσσω to renounce, give up.

ἆρα (introduces question).

ἀρετή f. goodness, virtue.

ἄρχω to begin.

ἀρχή f. beginning.

ἀρχιεπίσκοπος m. archbishop.

ἀρχιερεύς m. high priest.

ἄρχων m. ruler; Archon.

ἀσεβής impious.

ἀσθενής weak, without strength.

ἀσκός m. leather bag; wine-skin.

ἀσπάζομαι to greet.

ἀσπασμός m. greeting.

ἀσώματος incorporeal.

ἄτοπος odd, strange.

αὐξάνω to grow up.

ἀφελής simple.

βαλλάντιον n. purse.

βαπτίζω to baptize.

βάπτισμα n. baptism.

βάσανος f. torture, anguish.

βάσις f. course.

βῆμα n. platform, judgement seat.

βίος m. life.

βλάπτω to harm, injure.

βοήθεια f. help, aid, support.

γάρ for, since, because.

γενεά f. generation.

γένος n. race.

γραμματεύς m. secretary, scribe.

γραφή f. writing, scripture.

δαιμόνιον n. evil spirit; demoniac.

δαίμων m. evil spirit.

δέ but, however.

δεκανοί m.pl. the decans.

δήμιος m. executioner.

διάβολος m. the Devil.

διαθήκη f. will, testament, covenant.

διακονέω to wait on, serve.

διστάζω to hesitate.

δίκαιος just.

δικαιοσύνη f. justice.

δικαίωμα n. justice, ordinance.

δόγμα n. decree.

δοκιμάζω to prove, test.

δυνάστης m. ruler.

δῶρον n. gift.

ἔαρ n. springtime.

ἑβδομάς f. week.

ἔθνος n. nation, people.

εἰ μή τι if not, unless 30.10

εἶδος n. kind, sort.

εἰκών f. likeness.

εἰρήνη f. peace.

εἴτε ... εἴτε either (whether) ... or.

ἐκκλησία f. church.

ἕλος n. marsh.

ἐλπίζω to hope for.

ἐλπίς f. hope.

ἐνεργία f. function, action.

ἐνοχλέω to trouble, disturb.

ἐντολή f. command, commandment.

ἐξομολογέω to confess, acknowledge.

ἐξουσία f. power, authority.

ἐπεί since, because.

ἐπειδή since, because.

ἐπειδήπερ inasmuch as.

ἐπιβουλή f. plot.

ἐπιθυμέω to desire, be eager (for).

ἐπίσκοπος m. bishop.

ἐπιστολή f. letter, epistle.

ἐπιτιμάω to rebuke.

ἐρῆμος f. desert, wilderness.

ἐτάζω to examine, test.

ἔτι still, yet.

εὐαγγέλιον n. gospel.

εὐχαριστέω to give thanks.

ἤ or.

ἡγεμονία f. rule.

ἡγεμών m. governor.

ἡδονή f. pleasure, delight.

ἡλικία f. age, time of life.

ἥμερος mild, tame.

ἡσυχάζω to be still, quiet.

θάλασσα f. sea.
θεωρέω to observe, look at.
θλίβω to afflict, distress.
θρόνος m. throne.
θυσία f. offering, sacrifice.
θυσιαστήριον n. altar.

ἰδιώτης m. layman, uninformed person.

καθαρός pure.
καθηγέομαι to instruct.
καθολικός universal, catholic.
καὶ γάρ for surely.
καίτοι and yet, although, albeit.
κακία f. evil, badness.
καλῶς well.
κἄν (even) if.
καπνός m. smoke.
καρπός m. fruit.
κατά in accordance with; see 30.10.
καταλαλέω to slander.
καταλαλία f. slander.
κελεύω to order, bid, command.
κέραμος m. tile.
κεραστής f. horned-(viper).
κηρύσσω to announce, proclaim.
κινδυνεύω to be in danger.
κλάσμα n. piece.
κλῆρος m. portion, inheritance.
κοινωνός m. partner.
κόλασις f. punishment, correction.
κοσμικός worldly, secular.
κόσμος m. world.
κοῦφον n. (empty) vessel.

κράτιστος most excellent.
κρίνω to judge.
κρύσταλλος m. ice.
κτίσις f. world, creation.
κυριακή f. Sunday.

λαός m. people.
λύπη f. grief.

μαθητής m. pupil, disciple.
μακαρίζω to bless, deem blessed.
μακάριος blessed.
μάλιστα especially.
μέν ... δέ see 30.10.
μερίς f. portion, share.
μέρος n. part, member.
μεσίτης m. mediator, intercessor.
μετάνοια f. repentance; obeisance.
μετανοέω to repent.
μετέχω to partake (of: ε).
μέχρι even up to, even including.
μή (introduces question; 30.10).
μήποτε so that not (+ Conj.).
μήπως so that not (+ Conj.).
μήτι = μή.
μόγις with difficulty, hardly, scarcely.
μοναχός m. monk.
μόνον only, alone; but (w. neg.).
μορφή f. form, shape.
μυστήριον n. mystery.

νηστεία f. fasting.
νηστεύω to fast.
νοέω to think.

362

νομοδιδάσκαλος m. teacher of the law.

νόμος m. law.

νοῦς m. mind.

οἰκονόμος m. steward, manager.

οἰκουμένη f. world.

ὁλοκόττινος m. gold coin.

ὁλοσηρικός silken.

ὁμοίως adv. likewise.

ὁμολογία f. confession.

ὄργανον n. instrument.

ὀργή f. wrath.

ὀρεινή f. hill-country.

ὀρφανός m. orphan.

ὅσον as long as (+ Circum.), while.

ὅταν when, whenever, if (+ Cond.).

οὖν therefore.

οὐδέ and not, nor.

οὔτε ... οὔτε neither ... nor.

ὀψώνιον n. wages.

πάθος n. suffering.

πανοῦργος m. villain.

παντοκράτωρ m. the Almighty.

πάντως wholly, completely.

παραβολή f. parable.

παραγγέλλω to order, command.

παράγω to pass by, away.

παράδεισος m. Paradise, Eden.

παρακαλέω to exhort.

παράνομος lawless, unjust.

παρθένος f. virgin.

παρρησία f. freedom, openness.

πάσχα n. Passover.

πατριά f. family, clan, nation.

πείθω to persuade.

πειράζω to tempt, experience.

πειρασμός m. temptation.

περιεργάζομαι to be overly concerned.

περίχωρος f. surrounding country-side.

πίναξ m. writing-tablet.

πιστεύω to believe.

πίστις f. faith, trust.

πιστός faithful, true.

πλανάω to err.

πλάνη f. error, erring.

πλάσσω to form, mould.

πλήν except; but, however.

πνεῦμα n. spirit.

πνευματικά n. spiritual matters.

πόλις f. city.

πονηρός bad, wicked.

πόρνη f. prostitute.

ποτήριον n. wine-cup, cup of wine.

πρεσβύτερος m. elder.

προάστειον n. suburbs, environs.

προκόπτω to progress, advance.

πρός in accordance with.

προσευχή f. prayer.

προφητεύω to prophesy.

προφήτης m. prophet.

πύλη f. gate.

πῶς how? why?

σάββατον n. sabbath.

σαίτιον n. keg.

σάρξ f. flesh.

σεμνός holy, august.

σίκερα n. strong drink.

σκάνδαλον n. impediment; bad behavior.

σκεπάζω to cover, shelter.

σκηνή f. tent, "tabernacle".

σοφία f. wisdom.

σπέρμα n. seed, offspring.

σπήλαιον n. cave.

σταυρός m. the Cross.

στῆθος n. chest, breast.

στιγμή f. moment.

στρατιά f. army.

συγγενής m. kinsman.

συγκλητικός of noble rank.

σύμβολον n. mark, token.

συμβουλεύω to advise, give counsel.

σύμβουλος m. counsellor.

συναγωγή f. synagogue.

σχῆμα n. garb; monk's habit.

σῶμα n. body.

σωτήρ m. savior, redeemer.

ταλαίπωρος wretched, miserable.

τάξις f. order, rank, post.

τάφος m. tomb.

τάχα quickly.

τέλειος perfect, complete.

τελώνης m. tax-collector.

τελώνιον n. tax-house.

τετράρχης m. tetrarch, petty prince.

τεχνίτης m. craftsman.

τιμή f. price, value.

τότε then, thereupon.

τράπεζα f. table.

τροφή f. food, nourishment.

ὕλη f. woods, forest.

ὑμνέω to sing hymns.

ὑπηρέτης m. custodian.

ὑπομένω to be patient under, submit to.

ὑπομονή f. patience, endurance.

φαρισαῖοι m. the Pharisees.

φθόνος m. ill-will, jealousy.

φορέω to wear.

φυλή f. tribe, people, nation.

φύσει by nature, naturally.

φύσις f. nature.

χαῖρε Greetings!

χαλάω to lower, let down.

χαλινός m. bridle.

χάρις f. grace.

χήρα f. widow.

χιών f. snow.

χορός m. chorus, choir.

χράομαι to use.

χρεία f. need, necessity.

χρῆμα n. goods, money.

χρηστός useful, beneficial.

χριστός m. the Christ.

χώρα f. land, country.

ψάλλω to recite the psalter.

ψαλμός m. psalm.

ψυχή f. soul.

ὦ (vocative particle).

ὡς (see 30.10).

ὥστε (see 30.10).

ὠφελία f. advantage, profit.

364

The field of Coptic studies has never been a particularly
neglected area, and with the resurgence of interest brought
about by recent Manichaean and Gnostic finds, the bibliography of the field has expanded to enormous proportions.
We shall restrict ourselves here to mentioning a few essen-
tial bibliographical, grammatical, and lexical works with
which the student who wishes to continue his studies should
become familiar.

A. Bibliographical Works

Kammerer, W. *A Coptic Bibliography*. Ann Arbor, 1950.

Mallon, A. *Grammaire copte*. 4th ed. revised by M. Malinine;
Beirut: Imprimerie catholique, 1956. Contains a valuable bibliography pp. 254-398.

Scholer, D. M. *Nag Hammadi Bibliography 1948-1969*. Leiden:
E. J. Brill, 1971. This is updated annually in *Novum
Testamentum*.

Simon, J. "Contribution à la bibliographie copte des
années 1940-45," *Bulletin de la Société d'archéologie
copte* (Cairo) 11 (1945), 187-200.

_____. "Bibliographie copte," appears regularly in
Orientalia from 1949 onward.

B. Grammatical Works (including Dialect Studies)

Jernstedt, P. "Die koptische Praesens und die Anknüpfungs-
arten des näheren Objekts," *Doklady Akademii Nauk S. S. R.*
1927, pp. 69-74.

Kahle, P. E. *Bala⁽izah*. 2 vols.; London: Oxford University
Press, 1954.

Plumley, J. M. *An Introductory Coptic Grammar (Sahidic
Dialect)*. London, 1948.

Polotsky, H. J. *Études de syntaxe copte*. Cairo: Publications de la Société d'archéologie copte, 1944.

_____. "Modes grecs en copte?" *Coptic Studies in Honor of*

W. E. Crum. Boston, 1950.

_____. Review of W. Till, *Koptische Grammatik*, in *Orientalistische Literaturzeitung* 52 (1957), 219-34.

_____. "The Coptic Conjugation System," *Orientalia* 29 (1960), 392-422. (These and other articles are reprinted in H. J. Polotsky, *Collected Papers*. Jerusalem: Magnes Press, 1971.)

Steindorff, G. *Lehrbuch der koptischen Grammatik*. Chicago: University of Chicago Press, 1951.

Stern, L. *Koptische Grammatik*. Leipzig, 1880.

Till, W. C. *Koptische Grammatik (Saïdischer Dialekt)*. 2nd ed.; Leipzig: Harrassowitz, 1961.

_____. *Koptische Dialektgrammatik*. 2nd ed.; Munich, 1961.

Vergote, J. *Phonétique historique de l'égyptien: Les consonnes*. Louvain: Bureaux du Muséon, 1945.

_____. *Grammaire copte, Vol. Ia, Ib*. Louvain: Edit. Peeters, 1973.

Wilson, M. R. *Coptic Future Tenses: Syntactical Studies in Sahidic*. The Hague: Mouton, 1970.

Worrell, W. H. *Coptic Sounds*. Ann Arbor: University of Michigan Press, 1934.

C. Dictionaries and Concordances

Crum, W. E. *A Coptic Dictionary*. Oxford: Clarendon Press, 1939.

Spiegelberg, W. *Koptisches Handwörterbuch*. Heidelberg: C. Winters, 1912.

Wilmet, M. *Concordance du nouveau testament sahidique, II. Les mots autochtones*. *Corpus scriptorum christianorum orientalium; Subsidia*, vol. 11. Louvain, 1957.

Grammatical Index (Coptic)

(All references are to the numbered paragraphs of the Lessons unless "p." is specified.)

Table of Principal Verbal Conjugations

First Present · Rel. of Pres. I · Circumstantial[1]

First Present		Rel. of Pres. I		Circumstantial[1]	
ϯ	ⲧⲛ̄	ⲉϯ	ⲉⲧⲛ̄	ⲉⲓ	ⲉⲛ
ⲕ	ⲧⲉⲧⲛ̄	ⲉⲧⲕ̄	ⲉⲧⲉⲧⲛ̄	ⲉⲕ	ⲉⲧⲉⲧⲛ̄
ⲧⲉ(ⲣ), ⲧⲣ̄		ⲉⲧⲉ		ⲉⲣ(ⲉ)	
ϥ	ⲥⲉ, ⲥⲟⲩ	ⲉⲧϥ̄	ⲉⲧⲟⲩ	ⲉϥ	ⲉⲩ
ⲥ		ⲉⲧⲥ̄		ⲉⲥ	
zero-N		ⲉⲧⲉⲣⲉ-N		ⲉⲣⲉ-N	

Imperfect · Fut. I · Fut. II

Imperfect		Fut. I		Fut. II	
ⲛⲉⲓ	ⲛⲉⲛ	ϯⲛⲁ	ⲧⲛ̄(ⲛ)ⲁ	ⲉⲓⲛⲁ	ⲉⲛⲛⲁ
ⲛⲉⲕ	ⲛⲉⲧⲉⲧⲛ̄	ⲕⲛⲁ	ⲧⲉⲧⲛ̄(ⲛ)ⲁ	ⲉⲕⲛⲁ	ⲉⲧⲉⲧⲛ̄(ⲛ)ⲁ
ⲛⲉⲣⲉ		ⲧⲉⲛⲁ, ⲧⲉⲣⲁ		ⲉⲣⲉⲛⲁ	
ⲛⲉϥ	ⲛⲉⲩ	ϥⲛⲁ	ⲥⲉⲛⲁ	ⲉϥⲛⲁ	ⲉⲩⲛⲁ
ⲛⲉⲥ		ⲥⲛⲁ		ⲉⲥⲛⲁ	
ⲛⲉⲣⲉ-N		zero-N ⲛⲁ-		ⲉⲣⲉ-N ⲛⲁ-	

Fut. III · Neg. Fut. III · Imperf. of Fut.

Fut. III		Neg. Fut. III		Imperf. of Fut.	
ⲉⲓⲉ	ⲉⲛⲉ	ⲛ̄ⲛⲁ	ⲛ̄ⲛⲉⲛ	ⲛⲉⲓⲛⲁ	ⲛⲉⲛⲛⲁ
ⲉⲕⲉ	ⲉⲧⲉⲧⲛⲉ	ⲛ̄ⲛⲉⲕ	ⲛ̄ⲛⲉⲧⲛ̄	ⲛⲉⲕⲛⲁ	ⲛⲉⲧⲉⲧⲛ̄ⲛⲁ
ⲉⲣⲉ		ⲛ̄ⲛⲉ		ⲛⲉⲣⲉⲛⲁ	
ⲉϥⲉ	ⲉⲩⲉ	ⲛ̄ⲛⲉϥ	ⲛ̄ⲛⲉⲩ	ⲛⲉϥⲛⲁ	ⲛⲉⲩⲛⲁ
ⲉⲥⲉ		ⲛ̄ⲛⲉⲥ		ⲛⲉⲥⲛⲁ	
ⲉⲣⲉ-N		ⲛ̄ⲛⲉ-N		ⲛⲉⲣⲉ-N ⲛⲁ-	

Perfect I · Neg. Perf. I · Perfect II[2]

Perfect I		Neg. Perf. I		Perfect II[2]	
ⲁⲓ	ⲁⲛ	ⲙ̄ⲡⲓ	ⲙ̄ⲡⲛ̄	ⲛ̄ⲧⲁⲓ	ⲛ̄ⲧⲁⲛ
ⲁⲕ	ⲁⲧⲉⲧⲛ̄	ⲙ̄ⲡⲉⲕ	ⲙ̄ⲡⲉⲧⲛ̄	ⲛ̄ⲧⲁⲕ	ⲛ̄ⲧⲁⲧⲉⲧⲛ̄
ⲁⲣ(ⲉ), ⲁ		ⲙ̄ⲡⲉ(ⲣ), ⲙ̄ⲡⲟⲩ		ⲛ̄ⲧⲁⲣⲉ, ⲛ̄ⲧⲁ(ⲣ)	
ⲁϥ	ⲁⲩ	ⲙ̄ⲡⲉϥ	ⲙ̄ⲡⲟⲩ	ⲛ̄ⲧⲁϥ	ⲛ̄ⲧⲁⲩ
ⲁⲥ		ⲙ̄ⲡⲉⲥ		ⲛ̄ⲧⲁⲥ	
ⲁ-N		ⲙ̄ⲡⲉ-N		ⲛ̄ⲧⲁ-N	

---

[1] Second Present = Circumstantial.

[2] Relative of First Perfect = Second Perfect with or without prefixed ⲉ-.

Habitual		Negative Habitual		Injunctive	
ϣⲁⲓ	ϣⲁⲛ	ⲙⲉⲓ	ⲙⲉⲛ	ⲙⲁⲣⲓ	ⲙⲁⲣⲛ̄
ϣⲁⲕ	ϣⲁⲧⲉⲧⲛ̄	ⲙⲉⲕ	ⲙⲉⲧⲉⲧⲛ̄	———	———
ϣⲁⲣ(ⲉ)		ⲙⲉⲣⲉ		———	
ϣⲁϥ	ϣⲁⲩ	ⲙⲉϥ	ⲙⲉⲩ	ⲙⲁⲣⲉϥ	ⲙⲁⲣⲟⲩ
ϣⲁⲥ		ⲙⲉⲥ		ⲙⲁⲣⲉⲥ	
ϣⲁⲣⲉ-N		ⲙⲉⲣⲉ-N		ⲙⲁⲣⲉ-N	

Conditional		Conjunctive		Fut. Conj. of Res.[1]	
ⲉⲓϣⲁⲛ	ⲉⲛϣⲁⲛ	(ⲛ̄)ⲧⲁ	ⲛ̄ⲧⲛ̄	———	ⲧⲁⲣⲛ̄
ⲉⲕϣⲁⲛ	ⲉⲧⲉⲧⲛ̄ϣⲁⲛ	ⲛ̄ⲅ, ⲛ̄ⲕ̄	ⲛ̄ⲧⲉⲧⲛ̄	ⲧⲁⲣⲉⲕ	ⲧⲁⲣⲉⲧⲛ̄
ⲉⲣⲉϣⲁⲛ		ⲛ̄ⲧⲉ		ⲧⲁⲣⲉ	
ⲉϥϣⲁⲛ	ⲉⲩϣⲁⲛ	ⲛ̄ϥ, ⲛ̄ϥ̄	ⲛ̄ⲥⲉ	ⲧⲁⲣⲉϥ	ⲧⲁⲣⲟⲩ
ⲉⲥϣⲁⲛ		ⲛ̄ⲥ, ⲛ̄ⲥ̄		ⲧⲁⲣⲉⲥ	
ⲉⲣϣⲁⲛ-N		ⲛ̄ⲧⲉ-N		ⲧⲁⲣⲉ-N	

Temporal		"Until"		"Not yet"	
ⲛ̄ⲧⲉⲣⲓ	ⲛ̄ⲧⲉⲣⲛ̄	ϣⲁⲛϯ[2]	ϣⲁⲛⲧⲛ̄	ⲙ̄ⲡⲁϯ	ⲙ̄ⲡⲁⲧⲛ̄
ⲛ̄ⲧⲉⲣⲉⲕ	ⲛ̄ⲧⲉⲣⲉⲧⲛ̄	ϣⲁⲛⲧⲕ̄	ϣⲁⲛⲧⲉⲧⲛ̄	ⲙ̄ⲡⲁⲧⲕ̄	ⲙ̄ⲡⲁⲧⲉⲧⲛ̄
ⲛ̄ⲧⲉⲣⲉ		ϣⲁⲛⲧⲉ		ⲙ̄ⲡⲁⲧⲉ	
ⲛ̄ⲧⲉⲣⲉϥ	ⲛ̄ⲧⲉⲣⲟⲩ	ϣⲁⲛⲧϥ̄	ϣⲁⲛⲧⲟⲩ	ⲙ̄ⲡⲁⲧϥ̄	ⲙ̄ⲡⲁⲧⲟⲩ
ⲛ̄ⲧⲉⲣⲉⲥ		ϣⲁⲛⲧⲥ̄		ⲙ̄ⲡⲁⲧⲥ̄	
ⲛ̄ⲧⲉⲣⲉ-N		ϣⲁⲛⲧⲉ-N		ⲙ̄ⲡⲁⲧⲉ-N	

Inflected Infinitive

ⲧⲣⲁ	ⲧⲣⲉⲛ
ⲧⲣⲉⲕ	ⲧⲣⲉⲧⲉⲧⲛ̄
ⲧⲣⲉ	
ⲧⲣⲉϥ	ⲧⲣⲉⲩ
ⲧⲣⲉⲥ	
ⲧⲣⲉ-N	

---

[1] May have prefixed ⲛ̄-.

[2] Or ϣⲁⲛⲧⲁ.

Subject Index

(All references are to the numbered paragraphs of the
lessons unless "p." is specified.)

Achmimic dialect p. ix
adjectives 15.1
  "all" 16.4 "any" 16.3
  attributive 15.1
  comparative 29.3
  demonstrative 4.2; 30.8
  "each, every" 16.1
  Greek 15.1
  negative compound 27.1
  "other" 4.3
  predicate 15.2
  predicate inflected 29.2
  substantivized 15.1
adverbs
  directional 8.1
  with ₂ⲛ̄ ⲟⲩ- 21.3
  interrogative 14.2
  of static location 28.6
agent with passive 13.4
"all, entire" 16.4
alphabet p. x
anticipatory suffixed pronoun
  10.4
asyndeton 8.2
article
  definite 1.3
  indefinite 2.1
  omission (deletion) of 2.2; 4.3;
    15.3; 16.2; 18.1; 23.2; 26.1
assimilation p. xvi
Bipartite Conjugation 24.2

Bohairic dialect p. viii-ix
Causative Infinitive: see Inflected
  Infinitive
causative 30.4
  verbs of type ⲧⲁⲕⲟ 26.3
Circumstantial 23.1; 24.2
circumstantial: see clause types
circumstantial converter
  w. copulative clauses 25.1
  w. existential and possessive
    predications 25.1
  w. Fut. I 25.1
  w. Imperfect 24.2
  w. Habitual 28.1
  w. Perf. I 25.1
  w. Pres. I 24.2
clause types
  formal
    w. adjectival predicate 15.2;
      29.2
    w. adverbial predicate 1.4; 2.2
    w. existential predicate 2.2
    w. nominal predicate (copulative)
      5.1; 6.1; 6.2; 15.2
    w. possessive predicate 22.1
    w. verbal predicate 7.1
  functional
    circumstantial 23.1
    relative 3.1; 5.1; 12.1; 12.2;
      13.2; 19.1; 21.1
    purpose/result 27.4; 30.2